Encyclopedia of

Monasticism

Volume 2

M–Z

Encyclopedia of

Monasticism

Volume 2

M–Z

Editor

William M. Johnston

Photo Editor

Claire Renkin

Fitzroy Dearborn Publishers
Chicago and London

FITZROY DEARBORN PUBLISHERS
919 N. Michigan Avenue, Suite 760
Chicago, Illinois 60611
USA

or

FITZROY DEARBORN PUBLISHERS
310 Regent Street
London W1R 5AJ
England

British Library and Library of Congress Cataloging in Publication Data are available.

ISBN 1-57958-090-4

First published in the USA and UK 2000

Index prepared by AEIOU Inc., Pleasantville, New York
Typeset by Sheridan Books Inc., Ann Arbor, Michigan
Printed by Sheridan Books Inc., Ann Arbor, Michigan
Cover design by Peter Aristedes, Chicago Advertising and Design, Chicago, Illinois

Cover illustrations: Tibetan thangka, image courtesy of John C. Huntington, the Huntington Archive (Volume 1);
Jean Fouquet, *St. Bernard, Abbot of Clairvaux*, image courtesy of Giraudon/Art Resource, New York (Volume 2)

CONTENTS

ALPHABETICAL LIST OF ENTRIES

M

Macarian Homilies

The last quarter of the fourth century and opening years of the fifth saw the composition, collection, and, it seems, ecclesiastical condemnation of a body of monastic writings, including homilies, discourses, and correspondence, that escaped destruction at the censors' hands and continued to be handed down among Eastern Christian monks because they were sheltered under the famous name of Macarius the Great of Scete (c. 300–c. 390). The corpus survives today in four large collections compiled in the Byzantine Middle Ages (11th to 15th century), from which era we have the earliest Greek manuscripts, with earlier ones extant in Syriac and Arabic translations. The anonymous author wrote in Greek and lived in Upper Mesopotamia or perhaps southern Asia Minor. Like his exact contemporary, Evagrius Ponticus (346–399), he was familiar with the great Cappadocian Fathers, especially Gregory of Nyssa (c. 330–c. 395). In contrast to the case with Evagrius, it is also clear that the influence flowed in both directions. Gregory seems to have learned from Macarius and vice versa. Both Macarius and Evagrius comprise primary testimonies to and on influence on the formative phase of Eastern Christian monasticism and spirituality. From Diadochus of Photiki in the fifth century to Gregory Palamas (c. 1296–1359) and the Byzantine Hesychasts in the 14th and on to Nicodemus (c. 1749–1809) of the Holy Mountain's *Philokalia* and the Russian startsi (elders) of the 18th and 19th centuries, respectively, the Macarian impress, together with that of Evagrius, is unmistakable.

This "astonishing continuity," in the phrase of one modern scholar, appears to be all the more amazing in view of the several episcopal condemnations, culminating at the Ecumenical Council of Ephesus in 431, of the Messalian heresy with which the Macarian Homilies were linked. However, recent scholars, especially V. Desprez and C. Stewart, have convincingly demonstrated that much – and, in the case of Macarius, practically all – of the furor over Messalianism derived from what amounted to a cultural misunderstanding: Greek bishops were reacting reflexively against traditional emphases and idioms arising from the Semitic-Christian culture of Syria-Palestine. In fact, the Macariana turn out to have been one of the principal conduits through which the inheritance of Syriac-speaking Christianity was transmitted to the later monks of Byzantium and the Slavic countries.

The attraction that the Macarian Homilies exercised for Eastern monks lay in compelling witness to Christianity as renewal and transfiguration. God in Christ has entered into our world and, through the Baptism, into the believer's body and soul. Thus, the Christian is in potential the royal throne of Christ. To work toward the conscious fulfillment of that potential – that is, toward the loving awareness and even the inner vision of Christ's indwelling glory in the Holy Spirit – is the whole aim of Christian life on this side of the eschaton. Hope and longing for that encounter engage the monk in a total effort of moral and psychological reform, an effort that, once undertaken, reveals in turn the limitations of human effort and so the necessity of grace in overcoming the forces of sin rooted in the soul. Humility and continual prayer constitute the necessary ground for that emphasis on the visitation of grace for which the Macariana are mainly known: the light-filled experience (*peira*) of the divine presence within, "perceptibly and with complete assurance." The later Byzantine Hesychast defense of the "uncreated light of Tabor" stands in perfect continuity with this Macarian emphasis.

A much less noted but arguably nearly as important Macarian contribution is his coordination of the experience of God within the heart with the Church's liturgy and altar. His argument here is that the latter constitutes the former's divinely given and necessary image and thus constitutes its guide to the experience of the liturgy of heaven. This threefold relationship – heaven, altar, and heart – is adumbrated by earlier writings of Ephrem the Syrian (c. 306–373), rendered explicit by the anonymous *Liber Graduum*, and continues in Syriac texts of the fifth and sixth centuries. Through the *Macarian Homilies* it was taken up by such Greek writers as Dionysius the Pseudo-Areopagite (sixth century), Maximus Confessor (c. 580–662), Symeon the New Theologian (949–1022), Nicetas Stethatos (11th century), and Nicholas Cabasilas (14th century).

Hieromonk Alexander Golitzin

See also Asceticism: Christian Perspectives; Dionysius the Pseudo-Areopagite; Elders, Russian Monastic (Startsi); Gregory of Nyssa, St.; Hesychasm; Palamas, Gregory, St.; Philokalia; Spirituality: Eastern Christian; Symeon the New Theologian, St.; Visual Arts, Eastern Christian: Painting

Further Reading

Chatzopoulos, Athanasios, *Two Outstanding Cases in Byzantine Spirituality: The Macarian Homilies and Symeon the New Theologian*, Thessalonika: Patriarchal Institute of Patristic Studies at Moni Vlatadon, 1991
Desprez, V., "Le Baptême chez le Pseudo-Macaire," *Ecclesia Orans* 5 (1988)
Doerries, Hermann, *Symeon von Mesopotamien: Die Überlieferung des messalianischen Makarios Schriften*, Leipzig: Hinrichs, 1941
Doerries, Hermann, *Die Theologie des Makarios-Symeon*, Göttingen: Vandenhoeck und Ruprecht, 1978
Golitzin, Alexander, "Temple and Throne of the Divine Glory: Pseudo-Macarius and Purity of Heart," in *Purity of Heart in Early Ascetic and Monastic Literature: Essays in Honor of Juana Raasch, O.S.B.*, edited by Harriet Luckman and Linda Kulzer, Collegeville, Minnesota: Liturgical Press, 1999
Hausherr, I., "L'Erreur fondamentale et la logique du Messalianisme," *Orientalia Christiana Periodica* 1 (1935)
Pseudo-Macarius, *The Fifty Spiritual Homilies: The Great Letter*, translated by G. Maloney, New York: Paulist Press: 1992
Quispel, Gilles, *Makarius, das Thomasevangelium, and Das Lied von der Perle*, Leiden: Brill, 1967
Raasch, J., "The Monastic Concept of Purity of Heart and Its Sources V: Symeon-Macarius, the School of Evagrius Ponticus, and the Apophthegmata Patrum," *Studia Monastica* 12 (1970)
Staats, Reinhart, *Gregor von Nyssa und die Messalianer: Die Frage der Priorität zweier altkirchlicher Schriften*, Berlin: de Gruyter, 1968
Stewart, Columba, *"Working the Earth of the Heart": The Messalian Controversy in History, Texts, and Language to A.D. 431*, Oxford: Clarendon Press, and New York: Oxford University Press, 1991

Macarius of Alexandria, St. d. 394

Egyptian Christian hermit and leader at Kellia

Known as Macarius the Alexandrian or Macarius the Citizen (to distinguish him from another fourth-century monk, Macarius the Egyptian [c. 300–c. 390], also known as Macarius the Great), he was a leader at Kellia (the Cells), an important monastic settlement in the Nitrian desert. These epithets (the Alexandrian and the Citizen) also identified him in fourth-century Egypt as Greek speaking and perhaps of non-Egyptian ethnicity. Palladius (*Lausiac History*), who had personal knowledge of Macarius, is the main source for his life, but little is known about his early years or the reasons for his choice of the monastic life. Having left Alexandria, where he had been either a mime or a tradesman according to different sources, Macarius became a monk and settled at Kellia, an eremitic community 11 miles south of al-Barnuji. He also spent time in Nitria and Scetis (nearby eremitic communities in the Nitrian desert) and visited Pachomius (c. 290–346) in his cenobitic community in the Thebaid.

At Kellia the monks lived in individual cells but gathered on Saturdays and Sundays to worship together and share a meal. Such worship was one way that Macarius could influence his fellow monks, given that he was an ordained priest. In some sources he is termed the "priest of Kellia." The monks also met less formally for advice and encouragement, as their cells were not widely separated. This is the picture conveyed by the *Apophthegmata Patrum* (*Sayings of the Fathers*), and this would be another way that Macarius' teachings could have circulated. Only a few of the *Sayings* are attributed to Macarius the Alexandrian, a larger number to Macarius the Egyptian; some confusion might exist between the two in the sources.

Macarius did not leave any writings, although some texts were incorrectly attributed to him: a monastic rule (Migne, *Patrologia Graeca* 34.967–982) and a Greek treatise on the fate of souls after death. Thus, he influenced the development of monasticism through personal contacts with individuals who wrote extensively, especially Evagrius Ponticus (346–399) and Palladius (c. 364–420/30), and perhaps passed on some of his ideas.

Recent study has focused on separating the two Macarii in the sources to understand the contribution of each to monastic belief and practice. Evagrius Ponticus, also a monk at Kellia, might have modeled his very strict ascetic practices on those of Macarius the Alexandrian (including diet, vigils, and periods of prayer). The antirrhetical method, in which demon-inspired, sinful thoughts are resisted with biblical citations, might also have been practiced by Macarius and preserved by Evagrius in his *Antirrhetikos*. However, the antirrhetical method is found in other fourth-century sources: the Pachomian writings and the letters of Antony (251?–356), among others. Macarius is cited mainly by writers who became associated with the Origenist party in Egypt (Evagrius, Palladius, Rufinus, and Cassian) that was attacked and expelled from Egypt by Theophilus of Alexandria (d. 412) in 399. However, no evidence exists that Macarius adopted Origenist ideas or taught them. His influence seems to have been in the area of ascetic practice.

JANET TIMBIE

See also Cassian, John; Desert Fathers; Egypt; Evagrius Ponticus; Hermits: Eastern Christian; Origins: Comparative Perspectives

Biography

This Egyptian hermit lived near St. Antony and then settled as priest at Kellia. Although he left no writings, his sayings have been confused with those of Macarius the Great (c. 300–c. 390), to whom also the Macarian homilies were later attributed. His pattern of life may have influenced the writings of Evagrius Ponticus.

Further Reading

Bunge, Gabriel, "Évagre le Pontique et les deux Macaire," *Irénikon* 56 (1983)
Evelyn-White, Hugh G., *The Monasteries of the Wadi'n Natrun*, volume 2, New York: Arno Press, 1973
Guillaumont, Antoine, "Le problème des deux Macaire dans les Apophthegmata Patrum," *Irénikon* 48 (1979)

Meyer, R.T., translator, *Palladius: The Lausiac History*, volume 34, *Ancient Christian Writers*, Westminster, Maryland: Newman Press, 1965
Russell, Norman, translator, *The Lives of the Desert Fathers: The Historia Monachorum in Aegypto*, London: Mowbray, and Kalamazoo, Michigan: Cistercian Publications, 1981
Ward, Benedicta, translator, *The Sayings of the Desert Fathers*, London: Mowbray, and Kalamazoo, Michigan: Cistercian Publications, 1975

Machig Labdron. *See* Labdron, Machig

Macrina, St. c. 327–380

Cappadocian Christian leader of ascetic community for women

Macrina is often designated as "the Younger" to distinguish her from her grandmother of the same name who was a disciple of Gregory Thaumaturgus (c. 213–c. 270), the celebrated missionary and bishop of Neo-Caesarea in Cappadocia. Macrina the Elder (d. c. 340) was a foundationally important figure in the Christianity of her famous family and of the region in which they lived as wealthy benefactors and patrons.

Macrina the Younger was the oldest child of Basil and Emmelia, and her younger siblings included Basil (the Great; c. 330–379), bishop of Caesarea; Gregory (c. 330–c. 395), bishop of Nyssa; Peter, bishop of Sebaste; and a brother Naucratius, who died accidentally as a young man. Her father was a wealthy Cappadocian landowner and rhetorician. It seems that he gave careful attention to the education of his elder daughter and to that of his eldest son, Basil, who traveled extensively in the course of his education. At age 12 she was betrothed to a man, but the intended spouse died before the wedding. Macrina, claiming the support of Christian sentiment that was hostile to "second marriages" (betrothal counted as a first), was able to refuse familial pressure to be contracted in marriage again. Thus, at an early age she entered into an ascetic, virginal lifestyle at home. When her father died, she became the veritable support of the entire household, guiding her mother in practical affairs. She induced the family to relocate to the estates at Annesi, by the banks of the Iris River in Pontus. There she established an ascetic community, gathering a wider range of female disciples and presiding over the affairs of the estate and educating her younger siblings. When Basil returned from his formal education, it was her influence that persuaded him to abandon his plans for a secular career and to devote his talents to the Church in a celibate lifestyle. She possibly introduced him to Eustathius of Sebaste (c. 300–after 377), the charismatic and dynamic monk-bishop whose companion and disciple Basil became at this period. If this is correct, Macrina herself likely was a disciple of Eustathius, following his radical ideas of how the monastic state transcended social conventions and even local Church structures. That monastic program met with severe opposition from local hierarchs who felt that their authority was being threatened by Eustathius' "enthusiasm." The acts of the fourth-century Synod of Gangra tell part of the story and demonstrate how Macrina herself might fit into a time in Christian history when asceticism was still finding its place in the structures of the Christian Church. Her own stepping outside of aristocratic social convention through successful opposition to her family, as well as her view of the monastic state as involving labor even for the founders, is only hinted at in Gregory of Nyssa's accounts. Likewise the latter barely mention a certain kind of social leveling taking place in her household (Eustathius taught that Christian ascesis rendered slavery a defunct idiom).

Our knowledge of Macrina's history comes largely from Gregory's stylized biography of her (*Life of Macrina*), from his Letter 19, and also from a kind of platonic dialogue he wrote (On the Soul and Resurrection), in which he describes her as teaching him from her deathbed about the nature and destiny of the soul. Gregory describes her as the pivot of the Christian life of the family, although Basil himself never once mentions her in his extensive work, and Gregory of Nazianzus (c. 329–390), a contemporary theologian who was closely bound up with the affairs of this circle, gives merely a brief praiseworthy mention of her in his Letter 163. The latter is suspiciously formal, given the manner in which he is always ready to devote extensive encomia to other members of this circle of his Christian friends in Cappadocia. Recent work, especially that of Susanna Elm (1994), has been concerned with rediscovering the outlines of this shadowy but important and pioneering female ascetic. It seems an inescapable conclusion that she was one of the "casualties" of the hagiographers of the era. She has been remodeled extensively (even by Gregory of Nyssa, who was devoted to her and the only one who gave her memory sufficient honor). She was not alone in suffering a certain *damnatio memoriae*, an exile into Christian literary silence, for it was a fate suffered also by Eustathius of Sebaste and explicable in terms of the theological doctrine that Eustathius espoused and that the literary circle of male Cappadocian theologians felt was defective. Unable to anathematize mentors and family, they resorted to an economic silence. The fact that Macrina was herself a pioneering monastic founder was glossed over in the course of cultivating Basil's reputation as an originator of monastic life and rules.

John McGuckin

See also Basil the Great, St.; Cappadocia, Turkey; Desert Mothers; Gregory of Nazianzus, St.; Gregory of Nyssa, St.; Istanbul, Turkey; Origins: Eastern Christian; Theology, Eastern Christian; Women's Monasteries: Eastern Christian

Biography

The elder sister of St. Basil and St. Gregory of Nyssa, Macrina the Younger is to be distinguished from her paternal grandmother Macrina the Elder. She founded a Christian community of women on the family property in Pontus, and helped to persuade Basil to become a priest. She is known through Gregory's *Life* of his sister, which recounts their meeting at her deathbed.

Further Reading

Beagon, P.M., "The Cappadocian Fathers, Women, and Ecclesiastical Politics," *Vigiliae Christianae* 49:2 (1995)

Burrus, Virginia, *Chastity as Autonomy: Women in the Stories of the Apocryphal Arts*, Lewiston, New York: Edwin Mellen Press, 1987

Castelli, E., "Virginity and Its Meaning for Women's Sexuality in Early Christianity," *Journal of Feminist Studies in Religion* 2 (1986)

Elm, Susanna, *Virgins of God: The Making of Asceticism in Late Antiquity*, Oxford and New York: Oxford University Press, 1994

Laporte, Jean, *The Role of Women in Early Christianity*, New York: Edwin Mellen Press, 1982

Osborn, R.E., "I'm Looking Over a Four-Leafed Clover That I Overlooked Before: The Cappadocians Re-considered," *Impact* 8 (1995)

Sheather, M., "The Eulogies on Macrina and Gorgonia, Or: What Difference Did Christianity Make?" *Pacifica* 8 (1995)

van Loveren, A., "Once Again – The Monk and the Martyr: St. Antony and St. Macrina," *Studia Patristica* 17 (1973)

Wilson-Kastner, P., "Macrina, Virgin and Teacher," *Andrews University Seminary Studies* 17 (1979)

Woods Callahan, V., translator, "St. Gregory of Nyssa: On the Soul and the Resurrection," *Fathers of the Church* 58 (1967)

Woods Callahan, V., translator, "St. Gregory of Nyssa: The Life of Macrina," *Fathers of the Church* 58 (1967)

Mahāpajāpatī Gotamī c. sixth century–c. fifth century B.C.

Indian aunt and foster mother of Buddha and first Buddhist nun

Mahāpajāpatī Gotamī (Sanskrit, Mahāprajāpati), the Buddha's aunt and foster mother, is best known as the first nun (Pāli, *bhikkhunī*; Sanskrit, *bhikṣunī*) to be ordained in his incipient order. As such she set a precedent for women's ordination and is looked on in the literature of all schools of Buddhism and throughout its historical and geographic range as a model for ecclesiastical law (Vinaya). Her name and the aspects of her hagiography are referred to whenever disputes occur over women's ordination or the administration of the women's order.

The story of her ordination is recounted or mentioned in virtually identical form in almost every recension of extant Vinayas (the code of monastic rules and regulations that governs all aspects of monastic administration) of all schools of Buddhism. The story depicts Mahāpajāpatī approaching her nephew, who has become Buddha, the head of a rapidly expanding order of monks. Representing a large number of women (the text cites 500), she formally requests the ordination of women. He refuses a definitive three times and departs with his retinue of 500 monks (Pāli, *bhikkhu*; Sanskrit, *bhikṣu*) to take up residence in Vesali, a town some distance away. Mahāpajāpatī and the other women shave their heads, don the yellow robes of renunciation, and follow. Mahāpajāpatī then stations herself outside the gates of the monastery, travel-worn, dirty, and weeping. The Buddha's closest attendant, Ānanda, discerns the reason for her distress and takes up her cause with the Buddha. Again the Buddha rejects the petition with the definitive threefold denial. However, when Ānanda queries women's ability to attain the stages leading to *nibbāna* (Sanskrit, *nirvāṇa*, "awakening" or "enlightenment") and reminds the Buddha of the debt he owes his foster mother for nurturing him, the Buddha changes his mind, consenting to women's ordination on the condition that Mahāpajāpatī accept eight "weighty rules" (*garudhamma*). Ānanda conveys the condition to Mahāpajāpatī, who accepts them with joy, even though each of the *garudhamma* formally and permanently subordinates the order of nuns to that of monks.

This ordination stands as anomalous in Vinaya literature, which regulates in great detail both the qualifying characteristics of the candidate and the procedures by which ordination is conferred. The sixth of the eight *garudhamma* stipulates that *bhikkhunī*s must be ordained by a quorum of established *bhikkhunī*s and *bhikkhu*s. The Buddha himself confers ordination to male converts with the "*ehi bhikkhu*" (come monk) formula, but this was not used for Mahāpajāpatī, nor is there a corresponding "*ehi bhikkhunī*" formula for women converts. Rather, as the Buddha reaffirms when the legitimacy of Mahāpajāpatī's ordination is questioned by other *bhikkhunī*s, she was ordained the moment she accepted the eight rules (*Cullavagga* X 2.2).

The implicit controversy over this anomalous ordination anticipates the history of women's ordination in various branches of Buddhism. Today full ordination of women is recognized only in Mahāyāna communities; the Buddhism of Tibet (Vajrayāna) has never had a lineage of fully ordained women, and the lineage of Theravāda *bhikkhunī*s in Sri Lanka died out in the 11th century when there were an insufficient number of fully ordained *bhikkhunī*s to make up the necessary quorum.

However, the Pāli texts of Theravāda Buddhism reflect a vibrant community of women drawing on the example of Mahāpajāpatī for inspiration. The *Therīgāthā* (Verses of the Elder Nuns) and especially the *Therī-apadāna* (Stories of the Elder Nuns) convey a hagiography in which Mahāpajāpatī is revered as the leader of the *bhikkhunī-saṅgha*, who stands at the head of the community of women parallel to the Buddha at the head of the community of men. Indeed, as Jonathan Walters has recently argued, the shaping of Mahāpajāpatī Gotamī's story in the *Apadāna* is deliberately modeled on the biography of the Buddha to provide a feminine parallel of the path to *nibbāna* (Walters, 1994).

Later references in the Sri Lankan chronicles, the *Dīpavaṃsa* and *Mahāvaṃsa*, confirm Mahāpajāpatī's importance to generations of Buddhist women. A brother-and-sister team of missionaries from India, Mahinda and Sanghamittā, are reported to have converted the island's population to Buddhism and to have established prosperous monasteries for *bhikkhu*s and *bhikkhunī*s. Sanghamittā is credited with bringing a sapling from the Bodhi Tree (the tree under which the Buddha attained enlightenment), which to this day remains one of the most important pilgrimage sites in Sri Lanka and is still under the care of renunciant women. In the *Dīpavaṃsa*, a text possibly composed by women (Gunawardana, 1990), Sanghamittā's lineage is traced back to Mahāpajāpatī.

The lineage and the ordination precedent set by Mahāpajāpatī plays an important role in Chinese Mahāyāna *bhikṣunī* texts as well. The *Pi-ch'iu-ni chuan* (Biographies of Eminent Nuns), compiled around A.D. 516, records the travels of Sri Lankan *bhikkhunī*s to China to confer the Vinaya-prescribed ordination on women who had been ordained only by *bhikṣu*s. However, *bhikṣu*s and *bhiksunī*s in China argued that the *bhiksunī* lineage was in fact as valid as Mahāpajāpatī's, because, like her, they were ordained where the quorum of nuns was not possible. Still some *bhikṣunī*s did take a "second" ordination from the quorum of visiting Sri Lankan *bhikkhunī*s and Chinese *bhikṣu*s.

Today in Sri Lanka, where the *bhikkhunī* lineage has been ruptured, women follow the legacy of Mahāpajāpatī, living the lifestyle of nuns, shaving their heads, donning yellow robes, and following Vinaya prescriptions. Some of these women lobby for the reinstatement of formal ordination, arguing that the lineage continues through Chinese *bhikṣunī*s. Others, however, would reject such a reinstatement because formal ordination would bring to them the institutional subordination to the order of *bhikkhu*s that was the condition of Mahāpajāpatī's ordination. Living the legacy of Mahāpajāpatī when her petition for ordination was initially denied, they nonetheless revitalize it with their own modern decisions.

KATE BLACKSTONE

See also Buddha (Śākyamuni); Disciples, Early Buddhist; Gender Studies: Buddhist Perspectives; Holy Men/Holy Women: Buddhist Perspectives; Rules, Buddhist (Vinaya): Historical; Sri Lanka: History; Stūpa; Ten-Precept Mothers as Theravādin Nuns; Women's Monasteries: Buddhist

Biography

Known from Vinayas of all schools, Mahāpajāpatī, the Buddha's aunt, became his foster mother after his mother died young. Much later after his enlightenment, she approached him with a request to found an order of nuns. After he had refused three times, Ānanda intervened on her behalf and was thrice refused until the Buddha recalled his debt to his foster mother. She looms as the progenitor of Buddhist female monasticism and figures in all accounts of its rules.

Further Reading

Bartholomeusz, Tessa, *Women Under the Bo Tree: Buddhist Nuns in Sri Lanka*, Cambridge and New York: Cambridge University Press, 1994

Falk, Nancy, "The Case of the Vanishing Nuns: The Fruits of Ambivalence in Ancient Indian Buddhism," in *Unspoken Worlds: Women's Religious Lives in Non-Western Cultures*, edited by Nancy Falk and Rita Gross, San Francisco: Harper and Row, 1980; 3rd edition, as *Unspoken Worlds: Women's Religious Lives*, Belmont, California: Wadsworth, 1989

Gunawardana, R.A.L.H., "Subtile Silks of Ferreous Firmness: Buddhist Nuns in Ancient Sri Lanka and their Role in the Propagation of Buddhism," *Sri Lankan Journal of the Humanities* 14 (1988, published in 1990)

Horner, I.B., *Women Under Primitive Buddhism*, London: Routledge and Sons, and New York: Dutton, 1930; Delhi: Motilal Banarsidass, 1975

Karma Lekshe Tsomo, Bhiksuni, *Sisters in Solitude: Two Traditions of Buddhist Monastic Ethics for Women*, Albany: State University of New York Press, 1996

Karma Lekshe Tsomo, Bhiksuni, editor, *Buddhist Women Across Cultures*, Albany: State University of New York Press, 1999

Sponberg, Alan, "Attitudes toward Women and the Feminine in Early Buddhism," in *Buddhism, Sexuality, and Gender*, edited by Jose Cabezon, Albany: State University of New York Press, 1992

Walters, Jonathan, "A Voice from the Silence: The Buddha's Mother's Story," *History of Religions* 33 (1994)

Wilson, Elizabeth, *Charming Cadavers*, Chicago: University of Chicago Press, 1996

Mahāyāna

The Mahāyāna (Great Vehicle) designates a number of Buddhist movements and schools that originated in India and spread throughout much of Asia. Although most Buddhists in the world today are adherents of the Mahāyāna, the Great Vehicle began as a relatively small movement or group of movements in South Asia in the first or second century B.C. It then developed its major doctrines and practices over the next few hundred years. While the earliest Mahāyāna literature can be dated to the second century B.C., the Mahāyāna probably was not a distinct, self-conscious movement until between the second and fourth centuries A.D. The movement developed a number of different schools in India and spread to Tibet, central Asia, China, Korea, Japan, and Vietnam, changing and adapting to these different cultural environments and producing teachings, practices, and institutions unique to them. Thus, the Mahāyāna is not, and never has been, a unitary phenomenon but a complex of schools, texts, teachers, and movements that distinguished themselves from what they termed "Hīnayāna," the Lesser Vehicle, consisting of the older and more orthodox schools of Buddhism, today represented by the Theravāda.

The Mahāyāna introduced or popularized a number of novel doctrines and practices. In some Mahāyāna texts the Buddha is given a more exalted status as a divine or cosmic being who transcends space and time, in contradistinction to his depiction in the Pāli literature as a man, albeit an exceptional one, who achieved the maximal degree of wisdom and moral perfection possible. In some Mahāyāna accounts the Buddha is identified with the cosmos, and in some his appearance in the world as a man is merely a fictional apparition manifested to teach and inspire less developed people (those of the Hīnayāna) who would benefit from such an appearance. In some texts he is said to have an infinite life span, to be unlimited in space and time, and to have complete omniscience. Although some of these views were not exclusively Mahāyāna, it is the Mahāyāna sūtras (discourses) and philosophers that popularized and systematized them, making these doctrines normative for many Buddhists in mainly Mahāyāna countries.

Other innovations embraced and developed by some Mahāyāna texts and thinkers include a critique of the traditional emphasis on personal salvation as an escape from the wheel of rebirth. Instead, many Mahāyāna texts extol the ideal of the bodhisattva, a figure who remains indefinitely in the world of saṃsāra to help others achieve enlightenment. Rather than preaching the cessation of phenomenal existence entailed in achieving nirvāṇa, Mahāyāna texts often promote the goal of becoming a Buddha. With its appeal to the laity and its emphasis on compassion and remaining in the world of rebirth, the Mahāyāna tends toward a more world-affirming attitude than non-Mahāyāna schools. Along with the elevation of the Buddha Śākyamuni's status to something like a deity came an entire pantheon of supernatural beings that comprise a significant part of Mahāyāna devotion and cosmology. The Mahāyāna cosmos is immense, with numerous world-systems, each of which has its own Buddha and a host of celestial bodhisattvas. These Buddhas and bodhisattvas became objects of devotion for many Mahāyānists. Religious groups developed around the worship of particular ones, such as Amitābha, Maitreya, and Mañjuśrī, and their worship was common among monastics as well as laypeople.

Perhaps the most influential development in the Mahāyāna was its introduction of new sūtras. Although the earliest Mahāyāna sūtras were composed long after the Pāli canon had been established, the new sūtras claimed to contain the words of the Buddha. Although some of these sūtras contained teachings similar to those in the canon, many teachings (especially those mentioned previously) were innovative and considered heterodox. The style of these sūtras also differs substantially from that of the canonical texts. Often replete with visionary episodes and supernatural occurrences, they suggest an appeal to the popular and visionary imagination, even while they put forth subtle and complex philosophical doctrines accessible only to educated monastics.

Mahāyāna sūtras implicitly reject the notion that the orthodox *saṅgha* enjoys exclusive possession of the words of the Buddha and that monastics are more advanced on the Buddhist path than laity. The sūtras often elevate the laity to a higher status than do Hīnayāna texts, sometimes making laypeople rather than monks the heroes of sūtras, presenting them as having wisdom and insight superior to that of monastics. Nevertheless, despite their critiques of the Hīnayāna and their elevation of the laity's status, many adherents of the Mahāyāna were themselves monks and nuns who often lived and practiced alongside their more orthodox colleagues. Moreover, the composers of the many Mahāyāna sūtras and the developers of their complex philosophical doctrines were almost certainly educated monks rather than laity. Thus, notwithstanding its embracing of the laity, the Mahāyāna should not be construed as a mainly lay movement opposed to monastic Buddhism. In India, as well as in Tibet and East Asia, the vast majority of scholars and other shapers of the Mahāyāna traditions have been monks.

The common ground of all Buddhist monasticism, whether Hīnayāna or Mahāyāna, is the Vinaya, the code of conduct for monks and nuns. Although different Buddhist schools had different versions of the *Vinaya Piṭika*, the divergences were relatively minor. This applies to the Mahāyāna as well. While Mahāyāna schools developed doctrines that significantly departed from the non-Mahāyāna schools, they never developed a separate Vinaya. Mahāyāna monastics followed the Vinayas of either the Mahāsaṃghikas, Sthaviras, Sarvāstivādas, or Sammatīyas, all of which were themselves non-Mahāyāna schools. South Asian monasteries often housed both Mahāyāna and non-Mahāyāna monks and nuns, according to Chinese pilgrims who visited these regions from the fourth through the seventh century. Apparently, as long as the behavioral codes were the same, doctrinal differences between individuals were tolerated in many monasteries.

In India Mahāyāna monasticism prospered alongside non-Mahāyāna schools until the elimination of Buddhism in India in the 12th century with the Muslim invasions. It reached its height with the great Buddhist universities, such as Nālandā and Valabhī. These and other Buddhist monasteries became wealthy and powerful. Nālandā was an immense monastic school that taught a wide range of Buddhist philosophy and practice as well as the teachings of non-Buddhist traditions. It possessed a large library and housed over 3,000 monks. Part of the function of the school was to train missionaries to foreign countries, in many of which Buddhism eventually flourished.

In Tibet and parts of East Asia, the Mahāyāna thrived, while non-Mahāyāna schools met with minimal success. The monastic institution in Tibet took on a unique role in the history of Buddhism, enjoying unprecedented prestige and political power. Although the *saṅgha* had gained considerable power and status in India, it was in Tibet that its power eventually surpassed that of all other institutions, with monks becoming the ruling elite in the country. Monks from India and central Asia first brought Buddhism to Tibet in the seventh century. The dharma was initially given a mixed reception. According to traditional accounts, Buddhism was persecuted during the eighth century but was revived and became firmly established with the help of the Buddhist king, Khri Srong lDe bTsan. From the beginning Tibetan Buddhism developed from Indian Mahāyāna and its esoteric form, the Vajrayāna. The famous scholar-monks Śāntaraksita and Kamalaśīla are largely credited with establishing Mahāyāna Buddhism in Tibet and propagating its development along Indian lines. Tibetan accounts tell of Kamalaśīla defeating a Chan monk in a famous series of debates between 792 and 794, ensuring the success of a gradualist approach to enlightenment characteristic of Indian Mahāyāna over the Chan emphasis on sudden enlightenment.

If Kamalaśīla and Śāntaraksita represented the scholastic side of the Mahāyāna as it came to Tibet, Padmasambhava (eighth century) represented the shamanic, esoteric side embodied in the Vajrayāna. Tibetan accounts portray Padmasambhava as a Tantric master and exorcist who subdued and converted Tibet's demons to the role of protectors of the dharma. Although Vajrayāna Buddhism originated outside the monastic community and perhaps had an ambivalent relationship to it in India, in Tibet it became mainstream and was understood as the culmination of the Buddhist path. In fact, the thaumaturgy and exorcism that is a part of Tantra was a significant part of the appeal that helped Buddhism gain a foothold in Tibet. The mainstreaming of Tantric Buddhism, with its practices contrary to traditional notions of purity and impurity (sexual ritual, ingesting impure substances, and use of wrathful deities), necessarily entailed a turn toward a more symbolic interpretation of these practices among the celibate monks and nuns, who still followed the traditional Vinaya. Such rituals are often carried out by visualization or by substituting more acceptable substances and activities. However, physical practice of sexual and other "impure" rituals was not forbidden but reserved for those considered to have achieved the highest spiritual development.

In Tibet the growth of the *saṅgha*'s prestige increasingly implied privilege and political power. Monastic poverty was neither the rule nor the norm as monasteries involved themselves in trade and owned property. A number of large monasteries, such as Drepung and Ganden, became virtual cities, with their own economies, sharecroppers, and governments. Before the Chinese invasion Drepung housed some 10,000 monks. Moreover, the monks followed quite widely varying occupations. Only a relatively small percentage devoted themselves to intensive textual study and meditation, something for which they have become known in the modern West. A much more common vocation for monks was that of ritual specialist hired by members of the lay community to chant scripture and give blessings on various occasions, such as the birth of a child or the beginning of an important undertaking. Monks often sustained themselves by means of these fees and through family support. The monastic vocation is quite prestigious in Tibet, and those who are considered powerful ritualists, meditators, or scholars are especially respected and attract the most generous patronage. The place of nuns has been more restricted and less prestigious, although today an attempt is being made to revitalize the order of nuns in exile.

Perhaps the most important and unique feature of Mahāyāna monasticism in Tibet is the degree to which monks obtained political power. In no other Buddhist country have monks achieved and maintained sovereignty over a nation. Often throughout Tibetan history more than half the government officials were monks. The distinction between religion and politics in Tibet was always ambiguous, and Tibetans themselves often referred to their political system as *chos-srid gnyis-'brel*, or religion and politics combined. As the monasteries increased in wealth and prestige, their abbots grew in political influence, and by the 13th century monks constituted the ruling elite in Tibet. The *sprul-sku* (*tulku*) tradition became an essential component of this power and its transfer. A *tulku* is a reincarnation of a respected lama, often one who has given indications of the time and place of his next birth and is then sought out as a baby by his associates. Insofar as the monks were celibate, those who were rulers had no direct descendants to carry on a lineage. Such a dilemma led to this unique system of succession by reincarnation. In some traditions the position of abbot was transferred in this way, with the abbot of a monastery continuing his role in a succession of rebirths. The most important of these is in the Gelukpa school, which instituted the succession of Dalai Lamas, or monk-rulers who are considered embodiments of the bodhisattva of compassion (Avalokiteśvara), and have ruled Tibet for 14 generations. The fifth Dalai Lama (1617–1682) is largely responsible for bringing maximal power to the institution, working to ensure the ascendancy of the Gelukpa, accumulating great wealth for the sect and establishing the great Potala Palace in the capital, Lhasa.

The Gelukpa monks headed by the Dalai Lama remained the primary holders of power and the *saṅgha* the most prestigious institution in Tibet until the Chinese invasion in 1950. During the most destructive phases of the Chinese occupation, most of the monasteries of Tibet were destroyed, and many monks and nuns were imprisoned or killed. Today some monks and nuns in Tibet still practice their religion under Chinese occupation, but only a few monasteries are left standing, and the historical role of the monastic institution is gone. The present Dalai Lama (1935–) maintains his place as the leader of the Tibetans in exile, with his home now in Dharamsala, India. A number of Tibetan monasteries and centers now thrive in refugee communities in India, Nepal, Europe, and North America. Forms of Tibetan Buddhism still thrive as well in Bhutan, Mongolia, and parts of northern India, such as Ladakh and Sikkim.

Although Mahāyāna monasticism has not been as dominant an institution in other parts of Asia, it has been an important historical and cultural force in China, Japan, Korea, and Vietnam. Chinese Mahāyāna Buddhism provided the basis for Buddhism in other parts of East Asia. When Buddhism arrived in China from India in the first or second century A.D., it met unique challenges in adapting itself to this quite different culture. The Chinese had a well-organized, hierarchical society with well-established philosophy and ritual practices. Nationalism and suspicion of foreign practices and beliefs had prevented any imported religious tradition from surviving in China. The dominant Confucian ethic of filial piety – devotion to parents in life and worship after death – included an insistence on carrying on the family lineage. Buddhist monastic life, which included renouncing one's family and maintaining strict celibacy, was an affront to this ethic. Buddhists also were hesitant to pay homage traditionally due the emperor and often expected to be able to live with a greater degree of freedom from sovereignty than was acceptable in China.

Despite these challenges Buddhism eventually met with surprising success in China. Notwithstanding conflicts with the indigenous Confucian and Daoist traditions, Buddhism contained elements that appealed to both. Daoism liberally borrowed techniques of meditation as well as philosophical concepts, and Buddhism in turn made use of Daoist ideas. In the 11th and 12th centuries, neo-Confucianism incorporated certain Buddhist doctrines and practices while maintaining a somewhat tense relationship with Buddhism on the whole. One of the important ways in which the *saṅgha* adapted to Chinese society, with its emphasis on family and lineage, was to style itself as a surrogate family with the Buddha as its primary ancestor. The organizational structure of the monastery became akin to that of the Chinese family, with the abbot as a father, former abbot as grandfather, and monks as brothers.

This ordering of the *saṅgha* along familial lines also became an important factor in the organization of schools of Chinese Buddhism, each of which constructed a lineage tracing back to Gautama Buddha. For example, Chan traces a line of descent to the moment at which the Buddha transmitted the dharma to his disciple, Kāśyapa, by holding up a flower. Another important lineage was that of Tiantai, whose founder, Zhiyi (538–597), organized all the Buddhist sūtras available into a comprehensive hierarchy of teachings that the Buddha supposedly taught at different times to people with divergent levels of understanding. The Huayan lineage was based on the *Avataṃsaka Sūtra*, a lengthy set of texts composed in India and central Asia. This sūtra contains lavish descriptions of the pure lands of various Buddhas and their complete interpenetration with the world of ordinary phenomena. Ching-t'u, or Pure Land Buddhism, became quite popular as well. Founded by Huiyuan (334–416), this school focused on Amitābha Buddha, who created a paradisiacal pure land where his devotees can be reborn through faith in him and by relying on his pure karma and grace rather than on their own power. All these lineages maintained their own monastic communities, and each monastery was generally independent of the others, except when some were branches of a larger one.

Chinese Buddhism followed and developed many of the Mahāyāna themes introduced in India, such as an emphasis on Buddhahood and bodhisattvas. Some of the favorite sūtras of China, for example, the *Lotus* and the *Vimalakīrti-nirdeśa*, exalted the laity and relegated the Hīnayāna teachings to expedient means (*upāya*) for teaching spiritually undeveloped people. Chan fused the Daoist reverence for nature with Buddhist concepts, such as the nondifference of saṃsāra and nirvāṇa, creating a Buddhism more favorably disposed to the cyclical processes of nature. Despite the praise of the laity and the natural world (traditionally nonmonastic concerns) Chinese Buddhism remained firmly rooted in the monastic community. Although the *saṅgha* never reached the status and power that it achieved in Tibet, monasteries did gain considerable prestige and wealth at different times in Chinese history, especially during the Tang dynasty (618–907), when they became quite powerful, controlling a great deal of land and enjoying the support of various emperors. Today under Communist rule the *saṅgha* in China has been diminished considerably, both in numbers and social role.

The Mahāyāna in Japan, Korea, and Vietnam developed largely along the lines of Chinese Buddhism, although unique elements are present in each area. Of all the countries in which Mahāyāna Buddhism flourishes, Japan places the least importance on the distinctions between monastics and the laity. Saichō (767–822), the founder of the Tendai school (Chinese, Tiantai), introduced a more relaxed monastic code for Tendai monks, and Shinran (1173–1262), the founder of the Jōdo-shin school, was himself married as a monk. Many monks of other schools followed this precedent, and after the Meiji restoration in 1868 the government decreed that all Buddhist monks could marry. Presently, most Japanese priests marry, monastic celibacy being reserved mostly for youth in training for the priesthood. Japanese Buddhist priests now function mainly to perform funerals and other rituals. However, Zen monks maintain some of the roles and lifestyle of the traditional Buddhist monk who specializes in meditation, albeit celibacy is seldom a requirement. Nuns have traditionally maintained celibacy and have not fulfilled the roles of Buddhist priests, but this is changing in the more liberal attitudes of post–World War II Japan.

David L. McMahan

See also Buddhism: Overview; Buddhist Schools/Traditions: Japan; Buddhist Schools/Traditions: South Asia; Buddhology; China; Daoism: Influence on Buddhism; Deities, Buddhist; Dharamsala, India (Tibetan); Discourses (Sūtras): Mahāyāna; Holy Men in Power (Hierocrats), Buddhist; Images: Buddhist Perspectives; Japan: History; Laicization of Spirituality: Buddhist Perspectives; Lhasa, Tibet; Mantras; Monasticism, Definitions of: Buddhist Perspectives; Nālandā, India; Pure Land Buddhism; Repentance Rituals, Buddhist; Rules, Buddhist (Vinaya); Sexuality: Buddhist Perspectives; Tibet; Tibetan Lineages; Virtues, Buddhist

Further Reading

Buswell, Robert E., Jr., *The Zen Monastic Experience: Buddhist Practice in Contemporary Korea*, Princeton, New Jersey: Princeton University Press, 1992

Ch'ên, Kenneth, *Buddhism in China: A Historical Survey*, Princeton, New Jersey: Princeton University Press, 1964

Conze, Edward, *Buddhist Thought in India*, London: Allen and Unwin, 1962; Ann Arbor: University of Michigan Press, 1967

Dutt, Sukumar, *Buddhist Monks and Monasteries of India*, London: Allen and Unwin, 1962

Harrison, Paul, "Who Gets to Ride in the Great Vehicle? Self-Image and Identity among the Followers of the Early Mahāyāna," *Journal of the International Association of Buddhist Studies* 10:1 (1987)

Samuel, Geoffrey, *Civilized Shamans: Buddhism in Tibetan Societies*, Washington, D.C.: Smithsonian Institution Press, 1993

Snellgrove, David L., *Indo-Tibetan Buddhism: Indian Buddhists and Their Tibetan Successors*, Boston: Shambala Press, and London: Serindia, 1987

Suzuki, D.T., *The Training of a Zen Buddhist Monk*, New York: University Books, 1959

Williams, Paul, *Mahāyāna Buddhism: The Doctrinal Foundations*, London and New York: Routledge and Kegan Paul, 1989

Main, John 1926–1982

British Benedictine pioneer in disseminating Christian meditation

A major turning point in John Main's life took place in 1954 in Malaya, where he was stationed in the British Foreign Service. There he met the holy man Swami Satyananda, a Hindu master of meditation, and subsequently went every week for 18 months to meditate with him. Returning to Dublin to a lectureship at Trinity College, he sought to structure his life on meditation by becoming a monk. In 1959 he was accepted into the Order of St. Benedict at Ealing Abbey in London. The new novice was shocked to find that he was forbidden to use his method of meditation, as the practice was not deemed to be part of the Christian tradition of prayer.

While Main was serving as headmaster of St. Anselm's Abbey School in Washington, D.C., in 1970, a troubled young man consulted him about prayer. He gave the young man Augustine Baker's *Holy Wisdom* (1657), thinking this book would keep him busy for some weeks. The youth responded with such enthusiasm that Main reread the book, only to discover Baker's description of silent, imageless prayer. Recalled to Ealing in 1974, Main began to research the sources of the mantra in the Benedictine tradition. Augustine Baker (1575–1641) led him back to the fourth-century desert monk John Cassian (c. 360–after 430).

John Main, O.S.B.
Photo courtesy of Jill Black

Wrote Main: "Baker's frequent reminder of the emphatic insistence St. Benedict lays upon Cassian's *Conferences* sent me to them seriously for the first time" (see Main, 1983). In the Tenth Conference, Cassian consults Abbot Isaac, who says,

> What follows now is the prayer formula for which you are searching. Every monk who wants to think continuously about God should get accustomed to meditating endlessly on it [the prayer phrase] and to banishing all other thoughts for its sake.

Thus John Main was able to reconcile his experience of Eastern meditation with the Benedictine tradition, and he returned to his practice of meditation.

His first meditation groups formed rapidly in and around Ealing. Laurence Freeman, Main's closest associate in the teaching of meditation, joined him there. Main's essential teaching was, "Sit down, sit still, sit upright and continue to say your mantra from the beginning to the end of your meditation" (see McKenty, 1986). The mantra he recommended was the Aramaic word *Maranatha*, meaning "Lord Come," arguably the most ancient prayer in the church. Through the continual silent repetition of the mantra, Main taught, the meditator can move beyond distractions into the silence where peace and love abound. Once the rational mind has been stilled, one's consciousness can open to the Spirit of God and experience the real presence of Christ.

In 1977 Main was invited by the Archbishop of Montreal to found there a Benedictine community entirely focused on the teaching of Christian meditation. Freeman accompanied him. The community was to be an experiment in a new type of monasticism. Lay people and oblates, single and married persons, formed an integral part of the monastic community. The Benedictine vocations, however, never did materialize. The Montreal priory became the hub of a vast worldwide community of predominantly lay people meeting weekly in meditation groups and held together solely by their twice daily commitment to meditation.

Following John Main's untimely death in 1982, it became increasingly difficult to sustain an authentic Benedictine life at the priory due to lack of vocations. In 1991 the prior of nearby Mt. Saviour's closed the Montreal foundation. Laurence Freeman joined the Benedictine monastery of Christ the King in London, and subsequently set up an international meditation center in Kensington. The late Bede Griffiths (1907–1993) assisted him in drawing up a covenant for the World Community for Christian Meditation, a structure that came into being at the annual John Main Seminar in 1991. Griffiths wrote, "In my experience John Main is the most important spiritual guide in the Church today . . . because his teaching meets the critical needs of modern people in their search for a deeper experience of God" (see Griffiths, 1992).

JILL BLACK

See also Baker, Augustine; Cassian, John; Chapman, John; England: History; Meditation: Christian Perspectives

Biography

Having learned Hindu meditation in Malaya in 1954–1955, John Main entered the Benedictine Abbey of Ealing (London) in 1959. At first frustrated, he gained access to the use of a mantra by Christians through reading in 1970 Augustine Baker's *Holy Wisdom.* Thereafter Main pioneered Christian meditation in and around Ealing Abbey until invited in 1977 to Montreal to found a Benedictine community focused on Christian meditation. Following Main's untimely death in 1982, others including Bede Griffiths organized a World Community for Christian Meditation.

Major Works

Word into Silence, 1980
Community of Love, 1983
Moment of Christ, 1984

Further Reading

Cassian, John, *Conferences*, New York: Paulist Press, 1985
Griffiths, Bede, *The New Creation in Christ* (talks given at the John Main Seminar, 1991), London: Darton, Longman and Todd, and Springfield, Illinois: Templegate, 1992
Main, John, "The Monastic Adventure," in his *Community of Love*, Montreal: Benedictine Priory of Montreal, 1983
McKenty, Neil, *In the Stillness Dancing: The Journey of John Main*, London: Darton, Longman and Todd, 1986

Maṇḍala

In monastic Buddhism a maṇḍala is the epitome of sacred space. Literally the word *maṇḍala* means "circle." In the Buddhist context the term refers to a meditational diagram that explicates the methodology of attaining enlightenment. By definition all maṇḍalas are envisioned as elaborate, bejeweled three-dimensional palaces atop Mount Meru, the imagined center of the Buddhist world system. Because of the conflation between a maṇḍala and Mount Meru, the latter is essentially the perfected environment within which all realizations take place. Envisioned at the top of the mountain, the maṇḍala is also instinctively understood to be located in each individual's *citta*, or heart-mind. In the *citta* the structure is understood as a seed ready for germination, with the ability to blossom into the realizations leading to individual enlightenment.

When a maṇḍala is envisioned in three-dimensional form, it is generally seen as a jewel-encrusted palace, raised above a four-sided platform that represents the slopes of Mount Meru. From each side emerge the prongs of an object known as a *viśvavajra* (Fig. 1). The *viśvavajra* is a complex device and a symbol of the absolute, adamantine nature of enlightenment. At the very core of the *viśvavajra* is a single point that represents the unconditioned potentiality from which all phenomena arise. The structural components of the *viśvavajra* that appear to radiate out of this infinitesimal core symbolize all aspects of phenomenal existence. Specifically each of the four prongs and the center of the *viśvavajra* represent one of five *jina*, or victor, Buddhas. Each of these Buddhas presides over a *kula*, or family, to which all living creatures in the Buddhist world system belong.

The five Buddhas are themselves organized into a diagram known as the *pañca jina* maṇḍala (Fig. 2). Each Buddha is designated to one of the four cardinal directions as well as the zenith. Each is also identified by a distinct color and specific mudra, or hand gesture. The *pañca jina* maṇḍala forms the basis of every other maṇḍalic diagram, and the presence of the *jina* Buddhas may be indicated in the maṇḍala through anthropomorphic representations, specific attributes, or merely color designations. Since all phenomena, including all the deities of the Buddhist pantheon, belong to the *kula* of one of the *jina* Buddhas, the *pañca jina* maṇḍala forms the core over which other maṇḍalic diagrams are layered. No matter which maṇḍala or deity is represented, each is positioned within the four quadrants and the center, presided over by each of the corresponding Buddhas.

Starting at the east (by definition at the bottom of all maṇḍalas in the Asian context) is the *jina* Buddha Akṣobhya, who is blue in color and makes the *bhūmisparśa* mudra, or earth-touching gesture. Moving clockwise to the south is Ratnasambhava, who is yellow and makes the *varada* mudra, or bestowal gesture. At the top of the diagram, on the west, is Amitābha, who is red in color. He sits making *dhyāna* mudra, or the gesture of meditation. Next Amoghasiddhi occupies the north and is green in color. He makes *abhaya* mudra, the gesture of dispelling the fear of death. Finally, in the center, envisioned as the top or the pinnacle of Mount Meru, is Vairocana, who is white in color. He makes the *Dharmacakra* mudra, which signifies teaching by putting into motion the *Dharmacakra*, or wheel of the Dharma.

The five Buddhas each characterize a *jñāna*, or transcendental insight, that together define enlightenment. The five insights are as follows:

Akṣobhya, *Ādarśanajñāna*, "Mirror [-like] transcendental-insight": The ability to see and understand all phenomena without egoistic coloration, as if it were a reflection in a perfect mirror
Ratnasambhava, *Samātajñāna*, "Sameness transcendental-insight": The ability to recognize the underlying oneness of all phenomena
Amitābha, *Pratyavekśājñāna*, "Discriminating transcendental-insight": The ability to understand the ways in which the unified state of all phenomena manifests itself in apparent diversity
Amoghasiddhi, *Kriyānusthānajñāna*, "Transcendental-insight into the Accomplishment of action": Essentially the teaching modality of a Buddha in which he or she guides others in the Dharma
Vairocana, *Dharmadhātujñāna*, "Transcendental-insight into the realm of Absolute Reality" (i.e., *śūnyatā*)

As such the *jina* Buddhas do not have a separate existence but are in fact components of the single, albeit unlimited, notion of absolute enlightenment. Together they represent an enlightened

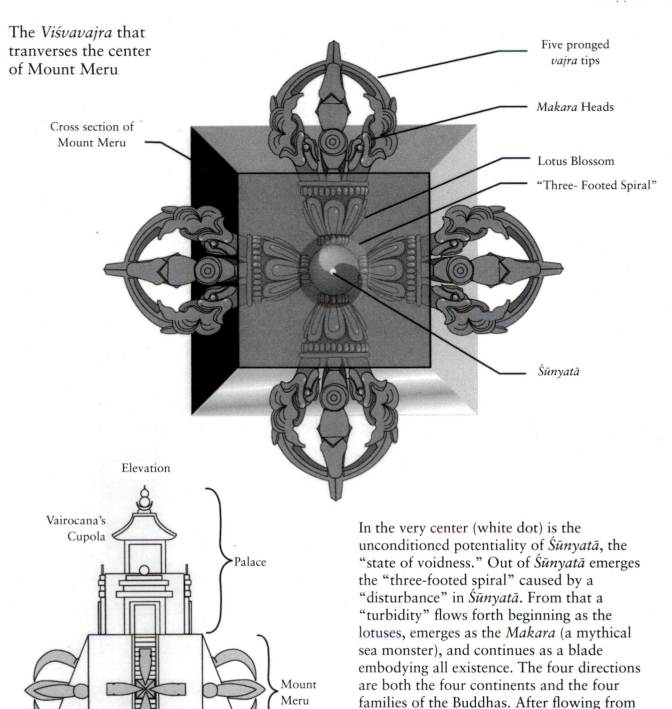

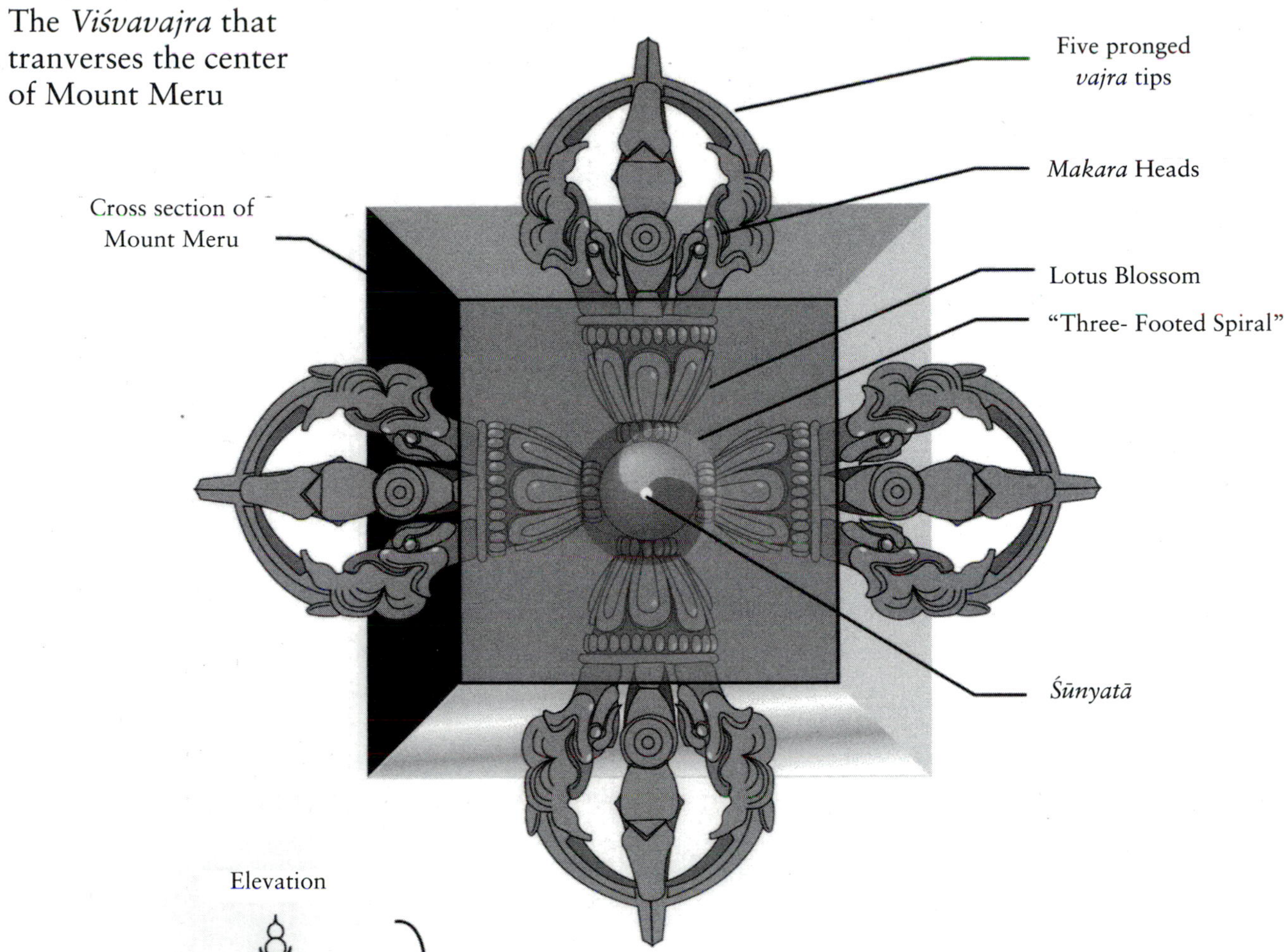

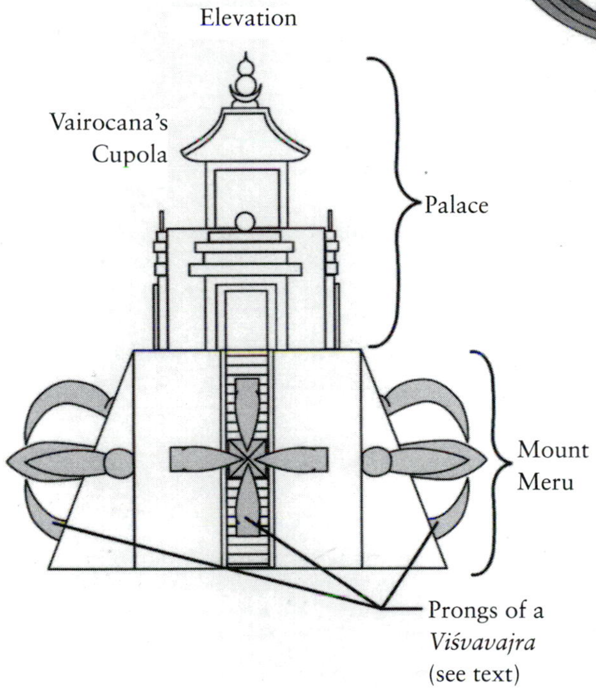

In the very center (white dot) is the unconditioned potentiality of *Śūnyatā*, the "state of voidness." Out of *Śūnyatā* emerges the "three-footed spiral" caused by a "disturbance" in *Śūnyatā*. From that a "turbidity" flows forth beginning as the lotuses, emerges as the *Makara* (a mythical sea monster), and continues as a blade embodying all existence. The four directions are both the four continents and the four families of the Buddhas. After flowing from the *Makaras*, these curve, through the Dharma, and return entering the central shaft of the *vajra*. The central shaft acts as a conduit of reintegration back into the central *Śūnyatā*.

Fig. 1
Drawing courtesy of John C. Huntington

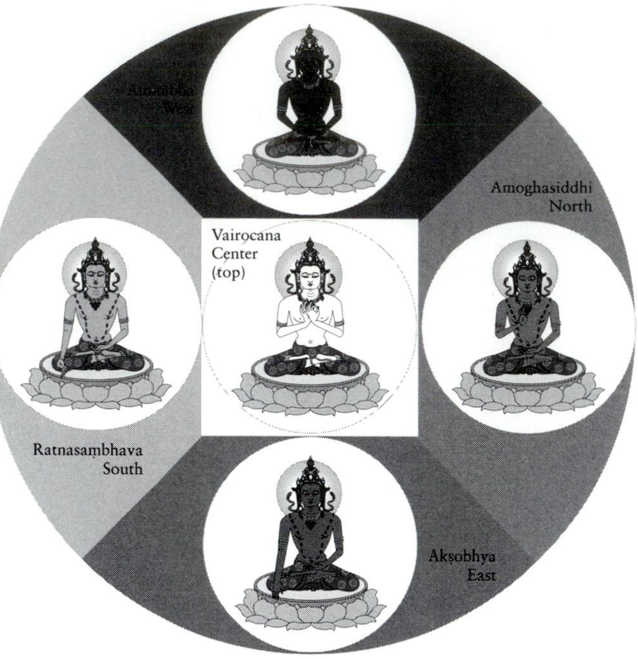

Fig. 2: The Pañcajinabuddha maṇḍala. Drawing courtesy of John C. Huntington

being's attainment of absolute reality, or *śūnyatā* – the "[unconditioned state of] void." It is important to note that the unconditioned state of void is identical to the single point at the core of the *viśvavajra* from which all phenomena manifest. This juxtaposition further underscores the interrelationship between maṇḍala diagrams, the *viśvajara*, and Mount Meru, all of which reside as purely imagined concepts within the core, or heart-mind, of a practitioner.

The *pañca jina* Buddhas also have specific technical roles that are relevant especially to the monastic context. They define the ideal path of a practitioner, specifying the steps one needs to take to reach the final goal. Each of the four directional Buddhas represents a stage in the development of the yogin, or practitioner. Buddha Akṣobhya, "he who is immutable [in resolve]," represents the awakening of *bodhicitta*, literally, "the heart-mind of [the resolve to attain] enlightenment." By entering the eastern gate of the *pañca jina* maṇḍala, the practitioner determines to dedicate his life (or lives) to seeking enlightenment.

The next stage is represented by Buddha Ratnasambhava, "Born of the Gem [of the teachings]." Making the *varada* mudra, he bestows the yogin with the right to be a *bhikṣu*, the mendicant practitioner of Buddhism. Because of this specific role of Ratnasambhava, in Nepal he is the patron of the *cūḍakarma*, or tonsure ceremony. The *cūḍakarma* is a passage rite in which it is mandatory for all young men of the Newar community to assume monkhood for a short period. As a *bhikṣu*, the practitioner can be initiated into the study and practices of esoteric Buddhist methodologies.

In the west, at the top of the diagram, Buddha Amitābha, "Light with-out end," is the gateway to enlightenment. Through the constant meditational practices of the *bhikṣu*, one attains enlightenment, or *bodhi*. At this stage the practitioner is advanced enough to become an enlightened Buddha. However, the ideal path calls for pursuing and fulfilling the subsequent stage to enlightenment. In Mahāyāna Buddhism a fully enlightened Buddha is known as a *samyaksambodhi*, or "perfected Attainment [of] Perfected Enlightenment" Buddha. By definition these Buddhas manifest perfect compassion and teach the Dharma to all beings. Lesser Buddhas, such as *pratyeka* Buddhas, or the Buddhas for oneself, do not teach but merely attain enlightenment and go to nirvāṇa.

In the north Buddha Amoghasiddi, "Immutable skill," manifests the ability of a practitioner to teach the Dharma, the duty of a fully enlightened being. He is the teaching modality of the compassionate enlightened Buddha. At this stage the practitioner fully realizes his potential as an enlightened being through the experiential dissemination of the Dharma.

Finally Buddha Vairocana, "Intensely Shining," represents the final stage of nirvāṇa. Depending on the teaching tradition, he may be either the *Dharmakāya*, "Essence being of the Dharma," or the *Sambhogakāya*, "Essence being of Ecstasy," representing the *Dharmakāya*. He resides in Akaniṣṭha paradise, the highest of the form worlds above Mount Meru. Thus, in the three-dimensional conception of the maṇḍala, Vairocana is at the pinnacle of the group and is the highest level of attainment, and he essentially is identical to *śūnyatā*, the unconditioned potentiality manifested by the point in the center of the *viśvavajra*. As such the path of a practitioner is layered onto the symbolism of the maṇḍala, *viśvavajra*, and Mount Meru alike.

The *trikāya* system is one of several means for describing the nature of a Buddha. It postulates three bodies (*kāya*) simultaneously extant in a Buddha: (1) *nirmāṇakāya*, the transformation body; (2) *sambhogakāya*, the essence being of ecstasy; and (3) *Dharmakāya*, the essence being of the Dharma. As *nirmāṇakāya* the Buddha exists in the realm of mortal beings. As *sambhogakāya* the Buddha exists in the meditational state of ecstasy as he or she explores the state of enlightenment. As *Dharmakāya* the Buddha is coincidental with the universality of the *Dharmadhātu*, or the realm of the Dharma, and thus is identical to *śūnyatā*.

Maṇḍala as works of art are created and used during ritual practices that require meditational diagrams. Especially as paintings, or pictures drawn with sand or colored powder, the three-dimensional maṇḍala palace atop Mount Meru is represented as a two-dimensional circular and square diagram (Fig. 3). Essentially the innermost circle houses the *pañca jina* Buddhas, with Vairocana in the center occupying the pinnacle of Mount Meru. The square that encloses the circle is the floor plan of the envisioned Meru palace. The four projections on each side of the square are the gateways leading into the palace, depicted in a conceptual, flattened manner. The gateways in two-dimensional maṇḍalas visually correlate with the projecting

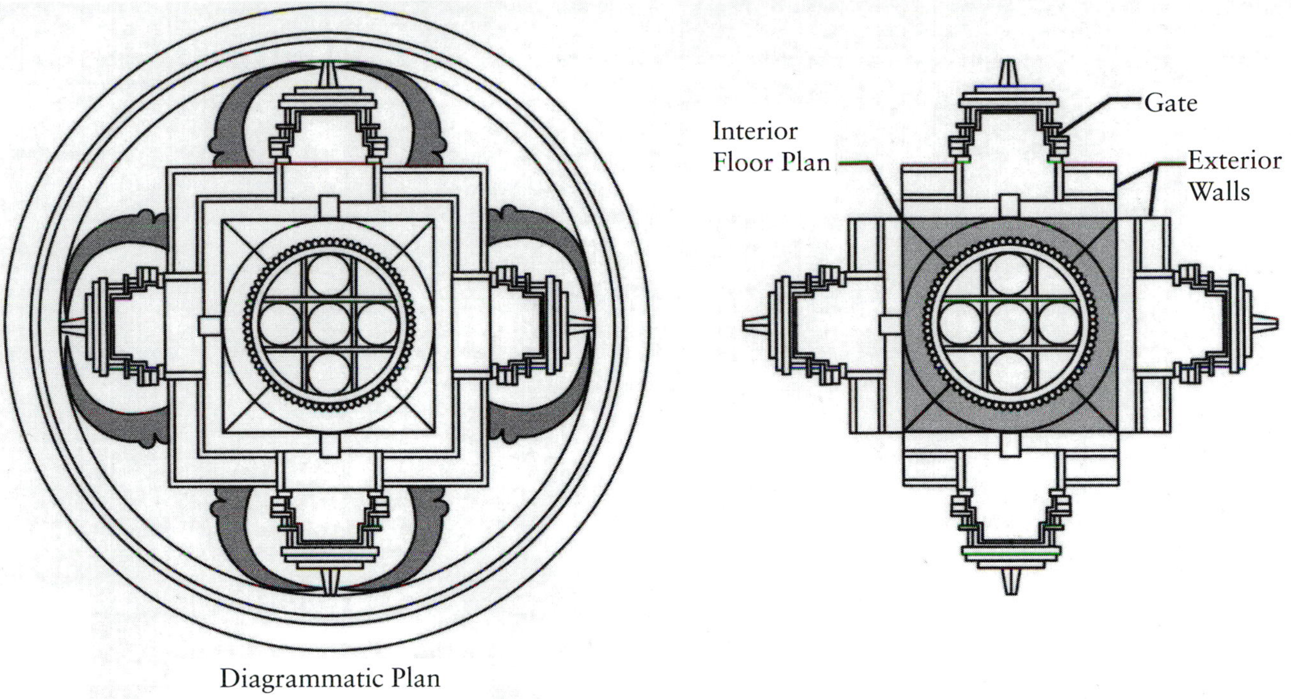

Fig. 3: In the diagrammatic view of the maṇḍala, an exterior view of walls surrounds the plan of interior (gray). The gates (*toraṇa*) are the doors to the palace that one reaches after ascending the stairs on the side of Mount Meru.
Drawing courtesy of John C. Huntington

viśvavajra prongs of the three-dimensional versions. The outer rings that encircle the entire configuration are purifying realms that a practitioner goes through before entering the sanctified space of the maṇḍala.

As many as 300 to 400 different maṇḍalas are known and practiced by various communities throughout the Buddhist world. Apart from the inherent presence of the *pañca jina* symbolism, it is axiomatic that there is a deity in the center of every maṇḍala and that he or she is envisioned as emanating the entire maṇḍalic system. Visual representations of maṇḍala can be as simple as portraying the central deity or may include a plethora of his or her emanations represented by subsidiary deities. Virtually any deity in the Buddhist system can serve as the central deity of a maṇḍala. In some maṇḍalas the central position is occupied by highly esoteric figures, such as Mahāvairocana or other *Ādi*, or primordial Buddhas that manifest the universal void, or *śūnyatā*. In others, relatively simple protective deities, such as Mahākāla, occupy the central position. The specific nature of the central figure of a maṇḍala is immaterial, as all deities are merely emanations of the *vajradhātu*, or the realm of the adamantine. Positioned in the center of the maṇḍala, the central deity essentially represents the final realization. This state, depicted at the heart of a maṇḍala diagram, at the core of Mount Meru and represented by the single point at the center of the *viśvavajra*, is the unconditioned potentiality from which all existence emerges. Thus, regardless of whether Mahāvairocana or Mahākāla occupies the center of the maṇḍala, each is a manifestation of absolute enlightenment. The inherent *pañca jina* maṇḍala serves simply to define the nature of the enlightenment of the central deity. Further, this identifies the central figure as being identical to Vairocana, who represents the final nirvāṇic stage.

Like many other aspects of Tantric methodologies in Buddhism, any specific maṇḍala is the product of an extremely detailed set of instructions and is rooted in profound philosophies. The complexity reflects the details of the meditation that is being practiced and the vision of the teachers who try to develop mechanisms through which the realizations can be made (see Geshe Kelsang Gyatso, *A Guide to Dakini Land*, 2nd edition, 1996).

Maṇḍalas in the Monastery

Although as an individual mental construct a maṇḍala does not require any physicality or physical environment in which it is practiced, artistic and architectural representations exist throughout the Buddhist world. Since at least as early as the sixth century in India, maṇḍalas have been inseparable from the monastic environment and religious life. Maṇḍalas were included into the iconographic programs of buildings from very early times. For example, one of the earliest known and conclusively identifiable examples of a diagrammatic maṇḍala occurs

Fig. 4: Aṣṭabodhisattva maṇḍala, Cave 12, Ellora, c. late sixth century. Photo courtesy of John C. Huntington

on the first floor of Cave 12 at Ellora in Maharashtra, India (Fig. 4). The rectangular panel is divided into nine units, each housing a deity. This is the maṇḍala of the *aṣṭamahābodhisattva*, or the eight great bodhisattvas. Although not visually similar to the circle-within-square format discussed previously, in concept this maṇḍala is identical to all maṇḍala diagrams. In the central unit of the panel is a Buddha, probably Amitābha, seated in the meditative posture. He is the progenitor of the eight bodhisattvas in the units arranged around the center.

Temples and monasteries also include maṇḍala diagrams in the fundamental design of the building. For example, Caves 6 and 7 at Aurangabad in Maharashtra, India, are reiterations of two esoteric maṇḍalas, namely, the Vajradhātu and Garbhadhātu (see John C. Huntington, "Cave Six at Aurangabad: A Tantrayana Monument?" in *Kalādarsana: American Studies in the Art of India*, edited by Joanna G. Williams, 1981). Although not always necessary for the existence of a maṇḍala, a temple or monastic setting provides the mental environment for realizing Buddhist attainments. The monastery itself is conceived as a heavenly realm above Mount Meru. When it is an excavated cave temple, it is understood as a cave in the side of Mount Meru, reaching the very core of the world-system axis. Thus,

Fig. 5: Śri Cakrasaṁvara maṇḍala, Tibet, c. 15th century.
Photo courtesy of John C. Huntington

Fig. 6: Base of colored powers and rice Mount Merus for the Vairocana maṇḍala of the Pañcajinabuddha of the Dharmadhātu Vagiśvara Mañjughoṣa maṇḍala as performed in 1996 at Ha Bahal Lalitput, Nepal.
Photo courtesy of John C. Huntington

Fig. 7: Placing the colored power Vairocana maṇḍala on top of the central Mount Meru illustrated in Fig. 6.
Photo courtesy of John C. Huntington

when a practitioner enters a monastery or a cave temple, he or she essentially enters the consecrated realm of Mount Meru.

In the sacred environment of a monastery, the practitioner prepares for experiencing the maṇḍala through specified rituals and initiations. Texts known as *sādhana* and *vidhi* contain detailed instructions for performing rituals and invoking deities. The deities relevant to a particular ritual are invoked into *kalaśa*, or water vessels, which house them for the duration of the ceremony. An image of a specific deity is then placed at the center of a maṇḍala and is offered various foods, flowers, incense, fire, water, and other substances specific to the ritual being performed. The practices and rituals are remarkably stable and similar across the entire world of esoteric Buddhism. This arises from the need for ritual correctness during the entire process of the maṇḍala offerings to validate the intent of the practitioner. Thus, the Shingon sect in Japan still practices the esoteric tradition introduced to the country by the priest Kūkai (774–835). He in turn closely followed the teachings of the Indian master Śubhakarasiṁha (636–735), who introduced esoteric Buddhism to China in 716. A similar phenomenon occurs in Nepal and Tibet as well. The Mahāsiddha traditions of the 6th through the 12th century of eastern and northern India are followed, with little change, to the present day in Nepal and Tibet.

Fig. 8: Caityaraj Vajracharya of Bu Bahal, performing the Vairocana realizations of the Dharmadhātu Vagiśvara Mañjughoṣa maṇḍala as performed in 1996 at Ha Bahal Lalitput, Nepal. He is dressed in a chasuble and white robe of Vairocana while he wears the Vajrasattva crown and performs the mudra of the various deities of the maṇḍala. Photo courtesy of John C. Huntington

The realization of a maṇḍala in monastic practice is often an elaborate event with many layers of meaning. Depending on who the *jajman*, or offerer, is and the purpose of the offering, the ritual may be very complex or very simple. These purposes range from high-level secret Tantric initiations to mundane offerings of thanks made by lay practitioners. The lay offerer may have little or no knowledge of the actual meaning of the ritual but simply offers it because of its presumed potency in effecting benefit to humanity. In preparing the space for a ritual to take place, a diagram of a lotus is drawn in rice powder on a clean floor. Then mounds of rice are made, each of them being the Mount Meru of a specific member of the maṇḍala configuration (Fig. 6). A maṇḍala drawn in colored powders on a board is then placed on the central mound (Fig. 7), situating it literally on top of Mount Meru. In this particular ritual vast amounts of foodstuffs were then placed around the maṇḍala, almost obscuring it. A priest dressed in the white robes of Vairocana and wearing a Vajrasattva crown (Fig. 8) performed the necessary rituals at this particular maṇḍala.

Fundamental to the practice of any maṇḍala is the notion of a state of being known as Vajrasattva/Sattvavajrī, or "[Purified] Adamantine Being." The dual nature of the deity signifies the union of wisdom and compassion on the path to enlightenment. Through a preliminary meditation, each practitioner establishes an identity transfer of his consciousness to that of the dual deity, Vajrasattva/Sattvavajrī. The practitioner then realizes him- or herself as identical with the deity. It is in this perfected state that the practitioner can undertake the realizations leading to attainment through the maṇḍala process. As Vajrasattva/Sattvavajrī the practitioner visualizes him- or herself as Mount Meru, with the *śūnyatā* core in the center of his or her heart-mind. The core is coincidental with his or her own *tathāgatagarbha* – the womb of his Buddha nature. Subsequently meditation on a specific maṇḍalic system takes place within the perfected practitioner's heart-mind. Whatever the maṇḍala and regardless of where it is located or practiced, it is essentially a conceptual map of one's own process of enlightenment.

JOHN C. HUNTINGTON

See also Buddhist Schools/Traditions; Cave Temples and Monasteries in India and China; Deities, Buddhist; Esoteric Buddhism in China and Japan; Meditation: Buddhist Perspectives; Mount Meru; Spirituality: Buddhist; Tibetan Lineages; Worship Space: Buddhist Perspectives

Further Reading

Brauen, Martin, *The Mandala: Sacred Circle in Tibetan Buddhism*, translated by Martin Willson, Boston: Shambhala, 1997

Saso, Michael R., *Homa Rites and Mandala Meditation in Tendai Buddhism*, New Delhi: International Academy of Indian Culture and Aditya Prakashan, 1991

Snodgrass, Adrian, *The Matrix and Diamond World Mandalas in Shingon Buddhism*, New Delhi: Aditya Prakashan, 1988

ten Grotenhuis, Elizabeth, *Japanese Mandalas: Representations of Sacred Geography*, Honolulu: University of Hawaii Press, 1999

Tharchin, Geshe Lobsang, *Offering of the Mandala*, Washington, D.C.: Mahayana Sutra and Tantra Center, 1981

Tucci, Giuseppe, *The Theory and Practice of the Mandala*, translated by A.H. Brodrick, London: Rider, 1969; New York: Weiser, 1970

Mantras

The use of mantras and *dhāraṇī*s are one of the major characteristics of Mahāyāna Buddhism and especially the esoteric tradition. The use of mantras and magical incantations were taken over from the Vedic tradition of Hinduism in the centuries following the death of Śākyamuni Buddha. Although the earliest sūtra tradition associated with so-called Hīnayāna Buddhism is ambivalent about whether their use is proper or improper, they are present in a limited way. It appears that their use became increasingly popular and would seem to have been rather widespread before the rise of Mahāyāna in the second century B.C. Perhaps this is not surprising, as the line distinguishing mantras from the practice of invoking the name of Buddha (*Buddhanusmṛtī*) is very thin indeed. However, the use of mantras and magical incantations in general was mainly popularized with the rise of Mahāyāna Buddhism. As such they occur in many of the most important nonesoteric sūtras of that tradition, including the *Saddharmapuṇḍarīka*, the *Laṅkāvatāra*, and the *Mahāparinirvāna* sūtra, as well as several of the later *prajñāpāramitā* sūtras. In due course mantras were also adapted by the Pure Land tradition, and they can be found appended to scriptures, such as the Longer and Shorter *Sukhāvatīvyūha* sūtra.

Different categories of mantras and *dhāraṇī*s exist, ranging from mere sounds (i.e., as having a phonetic value only) to fully developed semantic phrases or a combination of both. Although it has been argued that a difference exists between mantras and *dhāraṇī*s in terms of categorization, such a view makes little sense in the primary sources. The only real difference is the name. *Dhāraṇī*s tend to be longer than mantras, but in terms of their application, purpose, and function, the two are virtually identical.

The mantra of Avalokiteśvara (*Om mani padme-hum*) carved on a rock beside the circumambulatory path around the Dalai Lama's residence, Dharamsala, India.
Photo courtesy of John Powers

Many of the earliest known mantras and *dhāraṇī*s consist mainly of what can be described as "magical sounds" or "words of power." It is not possible to deduce any intelligible meaning, or at least very little, from these early mantras, nor were they intended to be read as literature. Their quality and power rests solely in the utterance of them. Although they are associated with having specific purposes, such as protecting the practitioner from demons, they are not bearers of meaning as such but of intent. The *Laṅkāvatāra* sūtra contains a chapter featuring *dhāraṇī*s of this type.

With the growing importance of esoteric Buddhism and the beginning of the Tantric tradition in the third century A.D., mantras became increasingly important. From having had a secondary and minor function in the standard sūtras, the mantras and *dhāraṇī*s became the central focus and raison d'être of a large number of esoteric sūtras that were composed between 300 and 600. They were sometimes considered so important that the entire sūtra or tantra could consist of mantras only. Because of the emphasis that it places on the mantra practice, esoteric Buddhism is sometimes referred to as Mantrayāna (i.e., the Mantra Vehicle). In the developed esoteric and Tantric traditions, mantras and *dhāraṇī*s can often be seen as having a semantic meaning, or at least central parts can be read and understood as literature. The readable parts are often the names of deities and protectors who are invoked through the utterance of the mantra. Mantras and *dhāraṇī*s often contain the so-called root syllables (*bija*) that make up the Sanskrit alphabet. The individual *bija*s were associated with the central Buddhas and deities worshiped in the esoteric tradition and were considered as the phonetic embodiment of the special quality of the deity.

In the standard Mahāyāna sūtras containing *dhāraṇī* and early esoteric scriptures, the incantations are normally used to seek a range of so-called worldly benefits. These might include the attainment of happiness and longevity, buried treasures, beautiful human and nonhuman women, the healing of diseases, or the protection against demons and other disasters. As the esoteric tradition developed, the focus of the mantras changed to include spiritual benefits as well. It now became possible with the aid of the mantras and *dhāraṇī*s to attain rebirth in the Pure Land of Amitābha Buddha or to be liberated from rebirth in the netherworld and ultimately to attain enlightenment. The mantras dealing with worldly benefits were generally available, and any Buddhist could take up this practice on his own. However, the *dhāraṇī*s that brought about spiritual benefits, including ones that gave the user magical powers, normally were transmitted by a master of esoteric Buddhism" an *ācārya*. Thus, the authorization to use especially powerful *dhāraṇī*s was transmitted in a secret ceremony from master to disciple and involved the taking of special vows on the part of the latter.

Mantras are normally used in conjunction with mudras (ritualized hand gestures) and visualization during the performance of rituals. As such they form part of the combined practice of body (mudra), speech (mantra), and mind (visualization) in traditional esoteric Buddhism. Certain mantras are known by all Buddhists of the Mahāyāna persuasion. They include the mantra from the *Hṛdaya* sūtra, the Avalokiteśvara mantra, *Om mani padme-huṃ*, and the Great Compassion Dhāraṇī from the *Nīlakaṇṭhaka* sūtra.

HENRIK H. SØRENSEN

See also Discourses (Sūtras): Mahāyāna; Esoteric Buddhism in China and Japan; Gestures, Buddhist; Liturgy: Buddhist; Meditation: Buddhist Perspectives; Prayer: Buddhist Perspectives; Repentance Rituals, Buddhist; Tibet: History

Further Reading

Alper, Harvey P., "The Cosmos as Śiva's Language-Game: 'Mantra' According to Kṣemarāja's *Śivasūtravimarśinī*," in *Mantra*, edited by Harvey P. Alper, Albany: State University of New York Press, 1989

Bechert, Heinz, and Richard Gombrich, editors, *The World of Buddhism*, London: Thames and Hudson, 1984; New York: Thames and Hudson, 1991

Dasgupta, Shashi Bhushan, *An Introduction to Tantric Buddhism*, Berkeley, California: Shambhala, 1974; 2nd edition, 1976

Gulik, R.H. van, *Siddham: An Essay on the History of Sanskrit Studies in China and Japan*, Nagpur: International Academy of Indian Culture, 1956

Hatta, Yukio, *Shingon jiten* (The Dictionary of Mantras), Tokyo: Hirakawa Shuppansha, 1985

Heinemann, Robert, *Kan-Bon Bon-kan darani yōgo yōku jiten, Chinese-Sanskrit Sanskrit-Chinese Dictionary of Words and Phrases as Used in Buddhist Dhāraṇī*, Tokyo: Meicho Fukyūkai, 1984

Lü Jianfu, *Zhongguo mijiao shi* (The History of Esoteric Buddhism in China), Beijing: Zhongguo shehui kexue chubanshe, 1995

Mevissen, Gerd J.R., "The Indian Connection: Images of Deified Spells in the Arts of Northern Buddhism, Part I," *Silk Road Art and Archaeology* 1 (1990); "Part II," 2 (1991/92)

Mikkyō daijiten (The Great Dictionary of Esoteric Buddhism), 6 vols., Kyoto: Hōzōkan, 1968–1970

Padoux, André, "Mantras – What Are They?," in *Mantra*, edited by Harvey P. Alper, Albany: State University of New York Press, 1989

Reis-Habito, Maria, "The Great Compassion Dhāraṇī," in *The Esoteric Buddhist Tradition*, edited by H.H. Sørensen, Copenhagen and Aarhus: Seminar for Buddhist Studies, 1994

Ryūken, Sawa et al., editors, *Mikkyō jiten: Zen*, Kyoto-shi: Hōzōkan, 1975

Skorupski, Tadeusz, translator, *The Sarvadurgatipariśodhana Tantra: Elimination of All Evil Destinies*, Delhi: Motilal Banarsidass, 1983

Snellgrove, David, *Indo-Tibetan Buddhism: Indian Buddhists and Their Tibetan Successors*, 2 vols., London: Serindia, and Boston and New York: Shambhala, 1987

Strickmann, Michel, *Mantras et mandarins: Le bouddhisme tantrique en Chine*, Paris: Gallimard, 1996

Xiao Dengfu, *Daojiao shuyi yu mijiao dianji* (Daoist Ritual Practices and Textual Sources of Esoteric Buddhism), Taipei: Xinwenfeng, 1993

Xiao Dengfu, *Daojiao yu mizong* (Daoism and Esoteric Buddhism), Taipei: Xinwenfeng, 1993

Manuscript Production: Buddhist

In accord with ancient Indian religious custom, the utterances of the Buddha were preserved by trained monks solely in an oral format throughout the initial phase of Buddhist history. However, a Sinhalese Theravāda chronicle, the *Mahāvaṃsa*, relates that during the reign of king Vaṭṭagāmāni (29–17 B.C.) almost 400 years after the death of the Buddha, dissension in the monastic order led to an assembly of 500 senior monks at the Ālokavihāra in Sri Lanka, where, "in order that the true doctrine might endure, they wrote it [the words of the Buddha] down in books." These first written texts, inscribed in Pāli on golden plates, were subsequently deposited in the Mahāvihāra monastery at Anurādhapura, becoming the basis for all later recensions. This tradition fits our knowledge of the period quite well, for, with the exception of ancient Indus valley script, writing in India (e.g., the edicts of Aśoka [c. 268–233 B.C.] and coins from the second century B.C.) pre-date the assembly by only a relatively short period. Writing on metals is also well attested around the time. For example, the original edition of the *Mahāvibhāsā*, a Buddhist Sarvāstivāda philosophical work composed around A.D.100 following a council sponsored by Kaniṣka, is said to have been inscribed on copper plates.

Prepared leaves (*pattra*) of various palms, notably the talipot (*Corypha umbraculifera*) and the palmyra (*Borassus flabellifer*), were the first widely disseminated writing materials among Buddhists in South India and Sri Lanka. Indeed they are still occasionally used today in southern and Southeast Asian countries for the transcription of sacred texts. The talipot furnishes a very resilient and uniform writing surface, but it seems to have been gradually superseded by the palmyra. The latter is certainly less tender and will survive in more northerly climates. In addition it has a variety of other uses, most notably in the production of toddy (*tāḍī*), an alcoholic beverage.

The young leaves at the top of the palm were harvested when young and just about to unfurl. They were blanched in boiling water, dried, and polished on both sides. Any piece up to about 20 feet in length was cut into rectangular strips of about three by 10 to 30 inches. The smaller sizes were employed for the copying of short texts, whereas the longer ones suited more extensive compositions. Both sides of the leaf were written on. In southern Asia the characters were inscribed with a sharp stylus, a wash of ink (usually of carbon) being then brushed over and the excess sanded off. However, in North India and central Asia characters were directly applied in ink by a thin brush. The surface of the leaf was regularly oiled to keep it pliable and to dispel insects, and the volume was generally bound by threading a cord (*sūtra* or *nāḍī*) through one or more holes punched near the middle of the leaves. The finished book, called a *pustaka* (Sanskrit) or *pothī* (Hindi), was held between wooden covers (*paṭa*) of roughly the same rectangular shape. Given the fact that most natural materials survive a surprisingly short time in the climatic conditions of monsoon Asia (such artifacts cannot be expected to last more than 200 years), only a few wooden covers have come down to us from ancient times.

The emergence of Mahāyāna Buddhism in the early first millennium A.D. seems to have accelerated the copying of sacred writings (sūtras), not least because it had few ordained monks able to sustain an oral tradition. Many of its early texts praised the copyist's art as highly meritorious, the *Perfection of Wisdom Sūtra in Eight Thousand Lines* stating, "If a good man or woman cannot receive and keep the . . . [sūtra], read and recite it, or practice as it preaches, he or she should copy it." Thus, we should not assume that such scribal work was uniquely the preserve of the ordained monk.

Mahāyāna texts were certainly available in central Asia by the middle of the third century, although when the Chinese pilgrim Faxian visited northwestern India in the late fourth century, he found no written texts. Memorization and the oral tradition must still have been the order of the day in this region.

In those parts of Buddhist Asia that have cooler climates, such as northwestern India and central Asia, birch bark, cloth, animal hides, and occasionally copper plates were also employed for the transcription of sacred literature. It seems that originally the Sogdians and Uygurs used imported palm leaves but switched to the paper scroll, probably adopted from China, toward the end of the third century. The earliest extant central Asian manuscript, found at Kizil and containing fragments of the work of Aśvaghoṣa, dates from the second century A.D., demonstrating how much longer a manuscript can survive in a fresher, drier environment.

An important collection of documents was found in 1931 at Gilgit in northern Kashmir by Sir Aurel Stein, consisting mainly of Buddhist texts on birch bark, palm leaves, and paper dating from the sixth to the tenth century. Interestingly very little evidence exists of illumination in these manuscripts, with the exception of the odd stylized lotus or roundel. However, from the ninth century, especially in texts translated into Khotanese and in those that circulated among the Uygurs, we find Buddha images appearing in the margins of a few texts. The color red also seems to have been introduced for decorative purposes at about this time. The lack of illumination in early North Indian and central Asian manuscripts seems mainly due to the difficulty of rendering a colored image on birch bark. However, illuminated palm leaf manuscripts are also uncommon in these areas before the 11th century. The occurrence of manuscript illumination on the Indian subcontinent from the late tenth century is probably related to the rise of Tantrism, especially in the monasteries of Nepal and eastern India. The oldest Tibetan texts, representing the period of the first diffusion of the Buddhist doctrine (seventh to ninth century), were scrolls of yellow paper, probably made under Chinese influence. However, from the tenth century the Indian *pustaka* style came into fashion in Tibet, although the paper strips were cut considerably larger than their palm-leaf counterparts. Such texts are often illuminated with images of Indian and Tibetan masters or Tantric deities.

In all regions of Buddhist Asia, with the exception of the south and southeast, which did not succumb until the 19th century, traditional materials were eventually eclipsed by the use of paper, which, although used by the Chinese from the second century, was brought to India from Europe by the Muslim colonists of the 13th century. Nevertheless the traditional shape and binding of manuscript scriptures, deriving from the natural form of palm leaves, was retained, and modern Western book forms are a largely modern phenomenon.

Tradition holds that the earliest Indic texts arrived in China during the late Han period (c. 70). However, the first extant translations of Buddhist writings into Chinese were probably made by An Shigao (d. c. 170) and Lokakṣema (147–185). The first complete Chinese canon (*tripiṭaka*) was compiled sometime in the fourth century. From then on it became fashionable for rulers and wealthy people to donate painstakingly copied collections of Buddhist scriptures to temples. As more texts were translated from central Asian and Indian sources, these collections grew in size. For example, the *Kaiyuan Era Buddhist Catalogue*, compiled by Chih-sheng in 730, lists 1,076 sūtras in 5,048 fascicles. An unusual tradition of copying sūtras with ink made from one's own blood (watered down and usually taken from the tongue) is well attested in the Tiantai tradition and seems to have survived in China until the early 20th century.

Although in the beginning Chinese manuscripts were written to no set form, in time the practice of copying texts in lines of 17 characters became the norm. As a result the paper scroll declined in significance, and by the Tang period (618–906) two kinds of Buddhist manuscript form had evolved: the "Sanskrit clamped binding" (*fan jia zhuang*), based on Indic models and basically unsuited to developing traditions of Chinese orthography, and the "Sūtra folded binding" (*jing zhe zhuang*), which was basically a rectangular, bound book constructed from a concertinaed paper scroll. The first examples of illustration in Chinese Buddhists texts also date from the mid-Tang.

From the Song period (960–1126), printing from wooden blocks, often made from plum or pear, began to make an appearance on a large scale, although this did not stop the production of handwritten texts, especially given the high aesthetic and spiritual emphasis placed on calligraphy in eastern Asian cultures. Printing blocks were prepared by writing the text on thin paper and transferring this upside down to the block, where it was held in place by a glue of rice flour. The wood around the characters was then removed to a depth of a fifth of an inch or so. The printing process was completed by a careful laying of paper on the inked block.

A Chinese *Diamond Sūtra* scroll dated 868 and found in caves at Dunhuang, Gansu province, now in the British Library, was regarded as the oldest printed book in the world until 1966, when a copy of the *Dhāraṇī Sūtra* printed from wooden blocks and produced sometime before 751 was discovered at Pulguk Temple near Kyongju, Korea. Korean Buddhists also lay claim to having printed the first book with moveable type, *Selections from Sermons by Buddhist Masters*, dated 1377 and produced at Hungdok Temple in northern Ch'ungch'ong province. The first Japanese woodblock-printed text is the *One Million Pagoda Buddhist Dhāraṇī*, which was mass produced and enshrined in portable miniature pagodas during the reign of Emperor Shōtoku (764–770). From the end of the 11th century, the six great temples of Nara, such as the Tōdaiji, had become major printing concerns.

One of the earliest examples of Japanese calligraphy is a scroll containing the *Commentary on the Lotus Sūtra*, dated around 609 to 615. Sūtra copying (*shakyō*) slowly became part of the Japanese state bureaucracy with government offices dedicated to this task, such as the Kawaradera in Nara established by Emperor Temmu (r. 673–686). The earliest of these texts, also known as *shakyō*, consisted of scrolls made by pasting together individual pieces of paper on the old Chinese model. Copyists (*kyōsei*) were appointed on the basis of an examination system in which calligraphy and knowledge of Chinese characters were assessed. During the reign of Emperor Shōmu in the eighth century, 24 sets of the Buddhist Canon, each containing 5,048 volumes, were produced under the system. The increase in sūtra production during this period probably had political overtones, as it was explicitly connected to the official "pacifying and protecting the state" (*chingo kokka*) ideology.

In eighth-century Japan the copying of texts by private individuals, often on blue paper with ink containing powdered gold or silver, became popular, a practice probably imported from China. However, the regular paper for these purposes, made from either hemp or mulberry, was stained with a light yellow-brown dye that possessed insecticidal properties. In the Heian period (794–1185), official scriptoria were abandoned, and most major works of calligraphy at this time are ascribed to famous religious personages, such as Saichō (767–822) and Kūkai (774–835). Another major renewal in copying, probably associated with the rise of the cult of the *Lotus Sūtra*, occurred in the tenth century. The copying of the entire Tripiṭaka in one day became another specifically Japanese novelty. Thus, 13,315 monks of the Saishō-shitennō-in in Kyoto completed the task in the presence of Emperor Gotoba in a single day in 1211. In a related development the 12th-century courtier Fujiwara no Sadanobu is reported to have copied the entire Buddhist Canon single-handed (*ippitsu issaikyō*).

The earliest extant Pāli palm-leaf manuscript is a fragment of the Theravāda Vinaya preserved in the Singh Darbar, Kathmandu, dating from the eighth to the ninth century. However, older Pāli texts engraved on stone, gold, or silver have been found in India and Southeast Asia. One of the oldest of these, a Burmese gold-leaf votive manuscript of 20 leaves incised with extracts from the Vinaya and Abhidhamma in Telugu-Canarese script of South India, dates from the Pyu period (fifth century). All modern editions of Pāli texts are ultimately based on manuscripts that have been repeatedly copied in the southern and Southeast Asian Theravāda heartlands, although the continuous production of such complete-text manuscripts can be traced back only to the late 15th century. Nevertheless it is known that a complete set of the Tripiṭaka, costing almost twice the sum of construction of a typical pagoda, was copied in 1293 during the Burmese Pagan period. Burmese lay donors were especially astute in this regard, for some included in their wills monies for the planting of palm trees for the production of writing materials and the provision of slaves for their maintenance. Burmese scribes were generally itinerant laymen who lived in the monastery for the duration of their labors. Laws promulgated by the kings of the country ensured that their spelling mistakes and drunkenness were rigorously punished. Decoration of the resulting manuscripts was confined mainly to gilding on the edges of the leaves. The introduction of the printing press by missionaries in 1776 led to the gradual demise of palm-leaf books in Burma. However, after the Fifth Buddhist Council at Mandalay in 1871, King Mindon had the definitive text of the Pāli Buddhist scriptures carved onto 729 stelae, referred to by one commentator as the "biggest Bible in the world," and erected at Kuthodaw (Royal Merit) pagoda, where they can still be viewed.

IAN HARRIS

See also Anurādhapura, Sri Lanka; Discourses (Suttas): Theravāda; Nālandā, India; Sri Lanka: History

Further Reading

Fraser-Lu, Sylvia, *Burmese Crafts; Past and Present*, Kuala Lumpur and New York: Oxford University Press, 1994
Losty, Jeremiah P., *The Art of the Book in India*, London: British Library, 1982
Mizuno, Kogen, *Kyoten: Sono Seiritsu To Tenkai*, Tokyo: Kosei, 1980; as *Buddhist Sutras, Origin, Development, Transmission*, Tokyo: Kosei, 1982

Manuscript Production: Christian

"[Antony] so closely listened to what he heard read that he missed nothing and remembered everything, because of this memory he had no need of books" (Athanasius, *Vita* 3). Implicit in this statement is that every monk less holy than Antony did need books. Here the recurring monastic theme of "unlearned wisdom" is ironically recorded in writing – itself the presupposition of learning. Moreover books (i.e., the Scriptures) are at the heart of monastic reflection, prayer, and study. Monks needed books for the liturgy, as did all Christians, but especially for the word-based Liturgy of the Office. The identity of the monastery was generated through rules, maxims, and the material on monastic heroes (lives, conferences, and admonitions), and even in unscholarly houses these were read as part of the basic routine (e.g., Benedict's *Regula* 42). The monastery as a school of holiness was of necessity a basic school and so needed books, from basic texts on reading and spelling to works for teaching the next generation of theologians. For example, Cassiodorus' (485/90–c. 580) massive annotated bibliography for monastic

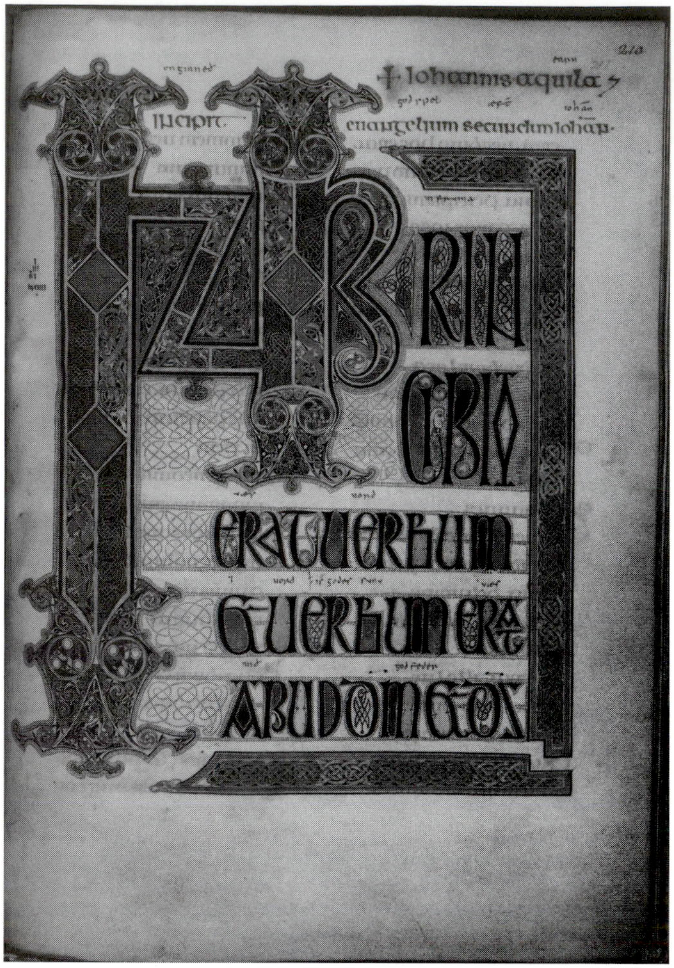

Eadfrith, initial page to St. John's Gospel, Lindisfarne Gospels, c. 698. The book was produced to mark the raising of St. Cuthbert's relics to the altar at Lindisfarne.
Photo by permission of the British Library, Cotton MS Nero D.iv, F.211.

education lists hundreds of works and became a desiderata list for monastic librarians. A monastery without a library became inconceivable, and building it up and caring for it were important tasks. Although we readily see this in the case of European medieval libraries (either extant, e.g., St. Gallen, or through catalogs that allow us to see what was valued), it was a trait present from the beginning. The Nag Hammadi library (probably mid–fourth century) belonged to a Pachomian-type community in Egypt, and the fourth-century Codex Alexandrinus (one of the most important parchment witnesses to the Christian scriptures) comes from St. Catherine's at Mount Sinai. Such attention to writings presupposed equal attention to their acquisition, an activity that involved the individual production, by hand, of each copy.

In the desert books were made mainly from papyrus (vegetable fibers pressed to make a paperlike material), although as the Codex Alexandrinus shows, parchment (skins prepared as a writing surface and virtually indestructible) was also used, probably for high-status texts where there was a demand for preservation and deluxe presentation. Parchment would have been produced commercially and then acquired by the monks. Moving northward papyrus gave way to parchment. Papyrus not only had to be imported from overseas (and was imported while Roman trading links continued) but proved unstable there because of its poor resistance to dampness. Moreover parchment, once the technology had been mastered, could be produced locally for each monastery, giving any with pasture for sheep or goats almost complete control over the whole cycle of book production. For example, seventh-century Iona enjoyed ready access to skins and cultivated a desire to build up the library (which supplied exemplars for copying) and to produce books for missionary work; in addition, monks wrote new works for a monastic audience.

In early monasteries book production does not appear to have been a specialist activity of a few monks but rather a task engaged in by many in accord with monastic ideals. Thus, Palladius (c. 364–420/30) refers to this on several occasions as work suited to monks, and he calls copying the Scriptures a particular form of asceticism (*Historia Lausiaca* 13.1). In his description of a Pachomian monastery, he mentions that the monks knew the Scriptures by heart, but still he notes "the copyist" among the skills (alongside, e.g., bakers, weavers, and shoemakers) that were needed in the community (32.12). One copyist was still at this work at the age of 80 (45.3), while he notes that his own

Scriptorium, Cistercian Abbey of Fontenay (Côte d'Or), 12th century.
Photo courtesy of Caroline Rose/CNMHS

teacher, the great monastic theorist Evagrius Ponticus (346–399) earned his food by copying and was famed for this skill. Although we associate ancient writing with men, it is noteworthy that Melania the Younger (383–439) not only was a great student of Scripture but also produced extracts that she distributed to encourage meditation. This approach esteemed the copying of texts as an activity in which the spiritual and material realms intermingled. It ensured that book production could be seen not only as a monastic necessity but, insofar as it made the Word known or enabled the liturgy to be performed, as a saintly one. Adomnán's *Vita Columbae* (c. 700) provides a good example of a founder-saint who produced books throughout his life: Columba (521–597) is called to check a book made by another monk for errors (which he can do miraculously) (1.23); is interrupted while working (2.29); produced many books, including psalters and hymnals for the Office (2.8–9); and continued work until just before death (3.23). His book production becomes symbolic of his life and a locus where his holy power resides.

After monasticism became an established part of Christian life, the monastery became a center of learning and a place for its preservation. Books were central, and the scriptorium (the place for copying them) became an integral part of the monastery (as shown in the ideal monastery plan from St. Gallen). Most scriptoria developed their own specific styles, and today many manuscripts' origins can be identified by the habits of the scriptorium they exhibit. Some were famous for deluxe works (e.g., Echternach) and others for accuracy (e.g., St. Gallen), whereas others emphasized the acquisition of works for copying, employing an intermonastery loan system (e.g., Corbie). In certain places book production became an important, sophisticated industry, and this did much to fuel the revival of learning in the ninth century. Although most of these books were plain texts, some of them, especially gospel books, are among the supreme artworks that have survived.

The rise of the cathedral schools shifted the focus of book production into the cities. When in the 15th century book production was a favored labor for the Brethren of the Common Life, it was no longer integral to their spirituality, as it had been in monasteries, but simply a job extrinsic to their devotions. Since printing, there has been another monastic involvement with earlier books through paleography: the greatest 17th-century historians, Jean Mabillon (1632–1707) and Bernard de Montfaucon (1655–1741), were Benedictines.

THOMAS O'LOUGHLIN

See also Alcuin; Antony, St.; Archives, Western Christian; Bede, St.; Columba, St.; Echternach, Luxembourg; Evagrius Ponticus; Humanism, Christian; Libraries: Eastern Christian; Libraries: Western Christian; Maurists; Origins: Eastern Christian; Visual Arts, Western Christian: Book Arts before the Renaissance

Further Reading

Becker, Gustav, *Catalogi Bibliothecarum Antiqui*, Bonn: Cohen, 1885

Bischoff, Bernhard, *Latin Palaeography: Antiquity and the Middle Ages*, translated by Dáibhí Ó Cróinín and David Ganz, Cambridge and New York: Cambridge University Press, 1990

Ganz, David, "The Preconditions for Caroline Minuscule," *Viator* 18 (1987)

Jones, Leslie W., "The Scriptorium at Corbie: I. The Library," *Speculum* 22 (1947)

Jones, Leslie W., "The Scriptorium at Corbie: II. The Script and the Problems," *Speculum* 22 (1947)

McDonald, Paul, "The Maurist Edition of Saint Augustine," *American Benedictine Review* 31 (1980)

McGurk, Patrick, *Latin Gospel Books from AD 400 to AD 800*, Paris: Éditions "Érasme," 1961

Metzger, Bruce M., *Manuscripts of the Greek Bible: An Introduction to Palaeography*, New York: Oxford University Press, 1981

O'Donnell, James J., *Cassiodorus*, Berkeley: University of California Press, 1979

O'Loughlin, Thomas, "The Library of Iona in the Late Seventh Century: The Evidence from Adomnán's *De Locis Sanctis*," *Ériu* 45 (1994)

Quain, Edwin A., "Palaeography, Manuscripts and Librarians," *American Benedictine Review* 26 (1975)

Marathon Monks

Among all Buddhist monastic practices, perhaps the most difficult and challenging asceticism is found among the Tendai monks, a Japanese Buddhist school founded in 788 by Saichō (767–822) at Mount Hiei in Shiga prefecture, Japan. Within the Tendai school, the *sennichi kaihōgyō* (the austerity of encircling the mountain for thousand days) is the preeminent monastic practice. It is a spiritual struggle between life and death.

Considering the ever-growing modernity of Japanese lifestyle and Buddhist religiosity, the very continuity of this asceticism from the time of Ennin (794–864) to the present incumbent at the head temple of Tendai school, Enryakuji, is rather remarkable. For understanding hidden features in Japanese Buddhist monasticism, this austerity is extremely valuable because it gives a completely different impression of Japanese Buddhism and religious devotion.

Kaihōgyō (the austerity of encircling the mountain) has become a standard expression in Japanese Buddhism to identify Tendai asceticism. In this religious practice the ascetic monk visits the 260 assigned sacred places on Mount Hiei and recites sūtras and mantras while performing esoteric mudras. The practitioner leads a very simple and austere life. He takes only two meals, consisting of noodles, potatoes, and tofu, and wears a white robe (the dress of the dead), a straw hat, and straw sandals. When he walks at night, he holds a lantern in his left hand while holding a rosary and a walking stick in his right hand. The ascetic starts his daily walking at 1:00 a.m. and finishes around 10:00 a.m. His pilgrimage becomes a combination of walking and running, praying and bowing, constituting a form of religious marathon. Once he begins his ordeal, neither in injury nor in sickness can he stop his religious commitment, even if it causes his death. This austerity lasts for seven years. In the first three years, the ascetic walks 100 days at a time, covering each day a circuit of more than 18 miles. In the fourth and fifth years, he covers the same route for 200 days. When the ascetic has completed successfully 700 days, he reaches a turning point in his spiritual journey. He is obligated to spend a nine-day retreat (*dōiri*) at Myōdō. During this retreat he neither sleeps, lies down, eats, nor drinks; he is constantly busy with reciting sūtras and chanting invocations to Fudō-myō-ō (Immobile One), a form of Dainich. Daily he departs Myōdō only once in the midnight to fetch water for use as an offering. This retreat demands extraordinary endurance. Next comes the *sekizan kugyō,* which includes walking 37 miles daily for about 15 hours for 100 days. In the final year, for 100 days, the ascetic walks 52 miles to Kyoto city. By encircling the mountain for 1,000 days, the ascetic completes walking more than 23,800 miles and thereby becomes a living Buddha (*ikibotoke*). A few such recent individuals are Utsumi Shunshō (1974–1979), Sakai Yūsai (1975–1987), and Mitsunāga Kakudō (1980–1990).

MAHINDA DEEGALLE

See also Asceticism: Buddhist Perspectives; Buddhist Schools/ Traditions: Japan; Ennin; Japan; Mount Hiei, Japan; Mountain Monasteries, Buddhist; Tiantai/Tendai: Japan

Further Reading

Ajari . . . yama no michi: Les mille jours ou la marche eternelle d'Ajari, a documentary film by Daniel Moreau, Paris: Dia Film Productions, 1999
Hagami, Shōchō, *Kaihōgyō no kokoro: Wagadōshin*, Tokyo: Shunjūsha, 1997
Hayashi, Takashi, and Mamoru Murakami, *Hokurei no hito: Hieizan sennichi kaihōgyōja Utsumi Shunshō*, Tokyo: Kōsei Shuppansha, 1983
Kikuchi, Tōta, and Shōsuke Nogi, *Nisennichi kaihōgyō: Daiajari Sakai Yūsai no sekai*, Tokyo: Kōsei Shuppansha, 1987
Mitsunāga, Kakudō, *Sennichi kaihōgyō*, Tokyo: Shunjūsha, 1996
Mitsunāga, Kakudō, *Kaihōgyō ima hito wa dō ikitara yoika*, Tokyo: Shunjūsha, 1998
Nagāo, Saburō, *Ikibotoke ni natta ochikobore: Sakai Yūsai Daiajari no nisennichi kaihōgyō*, Tokyo: Kōdansha, 1988
Stevens, John, *Marathon Monks of Mount Hiei*, Boston: Shambhala, 1988

Maria Laach, Germany

The Abbey of Maria Laach (St. Mary's Abbey on the Lake) in the Rheinland was founded in 1093 by Count Palatine Henry II of the House of Luxemburg-Salm and his consort, Adelheid of Orlamünde. The first monks came from the Abbey of St. Maximin in Trier and were joined later by a group from Affligem in Brabant. The impressive Rhenish Romanesque abbey church, begun within the first two years of the foundation, was consecrated by Bishop Hillin of Trier in 1156 during the tenure of Abbot Fulbert (1152–1177).

As a result of the French Revolution, the monastery was suppressed on 2 August 1802. The property was acquired by the Jesuits in 1862 for the major seminary of their German province. The Jesuits founded the periodical *Stimmen aus Maria Laach* in 1871 (since 1915 *Stimmen der Zeit*) and developed the neo-Scholastic *Philosophia Lacensis*. During the Kulturkampf the Jesuits themselves were forced to leave Maria Laach in December 1872.

Maria Laach was refounded as a Benedictine monastery by the monks of Beuron on 25 November 1892 after they had acquired the property from the Jesuits. At the beginning of the 20th century, Maria Laach entered on an especially auspicious and significant period of its history. The monastery enjoyed the patronage of Emperor Wilhelm II (1890–1918); the first abbot after the refoundation, Willibrord Benzler (1893–1901), was named bishop of Metz; and his successor, Fidelis von Stotzingen (1901–1913), was elected abbot primate of the entire Benedictine Confederation and abbot of the Primatial Abbey of St. Anselm in Rome (1913–1947).

However, the election of Abbot Ildefons Herwegen (1913–1946) marked the most significant turning point in history of Maria Laach in the 20th century. From the very beginning of his abbacy, Herwegen focused the entire activity of the monks of Maria Laach on the renewal of the Christian life through the Church's liturgy. To do so required first a solid scholarly foundation that gave birth to various liturgical periodicals: *Liturgiegeschichtliche Quellen* (1918–1927) and *Liturgiegeschichtliche Forschungen* (1919–1927), later *Liturgiegeschichtliche Quellen und Forschungen* (1928–1939); *Ecclesia Orans* (1918–1939); and *Jahrbuch für Liturgiewissenschaft* (1921–1941), later *Archiv für Liturgiewissenschaft* (1950–).

Three names characterize the fruitfulness of those years: Abbot Herwegen and his explanations of the liturgy as the objective basis on which to build Benedictine life; Kunibert Mohlberg (1878–1963), with his scholarly sources and research; and Odo Casel (1886–1948), whose thesis of the *Mysteriengegenwart* (presence of the mysteries) eventually acquired decisive significance. The dialogue Mass (with the altar facing the people), homily, and offertory procession was celebrated in the crypt of the abbey church beginning in 1921 and was the work of Albert Hammenstede, novice master, and of Simon Stricker, instructor of the lay brothers. In 1931 Abbot Herwegen founded at Maria Laach an academy for liturgical and monastic studies that trained such notable liturgists as Godfrey Diekmann, Balthasar Fischer, and Salvatore Marsili. The most significant publications from this period are Odo Casel's *Das christliche Kultmysterium* (1932; *The Mystery of Christian Worship*), Ildefons Herwegen's *Sinn und Geist der Benediktinerregel* (1944; The Meaning and Spirit of the Rule of Benedict), and Viktor Warnach's *Agape: Die Liebe als Grundmotiv der neutestamentlichen Theologie* (1951; Agape: Love as the Fundamental Theme of New Testament Theology).

In 1948, after the death of Herwegen, Abbot Basilius Ebel founded the Abt-Herwegen-Institut für liturgische und monastische Forschung (the Abbot Herwegen Institute for Liturgical and Monastic Research) to consolidate the work of the monks of Maria Laach. The Abt-Herwegen Institut published the series *Liturgie und Mönchtum* from 1948 to 1968 and continues the publication of *Beiträge zur Geschichte des alten Mönchtums und des Benediktinertums* (1912–). In 1999 the community numbered 65 monks, 32 of whom are priests.

Maria Laach, the abbey on the lake, is surrounded by fields and forests crisscrossed by hiking paths. The monastery welcomes pilgrims to the Mass and the Divine Office and provides them with opportunities for confession, spiritual direction, and retreats. The abbey offers all visitors an introduction to Maria Laach through a video in major European languages and a bookshop that specializes in art and religious articles.

KURT BELSOLE, O.S.B.

See also Abbot Primate, Benedictine; Architecture: Western Christian Monasteries; Beuron, Germany; Casel, Odo; Congregations, Benedictine; Guéranger, Prosper; Liturgical Movement 1830–1980; Liturgy: Western Christian

Further Reading

Bolger, Theodor, *Maria Laach Abbey*, 4th edition, translated by Margaret Senft-Howie and Radbert Kohlhaas, Munich: Schnell and Steiner, 1970

Casel, Odo, *The Mystery of Christian Worship and Other Writings*, edited by Burkhard Neunheuser, translated by J.T. Hale, with a preface by Charles Davis, Westminster, Maryland: Newman Press, 1962

Hammenstede, Albert, *Erinnerungen eines Laacher Mönches: Autobiographische Aufzeichnungen*, Benedictinerabtei Maria Laach: Maria Laach, 1996

Herwegen, Ildefons, *Sinn und Geist der Benediktinerregel*, Einsiedeln, Switzerland: Benzinger, 1944

Neunheuser, Burkhard, "Maria Laach Abbey: A Double Jubilee 1093–1993; 1892–1992," *Ecclesia Orans* 10 (1993)

Santagada, Osvaldo, "Dom Odo Casel," *Archiv für Liturgiewissenschaft* 10:1 (1967) (contains a complete bibliography of Casel)

Severus, Emmanuel von, "Maria Laach in neun Jahrhunderten (1093–1156–1956)," in *Enkainia: Gesammelte Arbeiten zum 800jährigen Weihegedächtnis der Abteikirche Maria Laach am 24. August 1956*, edited by Hilarius Emonds, Düsseldorf: Patmos-Verlag, 1956

Severus, Emmanuel von, "Die Wiederbesiedlung Maria Laachs durch die Benediktiner im Jahre 1892," in *Benedikt und Ignatius: Maria Laach als Collegium maximum der Gesellschaft Jesu 1863, 1872, 1892*, edited by Theodor Bolger, Maria Laach: Verlag Ars Liturgica, 1963

Severus, Emmanuel von, editor, *Ecclesia Lacensis*, Münster, Westphalia: Aschendorff, 1993

Warnach, Viktor, *Agape: Die Liebe als Grundmotiv der neutestamentlichen Theologie*, Düsseldorf: Patmos-Verlag, 1951

Marmion, Columba 1858–1923

Irish Benedictine theologian and leader of the Liturgical Movement

Dom Columba Marmion was born in Dublin, Ireland, on 1 April 1858. He was baptized Joseph, a name by which he was known for the first 28 years of his life. He changed his name to Columba when he entered the Benedictine abbey of Maredsous, Belgium, in November 1886. His father, William Marmion, whose family had lived in Ireland since the 13th century, was a successful businessman. His mother, Herminie Cordier, was a French woman, and had come to Ireland to learn English, when she met her future husband. They had nine children in all, Joseph being the third youngest.

Marmion received his elementary education with the Augustinian Fathers of John's Lane, Dublin. In 1869 he went to Belvedere College, run by the Jesuits. At the end of his secondary education, he successfully passed a scholarship examination, entitling him to a place in Holy Cross College, Clonliffe, the Dublin diocesan seminary. He spent the next five years studying philosophy and theology and was then sent to Rome to complete his priestly studies. The first real urgings toward a monastic life came to him during a visit to Monte Cassino in September 1880. As he said afterward to a friend, "It was in Monte Cassino that I first felt the call to the monastic life." However, he was already committed at this time to becoming a diocesan priest in Dublin and was ordained in Rome on 16 June 1881 at the hands of Monsignor Tobias Kirby, rector of the Irish College, Rome.

On his way back to Ireland from Rome in August 1881, Marmion visited the newly built Abbey of Maredsous, near Namur, in Belgium. He was greatly impressed by his reception there and by the atmosphere of this Benedictine monastery. He spent one year as a curate in Dundrum Parish (September 1881 to September 1882), County Dublin, and four years as professor of philosophy in Clonliffe College, Dublin. Throughout these five years he repeatedly asked his archbishop's permission to enter the Abbey of Maredsous, as no Benedictine monasteries existed in Ireland at this time. Finally, in 1885, Archbishop William Walsh gave Marmion the necessary permission. A year later, in November 1886, he entered Maredsous as a novice.

His first years as a monk in a Belgian monastery were not easy, but he persevered and soon built up for himself a reputation as a man of God and a man of prayer. In 1899 he was sent from Maredsous to a new Benedictine foundation in Louvain, called Mont-César. He remained in Louvain for the next ten years as prior and professor of theology. During these Louvain years he deepened his understanding of the monastic life and was looked on as an ideal monk. He summarized his main aim in life as follows: To bring people to God and to bring God to people. He was one of the first to use the expression the "Liturgical Movement" and believed that the Mass and the sacraments should be made more accessible to laity. He was also very interested in the sacred Scriptures, having made a special study of the Psalms and Epistles of St. Paul. He found his monastic life to be a source of great inner personal richness, above all in the daily recitation of the Divine Office, the *lectio divina* (holy reading), and the practice of the Rule of St. Benedict.

In 1909 he was elected the third abbot of Maredsous. By this time he had become well known as a preacher of retreats to religious men and women in Belgium, France, England, and Ireland. When World War I broke out in 1914, much of Belgium, including the area around Maredsous, was occupied by the Germans. Marmion took some of his younger monks to Ireland and found asylum for them at Edermine, County Wexford. He remained in Ireland until mid-1916, when he returned to Maredsous.

Wishing to bring his message of monastic living to a wider audience, between 1917 and 1922 he produced three volumes of spiritual writings: *Le Christ, vie de l'âme* (*Christ, the Life of the Soul*), *Le Christ dans ses mystères* (*Christ in His Mysteries*), and *Le Christ, idéal du moine* (*Christ, the Ideal of the Monk*). These have since been recognized as spiritual classics and translated into 15 languages, including Korean and Japanese. He has been called "the Doctor of Divine Adoption." His writings exerted considerable influence on the Fathers of the Second Vatican Council (1962–1965), especially in drawing up the Constitution on the Sacred Liturgy.

After World War I, with anti-German feeling still running high in Belgium, the Abbey of Maredsous could no longer remain in the German Confederation of Benedictine monasteries. Marmion was chosen to set in motion the process of separation from the Beuronese (German) Congregation. Within a few years he had established the Belgian Congregation, now known as the Congregation of the Annunciation.

Possibly the most influential Irish monastic of the 20th century, Marmion died in Maredsous after a short illness on 30 January 1923, in his 65th year. Soon after his death innumerable petitions were received in Maredsous, requesting that the cause for his beatification be introduced in Rome. Thousands of letters gave evidence of favors obtained through his intercession. However, it was only in 1957 that the bishop of Namur began the diocesan enquiry, when some 47 people who had known Marmion were asked to give their opinions on his character and holiness of life. On 27 March 1962 the canonical proceedings for his beatification were opened in Rome, and Marmion was declared to be worthy of the title Servant of God. The process of beatification is a lengthy one, requiring the production of several volumes of evidence. It was only on 28 June 1999 that Marmion was declared venerable, in a ceremony in the Vatican, presided over by Pope John Paul II. All is now on course for his beatification on 3 September 2000, the Jubilee Year.

MARK TIERNEY, O.S.B.

See also Belgium; Ireland: History; Lectio Divina; Liturgical Movement 1830–1980; Liturgy: Western Christian; Monte Cassino, Italy

Biography

Born in Dublin, the Irish Benedictine lived from 1886 at abbeys in Belgium, first at Maredsous from 1886 to 1899, then as prior of Mont-César, Louvain, from 1899 to 1909, and finally as abbot of Maredsous from 1909 until his death in 1923. From 1914 to 1916 he took refuge from World War I in Ireland, and after the war negotiated the separation of Maredsous from the (German) Congregation of Beuron. A pioneer of the Liturgical Movement (a phrase which he helped to circulate), Columba Marmion is scheduled to be canonized in the year 2000.

Major Works

Le Christ, vie de l'âme, 1918; as *Christ, the Life of the Soul*, translated by a nun of Tyburn Convent, 9th edition, 1940
Le Christ dans ses mystères, 1919; as *Christ in His Mysteries*, translated by Mother M. St. Thomas, 8th edition, 1939
Le Christ, idéal du moine, 1922; as *Christ, the Ideal of the Monk*, translated by a nun of Tyburn Convent, 8th edition, 1964
Spiritual Writings, edited by P. Lethielleux and Abbey Maredsous, 1998

Further Reading

Thibaut, Raymond, *Abbot Columba Marmion: A Master of the Spiritual Life, 1858–1923*, translated by Mother Mary St. Thomas, London: Sands, and St. Louis, Missouri: Herder, 1932
Tierney, Mark, *Dom Columba Marmion: A Biography*, Dublin: Columba Press, 1994

Maronites

The ancient Roman province of Syria Secunda, a region that makes up modern Lebanon and central Syria, was the homeland of many ascetics during the fourth and fifth centuries. One of these ascetics, named Maron, is the spiritual father of the Maronite Church. After the holy man's death, his disciples transferred Maron's body to a site near Apameia on the Orontes River, the capital of Syria Secunda. Here they built a tomb and founded a monastery, known as Bait-Maroun ("The House of Maron"). The Maronite tradition claims direct descent from the monks who ministered to the men and women of the region.

By the beginning of the seventh century, several monasteries had been dedicated to St. Maron in the region of Syria Secunda. Then a catastrophic event occurred. A Persian invasion swept over the region, and from 609 to 628, during the Persian occupation, every monastery became a tempting goal for looting, and the orderly life that monasticism requires disappeared. The disaster to monastic life was remedied when the Byzantine Emperor Heraklios (610–641) reclaimed Syria for Constantinople. Critics of the Maronite view of events claim that around this time the Maronites migrated into Syria from the southern Arabian Peninsula and joined themselves to the Christians, who had allied themselves with the monks of St. Maron.

Because Heraklios hoped to reconcile the large number of monks who had embraced Monophysitism, a doctrine that held that there was only one nature in Jesus, the emperor tried as best he could to win over the Syrians to a compromise. This was known as monotheletism, the idea that Jesus had only one divine will. The monks of Bait-Maroun and their followers accepted the imperial theology.

The eighth century, after the Muslim Arabs had become masters of Syria Secunda, marks the beginning of a distinct Maronite Church. It is probable that around 745 the abbot of Bait-Maroun, having obtained episcopal consecration, began to assert that he was the legitimate patriarch of Antioch. Later, in the first quarter of the tenth century, Bait-Maroun was abandoned, and the Maronite patriarch went with his monks to the security of Mount Lebanon, where they may have joined an existing community. By residing on the mountain, cut off from the events of the Muslim world, the patriarch could enjoy both spiritual and temporal authority over his community.

Monks who settled on the mountain lived very simple lives of prayer, fasting, total abstinence from meat, and manual labor. Most monasteries were small, containing four to ten people (with a few communities of 30), under the direction of an abbot bearing the title of archimandrite. The monks grew their own food and prepared their own meals with little sense of community; in fact, many adopted the hermetic life. No specific monastic rules needed to be followed, allowing each member to choose those ascetic practices that he felt might bring him closer to God. The monks' only guide were the Scriptures and the writings and examples of the holy men and women who preceded them. Women living the monastic life are first mentioned in 13th-century documents.

In the spring of 1099, the isolation of the Maronite monks came to an end with the arrival of the warriors of the First Crusade. The Maronites welcomed the Latins, for they found allies among them and willingly enlisted in the Western armies. In 1181 their unofficial alliance with the Catholic leadership in Antioch led to full union when the Maronite patriarch swore obedience to the Roman pope.

Rome kept in touch with the Maronites over the following decades through visitations by Dominican and Franciscan friars who toured the villages of Mount Lebanon and enjoyed the hospitality of the monastic communities. Then, from 1289 to 1291, catastrophe struck the Maronite monasteries once again. Egyptian Mamluk armies descended on Mount Lebanon, and not a monastery, church, or fort was saved from destruction.

In 1516 the Ottoman Turks, after a decisive defeat of the Mamluks, became the new rulers of Mount Lebanon. The Ottomans did not try to change the social order in Lebanon. Although the sultan's administration usually gave official letters of appointment (*berats*) to Christian ecclesiastics to confirm them in their office, the Maronite patriarch was not included among them.

Later in the 16th century, Pope Gregory XIII (1572–1585) for the first time sent Jesuits to Mount Lebanon. Their goal was to bring the Maronite Church and its monasteries into conformity with the decisions made at the Council of Trent (1545–1563). In 1695 three Maronites of Aleppo – 'Abd-allah Kar'ali, Jibra'il Hawa, and Yusuf El-Betn – founded a Maronite monastic community that took as its model the structure of the Society of Jesus. A written constitution regulated all the activities of the monks in great detail. The community was to have a father-general, elected for a three-year term, and a council of four assistants. Every four years a general chapter would discuss and vote on common interests. The father-general was to appoint the abbots of the monasteries. Such a centralization of authority was completely foreign to Maronite tradition, but so strong was the Western influence in Lebanon and Syria that novices flocked to the new community.

In 1736 further Latinization of the Maronite Church occurred at a council held at al-Luwayzah monastery. One of the issues addressed was that of the Maronite double monasteries. The double monastery was a custom in the Maronite Church that seems to have begun in the 15th century when men and women of the same family combined their efforts to establish a common residence. Monks and nuns shared the same church for the liturgy, a kitchen, and sometimes the dining room. Rome was not pleased with this arrangement and demanded that monasteries and convents be placed at separate locations. However, the double monasteries did not disappear until more than a century later.

Midway through the 18th century, a dispute broke out that divided the Maronite monastic communities. The traditionalists, drawn from peasant families on the mountain, had little in common with monks coming from urban backgrounds. The traditionalists, known as Baladites, appealed to Rome for a separate organization. In July 1770 Pope Clement XIV (1769–1774) approved a division. Sixty-one monks joined what became known as the Aleppan Maronites, now known as the Maronite Order of Mary; 91 went to the Baladites, who called themselves the Lebanese Order of St. Anthony; and St. Isaiah's monastery, which had kept aloof from the controversy, opted for autonomy under the name of the Maronite Antonines. All three orders continued to follow what was believed to be a rule left by St. Antony (251?–356), the founder of Egyptian monasticism. A small group of hermits and monks of the old order continued to lead a traditional way of life but disappeared during the following decades.

Today Maronite monks and nuns resemble the Catholic religious orders of the West and are actively engaged in education and a variety of public ministries. In 1990 the Vatican issued the *Code of Canons for the Oriental Churches*, a constitution that currently governs the lives of the 700 monks and 900 nuns of the Maronite Church.

CHARLES A. FRAZEE

See also Crusades; Israel/Palestine; Syria; Women's Monasteries: Eastern Christian

Further Reading

Breydy, Michael, *Geschichte der Syro-Arabischen Literatur der Maroniten vom VII. bis XVI. Jahrhundert*, Opladen: Westdeutscher, 1985
Cragg, Kenneth, *The Arab Christian: A History in the Middle East*, London: Mowbray, 1992
Dib, Pierre, *Histoire de l'église maronite*, Beirut: Éditions "La Sagesse," 1962
Frazee, Charles, "The Maronite Middle Ages," *Eastern Churches Review* 10:1–2 (1978)
Leroy, Jules, *Monks and Monasteries of the Near East*, London: Harrap, 1963
Mahfoud, Georges-Joseph, *L'organisation monastique dans l'église maronite: Étude historique*, Beirut: Bibliothèque de l'Université Saint-Espirit, 1967
Moosa, Matti, *The Maronites in History*, Syracuse, New York: Syracuse University Press, 1986
van Leeuwen, Richard, *Notables and Clergy in Mount Lebanon: The Khâzin Sheiks and the Maronite Church (1736–1840)*, Leiden and New York: Brill, 1994

Related Web Site

http://maronites.org/

Martin of Tours, St. c. 315/36–397

Christian soldier, founder of monasteries in France, and bishop of Tours

Born in Pannonia of well-to-do pagan parents and brought up in northern Italy, Martin followed his father into the Roman army. While serving in Gaul he came under the influence of Hilary, bishop of Poitiers, with whom he was to be associated until the latter's death in 367. When Hilary went into exile in 356, Martin left the army and followed him, spending much of the time again in northern Italy, where he crossed swords with the Arian heretics and founded a monastery near Milan. Returning to Gaul in 360, he founded another monastery at Ligugé, near Poitiers, having by this time acquired a reputation as a miracle worker, as one who saw visions and communed with angels and demons, and as a follower of the austere, ascetic monastic tradition of the East. In 371 he became bishop of Tours, where he remained until his death in 397. He defended the city against internal and external threats, founded another monastery on the outskirts at Marmoutier, aggressively confronted paganism, and brought Christianity, together with a rudimentary parochial system, to the surrounding countryside. By the time of his death, his reputation was such that two cities, Tours and Poitiers, quarreled over the right to receive his body. Two thousand monks are said to have attended his funeral, continuing miracles assured his elevation to sainthood, and his cult then began in earnest.

The primary source for Martin's life and career is the *Vita* composed by his friend Sulpicius Severus (c. 360–c. 430) that was written while the saint was still alive and quickly attracted a readership that extended well beyond the boundaries of Gaul. Although claiming to be a factual account, it is clearly the work of a disciple and was criticized as such by many of its contemporaries. It certainly bears the marks of its author's considerable literary and rhetorical skills. Sulpicius later added three Letters, which contain an account of Martin's death and funeral, and some *Dialogues* that deal with his powers as a healer. The *Vita* and *Dialogues* were versified by the fifth-century poet Paulinus of Périgueux and again in the late sixth century by Venantius Fortunatus (c. 530–c. 610). Gregory of Tours (538/39–594), a friend of Venantius, having succeeded to Martin's see, composed the *De Virtutibus S. Martini*, drawing on these earlier works and on accounts of more recent miracles associated with the saint's tomb.

Martin's first monastery, established near Milan in the late 350s, appears to have been unsuccessful, although whether this was simply the result of Arian opposition can be doubted. Perhaps, as has been suggested, his austere rather stern approach was less acceptable here than was the more relaxed, more cultured atmosphere of communities such as that of Paulinus at Nola a generation later. For all their simplicity, these owed more to the traditional otium of the Roman well-to-do than to the self-denying rules and regimes more common in the East. It was to this same rather comfortable Western tradition that the earliest communities in Gaul seem generally to have belonged, established as they were in country houses rather than in localities remote from the centers of population. Therefore, it might have been by way of a compromise that Martin's second monastery, at Ligugé, a few miles south of Poitiers, was set up on one of Hilary's estates in what can only have been a villa. However, excavations on the site suggest that the building may have undergone some extensive alterations at an early stage. How this affected the community's character is not possible to say, but it has been suggested that the villa was rapidly converted to a monastery rather than undergoing a gradual evolution.

The final foundation at Marmoutier, even if we make allowances for the rather overdramatized description of it by Sulpicius, would seem to mark a further stage of development. Again it is within walking distance of the city so that the site, although secluded, is hardly remote, and again archaeological evidence suggests that the monastery occupied or replaced an existing substantial building. However, this time the emphasis falls on the primitive simplicity of the individual cells, that of Martin himself being built of wood and those of other monks cut out as caves at the base of a cliff. The description of the site, if not its precise layout, is clearly modeled on the "communities of recluses" of the Judaean desert and elsewhere in the East, and although neither here nor at Ligugé are we given any reliable information regarding the regime under which the community lived, we likely are justified in seeing here the final working out of the more genuinely ascetic model to which Martin had originally been attracted.

However, it was not simply as a founder of monasteries that Martin was to be remembered and commemorated. The dispute over his body was won, supposedly after divine intervention, by Tours. His tomb, contained within a small church constructed by his successor, Brictio (St. Brice), became a center of pilgrimage, and in the mid–fifth century another successor, Perpetuus, replaced the church with a much larger one, commissioning frescoes and poems from the leading writers of the day. This church, together with the cathedral in which Martin had celebrated Mass and with the monastery at Marmoutier, became the focus of his rapidly growing cult, remaining so until both cathedral and church were seriously damaged by fire in 558. Their restoration and the revival of the cult were the work of Gregory, who became bishop in 573. Before long the city, with these three holy places and, most important, the body of the saint himself, became one of the leading religious centers of Western Europe. Martin was to become one of the patron saints of France.

As a monk who was also a bishop and a leading public figure and as the founder of monasteries rather than of an order as such, Martin influenced the development of monasticism in ways that are difficult to disentangle. He left no rule (indeed, no writings of any kind), and a certain irony exists in the fact that in the early medieval period his monasteries and the bishops who succeeded him competed rather than collaborated in spreading his cult. However, as the result of actions rather than words, he emerges as a figure of challenge at an early stage in the development of monasticism in the Roman West, and although it would be rash to claim that he exerted any direct influence on the major monastic developments of the succeeding centuries – whether on Cassian, Columban, or the Jura fathers – he can certainly be credited with setting an agenda, asking basic questions, and in this sense preparing the ground for such developments.

JOHN PERCIVAL

See also Asceticism: Christian Perspectives; Cassian, John; France: History; Hermits: Western Christian; Missionaries: Christian; Monte Cassino, Italy; Origins: Comparative Perspectives; Origins: Western Christian

Biography

Born into a soldier's family in Szombathely, Hungary, Martin remained a soldier until 356. After travels and a period as a hermit, he joined Hilary at Poitiers and founded nearby the monastery of Ligugé, the earliest one north of the Alps. Elected Bishop of Tours in 371, Martin founded further monasteries and resisted secular interference in the Church. St. Martin is the patron saint of France.

Further Reading

Delehaye, Hippolyte, "Saint Martin et Sulpice Sévère," *Analecta Bollandiana* 38 (1920)

Farmer, Sharon, *Communities of Saint Martin: Legend and Ritual in Medieval Tours*, Ithaca, New York: Cornell University Press, 1991

Griffe, Elie, "Saint Martin et le monachisme gaulois," *Studia Anselmiana* 46 (1961)

Percival, John, "Villas and Monasteries in Late Roman Gaul," *The Journal of Ecclesiastical History* 48 (1997)

Prinz, Friedrich, *Frühes Mönchtum im Frankenreich: Kultur und Gesellschaft in Gallien, den Rheinlanden und Bayern am Beispiel der monastischen Entwicklung (4. bis 8. Jahrhundert) Mit einem Kartenanhang*, Vienna: Oldenbourg, 1965

Severus, Sulpicius, *Vie de Saint Martin*, Paris: Éditions du Cerf, 1967

Van Dam, Raymond, *Leadership and Community in Late Antique Gaul*, Berkeley: University of California Press, 1985

Martyrs: Eastern Christian

The Greek word *martyr* or *martys* means "witness" in a legal contest (e.g., a witness called in a court of law). In Acts Luke employed the word to refer to the apostles who were witnesses to the ministry and Resurrection of Christ. The Orthodox Church continues to preserve a partiality for this less frequently used, early definition of "martyrdom," which should not be overlooked: persons who witness to Christ with their lives perform *martyria* (testimonies or proofs), so they are, by definition, martyrs. This witnessing may take place in a number of ways, including apostolic activity, a "righteous" life of monasticism, and confessing the faith. As a result, in the general commemoration of saints many different types of martyrs are remembered along with apostles, prophets, hierarchs, and righteous ascetics (e.g., in the services of vespers and matins and All Saints Sunday). The groups tend to be clumped together without overly precise definitions of their means to holiness but with an agreed insistence on their goals – the goals shared by all saints.

"Martyr," in the popular sense of the word, connotes a voluntary choice of death. This association was made early in the life of the Church as persecution of Christians spread. A martyr was identified, through the sacrifice of life, as one who bore testimony to Christ's victory over death. In Jesus' words, "No one has greater love than this, to lay down one's life for one's friends" (John 15:13). Martyrdom provided the earliest heroes of the Church, both male and female. Eastern tradition dictates that martyrs for the faith, through their "tour de force" of holiness, are automatically recognized as saints without necessarily being canonized by ecclesiastical authorities. The practice has the distinct advantage of affirming the singularity of this type of sanctity and proclaiming the "guaranteed entry" into the Kingdom of Heaven that goes along with martyrdom. It has the disadvantage of not formalizing the writing of a vita and not assigning that martyr a specific day, although ecclesiastical authorities might enact these at a later date. A victim's sanctity and the praiseworthiness of his or her life are rarely disputed (as they have been, however, in recent debates about Czar Nicholas II [d. 1918]). Under such circumstances it is not surprising that the bulk of martyrologies, as reported by Eusebius of Caesarea (c. 260–c. 340) and throughout the first millennium of Christianity, were extremely terse. What was evaluated as all important in their lives was, ironically, their deaths. With the cessation of state persecution of the Church under Emperor Constantine I (306–337), monasticism became identified as "bloodless (or "white") martyrdom."

Recent centuries, especially in 20th-century Soviet Russia, Greece, Armenia, and the Balkans, have produced "new martyrs," showing that martyrdom is a real, present-day possibility. Indeed some theologians believe that the greatest contribution of the Orthodox Church to the 20th century has been its long suffering. Unfortunately information about Christian victimizations – or the very fact of the murders themselves – has been occasionally suppressed, often for political reasons. Examples of this include the genocides of Armenians by the Turks during World War I and of Serbs by the Croats during World War II. In both cases religious affiliation played a role, and many of those killed could be considered martyrs. Accordingly one wonders whether the Nazi atrocities against the Jews would have been possible without the "historical silence" attending previous similar crimes. These earlier genocides proved that, because of a historical precedent of silence, savagery of this magnitude might be committed and hidden.

Another type of political silence surrounded mass deaths in the Soviet Union under Lenin and Stalin, the full extent of which will not be known until the KGB files are opened. Among the estimated 25 million people killed during this period (over and above the World War II casualties), approximately 40,000 bishops, priests, and monastics were executed. Many experts agree that the number of martyrdoms under the totalitarian Communist regime of the Soviet Union exceeded all the Christian martyrdoms of all preceding centuries combined. All the names will never be known. It is difficult to comprehend or assess such a reality.

The liturgical prayers of the Eastern Church contain the following general services to saints who have suffered martyrdom in addition to services specifically written to better-known biblical victims, such as St. John the Baptist or St. Peter and St. Paul. The general services are to (1) one martyr, (2) two or more martyrs, (3) one *hieromartyr* (clergy-martyr), (4) two or more *hieromartyrs*, (5) one monk-martyr, (6) two or more monk-martyrs, (7) one female martyr, (8) two or more female martyrs, (9) a nun-martyr, and (10) a *hiero-confessor* or a *monk-confessor* (*The General Menaion*, translated by Nicolas Orloff, 1899). A *hiero-confessor* connotes a clergyman who has rightly taught the faith before suffering, whereas the *monk-confessor* is an unordained monastic who has done the same. It should be noted that in the Eastern Church, according to ancient custom, monastics are not ordained clergy in most cases. They are considered laity, thus the distinctions outlined here between monk-martyrs and *hieromartyrs*. In the case of a bishop or *hieromonk* (priest-monk), the individual is given both titles.

Eastern martyrologies are not as easy to locate in collections as are their Western counterparts, and only a limited number exist in English. The reasons for this are not theological. First, the Western genre "book of martyrs," as popularized by John Foxe (1516–1587), Alban Butler (1710–1773), the Bollandists, and others, never caught on in the East. Second, no comprehensive collection exists in any language of all the recognized martyrs of the Orthodox Church, mainly because the *diptychs*, or lists of names, are determined and kept by each local church, and martyrs are not separated out from other saints, as was explained previously.

A representative selection of resources for locating and reading second-millennium martyrs' lives in the East are the following (fully referenced in the Further Reading section that follows this article). Each regional Orthodox Church compiles its own *Synaxarion*, a hagiography usually several volumes in length. For example, the *Great Synaxarion* of the Church of Greece is 14 volumes, and the more recent Serbian *Lives of the Saints* by Justin Popovich is 12. The Church Slavic and Russian vitae seem to have been documented first in various ancient regional, historical chronicles (three of which are now available in English) as well as in regional collections of *Paterica*, usually monastic saints' lives. A later style of Church Slavic hagiography was formulated in the 15th century by Epiphanius the Wise and Pachomius the Serb. The standard Russian collection was codified in 1705 by Dmitrii of Rostov and consists of 12 thick volumes, one for each month. Shorter compilations are available, such as the abbreviated *Synaxarion* (four volumes) by Nicodemus (c. 1749–1809) of the Holy Mountain or the shortened vitae in Bulgakov's *Nastolnaia Kniga*. None of these presently exists in its entirety in English.

A note regarding use of these resources is in order. Most of the collections are arranged according to the ecclesiastical calendar. This means that each saint's life is listed by calendar date (or dates if someone is commemorated more than once a year) corresponding to the martyr's ecclesiastical feast day, usually the date of death. An alphabetized index is sometimes appended to the final volume. In the case of the ancient Slavic *Chronicles* (often containing primary sources) the material is arranged exclusively by absolute chronology – "years after Creation" – to which compassionate editors frequently append dates anno Domini. The genres in use in the East are comparable to those used in the West in the fourth century, for example, Filocalus' "Chronographer of 354," *Despositio episcoporum*, and *Despositio martyrum*. Thus, locating Eastern martyrs' lives is not always a simple task, even with the proper resources, and critical texts are few. Fortunately many an individual vita has been translated into English and might be found in the library by title under the saint's name, in religious encyclopedias and dictionaries, and in collections.

The remainder of this article is concerned mainly with an overview of martyrs in the Eastern Church in the second millennium of Christianity. The names listed have been selected almost exclusively by Nicolas Zernov and approved by Archbishop Germanos of Thyatira for the tenth impression of *A Manual of Eastern Orthodox Prayers*. They represent martyred saints of many different backgrounds and cultures. Numbers in parentheses following certain names correspond to the liturgical categories of martyrs numbered previously. No attempt has been made to include the exceedingly long lists from the Communist period (see Dixon, 1993).

1015 – Saints Boris and Gleb (2)

These siblings, sons of Prince Vladimir of Kiev, were victims of feudal strife and were murdered by their older brother, Sviatopolk "the Damned," who in turn was killed by another brother, Iaroslav "the Wise." Boris and Gleb accomplished no heroic martyrdom; they neither sought nor desired death, as the ancient martyrs did. These holy sufferers are remembered not for their attachment to religion but for voluntary suffering through nonresistance, for sacrifice, however tenuous, in the face of fratricide. As the first canonized martyrs of Kievan Russ, an entire library exists (in English and Russian) on their martyrdom and its interpretation (Fedotov, 1946).

1094–1396 – The Crusades

One finds little to no evidence on the canonization of Eastern martyrs in connection with the period of the Crusades, not even with the Fourth Crusade (1204) against Constantinople and the sack and victimization of the city's churches, monasteries, and their residents. This might be attributed to the fact that a "theology of just war" has never developed in the East (i.e., the concept is explicitly denied as "theology" by the majority), and in the West it developed only in the 13th century with Thomas Aquinas (c. 1225–1274). Further, warriors in battle, even defensive battles for a homeland, were not given martyr status. This was true in the West as well, as late as the First Crusade (Morris, 1993).

1246 – Michael, prince of Chernigov, and his boyar Theodor (Russ)

1340 – John of Sochava (Yugoslavia)
1347 – Anthony, John, and their cousin Eustathius (Lithuania)
1472 – Abo (Georgia)
1472 – Isidor, presbyter, and 72 other martyrs of Derpt (Estonia)
1497 – Makarii, metropolitan of Kiev (Kievan Russ)
15th century – Jacob and John of Menuga, adolescent martyrs (Russ)
1515 – George, a goldsmith, new martyr (Bulgaria)
1526 – John, a tailor of Epirus (Greece)
1529 – John, martyr of Kazan (Russ)
1536 – Joasef, new martyr (Constantinople)

Circa 1550 – Marcella, Virgin (Chios, Greece) (7)
Marcella Mogias was a young woman who was tortured, murdered, and dismembered by her father as she fled his continual incestuous, mad pursuits. The "Tomb of St. Marcella" was associated with various miracles during World War II and in more recent times as well.

1551 – Nicodemus, Monk of Meteora (1)
Nicodemus was an ascetic in Thessaly who suffered martyrdom under the Ottomans.

1552 – Stephen and Peter, the Tatar martyrs of Kazan (Russia)

1569 – Philip, Metropolitan of Moscow (10)
Metropolitan Philip was imprisoned by Czar Ivan the Terrible (1533–1584) after remonstrating him face to face during the Divine Liturgy for injustice and murder, that is, for carrying on a war against his own people. The czar's secret police later killed him in prison. Philip is remembered as a *hiero-confessor* for his long-standing public opposition to Ivan as well as for his martyrdom (see Fedotov, 1978).

1582 – Ahmed, an architect and Turkish convert (Constantinople)
1601 – Seraphim, bishop of Phanar (Constantinople)
1622 – Luarsad, the king martyr (Georgia)

1624 – Ketvana, Queen of Georgia (7)
The deep piety of this empress and great-martyr was manifest in the particular attention she paid to the needs of the Georgian Church through the building of parishes, shelters, and homes for the needy. After the death of her husband, Ketvana settled into solitude. She refused the advances of Shah Abbas I to convert to Islam and then to marry him and as a result was tortured to death.

1657 – Parthenius III (3)
Parthenius III was one of the succession of 61 occupants forced onto the patriarchal throne of the Church of Constantinople by the Ottoman Empire during the 17th century. He is known for opposing the Confession of Peter Mogila (1596–1648) as unorthodox at a synod in Constantinople in 1656. The Turks put him to death for ostensibly conspiring with the czar of Russia.

1660 – Athanasius of Ikia (Turkey)

1678 – Makarii, Monk and Priest of the Kanevsk Monastery, Ukraine, and Belarus (3)
Thirty years of struggle in Belarussian and Ukrainian monasteries with competing Uniates gave this monk and priest a reputation for righteous and spiritual living, a life glorified by miracles and the gift of perspicacity. A Turkish incursion into the monastery demanded from him the treasury, and when he replied that his treasure was in heaven, he was tortured and killed.

1679 – Cyprian of Mount Athos

1680 – Stamatios of Thessaly (1)
A native of the city of Boleia, Stamatios was slandered and accused of apostasy. On confessing himself a Christian and not a Muslim, he was beheaded by the Ottomans in Constantinople.

1685 – Damianos, monk (Greece)
1686 – Elias, hairdresser (Greece)

1725 – Argyre, New Martyr (Greece) (7)
Living south of Constantinople, Argyre was a beautiful newlywed charged falsely for having rebuffed a local citizen's sexual advances. She was imprisoned by the Turks for 17 years and died in prison. Her relics, considered uncorrupted, are venerated in the church of St. Paraskeva.

1726 – Sabba Nigdelinus (Constantinople)
1754 – Nicholas of Chios (Greece)
1763 – Dimas, fisherman (Smyrna)

1770 – Michael, a Gardener (Greece) (1)
Michael suffered and died in Athens under the Turks for confessing the Christian faith.

1771 – Damascene, new martyr (Bulgaria)
1772 – Michael, a plumber (Smyrna)
1776 – Peter of the Peloponnese (Greece)
1779 – Cosma, missionary (Albania)
1794 – Alexander, a former Dervish (Smyrna)
1794 – Anastasius, new martyr (Bulgaria)

1795 – Chrysa, Virgin, New Martyr of Bulgaria (7)
The great-martyr Chrysa (or Zlata in Slavic) was born and lived in the Bulgarian village of Slatino, which was under Turkish rule. Known for her unusually strong character, beauty, chastity, and firm faith in Christ, she was imprisoned and tortured to death over many months for refusing to accept Islam.

1807 – George of Chios (Greece)
1808 – Nicetas, new martyr (Albania)

1814 – Ignatius, new martyr (Bulgaria)
1814 – Euthymius, new martyr (Greece)
1818 – Anuphrius, new martyr (Bulgaria)

1945 – Mother Maria Skobtsova (9)
Mother Maria was a poet and social activist involved in the Russian Student Christian Movement. Well known to the Russian intelligentsia of Paris, she was deported to the Nazi death camp at Ravensbrück because of aid she supplied to Jews through Orthodox action (Hackel, 1965, 1982).

1990 – Alexander Men, priest (Russia)

MICHAEL PROKURAT

See also Hagiography: Eastern Christian; Historiography, Recent: Eastern Christian; Holy Men/Holy Women: Christian Perspectives; Hymnographers; Liturgy: Eastern Christian; Orthodox Monasticism: Slavic; Persecution: Christian Perspectives; Relics, Christian Monastic; Spirituality: Eastern Christian; Theology, Eastern Christian

Further Reading

Atiya, Aziz S., *The Crusade in the Later Middle Ages*, London: Methuen, 1938; 2nd edition, New York: Kraus Reprint, 1965
Bergman, Susan, editor, *Martyrs: Contemporary Writers on Modern Lives of Faith*, San Francisco: HarperSanFrancisco, 1996
Bulgakov, Sergei Vasilevich, *Nastolnaia Kniga dlia Sviashchenno-Tserkovno-Sluzhitelei* (Handbook for Church Clergy), Kharkov: Tipografiia Gybernskago Pravleniia, 1900
The Chronicle of Novgorod, 1016–1471 (Camden Third Series, volume 25), translated by Robert Michell and Nevill Forbes, London: Offices of the Society, 1914; Hattiesburg, Mississippi: Academic International, 1970
Craig, Mary, *Candles in the Dark: Six Modern Martyrs*, London: Hodder and Stoughton, 1984; as *Six Modern Martyrs*, New York: Crossroad, 1985
Cross, Samuel Hazzard, editor and translator, *The Russian Primary Chronicle: Laurentian Text*, Cambridge, Massachusetts: Harvard University Press, 1930
Dixon, Simon, "Reflections on Modern Russian Martyrdom," in *Martyrs and Martyrologies: Papers Read at the 1992 Summer Meeting and the 1993 Winter Meeting of the Ecclesiastical History Society* (Studies in Church History, volume 30), edited by Diana Wood, Cambridge, Massachusetts, and Oxford: Blackwell, 1993
Dmitrii, Saint, Metropolitan of Rostov, *Zhitiia sviatykh na russkom iazyke* (Lives of the Saints in the Russian Language), 12 vols., Moscow: Izd. Vvedenskoi Optinoi Pustyni, 1900
Fedotov, G.P., *The Russian Religious Mind*, volume 1: *Kievan Christianity, the 10th to the 13th Centuries*, Cambridge, Massachusetts: Harvard University Press, 1946
Fedotov, G.P., *St. Filipp, Metropolitan of Moscow: Encounter with Ivan the Terrible* (Collected Works of George P. Fedotov, volume 1), translated by Richard Haugh and Nickolas Lupinin, edited by Haugh, Belmont, Massachusetts: Nordland, 1978
Golubinskii, Evgenii, *Istoriia kanonizatsii sviatykh' v' russkoi tserkvi – History of the Canonization of Saints in the Russian Church*, Moscow: Universitetskaia tip., 1903; reprint, Farnborough, Hampshire: Gregg, 1969
Grunwald, Constantin de, *Saints of Russia*, translated by Roger Capel, New York: Macmillan, and London: Hutchinson, 1960
Hackel, Sergei, *One, of Great Price: The Life of Mother Maria Skobtsova, Martyr of Ravensbrück* (Libra Books, 1009), London: Darton, Longman and Todd, 1965; revised as *Pearl of Great Price: The Life of Mother Maria Skobtsova, 1891–1945*, London: Darton, Longman and Todd, and Crestwood, New York: St. Vladimir's Seminary Press, 1982
Kliuchevskii, V.O., *Drevnerusskiia zhitiia sviatykh kak istoricheskii istochnik* (The Old Russian Lives of the Saints as a Historical Source), Moscow: Izd. K. Soldatenkova, 1871; reprint, The Hague and Paris: Mouton, 1968; Farnborough, Hampshire: Gregg, 1969
Langes, Matthaios, editor, *Ho Megas synaxaristes tes Orthodoxou Ekklesias* (The Great Synaxarion of the Orthodox Church), 14 vols., Athens: Ekd. Hieras Mones Metamorphoseos Kouvara Attikes, 1980–1984
Lenhoff, Gail, *The Martyred Princes Boris and Gleb: A Social-Cultural Study of the Cult and the Texts* (UCLA Slavic Studies, volume 19), Columbus, Ohio: Slavica, 1989
Menaion tou Septemvriou, [etc.]: periechon hapasan ten anekoysan auto akolouthian meta tes prosthekes tou typikou . . ., 12 vols., Athens: Saliverou, 1904
Morris, Colin, "Martyrs on the Field of Battle before and during the First Crusade," in *Martyrs and Martyrologies: Papers Read at the 1992 Summer Meeting and the 1993 Winter Meeting of the Ecclesiastical History Society* (Studies in Church History, volume 30), edited by Diana Wood, Cambridge, Massachusetts, and Oxford: Blackwell, 1993
Orthodox Eastern Church, *The General Menaion; or, The Book of Services Common to the Festivals of Our Lord Jesus of the Holy Virgin and of the Different Orders of Saints*, translated by Nicolas Orloff, London: Davy, 1899; New York: AMS Press, 1969
Vaporis, Nomikos, *Witnesses for Christ: Orthodox Christian Neomartyrs of the Ottoman Period, 1437–1860*, Crestwood, New York: St. Vladimir's Seminary Press, 2000
Wood, Diana, editor, *Martyrs and Martyrologies: Papers Read at the 1992 Summer Meeting and the 1993 Winter Meeting of the Ecclesiastical History Society* (Studies in Church History, volume 30), Cambridge, Massachusetts, and Oxford: Blackwell, 1993
Zenkovsky, Serge A., editor, *The Nikonian Chronicle*, 5 vols., translated by Serge A. Zenkovsky and Betty Jean Zenkovsky, Princeton, New Jersey: Kingston Press, 1984–1989
Zernov, Nicolas, editor, *A Manual of Eastern Orthodox Prayers*, London: SPCK, 1945; Crestwood, New York: St. Vladimir's Seminary Press, 1983

Related Web Sites

http://www.goarch.org/access/Companion_to_Orthodox_Church/SAINTS (Greek Orthodox Archdiocese of America, "The Saints of the Orthodox Church")

http://www.oca.org/Feasts-and-Saints/ (Orthodox Church in America, "Feasts and Saints of the Orthodox Church")

Martyrs: Western Christian

The notion of martyr has no direct link with monasticism. This reflects the classic Western view that it is not the fact of being killed as a Christian but the reason why one is killed that makes a martyr – "it is not the suffering, but its cause, that makes the martyr" (St. Augustine). Thus, although many monastics are considered martyrs (e.g., St. Boniface was martyred in Germany in 754, monks were killed when their monasteries were suppressed by civil authorities either during the Reformation period or the French Revolution, and Charles de Foucauld was killed in his Saharan hermitage in 1916), in these cases they were killed because they were Christians, Catholics, or religious and not because they were monastics. However, there is a long-standing link between martyrdom and monasticism that honors the latter as a type of and substitute for the former.

One of the original inspirations for going into the desert as hermits was that once Christianity had become "a lawful religion" (313), martyrdom (seen as "the crown" of Christian witness) was no longer available. Thus, a life of solitude fighting demons became a substitute for those brave enough to take on such a life. Thus, just as the martyr in the arena "confessed Christ," so the monk took on a life of renunciation that publicly professed Christian beliefs about life and society. Early monastics consciously saw their lives as a prolonged martyrdom. As such they became the new heroes of the Christian warfare, no longer contending with "rulers and authorities" (Luke 12:11) but rather with "the principalities and powers in the heavenly places" (Eph. 3:11). The spiritual high ground once held by martyrs was now reserved for monks, and this did much to propagate the notion of monks as a spiritual elite among Christians, possessing that intrinsic authority in the Church held earlier by *confessores* who had been willing to endure persecution. The "death" endured by the monk involved the death of the old self of sin through penance and celibacy and the renunciation of will through obedience. This theme, monasticism as the death of the self for life in Christ, remained present in monastic writings until the 20th century.

In early medieval writings the linking of martyrdom with monasticism became one of the most common themes in the construction of the image of the ideal monk/Christian. Two early and influential examples that show how the cult of martyrs became a major feature of monastic reading and prayer are Gregory of Tours' (538/39–594) *In gloriam martyrum* (*Miraculorum libri* 1) (On the Glory of the Martyrs [Books of Miracles, Book 1]) and Gregory the Great's (590–604) *Dialogi*. The first work celebrates the miracles of Jesus, the apostles, and many Gallic martyrs and especially the wonders connected with their cult. The second work, written with a monastic audience in mind and one of the most influential works in Western monasticism, testifies to the extent of monastic interest in martyrs in the late sixth century and contributed to an increase in that devotion. The connection of the monastery with the martyrs through their invocation and through possession of their relics was seen as securing protection on earth and intercession in heaven. The martyrs who were invoked acted as guarantors of the monastery's spiritual power, for the monks became their successors undergoing spiritual martyrdom.

Perhaps the clearest expression of martyrdom as a metaphor for the monastic life comes from an Irish homily (known as "the Cambrai homily") copied on the Continent in the eighth century. Its opening text is Matthew 16:24: "If any man would come after me, let him deny himself and take up his cross and follow me." The homily then identifies taking the cross with "loss and martyrdom" and goes on to distinguish three types of martyrdom, "which can count as a cross": first, "white martyrdom when a man leaves all he loves for God, although he does not undergo fasting nor labour in the process"; second, "green martyrdom when through fasting and labour, a man separates from his desires, and suffers toil in penance and repentance"; and third, "red martyrdom which is a cross and destruction for Christ's sake as happened to the apostles." Although this is not explicitly monastic, its context – in use by Irish monks in northeastern France – shows that the various trials of monasticism were explained with reference to martyrdom and were seen as a way "to obtain the rewards" of martyrdom. The monk who has left home and family undergoes white martyrdom and, through asceticism, green martyrdom.

The cult of martyrs also had a place in the monastic day – quite apart from the liturgical commemoration of martyrs' feasts within the liturgical year – for the reading of the martyrology (which included other saints but whose primary focus fell on martyrs) was read daily in common, and many martyrologies survive from medieval monasteries. Equally, monastic rules (e.g., the *Regula s. Benedicti*, chap. 42) specified that saints' lives be read when the monks had assembled, and among these the passions of the martyrs held a prominent and elevated place. In these ways, although the historic "age of the martyrs" was receding ever further into the past, the monastic, through the periodically "reformed" ideal of asceticism, remained the successor of the martyr.

In recent times, perhaps because the 20th century produced slaughter in the name of many causes like no period before it, there has been a hesitation to use images of martyrdom as metaphors: too many have suffered too deeply for such a metaphor to be used lightly. Indeed in the aftermath of various genocides, to compare a voluntary life of asceticism to undergoing death for one's beliefs seems exploitative, even derisive. However, at the same time many recent justifications of monasticism assert that its lifestyle provides a witness (the original meaning of *martus* in Greek) to the Christian mystery.

THOMAS O'LOUGHLIN

Francisco de Zurbarán, *Saint Serapion*, oil on canvas, 1628. Scottish by birth, St. Serapion joined the Mercedarian Order in 1222 and was martyred in Algiers in 1240.
Photo courtesy of the Wadsworth Atheneum, Hartford, Connecticut, The Ella Gallup Sumner and Mary Catlin Sumner Collection Fund

See also Asceticism: Christian Perspectives; Celtic Monasticism; Devotions, Western Christian; Dissolution of Monasteries; Holy Men/Holy Women: Christian Perspectives; Persecution: Christian Perspectives; Pilgrimages, Christian: Western Europe; Relics, Christian Monastic

Further Reading

Delehaye, Hippolyte, *Les Origines du culte des martyrs*, Brussels: Société des Bollandistes, 1912; 2nd edition, 1933; reprint, New York: AMS Press, 1980
Malone, Edward E., *The Monk and the Martyr: The Monk as the Successor of the Martyr*, Washington, D.C.: Catholic University of America Press, 1950
Ní Chatháin, Próinséas, "A Reading in the Cambrai Homily," *Celtica* 21 (1990)
Ó Néill, Pádraig, "The Background to the Cambrai Homily," *Ériu* 32 (1981)
Petersen, Joan M., *The Dialogues of Gregory the Great in Their Late Antique Cultural Background* (Studies and Texts, 69), Toronto: Pontifical Institute of Mediaeval Studies, 1984
Stancliffe, Claire, "Red, White and Blue Martyrdom," in *Ireland in Early Medieval Europe*, edited by Dorothy Whitelock, Rosamund McKitterick, and David Dumville, Cambridge: Cambridge University Press, 1982
Stokes, Whitley, and John Strachan, editors, *Thesaurus Palaeohibernicus: A Collection of Old-Irish Glosses, Scholia, Prose, and Verse*, volume 2, Cambridge: Cambridge University Press, 1901

Master and Pupil: Buddhist Perspectives

Master-disciple relationships are critical in any religious tradition. They enhance the personal quality of a faith not only in a theistic tradition with a personal God incarnate but also in atheistic Buddhism, which is mistakenly thought to be uniformly impersonal. In fact being what Weber calls an "exemplary prophet" (in contrast to the biblical "emissary prophet"), the Buddha had more reason to make himself into a personable example to emulate. Such intimacy is natural to monastic spirituality, both Christian and Buddhist. Nor is it true that Buddhism knows no emissary, mediator, or personal savior. Buddhism is not exclusively a reclusive tradition. As its *vihāra* cloisters grew into large, public *saṅghārama* temples, more monks acted as clerics (i.e., "priests") to serve the laity than meditated in quiet; and as savior Buddhas emerged in Mahāyāna, the relationship between the laity, the dharma masters, and the Buddha took on still more subtle shades.

According to the early records, the Buddha was eminently approachable. He had renounced strict eremitism to found the first known monastic order in the world. As head of this community, he was mentor to his spiritual sons who were brothers to one another. So democratic was the community that no hint of a future papal structure could be seen and, initially, not even a unified authority. For example, a follower of Mahāvira, the Jain leader, became a disciple of the Buddha. The Buddha made him welcome and did not require him to repudiate his former loyalty, saying that he should still serve his Jain master. When the great Kaśyapa was converted by the Buddha, his disciples who did the same still regarded Kaśyapa their leader. Thus, a truth seeker in early Buddhism can serve more than one master. Individual monasteries remained fairly egalitarian. Each community administered itself, networking with others into larger lineage confederations, all coming under a singular Saṅgha Jewel. However, later a "majestic *saṅgha*" would be superimposed on that republican structure not only because the Buddha was becoming increasingly regal but also because royal patronage under King Aśoka would seek to organize the *saṅgha* from top down.

Even before that ideological boundaries were being drawn. The formula for taking refuge is as follows: "I take refuge in the Buddha, the Dharma, and the Saṅgha" to underscore that it is the Buddha's dharma, not just any dharma, that then defines the *saṅgha*. As the Buddha became elevated to transmundane height, no man could any longer claim to emulate him in full. However, like the "absent God" the remote Buddha can sometimes make the heart grow fonder, for whereas when the Buddha was alive he had ruled out faith as a means to liberation (except for one disciple who apparently could do nothing else), the transmundane Buddha in Mahāyāna can now render aid to all the faithful. Thus, just as *devotio moderna* would return the "overly majestic" Christ to being once more an intimate other, "high Buddhology" could also bring men closer to the lofty Buddha. Just as the Pietists recalled the old Hebraic God who "is my shepherd . . . and companion" by singing "I have a friend in Jesus," so Zen and Pure Land Buddhism could make the *alst andere* ("utterly other" in Kierkegaard's phrase) Lord a familiar "master and companion."

Of the three monastic offices in Buddhism, the abbot is in charge of the order, the housekeeping monk the finances, and the rector the room and duty assignments. At one time reference was made to masters of the sūtra, of the monastic rules, and of the commentarial tradition. These went with specialization into the three baskets of the canon. Although a novice might benefit from a warm master-disciple relationship with the abbot or with a resident authority on the canon, usually he sustained personal ties to two other figures: his precept master and his spiritual master. The former sponsored his admission into the order, guiding and mentoring him through the years. To him the inductee owes eternal gratitude, and he would mourn his passing dutifully like a son. The early monastic code allowed any fully ordained monk to recruit novices on his own. (However, it limited the number of young pages to two in conservative Theravāda and three in liberal Mahāsaṇghika.) The inductee might take the full monk precepts later. Usually this ceremony took place at a larger temple and was much more formal (with a minimum quota of ten full monks present) and required preparation and registration. In the Far East this involves securing the necessary "monk certificates" from the issuing authorities. Important as that rite of passage might be – it could be enacted for hundreds of candidates by some grand master of the precepts – discipleship at that level does not necessarily measure up to the warmer, closer, and longer relationship with one's initial precept master. Thus, a monk is not duty bound personally to attend the funeral of that grand master.

The other intimate master-disciple relationship involves the spiritual master, of whom there is sometimes more than one. As in Christian monasteries the spiritual master is not necessarily (more often he is not) the abbot, nor is he one of those authorities on the canon. He need not reside nearby. One might have to go wayfaring, "like cloud and water," looking for him. The spiritual master can guide one through the spiritual exercises because he has traveled on that very road himself, knowing from firsthand experience – not from words in a book, although special meditation manuals might be available – the uncharted and unchartable highways and byways of the mystical path. Myths abound on where such masters are to be found, up mountains or in caves (the haunts of "forest recluses"), or he might turn out to be the illiterate cook in the kitchen or be a fabled layman, such as Vimalakīrti, living in the lap of luxury at the mercantile city of Vaiśālī. He might even dwell in whorehouses (if you believe the pilgrimage undertaken by a youthful Sudāna). Whatever that might mean, it seems that at the end of Mahāyāna development, namely, in Tantric Tibet and Chan/Zenist China, a claim is lodged about a secret lineage of spiritual masters that would remake the monastic order, create a new master-disciple relationship, and bring a "high Buddhology" down to kindle enlightenment in the "here and now." That historic myth needs a deconstructive but sympathetic retelling.

Chan/Zen claims to have inherited its teaching from a hitherto hidden lineage of spiritual masters (called patriarchs) going back to the first Chan encounter of its kind between the Buddha and Kaśyapa. In repeating that encounter between himself and his master, the Chan student is transported back in time by way of that unbroken mind-to-mind transmission to be an equal of the Buddha himself. Claiming to locate this transmission "outside the written scriptures" gives Chan/Zen an incontestable (if noncanonical) authority. With that Chan/Zen was able to remake monastic life: now the abbot is the spiritual master. This bold reform returned the *saṅgha* to its pristine ideal, when the Buddha was the abbot. Now the abbot is the Buddha. What the rhetoric hides is a revolt of the spiritual masters against the physical institution – a call to liberate the true fellowship from some captivity.

A patriarch of the Chogye Order at Chogye-sa Temple in South Korea. Photo courtesy of John Powers

The Chan/Zen claim to being heir to a patriarchal but noncanonical ("outside the scripture") lineage is a myth. However, no text is ever original; all texts are built on prior texts, and the Zen text here is no exception. Such a patriarchal lineage exists, and Chan/Zen got it from some written source. To unpack this we have to see how the myth arose. We noted earlier that the historical Buddha, at his death, never chose a successor. "Follow the Dharma," he had taught, "not the Person." No attestable papal institution exists, such as the biblical account of Jesus founding the Church on the Rock that was Peter. However, an institution akin to, and later a myth of, a papal succession actually existed. The monk-*saṅgha* was built on the "monastic precepts." The vinaya is the rock on which the *saṅgha* is built, and this is still believed today. Now the Theravāda lineage in Sri Lanka claimed to have inherited it unbroken from the Buddha. It came down by way of Kaśyapa and so on through the Great Tissa, who chaired the Buddhist Council under King Aśoka, whose son Rahula then supposedly came to Sri Lanka as a monk. Every respectable national *saṅgharāja* (leader or king of the *saṅgha*) in Southeast Asia can place himself in that Theravāda line of succession – no more and no less than every Chan/Zen abbot can trace himself back now to the sixth patriarch and on back to the Buddha. Even now all Theravāda ordinations of monks have to exhibit proof of this historical linkage. The linkage for nuns being broken, it has been retrieved through a Chinese line of succession, and not without controversy. China knew such succession. In the early sixth century, it received one such sacred vinaya text that has some dots appended at the end. Supposedly keepers of this "Dotted Record" had successively added one dot for every one year removed from the time of the Buddha's *parinirvāṇa* to attest to a datable tie to him. (The number of dots is used by one modern Japanese scholar to recover the historical date of the Buddha.) Theravāda used such a lineage to justify the claim of having inherited the whole Buddha dharma. From the Aśokan Council came the doctrinal settlement told in the *Kathāvastu*. Other schools in India also used the same lineage (up to a certain point) to justify their own claim to orthodoxy. For example, Mahāsaṇghika claimed the *Mahāvastu* as its own preceptory text that came out of a Fourth Council chaired by King Kanishka in the north. Early Chan/Zen in China came up with its own patriarchal lineage by tapping into a Kashmirean line of meditative masters and rewrote a report of the end of an Indian patriarchal succession – the last patriarch was killed by an evil king – to come up with a story of Bodhidharma, foreseeing chaos in India and bringing the dharma to China. So the uniqueness lies not with the Chan/Zen claim to a hidden lineage but elsewhere.

Theravāda used the patriarchal succession as its genealogical link to a sacred past. It honors first the vinaya and its upholder: the abbot. This is comparable to reciting all the names of the popes from St. Peter down to the current one to validate the sacradotal institution by way of the apostolic laying on of hands. It places all Theravāda *saṅgharājas* in the approved line. Chan/Zen cared less about that legitimization of the "physical" Church or *saṅgha*. Its goal was to revive true "spiritual" discipleship. Chan/Zen was not interested in a list of names. It fabricated typical stories and encounter dialogues for every one of those 28 Indian patriarchs. It sought not the "historical" succession but "spiritual" empathy. To borrow an anti-Hegelian/historicist term from Kierkegaard, the Buddhological narrative – like the Christological drama – is not an event "back then." It is an event "made present" again so that one can feel that one is "contemporaneous" with the Lord Buddha or with Lord Christ. A meeting of minds between master and disciple now replicates the first such Chan/Zen encounter between the Buddha and Kaśyapa. We smile with Kaśyapa once again just as "we walk with God/from this day on." The Chan/Zen master becomes that "helping hand/the disciple can lean upon." This is the new master-disciple relationship ushered in by Chan/Zen.

WHALEN LAI

See also Bodhidharma; Buddhadāsa; Buddhism: Overview; Buddhist Schools/Traditions: Japan; Buddhist Schools/Traditions: Tibet; Chan/Zen: China; Chan/Zen: Japan; Deities, Buddhist; Dialogue, Intermonastic: Buddhist Perspectives; Disciples, Early Buddhist; Dōgen; Gestures, Buddhist; Initiation: Buddhist Perspectives; Origins: Comparative Perspectives; Prophethood, Japanese Buddhist; Saichō; Shinran; Spirituality: Buddhist; Tibetan Lineages: Gelukpa

Further Reading

Hui Neng, *The Platform Sutra of the Sixth Patriarch*, translated by Philip Yampolsky, New York: Columbia University Press, 1967

McRae, John, *The Northern School and the Formation of Early Ch'an Buddhism*, Honolulu: University of Hawaii Press, 1986

Master and Pupil: Christian Perspectives

The relationship of master-pupil/disciple (Latin, *discipulus*; Greek, *mathētes*; Hebrew, *talmid*) is a basic organizing principle in Christianity, with a specific manifestation within monasticism. The first followers of Jesus saw themselves as disciples of a master/teacher, and ever since "to be a disciple" has been a means of expressing connection to him. Moreover in monasticism the notion inspired both a spiritual and an organizational form: the life of the monastery.

Biblical Roots

When early monks read the Old Testament, and the wisdom literature in particular, they found many examples of a relationship between a wise, older teacher and a young learner who sought wisdom, a way of life, and a path to righteousness. They construed the latter to mean a life of holiness. This notion of the search for wisdom, which the Hebrew writers had taken from Egyptian reflection, provided a paradigm for the pursuit of the wisdom of holiness in monasteries. The Book of Proverbs is a good example of this. It takes over many long passages from the Egyptian *Wisdom of Amenemope* (e.g., Prov. 22), presenting its teaching as that given by a father figure to his "son" whom he wishes to lead toward the good life ("my son" signals a piece of teaching on 24 occasions). In turn this teaching was taken over as an example of the relationship between the father (abbot) of the monastery and his sons (disciples/monks) as we see in the opening words of the Rule of St. Benedict: "My son, listen to the words of the master and give me the ear of your heart" (Prov. 4:20). When such texts (e.g., those from Sirach) are brought together and linked with the theme of the righteous teacher (e.g., Dan. 12:3) and with the image of a teacher based on Ezra (Ezra 7:10, Neh. 8), a picture of the path to holiness emerges as one that is handed on from one generation to the next through discipleship. If one wants to know the Lord, then find a wise teacher (wisdom seen as holiness) and attach oneself to him as a disciple, as a son to a father.

Although many of the images of discipleship derived from the Old Testament, to understand the power invested in this relationship one must turn to what was seen as its perfect exemplar: Jesus with his first followers. In the New Testament several religious leaders have disciples: the Pharisees are seen to present themselves as "the disciples of Moses" (John 9:28) with the clear implication in the text that the Christians have made a decision to be disciples of Christ (John 9:2); the Pharisees have their own disciples and send them to investigate the other teacher, Jesus (Matt. 22:16); and John the Baptist too has disciples (Mark 2:18), as have Christian teachers such as Paul (Acts 9:25). What this "discipleship" means is not reducible to being merely students or apprentices, for disciples function as members of the master's party, his companions, his assistants, and his runners, and crucially they live within a tradition from which they derive wisdom and identity (Matt. 11:2, 22:16; Luke 7:18). As disciples they pursue a distinctive way of life with distinctive religious practices, such as group eating and fasting (Mark 2:18, 9:14; Luke 5:33) and distinctive group liturgy: for example, John the Baptist taught a particular way of prayer (Luke 11:1). In comparison, Jesus is the unique perfect teacher (Matt. 23:8), usually addressed as such or else as "rabbi" (defined as "teacher" in John 1:38). He calls all who accept his message "disciples." These include not only the select inner group ("the 12") but all his followers as well.

The disciples of Jesus were like other disciples in terms of learning and companionship, but in addition they were seen as being prepared to share the master's fate (Matt. 10:24–25). Indeed to be a disciple is to follow Jesus in his suffering: the one who "does not bear his own cross and come after me, cannot be my disciple" (Luke 14:27). So conceived, discipleship leads to the full Christian life and to identification with Jesus (Luke 6:40:

"A disciple is not above his teacher, but every one when he is fully taught will be like his teacher"), and the command to preach is posed in terms of discipleship: "Go make disciples of all nations" (Matt. 28:19). Discipleship is the perfect following of Christ, and naturally it became the paradigm for the monastic life. Just as Israel was a disciple of the law and the Church a disciple of Christ, so the monk is the disciple within the monastery growing toward a perfect relationship with God.

In Early Monasticism

One common feature of all our accounts of early monasticism in Egypt and Palestine (Athanasius and Jerome but especially Cassian and Palladius) is that they present the beginnings of a person's monastic life as that of becoming a disciple of a master. One attaches oneself to a holy man as an apprentice and under his tutelage learns how to be a monk and to deal with spiritual enemies. The elder monk is addressed as "abba" (cf. Rom. 8:15 et al. with the meaning of "father" or "master"), and the younger monk is the son, the learner. This can be seen very clearly in the form in which John Cassian (c. 360–after 430) casts the teaching of his *Conlationes* (*Conferences*). Wishing to learn the wisdom of the elders, the new monks go and live with them, question them, and record their teaching not as a report but as truth that they must absorb. Having shared the life of each of the fathers and heard them speak, the young become fit to succeed them.

This process requires not so much teaching (in the sense of an academic activity) but rather imitation. Paul's "Be imitators of me, as I am of Christ" (1 Cor. 11:1) set the scene: the father-monk has become an imitation of Christ, almost to the point of identification, and so the disciple imitates him in life, action, and knowledge. Thus, we find in the relationship of abbot to monk two recurrent motifs: first, the abbot is the very expression of the tradition that he himself has received and so can characterize his relationship to the disciple as one of teaching and giving; second, the monk is the one who is receiving the tradition, and so his work, obedience, and imitation can be expressed as learning. The monastery is a school of holiness, a place of disciples/discipline, where an elder welcomes those who seek to learn and teaches by sharing his life with them.

Insofar as the essence of monastic life and the wisdom of the elders can be expressed in writing, it can be asserted that the rule becomes a master, and every monk is its disciple, thus, the imagery of many rules (e.g., "The Rule of the Master"). However, the book never supplants the person: learning always involved a communication of the life from one person, the master, to another. The rule embodied the frozen teaching of a master administered by a novice-master to the young monks. In this process the element of handing on was central: one must have been a disciple before one can become a teacher.

The monastic relationship of master-pupil is more complex than is its secular counterpart, that of master-apprentice. The monastic pupil does not leave his master to become a distinct master but rather becomes a master in place of his teacher. Both belong to a larger corporate personality that is ultimately identified as the body of Christ. Each master is a part of this larger body and embodies its wisdom – thus, reverence for the master means reverence for the whole tradition – and speaks not as an individual but as a mouthpiece for a tradition that is greater than either master or pupil. In absorbing the wisdom of the elders through his teacher, the disciple does so in order that he himself can be absorbed into the tradition and become, in time, its mouthpiece. Thus, a succession exists in monastic authority and teaching that is analogous to the succession in authority that communicates the very teaching of the Church. Significantly the latter was termed *magisterium* in Latin. Baptism conveys a similar succession in participation in the life of Christ that results from baptism (see Matt. 28:19).

The Relationship as a Motif

The significance of this relationship is best assessed in terms of it diverse manifestations. One of the preferred literary conventions in early monastic theology is that of master-pupil dialogue. The disciple questions and craves knowledge, and the master replies and dispenses it. Such question-and-answer texts cover the liberal arts, theology, scriptural exegesis, monastic training (e.g., in Cassian), and even the history of the monastery (e.g., in Gregory the Great's *Dialogues*). The format is often marked out in the manuscripts with "D" for *discipulus* or "M" for *mathétes* beside the question and "M" for *magister* or "D" for *didaskalos* beside the answer. Equally in prescriptive texts it was necessary to present the person drawing up the rules as one in harmony with the tradition of the elders and who acts now as a father toward children or as a physician to a patient (see Finnian's *Penitential*). Eventually the disciple motif became a force promoting conservatism within monastic theology. For Vincent of Lérins (d. before 450), the work of any Christian teacher is that of the disciple to the master, conceived as the collectivity of the tradition. Success means losing nothing (forgetfulness is related to sin) and not innovating beyond what one has received. In this manner one is assured of adhering to the truth by staying close to one's teachers, and one is not led astray by a pride that thinks itself greater than the masters. As a result excellence was seen to consist in the reiteration of earlier forms no matter what the changes in cultural milieu.

This model permeated monastic spirituality by validating obedience as key to holiness: the pupil depends on the master, the individual on the Church, and the Church on Christ. Jesus' words "learn [*mathete/discite*] from me . . . and you will find rest for your souls" (Matt. 11:29) provided a starting point for a sequence of relationships in the first of which a pupil-monk becomes obedient to his master and becomes identified with him (see Palladius' letter to Lausus). In turn this involves learning from Christ – himself the model of obedience (Phil. 2:8) – and listening to the Father (John 15:15), from which one should grow into union with him. Thus, the relationship supplies a means to union with Christ that brings about a union with God more perfect than that of master to pupil. It is folly to imagine that one does not need a teacher, and such an error can lead one to fall away, "for God alone is untaught" (Palladius to Lausus).

A Caveat: Contemporary Problems with the Notion of "Master-Disciple"

Despite its antiquity this relationship is moribund in Christianity today, except as a metaphor. Its central idea that tradition is greater than the individual conflicts with the demands of individual expression, and the values of a master-pupil culture are dismissed as constraining. The relationship of master to pupil was necessarily unequal: the one gives knowledge, and the other obeys, learns, and gives respect. This hierarchical model of teaching is rejected by modern Western theory and must be disguised wherever it is still used (e.g., in Church pronouncements). The crisis of authority structures in Christianity – for example, in the notion of the papacy as the "teaching church" (*ecclesia docens*) and those whom it teaches as the "learning listening church" (*ecclesia discens*) – can be seen as a rejection of this model. The master was esteemed as a spiritual hero, and with that went the notion of a fixed list of illustrious teachers to be emulated because they knew the truth. Modern rejection of "the hero" and of the related notion that truth requires fully remembering a past jettisons two key beliefs that underpinned the master-pupil relationship in monasticism.

THOMAS O'LOUGHLIN

See also Biblical Figures and Practices; Cassian, John; Elders, Russian Monastic (Startsi); Hagiography: Christian Perspectives; Lérins, France; Origins: Eastern Christian; Spirituality: Eastern Christian

Further Reading

Bardy, Gustave, "La littérature patristique des 'Quaestiones et responsiones' sur l'écriture sainte," *Revue Biblique* 41 (1932) and 42 (1933)

Louth, Andrew, "A Christian Theologian at the Court of the Caliph: Some Cross-Cultural Reflections," *Dialogos: Hellenic Studies Review* 3 (1996)

O'Loughlin, Thomas, "Individual Anonymity and Collective Identity: The Enigma of Early Medieval Latin Theologians," *Recherches de théologie et philosophie médiévale* 64 (1997)

O'Loughlin, Thomas, *Teachers and Code-Breakers: The Latin Genesis Tradition, 430–800*, Turnhout: Brepols, 1999

Stewart, Columba, *Cassian the Monk*, New York: Oxford University Press, 1998

Weder, Hans, "Disciple, Discipleship," in *The Anchor Bible Dictionary*, volume 2, edited by David Noel Freedman, New York and London: Doubleday, 1992

Mathurins. *See* Trinitarians

Maurists

The Benedictine Congregation of St.-Maur emerged as part of a monastic revival within the Catholic Church following the Protestant Reformation. In Protestant lands during the 16th century, monastic ideals and practices had come under severe criticism and were often rejected outright. Hundreds of monasteries were suppressed, above all in northern Germany, Switzerland, Holland, and England. The number of monks sank to less than half of pre-Reformation levels, and the spiritual condition of many of the surviving monasteries had badly deteriorated. The religious wars that erupted in many European lands only accelerated the decline.

As the centerpiece of Catholic response to the Reformation, the Council of Trent (1545–1563) decreed a major change in how monasteries were organized. Individual monasteries were ordered to merge into new regional congregations of ten or more houses under an elected superior general. This consolidation of authority was judged essential to correcting specific abuses, such as a widespread laxity in adherence to monastic vows, especially the rule of poverty.

Monastic confederations of this type soon sprang up across Catholic Europe. In France the major congregation was that of St.-Maur, composed originally of several monasteries in and around Paris. Influenced by congregations such as that of St.-Vannes at Verdun, the Maurists adopted an austere style of monastic life. An elected superior general was charged with implementing the necessary reforms. Every monk was to embrace fully the life of poverty, abstain from meat, work daily with his hands, and participate actively in the canonical liturgies of the monastic day. Finally, the Maurist constitution encouraged each monk to cultivate a scholarly interest. Study and research were legitimized as forms of manual labor.

During the 17th century three Maurists were most instrumental in promoting the values of learning and intellectual activity that would characterize the Maurist congregation: Dom Grégoire Tarrisse, Dom Luc d'Achery, and Dom Jean Mabillon.

Dom Tarrisse (1575–1648) had been a soldier before becoming a Maurist Benedictine at the age of 49. As elected superior general from 1630 to his death, he steered the infant Maurist community in directions that would define its mature outlook. To make education a central element in the Maurist tradition, Tarrisse installed a challenging program of academic studies for all prospective Maurists. The path to ordination took eight years, five of which involved not only courses in theology and philosophy but also intensive training in the often neglected disciplines of history and the classics. This broad curriculum was designed to promote scholarly interests, and it clearly succeeded. Meanwhile, the Congregation grew apace. By 1675 it comprised some 3,000 monks in close to 180 houses spread across France.

Another significant decision of Tarrisse was to make the ancient abbey of St.-Germain-des-Prés in Paris the headquarters of the Congregation. This was the Paris of the Sun King Louis XIV (1643–1715). With its major libraries and eminent writers and scholars, it had become the glittering capital of European cultural life. Paris would offer an ideal environment for the enterprises that Maurist scholars took in hand. Finally, Tarrisse conceived of a definitive history of the Benedictine Order and its achievements over the centuries, although mobilization of the necessary manpower and materials had only begun by the time of his death in 1648.

It was left to Tarrisse's protégé Dom Luc d'Achery (1609–1685) to carry forward his scholarly agenda. D'Achery spent virtually his whole career after his ordination in 1632 at the St.-Germain abbey in Paris, where, as chief librarian and as counselor to the superior general, he enlisted fellow monks in preparing the history of the Benedictine Order. He also undertook a multivolume set of biographies of monastic saints and martyrs and edited writings of medieval monastic historians. Finally, he sponsored at St.-Germain weekly meetings in which leading scholars and intellectuals of Paris discussed their work and the issues of the day.

This was the atmosphere that nurtured Dom Jean Mabillon (1632–1707), the greatest of Maurist scholars. After completing the celebrated Maurist curriculum, Mabillon was ordained in 1660. In 1664 d'Achery brought Mabillon to St.-Germain, where over the next two generations he would bring to bounteous fruition the seeds sown by Tarrisse and d'Achery. In addition Mabillon's pioneering work on methods of authenticating documents placed the study of medieval history, monastic and secular, on new foundations.

Mabillon wove the masses of evidence collected by his predecessors into a masterful narrative history of the Benedictine Order. He did likewise in writing lives of the monastic saints and martyrs. He placed each individual in historical context and carefully distinguished documented facts from edifying fables. As he wrote, "[the historian] must state frankly what he knows to be true. . . . Piety and truth must never be . . . separable, for honest and genuine piety can never conflict with the truth."

Then in 1681 Mabillon published a book that would bring him celebrity all across Europe. The *De Re Diplomatica* (*On Documents*) set forth the principles and methods through which charters, letters, and other old documents could be authenticated. Through careful examination of a manuscript's handwriting (paleography), dating, style and provenance, and so on, its degree of reliability could be established. The "auxiliary" disciplines of history, especially paleography, now came into their own.

Long before his death in 1707, Mabillon was regarded not only as the preeminent scholar of the day but also as the model of what the Maurist form of monasticism was all about: a monk, at once devout, modest, and congenial, who followed the Benedictine Rule to the letter.

In subsequent decades other Maurists would continue to produce important works on monastic and other topics, but after 1700 the sense of mission and collegial harmony of the great Maurists of the 17th century seemed gradually to fade in the face of mounting internal disputes and severe disruptions in society at large. For example, in some Maurist houses elements of puritan Jansenism confronted currents of secular rationalism in ways that sparked disruptive factionalism. Tendencies to relax the strict observance of the Rule existed as well.

The beginning of the end for the Maurists came in 1790, when the new anticlerical government of revolutionary France suppressed the Maurist Congregation. Shortly thereafter, in 1792, the last Maurist superior general was guillotined in Paris for refusing to swear allegiance to the revolutionary state. Recognizing the futility of attempting its revival, Pope Pius VII (1800–1823) officially dissolved the Maurist Congregation in 1818.

In the two centuries that the Congregation of St.-Maur endured, it made memorable contributions both to monastic culture and to the intellectual life of the age. Through meticulous source collections and writings in such fields as theology, patrology, liturgy, paleography, and history, the worlds of ancient and medieval monasticism were opened to detailed investigation. The Maurist legacy would be unique within the Benedictine Order, and for a time Maurist Benedictines gave eloquent proof that piety and learning can coexist.

DONALD D. SULLIVAN

See also Benedictines: General or Male; Congregations, Benedictine; France; Hagiography: Western Christian; Historiography, Recent: Western Christian; Humanism, Christian; Knowles, M. David; Manuscript Production: Christian; Scholars, Benedictine; Solesmes, France

Further Reading

Aris, Rutherford, "Jean Mabillon," in *Medieval Scholarship: Biographical Studies in the Formation of a Discipline*, edited by Helen Damico and Joseph B. Zavadil, New York and London: Garland, 1995

Barret-Kreigel, Blandine, *Jean Mabillon*, Paris: Presses Universitaire de France, 1988

Baudot, Jules, "Mauristes," in *Dictionnaire de Théologie Catholique*, volume 10, Paris: Letouzey et Ané, 1928

Bergkamp, Joseph, *Dom Jean Mabillon and the Benedictine Historical School of Saint-Maur*, Washington, D.C.: Catholic University of America Press, 1929

Chaussy, Yves, *Les Bénédictins de Saint Maur*, 2 vols., Paris: Études Augustiniennes, 1989, 1991

Knowles, David, "Jean Mabillon," in his *Historians and Character and Other Essays by David Knowles*, Cambridge: Cambridge University Press, 1963

Knowles, David, "Maurists," in his *Great Historical Enterprises: Problems in Monastic History*, London and New York: Nelson, 1963

Leclercq, Henri, *Mabillon*, 2 vols., Paris: Letouzey et Ané, 1953, 1957

Martène, Edmond, *Histoire de la Congrégation de Saint-Maur*, 9 vols., Paris: Picard, 1928–1943

Tassin, René, *Histoire Littéraire de la Congrégation de Saint-Maur*, Brussels: Chez Humblot, 1770; reprint, Ridgewood, New Jersey: Gregg Press, 1965

Maximus the Greek, St. c. 1470–1555

Greek Dominican friar, then Orthodox monk, polemicist, and translator in Russia

Maximus, in the world Michael Trivolis, was born in Arta (Epira), the son of an aristocratic family. He is one of very few churchmen of the 15th to 16th century who experienced the

Christian life of that time in its three major forms: Latin (Roman Catholic), Greek Orthodox, and Russian Orthodox. His main contribution was to Russian monasticism during the last part of his life, although he suffered prosecutions from the Russian Orthodox hierarchy for his pioneer work in the revision of Church-Slavonic translations and for his position in the quarrel about monastic wealth.

In the years from 1491 to 1504, the young Trivolis visited the main towns and abbeys of northern and central Italy (Florence, Bologna, Padua, Milan, and Venice), where he became acquainted with such bright personalities as Marsilio Ficino (1433–1499), Giovanni Lascaris, Aldo Manucio, and Girolamo Savonarola (1452–1498) and became a Dominican friar. From this early period we have only six letters of Maximus, but the imprint of humanistic thought can be felt in many his later works. In 1504 he left the Latin world for Mount Athos, where he changed his name to Maximus and devoted himself to theology. He stayed in Vatopedi abbey until 1516, when he was invited to Moscow by Grand Prince Basil (Vasilii) III (1505–1533) to translate the *Moralized Psalter* (*Tolkovaia Psaltir'*) into Church-Slavonic.

Maximus' fortunes in Muscovy show how ambivalent the Russians already were toward the Greeks. Maximus was welcomed as a learned monk and gathered a little intellectual circle in his cell at the Miracle (Chudov) monastery. His talents were held in such high esteem that after his first translation was completed (around 1522), he was denied authorization to return to Mount Athos. He supervised the revision of previous biblical and patristic translations and wrote some guidelines about how to correct old Church-Slavonic manuscripts. Meanwhile, every rephrasing of the traditional Russian religious texts could be and, in the end, was used against him because the Russian Church, autocephalous since 1448, thought that it was the keeper of the truest "Greek faith." A century later this attitude was of crucial importance when Patriarch Nikon (1652–1658) tried to correct crucial parts of the Russian liturgy according to the Greek model. Some Russian priests and their flock refused to comply, standing by the "true faith of [their] ancestors." Thus, they became known as "schismatics" (*raskol'niki*) or, as they put it themselves, "Old Believers" (*Staroobriadtsy*).

Maximus also endangered himself by indulging in polemics. He composed epistles against the Latins and the non-Christians but most of all against monastic property. Those works brought him close to the Non-Possessors (*nestiazhateli*), a group within the Russian Church who opposed ecclesiastical wealth. Their doctrine is often traced back to Nilus of Sora (Nil Maikov, c.1433–1508), a famous monastic publicist who praised eremitism as the supreme form of monastic life but did not condemn cenobitism and large monastic estates. Nilus seems indeed to have collaborated on the *Illuminator* (*Prosvetitel'*), the main treatise written by Joseph of Volokolamsk (Iosif Sanin, 1439/40–1515), the most articulate advocate of the "rich Church." At the time of Maximus' staying in Russia, the leader of the Non-Possessors was Vassian Patrikeev, the son of a very influential Muscovite boyar who had been forcibly tonsured in 1499 because of a political fall from grace. Vassian spent some years in St.-Cyrill of Beloozero abbey, a rich monastery but of austere standing, not far from Nilus of Sora's own hermitage. Around 1509 Vassian could return to Moscow and started criticizing monastic wealth, apparently with the (tacit) approbation of Basil III. The opposite side was headed by Daniel, a disciple of Joseph of Volokolamsk, who became metropolitan of the Russian Church in 1522. Thanks to Daniel, Maximus was twice condemned for heresy, first in 1525 and then in 1531, together with Vassian. Maximus' revised translation of the *Nomocanon* was especially at stake in the process; he was convicted of doubting the double nature of God (which he did not).

Whereas Vassian seems to have died soon after this, Maximus was subjected to a mild confinement first in Tver and then at the Trinity St.-Sergius monastery (from 1547 to c. 1548). There he was protected by Abbot Artem, who was, to put it simply, a partisan of monastic poverty while serving at the head of a very rich community. In rapid succession Artem abandoned his abbacy (1552), was condemned for heresy, and fled to Lithuania (1555). Meanwhile Maximus experienced a kind of rehabilitation. Indeed in his later days his teaching was again in favor, as Ivan IV the Terrible (1533–1584) opposed the extension of ecclesiastical property, which was officially forbidden during the 1551 Hundred Chapters (Stoglav) Synod. The translations and original epistles composed by Maximus gained renown: in Russia up to 130 manuscript anthologies of his works are extant, dating from the middle of the 16th to the end of the 19th century.

These circumstances explain why a "heretic" was turned into a Russian saint. As early as 1564 Maximus appears on the frescoes of the Moscow Kremlin Archangel Michael's church figuring among the great antique writers and philosophers. Although at the end of the 16th century some icons represent him as a saint, he was formally canonized by the Russian Church only in 1988.

Pierre Gonneau

See also Libraries: Eastern Christian; Moscow, Russia; Mount Athos, Greece; Russia: History; Savonarola, Girolamo

Biography

Born into a Byzantine family, Michael Trivolis moved at an early age to Corfu and then in 1492 to Florence, where he knew Ficino and Savonarola. In 1502 he entered the Dominican Order in Italy, only to leave it in 1504. Two years later he became a monk at Mount Athos. When the ruler of Muscovy requested a Slavonic translation of Greek texts, Maximus traveled to Moscow in 1518 to accept the task. His recommendation that the Russian church return to obedience to Constantinople led in 1525 and again in 1531 to his condemnation and imprisonment. By 1548 he was released and spent the rest of his life at the monastery of the Holy Trinity-St. Sergius near Moscow.

Major Works

Maxiumus' major works include translations of biblical texts (and comments on them), patristic literature (Basil the Great, Gregory the Theologian, John Chrysostom), the *Nomocanon*, and extracts from Symeon Metaphrast's

Menologe; epistles on the correction of Russian books, on the correction of books, and on the alphabetical order; and epistles on repentance, on pagan seduction, on monastic life, and against Armenians, Catholics, and Lutherans. See Denissoff in the Further Reading section for a selection of translations from the Greek and Church-Slavonic works.

Sochineniia prepodobnogo Maksima Greka (Works of St. Maximus the Greek), 2 vols., 1859–1862
Maksim Grek Tvoreniia (Works), 3 vols., 1996 (in Russian translation)

Further Reading

Bushkovitch, Paul, *Religion and Society in Russia: The Sixteenth and Seventeenth Centuries*, New York: Oxford University Press, 1992
Denissoff, Elie, *Maxime le Grec et l'Occident: Contribution à l'histoire de la pensée religieuse et philosophique de Michel Trivolis*, Louvain: Bibliothèque de l'Université, and Paris, Desclée de Brouwer, 1943
Haney, Jack A.V., *From Italy to Muscovy: The Life and Works of Maksim the Greek*, Munich: Fink, 1973
Ivanov, Aleksei I., *Literaturnoe nasledie Maksima Greka: Kharakteristika, atribucii, bibliografiia* (The Literary Heritage of Maximus the Greek: Characterization, Attributions, and Bibliography), Leningrad: Nauka, 1969
Obolensky, Dimitri, "Italy, Mount Athos and Muscovy: The Three Worlds of Maximos the Greek," *Proceedings of the British Academy* 67 (1981)
Olmsted, Hugh M., "A Learned Greek Monk in Muscovite Exile: Maksim Greek and the Old Testament Prophets," *Modern Greek Studies Yearbook* 3 (1987)
Schulze, Bernhard, *Maksim Grek als Theologe*, Rome: Pontifical Oriental Institute, 1963
Sinitsyna, Nina V., *Maksim Grek v Rossii* (Maximus the Greek in Russia), Moscow: Nauka, 1977

McInerney, Michael Joseph Vincent 1877–1963

U.S. Benedictine architect

Michael Joseph Vincent McInerney, a Benedictine monk and Catholic priest, was a prolific architect who rooted his design concepts in his own monastic values. Through a career of more than six decades, the McInerney style blended art and austerity, symbols and simplicity, and efficiency and elegance to enrich American churches and cloisters.

Born Joseph Vincent McInerney in McKeesport, Pennsylvania, he was apprenticed at age 15 (1892) to the British-born architect W.A. Thomas, then working in Pittsburgh, Pennsylvania. Showing exceptional gifts and a rare art, Joseph was made a partner in Thomas' firm after only two years of work. Nevertheless, dissatisfied with his accomplishment, McInerney decided to resign his position (1900), intending to enrich his art by the study of classics.

In Hilary term of 1900, Joseph enrolled at the college of the Benedictine monks in North Carolina. Concealing his architectural experience, he led the life of an ordinary student until, five months into his studies, the college was ravaged by fire. The resultant need for the school's reconstruction induced McInerney to confess his expertise and offer his professional services. Edified in these labors by the monks whom he assisted, McInerney determined to enter the Benedictine novitiate (1902). With his vocation came an eloquent redefinition of his art: McInerney's architecture began to draw its substance from the values he learned in the cloister. His style was soon made more austere: in construction he came to rely on natural elements and uncluttered surfaces, and he grew attentive to St. Benedict's admonition that the artisans of the monastery should glorify God in all things (RB 57.9).

McInerney's greatest achievement in ecclesial architecture was St. Michael Church (1952) in Wheeling, West Virginia. Behind its conventional exterior stood an oratory of rare art, articulated in the neo-Gothic style. This photograph shows a side aisle, a passageway made eloquent by McInerney's characteristic blend of simplicity, solid materials, and aesthetic composition.
Photo courtesy of Belmont Abbey Archives

Michael McInerney created an architectural style – a variation on Gothic Revival – that he called "American Benedictine" because of its adoption by so many American monasteries. Its classic statement is Saint Leo Hall (1906, seen here) at Belmont Abbey College in North Carolina. Photo courtesy of Belmont Abbey Archives

Taking the name Michael in religion, McInerney was soon professed (1903), admitted to solemn vows (1906), and ordained a priest (1907). Concurrent with his final monastic commitment, Fr. Michael unveiled an architectural style that he called American Benedictine. It reflected his determination to bring art to the "boxes" that financial constraints often imposed on his designs. American Benedictine architecture adapted these boxes by heightening them visually and varying the configuration of the masonry to suggest "towers." Its classic statement is found in McInerney's St. Leo Hall (1906) at Belmont Abbey in North Carolina. This style won immediate acceptance in the United States, earning widespread employment and imitation.

In later years, Dom Michael's architectural designs varied increasingly, and his art expanded into other media, including church paraphernalia, tombstones, and accoutrements of monastic, priestly, and academic life. However, architecture remained his primary focus. Overall, he designed more than 500 structures, virtually all for Roman Catholic institutional use in the United States. These included more than 220 churches, missions, and chapels; 78 schools and orphan asylums; 27 hospitals and infirmaries; 18 convents and monasteries; at least 10 freestanding gymnasiums, and countless auxiliary and support facilities, ranging from grandstands to barns. McInerney's work at his own monastery provides a microcosm of his creative expression: his designs for the Carolina campus included such structures as an imposing multi-arched portecochere (1902) that transformed the plain facade of his monastery; the American-Benedictine-styled St. Leo Hall (1906); brick, Gothic Revival cattle barns (1916); a well house outfitted with dormer windows, inlaid brick crosses, and a cloaked doorway, all proportioned on the model of a child's playhouse (c. 1922); an elegant Gothic fortress gymnasium (1929); and a versatile, austere, postmodern library (1957). His best church design is probably the neo-Gothic oratory of St. Michael (Wheeling, West Virginia, 1952), with its deceptively conventional brick exterior that opens on an imposingly austere, Gothic-themed marble interior.

In addition to his architectural work, McInerney served on the faculty of Belmont Abbey College for more than half a century. Publications included contributions to reference works and commentaries on art glass and hospital architecture. In his lifetime he was honored by various learned and architectural societies and received an honorary doctorate (St. Vincent College, Pennsylvania, 1959) that recognized and cited his contribution

Dom Michael Joseph Vincent McInerney, O.S.B. (1877–1963): architect, Benedictine monk, Catholic priest, educator, writer. Photo courtesy of Belmont Abbey Archives

to art and architecture that he accomplished within the context of his monastic and priestly vocation.

McInerney died on 3 March 1963 and was buried in the cemetery he had designed for his Carolina monastery.

PASCHAL BAUMSTEIN, O.S.B.

See also Architecture: Western Christian Monasteries; United States: Western Christian

Biography

Pennsylvania-born McInerney was apprenticed at age 15 to a Pittsburgh architect. At age 23 he resigned to study at the Benedictine College at Belmont, North Carolina. A need to rebuild the college after a fire brought out McInerney's training as an architect, and in 1902 he entered the novitiate. Over a career of more than six decades and 500 structures, he pioneered the "American Benedictine" style of architecture.

Further Reading

Baumstein, Paschal, *The Art of Michael McInerney*, Belmont, North Carolina: Archives of Belmont Abbey, 1997

"A Church Should Make People Mindful of God," in *The Abbey Message*, Subiaco, Arkansas: Subiaco Abbey, 1951

Lewis, Clifford, "A Jesuit Institution – A Benedictine Architect," *Wheeling Chronicle* (June 1980)

McInerney, Michael, "Antique Stained Glass and Religious Atmosphere," *Homiletic and Pastoral Review* (July 1956)

The 24 January 1942 edition of the *Georgia Bulletin* (Catholic newspaper) is dedicated to McInerney and his career and contains photographs of his designs and a partial inventory of his buildings. The McInerney papers have been collected in the Archives of Belmont Abbey (North Carolina).

Medicine, Buddhist

The healing and medical arts have been part of Buddhist monastic life since the beginning of the community. Evidence for this is preserved in Buddhist monastic documents in Pāli, Sanskrit, Tibetan, and Chinese. The most important of these are the canonical Vinaya collections. In English, the best sources on early monastic medicine are Horner's (1949) translation of the Pāli Vinaya and Zysk's (1991) excellent study of Buddhist monastic medicine. Other sources in Western languages include many new studies on Tibetan and Chinese medical systems, although the latter are not restricted to medical practices in monasteries.

The Buddha's original followers had two sources for medical theories and applications: theological formulas derived from Vedic texts and the remedies of nontraditional, or nonbrahmanical, wandering ascetics (*śramaṇa*). Vedic formulas, largely from the *Atharva Veda*, involved ritual practices that invoked the power of the gods to remedy human problems. Brahmin priests usually functioned as intermediaries. However, around the sixth century B.C. the prominence of the brahmin priests gave way to a new kind of religious inquiry, one that looked for religious answers in the constituent parts of the world and human body. Human functions and dysfunctions were subject to introspective analysis and treatment instead of external appeals to Vedic deities. This development involved analysis and rejection of ancient social institutions in favor of new ascetic lifestyles, such as that of the Buddhists, that centered around religious inquiry. In addition to these Indian religious and social forces, the ancient pre-Buddhist tradition may have been influenced by the medical ideas of the Greeks, the Chinese, and others.

Buddhist monastic medicine, like the earliest community itself, originated among wandering ascetics who sought cures and religious enlightenment through analysis of the constituent parts of the human body and the world. As the numbers of these wanderers grew, begging and wandering became impractical in India's village-based, agrarian culture. In response, medical and religious practitioners gradually established sedentary, cenobitic institutions. Medicine eventually became part of the monastic curriculum and after centuries of development evolved into a recognized branch of monastic education with specialists, pharmacopoeia, and a literary corpus.

A sick man walking toward Zenkōji Temple, Nagano, Japan. Photo courtesy of David Moore

Medical practice in Buddhist monasteries flourished because it was consistent with Buddhist doctrines. The Buddhist "middle way" between complete rejection and realistic affirmation of worldly conventions made medical therapies acceptable and even desirable. Although not parallel, the Buddhist Four Noble Truths contain an implicit validation of medical therapy. The First Noble Truth asserts that existence is pervaded by physical and psychological suffering. The other three Truths lay out the cause, the end, and the path to the end of suffering. Activities that alleviate the suffering of other beings are at once good for those beings and produce merit for the caregiver. Given these doctrinal considerations, the practice of treating diseases was institutionalized very early in the history of Buddhism. Some evidence of this success is in the Vinaya literature, in which an entire section is devoted to medical treatments and medical treatments are often indicated as proper activity. The early Vinaya attests to the importance of medicine and healing by allowing monks four necessary things: alms food, robes, lodging, and cow's urine as medicine.

The earliest medical procedures were administered by monks to other monks. Eventually monks were allowed to treat laypeople, and soon adepts in medicine treated donors and prominent citizens in their communities. Medical practice demonstrated Buddhist principles in action and, if effective, could win support from the lay community. Patients were originally treated in their own living quarters and later in sickrooms. Hospices were not widespread until the appearance of large Buddhist monastic universities in the Gupta period (320–c. 535). The large monasteries developed elaborate medical traditions with separate curricula, libraries, pharmacies, and treatment protocols.

Like its Indian predecessors Buddhist medical theory is based on the theory of "humors," i.e. the by-products of natural processes necessary for the physical operations of the body. These are wind, bile, and phlegm. The body itself was thought to be made up of combinations of five elemental substances (air, earth, fire, water, and space). Disease results from improper amounts of the humors and the resulting imbalances of the elements. Diseases can be the result of previous negative actions (*karma*) but can also be caused by excesses of heat or cold, environmental factors, improper levels of daily activity, and stress.

The Buddhist medical system rests on an accurate understanding of human anatomy. Late medical charts show the circulatory system, the skeletal system, and all internal organs in precise detail. Buddhists certainly observed anatomical functions and very likely engaged in postmortem dissection.

The Vinaya recalls that when the Buddha met some of his disciples who were in a wretched state of health, he allowed them to use medicines. The earliest allowable medicine was cow's urine, but this was soon expanded to include five fundamental medicines. These were ghee (clarified butter), fresh butter, oil, honey, and molasses. Allowable medicines were soon expanded to include a very wide range of herbs, spices, foods, and healing techniques that demonstrate the Buddhist commitment to medicine and healing. Because the allowable medicines were so numerous, Buddhist monasteries soon established special storage places and specialists for dispensing medicines.

As Buddhist philosophy and ritual practice developed, medical therapies expanded to include devotions, mantras, and worship of buddhas and bodhisattvas associated with healing. The Buddhist traditions in China and Tibet imported the figure of the Healing Buddha, Bhaiṣajyaguru. These traditions sometimes attempted to find causes of physical diseases in the mind and vice versa; the distinction between mental and physical became blurred. Similarly, both internal and external causes and conditions could generate both disease and healing therapy. Elaborate external rituals with corresponding internal meditations were used extensively in the treatment of psychological and physical diseases.

All these techniques, especially meditation, have received much attention in recent scholarship. Herbal remedies and naturopathic treatments based on theories of mental and physical

An image of an arhat (Japanese, *rakan*) at Zenkōji Temple, Nagano, Japan. Rubbing any spot on the image's body is said to heal that spot in the pilgrim.
Photo courtesy of David Moore

imbalances are often considered alternatives to more aggressive or invasive modern methods. Meditation practices for the treatment of diseases such as hypertension have received much attention in recent years and often prove effective, especially when used in conjunction with lifestyle and dietary changes that are not, in certain essential aspects, far removed from the renunciative lifestyles of early Buddhist monks.

PAUL NIETUPSKI

See also Ashram, Influence of; Gestures, Buddhist; Hygiene: Buddhist Perspectives; Rules, Buddhist (Vinaya); Social Services: Buddhist

Further Reading

Aris, Anthony, et al., editors, *Tibetan Medical Paintings: Illustrations to the Blue Beryl Treatise of Sangye Gyamtso (1653–1705)*, New York: Abrams, and London: Serindia, 1992

Horner, Isaline B., translator, *Book of the Discipline*, London: Pali Text Society, 1949; reprint, 1992

Van Alphen, Jan, and Anthony Aris, editors, *Oriental Medicine: An Illustrated Guide to the Asian Arts of Healing*, London: Serindia, 1995; Boston: Shambala, 1996

Zysk, Kenneth G., *Asceticism and Healing in Ancient India: Medicine in the Buddhist Monastery*, New York: Oxford University Press, 1991

Medicine, Christian. *See* Pharmacology

Meditation: Buddhist Perspectives

In Buddhism meditation is the central spiritual discipline. Siddhārtha Gautama was meditating when his enlightenment experience occurred, transforming him into the Buddha; ever since his followers have done likewise to become awakened themselves. The Buddha's enlightenment solved his own problems, but it does not solve the spiritual problems of Buddhists who follow him. They must experience the nature of reality for themselves. Buddhists consistently affirm that intellectual understanding, by itself, cannot substitute for direct personal experience. Nor can performing rituals or even following Buddhism's ethical code bring one to enlightenment. Meditation is the surest route to that transformative experience. Thus, the Buddha taught his disciples how to do the very meditations that he had done, and he still serves as an example of how meditation can awaken anyone to full understanding of "things as they are."

Thus, it is no accident that meditation is included in the Eightfold Path, the basic guideline for living and becoming enlightened that was developed in early Buddhism and that remains important in all forms of Buddhism to the present day. The seventh and eighth components of the path, mindfulness (*sati*) and concentration (*samādhi*), concern how to meditate. Likewise in Mahāyāna Buddhism, a later movement that advocates the path of bodhisattva training in addition to the Eightfold Path, the fifth *pāramitā* (transcendent virtue) to be practiced by a bodhisattva is *dhyāna* (meditation). Esoteric Vajrayāna Buddhism developed additional meditation practices. In all Buddhist countries and all varieties of Buddhism, with the exception of Pure Land Buddhism, meditation remains central.

In classical Buddhism meditation was often regarded mainly as a discipline for monastics, for whom it was essential. Lay Buddhists were thought to be too busy for serious meditation and not likely to be interested in it. However, in contemporary times, both in Asia and the West, lay meditation movements are growing in popularity.

Because the word "meditation" can mean different things in different religious contexts, it is important to clarify the essentials of Buddhist meditation. There are two forms: contentless meditations on the breath and meditations with content or "form." Of these meditations using the breath is more basic and more widespread. Meditations with content are especially associated with Tantric forms of Buddhism, whether Tibetan or Japanese. Basic meditations on the breath are "contentless" because they involve no intellectual, verbal, or doctrinal content. Thus, they can be – and especially in contemporary times – often are done by non-Buddhists and by people of any religious or secular orientation. By contrast form meditations involve fixing one's attention on a symbol, a meditation deity, a mantra, or some other content. Unlike formless meditations, they are not religiously neutral.

Because formless meditations using the breath comprise the earliest and most basic type of Buddhist meditation, they are common throughout the Buddhist world, although precise instructions vary in the different Buddhist schools. The most common and best-known techniques today include Zen meditation,

Seated Buddha Śākyamuni in meditation, Gal Vihāra, Poḷonnaruva, Sri Lanka, colossal stone relief (about seven meters in height), reign of Parākramabāhu I (A.D. 1153–1186).
Photo courtesy of Marylin M. Rhie

often associated with Japan, although Korean, Chinese, and Vietnamese forms are also important; Vipassanā meditation, which is widespread in Southeast Asian Theravāda Buddhism; and *śamatha-vipaśyanā* (mindfulness-awareness) meditation taught by Tibetan teachers. Today all these forms of meditation are readily available in the Western world in the wake of many Asian Buddhist teachers, both monastic and lay, who began teaching widely in the West beginning in the 1960s.

Although many books describe how to do these various meditation techniques, all schools of meditation agree that personal instruction or at least instruction by videotape is preferable to learning meditation from a book. Instruction in basic breath meditations begins with attention to the body and posture. The famous cross-legged position (although not necessarily full lotus) is preferred by most teachers, but other postures also work if the cross-legged posture proves too difficult. How precise and motionless one's posture should be varies from school to school, with Zen being the most rigorous. The central aspect of meditation technique deals with the breath. Attention is brought to the breath, and an attempt is made to maintain that focus. Exactly how this focus on breath is achieved varies from school to school, but the breath is universally chosen for several reasons: it is always available, it is neutral rather than having any specific religious or spiritual content, and it is the indicator of life. Finally, meditation techniques must deal with mental chatter – with the flow of thoughts, emotions, and sense impressions. It is commonly thought that one goal of meditation is to stop thinking, but that is not usually what happens. Rather the goal is in how one works with thoughts. Buddhist meditation techniques universally involved noticing thoughts but not acting on them and especially not evaluating or judging them. When the mind strays and gets lost in thought – in fantasies of the future or memories of the past – one simply returns one's awareness to the breath, to the exact present moment.

Two monks receiving meditation instruction from Babta Sunim, abbot of Unhae-sa Monastery in North Kyŏngsang province, South Korea. Photo courtesy of John Powers

People often wonder what is the point of such meditation. It is not to relax or to achieve a "higher state of consciousness," nor is it to go into a trance in which one withdraws from awareness of the external world. Rather one becomes more mindful of one's body, sensations, emotions, and thoughts and more aware of the whole situation in which they exist without reacting to or becoming attached to anything that occurs in meditation. According to Buddhism such equanimity and detachment prove valuable not only in formal meditation but also in daily life. In fact the point of meditation is to be able to maintain equanimity and detachment in daily life, not only in periods of sitting meditation. Formal meditation is not an end in itself but rather the most reliable method of developing ongoing awareness. This mental state is the route to seeing things "as they are" rather than as we fabricate them and thus is essential to enlightenment.

On the basis of this formless meditation technique, other kinds of meditation can be attempted. Because compassion and lovingkindness are so essential to Buddhism, contemplative meditations to develop them are frequently emphasized. Sometimes these meditations are done in the rhythm of the breathing: on the outbreath think of giving compassionate help; on the inbreath think of taking other people's misery into oneself. Other times they are not synchronized with the breathing but are simply mental activities. Clearly this type of meditation is different from formless meditation; instead of noticing thoughts without dwelling on them, specific thoughts are cultivated as a way gradually for the thinker to change. However, without the foundation of formless meditation on the breath, it is unlikely that one would be able to maintain any continuity of contemplation. In these meditations on lovingkindness and compassion, the meditation begins with extending compassion to those whom one cares about, then to those toward whom one is neutral, and finally to those whom one might regard as enemies or competitors. An advanced form of this meditation would involve seeing the emptiness and nonduality of the giver of compassion, the recipient, and the act of compassion itself.

Another contemplative meditation is more analytical and intellectual. One investigates thoughts and phenomena. Where do thoughts come from, and where do they go? Do they have any real substantiality? Can one locate them or capture them? Of what are phenomena composed? Do they form a whole entity apart from their parts, or are they just a collection of parts? Can the parts be further subdivided so that we can find a partless part? Do phenomena exist separate from the perceiver of phenomena? Do they have independent reality? Do they have permanence? These investigative meditations gradually convince the meditator of the truth of egolessness (*anātman*) and emptiness (*śūnyatā*), the central components of the Buddhist philosophical worldview.

More esoteric and much more complicated are the form meditations typical of Tantric Buddhism, both in Tibet and in Japan. The meditator's complete body, speech, and mind are taken over in these meditations. The mind is occupied with ongoing visualizations, speech with chanting a liturgy or reciting a mantra, and the body with both sitting posture and numerous ritual gestures that punctuate the meditation, often to the accompaniment of musical instruments. This style of meditation often alternates with formless sitting meditation, which is the essential counterpart of the complex form meditations.

Visualization practice often involves maintaining one's attention on a *yidam* (meditation deity), an anthropomorphic, personified portrayal of the meditator's own enlightened mind. There are many *yidam*s in the Tantric Buddhist pantheon; the *yidam* that is the focus of one's meditation is assigned in an initiation ritual in which the guru empowers the student to practice this form of meditation and teaches him or her how to do it. The chanted liturgy describes the visualization in great detail, elaborating the symbolic meanings of each detail of the visualization. When the liturgy has completely described the visualization, a period of mantra recitation follows. A mantra is a short string of syllables, usually in Sanskrit. Because the verbal meaning of a mantra is irrelevant, it is not translated from Sanskrit into any of the Buddhist vernaculars. The mantra's meaning is that it encapsulates the visualization in sound so that the mantra, and especially its most important syllable, becomes the aural form the *yidam*. Finally, a sign language of hand gestures is used to accentuate parts of the liturgy to exteriorize its meaning while also proclaiming that meaning.

These complex meditations serve the purpose of transforming both the meditator and the world that he or she perceives from a mundane form into the true, sacred form. This transformation is a matter of purifying the meditator's perceptions and developing a sacred outlook through these meditations. One's self and the world appear one way to those who have not practiced meditation and another way to those who have practiced meditation intensively for a long time. According to Buddhist perspective the meditator's perceptions correspond to things "as they are." Discovering things "as they are" is always the point of Buddhist meditation or philosophy.

Meditation, the central spiritual discipline of Buddhism, must be practiced regularly and intensively to be effective. Monasteries and nunneries can be dedicated to this discipline; for laypeople who have jobs and family responsibilities, finding time for this discipline can be much more difficult, but many nevertheless do take on these disciplines. In the context of monastic institutions or the meditation centers that often replace them in the West, the minimal schedule of meditation would include two periods of meditation, one in the morning and one at sunset or in the evening. Each school of Buddhism recommends different meditation intensives, but all schools agree that it is imperative to spend longer periods of time in which one meditates all day. The Vipassanā movement requires a minimum of a ten-day retreat. Vipassanā centers hold three-month retreats periodically. Zen Buddhists frequently participate in *sesshin*. These intensives can be of varying lengths. Five- or seven-day *sesshins* are common, and some Zen monasteries offer yearlong training periods. Tibetan Vajrayāna Buddhism has a large repertoire of meditation intensives. In Tibet it was quite common for the greatest meditation masters to spend years in solitary retreat in the mountains. All fully trained monastic meditators completed the traditional three-year, three-month, and three-day retreats, which is often a prerequisite for becoming a teacher. Western Vajrayāna centers host retreats of many lengths, including the traditional three-year retreat. Week- or month-long intensives are frequently undertaken and are required of more serious students by many meditation teachers. However, in every case it is also emphasized that daily practice is essential for success at meditation.

RITA M. GROSS

See also Body: Buddhist Perspectives; Buddhism: Western; Celibacy: Buddhist; Chan/Zen: Japan; Deities, Buddhist; Dialogue, Intermonastic: Buddhist Perspectives; Ennin; Gestures, Buddhist; Hakuin; Kōan; Mount Meru; Prayer: Buddhist Perspectives; Saichō; Stūpa; Zen, Arts of

Further Reading

Blofeld, John, *The Tantric Mysticism of Tibet*, New York: Dutton, 1970
Nyanaponika, Thera, *The Heart of Buddhist Meditation*, New York: Samuel Weiser, 1973; London: Rider, 1983
Sekida, Katsuki, *Zen Training: Methods and Philosophy*, New York: Weatherhill, 1975
Trungpa, Chogyam, *Shambhala: The Sacred Path of the Warrior*, Boulder, Colorado: Shambhala, 1984
Yamasaki, Taiko, *Shingon: Japanese Esoteric Buddhism*, Boston: Shambhala, 1988
Yeshe, Thubten, *Introduction to Tantra: A Vision of Totality*, Boston: Wisdom, 1987

Meditation: Christian Perspectives

In the Christian tradition the term *meditation* currently refers to the entire process of contemplative prayer. Under the influence of various forms of meditation characteristic especially of Buddhism and Hinduism, the term has recently been reappropriated in a Christian context to designate a similar spectrum of processes and practices long taught in the Western monastic tradition. These had become obscured since the 16th century by restricting the term *meditation* to activities of thinking, reflecting, reasoning, imagining, and resolving. Thus, within classical Christian texts the word *meditation* might refer to one among many practices that promote contemplative experience. In a broader sense the term denotes any practice for focusing intention and attention that disposes the seeker to be aware of the

Divine Presence and as a result to become receptive to transformation of consciousness and action.

The Latin word *meditatio* translates the Hebrew word *haga*, which denotes recitation of the word of God in a somatic, rhythmic process that facilitates being affected by that word and by God. This ancient Jewish practice of recitation, memorization, and repetition of a word or phrase is found in many other religious traditions. Examples include *dhikr* among the Sufis, mantras among the Hindus, and the "brief prayer" discovered by John Cassian (c. 360–after 430) in the Egyptian desert and recommended in his *Conferences*. Western monasticism developed this form of meditation through the fourfold organic process of *lectio divina* and later in a musical form in Gregorian chant. Popular piety retained elements of these meditative practices through the recitation of litanies and the rosary.

The Greeks translated *haga* with the word *melete*, implying a movement into the depths of the human heart, thereby opening the self to the action of the Spirit. Recitation of the word-prayer in the heart continued in an unbroken lineage in Greek and Russian Hesychasm, where it was known as the Jesus Prayer. In the 20th century the anonymous *Way of the Pilgrim* reintroduced this practice to the West in its Russian eremetical form. In this practice some form of the name of Jesus or the entire phrase "Lord Jesus Christ, have mercy on me a sinner" becomes the word focus. The 14th-century author of *The Cloud of Unknowing* recommended a focus word of only one syllable, such as "God" or "love," rather than a lengthy phrase. In the 20th century two Cistercians, Basil Pennington and Thomas Keating (b. 1923), have taught and promoted this practice under the name of "centering prayer." A Benedictine, John Main (1926–1982), and his disciple Laurence Freeman have likewise taught a Christian form of meditation based on the recitation of a single mantra, "Maranatha," largely influenced by Hindu mantra practice. This monologistic form of prayer represents a simplification by the meditator, thus increasing receptivity to the Spirit's action and presence. The focus word provides a transition into the experience of contemplation – a resting in God or a simple experience of peaceful quiet in the self amid a sense of God's presence.

Within Christian contemplative practice reading aloud or silently in a meditative attitude is rooted in the entire practice of religion. This requires three elements: an ethical way of living, a form of public worship in the liturgy that is expressed not only in words but in a wide variety of religious art forms, and a community life focused on love of God and love of neighbor. These specialized processes related to assimilating a "word" presuppose an intense desire to live in harmony with God and to seek experience of the presence of God. Unlike Buddhism, Christian meditation has not emphasized the attainment of specific states of consciousness that are likely to result from correct and diligent performance of a meditative practice as much as it has emphasized a focus away from self-absorption, self-centeredness, and ego preoccupations. Focus on the word promotes listening to God's speech, as recorded in sacred texts and incarnated in the life, actions, and teachings of Jesus. The focus falls on a form of God absorption through attentiveness either to God's utterance or to His incarnation until the meditator becomes Godlike or Jesuslike in thought, behavior, and presence. Spiritual teachers such as the ancient imas and abbas of the Egyptian desert could also mediate the divine by speaking a personalized word to their disciples, who in turn took this word back to meditation.

Another way of using a word or phrase is responsive rather than receptive. Here the meditator repeats a word or phrase that he or she has adopted as an effective prayer from the Scriptures or some other text. Through such a phrase the meditator seeks something from God in an open and receptive way but, even more important, becomes present to God. He allows himself to be affected as much by God's reciprocal presence in consciousness as by the fulfillment of the prayer desire.

Contemporary psychological studies analyze and describe common features of meditation practices from all religious traditions. Studies in consciousness and structural analysis of the practices have provided some of the most fruitful areas of interreligious monastic exploration. Notwithstanding the emphasis on method and technique characteristic of the Western cultures, these studies recognize that men and women who have practiced the disciplines of meditation escape the conditioned self of ego consciousness and thereby open themselves to other realms of experience resulting in personal transformation. Thus, it is important to recognize that both Eastern and Western meditation have a goal beyond particular procedure. Naranjo and Ornstein (1971) assert,

> If we take this step beyond a behavioral definition of meditation in terms of a *procedure*, external or even internal, we may be able to see that meditation cannot be equated with thinking or non-thinking, with sitting still or dancing, with withdrawing from the senses or waking up the senses: meditation is concerned with the development of a *presence*, a modality of being, which may be expressed or developed in whatever situation the individual may be involved.

As contemporary commentators on mysticism have noted, texts that discuss contemplative prayer or describe mystical experience have a performative aspect. Their authors intend not only to offer ideas about prayer, contemplation, or meditation but also invite or incite the reader to a similar experience.

Christianity recognizes that a wide variety of practices might achieve roughly the same results. Some of these practices are graduated according to a meditator's spiritual development acquired through concentrating attention on a particular object of consciousness while focusing intention toward relationship with God. Other practices might be appropriate at any stage of spiritual development but will be pursued to ever greater degrees by a person with real facility for focusing attention and relaxing ego control. Meditation practices in both the East and the West seek first to develop concentration and focused attention and then proceed to deconstruct conditioning and false consciousness. Meditative practices can themselves become a form of condition-

Discalced Carmelite nun in meditation.
Photo courtesy of Jim Young

ing that needs to be changed from time to time to release the meditator from habitual emotional, physical, and mental attitudes that might have developed.

Lectio divina merits further elaboration. Guigo II's (d. c. 1188) *The Ladder of Monks* (late 12th century) names the four stages of the process as *lectio*, *meditatio*, *oratio*, and *contemplatio*. These he compares to four rungs of a ladder connecting earth to heaven by which the monk can "touch heavenly secrets." He then describes each of the stages of the process circling through them several times, elaborating different facets of the stage and offering an extended example using one of the Beatitudes:

> Reading is the careful study of the Scriptures, concentrating all one's powers on it. Meditation is the busy application of the mind to seek with the help of one's own reason for knowledge of hidden truth. Prayer is the heart's devoted turning to God to drive away evil and obtain what is good. Contemplation is when the mind is in some sort lifted up to God and held above itself, so that it tastes the joys of everlasting sweetness. . . .
>
> Reading seeks for the sweetness of a blessed life, meditation perceives it, prayer asks for it, contemplation tastes it. Reading, as it were, puts food whole into the mouth, meditation chews it and breaks it up, prayer extracts its flavor, contemplation is the sweetness itself which gladdens and refreshes. Reading works on the outside, meditation on the pith, prayer asks for what we long for, contemplation gives us delight in the sweetness which we have found.

Within the monastic setting the text so chosen emerged either from public recitation or chanting of the Psalms or from other readings from the liturgy. It might also come from a monastic's personal reading of texts in this slow and deliberate fashion. Thus, in the Rule of St. Benedict the monastic was encouraged to savor a word or text that had touched the heart in the Divine Office and continue afterward in private contemplation. The monastic schedule specified time to be given to the practice of *lectio*. The text was often vocalized aloud, repeated, and memorized as part of the process. This assimilation of key passages and phrases literally permeated the entire consciousness of the monastic. The *meditatio* phase included not only apprehending the meaning of the text but also placing oneself in the narrative, imaging the scene interiorly, or contemplating a painting in the monastery or in an illuminated manuscript. Monastic calligraphers continued their meditation in the scribal process and in designing their illuminations. These first two phases lead to the personal response of *oratio*, either praise or petition. Finally, after words and feelings of response have subsided, the monastic simply rests in God, savoring the Divine presence. This fourfold process constitutes one organic whole. As the contemplative process develops, more time is spent in the latter phases of *contemplatio*, which Christian tradition considers to result from God's gift rather than from human effort. The *oratio* phase tends to become very simple, focusing on the single word, phrase, or sentence described previously. Thus, for Christian monastics meditation can be defined as that part of the prayer process initiated and sustained through human effort, whereas contemplation is God's response to that effort. Only from the 12th century on did these practices become somewhat systematized and mystical states or experiences categorized and described. From the 16th century on, methods of prayer that overemphasized thought, reflection, or imagination gradually eclipsed the understanding of meditation in a more holistic sense.

Naranjo discovered that a trait characteristic of all types of meditation at the procedural level is "a *dwelling upon* something." Generally, meditative practices involve focusing attention "upon a single object, sensation, utterance, issue, mental state, or activity." In Eastern meditation practice this focusing of attention is sometimes called "one-pointing" or "mindfulness." It results in integrating and concentrating the mind. In this process other states of awareness open up. Western monastic experience employed a variety of such techniques but embedded them in a whole way of life. Monastic treatises on prayer and meditation tended to focus on a limited range of these practices.

Naranjo helpfully described three distinct types of meditation practice. Various monastic traditions tended to specialize in one or another of these types, teaching only one explicitly while sometimes employing another in a less conscious and explicit way. He named these types the Way of Forms, the Expressive Way, and the Negative Way. The Way of Forms refers to meditations on externally given symbolic objects. This way contrasts with the Expressive Way, which focuses attention on spontaneously arising contents of consciousness. In the first way one confronts an other (e.g., a symbol or God) and eventually discovers oneself as related to or a reflection of the other. In the Expressive Way one identifies oneself with the mirror of the symbol, seeking the formless ground from which all images emerge in an unprogrammed spontaneity. In contrast to these two types, the third is a purely negative way. This is not a "reaching out or a reaching in but a self-emptying." This type cultivates detachment from all contents of consciousness and from psychological processes altogether.

This threefold typology interprets monastic arts and other expressive forms, such a visions and movement, as legitimate forms of meditation practice. As practices from Asian monasticism are embraced in the West, traditional Western monastic practices are too easily overlooked.

Janet K. Ruffing

See also Cassian, John; Devotions, Western Christian; Dialogue, Intermonastic: Buddhist Perspectives; Hesychasm; Keating, Thomas; Lectio Divina; Liturgy: Eastern Christian; Main, John; Mantras; Vision, Mystical: Eastern Christian

Further Reading

Cassian, John, *Conferences*, translated by Colm Luibheid, New York: Paulist Press, 1985

The Cloud of Unknowing, edited by James Walsh, New York: Paulist Press, and London: SPCK, 1981

Freeman, Lawrence, "Meditation" in *The New Dictionary of Catholic Spirituality*, edited by Michael Downey, Collegeville, Minnesota: Liturgical Press, 1993

Guigo II, *The Ladder of Monks: A Letter on the Contemplative Life and Twelve Meditations*, translated by Edmund Colledge and James Walsh, Garden City, New York: Image Books, and London: Mowbray, 1978

Kaisch, Ken, *Finding God: A Handbook of Christian Meditation*, New York: Paulist Press, 1994

Keating, Thomas, *Intimacy with God*, New York: Crossroad, 1994

Main, John, *The Word into Silence*, London: Darton, Longman and Todd, 1980; New York: Paulist Press, 1981

Naranjo, Claudio, and Robert F. Ornstein, *On the Psychology of Meditation*, New York: Viking Press, and London: Allen and Unwin, 1971

Palmer, G., P. Sherrard, and K. Ware, translators, *The Philokalia*, 3 vols., Boston: Faber and Faber, 1981

The Way of the Pilgrim, edited and translated by R.M. French, New York: Seabury Press, and London: SPCK, 1965

Melk, Austria

Sprawled majestically on a high, rocky promontory overlooking the Danube River in lower Austria, the Benedictine abbey of Melk is today most celebrated for its vast complex of palatial, 18th-century buildings and regarded by many as the epitome of the Austrian High Baroque.

However, because of its strategic position and defensive possibilities, the site, first mentioned in 831, was originally occupied by a fortress, and its Benedictine history did not begin until 1089. In March of that year, the Babenberg ruler of Austria, Leopold II (1075–1095), brought a colony of monks from Lambach (in upper Austria) to replace the secular canons who had hitherto cared for the church at Melk, with its relics (of the Irish saint, Colman, and of the Holy Cross) and its Babenberg family tombs. Generously endowed with lands and secure in a papal exemption, the monastery continued to flourish even after the ruling family had transferred its residence to Vienna. A school is mentioned in 1160, and a scriptorium was certainly active dur-

Melk Abbey (Benedictine), Lower Austria, rebuilt early 18th century.
Photo courtesy of the Austrian National Tourist Office

ing the time of Abbot Erchenfried (1121–1163). However, a disastrous fire in 1297 ushered in a difficult century for Melk despite a successful rebuilding of the abbey complex by Abbot Ulrich II (1306–1324).

The impetus given to ecclesiastical reform by the Council of Constance (1414–1418) led to the installation of Nicholas Seyringer, a monk who had been trained at Subiaco in Italy, as abbot of Melk (1418–1425), thus beginning what was arguably the most glorious page in the abbey's history and certainly the period in which it had most impact on the wider Benedictine world. The so-called Melk Reform influenced monasteries throughout Austria and southern Germany not only in terms of regular discipline but also in their liturgy, music, and general intellectual life. (At Melk, nearly 800 manuscripts survive from the 15th century alone.)

By contrast, the rapid spread of Lutheran ideas in the following century almost spelled the end of the monastery. In 1549 only three monks remained. Only the introduction of new blood from German abbeys and the training of recruits in strict Counter-Reformation ideals in Vienna salvaged the situation. The long period in office of Abbot Caspar Hofmann (1587–1623) marked a decisive turning point. However, the abbey's steadily improving financial position faced a new challenge in 1700 with the election of the 30-year-old Berthold Dietmayr as abbot. Able, ambitious, and domineering, he successfully carried through a complete rebuilding of the monastery by one of the greatest of Baroque architects, Jakob Prandtauer. Dietmayr's successors continued to embellish his splendid new buildings but seldom lived there, preferring the Melkerhof (the abbey's house in Vienna) so that they could be close to the imperial court.

Already in 1778 the old Latin school at Melk had been transformed, at government directive, into a public high school, but during the reign of Emperor Joseph II (1780–1790) the policies of "enlightened despotism" became even more dominant at the Habsburg court. Monastic communities now had to prove their "usefulness" to society at large or face suppression, and Melk was obliged to take on, staff, and financially maintain about a dozen new parishes in addition to those in its patronage, which (like other Austrian monasteries since the Late Middle Ages) it had already stationed with its own monks. In the 19th and 20th centuries, obliged to staff almost 30 parishes, most of the community lived outside the monastery. This is still the case, although some parishes have now been relinquished, given the decline in the size of the community. (In 1935, there were 66 professed monks of the abbey, 57 of whom were priests; in 1995, there were 34 monks, 26 of whom were priests.) Today the school is a coeducational establishment of more than 600 pupils in which only a few of the monks teach.

The greatest abbot of the 19th century undoubtedly was Wilhelm Eder (1838–1866), who salvaged the monastery's financial situation after the abolition of feudal land ownership in 1848. His successors in the 20th century reflected the varying attitudes within the monastic community itself. The spirit of Josephinism, with its close identification of church and state (and emphasis on social utility), lived on until the death of Abbot Amand John in 1942 (at which time the Nazi regime had confiscated most of the abbey buildings). Subsequently, monks who were trained at the Jesuit Canisianum in Innsbruck and those (a younger generation) at the Benedictine college at St. Peter's in Salzburg have each seen the role of the monastery somewhat differently.

Courtyard and church facade, Melk Abbey (Benedictine), Lower Austria, rebuilt early 18th century.
Photo courtesy of the Austrian National Tourist Office

**Melk Abbey (Benedictine), Lower Austria, rebuilt early 18th century.
Photo courtesy of the Austrian National Tourist Office**

The visitor approaches Melk at the point farthest from the Danube, passes between mighty bastions, and proceeds across a forecourt and beneath the eastern facade of the monastery to then stand in the great Prelate's Court, with its central fountain. (To the north and northwest are three other courts that are centers of life for the monastic community and the school and thus inaccessible to the tourist.) Instead, the visitor climbs the so-called Emperor's Staircase into the immense southern wing, half of which was given over to sumptuous accommodation for the emperor and his suite when visiting the abbey. The so-called Emperor's Gallery, a 650-foot-long corridor with portraits of every Austrian ruler from the 10th century to the early 20th century, culminates in the light-filled Marble Hall (*Marmorsaal*), containing full-length windows, reddish pilasters, and chocolate-brown, atlantean figures with gold turbans. On its coved ceiling is an immense fresco, the *Triumph of Reason* (the goddess Pallas Athene in a lion-drawn chariot), finished by Paul Troger in 1731.

The visitor then proceeds outside to a wide, sweeping terrace that follows the curve of the cliff edge. On the right are a forecourt and the thrusting towers and cupola of the abbey church. To the left, far down below, are the waters of the Danube. This is the dramatic, vertiginous climax to Prandtauer's whole design. At the other end of the terrace is the abbey library, in a great pavilion that exactly matches that of the *Marmorsaal* and contains the second of Troger's ceiling frescoes: the *Triumph of Faith*. Altogether Melk has around 100,000 books and 2,000 manuscripts.

Between the northern and southern pavilions is the abbey church (over 200 feet high to the top of its cupola). Its interior of ochre, pink, and gold – with convex and concave cornices, balustrades, balconies, pulpit, and organ loft – conveys a rhythmic rise and fall and a marked air of theatricality.

However, for all its stately architecture, its lavish interiors, and the precious contents of its sacristy and picture gallery, Melk is not only a treasure house of art or of antique learning but also the home of a still-living and vibrant monastic community.

TERENCE KAVENAGH

See also Austria; Benedictines: General or Male; Vienna, Austria

Further Reading

Bruckmüller, Ernst, et al., editors, *900 Jahre Benediktiner in Melk: Jubiläumsausstellung 1989*, Melk: Das Stift, 1989

Ellegast, Burkhard, *Stift Melk*, translated into English by Roger Klassen, Melk: Stift Melk, 1977; 3rd edition, 1986

Flossmann, Gerhard, "Abt Caspar Hofmann," in *Stift Melk: Geschichte und Gegenwart*, volume 2, edited by Wilfried Kowarik, St. Pölten-Vienna: Niederösterreichisches Pressehaus, 1980

Flossmann, Gerhard, and Wolfgang Hilger, *Stift Melk und seine Kunstschätze*, St. Pölten-Vienna: Niederösterreichisches Pressehaus, 1976

Glassner, Gottfried, "Christian Ethos and Monastic Book Culture: The History of the Melk Abbey Library as a Guidepost to a Lifestyle in Conformity with the Horizon of Christian Values," *American Benedictine Review* 45:4 (1994)

Keiblinger, Ignaz Franz, *Geschichte des Benediktiner-Stiftes Melk in Niederösterreich*, 2 vols., Vienna: Fr. Beck's Universitäts-Buchhandlung, 1851

Niederkorn-Bruck, Meta, *Die Melker Reform im Spiegel der Visitationen*, Vienna: Oldenbourg, 1994

Melkite Monasticism

Melkite (from Syriac *malkaya*, "royalist") designates Christians in Syria and Egypt who accepted the Christological formula of the Council of Chalcedon of 451 and thus remained in communion with Constantinople, the imperial see. Parallel churches and monasteries developed in areas where anti-Chalcedonian Christians (also known as Monophysites) were also present. From the beginning the Melkites were a small minority in Egypt, with larger numbers in Syria and Palestine. In the 18th century some Melkite groups became allied to Rome; these Byzantine-rite Eastern Catholics are under the jurisdiction of the Melkite patriarch of Antioch, Alexandria, Jerusalem, and All the East. The Melkite Orthodox follow the patriarch of Antioch and All the East. Orthodox and Catholic Melkites live in modern Egypt, Israel, Jordan, Lebanon, and Syria and in even larger numbers in a worldwide diaspora.

Melkite monasticism has maintained a continuous presence at important sites in the Near East since the fifth century, and leading Melkite monks (Sabas, John of Damascus, and Theodore Abu Qurrah, among others) influenced Christian belief and practice beyond the Melkite community.

Prior to the Council of Chalcedon, the monasteries of the Eastern Church maintained a certain informal unity of belief and practice. Egypt, Syria, and Palestine had both cenobitic and anchoritic forms of monasticism, and the teaching of the Council of Nicaea of 325 provided a basis for doctrinal consensus. In the late fourth and early fifth centuries, monastic writers from the Latin-speaking West, such as Cassian, Jerome, and Rufinus, could move freely between monastic communities in Egypt, Syria, and Palestine. This unity was disrupted in the aftermath of the Council of Chalcedon; Melkite and Monophysite monasteries began to follow parallel tracks with less mutual influence.

Each region underwent a somewhat different experience in the period between Chalcedon and the Arab conquest in the seventh century. Egypt remained intensely loyal to the doctrine of Cyril of Alexandria (patriarch 412–444) and largely rejected Chalcedon; thus, the monasteries were overwhelmingly Monophysite and became part of the developing Coptic Orthodox Church. Sporadic efforts by Byzantine authorities to suppress Monophysitism (a conflict described in the *History of the Patriarchs*; see the patriarchate of Benjamin I [622–661]) were ineffective but did lead to the dissolution of some monasteries. Melkites remained a small minority in Egypt, although Melkite monks are known to have settled in the Monastery of St. Antony, on the Red Sea, in the seventh and eighth centuries.

In Syria and Palestine, Chalcedon led to the same growth of parallel churches: Melkite and Monophysite. However, the Melkite presence in Palestinian monasteries was larger, perhaps because of their international character. The Holy Land drew pilgrims and would-be monks from throughout the Christian world, and this role in turn attracted the attention and financial support of the Byzantine emperors. Certain monasteries accepted the doctrine of Chalcedon and became important centers of the Melkite Church in Palestine. Thus, the Great Lavra (in the Judaean desert southeast of Jerusalem; also known as Mar Sabas), founded in 483 by Sabas, continued to lead even after the Arab conquest (Damascus in 635 and Jerusalem in 638) and was at the center of the transition from Greek to Arabic for Christian expression in the Near East. John of Damascus (665–749), a monk of Mar Sabas, wrote the *Fount of Knowledge* to clarify Melkite doctrine in relation to other Christian positions and in relation to Islam. He also defended the use of icons (*Three Orations*) and wrote a refutation of Islam in Greek. Theodore Abu Qurrah (c. 750–825), a monk from Mar Sabas who became the Melkite bishop of Harran, wrote in Syriac,

Greek, and Arabic in defense of Chalcedon and of icon veneration. He also wrote in response to the claims of Islam, using the Arabic language and phraseology of Muslim writers. The Monastery of St. Catherine on Mount Sinai, a site inhabited by Christian hermits since the fourth century, was established by Emperor Justinian (527–565) as a Melkite community, and it has remained an important center of pilgrimage and manuscript production and preservation into the modern era. John Climacus (c. 579–649), Sinai monk and ascetic writer, wrote *The Ladder of Divine Ascent* in Greek as a guide to ascetic life; later it was translated into other languages of the Christian Near East and into Latin.

The early history of Melkite monasticism, especially in Palestine, is impressive, but the Arab conquest eventually took a toll. All Christians were somewhat disadvantaged, but Melkites were more so because of their supposed loyalty to the imperial Church in Constantinople. Deprived of the intellectual and material support of the Byzantine Empire, with only brief respite during the Crusades, Melkite monasteries steadily declined, and some disappeared between the 10th and 13th centuries. Thus, in Syria, Arabic sources mention Melkite monasteries near Bosra and Damascus (Deir Murran) in the early medieval period, but after the 13th century there is very little evidence. In Egypt the Melkite monasteries of Deir Mar Hanna, Deir Mar Marco, and Deir al Qusair cease to function at the beginning of the 13th century.

Under Ottoman rule, with increased contact with the West, Melkite monasticism revived in Lebanon, first among those Melkites who had accepted communion with the Roman Catholic Church (beginning in 1724). Monastic orders for men and women were founded that followed the Rule of St. Basil, and these later divided along territorial lines. The same trend continued into the 20th century: new orders were founded in Lebanon, and a new monastery opened in 1980 (Monastery of the Resurrection in Faraya). Westerners attracted to the Melkite Catholic tradition have founded monasteries that are affiliated with the Melkite Church: St. John of the Desert in Jerusalem and others in Morocco and France. Melkite Orthodox monasticism has experienced a smaller revival in the 20th century, with new monasteries founded (St. George al Harf in Lebanon and St. George al Humeyra in Syria); some ancient ones continue with ties to the Greek patriarchate of Jerusalem. Mar Sabas and the monasteries of Theodosius, Choziba, Douka, Gerasimus, and St. John the Baptist are ancient monastic sites that were restored by the Greek patriarchate in the 19th century.

JANET TIMBIE

See also Climacus, John, St.; Egypt; Iconoclasm (Controversy); Israel/Palestine; John of Damascus, St.; Mount Sinai, Egypt; Sabas, St.; Syria

Further Reading

Atiya, Aziz S., *A History of Eastern Christianity*, Notre Dame, Indiana: University of Notre Dame Press, 1967; London: Methuen, 1968; enlarged edition, Millwood, New York: Kraus Reprint, 1980

Dick, Ignace, *Les Melkites: grecs-orthodoxes et grecs catholiques des patriarcats d'Antioche, d'Alexandrie et de Jérusalem* (Fils d'Abraham), Turnhout: Brepols, 1994

Griffith, Sidney H., *Arabic Christianity in the Monasteries of Ninth-Century Palestine* (Collected Studies Series, CS380), Aldershot, Hampshire, and Brookfield, Vermont: Variorum, 1992

Hirschfeld, Yizhar, *The Judean Desert Monasteries in the Byzantine Period*, New Haven, Connecticut: Yale University Press, 1992

Janin, Raymond, *Les églises orientales et les rites orientaux*, Paris: Maison de la bonne presse, 1914; 5th edition, Paris: Letouzey and Ané, 1997

Leroy, Jules, *Monks and Monasteries of the Near East*, translated by Peter Collin, London: Harrap, 1963

Roberson, Ronald, *The Eastern Christian Churches: A Brief Survey*, Rome: Editrice Pontificia Università Gregoriana, 1986; 6th edition, Rome: Pontificio Instituto Orientale, 1999

Mercedarians

The Mercedarians were founded by St. Peter Nolasco (d. 1245) to ransom Christians captured and enslaved by Muslims during the wars of the medieval Iberian *reconquista*. Although the order's traditions date the foundation in 1218 or 1222, Nolasco's earliest documented appearance is in 1230, or just after the Aragonese king, James I, began his conquest of the Muslim Balearics. Pope Gregory IX (1227–1241) granted his recognition in 1235 and assigned the Augustinian rule. Efforts to classify the Mercedarians as a military or mendicant order have been problematic, as Nolasco's followers were neither knights nor preachers; in terms of function and organization, they are most similar to the membership of caritative orders, such as the Antonines, Trinitarians, or Brothers of the Holy Spirit. During the 13th century, Mercedarians were for the most part not ordained as priests. They established several dozen residences within the crown of Aragon (Aragon, Catalonia, Valencia, and the Balearics) and a few others in Castile and Languedoc, from which they sought funds to subsidize the ransoms of needy countrymen or to finance the expeditions of Mercedarians to Muslim lands to redeem Christians. By the late 16th century, friars took a vow of redemption that required them to trade their own freedom for that of captives, but it is not clear whether this fourth vow had been a medieval practice.

The order's first constitutions were promulgated by Pere d'Amer (d. 1301) in 1272 to codify developing custom. A second set, those of Ramon Albert (d. 1330) in 1327, established a provincial structure (Aragon/Navarre, Catalonia, Valencia, Provence/Balearics, and Castile/Portugal) and formalized the order's transition from laic to clerical leadership. Several disputed elections for the mastership led the papacy to claim the power of appointment. Without directly challenging papal prerogatives, Kings James II (1291–1327) and Peter IV (1336–1387) of Aragon also claimed special rights over the order's revenues and members on the basis that King James I was the real

Lower level of a two-sided cloister, La Merced, Peru, 1653–1669. Photo courtesy of Chris Schabel

founder of the order. Specifically, it was on this basis that Peter IV, after the Black Death, successfully blocked an effort by the master, Ponce de Barelis (d. 1364), to consolidate the Mercedarians with the other redemptionist order, the Trinitarians. An agreement in 1467 granted each province institutional autonomy and marked the rise of Castile as the most important arena of Mercedarian activity. At the same time, the order gained exemption from episcopal authority and a century later established a house in Rome to represent the order before the papacy. The Chapter of 1574, which sought to implement the Tridentine reforms, replaced the lifetime tenure of the master general with a six-year term.

In 1317 more than 200 Mercedarians were divided among some 57 houses. In 1474 this had increased to 550 brethren in 62 houses. By the 16th century more than 900 brothers resided at 106 centers and in 1770, just past the order's apogee, 4,495 Mercedarians in 228 houses. Much of the growth that was experienced in the 16th and 17th centuries can be attributed to the order's expansion into the Americas. From the initial foundation at Panama, the Mercedarians established provinces in Guatemala, Lima, Cuzco, Chile, Argentina, and Mexico that by the 18th century surpassed in size the original Iberian provinces. In 1532 the province of Castile was given juridical control over all New World dependencies. Other Mercedarian houses were established in Granada, North Africa, and Italy.

Early modern Mercedarians engaged in a variety of apostolates. Ransoming reached its apogee in the 16th and 17th centuries. The Chapter of 1612 claimed 2,710 liberations during the previous half century, and over 800 captives were freed between 1604 and 1615. The liberation of 830 Sardinians from Tunis in 1798 brought this tradition of ransoming to a close. In the New World, Mercedarians were evangelists and teachers. Within Iberia the early modern era was a golden age of Mercedarian letters. Mercedarian colleges were established at the Universities of Salamanca and Alcalá, and the order produced a number of noted historians, theologians, and literary figures, of whom the most famous is the playwright Gabriel Téllez (Tirso de Molina, d. 1648).

The Chapter of 1603 granted permission for brothers to establish reformed houses, and these led to the emergence of a Discalced branch of the order, led by Juan Bautista González (d. 1618), that by 1800 had 42 houses in Spain, Sicily, and Italy. In addition, a dozen female communities were in existence; this marks the emergence of Mercedarian nuns, although Maria de Cervellón, who is said to have consecrated herself to the order in 1265, is counted as the first Mercedarian sister. Although more centered on an ascetic and mystical spirituality, the reformed order began to conduct its own ransomings in 1633 and cooperated with the Trinitarians and original Mercedarians in several expeditions throughout the 18th century.

Reform, war, and revolution wreaked devastation on the Mercedarians at the beginning of the 19th century. In 1773 Charles III (1759–1788) of Spain placed strict restrictions on the reception of new members, and Joseph Bonaparte, as king of Spain, suppressed the Order in 1809. Although restored in 1814, the Mercedarians lost their smaller Spanish houses in 1820 and, like all religious orders, were legislated out of existence in 1836 by the Spanish government. Until the Mercedarians were restored in Spain in 1886, surviving members in Europe and America were subject to a vicar general who was resident in Rome and named by the Holy See. Latin American independence meant a realignment of the order's provinces to reflect national boundaries and confiscation of houses and property, especially in Mexico. Just prior to its Iberian restoration, membership had reached a low of 243 but by 1911 recovered to 450 brothers in 40 houses. Although the Spanish provinces produced two distinguished historians, in F.D. Gazulla (1879–1938) and Guillermo Vázquez (1884–1936), the civil war caused severe losses, including 54 Mercedarians killed. Currently, about 750 Mercedarians are organized into eight provinces and serve in 22 countries with 159 houses. In constitutions promulgated in 1970 and 1986, the order has reinterpreted its redemptionist mission as one to serve the unchurched and those whose captivity is of a social, political, or psychological character.

James W. Brodman

See also Augustinian Rule; Crusades; Latin America; Spain: History; Trinitarians (Mathurins); Warrior Monks: Christian

Further Reading

Brodman, James W., *Ransoming Captives in Crusader Spain: The Order of Merced on the Christian-Islamic Frontier*, Philadelphia: University of Pennsylvania Press, 1986
Brodman, James W., "Fable and Royal Power: The Origins of the Mercedarian Foundation Story," *Journal of Medieval History* 25 (1999)
Gazulla Galve, Faustino D., *La Orden de Nuestra Señora de la Merced: Estudios históricocríticos*, Barcelona: Gili, 1934
Millán Rubio, Joaquín, *La Orden de Nuestra Señora de la Merced (1301–1400)*, Rome: Instituto Histórico de la Merced, 1992
Tourón, Eliseo, "Desarrollo histórico de la Merced (siglos XIV–XX), Ensayo hermenéutico-histórico," in *Las dos ordenes redentoras en la Iglesia: Actas del I Encuentro Trinitario-Mercedario*, Madrid: Offo, 1989
Vázquez Nuñez, Guillermo, *Manual de historia de la Orden de Nuestra Señora de la Merced*, Toledo: Editorial Catolica Toledana, 1931

Merton, Thomas 1915–1968

U.S. Trappist monk and prolific author

Thomas Merton, known in the monastery as Father Louis, was born on 31 January 1915 in Prades, southern France, in the diocese of Perpignan. His parents, both artists (his father a landscape painter from New Zealand and his mother a former student of interior design and modern dance from the United States), met in the Tudor-Hart Studios in Paris and, after their marriage in London, settled down in Prades at the foothills of the Pyrenees Mountains not far from the Spanish border.

The young Merton attended schools in France, England, and the United States. After a chaotic year at Clare College, Cambridge (on a scholarship from Oakham School), in England, he was urged by his guardian, Dr. Tom Bennet, to go to the United States and live with the Jenkins family, his maternal grandparents, who had funded his education. There he enrolled at Columbia University and fortunately came under the influence of some remarkable teachers of literature, including Mark Van Doren, Daniel C. Walsh, Joseph Wood Krutch, and a number of stimulating classmates, including Robert Lax, Edward Rice, Seymour Freedgood, and Ad Reinhardt. Merton entered the Catholic Church in 1938 after a rather dramatic conversion experience. Shortly after completing his masters thesis, "On Nature and Art in William Blake," he began work on a doctorate on the poetry of Gerard Manley Hopkins that he never completed.

Following some teaching at Columbia University Extension in New York and a year and a half at St. Bonaventure's College in Olean in upstate New York, on 10 December 1941 he entered the monastic community of the Abbey of Gethsemani at Trappist, Kentucky. He was received by Abbot Frederic Dunne, who, having come from a family of printers, appreciated the power of the printed word. It was not long before the abbot encouraged the young Frater Louis to translate works from the Cistercian tradition and write historical biographies to make the order better known. One of these was the life of St. Lutgarde (1182–1246), an early Flemish Cistercian mystic, which he called *What Are These Wounds?* Another such biography, *Exile Ends in Glory*, told the story of Mother Berchmans, a French nun exiled in the Far East.

The abbot urged the young monk to write his autobiography, which was published under the title *The Seven Storey Mountain* (1948) and became a best-seller and a classic. It made him a renowned religious figure and established him as a Catholic writer. During the next 20 years, he wrote prolifically on a vast range of topics, including the contemplative life, prayer, and religious biographies. His writings would later take up controversial issues (e.g., social problems and Christian responsibility: race relations, violence, nuclear war, and economic injustice) and a developing ecumenical concern. He was one of the first Catholics to commend the great religions of the East to Roman Catholic Christians in the West.

Merton died by accidental electrocution in Bangkok, Thailand, while attending a meeting of religious leaders on 10 December 1968, just 27 years to the day after his entrance into the Abbey of Gethsemani.

Many esteem Merton as a spiritual master, a brilliant writer, and a man who embodied the quest for God and for human solidarity. Since his death, many volumes by him have been published, including five volumes of his letters and seven volumes of his personal journals. According to present counting, more than 60 volumes of Merton's writings are in print in English, not counting the numerous doctoral dissertations and books about the man, his life, and his writings. Most of his important writings are available in English and in translations into French, German, Italian, Portuguese, Spanish, and languages of the Far East.

On 30 May 1987 the International Thomas Merton Society (ITMS) was formed at the Merton Center of Bellarmine College in Louisville, Kentucky. Its purpose is to promote understanding and appreciation of Thomas Merton and to encourage study that would help make better known the unique contribution he has made to the literature of spirituality as well as to American literature in general. Local chapters of the ITMS have been organized in various cities in the United States as well as in Canada, Brazil, Belgium, France, Spain, Great Britain, Ireland, and, most recently, Russia. Besides making Thomas Merton and his writings known to a new generation through conferences and other programs, the ITMS encourages the translation of Merton's writings throughout the world.

In his autobiography *Freedom in Exile* (1990), the Dalai Lama (1935–) wrote of Merton as being the first Christian he had met who exemplified the contemplative side of churches in the West. The latter, he thought, are better known for active works of ministry, such as building schools and hospitals and running efficient parishes for the faithful. He wrote, "This was the first time that I had been struck by such a feeling of spirituality in anyone who professed Christianity . . . it was Merton who introduced me to the real meaning of the word 'Christian.'" Since that was written, the Dalai Lama has visited Gethsemani and repeated the same at a meeting in 1996 of 25 Buddhist monks and 25 Christians (mostly Benedictines and Cistercians). This memorable conference probably could never have happened had the Dalai Lama not had such an in-depth meeting with Merton in the fall of 1968, just a few months before the latter's death.

Patrick Hart, O.C.S.O.

See also Dalai Lama (Tenzin Gyatso); Dialogue, Intermonastic: Christian Perspectives; Gethsemani, Kentucky; Jerome, St.; Keating, Thomas

Biography

Born in France of a New Zealander father and American mother, and educated in England, Merton attended Columbia University in New York City before joining the Trappist community at Gethsemani Abbey in Kentucky in 1941. One of the most prolific and influential monastic writers of the 20th century, Merton digested Trappist spirituality, aligning its themes with those of Buddhism and of various social issues. He died on 10 December 1968 by accidental electrocution while attending an inter-religious meeting in Bangkok, Thailand. He is perhaps the most widely read of 20th-century Christian monastics.

Selected Works

The Seven Storey Mountain, 1948
Seeds of Contemplation, 1949
The Waters of Siloe, 1949
The Sign of Jonas, 1953
Wisdom of the Desert, 1961
Mystics and Zen Masters, 1967
Climate of Monastic Prayer, 1968
Zen and the Birds of Appetite, 1968
Collected Poems, 1977
Literary Essays, 1981
Letters (5 volumes), 1985–1994
Journals (7 volumes), 1995–1998
The Intimate Merton, 1999

Further Reading

Dalai Lama, *Freedom in Exile: The Autobiography of the Dalai Lama*, New York: HarperCollins, and London: Stodder and Houghton, 1990
Hart, Patrick, *Thomas Merton, Monk: A Monastic Tribute*, New York: Sheed and Ward, 1974; reprint, Kalamazoo, Michigan: Cistercian Publications, 1983
Inchausti, Robert, *Thomas Merton's American Prophecy*, Albany, New York: SUNY Press, 1998
Mott, Michael, *The Seven Mountains of Thomas Merton*, Boston: Houghton Mifflin, 1984
Shannon, William, *The Silent Lamp: The Thomas Merton Story*, New York: Crossroad, 1992; London: SCM, 1993

Meteora, Thessaly, Greece

Where the cultivated landscape of the Thessalian plain mingles with the foothills of the majestic mountains of central Greece, the Khasia and Pindos ranges, one comes suddenly on the sight of a spectacular cluster of pillars on the top of which are perched the 14th-century Byzantine monasteries of Meteora, located about 190 miles northwest of Athens. The impression that these monasteries give of hanging from the sky gives Meteora its name (from Greek *meteoros*, "suspended").

No definite explanation exists to account for the genesis of these rocks, although geologists have advanced different theories to explain this unique phenomenon. The most convincing is that millions of years ago, a large river debouched into the deep and narrow gulf of the sea that at that time covered Thessaly. At its outlet the river deposited a thick layer of silt and stones, and in the course of geological ages parts of this deposit compacted into solid masses of limestone conglomerate. When the continental platform rose and the seawater drained away, these masses were washed clean and left standing on their own.

This wild and inaccessible terrain made Meteora the refuge of men fleeing the various invaders who over the centuries pushed into Thessaly. The awe-inspiring untenanted rocks attracted hermits and, later, monks who, forsaking the world, hoped to see God more clearly in the thin blue air of the summits. Dwelling there in giddiness, privation, loneliness, and discomfort, they sought lives of Christian perfection. In the beginning these hermits lived solitary lives, praying alone in rudimentary chapels, but in the course of time they saw advantage in sharing a more fully Christian life together in small monasteries called *sketes*.

We do not know exactly when Meteora was first settled, for the earliest surviving sources describe monastic life as already organized there. Some Byzantinologists maintain that *sketes* already existed by the end of the first millennium. According to one tradition the first monk to settle Meteora was a tenth-century hermit named Barnabas, who lived in one of the caves that pit the Meteora cliffs. It was Barnabas who between A.D. 950 and 970 founded the ancient *skete* of the Holy Spirit (Agio Pneuma). During the next two centuries, more monks came to Meteora and lived as hermits in other caves. Among them was Andronicus, a Cretan monk who in 1020 founded the *skete* of the Transfiguration (Metamorphoseos tou Sotiros). Some of the earliest settlements were on Doupiani, the sugar loaf, which has innumerable small caves. In time the monks living on Doupiani built a chapel to the Virgin Mary (the Theotokos). Heavily restored in 1861, this chapel can still be visited today. The *skete* of Doupiani or Stagion (1160) was the first organized monastic community of Meteora. In the middle of the 14th century, the prior (*hegumenos*) of the *skete* of Stagion, named Nilos, became afraid of brigands' raids. Having received financial support from the basileus (ruler) of the province of Thessaly, Symeon Uroîs Palaiologos (half brother of Stephen Dûsan), Nilos undertook the task of gathering all the solitaries together and organizing them into four basic monastic centers. He built more permanent settlements and reorganized administratively the monastic community. It was St. Athanasius the Meteorite (1305–1385) who first introduced the communal (cenobitic) form of monasticism to Meteora. On the basis of the *Diatyposis* of St. Athanasius the Athonite (c. 920–1003), Athanasius drew up a document of the liturgical and the disciplinary regulations to be followed by all the monasteries of Meteora.

On the advice of the bishop of Serbia, Athanasius came to settle Meteora and in about 1362 founded on the summit of a broad rock the monastery of the Transfiguration, or the Great Meteoron. This is the oldest and the largest church among the six that are still inhabited today. In time three other churches were added on the same rock – those of St. Athanasius, St. Constantine and St. Helen (1789), and St. John the Baptist (1600) – all of which were built at different dates.

In 1373 John Uroîs Palaiologos, son of the emperor of Serbia, brought with him a good portion of his personal fortune and retired to the Great Meteoron to live out his days as the monk Joasaph. On the death of St. Athanasius in 1383, Joasaph took charge of monastery and in 1388 financed the expansion of the church, an event recorded in an inscription still to be seen there. The wealth of Joasaph together with his royal connections ensured the Great Meteoron supremacy over the other monasteries that were founded thereafter on nearby rocks. According to one tradition Joasaph's own royal sister founded a convent (later destroyed completely by the Turks) on the adjacent rock of Hypselotera. This was the first nunnery established in the Meteora. Joasaph's influence was such that he is regarded as cofounder with Athanasius of the Great Meteoron, and he is depicted as such in more than one portrait in the church.

Much of the Great Meteoron's Church of the Transfiguration dates from a 16th-century rebuilding in which expansion and refurbishment work was carried out by the monk Symeon. This church sufficiently resembles churches of the same period on Mount Athos to suggest that the architect might have come from there. It is an impressive building with a large 12-sided central dome and a smaller one over the sanctuary. The sanctuary is decorated with frescoes, the oldest of which date from the end of the 15th century and follow the tradition of the Macedonian school of art. Other wall paintings are indicative of the so-called Cretan school of painters.

Among the monastery's many treasures are silver reliquaries containing the heads of its two founders; the first abbot's gold-embroidered miter; a chasuble embroidered with gold and pearls and a gold cup belonging, respectively, to members of the Palaiologos and Cantacuzene families, both former patrons of the monastery; and a fine library holding more than 500 books. The church also contains an exceptionally lovely 14th-century icon – a diptych showing the mourning Virgin Mary with the dead Christ; some believe that this was painted by an artist who worked on the frescoes of the church of Peribleptos at Mistra.

East of the Great Meteoron stands the monastery of Barlaam on the top of a rock. This is the richest among the currently inhabited monasteries. The first inhabitant of this rock was the ordained monk Barlaam, who around 1350 built the small chapel to the Three Hierarchs (Trion Ierarchon) and a few cells. After his death the site was deserted for about 200 years, and the building fell into ruins. However, in 1518 two brothers from one of the leading families of Ioannina, namely, Nektarios and Theophanes Apsara, scaled the rock, rebuilt and enlarged Barlaam's chapel, and a little later added the churches of All Saints (Agion Pandon) and of St. John the Baptist. The church of the Three Hierarchs was rebuilt in 1627 and decorated ten years later by the monks Cyril and Sergios. Some frescoes dating from the 16th century are still to be seen in the church, and a small museum in the refectory houses important manuscripts and ecclesiastical articles.

Gazing from the courtyard of Barlaam, one can see the monastery of Rousanou to the south at the end of a chain of lofty rocks. The monastery stands on an isolated and precipitous rock. According to various old texts, the monastery was founded by the monks Nikodemos and Benedict in 1380. They might have called it Rousanou after an earlier hermit, perhaps the first to settle here. Around 1545 another pair of monks from Ioannina, Maximos and Joasaph, rebuilt and enlarged it, but it never achieved the wealth of its neighbor. Today a small group of nuns live here and offer simple hospitality to visitors.

Another currently inhabited monastery is that of the Holy Trinity (Agias Triadas), crowning a delicate cliff-pinnacle. Although the exact date of the monastery's foundation is not known, some historical evidence suggests that it was built between 1458 and 1476, possibly by a monk named Dometions. The church of the Holy Trinity is a cruciform Byzantine building with a low dome supported by two internal columns. It contains a notable wall painting of 1692 and a collection of later icons. A tiny vaulted church hollowed out of the rock on the left of the monastery's entrance was probably once a *skete* that was later transformed into a chapel. Its wall paintings were carried out by the monks Damaskinos, Jonas, and Arsenious. Today only one monk is in residence, although for much of the Holy Trinity's history it was the home of numerous monks who lived as hermits in its caves and crevices.

Clinging to the top of an enormous weather-beaten rock that stands west of those carrying the monasteries of Barlaam and of the Transfiguration stands another still inhabited monastery, that of St. Nicholas Anapavsas. Built in 1527 by Dionysios, archbishop of Larisa, the monastery contains superb wall paintings by a famous post-Byzantine artist, the Cretan monk Theophanes. These suffered badly during the long years that the monastery remained uninhabited but, after being in danger of disappearing, recently have been restored.

The last of the six currently inhabited monasteries is that of St. Stephen. Now a convent, the monastery was found in the 14th century by the Byzantino-Serbian ruler Antonious Cantacuzene, who was probably a son of Nikephoros II of Epirus and a grandson of the Emperor John VI. The rock is likely to have been settled earlier, probably before 1200. This theory is supported by the fact that of the two churches that now exist inside the monastery, the older one of St. Stephen Martyr is said to have been built in 1300 by the monk Jeremias. The newer church of St. Charalambos was built by Fathers Theophanes and

Ambrose in 1798. Some historical evidence suggests that Byzantine Emperor Andronikos III Palaiologos (1328–1341) lived in the monastery for a short time in 1333 and thereafter it was considered a royal and patriarchal foundation. As a result it was generously endowed and was at one time the richest monastery in the Meteora. However, the possibility of Antonious Cantacuzene being the founder cannot be dismissed, as he is depicted as a monk in a portrait still to be seen in the church of St. Stephen. The church's treasury contains many precious articles and saintly relics.

Unfortunately the principal buildings of St. Stephen were badly damaged during both World War II and the civil war, and many frescoes were defaced. However, the monastery still has its principal relic: the head of St. Charalambos. Legend has is that this sacred relic was a gift of Prince Vladimir of Hungary, although it seems more likely that it was not he but Vladislav III, Voivode of Wallachia, who donated the sacred head. In any event these stories speak to an era when the monastery of St. Stephen, like the Great Meteoron, had extensive holdings in Romania.

In the historical development of the Meteorite monasticism, the 15th and 16th centuries marked the rise, advancement, and reorganization of the Meteorite monasticism. This was due mainly to the more secure and stable conditions that prevailed in the region after the Turkish occupation as well as to the moral and material support that the monasteries of Meteora received from the declining Byzantino-Serbian aristocracy of Epirus and Thessaly. These native donors and patrons came to be replaced in the heyday of the Meteorite monasticism (the 17th century) by the rulers of Wallachia and Moldavia. During that time the monastic federation of Meteora received endowments from these leading foreign patrons, who granted many privileges, including extensive and fertile holdings in the Danubian principalities. At the same time it became common practice for the monks of the monasteries to travel from time to time to Wallachia, Moldavia, or Russia, carrying with them saintly relics or miraculous icons and to ask for alms and economic support.

At the height of its prosperity, the community housed very large numbers of monks and hermits and included a large number of monasteries, most of which can be seen today in ruins scattered at the top of the rocks. The decline of Meteorite monasticism started gradually during the 18th century and was triggered by the insecurity, disorder, and anarchy that followed raids by Albanian brigands in the region. Later, in 1770, Turko-Albanian troops returning from Peloponnese to their country damaged the monasteries and terrorized the region of Thessaly for more than a decade. During the Ali Pasha years, the conditions became worse: seeking for reprisals, he did not hesitate to bombard the monasteries and punish the monks. Meteora suffered severe damage in the wake of the Greek revolution for independence of 1821, World War II, and the Greek civil war. German and Italian troops plundered the monasteries and stripped them of their treasuries, and many icons and precious manuscripts were burned.

Today the old days of glory are distant, and the monasteries of Meteora depend more on the charity of tourists, pious pilgrims, and visitors than on rich holdings or generous gifts from benefactors. Moreover only a handful of monks and nuns live today at Meteora, and most of the once flourishing 24 monasteries have fallen into disrepair. Recently the site has attracted a new archaeological interest while extensive restoration programs aim both to refurbish the six standing monasteries and to preserve the community's libraries and treasuries.

MARIA ROUMBALOU

See also Architecture: Eastern Christian Monasteries; Greece; Mount Athos, Greece; Orthodox Monasticism: Byzantine; Pilgrimages, Christian: Near East; Romania; Visual Arts, Eastern Christian: Painting

Further Reading

Beidiceanu, N., and P.C. Nâsturel, "La Thessalie entre 1454/55 et 1506," *Byzantion* 53 (1963)

Didron, (Ainè), "Voyage en Grèce – Les Météores," *Annales Archéologiques* 1 (1844)

Galatoriou, Catia, "Byzantine Ktetorika Typika: A Comparative Study," *Revue des Études Byzantines* 45 (1987)

Heuzey L., "Les couvents des Météores en Thessalie d'après un manuscript grec," *Revue Archéologique*, new series, 9 (1864)

Heuzey, L., and H. Daumet, *Mission Archéologique de Macédoine*, 2 vols., Paris, 1876

Kotopoulis, F., *Ta Metéora*, Athens: Difros, 1958

Nicol, Donald M., *Meteora: The Rock Monasteries of Thessaly*, London: Chapman and Hall, 1963; revised edition, London: Variorum, 1975

Nikonanos, N., *Metéora: Ta Monastiria kai he historia nous*, Athens: Ekdotike Athenon, 1987; English translation, Athens: Ekdotike Athenon, 1989

Milarepa 1040–1123

Tibetan Buddhist monk and poet

Cotton-clad Milarepa is Tibet's best-loved poet-saint. A key figure in the early history of the Kagyü lineage of Tibetan Buddhism, he was the foremost student of Marpa the Translator, who was instrumental in the second transmission of Buddhism from India to Tibet. Milarepa was also guru to Gampopa (1079–1153), who began the monastic order within the Kagyü lineage, but he is best known and most loved as a prolific poet who wrote songs of realization that are studied and sung to the present day. He is also loved and venerated because his life story demonstrates that anyone, even someone proficient enough at black magic to cause the death of his enemies, can attain enlightenment in a single lifetime if heart and mind are set fully to that task. Therefore, he is one of the most important role models among Tibetan Buddhists, not for his evil deeds but for the example of his zealous practice. Everyone knows his story, which is sung by wandering storytellers and acted out in folk operas to the present day, not least among communities of Tibetan refugees.

The beginning of Mila's story is quite ordinary. He was born the son of a moderately wealthy family and in his early years experienced love and gentleness from his parents. However, fortunes soon turned, and Mila's father died when the boy was about seven years old. His father took great care to put his affairs in order before his death, making a public will in which he entrusted all his property together with his children and wife to his brother until Mila came of age, at which time all the property was to revert to Mila. But Mila's uncle and aunt refused to honor the will. Instead the mother, brother, and sister were treated as slaves, and when Mila was old enough to receive his inheritance, the aunt and uncle claimed that the property had always been theirs. They asserted that they had loaned it to Mila's father during his life and were now reclaiming it as their own.

Mila's distraught mother begged him to learn black magic so that the family would have some power with which to combat the aunt and uncle. Somehow his mother managed to find the material resources he would need to apprentice himself to a powerful teacher of black magic. Mila, who was very devoted to his mother, consented and went off to complete the necessary training. He was only too successful. After some training he managed to cause the house in which a wedding feast was being celebrated to collapse, killing 35 people, including his uncle's sons and daughters-in-law and many who had sided with the uncle. His mother sang a song of triumph at this turn of events, but the villagers turned against her in disgust. In response she asked Mila to cause a hailstorm that would ruin their crops for the entire season. Again he was successful.

At this point Mila began to reflect on the karmic consequences of his actions and sought the path of Buddhist practice as an antidote to his evil deeds. Quickly realizing that his true teacher was Marpa the Translator, he apprenticed himself to Marpa with zeal exceeding that with which he had studied under his teachers of black magic. This is the point at which his life story becomes a role model for Tibetan Buddhists, whether monastic or lay. Marpa recognized that Milarepa was his successor, his dharma-heir, but he also realized that Mila had to be purified from his evil deeds before he would be fit to understand and pass on the teachings. The ordeals that Milarepa underwent before he was finally initiated into Vajrayāna teachings and practices were gargantuan. Repeatedly he would be told by Marpa to build a tower and then, when it was almost complete, to tear it down, to return all the stones to their original places, and to build a different tower in a different place. Every student of Vajrayāna Buddhism, whether monastic or lay, goes through similar trials, and Mila's persistence in the face of overwhelming demands from his guru proves inspiring to all such students.

Mila recognized that his intense trials were the karmic result of his previous deeds, but he still reached a point of being near suicide before Marpa finally relented and initiated him. Immediately afterward, as is the customary practice, Mila went into retreat to practice the spiritual disciplines to which he had just been initiated. For some years he practiced near Marpa's residence so that he could periodically confer with his guru, but finally he realized that he wanted to see his mother once more. Marpa predicted that if he left, they would never see each other alive again. Mila left for his village nevertheless. He found his former home in ruins, with the bones of his mother scattered about in the collapsed house. Meditating among his mother's bones, he realized more clearly than ever the impermanent nature of all things and vowed to spend the rest of his life in solitary practice in mountain caves, pursuing enlightenment far from ordinary human occupations.

The stories of his years of intense ascetic practice in the mountains also offer important role models for aspiring monastic and lay students of Tibetan Buddhism. Half-measures do not bring one to enlightenment, and Mila's story demonstrates what can be involved in staying the course. However, because Mila did attain enlightenment notwithstanding his earlier history, his story also brings encouragement to desponding students of Buddhist teachings and practices. In those years he became an emaciated solitary beggar, subsisting on nettle soup when nothing else was available. But those years were also replete with the luminous songs of realization that make him Tibet's greatest and most beloved poet.

Eventually students gathered around Milarepa, and although he never participated in the lavish institutional formats of Tibetan Buddhism, he attracted a large and loyal following. He transmitted what he had learned from Marpa, who had learned it in India from Naropa, who had learned it from Tilopa. Milarepa's close disciples later transmitted it to others in an unbroken lineage to the present day. When he died, everyone was aware that a great being had passed on to another level. Milarepa's impact on Tibetan Buddhism in all its forms, whether monastic or lay, is incalculable.

Rita M. Gross

See also Buddhist Schools/Traditions: Tibet; Ladakh, India; Tibetan Lineages: Kagyü

Biography

An early holder of the Kagyü lineage in Tibet, Milarepa is known mostly from legends. They tell of his powers as an evil magician and of his subsequent repentance and study with the translator Marpa. During years of ascetic practice he suffered ordeals of every sort. Tales of the obstacles he overcame make him a model for Tibetans, not least those under persecution.

Major Works

The Hundred Thousand Songs of Milarepa, 2 vols., translated by Garma C.C. Chang, 1977

Further Reading

Lama Kunga, Rimpoche, and Brian Cutillo, translators, *Drinking the Mountain Stream: Further Stories and Songs by Milarepa*, New York: Lotsawa, 1978

Lhalungpa, Lobsang P., translator, *The Life of Milarepa*, New York: Dutton, 1977

Nālandā Translation Committee, *The Rain of Wisdom . . . The Vajra Songs of the Kagyü Gurus*, Boulder, Colorado: Shambhala, 1980; London: Shambhala, 1981

Military Orders. *See* Hospitallers (Knights of Malta since 1530); Mercedarians; Templars; Teutonic Order

Missionaries: Buddhist

As Buddhism is a so-called universal religion, missionary activity – by which is understood the more or less organized form of proselytizing a certain region mainly but not exclusively by clerical members from another region – over the nearer boundaries of its homeland (in the North Indian regions of Kosala and Magadha) can be discerned in the texts from a very early stage of the religion's history. It is certainly not wrong to say that the Buddha himself, like other founders of religious movements, and his disciples – not least due to their life as begging (*bhikṣu*) mendicants (*śramaṇa*) – were engaged in missionary activities when they converted people from all social strata to take refuge to the Three Jewels, or *triratna*: the Buddha, the teaching (*dharma*), and the community (*saṅgha*). There is an often-cited passage in the canon (*Vinaya* 11.139: *Cullavagga* 5.33) that is usually seen as a kind of mission-order to the community of monks (*saṅgha*) to expound or to preach the Buddhist teaching in the vernacular of the regions. Use of the vernacular certainly contributed to the success of Buddhism not only in India but also in other Asian regions, such as central Asia, China, and Tibet, in the following centuries.

It is clear from archaeological and, indirectly, scriptural evidence that Buddhism had spread in the first centuries after the *parinirvāṇa* of the Buddha to regions such as Mathurā and northwestern India, known as Gandhāra in later times. The rapidly growing *saṅgha* of new adherents to the dharma – monks (*bhikṣu*), nuns (*bhikṣuṇī*), laymen (*upāsaka*), and laywomen (*upāsikā*) – was stabilized by the simultaneously evolving infrastructure of monastic institutions: monastic settlements (*vihāra*), *saṅghārāma*, and the set of rules regulating the life there (*vinaya*). Clear references to the spread of the Buddhist teaching, the dharma, are then found in the historical accounts on the missions sent abroad by Mauryan Emperor Aśoka (third century B.C.); because of his activities in promulgating the dharma, Kashmir, Sri Lanka (the latter, according to the Pāli chronicles *Dīpavaṃsa* and *Mahāvaṃsa*, being converted by Aśoka's son Mahinda), parts of South India, and other border regions became partly or mainly Buddhist (*Mahāvaṃsa*, *Dīpavaṃsa*, Rock Edict II). One main road for the expansion of the Buddhist religion was through the northwest (*Gandhāra*, Swat) into regions corresponding to present-day Afghanistan, northern Iran, and central Turkestan (Chinese Autonomous Region of Xinjiang). The spread was aided by the fact that parts of central Asia and northern India were ruled then by the powerful Kuṣāṇa dynasty (fl. first to third centuries A.D.), whose rulers, with Kaniṣka as an outstanding example, were at least tolerant toward Buddhism. Other routes to the Far East, although only scarcely documented for this early period, ran overland by way of continental Southeast Asia and by way of sea routes to and through the Southeast Asian archipelago.

From the first century A.D. on, textual evidence exists from Chinese sources that Buddhism had begun to spread into China proper; the main sources for these missionary events are the Chinese collections of monk hagiobiographies (e.g., the *Gaoseng-zhuan*, "Biographies of Eminent Monks," by Huijiao). The first missionaries to arrive in China were, according to the Chinese legend of the coming of the dharma, two Indian monks, Kāśyapa Mātaṅga and Dharmaratna, brought to China by an envoy who had been sent to India after Han Emperor Mingdi had dreamt of a golden man who was explained to him as the Buddha. According to this legend these monks also brought the first Buddhist scripture to China, the "Sūtra in Forty-Two Sections" (*Sishier-zhang-jing*), a narrative report that shows the high esteem that the Chinese had for scriptural traditions without claiming to be historical reality. It becomes evident from the monk biographies that proselytizing activities were executed both by Indian monks and by central Asians, such as the famous Parthian nobleman An Shigao. The texts indicate that in the beginning the majority of followers were laymen. Until the third century A.D., relatively few Chinese were ordained as full-fledged monks (*bhikṣu*). This was due not least to the fact that the corpus of monastic rules, the vinaya in its different denominational versions (*Sarvāstivādin*, *Mahāsāṅghika*, *Dharmaguptaka*, and *Mahīśāsaka*), was not translated in its important parts and as a whole into Chinese until the beginning of the fifth century A.D. The first complete vinaya of the school of the Sarvāstivādin (Shisong-lü?) was translated into Chinese by Puṇyatāra and the famous Kumārajīva in the first years of the fifth century. The consequence is that the early Buddhist missionaries in China – not only Indians but also a high number of monks from central Asian monastic centers, such as Khotan and Kucha – were in the first centuries concerned mainly with the translation, exegesis, and interpretation of the Buddhist texts. They do not appear to have been heavily involved in the organizational process of the Buddhist *saṅgha*, which obviously was dominated by eminent Chinese monks, such as Shi Daoan or Huiyuan (334–416). Ordination according to the correct monastic rules remained a main point of attention for Chinese Buddhists. The order of *bhikṣuni* (nuns) was established in China by the advent of nuns from Sri Lanka in the fifth century. Procedural nicety was also in the interest of the Chinese state, which had a keen interest in keeping control over the *saṅgha* by correct procedures of ordination and registration controlled by special officials from the fifth century on. The last foreign missionaries arrived with the wave of exiled monks fleeing from Muslim-conquered India to different Asian areas. Some of them were adherents of the esoteric Tantric school of Buddhism, which had already been brought to China by renowned Indian missionaries such as Śubhakarasiṃha and Vajrabodhi (eighth century). Their activities sometimes met with resistance from the Chinese *saṅgha*. With the interruption of contact between India and China and with the Mongolian domination of China through the reign of the Yuan dynasty, a new flow of Tibetan monks arrived in the big centers of the Chinese Empire, but the impact of Buddhism on Chinese culture was already in decline, and the Tibetan influence on the Chinese was relatively small.

Korea received the first transmission of the dharma at the end of the fourth century A.D. by Chinese monks dispatched from the tribal (barbarian) rulers of northern China. The fact that not only religion but other cultural and administrative achievements were brought from the powerful and impressive neighbor China led to an early active search for Buddhist teaching by Korean monks in China so that missionaries played a far less important role than in the case of China. The same is true for the transmission of Buddhism to Japan: after the first venture of Buddhism to Japan from Korea and later on from China, it was mainly Japanese monks who went to China to study Buddhism, and only a few Chinese masters went to Japan, often only reluctantly, during the Nara, Heian, and Kamakura periods.

Tibet's conversion to Buddhism owed mainly to Indian monks. The most famous of these missionaries and earliest were Śāntarakṣita and Padmasambhava. From the 11th century on – after a period of persecution and destruction of Buddhism by the Tibetan King Lang Darma – a second wave of Indian monks began arriving in Tibet, mainly from the Buddhist centers in Bengal. Some were fleeing their motherland following the conquest of North India by Muslim invaders who committed atrocities against the Buddhist religion and culture; the most famous of them was Atiśa. Later on Buddhism was also brought from Tibet to central Asian regions, such as Mongolia and Manchuria, which, until recently, were part of the former Soviet Union.

The countries of Southeast Asia received their first Buddhist impact during the course of Indianization, which brought them under either Hinduist or Buddhist influence (or both). In the early periods all three of the Buddhist main traditions were present: Hīnayāna, Mahāyāna, and Vajrayāna (Tantrism). However, the still surviving tradition on the Southeast Asian mainland is that of Theravāda Buddhism. For the northern countries of the region (Vietnam), there was also a concurrent activity by Chinese Mahāyāna Buddhists.

A new period of Buddhist mission brought the transmission of the dharma to the West, to the United States and Europe. After Buddhism had first attracted the attention mainly of intellectuals and Orientalists, there was also some embracing of the religion by Westerners, instigated not least by the activity of the Theosophical Society and the World's Parliament of Religions in Chicago in 1893. However, there was no active missionary activity of Buddhist clerics, with the exception of Lamaist activities in Czarist Russia, until the end of World War II in the West. The postwar period saw the arrival of larger emigrant or refugee communities from all parts of Asia and the active reception of Buddhism by westerners. One of the consequences was – in the case of Buddhist denominational groups with monastic traditions, such as Tibetans, Burmese, Sri Lankans, and other Southeast Asian communities or, to a lesser degree, the Chinese and Koreans (Japanese Buddhism was spread mainly by Buddhist lay organizations) – the foundation of retreat centers or genuine monastic facilities that promote more or less strong missionary activities.

Max Deeg

See also Asia, Central; Aśoka; Buddhism: Overview; China; Disciples, Early Buddhist; Huiyuan (Hui-yüan); Korea: History; Padmasambhava; Pilgrims to India, Chinese; Sri Lanka: History; Tibet: History; United States: Buddhist

Further Reading

Overview

Zürcher, Erik, "Missions – Buddhist Missions," in *The Encyclopedia of Religion*, volume 9, 570a–573b, New York: Macmillan, 1987

Early Period, India and Ceylon

Hirakawa, Akira, *A History of Indian Buddhism: From Śākyamuni to Early Mahāyāna* (Asian Studies at Hawaii, number 36), Honolulu: University of Hawaii Press, 1990; reprint, Delhi: Motilal Banarsidass, 1993

Lamotte, Etienne, *History of Indian Buddhism: From the Origins to the Śaka Era* (Publications de l'Institut orientaliste de Louvain, 36), Louvain-la-Neuve: Université Catholique de Louvain, Institut orientaliste, 1988

Rahula, Walpola, *History of Buddhism in Ceylon: The Anuradhapura Period, 3d Century* B.C.*–10th Century* A.C., Colombo: Gunasena, 1956; 3rd edition, Dehiwala, Sri Lanka: Buddhist Cultural Centre, 1993

Central Asia, China

Bagchi, Prabodh Chandra, *India and China* (Greater Indian Society, 2), Calcutta: Greater Indian Society, 1926; 2nd edition, Bombay: Hind Kitabs, 1950; New York: Philosophical Library, 1951

Bagchi, Prabodh Chandra, *India and Central Asia*, Calcutta: National Council of Education, Bengal, 1955

Ch'ên, Kenneth Kuan Shêng, *Buddhism in China, a Historical Survey* (Virginia and Richard Stewart Memorial Lectures, 1961), Princeton, New Jersey: Princeton University Press, 1964

Gaulier, Simone, Robert Jera-Bezard, and Monique Maillard, *Buddhism in Afghanistan and Central Asia* (Iconography of Religions, section 13, Indian Religions, fascicle 14), 2 vols., Leiden: Brill, 1976

Puri, Baij Nath, *Buddhism in Central Asia* (Buddhist Traditions, volume 4), Delhi: Motilal Banarsidass, 1987

Tsukamoto, Zenryu, *A History of Early Chinese Buddhism: From Its Introduction to the Death of Hui-yüan*, 2 vols., translated by Leon Hurvitz, New York: Kodansha International, 1985

Zürcher, Erik, *The Buddhist Conquest of China: The Spread and Adaptation of Buddhism in Early Medieval China* (Sinica Leidensia, volume 11), 2 vols., New York: Humanities Press, 1959

Korea and Japan

Lancaster, Lewis, and Chai-Shin Yu, editors, *Introduction of Buddhism to Korea: New Cultural Patterns* (Studies in

Korean Religions and Culture, volume 3), Berkeley, California: Asian Humanities Press, 1989
Matsunaga, Daigan, and Alicia Matsunaga, *Foundation of Japanese Buddhism*, volume 1, Los Angeles: Buddhist Books International, 1974

Tibet
Bell, Charles Alfred, *The Religion of Tibet*, Oxford: Clarendon Press, 1931; New York: Gordon Press, 1981
Snellgrove, David, and Hugh Edward Richardson, *A Cultural History of Tibet*, New York: Praeger, and London: Weidenfeld and Nicolson, 1968; revised edition, Boulder, Colorado: Prajña Press, and London: Routledge and Kegan Paul, 1980
Tucci, Giuseppe, *The Religions of Tibet*, Berkeley: University of California Press, and London: Routledge and Kegan Paul, 1980

Southeast Asia
Cœdès, George, *The Indianized States of Southeast Asia*, Honolulu, Hawaii: East-West Center Press, 1968
Lester, Robert C., *Theravada Buddhism in Southeast Asia*, Ann Arbor: University of Michigan Press, 1973

The West
Batchelor, Stephen, *The Awakening of the West: The Encounter of Buddhism and Western Culture*, Berkeley, California: Parallax Press, and London: Aquarian, 1994
Baumann, Martin, *Deutsche Buddhisten: Geschichte und Gemeinschaften* (Religionswissenschaftliche Reihe, 5), Marburg: Diagonal-Verlag, 1993; 2nd edition, 1995
Fields, Rick, *How the Swans Came to the Lake: A Narrative History of Buddhism in America*, Boulder, Colorado: Shambhala, 1981; 3rd edition, Boston: Shambhala, 1992
Prebish, Charles S., and Kenneth K. Tanaka, editors, *The Faces of Buddhism in America*, Berkeley: University of California Press, 1998
Snelling, John, *Buddhism in Russia: The Story of Agvan Dorzhiev, Lhasa's Emissary to the Tzar*, Shaftesbury, Dorset, and Rockport, Massachusetts: Element, 1993

Missionaries: Christian

Christian missionary work and Christian monasticism can be traced back to a common ideal: maintenance of the apostolic way of life. Whether this ideal led to missionizing, monasticism, or both depended on how the apostolic life was understood at a given time and place. Nevertheless the concept of the Christian missionary – one who seeks to bring the Christian truth to non-Christians – preceded by several centuries that of the Christian monk. In the so-called Great Commissioning (Matt. 28:16–20) and throughout the Acts of the Apostles and the Pauline Epistles, Christians could discern an obligation to spread the good news of Jesus Christ. Almost inevitably, then, whoever claimed to represent the apostles' successors had to address this obligation.

The earliest Christian monks held this obligation in tension with their efforts to flee from the world. The *Life of Antony*, attributed to Athanasius of Alexandria, asserts that its hero "persuaded many to embrace the solitary life. And thus it happened in the end that cells arose even in the mountains, and the desert was colonized by monks, who came forth from their own people, and enrolled themselves for the citizenship in the heavens." Antony also returned to the city to seek martyrdom unsuccessfully, to debate Arian heretics, and to convert numerous pagans in passing: "Assuredly as many became Christians in those few days as one would have seen made in a year." However, he debated several Greek philosophers without attempting to win them to Christianity and ultimately chose to move farther and farther away from the press of duties associated with urban or even cenobitic life.

From the beginning, then, the "solitary life" implied by the word *monachos* often turned outward, although this placed it in tension with its stated aim. Before long the colonization of the desert by monks led to cenobitic communities where repentant robbers and wayfarers could receive penance. From these communities and solitary cells, a few spiritual virtuosos went out to the city or simply wrote voluminously in order to rebuke idol worshipers or heretical Christians. Some of these "soldiers of Christ" used their education (often, but not always, acquired prior to monastic vocation) in order to outwit their human foes; others caused conversions by feats of asceticism and well-timed miracles. The notorious ascetic Simeon Stylites inspired a tribe of Bedouins to abandon their previous devotion to "Aphrodite" and cluster around his pillar. Monasticism could also be understood as a type of living martyrdom; as with Antony, however, desire for a more standard martyrdom also provided an inducement to missionary activity.

From this beginning the roles of monk and bishop put forward competing claims to represent the true apostolic life. Martyrdom aside there was considerable overlap early on: Athanasius spent six years in a monastery, and his *Life of Antony* concludes with an exhortation to read it even to non-Christians as an example of the powers that Christ confers on believers. It was not long before Christian communities began trying to "capture" leading monks by ordaining them as priests or bishops; these offices required a greater degree of contact with non- or semi-Christians, even when the honoree succeeded in living a relatively monastic life within his diocese. Monks such as Basil of Nyssa (c. 330–379) and Augustine of Hippo (354–430) spent their terms as bishops vigorously defending their own brands of Christian orthodoxy against heretics and pagans alike. The extent to which these actions can be described as "missionary" is open to debate, of course, but these men certainly managed to spread the Christian truth while retaining a sense of monastic vocation.

The doctrinal controversies of the third, fourth, and fifth centuries A.D. led to the fragmentation of the Church into Chalcedonian and non-Chalcedonian camps; however, these splits did not slow the transformation of the apostolic ideal from an episcopal to a monastic one, and missionary activity was increasingly centered on bishops who were or had been monks. Sulpicius Severus' *Life of St. Martin*, a fourth-century best-seller, recounts how its hero evangelized portions of western Gaul in sallies from the monastery he had founded at Ligugé. When the citizens of Tours succeeded in making him their bishop, Martin (d. 397) promptly formed a new monastery outside the city at modern-day Marmoutier and continued his idol smashing and miracle working in the surrounding countryside. Gallic monastic foundations such as Lérins and Auxerre also trained missionaries who traveled into Britain and Ireland, although it is not clear whether the famous Patrick was so trained.

In the East, Christian expansion was rendered more difficult by the large, well-organized, and relatively hostile Persian Empire. Nevertheless the Eastern Syrian, or "Nestorian," Church rose to the challenge with monk-missionaries who established Christian minorities throughout the Middle East and Asia; they penetrated into China and Mongolia, set up as many as five bishoprics in Afghanistan, and created a lasting Christian community in India. Many of these advances were wiped out by the Mongol invasions of the 12th and 13th centuries. On a more local level, Jacob Bardaeus, a sixth-century Syrian monk turned Monophysite bishop of Edessa, almost single-handedly created the Syrian Orthodox, or "Jacobite," Church by his ceaseless ordination of priests and deacons – contemporaries estimate that he created 80,000 to 100,000 new clerics – and by his prowess in working miracles to convert potential clerics to his Christology.

Indeed the sixth through the ninth centuries marked a golden age for monastic missionaries throughout Europe and Asia. The Byzantine Church, which spent most of those centuries falling in and out of union with its Roman counterpart and trying to counter the spread of Islam to its east and south, sent out monks in an effort to Christianize the Slavic peoples to its north and west. Both Cyril and Methodius, the famous ninth-century "apostles to the Slavs," had given up earlier careers to enter the same monastery at Mount Olympus before they were selected for the politically and theologically sensitive task of encouraging Khazaria, Moravia, and eventually Kievan Russia to embrace their brand of Christianity. However, this "golden age" soon ended: the Orthodox monastic tradition's increasing turn toward prayer and theology, its avoidance of the structuring orders found in Catholicism, and its position near or within hostile Muslim empires made an overtly missionary orientation unlikely in the following centuries.

On their western frontier, however, Orthodox monks might encounter their Scotto-Irish counterparts. The Irish, or Celtic, Church centered around monasticism from the beginning, although it remains unclear whether Irish monasticism was imported or entirely indigenous. Here the concept of *peregrinatio pro Christo* (pilgrimage for Christ) was the driving force behind the Irish monks' missionary activities: instead of fleeing into deserts, they established new monasteries in Britain and Gaul, from where they evangelized the surrounding areas. Indeed the Irish movement can be traced from foundation to foundation: Columba's (c. 521–597) sixth-century island monastery at Iona off the Scottish coast trained men who evangelized most of the Saxon kingdoms, most notably Aidan of Northumbria. Another product of Irish monastic training, Columban (d. 615), created monasteries in Burgundy, Neustria, Austrasia, and finally Italy in the early seventh century; the Burgundian foundation of Luxueil in turn trained other missionaries. By the mid–seventh century it seemed that the Irish monks were everywhere in Western Europe. They cheerfully converted pagan and Arian Germanic peoples to their understanding of Christianity and to their forms of monastic life.

Meanwhile monasticism near Rome was undergoing a sea change with the adoption of the Benedictine Rule. This vision of monastic enterprise did not emphasize missionary activity – indeed its vow of stability could be read as a mandate for enclosure and cloistering of monks and nuns alike – but it did mitigate the harsh asceticism of early monasticism and provide an organizational basis for multiplying foundations. Pope Gregory I (the Great; 590–604) extended his advocacy of Benedict's Rule across the English Channel when he sent Augustine, the prior of Gregory's own foundation of St. Andrew in Rome, to form a new monastery in Britain. This vision of missionary monasticism still entailed a good deal of overlap with episcopal function – Augustine soon became both an abbot and an archbishop, and his mission had been initiated by the bishop of Rome – but Benedictine monk-missionaries had begun to crisscross the areas being covered by their Irish coreligionists.

After training at the Benedictine monastery of Nhutscelle in the eighth century, the Saxon monk Wynfrith of Wessex traveled initially to Frisia and later (after refusing the abbacy of Nhutscelle) into Hesse and Thuringia, where he became known to posterity as Boniface (c. 673–754). To Boniface the best way to ensure that a newly converted populace would remain Christian was to plant a monastery in that region that would serve as a material and cultural resource for missionary endeavors. Thus, Boniface was responsible for at least nine major foundations, most famously that of Fulda. In the pattern that had become typical at this point, he became archbishop of Mainz before achieving a martyr's death at an advanced age while trying to convert yet another group of pagans.

It is worth noting that many of Boniface's foundations were nunneries or double monasteries and that a group of nuns accompanied Boniface on his initial journeys. Lioba, Boniface's relative, became the abbess of Tauberbischofsheim, and a group of other Saxon women adopted leadership positions in the new foundations. The historical record is remarkably quiet about the extent to which nuns were active in missionary work before or during this period, but in this case it is clear that they worked alongside male monks in the effort to convert the German peoples.

Benedictine missionaries continued to penetrate throughout Western Europe, and most of the Irish foundations changed their rule to Benedict's as Rome grew increasingly cool toward the Irish traditions. Some of them maintained a relatively strong missionary orientation, but most were content to serve as centers for the contemplative life in increasingly turbulent times. When the monk Ansgar left Corvey (a daughter monastery of Corbie, itself founded by missionaries from Luxueil, now Benedictinized) to preach the gospel throughout Denmark and into Sweden in the ninth century, he encountered disbelief and even a little opposition from his fellow monks. Ansgar's mission was sponsored by Carolingian King Louis the Pious (814–843), but it was also inspired by visions urging Ansgar to teach all nations and become a martyr – in which he succeeded. His missions in Denmark and Sweden, however, were abandoned after his death in 865: both monasticism and the Carolingian Empire were in decline and could not spare the resources to maintain Ansgar's outposts.

The Cluniac reforms of the following century strengthened the organization and moral standards of monasteries but made no provision for any missionary work. Indeed Cluniac efforts to return to strict monastic observance emphasized the extent to which monks should be cut off from the outside world – an ideal that made missionary work nearly impossible. A somewhat more activist stance was taken by the 12th-century Cistercian reformers: Bernard of Clairvaux (1090–1153), the early Order's most famous theologian and preacher, left his monastery regularly to combat heretics or help preach the Second Crusade. Toward the beginning of the 13th century, Cistercian monks worked together with the Teutonic Knights in the effort to Christianize East Prussia. Nevertheless the Cistercian monasteries never became sources of missionary activity; Bernard even discouraged his monks from going on crusades, reminding them that they could serve the world far better by reciting the Divine Office than by accompanying military campaigns.

Still the Cistercian movement did not preach total withdrawal from the world as did other contemporary monastic reforms. The popularity of Cistercian monasticism might have encouraged the development of the mendicant orders from the early 13th century onward. Certainly the mendicant orders were not "monastic" in the strictly Benedictine sense, but their vows, their habits, and their communal lifestyle were clearly meant to evoke monastic ideals. Perhaps most critically they saw themselves as embodying an even purer form of the apostolic life that entailed both monastic asceticism and missionary activity.

Whereas the Dominicans were founded during the effort to bring heretics back to Christianity, the Franciscans could boast a founder and some very early members who desired martyrdom in exchange for preaching the gospel to non-Christians. Francis' Rule of 1221, written after five Franciscans had lost their lives in Morocco while Francis himself tried to convert the sultan at Damietta, emphasizes the missionary vocation as a path toward martyrdom but counsels confession of Christianity and simple preaching rather than argument or confrontation. Although this advice was not always followed – the urge for martyrdom was correspondingly great – it proved to be a good foundation for mendicant missionary efforts. Increasingly the mendicant orders set themselves apart from traditional Benedictine monasticism less by their mendicancy than by their rapid spread into the Christian and non-Christian worlds alike.

Both Dominicans and Franciscans adopted the Cistercian model of multiple foundations under a centralizing authority, and both moved very early into non-Christian parts of the world. Within a few decades they took over from the Cistercians in East Prussia. Early in the 14th century, a papal bull divided the remaining mission fields of what was then the known world: Franciscans were to missionize in China, Armenia, northern Asia, and Asia Minor, whereas Dominicans were to devote themselves to Persia, southern Asia, and India. No room was allotted to the Cistercian and Benedictine orders, whereas monks of other Christian denominations were clearly "schismatics" and in need of evangelization themselves. Successive Franciscan reforms led to the Observants and, later, the Capuchins, both groups striving to return to Francis' Rule and including a strong missionary bent.

Another mendicant missionary order grew directly out of and away from monastic or semi-monastic foundations. The Augustinian Hermits or Friars were organized in 1256 by combining a host of previously unaffiliated monasteries. Although most of these congregations had been contemplative in orientation, the new order was distinctively active after the model of the Franciscans and Dominicans, and its nominally eremitic members shortly became known as friars. It spread rapidly during the 13th and 14th centuries, sending a few members to preach the gospel in Africa. However, 15th-century reform brought it even closer to the other mendicant orders, and it was in this guise the Augustinians established missions throughout Spanish territories in the New World.

The Augustinian reform also gave rise to Protestantism in the person of one Martin Luther (1483–1546); Luther, however, rejected monasticism and missionary activity alike. He maintained that the call to universal mission was confined to the generation of the apostles, and it was not until the second-generation reformer Hadrian Saravia argued that Jesus' call extended to the present that Protestant missionaries began their decidedly nonmonastic work. The only possible exception to this rule, the Moravian Church, or Unitas Fratrum, evangelized Native Americans with great success while maintaining semi-monastic communities in which unmarried men and unmarried women occupied separate dormitories and property was sometimes held in common.

On the Catholic side the 16th century saw a tightening of restrictions on the enclosure of religious women. The early mendicant organizations had included not only cloistered nuns but also "tertiaries," lay members of both sexes who lived under less strict supervision. While male tertiaries might accompany friars on missionizing trips, female tertiaries were sometimes able to move within a wider community, devoting themselves to works of charity that could also save the souls of nominal Christians. In 1563, however, the Council of Trent (1545–1563) decreed that all nuns should observe strict enclosure; in 1566, Pope Pius V (1566–1572) extended this prescription to female tertiaries. The few groups of *religieuses* who left for the New World or other mission fields were expected to confine their duties to the education of other women.

At the same time the world of male missionaries shifted to an entirely "secular" one with the advent of the Society of Jesus. Founded in 1541, the Jesuit Order consisted of secular priests, and its organizational structure evoked military rather than monastic comparisons. It was also devoted to a new vision of apostolic life: mission and education in the service of the Roman Catholic Church. Later orders of specifically missionary priests and sisters had little or no interest in the monastic paradigm; although the mendicants continued their missionary work as well, the new orders were largely based on the successful Jesuits.

The 17th, 18th, and 19th centuries were great ages for Christian mission, but few of those missions derived from monastic sources. A handful of Benedictine and Cistercian foundations existed in regions hostile to more overt Catholic evangelism. At the same time monasteries in Europe were being emptied and destroyed in the wake of 18th- and 19th-century revolutions, and Catholics were losing ground to evangelical Protestant missionaries. However, monastic revivals in the second half of the 19th century did not ignore the theme of missionary activity. Andreas Amrhein, a monk from Beuron (Swabia), founded a community of missionary Benedictines at Emming-St. Ottilien in Upper Bavaria. The Congregation of St. Ottilien was rapidly given mission territory in eastern Africa, followed by missions in Korea, China, and the Philippines. Monasteries in Europe and the Americas helped support the African and Asian missions. Currently the monks of St. Ottilien number approximately 1,060 with 20 independent monasteries and foundations. A group of women religious separated from St. Ottilien and formed the Congregation of Missionary Benedictine Sisters of Tutzing.

It was also in the 19th century that the Anglican Church began to sponsor monastic orders. Numerous Anglican Benedictine communities for men and for women exist today, some primarily contemplative and others oriented toward assorted forms of Christian mission. Many other Anglican communities practice monastic life and missionary activity simultaneously – some from traditional orders, such as the Cistercians, and others recently created, such as the Order of St. Helena.

The 20th-century movement toward Christian ecumenism has led to the formation of a substantial literature on missionary activity and to the study of missiology as a scholarly topic. It has also led to another shift in views of the apostolic life: the Second Vatican Council (1962–1965) emphasized the apostolic duty of all Christians. It is impossible to say what role missionary activity will play in Christianity's third millennium, but monasticism is most unlikely to be absent from the picture.

WENDY LOVE ANDERSON

See also Anglican Monasticism; Antony, St.; Basil the Great, St.; Benedictines: General or Male; Beuron, Germany; Boniface, St.; Celtic Monasticism; Cistercians: General or Male; Cluniacs; Columba, St.; Columban, St.; Dominicans: General or Male; France: History; Franciscans: General or Male; Fulda, Germany; Gregory VII; Martin of Tours, St.; Monastics and the World, Medieval; Poland; Russia; Schools and Universities, Benedictine; Stylites; Ukraine

Further Reading

Addison, James, *The Medieval Missionary: A Study of the Conversion of Northern Europe A.D. 500–1300*, Philadelphia: Porcupine Press, 1976

Camps, A., L.A. Hoedemaker, M.R. Spindler, and F.J. Verstraelen, editors, *Missiology, An Ecumenical Introduction: Texts and Contexts of Global Christianity*, Grand Rapids, Michigan: Eerdmans, 1995

Daniel, E. Randolph, *The Franciscan Concept of Mission in the High Middle Ages*, St. Bonaventure, New York: Franciscan Institute, 1975

Doppelfeld, Basilius, *Missionarisches Mönchtum: Idee, Geschichte, Spiritualität*, Münsterschwarzach: Vier-Türme-Verlag, 1996

Farmer, David Hugh, editor, *Benedict's Disciples*, Leominster: Wright, 1980; 2nd edition, Leominster and Harrisburg, Pennsylvania: Gracewing, 1995

Leclerq, Jean, "Monachisme chrétien et missions," *Studia Missionalia* 28 (1979); volume published as *Monasticism in Christianity and Other Religions*, Rome: Gregorian University Press, 1979

McNamara, Jo Ann, *Sisters in Arms: Catholic Nuns through Two Millennia*, Cambridge, Massachusetts: Harvard University Press, 1996

Vaulx, Bernard de, *History of the Missions: From the Beginning to Benedict XV (1914)*, translated by Reginald F. Trevett, New York: Hawthorn, and London: Burns and Oates, 1961

Monastery, Christian

The monastic impulse antedates Christianity and can be found in many religions. Generically, monastic life involves the single-minded pursuit of whatever gives ultimate meaning and purpose to life. Such a search requires separation and solitude because necessarily the quest is personal and interior. Shared experience, learned by trial and error, led in time to the development of rules and patterns of organization that exhibit a remarkable number of similarities. Because monasticism cannot flourish as a distinct alternative without separation from the everyday world of men and women, celibacy and the renunciation of possessions are commonly required. Celibacy separates one from the social and economic involvements that marriage and family entail. Renunciation aims at detachment not only from actual possessions but also from the materialistic urge to acquire more. Monastic separation is protected by admissions requirements for candidates and rites of initiation as well as by distinctive dress and rules of deportment. The desire for separation is also reflected in the remote location of many monasteries and in the restriction of at least some monastic spaces to members only, the practice known as monastic enclosure or claustration. Withdrawal and renunciation are intended to free a person for the wholehearted pursuit of the goal. Perseverance in that effort requires fidelity to prayer and meditation and to daily practice of self-denial. Separation, solitude, detachment, prayer, and asceticism are all common features of monasticism as such, but each religion has its own way of specifying the goal. For Christian monasticism the goal is salvation in Christ, which has been expressed in such images as the search for God, the following of Christ, and the angelic life.

In Christianity the term *monastery* can be applied to any place where men or women pursue monastic life. Even a hermit's cell, originally a hut or a cave, can properly be called a monastery (*monasterion*) because the occupant lives there alone (*monos*). The eremitic life was perhaps the earliest form of Christian monasticism. Other hermits lived under a superior in a monastic settlement called a *lavra*, consisting of a complex of buildings – typically a church, a refectory, a bakery, storerooms, and a guest house – and of a number of private or semiprivate cells randomly located in the same area. The Greek word *laura*, meaning "lane" or "alley," refers to the paths connecting the cells to the main complex. During the week the monks prayed, worked, and ate in their cells. On Saturday and Sunday they attended services together in the church and then returned to their cells carrying the supplies they would need for the week. In Palestine a monk was not allowed to occupy a cell in a *lavra* without prior training in a cenobium (*koinobion*, literally, "common life"). Basil the Great (c. 330–379) and Benedict of Nursia (c. 480–550) are honored as the patriarchs of Eastern and Western monasticism, respectively, and are credited with establishing cenobitic monasticism as a permanent calling. However, unlike Basil, who was opposed to solitary life, Benedict treats it as a possible exception (RB 1.3–5; Prol. 50, 72.11). In time cenobitic monasticism became the dominant form of monastic life, with the result that in the East the term *lavra* began to be applied to large cenobitic monasteries, such as the Great Lavra on Mount Athos.

No early monastic rule provides a plan for the spaces and buildings that a monastery needs. The design and arrangement of the spaces must be inferred from the activities that make up the community's day. A cenobitic community, living under one roof or at least in one complex of buildings, must have a space to meet several times a day for prayer (church), a space to keep things needed for worship (sacristy), a space where all meals can be taken in common (refectory), a kitchen, a place to sleep (either private or semiprivate cells or a dormitory), a space to accommodate guests, a space for the sick (infirmary), a space suitable for reading and study, and a variety of shops and storerooms. Both Basil and Benedict wanted monks to earn their living and to be as self-sufficient as possible so as to minimize the need for anyone to leave the monastic compound or to have contact with outsiders. Archaeological remains show that the earliest monasteries resembled Mediterranean farm-villas. The buildings, one or two stories high, were arranged around a rectangular, open-air courtyard that was faced on all sides by a covered walk that provided connected and sheltered access to rooms on the ground floor. This arrangement, called a cloister, is the most familiar and enduring feature of monastic architecture. All Byzantine monasteries are of that design. The church is located in the courtyard. In front of the church is usually a font, and the refectory generally faces the church, across the courtyard. Beyond that no uniform plan exists to the way space is organized in Eastern monasteries.

In the West the same age that produced the castles and the cathedrals also built the great monasteries. These structures testify to the remarkable ability of medieval designers to solve a multitude of problems and to organize the results into a logical, coherent, and hierarchically ordered whole. For monastic architecture the ninth-century plan of St. Gall offers a model for the ideal monastery. According to that ideal, space had to be provided for every function mentioned in the Rule of Benedict, with monastic areas clearly separated from guest areas. The placement of spaces had to be coordinated with the flow of life in the monastery, and each space had to have a size and an appearance to reflect its status in the ensemble, beginning with the church. Thus, for example, because the Word of God is heard and food and drink are shared in both church and refectory, the refectory had to be visibly related to the church in size and design. The Rule of Benedict called for two spaces in particular that would have a long-term effect on monastic life and on monastery design. The one, introduced it seems by Benedict, was a separate area in the monastery for formation where novices were to study, eat, and sleep (RB 58.5), and the other was a common dormitory for the community (RB 22). The early history of monasticism can be traced through the steps that led from the hermit's solitary cell to the cluster of cells in the *lavra*, to cells under one roof in the cenobium, to partitions instead of walls, and to a dormitory without partitions. The private or semiprivate cell was certainly more conducive to contemplative prayer, but it could also conceal idleness and violations of poverty and chastity. By the beginning of the sixth century, to discourage such lapses of discipline and to ensure a more uniform level of observance, the common dormitory was increasingly preferred. Benedict was simply following that trend when he wrote his Rule around 540. In 535 Justinian (527–565) mandated dormitories for monasteries in the Roman Empire.

During the Middle Ages in both East and West, gifts of land, with peasants attached, made monasteries prosperous and allowed them to grow in size while freeing monks from the need to work for a living. In stark contrast to those large, propertied monasteries, another form of monasticism took hold on Mount Athos in the late 14th century, a form known as idiorrhythmic, meaning "self-regulated." Under this system two or three monks live together, but each retains the right to personal property and the use of money. Idiorrhythmia first appeared in the fifth century and was denounced early (see RB 1.6–9) and often as a perversion of the cenobitic ideal of holding all things in common. However, it gained acceptance in the late Byzantine period and became a way to survive when monastery lands were confiscated by the Turks. In Greece since the 1960s, cenobitic monasteries have been absorbing the remaining idiorrhythmic monks. Apart from those medieval developments, Eastern monasticism has remained relatively unchanged down to the present. This has not been the case with Western monasticism.

In the West the character of the community itself changed in the centuries after Benedict. Medieval monasteries admitted chiefly men or women of aristocratic birth whose day was spent in liturgical exercises conducted in Latin and in work that was intellectual or artistic in nature. In male communities members were increasingly ordained. Peasants did the manual work, but from the 12th century the chores were done largely by lay associates called *conversi*. They lived in the monastery, but in their own separate quarters, and followed their own devotional exercises. Large, landowning monasteries exerted a significant impact on local economies, and their abbots could wield considerable influence in public affairs. In both the East and the West, the wealth and power of the monasteries gave rise at times to reform movements but also to forcible seizures of monastery property. The reform movements of the West tended to result in new and distinct religious orders, such as the Camaldolese and the Cistercians. The last wholesale suppression of religious life in Europe occurred as a consequence of the French Revolution, at end of the 18th century and the beginning of the 19th.

Today Benedictine monasteries exhibit a considerable diversity, ranging from those without external apostolates to those that are actively engaged in evangelization, education, and/or parochial ministry. Benedictines came to the United States from Europe in the mid–19th century to help Catholic immigrant populations retain their faith amid new and unfamiliar surroundings. This involved the Benedictines heavily in education and in pastoral ministry. Since the 1960s, because of demographic changes, declining vocations, and aging membership, communities staff far fewer parishes, and the operation of schools has increasingly been turned over to laypeople. The onset of those changes just happened to coincide with the Second Vatican Council's (1962–1965) call for the renewal of religious life, a call that set off seemingly endless discussions about monastic identity and the meaning of monasticism for today. In many ways the changes that ensued reflect the changes that occurred in the Roman Catholic Church. Now more emphasis is placed on monastic community and much less on monasticism as an institution. Use of the vernacular replaced Latin in public prayer, many external observances were abandoned, and the community has become less hierarchical and more integrated. People in formation are no longer strictly separated, and many of the distinctions that set ordained apart from nonordained have been eliminated. The last traces of the dormitory disappeared, and everyone now has a private room. Monasteries have also become more open to guests, welcoming them in the name of hospitality into areas that formerly were part of the enclosure. All these changes have left their mark on recent American Benedictine architecture.

The path ahead will require an honest assessment of how these changes in monastery life have affected the search for God. In the past the degree of participation in community exercises was the standard by which monastic commitment was measured. However, because scheduled activities for the community take up only three or four hours of the day, today a better indicator would probably be how the rest of the day is spent. To move from the dormitory back to individual rooms required centuries, but it happened largely in response to Western society's growing demand for privacy. This change will truly advance monastic life if the room is treated as a privileged space for personal prayer and communion with God. In any case it would be unwise to forget that private cells got eliminated for monastic and not for cultural reasons.

In the first seven questions of the Long Rules, Basil the Great presents cenobitic monasticism as an ideal way to fulfill Jesus' twofold commandment of love (Matt. 22:37–39): love of God, he says, requires separation from the world and solitude (q. 6); love of neighbor requires community (q. 7). The perennial challenge for Christian monasticism is to find a combination of separation, solitude, and community that best nourishes the search for God.

PHILIP TIMKO, O.S.B.

See also Architecture: Western Christian Monasteries; Augustinian Rule; Benedict of Nursia, St.; Camaldolese; Celibacy: Christian; Cistercians; Claustration (Cloister), Rules of; Cluniacs; Contemporary Issues: Western Christian; Critiques of Western Christian Monasticism; Desert Fathers; Double Houses, Western Christian; Hermits: Eastern Christian; Island Monasteries, Christian; Israel/Palestine; Lavra; Libraries: Western Christian; Mount Athos, Greece; Spirituality: Eastern Christian; Women's Monasteries: Eastern Christian; Women's Monasteries: Western Christian

Further Reading

Bauer, Nancy, "Monasticism After Dark: From Dormitory to Cell," *The American Benedictine Review* 38:1 (1987)
Braunfels, Wolfgang, *Monasteries of Western Europe: The Architecture of the Orders*, London: Thames and Hudson, 1972; New York: Thames and Hudson, 1993
Hellier, Chris, *Monasteries of Greece*, London: Tauris Parke Books, and New York: St. Martin's Press, 1996
Hirschfeld, Yizhar, *The Judean Desert Monasteries in the Byzantine Period*, New Haven, Connecticut: Yale University Press, 1992
Pennington, M. Basil, *Monastery: Prayer, Work, Community*, with photographs by Nicholas Sapieha, San Francisco: Harper and Row, 1983
Seasoltz, R. Kevin, "Contemporary Monastic Architecture and Life in America," in *Monasticism and the Arts*, edited by Timothy Gregory Verdon with John Dally, Syracuse, New York: Syracuse University Press, 1984
Vogüé, Adalbert de, "Histoire de l'institution: de la cellule au dortoir," in *La Règle de saint Benoît*, volume 5, Paris: Editions du Cerf, 1971

Monasticism, Definitions of: Buddhist Perspectives

Any definition of *monasticism* must take into account its two related terms – *monastic* and *monastery* – which are widely used in the West to denote the ascetic religious movements of the Desert Fathers that subsequently gave birth to Christian monastic orders, such as the Benedictines, founded by Benedict of Nursia (c. 480–c. 550). Western preunderstandings of Christian monasticism have influenced the scholarship on the development of Buddhist monasticism in India and elsewhere. The existing standard definitions of Buddhist monasticism and descriptions of its related practices reflect such preunderstandings.

The English term *monastery* derives from two Greek words: *monazein* (to live alone) and *monos* (alone). Thus, the aspect of living "alone" dominated the understanding of monasticism.

However, "monastery" was increasingly perceived as a "community of persons" who were "bound by religious vows" and were "living in partial or complete seclusion." While identifying each practitioner as a monastic, the institutionalized lifestyle came to be known as monasticism. The "monastic life," thus perceived, was a "secluded" lifestyle devoted to contemplative activities of continuous prayer, study, and manual labor. Because all aspects of life were strictly regulated by monastic rules, a monastery functioned as an ideal place for practicing austerities.

In understanding Buddhist monasticism, one should be aware of the limitations of these preunderstandings. Preunderstandings of the lifestyles of the Benedictine, Franciscan, Dominican, and similar monastic orders functioned as a prototype for the study of Asian monasticisms. In the case of Buddhism, beginning with Dutt's pioneering work (1924), it was assumed that the eremitic lifestyle preceded the cenobitic one, the former leading to the latter. Recent scholarship has demonstrated that these assumptions are inadequate. In the early Buddhist traditions, the eremitic and cenobitic lifestyles coexisted simultaneously. Rather than developing from one lifestyle to the other, Buddhist monasticism genuinely combined both traveling and dwelling while giving priority to preaching the teachings of the Buddha.

Searching for equivalent indigenous terms for monastic terminology in English becomes extremely difficult. Although Christianity-specific English terms have been widely used to describe Buddhist monasticism, we should proceed with caution.

Buddhist monasticism is perhaps the oldest active monastic system in the world. It began in India in the sixth century B.C. as a movement of wandering ascetics seeking religious salvation from human suffering. The religious path that eventually came to be called "Buddhism" and the monastic system devised by the Buddha, who flourished between about 566 and 486 B.C. (or 448–368 B.C.), included a basic community lifestyle with ample freedom for individual searching. Both male and female renunciants from various social backgrounds joined him with an urgent need to be free from conditions that cause suffering. The Buddha's teaching and his spiritual community, which was governed by a monastic code, spread beyond its birthplace to several countries in Asia – to the south to Sri Lanka; to the southeast to Burma, Thailand, Cambodia, Laos, and Vietnam; and to the north to Tibet, China, Korea, and Japan. The spread of Buddhist monasticism in Asia really began only after the Buddha's death with the royal patronage of Emperor Aśoka (272–232 B.C.).

From the third century B.C. on, Sri Lanka became the home for Theravāda Buddhist monasticism. The monastic ideal as envisaged by the "Way of the Elders" (Theravāda) can be seen textually in the Pāli Canon and institutionally in a variety of institutions that emerged in Sri Lanka. Having Mahāvihāra as the center, important religious activities, such as the writing down the Pāli Canon on palm leaves during the reign of Vaṭṭagāmaṇī Abhaya (c. 89–77 B.C.) and the translation of Sinhala commentaries into Pāli by Buddhaghosa and others (beginning in the fifth century A.D.), took place in Sri Lanka. These monastic efforts strengthened the Theravāda ideology and its monastic institutions, making Mahāvihāra the sole inspiration in the expansion of Theravāda into Southeast Asia, beginning from the 11th century. Firmly established Theravāda monasticism became the mainstream of religious influence in Burma, Thailand, Laos, and Cambodia. Mahāyāna Buddhist institutions spread from India to central Asia and then to China and subsequently to Korea, Japan, Vietnam, and Tibet, where they became an essential cultural and civilizational force. In the meantime, although Buddhist monastic institutions in India were fatally damaged by Hindu assimilation and Islamic invasions during the 12th century (e.g., Nālandā and Vikramaśilā were destroyed in 1197 and 1203, respectively), in the rest of Asia both Theravāda and Mahāyāna monastic institutions continued to flourish as a civilizational force and religious inspiration for both the people and the state.

Both Jainism, founded by Mahāvīra, and Buddhism, founded by Siddhārtha Gautama, stipulated a codified monastic rule for their fully committed members. The monastic community that the Buddha founded when renunciants joined him came to be known as the *saṅgha* (literally, "assembly"). This monastic community included two groups: monks (*bhikkhu*) and nuns (*bhikkhuṇī*). Unlike the Mahāyāna schools Theravāda traditions did not incorporate lay followers within the *saṅgha*, which remained exclusively a monastic community of fully committed members. The community spirit and one's right to monastic property as a member of that community are clearly expressed in the Sri Lankan inscriptions as "the community of the Four Quarters" (*cātuddisa bhikkhusaṅgha*). Although the order of nuns (*bhikkhuṇī*) began within the lifetime of the Buddha, it died out in the medieval period with the breakdown of the higher ordination (*upasampadā*) lineage. Thus, the ordination of new nuns within Theravāda has become problematic, as monastic law stipulates that new nuns can be ordained only when orders of properly ordained monks and nuns are both actively present.

The monastic code contained in the Vinaya-piṭaka was the foundation for the systematic growth of the Buddhist monastic community. The Pātimokkha (binding together) rules regulated monastic daily life. The number of disciplinary rules gradually increased through the attempts to conform to the social and religious conditions of the time. Whereas the Pāli Canon contained 227 rules, the Chinese and Tibetan Canons had 250 and 253 rules respectively. The Buddha's attitude toward rules was that they should be amended whenever changing religious conditions necessitated.

From very early on Buddhist monasticism devised democratic means to govern life within monasteries. Previous scholars have praised democratic aspects of the *saṅgha*'s administration. Because the Buddha himself admired unity within the *saṅgha* as a cause of great happiness, to ensure harmony and unity among its members democratic measures were introduced in certain ecclesiastical functions. For example, to perform a legal act (*saṅghakamma*), it was absolutely necessary that all members of a monastic community be present and cast their votes. After reading a motion three times, it was necessary to cast votes to ensure the unanimity of all members. In principle, except for the sick, the entire community of all fully ordained monastics living within an ecclesiastical boundary (*sīma*) were required to be present for the *uposatha* (confession) ceremony held every other week.

Although as in other monastic systems physical and psychological renunciation was important, Buddhism did not consider "renunciation" an escape but rather a first step in a religious training that leads to removal of real causes of pain. In other words Buddhism emphasized not physical renunciation itself but the better life that ensues after one renounces the lay life. From the Buddhist perspective the essential thing was to enter the religious life as a monk or nun. The rite of passage of taking monastic vows that initiates one to the life of purity (*brahmacariya*) is called the minor ordination (*pabbajjā*). As a novice, when one has completed the necessary training and has reached 20 years of age, that person becomes eligible to receive the higher ordination (*upasampadā*). Buddhist monasticism encouraged renunciation of lay life as early as possible, and as an institution it preferred the young over the old because monastic life was a period of training that required a great deal of flexibility.

An important difference appears in the way in which early Buddhism and early Christianity viewed the idea of monasticism. In the Buddhist tradition the monk or nun is not an independent ascetic who has given up all contacts either with the human world or with fellow seekers. In theory as well as in practice, the Buddhist monastics were not hermits. They often moved with companions and led communal lives. They were required to settle down neither too far nor too close to human settlements, as accessibility was a crucial factor both for their survival and for their success in disseminating the Buddha's teachings. Although they had formally given up all ties to society, they were not loners but social beings who functioned as members of a religious community. The Christian practice of solitary living scarcely exists in Buddhism.

The theoretical foundations and practices of Buddhist monastic traditions in Asia differed from country to country. Although the core feature of pan-Asian Buddhist monasticism was the fundamental teachings of Gautama Buddha (e.g., the doctrine of impermanence), significant diversity and innovations emerged in particular historical contexts. For example, the saffron robe of Theravāda monks differs from the black robes of Zen monastics in Japan, where the original Buddhist robe became a symbol to be worn only occasionally by them. When monastic daily routine in Theravāda and Mahāyāna is examined, further differences appear, especially in their attitudes toward manual labor. As a legacy of the Confucian critique of Buddhist monastic practices in China, Zen made a virtue of manual labor. Highlighting this positive aspect the prominent Chinese Zen master Pai-chang Huai-hai (Baizhang Huaihai, 720–814) stated that "a day without work is a day without food." However, Theravāda and most Mahāyāna traditions still refrain from engaging in manual labor.

Until recent times most Buddhist monastic traditions maintained that the ideal Buddhist is by definition a monk or nun. Reactions have arisen against this exclusive monastic vision. The medieval Japanese reformer Shinran (1173–1262) challenged the established Japanese Buddhist schools to reject the vows of celibacy and to choose to live among the poorest of the poor by dedicating his own life to devotion to the Buddha Amitābha. This reaction of Shinran within Tendai monasticism unleashed interesting developments within Japanese Buddhism. Recent lay reactions against exclusive monasticism that have sought religious happiness within the household lives include several powerful new Buddhist religious groups based on the *Lotus Sūtra*, such as Reiyūkai (fl. 1924, "Society of Companions of the Spirits"), Sōka Gakkai (fl. 1930, "Value Creation Society"), and Risshō Kōseikai (fl. 1938, "Society for Establishing Righteousness and Personal Perfection through Fellowship"). Within Sri Lankan Theravāda the Vinayavardhana movement (fl. 1938, "Persons Committed to Reviving the Discipline") is one example of a lay campaign that attempted to reform monastic values and virtues by educating the people in monastic rules and the life of purity.

The centrality of the monastic remains visible within Theravāda Buddhist traditions. Historically, because the monastic community handed down Buddhist scriptures from generation to generation through teacher-pupil lineages, the latter's undisputed authority in the preservation of Buddhism as an intellectual and spiritual tradition is acknowledged in the Theravāda countries of Sri Lanka, Burma, Thailand, Cambodia, and Laos. In these countries, as religious virtuosos, the monastics hold an elevated position within their societies and help the needy within monastic and nonmonastic circles on many occasions, ranging from rites of passage to soteriological solace.

MAHINDA DEEGALLE

See also Buddhism: Overview; Initiation: Buddhist Perspectives; Japan: History; Novices, Theravādin Rituals for; Origins: Comparative Perspectives; Regulations: Buddhist Perspectives; Rules, Buddhist (Vinaya); Saichō; Saṅgha; Sri Lanka: History; Women's Monasteries: Buddhist

Further Reading

Bechert, Heinz, and Richard Gombrich, editors, *The World of Buddhism: Buddhist Monks and Nuns in Society and Culture*, London: Thames and Hudson, and New York: Facts on File, 1984

Buswell, Robert E., *The Zen Monastic Experience: Buddhist Practice in Contemporary Korea*, Princeton, New Jersey: Princeton University Press, 1992

Deegalle, Mahinda, "Buddhist Principles of Democracy: An Exploration of Ethical and Philosophical Foundations," *Buddhist Studies (Bukkyō Kenkyū)* 26 (1997)

Dhirasekara, Jotiya, *Buddhist Monastic Discipline: A Study of Its Origin and Development in Relation to the Sutta and Vinaya Piṭakas* (Ministry of Higher Education Research Publication Series), Colombo: Ministry of Higher Education, 1982

Dutt, Sukumar, *Early Buddhist Monachism: 600 B.C.–100 B.C.* (Trubner's Oriental Series), London and New York: Kegan Paul, Trench, Trubner, Dutton, 1924; revised edition, London and New York: Asia Publishing House, 1960

Gombrich, Richard F., *Precept and Practice: Traditional Buddhism in the Rural Highlands of Ceylon*, Oxford:

Clarendon Press, 1971; 2nd edition as *Buddhist Precept and Practice: Traditional Buddhism in the Rural Highlands of Ceylon*, Delhi: Motilal Banarsidass, 1991; New York: Columbia University Press, and London: Kegan Paul International, 1995

Gothóni, René, *Modes of Life of Theravāda Monks: A Case Study of Buddhist Monasticism in Sri Lanka* (Studia Orientalia, volume 52), Helsinki: Societas Orientalis Fennica, 1972

Holt, John, *Discipline: The Canonical Buddhism of the Vinayapitaka*, Delhi: Motilal Banarsidass, 1981; Columbia, Missouri: South Asia Books, 1983; 2nd edition, Delhi: Motilal Banarsidass, 1995

Ishii, Yoneo, *Sangha, State, and Society: Thai Buddhism in History* (Monographs of the Center for Southeast Asian Studies, Kyoto University, 16), Honolulu: University Press of Hawaii, 1985

Malalgoda, Kitsiri, *Buddhism in Sinhalese Society, 1750–1900: A Study of Religious Revival and Change*, Berkeley: University of California Press, 1976

Olivelle, Patrick, *The Origin and the Early Development of Buddhist Monachism*, Colombo: Gunasena, 1974

Rahula, Walpola, *The Heritage of the Bhikkhu: A Short History of the Bhikkhu in Educational, Cultural, Social, and Political Life*, New York: Grove Press, 1974

Southwold, Martin, *Buddhism in Life: The Anthropological Study of Religion and the Sinhalese Practice of Buddhism* (Themes in Social Anthropology), Manchester, Greater Manchester, and Dover, New Hampshire: Manchester University Press, 1983

Spiro, Melford E., *Buddhism and Society: A Great Tradition and Its Burmese Vicissitudes*, New York: Harper and Row, 1970; London: Allen and Unwin, 1971; 2nd edition, Berkeley: University of California Press, 1982

Tambiah, Stanley J., *The Buddhist Saints of the Forest and the Cult of Amulets: A Study in Charisma, Hagiography, Sectarianism, and Millennial Buddhism* (Cambridge Studies in Social Anthropology, number 49), Cambridge and New York: Cambridge University Press, 1984

Wijayaratna, Môhan, *Buddhist Monastic Life: According to the Texts of the Theravada Tradition*, translated by Claude Grangier and Steven Collins, Cambridge and New York: Cambridge University Press, 1990

Monasticism, Definitions of: Christian Perspectives

Distinctions in Canon Law

According to the Code of Canon Law current in the Roman Catholic Church (as revised in 1983), a consecrated form of life entered

> by the profession of the evangelical counsels [poverty, chastity, and obedience] is a stable form of living by which faithful, following Christ more closely under the action of the Holy Spirit, are totally dedicated to God who is loved most of all, so that, having dedicated themselves to His honor, to the upbuilding of the Church and the salvation of the world by a new and special title, they strive for the perfection of charity in service to the Kingdom of God and, having become an outstanding sign in the Church, they may foretell the heavenly glory. (Canon 573.1)

The code then proceeds to differentiate the forms of consecrated life religious life according to (1) the intention of the founder; (2) the nature, purpose, spirit, and character of the institute; and (3) its wholesome traditions (578). By its very nature consecrated life is neither clerical nor lay (588). The code distinguishes various sorts of consecrated life. Religious institutes, which are approved by the papacy or the local bishop (593/94), whose members make public, perpetual vows and live the common life (607.2), may be wholly ordered to contemplation or dedicated to works of the apostolate (674/75).

Besides religious institutes the Church recognizes the eremitic or anchoritic life by which the Christian faithful devote their life to praise of God and salvation of the world through a stricter separation from the world and the silence of solitude and assiduous prayer and penance (603). Similar to the eremitic life is the order of virgins (604).

In a secular institute Christians living in the world strive for the perfection of charity and work for the sanctification of the world, especially from within (710). They promise chastity. They keep their own money but live in a spirit of poverty (710).

Comparable to institutes of consecrated life are societies of apostolic life whose members without religious vows pursue the particular apostolic purpose of the society and, while leading a life as brothers or sisters in common, strive for the perfection of charity through the observance of their constitutions. Among these are societies in which the members embrace the evangelical counsels by some bond defined in the constitutions (731).

Thus, consecrated life is divided into (1) religious life, which involves communal living and the profession of poverty, chastity, and obedience in institutes approved by the Church, which are usually said to take three forms: (a) monastic (community life and celebration of the liturgical hours, e.g., Benedictines and Trappists), (b) mendicant (emphasis on poverty and a structure that provides for mobility of it members to minister where needed, e.g., Dominicans, Franciscans, and Carmelites), (c) apostolic communities (founded for specific apostolic works, e.g., Brothers of Christian Schools and Ursulines); (2) secular institutes (Opus Dei and Madonna House); (3) hermits; (4) consecrated virgins; and (5) other societies without vows. Categories 1a, 3, and 4 would be considered "monastic" by most writers today; this encyclopedia includes also those in category 1b. However, the distinctions are precarious, and the word "monastic" is sometimes used to refer to all forms of consecrated life. The following discusses the origins of monasticism around the fourth century, the organization of monasticism according to the Benedictine Rule, and the development of other religious orders after 1050.

Origins in the East

The origins of Christian monasticism are obscure. The description of the earliest Christians in Jerusalem (Acts 2–4) served as a model, as did Christ himself, living as a celibate preacher with no fixed abode, his life dedicated to inaugurating the Kingdom of God. The earliest forerunners of the monastic movement seem to have been chaste women who chose to live celibately in their own dwellings or in dwellings shared with male clergy. These women devoted themselves to prayer and to service of the Church. In the third or fourth century, Christian men and women began to go to deserted places to live celibate lives dedicated to Christ, either as hermits (e.g., St. Antony, c. 251–356) or in community (e.g., St. Pachomius, c. 290–346). Saint Basil (c. 330–379) assigned monks to works of social service, and St. Augustine (354–430) invited his clergy to a monastic lifestyle. Saint Basil's Rules, which consist mainly of exhortations from the Bible, became the basis of Eastern Christian monasticism.

The Rule of St. Benedict

Saint Benedict's Rule, which along with several rules attributed to St. Augustine was to exercise preponderant influence in the medieval West, reflects many of the same values embraced by the early Desert Fathers: celibacy and a counterculture emphasizing dispossession of self and property through a life of humility, obedience, discretion, taciturnity, hospitality, and regularity at prayer in which the Psalms have a large place.

One can see Benedict's practical arrangements as archetypal for cenobitic monasticism. If Christians want to form a community dedicated especially to serving God, celibacy frees them from distracting marital and parental and social and economic involvements. Both to support themselves and to free themselves from economic concerns, they entrust themselves to God and one another by promising to pool their income from work or donations. They assign times and places for prayer, work, reading, sleep, eating, and guests. They provide for socializing new members. Evidently using the Roman villa or country house as a model, Benedict's followers soon developed a basic architectural arrangement of the necessary spaces.

Benedict confronted many options among the actual and potential forms contained in earlier monasticism. In many cases the Rule of Benedict often favors one option while not entirely ruling out the opposing choice(s). In some instances the followers of Benedict waited until others (e.g., the friars) had developed a possibility before embracing it themselves. Thus, (1) Benedict chose community, not the solitary life of the hermit, but he made provision for monks to advance from community to solitude. (2) The Rule of Benedict envisages a fairly strict separation between monks and their neighbors, but Benedictine monasteries (e.g., the large Carolingian communities) often have attracted larger religious, economic, social, and educational families that included laypeople. (3) Benedict did not provide for juridical connections among monasteries, but he did not exclude them either. The Cluniacs, the Cistercians, and the Canons Regular of Prémontré laid the basis for the modern congregational groupings of monasteries that provide mutual support. (4) The Rule of Benedict insisted on lifetime commitment, but there is no intrinsic reason why a person could not pledge to be a monk for a limited period. (5) Benedict's Rule gives no indication that in his monasteries men and women would be associated, although he does not prohibit it either. In the Middle Ages it was common to have double monasteries of various sorts. (6) Benedict chose an internal government that was autocratic in structure but held in check by the election of the abbot, obligatory consultation of the community, primacy of the Rule, and in some unspecified way oversight by outsiders (bishops and abbots). Benedict insisted that monks be answerable to someone. (7) Benedict preferred that a monastery be self-contained economically. In feudal times monasteries became entwined in local economies, and in other cases monks have worked at outside jobs. More important, monasteries provided to nonmonastics education, hospitality, sanctuary, and medical services when no other institutions could. (8) Benedict does not seem to have been a priest. Although he was somewhat reluctant to admit priests to his monastery, he does provide both for the ordination of monks and for the admittance of the ordained to the monastery. (9) Similarly the Rule of Benedict chose not to tie monasticism closely to the work of the ordained ministry of the Church, although he did not explicitly exclude monks from involvement in Church ministry. According to the *Life of Benedict* in book 2 of Gregory's *Dialogues*, Benedict himself seems to have done some preaching around Monte Cassino. English Benedictines later served as cathedral clergy in England and as missionaries to much of northern Europe. (10) Benedict created a life in which public prayer, work, *lectio*, and private prayer were balanced, but he said that those who were unsuited to reading could be given additional work. Later monks have altered the balance, almost always in the direction of increasing portions of liturgy or work. (11) Although Benedict does not use the terms, medieval monastic writers were almost unanimous in declaring every Christian's life to be a mixture of action and contemplation. With some inconsistency medieval monastics liked to claim the high ground of the "contemplative life" as their own.

New Religious Orders after 1050

Benedictine monks enjoyed a quasi-monopoly in the consecrated life of Europe between 800 and 1100. At their founding in 1098, the Cistercians, while seeking greater isolation and greater austerity than that embraced by most previous followers of the Rule of Benedict, pioneered closer connections among their monasteries. The Premonstratensians (representatives of those who came to be called Canons Regular) adopted the Rule of Augustine and the customs of the Cistercians and perfected the organizational links that the latter had pioneered. These Canons Regular seem to have stood on the road that led to a closer integration of monasticism with ordained ministry without actually proceeding down that road. The "friars" of the 13th century did proceed down the road, although they attracted both ordained and nonordained members. The Franciscans (Friars Minor) embraced radical dispossession. The Dominicans (Friars Preachers) shared the Franciscan desire for radical dispossession and service of the poor but, by their dedication to preaching, tilted their life toward study and ordained ministry. Both groups soon sought university education for their members. Later religious orders and societies would loosen the bonds of communal prayer and living in favor of ministerial flexibility (Jesuits). In the 20th century, centers such as Taizé and Bose have developed ecumenical forms of monastic life.

Until modern times women were restricted mostly to a cloistered, prayer-centered model of vowed celibate life. One exception was the beguines, devout women who lived celibate lives (without binding vows), usually in groups, supporting themselves by urban occupations and ministries. Eventually females with lifelong religious vows earned the right to work among the populace as nurses, teachers, and social workers. The period from 1830 to 1965 witnessed a great flowering of such "active" female orders. The same period saw a growth in the number and variety of religious orders of men.

Return to Origins versus Innovation

All these groups have been developing possibilities that are inherent in Christianity. As we have seen St. Benedict and his Rule are quite flexible, so that, for example, some Benedictine monks were eager missionaries in eighth-century Saxony and Frisia and in 19th- and 20th-century Africa and the Dakotas, yet others were rather strictly enclosed and held aloof from pastoral ministry. Religious orders who define their mission more narrowly must redefine or reconstitute themselves when it is necessary to take on a new mission, or else adapt to new situations. That some vowed celibates who follow one form of life are called "monks" and others "friars" or "clerks regular" is largely an accident of history. They all find their inspiration in Jesus and the early Christian community at Jerusalem. Most draw some inspiration from the Desert Fathers. They all select from the same range of choices that are there for any person who wants to follow Christ as a celibate for a time or for always.

During the last 1,500 years or so, discourse about developments in the monastic life has been dominated by two notions. The first is that of reform. When discipline and commitment begin to grow slack in a given religious community, members are called to return to the original form of the founders' intentions, to their rule, and ultimately to the New Testament. The second idea is that new situations call forth new forms of vowed celibate life. For example, faced with a landless proletariat, the Franciscans adopted a life that was radically poor, very mobile, and adapted to urban living. Mother Teresa's missionaries made similar choices. The reform model emphasizes continuity. When reform is the dominant metaphor, existing communities or orders continue, but with changes that aim to renew communities so that they recover the zeal and discipline of earlier times. The second model, adaptation, often spawns new orders and congregations. Although always bearing the stamp of earlier monastic history, they often bring something genuinely new. Often, when new orders find a suitable adaptation to current conditions, the older orders will be stimulated to discover new possibilities for themselves. Thus, after 1100 Benedictines learned from the organizational structures of the Cistercians and later more centralized orders, just as they learned from the mendicants the possibility of educating their members at the universities and ways of combining conventual life with ordained ministry. One can look at such adaptations as deflections from the original vision of the founder and/or as discovering new possibilities within a rich and fluid tradition.

Currently in Europe and North America, Christian monasticism suffers a decline in numbers. This decline does not seem to be related to lack of discipline in monastic communities. In most cases discipline is better now than it was in most centuries of the past. In fact nonmonastic Christians and other seekers very much admire monastic communities and frequently seek some sort of association with them. At the same time monastics and others are questioning their practices and experimenting in numerous ways. These include forms of prayer, relationships between the monastery and the larger Christian community, forms of governance within each community, the relation of the core of lifelong celibates to others who might want to associate with the community, the place of monasticism in the mission of the Church and of ordained members in the monastic community, and gender relationships among celibates. Celibacy for the Kingdom of God, creation of a counterculture, and dispossession remain the defining characteristics of the monk, but almost everything else is being put to the test as monastics, perhaps like canaries in a coal mine, feel the effects of the winds blowing toward them from an unknown future.

HUGH FEISS, O.S.B.

See also Antony, St.; Beguines; Benedict of Nursia, St.; Cistercians; Cluny, France; Congregations, Benedictine; Contemporary Issues: Western Christian; Desert Fathers; Double Houses, Western Christian; Missionaries: Christian; Orders (Religious), Origin of; Origins: Comparative Perspectives; Origins: Eastern Christian; Premonstratensian Canons; Regulations: Christian Perspectives

Further Reading

Athanasius, *The Life of Antony and the Letter to Marcellinus*, New York: Paulist Press, and London: SPCK, 1980

Brown, Peter, *The Body and Society: Men, Women and Sexual Renunciation in Early Christianity*, New York: Columbia University Press, 1988; London: Faber, 1989

Coriden, James A., Thomas J. Green, and Donald E. Heintschel, editors, *The Code of Canon Law: A Text and Commentary*, New York: Paulist Press, and London: Chapman, 1985

Feiss, Hugh, *Essential Monastic Wisdom*, San Francisco: HarperSanFrancisco, 1999

Frank, Karl Suso, *With Greater Liberty: A Short History of Christian Monasticism and Religious Orders*, Kalamazoo, Michigan: Cistercian Publications, 1993

Hostie, Raymond, *The Life and Death of Religious Orders*, Washington, D.C.: CARA, 1983

Kardong, Terrence, *Benedict's Rule: A Translation and Commentary*, Collegeville, Minnesota: Liturgical Press, 1996
Knowles, David, *From Pachomius to Ignatius: A Study in the Constitutional History of the Religious Orders*, Oxford: Clarendon Press, 1966
Lawrence, C.H., *Medieval Monasticism: Forms of Religious Life in Western Europe in the Middle Ages*, London and New York: Longman, 1984
The Life of Saint Benedict – Gregory the Great, commentary by Adalbert de Vogüé, translated by Hilary Costello and Eoin de Bhaldraithe, Petersham, Massachusetts: St. Bede's, 1993
McNamara, JoAnn, *Sisters in Arms: Catholic Nuns through Two Millennia*, Cambridge, Massachusetts: Harvard University Press, 1996

Monastics and the World, Medieval

From its origins in the Egyptian and Syrian deserts, European monasticism has always included a strong element of withdrawal, at least from the cares of secular society, if not from all contact with "the world." Because early and medieval Christian teaching strongly emphasized that the world outside the monastery was at best distracting and at worst polluting, both monks and nuns were encouraged to avoid its snares. However, at the same time monastics could not completely dismiss the world. Monastics came out of the world and could not easily rid themselves of all family ties; monasteries also needed the support of secular patrons and usually the labor of nonmonks. Even if a monastery could be completely self-sufficient, there remained a series of gospel passages that appear to enjoin activity in the world, including the great commandment to "love your neighbor as yourself" (Matt. 22:39) and the precept to "go forth and teach all nations" (Matt. 28:19). How to focus monastic life completely on God while showing proper charity to the world beyond the cloister walls has always been an important theme in monastic spirituality and at times in the European Middle Ages became a central problem.

The fathers of monasticism recognized that physical withdrawal from secular life helped prevent distractions. However, what was important was not merely physical but rather mental distancing from the world. As the tales of the Desert Fathers show, isolation was often interrupted by intervention in ecclesiastical or lay affairs and regularly punctuated by visits from nonmonastics seeking spiritual advice. Antony (c. 251–356) preached against Arianism in Alexandria; Simeon Stylites (c. 390–459) even converted a nomad tribe from the top of his pillar. As Peter Brown has shown in his seminal article "The Role and Function of the Holy Man in Late Antiquity," the fact that these protomonks spent most of their time in retreat from the world won them veneration and the power to intervene effectively when the world needed them. Indeed early monks were so successful in winning over city crowds to various causes that ecclesiastical authorities became wary of their influence. In 451 the Council of Chalcedon decreed that the proper place for monks was living a stable life in their monasteries under a bishop's authority rather than intervening in work more appropriate to the secular clergy.

However, some monks continued to be drawn into secular affairs in a variety of ways. Partly this was caused by a shortage of secular clergy. Bishops often forced monks into positions of pastoral care; as John Cassian (c. 360–after 430) said, the monk should above all flee women and bishops – women because of temptation, bishops because they force monks back into the cares of the world. In due course monks entered the episcopate but were then widely believed to suffer a diminution of spiritual vigor because of inevitable worldly contacts. Sulpicius Severus summed this attitude up well, reporting that Martin of Tours (d. 397) worked fewer miracles as a bishop than he had when still a simple monk. However, Pope Gregory the Great (590–604) was the first to express a theology of monks acting in the broader world. As the first monk elected to the papacy, Gregory found it especially difficult to reconcile his monastic vocation with the active life that he led as papal legate and then pope. His response, enunciated in his treatise *Pastoral Care* (*Regula pastoralis*), explains that the needs of the Christian people must take precedence over the individual monastic's longing for quiet and contemplation. When summoned by duly constituted authority, a monk must act. Gregory, however, held out hope for monks in such a situation, advocating a life that alternated between contemplation and action, the periods of contemplation giving strength and focus that would enable monks to survive the onslaughts of the world.

Monks often took up pastoral functions of their own will because the secular clergy were inadequate in quality or quantity. This appears to have been the case in the early Irish Church, when monasteries extended care not only to monastic servants but to the surrounding countryside as well. Shortage of secular clergy is also the likeliest explanation to be found for the many missionary activities of early Irish monks who evangelized as far as the modern Czech Republic. Although in many if not most cases Irish monks, such as Columcille (d. 597) and Columban (d. 615), desired to separate themselves from their homeland as an ascetic practice similar to that of early monks in the desert, they were very frequently drawn into the work of conversion, ecclesiastical reform, and even regular pastoral care. This willingness to undertake missionary work was carried further by the Anglo-Saxon monks and nuns of the eighth century who made their way to Frisia and Francia with conversion as their main goal.

Already by the death of the greatest monk-missionary, Boniface (c. 675–754), the tide was turning against such extra-claustral activity by monks. Although monks continued as missionaries in Saxony for at least another generation, they were soon replaced by the beginnings of parochial organization. Partly this was because regular episcopal jurisdiction was gradually imposed in the frontier areas where monks had been most active. Besides this, in the Middle Ages, work as parish priests was rarely considered appropriate for monks, as parish clergy were of much lower status; even parishes controlled by monasteries normally employed secular priests appointed by the monastery. However, the greatest hindrance to monks undertaking service to the secular Church was the triumph of the Benedictine Rule as the standard for monastic practice in much of Europe. Benedict of Nursia (c. 480–c. 550) was a firm advocate of monastic withdrawal from the world. His Rule orders that stability continue within the monastery of profession, that the monastery be located in an area with adequate water supply and all other necessities (so monks need not consort with people in the surrounding region), that monks avoid even speaking to visitors in the monastery, that the porter be an old man (so that he is unable to wander far), and that other limitations on contact with the world be observed. Especially abhorrent is the idea of the gyrovague, a monk who wanders from place to place. Benedict goes further than most monastic legislators in institutionalizing separation from secular society. The dominance of Benedict's Rule was ensured by the series of reforming councils called by Emperor Louis the Pious (814–840) and Benedict of Aniane (c. 750–821) in 816 and 817. Indeed the Anianian legislation goes well beyond the Rule itself in its efforts to cut monks off from secular lures. The ninth-century commentaries on the Rule, inspired by the Anianian reform, paint a picture of strict separation from the world, including special prayers for monks who have to leave the cloister for any reason and the proscription of monastics serving as godparents. This new emphasis on monastic withdrawal was especially motivated by concern for the ritual purity of the monastics, often likened to that of the Levites in Hebrew scripture. For their prayers to be heard, monks and nuns must be unpolluted by the world around them. This attitude is best summed up in the mid–ninth century by Rabanus Maurus (c. 780–856), who in his treatise defending child oblation (*De oblatione puerorum*) proclaimed that there is no safety outside the monastery, "nor can there be security sleeping with a serpent close by."

The difficulty of combining missionary work with strict adherence to the Benedictine Rule is clear in Rimbertus' *Vita* of Ansgar of Corvey (d. 865), a monk who did extensive missionary work in Denmark and Sweden, eventually serving as first archbishop of Hamburg-Bremen. Rimbertus made a long defense of Ansgar, trying to explain that his hero's life was indeed compatible with Benedictine monasticism. Finally Rimbertus had to have recourse to Ansgar's visions to argue for direct divine command, as proof that Ansgar was neither unstable nor a gyrovague, in violation of his vows. It is noteworthy that, after Rimbertus himself, Ansgar had no monks to follow in his work and always suffered from a critical shortage of personnel.

During the period when the Benedictine Rule reigned supreme, ritual separation from the pollutions of the outside world remained the monastic ideal. Although it is usually impossible to tell how closely reality lived up to aspiration, the general impression from the sources is that, aside from monastic officers, monastics had little to do with secular society. Abbots and, to some extent, abbesses were political figures, personifying the liaisons between cloister and world. However, customaries make it plain that most monastics rarely left the monastery and that even obedientiaries were not supposed to enjoy the experience. Laypeople were often present within the monasteries; the norm was to allocate one-tenth of monastic income for the care of visitors and another one-ninth for the poor in recognition of Benedict's command to care for others. However, ordinary monastics should not even speak to these visitors. When monastics did have direct contact with the poor, it was in a carefully ritualized context, such as the Maundy Thursday washing of a carefully selected symbolic number of poor people, accompanied by psalms. Visitors were not to enter the cloister, and often the monastery had a separate church to accommodate laypeople. Indeed at Cluny even lay servants were not allowed into the monks' private quarters.

This is not to deny that monasteries performed an absolutely vital service for the rest of Christian society. They prayed. The carefully guarded purity of monastics ensured that their prayers would be heard in heaven. Donors showered monasteries with donations in return for prayer and gave up their children to be monks and nuns in the certitude that, if they were going to be saved, it would be through the prayers of monks. Monasteries maintained great necrologies, lists sometimes of tens of thousands of donors, to make sure that the promised prayers were carried out. The great Cluniac confederation even gave a magnificent gift to all Christian society by instituting the feast of All Souls, on which they prayed for the souls of all Christian dead, whether associated with the monastery or not. As Emperor Henry III (1039–1056) said, "Has anyone ever *not* wished for the prayers of Cluny?"

The major exception to seclusion from the world for a well-regulated monastery was when a monk was forced to leave in order to serve the greater needs of the Christian community. Thus, in the 10th and 11th centuries, many monks of the Cluniac and Gorzian reform communities left the monastery to become bishops. Other monks left the cloister to serve various kings – especially necessary in the German system of monastic dependence on the ruler. In this way several Gorzian monks were sent as missionaries to lands conquered by the Ottonian rulers of Germany. Some vehemently protested this upheaval in their lives (the most notorious case is that of Adalbert of Magdeburg, who much against his will was sent to Kiev in 961); for most no evidence exists regarding how they felt about the matter. However, the Gorzian reformers were always more open to intervention in the world than were Cluniacs or Anianian monasteries in the ninth century, largely because of the very fruitful alliance between German rulers and leaders of the Church. This certainly helped German monks to evolve the idea that such extraclaustral work had a claim above the strictures of the Rule and that a monk could be called directly by God to intervene in the world as well as to act in obedience to episcopal or imperial authority. By around 970 it is possible to trace growing monastic enthusiasm for mission. By the turn of the millennium, at least a few highly visible monks were going out into the world of their own volition, trusting in their own religious expertise to guide them amid the shoals of lay culture.

Already around 930 Abbot Odo of Cluny (c. 879–942) had proclaimed the duty of monks to speak out against sin, quoting

Jeremiah 48:10: "Cursed is he who keeps back his sword from bloodshed." In the next century this became a key text in redefining monastic roles in relation to the world. No one *wanted* to be active in the world (or at least no one admitted to it), but the world needed people of superior religious insight to convert the pagans, to deepen the faith of the nominally Christian, and increasingly to combat the twin monsters of 11th-century reform – simony and clerical marriage. The extant writings about monks engaged in this work are full of apology for their improper level of activity; clearly such work was an embarrassment to many. However, Bruno of Querfurt (c. 974–1009) addresses the worry that missionary monks are acting improperly from vainglory by pointing out that souls will be damned if the monks do not help (*Vita Quinque Fratrum* [Life of the Five Brothers]). Monastic leaders of the early 11th century, such as Romuald of Ravenna (c. 950–1027), began proclaiming their desire to convert the entire world to a godly life. Perhaps most affecting, a letter of Guido of Arezzo (c. 992–1050) from sometime between 1023 and 1033 urging a bishop to halt his simoniacal practices, acknowledges that a monk is properly dead to the world but points out that anyone who sees a brother doing evil and fails to speak up will be damned. For Guido brotherhood clearly extended beyond the monastic community to the world.

In some cases the new 11th-century openness to the world can be seen in a greater willingness to admit laypeople to the monastery. This was the first great age of pilgrimage, and monasteries housed many important relics. Whereas some monasteries, such as Conques, tried to keep the laity at a distance, other abbots opened their gates to thousands of pilgrims, sometimes with disastrous results for the monastic regimen. In general the argument was that monks could not refuse the laity access to the means of salvation. Lotharingian reformers of the 11th century even allowed laypeople to join in monastic processions and meals in the refectory – to the scandal of outside observers, who agreed with the ninth- and tenth-century norm that such contacts would most likely lead to temptation for the monks.

It should be noted that these paths into the broader world were not open to nuns. Until this time monks and nuns had shared an essentially similar conception of their relation to lay society. Both groups engaged in the same charitable works with the same controls, and both valued strong seclusion in the cloister; monks as well as nuns even appointed lay "advocates" to act for the community in lay affairs. Women, however, were forbidden to preach or teach and so were by definition closed out of missionary activities, whether they took place within Christendom or among the pagans. Even the nuns involved in the eighth century in Boniface's mission were relegated to support services behind the lines. It was also more difficult for nuns to allow laymen into their churches because of possible scandal and the simple fact that most nunneries were poorer than their male counterparts, with fewer resources for entertaining and fewer first-class relics. In the 11th century, when a male celibate clergy rapidly eroded the position of women in the Church, nuns were left with little public role. Even their traditional contact with the world was further cut back, as when, for example, Pope Eugenius III (1145–1153) forbade nuns to leave their houses even to work in their own fields.

A surprising number of monks became involved in the ecclesiastical reform movement of the 11th century. Although beginning with concern over how simony could affect monastic observance, monks soon became involved in issues far beyond the cloister, preaching publicly on reform issues. The Vallombrosans went so far as to rouse Florence against its simonist bishop in the 1060s, in a propaganda tour de force that included the monk Peter "Igneus" ("fiery") walking through fire to prove the bishop's guilt. By the pontificate of Gregory VII (1073–1085), monks served as wandering public preachers by papal license. Although most of this work was done by individual monks, at least two whole monastic confederations – Vallombrosa in northern Italy and Hirsau in Germany – were active in reform, the Vallombrosans in particular acting independently of the more centralized papal reform. All this activity in the world led to a major polemic within the ranks of the monastic world, the active monks arguing New Testament authority against the more conservative monks who pointed to violations of both the Benedictine Rule and tradition.

The 11th and 12th centuries saw the formation of new religious orders that were increasingly defined by their contact with secular society. At one end of the spectrum, Carthusians and Cistercians advocated careful separation from secular influences, the early Cistercians even using lay brethren (semi-monks) to avoid reliance on estates worked by the laity and in some cases building their monasteries far from urban areas. At the other end of the spectrum rose new orders of canons regular who combined the life and activities of secular clergy and monks. Traditional Benedictines remained rather uncomfortably in the middle, advocating moderate withdrawal from the world and accepting that, especially for the sake of obedience to a higher authority, some interaction with the world outside the cloister was necessary.

However, the most important shift was one of attitude. The Benedictine centuries had emphasized physical stability, as well as physical withdrawal from a very tangible pollution. Beginning in the 11th century, evidence exists of a return to the spirituality of the Egyptian desert, including the belief that a monastic's state of mind rather than physical location constituted true separation from the world. By the middle of the 12th century, when the canon Hugh of Fouilloy wrote *De claustro animae* (On the Cloister of the Soul), monastic attitudes toward the world had come full circle. A true monk, it was thought, could maintain his focus on God even in the midst of crowds.

PHYLLIS G. JESTICE

See also Asceticism: Christian Perspectives; Boniface, St.; Claustration (Cloister), Rules of; Cluny, Abbots of; German Benedictine Reform, Medieval; Gregory I (the Great), St.; Gregory VII; Hospitality, Christian; Pilgrimages, Christian: Western Europe; Rabanus Maurus; Regulations: Christian Perspectives; Relics, Christian Monastic; Solitude: Christian Perspectives

Further Reading

Baker, Derek, "Crossroads and Crises in the Religious Life of the Later Eleventh Century," in his *The Church in Town and Countryside: Papers Read at the Seventeenth Summer Meeting and the Eighteenth Winter Meeting of the Ecclesiastical History Society* (Studies in Church History, volume 16), Oxford: Blackwell, 1979

Gregory I, Pope, *Pastoral Care* (Ancient Christian Writers, number 11), translated by Henry Davis, New York: Newman Press, 1950

Jestice, Phyllis G., *Wayward Monks and the Religious Revolution of the Eleventh Century* (Brill's Studies in Intellectual History, volume 76), New York: Brill, 1997

Miccoli, Giovanni, *Pietro Igneo; Studi sull'età Gregoriana* (Istituto storico Italiano per il Medio Evo. Studi storici, fascicles 40–41), Rome: Nella sede dell'Istituto, 1960

Mollat, Michel, editor, *Études sur l'histoire de la pauvreté [Moyen age–XVIe siècle]* (Publications de la Sorbonne. Série "Études," 8), 2 vols., Paris: Université de Paris, 1974

Rosenwein, Barbara H., *To Be the Neighbor of Saint Peter: The Social Meaning of Cluny's Property, 909–1049*, Ithaca, New York: Cornell University Press, 1989

Rousseau, Philip, *Ascetics, Authority, and the Church in the Age of Jerome and Cassian* (Oxford Historical Monographs), Oxford and New York: Oxford University Press, 1978

The Sayings of the Desert Fathers: The Alphabetical Collection (Cistercian Studies Series, number 59), translated by Benedicta Ward, Kalamazoo, Michigan: Cistercian Publications, and London: Mowbray, 1975; revised edition, London: Mowbray, 1981; Kalamazoo, Michigan: Cistercian Publications, 1984

Straw, Carole, *Gregory the Great: Perfection in Imperfection* (Transformation of the Classical Heritage, 14), Berkeley: University of California Press, 1988; Aldershot, Hampshire: Variorum, 1996

Wollasch, Joachim, *Mönchtum des Mittelalters zwischen Kirche und Welt* (Münstersche Mittelalter-Schriften, 7), Munich: Fink, 1973

Mongkut 1804–1868

Siamese king and Buddhist monastic reformer

The 19th century was a time of tumultuous change in the religious and political history of Siam (now Thailand). Born in 1804, Mongkut – the grandson of the founder of the still-in-place Chakri dynasty – was a primary actor in the "modernizing" developments that took place within the Buddhist monastic community on the one hand and within the closely related political and social order on the other.

In 1824, when Prince Mongkut was 20 years old, his father announced that the time had come for him to be ordained as a Buddhist monk and that this should be done immediately. In itself ordination was not especially unusual, as in Siam young men regularly became monks for a short period of time as part of the normal process of entering adulthood. However, the fact that Mongkut had not yet reached the appropriate age of 21 and that the ordination was done the very next day without any of the elaborate rituals usually associated with ordinations in the royal family strongly suggests that unusual factors were at work.

Within a week Mongkut's father had become severely ill, and before the month was out he had passed away. Immediately following his death a meeting of high court officials was convened, and Mongkut's older and powerfully situated half brother Rama III (1824–1851) was invited to assume the throne. Because in purely genealogical terms Mongkut himself had a very strong claim to the succession (his mother, unlike the mother of his half brother, had been a queen of royal lineage), his status as a monk protected him from involvement in a political struggle that he was not in any position to win.

Whether or not Mongkut's entrance into the monkhood was motivated by a desire to avert a potentially disastrous dynastic confrontation, it certainly enabled him creatively to exercise his many talents without directly challenging the authority of the new king. During the early segment of Mongkut's monastic career, he undertook meditational practice at a monastery outside the capital. Subsequently he returned to a monastery near the royal palace that placed a strong emphasis on the study of Pāli, the language in which the sacred texts of the Theravāda tradition (the dominant Buddhist tradition in Sri Lanka and mainland Southeast Asia) were preserved.

During Mongkut's stay in the main monastery of the capital, he became renowned both for his intellectual achievements in the study of Pāli texts and for his interest in new forms of knowledge and technology that were being introduced from the West. During this time he came to the conclusion that the Thai monastic community of his day had deviated from the rationally defensible teachings and strict disciplinary practices set forth in the teachings of the Buddha as these were recorded in the earliest Pāli texts. At the same time he became convinced that if Buddhism were to maintain its integrity and its influence in the modern world, major scripturally based reforms would be needed.

During the early stages of Mongkut's monastic career, he engaged in extended correspondence with monastics in Sri Lanka who had similar scripturalist and modernist aims. At a crucial point in his religious quest, Mongkut came into contact with the head of the Mon sect in Siam. The Mon were a minority community in Siam that had maintained an independent version of the Theravāda tradition. In the course of discussions with their head, Mongkut became convinced that this Mon version of the Theravāda tradition had preserved the Buddha's teaching and practices in their purest and most rationally compelling form. During the 1830s Mongkut gathered a group of followers and founded a new Mon-based Theravāda lineage that came to be known as the Thammayutika Nikāya. Between 1833, when Mongkut and his followers were reordained according to the Mon pattern, and 1851, when Mongkut left the monastic order, the Thammayut Nikāya emerged as an influential reformist movement within the Thai Buddhist community.

In 1851, 27 years after Mongkut's ordination, his half brother died, and Mongkut was chosen to be his successor as

Rama IV. During Mongkut's 17-year reign (1851–1868), he gave royal support both to the Mahanikāya (the "Great" Nikāya, to which the great majority of Thai monks continued to belong) and to the Thammayutika Nikāya, which he had founded. He and his immediate royal successors clearly favored the Thammayutika Nikāya and worked with its leaders to implement scripturally based and modernist reforms that exerted important effects not only within the Thai monastic community but within the broader Thai polity and society as well.

FRANK REYNOLDS

See also Bangkok, Thailand; Forest Masters; Thailand

Biography

Son of King Rama II (r. 1809–1824) of Siam (Thailand), Prince Mongkut was obliged to be ordained a Buddhist monk just days before his father took ill and died. Mongkut's position as a monk sheltered him from a dynastic struggle, in which his older brother Rama III (r. 1824–1851) became king. For 27 years Mongkut worked to update monastic regulations in Thailand, basing his reforms on those of a small Mon sect. In 1851 Mongkut succeeded his half-brother as king of Siam, reigning as Rama IV (1851–1868). His son Rama V (1868–1910) is known not least through his English governess Anna, who inspired the musical *The King and I*.

Further Reading

Griswold, Alexander B., *King Mongkut of Siam*, New York: Asia Society, 1961

Johnson, Paul, "'Rationality' in the Biography of a Buddhist King: Mongkut, King of Siam," in *Sacred Biography in the Buddhist Traditions of South and Southeast Asia*, edited by Juliane Schober, Honolulu: University of Hawaii Press, 1997

Lingat, Robert, "La Vie religieuse du Roi Mongkut," *Journal of the Siam Society* 20:2 (1926)

Lingat, Robert, "History of Wat Mahathat," *Journal of the Siam Society* 24:1 (1930)

Lingat, Robert, "History of Wat Pavaraniveca," *Journal of the Siam Society* 26 (1932)

Moffat, Abbot L., *Mongkut, the King of Siam*, Ithaca, New York: Cornell University Press, 1961

Mongolia. *See* Asia, Central

Monk-Bishops

Originally monasticism was a lay movement. The growing needs of the Church and society as well as the increasing importance of the liturgy in monastic life resulted in progressing clericalization of monks. This process proceeded much faster and was stronger in the Christian West than in the East, where it was successfully curbed by the strong anchoritic and eremitic tradition.

The education of some monks (especially in theology), their participation in doctrinal disputes, the scarcity of secular clergy, and the need to conduct missionary and evangelizing work and to fight heresies resulted in an increasing number of monks being appointed bishops. The development and popularity of monasticism influenced the formation of a model of priest and bishop that emphasized typically monastic features, such as celibacy.

While recommending celibacy the ancient and early medieval Church nevertheless accepted married priests. Only bishops had to stay celibate, a requirement that in the case of a married candidate required separation and his wife's entrance into a distant monastery. Under these circumstances, monks, who were by definition celibate, were at an advantage (as compared with secular clergy) as candidates for the position of bishop. This was an important reason behind the dominance of monk-bishops among the episcopate of the Eastern Church and the development of the tradition that was to lead to the complete monachism of the Orthodox episcopate.

From the beginning the attitude of the Western Church has been more restrictive. In the 11th and 12th centuries, all candidates for holy orders were gradually required to abide by celibacy. From the eighth and ninth centuries, canons slowly emerged as a category of secular clergy in a bishop's entourage. Taken together these two processes contributed to the increasing importance of secular clergy, who gradually won a dominant position within the Church.

As a result, in the West, from at least the 12th century the number of monk-bishops declined. In the 13th century members of mendicant orders gained popularity and importance among episcopates, and later, from the end of the 16th century, the same was true for clerks regular (such as the Jesuits). However, in the West monk-bishops would never again attain such importance or hold such a large proportion of episcopates as they did in the early Middle Ages, when most bishops were recruited from among monks.

From the beginning of monasticism in the West, there was a trend to recruit candidates for the position of bishop from among monks. The trend gained strength from the seventh century owing to the growing preoccupation with liturgy within the monastic movement and the Church in general as well as to the papal campaign to enlist monks in the Christianization of Europe. Of great importance was the growing influence on the Continent of Celtic monasticism, of which monastery-bishoprics were a typical feature.

Several varieties of bishop-monks emerged at that time, only to disappear soon after. In the seventh century the institution of "claustral bishops," subordinate to the abbot, emerged under the influence of "itinerant" Irish monk-bishops of obscure legal standing. Missions were undertaken by some monasteries in territories lacking established diocesan organization. Monks elected in an abbey and were ordained bishops by a bishop from a neighboring diocese. Their area of responsibility was limited to the boundaries of the abbey and its dependencies.

The institution of "abbot-bishops," widespread in the British Isles in the early Middle Ages, also derived from Celtic monasticism. An abbot-bishop was the superior of a monastic diocese whose episcopal authority extended over the area of influence of the monastic *familia*, that is, over the abbey and its filial monasteries but not over the defined territory of a diocese. This function was usually, but not exclusively, performed by the abbot. On the Continent this institution appeared only in Brittany.

Similar to the position of the superior of a monastic diocese (i.e., the abbot-bishop) was that of a monk-bishop, whose episcopal dignity resembled that of the abbot in a monastery independent of the diocese. Most of the early medieval missionary bishops belonged in this category. Their jurisdiction was in newly Christianized territories, and their subsequent seats were in abbeys founded as the mission progressed.

On very rare occasions the pope would grant a meritorious abbot a purely honorary bishop's title to which neither a specific seat nor jurisdiction was attached. Much more often monasteries housed former monk-bishops or bishops who had decided to become professed monks after voluntary or forced renunciation of their dignity. Although these monks retained their former title, they lost their former jurisdiction and had to obey the superior of the monastery.

The most common form of monk-bishop occurs when a monk or an abbot is appointed bishop in a diocese. Such situations continue to occur today.

Being ordained priest does not affect a monk's legal status, even if the *cura animarum* is involved. However, the difference between the responsibilities and legal status of a monk and those of a bishop is so pronounced that these roles cannot be combined into one without the monk/bishop relinquishing some of the responsibilities and rights associated with each position. The bishop's dignity impedes or even makes impossible the maintenance of monastic observance, and it exempts the monk-bishop from his superiors' authority. Moreover, a bishop is involved in the management of church property – a serious hindrance for members of the mendicant orders.

In the practice of canon law, the monk-bishop issue emerged slowly, with specific solutions being employed as late as the 12th to 14th centuries. Rules established at that time have been in force until now with only minute changes.

A monk appointed bishop remains a monk. He still abides by his monastic vows, he is a member of his order, and his are the rights and responsibilities of a monk, except for modifications prescribed by law in matters of vows of obedience and poverty and voting rights (which he no longer has). The monk-bishop should abide, as far as possible, by monastic observance. The earlier practice is reflected in the wording used in the current *Codex Iuris Canonici* (*CIC*): the monk-bishop is relieved from monastic obligations "which at his reasonable discretion cannot be reconciled with his status" (canon 705). From the Fourth Lateran Council (1215), he was required to wear the habit of his order.

Notwithstanding his profession a monk-bishop enjoys the right of use, usufruct, and administration of property. This disposition is important for bishops belonging to the mendicant orders.

A monk can be appointed bishop only with the consent of his superior and monastic authorities. However, the pope can create bishops at will and also from among monks. A monk, once ordained bishop, is relieved from obedience to his monastic superiors; monk-bishops, like all bishops, are subordinate to the pope.

Canon law does not prescribe conditions that a monk must meet in order to be appointed bishop. Nevertheless this appointment results in severing material, organizational, and disciplinary ties between the monk-bishop and his former monastery. This severing of ties is connected with the issue of combining the dignities of bishop and abbot. For a long time the accumulation of benefices by bishops was not formally forbidden (although neither was it recommended). Therefore, many abbots, when appointed bishops, continued to exercise authority in their abbeys, and some even became abbots of other monasteries. This practice used to be common, especially in the early Middle Ages. Later it returned with abbots *ad commendam* and the custom of granting bishops, especially those of impoverished dioceses, abbeys as additional benefices.

The current *CIC* gives to retired monk-bishops the right to select their "place of residence, also outside the house of their Institute, unless the Apostolic See has stipulated for something else." Earlier practice and legislation required the monk-bishop to return to his monastery upon leaving his bishopric.

MAREK DERWICH

See also Bishops: Jurisdiction and Role; Celibacy: Christian; Hume, Basil; Monastics and the World, Medieval; Origins: Western Christian; Patrons, Christian: Royal; Regulations: Christian Perspectives

Further Reading

de Meester, P., *De monachico statu iuxta disciplinam byzantinam*, Vatican: Typis Polyglottis Vaticanis, 1942
Frank, Hieronymus, *Die klosterbischöfe des Frankenreiches*, Münster in Westf.: Aschendorff, 1932
Gallen, Joseph F., *Canon Law for Religious*, New York: Alba House, 1983
Haines, R.M., "The Episcopate of a Benedictine Monk: Hamo de Hethe, Bishop of Rochester (1317–1352)," *Revue Bénédictine* 102 (1992)
Hourlier, Jacques, *L'âge classique (1150–1378): Les religieux*, Paris: Cujas, 1973
Lesage, G., and G. Rocca, "Vescovo religioso," in *Dizionario degli istituti di perfezione*, edited by G. Pellicca and G. Rocca, volume 9, Rome: Edizioni Paoline, 1997
Marositz, Joseph J., *Obligations and Privileges of Religious Promoted to the Episcopal or Cardinalitial Dignities*, Washington, D.C.: Catholic University of America, 1948
McDermott, R.M., "Religious Raised to the Episcopate (c. 705–707)," in *The Code of Canon Law*, New York: Paulist Press, 1985
Oliger, Paul Remy, *Les évêques réguliers: Recherche sur leur condition juridique depuis les origines du monachisme jusqu'à la fin du moyen-âge*, Paris: Desclée de Brouwer, 1958
Rencontre d'histoire religieuse, *L'évêque dans l'histoire de l'église: Actes de la Septième rencontre . . . à Fontevraud . . .*, Angers: Presses de l'Université d'Angers, 1984

Mont-St.-Michel, France

The monastery of Mont-St.-Michel stands on top of a granite outcrop, 250 feet high, about a mile offshore at the junction of Normandy and Brittany in northwestern France. Its isolation and dramatic beauty make this site well suited to monastic life. The monastery is usually surrounded by sandbanks, but the tide

Benedictine Abbey of Mont-St.-Michel (Manche), 12th–13th century.
Photo courtesy of J. Feuillie/CNMHS

can very quickly rise 40 feet. Although earlier groups of hermits likely existed at the Mont, the origin of the monastery dates to the eighth century, when Autbert, bishop of Avranches, established a small cenobitic community there in honor of St. Michael. According to the foundation legend, the archangel appeared to Autbert in a dream, instructing him to establish the monastery, but Autbert dismissed the dream when he awoke. Saint Michael repeated his instruction on two subsequent nights during Autbert's sleep, finally tapping the bishop's head with his finger to emphasize his point. Autbert awoke and obeyed St. Michael when he discovered a small hole in his head from the archangel's finger. The hole can still be seen in Bishop Autbert's skull, which is on display at the museum of Avranches, across the bay from Mont-St.-Michel.

Little is known about the first three centuries of monastic life at Mont-St.-Michel. This area of France was not central to the Carolingian realm, and the king offered no aid during the Viking raids of the ninth and tenth centuries. However, Mont-St.-Michel commands a naturally fortified position on its rock, surrounded by rushing tides and treacherous sands. Unlike many other monastic communities, the monks of Mont-St.-Michel did not abandon their abbey to the Vikings. Over the course of the tenth century, Vikings began settling permanently along the rivers and waterways of northern France. The most important of these groups was a band of Vikings led by Rollo (d. 931) that took up residence along the Seine River in the area of Rouen. These Vikings received permission from French King Charles III (893–923) to remain, on the understanding that they would convert to Christianity and that any further expansion of their territory would be toward the west, away from Paris and the heartland of France. Because the French called the Vikings *northmanni*, the area that Rollo's men controlled became known as *Northmannia*, or Normandy. By the end of the tenth century, Normandy had spread through conquest, alliance, and intermarriage from Rouen to the environs of Mont-St.-Michel.

In 966 Rollo's grandson Richard I sought royal approval for the "restoration" of monastic life at Mont-St.-Michel. Mainard, the abbot of St. Wandrille, was sent west with a group of monks to revive and reform monastic observance at the Mont. Later legends relate that Mainard found a decadent community when he arrived at Mont-St.-Michel, mere "canons" who spent more time feasting and hunting than in prayer. However, such accusations of corruption were often made by later Benedictines to justify their takeover of communities. In this case the original

Celebration of the 1,000th anniversary of the Benedictine Abbey of Mont-St.-Michel in 1966. The church dates from the 13th century.
Photo courtesy of J. Feuillie/CNMHS

Refectory of the Benedictine Abbey of Mont-St.-Michel (Manche), 12th–13th century. Photo courtesy of J. Feuillie/CNMHS

monks probably followed a mixed or Irish rule before the Benedictines arrived.

Lists of monks and records of property indicate strong Breton connections at Mont-St.-Michel during the 10th and early 11th centuries. The counts of Brittany were generous patrons of the abbey, and at least two chose to be buried there. Local inhabitants gave gifts to the monks in exchange for spiritual benefits as well as material support, even on occasion seeking refuge there in time of war. However, Mont-St.-Michel's importance as a religious center transcended local ties. Pilgrims came from all over Europe to visit the Mont, and their gifts brought the monastery wide-flung estates in the 11th century and beyond. Because of the danger posed by its tides, Mont-St.-Michel was sometimes called "Saint Michael in Peril from the Sea."

The Norman dukes sought to claim Mont-St.-Michel as a Norman monastery, but the community stubbornly maintained its broader affiliations. Nevertheless Mont-St.-Michel joined the other Norman monasteries in providing ships to Duke William on the eve of the conquest of England in 1066. The next three centuries witnessed increased wealth and prestige for the Mont despite considerable political turmoil. From 1154 to 1186 Mont-St.-Michel was under the authority of Abbot Robert of Torigny, who greatly expanded the monastery's library. The late 12th century and early 13th centuries saw ambitious building projects on the Mont. Mont-St.-Michel enjoyed close ties with the English monarchs during the Angevin Empire, but after 1203 the monastery was under the control of the French kings.

During the English invasion and occupation of the Hundred Years' War (1337–1453), the Mont remained impregnable despite a determined siege by the English in the 15th century. The wars of religion in the next century brought renewed violence as Protestants attempted to capture the monastery. The Mont resisted these attacks, but monastic life fell into decline during the 16th and 17th centuries. Kings appointed unscrupulous laymen as abbots. Discipline became lax, buildings fell into disrepair, and the monastery was used increasingly to incarcerate political prisoners. During the French Revolution the monks were expelled, and Mont-St.-Michel was officially turned into a prison.

In 1874 the French state declared the Mont a historic monument and undertook massive repairs. A small community of monks restored religious life, but during the 20th century Mont-St.-Michel served mainly as a tourist attraction. It remains a magnificent site: most impressive are the 13th-century buildings on the north side of the rock. They are designed to reflect the spiritual hierarchy, with the almonry on the first floor, the Knights' Hall for aristocratic visitors on the second, and the cloister and refectory for the monks on the third. The church, built between the 12th and 15th centuries, demonstrates the transition from Romanesque to Gothic as one travels from the nave to the chancel. The festival of the archangel St. Michael is still celebrated each year on the last Sunday of September.

CASSANDRA POTTS

See also Architecture: Western Christian Monasteries; England: History; France; Island Monasteries, Christian; Pilgrimages, Christian: Western Europe

Further Reading

Alexander, J.J.G., *Norman Illumination at Mont St. Michel, 966–1100*, Oxford: Clarendon Press, 1970

Bély, Lucien, *Wonderful Mont-Saint-Michel*, translated by Angela Moyon, Rennes: Ouest-France, 1986

Déceneux, Marc, *Mont-Saint-Michel: Histoire d'un mythe*, Rennes: Ouest-France, 1997

Dosdat, Monique, *L'enluminure romane au Mont-Saint-Michel, Xe–XIIe siècles*, Rennes: Ouest-France, 1991

Millénaire monastique du Mont-Saint-Michel, 966–1966, 4 vols., Paris: Lethielleux, 1966–1967

Potts, Cassandra, *Monastic Revival and Regional Identity in Early Normandy*, Woodbridge, Suffolk, and Rochester, New York: Boydell Press, 1997

Quétel, Claude, *Le Mont-Saint-Michel*, Paris: Bordas, 1991

Smith, T.D. Wilson, "The Millennium of Mont-Saint-Michel," *Downside Review* 84 (1966)

Monte Cassino, Italy

Monte Cassino is located 80 miles south of Rome in a strategic location on the Liri River. After St. Benedict of Nursia had founded 12 communities, he left Subiaco 40 miles east of Rome and went south to what Dante referred to in the Paradisio XXII as "a cui Cassino è nella costa" ("that mount on whose slope lies Cassino"). Here he founded the monastery of Monte Cassino in 529; his sister Scholastica lived at the foot of the hill with a community of women who probably followed the rule that Benedict wrote here. Monte Cassino became a symbol of the triumph of Christianity; in the same year it was founded, Emperor Justinian (527–565) closed the last of the pagan schools. Monte Cassino lay at the origin of Benedictine monasticism in Western Europe. The Benedictine emphasis on *ora et labora* (pray and work) provided the basis of medieval learning and revitalized medieval economic life. So important a symbol is Monte Cassino that many scholars date the beginning of the Middle Ages from its foundation.

As in the case of many other Christian sites, Monte Cassino was built on the ruins of a pagan temple, and the cult of Apollo was still being practiced on the mountaintop when the abbey was first built. Benedict transformed the temple into an oratory and dedicated it to St. Martin of Tours (d. 397). Benedict would later die in this oratory, with arms upraised in prayer after having received Holy Communion. Today this event is commemorated with a bronze statue at the entrance cloister, which is in the same location as the original oratory. Benedict's death is usually placed in 543, the only certain date in Benedict's life and the same year in which he was visited by Ostrogothic King Totila (541–552).

Just as Benedict had predicted, the monastery was destroyed by the Lombards in 585. Ironically in 717 the Lombards helped the Brescian Petronax, commissioned by Pope Gregory II (715–731), to rebuild the monastery. Many prominent figures in the history of Western Europe came here during this period, including the great Lombard historian Paul the Deacon (c. 720–c. 800); Sturmius, who was a disciple of Boniface and the founder of Fulda and of German monasticism; the Anglo-Saxon Willibald (700–786), who later became a disciple of Boniface; and Anselm, who was later abbot of Nonantola. Monte Cassino continued to serve as a symbol of peace when two warring kings, Ratchis, king of the Lombards, and Carloman, brother of Pepin and king of the Franks, entered the monastery as brothers in Christ. Charlemagne (768–814) also visited the abbey in 787 and granted it extensive privileges.

In 856 Bertharius became abbot, during a period when the expansion of Islam threatened the security of Europe. Bertharius fortified Monte Cassino and its holdings and created the medieval town of San Germano. Despite his efforts the monastery was sacked in 884 by the Saracens, who killed Bertharius at the altar of St. Martin. Many survivors fled to Teano and later to Capua. In the tenth century monastic life once again resumed at Monte Cassino, largely through the efforts of Abbot Aligernus. During his reign St. Romuald (c. 950–1027) and German Emperor Otto III (983–1002) visited the abbey. In the 11th century Monte Cassino again entered a period of greatness under the reign of such abbots as Theobald, Richerius, and Frederick of Lorraine, who later became Pope Stephen X (1057–1058). The Normans were a threat during this period, and despite the efforts of Richerius they sacked the abbey in 1046. The abbey reached the height of its greatness under the reign of the Desiderius, who became abbot in 1058. When the basilica was consecrated in 1071, his friend Cardinal Hildebrand, who later became Pope Gregory VII (1073–1085), was present. The basilica was rebuilt during Desiderius' tenure as abbot, and the monastery obtained numerous works of art, such as the middle bronze door to the basilica. The inscriptions on the door and its two companions list the churches and extensive possessions that were dependent on the monastery. Under Desiderius the state of San Germano became a model of civic order. It continues to thrive today in the 22 principalities governed by Monte Cassino. Desiderius assisted Gregory VII in his struggle to free the Church from the control of the state and later succeeded him as Pope Victor III (1086–1087).

The abbey's strategic location made it especially vulnerable to warring parties in the conflict between the empire and the papacy. Even in the midst of chaos, Monte Cassino continued to educate such brilliant minds as Thomas Aquinas (c. 1225–1274), who studied there before going to Naples in 1236. In July 1239 Emperor Frederick II (1212–1250) banished from the kingdom all monks born elsewhere, and Monte Cassino was left desolate, inhabited by only eight monks.

In 1349 Monte Cassino was again destroyed, this time by an earthquake. A few walls and a door were all that remained of Abbot Desiderius' building. The abbey was again rebuilt with many additions under the guidance of Benedictine Pope Urban V (1362–1370). It entered another period of greatness in the 16th century, symbolized by the cloister named for the Renaissance architect Bramante. During the 17th century Monte Cassino was an important center of pilgrimage, attracting as many as 47,000 pilgrims a year. During the Napoleonic Wars the abbey suffered another setback when 1,500 French soldiers retreating from Italy in 1799 sacked the abbey, leaving only the walls standing. When religious life was suppressed during the 19th-century Risorgimento, Monte Cassino became the property of the state and was declared a national monument with the monks as its custodians.

By the 14th centenary of Benedict's birth in 1880, a series of reforming abbots had renewed monastic fervor, and the monastery once again was a thriving cultural center. However, on 15 February 1944 the abbey was once again destroyed as it became yet another casualty of World War II. Convinced that Nazis were using the abbey to store munitions, American troops destroyed it in less than three hours. Not only were no munitions found in the abbey, but the hundreds of refugees there met their deaths. Miraculously the bronze urn containing the remains of Benedict and Scholastica was undamaged; an artillery shell that was stuck between the two steps in front of the altar never exploded. Among the items destroyed were the famous statue of Scholastica by P. Ciompi in the Bramante cloister and the Beuronese murals in the crypt. The abbey was liberated on 18 May 1944, and today one can see from the Bramante cloister the cemetery on a neighboring hill where thousands of Polish soldiers who gave their lives in the battle are buried. Once again the abbey was rebuilt, this time under the guidance of Abbot Ildefonso Rea, who insisted that the original architectural pattern be followed according to his "where and as was" philosophy. The facade of the basilica dates from this period, and the basilica itself was rebuilt according to the 17th-century plan of Fansago, who had designed the high altar in 1645.

A large oak tree in the abbey symbolizes the turbulent history of the community; just as a tree is cut down and grows green and strong again, so too the abbey has always recovered from destruction and continues to stand as a symbol of peace. During the ten-year reconstruction process after World War II, traces of the original oratory were found, the tomb of Benedict and Scholastica was opened, and their remains were subjected to examinations that reconfirmed the authenticity of the relics. Pope

Donato Bramante, courtyard (early 16th century) of the Monastery of St. Benedict, Monte Cassino, Italy, restored in the 1950s. Photo courtesy of the Editor

Foundations of the Monastery of St. Benedict, Monte Cassino, Italy, restored in the 1950s.
Photo courtesy of the Editor

Paul VI (1963–1978) reconsecrated the abbey on 24 October 1964 and proclaimed Benedict the patron saint of Europe. He referred to him as the "Messenger of Peace, Unifier, Master of Civilization, and in particular Herald of Faith and Initiator of monastic life in western Europe." In his reflection in 1993 on the 50th anniversary of the destruction of Monte Cassino, Pope John Paul II (1978–) saw the abbey as the symbol of the creation of a new united Europe built on the ideals of its Christian past. Today Monte Cassino stands as a monument to the grandeur of its past and as a testament to the enduring values of the Benedictine tradition.

DEBORAH VESS

See also Archives, Western Christian; Benedict of Nursia, St.; Benedictines: General or Male; Bobbio, Italy; Congregations, Benedictine; Libraries: Western Christian; Office, Daily: Western Christian; Pilgrimages, Christian: Western Europe; Schools and Universities, Benedictine; Subiaco, Italy

Further Reading

Bloch, Herbert, *Monte Cassino in the Middle Ages*, 3 vols., Cambridge, Massachusetts: Harvard University Press, 1986

Fabinai, L., *La Terra di S. Benedetto, Miscellanea Cassinese*, Badia di Montecassino: Pubblicazioni cassinesi, 1968

Gattola, Erasmo, *Historia Abbatiae Casinensis*, Venice: Apud Sebastianum Coleti, 1733

Hapgood, David, and David Richardson, *Monte Cassino*, London: Angus and Robertson, 1984

Hassel, Sven, *Monte Cassino*, London: Corgi Books, 1969

Hoffman, H., editor, *Chronica Casinensis*, in *Monumenta Germania Historiae SS* 34, Hannover 1980

Leccisotti, Tomass, *Monte Cassino*, edited and translated by Armond Citarella, Monte Cassino: Pubblicazioni cassinesi, 1987

Leclercq, Jean, *The Love of Learning and the Desire for God*, New York: Fordham University Press, 1961; reprint, London: SPCK, 1978

Tosti, Luigi, *Storia della Badia di Montecassino*, Rome: Pasqualucci, 1887

Vauchez, André, *The Spirituality of the Medieval West: The Eighth to the Twelfth Centuries*, Kalamazoo, Michigan: Cistercian Publications, 1993

Vogüé, Adalbert de, *The Rule of Saint Benedict: A Doctrinal and Spiritual Commentary*, translated by John Baptist Hasbrouck, Kalamazoo, Michigan: Cistercian Publications, 1983

Related Web Site

http://www.officine.it/montecassino/main_e.html (Official Web Site of Monte Cassino)

More, Gertrude 1606–1633

English Benedictine author and disciple of Dom Augustine Baker

Helen (Dame Gertrude) More was the daughter of Crisacre More, great-grandson of St. Thomas More (1478–1535). After the dissolution of the English monasteries under Henry VIII (1509–1547), it was common for wealthy Catholic families to send their children to other European countries for religious education or to join religious communities. When Gertrude was in her teens, she was encouraged by a confessor to leave her widowed father and pursue the religious life in France, but she showed little desire for or understanding of a monastic vocation. Eventually Gertrude's father was persuaded to provide assistance to endow a women's monastery under the English Benedictines of Douai. In 1623 Gertrude and eight companions went to Cambrai, where three Benedictine nuns from Brussels assisted in establishing the community.

In her later writing Gertrude makes no secret of the fact that she was a reluctant nun. She suffered physical illness, indifference and even hostility toward the life, and much interior restlessness. She continued nevertheless, struggling to accept both her own desire for God and the seemingly impossible conflicts between her own nature and the demands of monastic life. The young religious of the new community also seem to have had great need of education and grounding in their understanding of Benedictinism and its traditions. Some time around her profession of vows, Gertrude began to receive spiritual guidance from Dom Augustine Baker (1575–1641). Through this relationship she was able to come to understanding and acceptance of the monastic ideal as he envisioned it.

Dom Augustine was noted for his teachings on the mystical way of direct relationship with God. He associated the structures of the monastic way of life with discernment of and obedience to the will of God. He encouraged the practices of monastic life that would lead to an environment of contemplative listening, such as silence. Both Baker and his female disciple became known for their enthusiastic articulation and restoration of Benedictine spirituality, but this achievement was not without controversy and detractors. Many feared that his way of prayer was too affective and allowed for too much personal authority.

Dame Gertrude died an early death in 1633 while the debate still went on, but she continued to be a part of the developing story. After her death several writings by her, including her "Confession of a Loving Soul" and an apologia, were found and circulated. Baker took advantage of this in writing a biography of her, *The Inner Life of Dame Gertrude More*. Before it could be published the manuscript disappeared. The first half was recovered in Germany c. 1850 and now resides at Stanbrook Abbey, near Worcester. A somewhat shortened copy of the whole is at Ampleforth Abbey. In this work Baker examines in great detail her struggles with her vocation, the nature of her personality and spirit, and the holiness that she exemplified. The book offers an outstanding example of all that was good and beneficial about his concept of Benedictine life. More's writing and spirituality became known to many despite her short and obscure life, and Benedictine life did revive and prosper. When conditions in England improved, the monastic community was able to relocate to Stanbrook Abbey, where the Benedictine spirit continues to flourish.

Judith Sutera, O.S.B.

See also Baker, Augustine; Belgium: History; Benedictines: Female; Dissolution of Monasteries: England, Ireland, and Wales; England: History; Exile, Western Christian; Spirituality: Western Christian

Biography

Directly descended from Thomas More, Gertrude entered the Benedictine house at Cambrai in 1623. Dom Augustine Baker (1575–1641), while serving as chaplain to the house, helped settle her doubts. His *The Inner Life of Dame Gertrude More* was published only in 1910. At age 23 Gertrude became abbess, only to die of smallpox four years later.

Major Works

The Holy Practices of a Divine Lover, or the Saintly Idiot's Devotions, 1657
Confessiones Amantis, 1658
The Writings of Dame Gertrude More, edited by Edward Weld-Blundell, 1910

Further Reading

Baker, Augustine, *The Inner Life of Dame Gertrude More*, London: Washbourne, 1910
Nun of Stanbrook, *Stanbrook Abbey, A Sketch of Its History, 1625–1925*, London: Burns, Oates, and Washbourne, 1925
Nun of Stanbrook, "Cambrai: Dame Catherine Gascoigne (1600–1676)," in *In a Great Tradition: Tribute to Dame Laurentia McLachlan*, London: John Murray, 1956

Moscow, Russia

As soon as Moscow became a capital under one ruling family starting with Prince Daniel (d. 1303), the younger son of Alexander Nevskii (1236–1263), the city had to be endowed with a monastery to care for the souls of the deceased members of the dynasty. The ecclesiastical vocation of Moscow grew steadily after Metropolitan Peter, head of the Russian Church, died and was buried in the city (1326) and his successor, Theognost, chose Moscow as his permanent residence (1328). Peter's resting place was the Dormition Cathedral in Moscow's Kremlin, not a monastery, but soon there was to be a Muscovite metropolitan abbey. Other members of the Muscovite elite also had their own foundations for both men and women. The wave of new cenobitic monasteries inaugurated in the second half of the 14th century at the initiative of St. Sergius of Radonezh (c. 1322–1392) and Metropolitan Alexis (head of the Russian Church between 1354 and 1378) added some new important abbeys a few miles away from the medieval city. From the 15th to the 17th century, the number of Muscovite monasteries, both outside and inside the walls, grew steadily. Some of them resulted from vows formulated in time of military danger. They served as testimony to God's grace and as supplementary defenses of the city after they were erected. Also, because the state and the Church needed more books and more learned men, schools were established in some existing abbeys, and to a large extent the development of printing can be credited to monks. The translation of the capital to St. Petersburg in the 18th century did not diminish the religious significance of Moscow, although some rich patrons moved to the banks of the Neva River. Urban development and great catastrophes (such as the fire brought by the Napoleonic invasion in 1812) destroyed some buildings, but most of the Muscovite monasteries were still standing at the time of the 1917 revolution.

Under the Soviet regime, on the contrary, dramatic changes occurred in the urban landscape and in the religious life of Moscow. From the 1920s to 1943, worshiping came to a virtual halt, and many monasteries were either destroyed or converted to museums, offices, collective apartments, or prisons. World War II saw a controlled revival of religious life in the city and also stimulated grandiose projects of reconstruction. While new

Former refectory (Trapeznaia), Andronikov Monastery, Moscow, Russia, 17th century.
Photo courtesy of Robert E. Jones

skyscrapers popped out on the surface, the underground train system changed the archaeological layers beyond recognition. With the Perestroika period, the state started giving back many churches and monastic compounds to the Russian Orthodox Church. Some of the most famous buildings have been restored and returned to religious life, but others still keep their status as museums.

A first group of Muscovite monasteries includes half a dozen foundations anterior to the second half of the 14th century, when the Trinity St. Sergius abbey became the flagship of the cenobitic reformation in Russia. Among these oldest monasteries following the patterns of the pre-Mongol period was St.-Daniel's (Danilov) abbey. Located on a little hill southeast of Moscow, it was probably founded by Daniel, the first prince of Moscow, as a "personal" monastery, but it is not known whether Daniel himself was buried there. The abbey's existence is documented from the year 1330, when, however, it lost most of its significance because its abbot lost the title of archimandrite. At that time only one archimandrite was present in each major city (e.g., Novgorod, Smolensk, and Moscow), and he was a spokesman for all monastic communities to the bishop. From the 15th to the 16th century, St. Daniel's was used as a necropolis until from 1550 to the 1560s the abbey was solemnly restored by Ivan IV the Terrible (1533–1584). The legend of Prince Daniel was also developed at that time, and in the middle of the 17th century (in 1652, according to some sources), the invention of his relics occurred. From 1771 to the 1930s, Danilov's cemetery was a famous place of burial. The abbey was then turned into a state prison. It was given back to the Church in 1983 and restored over a period of six years. It is now the official residence of the patriarch, head of the Russian Church.

The monastery of the Miracle of Archangel Michael (Chudov monastyr', or Chudo arkhangela Mikhaila) was founded in 1365 by Metropolitan Alexis, within the Kremlin walls, and was the main metropolitan foundation in Moscow. There, in 1601–1602, under Czar Boris Godunov (1598–1605), the young monk Grigorii Otrep'ev became a deacon and showed some literary talent. He started also pretending to be the czarevitch Dimitri, the son of Ivan the Terrible and legitimate heir to the crown of Russia. The real Dimitri had died, in suspect circumstances, in 1591. Grigorii/Dimitri had to flee to Poland to establish his claim, but the Chudov was the starting point of his adventure. The buildings of the Miracle monastery were destroyed in the 1930s. Other monasteries were built within the Kremlin walls during the 14th century or at the beginning of the 15th: the Savior in the forest (Spas na Boru), St. Athanasius (Afanas'evskii), and the Ascension (Voznesenskii). By the 15th century some important Russian abbeys, such as the Trinity St. Sergius, also acquired a house or mansion (*dvor*; *podvor'e*) within the Kremlin walls. Saint Athanasius eventually became the *dvor* of St. Cyrill of Beloozero abbey.

Two important Muscovite abbeys are closely associated with Sergius of Radonezh (c. 1314–1392) himself, the charismatic founder of the Trinity monastery. The Simonov monastery was founded around 1360–1365 by Sergius' nephew Theodore, on the left bank of the Moskva River, about three miles southeast of

Church, Andronikov Monastery, Moscow, Russia, 14th–15th century. The icon painter Andrei Rublev (c. 1360/70–1427/30) lived here. Photo courtesy of Robert E. Jones

the Kremlin. It soon developed into a rich landowner and provided the Russian Church with many bishops. It was fortified in the middle of the 15th century and protected Moscow from the Crimean Tatars in 1591 and from rebel peasants in 1606. New walls were built during the 17th century. More than half the site was destroyed in the 1930s to build the Likhachev workers' quarter, but one can still visit the church of the Icon of the Virgin of Tikhvin (1680–1686). This monument is an example of "Naryshkin baroque," named after the family of the mother of Peter the Great, who favored artistic innovations in Moscow.

The Savior St. Andronic (Spas-Andronikov) abbey was founded in the 1360s by Metropolitan Alexis. Its first abbot, Andronic, was a disciple of Sergius who ended his career on Mount Athos. Saint Andronic abbey was located on the left bank of the Iauza River, east of the medieval city. Restored many times, the Savior's abbey-church is the only one dating from late 14th to early 15th century that is still preserved in Moscow. Its frescoes are due to the celebrated monk-painters Daniel and Andrei Rublev (c. 1428). As in the case of the Danilov abbey, the Andronikov cemetery was a place of choice for burial from the 18th to the 19th century. Part of the monastery compound was destroyed in the 1930s. It is now home of the Andrei Rublev museum of Russian medieval culture and art, which possesses the finest collection of icons in Moscow after the Tretiakov Gallery.

The New Convent of the Virgins (Novodevichii) was created as a nunnery in 1524 on the banks of the Moskva River southwest of Moscow. It hosted prominent female members of the Russian ruling families, among them Irina, widow of Czar Fedor (1584–1598) and sister of Boris Godunov, and a century later Sofia, step-sister of Peter the Great and regent of Russia for seven years, who was kept there after she lost power in 1689. The two most interesting churches are the abbey-church, erected in the 1550s and devoted to the Icon of the Virgin of Smolensk, and the church of the Transfiguration (1688; another typical example of Naryshkin baroque).

The Savior "beyond the icons shops" (Zaikonospasskij monastyr') on St. Nicholas Street in the neighborhood of Kitai Gorod north of the Kremlin was founded by Czar Boris Godunov (1598–1605) at the end of the 16th century. On the same street stood two other abbeys (The Epiphany [Bogoiavlenskii] and St. Nicholas) hosting the little colony of learned Greek monks living in Moscow in the 17th century. The Printing Hall (Pechatnyi dvor), the one and only official Russian publisher, moved also to St. Nicholas Street in 1620. Thus, for some decades this part of Moscow was a kind of equivalent to the "Latin Quarter" in Paris. Around 1665 a school was opened in the Zaikonospasskij abbey to teach Greek and Latin to selected clergymen. It was headed by two important religious writers of that time: Simeon of Polotsk (1629–1680) and Sylvester Medvedev (1641–1691). In 1687 the school was turned into the famous Slavonic-Greek-Latin Academy (Slaviano Greko Latinskaia Akademiia), the first higher-education institution in Russia. Its methods and teaching personnel were borrowed first from Greek experience (the Likhudes brothers were the regents of the academy until 1694) and then from the Mohyla College (later Mohyla Academy). The latter had been established in Kiev in 1635 to give Ruthenian Orthodox an opportunity to combat the Jesuits using their own scholarly weapons. The Slavonic-Greek-Latin Academy educated not only clergymen but also many notable lay personalities, such as the 18th-century Russian writers Mikhail Lomonosov (1711–1765) and Vasilii Trediakovskii (1703–1768). It lost its monopoly on higher education with the creation of the Academy of Sciences in St. Peterburg (1725) and the foundation of Moscow University (1755). Following the fire of 1812, which damaged the Zaikonospasskij abbey, the Slavonic-Greek-Latin Academy was transferred, under the name of Moscow Theological Academy, to the Trinity St. Sergius abbey.

The monastery of the Icon of the Virgin of the Don (Donskoi) was founded in 1591 south of Moscow on the very spot where the Russian army had built its camp to face the Crimean Tatars. The old one-dome abbey-church (*staryi sobor*) was erected in 1593, whereas the new five-dome one (*novyi sobor*) dates from 1684 to 1698 and exemplifies again Naryshkin baroque. Its iconostasis features Russian icons of the 17th-century style, but the ceiling and the vaults were painted by an Italian artist at the end of the 18th century. The abbey also has a large cemetery. From 1934 to 1992 the Donskoi monastery was used as a museum of architecture.

One cannot fail to mention two unusual communities that complete the monastic landscape of Moscow, the so-called cemeteries of Preobrazhenskoe and Rogozhskoe. Both appeared outside the city limits in September 1771 when Old Believers offered to help in burying the victims of a major plague that had overwhelmed the local authorities. Catherine the Great (1762–1796) authorized the opening of the cemeteries, which quickly got organized as paramonastic communities for the defenders of the Old Faith. Rogozhskoe (east of Moscow between Nizhegorodskaia ulitsa and Shosse Entuziastov) became the main center of the "Presbyterians" (Popovtsy), who maintained a clergy among them. Preobrazhenskoe (northeast of Moscow near the Bolshaia Cherkizovskaia ulitsa) was the home of the "Priestless" (Bespopovtsy), who considered that the Church had disappeared with the reforms brought by Patriarch Nikon (1652–1658) and later confirmed by a special council (1666–1667). Men and women were segregated until 1854, when the imperial administration seized half the compound and gave it to a new, more docile "Uniate" Church (Edinoverie). Under the name of St. Nicholas monastery, it was used as an outpost for the "conversion" of the Old Believers. As both Presbyterians and Priestless treasured the entire Russian heritage anterior to the Nikonian reforms and had among them rich merchants, they collected very valuable manuscripts and icons in Preobrazhenskoe and Rogozhskoe.

PIERRE GONNEAU

See also Archaeology: Russia; Elders, Russian Monastic (Startsi); Libraries: Eastern Christian; Mount Athos, Greece; Orthodox Monasticism: Slavic; Pilgrimages, Christian: Eastern Europe; Russia: History; Sergius of Radonezh, St.

Further Reading

Beliiaev, Leonid A., *Drevnie monastyri Moskvy (kon. XIII-nach. XV vv.) po dannym arkheologii* (Old Monasteries of Moscow [End of the 13th to the 15th century] According to Archaeological Data), Moscow: Institut arkheologii, 1994

Istoriia Moskvy (A History of Moscow), 6 vols., Moskva: Izd-vo Akademii nauk, 1952

Moscou: Patrimoine architectural, dir. D. Chvidkovski, J.-M. Pérouse de Montclos, Paris: Editions du patrimoine: Flammarion 1997

Palamarchuk, Petr G., *Sorok sorokov: Al'bom-ukazatel' vsekh moskovskikh tserkvei v chetyrekh tomakh* (Forty Times Forty: An Album-Index to All the Churches of Moscow), 4 vols., Moscow: "Kniga i biznes" and "Krom," 1992–1995

Zabelin, Ivan E., *Istoria goroda Moskvy* (A History of Moscow City), Moscow, 1905; reprint, Moscow: Stolitsa, 1990

Mount Athos, Greece

Mount Athos is a transnational Orthodox holy land and place of pilgrimage, consisting of the easternmost peninsula of the Chalcidice in Thrace (northeastern Greece). At its southern tip is the towering mountain for which it is named, whose cave-riddled cliffs rise precipitously from the Aegean Sea. Since its official dedication to the Virgin Mary in 963 by Byzantine Emperor Nicephoras Phocas (963–969), it has been a land of hermits and monks who preserve it as an Edenic paradise, the "Garden of the Panaghia" (traditional epithet for the Virgin). According to medieval Athonite legend, the Virgin herself selected this place to be a monastic holy land after the ship on which she was traveling ran aground there in a storm, saving her and her fellow travelers from death at sea. Her divine son gave it to her that it might continue to be a paradise and haven of salvation. Today this monastic territory, a protectorate of Greece, is noted for its observance of the medieval *abaton*, the sacred tradition of exclusion of women and female domestic animals.

Mount Athos remains for the modern world, as it was throughout the Middle Ages, the conservative, mystical, and theological heart of Eastern Orthodoxy. As a place of pilgrimage, its monasteries receive up to 400 pilgrims, suppliants, and other male visitors per day. It is a training ground for priests and host to a variety of Orthodox religious programs, retreats, and conferences. For administrative purposes the monastic territory is apportioned among its 20 independent royal and "stavropegiac" monasteries, that is, monasteries under the jurisdiction of the ecumenical patriarch. Their representatives constitute the Holy Community, the 20-member legislative and administrative body of this autonomous republic. The executive body is the Holy Epistasia, a four-member board whose membership changes yearly in a five-year rotation in the course of which all 20 monasteries are represented as follows:

Year 1: Lavra, Docheiariou, Xenophontos, Esphigmenou
Year 2: Vatopedi, Koutloumousiou, Karakallou, Stavronikita
Year 3: Iviron, Pantokratoros, Philotheou, Simonopetra
Year 4: Chilandari, Xeropotamou, Agiou Pavlou, Gregoriou
Year 5: Dionysiou, Zographou, Panteleimonos, Kastamonitou

History

After abandonment of the Athonite towns of the Roman era due to persistent depredations by pirates, the peninsula became attractive to hermits practicing the early Christian traditions of asceticism. Some lived in caves, and others formed loosely organized monastic communities called *lavras*, in which monks living in individual hermitages called cells would assemble for services on Sundays and holidays. During the later phase of the Iconoclastic Controversy (726–843), the Athonite peninsula is said to have become a place of refuge from persecution for monks who refused to abandon the traditional veneration of icons. Central government resided in the ancient office of the *protos* (primate), elected for life by the elders among the Athonite *lavras*. It was not until 885 that Byzantine Emperor Basil I (867–886) issued a charter recognizing Athos as an exclusively monastic territory. In 963 Emperor Nicephoras Phocas provided funding for his confessor and friend, Athanasius (c. 920–1003), later known as "the Athonite," to establish the first cenobitic (common-life) monastery. Although opposed by hermits and lavriotes already resident there, Athanasius built the Megisti Lavra (Greatest Lavra) near the southeastern tip of the peninsula, introducing the rigorous monastic regimen developed in the *typikon* (rule) of the Monastery of Stoudios in Constantinople.

With the advent of large monasteries, the power of the *protos* declined, and the council with representatives from the large monasteries played a greater role. The seat of government was moved to its present central location, the village of Karyes, identified in early documents as a *lavra* and sometimes called the Protaton. In 972 Mount Athos was recognized in a charter issued by Emperor John Tsimiskis (969–976) as an independent monastic state where all three monastic lifestyles were practiced. Known from this time on as Hagion Oros (Holy Mountain, hence the term Hagiorite), it was one among many such holy mountains that attracted communities of monks and hermits, such as Mount Sinai (site of St. Catherine's Monastery), Meteora in central Greece, and Mount Olympus, not to mention the Holy Mountain of St. Auxentius in Bithynia (today north-central Turkey), Mount Papikion in Thrace, and Mount Menoikion near Serres.

Monasteries and hermitages multiplied there between 963 and 1204. The second *typikon* (charter) of the Holy Mountain (1046) identifies 180 monasteries, and some 300 of varying size and character existed by the eve of the Fourth Crusade (1204).

By that time the transnational character of the territory had been solidly established. Among the earliest of the monastic foundations was the Monastery of the Georgians (Iviron), the Bulgarian Monastery of Zographou (both founded in the mid–tenth century), and a hermitage founded by 1016 called the Monastery of the Russian. By 1169 a Russian brotherhood had outgrown the monastery called Xylourgou and moved to the more spacious present Russian Monastery of Panteleimonos. At the end of the 12th century, Stephen Nemanja and St. Sava founded the Serbian monastery Chilandar. These monasteries played a major role in the spread of Orthodoxy to the Balkan peoples. They became centers of translation, and copies of Byzantine monastic and liturgical literature circulated to the growing numbers of monasteries in those countries. Many of the Greek monasteries acquired as endowments farms, villages, and small monastic houses in the upper Strymon River valley, contributing to the extension of Athonite influence among the Slavs of the northern Balkans. The cenobitic monasteries of the mountainous country between the Strymon and Vardar Rivers, the heartland of south Slav monasticism, were founded and organized on the Athonite model.

This development on Mount Athos during the 11th and 12th centuries was fueled by a combination of economic and demographic factors described in Athonite archival documents. Population increase during this period meant greater agricultural productivity with more peasants working the lands that made up the expanding monastic endowments. Increasing investment in agricultural properties – expansion of vineyards and gardens and implementation of irrigation systems – enhanced agricultural productivity. Increasing commercial ventures by the monasteries, especially the sale of wine, followed from the growing productivity of their landholdings. As the larger, earlier foundations expanded, so did many of the originally small brotherhoods, which, having gained royal or other patronage, developed into cenobitic monasteries with walls and defensive towers for protection from persistent Aegean piracy. Xenophontos, attested in Athonite archival documents for the first time in this period, grew into a prosperous monastery with private and imperial patronage. Xeropotamou became one of the richest monasteries on the Holy Mountain in the course of the 11th century. Philotheou, a tenth-century hermitage that had been abandoned, was reconstituted as a monastery in 1141 by a Constantinopolitan canonist, Arsenius, about whom little is known. The transnational character of the Holy Mountain is strikingly illustrated by a Catholic foundation, the Monastery of the Amalfitans, which flourished during this period not far from the original Lavra of Athanasius.

The Latin occupation of Constantinople following the Fourth Crusade (1204–1261) was disastrous for the Athonite monasteries, which were caught up in the struggles for control of the Byzantine Empire among the Latin crusader lords, the Greeks under Theodore of Epirus, the Greeks of the Nicaean kingdom in Anatolia, the Bulgarians who declared themselves protectors of Mount Athos, and the Serbs who maintained a strong presence at Chilandar on the Holy Mountain. In the aftermath of these conflicts, roving bands of Greek and other mercenaries, such as the Catalans, added to the woes of the Hagiorites.

Mount Athos was placed under the jurisdiction of Boniface of Montferrat as part of the Latin kingdom of Thessaloniki, which was formed from the division of the Byzantine Empire by the victorious Latins. Latin pressure on the Holy Mountain to submit to the pope and accept union of the Eastern and Western Churches was so strong that some monks chose to leave. When Theodore defeated the Latins, taking over Thessaloniki in 1225 and with it the Holy Mountain, Athonite loyalties, however, lay with the Nicaean kingdom and with the Bulgarians and Serbs, their spiritual children to the north. After the Latins were driven out of Constantinople in 1261, the new emperor, Michael VIII Palaeologos (1261–1282), faced with a serious threat of Latin reconquest by Charles of Anjou, was forced to submit to papal supremacy at the Council of Lyons in 1274 to gain papal restraint of Charles. The monks of Mount Athos denounced Michael's submission at the council as heretical, even though Michael courted their consent with lavish patronage of the monasteries. When a new pope, Innocent V (1276), put increasing pressure on Michael to impose Church union on his subjects, Michael turned to persecuting his opponents, including the Athonite monks. Several monasteries were attacked. Twenty-six monks at Zographou were tortured and killed; resistors at the Megisti Lavra were caught and executed, as were others at the Protaton and Vatopedi. Modern anti-Catholic sentiments of the

Athonite monks date from these events, whose martyrs are still commemorated on the Holy Mountain.

The 14th century (the Palaeologan era, named for the Palaeologan dynasty) brought new prosperity to Mount Athos. Bulgarian, Serb, and Byzantine patronage helped restore the damaged monasteries and their defenses. Over a third of the current 20 ruling monasteries were established or refounded during the 14th and early 15th centuries, not to mention many others that have not survived to the present:

> Dionysiou, named for its founder, a monk from Kastoria, brother of the metropolitan of Trebizond, through whose help he gained patronage from the grand comnenos of Trebizond, Alexios III
>
> Pantocrator, founded with patronage from the brothers Alexios and John, adventurers from Bithynia who carved out a principality for themselves consisting of the region of the lower Strymon around Christoupolis (present-day Kavalla) and the island of Thassos and then formed an alliance through marriage with the Palaeologan dynasty
>
> Simonopetra, founded with patronage from Serbian despot of Serres, John Ugliesa (1365–1371)
>
> Grigoriou, founded by Gregory of Syria, through whose Serbian connections the monastery gained patronage and came to be a Serbian monastery by the end of the 15th century
>
> Koutloumousiou, an 11th-century foundation later in dire economic straits, whose abbot cultivated the voivodes of Wallachia Alexander Basarab (1352–1364) and John Vladislav (1364–2374), thus developing it as a Romanian monastery
>
> Kastamonitou, a small hermitage in the late 12th century that gradually grew through the 13th, then was refounded in the 15th following a disastrous fire with patronage from Serbian Grand Celnik (general-in-chief) Radíc with endowments received from Serbian despot George Brankovich and the princess of Serbia, Anne the Philanthropic
>
> Saint Paul, under the leadership of Serbian nobles from Kastoria, Gerasimos Radonias, and Antonios-Arsenios Pagasis, who gained both Serbian and Byzantine patronage to develop it from a hermitage into a major Serbian monastery

In this context of prosperity, the Hesychastic (quietistic) movement emerged under the leadership of Gregory Palamas (c. 1296–1359) to play a major role in shaping Orthodox mystical theology. Palamas articulated an Orthodox rationale for Hesychastic mysticism and the Athonite practice of meditative or contemplative prayer. The latter involves internally focused attention through controlled breathing and repetition of the Jesus Prayer ("Lord Jesus Christ, Son of God, have mercy on me"). He argued that human beings can experience mystically the divine energy that they observe in the form of light, which is to be distinguished from the divine essence. Ridiculed by the Platonist Calabrian monk Barlaam (c. 1290–1348), who restricted prayer to an intellectual function, was condemned by two synods, and then was excommunicated in 1344, Palamas persisted among his Athonite supporters, demonstrating the legitimacy and antiquity of Athonite Hesychasm from the writings of the Church fathers. The orthodoxy of his teaching and of the Athonite practice of prayer was finally affirmed in 1351, and Gregory was canonized as a father and doctor of the Church in the 1368 Synod of Constantinople.

Athonite prosperity and growth, combined with persistent opposition to Latinization, continued right up to the fall of the Byzantine Empire to the Ottoman Turks in 1453. Hagiorite opposition to the West was reinforced in the 14th century by Western resistance to Athonite mysticism of the period.

In 1423, even before Thessaloniki fell to the Turks (1430), the Athonite Monks had the foresight to submit peacefully. Thus, the Ottoman sultans, from Orkhan (1326–1362) through the 15th century, recognized the endowed properties of the monasteries and left them in relative peace, observing Koranic injunctions of toleration toward Jews and Christians. Initially Mount Athos flourished under the Ottoman regime. Nobles and other persons of wealth (e.g., Serbian Grand Celnik Radíc, fl. 1425–1441) deposited their assets with the monasteries, and many took vows to be assured of freedom from harassment and enjoyment of their wealth. Idiorhythmism, introduced at Koutloumousi in the 14th century by monks from Hungro-Wallachia, became widespread in the 15th, accommodating increasing numbers of monks from the northern Balkans and wealthy individuals seeking to maintain independent lifestyles. Idiorhythmism was also a way of circumventing increasingly heavy taxation by the Ottoman Turks.

The Ottoman defeat of the Serbs in 1441 sent another surge of émigrés to Mount Athos, where they too contributed both human and fiscal resources to the Athonite economy. However, by the 16th century, as Ottoman confidence weakened, a policy of enforced Islamization went into effect with the banning of the Orthodox liturgy and teaching everywhere but at the Holy Mountain. Many educated Greeks who could not afford to emigrate to Italy to devote themselves to printing liturgical books and Greek patristic literature took refuge in Athonite monasteries. There they trained as priests and teachers, producing liturgical manuscripts in large numbers to take on sacrificial missions to the subjugated Greek-speaking world. It was the era of the neomartyrs.

The age of the Enlightenment brought exposure to North European Protestantism and philosophy and, in reaction, a renewed emphasis on traditional Athonite spirituality and the cenobitic regimen. The Athoniada academy was founded at Vatopedi Monastery by Patriarch Cyril V in 1749 as a college of higher learning and put under the direction of European-trained philosopher Eugenios Voulgaris in 1753. Connected with the school was the establishment of an Athonite press. Voulgaris framed the study of contemporary English and Continental rationalist philosophy and contemporary Copernican astronomy in a broader context of respect and appreciation for traditional Orthodox theology. Nevertheless the faculty and students were split by factions that, although contributing to the intensity of the intellectual life there, soon led to Voulgaris' departure. The Kollyvades controversy over the timing of the Saturday commemoration of the dead, celebrated on Sundays at some *sketes* to accommodate the monks' work schedules and their need to market their produce on Saturdays, was seen as a serious violation of monastic tradition. A capitulation to the demands of life in "the world," it undermined the symbolism of Sunday as the day of resurrection to new life. Athonite resistance to worldly influences was manifested simultaneously by the return to the classic cenobitic monastic life and by the renewal of Hesychastic spirituality evidenced in the outpouring of publications such as Nikodemus the Hagiorite's (c. 1749–1809) phenomenally successful edition of the *Philokalia* (Venice, 1782), a collection of traditional inspirational texts derived from earlier Hagiorite anthologies.

The rise of nationalism in Europe also affected Mount Athos at the beginning of the 19th century, reversing the long Hagiorite tradition of transnationalism. Paisi of Chilandar and later Zographou wrote his *Slavobulgarian History* to revive awareness of the former greatness of the Bulgarian nation at the same time that the patriarch and the Athonite community adopted a policy of rapprochement to the czars in the course of the Russo-Turkish wars (1682, 1730, and 1770). The increase of nationalism, in part a response to Ottoman Islamization, laid the foundation for Athonite activism in the years leading up to the Greek Revolution of 1822, when Athonite factories were producing firearms for the Greek fighters. When Turkish troops invaded the peninsula in 1821, the Holy Mountain suffered severe depopulation as monks fled or joined Greek military units. The resulting impoverishment and decline of monastic life continued for over a century.

In the last half of the 20th century, Mount Athos enjoyed a revival of monastic life, fueled once again by economic and demographic factors. Depopulation of remoter villages as well as crowding, pollution, and turbulent conditions in major cities, combined with worldwide revival of conservative religion and spirituality, fostered renewed interest in monastic life at the end of the second millennium. The Athonite monasteries entered their second millennium (1963) by founding numerous *metochia* (monastic dependencies, including subordinate monasteries and other properties) in the Western Hemisphere and Western Europe, hosting retreats devoted to theological education and furtherance of popular piety grounded in Palamite theology and the *Philokalia* and conducting an energetic program of publication of traditional patristic and gnomic literature as well as of contemporary inspirational and evangelistic writing.

Today Mount Athos attracts worldwide attention because of its rich history; its continuation of medieval liturgical, musical, and other traditions; its relics and miraculous icons; its wealth of manuscripts, archival documents, and early imprints; and its Byzantine and post-Byzantine architecture, icons, embroideries, and other antiquities. These treasures have served to draw attention to the Hesychastic traditions that continue to flourish there and to define the Athonite mission in the modern world.

ROBERT W. ALLISON

See also Archaeology: Near East; Architecture: Eastern Christian Monasteries; Hagiography: Eastern Christian; Hesychasm; Iconoclasm (Controversy); Images: Christian Perspectives; Isaac the Syrian (Isaac of Nineveh), St.; Island Monasteries, Christian; Lavra; Libraries: Eastern Christian; Maximus the Greek, St.; Meteora, Thessaly, Greece; Monastery, Christian; Orthodox Monasticism: Slavic; Paisy Velichkovsky; Palamas, Gregory, St.; Philokalia; Pilgrimages, Christian: Eastern Europe; Pilgrimages, Christian: Near East; Serbia; Theology, Eastern Christian; Vision, Mystical: Eastern Christian; Visual Arts, Eastern Christian: Painting

Further Reading

Bryer, Anthony, and Mary Cunningham, editors, *Mount Athos and Byzantine Monasticism: Papers from the Twenty-Eighth Spring Symposium of Byzantine Studies, Birmingham, March 1994* (Society for the Promotion of Byzantine Studies, 4), Aldershot, Hampshire, and Brookfield, Vermont: Variorum, 1996

Gothóni, René, *Paradise within Reach: Monasticism and Pilgrimage on Mt. Athos*, Helsinki: Helsinki University Press, 1993

Hellier, Chris, *Monasteries of Greece*, London: Tauris Parke Books, and New York: St. Martin's Press, 1996

Kadas, Sotiris, *Mount Athos: An Illustrated Guide to the Monasteries and Their History*, Athens: Ekdotike athenon, 1979

Le Millénaire du Mont Athos, 963–1963: Études et mélanges, 2 vols., Chevetogne: Éditions de Chevetogne, 1963–1964

Sherrard, Philip, *Athos, the Mountain of Silence*, London and New York: Oxford University Press, 1960

Sherrard Philip, *Athos, the Holy Mountain*, London: Sidgwick and Jackson, 1982; Woodstock, New York: Overlook Press, 1985

Theocharides, Ploutarchos, et al., *Mount Athos* (Greek Traditional Architecture), Athens: Melissa Publishing House, 1992

Related Web Site

http://www.medialab.ntua.gr/athos.html (a guide to all 20 monasteries, in Greek and English)

Mount Hiei, Japan

The Tendai monastery Enryakuji on Mount Hiei, located between the northeast of Kyoto and Lake Biwa, not only constitutes one of the most important Buddhist centers in Japanese history but also exemplifies Tendai syncretism incorporating various Buddhist practices and teachings as well as Shintoism. The importance of Mount Hiei is underscored by the fact that the founders of the Kamakura schools of Pure Land Buddhism (Japanese, Jōdō), Zen, and Nichiren Buddhism – Hōnen (1133–

1212), Eisai (1141–1215), Shinran (1173–1262), Dōgen (1200–1253), and Nichiren (1222–1282) – had spent a considerable time of their monastic training on Mount Hiei.

After his ordination in Nara, Saichō (767–822) retreated to Mount Hiei, where in 788 he carved a statue of Yakushi Nyorai and built Hieizanji (which he later called Ichijō Shikanin and which today carries the name Enryakuji) to devote himself wholeheartedly to the bodhisattva precepts of Mahāyāna Buddhism. This move to Mount Hiei embodied Saichō's criticism of the primacy of the ordination platform (Japanese, *kaidan*) in the capital Nara as well as the political corruption of Nara Buddhism in general. Sponsored by Emperor Kammu (r. 781–806), Saichō went to China in 804 in order to bring to Japan the pure teaching of Tiantai Buddhism. On his return Mount Hiei became the center of the new Tendai school, also known as the one vehicle of the *Lotus Sūtra* (Japanese, *hokke ichijō*), which combined Chinese Tiantai teaching with a variety of other Buddhist practices, mainly esoteric Buddhism. Saichō received the *abhiṣeka*, the initiation to esoteric Buddhism, from Shun-hsiao in 805 and from Kūkai (774–835) in 812. In 806 Emperor Kammu allotted Saichō's Tendai Buddhism two ordinants per year. While Saichō struggled to establish Tendai as one-vehicle Buddhism (Sanskrit, *ekayāna*; Japanese, *ichijō*), his friendship with Kūkai deteriorated over their interpretation of the Shingon initiations, over Kūkai's refusal to lend Saichō sūtras in 813, and over the defection of Saichō's disciple Taihan to Kūkai. After Saichō's death Mount Hiei was granted a distinct Mahāyāna ordination platform, for which Saichō had fought all his life. However, the monastic community on Mount Hiei faced increasing strive and disunity. Ryōgen's (912–985) effort to unify the monastic community on Mount Hiei in the years from 970 to 980 led to the schism between the Sammon and Jimmon sects of Tendai Buddhism, with the former, following the transmission lineage of Saichō and Ennin (792–862), staying in control of Mount Hiei. Ryōgen's expulsion of the Genshin (781–833)-Enchin (814–889) lineage of the Jimmon sect not only set a precedent for the use of priest-soldiers (Japanese, *sōhei*) to resolve temple disputes but also exaggerated the schism between Sammon and Jimmon and their fight over the control of Mount Hiei and its ordination platform (Japanese, *kaidan*). This conflict culminated in 1571, when the troops of Oda Nobunaga destroyed Enryakuji. After its restoration between 1585 and 1650, life on Mount Hiei slowly normalized. While the political climate of the Tokugawa (1600–1868) and Meiji (1868–1912) periods hindered the growth of Buddhist practice and monasteries in general, Mount Hiei, which celebrated its 1,200th anniversary in 1987 and was the host to a religious summit in the same year, constitutes a flourishing monastic community and religious center today.

Tendai syncretism is reflected not only in the one-vehicle doctrine but also in a multitude of practices present on Mount Hiei. On the one hand Tendai syncretism is expressed in the performance of esoteric practices, the *nembutsu*, sūtra chanting, and meditation (Japanese, zen). On the other hand Tendai Buddhism emphasizes Zhiyi's practice of *maka shikan* – great cessation and insight (Chinese, *moho chih kuan*) – and the classic quaternity of mediation consisting of continuous sitting meditation (Japanese, *jōza sammai*), continuous moving meditation (Japanese, *jōgyō sammai*), half moving and half sitting meditation (Japanese, *hangyō hanza sammai*), and neither moving nor sitting meditation (Japanese, *higyō hiza sammai*). Candidates for priesthood undergo a 60-day training period, whereas an abbot (Japanese, *jūshoku*) must conclude a three-year retreat (Japanese, *sannenrōzan*). Most of all, however, Mount Hiei is known for its uncompromising practice regimens, such as the 12-year retreat (Japanese, *jūninenrōzan*) in the Jōdō-in on Mount Hiei, instituted by Saichō himself, and the legendary 1,000-day mountain pilgrimage (Japanese, *issennichi kaihōgyō*), which is attributed to Sō-ō (831–918). A recent documentary by the NHK (Japan Broadcasting Corporation), which partially aired during the coverage of the Winter Olympics at Nagano in 1998, and books such as John Stevens' *The Marathon Monks of Mount Hiei* (1988) have called attention to the 1,000-day mountain retreat and its recent practitioners, Utsumi Shunshō and Sakai Yusai. In its present form the 1,000-day mountain pilgrimage includes 1,000 days of running between 18 and 52 miles per day over seven years and a nine-day fasting period during which the practitioner (Japanese, *gyōja*) neither eats, drinks, nor sleeps (Japanese, *dōiri*). During each day of running-meditation, the practitioner worships at up to 260 stations. Practitioners who have concluded the 1,000-day pilgrimage successfully are revered as living Buddhas.

Gereon Kopf

See also Buddhist Schools/Traditions: Japan; Dōgen; Eisai (Yosai); Ennin; Esoteric Buddhism in China and Japan; Fasting: Buddhist; Hōnen; Japan; Kūkai; Kyoto, Japan; Libraries: Buddhist; Marathon Monks; Mount Kōya, Japan; Mountain Monasteries, Buddhist; Nara, Japan; Nation-Building and Japanese Buddhism; Nembutsu; Pure Land Buddhism; Rennyo; Saichō; Shinran; Syncretism in Japan, Buddhist; Tiantai/Tendai: Japan; Visual Arts, Buddhist: Japan; Warrior Monks: Buddhist; Zhiyi (Chih-i)

Further Reading

Abe, Rūyichi, "Saichō and Kūkai: A Conflict of Interpretations," *Japanese Journal of Religious Studies* 1:2 (1995)

Kageyama, Haruki, *Hieizan*, volume 1: *1200-nen no ayumi*, Tokyo: Osaka Shoseki, 1986

McMullin, Neil, "The Sanmon-Jimon Schism in the Tendai School of Buddhism: A Preliminary Analysis," *Journal of the International Association of Buddhist Studies* 7 (1984)

Murayama, Shuichi, *Hieizan shi: Tatakai to Inori no Seiiki*, Tokyo: Shohan, 1994

Stevens, John, *The Marathon Monks of Mount Hiei*, Boston: Shambhala, 1988

Watanabe, Shujun, *Hieizan*, Tokyo: Hōzōkan, 1987

Mount Kōya, Japan

Mount Kōya (Kōya-san) was founded in 816 by imperial decree for Kūkai or Kōbō Daishi (774–835), who had returned from the Tang dynasty capital of Chang-an imbued with Chinese

Moss-covered vermilion Shintō shrine on Kōya-san, not unusual amid Shingon temples because of Kūkai's ecumenism.
Photo courtesy of Steve McCarty

civilization and Indian Mantrayāna Buddhism. To believers Kūkai sits inside a locked Kōya-san temple in a meditative state that may be compared to the Buddha's Parinirvāṇa. Kōya-san remains the headquarters of Kūkai's Shingon Buddhism, with Kongōbuji the head temple of the sect. Today Kōya-san remains a mountaintop monastic town in Wakayama prefecture near southern Nara prefecture. Despite the remote location a train runs to Mount Kōya from Umeda in downtown Ōsaka, making for a convenient day trip. Unlike the cities of Kyoto and Nara, Mount Kōya consists almost entirely of monasteries and religious sites set in nature. Towering evergreen forests provide relief from Japan's long sultry summer, but the winter is freezing, and cryptomeria allergy is common before spring. The library of Kōya-san University publishes books and journals on esoteric Buddhism.

On an inhospitable plateau periodically ravaged by fires, the monasteries of Kōya-san have been nearly abandoned at times. Kūkai attracted a great number of disciples, including his relatives from Shikoku Island. However, although he innovated in the critical classification of doctrines among Asian religions of his era, he insisted that Shingon monks obey all the precepts harking back to the historical Buddha. Combining such ethical integrity with erudition in Chinese and Sanskrit, the historical Kūkai set a standard that the following generations who remained in Japan found that they could not attain. Thus, it became necessary for Kūkai to abide with believers soteriologically as Kōbō Daishi. Shingon was also able to adapt to changing trends with a syncretism going back to Kūkai himself, whose calligraphy includes a "Namu Amida Butsu" scroll long before Amidism began to eclipse the Asian mainland style of monasticism in Japan. Holy men known as Kōya Hijiri mixed Shingon creatively with Amidism as they roamed the Japanese countryside, where Buddhism was for the first time becoming a mass religion. The Kōya-san Holy Men told tales that beatified Kūkai while subtly warning the public to take care of the Great Saint's messengers. They popularized the pilgrimage of the 88 sacred places of Shikoku Island that purportedly recapitulate the life of Kūkai from birth to enlightenment. With the idea that St. Kūkai walked together with the pilgrim (*dōgyō ninin*), the celebrated pilgrimage of Shikoku gave new impetus to sustain the Shingon sect through the medieval period of civil warfare. Thus, today with 13 million nominal members, Shingon is the only large sect surviving from the classical Nara and Heian periods.

Closed to women until recently, Mount Kōya now has accommodations in about 50 of more than 100 temples, with vegetarian fare featuring Kōya-style tofu. Some visitors find the sprawling graveyards of interest for the historical figures who sought a resting place on such sacred ground. Many designated national treasures can be seen, including Buddha images and temple buildings that were spared from fire. A day trip, prefer-

Pagoda for treasured manuscripts at the Kongō Sammai-in Temple on Kōya-san, itself a designated national treasure.
Photo courtesy of Steve McCarty

Hongan-in, a Shingon temple at Daimyō-ō-in on Mount Kōya, Japan, now used as a guest house. Photo courtesy of David Moore

ably with a guide who is bilingual in Japanese and associated with the Shingon religion, is recommended. One can write to the Research Institute of Esoteric Buddhist Culture, Kōyasan University, Kōyasan, Wakayama-ken, 648-02, Japan.

STEVE MCCARTY

See also Buddhist Schools/Traditions: Japan; Esoteric Buddhism in China and Japan; Japan: Sites; Kūkai; Mountain Monasteries, Buddhist; Shikoku, the Pilgrimage Island of Japan; Visual Arts, Buddhist: Japan

Further Reading

Hakeda, Yoshito, *Kūkai: Major Works*, New York: Columbia University Press, 1972
Ishida, Shōhō, "Mikkyō-ga," in *Nihon no Bijutsu* 1:33, Tokyo: Shibundō, 1969
Kitagawa, Joseph, "Kūkai as Master and Savior," in *The Biographical Process: Studies in the History and Psychology of Religion*, edited by Frank Reynolds and Donald Capps, The Hague: Mouton, 1976
Matsunaga, Yūkei, *Himitsu no Kura o Hiraku: Mikkyo Kyoten Rishukyo*, Tokyo: Shueisha, 1984
Moriya, Kenrō, editor, *Kūkai to Shingon Mikkyō*, Tokyo: Yomiuri Shimbunsha, 1982
Sōga, Tetsuo, *Tōji to Kōya-san*, Tokyo: Shōgakkan, 1981
Yamamoto, Chikyō, *Kōbō Daishi Kūkai*, Tokyo: Kōdansha, 1973
Yamasaki, Taikō, *Shingon: Japanese Esoteric Buddhism*, Boston: Shambhala, 1988

Related Web Sites

http://www.ccil.org/~cneal/view.html (a brief scholarly view of Shingon)
http://www.wsu.edu:8000/~dee/ANCJAPAN/KUKAI.HTM (Kūkai)
http://www.shingon.org/home.html (Shingon Buddhist International Institute)

Mount Meru

Introduction

One of the most fundamental cosmogonic notions in Buddhism is the imagined Mount Meru or Mount Sumeru (*Sumeru* means "good" or "excellent," and *Meru* and is an honorific appellation) world system where virtually all Buddhist meditational attainments take place. In order to express the totality of an individual's attainment, the world system includes a central mountain and a field in which all samsaric phenomena exist. This system has taken a number of physically different forms throughout the Buddhist world, but its messages, described here, have remained the same.

In popular Western-language Buddhist writings, the Mount Meru system is frequently misconstrued as "the Buddhist Universe." However, each individual envisions Mount Meru within his or her own *citta*, or heart-mind, and uses it to provide a position and place for all phenomena at all levels of existence. Accordingly Mount Meru is better understood as a practitioner's own world system. Thus, rather than a singular universe, there are infinite Mount Meru world systems, each in the individual heart-mind of beings throughout all space and time.

The purely conceptual system, having no physicality or geographic location, is envisioned as a central mountain encircled by mountain ranges, seas, and continents (Figs. 1 and 2). Jambu, the continent to the south, is understood to be South Asia, the realm of human and animal existence and the center of all Buddhist practice. Above the mountain rise a series of heavens growing increasingly ethereal as they ascend, and below are a series of torturous hells. A linear vertical axis that extends infinitely in both directions is understood to run through the center of the mountain and is the only immutable element in the system. The description of the mountain as recorded in the *Abhidharmakośaśāstra* of Vasubandhu, the fourth-century commentator and exegete, is summarized here.

Part One: An Overview of the Meru System

(The following description has been compiled from the Louis de La Valleé Poussin, *Abhidharmakośabhāṣyam*, vol. 2 [1988], chapter 3 passim, and especially pp. 451–467. All Pāli terms are from Maurice Walshe, *Thus I Have Heard: The Long Discourses of the Buddha* [1987], pp. 37–43.) (Figs. 1 and 2)

I. Kāmadhātu, "Desire Realms," includes 20 lower states of being (2.365)
(Starting at the lowest level, there are as follows:)
  A. Aṣṭaniraya, Eight Hot Hells (Pāli, Niraya). Beginning with the lowest they are:
    1. Avīci 2. Pratāpana 3. Tapana 4. Mahārauravba 5. Raurava 6. Saṁghāta 7. Kālasūtra 8. Saṁjīva
  (A1. Eight Cold Hells. Even though given in the ADK, the Eight Cold Hells are not included in the 20 states. Beginning with the lowest, they are:
    1. Arbuda 2. Nirarbuda 3. Aṭaṭa 4. Hahava 5. Huhuva 6. Utpala 7. Padma 8. Mahāpadma)
  B. Pretaloka (Pāli, Peta loka), "World of Preta (hungry ghosts)," is located directly below Jambu continent. This realm is presided over by Yama, the god of the underworld.
  C. Tiryagyoni gati Birth as Animals (Pāli, Tiracchāna Yoni). Excluding humans, this realm includes all other land, water, and air creatures.
  D. Mānuṣya Gati Human Birth (Pāli, Manussa) (see Bhājanaloka description below)
  E. (Lower three terraces of Mount Meru are not counted among the 20 states in the ADK but are described as follows:)
    1. Karoṭapāṇis ("Pitcher in Hand") reside on the first terrace, which is 1/8 the height of Meru or 10,000 *yojanas* (a day's journey) above the ground.
    2. Mālādhāras ("Bearers of Garlands") reside at 1/4 the height of Meru or 20,000 *yojanas*.
    3. Sadāmattas ("Always Ecstatic") reside at 3/8 the height of Meru or 30,000 *yojanas*.
  F. "Realms of Those Who Taste Pleasure"
    1. Cāturmahārājaikas (also known as Mahārājikas; Pāli, Catumahārājikā devās), Four Great Kings who reside on the fourth terrace of Mount Meru at 1/2 the height of Meru (40,000 *yojanas*)
    2. Trāyastriṁśās (Pāli, Tāvatiṁsa devās), (place of the) 33 Vedic gods who reside in a vast plain on the very pinnacle of Mount Meru, which is 80,000 *yojanas* above the ground of the mundane world
    3. Yama deva loka (Pāli, Yāmā devā), world of Yama devās who reside at 160,000 *yojanas* above the ground, i.e., 80,000 *yojanas* into space above Mount Meru
    4. Tuṣita (Pāli, Tusitā), contented devās who reside at 320,000 *yojanas* above the ground
    5. Nirmāṇarati (Pāli, Nimmānaratī devās), devās delighting in transformation who reside at 640,000 *yojanas* above the ground
    6. Paranirmitavaśavartins (Pāli, Paranimmitavasavattī devās), "Devās Holding Power Over Others' Creations," who reside at

II. The Rūpadhātu or "Form Realm" consists of 17 states of physical existence without lust/desire and exist above the Kāmadhātu. The 17 states of existence consist of four *dhyānas* ("meditations"). The first three *dhyānas* are further divided into three separate stages. The fourth *dhyāna* is divided into eight stages.
  A. The first *dhyāna*
    1. Bhramakāyikas (Pāli, Brahma- Parisajjā devās), Retinue of Brahmā who reside 2,560,000 *yojanas* above the ground
    2. Brahma purohitas (Pāli, Brahma purohitā devās), ritual specialists (on behalf of) Brahmā, i.e. the Brahmin caste of priests, who reside 5,120,000 *yojanas* above the ground
    3. Mahābrahmanus (Pāli, Mahā Brahmās), Great Brahmā who reside 10,240,000 *yojanas* above the ground
  B. The second *dhyāna*
    1. Parīttābhas (Pāli, Parittabhā devās), devās of limited radiance who reside 20,480,000 *yojanas* above the ground

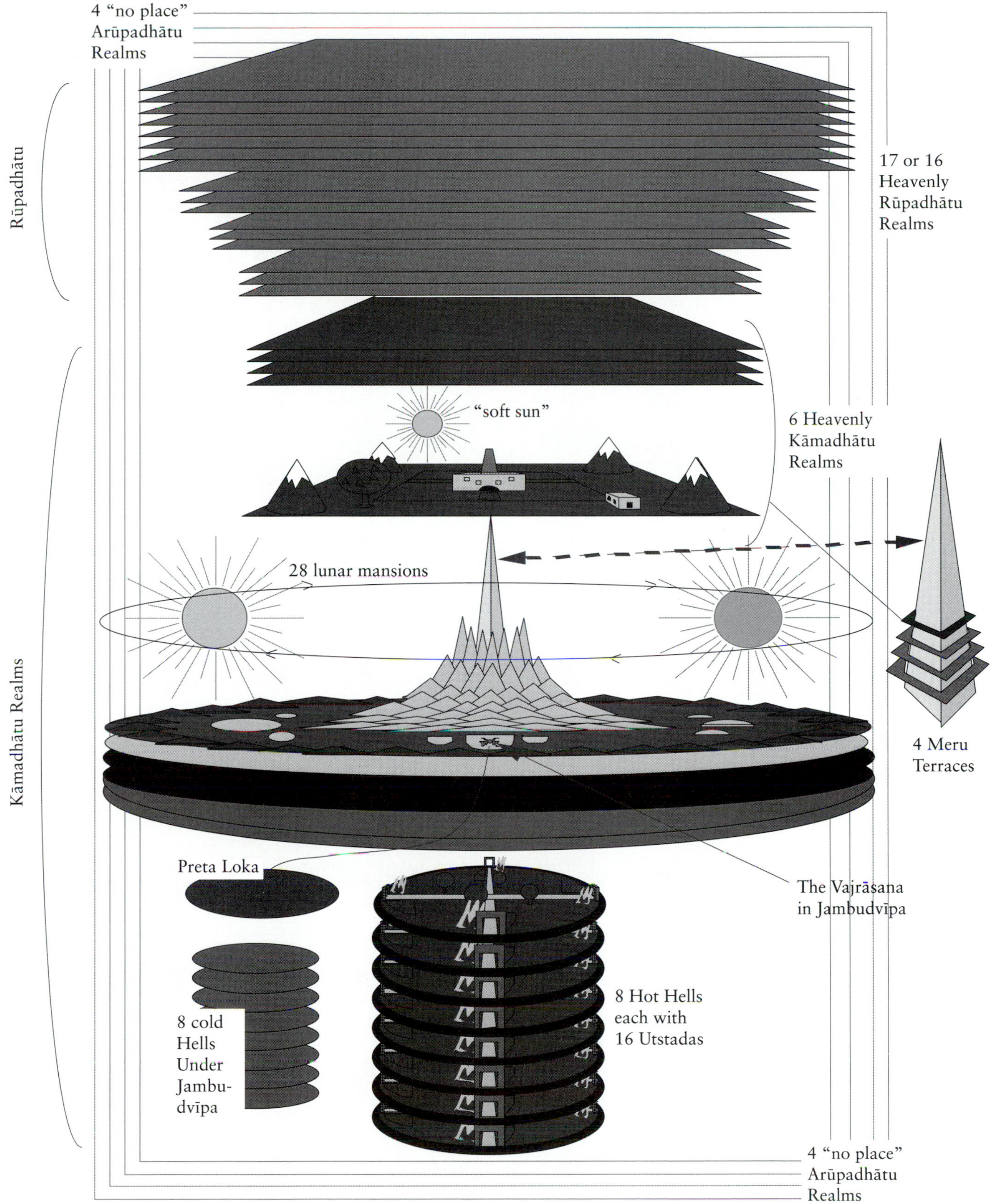

Fig. 1: Mount Meru diagram based on an analysis of Vasubandhu's *Abhidharmakośa*. Drawing courtesy of John C. Huntington, the Huntington Archive

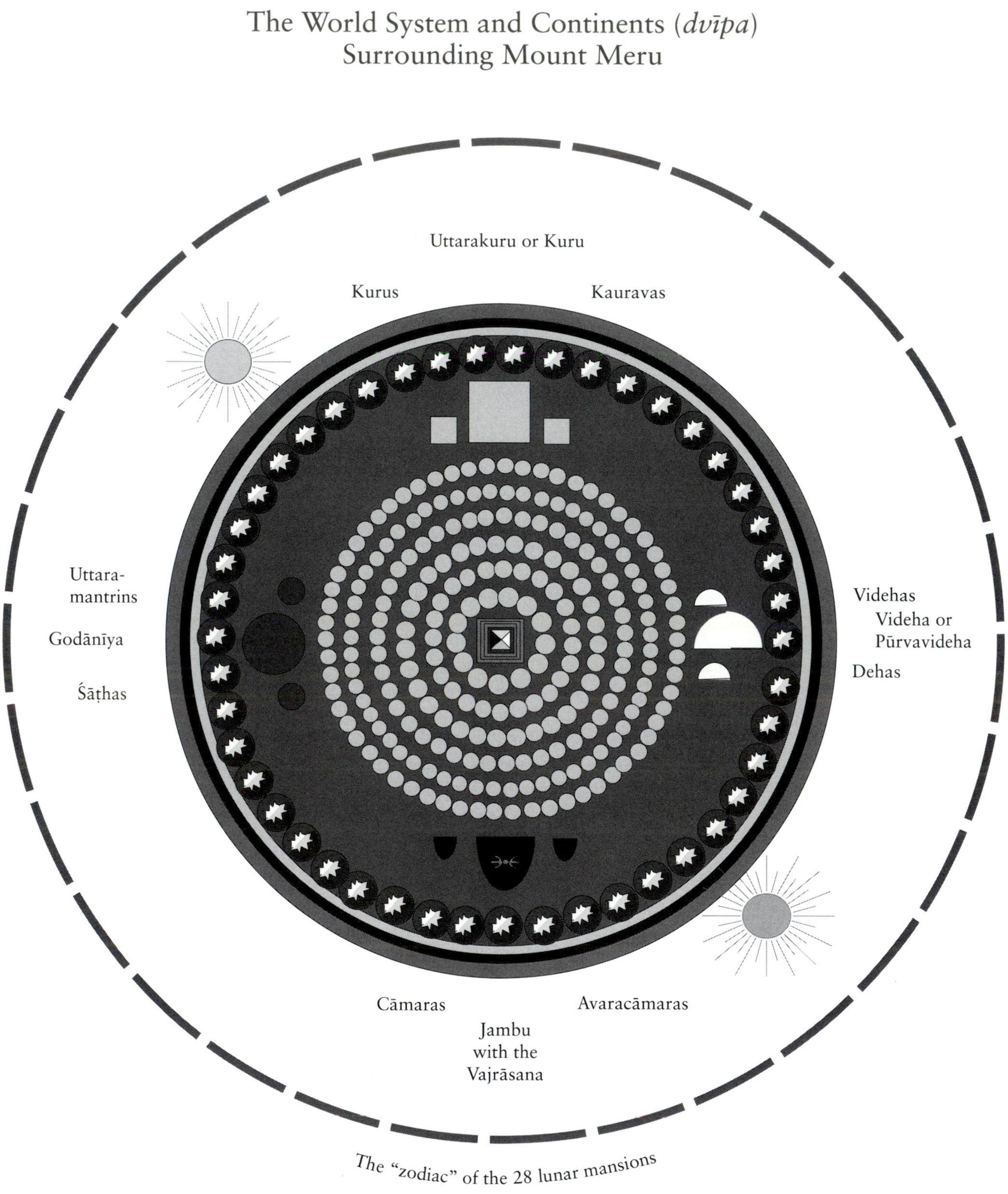

Fig. 2: "Map" of Mount Meru and the plane of saṃsāric existence based on an analysis of Vasubandhu's *Abhidharmakośa*. Drawing courtesy of John C. Huntington, the Huntington Archive

2. Apramānābhas (Pāli, Appamāṇabhā devās), devās of unbounded radiance who reside 40,960,000 *yojanas* above the ground
3. Ābhāsvaras (Pāli, Abhassarā devās), devās of streaming radiance who reside 81,920,000 *yojanas* above the ground

C. The third *dhyāna*
1. Parīttaśubhas (Pāli, Parittasubhā devās), devās of limited glory
2. Apramāṇaśubhas (Pāli, Appamāṇasubhā devās), devās of unbounded glory
3. Śubhakṛtsnas (Pāli, Subhakiṇṇā devās), devās of refulgent glory

D. The fourth *dhyāna*
1. Anabhrakas, devas without clouds (no counterpart in the Pāli lists)
2. Puṇyaprasavas, devas born of merit (no counterpart in the Pāli lists)
3. Bṛhatphalas (Pāli, Asaññasattā devās), devās (attainment of the) Great Fruit
4. The five Śuddhāvāsikas, "pure abodes"
   a. Avṛhas (Pāli, Avihā devās), un-hindered or unstoppable devās
   b. Atapas (Pāli, Atappā devās), without religious observance devās (because they have accomplished all)
   c. Sudṛśas (Pāli, Sudassā devās), beautiful ("clearly visible") devās
   d. Sudarśana (Pāli, Sudassī devās), clear sighted devās
   e. Akaniṣṭha (Pāli, Akaniṭṭhā devā), devās all of equal age who reside at 167,772,160,000 *yojanas* above the ground

III. The Arūpadhātu "Formless realms" consist of four divisions. These realms are not "places" (ADK 2.366) and the beings born there are all-pervading essences that permeate the infinity of space (Sanskrit, Ākāśa).

A. Ākāśānantyāyatana (Pāli, Āsāsānañcāyatanūpagā devās), devās of the sphere of the infinity of space

B. Vijñānānantyāyatana (Pāli, Viññāṇañcāyatanūpagā devās), devās of the infinity of Consciousness

C. Ākiṁcanyāyatana (Pāli, Ākiñcaññañāyatanūpagā devās), devās of the Sphere of No-thing-ness

D. Naivasaṁjñānāsaṁjñāyatana (or Bhavāgra; Pāli, Nevasaññāsaññāyatanūpagā devās), devās of the Neither-Perception-nor-non-Perception

Part Two: The Bhājanaloka "Physical world" (Fig. 2)

I. Descriptions of the Bhājanaloka (Physical world), ADK 2.451 (the Kāmadhātu)

A. At the bottom a circle of wind infinite in size and 16,000 *yojanas* thick

B. Above that is a circle of water

C. Above that is a circle of gold

D. Above that is a sphere of gold

E. On the gold sphere are nine mountain (ranges)

F. Meru is in the center (made of the four jewels); it is square with four faces: gold, Lapis, silver, crystal

G. Plane of Saṃsāric existence
1. Six mountain rings of gold
   a. Yugandhara b. Īṣādhara c. Khadiraka d. Sudarśana e. Aśvakarṇa f. Vinataka
7. Surrounding all is Mount Nimindhara
8. Then are the continents
9. Surrounding all is the Iron mountain Cakravāḍa

H. Meru is immersed in water

I. There are seven *sītās* (Oceans) between the rings of mountains; these are called the inner oceans

J. Between Nimindhara and Cakravāḍa is the outer ocean; it is a salt sea

K. In the salt sea are the four continents (*dvīpas*)
1. To the south is Jambu, which is shaped like a cart. In its center is the Vajrāsana. Next to it are the intermediate continents Cāmaras and Avaracāmaras.
2. To the East is Videha or Pūrvavideha, which is shaped like a half moon. Next to it are the intermediate continents Dehas and Videhas
3. To the west is Godānīya, which is round. Next to it are the intermediate continents Śāṭhas and Uttaramantrins
4. To the north of Meru is Uttarakuru or Kuru, which is square. Next to it are the intermediate continents Kurus and Kauravas

Redundancy of Mount Meru Symbolism

In Mahāyāna Buddhist thought, every Buddha is envisioned as seated atop Mount Meru (Figs. 3 and 4). Every stūpa is a reiteration of Mount Meru, and every monastery is a palace of the gods atop Mount Meru. Every practitioner, with the potential of Buddhahood within him or herself, is also understood as containing Mount Meru within his or her heart-mind and, during certain meditations, as being coincidental with Mount Meru (Fig. 5). The concept permeates every aspect and manifestation of the religious methodology. Mount Meru symbolism is inherent in nearly all Buddhist architecture, sculpture, painting, ephemeral representations, rituals, and practices. Its compelling redundancy is further evident in that almost every Buddha image, subsidiary deity, stūpa, temple, monastery, and maṇḍala communicate the idea of the mountain. Repeated over and over in these contexts, Mount Meru serves to create and sustain a suitable sacred environment within which a practitioner may progress toward his or her religious goal.

Stūpas, temples, and monasteries represent, symbolize, and communicate varying aspects of the Mount Meru concept. Stūpas are literally sculptural and architectural replicas of Mount Meru. In inscriptions as early as the first century A.D., stūpas are known as *eka kuṭa*, or "one mountain" (see Stanislaw J. Czuma, *Kushan*

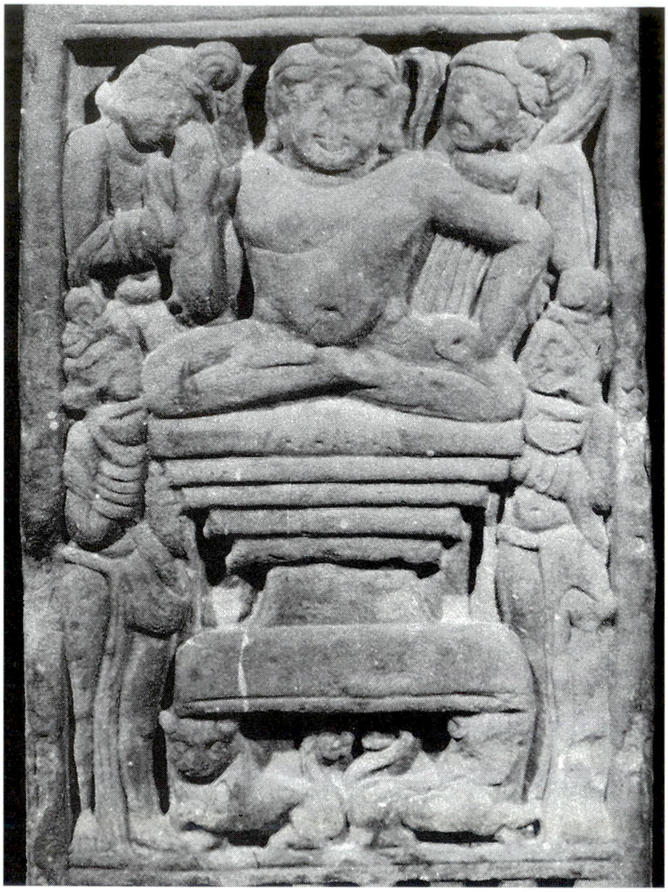

Fig. 3: Buddha on Mount Meru receiving the gift of four bowls offered by the Cāturmahārāja, Mathura, India, c. first century B.C.E., Mathura Museum.
Photo courtesy of John C. Huntington, the Huntington Archive

Sculpture: Images from Early India [1986], pp. 165–168, and citation of H.W. Bailey's translation of the inscription, p. 168). In the sense of "one" as the "universal," this is undoubtedly a reference to the stūpa as Mount Meru. Moreover the structural features of a stūpa also symbolize Mount Meru. The notion of an imagined mountain world system appears to have been an extant presupposition in Indic thought from the earliest layers of religious history. Subsequently the concept appears to have been adopted into specific religious methodologies. For example, in Buddhism Mount Meru serves as the Buddhist world ordering. Similarly Mount Kailāsa, the absolute religious core in Hinduism, is also envisioned as a transcendent mountain. The virtually identical symbolism in both religions suggests that the concept of the transcendent "Inner Mountain" was probably a common postulate in pre-Buddhist and Hindu thought.

Cave temples throughout the Buddhist world are reiterations of the conceptual cave located along the vertical axis at the core of Mount Meru. In Buddhist thought the cave at the center of the mountain is equated to an entry into an individual's heart-mind (Sanskrit, *citta*). Thus, when devotees enter a cave temple, they are understood as walking into the cave that reaches into the core of Mount Meru within their own heart-minds. The Buddha image housed within the confines of the temple then reflects the latent Buddha nature within the devotee's very own heart-mind.

In structural temples the plinth on which the monument rests is understood to be Mount Meru. The temple structure itself is a palace, or one of the paradises, atop the system. A temple can represent Trāyastriṁśa, Akaniṣṭha, or Tuṣita Paradises. Specifically which of the three paradises is intended may be indicated by the iconographic details of the temple. Often an emphasis on verticality or the mainly pyramidal shapes of temple superstruc-

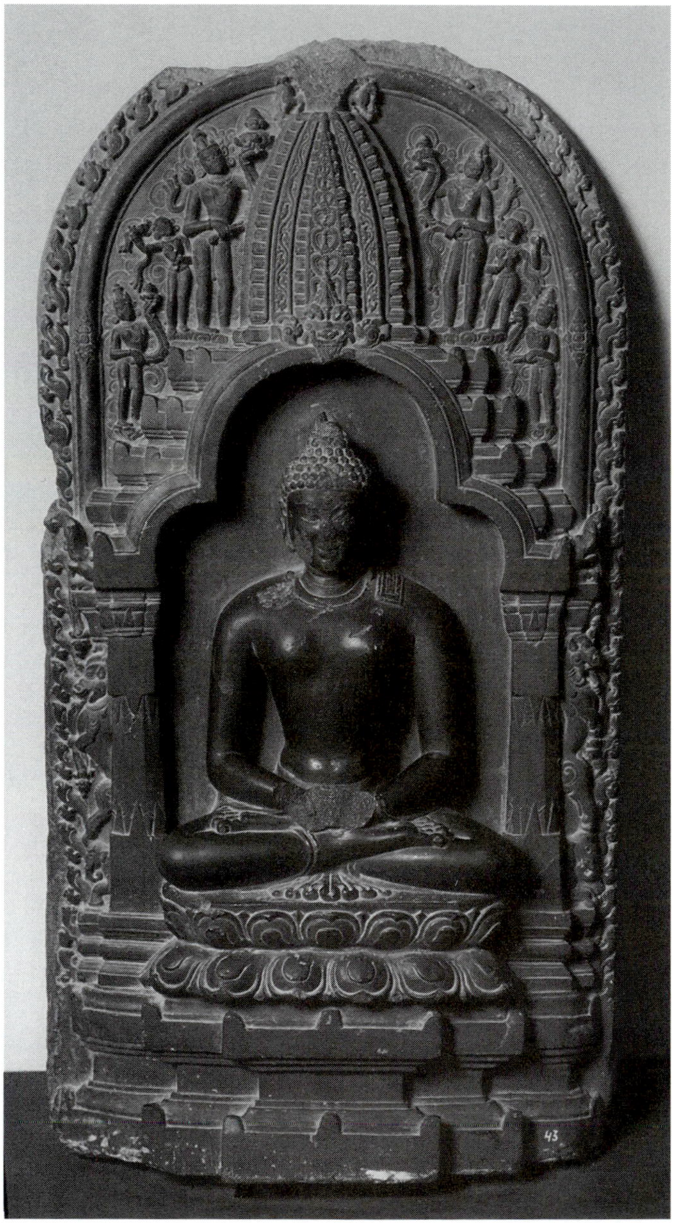

Fig. 4: Buddha Amitābha in Sukhāvati depicted as though both temple and the Buddha are on a Mount Meru platform, Mahakali, Bangladesh, Pāla period, c. 11th century, Bangladesh National Museum.
Photo courtesy of John C. Huntington, the Huntington Archive

Fig. 5: Buddhist yogin wearing the four continents chasuble, his hair in a *merujaṭā* and showing the position of the Mount Meru system as envisioned in this particular meditation. The internal *cakra*s are shown at their respective elevations.
Photo courtesy of John C. Huntington, the Huntington Archive

tures further echo the concept of the mountain. Thus, when a devotee enters a temple complex he or she is physically present in the sacred space marked by Mount Meru and is understood to actually enter a palace atop Mount Meru presided over by a buddha.

Images within a temple manifest the presiding deity of the paradise and his or her entourage. The images are generally elevated on a platform that is conceptually Mount Meru. Further, the pedestals directly under the images are also understood as Mount Meru. As is frequently the case in many Buddhist temples, there might be images of buddhas, bodhisattvas, and other subsidiary figures, many of which, if not all, are atop their respective Mount Meru bases. Thus, the deities are conceptually above the mountain.

In Tantric methodologies, in which meditations and rituals frequently require maṇḍalas, the redundancy of Mount Meru symbolism is carried even further. Axiomatically every maṇḍala is visualized as a three-dimensional palace located at the top of Mount Meru. In addition the devās, or deities of the maṇḍalas, are all inherently invested with Mount Meru in their respective heart-minds. For example, in one well-known Tantric meditation, the practitioner visualizes his personal *mūlaguru*, or "root teacher," in his or her heart-mind. Further, the Buddha Śākyamuni is visualized in his guru's heart-mind. In the Buddha Śākyamuni's heart-mind is the Ādibuddha, Vajradhara, who is the demonstration of the essence of the practitioner's attainment of *śūnyatā*. Each is understood coincidental with the others and are all located at the top of the Mount Meru system, usually in Akaniṣṭha heaven.

This redundancy is considered both sequential and simultaneous and thereby outside of, or transcending, normal linear time. The iconology of the *vajrāsana*, or adamantine seat of the Buddha's place of enlightenment, further illustrates the transliminality of Mount Meru symbolism. In the *vajrāsana* realizations the seat exists simultaneously in two locations. By the Meru geographic definition in the *Abhidharmakośa*, the *vajrāsana* is situated at Bodhgāya, in the heart of Jambu continent, to the south of Mount Meru. However, according to some teachings, at the moment of Buddha Śākyamuni's enlightenment, he appeared, still seated on the *vajrāsana*, in Akaniṣṭha paradise, the highest of the "Form Realms," to preach the *Avataṃsaka Sūtra*. The implication is that the *vajrāsana* at Bodhgāya is simultaneously both far to the south in Jambu and centrally atop Mount Meru.

In conclusion Mount Meru is the visualization through which an individual is related and integrated into his or her world system. The practitioner is centered directly on the vertical axis, either on the pinnacle of the mountain or deep within it. As such this comprehension parallels and reifies the Upanisadic notion of *tat tvaṁ asi*, or "that thou art." It is the mechanism through which the individual reintegrates into the absolute. Once the *tathāgatagarbha* within an individual's heart-mind is awakened, he or she begins to realize the true nature of Mount Meru as noumenon. Subsequently, when Mount Meru is experienced, as both an infinite world system and the infinitesimal core of the heart-mind, the practitioner approaches the final stages of perfection.

JOHN C. HUNTINGTON

See also Architecture: Buddhist Monasteries in Southern Asia; Cave Temples and Monasteries in India and China; Images: Buddhist Perspectives; Liturgy: Buddhist; Maṇḍala; Meditation: Buddhist Perspectives; Nepal: History; Spirituality: Buddhist; Stūpa; Temple, Buddhist; Vajrayāna Buddhism in Nepal; Visual Arts, Buddhist; Worship Space: Buddhist Perspectives

Further Reading

Jamgön Kongtrul Lodrö Tayé (Kong-sprul Blo-gros-mtha'-yas), *Myriad Worlds: Buddhist Cosmology in Abhidharma, Kalacakra and Dzog-chen*, Ithaca, New York: Snow Lion, 1995

Kloetzli, Randy, *Buddhist Cosmology: From Single World System to Pure Land: Science and Theology in the Images of Motion and Light*, Delhi: Motilal Banarsidass, 1983

Sadakata, Akira, *Buddhist Cosmology: Philosophy and Origins*, translated by Gaynor Sekimori, Tokyo: Kosei, 1997

Vasubandhu, *Abhidharmakosabhasyam*, original translation by Louis de La Vallée Poussin, English translation by Leo M. Pruden, volume 1, Berkeley, California: Asian Humanities Press, 1988

Mount Sinai, Egypt

Rising to a height of about 7,500 feet and located in the middle of a mountain range in the plateau at the southern end of the Sinai Peninsula, Mount Sinai (Jebel Musa or the Mountain of Moses) has a monastic tradition dating possibly as early as the third century. Various sources say that Moses first encountered God in the burning bush here. He returned to the mountain, called by its alternate name Horeb (the Mount of God), to ascend the clouded peak and descend with the Law. It was also Horeb where Elijah encountered a less dramatic theophany in God's "still small voice" (or "sound of sheer silence"; NRSV 1 Kings 19:12). However, the exact mountain where these events occurred is often questioned. A still-current tradition says Horeb is Mount Serbal (Jebel Sufsafeh), an adjacent mountain to the northwest of Jebel Musa. About Elijah the Scriptures say only that he walked 40 days and nights from Beersheba but do not specify in which direction. Scholars propose eight possible routes taken by the Children of Israel in their flight from Egypt, inferring eight possible mountains of God, including the traditional one. Indeed, the early history of Mount Sinai and its vicinity is rich and confusing because so much of it rests solely on tradition and legend. Thus, what follows should be viewed with a critical eye.

The earliest monks on the mountain (i.e., hermits who withdrew from society) regarded Jebel Musa as the mountain of God's revelations and were drawn there by its holiness. The Egyptian monk Paphnutius (d. c. 390) encountered the hermit Onophrius living in a hut in wadi Leyan close to the mountain. Onophrius had lived 70 years in the desert, sustaining himself on dates. One of the earliest records of a hermit living on Mount Sinai is in the *Dialogues* of Severus describing the experience of the Italian pilgrim Postumianus in the late fourth century. He went there to seek out the council of a hermit who had avoided human contact for almost 50 years. Postumianus climbed to a point below the summit of Mount Sinai that he called *jugum Sina Montis*, where the hermit was said to be dwelling in its recesses. However, both the hermit and the summit eluded the pilgrim. The hermit was said to have been completely naked except for the hair growing on his body. Sometime around the middle of the fourth century, the Syrian ascetic Julian Sabas of Edessa (fourth century) is reported to have founded the church on the peak of the mountain Symeon the Ancient, another Syrian pilgrim, is also reported to have visited in the fourth century. The pilgrim Egeria, who was possibly a nun or an abbess from Gaul or Spain, visited Mount Sinai sometime between 381 and 384. She describes a church – possibly the one built by Julian – and the cave at the top of the mountain, the church and cave of Elijah, and a church near the burning bush at the base of the mountain. She might have encountered Silvanus the Palestinian, who had brought his community of 12 disciples to Mount Sinai from Scetis around 380. He rejected excessive austerity and promoted physical labor, especially by working in the community's garden. It is not known when Silvanus and his disciples departed the mountain to return to Palestine.

Scant record is preserved of monastic activity on Mount Sinai during the fifth century, although a letter has survived, dated about 451, from Emperor Marcian (450–457) to the bishop of Sinai, Archimandrite Macarius, and his monks. In addition, stories survive about the fifth-century monk Abba Nilus, who left observations about the cults of the "Saracens" (i.e., Arabs) and whose son was captured by them and almost sacrificed to the morning star by them. According to Nilus, the Arabs attacked Mount Sinai and environs after the death of their king. The monks undoubtedly negotiated a truce once the new king was installed.

In 536 monks from Sinai took part in theological deliberations at Constantinople. John Moschus (c. 550–619/34), in his collection *The Spiritual Meadow*, tells the story of Hegumen (abbot) George, who had not left Mount Sinai for 70 years and then miraculously appeared in the Church of the Holy Resurrection at Jerusalem at Easter in 551 or 552. Patriarch Peter of Jerusalem wrote to Bishop Photios of Paran about the event, and it is apparent from the letter that the monks of Mount Sinai were under the ecclesiastical jurisdiction of the see of Paran, which in turn was under the authority of the patriarch. Moschus also relates the story of Abba Zosimos the Cilician, who was one of George's emissaries to Patriarch Peter. He had been made bishop of Cairo by Pope Apollinarius of Alexandria (551–570) but later withdrew and returned to Sinai. In 570 the anonymous pilgrim from Placentia (Piacenza, Italy) visited the mountain. His estimate of 12,000 Saracens (Arabs) in Sinai appears to be exaggerated, but his description of their extreme poverty does not. Their tribes often threatened the monastery, and the pilgrim mentions that the area was protected by the presence of a military garrison. He also describes a ceremony of an Aral moon cult performed on Mount Sinai or nearby. The monks eventually converted many of these Arabs, who had been idol worshipers but who then readily accepted Islam after the Muslim conquest. On the other hand, the Muslim conquest brought a period of durable peace to the monastery, whose presence was tolerated by the invaders.

The previously mentioned John Moschus lived in the *lavra* (monastic center) of the Aeliotes on Mount Sinai for ten years from around 584 to 594. His collection *The Spiritual Meadow* is valuable for its brief studies of a number of monks from the mountain. In addition to George and Zosimos, he describes Abba Stephan the Cappadocian, priest of the Aeliotes Lavra; Abba Theodosios the solitary; Abba Anthony, the superior and builder of the Aeliotes Lavra; Abba Theodosios the solitary; Abba John about Theodore the anchorite; Abba Sergios the anchorite; and Abba Orentes.

Sometime around the late sixth century, John Climacus (c. 570–649), the hesychast and author of *The Ladder of Divine Ascent*, was tonsured at the monastery of Mount Sinai at the age of 16. He remained there for three years under the spiritual eldership of Abba Martyrius before retiring to the life of a hermit in a place in the wilderness some five miles from the monastery. After 40 years as a solitary, he returned to the monastery to become its abbot. It was as abbot that he composed his very influential book.

Following in the Sinaite hesychastic tradition of Climacus is Abba Hesychius of Sinai (c. eighth to ninth century), the author of the "centuries" of ascetic maxims that were for many years included in the works of St. Hesychius of Jerusalem (fifth century). He was the abbot of the Monastery of the Mother of God of the Burning Bush (*Vatos*). His writings are especially helpful on watchfulness, inner attentiveness, and guarding of the heart. Philotheus of Sinai (c. ninth to tenth century) was probably a monk of Mount Sinai. In the 13th century another hesychast, Gregory Sinaite (c. 1265–1346), received his full monastic profession at St. Catherine's and later settled on Mount Athos.

St. Catherine's Monastery did not fare well after the Muslim conquest. As subjects of the Muslim rulers, the monks no longer had autonomy. Over the years the monastery became dilapidated as the number of monks dwindled. It was even abandoned several times during the 15th and 16th centuries. The monastery still possessed great treasures and attracted many pilgrims, but it was flagging as a monastic venture. When two of Napoleon Bonaparte's officers visited in 1798, they found only six monks in residence. A section of the surrounding wall, some towers, and several buildings had collapsed. In response Napoleon sent masons from Cairo to make repairs and improvements, including the construction of the Kleber tower in the middle of the northeastern outer wall. When the English ousted the French from Egypt in 1802, Sinai was returned to Turkish rule. However, the reports of Napoleon's Egyptian expeditionary force stimulated an increasing number of Western travelers to visit the monastery during the 19th century.

One of the more notorious 19th-century visitors was Constantin Tischendorf (1815–1874), the New Testament textual critic from Germany. He visited St. Catherine's three times between 1844 and 1859. During the visits he uncovered the Codex Sinaiticus, the famous manuscript of the Greek Bible that might be of Egyptian origin and possibly was copied around the middle of the fourth century. It was known to have been in Caesaria, Palestine, in the sixth century. Tischendorf borrowed the work from the monastery and never returned it, insinuating that the monks were too ignorant and inept to be caretakers of such valuables. It remained in St. Petersburg from 1859 to 1933, when it was purchased for the British Museum.

About the physical development of the monastery, Eutychios, patriarch of Alexandria (early tenth century), tells the story of how Emperor Constantine (306–337) and his mother, Helen, traveled to Sinai in 327. Helen was so impressed by the site of the burning bush that she ordered a small chapel to be built dedicated to the Mother of God (*Theotokos*). It was completed in 330. Beside it she had a fortified tower erected as a refuge for the hermits. However, this story has no factual basis. According to Patriarch Eutychios, in 556–557, during the time of Hegumen Doulas, Emperor Justinian (527–565) completed the construction of a fortress to surround the existing church and built a second church also consecrated to Mary. The walls of the fortress were constructed in such a way as to defend the burning bush perhaps more than to protect the monks. Justinian also provided troops to defend the area. The period 565–567 marks the completion of the wonderful mosaic of the Transfiguration in the apse of the church, which later became the Church of the Transfiguration. Hegumen Longinus and his deacon John are depicted in the mosaic. Longinus probably died not long after his portrait because Justinian II (685–695) soon sent Gregory of Fara to be *hegumen*. This is a period when Mount Sinai came under siege from the Arabs, and Gregory was able to conclude a truce with them. Although the process is not documented, the fortress walls gradually ceased to fill a military function and became the monastic center for the hermits of Mount Sinai, perhaps as a result of peaceful conditions.

Byzantine sources suggest that the monastery was not dedicated to St. Catherine of Alexandria until the Middle Ages. Of St. Catherine (whose alleged existence in the fourth century is now discredited), tradition says that angels miraculously transported her body to Sinai after her martyrdom. The Chapel of the Burning Bush is considered the most sacred part of the monastery. It was probably built around the turn of the 13th century and is located in the area where the bush once grew, below and behind the altar of the Church of the Transfiguration. The sacred bush that is now protected by a stone wall is not native to Sinai. The monks converted a guest house in the compound into a mosque around 1106. One of the legends surrounding it tells how the leader of an attacking Muslim army spared the monastery in exchange for having the mosque built. To appease his forces he spread a rumor that Muhammad had been a guest there. Much has already been said about the dilapidated condition of the monastery by the early 19th century. Intensive building and restoration activity did not begin until the late 19th century, and effort was redoubled in the 20th.

Saint Catherine's Monastery is part of the Church of Sinai, which is the smallest autonomous Church in the Orthodox Communion. The archbishop of Mount Sinai, who is the abbot of St. Catherine's, is the head of the Church and wields jurisdiction over several daughter houses, some hermit cells, and a small number of Arabs who live near the monastery. The Church of Sinai claimed its independence in 1575, but the claim was not confirmed until 1782. The patriarch of Jerusalem is solely responsible for consecrating the archbishop of Mount Sinai. Because Sinai was at one time under his ecclesiastical jurisdiction, the patriarch has frequently attempted, unsuccessfully, to assert his rule over the Church. The monastery rule is based on St. Basil's *Regula* and the ancient anchoritic precepts of Sinai.

MICHAEL D. PETERSON

See also Archaeology: Near East; Architecture: Eastern Christian Monasteries; Basil the Great, St.; Climacus, John, St.; Desert Fathers; Egypt; Hermits: Eastern Christian; Iconoclasm (Controversy); Images: Christian Perspectives; Jerusalem, Israel; Origins: Eastern Christian; Pilgrimages, Christian: Near East; Visual Arts, Eastern Christian: Painting

Further Reading

Chitty, Derwas, *The Desert a City: An Introduction to the Study of Egyptian and Palestinian Monasticism under the*

Christian Empire, Oxford: Basil Blackwell, and Crestwood, New York: St. Vladimir's Seminary Press, 1966
Climacus, John, *The Ladder of Divine Ascent*, translated by Archimandrite Lazarus Moore, New York: Harper, and London: Faber and Faber, 1959
Eckenstein, Lina, *A History of Sinai*, London and New York: SPCK, 1921
Egeria, *Egeria's Travels to the Holy Land*, translated with supporting documents and notes by John Wilkinson, Warminster: Aris and Phillips, 1981
Galey, John, *Sinai and the Monastery of St. Catherine*, London: Chatto and Windus, and Garden City, New York: Doubleday, 1980 (contains superb photographs)
Kamil, Jill, *The Monastery of Saint Catherine in Sinai: History and Guide*, Cairo: American University in Cairo Press, 1991
Moscos, John, *The Spiritual Meadow*, with introduction, translation, and notes by John Wortley, Kalamazoo, Michigan: Cistercian Publications, 1992
Papaioannou, Evangelos, *The Monastery of St. Catherine Sinai*, Sinai: St. Catherine's Monastery, 1976
Tsafrir, Uorum, "Monks and Monasteries in Southern Sinai," in *Ancient Churches Revealed*, edited by Yoram Tsafrir, Jerusalem: Israel Exploration Society, 1993

Mount Wutai, China

Wutai-shan, the mountain of the Five Terraces, is named after five domed peaks shaped like terraces (*tai*), four more than 9,000 feet, that dominate a highland district of some 96 square miles in northern Shanxi province. Its sanctity was created by its identification with the legendary northeastern Chill Clarity Mountains (*Qingliang-shan*) of the *Avataṃsaka Sūtra* (Chinese, *Huayan-jing*, translated between A.D. 418 and 420). This was the home of the bodhisattva Mañjuśrī, symbol of wisdom, and his retinue of 10,000. This homology was completed by the Sinifying emperor Xiaowen (r. 471–499) of the Northern Wei, possibly after he shifted his capital to Luoyang in 494. Wutai was to the northeast of this capital and was chilly, even in summer, and he founded a monastery there. In 516 the monk Lingbian retreated to the Qingliang Monastery, where he wrote, with the assistance of Mañjuśrī, the first commentary on the *Huayan-jing*, which focuses on the manifestations of the buddhas. This faith and the numbers of monasteries burgeoned despite the setbacks of the Northern Zhou persecution (574–578) and the destruction wrought by the wars waged to found the Tang dynasty. Seventy-two monasteries survived, and several of these, such as Foguang and Qingliang, in rebuilt form, still stand today. The mountain was also called Qingliang, and pilgrims came from throughout China and from as far as India, Tibet, Korea, and Japan. Many reported visions of Mañjuśrī as an avatar; as a bodhisattva surrounded by his retinue in a chimerical, golden monastic complex; or simply as a radiance or unusual clouds. These visions and prodigies attracted some of the most famous Tang Buddhist scholars and innovators, such as Amoghavajra (705–774), the esoteric Buddhist translator who spread the cult of Mañjuśrī throughout China and induced the court to build Jin'ge Monastery there, with gilded tile roofs, based on a vision. The Japanese pilgrim Ennin (794–864) recorded its glory during his visit in 840.

Soon after, in 844, a persecution led to the decline of Wutai, and although it was partially restored, its location in the marchlands meant that it was frequently occupied by the northern nomads: the Khitan, Jurchen, and Mongols. For the Chinese it was both a spiritual barrier against and a bridge to these northern invaders, and this lent Wutai greater sublimity in its political role. The Mongol Yüan dynasty introduced Tibetan Buddhism (Lamaism) to Wutai, but this remained a religion of the Mongol elite. The succeeding Chinese Ming dynasty were not enthusiastic patrons and even forced the Wutai monks into military service and deforested its rich stands. In the 1570s the Mongol leader Altan Khan converted to Lamaism and made peace with the Ming. When the Ming empress dowager built the great white stūpa (*chorten*) that still dominates Taihuaizhen, the main monastic town in Wutai, Altan Khan led his followers there on pilgrimage, signaling a conversion of the Mongols to Buddhism. Meanwhile the Manchus, whose name is supposedly derived from "Mañju(śrī)," began their conquest of China and to appease the Mongols gave special privileges to Wutai-shan by building monasteries and appointing lamas as abbots. Several of the most powerful emperors made repeated pilgrimages to the mountain sanctuary, and this promoted the Wutai-shan faith among the Mongols and Manchus. Pilgrims streamed there from the steppes, giving it a Lamaist coloration that remains, although after 1917 many Mongols were prevented from coming by the creation of the communist state in Outer Mongolia.

Up until the foundation of the People's Republic of China, more than 1,000 monks lived there, divided broadly into followers of Chinese Chan or Tibetan Buddhism. The Cultural Revolution destroyed many monasteries, but some have been restored, and 76 remain. The oldest wooden-frame buildings in China are on Wutai: the Nanchan Monastery of 782 and the Foguang Monastery of 857, the latter also displaying Tang statuary and murals. Khitan Jin–dynasty art can be seen at Yanshan Monastery, and Guangji Monastery has a Yüan-dynasty building. The greatest structure is the Buddha Hall of Xiantong Monastery. Although there are several routes to the mountain, the most convenient is by daily bus from Taiyuan.

Wutai-shan was a pilgrimage site for all of East Asia and especially for the Mongols; for those who could not go, imitations or homologues were built in Korea (Odae-san, or Wutai-shan, at the command of Mañjuśrī to Chajang in 636), Seiryōji (Qingliang Monastery) in Kyoto, and in Central Asia. Its Mañjuśrī faith inspired people without regard of ethnicity or Buddhist affiliation, making it the prime pilgrimage destination of East and Central Asian Buddhism.

JOHN JORGENSEN

See also Asia, Central; Buddhist Schools/Traditions: China; China; Ennin; Mountain Monasteries: Buddhist; Pilgrimages, Buddhist; Tibet: History

View of Taihuai from Pusading, Wutai-shan (sacred site of Mañjuśrī [Wenshu] Bodhisattva), Shanxi province, China.
Photo courtesy of Marylin M. Rhie

Further Reading

Birnbaum, Raoul, "The Manifestation of a Monastery: Shen-ying's Experiences on Mount Wu-t'ai in Tang Context," *Journal of the American Oriental Society* 106:1 (1986)

Chen Shunxuan, Zhang Lechu, Wu Huiqing, and He Chuxiang, *Zhongguo simiao yu pusa*, Nanning: Guangxi Renmin chubanshe, 1990

Gimello, Robert M., "Changing Shang-ying on Wu-t'ai Shan," in *Pilgrims and Sacred Sites in China* (Studies on China, 15), edited by Susan Naquin and Chün-fang Yü, Berkeley: University of California Press, 1992

Gimello, Robert M., "Wu-t'ai Shan during the Early Chin Dynasty: The Testimony of Chu Pien," *Zhonghua Foxue xuebao (Chung-Hwa Buddhist Journal)* 7 (1994)

Hibino, Takeo, and Katsutoshi Ono, *Godaisan*, Tokyo: Zayuho Kankokai, 1942

Karetzky, Patricia Eichenbaum, "The Recently Discovered Chin Dynasty Murals Illustrating the Life of the Buddha at Yen-shang ssu, Shansi," *Artibus Asiae* 42 (1980)

Reischauer, Edwin O., *Ennin's Travels in T'ang China*, New York: Ronald Press, 1955

Rhie, Marylin M., *The Fo-kuang ssu: Literary Evidences and Buddhist Images* (Outstanding Dissertations in the Fine Arts), New York: Garland, 1977

Sickman, Laurence, and Alexander Soper, *The Art and Architecture of China* (Pelican History of Art, Z10), Baltimore, Maryland: Penguin, 1956; 2nd edition, Harmondsworth, Middlesex: Penguin, 1960; 3rd edition, Baltimore, Maryland, and Harmondsworth, Middlesex: Penguin, 1968

Weinstein, Stanley, *Buddhism under the T'ang* (Cambridge Studies in Chinese History, Literature, and Institutions), Cambridge and New York: Cambridge University Press, 1987

Mountain Monasteries, Buddhist

Mountains, both real and imagined, have long been important to Buddhist conceptions of sacred space. According to traditional Buddhist cosmology, the mythic Mount Meru is the cosmic center, or *axis mundi*, of the Buddhist universe. In ancient

India sacred relics of the historical Buddha were housed in stone mounds – inspired by mountainous forms – known as stūpas. Thus, it is not surprising that Buddhist monasteries are often situated in mountain settings, especially because of the identification of mountains with sacredness. Despite the tradition of venerating mountains as holy places in Buddhist countries, considerable variation exists from country to country in the location and configuration of mountain monasteries. In a mountainous region such as Tibet, layers of peaks figure differently, in both visual and religious terms, than in Japan, where mountains ascend amid expanses of flat land. In a brief overview of the significance of mountain monasteries past and present in an eastern Asian context, this article focuses on China and Japan.

Although mountains do not always share the same symbolic valence in all cultures, mountains have nevertheless been a potent source of imagery about the sacred; this is certainly true of eastern Asia. In China mountains have long been associated with sacred power and with Daoist (Taoist) immortals. In Japan mountains are considered sacred both because they are a space that the gods (*kami*) inhabit and because they are an abode of the dead. Thus, Buddhist mountain monasteries sometimes tap into a collective cultural view of mountains as having a sacred quality that in turn heightens the spiritual prestige of the monastery.

The Fundamental Great Pagoda at the Central Compound (Garan), Mount Kōya, Japan. This one of the two main temples there represents the active side of Vairocana.
Photo courtesy of David Moore

Mountain monasteries usually have a denominational identity. However, in the case of important mountain centers they often transcend sectarian boundaries because of their popularity with pilgrims who visit the sacred precincts without concern for sectarian connections. Pilgrims make the journey because the mountain is considered sacred, and access to its sacred power can be gained through travel to the mountain. This notion of the mountain as a holy place is strengthened by the existence of monasteries and the monks who dwell within, some of whom are considered spiritual adepts.

Pilgrimage is a central activity at many Buddhist mountain monasteries. Often monasteries located among mountain peaks are the destinations of pilgrims seeking to commune with the numinous power thought to reside in mountains as well as with the holiness imparted to mountain precincts by the pious people who practice there. Sacred mountains are often associated with a bodhisattva who is believed to reside there, who protects the space, and whose spiritual presence is manifest and active. Both monastics and pilgrims seek to tap into this sacred power.

Pilgrimage has been a vital aspect of Buddhist religiosity since early in the tradition's history. Originally, faithful Buddhists traveled to sites associated with the life of the historical Buddha, but as Buddhism spread throughout Asia pilgrimage became localized and often focused on sites linked to important monastics or significant events. Often these places have been located in mountainous regions.

Two representative Buddhist mountain monasteries – the monastic complexes on Mount Wutai (Wutaishan or Wu-t'ai Shan, "Mountain of the Five Terraces") in China and Mount Hiei in Japan – are paradigms of at least some of the functions that mountain monasteries perform in Buddhist traditions.

Mount Wutai is one of Chinese Buddhism's most sacred sites. Although originally associated with Daoism, by the seventh century Mount Wutai became an important center for Buddhist thought and practice. For centuries Mount Wutai has been a locus of Buddhist monastic and ascetic activity with sectarian connections to the Huayan (Hua-yen), Zhenyan (Chen-yen), and Chan (Ch'an) Buddhist schools.

Wutai's holiness and appeal as a monastic center is due largely to its association with Mañjuśrī, a bodhisattva symbolic of supreme wisdom who is said to reside there, presenting himself to the faithful. Chinese Buddhist literature is filled with stories chronicling miraculous events that occurred as a result of Mañjuśrī's activities on the mountain. Historically Mount Wutai was sacred not just to the Chinese: Indian, Tibetan, central Asian, Korean, and Japanese Buddhists also considered Mount Wutai a pilgrimage destination. The Japanese pilgrim Ennin (794–864) has left us with a vivid account of monastic life on Wutai in a detailed diary, the *Nittō guhō junrei gyōki* (Record of

A mountain god (non-Buddhist in origin) at the mountain god shrine customary in Korean monasteries. This one is located at Paekjong-am in South Kyŏngsang province, South Korea.
Photo courtesy of John Powers

a Pilgrimage to Tang [T'ang] China in Search of the Dharma). The association of Mount Wutai with Mañjuśrī was also related to the Buddhist eschatological idea of the end of the dharma, or Buddhist law, a period of time in which it would be nearly impossible to achieve Buddhahood without the divine assistance of salvific figures such as Mañjuśrī. Thus, through connections to the Mañjuśrī cult this Chinese mountain, originally on the periphery of Buddhist worship, become a major cultic center for Buddhists across Asia.

In Japan Mount Hiei is the site of the Tendai monastic complex centered at the Enryakuji temple. Originally associated with Shintō gods (*kami*), in the early ninth century this mountain became the location of a monastic complex that would number over 3,000 temples and other buildings at its apex. The Japanese monk Saichō founded this monastic center, and it quickly became an important place for Tendai (Chinese, Tiantai/T'ien-t'ai) monastic practice, doctrinal study, and pious austerities. One of the distinctive characteristics of Tendai Buddhism is its embrace of a wide array of Buddhist practices, including ritual and meditative techniques culled from Tendai, Zen, Shingon (esoteric Buddhism), and Pure Land traditions. Although much of the thriving monastic community was destroyed in 1571 by Oda Nobunaga in his quest to control Japan, Mount Hiei remains an important site for Japanese monastics and pilgrims.

Mount Hiei cultivated an active monastic community but also served as an important pilgrimage site, attracting both aristocrats and commoners to its sacred precincts. Perhaps the most famous religious practice associated with Mount Hiei is the *kaihōgyō*, or mountain circumambulation practice, an intense, physically demanding ascetic ritual. This practice originated with the Tendai monk Sōō, who in the ninth century inaugurated the mountain circumambulation to sacred sites at various locations on the mountain. Today one either undertakes a 100- or a 1,000-day practice. The 100-day practice is required of all monastics who want to become temple head priests. The 1,000-day practice, which requires seven years to complete and marks a significant commitment to an austere monastic life, is undertaken by very few. Those who have completed this arduous practice are seen as spiritual adepts imbued with an aura of sacred power.

Buddhist monasteries located in Chinese and Japanese mountain settings offer monastics a refuge and pilgrims access to the sacred. Because the temptations and distractions of daily life are at least partially reduced, mountains are viewed as especially suited to the concentration demanded by monastic study and ascetic discipline. Through the rigors of mountain living and the reclusive nature of mountain hermitages, mountains have become associated with ascetic practice. Both lay and monastic Buddhists have sought spiritual progress in the mountains, believing that encounters with the sacred are more feasible away from secular temptations and the defilements of daily life. Throughout history and in several Buddhist countries, mountain monasteries have provided an ideal environment for spiritual advancement.

William E. Deal

See also Chinul; Dōgen; Ennin; Esoteric Buddhism in China and Japan; Kūkai; Ladakh, India; Marathon Monks; Mount Hiei, Japan; Mount Kōya, Japan; Mount Meru; Nepal; Pilgrimages, Buddhist; Saichō; Stūpa; Tibet: Sites; Topography, Sacred (Buddhist)

Further Reading

Bernbaum, Edwin, *Sacred Mountains of the World*, San Francisco: Sierra Club Books, 1990
Birnbaum, Raoul, *Studies on the Mysteries of Mañjuśrī: A Group of East Asian Mandalas and Their Traditional Symbolism* (Society for the Study of Chinese Religions Monograph Series, number 2), Boulder, Colorado: Society for the Study of Chinese Religions, 1983
Birnbaum, Raoul, "The Manifestation of a Monastery: Shen-ying's Experiences on Mount Wu-T'ai in a T'ang Context," *Journal of the American Oriental Society* 106:1 (1986)
Einarsen, John, editor, *The Sacred Mountains of Asia*, Boston: Shambhala, 1995
Gimello, Robert M., "Changing Shang-ying on Wu-tai Shan," in *Pilgrims and Sacred Sites in China* (Studies on China, 15), edited by Susan Naquin and Chün-fang Yü, Berkeley: University of California Press, 1992
Grapard, Allan G., "Flying Mountains and Walkers of Emptiness: Toward a Definition of Sacred Space in Japanese Religions," *History of Religions* 21:3 (1982)
Naquin, Susan, and Chün-fang Yü, editors, *Pilgrims and Sacred Sites in China* (Studies on China, 15), Berkeley: University of California Press, 1992
Reischauer, Edwin O., *Ennin's Travels in T'ang China*, New York: Ronald Press, 1955
Reischauer, Edwin O., translator, *Ennin's Diary: The Record of a Pilgrimage to China in Search of the Law*, New York: Ronald Press, 1955
Stevens, John, *The Marathon Monks of Mount Hiei*, Boston: Shambhala, 1988
Tobias, Michael Charles, and Harold Drasdo, editors, *The Mountain Spirit*, Woodstock, New York: Overlook Press, 1979; London: Gollancz, 1980

Mun, Ajahn 1871–1949

Thai Buddhist monk and founder of forest masters lineage

A prominent feature of the early 20th-century Buddhist monastic community in Thailand has been the emergence of a lineage of monks noted for a lifestyle that places a premium on wandering in the forest. These forest masters are known for the zeal of their ascetic practices and for a high level of meditational attainment. The monk who is recognized as the founder of this particular lineage is Ajahn/Acharn (Teacher) Mun/Man (his birth name) Purithat/Phuuurithatto (his monastic name).

Although our knowledge of the life of Ajahn Mun is filtered through the memories and writings of his disciples, some basic patterns are clear. It is generally agreed that Mun was born in 1870 or 1871 in the Lao area of northeastern Thailand, that between the ages of 15 and 17 he was a novice at the local monastery, and that at the age of 22 he was ordained a monk in the local Lao tradition. The available sources also agree that soon thereafter he was reordained in the reformist Thammayut lineage that had been established in central Thailand in the middle decades of the 19th century and that he adopted a particular Buddhist lifestyle associated with so-called *thudong* monks. This lifestyle combined external adherence to a set of 13 ascetic rules (including the wearing of rag robes and dwelling in the forest) with traditional forms of intensive meditational practice.

After spending some time in northeastern Thailand, Mun began to wander much more widely through Laos, Thailand, and Burma. He sought out contacts with leading teachers, stayed for periods of time in remote forests, and focused on developing his own meditational prowess. As time passed, his reputation for spiritual attainment grew, and he attracted an impressive group of disciples who accepted the *thudong* discipline, followed his teachings, and practiced the forms of meditational practice that he advocated. Before Mun's death in 1949, many of his followers came to the conclusion that he – and perhaps one or two of his leading disciples – had achieved the status of an arhat, or fully perfected saint. This is the highest level of spiritual attainment that is recognized within the Theravāda tradition.

Since Acharn Mun's death the lineage that he founded has continued, but many changes have occurred. Pressures from the national Buddhist establishment and the ever increasing deforestation of the landscape in northeastern Thailand have resulted in a shift away from the wandering lifestyle of the *thudong* tradition to one that is almost completely domesticated and settled. Concurrently the spiritual attainments and reputations of the monks who have extended the lineage have led to their emergence as nationally renowned sources of religious charisma. They have been heavily patronized by members of the Bangkok-based political and economic elite who seek religious legitimacy and protective power. At the same time the monks have become active in producing and blessing amulets that play a central role in the religious life of all segments of the population.

FRANK REYNOLDS

See also Bangkok, Thailand; Buddhadāsa; Forest Masters; Thailand

Biography

Born in northeastern Thailand, Mun lived in a local monastery and was ordained as a monk at age 22. Re-ordained in the reformist Thammayut lineage, he wandered all over Laos, Thailand, and Burma. As a forest elder he deepened his practice of meditation and attracted many disciples. Mun renewed the tradition of Thai forest masters.

Further Reading

Boowa, Nanasampanno, *The Venerable Phra acharn Mun Bhuridatta Thera, Meditation Master*, translated by Siri Buddhasukh, Bangkok: Mahamakut Rajavidynlaya Press, 1976

Keyes, Charles, "Death of Two Buddhist Saints in Thailand," *Journal of the American Academy of Religion, Thematic Studies* 48:3–4 (1982)

Tambiah, Stanley, *The Buddhist Saints of the Forest and the Cult of the Amulets*, Cambridge and New York: Cambridge University Press, 1984

Taylor, James, *Forest Monks and the Nation-State: An Anthropological and Historical Study in Northeastern Thailand*, Singapore: Institute of Southeast Asian Studies, 1993

Taylor, James, "The Textualization of a Monastic Tradition: Forest Monks, Lineage and Biographical Process in Thailand," in *Sacred Biography in the Buddhist Traditions of South and Southeast Asia*, edited by Juliane Schober, Honolulu: University of Hawaii Press, 1997

Tiyavanich, Kamala, *Forest Recollections: Wandering Monks in Twentieth-Century Thailand*, Honolulu: University of Hawaii Press, 1997

Music: Buddhist Perspectives

From strict textual interpretations of certain Buddhist canons one might conclude that music has no religiously significant place within Buddhist traditions. Lack of research illustrates that Buddhologists and ethnomusicologists have not paid adequate attention to the role of music in Buddhist traditions. Although several anthropological works exist on Sinhala Buddhist rituals, the space given in them to music is at best minimal. A major reason for this scholarly neglect is that certain scholars have attempted to demonstrate that Buddhism as a whole eschews or

Gyuto monks (Gelukpa lineage) chanting in a public ceremony in 1998 at Royal Albert Hall, Canberra, Australia.
Photo courtesy of John Powers

even prohibits music. To show the existence of negative attitudes embedded within the early tradition itself, scriptures can be quoted in which the Buddha himself downplayed the importance of music for the realization of nirvāṇa (which is the soteriological goal prescribed by Theravāda Buddhists). Apparently, this classical textual tradition conflicts with the realities of popular traditions in contemporary Buddhist societies. Two conflicting tendencies – the negative attitudes of the early tradition and the extensive use of music in modern popular Buddhist practices – must be dealt with to gain a proper understanding of Buddhist attitudes toward music.

Modern socioreligious research shows that various forms of music – religious chants, devotional hymns, pious songs, and enchanting performances of musical instruments – abound in Buddhist rituals as intrinsic parts of Buddhist religiosity. They become enriched, enhanced, and preserved by Buddhist monastics, laity, and Buddhist institutions.

From the inception of Indian Buddhist monasticism, a clear distinction had been made between the living patterns that are prescribed for regular monastic life and the religious guidelines that are provided for laymen and laywomen who led secular lives. Unacceptable behavior for monastics is clearly outlined in regulations given in the vinaya (disciplinary) texts. In examining Buddhist attitude toward music, differences between these two modes of life must be analyzed as well.

From the Theravāda perspective a disjunction can be seen between the disciplinary rules for the monastics and music. Buddhist monastic discipline is rigid and strict; to achieve a contemplative life, it recommends physical restraint, verbal silence, and mental concentration. The purpose of monastic discipline is to produce an atmosphere in which the five senses are shielded. Although music appeals to the sense of hearing, it is often perceived as a distraction rather than an aid to concentration. Yet it is only for the unawakened that music becomes a distraction, for it does not pose a threat to the awakened. The traditional precept is that if music arouses sensuality, music must be put aside. Often monastic discipline and music are seen as not mutually enhancing. In comparing this position with that of Christianity, a clear contrast emerges. Unlike in Buddhist traditions, in medieval Christian monasticism music was almost exclusively the domain of learned monks. For example, Gregorian chant was a creation of the monks and played an important role in the development of Christian monasticism.

Although scriptural statements are often negative toward the use of music, when music and song are placed in the proper religious context of elucidating *dhamma*, they become religiously supportive devices for the spiritual growth of the laity as well as that of the monastics. An example of such a context is the two-pulpit preaching (*āsana dekē baṇa*) tradition of the 18th century Sri Lanka.

Straw chanting center, Anurādhapura, Sri Lanka, rebuilt 20th century. Photo courtesy of John C. Huntington, the Huntington Archive

In many Asian Buddhist societies, both liturgical and nonliturgical music have found a place. Although music has no formal role in established ritual procedures (apart from stereotypical chanting in scriptural languages such as Pāli and Sanskrit or in the vernaculars), music has found a place when the themes are Buddhist. In a word, music becomes legitimate when it enhances the religious message. All sorts of musical compositions and musical instruments are recognized as authentic when they point beyond their artistic form, that is, when they enhance a religious message.

If music is interpreted as "humanly organized sound," the full-scale choral chantings of Buddhist monastics can be regarded as a form of music descended from the early tradition. In ethnomusicological terms such religious chanting clearly falls within the definition of music. The Pāli canon contains an extensive portion of verse (*gāthā*) texts, such as the *Theragāthā*, *Therigāthā*, *Suttanipāta*, and *Dhammapada*. Some were actual recitations by early Buddhist monks and nuns, whereas the remainder were scriptures used for recitation and chanting in monastic contemplative life. Such texts demonstrate that early Buddhists possessed a sense of beauty and that they expressed it in words during the course of attaining nirvāṇa.

In modern Theravāda societies the *paritta* (protection) recitation functions as an all-night practice. At the very outset drumming and instrumental music are used in the *paritta* ritual to invoke deities. Even in the midst of the recitation, for example, of the *Dhammacakkappavattana Sutta* (The Discourse on the Turning of the Wheel of *Dhamma*, i.e., the first sermon delivered by the historical Buddha), drumming and instrumental music accompany the monks' recitation. Similarly, during a variety of ritual offerings (*pūjā*s) held in Buddhist monasteries and at religious festivals, such as the annual procession in the Temple of the Tooth in Kandy, ritual drumming and instrumental music have become intrinsic parts of Buddhist ritual.

In the 20th century Buddhist attitudes toward music have changed drastically. Although it is not certain whether the changes are due to Western and Christian influences on Buddhist societies, today increasingly more hymnals are being produced by Buddhist groups, especially by Japanese Buddhist groups, such as Jōdō Shinshū (Pure Land school). All across Buddhist societies positive attitudes toward music have recently increased. Especially within Theravāda the 20th century has brought gradual acceptance and appreciation of music within Buddhist religious services.

MAHINDA DEEGALLE

See also Kandy, Sri Lanka; Liturgy: Buddhist; Mantras; Plainchant; Rules, Buddhist (Vinaya)

Further Reading

Carter, John Ross, *On Understanding Buddhists: Essays on the Theravāda Tradition of Sri Lanka*, Albany: State University of New York Press, 1993

Deegalle, Mahinda, "Marathon Preachers: The Two-Pulpit Tradition in Sri Lanka," *Asiatische Studien: Études Asiatiques* 52:1 (1998)

Gombrich, Richard F., "A New Theravadin Liturgy," *Journal of the Pali Text Society* 9 (1981)

Kulatillake, Cyril de Silva, "Buddhist Chant in Sri Lanka, Its Structure and Musical Elements," *Jahrbuch für musikalische Volks-und Völkerkunde* 10 (1982)

Palihawadana, Mahinda, "Pali *Sajjhāya* and Sanskrit *Svādhyāya*: An Inquiry into the Historical Origins of *Parittāna* Recitation," in *Recent Researches in Buddhist Studies: Essays in Honour of Professor Y. Karunadasa*, edited by K. Dhammajoti, A. Tilakaratne, and K. Abhayawansa, Colombo, Sri Lanka, and Hong Kong: Y. Karunadasa Felicitation Committee and Chi Ying Foundation, 1997

Seneviratna, Anuradha, "Musical Rituals of Dalada Maligawa," *Sangeet Natak* 36 (1975)

Seneviratna, Anuradha, "*Pañcatūrya Nāda* and the *Hewisi Pūjā*," *Ethnomusicology* 23:1 (1979)

Seneviratne, H.L., and Swarna Wickremeratne, "*Bodhipūjā*: Collective Representations of Sri Lanka Youth," *American Ethnologist* 7:4 (1980)

Music: Christian Perspectives

The medieval monastic liturgy involved two modes of verbal performance: "reading" and "singing." To modern ears, both singing and reading are "musical" endeavors, involving the vocalization of words on discrete pitches, yet early monastic writings consistently distinguish these two practices. To find out what music meant to monastic communities, we must first understand what singing meant. Although many texts performed by singing, such as antiphons and responsories, involve more florid melodies than those performed by reading, the complexity of melodic style alone does not distinguish them, as the melodic formulas used to "read" the Gospel or Epistle were often more florid than those used to "sing" the Psalms. The distinction pertains rather to how these performative modes functioned within the liturgy and, further, to how these ritual speech acts served to articulate relationships within both the monastic community and the greater Christian community.

Singing and reading both enact and configure threefold relationships among the verbal text, its performer(s), and its hearers or witnesses within ritual space and time, but they do so in different ways. Reading constitutes a quasi-juridical act, the publication (i.e., "making public" by reading aloud) of God's Word as given to humanity in the form of sacred Scripture and the lives of his saints. Reading further ritualizes the clerical privilege of literacy itself, the sacred knowledge that enabled the cleric to decode as well as interpret the Word for the Christian community. As such it was generally performed by a single person, reading from a book, to which the rest of the community bore witness.

Singing, by contrast, articulates relations within the community before God. Texts were sung by a unison choir, responsorially between soloist and choir, or antiphonally between sides of the choir. Ideally, they were sung from memory rather than from a book. If reading focuses attention on the enunciation and origin of the texts that underlie the Christian community, singing focuses attention on the monastic community's internalization of the those texts and on the potential to allow the members of that community to sing as one body. So constituted, the monastic choir functioned as mediators between the entire Christian community and God. Whatever devotional desires they might bring to their singing, the intercessory role of communal song was clear. The sanctity of the *opus Dei*, or work of God, depended on their unified will in performance: memorization of texts, careful pronunciation of syllables, synchronization of pauses, and agreement in pitch were highly valued as expressions of this unity. To be sure, new forms of musical notation and the introduction of polyphony into the liturgical repertoire complicated the distinction between reading and singing by lending heightened prestige to notational literacy and by requiring the use of soloists and books in performance. Nevertheless the ideals behind singing and reading remained.

Writers who theorized the use of music, from Boethius (c. 480–c. 524) and Augustine (354–430) on, argued that the nature of music allows the choral body to commune with more universal structures as well. Invoking the Neoplatonic concept of *musica mundana*, they conceived of the cosmos in terms of universal forms. The fundamental unity and perfection of these forms could be perceived in their harmonious relations to one another, relations that could be discerned in terms of arithmetical proportions or ratios. Such ratios could be heard in the intervallic relationships between musical pitches, as a string divided in half, giving a ratio of 2 to 1, sounds the interval of an octave. It is precisely this knowledge of cosmic relations, according to Boethius, that distinguishes the mere *cantor* – the singer who parrots what he or she has heard by rote – from the *musicus* – the musician aware of his or her participation in divine forms. This knowledge imparts to the musician greater knowledge of God. According to the 12th-century mystic and abbess Hildegard of Bingen (1098–1179), Adam possessed the knowledge to speak with a divine voice before the Fall. Singing, performing the liturgy *cum nota* as opposed to speaking it, is the closest humans come in a fallen world to that divine voice.

Augustine presents a similar sentiment when he acknowledges that words sung stir the heart to devotion more than words spoken, an attitude stemming from Greek conceptions of musical modes and their ability to induce emotion directly. Yet this acknowledgment is tempered by his Neoplatonic suspicion of any practice involving the senses. To be swayed by the sound of melodious voices would be a species of *amor mundi*, the love of sound for its own sake rather than for the presence of God expressed therein. For singers themselves such love could become a vehicle of pride. Frequent are monastic admonitions against taking too much pleasure in one's own voice, against singing higher or more loudly than others in the choir, against placing the self above the community as it presents itself before God.

Although such suspicion lingered, the sensible dimension of music was gradually brought into the realm of the intelligible as increasingly complex liturgies used melody as part of their signifying systems. The psalms, arranged in a regular weekly cycle, came to be framed by antiphons, or shorter pieces with texts appropriate to particular feasts or seasons. The verbal relationships suggested by the pairing of antiphons and psalms were enhanced by the fact that the musical mode of the antiphon determined the tone on which the psalm was sung. William Durandus (c. 1230–1296), a 13th-century canon lawyer and commentator on the liturgy, allegorized further, stating that whereas psalms represent good works, antiphons represent charity, as charity ought to inform all good works. Tunes as well as modes could be used to suggest significant relationships, as when the melody of one hymn was sung to the text of another. Such interdependent signification of text and music led Dom André Mocquereau (1849–1930), leader of the 19th-century revival of chant at Solesmes, to say, "Even as a healthy body is an instrument perfectly fitted to serve the soul, and interpret its workings, so the chant interprets the truth, and gives it a certain completeness which words alone could not achieve."

KATHERINE ZIEMAN

See also Augustinian Rule; Benedict of Nursia, St.; Guéranger, Prosper; Hildegard of Bingen, St.; Hymnographers; Liturgy: Western Christian; Plainchant; Solesmes, France

Further Reading

Bergeron, Katherine, *Decadent Enchantments: The Revivial of Gregorian Chant at Solesmes*, Berkeley: University of California Press, 1998
Boethius, *Fundamentals of Music (De institutione musica)*, translated by Calvin M. Bower, New Haven, Connecticut: Yale University Press, 1989
Durandus, William, *Guillelmi Duranti Rationale divinorum officiorum*, edited by Anselmus Davril and Timothy M. Thibodeau, Turnholti: Brepols, 1998
Ekenberg, Anders, *Cur cantatur?: Die Funktionen des liturgischen Gesanges nach den Autoren der Karolingerzeit*, Stockholm: Almquist and Wiksell, 1987
Hiley, David, *Western Plainchant: A Handbook*, Oxford: Clarendon Press, 1992; New York: Oxford University Press, 1993
Hughes, Andrew, *Medieval Music: The Sixth Liberal Art*, revised edition, Toronto and Buffalo: University of Toronto Press, 1980
Hughes, Andrew, *Medieval Manuscripts for Mass and Office: A Guide to Their Organization and Terminology*, Toronto and Buffalo: University of Toronto Press, 1982
Jeffery, Peter, *Re-Envisioning Past Musical Cultures: Ethnomusicology in the Study of Gregorian Chant*, Chicago: University of Chicago Press, 1992
McKinnon, James, *The Temple, the Church Fathers, and Early Western Chant*, Aldershot, Hampshire, and Brookfield, Vermont: Ashgate, 1998
Meyer, Hans Bernhard, et al., editors, *Gestalt des Gottesdienstes: Sprachliche und Nichtsprachliche Ausdrucksformen*, Regensburg: Pustet, 1987
Mocquereau, dom André, "L'Art Grégorien: Son but, ses procédés, ses caractères," *Études Gregoriennes* 25 (1997)

Spitzer, Leo, *Classical and Christian Ideas of World Harmony: Prolegomena to an Interpretation of the Word "Stimmung,"* edited by Anna Granville Hatcher, Baltimore, Maryland: Johns Hopkins University Press, 1963

Myanmar. *See* Burma (Myanmar)

Mystical Vision. *See* Vision, Mystical

Mystics, German Monastic: Female

The mystical tradition among German monastic women, which reached its zenith in the 13th and 14th centuries, notably at Helfta, allowed women to develop their own, often unique expression of piety. The experience provided a means of spiritual empowerment at a time when women's authority within the ecclesiastical hierarchy had been sharply curtailed. A number of women of the traditional orders – as well as those who took vows in the newly established mendicant orders and others who adopted an extraregular lifestyle (e.g., beguines) – embraced the mystical tradition. Following the example of the female prophets of the Old and New Testaments, the German women mystics disclosed the divine visions and auditions they experienced as they sought spiritual union with God (*unio mystica*); in addition, they attempted to imitate the life of Christ (*imitatio Christi*) through acts of penitential asceticism, such as fasting and mortification of the flesh. Paramount for the women is Christ's humanity, and in their writings they frequently make reference to the Christ Child and the suffering of Christ. Their works are replete with maternal imagery and references to the tradition of bride mysticism (*Brautmystik*) derived from the *Song of Songs* and fostered by Bernard of Clairvaux (1090–1153). Male religious served as the confessors, spiritual advisers, and personal friends of the women mystics, whose orthodoxy was almost always above suspicion. The men encouraged and sometimes assisted the women in recording the religious experiences.

The German mystical tradition began in the 12th century with the Benedictine abbess Hildegard of Bingen (1098–1179). More a prophet than an ecstatic mystic, Hildegard experienced visions of salvation history and served as God's herald to both ecclesiastical and secular leaders of her time. Hildegard's somewhat younger contemporary Elizabeth of Schönau (1129–1164) also was called by God to record her visionary experiences; she accomplished this with the assistance of her brother Eckbert. Given the number of extant manuscripts, it is clear that Elizabeth enjoyed greater popularity in the Middle Ages than did Hildegard, probably because many readers found Hildegard's visions difficult to comprehend.

In the 13th century the community of Helfta became the center of mysticism in the German-speaking territories. Originally established at Mansfeld in 1229 by and for the Thuringian nobility, the community moved to Helfta near Eisleben in 1258. Technically Benedictines, the nuns lived according to the Cistercian rule but received spiritual direction from the Dominicans in nearby Halle. During the second half of the century, the Helfta community was the residence of four remarkable women: Gertrude of Hackeborn, her sister Mechthild of Hackeborn, Gertrude the Great (of Helfta), and Mechthild of Magdeburg. Gertrude of Hackeborn (1232–1291/92) became abbess in 1251; no writings by her are extant, but she was renowned for her erudition and her encouragement of the study of the *artes liberales* among the Helfta nuns. Mechthild of Hackeborn (1214–1298/99) experienced visions and auditions beginning around the age of 50; these experiences were recorded in the *Liber specialis gratiae* (Book of Special Grace), a work notable for its veneration of the heart of Christ. This type of Eucharistic piety embraced by the Helfta sisters and inspired by meditation on Christ's wounds gave rise to the devotion of the Sacred Heart. Gertrude the Great (1256–1301/02) was educated in the Helfta community. Her writings provided spiritual instruction to the community and documented her visionary experiences, which began when she was about 25. Meditations, rituals, and prayers strongly influenced by the Liturgy, especially the celebration of the Eucharist, comprise her *Exercitia spiritualia* (Spiritual Exercises). The exercises direct the nuns along the path from spiritual rebirth to the mystical union and beyond. The *Legatus divinae pietatis* (The Herald of Divine Love), much of which probably was written by other Helfta nuns after Gertrude's death, characterizes the gifts of divine grace, love, and revelations that Gertrude experienced during her lifetime.

Mechthild of Magdeburg (c. 1207–c. 1282), a well-born woman from Lower Saxony, spent most of her life as a beguine in the town of Magdeburg. Perhaps because of the questionable status of beguines, around 1270 Mechthild chose to enter the Helfta community, where she spent her remaining years and where *Das fließende Licht der Gottheit* (The Flowing Light of the Godhead) was recorded. This work consists of seven books in which Mechthild combines prose and verse and monologue and dialogue in her description of the relationship between the bride/soul and the Bridegroom/Christ. Her language is inspired by that of the German poets of courtly love (*Minnesänger*). Mechthild first recorded her work in Low German with the assistance of her Dominican confessor Henry of Halle; before her death Latin translations were prepared. However, the work was circulated among religious communities in the 14th century by way of a translation into the Alemannic dialect accomplished under the direction of Henry of Nördlingen, a secular priest who served as spiritual adviser to Dominican nuns.

The center of religious fervor in the 14th century was the Dominican province of Teutonia (southern Germany and Switzerland), where men such as Meister Eckhart (c. 1260–c. 1328), John Tauler (c. 1300–1361), and Henry Suso (c. 1295–1366) preached, heard confessions, and mentored the religious women in their spiritual care. A remarkable number of 14th-century

Dominican nuns, such as Christina Ebner (1277–1356), Margaret Ebner (1291–1351), and Adelheid Langmann (1306–1375), were blessed with ecstatic experiences that they described in the vernacular in autobiographies and letters. Nine women's communities in Teutonia produced a distinctive literary form known as the sister book (*Schwesternbuch*), in which they chronicled the history of their house through biographies of its spiritually blessed residents. Among these are the chronicle of Adelhausen in Freiburg, written by Anna of Munzingen, and the *Tößer Schwesternbuch* (The Töß Sister Book), which might have been written in part by Elsbeth Stagel, spiritual daughter of Henry Suso and possible contributor to his *Vita*.

By the 15th century the mystical tradition among religious women in Germany had waned, but the reform movements fostered an interest in the ascetic lives of the women mystics that led to the preservation of their texts. In subsequent centuries the women and their works were again relegated to obscurity, but recently scholars have rediscovered the literary accomplishments of the German women mystics and reevaluated the nature of their piety.

DEBRA L. STOUDT

See also Benedictines: Female; Devotions, Western Christian; Germany: History; Hildegard of Bingen, St.; Liturgy: Western Christian; Spirituality: Western Christian; Vision, Mystical: Western Christian; Women's Monasteries: Western Christian

Further Reading

Bynum, Caroline Walker, "Women Mystics in the Thirteenth Century: The Case of the Nuns of Helfta," in *Jesus as Mother: Studies in the Spirituality of the High Middle Ages*, edited by Bynum, Berkeley: University of California Press, 1982
Coakley, John, "Gender and the Authority of the Friars: The Significance of Holy Women for Thirteenth-Century Franciscans and Dominicans," *Church History* 60 (1991)
Finnegan, Mary Jeremy, *The Women of Helfta: Scholars and Mystics*, Athens: University of Georgia Press, 1991
Hindsley, Leonard P., translator and editor, *Margaret Ebner: Major Works*, New York: Paulist Press, 1993
Lewis, Gertrud Jaron, *Bibliographie zur deutschen Frauenmystik des Mittelalters*, Berlin: Schmidt, 1989
Lewis, Gertrud Jaron, *By Women, for Women, about Women: The Sister-Books of Fourteenth-Century Germany*, Toronto: Pontifical Institute of Mediaeval Studies, 1996
McGinn, Bernard, *The Flowering of Mysticism: Men and Women in the New Mysticism (1200–1350)*, New York: Crossroad, 1998
Peters, Ursula, *Religiöse Erfahrung als literarisches Faktum: Zur Vorgeschichte und Genese frauenmystischer Texte des 13. und 14. Jahrhunderts*, Tübingen: Niemeyer, 1988
Ringler, Siegfried, *Viten- und Offenbarungsliteratur in Frauenklöstern des Mittelalters: Quellen und Studien*, Munich: Artemis, 1980
Spitzlei, Sabine B., *Erfahrungsraum Herz: Zur Mystik des Zisterzienserinnenklosters Helfta im 13. Jahrhundert*, Stuttgart-Bad Cannstatt: Frommann-Holzboog, 1991
Tobin, Frank, *Mechthild von Magdeburg: A Medieval Mystic in Modern Eyes*, Columbia, South Carolina: Camden House, 1995
Weeks, Andrew, *German Mysticism from Hildegard of Bingen to Ludwig Wittgenstein: A Literary and Intellectual History*, Albany: State University of New York Press, 1993

Mystics, German Monastic: Male

Within the Western Christian tradition, the culmination of the mystical experience is unity with the Divine, a unity most frequently achieved through contemplation. The growth of the Dominican Order, with its emphasis on the meditative as well as the apostolic aspects of spiritual life, served as fertile soil for the flowering of mysticism in 14th-century Germany.

The German mystical tradition established itself in the 12th century and was grounded in the Christocentric ideas of Bernard of Clairvaux (1090–1153) and Neoplatonic teachings, especially those derived from the writings of Dionysius the Pseudo-Areopagite. Cologne served as the center of religious study in 13th-century Germany; in the 14th century study was pursued mainly in the upper Rhine region (Strasbourg and northern Switzerland). The writings of Albertus Magnus (c. 1200–1280) concerning the act of contemplation influenced fellow Dominicans, such as Dietrich of Freiburg (c. 1250–c. 1318/20), whose views on the relationship between the intellect and the soul inspired Meister Eckhart. The ideas of Thomas Aquinas (1225–1274) regarding the gifts of the Holy Spirit and the doctrine of grace exerted a significant impact on John Sterngassen (d. after 1327), a teacher of John Tauler.

The German Franciscans were involved to a lesser extent in the promulgation of mystical ideals. An adherent of speculative mystical theology, David of Augsburg (1200–1272) exercised a profound influence on contemporary and subsequent generations through his vernacular and Latin tracts characterizing the threefold way to spiritual perfection. Many of David's treatises focus on higher levels of contemplation and prayer and reflect the influence of Bernard of Clairvaux and William of St. Thierry (1075/80–1148).

In part as a reaction against the political upheaval, ecclesiastical dissent, and natural calamities of the 14th century, pious individuals sought to attain religious fulfillment through contemplation and the imitation of Christ. Guiding both laity and religious on this spiritual journey were three prominent Dominicans: Meister Eckhart, Henry Suso, and John Tauler.

Meister Eckhart (c. 1260–1327/28) is the greatest luminary among medieval Christian mystics. The theological-philosophical works that he prepared for his colleagues and the sermons that he often preached to audiences of laypersons or religious women exemplify the tradition of speculative mysticism. Central to Eckhart's understanding of the mystical experience is the spark of the soul (*Seelenfünklein*), through which or in which one can experience and have knowledge of the Divine. A misunderstanding of this concept and others dealing with the nature of the union of the soul with the Divine led to charges of heresy against Eckhart. For this reason Eckhart's Dominican successors, who may have been his students in Cologne, distanced themselves from the master's speculative ideas.

On completion of the *studium generale* in Cologne, Henry Suso (c. 1295–1366) returned to monastic life in Constance, where he had begun his religious life at age 13. After more than 20 years of ascetic living, Suso felt called to direct others on their journey toward divine union; at this time he began his career as spiritual adviser to the laity and especially to Dominican women in various houses in Teutonia, in particular the community of Töss near Winterthur, Switzerland. Suso's devotional works the *Büchlein der Wahrheit* (Little Book of Truth) and the *Büchlein der ewigen Weisheit* (Little Book of Eternal Wisdom) were among the most popular writings of the late Middle Ages. The works take the form of a dialogue between the Eternal Servant (Suso himself) and the allegorical figures of Truth and Eternal Wisdom. His lyric style, punctuated with images from the tradition of bride mysticism and the language of the German courtly poets (*Minnesänger*), stands in stark contrast to the complex, philosophical prose of Meister Eckhart.

John Tauler (c. 1300–1361), the third in the triumvirate of Dominican male mystics of the 14th century, earned a reputation as a great preacher. He was born in Strasbourg, where he also received his early education. Details of his life are scant; he was forced to leave Strasbourg between 1339 and 1343 when Pope John XXII (1316–1334) placed an interdict on the city. Tauler undertook a number of journeys throughout his life in conjunction with his responsibilities as preacher to the laity and the religious and as spiritual director to Dominican women. In his vernacular sermons, which are his only extant works, Tauler frequently describes the purgative way (*via purgativa*), which leads to the purification of the soul. For Tauler the ground of the soul (*Seelengrund*), the soul in its "emptied" state, is central to the spiritual journey. Tauler's mystical tenets have a practical orientation that is reflected in a simple, idiomatic manner of expression.

Both Suso and Tauler as well as the Franciscans Otto of Passau and Marquard of Lindau (1320/30–1392) were associated with the Friends of God (*Gottesfreunde*). This loosely knit group of religious and laypersons was attracted by mystical ideals and the apostolic life and was active in and around Cologne as well as along the upper Rhine. Numbered among this group was Rulman Merswin (1307–1382), a successful Strasbourg merchant who took up the religious life at age 40 and produced about 20 devotional tracts. The accomplishments of the followers of the Friends of God also include the *Theologia Deutsch*, an anonymous tract that advocates the union with God through the imitation of Christ, which requires complete surrender of the human will.

Charged with the care of religious women (*cura monialium*), the German male mystics of the 14th century exercised a profound effect on the spiritual lives of religious women; many of their writings were written for nuns, beguines, and female Friends of God. They corresponded with their spiritual daughters, who posed questions and revealed to the confessors something of the nature of their mystical experiences, which in turn inspired the Dominican males.

The 14th-century German mystics exerted substantial influence on subsequent generations of religious, such as the followers of the spiritual movement prevalent in the Low Countries in the 14th and 15th centuries known as the *Devotio moderna* (New [Modern] Devotion). Affected as well were individuals such as Nicholas of Cusa (1401–1464) and Martin Luther (1483–1546), who knew the works of Tauler, the *Theologia Deutsch* (which he edited in 1518), and possibly the writings of Eckhart as well. The 17th-century Pietists and the 19th-century Romantics also owe much to the legacy of the medieval German mystics.

Debra L. Stoudt

See also Dialogue, Intermonastic; Germany: History; Vision, Mystical: Western Christian

Further Reading

Clark, James Midgley, *The Great German Mystics: Eckhart, Tauler and Suso*, Oxford: Blackwell, 1949; New York: Russell and Russell, 1970

Greith, Carl, *Die deutsche Mystik im Prediger-Orden (von 1250–1350) nach ihren Grundlehren, Liedern und Lebensbildern aus handschriftlichen Quellen*, Freiburg/Breisgau: Herder, 1861; Amsterdam: Rodopi, 1965

Haas, Alois M., *Sermo mysticus: Studien zu Theologie und Sprache der deutschen Mystik*, Freiburg, Switzerland: Universitätsverlag, 1979

Jones, Rufus M., *The Flowering of Mysticism: The Friends of God in the Fourteenth Century*, New York: Macmillan, 1939

McGinn, Bernard, *The Flowering of Mysticism: Men and Women in the New Mysticism (1200–1350)*, New York: Crossroad, 1998

Preger, Wilhelm, *Geschichte der deutschen Mystik im Mittelalter*, 3 vols., Leipzig: Dörffling and Franke, 1874, 1893; as *Geschichte der deutschen Mystik im Mittelalter, nach den Quellen untersucht und dargestellt*, Aalen: Zeller, 1962

Seesholtz, Anna Groh, *Friends of God: Practical Mystics of the Fourteenth Century*, New York: Columbia University Press, 1934; reprint, New York: AMS Press, 1970

Weeks, Andrew, *German Mysticism from Hildegard of Bingen to Ludwig Wittgenstein: A Literary and Intellectual History*, Albany: State University of New York Press, 1993

Wentzlaff-Eggebert, Friedrich-Wilhelm, *Deutsche Mystik zwischen Mittelalter und Neuzeit: Einheit und Wandlung ihrer Erscheinungsformen*, Berlin: de Gruyter, 1944; 3rd expanded edition, 1969

N

Nagano, Japan

The modern city of Nagano, capital of Nagano prefecture, is the location of one of the most important religious establishments in Japan, the temple called Zenkōji. Set in the mountainous area of central Honshu, Nagano was thought of as a very remote and inaccessible area in premodern times. Nevertheless in both past times and more recently, large numbers of people visited Zenkōji, and at present several million individuals come each year, some specifically as pilgrims and others as tourists, although even the latter tend to pay their respects and leave a donation. The reason for this great enthusiasm is the presence at Zenkōji of an extraordinary sculptural icon, an Amida Triad, which is believed by many to be a "Living Buddha." A lengthy narrative, *Zenkōji engi* (Legends of Zenkōji), explains how the Amida Triad came into existence in ancient India, flew magically to Korea in the sixth century, and then was taken by ship to the Japanese court in Yamato before finally being transported to Shinano province (present-day Nagano prefecture) during the seventh century. Although this account is legendary, evidence exists for a temple at the site by the end of the seventh century, and it is possible that a gilt-bronze triad of a type common on the Korean peninsula was this early temple's principal icon. Despite the likely existence of an early, proto- Zenkōji, firm evidence for an institution related to the historical Zenkōji does not appear until the later Heian period (11th to 12th century), and in fact the temple did not become a flourishing religious center until the following Kamakura period (1185–1336). Shinano Zenkōji became the focal point for a nationwide cult from about the middle of the 13th century, with replications of its Living Buddha distributed to temples called Shin Zenkōji (New Zenkōji) in most areas of Japan. In fact the cult of the Zenkōji Amida Triad became one of the most important aspects of the development in medieval Japanese religion referred to as popular Buddhism. This tendency has continued to the recent time, with a Zenkōji presence in virtually all prefectures.

Naturally the original temple in Nagano City continues to have the highest status. Its Hondō (Main Hall), the second-largest wooden temple structure in the country after the Great Buddha Hall of Tōdaiji, enshrines the Amida Triad, the Living Buddha, as a "secret image" (*hibutsu*). Although some icons classified as *hibutsu* are periodically shown to the worshipers, the Amida Triad of Zenkōji is never revealed and thus functions as a mysterious, sacred presence unavailable to human eyes. This Buddha is believed to be able to save the faithful from descent into hell, with the result that rebirth in the Western Paradise of Amida is possible. The blessings of the deity are conveyed by direct physical actions, such as the pressing of a sacred seal on the forehead of the devotee. Especially interesting is the practice of *kaidan meguri*, whereby the worshipers descend into a totally dark, subterranean passage that passes below the shrine of the Living Buddha; partway through the passage is a lock on the wall that is said to be the lock on the door leading to paradise, and if a person rattles this lock, rebirth in paradise in ensured.

The ecclesiastical organization of Shinano Zenkōji is most unusual in that it does not follow the normal pattern of Japanese temples, which are almost invariably associated with only one school of Buddhism. At present the Hondō does not have a specific sectarian affiliation, but two principal subtemples are sectarian: the Daikanjin is presided over by an abbot and is of the Tendai school, whereas the Daihongan has an abbess and is of the Jōdo school. This bifurcation of religious authority appears to derive from an early practice, perhaps associated with shamanistic origins. Operating under each of the principal subtemples is a group of smaller subtemples, each presided over by a resident priest; normally all these priests are married and have families. The abbot, who is appointed by the Tendai headquarters, is assisted by several priests resident at the Daikanjin; both the abbot and his assistants are also usually married. Traditionally the abbess has come from either the imperial family or one of the great aristocratic lines, and she and the women who serve under her are celibate. On those grounds they may reasonably be called nuns, although the term *monk* seems inappropriate for the married priesthood of the Tendai group.

Ritual activity at Zenkōji centers on the worship of the Living Buddha. Each morning the abbot and abbess, accompanied by their followers, officiate at a regular service. The Tendai service of the abbot is held first, followed by the Jōdo service of the abbess; no interaction takes place between the two sects at these regular services because as one group is exiting from the front of the hall, the other is entering from the back. Most of the worshipers have spent the night in one of the smaller subtemples, and they go as a group to the morning service. A second regular service is held at midday, and between these services individuals can have specific rituals performed at their own request: these rituals include prayers for health and success and the blessing of the remains of deceased relatives. In addition to the daily ritual activity is a cycle of annual events spread throughout the year, culminating in a highly complex sequence of rituals welcoming the new year. Pilgrims who visit the temple from the last minutes of 31 December through the first minutes of 1 January are deemed to have performed a "two years' pilgrimage" (*Ninen mairi*), thereby accumulating double merit. Hundreds of thousands of pilgrims participate in this event each year, with the temple receiving substantial donations.

Although most Japanese have heard of Zenkōji and a significant number have visited it, the temple achieved international fame only in 1998 because of its close association with the Nagano Winter Olympic Games. The official opening ceremonies began with the ringing of the temple bell, and the Main Hall was a constant background element in the television coverage because the studio was located on the temple grounds directly in front of that structure.

DONALD F. MCCALLUM

See also Buddhist Schools/Traditions: Japan; Deities, Buddhist; Japan; Medicine, Buddhist; Pure Land Buddhism; Temple, Buddhist; Tiantai/Tendai: Japan; Visual Arts, Buddhist: Japan

Further Reading

Asami, Ryusuke, "Zenkōji shiki Amida Nyorai zō nirei: Tokyo Kokuritsu Hakubutsukan chūzon zō to Fukushima Iwaki shi shōzō sanzon zō" (Two Examples of the Zenkōji Style Amitabha [Amida Nyorai] Images – The Former Trinity Central Figure of the Tokyo National Museum and the Amitabha Trinity of Iwaki City, Fukushima), *Museum* 558 (1999)

Gorai, Shigeru, *Zenkōji mairi* (Pilgrimage to Zenkōji), Tokyo: Heibonsha, 1988

Itō Nobuo, et al., editors, *Zenkōji: Kokoro to katachi* (Zenkōji: Spirit and Form), Tokyo: Daiichi Hōki, 1991

Kobayashi Ichirō, *Zenkōji Nyorai engi: Genroku gonen ban* (The *Zenkōji Nyorai Engi*: The Version of Genroku 5), Nagano: Ginga Shobō, 1985

Kobayashi, Keiichirō, *Zenkōji san*, 2nd edition, Nagano: Ginga Shobō, 1979

McCallum, Donald F., *Zenkōji and Its Icon: A Study in Medieval Japanese Religious Art*, Princeton, New Jersey: Princeton University Press, 1994

McCallum, Donald F., "The Buddhist Triad in Three Kingdoms Sculpture," *Korean Culture* 16:4 (1995)

McCallum, Donald F., "The Replication of Miraculous Images: The Zenkōji Amida and the Seiryōji Shaka," in *Images, Miracles, and Authority in Asian Religious Traditions*, edited by Richard H. Davis, Boulder, Colorado: Westview Press, 1998

Nagano Kenritsu Rekishikan, *Shinano fūdo to rekishi: Chūsei no Shinano* (Topography and History of Shinano: The Medieval Period), Nagano, 1997

Nagano Shiritsu Hakubutsukan, *Zenkōji shinkō to Hoku Shinano* (The Zenkōji Cult and Northern Shinano Province), Nagano, 1997

Sakai, Kōhei, *Zenkōji shi* (History of Zenkōji), 2 vols., Tokyo: Tokyo Bijutsu, 1969

Suda, Osamu, *Romanteikku Zenkōji* (Romantic Zenkōji), Nagano: Shinano Mainichi Shinbunsha, 1997

Ushiyama, Yoshiyuki, "Shinano Zenkōji shi kankei bunken mokuroku" (Catalogue of Publications Related to the History of Shinano Zenkōji), *Jiin shi kenkyū* 2 (1991)

Ushiyama, Yoshiyuki, "Shinano Zenkōji kankei bunken mokuroku hoi – Son ichi" (Supplement to Catalogue of Publications Related to the History of Shinano Zenkōji, Part 1), *Jiin shi kenkyū* 5 (1996)

Nālandā, India

The greatest center of Buddhist scholarship in medieval India was located near Bargaon, Bihar state. Nālandā's origins are obscure, although it certainly flourished from the fifth century A.D. Its influence grew under the Guptas (c. 300–c. 550), reaching a zenith during the Pāla dynasty. Textual sources indicate that a number of separate monasteries occupying the site by the early seventh century were later unified into one great monastic and university complex (*mahāvihāra*), although this is not fully confirmed by current archaeology.

The Buddha is said to have visited Nālandā on several occasions, and the area also seems to have been an early stronghold of Jainism. Nālandā's connection with learning is reinforced by the tradition that the original Mahāyāna Sūtras were brought here after they were recovered from the mythical Nāgā (serpent) realm. Prominent Mahāyāna scholar-sages later associated with the university include Nāgārjuna, Āryadeva, Vasubandhu, Asaṅga, Dharmapāla, and Dignāga, the founder of Buddhist logic. Tantric thought and practice began to dominate Nālandā from the eighth century.

When the Chinese pilgrim Xuanzang visited around 637, he described an assorted population of about 6,000 at Nālandā. The university's "principal scholar" was Śīlabhadra, a 106-year-old authority on Yogācāra philosophy. Lectures took place every day on a wide variety of Buddhist and non-Buddhist subjects. Admission was by way of a stiff verbal examination administered by the monastery doorkeeper. The term of residence was not fixed, and no degree seems to have been awarded. The monastery appears to have been materially supported by the revenues from some 200 villages, its campus including eight lecture halls, five temples, many stūpas, an observatory, ten ponds, and three multistory libraries.

In its heyday Nālandā became a considerable magnet for Buddhists from different parts of Asia. For example, a Javanese king built a hostel to accommodate monks from his kingdom there around 860. However, other centers of Buddhist learning, such as Valabhī in western and Vikramaśilā in eastern India, were beginning to challenge the supremacy of Nālandā by this time, and with the foundation of nearby Uddaṇḍapura in the mid–eighth century, Nālandā gradually declined.

In 1202 the Muslim Muhammed Bhaktiyar Khilji devastated Nālandā, although it seems to have been plundered a number of

Remains of the Great Stūpa, Buddhist Monastic University, Nālandā, India, Gupta period, c. fifth–sixth century.
Photo courtesy of Marylin M. Rhie

Stūpa, Temple 3, Nālandā, India, fifth to seventh century.
Photo courtesy of John C. Huntington, the Huntington Archive

West wall, stūpa, Temple 3, Nālandā, India, seventh century.
Photo courtesy of John C. Huntington, the Huntington Archive

times before. When the Tibetan monk Dharmasvāmin visited the site in 1235, he found that all the manuscripts had been destroyed and that only one old monk remained, teaching Sanskrit to a class of 70 pupils. Nālandā is now an important archaeological and pilgrimage site. A center for postgraduate Pāli and Buddhist studies was established there in 1951.

IAN HARRIS

See also Architecture: Buddhist Monasteries in Southern Asia; Libraries: Buddhist; Patrons, Buddhist: India; Pilgrims to India, Chinese

Further Reading

Barua, Dipak Kumar, *Viharas in Ancient India: A Survey of Buddhist Monasteries*, Calcutta: Indian Publications, 1969
Dutt, Sukumar, *Buddhist Monks and Monasteries of India: Their History and Their Contribution to Indian Culture*, London: Allen and Unwin, 1962
Ghosh, A., *A Guide to Nalanda*, Delhi: Manager of Publications, 1939; 6th edition, New Delhi: Director of Publications, Archaeological Survey of India, 1986
Paul, Debjani, *The Art of Nalanda: Development of Buddhist Sculpture, A.D. 600–1200*, New Delhi: Munshiram Manoharlal, 1995
Sankalia, Hasmukhlal Dhirajlal, *The University of Nalanda*, Madras: n.p., 1934; 2nd edition, Delhi: Oriental Publishers, 1972
Stewart, Mary L., *Nalanda Mahavihara: A Study of an Indian Pala Period Buddhist Site and British Historical Archaeology, 1861–1938*, Oxford: BAR, 1989

Nara, Japan

The capital of the Japanese state from 710 to 784, Nara (old Heijō) city, is located in the north of Nara prefecture on the northern edge of the Nara basin. Originally Yamato province, the basin was the heartland of Japanese culture from well before the introduction of Buddhism in the middle of the sixth century A.D. to the transfer of the capital to Heian (Kyoto) in 794. The ideographs used then, meaning "level castle" and usually pronounced "Heijō," in fact were probably first pronounced "Nara." The currently used ideographs for "Nara" have no real meaning and were adopted merely for their phonetic value.

Nara was designed to conform to Chinese geomantic specifications and laid out like the Chinese capital cities on a grid plan aligned with the cardinal directions. The Nara hills lie on the north, the Kasuga and Wakakusa mountains on the east, and Mount Ikoma on the west. The Saho and Akishino Rivers flow through the east and west sides of the city, the two meeting just to its south.

The city was larger than its predecessor, Fujiwara, which had been used for only 16 years. Based on the measurement unit for land allotments at the time, *chō* (about 400 feet), it was 36 *chō* north to south by 32 *chō* east to west (about 3 by 2.7 miles), or nine by eight large blocks, each block then subdivided into 16 *tsubo* (about 100 by 100 feet). The last was the square given to a commoner's family, whereas upper officials received up to four subblocks, or land quite large enough to constitute an estate with servants' quarters and substantial vegetable gardens.

In the north lay a huge enclosure for the palace occupying about four large blocks where, toward the end of the century, two palaces might have stood side by side, the west one for the emperor and the east one for the crown prince. More excavations will make the relationship clearer. The Sujaku (Red Bird) Gate was the main entrance to the city, and its wide street led directly north to the palace complex. Toward the south were the east and west markets. The west half of the city was called Ukyō (right capital) and the east half Sakyō (left capital), named as seen by the emperor sitting on his throne. Such a city existed exclusively as a support system for the palace and court, its plan designed to further hierarchical management and population control. Its successful operation depended on the steady collection of taxes in foods and raw materials and the conversion of the latter to useful commodities in city or palace workshops.

Over time the population – which probably never exceeded 100,000 – gravitated toward the better water supplies in the east. Large western areas reverted to rice fields, which, until the post–World War II pressures on space, left much land available for archaeology. Investigations of the palace area started in 1928, but not until 1953 were continuous excavations begun, much attention being devoted to the problems of palace construction and reconstruction. Quantities of artifacts of all kinds include thousands of discarded inscribed wooden tallies (*mokkan*), many of which are dated, recording primarily tax receipts. These have provided valuable information on the support system, trade network, and the production of goods.

Temples had been classified by the government for control and support into three categories: *kan-ji* (official temples), which received full government subsidies; *uji-dera* (clan, house, or aristocratic family temples); and *chishiki-dera* (clergy-built temples or temples erected by a related family). Initially the government reserved the right to appoint administrators for all of them, but for economic reasons this was limited in 680 to official temples only, a move that opened the way for the temples to become independent, wealthy, and politically powerful entities.

Niō (Door Guardian), entrance gate, Hōryūji temple, Nara, Japan, clay, over life size, early eighth century, Hakuhō (Nara) period.
Photo courtesy of Marylin M. Rhie

When Nara was built, it was planned that the major existing temples associated with the Fujiwara capital would be moved up. Dismantling and rebuilding was not an unusual procedure. New sets of roof tiles were usually necessary. The Yakushi-ji and Daikandai-ji (called Daian-ji in Heijō) were given prominent locations similar to what they had enjoyed at Fujiwara. The Asuka-dera was transferred around 718 and called Gankō-ji. The Fujiwara family temple, Kōfuku-ji, was moved in from Yamashina near Lake Biwa. The consort of Emperor Shōmu (r. 724–749) built the Kairyō-ji in 731, the Shin-yakushi-ji from 747, and the Hokke-ji around 750, the last to be the headquarters of the country's provincial nunneries and a place where she could become a nun and retire. Emperor Shōmu added extra city blocks in the northeast and built the vast Tōdai-ji, its Daibutsuden – still said to be the world's largest wooden building, but now only two-thirds its original size – erected to house the immense bronze Vairocana (J. Roshana) Buddha (Daibutsu) that he was having cast. After several years spent solving technical problems, the "eye-opening" ceremony for the 52-foot-high statue was held in 752 in the huge temple courtyard in the presence of the ailing emperor and 10,000 attendants.

Other monumental Buddhist establishments were the Saidai-ji, started by the empress in 765, and the Akishino-dera, begun by Emperor Konin (r. 770–781) in 780. These and the other imperial temples were grand but extravagant two-pagoda complexes, erected for one of three reasons: supplication to Buddhist deities to secure recovery from a sickness, the peaceful rest of an ancestor's soul, or national protection. A document from 720 speaks of 48 temples in the Heijō capital. Because all of these needed full complements of Buddhist images and didactic materials, palace and temple workshops, following Chinese models, produced some of the finest arts seen in Japan, excelling in both technique and style.

To Shōmu the city's politics were unmanageable and even threatening, and he moved the capital to Kuni in 740, causing much dislocation. He tried Naniwa (Osaka) in 743, but within two years the buildings were being dismantled and hauled back to Nara. He also tried Shigaraki (Shiga prefecture). The economy never quite recovered from such prodigal ways and slowly deteriorated through the latter part of the century. Shōmu is also remembered for an exotic collection of art assembled from international sources that forms the nucleus of the material in the Shōsō-in, the storehouse in the precincts of the Tōdai-ji.

Shōmu ordered all 66 provinces each to construct a provincial monastery and nunnery (*kokubun-ji* and *kokubunni-ji*) in 741, just three years after a smallpox plague had decimated the country. They were to be staffed by 20 monks and 10 nuns each and were to read and keep ten copies of the *Konkōmyō-saishō-ō-kyō* (*Suvarna-prabhasa-sūtra*, "State-Protecting Sūtra") in their pagodas. This effort by the state to impose Buddhist practices on rural areas met with considerable hostility. At one point the clerics were told to stay indoors for their own safety, and by the ninth century many of these establishments had disappeared as functioning religious institutions due to the arson of peasant uprisings against symbols of an oppressive government.

Nara remained a special goal of pilgrims after the capital was moved in 794 to Heian (Kyoto), and many of its large temples were reasonably intact until 1180, at the start of the war that saw the disintegration of the Fujiwara regime. In later centuries small businesses, especially textile crafts, earned a good reputation for the city. Civil strife, pernicious arson, and natural fires in medieval centuries took their toll, but enough of the old culture survived to make Nara a remarkable repository of early Buddhist art. Over 14 million pilgrims and tourists visit each year, and greater Nara city, with a population of about 350,000, is a thriving bedtown area for people working in Osaka.

J. Edward Kidder, Jr.

See also Architecture: Structural Monasteries in East Asia; Buddhist Schools/Traditions: Japan; China; Fujii, Nichidatsu (Nittatsu); Kyoto, Japan; Nation-Building and Japanese Buddhism; Patrons, Buddhist: Japan; Pilgrimages, Buddhist; Temple, Buddhist; Visual Arts, Buddhist: Japan; Warrior Monks: Buddhist

Further Reading

Farris, William, *Sacred Texts and Buried Treasures: Issues in the Historical Archaeology of Ancient Japan*, Honolulu: University of Hawaii Press, 1998

Kidder, J. Edward, *Early Buddhist Japan*, London: Thames and Hudson, 1972

Tsuboi, Kiyotari, and Migaku Tanaka, *The Historic City of Nara: An Archaeological Approach*, translated by David Hughes and Gina Barnes, Paris and Tokyo: Centre for East Asian Cultural Studies/UNESCO, 1991

Wheatley, Paul, and Thomas See, *From Court to Capital: A Tentative Interpretation of the Origins of the Japanese Urban Tradition*, Chicago: University of Chicago Press, 1978

Nation-Building and Japanese Buddhism

From its introduction to Japan in the mid–sixth century through the early modern period (1600–1867), Buddhist monasticism was closely associated with the nascent state, whether led by the imperial family or by shogunal regimes. Although Buddhism was attacked by the Meiji imperial regime (1868–1912) as part of its efforts to construct a modern nation-state based on Shintō and Confucian doctrines, Buddhist monasticism had been the most politically active and theoretically articulate religious institution during successive stages of premodern nation building in Japan.

Buddhism did not enter Japan because of the soteriological efforts of missionaries intent on spreading the religion. Rather the king of Paekche, one of three Korean kingdoms contending for supremacy on the peninsula, sent Buddhist texts, monks, artists, and artisans as part of his effort to forge an alliance with the so-called Yamato court ruling the central area of Honshu, Japan. Although nothing came of the alliance with Paekche, Buddhism did develop exceptionally close ties with the Yamato court. Of the various writings that penetrated ancient Japan, the *Konkō myō saishō ō gyō* (Sūtra of the Sovereign Kings of the Golden Light) was the most politically oriented. In part it affirmed that any ruler who promoted Buddhism, doctrinally and institutionally, would be protected by heavenly kings who pledged to provide peace and prosperity for the secular realm otherwise embracing Buddhism.

Seeking to reap such rewards, the Yamato court as led by Prince Shōtoku (573–621) supposedly sponsored construction of a major Buddhist monastery, the Shitennōji, dedicated to the worship of the heavenly kings. In the seventh century Emperor Temmu justified his seizure of the throne in 672 by appeal to a Buddhist theory of divine right similar to that in the *Konkō myō saishō ō gyō*, thus legitimizing his rule by appeal to his alleged support of the religion and its monasteries. In the mid–eighth century Emperor Shōmu had the Tōdai temple constructed in the new imperial capital, Nara, along with an enormous bronze statue of the universal Buddha as its central icon. Shōmu further decreed that a pagoda, a guardian temple, and an atonement nunnery be built in each provincial capital. Thus, in search of the earthly benefits promised by way of celestial agency in the *Konkō myō saishō ō gyō*, Japanese rulers early on promoted Buddhist icons, architecture, and monasticism throughout their realm. In doing so they also extended their political power under a legitimizing, religious guise.

One significant exception to the positive role of Buddhist monasticism for state building in the Nara period (710–784) was the so-called Dōkyō incident, which involved the Buddhist monk Dōkyō and the Empress Shōtoku (r. 764–770). Traditional accounts suggest that Dōkyō romanced the empress into elevating him into the upper echelons of religious and political power. Critics suspected that Dōkyō intended to supplant the imperial state with a Buddhist theocracy, one that would have accorded monastics sovereign power. On Empress Shōtoku's death Dōkyō fell abruptly. The imperial family soon moved its capital away from Nara, which had become a stronghold of Buddhist monasticism and was thus viewed as a serious threat to the integrity of the imperial regime. Ultimately the capital was relocated in Heian, or modern Kyoto. Although chosen in part because of its lack of entrenched and politically ambitious monasteries, Heian soon became the center of a new form of Buddhist monasticism, that of the Tendai sect, which promptly became closely associated with the imperial state.

During the Heian period (794–1185), the Tendai writings of Saichō (768–822) directly linked monastic training to the fate of the emerging imperial state. In writings such as *Chingo kokka* (Preserving the Realm) and *Shugo kokkai shō* (Commentary on the Sūtra for Protection of the Realm), Saichō argued that if Buddhism were affirmed, it would serve as an aid in ruling "the Great Japanese nation" (*Dai Nippon koku*). He also admonished that if Buddhist teachings were ignored, sociopolitical chaos would ensue. Seeking to portray the Tendai monastic order as a source of national security, Saichō's *Sanga gakusei shiki* (Regulations for Students of the Mountain School) defined bodhisattvas, or Buddhist saints, in terms of monastic training and their consequent ability to serve the realm. The "nation's teachers" (*koku no shi*) were, according to Saichō, bodhisattvas capable in speech but not action. "Administrators of the nation" (*koku no yō*) were those capable in action but not speech. Bodhisattvas who ranked as "treasures of the nation" (*koku no hō*) were capable in both and because of their special talents were to remain at Tendai monasteries to train others. In significant ways Saichō envisioned the Tendai monastic order as a religious bulwark for the imperial state: he referred to Mount Hiei, the center of Tendai monasticism, as "a sanctuary defending the national realm" (*shugo kokkai no dōjō*).

In the Kamakura period (1185–1336), novel developments in Buddhist doctrine were accompanied by claims that promotion of new forms of monasticism would benefit the realm, whereas the opposite would leave it vulnerable to severe calamities. Nichiren (1222–1282), founder of the Lotus school, advanced such arguments in his *Risshō ankoku ron* (Establishing the True Doctrine to Pacify the Realm) and *Shugo kokka ron* (On the Religious Protection of the Realm). However, rather than the Lotus school successive shogunal regimes based in Kamakura and Heian favored the Rinzai Zen sect of Buddhism through support for its "five mountain" (*gozan*) system of monastic organization. In doing so these samurai regimes implicitly endorsed the earlier claims of Myōan Eisai (1141–1215) made in *Kōzen gokoku ron* (Propagation of Zen for the Defense of the Realm). There Eisai explained that patronage of Zen, doctrinally and institutionally, would enhance the realm, whereas persecution of it would invite national ruin. Despite such long-standing claims, warlords in the late 16th century, confronting chronic civil war resulting from the degeneration of the Ashikaga shogunate (1336–1573), consolidated their military control of the realm by brutally punishing any monastic orders that challenged their authority. Oda Nobunaga's (1534–1582) burning of Mount Hiei's Tendai compound exemplified this process in the struggle for political supremacy. The result was a severely weakened Buddhist presence, especially on the political scene.

Nevertheless during the Tokugawa period (1600–1867), Buddhism was promoted along with Shintō and neo-Confucianism as part of the shogunal regime's multifaceted religio-ideological efforts to legitimize itself, spiritually and politically. Perhaps the most significant role accorded Buddhist temples was that of religious registration (*terauke*) of the population. The Tokugawa regime required such registration not to guarantee Buddhist beliefs among the masses but rather as part of its efforts to eradicate Christianity from the archipelago. Again Buddhist monasticism served as an auxiliary agency facilitating state control of the population and the construction of an early modern state. Ironically during the Meiji period (1868–1912), Buddhism fell victim, doctrinally and institutionally, to systematic state persecution as the restored imperial state sought to ally itself religiously with Shintō.

JOHN ALLEN TUCKER

See also Bodhisattva; Buddhism: Inculturation; Buddhist Schools/Traditions: Japan; Chan/Zen: Japan; Critiques of Buddhist Monasticism: Confucian; Japan: History; Korea: History; Mount Hiei, Japan; Prophethood, Japanese Buddhist; Saichō; Tiantai/Tendai: Japan

Further Reading

Bellah, Robert N., *Tokugawa Religion: The Values of Pre-Industrial Japan*, Glencoe, Illinois: Free Press, 1957; as *Tokugawa Religion: The Cultural Roots of Modern Japan*, New York: Free Press, and London: Collier Macmillan, 1985

Collcutt, Martin, *Five Mountains: The Rinzai Zen Monastic Institution in Medieval Japan*, Cambridge, Massachusetts: Council on East Asian Studies, Harvard University, 1981

De Bary, William Theodore, *The Buddhist Tradition in India, China, and Japan*, New York: Modern Library, 1969

Goodwin, Janet R., *Alms and Vagabonds: Buddhist Temples and Popular Patronage in Medieval Japan*, Honolulu: University of Hawaii Press, 1994
Ketelaar, James Edward, *Of Heretics and Martyrs in Meiji Japan: Buddhism and Its Persecution*, Princeton, New Jersey: Princeton University Press, 1990
Kitagawa, Joseph M., *On Understanding Japanese Religion*, Princeton, New Jersey: Princeton University Press, 1987
Morrell, Robert E., *Early Kamakura Buddhism: A Minority Report*, Berkeley, California: Asian Humanities Press, 1987
Payne, Richard K., *Re-Visioning "Kamakura" Buddhism*, Honolulu: University of Hawaii Press, 1998
Saunders, Ernest Dale, *Buddhism in Japan*, Philadelphia: University of Pennsylvania Press, 1964
Tsunoda, Ryusaku, *Sources of the Japanese Tradition*, New York: Columbia University Press, 1958
Visser, Marinus Willem de, *Ancient Buddhism in Japan*, 2 vols., Paris: Geuher, 1928

Nembutsu

The term *nembutsu* (Chinese; *nian fo*) refers to several practices oriented toward Amitābha, the buddha of the Western Pure Land. The ambiguity of the first of the two Chinese characters (*nem*) has served to provide for several modes of practice.

First, the term means "to contemplate" and originally meant "to meditate on the image of the Buddha," contemplating all his excellent qualities. In China this was the sense in which the Tiantai (T'ien-t'ai) school understood the practice. This school's "constantly walking samādhi" involved circumambulating an image of Amitābha for 90 days, keeping an eidetic image of the Buddha in the mind at all times until he actually appeared.

Second, the term also means "to recite aloud," and this reading gave rise to the practice of calling the Buddha's name, either orally or mentally. This is the sense in which the practice is understood by the Pure Land traditions of China, Japan, and Korea.

Within the meaning of *nembutsu* as mental or oral invocation are two more subdivisions related to the purpose of one's practice. In the first, one recites the name of the Buddha to purify and concentrate one's mind and to create links to the Buddha and his Pure Land to ensure rebirth there after one dies. When this is the purpose, one practices constantly and vigorously.

This is the dominant conception of *nembutsu* practice in Chinese Pure Land Buddhism. Most authors in this tradition emphasize the need for constant practice for two reasons. First, and most important, one does not know when one is going to die, and if the mind is not set on the Buddha at that moment, one will not attain rebirth in the Pure Land. Second, constant practice reinforces the mental habit of maintaining one's mindfulness of the Buddha, making it more likely that one will be in tune with the Pure Land at the critical moment.

The practices outlined here are based on the notion of "self-power" (Chinese, *zi li*; Japanese, *jiriki*), in which the practitioner works to achieve certain results. The second way of looking at oral and mental invocation is in terms of "other-power" (Chinese, *ta li*; Japanese, *tariki*). This idea is based on a set of vows undertaken by the Buddha Amitābha prior to his attaining Buddhahood. A passage from the Longer Sukhāvatīvyūha Sūtra reads, "If, when I attain Buddhahood, sentient beings in the lands of the ten directions who . . . desire to be born in my land, and call my name even ten times should not be born there, may I not attain perfect Enlightenment." Because he did indeed become a buddha, this vow must have been fulfilled, meaning that practitioners, having little confidence in their own abilities, can call on the Buddha's name and attain rebirth in the Pure Land.

Although the Chinese tradition acknowledges this understanding of *nembutsu* as necessary for some, it still maintains that the practitioner should work toward rebirth in the Pure Land to the best of his or her abilities. By contrast, the Japanese tradition emphasizes the believer's powerlessness to effect his or her own liberation and sees practice entirely in terms of invoking Amitābha's name in dependence on "other-power."

CHARLES B. JONES

See also Buddhist Schools/Traditions: China; Buddhist Schools/Traditions: Japan; Chan/Zen: Japan; China; Ennin; Hōnen; Ippen; Japan: History; Kyoto, Japan; Mantras; Prayer: Buddhist Perspectives; Pure Land Buddhism; Rennyo; Shinran; Tiantai/Tendai: Japan

Further Reading

Foard, James, Michael Solomon, and Richard K. Payne, editors, *The Pure Land Tradition: History and Development*, Berkeley: Regents of the University of California, 1996
Gómez, Luis O., translator, *The Land of Bliss: The Paradise of the Buddha of Measureless Light: Sanskrit and Chinese Versions of the Sukhavativyuha Sutras*, Honolulu: University of Hawaii Press, 1996
Hirota, Dennis, translator, *No Abode: The Record of Ippen*, Kyoto, Japan, and San Francisco: Ryukoku University, 1986; revised edition, Honolulu: University of Hawaii Press, 1997
Pas, Julian, *Visions of Sukhavati: Shan-tao's Commentary on the Kuan Wu-liang Shou-fo Ching*, Albany: State University of New York Press, 1995
Tanaka, Kenneth K., *The Dawn of Chinese Pure Land Buddhist Doctrine: Ching-ying Hui-yuan's Commentary on the Visualization Sutra*, Albany: State University of New York Press, 1990
Unno, Taitetsu, translator, *Tannisho: A Shin Buddhist Classic*, Honolulu, Hawaii: Buddhist Study Center Press, 1984

Nepal: History

Until 1769, when the modern state adopted "Nepal" to name its newly unified territory roughly 100 miles wide spanning 500 miles of the central Himalayan region, the name referred to the Kathmandu Valley alone. Because little historical information is available about the other regions, this article focuses mainly on the early history of monasticism in the premodern Kathmandu Valley and sketches the rise of Tibetan monasticism in the mid-montane and highland regions that fall within the modern state.

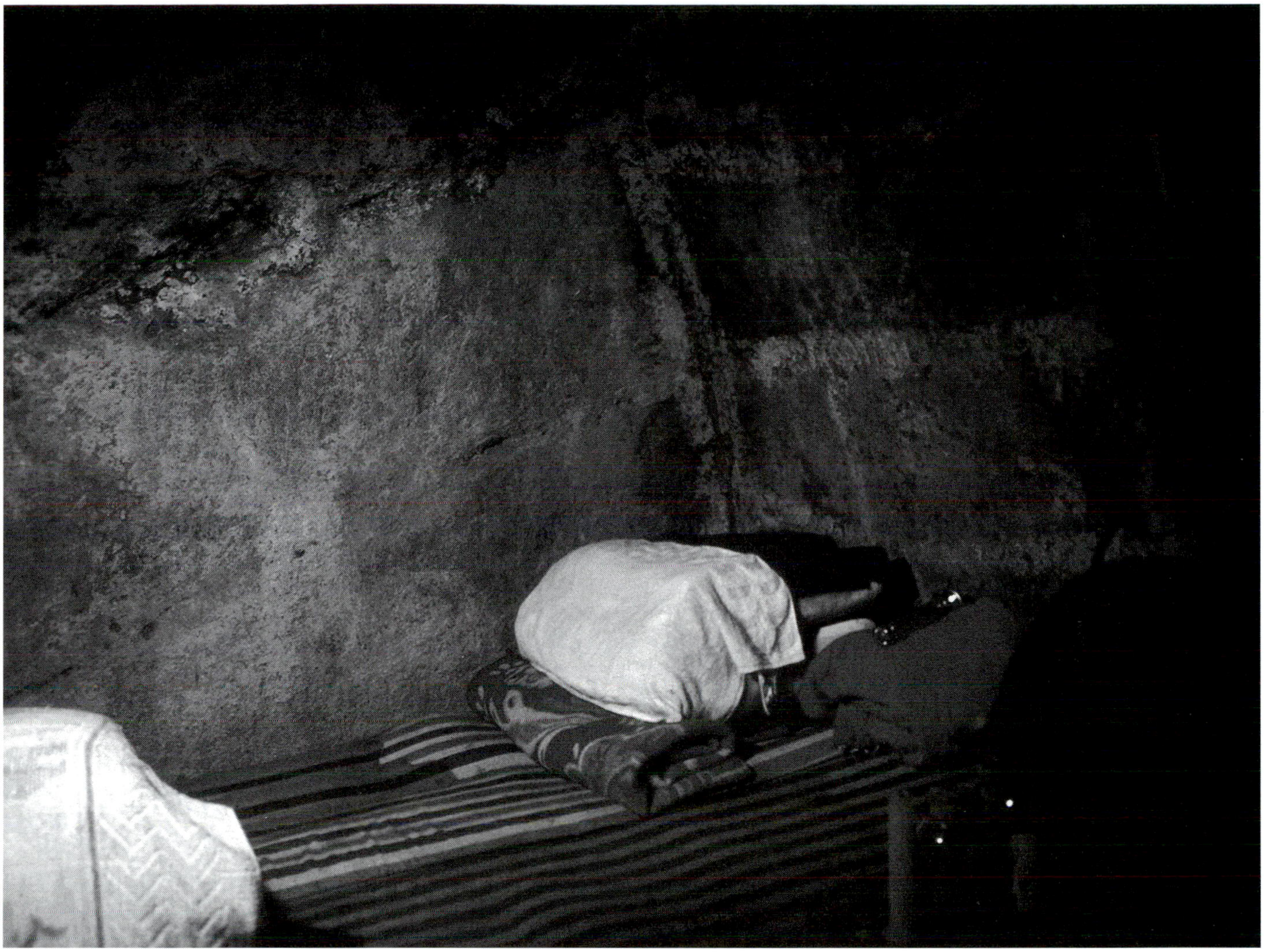

Monks' cell, interior of a rock-cut cave, Khaḍgayoginī Shrine Complex, near Gum Bahal, Nepal. The shrine (second century B.C.) was reconstructed after a 1934 earthquake.
Photo courtesy of John C. Huntington, the Huntington Archive

Kathmandu Valley

Like the Himalayan region overall, the valley comprising early Nepal was a frontier zone, absorbing and interpreting Indic cultural influences from the south and, later, from Tibetan cultural regions to the north. The earliest records of the Nepal Valley are Sanskrit inscriptions by kings of a ruling dynasty that adopted the name Licchavi. These indicate Hindu monastic institutions existing alongside Buddhist monastic traditions, a harmonious relationship existing up to the present day and confirmed by the Chinese pilgrim Hsüan-tsang around 640.

Hindu Monasteries (464–1750)

The earliest epigraph from Nepal is from the Changu Narayan temple, where in 464 a King Manadeva built a hilltop temple dedicated to Viṣṇu. Inscriptions also mention the *mandali*, a Śaivite institution for Hindu monks who performed the daily rituals for Śiva shrines while also assuming the secular management of specific settlements, mainly collecting taxes and ensuring the performance of corvée labor. Later texts assert that the great Hindu philosopher and monastic founder Śaṅkarācārya (d. 718) came to the valley to undermine Buddhism, but no early records that document this visit exist, nor did monastic institutions in the valley become part of monastic order he founded.

By the Malla era (1382–1769), records refer to Hindu monasteries as *maṭha*s. Most retain their autonomy and the responsibility for collecting corvée labor and taxes from their tenants. One especially significant activity in these institutions was manuscript copying, as monastic libraries in the Kathmandu Valley became repositories for thousands of Sanskrit texts, some of which did not survive elsewhere in the Indian subcontinent. Hindu monks and pandits in the valley were also active in making vernacular redactions of the classic Sanskritic epics, ritual texts, and tantras originating from India.

One sectarian Hindu group with a tantric identity became especially influential in the early Malla era: the Nātha sect, tracing its origins to the teachers Gorakṣa and Matsyendranāth (who

Buddhist nun in front of rock-cut cave, Khaḍgayoginī Shrine Complex, near Gum Bahal, Nepal. A reconstruction following the 1934 earthquake.
Photo courtesy of John C. Huntington, the Huntington Archive

lived around 1200). Hindu monks following their tradition, called Kāṇphaṭa yogins, later developed a following among the Newar kings, who donated city rest houses to them. (The most famous such building is the Kāstamandapa, the immense building from which the name "Kathmandu" originates.) Although their descendants became householders and assimilated into the local society, Kāṇphaṭa monasteries still exist in Pharping and in the precincts of the Paśupatinātha temple complex. Other Hindu monasteries established in the valley near this same temple are the Śaivite Paśupata *maṭhas*.

Buddhist Monasticism (500–1769)

The Licchavi inscriptions also reveal a strong and clear connection linking Nepal to the ancient Buddhist monastic traditions and patronage originating across the Gangetic plain. Among more than 200 recorded inscriptions, there are references to monks and nuns who as members of over a dozen discrete *saṅghas* (monastic communities sharing common residence) reside in landowning *vihāras* (monasteries) and enjoy support given by prominent local merchants and caravan leaders. (The most mentioned *saṅgha* is that of the Mahāsamghikas.)

These early monasteries were centers of a dominantly Mahāyāna culture, with the inscriptions providing only a few hints of Vajrayāna practice. Monastic precincts reveal verses of praise addressed toŚākyamuni and other Buddhas as well as shrines to the celestial bodhisattvas Mañjuśrī, Vajrapani, Samantabhadra, and most frequently Arya Avalokiteśvara. Unusual for Buddhist monasticism elsewhere, however, was the custom of monks in ancient Nepal's monasteries (e.g., the Hindu *mandali*s) being responsible for the maintenance of law and civic order in settlements built on lands donated to them.

By the early Malla era, the valley had become an important regional center active in propagating Mahāyāna Buddhism. Nepalese monks developed a highly ritualized Buddhist culture among the Newars whose life cycle rites, Mahāyāna festivals, and temple ritualism reached high levels of articulation. It was Vajrayāna Buddhism and tantric initiation that assumed the highest position in local understanding. Monastic architecture reflects this development: in the large courtyards that define the monastic space, the shrines facing the entrance have on the ground floor an image of Śākyamuni, but on the first floor above is the *āgama*, a shrine with a Vajrayāna deity, with access limited to those with a tantric initiation.

By the later Malla era (1425–1769), when Hindu shrines and law were in the ascendancy, Newar Buddhism underwent many changes and assumed roughly the form still extant today. This era was one marked by the building of many new *vihāras*, but there was also a domestication of *saṅgha* as monks became householders. These Newar "householder monks" called themselves *Bare* and adopted the caste names *sākyabhikṣus* and *vajrācāryas*. Many of the monasteries, especially in Patan, still bear the name of their founding patrons, some dating back to the early Malla period. Local Buddhist monks, like Hindu monks, were especially active in manuscript copying; Buddhist monastic libraries became by the modern era a vast repository of Sanskrit texts.

By the early Malla era and in the following centuries, Tibetan monks came to acquire from Newar masters tantric initiations, ritual practices, and texts – traditions that they conveyed up to the highlands. Some Tibetan monks also established in the valley many branch monasteries affiliated with the main Tibetan schools, the first sited around the monumental stūpas at Svayambhū and Bauddha.

Tibetan Monasticism across the Himalayan Highlands

Numerous Tibetan Buddhist texts recount the establishment of Buddhism on the Tibetan plateau as the result of great Indian sages coming up through the Nepal Himalayas with stories of their subduing demons and establishing communities of devotees. Although the history of these first Himalayan monasteries remains obscure, it is certain that some were established by the great saints Padmasambhava (active c. 750), Atiśa (982–1057), and Marpa (1012–1096).

Maṇḍala initiation ceremony (Dharmadattu Vagiśvari), Svayambhū Mahācaitya, Kathmandu, Nepal.
Photo courtesy of John C. Huntington, the Huntington Archive

Once Buddhism was firmly established in central Tibet as a result of its second introduction (after 1000), the northernmost settlements of current Nepal became sites where monasteries were founded by most major schools of Tibetan Buddhism. These areas include Humla in the far west as well as (from west to east) Dolpo, Lo-Mustang, Nyeshang, Nupri, Langtang, Helambu, Solu-Khumbu, and Walung. Local boys interested in training to become monks would travel to central Tibet and return to maintain local institutions that typically sheltered, at most, only a dozen or so inmates and whose main occupation was ritual service. This same pattern occurred for the Bön faith in a few of these regions.

Finally, among the peoples speaking the Tibeto-Burman language living in the midhills (whose villages are typically lower than 9,000 feet) – Magars, Gurungs, Tamangs, and Sherpas – there was a "second tier" of connection with the monastic networks of the Tibetan Buddhist world. Many of these peoples followed the Nyingma school and relied on householder lamas to perform Buddhist rituals for their villages. To train for this service, young men typically lived for several years as apprentices in the regional highland monasteries. They returned to marry and maintain shrines established as their family's own property. Thus, most "Buddhist monasteries" among Tibeto-Burman peoples were (and are) family shrine-residences, and sons usually continue to follow their fathers as the local Buddhist ritualists.

Although the Hindu state of Nepal (1769 to present) did not favor Buddhism and tried to have Buddhists conform to brahmanic laws, the faith of the peoples endured, as did these family-based monasteries. In recent years the strength of Buddhist identity held together by these institutions among the Tibeto-Burman groups has become the basis of post-1990 ethnic nationalism directed against the high caste-dominated Hindu state.

Todd T. Lewis

See also Bön Monasticism; Kathmandu Valley, Nepal; Ladakh, India; Libraries: Buddhist; Mahāyāna; Mount Meru; Nepal: Sites; Padmasambhava; Stūpa; Tibetan Lineages: Nyingma; Vajrayāna Buddhism in Nepal; Visual Arts, Buddhist: Nepal

Further Reading

Dowman, Keith, "A Buddhist Guide to the Power Places of the Kathmandu Valley," *Kailash* 8:3–4 (1982)

Lewis, Todd T., "Newars and Tibetans in the Kathmandu Valley: Ethnic Boundaries and Religious History," *Journal of Asian and African Studies* 38 (1989)

Lewis, Todd T., and Theodore Riccardi, Jr., *The Himalayas: A Syllabus of the Region's History, Anthropology, and Religion* (Occasional Paper, Association for Asian Studies), Ann Arbor, Michigan: Association for Asian Studies, 1995

Riccardi, Theodore, Jr., "Buddhism in Ancient and Early Medieval Nepal," in *Studies in History of Buddhism: Papers Presented at the International Conference on the History of Buddhism at the University of Wisconsin, Madison, WIS, USA, August 19–21, 1976*, edited by A.K. Narain, New Delhi: B.R. Publishing, 1980

Slusser, Mary S., *Nepal Mandala: A Cultural Study of the Kathmandu Valley*, 2 vols., Princeton, New Jersey: Princeton University Press, 1980

Nepal: Sites

Hindu Maṭhas *and Ashrams*

In the Newar settlements today in Kathmandu Valley, 35 *maṭha*s established in the Malla era are still extant. Thirteen are in the mainly Hindu city Bhaktapur, most in the eastern section of the old town; Patan has six, and the remainder are isolated in scattered settlements. As monasteries most are defunct as institutions promoting yoga, meditation, and textual study. The *maṭha* leaders, still designated by the Sanskrit title Mahant, are in most cases householders who through their seniority are heads of extended families who claim ownership of the buildings. Their religious roles are confined to maintaining rituals to the deities housed within their compounds.

These Newar *maṭha*s are large houses built around a courtyard, all containing a shrine complex that houses images of Śiva, Viṣṇu, and so on and some of which differ from secular houses only by the elaborate wood carvings that embellish windows and doorways with religious scenes. As with the Buddhist monasteries, some of these buildings still display some of the finest wood carving in Asia. The most successful *maṭha*s expanded to connect several courtyards, and some had multiple shrines, libraries, and rooms decorated with religious paintings illustrating Hindu stories.

Other Hindu monasteries in Nepal are not confined to the Newar community. In the Kathmandu Valley there are a number of the Śaivite Paśupata *maṭha*s. Today they are found in Mrigasthali near the Paśupati temple complex, near Balaju Park, and in both Kathmandu and Patan. These are allied with other institutions in India, serving as hostels for sannyasins of this sect, most of whom are Indians who come on pilgrimage from the plains.

Still other Hindu institutions, most modest in scale, are found outside the Kathmandu Valley. Some were founded by the state to promote Sanskrit study, such as those in Gorkha and Dingla. Others were created mainly to assist Hindu pilgrims from India and Nepal, such as those in Janakpur, Ridi, and Muktinath. There is nothing distinctive in architecture or function to differentiate these Nepalese institutions from those in India.

Amogasiddhi Pūjā, Svayambhū Stūpa, Nepal.
Photo courtesy of John C. Huntington, the Huntington Archive

Buddhist Monasteries

1. Tibetan Buddhism

Across the modern state are Tibetan monasteries (called *gombas*). These include major institutions linked to the large schools located in the highlands of the formerly independent Tibet, as found in the Kathmandu Valley. There are important regional monasteries in Humla, Mustang, Manang, Langtang, Helambu, Solu-Khumbu, and Walung. Finally, there are the village monasteries controlled by families who serve as local Buddhist ritualists among the Tibeto-Burman peoples, such as the Magars, Tamangs, Gurungs, and Sherpas.

Of recent importance has been the migration of refugees into areas that were formerly on the far periphery of the Tibetan Buddhist monastic network. In scattered sites across the midmontane region, refugee lamas have established celibate institutions

Sat Pūjā, Svayambhū Stūpa, Nepal.
Photo courtesy of John C. Huntington, the Huntington Archive

where before only a family shrine-ritualist tradition had been found.

The Kathmandu Valley has been especially affected by this diaspora of Tibetan teachers, making it now one of the most important centers of Tibetan Buddhism in the world. Every major school is found there, as refugees, migrants from the Tibeto-Burman ethnic groups, and westerners have converged to create many new institutions. Except for the use of local building materials, these institutions are no different from those of the highlands in their layout, religious purpose, iconography, or decoration.

2. Newar Buddhism

Buddhism has been an important religion among the Newars of the Kathmandu Valley dating back to the Licchavi period (464–900). Since the Malla era the Newar adaptation of Buddhist monasticism has, like the Nyingma school of Tibet, sanctioned a householder monastic community. The Newar *saṅgha* became a two-division caste (*sākyabhikṣu* and *vajrācārya*) that serves the community's ritual needs while dwelling in monasteries that have become family property. Although the Shah era (1769 to the present) has seen the decline of Newar Buddhism, including the decline of the monasteries as buildings and institutions, much has been preserved in monastic architecture, texts, and cultural observances. For example, in Kathmandu's Itum Bāhā, one can still see the ritual of marking time by rapping on a wooden gong, a monastic custom begun over 2,000 years ago in ancient India.

The typical Newar *bāhā* is arrayed around a courtyard. The main entrance, often ornamented by a tympanum, usually has small shrines to the guardians Ganesh and Mahākāla flanking the passageway leading into the main courtyard. Opposite the entrance is the main shrine building. On the ground floor is the *kwapa dyah*, usually Śākyamuni Buddha, flanked by images of his two great human disciples, Moggallāna and Sāriputra. In the shrine above, reached by stairs, is the *āgama*, the tantric shrine that is opened only to adults who have received the appropriate *vajrayāna* initiation. There is often elaborate wood carving to adorn the windows and door, including another tympanum. Each member of the *saṅgha* of this *bāhā* has to serve as the shrine attendant and do the morning rituals inside and around the stūpas usually located in the *bāhā* courtyard.

3. Extra-Valley Newar Buddhism in the Shah Era

One of the most important changes that Shah rule brought to the midhill regions of the country was the expansion of trade, and this was commonly in the hands of Newars who migrated to trade towns. With them went their culture, preeminently Buddhist. Thus, in towns such as (from east to west) Daran, Dhankuta, Chainpur, Bhojpur, Dolakha, Trisuli, Bandipur, Pokhara, Palpa, and Baglung, Newar Buddhists built *bāhā*s as branch institutions of those in their home cities.

4. Theravāda Buddhism

Since midcentury Newars disenchanted with their form of Mahāyāna monasticism have supported the establishment of Theravāda Buddhist reform institutions in the Kathmandu Valley. Monks from Sri Lanka, nuns from Burma, and lay teachers from India (Goenka) have founded institutions dedicated to the revival of Buddhism based on textual study, popular preaching, and lay meditation. Kathmandu and Svayambhū hill have been at the center of this movement, but with monasteries and meditation centers found in most major towns.

5. Lumbinī

Since 1956 both Nepalese and international efforts have sought the development of this site in southern Nepal, which archaeological remains have identified as the venue long recognized by Buddhists as the site of Śākyamuni Buddha's birth. Since 1985 many *saṅgha*s from Buddhist countries around the world have established monasteries around the site.

Monasteries to Visit

Kathmandu City and Environs

Newar Buddhism: Chusya Bāhā, Jana Bāhā, Tha Bāhi (Thamel); Theravāda Buddhism: Dharmakīrti Vihāra in the Kathisimbhū compound, Anandakuti Vihāra at Svayambhū; Tibetan Buddhism: Sikkimese Gomba at Svayambhū; Bauddha; Nagi Gomba

East face, Svayambhū Stūpa, Nepal. The ancient stūpa was reconstructed following the 1934 earthquake.
Photo courtesy of John C. Huntington, the Huntington Archive

Kirtipur: Thai Theravāda Vihāra
Patan: Oku Bāhā and Kwa Bāhā
Bhaktapur: Pujāri Maṭha and Kutu Maṭha

Tibetan Buddhist Monasteries outside the Kathmandu Valley
Tengboche in Khumbu; Shey Gomba, Shimen, Karang in Dolpo; Lo-Gekar and Gomba-K'ang in Mustang

TODD T. LEWIS

See also Buddhist Schools/Traditions: Tibet; Kathmandu Valley, Nepal; Nepal: History; Tibet: History; Vajrayāna Buddhism in Nepal; Visual Arts, Buddhist: Nepal

Further Reading

Boullier, Véronique, "The Sannyasi Monasteries of Patan: A Brief Survey," *European Bulletin of Himalayan Research* 15–16 (1998–1999)

Hutt, Michael, *Nepal: A Guide to the Art and Architecture of the Kathmandu Valley*, Gartmore: Kiscadale, 1994; Boston: Shambhala, 1995

Lewis, Todd T., and Daya Ratna Shakya, "Contributions to the History of Nepal: Eastern Newar Diaspora Settlements," *Contributions to Nepalese Studies* 15:1 (1988)

Locke, John K., *Buddhist Monasteries of Nepal: A Survey of the Bahas and Bahis of the Kathmandu Valley*, Kathmandu: Sahayogi Press, 1985

Locke, John K., "The Vajrayana Buddhism in the Kathmandu Valley," in *The Buddhist Heritage of Nepal: Souvenir of the 15th General Conference of the World Fellowship of Buddhists, Kathmandu, Nepal, 27 November–2nd December 1986*, Kathmandu: Souvenir Committee, 15th General Conference of W.F.B., 1986

Mumford, Stanley, *Himalayan Dialogue: Tibetan Lamas and Gurung Shamans in Nepal* (New Directions in Anthropological Writing), Madison: University of Wisconsin Press, 1989

Snellgrove, David L., *Himalayan Pilgrimage: A Study of Tibetan Religion*, Oxford: Cassirer, 1961; 2nd edition as *Himalayan Pilgrimage: A Study of Tibetan Religion by a Traveller through Western Nepal*, Boulder, Colorado: Prajña Press, 1981

Nestorian Monasticism

Monasticism of the Nestorian Church, also known today as the Church of the East, is properly the monasticism practiced by those Christians who identified themselves with the dyophysite (two-natures) teachings of Nestorius (after 351–after 451) and his successors, especially Diodore of Tarsus (d. c. 390) and Theodore of Mopsuestia (c. 350–428). The Nestorians, in reaction to the Monophysite position of the complete union of the two natures of Christ, accepted only a prosopic (persona-based) unity of the two persons, rejecting the hypostatic union (total fusion); they rejected as well the epithet "Theotokos" (God bearer) in favor of "Christotokos" (Christ bearer) for Mary, the mother of Jesus. The Nestorian church is a Syrian-rite church that had its earliest roots in Antiochian theology and monastic practices. Because of their firm rejection of orthodox Byzantine theology, the Nestorians moved to the eastern regions of the empire and eventually located in the famous school of Edessa (present-day Urfa in southeastern Turkey). Gradually they moved farther east, and their foremost theology faculty was forced to flee from Edessa when Emperor Zeno (474–491) forcibly closed down the school in 489. Thus, by end of the fifth century the Nestorian Church found itself located entirely outside the Byzantine Empire and quickly became a national Persian Church under the Sassanian rulers. This was advantageous both to the Persians, who now ruled Christians who were not loyal to the Byzantine Empire, and to the Nestorians, who, at least in the beginning, enjoyed freedom to practice Christianity without persecution. The Nestorian Church later received this same recognition from the Islamic Caliph, a benefit that also ensured its continued existence.

In the mid–ninth century, Ishô'denah of Basra wrote a short account of the first beginnings of monasticism in Syria and Persia. According to this account a certain Mar Awgên, a native of Egypt and a dealer in pearls for some 25 years, entered monastic life in a Pachomian monastery. After living this lifestyle for some time, he felt the call to do monastic missionary work and, setting out with 70 disciples (the more traditional of several numbers found in the sources), entered Persian territory and set up monastic life in a cave on Mount Izla, just outside the city of Nisibis (present-day Nusaybin in southeastern Turkey). While he remained here and eventually gained numerous adherents, his disciples dispersed from there and founded numerous other monasteries in the surrounding regions. Awgên, who reportedly cultivated friendly relationships with both the Byzantine Constantine (306–337) and the Sassanian Shapur II, died around 363. This account of Ishô'denah has colored all subsequent monastic history of Persia and has only recently been corrected. More recent research shows that such rewriting of sources in order to create Byzantine roots of essentially native practices is a too common topos in Oriental sources; in this case no other trace of Ishô'denah's version of the beginnings of monasticism in Persia can be found prior to his. A careful reckoning of the monasteries that Ishô'denah enumerates demonstrates that this tradition ascribes Egyptian roots to what was probably a native Nestorian expansion, although some think that it might reflect Nestorian occupation of monasteries that had already been abandoned by the Syrian Monophysites. A more critical view of the sources shows that although the historical personages and the chronology of Ishô'denah's account are almost totally fabricated, the account nonetheless announces three important developments: the great and rapid expansion of Nestorian monasticism, its strong missionary aspect, and the chronological and hierarchical importance of Mount Izla to its monastic structure.

In actual fact the early history of Nestorian monasticism is inextricably linked with that of its new Zoroastrian neighbors. Unable to see any value in virginity or celibacy, the Sassanian rulers tried to insist that their new Christian allies adopt their own views on marriage. Many refused, but, apparently because

Nestorian parish church in Gothic style, Famagusta, Cyprus, 14th century.
Photo courtesy of Chris Schabel

of clandestine dealings of Barsauma of Nisibis with the Sassanian authorities, a certain rapprochement was reached such that later, at the Council of Acacius in 486, it was decreed that monks not only could be married but in certain cases were even forced to be. An especially important witness to Nestorian monasticism is the *Book of Governors* of Thomas of Marga, a lengthy ninth-century account of the lives of the abbots and some of the monks of the monasteries of Beth Abê (Books I–V) and of Rabban Cyprian (Book VI). Thomas himself entered the monastery, located approximately 100 miles northeast of Mosul, in 832 and soon became secretary to Patriarch Abraham, who in turn appointed Thomas bishop of Marga. His account begins with the deplorable state of these early monasteries: many monks kept their wives and children in their cells. Apparently the monasteries were of such size or had such lack of communal contact that this cohabitation and procreation often passed unknown to the abbot. The first attempts at dealing with this new issue seem to have come from such men as Abdâ and his disciples, especially Ahai and Abdishô, in the late fourth and early fifth centuries. The latter tried to convince others, by his own example of not taking a wife, that celibacy was an integral element of monastic life. These three, along with certain other like-minded monks, expended great energy and managed to establish a few celibate monasteries throughout Persia. However, the fundamental call to reform was sounded by Abraham of Kashkar (c. 500–588), known as "the Great" for his singularly important role in Nestorian monasticism. Abraham was trained in the school of Nisibis and for a short time practiced the monastic life among the monks of Scetis. Abraham returned to his native land and engaged in missionary work among the Arabs in al-Hira, after which he retired to a cave on Mount Izla and eventually constructed a monastery there to accommodate the large number of disciples who came to him. It was because of Abraham's influence that Mount Izla became a monastery of such central importance for Nestorians: Thomas of Marga says that "it is for monks what Athens was for philosophers." Abraham then set about reforming monastic life among the Nestorians. His reforms, along with the further reforms by his successor Dadishô, were so successful that they stimulated not only an upsurge of hundreds of new monasteries but increases of four- and fivefold in membership of already existing monasteries. Monks were again bound to practice celibacy, and this led to the expulsion of numerous monks. Now every monk had to take an oath that he would profess the teachings of the three great Nestorian doctors: Nestorius, Diodore of Tarsus, and Theodore of Mopsuestia. Strong measures were instituted to ensure obedience to the superior, and, perhaps most significant, no one was admitted into a monastery who could not demonstrate an ability to read. These rules for monks also provide a concrete glimpse into the daily life of a Nestorian monk. In addition to the obligatory prayer and fasting, Nestorian monasticism distinguished itself for its production of manuscripts and for its concentration on biblical study. These two traits, education and proselytism, were essential characteristics of Nestorian monasticism.

It was also at this time that Nestorian monasticism underwent its greatest growth. Advancement was made into Khurdistan, especially by Rabban Hormizd (c. 600–c. 665) and his disciples, who set up monasteries in and around Alqosh, near Mosul, which became largely populated by many native Arabs, whose language still retains a number of Syriac words in its monastic vocabulary. Many monks continued to advance eastward. Thus, although the Nestorian center of action was in the Greater Persian Empire (modern Iraq, eastern Syria and Turkey, and western Iran), its missionary enterprises, undertaken almost entirely by the monks, reached into central Asia, Tibet, India, and China as well as into Cyprus, Manchuria, and even the islands of Java and Sumatra. The famous inscription of Sigan-Fu, erected in northwestern China in 781, is testimony to the education and the missionary zeal of the Nestorian monks.

One cannot underestimate the influence that the school of Nisibis exercised on the history of Nestorian monasticism; its impact here was no less important than its impact on the subsequent development of Nestorian theology. Its graduates became monks and helped spread the monastic life not only within Persian borders but also eastward through central Asia and even into China. Within Persia the monasteries were often the only means of gaining an education, and some of these monastic schools claimed as many as several hundred students at their height. The life of many Nestorian monks, both spiritual and intellectual, was formed in the school of Nisibis. Abbots and teachers in the other monastic schools almost always had connections to the school of Nisibis, and its students and teachers comprise the great names of the Nestorian Church. Nearly every head of the school left commentaries on most, if not all, of the books of the Bible. Unfortunately, apart from a few translations of the commentaries of Theodore of Mopsuestia and the hymnic commentaries of Narsai (d. c. 503), most have not survived. However, from the eighth and ninth centuries a number of anonymous commentaries survive, as does a *Book of Questions* on the biblical books compiled by Ishô bar Nun and another such book incorporated into Theodore bar Konai's *Book of Scholia*. In addition to these we have a complete cycle of biblical commentaries written by Isho'dad of Merw, a work that seems to represent a kind of summit of Nestorian exegesis as well as preserving a number of traditions from the lost commentaries of his predecessors. His citations from Hebrew and Greek versions and other references not only betray a very learned community but also indicate that monasteries were often equipped with both religious and pagan books. A recent scholar has estimated that at the time of Thomas of Marga, the library of the Beth Abê monastery contained nearly 1,000 manuscripts.

Nestorian monastic life was also notable for inspiring a very high level of intellectual mysticism. Faithful to the traditions of the Fathers, including Ephrem (c. 306–373) and the Byzantine mystical tradition, especially the works of Evagrius Ponticus and Pseudo-Macarius, one finds the beginnings of this development in the syntheses of Abraham of Nathpar in the sixth century and in the work of John of Apamea, or John the Solitary (early fifth century). However, in the next two centuries there is a blossoming of a distinctive Nestorian mysticism in the writings of the greatest of the Nestorian mystics: in the seventh century Sahdona, Isaac the Syrian (d. c. 700), Dadisho' of Qatar, John bar Penkayê, and Simon of Taybutheh and in the eighth century John of Dalyatha and Joseph Hazzayâ (the Seer). A number of contemporary specialists in Muslim mysticism have argued that Nestorian mystical teachings influenced certain forms of Arab mysticism, especially Sufism.

Although neither the designations nor the proponents are consistent, there was nonetheless a rather constant threefold distinction to the spiritual life, following the general lines of the Pauline threefold distinction of physical, pneumatic, and spiritual. The first stage was characterized by fear of punishment and even a physical notion of God, the second was characterized by a greater commitment to penitence and asceticism and to leave behind the world in order to do battle with one's interior passions, and the third was marked by the attaining of purity, or limpidity (Syriac, *shaphyutâ*), of heart or thoughts. Now tears became tears of joy, as the monk was now a friend of God, not a servant. This purity of heart also signified that the monk's prayer was no longer an activity but a state that allowed the soul to see the mysteries of the other world.

Although there survive hints of hermits in various spots, the dominant style of Nestorian monasticism was the cenobitic, even though the elder monks often lived in nearby caves that thus resembled the Palestinian *lavra* system. Most of the monasteries were forcibly emptied or destroyed during the Mongol occupations; the few that have survived to the present day stand as monuments to their former culture. The single Nestorian monastery that still functions today is the Monastery of Rabban Hormizd near Mosul. Alas it no longer houses Nestorian monks; instead dwelling there are monks of the Chaldean Church, as those Nestorians who united themselves to the Roman Catholic Church are known.

EDWARD G. MATHEWS, JR.

See also Evagrius Ponticus; Isaac the Syrian (Isaac of Nineveh), St.; Lavra; Macarian Homilies; Origins: Eastern Christian; Pachomius, St.; Spirituality: Eastern Christian; Syria

Further Reading

Beulay, Robert, *La Lumière sans forme: Introduction à l'étude de la mystique chrétienne syro-orientale*, Chevetogne: Éditions de Chevetogne, 1987

Brock, Sebastian P., "The Prayer of the Heart in Syriac Tradition," *Sobornost* 4 (1982)

Brock, Sebastian P., *The Syriac Fathers on Prayer and the Spiritual Life* (Cistercian Studies Series, 101), Kalamazoo, Michigan: Cistercian Publications, 1987

Budge, Ernest A. Wallis, editor and translator, *The Book of Governors: The Historia Monastica of Thomas, Bishop of Marga, A.D. 840*, 2 vols., London: Kegan Paul, Trench, Trübner, 1893

Chabot, Jean-Baptiste, editor and translator, "Le Livre de la Chasteté composé par Jésusdenah, évêque de Baçrah," *Mélanges d'archéologie et d'histoire* 16 (1896)

Fiey, Jean Maurice, *Jalons pour une histoire de l'église en Iraq* (Corpus Scriptorum Christianorum Orientalium, 310), Louvain: Peeters, 1970

Hendriks, Otto, "L'activité apostoloque du monachisme monophysite et nestorien," *Proche-Orient Chrétien* 10 (1960)

Hendriks, Otto, "La vie quotidienne du moine syrien oriental," *L'Orient Syrien* 5 (1960)

Miller, Dana, translator, *The Ascetical Homilies of Saint Isaac the Syrian*, Boston: Holy Transfiguration Monastery, 1984

Peña, Ignacio, Pascal Castellana, and Romuald Fernandez, *Les Cénobites Syriens* (Studium Biblicum Franciscanum Collectio Minor, 28), Jerusalem: Franciscan Printing, 1983

Tisserant, Eugene, "L'église nestorienne," in *Dictionnaire de théologie catholique*, volume 11, Paris: Letouzey et Ané, 1928; reprinted in Sever Pop, et al., editors, *Recueil Cardinal Eugène Tisserant "Ab Oriente et Occidente,"* Louvain: Centre International de Dialectologie Générale, 1955

Vööbus, Arthur, *History of Asceticism in the Syrian Orient I–III* (Corpus Scriptorum Christianorum Orientalium, 184, 197, 500), Louvain: Peeters, 1958, 1960, 1988

Netherlands

Although the dawn of Dutch civilization coincides with the birth of Christianity, it took another three centuries for Christianity to make itself known. Although it was the Romans who colonized the Low Countries, around the time of Christ's birth, it was Byzantine Christianity that came first to the land, traveling by way of the Danube. The Low Countries' first bishop was Byzantine Armenian, St. Servatius (Servaas), who arrived around 300 and founded the Low Countries' first monastery at Tonergren on the banks of the Maas. As bishop, Servatius attended the Council of Sardica in the Balkans in 343, siding with the majority in condemning the Arian heresy. Sometime thereafter Servatius transferred the seat of his bishopric to Maastricht to secure greater safety from the growing Germanic menace to the north. After he died in 384, he was so greatly revered throughout central Europe that he inspired churches and monasteries in Duisburg, Worms, Augsburg, Regensburg, Passau, and Salzburg. In time Servatius' monastery at Maastricht grew into a leading European center of learning.

Another 100 years passed before things settled down enough for Christianity to begin to take hold in the southern regions of the Low Countries. Clovis (Chlodwig, 481–511), founder of the kingdom of the Franks, accepted Christian baptism in 496 and with un-Christian ruthlessness set out to consolidate all Frankish lands in Gaul and the Netherlands, all the while giving the Church his support for missionary endeavors in the land. Under Clotair II (613–623) and his son Dagobert I (623–639), serious effort was made to contain the Saxons and Frisians to the north. It was during this period of treachery, deceit, and fratricide, so graphically detailed by St. Gregory of Tours, that Christianity came into its own in the southern regions of the Low Countries. Saint Amandus began to preach the gospel to the Frisians on the Scheldt, along with St. Bavon and Florbert, founding two Benedictine monasteries near Gent. After him came St. Livinus the Martyr (d. 655) and another martyr, St. Eligius (Eloi), bishop of Noyon and all of Flanders, along with the founding of monastic seminaries and new bishoprics at Cambrai, Tournai, Arras, and Thérouanne. As the Low Countries became increasingly Christianized, they became a bridge between the barbarian northlands and the civilized countries to the south, playing host to a constant flow of people. As inns were few and far between, monasteries provided hospitality, and in the exchange of ideas within the walls sowed the seeds of scholarship. Soon scholar monks from Italy and the British Isles arrived to teach local monastics and to establish libraries.

Under Dagobert I the first serious effort was made to introduce Christianity among the northern Frisians, although it was not until the time of the Carolingians that Christianity made any serious inroads. The spread of Christianity went hand in hand with the submission of the people of the Low Countries to the Franks. As the Franks moved northward, their ruthless footsteps were followed by Frankish, Anglo-Saxon, and Irish missionaries, who brought a message of love and accommodation, planting stability among an hitherto restless people. With the blessing of Pope Gregory I (590–604), heathen beliefs and sites were Christianized rather than destroyed. Pagan wells and hilltops honoring the deities of the Old Way were rededicated to Christ, thereby becoming the sites of new churches and monasteries. Wilfrid (634–709) came first, followed by his disciple Willibrord (Clement, 658–739), "The Apostle of the Frisians," who with 11 monks from Ireland (692) set about converting Friesland. At Trajectum, near the ruins of a small chapel dating from Dagobert's time, he founded the monastery and church of the Holy Savior followed by St. Martin's. During his second trip to Rome, he was named bishop of the Frisians with his see at Utrecht. Willibrord and his disciples traveled throughout the region, founding churches, monasteries, and convents, the greatest being that of Echternach in Luxembourg. Following the death of Pepin in 714, the Frisian king, Radbod destroyed the foundations that Willibrord had established. Winfrid (Wynfrith), the Anglo-Saxon known to us as St. Boniface (c. 673–754), "The Apostle to Germany," preached briefly in 716 at Trajectum and, finding little fruit, returned to Germany. On 5 June 754, over 70 years old, preaching once again among the Frisians, Winfrid was met at Dokküm by a hostile band set on plunder as he was confirming new Christians. Forbidden by him to take up arms, they were all massacred, so incensing the other Christian Frisians that they later fell on the band, now drunk and fighting among themselves, and slew them.

Others were to follow in the footsteps, including his disciple Gregory, abbot of Willibrord's monastery of the Holy Savior, who was the first to carry the gospel to the west of the Lauwers. Gregory's disciples are prominent in the ecclesiastical history of the Low Countries, including such notables as the Frisian Liudger, founder of the great monastery of Werden on the Ruhr and the first bishop of Münster. It was during this time that the realm of the Franks was consolidated under the succession to the Frankish throne of the Netherlands-born Charlemagne in 768. Later Norman raids (810, 834–837, and 880–882) brought devastation to monasteries, including those at Egmont, Maastricht, and Utrecht.

In the ninth century the Norse conquered Friesland, and the dynasty of Heriold was established. The dynasty lasted until Godfried (Godfrey) was murdered in 885. Christianity was thrown into confusion as church and monastery were pillaged by the Northmen. Although Godfried converted to Christianity in 882, he treated his Frisian subjects not much better than slaves, and throughout the land monasteries and churches continued to lie in ruin. Following his death the monastic foundations began slowly to rebuild.

From 925 until the dissolution of the German Empire in 1806, the Low Countries were part of the German Empire. In conformity with the Ottonian-Salic system, the bishops of

Utrecht and Liège in the 10th and 11th centuries found themselves endowed with secular rights and privileges, making their dioceses mini-states. As the monastic system was closely tied to that of the bishopric, monasteries gained in power, leading to political feuds and ecclesiastical abuse. Some monasteries, such as Thorn and Elten, even became political mini-states. The Diocese of Utrecht, especially its monasteries, staunchly resisted Gregorian reform, with the bishop becoming party to the act of deposition of Pope Gregory VII (1073–1085). Saint Paul's Abbey in Utrecht and Egmont Abbey, abbeys that had rebuffed Cluniac reform, refused allegiance to Gregory. It was not until 1140 that the owner of Egmont Abbey, Count Diederick VI, transferred possession to the Holy See.

The northern Low Countries were more interested in moral reform than political, taking their inspiration from the rediscovered "Apostolic" ideas of poverty and preaching. Among the chief proponents of this renewal was St. Norbert of Xanten (c. 1080–1134), founder of the Premonstratensians. The Canons Regular of St. Augustine, especially at Rolduc, and the Benedictines were also involved. Up to the 12th century, only three monasteries had existed in the north, but the evangelical fervor of the renewal brought a rapid increase and engendered enthusiasm among the laity.

Before the 15th century most attempts at monastic reform, such as the Cluniac, were imported from the south. Even so the Dutch influenced the reform movement. In 1271 the Flemish poet Jacob van Maerlant wrote a prose version of the Bible, *Rijmbibe*, in the common language, translating not the Vulgate but Petrus Comestor's *Historia Scholasticia*. The prose Bible became a tool in the hands of the monastic reform movement, giving impetus to another reform movement, the beguinages (nonmonastic communities of women). The first of these communities was established by Lambert le Bègue in the middle of the 12th century at Liège. Seeking to control the doctrinal vagaries of the women, the Dominicans encouraged the spread of mystical texts in the vernacular. This stimulated Dutch literature, for in the mystical poetry and prose of the late medieval period Dutch literature reached its apogee.

Always a breeding ground for mysticism, first among beguines and then among men, the 13th-century southern Netherlands produced the mystical love songs of the Flemish Hadewijch, believed to be a nun, followed by the great mystic hermit Jan van Ruusbroeck (Ruysbroeck, 1293–1381) of Brabant, near Brussels. It has been said that with Ruusbroeck medieval mysticism peaked with a flourish. A frequent caller on Ruusbroeck was Geert Groote (d. 1384), founder of the Brethren of the Common Life, who redirected Ruusbroek's mysticism "outward" toward the solving of social ills. The chief aim of Groote and the Brethren was to encourage practical Christianity through imitation of the early apostolic Church. Throughout the Middle Ages the care of the poor and infirm had fallen to the monastic orders, which performed care with little thought to root causes. Groote was concerned about root causes of distress, which he blamed on the monastic orders because they had deviated from the apostolic example of humility. Groote's movement, known as the "New Devotion," moved rapidly into the northern Netherlands and throughout Germany, producing St. Thomas a Kempis' *Imitatio*, which many scholars believe is a reformulation of a work originally written by Groote. Martin Luther (1483–1546) for a brief while studied under the Brethren, and although nowhere in their philosophy is to be found any opposition to the Roman Church, it is possibly from the Brethren that he derived his emphasis on *sola scriptura*.

The Brethren lived together as a *stift* (a community that requires no vows or adherence to any monastic rule), seeking humbly to imitate the manner of apostolic life. Under Florentius Radewijns, Groote's successor, the Brethren also instituted *stifts* for the Sisters of the Common Life. Desiring a rule, some of the Brethren withdrew to the monastery of Windesheim, submitting themselves to the Canons of St. Augustine. The Windesheim initiative met with acclaim and served as the model for much monastic reform throughout the Netherlands. The "reformed" houses organized themselves as the "Windesheim Congregation." A papal delegation to the Netherlands in 1450 was so impressed by the piety of the Congregation that the latter was put in charge of much of German monastic and bishopric reform.

The steady rise of the Congregation and the Brethren earned them the animosity of the mendicant orders, the Franciscans and Dominicans, who saw their own influence being weakened. Nevertheless the movement served as a catalyst for the Minorites to begin reform. The supporters of this reform were called the Observants and the opponents the Conventuals. One of the leading Dutch Observants was the Franciscan Johannes Brugman, who from the convent of St. Francis at St. Omer, an Observant stronghold, traveled throughout the northern Netherlands preaching monastic reform.

Neither the Low Countries nor its churches and monasteries could escape the ravages of the guild movement of the 14th century, a movement in part fueled by the "democratic" mysticism of the Brethren and others. The Church, in need of reformation and enduring feuding among its members, had little power to curb abuses. Nowhere was this more severely felt than in Liège. On 13 August 1312 the church of St. Martin was burned to the ground, and hundreds of nobles lost their lives at the hands of the guilds. Finally, in June 1315, the Peace of Fexhe, mediated by Bishop Adolf de la Mark, brought a halt to the rampages. The Peace led to the foundation of Liège Liberties, which among other things established the Church's oversight over the guild chapter of St. Lambert. However, the guilds were to exert their power again and again against the Roman Church, leading eventually to the revolt of 1417. Although the Church was able to maintain the upper hand, the democratic movement continued to fester, reviving itself in the Reformation and in William of Orange, who delivered his fellow countrymen from both Spanish rule and papal authority. In January 1579 the seven northern provinces formed the Utrecht Union, which became the nucleus of the largely Protestant Dutch Republic.

However, between 1417 and 1579 there was still hope among the Reformers for a revitalized Church. Erasmus was gaining support for his ideas on monastic reform, and the

Dutchman Adrian VI was named pope in 1522. Both were disciples of the Brethren. Erasmus had studied at the Brethren center of Deventer and at the monastery of Steyn, a congregation of Windesheim. The Utrecht-born Adrian was the vice chancellor of the University of Louvain, tutor and friend of the young Emperor Charles V (1519–1556), and it was this friendship that propelled him toward the papacy. Adrian became pope by default; not even in the running, he was elected on the failure of the College of Cardinals to decide on one of the preferred choices. As pope for a year, however much Adrian sought to curb abuses amid the petty jealousies of the cardinals, the latter considered him a country bumpkin and blocked reform.

From the ascendancy of the Reformed Church until the Netherlands became the Batavian Republic (1795), Catholicism retained an unfavorable position and was cut off from Rome in 1702. On 5 August 1796 the Batavian National Assembly ended the privileged position of the Reformed Church, and with the introduction of the principles of toleration of the French Revolution, Catholics were legally emancipated. Churches and monasteries were restored, and theological seminaries were founded in Breda, Bois-le-Duc, Warmond, and 's-Heerenberg. For a while the French Concordat of 1801 sought to establish a national church under government supervision. In 1827 King William I (1814–1840), a supporter of the Concordat, became concerned with the rise of Febronianism, which promoted diocesan power independent of the Holy See, and asked for a new concordat. This concordat established new dioceses, which, because of opposition, were never put into effect. King William II (1840–1849), influenced by the Tilburg priest, Johannes Zwijsen, encouraged the foundation of new monasteries and new institutions for education and social welfare but did not enforce the Concordat of 1827 against combined Catholic and Protestant opposition. The 20th century has seen a revival of Catholicism, including the building of several new monasteries. Today there are about 40, 000 religious in around 1,500 houses.

Sites

Of unusual interest is the tenth-century abbey at Thorn founded by Ansfried, a count from the Meuse district who later became bishop of Utrecht. The abbey functioned as a sovereign state within the German Empire. Here the aristocracy founded a convent for their unmarried daughters. The abbess of the convent, or *stift* (for it required no vows), ranked as the reigning monarch and lived in a small palace. The women themselves lived in luxurious white houses, being attended by servants and owning property. After marriage they left the order. The abbey's chapter of canons and canonesses served as the state administrators. Of the abbey's original buildings, only the church remains.

Ruins of St. Bavon's Monastery, Gent

Ruins of several monasteries in the Parish of St.-Martin include those perhaps visited by Charlemagne. The parish was founded in the seventh century. In the vicinity of Moorsel, an ancient Benedictine monastery still thrives.

FRANK A. MILLS

See also Beguines; Belgium; Boniface, St.; Echternach, Luxembourg; France: History; Gregory VII; Luther, Martin; Wilfrid, St.; Willibrord, St.

Further Reading

To fully understand the complexities of the monastic history of the Netherlands it is essential to first understand the political history, as the two go hand-in-hand. An excellent works is:

Blok, Petrus Johannes, *History of the People of the Netherlands*, translated by Oscar Bierstadt and Ruth Putnam, New York: AMS Press, n.d. (5-volume reprint of the 1898–1912 edition)

Other sources:

Acta Sanctorium ("Lives of the Saints"), published by Antwerp Jesuit John Bolland and his successors from 1643 to present time

Borchert, Bruno, *Mysticism: Its History and Challenge*, York Beach, Maine: Weiser, 1994 (translation of the original Dutch language edition, 1989)

Monumenta Germaniae, "Scriptores" (contains the *Annales of Laurissenses majores*, *Mosellani*, *Xantenses*, *Egmundani*, and *Rodenses* and the *Chronicon Egmundanum*) (see also Muller, *Lists of North Netherland Chronicles*)

North Dutch Book of Hours, The Brethren of the Common Life, c. 1470–1500 (abstracts available from the Richard C. Kessler Reformation Collection, Pitts Theological Library, Archives and Manuscript Department, Emory University, manuscript number: 086; *www.pitts.emory.edu/text/mss086.html*)

New Skete, New York

The New Skete communities of Cambridge, New York, are stavropighial (i.e., under the jurisdiction of the Primate rather than the local bishop) monasteries under the jurisdiction of the metropolitan of the Orthodox Church in America (OCA). The word *skete* derives from the Greek word *asketes*, meaning "monk" or "hermit." A *skete* is traditionally a small monastic village dependent on a monastery. It is self-governed and subject to the authority of the monastery and its visitor (i.e., patriarch or metropolitan). However, New Skete is not technically a *skete* at all; rather it is several cenobitic monasteries. New Skete derives its name not from the traditional definition but from the fourth-century Egyptian monastic settlement at Scetis, renown for its spiritual athletes.

New Skete consists of three communities: New Skete Monastery for Men, Our Lady of the Sign Monastery for Women, and Emmaus House for Married Couples (Companions of New Skete). The abbot of the Monks, Nuns, and Companions of New Skete is Archimandrite Laurence Mancuso, who founded the group in 1966. The monks had been affiliated with the Slav-Byzantine Rite Custody of the Franciscan Order. From the outset the monks were involved in monastic and liturgical reforms to recover an earlier, more authentic tradition. Father Laurence compiled a *typikon* that was reflective of Orthodox liturgical practice. The *typikon* was formally adopted by the Custody in 1963 and observed by its two monasteries. At first the language used was Church Slavonic; in 1964 the two monasteries began using English for the Daily Office and the Divine Liturgy. In 1965, while still in the Custody, the monks compiled a Book of Hours (all the monastic divine offices in English) that was based on Byzantine Constantinopolitan liturgical forms from the 10th to the 12th century. Their Book of Hours resulted from intensive consultations with Fr. Juan Mateos, a specialist in the Oriental divine office and consultor to the Roman liturgical consilium. Some of the monks attended his Fordham University summer lectures around 1964 to 1965. They absorbed his published and unpublished essays and notes. In 1965 Fr. Mateos visited the monks for several days in New Canaan, Connecticut. Father Mateos thus influenced them to publish the initial version of the Book of Hours, which, 12 years later, evolved into their Prayerbook (1976).

Increasingly steeped in the ways of Orthodox monasticism, the group approached the Custody to establish an experimental *skete* but was refused. In 1966 they separated from the Order. The New Skete venture was begun under the leadership of Fr. Laurence and a group of 12 monks, officially known as the Monks of the Brotherhood of St. Francis. They eventually came under the canonical jurisdiction of the Roman Catholic bishop of Albany, New York, and continued to follow the Byzantine Rite. Their first home was a cabin in Utica, New York. From there they moved to a hunting lodge in Ridgway, Pennsylvania, where they remained for six months. The monks began Liturgy & Art publications in 1966.

On 1 January 1967 the monks, 14 in number, moved to a farm near Cambridge, New York. Their existence there was humble: the Divine Liturgy was celebrated in the common room that also served as the refectory. They maintained themselves by tending livestock and working the land. However, the farmhouse was located on a busy road, and privacy and quiet were difficult to maintain. They soon moved to their present location on a 400-acre site on a mountain at the opposite end of the village from the farmhouse. By the Easter of 1968, they had constructed two buildings. The rugged terrain was not suitable for livestock, so the monks sustained themselves as butchers, carpenters,

Temple of the Transfiguration at New Skete, New York, designed and built by the monks in 1969. Bell tower (on right) was designed and built by the monks in 1978.
Photo courtesy of Monks of New Skete

and – their most renowned endeavor – the breeding and raising of pedigreed German shepherd dogs, which started in 1969. They also started their New Skete Farms mail order in 1969.

In the summer of 1969, the monks were joined by a small group of nuns – formerly Sisters of St. Claire – who at first were housed in the art-shop building. By Thanksgiving of that year, the sisters were able to purchase a small farmhouse about five miles from New Skete. Their permanent housing was completed in the fall of 1970, at the same time that the monks' first chapel, the Temple of the Transfiguration, was finished. The chapel was completed in 78 working days and was dedicated in November 1970, with Roman Catholic Bishop Edwin Broderick of Albany presiding at the service. A bell tower with 16 bells was built in 1978, and a second, larger church was built in 1984. Emmaus House was started in 1984, made up of lay members of the parish at New Skete.

With the encouragement and help of Frs. Alexander Schmemann and John Meyendorff, the monks and nuns were received into the OCA in 1979. As members of the OCA, their first monastic *typikon* was published in 1980. It "emphasizes the primitive simplicity and ideals of the early Desert Fathers, especially the vital dimension of community life (cenobitic) in work, liturgy, meals, stability, and hospitality with guests. . . . The liturgical typicon of New Skete is based on extensive study of recent liturgical scholarship, with emphasis on clarity and simplicity of the divine offices, choral singing by all the monastics, chanting aloud of the priestly prayers which are distributed throughout the services, and the recovery of the balance toward use of Scripture. All is done in modern literary English, their own translations (beginning with the Psalter) and adaptations of traditional chant melodies and harmonies for mixed choir (Monks, Nuns, and Companions)" (from e-mail communication with Fr. Marc).

The brothers have edited and translated a number of liturgical texts for use at New Skete. They include *Temple for Yahweh* (texts for dedication of a church, 1970); *Office for the Dead* (Panychida, 1973); liturgical music (principally traditional Byzantine chants harmonized for mixed or men's chorus, including selections for vespers, matins, and liturgy; dogmatica and other selections, 1975); *Prayerbook* (book of hours, a variant of the Byzantine rite horologion, 1976); *Service Book* (1978); *Psalter* (1984); troparia and kondakia (including exapostilaria and the stikhira, 1984); *Book of Prayers* (including prayers, order of vespers, order of Great Vigil, order of matins, order of the little hours, dismissals, exaltations, trisagion for the dead, special petitions, and prayers for New Year's Day, 1988); a second, revised edition of their monastic *typikon* (1988); *Vespers and Matins* (1993); *Divine Liturgy of Our Father among the Saints, John Chrysostom* (1994); *Passion and Resurrection* (1995); and *Divine Liturgy of Our Father among the Saints, St. James of Jerusalem* (edited by Laurence Mancuso, 1996). On 6 August 1998 they recorded a videocassette, *Transfiguration Divine Liturgy* (the Festal Liturgy at New Skete), and in November 1999 Little, Brown publishers of Boston published New Skete's *In the Spirit of Happiness*, an exposition on the ways of spiritual life in the world.

In 1973 the monks began a journal, *Gleanings*, which was begun to commemorate the life of a New Skete monk who had died in an automobile accident. The journal continued publication until 1978, concluding with a final issue in 1981. As part of New Skete's attempt to achieve liturgical restoration, Br. Stavros translated M. Arranz's "N.D. Uspensky: The Office of the All-Night Vigil in the Greek Church and in the Russian Church" (*St. Vladimir's Theological Quarterly* 24 [1980]). Their nontheological publications include *The Art of Raising a Puppy* (1991), *How to Be Your Dog's Best Friend: A Training Manual for Dog Owners* (1978), and *Raising Your Dog with the Monks of New Skete* (1996, three videocassettes).

MICHAEL D. PETERSON

This article would not have been possible without the generous assistance of Fr. Marc of New Skete.

See also Liturgy: Eastern Christian; Office, Daily: Eastern Christian; Orthodox Monasticism: Slavic; Seasons, Liturgical: Eastern Christian; Spirituality: Eastern Christian

Further Reading

Monks of New Skete, *New Skete Communities*, Cambridge, New York: Monks of New Skete, 1985

Oliver, Rose, "The Journey Home," *Gleanings: The Journal of New Skete* 1:1 (Winter 1973)

Stavros, Brother, "The Restored Office of New Skete," *Gleanings: The Journal of New Skete* 1:1 (Winter 1973)

Stavros, Brother, "The Restored Liturgy of New Skete," *Gleanings: The Journal of New Skete* 4:1 (Spring 1976)

Taft, Robert, "The Byzantine Office in the *Prayerbook* of New Skete: Evaluation of a Proposed Reform," *Orientalia Christiana Periodica* 48 (1982)

Related Web Sites

http://www.acs.ucalgary.ca~simmins/Cincinnati.paper.html (Simmins, Geoffrey, "Atavism and Accommodation in Selected Recent North American Places of Worship," paper presented at the Cincinnati Conference on Sacred Spaces, October 1997)

http://www.newskete.com ("New Skete Monasteries")

http://www.oca.org/OCA/pim/oca-st-camnsm.htm ("Monks of New Skete [1966], Cambridge, New York")

Nhát Hanh, Thích 1926–

Vietnamese Buddhist monk, scholar, and advocate of Engaged Buddhism

The life and teaching of Thích Nhát Hanh constitutes an example of both Buddhist nondualism and the sociopolitical dimension of Engaged Buddhism.

Nhát Hanh, who was born in 1926 as Nguyën Xuân Bao and joined monkhood in 1932 to study under the Lâm Té master Thanh Qúy (Thích Chân Thât), gained prominence within the

Buddhist community in Vietnam when he founded the Ung Quang Temple one year after his ordination in 1950, the monastic community at Phúóng Bói in 1956, the Vanh Hanh University and the Youth for Social Service in 1964, and the Tiép Hiên Order (Order of Interbeing) – a branch of the Lâm Té (Chinese, Lin Chi; Japanese, Rinzai) school of Zen Buddhism – in 1965. Nhát Hanh entered public awareness in the United States when he lectured on contemporary Buddhism at Columbia University in 1963 and represented the Unified Buddhist Church (UBC) of Vietnam to the United States government and the United Nations in 1963 and 1966. Unable to return to Vietnam in 1966, Nhát Hanh represented the UBC during the peace talks in Paris in 1968, retreated to rural France to practice meditation thereafter, organized efforts to help the boat people in the wake of North Vietnam's takeover of South Vietnam between 1975 and 1977, and cofounded Plum Village in the Dordogne region of southern France together with Cao Ngoc Phúóng in 1982.

Nhát Hanh's "Engaged Buddhism" (Vietnamese, Nhan Gian Phât Giáo) emphasizes the sociopolitical implications of Mahāyāna Buddhist nondualism. Kenneth Kraft, in *Inner Peace, World Peace: Essays on Buddhism and Non-Violence* (1992), traces the first mention of "engaged Buddhism" to a book with this title written by Nhát Hanh, whereas Nhát Hanh, in *Vietnam: Lotus in a Sea of Fire* (1967), himself attributes the term to Do Nam Tui and Thien Chieu, who discussed this "school" of Buddhism in articles published in the journal *Duoc Tue* in the 1930s. In his theoretical work, which is strongly grounded in basic Buddhist tenets, such as the Four Noble Truths and the doctrine of codependent arising (Sanskrit, *pratītya samutpāda*) as well as the doctrine of emptiness (Sanskrit, *śūnyatā*) and the twofold truth of Mahāyāna Buddhism, Nhát Hanh develops four aspects of nondualism that are programmatic for his spiritual and his social teachings. (1) The nondualism of opposites: Following the "logic" of the Buddhist wisdom literature, the *Prajñāpāramitā Sūtras* (most notably the *Diamond Sūtra*), Nhát Hanh rejects the logic of noncontradiction and its conceptual and ethical implications. In short he rejects the belief that the self-identity of A qua A = A is tautological and simultaneously independent of not-A. On the contrary, Nhát Hanh postulates an interdependence of A and not-A. (2) The nondualism of self and no-self: Nhát Hanh utilizes this "logic" of *pratītya samutpāda* not only to affirm the Buddhist notions of impermanence and the selflessness of all existents but also, and more important, to argue a necessary interconnectedness of all beings and concepts. In this sense Nhát Hanh argues that a flower neither exists nor can be conceived to exist independent of nonflower elements, such as soil, sun, and water. In the same sense Nhát Hanh argues that it is impossible to conceive of the individual human subject who is dependent on oxygen, food, sun, and so on as an independent, self-sufficient entity. Following this reasoning Nhát Hanh concludes that the human subject and the nonhuman elements on which it depends are nondifferent. (3) The nondualism of self and other: Nhát Hanh observes a similar interdependence between self and no-self with regards to the interpersonal relationships. In a heart-wrenching and often-cited passage of *Being Peace* (1987), Nhát Hanh relates the story of a 12-year-old boatgirl who, after being raped during an assault by pirates, took her own life. Nhát Hanh argues that although it would be easy to take sides in this case, there is a causal dependence between the judging bystander and the girl, the pirate, and the political situation causing the mass exodus of the boat people. Evoking philosophically, economically, psychologically, and politically the nondifference of self and other in such a way, Nhát Hanh rejects the notion of the isolated individual and postulates the nondualism of the individual person and the human community in toto. (4) The nondualism of practice and nonpractice: Defining meditation as mindfulness of the nondualisms of self and other, individual and society, and individual and environment, Nhát Hanh argues that practice and nonpractice are nondifferent. This last nondualism reflects the Mahāyāna dictum that "saṃsāra is nondifferent from nirvāṇa, and nirvāṇa is nondifferent from saṃsāra." Furthermore, Nhát Hanh's nondualism of practice and nonpractice emphasizes two aspects of mindfulness – cessation (Sanskrit, *samādhi*), quite literally in the sense of stopping to act and think, and insight (Sanskrit, *vipaśyanā*) into the interconnectedness and nondifferentiation of human individuals – an attitude that evokes responsibility and urges social justice.

This philosophy of the Middle Path can be seen clearly in Buddhist insistence on political neutrality during the second Vietnam War and in the precepts of the Tiép Hiên Order. These precepts, which are formulated in *Stepping into Freedom* (1997) and *Interbeing* (1987), reflect the two basic notions of mindfulness and nonattachment to views. Whereas the former evokes awareness of the four aspects of nondifference, the latter is based on the Mahāyāna Buddhist tenet that all intellectual positions are ultimately empty. However, Nhát Hanh interprets this nonattachment to views, including Buddhism itself, not only soteriologically as detachment from detachment and karmic efficacy but also socially and politically as the fundamental step toward "being peace." In this sense Nhát Hanh cannot but conceive of his Order of Interbeing in particular and the Buddhist *saṅgha* in general as a community that is simultaneously contemplative and socially engaged. The 14 principles of "interbeing" can be understood both as the precepts of a monastic community and as the foundation for a sociopolitical program. In other words suffering and its release is not merely a spiritual matter but also a political one. Although Nhát Hanh tends to be a scholar and spiritual teacher rather than a political leader, his interpretations of Buddhist teachings and precepts as the theory of "interbeing," his participation in the UBC, and his commitment to the boat people and the Vietnamese community in exile serve as an impressive example of his nondualism of practice and nonpractice.

GEREON KOPF

See also Buddhadāsa; Buddhism: Western; Peace Movements, Buddhist; Persecution: Buddhist Perspectives; Social Services: Buddhist; Vietnam

Biography

A leader of "Engaged Buddhism" in Vietnam and later in France, Nhát Hanh was ordained in the Rinzai Zen monastic order in 1950 and founded the Tiếp Hiên Order in 1965. He represented the United Buddhist Church of Vietnam to the United States government in 1963 and at the Paris peace talks in 1968. He has interpreted the concept of Interbeing as a foundation for both monasticism and peace initiatives.

Major Works

Vietnam: Lotus in a Sea of Fire, 1967
The Miracle of Mindfulness: A Manual on Meditation, 1975
Being Peace, 1987
Interbeing: Commentaries on the Tiếp Hiên Precepts, 1987
Stepping into Freedom: An Introduction to Buddhist Monastic Training, 1997
The Heart of the Buddha's Teaching: Transforming Suffering into Peace, Joy and Liberation, 1999

Further Reading

While the press release of Parallax Press identifies 1964 as the founding year of the School of Youth for Social Service, Chan Kong (Cao Ngoc Phúóng), *Learning True Love* (Berkeley, California: Parallax Press, 1993), locates the beginning of the school in the year 1965.

Kenneth Kraft, *Inner Peace, World Peace: Essays on Buddhism and Non-Violence* (Albany: State University of New York Press, 1992), page 18, traces the first mention of "engaged Buddhism" to a book with this title written by Nhát Hanh, while Thích Nhát Hanh, *Vietnam: Lotus in a Sea of Fire* (New York: Hill and Wang, and London: SCM Press, 1967), page 42, himself attributes the term to Do Nam Tui and Thien Chieu who discussed this "school" of Buddhism in articles published in the journal *Duoc Tue* in the 1930s.

The centrality of the non-dualistic principle to Nhát Hanh's work is indicated by the title of Sallie B. King's "Thích Nhát Hanh and the Unified Buddhist Church: Nondualism in Action," in *Engaged Buddhism: Buddhist Liberation Movements in Asia*, edited by Sallie B. King and Christopher Queen (Albany: State University of New York Press, 1996). On page 342 King argues that relieving suffering is the primary concern and most basic principle of Nhát Hanh's Engaged Buddhism.

Nichiren. *See* Prophethood, Japanese Buddhist

Nilus of Sora, St. c. 1433–1508

Russian Orthodox monk, advocate of Hesychasm, and leader of "Non-Possessors" movement

Nilus of Sora, frequently transliterated as Nil Sorskii, established *skete* monasticism (from the Egyptian desert tradition, a Greek word, and later used in Church Slavic) in Muscovy in imitation of his personal experience in Greece. *Skete* monasticism is generally defined as a monastic settlement that depends on a larger, parent monastery, with the brethren inhabiting small cottages gathered around a chapel. Nilus' religious commitment included formation in continuity with Byzantine Hesychasm, characterized by the practiced repetition of the Jesus Prayer. In addition he advocated only limited monastic holdings of land and thus became associated with the "Non-Possessors." Because the "Possessors," led by Joseph of Volokolamsk (1439/40–1515), achieved spiritual and political dominance in 16th-century Russia, a dominance that lasted for about three centuries, it is believed that Nilus' *Vita*, along with all biographical information, was lost or suppressed. Despite the fact that he did not make this claim for himself, Nilus was unmistakably a spiritual director or "elder" (Russian, *starets*; Greek, *geron*).

Little is known of the elder's life or his possible peasant origins. His family name was Maikov, and he was a copyist who was tonsured young. He entered the great northern monastery of St. Cyril at Beloozero but soon traveled with a disciple to a Hesychast monastery on Mount Athos, only to return to a wilderness about ten miles from St. Cyril's. Because he settled with some friends beyond the Volga River (c. 1470s–1480s), the group was later referred to as the Trans-Volgan Elders of the Northern Thebaid. None of them, except Nilus, left any writings. Nilus himself settled near the River Sora (thus his eponym). He is known to have attended local councils in Moscow in 1490 and 1503. At the latter council he unexpectedly denounced monastic landholdings and the monastic ownership of serfs who occupied and worked those lands, thereby becoming a chief proponent of Non-Possession.

The rest of Nilus' life can be gleaned from his writings, which include: a monastic rule, or rather a treatise on spiritual matters based on Egyptian, Latin, and Greek fathers and mothers, with a preface ("The Tradition") to his disciples; some personal letters; a last will; and two hagiographic manuscripts. Other aspects of his life can be inferred from the later history surrounding his disciples (especially Vassian Patrikeev), many of whom were persecuted by the grand princes of Muscovy. Nilus was canonized in Russia in the 19th century, much later than were his Possessor rivals, at a time when sensibilities about the wisdom of ownership of human beings and the accumulation of Church wealth were again called into question.

Although frequently viewed as a foil to the Possessor movement of Joseph of Volokolamsk, Nilus and the Non-Possessor movement display an autonomous spiritual importance that is not contingent on surrounding historical circumstances. The spiritual legacy of Nilus is quite distinctive both in its particulars and in its totality:

1. Monastic organization: By the 15th century the Slavs had established traditions of both eremitic and cenobitic monasticism, but the *sketes* introduced by Nilus, consisting of two- to four-person clusters of monks observing silence, were new to the region. Nilus had so little use for religious or political authority that he neither asserted nor organized any leadership whatsoever

in the *sketes*. (This renunciation of power put all the Non-Possessors out of step with the rising centralization of Muscovy during the 16th century.) Thus, Nilus allowed no priority among the brothers of these *sketes*, seeing the members as only an association of friends who were admonished by one another. The brothers progressed by sharing their experiences. Their authorities were solely Holy Scripture and the "divine writings," the latter connoting the collective tradition of the Church. Nilus even offered a Christian solution to the problem of capitalism (without however advocating another political system or falling into utopianism): Christians may buy and sell goods, but they should do so at a loss, not bargaining to the disadvantage of others.

2. Hesychasm: Everyone in the *sketes* practiced a version of the Hesychast prayer of the heart, "Lord Jesus Christ, be merciful to me a sinner." It is rooted in the prayer of the publican in the Gospel of Luke (18:13), and practiced according to the admonition of St. Paul to "pray without ceasing" (1 Thess. 5:17). The rhythm of the prayer follows one's breathing (possibly originating from Indian influence) and is a continuous part of daily life. The practice of the aforementioned Jesus Prayer puts Nilus in continuity with fathers such as Symeon the New Theologian (949–1022), Theodosius of the Kievan Caves, and Gregory Palamas (c. 1296–1359), as well as later figures such as Paisy Velichkovsky (1722–1794) and Seraphim of Sarov (1759–1833).

3. "Kenoticism": Once Nilus had combined the two previous characteristics, either of which could exist independently, the result was something new. This tradition has been identified repeatedly by G. Fedotov and others with the so-called kenotic Christ (from the Greek *kenosis*). Slavic kenoticism is characterized by self-sacrificing humility directed toward social conscience and at the same time is animated by active interior prayer.

The often austere egalitarian particularities of Nilus' spirituality are characteristic neither of his time nor of his Slavic heritage. They resonate better with later Reformation debates, if not late 20th-century democratic sensibilities. First, at a time when many of Nilus' European and Slavic contemporaries shared an admiration for the Spanish Inquisition, he showed respect for human intellect and freedom and believed that heretics should not be persecuted or compelled in their beliefs. Second, his resistance to church ornamentation, supported by little-known, ancient authorities, is akin to later Protestant insistence on the simplicity of church adornment. This renunciation was so uncharacteristic as to seem peculiar to Russians. Third, just as was St. John Climacus (c. 570–c. 649), Nilus is explicit and detailed in analyzing the "movements of the heart," the interior spiritual life.

MICHAEL PROKURAT

See also Climacus, John, St.; Elders, Russian Monastic (Startsi); Isaac the Syrian (Isaac of Nineveh), St.; Joseph of Volokolamsk, St.; Orthodox Monasticism: Slavic; Palamas, Gregory, St.; Paisy Velichkovsky; Russia: History; Seraphim of Sarov, St.; Symeon the New Theologian, St.

Biography

Born into a noble family of Moscow, Nilus lived in the monastery of St. Cyril in northern Russia before he made an extended stay at Mount Athos. After returning to Muscovy, he settled in a *skete* ten miles from St. Cyril's. There he pioneered a Russian context for Hesychasm.

Selected Works

Nil Sorskii i Vassian Patrikeev (Nilus of Sora and Vassian Patrikeev), edited by A.S. Arkhangelski,, in *Pamiatniki drevnei pismennosti i iskusstva 35* (Monuments of Old Writings and Art 35), 1882

Nila Sorskago, Predanie i Ustav (Nilus of Sora's Tradition and Rule), in *Pamiatniki drevnei pismennosti i iskusstva 179* (Monuments of Old Writings and Art 179), edited by M.C. Borovkova-Maikova, 1912

"Poslaniia Nila Sorskago" (The Letters of Nilus of Sora), edited by G.M. Proxorov, in *Trudy otdela drevnerusskoi literatury 29* (Works of the Department of Old Russian Literature 29), 1974

Nilus' *Tradition*, *Rule*, and *Last Will* can be found in English in *A Treasury of Russian Spirituality*, edited and compiled by George P. Fedotov, 1975

Further Reading

Fedotov, G.P., *The Russian Religious Mind*, volume 2: *The Middle Ages, 13th to the 15th Centuries*, edited by John Meyendorff, Cambridge, Massachusetts: Harvard University Press, 1966

Hackel, Sergei, "Late Medieval Russia: The Possessors and the Non-Possessors," in *Christian Spirituality: High Middle Ages and Reformation*, edited by Jill Raitt, New York: Crossroad, and London: Routledge and Kegan Paul, 1987

Lilienfeld, Fairy von, *Nil Sorskij und Seine Schriften: Die Krise der Tradition im Russland Ivans III*, Berlin: Evangelische Verlaganstalt, 1963

Maloney, George A., *Russian Hesychasm: The Spirituality of Nil Sorskij*, The Hague: Mouton, 1973

Maloney, George A., *Nilus of Sora: Classics of Western Spirituality*, New York: Paulist Press, 1999

Norway. *See* Scandinavia

Novices, Theravādin Rituals for

Shinpiyu is the Burmese name given to the ceremony through which one becomes a novice (Pāli, *pabbajjā*) within the Theravāda monastic tradition. Literally the term means "the making of a novice" (*shin*). In Myanmar and Thailand every man must become a novice for a period that can extend from one week to an entire lifetime. This contrasts with the Theravāda Buddhist tradition of Sri Lanka, in which entering the order is perceived as a lifetime commitment. Just as the Hindu *upanayana* ceremony, wherein every "twice-born" (*dvija*) is officially admitted as a member of his own class (*varṇa*), *shinpiyu* could be perceived as a *rite de passage* that marks admission into society. *Shinpiyu* is by far the most important ritual within Burmese and Thai societies. As early as seven years old, when the boy is old enough to scare crows and to pronounce intelligibly the Pāli verses necessary for being admitted into the monastic order, one can undergo *shinpiyu*. Because no age is fixed for this ceremony, novicehood could theoretically be entered at any time, although parents deem it crucial to see each of their sons enter the order, and it must necessarily be performed before marriage. Once admitted as a novice, the boy is free to decide when he will reintegrate into the laity, if at all. The ceremony of *shinpiyu* and the stage of novicehood that follows enable every man to live, at least for some time, the ideal lifestyle that constitutes monkhood within Theravāda countries.

Shinpiyu is the most auspicious ceremony that can be performed. On the one hand the boy must scrupulously follow the ten monastic precepts: to abstain from killing; from stealing; from indulging in sexual misconduct; from lying; from taking intoxicants; from eating after noon; from dancing, singing, or playing a musical instrument; from wearing flowers, perfumes, or any cosmetics; from using high and luxurious seats and beds; and from handling silver and gold (and, by extension, using money). This proper conduct (*sīla*) by itself ensures the acquisition of endless merits. Besides living this auspicious monastic life, the boy has the opportunity to learn the *piritta* (protective texts), to familiarize himself with the most important canonical texts, and to get acquainted with the basics of meditation practice. Depending on the lineage in which the boy is ordained, more emphasis will be laid on scholastic training (*pariyatti*) or meditation practice (*paṭipatti*). Whether or not the boy chooses to remain a novice and eventually to become a full-pledge monk (*bhikkhu*) through the ceremony of *upasampadā* after he reaches 20 years of age (age is counted from the moment of conception rather than of birth), the merits acquired will ensure, at the least, a positive rebirth; at the most his practice could enable him to realize the highest monastic ideal that constitutes *nibbāna*.

On the other hand the *shinpiyu* ceremony is highly auspicious for the parents themselves, for it is perceived as the culminating act of charity (*dāna*). The way to *nibbāna* is often described as the Eightfold Noble Path, itself divided into three major categories: morality (*sīla*), concentration (*samādhi*), and wisdom (*paññā*). However, it is often suggested that, for the laity, charity is a keystone quality that must be developed before perfecting any of the links of the Eightfold Path, thus its importance. The ordination ceremony itself might involve a substantial financial investment on the part of the parents, as a large meal is offered to the entire monastic community receiving the new novice, and robe, bowl, and other monastic paraphernalia are usually offered to each member of the *saṅgha* (monastic community). However, this financial contribution is minimal in light of a much larger concession made by the parents. Because in Burmese society, as in most Asian cultures, sons are expected to take care of the parents in their old age, the parents' offering of their son to the *saṅgha* can easily be interpreted as the uttermost act of charity and thus of merit making. A Burmese mentioned that the deepest sorrow of his mother is that his father had died before he became a novice and thus could not reap the merits associated with the ceremony. It is not uncommon for wealthy couples without a son to sponsor the *shinpiyu* for the son of a poor family; thus, by symbolically "adopting the child" (*katimatha*), they gain the same amount of merit as if they had sponsored the ordination of their own son.

The preparation for the event usually starts at least one week prior to the actual ceremony. Well in advance women of the household start cooking the food that will be served first to the members of the *saṅgha* and then to the guests once the monks have completed their meal; new dresses are prepared and costumes ironed. The novice-to-be goes to the monastery to receive instruction as to how to recite the Pāli formula required for the ceremony and to mentally prepare himself for the drastic changes that will soon occur in his lifestyle. Monks teach him the daily routine and the various rules that he will be expected to follow. On the day of the ceremony, the boy is dressed in a royal costume; an umbrella, the southern Asian symbol of monarchy, is held over his head, and the boy is carried around town in procession before reaching the monastery. In times past, rich families would have the boy carried by an elephant, another allusion to royalty. However, most families would use horses or bullocks. In the case of poor families, the boy could be carried on the father's shoulders. In modern times in urban areas, it is more common to see the boy carried in the back of a pickup truck or in a car. The father would follow behind his son carrying the monastic robes and the bowl (unless the child is on his shoulder, in which case an uncle would carry these items), whereas the mother would carry articles such as bedding and soap. On reaching the monastery the parents and the boy are presented to the *saṅgha*, and a monk is appointed to shave the boy's head. While his hair is being cut, the boy should meditate on the ephemeral (*anicca*) and "disgusting" (*asubha*) nature of the 32 parts of his body (the hair being one of them). Then, after the boy has requested permission to sit among the *saṅgha*, he offers the eight requisites of a novice (*parikkhāra*: a bowl, two upper robes, one under robe, a girdle, a razor, a needle, and a strainer) to the community and asks the community to return to him these items and to confer initiation so that he can attain *nibbāna*. Then the boy takes away the royal costume, wears the robe, and formally requests permission to enter the monastic order. If none of the members of the *saṅgha* object to the boy's request, he pledges to follow the ten precepts and takes refuge in the "three jewels" (the Buddha, the *dhamma*, and the *saṅgha*), and a preceptor is appointed to supervise the newly admitted novice. The ceremony officially closes with the parents paying respect to this individual who has just acquired a totally new status, well above that of his parents. Then, before noon, the meal is offered to the monastic community. After everyone has eaten, all return home, except the boy, who now resides within the monastic precinct until he decides to reintegrate into society.

In modern times most of the novicehood ordinations take place in April, when the school year ends. Thus, one would remain a novice until the beginning of the new school year. However, this is not a strict rule, for one can decide to extend the period of residence in the monastery. Because *shinpiyu* is considered highly meritorious, it is not unusual for an individual to undergo the process a few times in one's lifetime, especially as the period of novicehood is not perceived as unpleasant.

The *shinpiyu* ceremony plays a crucial role in maintaining the vitality of Buddhism in Myanmar and Thailand. On the one hand it is a ceremony that strengthens bonds within the community, whether those of a village or those of a microsociety within a larger urban setting. On the other hand it encourages every male to acquire an inside perspective of the monastic tradition and thus to develop deep respect for a lifestyle that he now knows to be difficult and worthy of homage. More important the *shinpiyu* ceremony reactualizes the hagiography of Siddhārtha Gautama, the Buddha. By comparing the novice-to-be to a royal prince who is being carried around town on a palanquin, performers reenact the great renunciation of Prince Siddhartha for all the lay and monastic communities witnessing the process; thus, every family is symbolically endowed with the honor of having, as its member, the very individual who became the Buddha.

Mathieu Boisvert

See also Body: Buddhist Perspectives; Burma (Myanmar); Clothing: Buddhist Perspectives; Economics: Buddhist; Examinations, Theravādin; Forest Masters; Gestures, Buddhist; Initiation: Buddhist Perspectives; Meditation: Buddhist Perspectives; Sri Lanka: History; Thailand; Virtues, Buddhist

Further Reading

Htun, Hmat Win, Sao, *The Initiation of Novicehood and the Ordination of Monkhood in the Burmese Buddhist Culture*, Rangoon, Burma: Department of Religious Affairs, 1986

Nyingma. *See* Tibetan Lineages: Nyingma

O

Oblates

An oblate is a young child offered (*oblatus*) to a monastery or nunnery by his or her parents. In ecclesiastical Latin the term evokes the idea of a sacrificial gift.

The only Western monastic rule to describe precisely the ritual of oblation is the Rule of St. Benedict: "let parents draw up the petition which we have mentioned above [a promise of stability, reformation of life, and obedience]; and at the oblation let them wrap the petition and the boy's hand in the altar cloth and so offer him [to God] . . . before witnesses." Benedict specifies that at this time nobles should disinherit their son or give his property to the monastery, that the less well to do should make a suitable offering, but that the rite itself should suffice for "those who have nothing at all." Medieval monks and modern scholars have debated the irrevocability of this commitment. It could be conditional on the dedicatee reaffirming monastic vows after reaching the age of responsibility, but in practice, even where such a reaffirmation is specified, the alternative of life in the world probably had few attractions to a monastically socialized child limited in his or her ability to reclaim a share of family property.

The sole medieval Western treatise devoted to this practice is Rabanus Maurus' (c. 780–856) *De Oblatione Puerorum* (*Patrologia Latina* 107.419–440). Rabanus cites biblical prototypes, including dedications and sacrifices of the firstborn, the dedication of the Levites to God, and more specifically the examples of Hannah's dedication of Samuel and Anne's of Mary. He equates the parents' promises with the binding vows mentioned in the Bible. This suggests that oblation should be construed within the early medieval Western Church's pronouncedly Old Testament mentality. Rabanus observes that both Benedict (c. 480–c. 550) and Gregory the Great (pope, 590–604) countenanced oblation. Assuming that monasteries are the purest remaining incarnation of the apostolic Church, he argues that oblation offers children their most perfect possible life.

Rabanus recognized correctly that oblation had its roots in ancient practices. In addition to the Hebrew prototypes that he cites, communities of celibate adults, such as the Essenes, trained children to ensure their continuity. In Rabbinic Judaism a man could vow that his son would become a Nazirite. One could also cite more distant analogies in pagan religions, such as young girls dedicated to be vestal virgins.

Nevertheless Latin oblation seems to have its proximate origins in Greek monasticism. Boys appear in paleomonastic communities. In the Rule of St. Basil (c. 330–379), they are definitely oblates, although he requires that they be ten years old before entering religious life and, unlike Benedict, he specifies the need for a personal rededication when they come of age. In the seventh century the Greek age of entrance was raised to 11. Presumably Fathers such as Athanasius, Jerome, and Cassian helped introduce and sanction this custom in the West. However, in its Latin development the parents' dedication became more binding, and institutions were more willing to accept very young children. A common scenario in Western miracle collections describes parents who vow to a saint that should their sick child recover he or she would be dedicated to that saint's monastery or convent.

Recent interest in medieval concepts of childhood has produced several studies on the education of oblates. These suggest that monks and nuns were often conscientious surrogate parents who tried to optimize the physical and educational situations of their charges.

Although oblation might have been the primary form of recruitment in Benedictine monasteries until the 11th century, it largely disappeared during the High Middle Ages. The "new monasteries" of the 12th century (the Carthusians, Cistercians, and various reformed groups of canons) recruited their members as adults. A few admitted children either as oblates or, together with their parents, as members of families, but these probably had more freedom to depart. Even the traditional Benedictine houses gradually changed. The monastery of Cluny, which had already limited the number of oblates it would accept, dropped the system entirely in 1300.

Perhaps one reason for the change was that it was not easy to combine childhood oblation with adult recruitment. Once new prosperity and alternative methods of schooling permitted an influx of *conversi,* any system that attempted to rely both on the traditional monastic child-rearing regime and on adult recruits would retain all the expenses and inconveniences of the former. At the same time it would lose much of its ability to control childhood socialization effectively once it had added to the mix the worldly vices of more adult recruits, who often felt contempt for the righteous innocence of monks raised in the monastery. Adult recruitment triumphed practically and idealistically: the

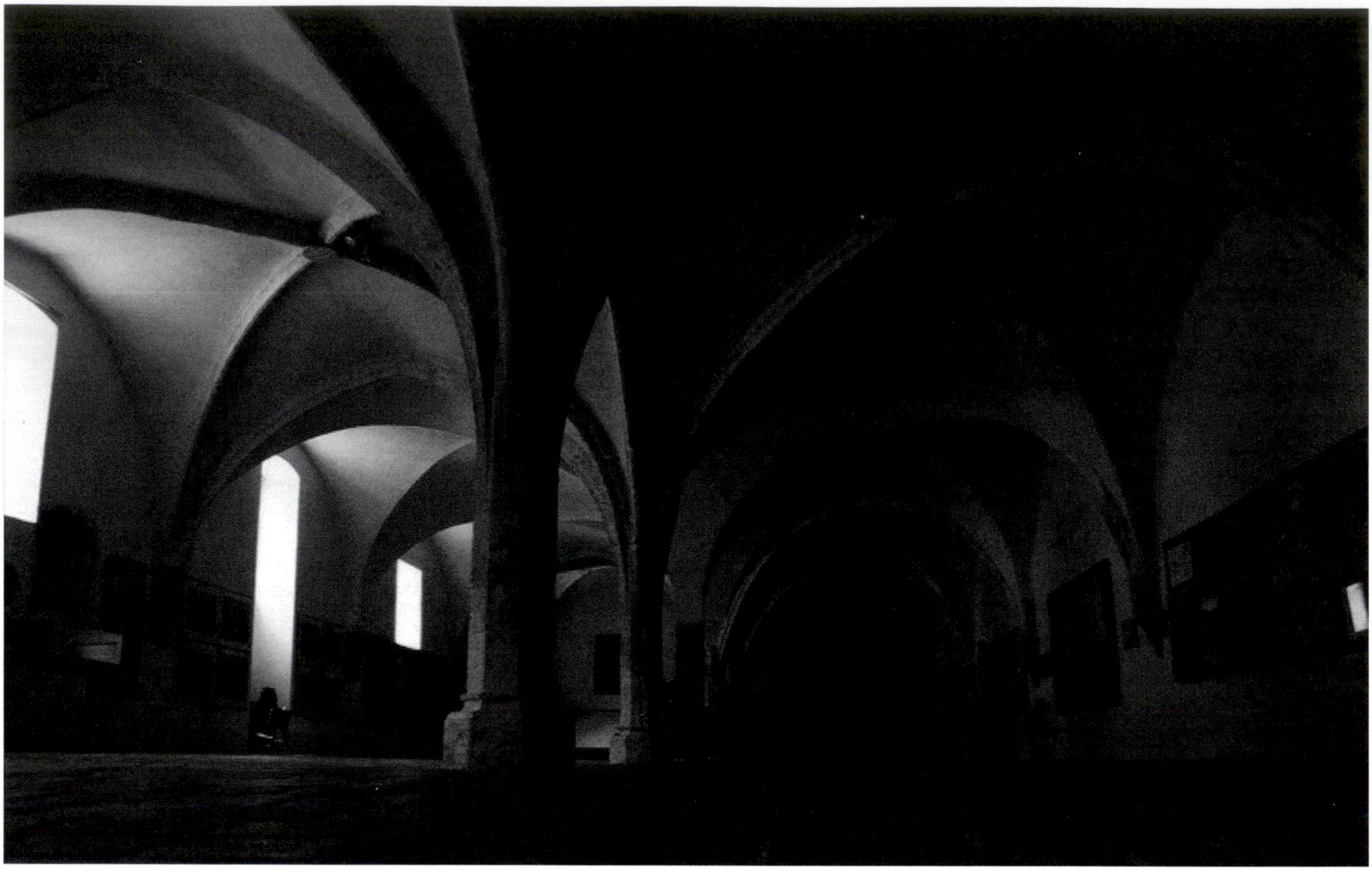

Lay brothers dormitory, Cistercian Abbey of Lilienfeld, Austria, 13th century.
Photo courtesy of Chris Schabel

economic advantages of leaving the burdens of child care to others reinforced the 12th century's greater concern for individual personality and individual rights.

The terms *oblates* and *oblation* are generally used in the context of Christian monasticism. In Eastern monastic traditions, boys and girls are associated with ascetic and monastic communities as servants, pupils, apprentices, and disciples. Oblation's emphases on the parents' sacrifice of the child, the vow of obedience to the abbot, the commitment to stability, and irrevocable vows in general do not have exact equivalents in systems such as the Buddhist *saṅgha*.

JOHN HOWE

See also Basil the Great, St.; Benedict of Nursia, St.; Benedictines: Female; Biblical Figures and Practices; Claustration (Cloister), Rules of; Cluny, France; Rabanus Maurus; Schools and Universities, Benedictine

Further Reading

Boswell, John, *The Kindness of Strangers: The Abandonment of Children in Western Europe from Late Antiquity to the Renaissance,* New York: Pantheon Books, and London: Penguin Press, 1988

De Jong, Mayke, "Growing Up in a Carolingian Monastery: Magister Hildemar and His Oblates," *Journal of Medieval History* 9 (1983)

De Jong, Mayke, *In Samuel's Image: Child Oblation in the Early Medieval West,* Leiden and New York: Brill, 1996

Lahaye-Geusen, Maria, *Das Opfer der Kinder: Ein Beitrag zur Liturgie- und Sozialgeschichte des Mönchtums im Hohen Mittelalter,* Altenberg: Oros, 1991

Lynch, Joseph H., *Simoniacal Entry into Religious Life from 1000 to 1260: A Social, Economic, and Legal Study,* Columbus: Ohio State University Press, 1976

Quinn, Patricia A., *Better Than the Sons of Kings: Boys and Monks in the Early Middle Ages,* New York: Peter Lang, 1989

Office, Daily: Eastern Christian

The Eastern Christian monastic Daily Office (*horai,* also called Liturgical Hours or Divine Office) is a series of daily prayer services that varies according to individual tradition. The Daily Office evolved from the early Christian practice of set times for private daily prayer, which in itself was a response to the New

Testament dictum to pray unceasingly. In addition the early Christian practice of continuous psalm reading anticipated the crucial role of psalmody in the Daily Office. Most of the Divine Offices are urban monastic hybrids; that is, they are a mixture of cathedral (nonmonastic) and monastic traditions.

In order of appearance, from the beginning to the end of the day, the services of the monastic Daily Office are as follows.

1. *Orthros,* or matins, is a service at daybreak to devote the day to God. *Orthros* and vespers were the two original hours celebrated in both monastic and cathedral offices. Both offices share the theme of light and of Christ the Light of the World. Cathedral usage established the liturgical elements of antiphons of psalms and canticles and their accompanying prayers, troparion, psalmody, great doxology, trisagion, gospel readings, and concluding prayers. Of special significance in its development as a monastic service is that beginning in the ninth century the Studite monks of Constantinople adopted *orthros* from the Palestinian monastic horologion. The Palestinian *orthros* contained a poetic canon of nine odes adopted from the ten biblical canticles. Originally the canticles themselves were used, then eventually replaced outside of Lent by the poetic canon. Only canticle 9, the Magnificat (Luke 1:46–55), was retained. The full canon gradually evolved from its use only in the Saturday all-night vigil (*agrypnia*) to become a permanent part of the non-Lenten daily service. In the Studite practice a reading from the Church fathers or the saints' lives was inserted after the third or sixth odes. In the 14th century the Athonite Hesychasts further hybridized *orthros* in their redaction of the Sabaitic *Typika,* a later Palestinian monastic liturgical manual. The Sabaitic *orthros* is the final developmental stage of the service. At the all-night service, the reading of the whole Psalter and all nine odes of the canon characterize Sabaitic *orthros*.

2. The "Little Hours" of the first, third, sixth, and ninth were added to the Daily Office in late fourth-century urban monasticism. The basic structure of the little hours on Ordinary days includes the priest's blessing "O Heavenly King," the Trisagion ("Holy God, Holy Mighty"), the Lord's Prayer, the Psalms, the Troparion of the day, the Theotokion, scripture verses, the Kontakion (a collect hymn), Prayer of the Hours, and a dismissal. The Trisagion and the Lord's Prayer occur before and after the psalms. The selection of psalms pertains to the particular hour. Psalms 5, 89, and 100 are used in the first hour; 16, 24, and 50 in the third; 53, 54, and 90 in the sixth; and 83, 84, and 85 in the ninth.

3. Vespers is an evening prayer service focused on giving thanks for the day's blessings and asking forgiveness for sins. It begins at sundown, the hour for lighting lamps, and thus shares with *orthros* the central theme of Christ the Light of the World. Also in common with *orthros* – the other original major hour – it is an urban monastic hybrid service combining Egyptian monastic and cathedral components. The cathedral service established the elements of variable psalmody, followed by Psalm 140 with troparion, responsory, three antiphons, litany, three Scriptural readings on certain days, troparion, and dismissal. Three monastic vesper services resulted from the hybrid service created in the final Sabaitic *Typika*. They are daily vespers, great vespers (celebrated when *orthros* includes a great doxology and distinguished by added introductory prayers and psalmody), and little vespers (a shortened vespers celebrated in some monasteries before certain feasts, which is intended to close the day prior to beginning the festive vigil with great vespers).

4. *Apodeipnon,* or compline, marks the completion of the monastic day. It is an invocation for a peaceful night, sinless and free from evil imaginings. It is first found in St. Basil's Longer Rules and is actually a monastic duplication of vespers, which was the original final hour. *Apodeipnon* consists of Psalm 90 (especially important to this service), more psalms, the doxology, the creed, a canon, the Trisagion, the Lord's Prayer, Troparia, 40 Kyrie eleisons, prayers, mutual pardon rite, and a concluding litany.

5. *Mesonyktikon,* or nocturns, is the monastic midnight service. It is composed of continuous psalmody and readings and is occasionally referred to as a self-contained vigil. Father Taft is of the opinion that "*mesonyktikon* is a later office added to fill the gap in the cursus caused by the fusion of the original nocturns with orthros" (Taft, 1986, 1993).

6. Vigils are of an occasional nature and might appear as all-night services before Sunday and feast-day Eucharistic services. They are of varying length and structure but normally consist of vespers, *Apodeipnon,* midnight office, and *Orthros*. Major, or "all-night," vigils, which include the commemoration of great feasts and a monastery's dedication feast, are solemn observances that can last from the 6 p.m. vespers until the third hour at 9 a.m. The present Byzantine midnight office (*mesonyktikon*) is omitted when an all-night vigil is celebrated. Instead vespers is directly followed by the *orthros* psalms.

Father Mateos, in his article "The Origins of the Daily Office," identifies four main stages in the development of the Daily Office. (1) From the first to the fourth century, Christians prayed in private, with emphasis on the important hours of the day, especially morning and evening. (2) The Egyptian monastic office celebrated daily in the morning and evening was established in the early fourth century. (3) In the second half of the fourth century, the ecclesiastical morning and evening offices were established for the secular churches. These offices are called the Cathedral Liturgy of the Hours. (4) The rise of urban monasticism in the latter half of the fourth century brought a hybrid Daily Office based mainly on ecclesiastical offices and tempered with elements from Egyptian monasticism. It was in this phase that additional hours came to be celebrated in accordance with the tradition of Christian private devotion.

The earliest extant evidence on the monastic Daily Office is from John Cassian's *De Institutis Coenobiorum* (c. 417–425) – parts of which the *Apothegmata Patrum* confirms – and the Pachomian sources. Cassian had been a monk in Scetis, the great monastic center in the desert of Lower Egypt, from around 380 to 399. According to the *Institutes* there were only two Daily Offices at Scetis: a night vigil in the early hours of the morning at cock crow (*orthros*) and another in the evening (vespers). Both had the same structure constructed around 12 varying psalms –

the number of psalms called the "Rule of the Angel" in Palladius' *Lausiac History* (c. 419) and later adapted by Cassian in the *Institutes*. The rule of the angel is the norm for psalmody in Egyptian monasticism. According to Cassian's account each psalm was interspersed with private prayer, prostration, and a "collected" prayer by the presider. The 12th psalm appears to have been an "alleluia psalm," which was then followed by "Glory to the Father . . ." and one reading each from the Old and the New Testament. On Saturday, Sunday, and during Paschaltide, the readings were from the Epistles or Acts and from the Gospels. On weekdays the monks celebrated the two offices in their cells. On Saturday and Sunday they gathered together in church for the offices, Eucharist, and a common meal. Thus, the monks at Scetis were semi-anchoritic.

The Pachomian monasteries founded by Pachomius (c. 290–346) were started around 320 at Tabennesi in the Nile valley north of Thebes (the "Thebaid"). According to the Pachomian sources, the Tabennesiot monks were cenobitic, and their two compulsory daily services, morning and evening office, were held in common. These two offices included six monks taking turns reading or reciting six scriptural readings but not necessarily psalmody, a common recitation of the Our Father standing with arms outstretched in cruciform manner, a penitential prostration, and silent prayer while standing. Once the sequence was completed, it was begun again. It is not known how many times the sequence was repeated. The Sunday office specifically included the responsory chanting of psalms as well as the Eucharist and two catechetical or spiritual conferences. In addition the Pachomian morning office began at the same hour used in cathedral practice, which was later than the hour of cock crow at Scetis.

The reason for only two offices in fourth-century Egyptian monasticism is much debated, although the rule of unceasing personal prayer appears to have been a strong factor. However, monastics living near urban centers in Palestine, Mesopotamia, Syria, and Cappadocia at the end of the fourth century were taking a different approach to the Daily Office. These monks maintained the psalmody tradition of the Egyptian desert while also absorbing elements of the cathedral office. According to Cassian's *Institutes* they included three psalms and prayers each for the third, sixth, and ninth hours (Little Hours) in addition to 12 psalms in a predawn office. At evening and morning services, the monks adopted a number of cathedral as well as innovative elements. Traditions tended to vary from place to place. For example, in the monastery at Bethlehem (where Cassian had been a monk from around 382 to 383), a two-part morning service was created to counteract the laziness of the monks. First the Little Hours were added to complement the standard Egyptian morning and evening services, then they added the innovation of a sunrise service. The sunrise service was instituted because the monks had fallen into the habit of returning to bed after the cock crow to dawn service and then sleeping until terce. The new service had the same structure as the Little Hours, consisting of three psalms (50, 62, 89) and three prayers.

Another example of the hybrid nature of the Divine Hours is the Studite *Typika* created under the influence of St. Theodore of Stoudios (759–826). This influential office borrowed from the Euchologion the prayers and diaconal litanies (*diakonika*) of the cathedral office at Constantinople and combined them with the psalmody and hymns of the monastic office at Jerusalem found in the Horologion. The influence of the Studite *Typika* was so great that by the 12th century it had spread throughout the Orthodox monastic world. In that century it was readopted by the monasteries of Palestine and synthesized into the Sabaitic *Typika*. Under the influence of the 14th-century Athonite Hesychasts, the Sabaitic Typika was once more transmuted to become the definitive liturgical *typika* for Byzantine monastic usage.

The daily services of the developed Byzantine and Russian monastic traditions are as follows: *Orthros* (dawn, lauds in the Latin, *utrenyya* in the Slavonic); the Little Hours of first (7 a.m., prime/*hora prote*/*tchas pierve*), third (9 a.m., terce/*hora trite*/*tchas trietie*), sixth (12 noon, sext/*hora hekte*/*tchas schiestie*), and ninth (3 p.m., none/*hora enate*/*tchas devyatie*); vespers (sunset, *lucernarium*/*hesperinos* or *luknikon*/*vetchernya*); *Apodeipnon* (late evening, compline/povecheriya); *Mesonyktikon* (midnight, compline/*polunoshtchnitza*); and occasional vigils (*agrypnia*, Greek, "wakefulness," consisting of vespers, *Apodeipnon*, *Mesonyktikon*, and *Orthros*).

In the Byzantine tradition during the fasts before the feasts of the Nativity and St. Peter and Paul, the monastic *mesoria* (intermediate hours) are said after each of the Little Hours. Great, or Imperial, Hours are added for Good Friday and the vigils of Nativity and Epiphany. These hours are distinguished by three Scripture readings: an Old Testament prophecy, an Epistle, and a Gospel. The Great Hours were derived from a Palestinian Good Friday vigil service at the ninth hour.

MICHAEL D. PETERSON

See also Cassian, John; Egypt; Hesychasm; Hymnographers; Liturgy: Eastern Christian; Mount Athos, Greece; New Skete, New York; Origins: Eastern Christian; Pachomius, St.; Seasons, Liturgical: Eastern Christian; Syria

Further Reading

Arranz, M., "N.D. Uspensky: The Office of the All-Night Vigil in the Greek Church and in the Russian Church," *St. Vladimir's Theological Quarterly* 24 (1980)

Bradshaw, Paul F., *The Origins of the Daily Office* (Alcuin: The Occasional Journal of the Alcuin Club), London: SPCK, 1978

Bradshaw, Paul F., *Daily Prayer in the Early Church: A Study of the Origin and Early Development of the Divine Office* (Alcuin Club Collections, number 63), London: SPCK, 1981; New York: Oxford University Press, 1982

Cassian, John, *A Select Library of Nicene and Post-Nicene Fathers of the Christian Church*, 2nd series, volume 11: *Sulpitius Severus. Vincent of Lerins. John Cassian*, translated and edited under the supervision of Philip Schaff and Henry Wace, Grand Rapids, Michigan: Eerdmans, and Edinburgh: Clark, 1986

Grisbrooke, W. Jardine, "The Formative Period: Cathedral and Monastic Offices," in *The Study of Liturgy*, edited by Cheslyn Jones, revised edition, New York: Oxford University Press, and London: SPCK, 1992

Mateos, Juan, "The Origins of the Divine Office," *Worship* 41:8 (October 1967)
Mateos, Juan, "The Morning and Evening Office," *Worship* 42:1 (January 1968)
Pachomian Koinonia (Cistercian Studies, numbers 45–47), translated and introduced by Armand Veilleux, 3 vols., Kalamazoo, Michigan: Cistercian Publications, 1980–1982
Schmeman, Alexander, *Introduction to Liturgical Theology* (Library of Orthodox Theology, number 4), translated by Ashleigh E. Moorhouse, London: Faith Press, and Portland, Maine: American Orthodox Press, 1966; 2nd edition, 1975; 3rd edition, Crestwood, New York: St. Vladimir's Seminary Press, 1986
Symeon, Archbishop of Thessalonike, Treatise on Prayer: *An Explanation of the Services Conducted in the Orthodox Church* (Archbishop Iakovos Library of Ecclesiastical and Historical Sources, number 9), translated by H.L.N. Simmons, Brookline, Massachusetts: Hellenic College Press, 1984
Taft, Robert F., "Praise in the Desert: The Coptic Monastic Office Yesterday and Today," *Worship* 56 (1982)
Taft, Robert, "*Quaestiones disputatae* in the History of the Liturgy of the Hours: The Origins of Nocturns, Matins, Prime," *Worship* 58 (1984)
Taft, Robert, *The Liturgy of the Hours in East and West: The Origins of the Divine Office and Its Meaning for Today*, Collegeville, Minnesota: Liturgical Press, 1986; 2nd edition, 1993
Taft, Robert, "Hours, Liturgical," in *The Oxford Dictionary of Byzantium*, edited by Alexander P. Kazhdan, New York: Oxford University Press, 1991
Uspenskii, Nicholas, *Evening Worship in the Orthodox Church*, translated and edited by Paul Lazor, Crestwood, New York: St. Vladimir's Seminary Press, 1985
Van der Mensbrugghe, A., "Prayer-time in Egyptian Monasticism (320–450)," *Studia Patristica* 2 (1957)

Office, Daily: Western Christian

The term "Divine Office" was in use by the sixth century to describe the structure of psalms, Scripture readings, hymns, and prayers, exclusive of the Mass, that formed the daily liturgy in Christian monasteries. These prayers constituted the major duty of the monk, as the Latin term *officium* suggests. In the classic formulation of the Rule of St. Benedict, they comprised the *opus Dei*, "the work of God," before which "nothing is to be preferred." Although the texts of the office varied greatly at different times and places, from the ninth century the structure of the office throughout Western Latin-rite monasticism displayed a remarkable and increasing uniformity.

A single principle directed the evolution of the monastic office: the New Testament injunction to "pray always" (1 Thess. 5:17). However, since early Christian times this admonition was interpreted as an obligation to pray at set intervals throughout each day and to fix these times with ever greater precision. This structure evolved into the seven "hours" of prayer that constituted the classic Divine Office: matins and lauds, or prayers in the middle of the night and at daybreak (Monastic matins was usually called "nocturnes," or "vigils," in the early Middle Ages; lauds was referred to as "matins." This nomenclature was retained in many monasteries into the modern period.); daytime prayer at the first (prime), the third (terce), the sixth (sext), and the ninth (nones) hour; and prayer at early evening (vespers) and before retiring (compline). This system was often justified as divinely inspired, quoting a verse from Psalm 118: "Seven times a day have I given praise unto thee."

No evidence pre-dating the fourth century describes in any detail either the structure or the content of daily prayer in Christian communities. By 350 the so-called cathedral office is clearly in existence, celebrated in the morning (lauds) and evening (vespers or lucenarium) by the bishop along with the clergy and the people. These services consisted mainly of fixed psalms that had become associated with certain times of the day: Psalm 62 and the "psalms of praise" (148–150) for the morning and Psalm 140 for the evening. In some places communal prayer was also celebrated at various other hours of the day.

The monastic office was much influenced by this cathedral office, but it also had a second important antecedent: the prayer

Oil lamp and lectern, Chapel of St. Bonaventure, Greggio (Lazio), Italy, early 13th century.
Photo courtesy of Mary Schaefer

practices of the first monks in the Egyptian desert. These eremitic monks argued that the recitation of specified prayers at certain times of the day simply encouraged the neglect of prayer at all other times. Thus, communal prayer in the famous Upper Egyptian monasteries of Pachomius (c. 290–346) was minimal and might not have existed at all as an identifiable entity. Practice flowed imperceptibly from constant private prayer into simple communal gatherings. The monks met together in the morning and again before retiring. At these "collects" individual monks recited memorized Scriptures, punctuated by a communal Lord's Prayer and prostrate silent prayer. The monks performed light manual labor as they meditated on the recitations and then moved easily into an organization of the day's work. Only on Sundays did the monks come together more formally and chant psalms in preparation for the weekly Eucharist. This insistence of the Desert Fathers on the importance of the monk's private prayer over against communal liturgy undergirded many later reforms of the monastic office.

Forty years later, around 385, John Cassian (c. 360–after 430), a monk from Bethlehem, visited the Egyptian monasteries and subsequently wrote a description of the liturgical prayer of the Egyptian monks in his *Institutes*, a famous text that much influenced the monastic office in the West. Cassian claimed to be describing the practices of the Pachomian monasteries but in fact was describing a much more structured liturgy centered in Lower Egypt. Cassian's "Egyptian" office had two parts. The first was a lengthy night prayer that extended into the morning, and the second was an evening prayer; both originally involved many psalms. These, said Cassian, had been reduced to 12 by the intervention of an angel. To this divinely appointed number of psalms the Egyptian fathers had added two optional readings, one from the Old Testament and one from the New. Cassian claimed that a new hour had been added after the night office because monks were returning to sleep until daybreak, contrary to the Egyptian desert traditions. Until recently scholars believed that this new hour represented the institution of prime, but recent research has concluded that it actually represents the adoption of the cathedral morning prayer of lauds. It consisted of psalms that are traditionally associated with that hour: Psalms 50, 62, and 118:147–148, and the three psalms of praise, 148, 149, and 150.

Cassian took up residence in southern Gaul after leaving Egypt around 410 and imposed this "ancient Egyptian" office on the monasteries that he founded around Marseilles, claiming the authority of the founders of monasticism. Cassian's office can plausibly be described as follows:

Matins: 12 or more psalms and two (optional) readings
Lauds: Psalms 50, 62, and 118:147–148, and the psalms of praise: 148, 149, and 150

Choir stalls, Church of the Cordeliers (Franciscan), Fribourg, Switzerland, 13th century. Photo courtesy of Mary Schaefer

Terce, sext, and nones: three psalms and concluding prayers
Vespers: 12 psalms and two readings

Except for the hour of lauds, borrowed from the cathedral tradition, the psalms of the hours were sung in sequence, following the order of their appearance in the Psalter, which became the distinctive monastic interpretation of "praying always." The hours of prime and compline, unmentioned by Cassian, probably had as yet no place in the daily round of monastic prayer.

Cassian also introduced a monastic vigil on Saturday/Sunday that originated in Palestine and was celebrated after the normal monastic night office ended. It consisted of three psalms followed by three readings. This pattern was likely repeated until an hour before daybreak. Owing to the influence of Cassian's writing, this Sunday vigil became a model for the third nocturn of the classic Benedictine night office.

The course of Cassian's influence on the evolution of the Western office can be traced with some precision. It begins at the monastery of Lérins, founded about 410 by Cassian's pupil, St. Honoratus (d. 429/30). Brief monastic rules from throughout the fifth century, plausibly connected to Lérins, do not provide detailed descriptions of liturgical practices, but some sections recall Pachomius and Cassian, whereas others look forward to the office of St. Caesarius of Arles (c. 470–542).

The French, or "Gallican," office of St. Caesarius of Arles is the first monastic office that can be described in detail. All seven traditional hours are presented with their classic elements: psalms, Scripture readings, hymns, and prayers. Although Caesarius claims to be following the Lérins and Cassian traditions, his office exhibited many original features that became part of the classic Benedictine monastic office. These included the inclusion of a hymn at every hour and the chanting of the Gospel canticles of Simeon (the Benedictus) and of Mary (the Magnificat) at lauds and vespers.

Although the Gallican office of Caesarius was widespread in the sixth century, it was not destined to play the leading role in the formation of the classic monastic office. This distinction went to Italy and involved developments in and around Rome. Around 550 the Rule for Monks of St. Benedict was written at Monte Cassino. Containing a detailed *ordo* for the recitation of the Divine Office, this Rule became the foundation document for the Western office until the present.

Benedict's office is indebted in its overall structure to Cassian and the Egyptian desert tradition, but many specific elements were borrowed from Roman monasteries, a source that Benedict repeatedly credits. Benedict was himself a Roman, and his monastic foundations were near that major urban center. Benedict's most significant borrowing from Rome was the weekly recitation of the Psalter, and in this matter Benedict's creativity is most evident. He slashed the number of psalms at matins from the 12 to 25 psalms of the Roman office to an invariable 12, arranged in two sections, or nocturns, thus restoring the "angelic number" set down in Cassian. Although Benedict shortened the psalmody at matins, he increased the readings: four lessons were read in the winter daily office, increasing to 12 on Sundays and major feasts. However, the reading in the shorter summer nights was reduced to two brief passages. Benedict is also the first to prescribe reading in the Fathers as well as the Scriptures, and he added a reading at all the other hours of the office as well. For Benedict's office, as for all monastic usages, the psalmody was the core of the liturgy, yet the prominence that he gave to readings is a fundamental source of the later Benedictine intellectual tradition. Finally, Benedict added a third nocturn as a Sunday vigil, consisting of three Old Testament canticles and four New Testament readings. This section borrows its structure from the Sunday vigils of Cassian and of Caesarius of Arles, but Benedict innovates here as well by substituting canticles for psalms, thus injecting some variety into the lengthy office. The hymns that he included in each hour provided another element of balance. Because the Italian traditions did not use hymns, Benedict probably borrowed them from the widespread Gallican office of Caesarius.

Benedict's creative balancing of elements is perhaps best seen in the morning hour of lauds. The psalmody consists mainly of fixed psalms and an Old Testament canticle, showing its origin in the secular cathedral tradition, but it also contains sequential psalmody, a typically monastic element. A short reading followed and a hymn preceded the climax of the hour: the chanting of the Benedictus or the Magnificat, a practice found both in the Roman monastic *cursus* and in Caesarius. The hour ended with another innovation, the recitation of the Our Father by the abbot. Benedict's vespers, the mirror hour of lauds, had the same elements after the psalmody, but as a monastic celebration it employed four sequential psalms instead of fixed psalmody. Sequential psalms also replaced the Roman invariable psalms in the daytime hours. This change was designed to finish the Psalter in a week, as Benedict had reduced the psalmody at the night office and to add variety to the day hours. Compline alone retained three fixed psalms (4, 90, and 135), an archaic usage suitable for a private prayer recited by heart when retiring.

Benedict's fusion of structures from many sources, as well as his own original contributions, created a balanced office of moderate length. Thus, his office had the potential for widespread adoption but was slow to extend its influence. Soon after the Rule was written, Benedict's abbey at Monte Cassino was destroyed by invading Lombards and lay in ruins for almost over a century. During that period (the late sixth to seventh century), the most widespread monastic liturgy was the Irish office of St. Columban (d. 615). Composed in the spirit of Irish penitential austerity, it contained a night office of 60 to 100 psalms. However, monasteries founded during the latter 600s from Irish centers in northern and eastern France increasingly tempered the austerities of Columban's rule with elements of the Rule of St. Benedict. Some elements of this mixed monastic life are well detailed, although the sources do not reveal the liturgical practices of such houses.

The Benedictine usage was at the same time penetrating the Frankish kingdom to the east. Anglo-Saxon missionaries to Germany followed the Benedictine liturgy, and the main monastic adviser to the Carolingian ruler, St. Boniface (c. 675–754), imposed the Benedictine Rule on the abbey that a disciple founded at Fulda in 744. He sent its first abbot to Monte Cassino to learn its usages, and thereafter Fulda became the center for monastic reform in the ever expanding Carolingian Empire.

The establishment of the Benedictine usage as the official liturgy in Frankish monasteries was the work of Benedict's namesake, Benedict of Aniane (750–821). Benedict shared the emperor's desire for a single monastic usage throughout the empire. Thus, at the Council of Aachen in 817, the Frankish bishops agreed to establish the Benedictine Rule, along with its liturgy, in all imperial abbeys. Official inspectors were sent out to ensure compliance with the edict. Although enforcement of the order ended with the swift decline of the Carolingians in the ninth century, the ideal of uniformity was gradually accepted, and by the time documentation reappears in the late tenth century, many more monasteries have adopted the Benedictine liturgy.

The most important of these was the abbey of Cluny in eastern France, founded in 909, whose first abbots established the Benedictine Rule and liturgy as interpreted by Benedict of Aniane. Over the next two centuries, Cluny came to dominate the monastic life of Western Europe, directly controlling over 200 monasteries and reforming many others. One result of this Cluniac "empire" was the establishment of the monastic office of Benedict in most Western European monasteries. However, that liturgy was established according to the interpretation of Benedict of Aniane, regarded by many in the Middle Ages as the authoritative explicator of Benedictine monasticism. Although Benedict was careful to retain the core structure of the founder's office, he made significant additions to it. These included recitation of the 15 "gradual" psalms (119–133) before the night office, the recitation of the seven penitential psalms after the various hours of the office, and the obligation to sing the office of the Dead, a semi-liturgical devotion usually consisting of matins, lauds, and vespers.

Benedict's additions provided a precedent for further augmentations: special psalms and prayers for the ruler and abbey's benefactors were added, called the *psalmi familiares*, at the end of every hour. Shifts in piety added further burdens to the liturgy: in the tenth century a devotional office appeared called the "office of the Blessed Virgin," or the *officium de Beata*, which was soon adopted in most monasteries. A popular anthem to the Virgin, usually employing the text *Salve Regina*, along with associated prayers, was appended to compline.

It was the burgeoning cult of the saints that most complicated the monastic liturgy. Saints' feasts competed with one another and with the older yearly cycle that celebrated Christ's life: the Nativity, the Epiphany, the Death and the Resurrection. Elaborate calculations became necessary to decide which celebration took precedence on a given day. If lesser-ranked feasts were omitted, their "commemorations" were added to the office of the day. On many occasions feasts of equal rank occurred on the same day, and so both offices or parts of both offices were chanted. A new "votive" office of all saints, consisting of vigils and vespers, was celebrated daily in many Cluniac houses, and a litany of the saints, accompanied by a procession, was recited at prime.

The rise of devotion to the saints caused two important alternations of the core office. Readings from the legends of the saints came increasingly to be substituted for the patristic readings and later for the scriptural readings as well, owing to the popularity of this genre. Moreover saints' feasts had their own set of psalms, so as saints' days filled the calendar, Benedict's basic structural principle of weekly recitation of the Psalter was rarely observed by the later Middle Ages.

Elaborate ritual movements and processions accompanied the offices, and beginning in the tenth century an increasingly complex and leisurely chant was used. At Easter and Christmas, dramatizations of the events of the feast were integrated into the night office, often involving theatrical action and invented dialogue. Voluminous choir cowls with sleeves sometimes reaching to the floor become common. The celebration of this liturgy reached such a degree of length and complexity that in some houses it continued night and day with different choirs working in shifts as *laus perennis*, or "perpetual praise."

Major revolts against this vision of monasticism arose in the late 11th and 12th centuries. Reformed Benedictine groups, such as the Cistercians and the Camaldolese, and new monastic orders, such as the Carthusians, abolished Cluniac additions to the office, simplified the chant, and restored the primacy of scriptural and patristic readings at matins. However, even these reformed groups retained the most popular liturgical devotions, such as the office of the Dead and of the Blessed Virgin. In the later Middle Ages, complaints about the length and complexity of the monastic office and its accretions also increased within the Cluniac houses. A new spirituality focusing on individual piety and a desire for more time to pursue intellectual work added to the dissatisfaction. Consequently the accretions to the office were gradually abolished, although observance of the more popular devotions, such as the office of the Dead, continued in many Benedictine houses into modern times.

Of the many important religious orders that emerged in the later medieval centuries, such as the Franciscans and Dominicans, not one adopted the monastic liturgy, although many lived in a monastic enclosure with a chanted choir office. The numerous and popular Franciscans adopted the office of the Roman Curia, a shorter and more simply celebrated office than Benedict's. They spread this papal office to all parts of Europe, and in 1568 a centralizing papacy imposed a reformed version of this office, the *Breviarium Romanum*, on all the Western clergy while exempting older orders, such as the Benedictines.

Although the Benedictines were exempt from using the new papal office, many houses found it superior to the current monastic liturgy, especially in its restoration of the weekly recitation of the Psalter. Moreover a desire was growing for a common monastic office, a sentiment reflecting the centralizing tendencies of the early modern Church. However, most Benedictines favored a common office that would better preserve the traditional Benedictine elements than did the *Breviarium Romanum*. Such an office appeared in 1610, prepared by the monks of St. Gall, Switzerland. It adopted the Roman lectionary, its calendar of saints, and many of its texts while retaining the distinctive Benedictine arrangement of the Psalter. Most Benedictine monasteries adopted the breviary of St. Gall during the next century. This office, later known as the *Breviarium Monasticum*, became the liturgy for most Benedictines until the late 20th century, although the Cistercian Order retained its distinctive liturgy, as did many of the older Benedictine houses, most notably Cluny and its many dependent monasteries.

The most recent transformation of the monastic office occurred in the context of the Second Vatican Council (1962–1965). A major item on the council's agenda of *aggiornamento*, or modernization, was the reform of the Roman office. This reform was accomplished with the publication in 1972 of the *Liturgia Horarum* (Liturgy of the Hours). Although the traditional structure of the office was retained, major changes were made in its component parts: the recitation of the Psalter was spread over four weeks, the night office was transformed into an "office of Readings" that could be performed at any hour, its psalmody was drastically curtailed, its readings were reduced in number and extended in length, and many traditional texts were changed. The hour of prime was abolished and the remaining daytime hours reduced to a single "midday prayer." Use of the vernacular and of modern popular hymns was permitted. Benedictine monasteries quickly adopted a number of these changes, having long felt the need for such a reform. Although the Vatican encouraged monastic communities to retain the use of Gregorian chant and Latin for the office, a survey of male Benedictine houses in 1986 showed that most houses had abandoned both Latin and Gregorian chant except for the most traditional and popular elements, most notably the antiphon of the Blessed Virgin, the *Salve Regina*, after compline. However, the degree of experimentation varied greatly. Monasteries in the United States, in Germany, and in third-world countries innovated freely, using new music and texts, whereas in the Mediterranean countries many houses retained Latin and Gregorian chant. In many monasteries the parts of the office that are sung rather than recited have increased since the council's reforms.

The Benedictine Order also followed the Roman lead in reforming the structure and altering the texts of the monastic office. In 1977 the Benedictine abbots published the *Thesaurus Liturgiae Monasticae Horarum*. This provided a wide variety of texts and structures from which individual Benedictine houses could choose, depending on local circumstances (although some congregations have published complete monastic office books for individual countries). Perhaps most important was the provision by the *Thesaurus* of four different "schemes," whereby the recitation of the Psalter could be spread over one, two, or four weeks. In 1981 the abbey of Solesmes published the *Psalterium Monasticum* and in 1995 a new edition of the *Antiphonale Monasticum*; these publications allow the texts of the office from the *Thesaurus* to be chanted in historically researched Gregorian modes. The appearance of these books has caused some Benedictine houses to renew their traditions of using Gregorian chant and Latin for portions of the office. After the experimentation of the 1960s and 1970s, a reestablishment of more traditional structures and practices in the celebration of the monastic office seems to be occurring, although many exceptions and local variations exist. A number of monasteries make use of guitars and of the vernacular, have introduced newly composed hymns and antiphons, and have created novel structures for some hours. Thus, after centuries of increasing standardization and domination by Roman usages, the diversity and localism that characterized the monastic office in the early Middle Ages once again emerges as its distinguishing characteristic.

JOHN B. WICKSTROM

See also Benedict of Aniane, St.; Benedict of Nursia, St.; Benedictines; Boniface, St.; Caesarius of Arles, St.; Cassian, John; Christianity: Overview; Cluny, France; Egypt; Fulda, Germany; Humanism, Christian; Lérins, France; Liturgy: Western Christian; Martyrs: Western Christian; Monte Cassino, Italy; Music: Christian Perspectives; Origins: Eastern Christian; Pachomius, St.; Plainchant; Solesmes, France

Further Reading

Aethelwold, Saint, *The Monastic Agreement of the Monks and Nuns of the English Nation* (the *Regularis concordia*), edited by Thomas Symons, New York: Oxford University Press, 1953

Benedict, Saint, RB 1980: *The Rule of St. Benedict in Latin and English*, edited by Timothy Fry, Collegeville, Minnesota: Liturgical Press, 1981

Bradshaw, Paul, *Daily Prayer in the Early Church*, New York: Oxford University Press, and London: SPCK, 1981

Campbell, Stanislaus, *From Breviary to Liturgy of the Hours: The Structural Reform of the Roman Office: 1964–1971*, Collegeville, Minnesota: Liturgical Press, 1995

Evans, Joan, *Monastic Life at Cluny, 910–1157*, London: Oxford University Press, 1931; Hampden, Connecticut: Archon Books, 1968

Nicholson, David, editor, *Liturgical Music in Benedictine Monasticism: A Post-Vatican II Survey*, 2 vols., St. Benedict, Oregon: Mount Angel Abbey, 1986

Taft, Robert, *The Liturgy of the Hours in East and West*, Collegeville, Minnesota: Liturgical Press, 1986

Tolhurst, J.B.L., *Introduction to the English Monastic Breviaries*, Woodbridge, Suffolk, and Rochester, New York: Boydell and Brewer, 1993 (first published as volume 6 of *The Monastic Breviary of Hyde Abbey, Winchester*, London: Harrison, 1932–1942)

Officials: Buddhist

In speaking of Buddhist officials, we have to differentiate between the earlier phases for which the law books (*vinaya*) of the various Buddhist schools, the commentaries on these law books, and the reports of the Chinese pilgrims who traveled to India serve as sources and later developments in the different Buddhist countries up to modern times. Here only the earlier developments are dealt with.

During the lifetime of Gautama Buddha, he himself headed the whole Buddhist community (Sanskrit, Pāli, *saṅgha*) and determined the mode of living of Buddhist monks and nuns. On his deathbed the Buddha refused to designate a successor as head of the community after his demise. He ordered the monks and nuns to follow only the teaching (Sanskrit, *dharma*; Pāli, *dhamma*) and discipline (Sanskrit, Pāli, *vinaya*) as taught by him. Thus, the office of head of the whole Buddhist community does not exist in the earliest textual layers.

The local community is the acting unit regarding administrative and executive and sometimes also legislative affairs. A local community is defined in the Vinaya as the totality of monks (Sanskrit, *bhikṣu*; Pāli, *bhikkhu*) living within one and the same ecclesiastical boundary (Sanskrit, Pāli, *sīmā*). All the fully ordained (Pāli, *upasampanna*) members of the local community had the same right to vote and thus were responsible for the administration of the monastery. The office of head of these local communities is not mentioned in the law books. In the first centuries the age of higher ordination (Sanskrit, *upasaṃpadā*; Pāli, *upasampadā*) was the only factor relevant for the hierarchy within the local communities. However, the spread of Buddhism over a wide geographic area, the growth of the monasteries, the increasing number of monks, as well as the increase of the monasteries' property led to many differing models for administration. Nevertheless matters of daily life as well as judicial affairs had to be dealt with in all communities from the very beginning. Thus, there existed various offices common to most of the Buddhist schools. They were conferred on monks of a local community, not at a supraregional level.

To the basic offices belonged all tasks connected with robes. The Theravādin names are the "receiver of robes" (Pāli, *cīvarapaṭiggāhaka*), "storer of robes" (*cīvaranidāhaka*), and "distributor of robes" (*cīvarabhājaka*). Similarly there are several offices concerning food: "distributor of soft food" (Pāli, *bhattuddesaka*), "distributor of hard food" (Pāli, *khajjābhājaka*), "distributor of gruel" (Pāli, *yāgubhājaka*), and "distributor of fruit" (Pāli, *phalabhājaka*). A third group deals with lodgings: "assigner of lodgings" (Pāli, *senāsanaggāhāpaka*) and "assigner of beds" (Pāli, *senāsanapaññāpaka*). The "disposer of trifles" (Pāli, *appamattakavissajaka*) had to dispose of scissors, sandals, and other utensils used by the monks, and the "keeper of the storeroom" (*bhaṇḍagārika*) was responsible for the stores. When larger monasteries came into existence, some of the worldly affairs of the community were handled by slaves (Pāli, *dāsa*) or by laypeople "belonging to" the monasteries (Pāli, *ārāmika*). In that case the laypeople were supervised by monks, who were installed in the office of "supervisor of the ārāmikas" (Pāli, *ārāmikapesaka*). New building work or restoration projects were supervised by a "supervisor of new building activities" (Pāli, *navakammika*), and the work of novices was supervised by a "supervisor of novices" (Pāli, *sāmaṇerapesaka*). A similar office existed for religious affairs, namely, that of the "teacher of nuns" (Pāli, *bhikkhunovādaka*), an office relevant only as long as the nun's community existed.

New offices were introduced when there was need. Such new offices, not known to the Theravāda Vinaya but mentioned in the Vinaya of the Mūlasarvāstivāda school, are, for example, the "superintendent of servants" (Sanskrit, *upasthāyaka*) and the "guardian of material objects" (Sanskrit, *upadhivārika*) or, in the Mahāsāṃghika tradition, the office to care for the calendar (Sanskrit, *pakṣacārika* or *māsacārika*). Installation in these new offices followed the practice in use before. The persons chosen for the respective office had to be asked beforehand whether they were willing to accept the assignment. If they agreed they were installed in the office by the local community in a legal act, consisting of a motion and a single proclamation (Sanskrit, *jñaptidvitīyakarma*; Pāli, *ñattidutiyakamma*). According to the later Theravāda tradition (e.g., in the text Samantapāsādikā), a single monk could occupy up to 13 such functions. In the modern Thai tradition, it is recommended to choose one monk for related tasks and to install him, for example, in all three offices connected with robes.

The reports of the Chinese pilgrims I-ching and Hsuan-tsang, who traveled in India during the seventh century A.D., show that at that time there was no uniform model for the administration of monasteries in India. Most of them were headed by a "director," who was generally the eldest monk of the community (Sanskrit, *saṅghasthavira*), regardless of his learning. However, this was not valid for all monasteries. Some kept very strictly to the Vinaya rules and thus did not introduce such an office. In other communities "very learned" persons, often foreign monks with a great reputation, were asked to function as head of a monastery. In some cases the ruling king installed monks in the various offices (e.g., in Vikramaśīla).

According to I-ching's account, in some monasteries a subdirector (*karmadāna*) supervised the kitchen and announced religious ceremonies. The administration of greater monasteries, such as the famous Buddhist university Nālandā, with about 3,500 monks and more than 200 villages for its support, required a centralized and strictly hierarchically structured apparatus. I-ching tells us that the finance department in Nālandā consisted of a committee of several monks. This holds true also for the temple administration, for building activities, and so on.

Whereas in India Buddhism disappeared after the Muslim invasions during the 12th and 13th centuries, Buddhism survived as Theravāda Buddhism in Burma, Sri Lanka, Thailand, Laos, and Cambodia as well as in various forms, subsumed under the term Mahāyāna, in Tibet, China, Japan, and so on. These diverse traditions gave rise to very different offices. Mainly during the Middle Ages, offices of a supraregional type developed in some Buddhist countries. For example, in the Theravāda tradition of Sri Lanka the office of a head of the whole Buddhist community of Sri Lanka came into existence, an office that from the 14th century on was titled "king of the Buddhist community" (Pāli, *saṅgharāja*). This office also existed in Burma and in Thailand. In Tibet the offices of the Dalai Lama and the Panchen Lama originated.

In general it can be stated that the type and number of offices within one community, whether or not there existed hierarchically structured offices of head, vice head, and so on, depended to a considerable degree on the structure of the secular administration of the respective country and on the degree of interference of the state into religious affairs. However, these later developments are not based on the rules of the law books (*vinaya*) of the diverse Buddhist schools.

PETRA KIEFFER-PÜLZ

See also Abbot: Buddhist; Nālandā, India; Pilgrims to India, Chinese; Regulations: Buddhist Perspectives; Rules, Buddhist (Vinaya)

Further Reading

Joshi, Lal Mani, *Studies in the Buddhistic Culture of India (During the 7th and 8th centuries A.D.)*, Delhi: Motilal Banarsidass, 1967; 2nd edition, 1977

Karunatillake, P.V.B., "The Administrative Organization of the Nālandā Mahāvihāra from Sigillary Evidence," *Sri Lanka Journal of Humanities* 6 (1980)

Lahiri, Latika, translator, *Chinese Monks in India: Biography of Eminent Monks Who Went to the Western World in Search of the Law During the Great T'ang Dynasty*, Delhi: Motilal Banarsidass, 1986

Officials: Western Christian

Members of monastic communities shared various tasks related to the practical needs of monasteries, sometimes resorting to the assistance of hired laymen. The diversity of monastic life and of local conditions caused monastic offices to multiply and their responsibilities, terms of office, and place within the power structure to vary enormously. A pragmatic approach, typical of monks, caused offices to be created and abolished on the basis of local needs.

Officials were the monks performing specific offices in a monastery. The special task to which each official was assigned was called an "obedience," and he himself was referred to as an "obedientiary." Among officials were those "superior" who performed the most important functions and numerous "inferior" ones who discharged specialized duties.

The Rule of St. Benedict, written for a small community of monks, named two principal officials to assist the abbot: his lieutenant, i.e. the provost or prior (chap. 65), and the cellarer (31), who had complete control of the community's material resources. Besides these passing mention is made of deans (21), novice-master (58), guest-master (53), and councillors (3).

The gradual clericalization of monastic communities and of their tasks, resulting from an increasing role in society on the one hand and the growth and specialization of various orders and congregations on the other, added new offices to the list of principal ones.

Deans, superiors of groups of ten monks, first appeared in cenobitic communities of Egypt. Although St. Benedict favored them, the development of monastic offices led to the disappearance of deans.

A provost or prior was the abbot's deputy. The original name "provost" was gradually superseded by that of "prior." However, the name "provost" has been used, especially to the east of the Rhine, in reference to some offices (e.g., provost of a hospital or infirmarian) and in particular to the superiors of monastic dependencies. The position of the provost (in the latter sense) within the hierarchy of power was high. The title "provost" was also frequently used in monasteries of canons regular.

The gradual evolution of the position of abbot and his growing separation from the monastic community resulted in the emergence of an abbot's court with its own hierarchy of offices, mostly lay. An important role was played within it by the abbot's chaplains or secretaries (also called chancellors), usually recruited from among the monks. Such officials assisted priors as well.

The prior headed the monastic community, reporting to the abbot. With time functioning as *prior claustralis*, he represented the convent before the abbot. In large monasteries he had a deputy (subprior), who in turn could have deputies of his own (the third prior or even the fourth prior). His power was based on an indefinite number of seniors charged with supervision in the cloister and dormitory, known as the *circatores* or *custodes ordinis*.

One of the most important posts was that of the cellarer, the monastery's manager and general administrator, who was responsible for all matters not entrusted to other officials. He was in charge of the monastery's economy, including food supplies and the management of property and goods. In large monasteries there were the intern and extern cellarers as well as numerous specialized officers reporting to the cellarer. The most important among them were the kitchener, in charge of catering; the refectorer, in charge of the movable and immovable furnishings of the refectory (dining hall of the monks); the pittancer, responsible for the provision of all materials for the pittances (individual "extra" dishes); the gardener; the chancellor, in charge of the chancery; and specialized officials responsible for the supervision of goods and the monastery's legal cases judged in various courts. In mendicant orders (i.e., those not endowed with real estate), an official of great importance was *questarius*, a monk collecting funds for the monastery.

The chamberlain was the banker of the community, receiving its income and managing its funds. He was also to take care of the dormitory and the basic needs of the monks (e.g., their straw mattresses, hot water, soap, and razors). He was assisted by the master of the vestry, in charge of clothing and its cleanliness, and, for example, by a monk responsible for bringing lamps to dormitories every night and for hanging towels.

In a broad sense the liturgy was the responsibility of the cantor, also called provisor (sometimes *custos*) and the sacristan. The cantor was charged with training the monks in the chant and the proper celebration of the liturgy as well as with running the library and scriptorium, as liturgical books were kept and copied there. Under his authority were the numerous succentors who served as his assistants or deputies, and in this number also were the supervisors of the library and scriptorium (the *armarius*, i.e., the librarian).

The sacristan was initially responsible only for holy vessels, vestments, relics, and the treasury and later for the upkeep of the church, for example, for repairs, cleaning, heating (he provided glowing embers so that the monks saying mass could warm their

Chapter house, Cistercian Abbey of Lilienfeld, Austria, 13th century. Photo courtesy of Chris Schabel

hands), and lighting (often not only of the church). His duties included also providing for pilgrims. His assistant, the *capicerius*, was in charge of church vestments, altar cloths, and clothing of the monks. Another succentor's duty was keeping the Canonical Hours, ringing the bell, and winding clocks.

New tasks set for orders after the Council of Trent (1545–1563) necessitated the creation of the new offices of preacher and confessor, both of special importance among mendicants. At that time the role of the librarians grew.

The almoner distributed the charity of the house to regular and casual applicants for help. It was also his duty to visit deserving cases in the town or city and to distribute alms. The guest-master took care of guests of the monastery, providing food and shelter for them and their horses. The gate of the monastery was guarded by the gatekeeper, often a layman.

The infirmarian was responsible for the infirmary (i.e., the monastic hospital). In large monasteries the infirmary was a separate place with its own kitchen, refectory, chapel, and garden.

The care of novices was entrusted to the novice-master; the care of boy oblates staying in the monastery was entrusted to the children-master. Mendicant friars, especially the Dominicans, raised the importance of education and internal monastic schools. The office of lector of theology was regarded as very important and soon spread to other orders as well.

There were similar offices in female orders, where usually an important role was played by the "external" male staff. The principal officials were supported by monks assigned on a weekly basis (thus the name *hebdomadarii*) to provide basic services (e.g., cleaning, work in the kitchen, and serving the table).

Initially officials were appointed and removed by the abbot to whom they reported. Then a system in which the monastic chapter elected its officials for a prescribed term (usually for three years) became popular.

Gradually a system for supervising officials developed in the form of annual and final reports. In centralized congregations and orders, the review was assigned to the visitors, that is, monks conducting regular visitations in dependent monasteries or in those belonging to an order or congregation. An important supervising role was played by a group of councillors traditionally advising the superior of a monastery. In older orders there were, according to the Rule of St. Benedict, seniors, that is, monks with the longest monastic seniority. In new orders there were definitors.

At first, officials withdrew the means necessary to carry on their duties from the common fund of the abbey, that is, from the income of the so-called *mensa conventualis*, or the "table of the convent" (if it existed as a separate entity). However, soon the practice of assigning benefices to particular offices became widespread, mainly in reference to the highest-ranking ones (prior, cellarer, chamberlain, cantor, and sacristan) or to those responsible for independent areas (almoner and guest-master). Reformers of monastic life opposed this practice because of its adverse influence on the communal life of the convent.

With the emergence of centralized orders and Benedictine congregations, hierarchies within the central offices of a given order or congregation developed as well.

MAREK DERWICH

See also Abbot: Christian; Governance: Christian Perspectives; Monk-Bishops; Patrons, Christian: Royal; Timekeeping: Christian Perspectives

Further Reading

Borias, André, "Le cellérier bénédictin et sa communauté," *Regulae Benedicti Studia* 6:7 (1981)

Constable, Giles, "Cluniac Administration and Administrators in the Twelfth Century," in *Order and Innovation in the Middle Ages: Essays in Honor of Joseph R. Strayer*, Princeton, New Jersey: Princeton University Press, 1976; also in his *Cluniac Studies* (Collected Studies Series), London: Variorum, 1980

Gallen, Joseph F., *Canon Law for Religious: An Explanation*, New York: Alba House, 1983

Hanstein, Honorius, *Ordensrecht: Ein Grundriss für Studierende, Seelsorger, Klosterleitungen und Juristen*, Paderborn: Verlag Ferdinand Schöningh, 1970

Hourlier, Jacques, *L'âge classique, 1140–1378: les religieux* (Histoire du Droit des Institutions de l'Église en Occident, 10), Paris: Cujas, 1973

Jocqué, Luc, "Les structures de la population claustrale dans l'odre de Saint-Victor au XIIe siècle. Un essai d'analyse du *Liber Ordinis*," in *L'abbaye parisienne de Saint-Victor au Moyen Âge: Communications* (Bibliotheca Victorina, 1), edited by Jean Longère, Paris: Brepols, 1991

Knowles, David, *The Religious Orders in England,* 3 vols., Cambridge: University Press, 1948–1959; New York: Cambridge University Press, 1979

Lemoine, Robert, *Le droit des religieux du Concile de Trente aux Instituts séculiers*, Paris: Desclée, de Brouwer, 1956

Listl, Joseph, Hubert Müller, and Heribert Schmitz, *Handbuch des katholischen Kirchenrechts*, Regensburg: Pustet, 1983

Moulin, Léo, *La vie quotidienne des religieux au Moyen Âge Xe–XVe siècle*, Paris: Hachette, 1978

Primetshofer, Bruno, *Ordenrecht* (Rombach Hochschul Paperback, 89), Freiburg im Breisgau: Rombach, 1978; 3rd edition, 1988

Les religieuses dans le cloître et dans le monde des origines à nos jours: Actes du Deuxième Colloque International du C.E.R.C.O.R., Poitiers, 29 septembre– 2 octobre 1988 (C.E.R.C.O.R., Travaux et Recherches, 4), Saint-Étienne: Publications de l'Université de Saint-Étienne, 1994

Orders (Religious), Origin of

The term *religious order* often is applied anachronistically to earlier centuries, but such an institution appears only in the 12th century. It can be seen to reflect growing trends toward institutionalization and the use of written documents, something that is characteristic of what has often been called the "12th-century Renaissance." Although individual monastic houses and congregations of monastic communities existed before the 12th century in Western Europe, the religious order, an umbrella group of monastic communities with common practices enforced by a centralized administration, was a 12th-century invention. Indeed the term *order* (*ordo/ordinis*) did not begin to be used in the sense of a group to which one could belong until the 1140s; before that *ordo* designated a way of life, for example, that of the *ordo clericus* or *ordo laicus*. Eleventh-century groups might have belonged to congregations, but they had no overarching organizations other than monarchical or familial ones, such as that between the abbey of Cluny and its many dependent priories during the long reigns of its early abbots. Congregations were held together by strong, often charismatic leaders whose individual authority was more important than any written customaries or guidelines for the practice of monastic rules. For many new reform groups of the 12th century – Premonstratensians, Gilbertines, Grandmontines, and Carthusians – it is especially difficult to tell when they were transformed from a congregation into a religious order. Despite our tendency to talk as if they had been orders from the beginning, it is likely that none underwent such a transformation before the mid–12th century. Gradually the meaning of *ordo monasticus* begins to shift from meaning the regular life of monks and nuns to particular instances of the regular monastic or canonical way of life, such as the *ordo cisterciensis*, *ordo cluniacensis*, or *ordo praemonstratensis*, designating specific types of practices of liturgy and of economic and social organization within monasteries.

At the same time as the word *ordo* was taking on connotations of specific practices, groups of houses practicing one of these more specific ways of life were beginning to coalesce into larger, supramonastic bodies under the authority of heads, usually collective ones, often called general chapters. Such chapters varied considerably in their makeup. For example, 13th-century Cluniac general chapters were not assemblies of all heads of houses but rather of a smaller, select group. Cistercian general chapters of the same era were annual, universal legislative and juridical assemblies of the abbots of all member male abbeys; during the 13th century but certainly not later, there were also assemblies for all heads of Cistercian women's houses, although their powers were less extensive. By the 13th century Dominicans and Franciscans had orders in which there was a single head, a procurator general of some sort, as well as provincial chapters. This seems to have been the case from the beginning in the military-religious orders, such as the Hospitallers and the Templars.

Until recently it was believed that the Cistercians had invented the religious order early in the 12th century. In fact this gives too much credence to early foundation myths of the Cistercians, myths that attribute the first papal confirmation of the *ordo cisterciensis* to Calixtus II (1119–1124) in 1119 when in fact it likely occurred only with Alexander III (1159–1181) in 1165. Certainly by the time of the Fourth Lateran Council

Spinello Aretino (Spinello de Luca Spinello), Italian, act.1373–410/11, Pope Innocent III Sanctioning the Rule of Saint Francis, tempera on panel (poplar), 1390/1400, 88.7 x 62.9 cm, Mr. and Mrs. Martin A. Ryerson Collection, 1933.1031.
Photo courtesy of The Art Institute of Chicago

(1215), when it was declared that no new orders were to be founded, the Cistercians provided the model for all other monastic communities to organize themselves into orders. The Cistercians attributed the creation of the religious order to an early founder, Stephen Harding (d. 1134), and assumed that a variety of institutional innovations had been introduced when the first Cistercian daughter houses were founded. These assumptions mean that too little attention has been given to the 12th-century evolution of the order as an institution, to the contributions of other religious reformers, or to pressures from papal government for that invention.

Among the components of this new institution of the 12th century, we can point to (1) annual, universal assemblies of some sort; (2) notions of equality among member communities; (3) written liturgical handbooks and other legislation and constitutional documents often urging uniformity of types of endowment; (4) new economic and internal organization, including the incorporation of many adult converts to the religious life; (5) a flight from the cult of relics and the Liturgy of the Dead toward simplicity in the decoration of churches; (6) simplicity in interpretation of the Rule of St. Benedict; and (7) a variety of shared privileges, such as concessions of exemption from episcopal visitation or from payment of certain tithes (especially on animal husbandry). The religious order came to coalesce in the last years of the 12th century among the Cistercians and others in part because of pressure from the papacy and others who found it increasingly difficult to control so many monastic groups. Given that the order derived from such varied components and fulfilled a diversity of needs, not all its parts necessarily originated with the Cistercians but might have been contributed by different groups. Much needs to be reexamined in this history. For example, it might turn out that the earliest general chapters were those of Cluniac or Carthusian reformers rather than of the Cistercian reformers or that certain notions about the oversight of the founding house by daughters might have been borrowed by the Cistercians from the Premonstratensians.

CONSTANCE HOFFMAN BERMAN

See also Agriculture, Western Christian; Carthusians; Christianity: Overview; Cistercians; Cluniacs; Cluny, Abbots of; Congregations, Benedictine; German Benedictine Reform, Medieval; Gilbertines; Grandmontines; Hospitallers (Knights of Malta since 1530); Monastics and the World, Medieval; Officials: Western Christian; Premonstratensian Canons; Templars

Further Reading

Berman, Constance H., *The Cistercian Evolution: The Invention of a Religious Order in Twelfth-Century Europe*, Philadelphia: University of Pennsylvania Press, 2000

Constable, Giles, *Three Studies in Medieval Religious and Social Thought*, Cambridge and New York: Cambridge University Press, 1995 (see especially "Three Orders of Society")

Constable, Giles, *The Reformation of the Twelfth Century*, Cambridge and New York: Cambridge University Press, 1996

Falkenstein, Ludwig, *La papauté et les abbayes françaises aux XIe et XIIe siècles*, Paris: Champion, 1997

Hourlier, Jacques, *Le Chapitre Général jusqu'au moment du Grand Schisme*, Paris: Librairie du Recueil Sirey, 1936

Little, Lester K., *Religious Poverty and the Profit Economy in Medieval Europe*, Ithaca, New York: Cornell University Press, and London: Elek, 1978

Sayers, Jane, "The Judicial Activities of the General Chapters," *Journal of Ecclesiastical History* 15 (1964)

Origins: Comparative Perspectives

It seems that the drive to renounce the worldly life has emerged naturally in ardent practitioners of many of the faiths that we are familiar with today – Christianity, Buddhism, Hinduism, and Jainism, to name a few. What is interesting to note is that, despite the diversity and frequent divergences of these religions' belief systems, their monastic traditions share distinct and definite similarities that, when viewed objectively, appear to point to the existence of what we might call "pure monasticism." However, it is impossible to discern the characteristics of this pure monastic lifestyle without examining and comparing its manifestations within the different religious traditions. An analysis of every known monastic system would certainly reveal the qualities of pure monasticism; however, such an ambitious undertaking is far beyond the scope of this article. Instead it limits the inquiry to the world's two largest monastic traditions, understanding that the similarities noted here offer us remarkable insight into what it means to be a monastic.

Many of the beliefs on which Buddhism and Christianity are founded are antagonistic, for the teachings of these two traditions pivot around certain assumptions that are irreconcilable. For example, the concept of God, central to all Christian traditions, is nonexistent in Buddhism. By the term *God* this article does not refer to the various "gods" (*deva*) mentioned at many occasions in the Buddhist scriptures, as these "gods," being subjected to the law of karma, are not endowed with absolute power as is the Christian God. Moreover Buddhists specifically reject the notion of a Lord of the universe (*Issara*) who is responsible for the creation of the world in general and humanity in particular, is a source of knowledge that transcends the limits of ordinary human understanding, and is a factor in human salvation. Similarly Christianity takes for granted the existence of a soul, whereas Buddhism categorically rejects the presence of such an entity that lasts through time. However, despite their dogmatic differences, both Buddhism and Christianity are labeled "religion" and thus have many common features. The most important resides in the fact that each offers a distinct soteriology, that is, a method for attaining what is described as the absolute. Although the philosophy and theology found in Buddhism and Christianity are for the most part mutually exclusive, their goal is irrefutably the same: a relief from the vicissitudes of day-to-day life either through the attainment of *nibbāna* or through union with God.

Another common feature of these two religions lies in the fact that both have preserved a monastic heritage. By distinguishing the crucial characteristics of Christian and Buddhist monasticism, this article shows that monasticism itself constitutes a tradition of its own, a tradition that transcends the dogmas and beliefs of various religious orientations. Although a few traditions, such as Protestant denominations, Confucianism, and Shinto, have excluded the monastic vocation from their orientation, most religions can claim at least a few individuals following the monastic ideal, an ideal that will be clearly circumscribed by the end of this article.

This article analyzes and compares the practices of those first renunciants who sought to reach the ultimate goal within Christianity and Buddhism. Because neither of these traditions has a uniform shape and because both are divided into sundry churches and schools, the article is limited to a specific period and geographic area: the practices of the early Buddhist monastics of India, as portrayed in the Pāli Canon of the Theravāda tradition, and those of the Desert Fathers of Egypt and Syria, as these two movements are considered to have catalyzed the monastic tradition as such within both faiths. The comparison will not concern itself with ideologies or try to provide a reason for the rise of monasticism, as the aim is simply to arrive at a clearer understanding of the concept of monasticism by explaining certain practices common to both traditions.

At first approach the early forms of Christian and Buddhist monasticism seem incongruous. The image that arises in one's mind when thinking about the first Buddhist monastics takes the shape of a saffron-robed, shaven-headed Indian sitting under a tree in a cross-legged position, absorbed in silent meditation. Contrast this serene picture with one of the many possible images that we might conjure up when considering the Desert Fathers, such as St. Simeon the Stylite, who spent 25 years on a 55-foot-high column, or St. Antony and his various confrontations with demons. The static image of the Buddhist monastic sitting in meditation does not tally with the fabulous hagiographies surrounding the Desert Fathers. Furthermore the austerity of early Christian monastics was pushed to extremes (such as portrayed in the *Life* of Mary of Egypt, who, in her quest for purity, repeatedly washed her vagina with sand) that early Buddhists, followers of the Middle Path, had neither needed nor thought of.

However, perhaps the most crucial difference between Christian and Buddhist monasticism is that the former is peripheral to the tradition, whereas the latter is central. Yet proponents of early Christian monasticism did attempt to trace its origin back to Jesus' teaching. This is exemplified in Athanasius' biography of St. Antony, the founder of Christian monasticism (Athanasius, 1978, p. 196). A few months after the death of his parents, Antony was attending a church service when he was deeply affected on hearing a recitation of the evangelical saying, "If thou wilt be perfect, go and sell that thou hast, and give to the poor and thou shalt have treasure into heaven; and come and follow me" (Matt. 19:21). The impact of these words stimulated the young Antony to leave his village for the desert. Not long after his arrival there, the desert, literally swirling with monks, became a city. However, that this occurred about 300 years after Christ reinforces the fact that, unlike the Buddha, Jesus did not overtly start a monastic structure. On the other hand Buddhism could not have developed without its monastic order, which was present from the very beginning and is, in fact, the foundation of the tradition. According to the canonical Pāli texts (*Saṁyuttanikāya* 5.420), the formation of the Buddhist monastic community (*saṅgha*) occurred near Benares immediately following the first discourse of the Buddha to the five ascetics. These five ascetics had followed Siddhattha Gotama for the six years of asceticism preceding his enlightenment. Although they had not yet been formally ordained as "monks," the Theravāda texts refer to them as *bhikkhu*, a Pāli word usually translated as "monk." A few days later a rich young man (thus implying a nonascetic) named Yasa, along with some of his friends, joined this new religious movement (*Vinayapiṭaka, Mahāvagga*, volume 1, 1964, pp. 15–20), which grew so rapidly that within a year of the Buddha's enlightenment the saṅgha was already composed of many hundreds of monks (*bhikkhu*). Nuns were not permitted to join the order until later, when Ānanda earnestly requested the permission to admit women. (For more information on this subject, consult the *Cullavagga*, in the *Vinayapiṭaka*, volume 2, 1977, pp. 253–261.)

Although monasticism is central to Buddhism and merely peripheral to Christianity, we will see that the monastic practices of both traditions are rooted in a similar ideal. Leaving behind the dogmas and the theology that color them, these practices stand at the core and constitute the outlines of a certain discipline that is a common denominator of all existing monastic traditions.

Before entering into an analysis of the specific concepts governing the lifestyle of the first Christian monastics, it will be both interesting and useful to begin by examining the etymology of the words used to describe them. During the first three centuries of the Christian Church, the terms *monachoi* and *monachos*, from which the modern word *monk* has been derived, were widely used. As Bernard McGinn indicates, the word *monachos* itself was already extant in the apocryphal Gospel of Thomas "in the general sense of 'a solitary, or single-minded, or celibate person'" (Eliade, 1987, 10:44). This use of the term is conventional, as both *monachos* and *monachoi* are derived from the Greek root *monos*, meaning "one" and "one alone," thus implying a life of solitude and celibacy. However, these two words did not yet refer to those living in the desert: the massive movement toward the desert did not actually begin before the early fourth century, many decades after the writing of the Gospel of Thomas, the compilation date of which has been tentatively set around the third century.

According to Antoine Guillaumont the words *monachoi* and *monachos* are intimately related to the widely documented Syriac concept of *îhîdayâ* (Guillaumont, 1979, pp. 48–49). This latter term was often used to refer to monks, be they anchorites or cenobites. However, just as were the words *monachoi* and *monachos*, *îhîdayâ* was also widely used by the Mesopotamian Church even before monasticism began dramatically in Egypt and Syria, but its signification referred to another type of asceticism: the *îhîdayâ* were those who had renounced married life, who had vowed to live separately and to practice celibacy to realize the Christian ideal.

This practice of isolation and chastity was a characteristic of those called *b'nai qyama*, "the sons of the pact," who formed a special category of the faithful (Guillaumont, 1979, p. 49). Undoubtedly such practices were prevalent even before St. Antony decided to adopt the ascetic life, around 271 according to Lucien Regnault (1990, p. 309) because as early as the second century we can see an alteration of the meaning of the Greek word *anachorein*, which came to imply those living alone as hermits for the purpose of attaining inner wisdom. Before the second century the term *anachorein* was already widely used, but it referred to a slightly different concept: it designated tax evaders who ran away from the cities and hid in isolated places out of fear of being caught by the Roman fisc.

What then distinguishes the solitary and unmarried *b'nai qyama* and other early hermits from the "monastics" who started invading the desert at the beginning of the fourth century? Why are the former not considered "official" monastics by the Christian tradition, which traces the origin of monasticism back only to St. Antony and not earlier? Perhaps solitude and celibacy, although key characteristics of monasticism, are not sufficient to make one a monastic.

The essential aspects of early Christian monasticism can be further illuminated by a discussion of *monotropos*, a cognate to *monachoi* and *monachos*. As A. Bailly (1963) suggested, this Greek word implies celibacy. In the Christian tradition celibacy is important not because sexual activity is considered inherently evil but because intimate and intense relationships were deemed distracting. Without abstaining from sexual relations and all that they imply, one cannot be fully and only devoted to God. In the words of St. Paul, "But I would have you without carefulness. He that is unmarried careth for the things that belong to the Lord, how he may please the Lord. But he that is married careth for the things that are of the world, how he may please his wife" (1 Cor. 7:32–33). However, although celibacy is central to most traditions, it is surely not the concept around which the whole discipline revolves. Although celibacy is different from the practice of *monotropos*, the latter involves the former. *Monotropos* literally means "having a single aim" or, in other words, a single desire for the total commitment of self to God or any other spiritual aim. Consider this saying of St. Antony's:

> A truly intelligent man has only one care – wholeheartedly to obey Almighty God and to please Him. The one and only thing he teaches his soul is how best to do things agreeable to God, thanking Him for His merciful Providence in whatever may happen in his life. For just as it would be unseemly not to thank physicians for curing our body, even when they give us bitter and unpleasant remedies, so too would it be to remain ungrateful to God for things that appear to us painful, failing to understand that everything happens through His Providence for our good. In this understanding and this faith in God lie salvation and peace of soul. (*Early Fathers from the Philokalia*, 1981, p. 21)

The ideal of *monotropos* can be most accurately described by comparing it to a plant that constantly orients its leaves toward the sun, a process known as photo*tropism*. Like the plant the "monotrope" constantly directs his or her efforts toward God. Celibacy does not necessarily imply such single-mindedness, but it is nevertheless compulsory for the development of this mental state, which demands the eradication of any possible distraction to be totally God-minded.

Besides necessitating celibacy the practice of *monotropos* also calls for solitude and seclusion. Saint Paul praises chastity, for without it one will lose one's singleness of mind, becoming intent on pleasing one's partner rather than thoroughly directing all energy and efforts toward the realization of God. However, sexual activity is not the only practice that might divert the focus from God. According to Athanasius, St. Antony gave all his belongings away, apparently in response to St. Paul's recommendation: Antony renounced all property "in order not to be bothered by his possessions" (Athanasius, 1978, p. 196). To avoid being distracted and losing his singleness of mind, Antony distributed to the villagers what he had inherited from his parents, indicating that material possessions also constituted an obstacle on the path to union with God.

The practitioners of *monotropos* aim at eliminating all diversions that might take their mind away from God. However, pushed to an extreme the recommendation of unity toward the goal goes far beyond mere poverty and celibacy. Saint Paul's recommendation to avoid marriage, coupled with the precept of celibacy, can lead to a severe form of seclusion. Every relationship, in fact, demands a certain amount of effort and duty and requires the "establishment of ties," as St. Exupéry exemplified so magnificently in *The Little Prince*. These social ties and responsibilities scatter our energy and tend to distract us from the ideal of *monotropos* toward God. Thus, solitude is a quality that must be cultivated to be fully God minded. As Abba Evagrius instructed, "Solitude with love purifies the heart" (*Early Fathers from the Philokalia*, 1981, p. 115). This might be one of the reasons that many Desert Fathers avoided crowds, even the gathering of disciples around them.

The lives of the Desert Fathers are saturated with examples of certain monastics running away from the newly formed group of disciples and vanishing into more secluded places where they would reside for a few years until a new gathering of followers formed, necessitating another departure. Of course this practice was motivated also by the desire to be humble and not to drag a crowd of followers behind. A vivid example of this humility and quest for a more isolated lifestyle can be found in the biography of John Cassian. At the monastery in Bethlehem, Cassian was assigned to share a cell with his friend Germanus. Not long after his arrival, a third man, who had already attained a certain age and had sought permission to join the monastery as a novice, was also assigned to their cell. Cassian later found out that the "novice" was none other than Abba Pinufius, who had run away from his monastery to withdraw from the administrative functions that an abbot must fulfill.

At first glance solitude might not seem to be an intrinsic characteristic of early Christian monasticism, as the tradition soon became mainly cenobitic. However, at its birth Christian monasticism was eremitic in character. A change of orientation developed within a few years of the rise of the eremitic movement when Pachomius established one of the first cenobitic communities in Egypt. Pachomius, being an ex-military man, wanted to provide a better structure for the monastics both to diminish the difficulties and hazards that had been encountered by the anchorites and to provide communal support for the individual. Yet even before cenobitic practices were established, anchorites had been meeting at regular intervals. Most Christian hermits would gather weekly for a common meal and prayer (*agape*). Encountering other people following the same path certainly helps in consolidating the mental determination of the hermit. Although anchorites are, by definition, people who live in isolation, these meetings "recharged their batteries," so to speak, and provided further inspiration for their eremitic practices. However, these encounters were by no means designed to offer monastics an avenue whereby to escape solitude, which remained at the core of their practice, whether living in a cenobitic institution or not; rather they were meant to serve as a source of affirmation and inspiration.

The concept of *monotropos* also influenced another practice of the Desert Fathers and of later Christian monastics, that of *xênitêia*, or the practice of being constantly "on the road" to avoid creating any strong human bonds. The notion of *xênitêia* implies the feeling of living as a complete stranger to the world, a mere passerby in exile from one's land of origin. One of the reasons behind the practice of *xênitêia* is that, as Victor Monod argued, removing oneself from one's environment may help bring about a new perspective on life (Monod, 1936, pp. 385–399). A change of lifestyle is enabled by a change of milieu. Within certain churches of the Christian tradition, the practice of *xênitêia* was strikingly dominant. For example, early Irish monasticism revolved around this concept by demanding that the monk exile himself to spread the Christian faith and establish new monasteries.

Just as with many other terms found in the Christian monastic vocabulary, xênitêia seems to be of military origin, initially describing the journey of mercenaries out of their own country. However, in monastic literature this term refers to the discipline wherein monastics exiled themselves to a land where they would always have the impression of being strangers, thus allowing them to fulfill their function as "soldiers of Christ," as Evagrius and Cassian called them (*The Philokalia*, 1986, 1.31, 91). This practice was popular with the Desert Fathers, who traced its origin to the Bible itself. For example, Christ did not perform miracles among his own people, as "a prophet hath no honor in his own country" (John 4:44). In other words Jesus had to exile himself from his place of origin to be accepted as a prophet. However, even much earlier, in Genesis, God told Abraham, "Get Thee out of thy country, and from thy kindred, and from thy father's house, unto a land that I will shew thee" (Gen. 12:1). In an exegesis of this passage, John Cassian explains that three kinds of renunciation need to be perfected. According to him, "Get Thee out of thy country" means that one must cultivate material renunciation, a complete abnegation of worldly wealth. "From thy kindred" entails the renunciation of the old habits that we carry along and accumulate from birth and that are so associated with our personality that they become "part of our family." Finally, "from thy father's house" suggests that monastics must relinquish all memories of the world they have left (Cassian, 1955, 1.145–150). Thus, the goal of this personally inflicted exile is to free oneself from all the worries that might arise from the bond between an individual and his or her native place. Here again we notice traces of St. Paul's recommendation emphasizing the importance of *monotropos*: monastics wish to be liberated from worries to be fully available to God and to integrally pursue their goal. In *Des vertus des solitaires d'Orient*, Sulpicius Severus offers us a vivid example of such an extreme form of *xênitêia*:

> It is said that in the most secluded places on Mount Sinai there lives an anchorite whom I sought for a long time without success, and I am told that it is nearly fifty years since he gave up all conversation with his fellow men. For clothing he had only his hair, which covered his entire body, God thereby granting him a particular favour in affording the means of hiding his nakedness. When pious men made an attempt to meet him he removed himself to inaccessible places so as to avoid them. About five years ago, by the power of his faith, one man gained the extraordinary favour of making his acquaintance. In the course of several talks with him, he asked the reason why he took such pains to avoid conversation with humans. The anchorite replied that those who are visited by men could hardly receive the visits from the angels at the same time; which created the general impression that the angels did visit him. (Sulpicius Severus, quoted in Lacarrière, 1943, p. 143)

At first glance the concept of *xênitêia* seems to contradict the basic form of monastic discipline that was later developed by St. Benedict of Nursia in the sixth century. Of the three vows that Benedict had proposed – obedience, *conversatio moram*, and stability – the last leaves no room for any type of solitary wandering. We might even conclude that Benedict indirectly condemned this practice when he fiercely attacked the *gyrovagis*, those wandering monks constantly on the move who abused the hospitality of other monasteries and whom C.H. Lawrence calls "professional guests." Such an anti-wandering viewpoint can by no means be considered an innovation of Benedict's, as Antony himself warned us that "a monk out of his enclosure is a fish out of water" (Lawrence, 1989, p. 27). In fact this attitude was shared by most of the Egyptian Desert Fathers, as opposed to that of the Syrians, who adopted a much more itinerant lifestyle.

An anonymous apophthegm says that "just as a tree cannot bear fruit if it is constantly transplanted, a monk who travels from place to place cannot perfect virtue" (quoted in Guillaumont, 1979, pp. 108–109).

However, although *xênitêia* was overtly practiced by neither the Egyptian Desert Fathers nor the later Benedictine community, it may be suggested that it *was* practiced inwardly, in the sense that monastics who settled at one given place still strove to develop within themselves this feeling of being a stranger. After all, their whole effort was aimed at attaining the kingdom of God, and one way of realizing that was to alienate oneself from or "to die to" the world. By developing an internally solitary state of mind rather than an external change of location, these early Fathers and Benedictines became strangers to the world without being physically exiled from their community. A story from the *Apophthegmata Patrum* illustrates the point: "One day Abba Longinus questioned Abba Lucius about three thoughts saying first, 'I want to go into exile.' The old man said to him, 'If you cannot control your tongue, you will not be an exile anywhere. Therefore control your tongue here, and you will be an exile'" (*The Sayings of the Desert Fathers*, 1981, p. 122). John Cassian also reports a similar story regarding a certain Abba Apollo who lived near Cassian's village. One night the abba's brother arrived at Apollo's dwelling, requesting his assistance in rescuing a cow struck in a nearby swamp. The abba suggested that he instead ask their younger brother to help him. As their younger brother had died 15 years earlier, Apollo's brother reminded him of this fact, at which point the abba said, "Don't you know that I have also been dead to the world for twenty years and that from the tomb of this cell, I cannot be of any help for, at least, this present life?" (Cassian, 1955, 1.180).

These two examples of Abbas Lucius and Apollo illustrate that neither total withdrawal from the world nor complete isolation are imperative for the perfection of solitude and *xênitêia*. Rather, being states of mind, these perfections can be developed independently and regardless of the external situation in which monastics find themselves. Thus, monastics who do not practice the "external" *xênitêia* do and must cultivate the mental conviction of not belonging to this world, of not being settled, what became known in Latin medieval monasticism as *peregrinatio in stabilitate* (see Leclercq, 1964, pp. 35–90).

Another element of monasticism to be analyzed lies in the notion that early Christian monastics might have followed a practice that culminated formally in St. Benedict urging his monks to remind themselves daily of the presence of death (literally, "to keep death before their eyes"): *mortem cotidie ante oculos suspectam habere*. It seems that many Egyptian anchorites of the fourth and fifth centuries were involved, whether intentionally or not, in such a practice. Many paintings portray saints or Church fathers contemplating a human skull as a *memento mori*. It is interesting to note that this Latin locution, meaning "remember that you are mortal," was used as a form of greeting in certain later monastic orders, such as the Trappists. Moreover to protect themselves from the heat of the day and the trenchant cold of the night, early desert hermits found it necessary to locate makeshift shelters because not many facilities were at their disposal. In this harsh environment tombs provided just such adequate sources of shelter. Given this circumambience it is probable that monastics who resided in such places would have been indirectly submitted to the contemplation of death and of the transience of life. According to Athanasius, St. Antony himself temporarily made his abode in an abandoned tomb (Athanasius, 1978, p. 198). It is interesting to note that Antony also adopted this abode in an early stage of his ascetic career, only, if we may speculate, to overcome the strongest layers of attachment to life, to realize that death was also inescapable, and finally to impel his own symbolic death to the world.

The last aspect of early Christian monasticism to be analyzed is *hêsuchia*, a word that is often mistakenly translated as "solitude." This word actually implies peaceful meditation, a condition that is not automatically attained by dwelling in isolation. *Hêsuchia* is more correctly understood as a state free from all desires as well as from the multitude of distractions that emanate from them. Guillaumont describes this term as follows: "Hesuchia, that is calmness, retreat, a state of life in which the monk is distracted by nothing, not even, said Abba Arsenius, by the noise of the wind in the reeds, and therefore in which he finds the most favorable conditions for contemplation, for unification of his being" (Guillaumont, 1979, p. 236). We see that, no matter how free the monastic might be from external distraction, the goal lies even deeper: in taming the mind by calming the mental process or, if not yet possible, in at least not being distracted by the various thoughts that might arise. This goal alludes to Evagrius' concept of *praktikê*, or the fight against thoughts. According to Evagrius' terminology the natural outcome of *praktikê* is *apatheia*, the single element leading to internal peace. *Apatheia* is achieved in the complete and sole contemplation of God and the rejection of any other elements that might divert the monastic's attention. As Evagrius further elucidated, "By means of these virtues the new Adam is formed, made again according to the image of his Creator – an Adam in whom, thanks to dispassion [*apatheia*], there is 'neither male nor female' and, thanks to singleness of faith, there is 'neither Greek nor Jew, circumcision nor uncircumcision, barbarian, Scythian, bond nor free; but Christ in all and in all'" (Guillaumont, 1979, p. 236). Thus, monastics must also strive to attain *apatheia* to fulfill their ideal of *monotropos*.

So far we have seen that early Christian monasticism revolves around the concept of *monotropos*: being focused single-mindedly toward the realization of God. The quest for *monotropos* naturally leads to certain practices, such as celibacy, solitude, and perfecting the feeling of being a stranger to the world. Thus, could we say that someone following these practices would automatically be a "monastic"? A monastic in appearance, yes, but not a true monastic. According to Evagrius a distinction must be made between a "man-monk" and an "intellect-monk." One might appear to be a monk, but as long as the mind itself has not worn the monastic habit, so to speak, that person is not fully a monastic. As the popular adage says, *habitus non facit monachum*. True monastics must be endowed with a certain mental disposition that naturally calls for rather than imposes celibacy, solitude, and exile; this is *apatheia*. *Apatheia* allows monastics to focus their entire attention on the object of their contemplation, as it is a state of mind devoid of "diversion." Thus, by adding the rather subtle quality of *apatheia* to the more apparent and tangible practices described previously, the formula that designates the true monastic is complete.

To come up with some of the basic features of monasticism, this article will now examine similar practices within the Theravāda Buddhist tradition. Just as in Christianity specific terms are used to refer to monastics. The Pāli words *bhikkhu* and *bhikkhunī* are used to refer to monks and nuns, respectively. Although the usage of these two nouns undoubtedly refers to "monastics," no explicit definition of the terms can be found within the *sutta* literature itself; however, the *abhidhamma* literature sheds more light on the meaning of the terms. The *Vibhaṅga* states that a *bhikkhu* is one endowed with unity or harmony. We can easily recognize here a relation between the terms *monachoi* and *monachos*, cognate to the Greek root *monos*, and the *Vibhaṅga* definition of *bhikkhu*, as "unity" is a crucial factor in both concepts. Furthermore the *Vibhaṅga's* emphasis on "harmony" reminds us of the notion of *monotropos*, which implies a total unity and psychological harmony toward the goal to be accomplished.

Moving beyond strictly monastic terminology, it is interesting to note that the Pāli language possesses a word that might very well be a literal equivalent to *monotropos*. The term *brahmacariya*, which usually refers to the observance of religious precepts, especially chastity, implies more than just celibacy. It is worth noting that the third of "the five major precepts" (*pañcasilā*) in Buddhism is "wrong behavior toward sensual pleasures," traditionally interpreted for monastics as celibacy (*Kamesu micchacara veramaṇisikkhapadam samadiyami*). As for lay disciples *micchacara* implies sexual restraint and fidelity to one's spouse. On the other hand the third of "the eight precepts" (whose first five are virtually identical to "the five precepts") is usually translated as "celibacy" as well; however, its different wording literally points to abandoning the "nonbrahmacariyan" way of life). This indicates a certain nuance distinguishing *celibacy* from *brahmacariya*, a nuance that fortunately is further clarified in the Pāli Canon, where a wider interpretation of the word *brahmacariya* is offered: according to the *Majjhimanikāya*, the apex of *brahmacariya* is unshakable freedom of mind (*Majjhimanikāya: The Middle Length Sayings*, 1977, 1.205), a freedom that certainly cannot be attained through the mere practice of celibacy. *Brahmacariya* is also the term used to characterize the monastic lifestyle (Nyanatiloka, 1956, p. 32) in that it demands, just like *monotropos*, a *total* devotion to the quest for enlightenment by leading a life in which not a single activity obstructs the attainment of *nibbāna*. With emphasis on the concepts represented by the words *monotropos* and *brahmacariya*, we can realize that the activities of early monastics, be they early Buddhist monks and nuns or Desert Fathers, were oriented toward a single goal, the shape of which might have differed from tradition to tradition but whose realization demanded a single-mindedness and shared, in many instances, a similar path.

Just as was found with *monotropos*, *brahmacariya* is distinct from but implies celibacy, as one who yearns to dedicate oneself to the "holy life" and the pursuit of *nibbāna* must scrupulously follow the precept of celibacy to perfect the single-mindedness that he or she desires. The importance of this practice is emphasized in Buddhism not only by the inclusion of the vow of celibacy in the five basic precepts, which even the dedicated layperson must follow, but also in the uncompromising attitude of the Buddha regarding this aspect of the discipline. His immutability regarding the importance of celibacy proved to be unpopular with many nonfollowers, and during his lifetime the Buddha was often accused of extolling a way that would break up families, making the people childless and spouseless (*Mahāvagga*, 1964, 1.43). Despite this criticism it seems that the Buddha never even considered compromising this precept. He still encouraged monks to ordain young men, married or not, into the monastic community, the only prerequisite being that they leave their marital life behind and obtain the assent of their parents prior to their admission. Probably, as St. Paul pointed out, married monastics would have been more preoccupied in pleasing their spouses than in achieving the aim of religious life, which for the Buddhist is attaining *nibbāna*. The essentiality of celibacy is so strong in Buddhism that the tradition generally holds that no one can remain alive as an arahant, a fully liberated person, if that person has not dedicated his or her life to the monastic discipline and the various restrictions it implies. However, it seems that the Theravāda tradition was by no means uniform on the question of whether renouncing the household life is necessary for arahants. The *Kathāvatthu* says that renunciation is not necessary to become an arahant, but it also says that no one who becomes an arahant would wish to remain a householder. On the other hand the *Milindapañha* postulates a different theory. Nāgasena tells King Milinda that the number of arahants who have been monks is a small fraction compared to those who became arahants without ever renouncing the household life, either before or after achieving *nibbāna*. Not only have most arahants not renounced their families, Nāgasena says, but they have also not renounced their possessions. This prompts Milinda to ask why people become monks if becoming a monk is not necessary. Nāgasena replies that, although it is not necessary to be a monk in order to gain *nibbāna*, it is much easier for the monk, as he has fewer worries and distractions and has to make fewer moral compromises to be a monotrope. Just as in Christianity celibacy is a necessity for those wishing to perfect the *brahmacariya* (or *monotropos*) lifestyle.

Another crucial element for the cultivation of *brahmacariya* lies in the idea of solitude. For example, the whole *Khaggavisanasutta* promotes the ideal of solitary life and its advantages: "Leaving behind son and wife, and father and mother, and wealth and grain, and relatives, and sensual pleasures to the full extent that *one should wander solitary as a rhinoceros horn*" (*The Group of Discourses* [*Sutta-nipāta*], 1984, pp. 7–10). The final line of this verse, repeated at the end of all the 41 stanzas that constitute this *sutta*, emphasizes the importance of solitude. However, the commentary emphasizes that this ideal of solitude reflected the direct opinion not of Gotama the Buddha but rather of the "solitary," or *pacceka*, Buddhas who had lived long before Gotama. The Buddha himself did not adopt a strict position regarding "external" solitude. The *Vinayapiṭaka* (2.197) reminds us that the Buddha refused to uphold any single point of view on this matter; monastics were allowed to live either retired in the forest or close to the village. However, the *Bhaddekarattasutta* (*Majjhimanikāya*, 1977, 3.187) alludes to the auspicious state of "internal" solitude in a manner that reminds us of Cassian's exegesis of the last portion of Genesis 12:1: "The past should not be followed after, the future not desired. What is past is got rid of and the future has not come. But whoever has vision now here, now there, of a present thing, knowing that it is immovable, unshakable, let him cultivate it" (Cassian, 1955, 1.233). Although the text does not explicitly refer to solitude, this passage implies the necessity of severing oneself from previous and potential acquaintances to be able to focus on the sole reality, just as Cassian urged monastics to relinquish their memories of the world.

As with early Christian monasticism, the Buddhist practice of solitude does not seem to be integral to the tradition, for monastic orientation itself is usually perceived as cenobitic. Modern Buddhist monasticism is almost completely cenobitic, except in rare cases of forest monks or recluses, such as the *Thudong* monks of Thailand. These hermits follow some of the following 13 ascetic practices (*dhutaṅga*): (1) wearing patched-up robes, (2) wearing only three robes, (3) going for alms, (4) not omitting any house while going for alms, (5) eating at one sitting, (6) eating only from the alms bowl, (7) refusing all further food, (8) living in the forest, (9) living under a tree, (10) living in the open air, (11) living in a cemetery, (12) being satisfied with whatever dwelling, and (13) sleeping in the sitting position only. These extreme practices were described by the Buddha as not compulsory for monastics (*Vinayapiṭaka* [*Parivara*], volume 5, 1982, pp. 131, 193). However, the Buddha also described five types of "forest monastics" (*araññaka*), the fifth of which refers to those adopting such a lifestyle "because their wants are little, just for contentment, just to mark (their own faults), just for seclusion, just because it is the very thing" (*Gradual Sayings: Aṅgutaranikāya*, 1973, 3.161). This type of forest monastic is ranked as the highest of the five. Almost since its beginning Buddhist monasticism has revolved around the institution, or community, called the *saṅgha*. Buddhist monastics have traditionally met at regular intervals in a manner similar to the Christian anchorites, who gather weekly for a common meal and prayer. Members of the *saṅgha* were expected to gather every other week for the *uposatha*, a ceremony during which the code of discipline, the *paṭimokkha*, was read before the assembly of monastics. The *paṭimokkha* is composed of the 227 rules set forth in the *Suttavibhaṅga*.

However, despite this practice of *uposatha* Buddhism was eremitic in character in its early development. Only a few years after the ordination of the first monks, who were for the most part, as we will see, wandering mendicants, the Buddha laid down the rule that monastics should reside in the same dwelling for the entire rainy season (*vassa*). It seems that the Buddha did not originally wish to establish stable monastic communities at particular residences. However, when the *bhikkhu* and *bhikkhunī* were accused of carelessness because of their constant roaming during the rainy season, the Buddha had to make a compromise: "People looked down upon, criticized, spread it about, saying: 'How can these recluses, sons of the Sakyans, walk on tour during the cold weather and the hot weather and the rains, trampling down the crops and grasses, injuring life that is one-facultied and bringing many small creatures to destruction?'" (*The Book of Discipline, Vinayapiṭaka*, volume 4, 1982, p. 183). To remedy this criticism the Buddha instigated a new rule requiring that every monastic reside in only one place during the whole period of monsoon. This decision resulted in the beginning of the formal community of Buddhist monastics as such. We have to understand that the *saṅgha* existed prior to this event but was more of a theoretical communal body than a physical one.

Before the rule of *vassa* was initiated, it seems that Buddhist monastics lived as wandering ascetics who, although affiliated with a particular group (the *saṅgha*), followed a practice similar to most other Indian mendicants of the time. The itinerant lifestyle is strongly reminiscent of the *xênitêia* adopted by certain Desert Fathers and Irish monastics. Within the Indian tradition of the time, the concept of itinerancy was dominant. This is reflected by the most common term referring to ascetics: *paribbājaka*. Etymologically speaking this term means "going around" and refers to all wandering religious mendicants, including Buddhists. The first *bhikkhu* were emphatically urged by the Buddha to "walk" alone: as portrayed in his second discourse, "Walk, let not two go by one way" (*Vinayapiṭaka, Mahāvagga*, volume 1, 1964, p. 20).

We can further discern the incorporation of the *xênitêia* into the Buddhist monastic ideal by examining the two levels of ordination that are still performed in the Buddhist monastic tradition. The first, where the layperson is admitted as a novice, is called *pabbajja* and symbolizes, as the Pāli word implies, "going out," going out from home and, by entering the state of homelessness, leaving the world behind. This word also implies, as van der Leeuw suggests, a departure from and a renouncing of one's previous condition (van der Leeuw, 1948, pp. 257–258). The Buddha himself, on "hearing the call," left his country and his family to pursue his ideal. His life of voluntary exile as a wandering ascetic seems to have been a required condition for his attainment of *nibbāna*.

Whereas the *pabbajja* ordination as described previously implies external peregrinations, the second level or ordination entails a certain stability and association with a monastic body that might, and often does, restrict the wandering practice. This higher ordination, known as *upasampada* (taking on oneself), consists of full admission into the *saṅgha* and represents symbolically the formal and preferably stable "entry" into the "community." Thus, this higher ordination implies the acceptance of the individual into the monastic community; however, it does not exclude ipso facto the practice of *xênitêia*. We must remind ourselves that *xênitêia* was not always applied in the external sense. With reference to Cassian's tale of Abba Apollo, who, although residing near a village for many years, was completely dead to the world, we might recall that within Christianity the true practice of *xênitêia* is to develop the mental attitude of being a stranger to the world. The same also applies to Buddhism and is illustrated by the story of Mahasiva:

> In the Great Cave of Kurundaka, it seems, there was a lovely painting of the Renunciation of the Seven Buddhas. A number of Bhikkhus wandering about among the dwellings saw the painting and said "What a lovely painting, venerable sir!" The Elder said "For more than sixty years, friends, I have lived in the cave, and I did not know whether there was any painting there or not. Now, today, I know it through those who have eyes." The Elder, it seems, though he had lived there for so long, had never raised his eyes and looked up at the cave. And at the door of his cave there was a great ironwood tree. And the Elder had never looked up at that either. He knew it was in flower when he saw its petals on the ground each year. (*Visuddhimagga: The Path of Purification*, 1979, p. 38)

Although this depicts mainly a total absence of distraction, it also exemplifies the lifestyle of a monk who, although having stably resided for many years at the same location, never developed the feeling of being "at home," even so much as never to have noticed the physical appearance of his living quarters.

Similarly the Buddha himself explicitly stated that monastics should not be judged according to their practices: "Oh monks, I say that a robe-wearer is a [true] monk not simply by the virtue of wearing a robe, nor by being naked, nor by covering his body with dust and dirt, nor by performing ablution, nor by living at the foot of a tree" (*Majjhimanikāya*, 1977, 1.281). This passage alludes to two types of monastics: those who perform certain practices without really fulfilling the criteria of a true monastic and those who do not necessarily adopt these austerities yet are endowed with all the monastic qualities. This distinction reminds us of Evagrius' distinction between the "man-monk" and the "intellect-monk" discussed previously. Thus, we can deduce that the Buddha would have preferred his monastics to develop true internal *xênitêia* rather than only the external appearance of it.

However, it seems that during the early phases of the Buddha's ministry, the distinction between the two ordinations was not clearly delineated. As evinced in his first discourse, the *Dhammacakkappavattana*, the Buddha simultaneously ordained Aññātta Kondañña and the four other ascetics as *pabbajja* and *upasampada* simply by saying, "Come, oh monks" (*Vinayapiṭaka* 1.12). However, soon afterward the higher ordination became distinct from the novitiate, which later developed into a period of training under a preceptor, a practice employed by the Desert Fathers as well. For example, St. Antony of Egypt underwent a period of training under an elder, beginning when he was 20 years old (Lacarrière, 1943, p. 55). According to Athanasius (p. 196), Antony did not follow an elder as such but sought inspiration from many "good men." At that time he decided to leave his village of Qmân in Middle Egypt and live for a certain period at the outskirts of that village with an elder who was not, properly speaking, an anchorite but who had followed for many years some form of asceticism. According to Lacarrière this practice of leaving the household and following an ascetic discipline within a house or at the outskirts of the village was common. Because asceticism is a mental discipline as much as a physical exercise, postulants often place themselves under the strict supervision of an experienced elder. Although this was not a rule, it was a very important custom: one first had to obey someone else before being capable of obeying God (Lacarrière, 1943, p. 55).

Another aspect of Buddhist monasticism that shares intimate similarities with the Christian tradition lies in the contemplative practice of death, *maraṇānupassi*. The *Visuddhimagga* even offers us a stanza that emphasizes the importance of cultivating the awareness of death:

> Now when a man is truly wise,
> His constant task will surely be
> This recollection of death
> Blessed with such mighty potency. (*Visuddhimagga*, 1979, p. 259)

This practice might have derived from or influenced the contemplation of *asubha*, a Pāli word that literally means "not beautiful." The Buddha often exhorted his monks to cultivate a sense of repulsion toward their own bodies to stimulate detachment from their egos (*Majjhimanikāya*, 1977, 1.336). This was done by analytically observing the 32 parts of the body without a trace of vanity or clinging. The reflective aspect of this practice has been described in the *Satipaṭṭhānasutta*: "Again, a monk reviews this very body from the soles of the feet upwards and from the scalp downwards, enclosed by the skin and full of manifold impurities: 'In this body there are head-hairs, body-hairs, nails, teeth, skin, flesh, sinews, bones, bone-marrow, kidneys, heart, liver, pleura, spleen, lungs, mesentery, bowels, stomach, excrement, bile, phlegm, pus, blood, sweat, fat, tears, tallow, saliva, snot, synovic fluid, urine.'" Other portions of the *Satipaṭṭhānasutta* explicitly describe the further cultivation of repulsion (*asubha*): "Again, a monk, as if he were to see a corpse thrown aside in a charnel-ground, one, two or three days dead, bloated, discoloured, festering, compares this body with that, thinking: 'This body is of the same nature, it will become like that, it is not exempt from that fate'" (*Thus Have I Heard*, 1987, pp. 337, 338).

Such formulas were considered crucial for the monastic whose mind was not subtle enough to grasp the impermanence (*anicca*) of the world. According to Buddhism *anicca* is one of the three basic characteristics of existence. Impermanence (*anicca*), selflessness (*anatta*), and dissatisfaction (*dukkha*) are characteristics inherent to all entities, and an experiential understanding of them is essential for attaining *nibbāna*. By employing these techniques monastics can first acquire enough detachment to cultivate not only the awareness but also the conviction of the transience of the world and their own individual personality. These practices seem to have been designed as a tool to help develop the understanding of impermanence, eventually inducing a sense of being a passerby in this ever changing world. Such practices seem to lead to results similar to those intended by St. Benedict's *mortem cotidie ante oculos suspectam habere* discussed previously.

The final parallel between Buddhist and Christian monastic practices lies in the state of mind that every monastic ought to cultivate: one free of diversion. In Buddhism one of the ten *paramitas* (i.e., the qualities that one must cultivate to attain *nibbāna*) is *upekkha*, or equanimity. This is a practice that must be not only developed but also perfected if one is to achieve the goal of full liberation. *Upekkha* implies a certain stability of mind, "the neutral aspect of feeling, or zero-point between pain and pleasure, joy and sorrow" (Anuruddha, 1979, p. 66). However, *upekkha* cannot be cultivated without simultaneously reducing the function of the mental faculty of *saññā*. According to Buddhist doctrine this faculty of *saññā* represents the part of the mind that recognizes objects by imposing categories such as "good" and "bad" on our perceptions. Real *upekkha* is not present when one, although feeling pain, restrains his or her reaction merely at the intellectual level by giving the mind an autosuggestion that the pain is nonexistent. Real *upekkha* is achieved only when the *saññā* ceases to function, and pain and pleasure are not recognized as such anymore because the faculty that would normally process pleasure or pain has been turned off.

In this state a person dwells above the vicissitudes of life; owing to the complete absence of *saññā*, the individual dwelling in perfect *upekkha* is deprived of the necessary tools for conceptualizing and categorizing. In this sense we could say that perfect *upekkha* is no different from Evagrius' description of *apatheia*, a state of consciousness in which there is neither male nor female (discussed previously), or from St. Maximus' definition of *apatheia*: "When during prayer no conceptual image of anything worldly disturbs your intellect, then know that you are within the realm of dispassion (*apatheia*)" (*The Philokalia*, 1986, 2.63). *Upekkha* and *apatheia* permit total absorption, full contemplation that would be impossible to achieve without this state of tranquillity.

Both early Buddhist and early Christian monasticism share one essential element: single-mindedness toward the goal. *True* monastics will be completely and solely engaged in the fulfillment of their goal. This single-mindedness has given birth to different practices that were designed solely to strengthen it and that could be held as general characteristics of most monastic traditions.

Celibacy is essential for the monastics to avoid wasting energy in any relation other than the one with God or the striving toward *nibbāna*. Although celibacy is imposed by the tradition on both Christian and Buddhist monastics, this restriction seems to prevail only to assist the monastic in perfecting the ideal of *monotropos* or *brahmacariya*, an ideal that basically consists of a harmonious and undivided mind. Celibacy is claimed to be essential for those wishing to realize the monastic goal, as without it the practitioner will be forced to divide his or her energy and attention between the desire to please a spouse and the desire to fulfill the monastic objective. Pushed to an extreme this practice of celibacy naturally leads monastics to sever themselves from all human relationships, as they are sources of distraction and might interfere with their aim. Thus, the concept of solitude is an important aspect of both Buddhist and Christian monastic traditions and has given rise to the various wandering practices (*xênitêia* or that of the *paribbājaka*) found in other religions. However, solitude and the wandering practices need not necessarily be outwardly expressed. As pointed out these practices are representative of states of mind that need to be cultivated internally rather than simply followed externally by rote. Thus, in both traditions we find monastic communities residing permanently at a given place where monks and nuns strive to perfect the ideals of *monotropos* or *brahmacariya* by cultivating the feeling of being "strangers to the world" through their inner isolation and peregrinations.

To help cultivate the feeling of being a "stranger to the world," many early Christian monastics engaged in the contemplation of death, a practice that has its counterpart in Buddhist meditation on *maraṇānupassi* and *asubha*. By focusing on the imminence of death and the unpleasantness of life, a practitioner let layers of attachment to life and its pleasures gradually disintegrate until one realizes the transience of his or her own mortal being. This awareness reinforces the sense of alienation from a frail and insubstantial world and invigorates the feeling that attainment of the immutable must be strived for and achieved.

We finally saw that *monotropos* or *brahmacariya* ultimately culminates in a state of total contemplation that requires the cessation of the mind's discursive function. Through the attainment of *upekkha* and *apatheia*, Buddhist and Christian monastics were capable of fully concentrating their attention on the object of meditation and thereby obtaining the goal of *nibbāna* or union with God.

It is worth noting that, although defining characteristics of the early forms of Buddhist and Christian monasticism are numerous, all are linked to the concept of having a single goal, of being single-minded. However much Buddhist and Christian monasticism might have changed through history, these traditions still cherish this aim, which constitutes the foundation stone of monasticism as such.

MATHIEU BOISVERT

This text was first published by *Buddhist-Christian Studies* 12 (1992) and is now reprinted, with the authorization of the University of Hawaii Press, with minor modifications.

See also Antony, St.; Buddha (Śākyamuni); Buddhism: Overview; Cassian, John; Celibacy; Desert Fathers; Disciples, Early Buddhist; Discourses (Suttas): Theravāda; Egypt; Evagrius Ponticus; Hermits; Jain Monasticism and Buddhist Monasticism; Monasticism, Definitions of; Pachomius, St.; Regulations: Christian Perspectives; Syria

References

Anuruddha, *Abhidhammatthasaṅgaha: The Compendium of Philosophy*, translated by S.Z. Aung, London: Pali Text Society, 1979

Athanasius, St., *Select Writings and Letters of Athanasius, Bishop of Alexandria*, edited by Archibald Robertson, Grand Rapids, Michigan: Eerdmans, 1978
Bailly, A., *Dictionnaire grec-français*, Paris: Hachette, 1963
The Book of Discipline, Vinayapitaka, volume 4, translated by I.B. Horner, London: Pali Text Society, 1982
Cassian, John, *Conférences*, translated by Dom. Pickery, Paris: Cerf, 1955
Cullavagga, in the *Vinayapiṭaka*, volume 2, edited by Herman Oldenburg, London: Pali Text Society, 1977
Early Fathers from the Philokalia, translated by E. Kadloubovsky and G.E.H. Palmer, London: Faber, 1981
Eliade, Mircea, editor, *Encyclopedia of Religion*, New York: Macmillan, 1987
Gradual Sayings: Aṅgutaranikāya, translated by E.M. Hare, London: Pali Text Society, 1973
The Group of Discourses [*Sutta-nipāta*], translated by K.R. Norman, London: Pali Text Society, 1984
Guillaumont, Antoine, *Aux origines du monachisme chrétien*, Bégrolles en Mauges: (Maine and Loire): Abbaye de Bellefontaine, 1979
Lacarrière, Jacques, *The God-Possessed*, London: Allen and Unwin, 1943
Lawrence, C.H., *Medieval Monasticism*, New York: Longman, 1989
Leclercq, J., "Monachisme et pérégrination," in *Aux sources de la spiritualité occidentale*, Paris, 1964
Majjhimanikāya: The Middle Length Sayings, translated by I.B. Horner, London: Pali Text Society, 1977
Monod, Victor, "Les voyages, le déracinement de l'individu hors du milieu natal constituent-ils un des éléments déterminants de la conversion religieuse?" *Revue d'histoire et de philosophie religieuse* 16 (1936)
Nyanatiloka, *Buddhist Dictionary*, Colombo: Frewin, 1956
The Philokalia, translated by G.E.H. Palmer, Philip Sherrard, et al., London: Faber, 1986
Regnault, Lucien, *La Vie quotidienne des pères du désert*, Paris: Hachette, 1990
The Sayings of the Desert Fathers, translated by Benedicta Ward, London: Mowbray, 1981
Thus Have I Heard (Dīghanikāya), translated by Maurice Walshe, London: Wisdom, 1987
van der Leeuw, G., *La religion dans son essence et ses manifestations*, Paris, 1948
Vinayapiṭaka, Mahāvagga, volume 1, edited by Hermann Oldenburg, London: Pali Text Society, 1964
Vinayapiṭaka [*Parivara*], volume 5, edited by Herman Oldenburg, London: Pali Text Society, 1982
Visuddhimagga: The Path of Purification, translated by Bhikkhu Nanamoli, Kandy: Buddhist Publication Society, 1979

Origins: Eastern Christian

The origins of Christian monasticism – defined as a culture or society of its own, distinguished by the renunciation of private property and permanent celibate life, consciously set apart from ordinary people and completely devoted to God – are still obscure. Undoubtedly monasticism as an institution within the Church was first established in the East and only later transplanted to the West. The monastic tradition has its deeper roots in at least three distinct traditions, namely, Jewish apocalypticism, the radical social vision of the Gospels, and the ascetic practice of some of the schools within the Greek philosophical tradition. Christian ascetics are known from the first centuries mainly as itinerant preachers who, like Jesus' disciples, had cut off all relations to their families and homes. In early Syriac tradition a strong movement toward celibacy for all baptized Christians resulted in the emergence of a special group called the *Bnay*, or *Bnat Qyama* (Sons/Daughters of the Covenant). Although marriage was not questioned except in sectarian settings, an ascetic life and celibacy became an ideal for most Christians of the first centuries. The periods of persecution further strengthened the tendency to a radical Christian life separated from ordinary society. The theological and theoretical framework for a monastic interpretation of Christianity are found in Christian philosophers, such as Clement of Alexandria (c. 150–c. 215) and Origen (c. 185–c. 254), but also in Syriac ascetic writings, such as the *Liber Graduum* and in the works of Aphrahat of Mesopotamia. Important forerunners of monasticism are further prophetic and apocalyptic movements in early Christianity, the most famous being Montanism.

However, the most important background for the establishment of monasticism is the tradition of a celibate life, mainly of women, connected to a specific Church. Individual Christians consecrating their life to Christ and the Church and thereby refusing marriage and normal social obligations are attested to in the first centuries. Their special position in the local Church is defined and described in the earliest Church orders, for example, by Hippolytos (c. 170–c. 236). These virgins lived either independently within their own household or together in separate houses in the towns and cities and can be considered to have been a major model for the emergence of monasticism. Given this background good reasons exist to consider women, and perhaps especially women from the higher levels of society, as playing a decisive role in the transformation of private asceticism within the cities to communal life in a specifically monastic environment. With growing Christian communities and a gradual integration of these into ordinary city life, a radical interpretation of the gospel forced some ascetics to leave the community and to live as recluses.

The transformation of this type of Church-connected ascetics into monastic settlements seems to have its roots in the fierce persecution of the 310s and the subsequent changes resulting from the acceptance and even endorsement of the Church by Constantine (306–337). Persecutions gave additional significance and authority to charismatic individuals who had turned their backs on society, whereas the official recognition of the Church put an emphasis on structural leadership and integration into society. The rapid growth of a monastic movement in Egypt in the mid–fourth century and in Palestine, Syria, and Asia Minor a few decades later makes a causal connection indisputable between the establishment of a recognized Church on the one hand and the establishment of an independent monastic society on the other.

Although other examples might be found elsewhere, available sources point to Egypt and the first decades of the fourth century as the place and time when monasticism proper was born. The transformation from asceticism to monasticism in other areas cannot be documented earlier and is, usually in the literary sources although not exclusively, connected with Egyptian influence. Historical as well as geographical factors, the late and very violent persecutions, the sharp border between civilization and desert, and perhaps also the influence of Alexandrian philosophy can help explain Egypt's prominent role. In Egypt three figures stand out as the most important: St. Antony the Great, St. Pachomius, and St. Athanasius of Alexandria.

Saint Antony (c. 251–356) is credited with an almost complete break with society – that is, with the decisive movement from asceticism inside or on the outskirts of the village (or city) into asceticism in the desert, as well as with the organization and teaching of groups of disciples, thus establishing some of the first known monastic communities sometime before 320. As revealed by his letters, Antony's immediate model seems to have been ascetic teachers of philosophy, and his dependence on Alexandrian theological tradition is strongly manifest. However, in contrast to other teachers of religious philosophy and self-knowledge through ascetic practice, Antony decided to settle down in isolation, keeping his disciples and those seeking his help at a distance.

Saint Pachomius (c. 290–346) is credited with the first shaping of rules for a communal monastic life and the erection of building complexes for the monastic community beginning in the early 320s. As an army conscript impressed by the social concern of some local Christians, he had been baptized. His social concern forced him to develop strategies and structures to cope with tensions among ascetics living together, thus making it possible to establish a communal life. In contrast to the emphasis on self-knowledge and the highly individual life of Antony and his disciples, Pachomius consciously emphasized relations to others and a cenobitic, communal life. To Pachomius the monastery was a school as well as a common workshop, and his monasteries might well be regarded as the first examples of specifically Christian schools in which reading and writing were taught on the basis of the Bible.

Antony and Pachomius stand out as founders of monasticism partly because of Athanasius of Alexandria (c. 296–373), who played a decisive role in integrating the monastic movement into the Church. During his long episcopate Athanasius developed close links with the emergent monastic communities and began to consecrate monks as priests and bishops. In his writings, especially his *Life of Antony*, he strongly favored the growing monastic movement and described it as part of the Church, subordinate to the ministry of bishops, priests, and deacons.

Further developments in Egypt included an extremely rapid growth of monasticism in the second half of the fourth century in which differences between the cenobitic and the anchoritic were often blurred. The influence of Pachomius was naturally greater in Upper Egypt among Coptic-speaking monks who lived mainly in deserted areas in or on the border of the Nile valley. Because of the proximity to Alexandria and the widespread knowledge of Greek there, the anchoritic monks of Lower Egypt (living mainly in Kellia, Nitria, and Scetis in the desert between Alexandria and Cairo) had a seminal impact on the spread and development of monasticism. Visitors from Rome (Melania the elder, Rufinus), Dacia (John Cassian), Asia Minor (St. Basil, Evagrius of Pontus), Syria, and Palestine (St. Hilarion) were attracted to the so-called Desert Fathers (and Desert Mothers) and were later influential in the establishment of monasteries throughout the empire.

The origins of monasticism in Palestine go back to the poorly attested figure of St. Chariton, who is said to have settled in the Judaean desert in the mid–fourth century and attracted disciples to his semi-anchoritic life. The deep gorges of Judaea with their proximity to Jerusalem and its pilgrims soon attracted monks from everywhere. In 405 Euthymius (377–473), a young priest and native of Armenia, came to Jerusalem on a pilgrimage. Attracted to the desert he settled down and soon became the undisputed leader of Judaean monasticism until his death. Along the gorges a new kind of monastic establishment, the *lavra*, a string of monastic cells connected to a church but without common enclosure, was created. A special feature of Judaean monasticism is the strong influx of Christian ascetics coming to the Holy Land from the north (Syria, Armenia, Georgia, and Asia Minor) as well as from Rome. The importance of Jerusalem for imperial policy and its international character gave the monasteries of Jerusalem and Bethlehem, among them the Latin foundations of Melania, Rufinus, Paula, and Jerome, additional importance.

Because of good communications with Egypt, Gaza and its surroundings became important centers for the diffusion of Egyptian influence on Palestinian monasticism, especially after the expulsion of many leading monks from Nitria in 399. Tensions with the patriarchate, attacks by nomads, and a general decline in Egypt contributed to a gradual movement from Egypt by way of Sinai to Palestine. Good reasons exist to believe that the large collections of sayings of the Desert Fathers were actually compiled in Gaza in the period directly after the conflicts over the Council of Chalcedon (451).

In Syria Christian asceticism had strong roots, and the transformation into monasticism is almost impossible to date. The earliest reports about Syrian monks come from Theodoret of Cyrrhus (c. 393–c. 460), according to whom monasticism in Syria began in the mid–fourth century with solitary ascetics who often did not settle down but moved around in the wilderness radically rejecting the society. Monasteries and communities of monks were then established, mainly in the mountains between Antioch and Beroè (Aleppo). In lieu of a desert, other means of isolation were developed, including immurement and later the erection of pillars (stylites).

In Asia Minor the emergence of monasteries was connected with Eustathius of Sebaste (c. 300–after 377) and the family of St. Basil of Caesarea and St. Macrina (c. 327–380). Eustathius, who also inspired St. Basil, emerged in the mid–fourth century as the leader of Christian ascetics who demanded a more radical break with society and who advocated a more rigorous Church discipline. Against this several councils criticized the monks for making undue demands on ordinary people, including contempt for marriage and the sacraments. In the 360s St. Macrina reorganized the family estate into a dual monastery with monks as well as nuns. After becoming metropolitan of Caesarea, St. Basil, who early in his life had lived for some time as a monk in seclusion, reorganized and integrated monasticism into the structure of the Church, putting all emphasis on monasticism as part of the ministry of mercy. His ascetic writings, including the so-called rule, became normative for the Byzantine tradition. In Constantinople monasticism proper seems not to have been introduced until the 380s. Because of imperial interests and the position of the patriarch after the council of 381, the monasteries in Constantinople became rich and influential establishments. Their direct links with the court sometime occasioned conflict, as, for example, during the tenure of St. John Chrysostom (c. 347–407) as bishop.

SAMUEL RUBENSON

See also Antony, St.; Archives, Western Christian; Armenia; Basil the Great, St.; Cappadocia, Turkey; Cassian, John; Celibacy: Christian; Desert Fathers; Desert Mothers; Egypt; Hagiography: Eastern Christian; Hermits: Eastern Christian; Israel/Palestine; Istanbul, Turkey; Jerusalem, Israel; Lavra; Macrina, St.; Office, Daily: Western Christian; Origins: Comparative Perspectives; Pachomius, St.; Pilgrimages, Christian: Near East; Stylites; Syria; Women's Monasteries: Eastern Christian

Further Reading

AbouZayd, Shafiq, *Ihidayutha: A Study of the Life of Singleness in the Syrian Orient: From Ignatius of Antioch to Chalcedon 451 A.D.*, Oxford: ARAM Society for Syro-Mesopotamian Studies, 1993
Binns, John, *Ascetics and Ambassadors of Christ: The Monasteries of Palestine, 314–631*, Oxford: Clarendon Press, and New York: Oxford University Press, 1994
Brakke, David, *Athanasius and the Politics of Asceticism*, Oxford: Clarendon Press, and New York: Oxford University Press, 1995
Chitty, Derwas, *The Desert a City*, Oxford: Blackwell, 1966; Crestwood, New York: St. Vladimir's Seminary Press, 1966
Elm, Susanna, *'Virgins of God': The Making of Asceticism in Late Antiquity*, Oxford and New York: Oxford University Press, 1994
Gould, Graham, *The Desert Fathers on Monastic Community*, Oxford: Clarendon Press, 1993; New York: Oxford University Press, 1994
Guillaumont, Antoine, *Aux origines du monachisme chrétien*, Bégrolles en Mauges (Maine and Loire): Abbaye de Bellefontaine, 1979
Heussi, Karl, *Der Ursprung des Mönchtums*, Tübingen: Mohr, 1936
Rousseau, Philip, *Pachomius: The Making of a Community in Fourth-Century Egypt*, Berkeley: University of California Press, 1985; updated, 1999
Rubenson, Samuel, *The Letters of St. Antony: Monasticism and the Making of a Saint*, Minneapolis, Minnesota: Fortress Press, 1995
Vogüé, Adalbert de, *Histoire littéraire du mouvement monastique dans l'antiquité*, 5 vols., Paris: Éditions du Cerf, 1991–1998
Vööbus, Arthur, *History of Asceticism in the Syrian Orient*, 3 vols., Louvain: Secrétariat du Corpus SCO, 1958–1988

Origins: Western Christian

Already in the fourth century, various forms of monastic life are attested in Western Christianity. They sprang in part from local sources, common to all Christianity, and in part from the Eastern influence. At that time indigenous, anchoritic forms of monasticism could be found in most areas of the West: in the Apennine Mountains, in the Po Valley, in Gaul, and in the Iberian Peninsula. They were best developed on the Mediterranean seacoast and on islands, which were best suited for this way of life.

There is no doubt that the development of Western monasticism and especially the process of crystallization of the cenobitic movement was greatly influenced by numerous examples and inspiration coming from the East, which was leading the way in terms of the magnitude of this phenomenon and the degree of its organization as well as the development of monastic legislation and writing. The influence of the Desert Fathers was of crucial importance. This influence, combined with local monastic forms, climate conditions typical of the West, and local social needs, was ingeniously transformed, defining new directions of development. Conspicuous among these were four types: (1) "episcopal" monasticism, involved in social life; (2) apostolic monasticism, connected with the former; (3) missionary monasticism, promoted by the popes; and (4) Benedictine monasticism.

Rapid dissemination of monastic ideas was favored by the fact that Christian monasticism came into being in the territory of a single state: the Roman Empire. Business and trade trips, social and cultural contacts, Church councils and synods, as well as journeys undertaken by individual anchorites and groups of Eastern monks settling within the Mediterranean furthered the circulation of new ideas.

An example is provided by the career of St. Athanasius (c. 296–373), the metropolitan of Alexandria and later the author of the *Life of St. Antony* (c. 251–356), twice exiled to Trier (335–337) and Rome (339–346). Athanasius' stay in these places encouraged the development of local monasticism, including that of female monasticism in Rome, later supported by Jerome.

Already before 363 Egyptian monks led by Hilarion (c. 291–371) came to Sicily, laying the foundation of the development of Eastern monasticism in southern Italy, later closely linked with monastic centers in the Byzantine Empire. From there groups of monks entered Gaul and Spain. The activity of Cassiodorus (485/90–c. 580) and his "intellectual" monastery at

Vivarium was associated with monasticism of this type, shaped by the intellectual centers of Greece and Asia Minor. Simultaneously in the same area Latin monasticism was developing until the seventh century, nourished by exiles from North Africa, with its especially long tradition of asceticism and monasticism stretching all the way back to Typasius of Tigara (d. c. 298).

Similar, albeit much later, was the beginning of organized monasticism in the Iberian Peninsula, where anchoritic movement is attested from at least the fourth century. Already around 550, after returning from a pilgrimage to the East, St. Martin of Braga (d. after 579) founded several monasteries. Of great importance was the arrival of a group of intellectually distinguished African monks headed by Donatus around 570. The activity of his pupil Eutropius (d. c. 610); the two brothers from Seville, St. Leander (d. 601) and St. Isidore (c. 560–636); and St. Fructuosus of Braga (d. c. 660) endowed Iberian monasticism with its high level of culture.

An important role in spreading monastic ideas from the East in the West was played by pilgrimages to the native land of Jesus, increasingly popular from the fourth century. At the same time a "fashion" developed among the rich elite of Rome to undertake journeys and pilgrimages to the East, where monasteries and hermits were a curiosity. Among the first pilgrims was a Roman widow Melania the Elder (c. 342–c. 410), who visited Egyptian anchorites in 372, meeting Rufinus (c. 345–411), a friend of Jerome who was traveling with the same purpose in Nitra. Some of these pilgrims tried to implant this type of life in their countries, adapting it to local conditions.

This influenced the elitist character of one trend in Western monasticism. Monastic ways of life were developing (usually, but not only, in Italy) in a narrow circle of family and close friends of a person belonging to the Church or administrative elite. People leading an ascetic life, while remaining involved in family and society, made a decision to "break with the world," taking refuge in a deserted place either individually or with a few close friends, settling in the country, or locking themselves up in their homes. In many cases these endeavors resulted in the establishment of permanent monasteries.

For example, Anicius Paulinus, the governor of Campania, resigned his post in 393 to settle with his wife (from that moment they lived in celibacy) at the tomb of St. Felix the martyr near Nola, where together with friends he founded a monastery and was even ordained priest by a local bishop. A group lead by Rufinus near Aquileia followed a different way. Many of them, including Rufinus, finally chose monastic life in the East. These examples reflect the spontaneity and heterogeneity of the early stages of monastic life in the West, including Italy.

A promoter of Eastern forms of monasticism was Bishop Hilary of Poitiers (c. 315–367), who had encountered it while in exile in Asia Minor. Eventually he became the mentor of Martin of Tours (d. 397), who gave a new impulse to Western monasticism. Before Martin there had been anchorites and monks in Gaul, but only from his time dates a mass monastic movement, introduced by his pupils formed in monasteries in Ligugé and Marmoutier. An important novelty of these two communities, modeled on the Eastern *lavra*, was to combine an ascetic and communal life conducted in small groups with pastoral activity. Martin, elected bishop of Tours c. 371, retained his monastic dress, way of life, and simplicity and settled in Marmoutier, where he lived with his priests among monks as one of them. They all constituted one community of brother-monks composed of priests and laymen. Brother-priests helped Martin in his apostolic and missionary work and in ministry, whereas lay brothers worked, prayed, and copied manuscripts. This involvement of monks in matters of the world, alternating periods of monastic enclosure with activity outside its confines, was to become characteristic of Western monasticism. The *Life of St. Martin* by Sulpicius Severus (c. 360–c. 430), written after 400, became a classic of medieval hagiography and played a tremendous role in the history of Western monasticism.

Of special importance for the development of Western monasticism were its close ties with bishops and local churches and, by this token, with society and its needs. First steps in this direction were taken by bishop Eusebius of Vercelli (c. 285–371). Having learned the life of Eastern monks while in exile in Palestine and Cappadocia, on his return (c. 363) he strove to encourage monastic life in his diocese and together with his clergy led a communal life. In addition, St. Ambrose (c. 340–397), bishop of Milan, founded a monastery in this city, of which we know from St. Augustine of Hippo (c. 354–430). The work and writings of St. Augustine played another vital role. Communities of priests established by Augustine in Tagaste and Hippo in North Africa, in which menial labor was combined with intellectual activity, ministry, and work for the diocese, marked an important stage in the history of Western monasticism. The so-called Augustinian Rule played a decisive role in the development of Western monasticism.

Also important for the development of monasticism in the West were, from the end of the fourth century, the first Latin translations of writings devoted to Eastern monks. Already in 374 Evagrius of Antioch (c. 320–c. 394), a friend of Eusebius of Vercelli and of Jerome, translated the *Life of St. Antony*. Of special importance were the writings and life of a monk and intellectual, St. Jerome (c. 345–420), who translated the Rule of Pachomius (c. 290–346) and wrote a colorful *Life of Paul the Hermit*. A friend of Jerome, Rufinus of Aquileia translated the Rule of Basil and the *History of the Monks in Egypt*.

As regards the adoption and consolidation of the Eastern tradition, the establishment of permanent centers of monastic life in Provence played a crucial role. The earliest and most important of these was formed around 400 on one of the islands of Lérins opposite Cannes. It was founded by a hermit, St. Honoratus (d. 429). This aristocrat renounced, in accordance with the mood of the epoch, the temporal world to travel with his brother Venantius and a friend to the East to learn the life of monks. On his brother's death he returned to Gaul and established a monastery on an Eastern model on an island now called after him. The communal life was one of extreme asceticism with an opportunity of hermitage for monks ready for that. The rule written by Honoratus is no longer extant. In 426 Honoratus was appointed

Holy cave (*Sacro Speco*) occupied by St. Benedict as a young man, Monastery of St. Benedict, Subiaco, Italy. Photo courtesy of the Editor

bishop of Arles and continued to foster there a model of life similar to that of St. Augustine. Lérins produced many prominent figures of Gallic monasticism, including St. Hilary (401–449), the successor and biographer of Honoratus, and St. Eucarius, the bishop of Lyons (d. 450), as well as St. Caesarius of Arles (c. 470–542), who wrote a new monastic rule for men and the first monastic rule for women, employed, among others, by St. Radegunde (c. 518–587) in her famous monastery in Poitiers. The appearance of monks in the ranks of the episcopate marked the assimilation of monasticism into the ecclesiastical organism.

Another important center for this type of monasticism emerged in Marseilles, where St. John Cassian (c. 360–after 435) founded the monastery of St. Victor and a nunnery. Like Honoratus he also traveled to Egypt, where he lived for seven years among Egyptian monks. Twenty years later, after his return, he committed his experience and reflections to paper in two volumes (*Collationes* and *Institutiones*) of advice and instruction for the monks of Provence.

The program of monastic life outlined in the writings of Cassian and implemented in the monasteries of Lérins profoundly affected the direction in which Western monasticism developed, especially in Gaul and northern and central Italy. In this respect his influence was much stronger than that of the penetration of Eastern monasticism in southern Italy and Spain described previously. No writings or practical example comparable to those of Cassian and Lérins ever emerged there.

Simultaneously with monastic centers in Provence, monastic life was developing in the rest of Gaul. It is best known in the Jura, owing to the *Life of St. Roman* (c. 515). Having spent some time as a monk in a monastery near Lyons, around 430 Roman founded a community of monks in a deserted place of the Swiss Jura at Condatisco (now St. Claude), giving rise to a group of monasteries. Local customs, under the influence of Lérins, initially strictly following the example of Eastern monasticism but in time evolved slowly toward moderating the strict discipline typical of Eastern monks. A clear trend toward the "Europeanization" of monasticism to suit Western predilections and to adapt it to local climate can be seen. This was the general direction of the development of Western monasticism in the sixth century. Even in Provence the original customs of Honoratus and John Cassian were superseded by the more moderate rule of Caesarius of Arles. This trend was best reflected in the *Regula Magistri* and in the Rule of St. Benedict.

The extent of this ability to adapt the monastic idea to local customs is clearly visible in the example of Ireland. Monasticism, introduced there in the fifth century, quickly accommodated the needs of the local social structure. Entire clans assumed the monastic way of life. Their leaders founded monasteries and not infrequently assumed the dignity of abbot, governing monastic communities of up to several thousand. Functions of abbot and bishop and those of monks and priests amalgamated. Austere, ascetic life was accompanied by concern with liturgy and, as a consequence, by interest in the beauty of books and objects used in liturgy. This attitude proved conducive to a high level of achievement in language, writing, and craftsmanship. The notion of external missions as the highest form of renunciation impelled Irish monks to evangelize adjacent islets and Britain and then to reevangelize and evangelize the Continent.

The earliest local monastic rules appeared in the West from the beginning of the fifth century, but only the sixth century brought the true flourishing of "local" monastic rules written for various Western monastic centers. They attest the organizational progress and gradual stabilization of Western monasticism in this period.

At the end of the sixth century, monasticism in the West was already well developed and deeply rooted. The number of monasteries in Gaul at that time is estimated at over 200, and those with 100 monks or nuns were not rare. The situation in Italy and Spain was much the same. The privileged position of the Church in Germanic states meant no difficulty with recruiting new members. Quite the contrary: too many candidates entered monasteries for extraneous reasons, without real vocation, a fact that resulted in the declining level of monastic life. A role in reversing this trend of degeneration of monastic life was played by St. Columban (d. 615) and Irish monks.

Western monasticism was very heterogeneous. The fifth and sixth centuries brought diversity to monastic forms and rules and everyday practice and liturgy. Alongside semi-eremitic forms existed inadequately organized rural monasteries and in some areas also equally large communities of "urban" monasteries, founded mainly at tombs of martyrs and cathedral churches. They faced the responsibility of meeting demands arising from the progressive barbarization of the West.

From the fifth and sixth centuries, monasteries became the principal centers of culture in the West. For this reason, among others, bishops aimed at getting monastic communities involved in social service. Moreover, more and more bishops were chosen from among monks. Celebrating liturgy and communal singing of psalms in basilicas in towns was also becoming a monk's occupation. This in turn required the stabilization of monastic life and expansion of its base in order to provide an adequate number of manuscripts, liturgical vestments, and vessels.

A belief was slowly emerging that under exceptional circumstances a monk could be detached from his community, liturgy, and ascetic life and directed to other tasks. In this respect the influence of Pope Gregory I (590–604) was paramount. He decided, for the first time on such a large scale, to employ monks in missionary and apostolic work. Considering active life and private asceticism to be everyone's duty, he resolved to enlist monks in papal service. Under papal direction they were to perform apostolic activity, exerting influence through both words and the example of their own lives. Around 600 a new chapter in the history of Western monasticism began, bringing with it an active involvement of monks in the building of European civilization.

MAREK DERWICH

See also Ambrose, St.; Antony, St.; Augustinian Rule; Caesarius of Arles, St.; Cassian, John; Cassiodorus; Christianity: Overview; Desert Fathers; Desert Mothers; Isidore of Seville, St.; Jerome, St.; Lavra; Lérins, France; Martin of Tours, St.; Monasticism, Definitions of: Christian Perspectives; Pilgrimages, Christian: Near East

Further Reading

Biarne, Jacques, "La vie quotidienne des moines en Occident du IVe au VIe siècle," *Collectanea Cisterciensia* 49 (1987)

Biarne, Jacques, "Les origines du monachisme en Occident (IVe–VIe siècles)," *L'Information Historique* 54 (1992)

Centro italiano di studi sull'alto medioevo, *Il monachesimo nell'alto medioevo e la formazione della civiltà occidentale [settimana di studi] 8 –14 aprile, 1956* (Settimane di studio del centro italiano di studi sull'alto medioevo, 4), Spoleto, 1957

Colombás, García María, *El monacato primitivo*, volume 1: Hombres, *Hechos, Costumbres, Instituciones* (Biblioteca de Autores Cristianos); volume 2: *La espiritualidad* (Biblioteca de Autores Cristianos), Madrid: La Editorial Católica, 1974–1975; 2nd edition, Madrid: Biblioteca de Autores Cristianos, 1998

Duckett, Eleanor Shipley, *The Gateway to the Middle Ages*, volume 3: *Monasticism*, New York: Macmillan: 1938

Garrigues, Jean-Miguel, and Jean Legrez, *Moines dans l'assemblée des fidèles à l'époque des Pères, IVe–VIIIe siècle* (Théologie historique, 87), Paris: Beauchesne, 1992

Gobry, Ivan, *Les Moines en Occident*, 3 vols., Paris: Fayard, 1985–1987

Hen, Yitzhak, *Culture and Religion in Merovingian Gaul, A.D. 481–751* (Cultures, Beliefs, and Traditions, volume 1), New York: Brill, 1995

International Scientific Colloquium on Spirituality of Ancient Monasticism, *The Spirituality of Ancient Monasticism: Acts* (Pontificia Academia Theologica Cracoviensi, Facultas Theologica, volume 4, number 1), Tyniec, Poland: Wydawn Benedyktynów, 1995

Jenal, Georg, *Italia ascetica atque monastica: Das Asketen- und Mönchtum in Italien von den Anfängen bis zur Zeit der Langobarden (ca. 150/250–604)* (Monographien zur Geschichte des Mittelalters, 39), 2 vols., Stuttgart: Hiersemann, 1995

König, Dorothee, *Amt und Askese: Priesteramt und Mönchtum bei den lateinischen Kirchenvätern in vorbenediktinischer Zeit* (Regulae Benedicti Studia, Supplementa, 12), St. Ottilien: EOS Verlag, 1985

Lawrence, Clifford Hugh, *Medieval Monasticism: Forms of Religious Life in Western Europe in the Middle Ages*, London and New York: Longman, 1984; 2nd edition, 1989

Nürnberg, Rosemarie, *Askese als sozialer Impuls: Monastisch-asketische Spiritualität als Wurzel und Triebfeder sozialer Ideen und Aktivitäten der Kirche in Südgallien im 5. Jahrhundert* (Hereditas, 2), Bonn: Borengässer, 1988

Prinz, Friedrich, Frühes *Mönchtum im Frankenreich: Kultur und Gesellschaft in Gallien, den Rheinlanden und Bayern am Beispiel der monastischen Entwicklung (4. bis 8. Jahrhundert) mit einem Kartenanhang*, Vienna: Oldenbourg, 1965; 2nd edition, Munich: Oldenbourg, 1988
Starowieyski, Marek, "Évolution des structures monastiques: des ascètes aux ordres religieux," in his *La vie quotidienne des moines et chanoines réguliers au Moyen Âge et Temps modernes: Actes du Premier Colloque International du L.A.R.H.C.O.R.: Wroclaw-Ksiaz, 30 novembre–4 décembre 1994* (Travaux du L.A.R.H.C.O.R., Colloquia, 1), Wroclaw: Institut d'Histoire de l'Université de Wroclaw, 1995
Vogüé, Adalbert de, *Histoire littéraire du mouvement monastique dans l'antiquité*, 5 vols., Paris: Editions du Cerf, 1991–1998

Orthodox Monasticism: Byzantine

Byzantine Orthodox monasticism is a continuation of the early Christian monastic movement that began to flourish in the third century in the deserts, wildernesses, and remotely inhabited areas of Egypt, Palestine, Syria, and Anatolia. The Egyptian hermits St. Paul of Thebes (d. c. 340) and St. Antony the Great (c. 251–356) and the Syrian, Palestinian and Cappadocian hermits were ascetics who lived a solitary lifestyle. Eastern monastic life was organized and given a rule by Basil the Great (c. 330–379), who is considered the father of Eastern monasticism. The early monastic movement expressed itself in the desire of men and women to lead a more perfect Christian life. The monasticism of the hermits and anchorites was at first quite unstructured and individualistic, having been known for its extreme rigorism and asceticism. Soon disciples began to attach themselves to a spiritual father who formed the new monks by his example, advice, and personal magnetism. Under Basil and his predecessor, St. Pachomius of Egypt (c. 290–346), the severe austerities and the unstructured and individualistic characteristics of eremitic monasticism gave way to the organized common life under an abbot of cenobitic monasticism. Byzantine cenobitic monasticism was reorganized by St. Theodore of Stoudios (759–826), who also wrote liturgical commentaries and supported the veneration of icons during the final stage of the Iconoclastic controversy. Byzantine Orthodox monasticism, even down to its contemporary expression on Mount Athos, has been heir to both the eremitic and the cenobitic form of monastic life. Thus, most of the comments about "Byzantine" monasticism pertain as well to contemporary Orthodox monasticism.

The Byzantine monk wore the habit, as a distinctive form of dress, and the tonsure, originally the shaving or shearing of the head. Monastic profession was considered the entering on of an entirely new life of separation from the world, a second baptism, which was symbolized by receiving a new name. The three grades of the monastic life differed mainly in the degree of asceticism to which the monk pledged himself; in theory these were three stages in the monk's career: (1) The Rasophore (so named because he "wears the rason," or habit) was somewhat like the Western novice, and he committed himself to abide in the monastic life of asceticism until death. The monk might content himself to remain in this stage for the rest of his life. (2) The Microschemos (so named because he wears "the little habit") entered on the intermediate stage of monasticism by publicly professing vows and receiving the tonsure and the little habit. This stage corresponded roughly to the cenobitic ideal of Pachomius, Basil, and Theodore of Stoudios. (3) The Megaloschemos (so named because he wears "the great habit") was the highest grade of monasticism. It exemplified the austere asceticism of Antony's eremitic ideal, to which the monk of the great habit pledged himself by special fasting, more intense mortifications, and a more solitary life.

Byzantine monasticism, like its predecessors, was mainly a lay institution. Normally monks were not advanced to Holy Orders, but enough monks were ordained deacons and priests to provide for the liturgical and sacramental needs of the community. It became customary for bishops to be chosen from those in the monastic state, and this practice was legislated at the Quinisext Council (Trullan Synod) in 692. The reasoning supporting this development was that the bishops, as leaders of the local churches, should be chosen from among those who had achieved a certain level of spiritual and ascetic perfection through communion with God in the monastic life.

What was the daily routine of the Byzantine monk? Because prayer was the primary obligation of the monk, the day revolved around periods of private prayer and the communal chanting of the Divine Office: the liturgical hours of vespers, compline, nocturns, matins, and the first, third, sixth, and ninth hours. Symeon the New Theologian (949–1022), abbot of the cenobitic monastery of St. Mamas in Constantinople and a mystical writer who taught the vision of the Divine Light through prayer even in this earthly life, supplies us with the following outline in his 16th catechetical discourse. The monk rises at midnight and performs his private prayers, which have been mandated for him by his spiritual father. These private prayers would include praying the psalms, reading the Scriptures and the Fathers, and performing bodily prostrations with the saying of the Jesus Prayer ("Lord Jesus Christ, Son of God, have mercy upon me, a sinner"). Then in the wee hours after midnight, the night office (nocturns and matins and first hour) was celebrated communally in the monastic church, a service lasting about three hours. During the interlude of several hours, the monk retired to his cell for more private prayer or a brief morning siesta. Little interest was devoted to recovering a prolonged night's sleep, something that ill accords with a monastic vocation; rather, sleep was obtained through several naps of several hours. In the monastery of St. Mamas – this was not a universal custom – was a daily Eucharistic liturgy. At around 9:00 a.m. began the third and the sixth hours, and the Divine Liturgy (Mass) was celebrated, at which those monks who had prepared themselves devotionally received Holy Communion. Then the first, main meal of the day was taken in the monastic refectory, somewhat before noon. After table prayers, the meal was eaten in silence while one of the brethren read aloud devotional nourishment from patristic writings and scriptural commentaries and from the lives of the saints. After the meal the monks retired to their cells for more prayer, perhaps a brief nap, and then to manual labor, which occupied them until late afternoon. At around 4:00 p.m. the service of the ninth hour and vespers was celebrated. After this service a very light supper, the second meal of the day, was allowed for the brethren who felt a need for this sustenance. Then the monks returned to the church for compline. When this last service of the day was concluded, the monks venerated and kissed the holy icons throughout the church and received the abbot's blessing before retiring to their cells for the night. Each in his cell, the monks read devotional literature, the *lectio divina*, which customarily included the Scriptures, the writings of the Church fathers (especially monastic authors), and the lives of the saints. After private evening prayers and bodily prostrations, the monks gave themselves three hours sleep, before beginning the new day by rising again at midnight for private prayer in preparation for nocturns.

In addition to prayer rigorous fasting characterized the Byzantine Orthodox monastic vocation. To the normal Orthodox fast days of Wednesdays and Fridays, the monks added Monday. In addition to these weekdays throughout most of the year came four fasting periods: Great Lent before Easter, the Christmas Fast of 40 days before the Nativity of Christ, the Apostles' Fast from the Sunday after Pentecost until the Feast of St. Peter and St. Paul on 29 June, and the 14 days before the feast of the Dormition of the Mother of God on 15 August. The monks never ate flesh meat. On fast days the monks refrained also from dairy products, such as cheese and eggs, and from wine and olive oil. In effect the fast days involved vegetarian fare – soup and bread and water – often eaten unwarmed. Depending on the monastery and the piety of the monk, the variety and the quantity of the food were severely reduced. From the modern perspective this is a spartan but healthy diet; indeed it was not unusual for monks to reach nearly 100 years of age or even beyond. In contrast to much medieval Western monastic life, Byzantine monasticism was a "contemplative," not an "academic" monasticism. Byzantine monks did not normally operate schools or engage in innovative theology; rather, they read the written patrimony of Scripture and Tradition and followed unswervingly the legacy of the Fathers. Orthodox monasticism has always prided itself as the watchdog of doctrinal Orthodoxy, providing a conservative anchor to the ship of the Church.

This is not to say that no creativity existed in Byzantine monasticism. During the Byzantine era the monks engaged in spiritual and theological debates and in the Church councils. Monks were ardent advocates of the divinity of Christ during the Christological disputes of the ecumenical councils of Ephesus, Chalcedon, Constantinople II and III, and Nicaea II. Later, during the Iconoclastic controversies, they defended the veneration of the Virgin Mary and the saints and their painted images or icons. Theodore of Stoudios was a monastic reformer who, in addition to his vigorous defense of icon veneration, reorganized cenobitic monasticism and wrote numerous doctrinal and liturgical treatises.

From the monastic perspective the most controversial debate centered on Hesychasm. Hesychasm (from the Greek word for "quietness") was a method of interior private prayer the purpose of which was to achieve union with God through continuous prayer (as advocated by St. Paul in 1 Thessalonians) through the repetition of the Jesus Prayer. The repetition of prayer formulas such as this can be traced to the fourth century, in St. Gregory of Nyssa, and then later to St. John Climacus (c. 570–c. 649), whose *Ladder of Divine Ascent* describes this method as characteristic of the monks of Mount Sinai. Saint Maximus the Confessor (c. 580–662), St. Symeon the New Theologian, St. Gregory of Sinai, and St. Nicephorus of Mount Athos all advocated this method. However, Hesychasm became controversial in the 14th century. The Hesychasts advocated a psychosomatic form of the Jesus Prayer, holding that the prayer formula should be recited with head bowed and concentration focused on the heart and the interior of the body. The recitation of the prayer was timed to coincide with the rhythm of breathing. This "Prayer of the Heart" was considered the highest form of contemplative prayer designed to achieve union with God. Those who practiced this prayer could be granted even in this life the vision of God, and through the grace of the Holy Spirit they could see with their earthly eyes the uncreated light of the divine energies.

When this Hesychast prayer of the monks of Mount Athos was attacked in the 14th century by Barlaam of Calabria (c. 1290–1348), who ridiculed it as "navel gazing." St. Gregory Palamas (c. 1296–1359) rose to its defense in the *Hagioritic Tome* (1341) and the *Defense of the Holy Hesychasts* (c. 1338). Gregory distinguished between the transcendent uncreated divine essence and the divine energies (or operations or outward activities), by which God communicates Himself and by which humans can participate in the divine life even in this world. This vision of God was promised men in this life so that they can see the uncreated divine grace, the light that shone about Moses on Mount Sinai and especially about Jesus Christ on Mount Tabor. The distinction between the divine essence and the divine energies, a distinction that was rooted in patristic tradition as far back as Gregory of Nyssa (c. 330–c. 395), was formally sanctioned at councils in Constantinople in 1341, 1347, and 1351. This distinction became a part of Orthodox tradition, especially in its monastic expression, and it sparked controversy with strict Western Thomists, who viewed this distinction as destroying the simplicity of the Godhead. The Hesychast Prayer of the Heart is embodied in the texts of monastic and patristic sayings known as the *Philokalia*, collected by St. Nicodemus (c. 1749–1809) of Mount Athos.

In 1453 Constantinople, the "new Rome," was captured by the Ottoman Turks, who destroyed many monasteries and churches. Thereafter monastic life continued in the former Byzantine Empire but on a smaller scale. Slavic countries that had been under the ecclesiopolitical influence of Constantinople enjoyed a thriving monastic culture because of the missionary activity of Byzantium. The monks remained in frequent contact with the center of Orthodox monasticism at Mount Athos. As early as 1000 St. Anthony of the Kyiv (Kiev) Caves left Russia as a youth and journeyed to Mount Athos, where he was tonsured a monk, and his abbot sent him back to Kiev to share traditional Byzantine monastic spirituality and customs with his countrymen. In 1219 St. Sava of Serbia (c. 1175–1235), after he had spent the greater portion of his monastic life on Mount Athos, returned to his native Serbia to strengthen and reorganize the Church according to the teachings and traditions that he had learned on the Holy Mountain of Athos. In 1354 St. Sergius of Radonezh (c. 1314–1392), the enlightener of the Russian north, was in communication with the Ecumenical Patriarch Philotheus of Constantinople, who advised him to establish the cenobitic life in his monastery. As late as 1746 St. Paisy Velichkovsky (1722–1794), after having spent 17 years on Mount Athos, returned to his native Romania, where he translated many Greek theological and spiritual writings into Slavonic and Romanian. He helped disseminate Hesychasm into Romania and Russia.

Today a resurgence of Orthodox monasticism is occurring. In Greece women's monasteries are flourishing, and increasing numbers of young men are entering the monasteries on Mount Athos and throughout Greece and the Greek islands. A restoration of monasticism is taking place as well in many of the former communist countries, although even during the communist era an active, albeit restricted, monastic life was present. Moreover many small monastic communities are appearing in Western Europe and North America, populated by individual monks and nuns from Orthodox backgrounds as well as by converts. Thus, traditional Orthodox monasticism continues from its roots in the early Church and in the Byzantine era down to the present.

WAYNE JAMES JORGENSON

See also Antony, St.; Archaeology: Near East; Basil the Great, St.; Cappadocia, Turkey; Climacus, John, St.; Gregory of Nyssa, St.; Hagiography: Eastern Christian; Hermits: Eastern Christian; Hesychasm; Hymnographers; Iconoclasm (Controversy); Images: Christian Perspectives; Istanbul, Turkey; Italo-Greek Monasticism; Kiev (Kyiv), Ukraine; Lectio Divina; Meteora, Thessaly, Greece; Mount Athos, Greece; Mount Sinai, Egypt; Origins: Eastern Christian; Palamas, Gregory, St.; Philokalia; Sergius of Radonezh, St.; Spirituality: Eastern Christian; Symeon the New Theologian, St.; Theodore of Stoudios, St.; Theology, Eastern Christian; Visual Arts, Eastern Christian: Painting; Women's Monasteries: Eastern Christian

Further Reading

Cavarnos, Constantine, *The Holy Mountain*, Belmont, Massachusetts: Institute for Byzantine and Modern Greek Studies, 1973

Cavarnos, Constantine, *Anchored in God*, 2nd edition, Belmont, Massachusetts: Institute for Byzantine and Modern Greek Studies, 1975

Golitzin, Alexander, *The Living Witness of the Holy Mountain,* South Canaan, Pennsylvania: St. Tikhon's Press, 1996

Hester, David Paul, *Monasticism and the Spirituality of the Italo-Greeks*, Thessaloniki, Greece: Patriarchal Institute for Patristic Studies, 1991

Joanta, Seraphim, *Romania: Its Hesychast Tradition and Culture*, Wildwood, California: St. Xenia's Skete, 1992

The Lives of the Spiritual Mothers, Buena Vista, Colorado: Holy Apostles Convent, 1991

Meyendorff, John, *St. Gregory Palamas and Orthodox Spirituality*, Crestwood, New York: St. Vladimir Seminary Press, 1974

Petersen, Joan M., translator and editor, *Handmaids of the Lord: Contemporary Descriptions of Feminine Asceticism in the First Six Christian Centuries*, Kalamazoo, Michigan: Cistercian Publications, 1996

Robinson, N.F., *Monasticism in the Orthodox Churches*, London: Cope and Fenwick, and Milwaukee, Wisconsin: Young Churchmen, 1916; New York: American Review of Eastern Orthodoxy, 1964

Sherrard, Philip, *Athos – The Holy Mountain*, Woodstock, New York: Overlook Press, 1985

Orthodox Monasticism: Slavic

As this topic is very large, both historically and geographically, the approach herein is not comprehensive but simply an overview of the historical foundations and spread of Slavic monasticism from Saints Cyril and Methodius until the present. The focus is on consecutive regional developments and trends that retain spiritual and cultural significance for the Orthodox world.

Macedonia and Bulgaria – Apostolic Mission to the Slavs

Saint Cyril (c. 820/27–869), known in secular life as Constantine "The Philosopher," was a scholar and linguist and a colleague of the learned Patriarch Photius (c. 810–c. 895). He was entrusted at different times with the chair of philosophy at the imperial university, diplomatic missions to the Arabs and Khazars, and the administration of the patriarchal chancery. Methodius (c. 815–885), his older brother, had a calling to monastic life and entered a monastery on Mount Olympus, Bithynia, in 850. The two were asked in 863 to head a mission to the Slavic kingdom of Moravia, sponsored by its prince, Rastislav. Constantine-Cyril devised an alphabet for the Slavs, a script that survives under the name Glagolitic, and began the translation of the Scriptures and liturgical texts into Slavic. Frankish clergy, already missionizing the area on very different Western principles, resented the new competition and provided resistance in Moravia.

As a result of the opposition, the brothers traveled to Rome to seek the support of Pope Hadrian II (867–872). In their possession they had what they believed to be the relics of St. Clement of Rome (fl. c. 96) that they had gotten from the Khazars and that they bequeathed to the Roman Church. Constantine died in Rome and was tonsured Cyril on his deathbed. Pope Hadrian consecrated Methodius bishop, and this allowed him to continue the mission, translating and ordaining native clergy. However, the death of Prince Rastislav and the continued resentment of the Frankish clergy caused Methodius to withdraw to the territories of modern Croatia. At the time of his death, it was clear that the brothers had not succeeded in establishing a territorial church, although they did attract a small monastic following in the persons of Clement, Naum, Angelarius, Gorazd, and Sava.

When Methodius died in 885 his disciples Clement (c. 840–916) and Naum (830–910) were imprisoned and then exiled, their teachers' lifework apparently in ruins. The two missionaries traveled to a new patron, Boris of Bulgaria (852–889), and renewed their apostolic endeavors, which were supported by the Byzantine court. In 886 Clement went to Macedonia near Ochrid to baptize, serve the liturgy in Slavic, translate Church books, and train indigenous clergy. He was appointed bishop in 893, at which time Naum joined him.

Naum (also Nahum) was a monk and translator and is the probable originator of important work in the Cyrillic alphabet, whereas Clement continued to work in Glagolitic. The Bulgarians adopted the Cyrillic script, possibly following Naum's initiative. Naum founded a monastery, subsequently bearing his name, on Lake Ochrid around 905. He also translated liturgical and patristic texts into Church Slavic and was a major force in the Church of the emerging Bulgarian Empire.

Clement spent 30 years in Christian ministry, teaching in the environs of Ochrid and gathering about 3,500 disciples. Ochrid became a leading city of Slavic Christian culture in Europe. Clement is remembered as a founder of Slavic literary culture, an enemy of paganism, and an organizer of a school that anticipated later higher learning. His *Vita* was written by Archbishop Theophylact of Ochrid (c. 1090–1109). Both Clement and Naum were canonized and still attract active cults in Bulgaria. Bulgaria, Romania, Serbia, Russia, and Ukraine all owe their Christianity and their early language and literature to this monastic association.

Shortly after the establishment of urban monasticism in Bulgaria and Macedonia, the monk John (c. 876–946) founded a wilderness monastery in Rila in the mountains south of Sofia around 930. During his lifetime John was renowned for sanctity throughout the Balkan peninsula, having begun monastic life as a hermit, and ended as the head of a community. The Rila monastery quickly became and has remained the center and pattern of Bulgarian monasticism, wherein a contemplative eremite moves to a mountainous wilderness and founds a cenobitic house. John's cult increased following his death and canonization and eventually extended throughout the Eastern Christian world, as evidenced by his 12th-century life. The monastery was recently returned to the Bulgarian Church by the Communist government and remains a pilgrimage site.

Kievan Russ and Serbia – Byzantine and Athonite Continuity

The "golden ages" of Christianity in Kievan Russ (10th to 13th century) and in Serbia (12th to 14th century) share certain characteristics. Both peoples accepted Christianity not as a "grassroots" movement but "from the top down," through the baptism of the dominant princely families. In addition the respective periods end with protracted foreign invasion and occupation by the Mongols (or Tatars, a Turkic tribe) on the one hand and by the Ottoman Turks on the other.

Kievan Russ was baptized in 988 during the reign of Prince Vladimir (956–1015). The following three centuries were dominated mainly by internecine warfare among the princely families, the assimilation of Byzantine spirituality through translations from Greek into Slavic, and the establishment of Studite monasticism brought from Constantinople to Kiev. The latter two historical movements depended entirely on widespread monastic culture and communities.

Anthony (d. 1072) and Theodosius (d. 1074) are the best-known sainted monks of the Monastery of the Caves near Kiev in Pechersk. Anthony brought traditional eremiticism to Kievan Russ with "the blessing of the Holy Mountain." Athanasius of Athos (c. 920–1003), originally a monk of Bithynia, had founded 58 communities on Mount Athos with imperial support. Anthony accepted Theodosius as one of his disciples, and what we know of Anthony comes from Theodosius' *Vita* and the *Primary Chronicle*. Theodosius was not disposed to the solitary life and founded cenobitic monasticism in Pechersk. He became abbot (*hegumen*) of the community and based the corporate monastic life on the Rule of the Monastery of Stoudios in Constantinople, moving the community out of the caves and above ground. He counseled monks as spiritual director, preserved community order and obedience, constructed hospitality facilities for the needy, and maintained a spiritual and political advisory role with Kievan rulers – functions that were "institutionalized" in later Slavic monastic centers.

Theodosius' *Vita* was written soon after his death – and before his canonization – by the monk Nestor (1056–c. 1114) as the first hagiography among 30 early monastic lives from Pechersk. Nestor is best known as "the Chronicler" of Kievan Russ. Various chronicles or annals from different areas of ancient Russ circulated, many written by monks. The most historically significant and the premier literary work was the *Primary Chronicle* or *Tale of Bygone Years*, which began with the evolution of the Kievan state in the ninth century and was edited by Nestor in the 11th century. Monks also translated and copied the literature of the day, which focused on Scripture as a centerpiece. Sacred Scripture and apocryphal works were rivaled in popularity by translations of the lives of saints, followed by sermons and patristic exegeses. The largest and most popular literary corpuses of the period were religious and included the writings of early Egyptian and Palestinian monks known as the Desert Fathers and the Desert Mothers.

Serbian monasticism – actually any Serbian Christian foundation – is intrinsically linked to St. Sava (1175–1235). Rastko was born into the royal house of Stephan Nemanja, grand *zhupan* and "Imperial Majesty" of Serbia. Rastko left the court to be tonsured Sava at the Vatopedi Monastery of Mount Athos. His father abdicated to another son (*Sebastocrator* Stephan) in 1196 and took the name Symeon at the Serbian monastery in Studenica. In 1198 father and son founded the Serbian Monastery of Hilandar on Athos, the fourth important center of Slavo-Byzantine spirituality and literature there. (In the tenth century the Bulgarian Zographou Monastery had been established on Athos, followed by Russ' monasteries in 1016 and 1169, all of which translated spiritual writings from Greek into Slavic.) Today three of the four Slavic Athonite houses still exist: Zographou, St. Panteleimon, and Hilandar.

Macedonian, Bulgarian, and Byzantine monasticism appear to have exerted scant effect on Serbia prior to the 13th century, probably because of Serbia's political isolation and slow development. With Sava, Serbian monasticism came to be more in tune with Byzantine models. Hilandar used a variant of the Constantinopolitan Studite Rule. When Sava returned to Serbia and became abbot of Studenica, he adopted the same Rule. In 1219 he went to the Byzantine court (in exile, from the Fourth Crusade) and was consecrated the first archbishop of Serbia by Patriarch Manuel I. As primate of the Serbian Church, he journeyed to St. Sabas Monastery in Palestine and later included parts of their liturgy into the Serbian *typikon* (*ordo*). Thus, the literary and liturgical influences that prevailed in Kievan Russ – influences from Constantinople, Mount Athos, and Palestine – were present in Serbia as well.

The Studite communities that the Slavs encountered both in the imperial capital and on the Holy Mountain showed remarkable features. Studite cenobitic monasticism had been introduced on Mount Athos from Constantinople in the mid–tenth century. The founder and theologian of the Stoudios, St. Theodore (759–826), was known for his defense of icons and for his community's replete liturgy, the texts of which are profoundly theological. Thus, all Byzantine and Slavic monasteries adopting his Rule had three major traits, each of which can be discerned in monasticism down to the present: extensive iconography in both the temple and living quarters, a full liturgical cycle of changeable texts with a set *ordo* and about nine daily services, and well-developed literary and musical settings for all the liturgy.

To these one may add the disciplined recitation of the Jesus Prayer, "Lord Jesus Christ have mercy on me a sinner," and vigilance as to the presence and glory of God. These last items are sometimes treated under the topic of the Hesychast Movement Synods (1341, 1347, and 1351), St. Gregory of Sinai, and St. Gregory Palamas (c. 1296–1359). For decades, the question of Divine Grace was hotly debated in the Eastern Church on a very high theological level. One rarely finds this acknowledged in classical Western scholarship, which, on the question of Divine Grace, tends to jump from Aquinas to Luther. Monastic practitioners of this discipline and most experts are quick to point out a continuous historical devotion to prayer (here "prayer of the heart") and a vision of the Uncreated Light from the inception of Christian monasticism, if not before. All these rather intricate elements, as well as their prioritization, are constitutive of Slavic monasticism as it was instituted and experienced at various times and places.

Novgorod and Muscovy – Autonomy and Empire

The Mongols began conquering northern Russ in 1237, capturing Kiev in 1240 and maintained political dominance until 1480, an era known as the Appanage period. During the initial battles many of the Russ urban monasteries were destroyed along with the cities they served. Despite the tragedy of foreign domination, two promising signs remained: Novgorod and its environs escaped devastation, and, after the initial defeat of Russ, Mongol hegemony neither supplanted the populations nor repressed the peoples culturally. Consequently the church and culture continued many of their institutions, even if under heavy foreign taxation.

Novgorodian Russ may be considered a direct link between Kievan Russ and the Muscovite Empire, following a unique democratic political and ecclesiastical course from 1136 to 1471. Novgorod's culture, social classes, and government were similar to Kiev's, but they began electing their own archbishop independently in 1156. Because the archbishop administrated all ecclesiastical affairs, monasticism depended largely on him, and he enjoyed a considerable political role in the city-state. Under the direction of its archbishops, monastics in Novgorod participated in a glorious marriage between the religious life and high culture.

Novgorod's monasteries were strategically located on the perimeters of the city to supplement its constructed water defenses. These monastic fortresses allowed the city to resist over 50 crusader-type invasions from the West as well as from the Mongols. During the city's three-century flourishing, the monasteries developed church architecture and iconography to a degree that would serve as a standard of comparison in later years. Continued contacts with Constantinople facilitated the transplanting of the "Palaeologan Renaissance" to Novgorodian soil, and the religious literary corpus expanded because of widespread literacy. Both the oldest Church Slavic illuminated biblical manuscript, the Ostromirovo Gospel (1056–1057), and the first complete Old and New Testament, Gennadius' Bible (1499), were assembled and copied there. Writings of Church fathers and mothers, historical chronicles, and pilgrimage diaries proliferated as well.

The most famous Slavic monastic theological debate of the millennium, the Possessors versus the Non-Possessors, between Joseph of Volokolamsk (1439/40–1515) and Nilus of Sora (c. 1433–1508), took place within the context of the extended development of the Novgorodian tradition. Joseph propounded church and state cooperation, monastic possession of villages, and material wealth. Nilus separated church and state, supported monastic poverty, and looked at the world from an eschatological viewpoint. Finally, the monk Filofei of Pskov created what came to be understood as a religious if not political doctrine of "manifest destiny" in Russia when he wrote to Czar Basil III (1505–1533) and described Moscow as the "Third Rome," the new Eastern Christian capital after which there would be no other.

The rise of Muscovy is connected not only with Novgorodian culture and the regaining of the Kievan possessions but also with the spiritual legacy of St. Sergius of Radonezh (c. 1314–1392). Sergius was a priest-monk and ascetic who reestablished cenobitic monasticism in Russia. He began his life as a solitary monk in the forest and almost disappeared into anonymity, but his reputation attracted disciples who gathered around him in this "new wilderness." At the monastery site the forest was cleared, a

Church, Andronikov Monastery, Moscow, Russia, 14th–15th century. The icon painter Andrei Rublev (c. 1360/70–1427/30) lived here.
Photo courtesy of Robert E. Jones

road was made, and a village sprang up, and the eremitic life became a type of frontier monasticism. Sergius was ordained and made abbot but soon departed to a site deeper in the forest, establishing another monastery. The process continued, and in all he is credited with the foundation of about 40 communities, the most notable of which is Holy Trinity Monastery in Sergeyev Posad (Zagorsk), which functioned without interruption throughout the Communist period until today.

Sergius' formidable spiritual legacy included a reputation as a clairvoyant and mystic but with no particular human strengths besides charity. He did heal soul and body, although not as a popular healer. The rule of prayer that he and his monks observed left little time other than for necessary work, yet he expressed Christian love in service to others. He was known for giving sound advice and exercised enough influence to prevent four civil wars among the princes. Early Muscovite tradition bore Sergius' seal, disdaining internecine warfare and allowing Moscow to centralize its power. Last but not least, Sergius blessed Prince Dmitri Donskoy to battle the Mongols at Kulikovo Polye on 8 September 1380, marking the beginning of the end of Tatar appanage in Russia and introducing a theological distinction between defensive and offensive warfare.

Muscovite monasticism of the 16th to 17th century was firmly ensconced in Novgorodian and Kievan traditions and Possessor values, actively condemning the Non-Possessors and Protestants as heretics. Muscovite Councils in 1547 and 1549 canonized about 40 new Russian saints, improved ecclesiastical organization, and synthesized a type of nationally united political and religious self-identity. The Greek Catholic "Unia" and the Old Believer Schism (Russian, *Raskol*) distracted the Church theologically; less attention was given to the Byzantine legacy because of the fall of that empire in 1453.

Devotion to Athonite-style contemplation championed by the Non-Possessors was replaced as Metropolitan Macarius of Moscow began building a "Christian society" in the mid–16th century. He constructed the first printing press in Russia and published the lives of the saints, *The Great Reading Compendium*, and the *Biblical Codex*, models for Christian piety in the new society. In 1589 the autocephalous patriarchate of Moscow was established, joined by the ancient metropolitanate of Kiev in 1654. This marked not only a break from the Greeks but also new engagement with the West. Kiev had been dominated by Poland-Lithuania in the preceding centuries. Overwhelming influence there from the Roman Catholic Church in the Unia and Peter Mogila (1596–1646) would make its mark elsewhere.

The next convulsive change for monasticism and for the Church as a whole was the Spiritual Regulation (Russian, *Reglament*) of Peter the Great (1689–1725). Instituted in the context of the Westernization and reform of Russia, it embraced all government administrations (which meant the Russian Church and monasticism), the economy, education, and so on, and its effects lasted into the 20th century. When Archbishop Theophanes Prokopovich prepared the document for Peter, who issued it on 25 January 1721, uniform ecclesiastical schools were included. The archbishop, who had studied at the Greek Catholic College of Athanasius in Rome, took the Kievan Academy's "Latin learning" of Scholasticism as his model for theological education throughout Russia. Because of this, bishops from Ukraine opened ecclesiastical schools with Ukrainian teachers and students. In some cases only Ukrainian was spoken and only Ukrainians advanced to the episcopacy – a forced "Ukrainization" occurred. However, Latin and Scholasticism had little relevance to Orthodox life and were no longer a significant part of European culture either. The contradiction between praying in Church Slavic and theologizing in Latin was unwelcome.

In Prokopovich's Regulation the patriarchate was abolished and replaced by "The Most-Holy Ruling Synod." The Holy Synod was comprised of three bishops, four archimandrites, and four archpriests. Matters were settled by majority decision, but all decisions were subject to state control. Traditional Church government and discipline had been dislodged, if not destroyed. In addition Peter was an active adversary of monasticism. He tried to transform it into a state agency of educated social workers, as shown in the importance accorded to ecclesiastical education described previously. Contradictorily, unprecedented prohibitions against monks having books or writing materials in their cells aimed to curtail any thinking or writing that was not state approved! Happily the reforms in this regard went unheeded in monastic circles.

"Romania" – Answering Challenges to Traditionalism

In the face of Czar Peter's reforms and increased Westernization of the religious life, Paisy Velichkovsky (1722–1794) raised an opposing voice. A student at the Kievan Academy, he was disappointed with spiritual conditions and the curriculum. He scorned learning pagan mythology and higher Latin studies, complaining that the Church fathers were little read. Independently he began searching for true monastic life – which brought him to Mount Athos, where he lived 17 years, founding a monastery on the tradition of inner prayer.

Paisy did not reject knowledge but attempted to discern what sort of knowledge is valuable to the Christian life. On Athos he started collecting and checking Slavic translations of ascetic works in an exacting manner. He built another monastery, Niamets in Moldavia, where he continued his work. Niamets became a literary and theological center concerned with spiritual enlightenment and "intellectual construction." Velichkovsky's writing depended on the literary style of Nilus of Sora and continued his predecessor's interrupted work. Paisy's translation of the *Philokalia* or *Dobrotolubie* was a major event in Slavic monasticism and characterized the era that Elisabeth Behr-Sigel called "La renaissance philocalique." His disciples focused on translations from Greek but included Latin as well. The "Paisy movement" served as a catalyst for things to come, a return to monasticism's traditional sources. The sainted monk also established monasteries according to the Hesychast rule in Moldavia at Dragomirna and Sekul. This is but a small sample of the estimated 200 Orthodox monasteries and 100 *sketes* constructed in

Wallachia and Moldavia from the 14th to the 19th century, most of which still exist today.

Difficulties created by the Spiritual Regulation of Peter the Great continued throughout the 18th and 19th centuries. Russian monastic properties and Church lands were systematically confiscated by Catherine II (1762–1796). The government increasingly interfered in the intellectual and administrative life of the Church. There was no patriarch, the Holy Synod was controlled by the government's Ober-Procurator, and the social status and economic situation of clergy continued to deteriorate. Count Nikolai Protasov became Ober-Procurator of the Holy Synod (1836–1855) and strengthened the office, transforming the Church into an organ of the state, "The Department of the Orthodox Confession." Higher education and ecclesiastical freedom became irrelevant. All that was necessary was supplied by the czar, who was "the supreme defender and guardian of the dogmas of the ruling faith . . . the head of the church" (*Fundamental Laws*, 1832). Under this repressive system monasticism was disassociated from higher culture and learning and regarded as an institution of the peasant class. The Regulation's end came with the "reform movement" (1905–1918).

During the first quarter of the 20th century, Seraphim of Sarov (1759–1833), a traditional Orthodox monastic and ascetic, was recognized as a saint over the loud protests of the last Ober-Procurator, Pobedonostsev, and the Russian intelligentsia, who claimed that this was "a canonization of peasant ignorance." Seraphim became a most influential spiritual force over the succeeding decades. Added to this, the outpost of Orthodoxy in Russian America helped produce the next patriarch of Moscow and All-Russia, Tikhon Belavin, elected in 1918 as the first patriarch since the reign of Czar Peter the Great.

United States – Slavic Monastic Émigrés

Three exceptional men emigrated to the Western Hemisphere and were canonized because of their work there. It should be noted that in each case the man was interested mainly in evangelism and building up the Orthodox Church. None of their ministries resulted in the founding of a monastic community, but each was successful in an active evangelical witness in the New World.

Herman of Alaska (d. 1837) was the first Orthodox saint canonized in the United States (1970). He came from Valaam (Lake Ladoga) Monastery to Alaska in 1794 with a group of about a dozen monk-missionaries, half of whom perished within five years. In North American horticultural history, Herman is listed as the discoverer of a method of fertilization based on the harvest of "sea cabbages," and he was known for growing crops in Alaska where others had failed. Nevertheless Herman was better known for his spiritual achievements. In Kodiak he and the other monks laid the foundation of the Holy Resurrection Church and established a school where they taught catechism, history, mathematics, language, agriculture, and domestic science to the indigenous population. Native cultures were not suppressed, and there was an official directive to avoid cultural interference. This, along with thousands of baptisms, constituted the early success of the missionary party.

The monks came into serious conflict with the Russian-American Company over the treatment of natives. Herman went into seclusion on Spruce Island sometime in the decade between 1808 and 1818, when the governor of the Russian-American Company put the monks under house arrest. By 1823 he was the sole survivor of the original missionary group remaining in Alaska. He was never ordained, enjoyed a reputation for sanctity, and was recognized as *Apa* (elder) by the natives. His canonization in 1970 was predicated largely on his continued memory and cult among the Alaskan populace. Both the church that the monks built and a seminary still function today.

Father John Popov-Veniaminov (1798–1879) figured in the history of Alaska by scientifically recording flora, fauna, weather, and the tides. He made furniture, built clocks, and designed and built churches, including Alaska's historic Mission House and St. Michael's Cathedral in Sitka. An active proponent of education to train native clergy, he developed an Aleut alphabet and translated a catechism and the Gospel of Matthew with the assistance of Ivan Pankov. After his wife's death, Father Veniaminov took monastic vows as Innocent and became the first resident bishop of Alaska (1840–1858). He too advocated indigenous Christianity in Alaska before the Holy Synod of Russia.

In 1850 Russian history records his archbishopric and in 1852 the added responsibilities in Yakutsk in Asia. In the succeeding years he worked with Count Nicholas Muraviev for the annexation of the Amur River basin to the Russian Empire, which occurred through the Treaty of Argin in 1858. After a shipwreck in 1861, he spent time in Japan with the monk-priest Father Nikolai Kasatkin and served as an apostolic inspiration for him. Kasatkin was instrumental in establishing Orthodox Christianity as a legal religion in Japan and was later canonized as the archbishop of Tokyo and "Enlightener of Japan." In 1865 Veniaminov was appointed to the Holy Synod of Russia. With the sale of Alaska to the United States in 1867, Innocent made recommendations to the Holy Synod to establish the Orthodox Church in America with indigenous clergy and English as its native language. In 1868 Czar Alexander II (1855–1881) appointed him metropolitan of Moscow, and in 1870 the metropolitan organized the Imperial Mission Society. During the next 30 years, the Mission Society surpassed the U.S. government in financing the education of Native Americans in Alaska, supporting their languages and cultures – in marked contrast to later policies forced on the original Alaskans.

The third monastic saint, Basil Belavin (19 January 1865 to 7 April 1925), was tonsured, took the name Tikhon, and was ordained priest in 1891. He became rector of the Kazan and Kholm Theological Seminaries and in 1897 was consecrated bishop of Lublin, one of the youngest hierarchs of the Russian Church. In 1898 he was appointed bishop of the Aleutian Islands and Alaska, with the bishop's seat in San Francisco. He evaluated his assignment's difficult circumstances: the size of the Missionary Diocese encompassed Alaska, Canada, and the United States; the polity of the diocese was comprised of ethnic Orthodox from throughout the world; and there were no proper church buildings in New York, Chicago, or San Francisco. Two cathedrals were built in New York in 1902, one Russian and the other Syrian, and in 1903 Holy Trinity Cathedral in Chicago, designed by Louis Sullivan, was completed. In 1909 Holy Trinity Cathedral in San Francisco, one of the oldest Orthodox parishes in the Western Hemisphere, was constructed. In 1905 Tikhon helped found the first Orthodox seminary in the continental United States in Minneapolis. The next year he instituted his project for a multinational and autocephalous Orthodox Church for America and commissioned and published *The Service Book of the Holy Orthodox Catholic Church*, long the only comprehensive church service book in English. In 1907 he convened the first All-American Council in Mayfield, Pennsylvania, after which he was recalled to Russia for reassignment.

That year he was appointed to the See of Yaroslavl, Russia, and in 1914 to the See of Vilno. On 23 June 1917 he was elected to the See of Moscow by the diocesan assembly and granted the title of metropolitan. In 1917–1918 the Church Council elected Tikhon presiding bishop of the first general council of the Russian Church since the 17th century and elected him patriarch of Moscow and All-Russia on 18 November. The patriarchate had been abolished and forbidden from the time of Peter the Great. From 1918 to 1925 Patriarch Tikhon defended the Church and its people from the Bolsheviks' terror and political abuse and was himself imprisoned. He appealed for obedience to legitimate decrees of the Soviet state, although murder, imprisonment, and persecution had become commonplace. In the period between the two world wars, it is estimated that the Communists executed about 40,000 ordained clergy in the Orthodox Church alone.

Worldwide – Present Conditions

Soviet closures of monasteries during the 20th century were devastating. In 1914 there were 1,498 monasteries and convents in Russia, not including other nearby Slavic countries. Steady pressure against the Orthodox Church and all religions by Lenin and Stalin caused a general decline throughout every country eventually included in the Soviet Union. By the end of World War II, only 101 such institutions existed in the entirety of the Soviet Union. Within a decade the number decreased to 90. Under Khrushchev's persecution of religion, the scope and effectiveness of which were little known in the West, monastic communities in all Soviet bloc countries dwindled to a total of 17 in 10 years.

The current worldwide situation for Slavic monasticism indicates that it has not entirely recovered from the effects of Communism. Slavic monasteries on Mount Athos gained no new vocations during the Communist period and few following it. The Bulgarian monastery now has about a dozen monastics, the Romanian monastery over 30, the Russian monastery about 40, and the Serbian monastery about a dozen. These numbers have been relatively stable for the last decade.

Because many of the national churches do not publish statistics that are readily available, the information was culled from reports of traveling clergy and might not be up-to-date. In Bulgaria itself monasticism continues to be very weak with only a handful of vocations in few monasteries. The Czech Republic and Slovakia are in a similar situation. Poland has two Orthodox monasteries. In 1958 there were 10,000 male and female monastics in Romania. The figure dropped to 2,000 during the regime of Nicolae Ceausescu but has now risen again to 10,000.

At one time there were 1,300 churches and monasteries in the Kosovo region of Serbia (Yugoslavia), but now, at the end of the 20th century, there are less than 200 and few working monasteries. The Decani Monastery was made famous as a source of philanthropic work for the Kosovo population and for distributing information on the Internet before and during the 1999 NATO bombings. Under the present circumstances one cannot anticipate how many of the few men and women monastics or their monasteries will be left in the former Yugoslavia at the turn of the millennium.

The situation is quite different in Russia and some surrounding countries of the Commonwealth of Independent States (CIS), as evidenced by the following summary report of Patriarch Alexis II at the end of 1998:

> The number of [male and female] monasteries has reached 478, not counting 87 monastery annexes. Of these, 299 monasteries (151 male and 148 female) are located on Russian territory, plus 74 monastery annexes. On the territory of Ukraine there are 111 monasteries (51 male, 60 female) and nine monastery annexes. On the territory of the CIS there are 58 monasteries (25 male, 33 female) and two annexes. On the territory of the Baltic republics there are five monasteries (two male, three female) plus three *skete* annexes. Abroad there are five monasteries (two male, three female). In Moscow the number of monasteries has remained constant: four male and four female. Immediately under the control of the Patriarchate are another 24 *stauropegial* monasteries.

At present there are two small men's monasteries of Slavic Orthodox background functioning in the United States. St. Tikhon Monastery is in South Canaan, Pennsylvania, and Holy Trinity Monastery is in Jordanville, New York. The Holy Transfiguration Monastery for women is in Ellwood City, Pennsylvania.

MICHAEL PROKURAT

See also Bulgaria; Croatia (Hrvatska); Desert Fathers; Hagiography: Eastern Christian; Historiography, Recent: Eastern Christian; Images: Christian Perspectives; Istanbul, Turkey; Joseph of Volokolamsk, St.; Kiev (Kyiv), Ukraine; Mount Athos, Greece; Nilus of Sora, St.; Paisy Velichkovsky; Palamas, Gregory, St.; Philokalia; Romania; Russia: History; Seraphim of Sarov, St.; Serbia; Sergius of Radonezh, St.; Spirituality: Eastern Christian; Theodore of Stoudios, St.; Theodosius of Kiev, St.; Theology, Eastern Christian; Ukraine; Visual Arts, Eastern Christian: Painting; Women's Monasteries: Eastern Christian

Further Reading

Behr-Sigel, Elisabeth, "Le Monachisme Russe," in *Le Monachisme: Histoire et spiritualité* (Dictionnaire de Spiritualité, volume 9), Paris: Beauchesne, 1980

Cross, Samuel Hazzard, editor and translator, *The Russian Primary Chronicle: Laurentian Text*, Cambridge, Massachusetts: Harvard University Press, 1930

Dvornik, Francis, *Les Légendes de Constantin et de Méthode vues de Byzance* (Byzantinoslavica Supplementa, 1), Prague: Commissionnaire "Orbis," 1933; 2nd edition, Hattiesburg, Mississippi: Academic International, 1969

Featherstone, Jeffrey, translator, *The Life of Paisij Velyckovs'kyj* (Harvard Library of Early Ukrainian Literature, volume 4), Cambridge, Massachusetts: Harvard University Press, 1989

Iosif, Volotskii, Saint, *The Monastic Rule of Iosif Volotsky* (Cistercian Studies Series, number 36), edited and translated by David M. Goldfrank, Kalamazoo, Michigan: Cistercian Publications, 1983

Lenhoff, Gail, *Early Russian Hagiography: The Lives of Prince Fedor the Black* (Slavistische Veröffentlichungen, 82), Wiesbaden: Harrassowitz, 1997

Meyendorff, John, *Byzantium and the Rise of Russia: A Study of Byzantino-Russian Relations in the Fourteenth Century*, Cambridge and New York: Cambridge University Press, 1981

Obolensky, Dimitri, *The Byzantine Commonwealth: Eastern Europe, 500–1453* (History of Civilization), New York: Praeger, and London: Weidenfeld and Nicolson, 1971; new edition, London: Phoenix Giant, 1999

Obolensky, Dimitri, *Six Byzantine Portraits*, New York: Oxford University Press, and Oxford: Clarendon Press, 1988

Panchovski, Ivan, "Sv. Metodii Slavianoblgarski (Zhivot i deinost)" ("St. Methodius the Slavo-Bulgarian Apostle [Life and Works]"), in *Godishnik na Duxovnata Akademia "Sv. Kliment Oxridski"* (Annual of the Academy of Theology of St. Clement of Ochrid), Tom XXVIII, Sophia: Synodal Press, 1986

Plamadeala, Antonie, et al., editors, *Romanian Orthodox Church: An Album-Monograph*, translated by Remus Rus, Bucharest: Bible and Orthodox Mission Institute Publishing House of the Romanian Orthodox Church, 1987

Ridiger, Patriarch Alexis, II, "Annual Report to the Diocesan Council, 23 December 1998," Moscow Patriarchate Press Release

Robinson, N.F., *Monasticism in the Orthodox Churches*, Milwaukee, Wisconsin: Young Churchman, and London: Cope and Fenwick, 1916

Smolitsch, Igor, *Russisches Mönchtum: Entstehung, Entwicklung und Wesen, 988–1917* (Das östliche Christentum, Neue Folge 10–11), Würzburg: Augustinus, 1953

Tachiaos, Anthony-Emil, *Cyril and Methodius of Thessalonica*, Crestwood, New York: St. Vladimir's Seminary Press, 2000

Todorovich, Slavko P., *The Chilandarians: Serbian Monks on the Green Mountain* (East European Monographs, number 264), New York: Columbia University Press, 1989

Velimirovic, Nikolaj, *The Life of St. Sava*, Libertyville, Illinois: Serbian Eastern Orthodox Diocese for United States of America and Canada, 1951

Vlasto, A.P., *The Entry of the Slavs into Christendom: An Introduction to the Medieval History of the Slavs*, Cambridge: Cambridge University Press, 1970

Zernov, Nicolas, *St. Sergius: Builder of Russia*, London: SPCK, and New York: Macmillan, 1939

P

Pachomius, St. c. 290–346

Egyptian founder of Christian cenobitic monasticism

Pachomius, a native Egyptian convert to Christianity, is commonly regarded as a primary "founder" of Christian cenobitic monasticism, that form of ascetic existence in which emphasis is laid on community life, usually with an organized rule of the foundation and a regulated schedule for the day. Such life revolves around regular meetings for common prayer, work, and table fellowship, under the overall control of a superior (*hegumen* or abbot). Although to designate Pachomius the sole founder of cenobitic life cannot convey the complex developments of the various ascetic movements in fourth-century Egypt, at least it serves to highlight his importance in the development of the cenobitic model for future Christian monasticism.

As a young man Pachomius was conscripted from his village to serve in the army. In a moment of wretched loneliness, while passing through a Christian settlement, he experienced the practical charity of a Christian and later ascribed to this his conversion to the new religion. When he was dismissed from military service in 313, he returned to the Upper Egyptian village of Chenoboskion and was baptized into the Christian community there. Shortly afterward he took up the ascetic life under the eldership of the hermit Abba Palaemon. The nearly contemporary (First Greek) Life tells that in the early 320s he was collecting firewood at the deserted village of Tabennesi, in the Thebaid, near the Nile River, when he heard a voice (from a heavenly vision) telling him to settle and build a monastery in this place. He soon attracted many disciples to live the ascetic life in the form of communal coexistence, and after six years he had to establish a second foundation nearby at Pbou. This latter house was destined to grow into the largest monastery and became the center of a chain of Pachomian "federated" houses, as other monastic groups further afield began to associate themselves with his system along the great river in Upper Egypt. The existence of a chain of organized Christian communes, each capable of harnessing the collective work of its members, was an important factor in the establishment and growth of Christianity in Egypt in this era. The monasteries gained in economic and political weight while offering their members secure protection and mutual support.

Pachomius' military background is often said to have shaped his ideas of group organization, although some recent scholarship has pointed to the possible influence of Manichaean communities in the area. Pachomian settlements were characterized by a strict insistence on communal poverty, and discipline in the houses often bordered on the excessive, although in comparison to such as Shenoute of Atripe (c. 350–466), Pachomius was positively moderate. Like Shenoute, Pachomius seems to have been a charismatic and visionary personality. His foundational visionary and auditory experience aside, the Coptic sources suggest that visionary experiences and heavenly intuitions were a regular part of how he thought an inspired Christian leader should function in the elect community. The Greek sources underrepresented this aspect of Pachomius' life in the process of spreading his fame and example further afield in the international Greek-speaking Christian community.

In 345 Pachomius was censured by a synod of Egyptian bishops meeting at Latopolis. The ecclesiastical attack had little effect, mainly because his death soon followed but also because his supporters were sufficiently strong to rebuff it directly. It is an interesting indication, among several others from this period, of a growing tension between ascetic forms of Christianity and the traditional power of village and city bishops. It is reported that Athanasius (c. 296–373) was a constant supporter. When one considers that all the Nag Hammadi Gnostic finds of recent years emanated from the library of a Pachomian settlement, deliberately buried and hidden rather than being burned, the exact nature of the relation between these ascetic houses and the established structures of Christian village communities, with their episcopal and priestly hierarchy, becomes an interesting topic for speculation.

In 346 Pachomius died in the plague that ravaged settlements along the Nile. At that time he had nine male and two female monasteries under his authority. Palladius (c. 364–420/30) the historian, writing around 420, estimated that 3,000 monastics belonged to Pachomius' federation in his lifetime (*Historia Lausiaca* 26.18–20). By the fifth century the federation had entered into a process of dissolution, accelerated by divisive Christological controversies affecting the Church in the aftermath of Chalcedon (451). However, by that time Pachomius' modeling of cenobitic life had left an indelible mark on the consciousness of monastic organization elsewhere in the Christian world, such as at Mount Sinai, in Palestine, and in Cappadocia, and was to have long-lasting effects. The "Rules" of Pachomius are highly practical and based on common sense, embodying an active concept of the common good. Perhaps they were not written down until after Pachomius' death, but they represent the essential tenor of his system. They not only influenced Basil of Caesarea (c. 330–379) but, translated into Latin by St. Jerome (c. 345–420), were a strong influence on John Cassian (c. 360–after 430), Caesarius of Arles (c. 420–542), and Benedict (c. 480–c. 550) and thus played a role as an archetypal guide for cenobitic founders in both the Eastern and the Western Churches.

JOHN MCGUCKIN

See also Asceticism: Christian Perspectives; Basil the Great, St.; Cappadocia, Turkey; Cassian, John; Desert Fathers; Egypt; Ethiopia; Governance: Christian Perspectives; Hagiography: Eastern Christian; Hermits: Eastern Christian; Mount Sinai, Egypt; Office, Daily: Eastern Christian; Origins: Eastern Christian; Pilgrimages, Christian: Near East; Retreat, Christian; Shenoute of Atripe; Spirituality: Eastern Christian

Biography

Born in Upper Egypt of pagan parents, Pachomius served as a conscript in the Roman army before being baptized. After becoming a disciple of the hermit Palaemon, about 320 he founded what may have been the first cenobitic monastery. At Tabennisi in the Thebaid desert of Egypt, he attracted many followers and was ruling nine monasteries for men and two for women when he died in 346. Virtually every monastic order regards Pachomius as its ancestor.

Further Reading

Athanassakis, A.N., translator, *The Life of Pachomius: Vita prima Graeca*, Missoula, Montana: Scholars Press, 1975

Chitty, Derwas, *The Desert a City*, Oxford: Blackwell, and Crestwood, New York: St. Vladimir's Seminary Press, 1966

Goehring, J.E., "New Frontiers in Pachomian Studies," in *The Roots of Egyptian Christianity*, edited by Goehring and A. Pearson, Philadelphia: Fortress Press, 1986

Goehring, J.E., *The Letter of Ammon and Pachomian Monasticism*, Berlin and New York: de Gruyter, 1986

Rousseau, Phillip, *Pachomius: The Making of a Community in Fourth-Century Egypt*, Berkeley: University of California Press, 1985

Veilleux, Armand, *Pachomian Koinonia*, 3 vols., Kalamazoo, Michigan: Cistercian Publications, 1980–1982

Padmasambhava eighth century A.D.

Indian reputed founder of first Tibetan Buddhist monastery and the Nyingma lineage

No figure is more revered by Tibetan Buddhists than Padmasambhava, often known simply as Guru Rinpoche (precious master), the semi-legendary Indian meditation master, yogic practitioner, exorcist, and magician of the eighth century. Although his dates are uncertain and little is known about him historically, few doubt the existence of a historical person behind the legends. He is a major figure in the establishment of Buddhism in Tibet, not least because he is credited with helping found the first Tibetan Buddhist monastery, Samye. This story, which probably has some historical basis, narrates that Padmasambhava was invited to Tibet by King Thri-song-de-tsen on the advice of Śāntarakṣita, another Indian Buddhist already working to build the first monastery. Legends state that the scholar-monk Śāntarakṣita had been unsuccessful in building the monastery because local deities repeatedly destroyed his work. Thus, he suggested that Padmasambhava be invited to Tibet to tame the local deities and turn them from hostile forces into guardians of the dharma and the Buddhist religion. Padmasambhava was successful in this task, the monastery was completed, and the first Tibetan monks were ordained. Historically little is known of Padmasambhava subsequent to this feat. Some sources say that he was sent away almost immediately after the first monks were ordained because he performed magical acts that displeased the court, and other sources say that he remained in Tibet for 50 years. Nevertheless Tibetan Buddhists of all sects revere him as the founder of the Nyingma lineage, the oldest of Tibet's four major lineages.

However, for Tibetans and Tibetan Buddhism the historical facts about Padmasambhava matter little. Tibetan Buddhist literature is replete with sacred biographies of great practitioners who often perform acts that defy conventional ideas about what humans can accomplish. These sacred biographies are well known and frequently retold; both monastics and laypeople take them seriously both as inspirational models and as entertaining, exciting stories. The Padmasambhava of legend is the one that we must consider if we want to know about the religiously important Padmasambhava.

Padmasambhava's legendary life is miraculous from beginning to end. The stories of his deeds in India are no less wondrous than those of his deeds in Tibet. Whereas the Indian stories tell mainly about his training, the Tibetan stories tell about his accomplishments as subduer of demons and teacher. Revered as a "second Buddha," he is probably more immediate to most Tibetans than is the historical Buddha who founded the religion, and in many ways he is more wondrous than that first Buddha.

The name Padmasambhava means "Lotus born," and that describes his legendary mode of birth. He is said to have been discovered as a eight-year-old child seated in the center of a lotus blossom by King Indrabhuti, who raised the boy as his son. In line to inherit the kingdom, the youth realized that being king would not be of great service to the world and asked to renounce the world. His wish was not immediately granted, but once he did leave the householder life he practiced in the charnel grounds, a motif common in the stories of Tantric adepts. He received many Tantric practices from various superhuman teachers and also received monastic ordination. Although his manifestation as yogic practitioner is emphasized, it is said that his outer appearance was that of a monk wearing the ochre robes. One of his teachers in India was a great *ḍākiṇī* (supernatural female enlightened being) appearing in the form of a nun. She transformed him into a sacred syllable and swallowed him. In her body he received great empowerments and then was ejected through her vagina. He continued to study with all the great masters of his day and received all the teachings of both sūtra (public texts) and tantra (esoteric texts) until he understood everything there was to be known. He and his Indian consort, Mandarava, excelled at longevity practices, so that Padmasambhava attained power over the duration of his life. While in India he taught countless disciples, defeated non-Buddhist teachers in debates, and converted several kingdoms.

After he came to Tibet, his first deed was to subdue the local deities. The popular legends say that he traveled the length and breadth of Tibet, subduing all the local deities and consecrating sacred places. They also state that once the building of Samye monastery began, progress was very rapid because the oath-bound local deities built by night, whereas the human artisans built by day. After the completion of the monastery, the first monks were ordained, and the immense task of translating the corpus of Indian Buddhism into Tibetan began. Padmasambhava is said to have been among the translators. At the same time he imparted numerous Tantric empowerments to his Tibetan disciples, both male and female, thus inaugurating many important Tibetan lineages. Among his many disciples were 25 major ones, of whom none was more accomplished than the *ḍākiṇī* Yeshe Tsogyel, who accompanied him on many of his travels as the consort who supported his Tantric practices. He is also said to have founded many colleges for teaching both dialectical methods, preferred by monks, and Tantric methods, preferred by yogic practitioners.

For the future of Tibetan Buddhism, no task said to have been done by Guru Rinpoche was more important than that of composing and concealing texts in various hidden places in Tibet, to be discovered later when they would be needed or when people could understand them. These texts, called *terma* (hidden treasures), play a crucial role in Tibetan Buddhism. They have frequently been discovered throughout Tibetan history down to contemporary times. Often they are attributed to either Padmasambhava or Yeshe Tsogyel.

Even traditional sources concede that it is impossible to know how long Padmasambhava remained in Tibet. Some traditional authors say that even if he was in Tibet for only a short while, that does not disprove any of the accomplishments attributed to him because he was not an ordinary being and thus could have accomplished a great deal in a very short time. All sources agree that he departed to the southwest to tame demons there after having given detailed instructions to all classes of Tibetan practitioners, including monks and nuns. He is said to have departed riding a lion or a fine horse. After quelling the demon that he had set out to destroy, he materialized his Palace of Lotus Light on the Copper-Colored Mountain, which is his Buddha field. From there he sends out emanations whenever needed to teach and protect. Padmasambhava himself will remain there until the dissolution of the universe.

RITA M. GROSS

See also Buddhist Schools/Traditions: Tibet; Holy Men/Holy Women: Buddhist Perspectives; Missionaries: Buddhist; Tibetan Lineages: Nyingma; Visual Arts, Buddhist: Tibet

Biography

The "Lotus-Born" one was an Indian *siddha* invited to Tibet in the eighth century. There legends accumulated to recount the magical acts of "Guru Rinpoche" (Precious Teacher). As consort of Yeshe Tsogyel, he is renowned particularly for having concealed texts (*terma*) intended to be discovered in future centuries.

Further Reading

Chattopadhyaya, Alaka, *Atisa and Tibet*, Delhi: Motilal Barnasidass, 1981
The Nyingma School of Tibetan Buddhism: Its Fundamentals and History, 2 vols., Boston: Wisdom, 1991
Snellgrove, David, and High Richardson, *A Cultural History of Tibet*, Boulder, Colorado: Prajna Press, 1980
Attributed to Yeshe Tsogyel, *The Life and Liberation of Padmasambhava*, 2 vols., Berkeley, California: Dharma, 1978
Attributed to Yeshe Tsogyel, *Dakini Teachings: Padmasambhava's Oral Instructions to Lady Tsogyal*, Boston and New York: Shambhala, 1990
Attributed to Yeshe Tsogyel, *The Lotus Born: The Life Story of Padmasambhava*, Boston: Shambhala, 1993

Pagoda. *See* Architecture: Structural Monasteries in East Asia

Painting, Christian. *See* Visual Arts, Eastern Christian: Painting; Visual Arts, Western Christian: Painting

Paisy Velichkovsky 1722–1794

Ukranian Orthodox monk, translator, and exponent of the Hesychast tradition

Born in Poltava, Ukraine, named Peter in baptism, from his youth Velichkovsky showed a great interest in reading religious books and desired to become a monk. His father, John, the archpriest of Poltava, died when he was four, and his eldest brother became priest of the Church of the Dormition, where his father, grandfather, and great-grandfather had served. At the age of 13, his brother died, and his mother wanted him to become priest of the same church. He studied at the church school of Kiev until the age of 17 when he went to the monastery of Lyubetz on the Dneper River and then to the Medvedovsky monastery, where he was tonsured a rasophore monk and given the name Platon at age 19. When Roman Catholics took over the territory, he fled to Kiev, only to learn about the monasteries of Vlachia (modern Romania), where he stayed in various *sketes* from 1743–1746.

From 1746 to 1763 he dwelt on Mount Athos. At age 28 he was tonsured a monk and given the name Paisy. On Athos he observed that the Turkish domination had led to a general decline in monasticism, and, unable to find an elder to guide him, he lived alone, aided by some Slavic monks. A young Vlachian monk, Bessarion, came to Athos and asked Paisy to become his elder. Paisy, not wanting to be his superior, accepted him as a companion. To find guidance Paisy read patristic books in Slavonic, borrowed from the Athonite Serbian and Bulgarian monasteries. From 1754 Paisy began to gather disciples and was forced not only to expand the size of his monastery but also to be ordained priest to serve the community. Paisy gradually learned Greek and, translating the Fathers into Slavonic, began his labors in the collection, correction, and translation of texts. His interest influenced other Athonite monks to collect and study patristic texts.

In 1763 Paisy and 64 monks, Slavic and Moldavian, left Mount Athos and returned to Vlachia, where they took up residence in the Dragomirna Monastery in the Carpathian Mountains. Here he continued his work in the translation of patristic texts, got other monks to aid him, and used this work to give regular instruction to his monks. In 1775 this territory was taken over by Austrian rule, and Paisy and his monks were invited by the abbot of Sekoul to come to his monastery. With some 350 monks Paisy took up residence at Sekoul, faced with an enormous building project that lasted three years. Here his translating activity further developed by establishing schools for the instruction of young monks in Greek. In 1779 he wrote to the civil ruler asking for help, and to his surprise he and the monks were ordered to go to the monastery of Niamets, one of the largest and most influential monasteries in Moldavia.

While at Niamets, Paisy learned that Macarius of Corinth and Nicodemos the Hagiorite had published in 1782 a collection of ascetic patristic works in Greek, the *Philokalia*. Paisy sent a monk to Athos to get a copy of this work. In 1787 Paisy completed one of his most important works, the translation of the Ascetic Homilies of Isaac the Syrian. In 1790, after the Russians drove out invading Turkish forces, Paisy met an accompanying Russian archbishop who raised him to the rank of archimandrite. After a brief illness Paisy died on 15 November 1794.

Prior to this time Metropolitan Gabriel of Novgorod and Petersburg requested to publish the Slavonic translation of the *Philokalia* from the Greek that Paisy had made. Paisy sent the Greek and Slavonic texts, which were examined by him and other scholars and monastic spiritual elders. The corrected translation, published in the Moscow Synodal Printshop in 1793, received the Slavonic title *Dobrotolubiye*. Through the influence of the monks connected to Paisy, this work exerted an important impact on Russian monasticism in the 19th century, especially on the great monastic revival that flowered among the Elders of Optina Monastery.

DAVID PAUL HESTER

See also Elders, Russian Monastic (Startsi); Hesychasm; Isaac the Syrian (Isaac of Nineveh), St.; Mount Athos, Greece; Nilus of Sora, St.; Orthodox Monasticism; Philokalia; Romania; Russia: History

Biography

This Ukrainian monk from Poltava settled at the St. Elijah Skete on Mount Athos in 1746 and in 1763 moved his community to Moldavia. He promoted translation into Slavonic of Greek Fathers, whose texts he found at Mount Athos. He himself translated the *Philokalia* (1793) of St. Macarius and St. Nicodemus. As a spiritual director, he continued the Hesychast tradition.

Major Work

Slavonic translation in 1793 from the Greek of the *Philokalia* (1782) by St. Macarius of Corinth and St. Nicodemus of the Holy Mountain

Further Reading

Chetverikov, Sergii, *Starets Paisii Velichkovskii: His Life, Teachings, and Influence on Orthodox Monasticism*, Belmont, Massachusetts: Nordland, 1980

Meyendorff, John, *St. Gregory Palamas and Orthodox Spirituality*, Crestwood, New York: St. Vladimir's Seminary Press, 1974; reprint, 1998

Schema-monk Metrophan, *Blessed Paisius Velichkovsky*, Platina, California: Saint Herman of Alaska Brotherhood, 1976

Velichkovsky, Paisius, *Saint Paisius Velichkovsky*, Platina, California: St. Herman Press, 1994

Palamas, Gregory, St. c. 1296–1359

Byzantine Orthodox monk and apologist of Hesychasm

Gregory Palamas was born in the Byzantine capital of Constantinople. His father, a member of the aristocracy, was employed in the court of Emperor Andronicus II (1282–1328). Accordingly, Palamas' own early education was a thorough preparation for a similar career. However, after his father's death, when Palamas was about 20 years old, he abandoned all plans for high state office and instead became a monk at the monastery of the Great Lavra on Mount Athos (c. 1316). Here he lived the common life, except for short excursions to nearby Berrhoia and Thessalonica, where he was also ordained (1326). In 1335–1336 he moved to the Athonite cenobitic foundation of Esphigmenou, where he briefly served as abbot. Even so, Palamas was partial to the more contemplative Hesychast tradition of eremitic monasticism. He often preferred to live in near total solitude and seclusion in various hermitages, or *sketai*, both at Berrhoia and the Holy Mountain. Shifting from cenobitism to eremitism for a more austere life of prayer and asceticism was not unusual in Byzantine Orthodox monasticism. The barrier between the active and the contemplative life was flexible. This said, Palamas soon achieved a measure of fame as an ascetic and in 1337 became involved in a public exchange with the philosopher-monk Barlaam of Calabria (c. 1290–1348). It was the opening round of a controversy that eventually engulfed both the church and society. Essentially, Barlaam had argued that because of God's absolute transcendence, human theological reasoning is limited; even a personal experience of the divine was impossible. When Palamas rejected this approach to the problem of the knowledge of God in general and to the reality of communion with God in particular, Barlaam launched an abusive broadside against Hesychast spirituality.

Palamas' response is contained in his major theological treatise, the *Triads in Defense of the Holy Hesychasts*, and in a subsequent text (endorsed by the Athonite community) known as the *Hagioritic Tome*. The *One Hundred and Fifty Chapters* is a more concise, shorter statement of his theology. His teaching, also known as Palamism, is above all a theological defense of the patristic doctrine of human deification in Christ (*theosis*). At its center lies the conviction that genuine participation in divine life is both possible and accessible through contemplative prayer and the sacramental life of the church. Briefly, although God in his unique transcendent essence remains beyond all participation, humans are able to experience God's grace in his energies or operations. Through these uncreated, divine energies (as distinct from the unknowable and immutable divine essence), we are able to know God directly and thus be saved. This Palamite distinction between essence and energy also explains the vision of the uncreated Divine Light that the Hesychast seeks in a life of continual prayer of the heart. What the contemplative solitary experiences is not a subjective emotion, illusion, or symbol, as Barlaam had reasoned, but rather God's genuine self-communication – his gift of deifying grace to humanity.

Palamas' theology was formally approved by the church in the Constantinople councils of 1341, 1347, and 1351. His teaching regarding the fundamental distinction between the essence and the energies of God was declared dogma; it possessed ecumenical authority and as such was as binding as any conciliar definition. This ecclesial endorsement also implied acceptance of the theory and practice of contemplative mental prayer and the vision of Divine Light. To be sure, Palamism has had its critics. During the civil war of 1341–1347, Palamas was briefly imprisoned and even condemned. However, these developments were, in all essential respects, politically inspired. Predictably, the articulate anti-Palamite circle of prominent Byzantine humanists and Thomists often had its own agenda but, although highly vocal, remained a minority. As it happened, in 1347 Palamas was consecrated archbishop of Thessalonica. And after his death (14 November 1359), he was canonized as a saint (1368). The feast day is the second Sunday of Lent and 14 November.

As a synthesis of the patristic teaching on deification, Palamism knows few equals. This is not to say that its integration of the spiritual tradition of the Desert Fathers is of any less importance. Historically, Palamas' achievement brought a victory for Orthodox contemplative monasticism. Indeed, after 1347 a succession of Hesychasts found positions as bishops, abbots, and patriarchs within the Church of Constantinople. Their agenda, which was aimed at the wider world of Eastern Christendom, focused mainly on promoting church unity and the Athonite tradition. Before long, in fact, Slavonic translations of the texts of Hesychast literature found their way from Mount Athos to other Orthodox monasteries in the Balkans and beyond. The monastic revival in, for example, the distant Russian Lavra of the Holy Trinity of St. Sergius cannot be explained solely in terms of its local context. Increasingly, too, the diffusion of Hesychast mysticism was sustained by the development of a genuine international Athonite network. It was not unusual for monastic visitors or pilgrims to the Athonite peninsula to become active agents of Hesychast spirituality on returning home. Typically, contacts with both friends and spiritual masters on Mount Athos were continued and maintained long after these visits. More generally, the role played by Palamism and monastic Hesychasm in preserving the spiritual unity and identity of the Christian East during the bleak centuries of captivity following the fall of Constantinople was decisive. Down to the 20th century, it continued to inspire monastic revivals in the Orthodox world. The prolific literary achievement and authentic holiness of, say, St. Paisy Velichkovsky (1722–1794), St. Nicodemus the Hagiorite (1759–1809), St. Seraphim of Sarov (1759–1833), and St. John of Cronstadt (1829–1908) have helped to sustain this living spiritual tradition. This is equally the case with the phenomenon of elders, or *startsi*, represented by the Optino hermitage in central Russia during the 19th century. It is worth adding that the Hesychast devotion to the practice of interior prayer lies at the heart of the 19th-century Orthodox spiritual classic *The Way of a Pilgrim*. Its anonymous author, who quotes Palamas as his authority, argues that such prayer is for all Christians and not solely for those bound by monastic vows.

Aristeides Papadakis

See also Elders, Russian Monastic (Startsi); Hesychasm; Humanism, Christian; Macarian Homilies; Mount Athos, Greece; Nilus of Sora, St.; Orthodox Monasticism: Byzantine; Spirituality: Eastern Christian; Theology, Eastern Christian; Vision, Mystical: Eastern Christian

Biography

Born most likely at Constantinople into a noble family, Gregory went with his brothers c. 1318 to Mount Athos. Forced to flee by the advance of the Turks, he was ordained priest in Thessalonica in 1326. After living as a hermit near Berrhoia, he returned to Mount Athos in 1331 as a leader of the Hesychasts. He disputed with the Calabrian monk Barlaam, who upheld the unknowability of God against the Hesychasts' notion of human divinization (*theosis*). Gregory's doctrines (e.g., of seeing the Divine Light) were first condemned in 1344 but then affirmed at two Councils of Constantinople (1347 and 1351). From 1350 he served as Archbishop of Thessalonica, and in 1354 spent a year as a captive of the Turks. He is esteemed as the definitive formulator of Hesychasm.

Major Works

Triads in Defense of the Holy Hesychasts, c. 1338
One Hundred and Fifty Chapters

Further Reading

Chrestou, Panagiotes, editor, *Gregoriou tou Palama: Syngrammata*, 4 vols., Thessalonica, Greece, 1962–1970

Palamas, Gregory, *The Triads*, edited and with an introduction by John Meyendorff, partial translation by Nicholas Gendle, New York: Paulist Press, 1983

Lossky, Vladimir, "La théologie de la lumière chez saint Grégoire de Thessalonique," *Dieu Vivant* 1 (1945)

Meyendorff, John, *A Study of Gregory Palamas*, London: Faith Press, 1964; 2nd edition, 1974

Meyendorff, John, *St. Gregory Palamas and Orthodox Spirituality*, Crestwood, New York: St. Vladimir's Seminary Press, 1974

Meyendorff, John, editor and translator, *Défense des saints hésychastes*, 2 vols., Louvain, Belgium, 1959

Papadakis, Aristeides, and John Meyendorff, *The Christian East and the Rise of the Papacy: The Church 1071–1453 A.D.*, Crestwood, New York: St. Vladimirs Seminary Press, 1994

Sherrard, Philip, "The Revival of Hesychast Spirituality," in *Christian Spirituality: Post-Reformation and Modern*, edited by Louis Dupré and Don E. Saliers, volume 18 of *World Spirituality: An Encyclopedic History of the Religious Quest*, New York: Crossroad, 1989

Stiernon, D., "Bulletin sur le Palamisme," *Revue des études byzantines* 30 (1972)

Yannaras, Christos, "The Distinction between Essence and Energies and Its Importance for Theology," *St. Vladimir's Theological Quarterly* 19 (1975)

Palestine. *See* Israel/Palestine

Papacy: Monastic Popes

Of the approximately 263 bishops of Rome, at least 35 have been members of religious orders, all but one of them (Pope Paul IV [1555–1559], who was the cofounder of the Theatines) falling within the group of religious orders covered in this encyclopedia. There may well be more. The *Liber Pontificalis* reports of St. Telesphorus (pope c. 125–c. 136) that he was an "anchorite" or hermit: the term is anachronistic, although it did not prevent the Carmelites including him in their calendar of saints on the grounds that he must have been a hermit on Mount Carmel. With the exception of Gregory II (715–731), from John V, who became bishop of Rome in 685, to the death of St. Zacharias in 752, all the popes were either Greek or Syrian in origin, perhaps suggesting that some of these nine were monks, but they are not recorded as such in the *Liber Pontificalis*. A late version of the text of the *Liber* claims that the Sicilian Agatho (678–681) had been a monk, but there is no reason to give this credence over the earlier text, which makes no mention of it.

The case of the great reforming Pope Gregory VII (Hildebrand, 1073–1085) is more complicated. He was certainly "rector and treasurer" of the Roman monastery of St. Paul-without-the-Walls, but this of itself does not prove that he was himself a monk. There is indeed no unambiguous evidence that he ever was one, certainly none that he was a monk of Cluny, as a late tradition suggests. It would not have been surprising: Cluny was very much in the forefront of the reform movement with which Gregory was associated and had been so for a century. It is quite possible that Hildebrand visited Cluny, but the likelihood is that he was a monk from a young age at one of the Roman monasteries, which, if true, would account for the fact that very little is known of his early life.

Thus, apart from Paul IV, the list of "monastic" popes is as follows: Gregory I (590–604, monk of St. Andrew's on the Caelian Hill – his own family home); Adeodatus II (672–676, monk of St. Erasmus on the Caelian Hill); Stephen III (IV) (768–772, monk of St. Chrysogonus, Rome); Paschal I (817–824, abbot of St. Stephen's, Rome); Leo IV (847–855, monk of St. Martin-without-the-Walls); John IX (898–900, monk – possibly of a monastery in Tivoli); Silvester II (999–1003, monk of St. Géraud, Aurillac, France, later abbot of Bobbio); Stephen IX (X) (1057–1058, abbot of Monte Cassino, although he had fled there for his own safety only in 1055 and had not otherwise spent his life as a monk); Gregory VII (see above); Victor III (1086–1087, abbot of Monte Cassino); Urban II (1088–1099, monk of Cluny); Paschal II (1099–1118, certainly a monk from his youth, possibly at Cluny, but then abbot of St. Lawrence-without-the-Walls); Gelasius II (1118–1119, monk of Monte Cassino); Honorius II (1124–1130, canon regular of Bologna, then of the Lateran); Innocent II (1130–1143, canon regular of the Lateran); Lucius II (1144–1145, canon regular of Lucca, then of Santa Croce in Rome); Eugenius III (1145–1153, Cistercian); Anastasius IV (1153–1154, canon regular of St. Ruf of Avignon); Hadrian IV (1154–1159, canon regular of St. Ruf of Avignon); Gregory VIII (1187, canon regular of Laon); Innocent V (1276, Dominican); Nicholas IV (1288–1292, Franciscan); Celestine V (1294–1296, Benedictine monk, then hermit, then founder of the Celestines); Benedict XI (1303–1304, Dominican); Benedict XII (1334–1342, Cistercian, abbot of Fontfroide, near Narbonne); Clement VI (1342–1352, monk of La Chaise-Dieu, then abbot of Fécamp); Urban V (1362–1370, monk of St. Victor, Marseilles; then abbot of St. Germain, Auxerre; then abbot of St. Victor); Eugenius IV (1431–1447, canon regular); Sixtus IV (1471–1484, Franciscan); Pius V (1566–1572, Dominican); Sixtus V (1585–1590, Franciscan); Benedict XIII (1724–1730, Dominican); Clement XIV (1769–1774, Franciscan); Pius VII (1800–1823, Benedictine, eventually of Sant'Anselmo, Rome); and Gregory XVI (1831–1846, Camaldolese).

Three popes were founders of religious orders. Paul IV and Celestine V have already been mentioned. Pius II founded the Bethlehemites, a military order, to defend the Aegean against the Turks after the fall of Constantinople in 1453.

A number of monks and friars became antipopes. John XVI (997–998) was for a few years before his election to the papacy abbot of Nonantola, near Modena, and after his deposition was imprisoned in a monastery in Rome. Anacletus II (1130–1138) had been a monk of Cluny; Callistus III (1168–1178) was a monk of a Vallombrosan abbey, eventually being elected its abbot. Both Nicholas V (1328–1330) and Alexander V (1409–1410) were Franciscans, the former having abandoned his wife to join the Order.

The choice of members of religious orders to become bishops of Rome rarely follows a pattern. It is hardly surprising that there were so few in the first millennium of Christianity (unless, as suggested previously, those from John V to St. Zacharias were monks): during this period it was the practice to elect to the papacy those who were already in the service the Church of Rome, the vast majority of whom were not monks in the city. In the tenth century, even though the Cluniacs were turned to for help in restoring the religious life of Rome, no monk became pope. However, successive pontiffs in the middle of the century were supportive of their efforts. Silvester II, at the very end of that century, was both a monk and a very active reformer, and the reform of the Church at large, vigorously pursued from Gregory VII onward, at first very much depended on monastic popes and later on popes from the recently founded canons regular. Both these groups were themselves "reformed" clergy and could be expected to adhere to the policy pursued since Gregory VII.

MICHAEL J. WALSH

See also Carmelites; Cluniacs; Gregory I (the Great), St.; Gregory VII

Further Reading

Batiz, M., et al., "Papato," in *Dizionario degli Istituti di Perfezione*, volume 6, edited by Giancarlo Rocca, Rome: Edizioni Paoline, 1980

Davis, Raymond, translator, *The Book of Pontiffs (Liber Pontificalis)* (Translated Texts for Historians, Latin Series, 5), Liverpool, Merseyside: Liverpool University Press, 1989; 2nd edition as *The Book of Pontiffs: The Ancient Biographies of the First Ninety Roman Bishops to* A.D. *715* (Translated Texts for Historians, 6), 1999

Davis, Raymond, translator, *The Lives of the Eighth-Century Popes (Liber Pontificalis): The Ancient Biographies of Nine Popes from* A.D. *715 to* A.D. *817* (Translated Texts for Historians, 13), Liverpool, Merseyside: Liverpool University Press, 1992

Davis, Raymond, translator, *The Lives of the Ninth-Century Popes (Liber Pontificalis): The Ancient Biographies of Ten Popes from* A.D. *817–891* (Translated Texts for Historians, 20), Liverpool, Merseyside: Liverpool University Press, 1995

Kelly, J.N.D., *The Oxford Dictionary of Popes*, Oxford and New York: Oxford University Press, 1986

Levillain, Philippe, editor, *Dictionnaire historique de la papauté*, Paris: Fayard, 1994

Papacy: Papal Pronouncements

The earliest ecclesiastical legislation at a Church-wide level came not from the papacy but from councils. It began formally at the Council of Chalcedon (451), which, although it met specifically to settle a dispute about the nature of Christ, also legislated for men and women living a religious life. Sundry references were made to monks and some to virgins, forbidding both classes, for example, to contract marriage after consecrating themselves to God. There was also a provision against turning monasteries into "secular hostelries." Most important Chalcedon insisted that monasteries were to be under the jurisdiction of the local bishop and were not be established without his authority. This provision, still part of canon law, had to be repeated regularly in councils and synods.

If this was the norm, many instances developed to the contrary. In 628 the monastery of Bobbio was placed by Honorius I (625–638) under direct papal oversight. This – and similar rights granted to Fulda in 751 and St. Denis in 757 – is taken as the origin of what later came to be the important notion of monastic "exemption," although what Honorius was intending (he does not himself seem to have been a monk, although he was very sympathetic to monastic ideals) is unclear. It might be that he simply wished, as had his great model Gregory I (590–604) before him, to safeguard monasteries from unfair episcopal demands. In March 1027, after the exemption of Cluny had been attacked by French bishops at the Council of Anse, John XIX (1024–1032) reasserted the privileges of Cluny in a series of charters, insisting on the papacy as the sole source of ecclesiastical authority. Cluny, an agent of reform in the Church long before the papacy took up that task, was, said Gregory VII (1073–1085) at the synod of Rome in 1080, the papacy's "own particular property."

A further aspect of the reform movement was the development of new communities of canons living a religious life in common. This took numerous forms. However, in a bull of 1092 Urban II (1088–1099) distinguished between diocesan clergy and the new orders of canons by defining the latter as those who, unlike the diocesan priests, had no personal property. They were the "canons regular." The linking of religious life to the repudiation of private property went back to Chalcedon and was an ideal on which the papacy had constantly to insist.

Innocent III (1198–1216), powerful though he was, found the reform of religious life almost too much of a challenge. His efforts in 1203 to bring monastic superiors together on a regional basis came to nothing, as did his attempt to reform religious life for nuns in the city of Rome by bringing the communities together in one major monastery. His significant reforms had to be left to the Fourth Lateran Council of 1215. When the council was summoned, the pope had made a special point of requiring the presence of representatives of all varieties of religious communities: the topics for discussion were to touch them closely. One decision imposed on monastic orders the obligation of holding general chapters every three years – those who were not accustomed to this were recommended to seek the guidance of Cistercian abbots. "They shall treat carefully," declared the council, "of the reform of the order and the observance of the rule" (sec. 12). The same declaration required the appointment of visitors to ensure religious observance and emphasized the obligation on bishops to visit those religious houses under their jurisdiction.

The following section prohibited the creation of new religious orders. Innocent III had himself, of course, given verbal approval to the Franciscan rule in 1206. When he was approached to do likewise for the Dominicans immediately after the council, Innocent persuaded them to accept the already existing Augustinian rule. It was Innocent's successor, Honorius III (1216–1227), who gave formal approval to the Dominicans in December 1216 and January 1217, as he did in 1226 to the Carmelites. In 1243 Innocent IV (1243–1254) brought together all hermits living in Tuscany under one rule; in 1256, by uniting remaining groups in Italy living by the Augustinian rule, Alexander IV (1254–1261) created the Order of Hermits of St. Augustine.

The prescriptions of the Fourth Lateran Council were reiterated by Benedict XII (1334–1342), a Cistercian who, as a cardinal, had continued to wear his Cistercian habit. For example, *Summi Magistri* of 1335 urged monks to gather into some 30 or so (the exact figure is unclear) provinces whose superiors would meet every three years to examine the standard of observance in the houses of their province. It also impressed on the Benedictines the necessity of study.

If popes could create religious orders, they could also close them down. The suppression of the Knights Templar in 1312 was later to be taken as a historical precedent. The suppression itself took place during the Council of Vienne, although the bull *Vox in excelso* was the act of Clement V, forced on him by Philip IV the Fair (1285–1314) of France.

The papal involvement in religious life discussed here thus far has concentrated mainly on monks. However, at the end of the 13th century Boniface VIII (1294–1303) published a decree that deeply affected the life of nuns. *Periculoso* (1298) required strict enclosure of all women religious. This was not in itself new. Such a regulation had been imposed by Urban II in 1095, when he had issued a charter to the Cluniac nuns of Marcigny, and it was the rule in houses of Cistercian nuns. However, Boniface's decree applied to all women religious. Although required, strict enclosure was difficult to enforce and was repeated by Pius V (1566–1572) in 1566 in the wake of the Council of Trent (1545–1563). It had the result that those groups of women wishing to lead a religious form of life but at the same time to engage in an active apostolate could not be formally designated "religious" – at least until Leo XIII's constitution *Conditae* of 1900.

The problem of monks leaving their cloisters was not considered serious. Nonetheless religious living outside their houses was one of the scandals of the Middle Ages. In 1558, between the second and the third session of the Council of Trent, Paul IV (1555–1559) issued a bull against all living outside their houses without permission, depriving them of all benefices, even of academic rank, and committing those in the papal states to prison or the galleys.

In the period after Trent, the council's decrees were applied to the orders, most actively perhaps by Clement VIII (1592–1605), who undertook a visitation of the religious houses of Rome: he had all windows in convents that looked onto the street blocked up. He called together the superiors and instructed them to attend to the reform of their institutes. With *Regularis disciplina* of 1596, he forbade anyone to enter religious life for other than religious reasons, putting an end to a practice that had lasted a millennium. With *Quaecumque* of 1604, he also regulated the relationship between regular clergy and the local bishops in missionary territory, an issue that had become enormously important after the vast expansion of missionary activity that had occurred in the 16th century.

When Pius IX (1846–1878) issued his encyclical *Ubi Primum* in 1847, he addressed the question of reform of religious life throughout the world, not limiting his concern, as his predecessors had done, to the Papal States. The encyclical called on superiors to introduce – or reintroduce – common life into their institutes and to be more exacting in their acceptance of candidates and for religious to become more involved in pastoral activity and to take simple vows before solemn profession. This last was a major innovation that was not universally welcomed by all orders, partly for economic reasons, but the pope insisted.

In addressing all religious superiors, Pius IX was reflecting the centralizing tendency of the papacy, manifested in many of the pope's policies. An aspect of this centralization was the effort of Leo XIII (1878–1903) to unite varieties of religious orders, bringing together the diverse branches of the Franciscans, for example, into the Friars Minor. Leo also pressed rather reluctant Benedictines into creating in 1893 a federation of the various congregations and electing an abbot primate to reside in the College of Sant'Anselmo (on Rome's Aventine Hill), which the pope had brought back into being in 1888.

The Second Vatican Council (1962–1965) addressed reform of religious orders in the decree *Perfectae Caritatis*, which was approved, with only four dissenting voices, in October 1965. *Ecclesiae Sanctae*, "Norms of the implementation of the decree . . . ," was issued by Pope Paul VI (1963–1978) the following August. The criteria for renewal of religious life Paul defined as fidelity to the gospel, to the special insight (or charism) of the founder, and to the needs of the modern world. Several documents followed, issued by the Congregation for Religious. It was, as Pope Paul's apostolic constitution *Evangelica Testificatio* of June 1971 recognized, a destabilizing period in the life of many religious.

MICHAEL J. WALSH

See also Archives, Western Christian; Augustinian Friars/ Hermits; Benedictines: Female; Bishops: Jurisdiction and Role; Capuchins; Gregory I (the Great), St.; Gregory VII; Origins: Western Christian

Further Reading

Batiz, M., et al., "Papato," in *Dizionario degli Istituti di Perfezione*, volume 6, edited by Giancarlo Rocca, Rome: Edizioni Paoline, 1980

Cowdrey, H.E.J., *The Cluniacs and the Gregorian Reform*, Oxford: Clarendon Press, 1970

Flannery, Austin, editor, *Vatican Council II: The Conciliar and Post Conciliar Documents*, Northport, New York: Costello, and Dublin: Dominican, 1975; 2nd edition, 1996

Makowski, Elizabeth, *Canon Law and Cloistered Women: Periculoso and Its Commentators, 1298–1545* (Studies in

Medieval and Early Modern Canon Law, volume 5), Washington, D.C.: Catholic University of America Press, 1997
Morris, Colin, *The Papal Monarchy: The Western Church from 1050 to 1250* (Oxford History of the Christian Church), New York: Oxford University Press, and Oxford: Clarendon Press, 1989
Tanner, Norman P., editor, *Decrees of the Ecumenical Councils*, Washington, D.C.: Georgetown University Press, and London: Sheed and Ward, 1990

Patrons, Buddhist: China

Once he had achieved his insights, the historical Buddha Śākyamuni (563–483 B.C.) delivered his first sermon in Deer Park, where he enunciated the Four Noble Truths, the essence of his doctrine, and laid out the Middle Way of the Noble Eightfold Path to realize these truths. These were modes of correct behavior; but it can be said that what underlies all of them is the concept of "merit," which will ultimately gain enlightenment. This figures throughout the history of Buddhism, and one manifestation of it is the sponsorship of Buddhist artifacts that might range from the smallest votive image to an entire temple or monastery. From its earliest history to the present, Buddhism is rife with inscriptions and citations of the names of patrons of Buddhism, ranging from the lower classes, who are otherwise forgotten in history, to kings and emperors.

The fifth-century caves at Yungang in northern Shanxi province show this well. The rulers of the Northern Wei dynasty (386–535) received a petition from the then head of the Buddhist Church to erect five cave temples, each centering on a colossal figure (about 50 feet in height; Fig. 2). On the basis of the precedent of five colossal bronze figures (no longer extant) that had been earlier cast for a temple in the capital city of Pingcheng (present-day Datong) and that were said to be in honor of the first five emperors of the dynasty, it is logically assumed that the same rationale pertained to those carved in the sandstone cliffs at Yungang. Even earlier than that a former head of the Buddhists had said that he was bowing not before an emperor but before a Buddha. Thus, an equation was clearly made between the historical Buddha and his ostensible descendants in the form of emperors. This obviously had a double meaning. On the one hand it was testimony to the belief in Buddhism, but this had the purpose of persuading the court and the population generally that an emperor was superhuman and held supreme power. On the other hand almost the reverse was true: the emperor exercised political and other mundane authority just as the teachings of the Buddha had come to do in its homeland of India. The great Indian emperor Aśoka (272–232 B.C.) had drawn on Buddhism and its moral tenets as a part of his empire's legal code, but the Northern Wei emperors took this one step further by uniting the Buddha and his teachings in a single political and religious entity.

Some debate exists about the nature of Chinese patronage when it comes to larger enterprises such as cave temples. All would agree that the first five cave temples at Yungang (numbered 16–20) were backed by the central court. But 15 other large caves exist at the site, and these are quite different in many ways. Some are carefully planned and suggest a single sponsor or small group that insisted on a coherent plan; Buddhist associations (known as *yiyi*) can be included among the latter. Others are far more chaotic. For example, Caves 7 and 8 are characterized by systematic planning, and there is reason to believe that a rich court sycophant, a eunuch, sponsored the cave pair for himself, not for the court. (See Caswell, 1988; a Chinese scholar, Su Bai, agrees in part, but a Japanese scholar, Nagahiro Toshio, does not.) This derives from an admittedly somewhat questionable document of the 12th century that records an alleged inscription that was originally at the site but is no longer extant. Nevertheless the cave pair is distinctly different from the imperial five, and this in itself suggests a different order of patronage. In another case the inscription at the bottom of a large and prominent panel on the east wall of Cave 11 containing a multitude of images (dated to 483) says that it was sponsored by some 54 "faithful believers" (Fig. 4). The remainder of this cave (as

Fig. 1: Gongxian, Henan, Cave 1, interior wall with three registers of donor figures.
Photo courtesy of H. Iwata, Peking #25, Asian Art Archives

Fig. 2: Yungang, Shanxi, Cave 18, side view of central colossal standing Buddha figure with frontal view of flanking Buddha figure. Photo courtesy of John C. Huntington, the Huntington Archive

Fig. 3: Longmen, Henan, procession of female figures from the front wall of the Binyang dong (in the Nelson-Atkins Gallery, Kansas City, Missouri). Photo courtesy of Nelson-Atkins Museum of Art

well as other caves at the site) is a hodgepodge of images, large and small, squeezed into almost every available wall space (even on the exterior walls).

A contrary view is that almost all the large caves at Yungang were imperially sponsored (see Soper, 1966). A certain natural logic exists to this, as they are indeed significant enterprises that would have represented a considerable investment of labor and financing that would have been most easily accessed by the court. Yet the Northern Wei imperial history, the *Wei Shu*, laments the rampant construction of temples and monasteries throughout the empire, especially toward the end of its reign, and the waste of resources that resulted – although the historian regretfully concedes that this could not have been curbed. Finally one cannot ignore the fact that only the first five Yungang caves are mentioned in the *Wei Shu*, and it is entirely silent about any other such completed endeavors at Yungang or elsewhere throughout the empire.

Innumerable images in stone and gilded bronze date to the Northern Wei period as well as earlier and later. They vary greatly in size and complexity, but inscriptions of a rather special character are almost ubiquitous. Often these will list the names of the donor as well as his or her family line, seeking blessings on their behalf. Although the Buddhist adept should be separate from family attachments as an expression of Buddhist injunctions to sever ties of any kind with this world, the Chinese could not give up that bond to family that has been so fundamental to Chinese society throughout the ages. These sponsors would even include their portraits in the program of their icons, being further evidence as to their presence before the sacred (Fig. 3); and, like the inscriptions, these images could number in the scores and even more (Fig. 1).

The heyday of Buddhism in China was the Tang dynasty (618–907), which witnessed the construction of temples and monasteries, extensive Buddhist scholarship and libraries, and Chinese travelers going to India on pilgrimages and seeking texts and images. The most prominent monument that survives today is the Fengxian *si* at Longmen just outside Luoyang. It was built during the period 672–675 under the aegis of the redoubtable Wu Zetian, a consort of a weak Tang emperor who later declared herself emperor, the only woman to do so in the history of

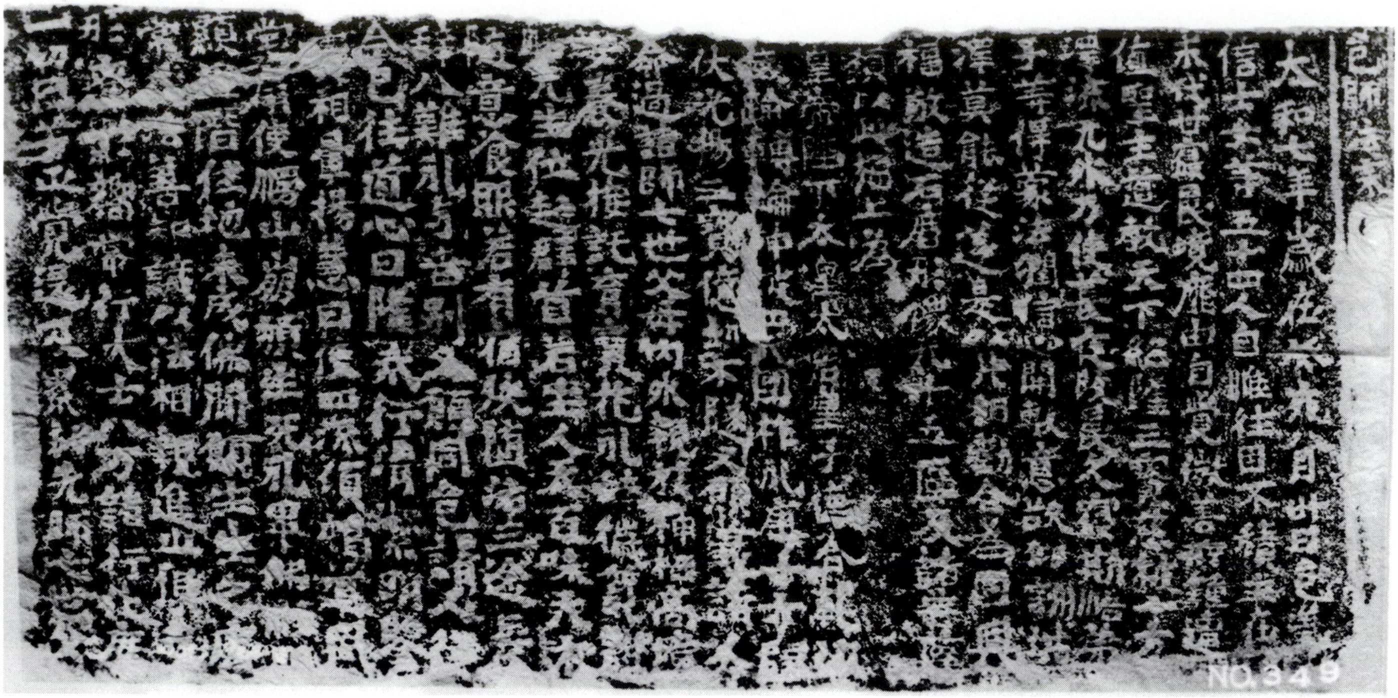

Fig. 4: Yungang, Shanxi, Cave 11, large panel on the upper east wall of the interior with an inscription dated 483. Photo courtesy of H. Iwata, Peking #349, Asian Art Archives

China. She reigned during the period 690–705 and even went so far as to have falsified written texts that identified her with a Bodhisattva, another version of the old Buddha-equals-emperor equation.

Thus, merit in the sponsorship of Buddhist icons and structures had several motivations in China, ranging from genuine piety to the machinations of the politically powerful. The end result, even after the depredations since, is visually rich. It shows how strongly Buddhism stirred the human imagination in its new milieu.

James O. Caswell

See also Cave Temples and Monasteries in India and China; China; Economics: Buddhist; Images: Buddhist Perspectives; Taiwan; Visual Arts, Buddhist: China

Further Reading

Brook, Timothy, *Praying for Power: Buddhism and the Formation of Gentry Society in Late Ming China*, Cambridge, Massachusetts: Harvard University Press, 1993

Caswell, James O., *Written and Unwritten: A New History of the Buddhist Caves at Yungang*, Vancouver: University of British Columbia Press, 1988

Nagahiro Toshio, "Shuku Haku shi no Unkō sekkutsu bunki ron o hakusu" (A Refutation of the Discussion of the Periodization of the Yungang Caves by Mr. Su Bai), *Tōhō gaku* 60 (1980)

Satō, Chisui, "The Character of Yün-kang Buddhism: A Look at the Emergence of a State-Supported Religion in China under the Northern Wei," *The Memoirs of Tōyō Bunkō* 36 (1978)

Soper, Alexander, "Imperial Cave-Chapels of the Northern Dynasties: Donors, Beneficiaries, Dates," *Artibus Asiae* 28:4 (1966)

Su Bai, "Yungang shiku fenqi shilun" (A Discussion of the Periodization of the Yungang Caves), *Kaogu xuebao* 1 (1978)

Weinstein, Stanley, "Imperial Patronage in the Formation of T'ang Buddhism," in *Perspectives on the T'ang*, edited by Arthur F. Wright and Denis Twitchett, New Haven, Connecticut: Yale University Press, 1973

Patrons, Buddhist: India

The Buddha established an order of wandering mendicants (the literal meaning of *bhikṣu*), who subsisted on alms given to them by the laity. Because they had no fixed abode and did not work for a living, such support was crucial to the survival of the order and of its individual members. In addition to the daily almsround, during which monks and nuns collected food for their daily needs, lay support was required for them to obtain clothing, medicines, and other necessities.

In the Indian society of the time, many other ascetic groups existed, all of which depended on the largesse of the community; thus, such support required a general public perception of sanctity. In addition to the daily gifts of food, clothing, and so on, Pāli sources report that a number of generous lay patrons provided not only basic necessities for the order (Pāli, *saṅgha*) but also more substantial support in the form of land and housing for the rainy-season retreat. In the Pāli Canon the most generous lay supporter of the *saṅgha* was said to be Anāthapiṇḍika (whose real name was Sudatta but was referred to as Anāthapiṇḍika, which means "Feeder of the Destitute"). He was a wealthy banker from Śrāvastī (Pāli, Sāvatthi) who donated the Jetavana Grove to the Buddha and his followers. This became the Buddha's favorite resting place, and he is said to have spent the last 25 rainy-season retreats of his life there.

Anāthapiṇḍika spent a large amount of money on Jetavana and subsequently spent much more building a monastic residence (*vihāra*). He is also said to have fed 100 monks every day at his house, and he provided food and other necessities for invalids, beggars, and so on. Anāthapiṇḍika's generosity was so great that he eventually gave away all his money and was reduced to poverty, but the tradition reports that he was rewarded by rebirth in Tuṣita heaven. The Buddha's appreciation of his liberality is evidenced by the fact that several discourses in the *Sutta-piṭaka* are addressed to him. The *saṅgha* received other donations of land for use as rainy-season retreats, including the Ambapālīvana in Vaiśālī, which was provided by the courtesan Ambapālī.

Although lay patronage was important for the Buddhist monastic community, royal patronage played an even more significant role, as it allowed the *saṅgha* to expand its numbers and to operate in areas whose rulers were sympathetic. In later centuries royal patronage aided Buddhism's expansion outside India. Pāli sources report that the *saṅgha*'s most munificent royal supporter during the Buddha's lifetime was Bimbisāra, the king of Magadha. He donated the Veṇuvana Ārāma, which was the first dwelling used by the early Buddhist community during the rainy season, and at the age of 30 he became a lay disciple. Another significant contribution that he made was convincing the Buddha to institute the twice-monthly recitation of monastic rules during the *uposatha* ceremony. He reportedly met a sad end when his son Ajātasattu (Sanskrit, Ajātaśatru), fearing that his father (who had willingly ceded the throne to him) presented a threat to his power, imprisoned him. He died of starvation while in prison.

Despite a sometimes acrimonious relationship with the Buddha, Ajātasattu also is said to have been an important supporter of Buddhism. He reportedly plotted with Devadatta (the Buddha's first cousin) to kill the Buddha, but he later reconciled with him and became a patron of the *saṅgha*. He is said to have presided over the distribution of the Buddha's relics after his cremation.

Following the Buddha's death, the fortunes of the order he founded often waxed or waned in accordance with the dispositions of Indian rulers. The most enthusiastic royal supporter of Buddhism was undoubtedly the third Mauryan king, Aśoka (r. 272–232 B.C.). A grandson of Candragupta Maurya, Aśoka is best known for his Rock Edicts, in which he enunciated his ruling philosophy and which were distributed throughout his vast realm. These stone pillars indicate that he sought to be a righteous monarch and that he was influenced by Buddhist philosophy. After a bloody war with the neighboring state of Kaliṅga, he renounced armed conquest and also reportedly became a Buddhist lay disciple in the Vibhajyavāda tradition (described in Rock Edict XIII).

Aśoka's most notable contribution to the expansion of Buddhism was a mission he sponsored to Sri Lanka, led by his son Mahinda, a Buddhist monk. According to traditional accounts, Mahinda and his sister Saṅghamittā (a Buddhist nun), together with several monks, traveled to the island and met with its king, Devānaṃpiya Tissa (r. 247–207 B.C.), who was converted to Buddhism. To facilitate its establishment on the island, he donated a tract of land near the capital, Anurādhapura, where a monastery named the Mahāvihāra was built. This later became the seat of Theravāda orthodoxy in Sri Lanka. Shortly after this the first Buddhist monks in Sri Lanka were ordained, and from this base Theravāda later spread throughout Southeast Asia.

Aśoka's other significant contribution to Buddhist history in India was his sponsorship of the Third Buddhist Council, which was held in his capital city of Pāṭaliputra under the direction of the monk Moggaliputta Tissa and attended by 1,000 monks. The council concluded that the doctrines and practices of the Vibhajyavāda tradition should be considered orthodox, and monks adhering to other systems were ordered to convert to it or else be expelled from the *saṅgha*.

In later centuries Buddhism experienced persecution during the rule of Puṣyamitra Śuṅga (r. c. 187–151 B.C.), but the Śuṅga dynasty (185–73 B.C.) was generally a period of prosperity for Buddhism. During this time some of India's greatest Buddhist monuments (including Sāñcī, Bhārhut, and Amarāvatī) were constructed, some of them with royal sponsorship. The Śuṅga dynasty came to an end as a result of a series of foreign invasions that brought armies of Greeks, Parthians, Kushans, and Scythians (Śakas) to India. Some of these were patrons of Buddhism, including the Kushan King Kaniṣka I (c. first to second century A.D.), who is reported to have sponsored the Fourth Buddhist Council at Gandhāra around 100. In later centuries large monastic universities – most notably Nālandā and Vikramaśīla – were either built or sustained by royal supporters of Buddhism. By the time of its final disappearance in India (c. 13th century), Buddhism had apparently lost much of its popular and royal support, and the final death knell for the tradition in the land of its origin resulted from Muslim invasions that destroyed the great monasteries of northern India.

C. JOHN POWERS

See also Anurādhapura, Sri Lanka; Aśoka; Buddha (Śākyamuni); Councils, Buddhist; Disciples, Early Buddhist; Discourses (Suttas): Theravāda; Missionaries: Buddhist; Nālandā, India; Saṅgha; Sri Lanka: History

Further Reading

Dutt, Sukumar, *Buddhist Monks and Monasteries of India: Their History and Their Contribution to Indian Culture*, London: Allen and Unwin, 1962

Gunawardana, R.A.L.H., *Robe and Plough: Monasticism and Economic Interest in Early Medieval Sri Lanka*, Tucson: University of Arizona Press, 1979

Prebish, Charles, *A Survey of Vinaya Literature*, Taipei: Jin Luen Publishing House, 1994

Patrons, Buddhist: Japan

Patronage for Buddhist monastic establishments in Japan began with the Soga family sponsoring the use of certain Buddhist articles brought by a mission from Paekche, a friendly kingdom in western Korea, soliciting military help against its neighbors. Official Japanese histories put the date at A.D. 552, when Emperor Kimmei was on the throne (r. c. 540–571). An earlier date appears in a less official text. Opposition from other court families, especially those involved with the formal Shintō ceremonies, delayed acceptance, but Emperor Yōmei (r. 585–587), a son of Kimmei, is noted as the first imperial believer, and a battle between the Soga family on one side and the Mononobe and Nakatomi families on the other that helped put Emperor Sushun (r. 587–592), the Soga selection, on the throne, eliminated the opposition. Soga women became imperial wives.

Empress Suiko (r. 592–628), daughter of Kimmei and a Soga wife, appointed Prince Shōtoku, Yōmei's son, as her regent shortly after taking the throne. Known as Shōtoku Taishi (Crown Prince of Sagely Virtue) (c. 573–622), he was an immensely popular, imposing individual, first in the accession line. However, the Soga, intolerant of the least suggestion of independence, had installed her as stakeholder to bypass him. A hardy, rather timeless person, she died at 75, outliving him by six years.

Suiko kept her palace in Asuka, Nara prefecture. He lived a few miles away, near Sakurai. By 601 the prince was assigned mainly to foreign affairs, presumably to reduce his influence in domestic politics, and he moved to a palace in Ikaruga in 605, about ten miles to the northwest. There he turned more and more to studying the Buddhist scriptures, soliciting the help of Korean monks.

The *Nihon-shoki* (Chronicles of Japan), the eighth-century history, says that the prince instituted the first 12-cap rank system (604); composed a 17-article "constitution" (604); studied, annotated, and lectured on two sūtras (other documents say three) (606); wrote histories of the imperial system and the country; compiled genealogical lists of the ranking families (620); and died there in 621. Other information indicates a death date of 622.

The so-called constitution consists of guidelines for moralistic behavior that include such traditional Confucian values as harmony, obedience to the emperor, honesty of officials, rewards for good service, and decisions made by consensus. It might have been included by eighth-century writers to enhance the prince's status. Scholars today see it as very suspect. Only the second article deals with Buddhism, which is an injunction to revere the Three Treasures: the Buddha, the law, and the priesthood. It seems strangely inadequate and even out of order.

Already in the eighth century, the *Nihon-shoki* writers had attributed some supernatural traits to the prince – for example, being able to speak like an adult at birth – but he was transformed into a full-fledged cult figure by Fujiwara Kanesuke in a "biography" that came out in 917 called *Shōtoku Taishi-denryaku*. It was written to enhance the prestige of the Hōryū-ji, one of the prince's temples. The prince became an introspective, gloomy interpreter of omens; a prognosticator and miracle worker; and the builder of scores of temples. This was the medieval picture of him, until 20th-century historians began to peel off the layers of mythology.

Several other documents speak of the Seven Temples of Prince Shōtoku. Only four of these can be positively identified with him, three in Nara prefecture: Shitennō-ji in Ōsaka, started about 593; Tachibana-dera in Asuka, probably 601; Ikaruga-dera (later rebuilt and called Hōryū-ji) in Ikaruga, 607; and Chūgū-ji, its neighboring nunnery, built about the same time. Of interest is that four in the usual list of seven either were or became convents: Chūgū-ji, Tachibana-dera, Hokke-ji, and Katsuragi-dera. Only the last of these is defunct today. The first known convent, Sakata-dera, was built as a retirement home for

Image of Shōtoku Taishi (d. 621/22) carved during his lifetime. He was the first royal patron of Buddhism in Japan.
Photo courtesy of David Moore

Empress Suiko by Tori Busshi, the distinguished sculptor for the Soga family, to repay her for a generous gift of rice fields after he had made a large bronze image of Buddha, but she did not live to use it.

However one views the mythology – and much of it is still accepted today – the prince's contributions were many and far-reaching. He took Buddhism out of the realm of pure magic and use as a clan deity – as used by the Soga in a Shintō way – and understood the potential of its intellectual and personal content, opening the door for exchanges on the cultural level with Korea and China. Learned Koreans were especially welcomed. He built monasteries and nunneries alike. By employing the best teams of Korean architects, bronze casters, tile makers, painters, and diviners, he set high standards for the Japanese to follow. All later sects of Japanese Buddhism claimed some association with the prince, the ultimate resort in validating their beliefs.

Every later era had its monastic patronage, although often more collective than individual: Emperor Shōmu (r. 724–749) and the exoteric Nara sects, builder of the Tōdai-ji and of the provincial monasteries and nunneries; Emperor Kammu (r. 781–806) and the esoteric sects, supporter of the Enryaku-ji; the Fujiwara family dictators, their imperial appointments, and their Amida temples; and the Hōjō regents and the Ashikaga shōguns of Kamakura and Kyoto and their Zen temples, the latter proving constructive insofar as the temples were on the right political side.

Closing out over four centuries (1180–1600) of intermittent warfare, Tokugawa Ieyasu (1542–1616) installed his regime in Edo (Tokyo) and indulged in selective rebuilding of supportive sects and temples. This relative Tokugawa beneficence ended abruptly with the Meiji Restoration of 1868, when Emperor Meiji (r. 1868–1912) was enthroned. Pacifistic and conservative Buddhism was viewed as antagonistic to the planned modernization. Shintō became the rallying point for national solidarity. In the *Haibutsu kishaku* (Throw Out the Buddhas) movement, numerous priests were forced out and many temples and their arts destroyed or confiscated. Not until 1877 did the turmoil settle. Buddhism now thrives on its local traditions. The rural temples are the local cemeteries, the scene of memorial services, and special ceremonies that link the living with the spirits of the dead.

J. EDWARD KIDDER, JR.

See also Buddhist Schools/Traditions: Japan; Death: Buddhist Perspectives; Eisai (Yosai); Ennin; Korea: History; Kūkai; Kyoto, Japan; Nara, Japan; Nation-Building and Japanese Buddhism; Saichō; Syncretism in Japan, Buddhist; Visual Arts, Buddhist: Japan

Further Reading

Anesaki, Masaharu, *Prince Shōtoku, the Sage Statesman*, Tokyo: Boonjudo Publishing House, 1948

Iwao, Seiichi, editor, *Biographical Dictionary of Japanese History*, translated by Burton Watson, Tokyo: Kodansha International, 1978

Kanaji, Isamu, "Three Stages in Shōtoku Taishi's Acceptance of Buddhism," in *Acta Asiatica*, 47, Tokyo: Tōhō Gakkai, 1985

Tamura, Enchō, "Japan and the Eastward Permeation of Buddhism," in *Acta Asiatica*, 47, Tokyo: Tōhō Gakkai, 1985

Patrons, Buddhist: Korea

During the Three Kingdoms period (c. 300–668), the main patrons of Buddhism in Korea were the royal houses and the highest nobility. Thus, the earliest temples and monasteries in Korea were established on the basis of royal patronage. By the time of Unified Silla (668–935), patrons of Buddhism reflected a wider spectrum of Korean society, including the nobility and the growing gentry class. Commoners also functioned as patrons but mainly as members of Buddhist societies organized by the temples. Both Pulguk Temple and the Sŏkkuram Grotto outside Kyŏngju were founded by a member of the highest nobility in the country, the minister Kim Taesŏng (700–774).

Buddhism reached the acme of its power and influence under the Koryŏ dynasty (918–1392). At that time most Koreans were followers of Buddhism. Most of the large monasteries in and around the capital, Kaesŏng (Kaegyŏng), were built by royal decree and with state funding. During this period patronage of Buddhism reached its absolute height in terms of extravagance and amount, and the temples grew into huge economic and politically powerful institutions. At some point during the dynasty, members of the royal house and the nobility competed with each other in extending patronage to the Buddhist temples. Their donations included precious metals, money, silk, cloth, provisions, and luxury goods, such as tea and incense. The temples owned large tracts of the best arable land that in many cases had been given them by the members of the upper class. Because the temples and monasteries were exempt from taxation, the state lost revenue because of these overgenerous donations of land.

During the Chosŏn dynasty (1392–1910), when Buddhism lost much of its political support and prestige in society, lay Buddhist patronage declined. In the early period of the dynasty, when Buddhism still was relatively influential, it was mainly queens, royal concubines, and upper-class women who continued to support the temples. However, as the power of Buddhism gradually diminished, most patrons became commoners and to some degree members of the lower gentry clans. At that time most Buddhist supporters hailed from the countryside. The continuation of patronage is reflected in inscriptions found on the beams of temple buildings or on commissioned votive paintings (*t'aenghwa*) as well as in association with the making of Buddhist images. Patronage was often organized by local associations, and the display of their support was celebrated on the occasion of Buddhist festivals and holidays. This practice continues in contemporary Korean Buddhism, in which almost all the temples depend entirely on donations from the faithful for their maintenance.

HENRIK H. SØRENSEN

See also Buddhist Schools/Traditions: Korea; Chan/Zen: Korea; Korea: History; Visual Arts, Buddhist: Korea

Further Reading

Buswell, Robert E., *The Zen Monastic Experience: Buddhist Practice in Contemporary Korea*, Princeton, New Jersey: Princeton University Press, 1992

Ch'oe, Pyŏnghŏn, "Koryŏ chunggi Yi Chahyŏn ŭi Sŏn kwa kosa pulgyo ŭi sŏnggyŏk" (Yi Chahyŏn's Sŏn and the Nature of Lay-Buddhism during the Mid-Koryŏ), in *Koryŏ ch'ogi pulgyo saron* (Essays on the History of Buddhism during the Middle and Late Koryŏ), Seoul: Minjŏksa, 1986

Ch'oe, Pyŏnghŏn, "The Founding of the Ch'ŏnt'ae School and the Reformation of Buddhism in 12th Century Korea," in *Religions in Traditional Korea*, Copenhagen: Seminar for Buddhist Studies, 1995

Choi, Byŏng-hŏn (Ch'oe, Pyŏnghŏn), "Significance of the Foundation of Susŏnsa in the History of Korean Buddhism," *Seoul Journal of Korean Studies* 1 (1988)

Han'guk Chogye chong ŭi sŏngni sa chŏk yŏngu (Studies in the History of the Formation of the Chogye School in Korea), Seoul: Minjŏksa, 1986

Hŏ Hŭngsik, *Koryŏ pulgyo sa yŏngu* (A Study of the History of Koryŏ Buddhism), Seoul: Ilcho kak, 1986

Ko Ikchin, *Hanguk kodae pulgyo sasang sa* (The History of Buddhist Thought in Ancient Korea), Seoul: Tongguk taehakkyo ch'ulp'anbu, 1989

Sørensen, Henrik H., "Lamaism in Korea During the Late Koryŏ Dynasty," *Korea Journal* 33:3 (1993)

Patrons, Christian: Lay

The first lay patrons of Christian communities include the rich young man (Luke 18:18), Nicodemus, the ruler who came by night (John 3), the women who supported Jesus and his followers (Luke 8:1–3), and Joseph of Arimathea (Luke 23:50), who gave Jesus his tomb. Later lay patrons were often those who yearned to join communities themselves but could not then make the commitment, granted that other benefactors sought economic or political advantages in founding or supporting religious communities. The conversion of the soldier Pachomius in the fourth century was sparked by the kindness of Egyptian villagers, and he settled down among them to form small Christian communities. Melania and Pinianus, a fabulously wealthy, young Roman couple fleeing the Goths, asked advice of Bishop Augustine of Hippo (354–430) on how to live a religious life, and he suggested that they make a pilgrimage through the Christian world endowing religious communities. Paulinus of Nola (355–431) and Cassiodorus (485/90–c. 580) also developed communities of rich and poor, married and single, on their ancestral Italian estates. Many late Roman ascetics were drafted as bishops and founded monasteries for men and women as Christian centers in a still-pagan world. Martin of Tours (d. 397) and Caesarius of Arles (c. 470–542), refusing to accrue episcopal fortunes, depended on lay entrants and supporters for bequests for monasteries, such as Ligugé, Marmoutier, and (for women) St. John at Arles. Caesarius took steps to ensure the independence of his foundations from both future bishops and lay lords by limiting lay and clerical contacts with the religious and insisting on free elections of superiors by the monks and nuns.

In the early Middle Ages, the laity led the way in the founding and endowment of monasteries. Monasteries, many of which later adopted the Benedictine Rule, were lay institutions with only a few priests to provide the sacraments. The men and women who entered kept close ties with their families, who continued to provide them support. Benedict of Aniane (c. 750–821), the Carolingian reformer, remarked on the generosity of laypeople who supported him and his brothers in their early days. Manuals of the Christian life directed to lay aristocrats, such as those of Jonas of Orleans and Dhuoda, advised princes to support monasteries and the poor and to live as much as possible a monastic life. Count Gerald of Aurillac (c. 855–909) was renowned for feeding the poor at his own table and turning his castle into a veritable monastery. Beginning in the tenth century, increasing numbers of surviving charters witness the eagerness of lay landholders (or sometimes their anxiety to make amends before judgment) to grant or restore lands to monastic institutions. The famous charter for Cluny shows William of Aquitaine in 909/910 granting his hunting lodge and estates to the new monastery of Cluny and permitting the monks to elect their own superior without interference from secular or episcopal authorities. This became a model for reformed Benedictine houses. In the tenth century the laity hastened to restore many ancient monasteries that had been either destroyed entirely or turned over to secular canons during the Norse invasions. In Tours the Abbey of St. Julien was founded by a bishop and his sister out of their ancestral estates, augmented by many of the local nobility. Around 1000 a later William of Aquitaine and his wife, Emma of Blois, established Gauzbert, a reforming relative of hers, as abbot of their new foundation of Bourgueil and its consortium of other monasteries. Count Odo of Blois and his wife, Bertha, restored monks and many gifts to the Abbey of Marmoutier, originally a foundation of St. Martin. Meteor fragments falling at their feet inspired Count Geoffrey Martel of Anjou and his wife, Agnes, to establish the Abbey of Holy Trinity, Vendôme. Agnes later endowed Notre Dame, Saintes, for women. Churches, bell towers, vestments, and sculptures given by the laity followed the initial foundations, not to mention vineyards, fields, forests, and families of serfs. Impressive reliquaries and Romanesque sculptures were given to churches along the pilgrimage routes, notably to the Basilica of St. Mary Magdalene, Vézelay, and St. Foy at Conques.

The laity sometimes profited directly from their gifts, which might be outright exchanges or veiled sales. They also profited indirectly, for the monasteries became the cultural centers of their communities. Regular liturgical services and brilliant feastday celebrations, libraries, schools, preaching in the vernacular, and centers of healing inspired by the relics of the saints were only a few of the benefits. Fortifications of a monastery provided physical protection in time of invasion and moral security in between. Patrons assured themselves of receiving prayers for their souls and for those of their ancestors after their deaths. If possible they acquired valuable relics for their shrines so as to make their towns centers of pilgrimage and trade.

Recent studies have shown the partnership of the laity in monastic foundations and reform movements. As princes assumed regalian rights where the kings were weak, they also took on the responsibility of restoring monasteries and churches that had previously existed. By associating itself with a monastery, an aristocratic family extended its authority. In return monastics often helped family members who wished to enter or hoped to be buried there.

In the High and later Middle Ages, castellans, knights, and even the middle class joined the aristocracy in giving to monasteries. In attracting gifts traditional black Benedictine houses had much competition from the newer Cistercian and mendicant orders and even from hermits and anchoresses.

The dissolution of the monasteries in Protestant countries radically diminished their numbers. Nonetheless lay patrons remained vital to those houses that survived. Convents became refuges for widows, orphans, and wealthy abandoned women who paid for the privilege of living there. Following the Council of Trent (1545–1563), women religious were allowed to live an active life in the world and to engage in teaching and nursing, with the result that those houses that remained purely contemplative attracted less support from the laity.

For example, during the French Revolution the nuns of the Holy Cross, Poitiers, took refuge in homes in the town, retaining a continuous existence since their seventh-century beginnings. Trappist monks and nuns wandered as refugees all over Europe, refusing to disband. After the French Revolution those houses that survived attracted fewer novices and professed and were forced to prove their usefulness to society by good works.

The 19th century was marked by a religious revival, and the Jesuit Order again numbered 2,000 by 1820. Compassion, work, penance, and prayer marked restored communities as the papacy sought to centralize religious houses into large congregations. Nonetheless many new local communities were founded at a diocesan level. Wealthy single women, such as Catherine McAuley (1778–1841) in Ireland, founded and joined several new vital, influential orders. Brothers and sisters have staffed colleges, schools, parishes, and hospitals throughout the 20th century, notwithstanding a steep decline of entrants from the late 1960s after the Second Vatican Council (1962–1965).

MARY S. SKINNER

See also Benedict of Aniane, St.; Benedictines: Female; Caesarius of Arles, St.; Cassiodorus; Cluniacs; France: History; German Benedictine Reform, Medieval; Holy Men/Holy Women: Christian Perspectives; Monastics and the World, Medieval; Pachomius, St.

Further Reading

Astell, Ann W., editor, *Lay Sanctity, Medieval and Modern: A Search for Models*, Notre Dame, Indiana: University of Notre Dame Press, 2000

Bouchard, Constance Brittain, *Sword, Miter, and Cloister: Nobility and the Church in Burgundy, 980–1198*, Ithaca, New York: Cornell University Press, 1987

Brown, Peter, *Body and Society: Men, Women, and Sexual Renunciation in Early Christianity*, New York: Columbia University Press, 1988; London: Faber, 1989

Cownie, Emma., *Religious Patronage in Anglo-Norman England, 1066–1135*, Rochester, New York: Boydell Press, 1998

Elder, E. Rozanne, editor, *Benedictus, Studies in Honor of St. Benedict of Nursia*, Kalamazoo, Michigan: Cistercian Publications, 1981

Frank, Suso, *Grundzüge der Geschichte des Christlichen Mönchtums*, Darmstadt: Wissenschaftliche Buchgesellsschaft, 1975; as *With Greater Liberty: A Short History of Christian Monasticism and Religious Orders*, translation of 4th edition by Joseph Lienhard, Kalamazoo, Michigan: Cistercian Publications, 1993; 5th edition, as *Geschichte des Christlichen Mönchtums*, Darmstadt: Wissenschaftliche Buchgesellschaft, 1993

Hill, Bennett, *English Cistercian Monasteries and Their Patrons in the Twelfth Century*, Urbana: University of Illinois Press, 1968

Johnson, Penelope, *Prayer, Patronage, and Power: The Abbey of la Trinité, Vendôme, 1032–1187*, New York: New York University Press, 1981

Johnson, Penelope, "Agnes of Burgundy: an Eleventh Century Woman as Monastic Patron," *Journal of Medieval History* 15:2 (1989)

Mellinger, Laura, "Prayer and Politics in Medieval Brittany: The Making of Saint-Georges," *American Benedictine Review* 47:4 (1996)

Miller, Maureen C., *The Formation of a Medieval Church: Ecclesiastical Change in Verona, 950–1150*, Ithaca: Cornell University Press, 1993

Nichols, John, and Lillian Thomas Shank, editors, *Distant Echoes: Medieval Religious Women*, volume 1, Kalamazoo, Michigan: Cistercian Publications, 1984

Potts, Cassandra, *Monastic Revival and Regional Identity in Early Normandy*, Woodbridge, United Kingdom, and Rochester, New York: Boydell Press, 1997

Reynes, Geneviève, *Couvents de Femmes: La Vie des Religieuses Contemplatives dans la France des XVIIe et XVIIIe Siècles*, Paris: Fayard, 1987

Sheingorn, Pamela, translator, *The Book of Sainte Foy*, Philadelphia: University of Pennsylvania Press, 1995

Skinner, Mary, "Aristocratic Families: Founders and Reformers of Monasteries in the Touraine, 930–1030," *Benedictus Studies in Honor of St. Benedict of Nursia*, edited by E. Rozanne Elder, Kalamazoo, Michigan: Cistercian Publications, 1981

Thompson, Sally, *Women Religious: The Founding of English Nunneries After the Norman Conquest*, Oxford: Clarendon Press, and New York: Oxford University Press 1991

Warren, Ann K., *Anchorites and their Patrons in Medieval England*, Berkeley: University of California Press, 1985

Wood, Susan, *English Monasteries and their Patrons in the Thirteenth Century*, London and New York: Oxford University Press, 1955

Patrons, Christian: Royal

The rapid development of monasticism occurred in the West to a large extent because of monarchs. It was a duty of a Christian monarch to protect the Church. In this way he was performing a basic responsibility, namely, to protect his subjects against the forces of evil and to secure eternal salvation for their souls. Monks could help by praying perpetually for the stability of the kingdom and the safety of the country. Founding new monasteries and protecting already existing ones legitimized the authority of a Christian monarch.

Personal piety of monarchs was of great importance as well. Because the prayers and mortifications of monks would carry weight with God, a monarch and his family strove to participate in the merit acquired by a monastic community. In turn monks prayed for the welfare of their founders and protectors, and when the latter died, monks buried their bodies in monastic churches and prayed for their souls. Beside these spiritual advantages, patrons sought to obtain temporal benefits from their foundations by utilizing their monasteries' influence in social, economic, and political life.

The Byzantine emperors were the first to extend their protection not only over imperial abbeys (i.e., those founded by emperors) but also over the others. In return, an emperor became the superior of the Church. Additionally, state legislation required newly founded monasteries to produce *typikon*s, a process that was overseen by the imperial administration. This allowed Byzantine emperors and later also Russian princes not only to oversee immense monastic estates but also to use at their discretion the manpower and cultural resources belonging to monastic communities.

The decline of central authority in the West after A.D. 500 meant that relations between the monarch and monasteries were formed on the basis of protection and property rights. Before long a notion of *Eigenkirche* (i.e., the proprietary church) came into being. An abbey was viewed simply as the property of its founder, like a manor. The founder-owner had both the responsibility and the right to protect the abbey as long as it remained under his patronage. He retained property rights over his real estate and thus over the monastery as well. He could continue to administer his estate or even transfer the usufruct to another person. The only restriction was that real estate, once given to the Church, would remain its property forever.

Already the Merovingians (481–752) were aware of the manifold importance of abbeys. By founding new monasteries and generously endowing those already existing, they made subordinate to themselves centers that were not only religious and cultural but also economic and administrative. The Merovingians eagerly granted monasteries various privileges, especially economic and court immunities (i.e., exemptions). These privileges became even more numerous under the Carolingians; in the tenth century all monasteries in the West enjoyed immunities. In central Europe the process of extending immunities over monastic real estate took place from the 11th to the 13th century.

In the early Middle Ages, immunities relieved a weak state administration of some of its responsibilities, transferring these responsibilities to abbeys. At the same time state administrations assisted monasteries in their often vigorous colonization and economic activities, thus furthering the country's development.

The last strong Merovingians and the mayors of the palace were aware of various advantages associated with exercising suzerainty (*dominium*) over a large number of abbeys. They also eagerly extended protection over abbeys not founded by them. These monasteries were designated royal abbeys (i.e., "private" abbeys of a monarch); they were dependent on their benefactor and enjoyed his protection in exchange for prescribed services, the so-called *servitium regis*. These services included military service, gifts, or sometimes financial aid and were demanded by the king to defray the cost of war or to meet some other crisis. In addition, a deceased abbot's private possessions became the property of the royal treasury. One of a monastery's most onerous obligations was that of offering hospitality to the king, his household, and his numerous retinues. In a later period these services were usually redeemable for a set monetary remittance. Wealthy abbeys with spacious buildings were also used as centers for national or regional assemblies.

A king often used a monastery to provide for members of his family. Sick children, those who might prove a threat to the dynasty, and women for whom no appropriate husband could be found were placed in a monastery. Sometimes a king would turn a part of monastic real estate into a special benefice to support a chosen individual. He could also order an abbey to provide worthy recipients with lifetime care or to pay them retirement benefits.

A monarch often controlled not only an abbey's real estate but also the office of abbot. He could transfer the office of abbot to a trusted person even if that person was not a monk. The abbot's attendance was required at court and at various meetings and also at country diets. Under the Carolingians (751–987) abbots were employed as the imperial *missi*, charged with the duty of visiting counties and investigating the conduct of counts and the emperor's other agents.

The collapse of central authority in the tenth century resulted in the transfer of some royal prerogatives to nobles through grants or usurpation. At that time the institution of monastery advocate (*advocatus monasterii*) became independent and important. Originally, the advocate was an officer, appointed by and reporting to the abbot, whose responsibility was to defend monastic property and rights against laymen. Soon it became a hereditary benefice and one of the channels through which laymen could exercise influence over monasteries. Only the Gregorian reforms (11th to 12th century) and a long struggle on the part of monasteries gradually curtailed the powers of advocate (*advocatus*), and by the late Middle Ages the office was finally abolished.

As a result of the Gregorian reforms, the notion of *Eigenkirche* disappeared, and patronage came in its place, a patron being no more and no less than a policeman. Of his former prerogatives the ruler-patron lost, among other powers, the right to control monastic property and to appoint "secular" abbots. Nevertheless his representative still supervised the election of abbots, and abbots needed to obtain the monarch's approval.

It was the growing power of the papacy and the emergence of large centralized orders that became the greatest threat to royal control of monastic life. Papal protection as well as assistance received from an order's central authorities effectively curbed the king's involvement in monastic matters. The king's power remained strongest over old and rich abbeys, including those of the Benedictines and Augustinian canons regular.

From the 12th century the king's ability to intervene in monastic life rested on three aspects of his power: as feudal lord, as suzerain, and as king (i.e., the highest authority in the state); over time the importance of the third aspect grew. As feudal lord the king held under his authority royal abbeys that he protected in return for certain benefits. As a suzerain he ruled over his vassals, abbots, and advocates (*advocati*). As a monarch he exercised general supervision and protection of the Church (including monastic life) in his realm. This supervision and protection extended over all monasteries and implied also the right to impose on them various duties.

It is difficult to overestimate the role played at court by the king's chaplains, preachers, and confessors, usually recruited from among monks. They not only shaped the king's spirituality but, as numerous examples show, influenced other aspects of his kingship as well.

MAREK DERWICH

See also France: History; Regulations: Christian Perspectives

Further Reading

Bernhardt, John W., *Itinerant Kingship and Royal Monasteries in Early Medieval Germany: c. 936–1075*, Cambridge and New York: Cambridge University Press, 1993
Boshof, Egon, "Untersuchungen zur Kirchenvogtei in Lothringen im 10. und 11. Jahrhundert," *Zeitschrift der Savigny-Stiftung für Rechtsgeschichte, Kanonistische Abteilung* 96 (1979)
Brooke, Christopher, "Princes and Kings as Patrons of Monasteries: Normandy and England," in *Il monachesimo e la riforma ecclesiastica (1049–1122)*, Atti della quarta Settimana internazionale di studio, Mendola, 23–29 agosto 1968, Milan: Societè Editrice Vita et Pensiero, 1971
D'Haenens, Albert, "Une abbaye bénédictine sous tutelle royale au XIVe siècle: Les gardiens de saint-Martin de Tournai de 1309 à 1348," *Revue d'Histoire Ecclésiastique* 54 (1959)
Didier, Noel, *La garde des églises au XIIIe siècle*, Grenoble: Allier Père et Fils, 1927
Gallen, Joseph F., *Canon Law for Religious*, New York: Alba House, 1983
Hourlier, Jacques, *L'âge classique (1150–1378): Les religieux*, Paris: Cujas, 1973
Michalowski, Roman, "Les fondations ecclésiatiques dans l'idéologie de la première monarchie piastienne," *Acta Poloniae Historica* 60 (1989)
"Le monachisme à Byzance et en Occident du VIIIe au Xe siècle: Aspects internes et relations avec la société, Actes du colloque international organisé par la Section d'Histoire de l'Université Libre de Bruxelles en collaboration avec l'Abbaye de Maredsous (14–16 mai 1992)," edited by Alain Dierkens, Daniel Misonne, and Jean-Marie Sansterre, *Revue Bénédictine* 103:1–2 (1993)
Naz, Raoul, "Avouerie, avoué," in *Dictionnaire de droit canonique*, volume 1, edited by Raoul Naz, Paris: Letouzey et Ané, 1935
Semmler, Josef, "Protezione reale (imperiale)," in *Dizionario degli istituti di perfezione*, edited by G. Pellicca and G. Rocca, volume 9, Rome: Edizioni Paoline, 1997
Senn, F., *L'institution des avoueries ecclésiastiques en France*, Paris: Rousseau, 1903
Warren, Ann K., *Anchorites and Their Patrons in Medieval England*, Berkeley: University of California Press, 1985
Wood, Susan, *The English Monasteries and Their Patrons in the Thirteenth Century*, London and New York: Oxford University Press, 1955

Peace Movements, Buddhist

Modern Buddhist peace movements arose when traditional Buddhist spirituality and values responded to the horrors of modern war, genocide, and invasion unleashed with unusual ferocity on Asia in the 20th century. Almost all the leaders of these movements have come from the monastic community. Four national examples will be mentioned.

The war in Southeast Asia spawned Buddhist peace movements of very different natures in Vietnam and in Cambodia. In Vietnam the peace movement began in a protest for religious freedom. In 1963 government soldiers of the pro-Catholic, anti-Buddhist Diem regime fired on a peaceful crowd gathered around a radio station that had failed to air an expected program celebrating the Buddha's birthday. In response the monk Thích Quang Duc burned himself to death at a Saigon crossroads. A wave of self-immolations and street protests followed in which protest for religious freedom for Buddhists and protest against the war and the government could scarcely be distinguished. At this time the various divisions of Vietnamese Buddhism joined in the Unified Buddhist Church of Vietnam to unify their strength to face this crisis.

The actions of the so-called Struggle Movement led by the monks to end the war fell into two broad categories: (1) work to end the war involved innumerable activities, such as developing antiwar poetry, music, and art; fasting; laymen shaving their heads (to look like monks) to protest the government's actions; holding street protests; placing family ancestor altars in the streets in the path of approaching tanks; staging strikes and boycotts; aiding deserters and draft resisters; protesting excessively pro-war governments and sometimes succeeding in bringing them down; and engaging in self-immolation; and (2) direct work to relieve suffering and heal wounds involved evacuating villages; establishing cease-fire lines outside of villages; reconstructing destroyed villages; and aiding war orphans. The preeminent principle underlying this work was to stop all killing and prevent all harm. A second basic principle was to avoid taking sides; the Buddhist Struggle Movement refused to side with either North or South and called itself the "Third Way," siding with life itself.

During and after the war, the Vietnamese monk Thích Nhát Hanh (1926–) emerged as an important leader. One of the principal theoreticians of the Struggle Movement, he spoke throughout the world in an effort to help others understand the situation in Vietnam and promote a quick end to the war. He headed the Vietnamese Buddhist Peace Delegation, which, although not seated at the Paris Peace Talks, kept an information office

Monastics of the Nipponzan Myōhōji Order chanting, 1998, Peace Pagoda, North Leverett, Massachusetts. Photo courtesy of the Editor

nearby. After the war he organized an effort to rescue Vietnamese boat people. Since then he has led retreats and workshops throughout the world in which he seeks to help people to "be peace" so that they might make peace in the world. He coined the term "engaged Buddhism" and is one of the foremost spiritual social activists in the world. He was nominated for the Nobel Peace Prize by Martin Luther King, Jr., who publicly opposed the war after speaking with Nhát Hanh. The government of Vietnam refuses to allow him to return to his country, where Buddhism continues to be severely restricted.

When the war in Vietnam spread into Cambodia, the bombing devastated traditional economic and social patterns of village life. When the bombing stopped, over two million (out of a total population of seven million) people had been displaced, and the traditional economy lay in ruins: 80 percent of the prewar paddy fields had been abandoned. Sihanouk estimated that 600,000 people had been killed and over a million seriously wounded. Starvation was rampant. Under these circumstances the Khmer Rouge successfully recruited many young men and built an organization that took control of the country. The utter devastation that followed is well known. The Cambodian holocaust of 1975–1979 took the lives of an estimated two to three million Cambodians, one-third of the population of the entire country in 1975. During this period Buddhism itself was directly targeted; virtually all Buddhist temples were destroyed, and all but 3,000 of the former 50,000 monks died or were killed.

During the holocaust itself no Buddhist peace movement was possible in Cambodia, but as soon as the grip of the Khmer Rouge was loosened a peace movement developed from the shreds of Buddhism that survived. In 1978 the monk Maha Ghosananda (1929–), who was in Thailand during the holocaust, returned to Cambodia and began to teach forgiveness and reconciliation to heal the wounds of individuals and country. His teaching is summed up in the lines from the *Dhammapada* that he frequently preaches:

> Hatred is never overcome by hatred;
> It is overcome by love.
> This is an eternal law.

The "law" is the law of karma, according to which every action sows a karmic seed that will bear appropriate fruit sometime in

A protest by Tibetan monks at the Capitol Building, Washington, D.C., on 10 March 1990 to commemorate the protest in Tibet on 10 March 1959 that led to the Dalai Lama's exile.
Photo courtesy of John Powers

the future. If the Cambodian people were to strike out and hurt their persecutors in the Khmer Rouge, this would sow karmic seeds that would redound on them or their descendants sometime in the future. To avoid future suffering the people of Cambodia must restrain themselves now, eschewing retaliation and vendetta. Thus taught Maha Ghosananda, and thus believed many Cambodian people, who out of enlightened self-interest restrained their urge to retaliate, allowing the rank-and-file Khmer Rouge soldiers to reintegrate into the society they had devastated. Whether the remaining leaders of the Khmer Rouge should be pardoned or tried for crimes against humanity remains a hotly debated question in Cambodia.

Maha Ghosananda was elected *Somteja*, the supreme patriarch of Cambodian Buddhism. He has worked tirelessly to heal the wounds of Cambodians at home and abroad. Called the "Gandhi of Cambodia," he is best known for instituting and leading a series of annual *Dhammayietra* (Walks for Peace and Reconciliation), beginning in 1992. These have variously accompanied refugees returning home; created an atmosphere of safety, thus making it possible for Cambodians to vote; and visited remote areas still under threat of hostilities so as to let villagers know that they are not forgotten and to bring the eyes of the world to them. Maha Ghosananda has been nominated several times for the Nobel Peace Prize and has won the Niwano Peace Prize.

Japan is the only country that has suffered atomic bombing. Consequently antiwar and antinuclear sentiment is unusually strong in Japan. The Nipponzan Myōhōji Order of Nichiren Buddhism is entirely devoted to eradicating war and nuclear weapons from the world. The Order was founded in Japan by the monk Nichidatsu Fujii (1885–1985) and has chapters in many countries. Fujii was an antiwar activist before World War II; his meeting with Mahatma Gandhi was a major inspiration to his life.

Today the Order is best known for two things. First, the Order has constructed Peace Pagodas, which are stūpas symbolizing nonviolence and peace, throughout the world; for example, the London city council erected a stūpa designed by the Venerable Fujii on the Thames River as a symbol of the city's declaration to be free from nuclear arms. Second, the Order is known for its peace marches led by monks and nuns of the Order, beating continuously on drums and chanting "Namu Myoho Renge Kyo" ("Praise to the Lotus Sūtra") and followed by long or short columns of supporters, both planned and spontaneous. Monks and nuns of the Order and their lay supporters march annually to Hiroshima and Nagasaki; they have traveled to Nanking to mourn those killed in the Nanking massacre and to build friendship between Japan and China; they have marched to Auschwitz and offered prayers there; they have marched together with Maha Ghosananda's *Dhammayietra*; and they have marched at most major sites of conflict in the world to pray for the dead, to appeal for peace, to dedicate themselves to work for peace, and to inspire others to do the same. Monks and nuns of the Order also frequently sit in protest or witness before sites of armament manufacture or war preparation, beating on their drums and chanting. They might witness in this way at sites where peace or disarmament talks are under way, such as at the United Nations. Occasionally they publicly fast for peace. Fujii often stated his passionately held view that war and the manufacture of weapons are criminal activities and urged his followers to find new and creative ways to eliminate war absolutely.

The Dalai Lama (1935–) leads the Tibetan Liberation Movement, a nonviolent effort to free Tibet of Chinese oppression. Because the Dalai Lama is traditionally the secular as well as spiritual head of Tibet, it is impossible to separate the political from the religious in Tibet. Under Chinese rule Buddhism has been directly attacked, with many monks and nuns killed or imprisoned for their support of the Dalai Lama or their opposition to the Chinese regime. Many have been forcibly defrocked, and many monasteries have been closed, destroyed, or reduced to a fraction of their former population. The suffering of the Tibetan people was especially acute during the Cultural Revolution, when death from torture, inhumane prison conditions, execution, and especially famine reached its peak. It is estimated that over one million Tibetans, one-fifth of its population, died during the Chinese occupation. Since that time the Chinese have embarked on a program called "cultural genocide" by its critics in which great numbers of ethnically Han Chinese are being moved into Tibet, with the result that the Tibetans are becoming a minority in their own country. At the same time severe repression of traditional religion and culture is taking place. As a consequence of these policies, Tibetan culture is engaged in an impropitious struggle for existence, and many realistically fear its extinction. Much of the hope for its preservation lies in the Tibetan refugee community outside Tibet.

The Dalai Lama is the spokesperson for the Tibetan cause. He does not insist on independence for Tibet. His most famous initiative has been the Five Point Peace Plan, which calls for the following:

1. transformation of the whole of Tibet into a zone of peace, free of armaments;
2. abandonment of China's population transfer policy;
3. respect for the Tibetan people's fundamental human rights and democratic freedoms;
4. restoration and protection of Tibet's natural environment; and
5. negotiations on the future of Tibet.

These and all other Tibetan proposals have borne no fruit. In such a struggle between unequals, the Dalai Lama has turned to the international community, relying on the moral integrity of the Tibetans' cause to generate support.

The Dalai Lama strongly advocates principled pacifism but does not condemn the Tibetan people when, in the severity of their suffering, they sometimes strike out violently against their oppressors. His own pacifism is so strict that he refuses to endorse a boycott against China, as that would be hurtful to the Chinese people. He points to the fact of interdependence and states that only a solution that is acceptable to all parties will provide a long-term resolution, whereas solutions reached through violence are fundamentally ineffective because the problem will return. He states that the correct attitude toward one's "enemy" is not anger but gratitude, as only the enemy can give one the opportunity to test one's inner strength. The Dalai Lama was awarded the Nobel Peace Prize in 1989. He is one of the best known and most beloved leaders for peace in the world.

The Buddhist response to crisis varies, depending on the circumstances being faced, but core moral and spiritual values are shared in all these cases: (1) principled nonviolence, coupled with a passionate concern to bring violence and suffering to an end; (2) compassionate concern for all, refusal to side with one group against another, and siding with life; and (3) emphasis on interdependence, reconciliation, and healing. The fact that in Vietnam, Cambodia, and Tibet Buddhist institutions, monks, and nuns have been directly attacked demonstrates both communism's antipathy toward Buddhism and the oppressors' fear of Buddhism's ability to move people to action.

SALLIE B. KING

See also Buddhadāsa; Buddhism: Western; Dalai Lama (Tenzin Gyatso); Dharamsala, India (Tibetan); Fujii, Nichidatsu (Nittatsu); Nhất Hanh, Thích; Persecution: Buddhist Perspectives; Self-Immolation, Buddhist; Tibet: History

Further Reading

Dalai Lama XIV, *Kindness, Clarity and Insight*, edited by J. Hopkins and E. Napper, Ithaca, New York: Snow Lion, 1984

Fujii, Nichidatsu, *The Time Has Come*, Tokyo: Japan-Bharat Sarvodaya Mitrata Sanga, 1982

Ghosananda, Maha, *Step by Step: Meditations on Wisdom and Compassion*, Berkeley, California: Parallax Press, 1992

Kraft, Kenneth, editor, *Inner Peace, World Peace: Essays on Buddhism and Nonviolence*, Albany: State University of New York Press, 1992

Nhất Hanh, Thích, *Vietnam: Lotus in a Sea of Fire*, New York: Hill and Wang, and London: SCM Press, 1967

Nhất Hanh, Thích, *Being Peace*, Berkeley, California: Parallax Press, 1987

Queen, Christopher S., and Sallie B. King, editors, *Engaged Buddhism: Buddhist Liberation Movements in Asia*, Albany: State University of New York Press, 1996

Penitential Books

These lists of sins, together with the fixed penances intended to help a sinner recover from his or her sin, are the most distinctive contribution of Celtic monasticism to Western Christianity. Having appeared likely first in Wales, they acquired their characteristic form in sixth-century Irish monasteries. Only a few early texts survive, but these show a new, highly sophisticated view of spiritual life.

About the time Christianity came to Ireland, the Latin Church faced two interconnected problems regarding sin: first, could formal "Public Penance" be used only once in a lifetime, and, second, because this was for only "the greatest sins" (e.g., murder, adultery, and apostasy), what of the accumulation of lesser sins? No solution emerged, and the result was a pastoral impasse. The penitentials' approach was driven by praxis, based on a combination of ideas from Irish law and the spiritual guidance of monks. The latter drew above all on John Cassian (c. 360–after 430) and his view of monastic life as a process toward perfection based on healing the ailments of sin. In Irish law a crime was an offense against someone's dignity and carried with it a price to be paid by the offender to the one injured. This debt varied with the offense and the status of the guilty and injured parties; once the debt had been paid, justice was restored. From monastic spirituality came another inspiration: penances were medicines to be applied to the Eight Capital Vices, thus making penitence into an ongoing therapy. As with a sickness, each sin required a particular mixture of medicine as its cure, made up of fasting, prayer, or service in fixed amounts and graded according to the severity of the wrong and the status of the offender. The principle was "contraries are healed by contraries," and the administrator viewed his work as that of a physician and a father dealing with disciples rather than as that of a judge dealing with criminals.

Although rooted in monasticism (and the early texts concentrate on the sins of monastics), from the start penitential books spread beyond the monks to everyone in their pastoral care and thence to the wider Church. Their impact was a more widespread understanding of how sin affected Christian life by teaching that someone could confront internal disorder using many paths and that the Christian struggle could be seen in therapeutic terms. Inherent in the practice was the notion that the key element in initiating restoration is awareness of the offense (as distinct from the crime) given to God: such awareness was manifested in sorrow, and this notion led later to emphasis on contrition. Moreover the pardoning of sin became private, each sin being seen as a distinct crime against God, so that process between penitent and priest could be repeated many times in a lifetime. Thus, the penitentials marked the crucial step in the transition from patristic practice to the later Sacrament of Penance ("Confession"). As a by-product they provided the basis from which the practice of indulgences developed in the 12th century.

THOMAS O'LOUGHLIN

See also Cassian, John; Celtic Monasticism; Fasting: Western Christian; Ireland: History; Island Monasteries, Christian; Liturgy: Celtic; Missionaries: Christian; Recluses, Western Christian; Spirituality: Western Christian; Wales

Further Reading

Bieler, Ludwig, editor, *The Irish Penitentials*, Dublin: Dublin Institute for Advanced Studies, 1975

Connolly, Hugh, *The Irish Penitentials and Their Significance for the Sacrament of Penance Today*, Dublin and Portland, Oregon: Four Courts Press, 1995

McNeill, John T., and Helena M. Gamer, translators, *Medieval Handbooks of Penance*, New York: Columbia University Press, 1938

O'Loughlin, Thomas, and Helen Conrad-O'Briain, "The 'Baptism of Tears' in Early Anglo-Saxon Sources," *Anglo-Saxon England* 22 (1993)

O'Loughlin, Thomas, "Penitentials and Pastoral Care," in *A History of Pastoral Care*, edited by G.R. Evans, London: Cassell, 1999

Payer, Pierre J., *Sex and the Penitentials: The Development of a Sexual Code 550–1150*, Toronto and Buffalo, New York: University of Toronto Press, 1984

Poschmann, Bernhard, *Penance and the Anointing of the Sick*, New York: Herder and Herder, 1964

Persecution: Buddhist Perspectives

Buddhist monasticism has suffered periods of persecution in one form or another in practically every region where Buddhism has become established in its long and complex history. These regions embrace the Indian subcontinent of its birth, where it was almost obliterated by Turkic Muslim invaders in the first millennium A.D., Sri Lanka, Southeast Asia, China, Tibet, central Asia, Mongolia, Korea, and Japan. The persecutors of the Buddhist faith have included adherents of competing faiths such as Islam, Christianity, and Hinduism and variants of Confucianism, Taoism, Shintoism, Western colonialism, and Communist ideology. Our knowledge about how Buddhist clergy of the various traditions perceived and responded to individual and institutional repression and violence in the distant past is often secondhand, obscure, and anecdotal. Much of this history was not well recorded, if at all, or has not survived the ravages of war, climate, and the passage of generations.

The 20th century was an unfortunate period of severe persecution of Buddhist clergy and the lay communities that have supported them. Persecution of Buddhism continues into the present. Policies of cultural and religious genocide, as in Cambodia and Tibet, are well documented, and acts of cruelty and injustice toward Buddhists are clearly recorded, sometimes while still in progress, thanks to the investigative reporting of global news agencies based in relatively open, democratic societies.

There is perhaps no better way to present a characteristically Buddhist response to persecution than to allow the leaders of persecuted Buddhist populations to speak for themselves in their own words. Among the most highly regarded exemplars of Buddhist teachings and practice today are those ordained leaders whose nations and cultures have experienced severe oppression by totalitarian regimes that have seized control of their countries. They are the internationally renowned Buddhist monks: the Venerable Tenzin Gyatso (1935–), the Fourteenth Dalai Lama of Tibet; Somdech Preah (Supreme Patriarch) Maha

Ghosananda (1929–) of Cambodia; and the exiled scholar-poet and activist the Venerable Thích Nhát Hanh (1926–) of Vietnam. Although the Buddhist traditions that they represent range from Tibetan Vajrayāna (Geluk sect) to Theravāda to Vietnamese Zen and the circumstances of their respective lands and their roles as Buddhist leaders differ widely, their responses to persecution converge in their evocation of basic Buddhist teachings emphasis on learning and practice. They speak for the many nameless men and women of their *saṅgha*s and lay communities whose suffering goes unwitnessed or whose voices have been permanently silenced by oppressors.

In the case of Tibet, Buddhist clergy and monastic institutions, as leaders of the traditionally religious society, have suffered continuous persecution by Communist China from the middle of the 20th century. Beijing leaders since Mao have claimed the long-independent Tibet to be part of China. The Communists view their military incursion into Tibet as the pacification of a local rebellion; they see the destruction of more than 6,000 monasteries, the deaths of approximately 1.2 million Tibetans (including many unarmed monks who were machine-gunned to death while at prayer in their temples), and the forced Sinicization of the remaining population as the "liberation" of the Tibetan people from an antiquated and parasitic class hierarchy. His Holiness the Dalai Lama fled to India in 1959 and heads a Tibetan government-in-exile with about 100,000 Tibetans who followed him over the Himalayas. A recipient of the Nobel Peace Prize in 1989 for his consistently firm yet nonviolent stance toward rapprochement with China, he has become a universally recognized paragon of spiritual endurance, equanimity, and insightful wisdom under oppression.

A few stanzas from a prayerlike poem called *Dentsik Mom-lam* in Tibetan ("A Prayer of Words of Truth") composed by the Dalai Lama shortly after his flight from Tibet captures the simple honesty and altruism of this Buddhist monk and head of state in exile. It is addressed to the "buddhas of the past, present and future, the bodhisattvas, great masters and their disciples" who care for human beings "as a mother cares for her only child":

> (3)
> Wretched beings are ceaselessly tormented by their
> sufferings,
> Driven by the dreadful force of their evil karmic acts –
> Please save them from unbearable terrors, sicknesses,
> wars, and famines,
> And refresh their spirits in your ocean of bliss and joy.
>
> (4)
> Please look at the religious people of the Land of Snows,
> Ruthlessly conquered by the cruel tactics of evil invaders,
> And let the might of your compassion swiftly arise
> To stop the terrible flow of their blood and tears.
>
> (5)
> The violent oppressors are also worthy of compassion.
> Crazed by demonic emotions, they do vicious deeds
> That bring total defeat to themselves as well as to others.
> Please grant them the insight into right and wrong,
> And bring them to know the glory of loving friendship.
>
> (excerpted from Dalai Lama, 1975)

Still in exile in 1993, more than three decades after this poem was written and no progress having been gained in relieving the bitter colonization of his country, His Holiness the Dalai Lama was asked whether he did not feel hatred against those who sought to destroy him. He responded,

> From a Buddhist point of view it is very important to understand the link which exists between the one who is causing harm and his victims. In reality, what is a person doing when, in a spirit of malevolence, he harms others through his destructive, negative acts? According to the Buddhist view, that person is preparing to endure great suffering and torment in the future as a karmic result of his malevolent acts. However, the one who suffers the other's evildoing and misfortunes is using up the karmic results of his past negative acts. He is purifying his karma, but while he is in the process of using up his past karma through suffering, he is not accumulating any new negative impressions. Consequently, far from considering the person who harms us as an enemy or an object of hatred, if we understand what suffering awaits him in the future he becomes for us a rather special object of compassion. To think in this way can be of great help.

As for an exemplary response to torture and imprisonment, the Dalai Lama adds,

> In India I recently met up with a man I had known long ago, the abbot of a monastery who spent twenty years of his life in prison and in labor camps in Tibet. While we were speaking he declared to me that during the entire time of his imprisonment in Chinese jails the greatest danger he had encountered was that of losing his compassion for the Chinese. I found his attitude most remarkable.
>
> If we look at the current situation in Tibet . . . the Tibetans are the oppressed and the Chinese are the oppressors. Up to now the Chinese have been successful in their work of oppression, and their desire for conquest has been fulfilled; they should be happy. But, in fact, the Tibetans seem much happier than their oppressors. This is yet another persuasive reason for fostering compassion for the Chinese, rather than hatred. (Dalai Lama, 1996)

In contrast to the ongoing colonization of Tibet by a foreign power, Cambodian Buddhism suffered near extinction at the hands of Cambodians themselves who tried to realize a radically Marxist vision in order to begin history anew under Pol Pot. Under Year Zero policies beginning in April 1975 of the Khmer Rouge era, almost all Cambodia's 3,600 temples were destroyed, and only some 3,000 of Cambodia's 50,000 monks survived hard labor, torture, starvation, and execution. There are no precise statistics on the fate of Cambodia nuns, but their persecution is well known.

Much-revered Supreme Patriarch of Cambodia Maha Ghosananda was able to survive the holocaust because he was on a many-years-long intensive meditation retreat in the forests of Thailand while the American bombing and total war in his country raged. Returning to the "killing fields" of Cambodia to help restore his country's ancient culture that had almost succumbed to extinction, the patriarch teaches his monks to leave their temples and practice in the world, walking the Buddhist path "step by step" in daily life, even as he has done by example in past years. He has led *Dhammayietra* peace marches through the minefields of rural Cambodia and even between battling patrols of government troops and Khmer Rouge insurgents. As founder of the Inter-Religious Mission for Peace in Cambodia, his message freely combines teachings from the Pāli *sutta*s with references to Christ and Gandhi.

The Venerable Maha Ghosananda (Great Joyful Proclaimer), paraphrasing a passage in the *Dhammapada*, offers a universal teaching rooted the Theravāda Buddhist culture that he wishes to reconstitute in his homeland:

> In those that harbor thoughts of blame and vengeance towards others, hatred will never cease. In those who do not harbor blame and vengeance, hatred will surely cease. For hatred is never appeased by hatred. Hatred is appeased by love. This is an eternal law. ("Prayer for Peace," in Maha Ghosananda, 1991)

Taking a philosophical overview that is both idealistic and shrewdly practical, the patriarch urges monks to commit to relieving suffering directly in front of them rather than retreating into passive contemplation:

> Many Buddhists are suffering – in Tibet, Laos, Burma, Vietnam, and elsewhere. The most important thing we Buddhists can do is to foster the liberation of the human spirit in every nation of the human family. We must use our religious heritage as a living resource. . . .
>
> What did the Buddha teach that we can use to heal and elevate the human condition? One of the Buddha's most courageous acts was to walk onto a battlefield to stop a conflict. He did not sit in his temple and wait for the opponents to approach him. . . . The opponent has our respect. We implicitly trust his or her human nature and understand that ill-will is caused by ignorance. By appealing to the best in each other, both of us achieve the satisfaction of peace. We both become peacemakers. Gandhi called this a "bilateral victory."
>
> We Buddhists must find the courage to leave our temples and enter the temples of human experience. . . . If we listen to the Buddha, Christ, or Gandhi, we can do nothing else. The refugee camps, the prisons, the ghettos, and the battlefields will then become our temples. We have so much work to do. . . .
>
> This will be a slow transformation, for many people throughout Asia have been trained to rely on the traditional monkhood . . . but we monks must answer the increasingly loud cries of suffering. We only need to remember that our temple is with us always. We *are* our temple. (Maha Ghosananda, 1991)

The integration of Buddhist thought and spiritual practice with commitment to relieve suffering in the midst of persecution is exemplified in the lives of many clergy and lay Buddhists in Vietnam. Suppressed by French colonialists and ruling Vietnamese Catholic administrations earlier in the 20th century, Buddhists in Vietnam sought to maintain neutrality and peace between the Vietcong in the north and U.S.-supported authoritarian governments in the south. This autonomous stance was deemed treasonous by both sides and occasioned sensational self-immolations by Buddhist clergy and laypersons who sacrificed themselves to call attention to the desperation of the Vietnamese masses who did not want their country torn apart by warring ideological factions. The victorious Communist regime still maintains a policy of persecution through house arrest and imprisonment of numerous members of the Unified Buddhist Church of Vietnam today.

Nominated for the Nobel Peace Prize by Martin Luther King, Jr., the Venerable Thích Nhát Hanh, founder of the Tiép Hiên Order (Order of Interbeing), has become an influential peace and reconciliation advocate in the West while he remains in exile from his native land. Like Maha Ghosananda and the Dalai Lama, Thích Nhát Hanh emphasizes the need for meditation and mindfulness practice in order to recognize experientially the shared identity of "the persecuted and the persecutors" so that activists will be able to actively embrace both when working for peace. Nhát Hanh's poem "Please Call Me by My True Names" shockingly juxtaposes victims and the victimizers to illustrate our (the speaker's) "karmic" interrelatedness and responsibility. Persecution and the suffering it produces is rooted in our ignorance of our common conditioning. We must recognize our "true names"; that is, we are responsible for "both sides," the victim as well as the perpetrator, before insight and selfless love for others can dawn within us.

> "Please Call Me by My True Names" (excerpts)
>
> Do not say I'll depart tomorrow
> because even today I still arrive.
>
> Look deeply: I arrive in every second
> to be a bud on a spring branch,
> to be a tiny bird, with wings still fragile,
> Learning to sing in my new nest,
> to be a caterpillar in the heart of flower,
> to be a jewel hiding itself in a stone.
>
> ***
>
> I am the child in Uganda, all skin and bones,
> my legs as thin as bamboo sticks,

and I am the arms merchant, selling deadly
weapons to Uganda.

I am the 12-year old girl, refugee
on a small boat,
Who throws herself into the ocean after
being raped by a sea pirate,
And I am the pirate, my heart not yet capable
of seeing and loving.

I am a member of the politburo, with
plenty of power in my hands,
and I am the man who has to pay his
"debt of blood" to my people,
dying slowly in a forced labor camp.

***

Please call me by my true names,
so I can hear all my cries and my laughs
at once,
so I can see that my joy and pain are one.

Please call me by my true names,
so I can wake up,
and so the door of my heart can be left open,
the door of compassion.

(Nhát Hanh, 1993)

Many erudite volumes would be required to document the persecution (and even holocausts) of Buddhism in detail and to analyze the causes and denouement of these tragic historic configurations in widely separated and linguistically diverse cultures over the last two millennia. Nevertheless, a basic Buddhist response to persecution, profoundly yet simply stated, hearkens back to the cultivation of a deeper comprehension and acceptance of Śākyamuni Buddha's original teaching of the nature of suffering and its roots in our ignorance and attachment to our interdependent and transient existence. As insight into the nature of suffering dawns, so does greater compassion for ourselves and for those who oppress us.

FRANK M. TEDESCO

See also Critiques of Buddhist Monasticism; Dalai Lama (Tenzin Gyatso); Korea: Sites; Nhát Hanh, Thích; Peace Movements, Buddhist; Self-Immolation, Buddhist; Social Services: Buddhist; Tibet: History; Vietnam

Further Reading

Bimal Bhikkhu, "Apropos the Future of the Chakmas," *Chakma Voice* 1:1 (April–June 1995)

Dalai Lama XIV, *A Prayer of Words of Truth by His Holiness the Dalai Lama and the Tibetan National Anthem*, Dharamsala: Library of Tibetan Works and Archives, 1975

Dalai Lama XIV, *Beyond Dogma: The Challenge of the Modern World*, translated by Alison Anderson, edited by Marianne Dresser, London: Souvenir Press, 1996; as *Beyond Dogma: Discourses and Dialogues*, translated by Alison Anderson, edited by Marianne Dresser, Berkeley, California: North Atlantic Books, 1996

Dalai Lama XIV, *Ethics for the New Millennium*, New York: Riverhead Books, 1999

Hsü-yün, *Empty Cloud: The Autobiography of the Chinese Zen Master, Hsu Yun*, translated by Charles Luk, Rochester, New York: Empty Cloud Press, 1974; as *Empty Cloud: The Autobiography of the Chinese Zen Master, Xu-Yun*, translated by Charles Luk, edited by Richard Hunn, Shaftesbury, Dorset: Element Books, 1988

Ketelaar, James E., *Of Heretics and Martyrs in Meiji Japan: Buddhism and Its Persecution*, Princeton, New Jersey: Princeton University Press, 1990

King, Sallie B., "Thích Nhát Hanh and the Unified Buddhist Church of Vietnam: Nondualism in Action," in *Engaged Buddhism: Buddhist Liberation Movements in Asia*, edited by King and Christopher S. Queen, Albany: State University of New York Press, 1996

Maha Ghosananda, *Step by Step: Meditations on Wisdom and Compassion*, edited by Jane Sharada Mahoney and Philip Edmonds, Berkeley, California: Parallax Press, 1991

Nhát Hanh, Thích, *Vietnam: Lotus in a Sea of Fire*, forward by Thomas Merton, New York: Hill and Wang, and London: SCM Press, 1967

Nhát Hanh, Thích, *Call Me by My True Names: The Collected Poems of Thích Nhát Hanh*, Berkeley, California: Parallax Press, 1993; Enfield, Greater London: Airlift, 1999

Nhát Hanh, Thích, *Love in Action: Writings on Nonviolent Social Change*, Berkeley, California: Parallax Press, 1993

Nhát Hanh, Thích, *Living Buddha, Living Christ*, New York: Riverhead Books, and London: Rider, 1995

Powers, John, "The Twentieth Century," in his *Introduction to Tibetan Buddhism*, Ithaca, New York: Snow Lion, 1995

Queen, Christopher S., and Sallie B. King, editors, *Engaged Buddhism: Buddhist Liberation Movements in Asia*, Albany: State University of New York Press, 1996

Tedesco, Frank M., "Questions for Buddhist and Christian Cooperation in Korea," in *Buddhist-Christian Studies*, volume 17, Honolulu: East-West Religions Project, University of Hawaii, 1997

Thurman, Robert A.F., "Tibet and the Monastic Army of Peace," in *Inner Peace, World Peace: Essays on Buddhism and Nonviolence* (SUNY Series in Buddhist Studies), edited by Kenneth Kraft, Albany: State University of New York Press, 1992

Topmiller, Robert J., "The Lotus Unleashed: The Buddhist Struggle Movement in South Vietnam, 1964–66," Ph.D. diss., University of Kentucky, 1998

Vietnam Committee on Human Rights, *Religious Intolerance in Viet Nam: Repression against the Unified Buddhist Church of Viet Nam*, Gennevilliers: International Buddhist Information Bureau of the Unified Church of Vietnam, 1994

Related Web Sites

http://home.earthlink.net/~crtp/ (about Soviet persecution of Buddhism in Mongolia)

http://iarf-religiousfreedom.org (International Association of Religious Freedom – Korea news)

http://www.bpf.org (Buddhist Peace Fellowship)

http://www.bpf.org/ineb (International Network of Engaged Buddhists)
http://www.fva.org (about the Unified Buddhist Church of Vietnam)
http://www.interfaith-center.org/oxford/press/niwano98.htm (about Maha Ghosananda)
http://www.plumvillage.org (about the Unified Buddhist Church of Vietnam)

Persecution: Christian Perspectives

Persecution, which for the Christian as Christian attains its culmination in death, or martyrdom, played a certain role both in the early spread of monasticism and in its self-definition. When Christianity was still being persecuted at the beginning of the fourth century, Egyptian Christians were fleeing to the desert for safety, and a number of them are said to have embraced an ascetic life there and thus to have contributed to the origins of monasticism in Egypt. However, when the persecution had ceased, largely after the publication of the so-called Edict of Milan in 313, Christians who craved the opportunities for moral heroism offered by a hostile regime now found an acceptable substitute in the rigors of monasticism. It is for this reason, among others, that the Christian monastic life in its earliest days was referred to quite regularly as a form of martyrdom. Thus, Sulpicius Severus (c. 360–c. 430) wrote of the bishop and monk Martin of Tours, shortly after his death in 397, that

> although the temper of the age was unable to offer him martyrdom, nonetheless he will not lack a martyr's glory, since by both desire and virtue he could have been a martyr and was willing to be one. . . . Even though he did not endure [the pains of martyrdom], still he attained to martyrdom, albeit in unbloody fashion. For what agonies of human sorrows did he not bear for the hope of eternity, in hunger, in vigils, in nakedness, in fastings, in the hard words of the envious, in persecutions of the unrighteous, in care for the sick, in concern for the imperiled? (from the "Letters of Sulpicius Severus on St. Martin")

Such testimony to the martyrlike quality of monasticism could easily be multiplied in the literature of the early Church.

Yet from the Christian perspective persecution is by no means a specifically monastic issue, although monastics have been subjects of persecution throughout the history of monasticism. Examples include a certain Egyptian monk named Apollonius, who died during the Diocletian persecution at the beginning of the fourth century; the Carthusians of the London charterhouse who were martyred under Henry VIII (1509–1547) in 1535; the Carmelite nuns of Compiègne who were guillotined during the French Revolution in 1794; and the French Trappists who were slain by Islamic fundamentalists in Algeria in 1996. If monks and nuns often seem to be specially selected for persecution, sometimes to the point of death, it is most likely because they appear to their persecutors in some way to epitomize Christianity or the Church or, at the very least, certain aspects of Christianity or the Church that are felt to be repugnant or threatening. No suggestion is being made here that those being persecuted are necessarily the purest representatives of Christianity (or the representatives of the purest Christianity) but rather that they represent it as no one else could, apart perhaps from clerics. To strike out at a monk or nun is to attack Christianity or the Church in a way that one could not if one were to strike out at a layperson.

However true it might be that monastics who are morally mediocre can be targeted for persecution, it is also true that monastic life, and perhaps even a mediocre monastic life, offers a singular preparation for suffering. Here one could cite three factors: monasticism's discipline, its cultivation of a spirit of acceptance or resignation, and its eschatological thrust. Ideally, these factors would make persecution at least somewhat more tolerable than it might be for nonmonastics, and the eschatological thrust, the strong sense of living for something beyond the present world, could even make it seem desirable.

However, for all that, persecution is not a specifically monastic issue. It is a Christian issue, and, as has already been suggested, if monks and nuns are persecuted and martyred, it is because they are Christians. In their own eyes their sufferings would have no value apart from that.

Regarding suffering, since Christianity's earliest days persecution has been understood to be a blessing. "Blessed are those who are persecuted for righteousness' sake, for theirs is the kingdom of heaven," Jesus declares in Matthew 5:10–12. "Blessed are you when men revile you and utter all kinds of evil against you falsely on my account. Rejoice and be glad, for your reward is great in heaven, for so men persecuted the prophets who were before you." These and similar words of encouragement and comfort served to help steady the early Christians in their various moments of trial, yet other words seemed to say just the opposite. As Jesus also declares in Matthew 10:23, "When they persecute you in one town, flee to the next." It would appear that this passage counseled not steadfastness but flight.

The early Church, which was the first to interpret Jesus' sayings, did not see these two different kinds of pronouncements as contradictory. Rather, together they implied that although it was a blessing to suffer on behalf of Christ and righteousness, it was not something that should be grasped at. That is, such a gift, a charism, was not something that could be obtained by one's own efforts. Flight would guarantee the purity of the gift: if the charism of suffering were really to be one's lot, it would occur when God had determined, when no more flight could occur, or when it was clear that no more suffering should take place. On the other hand, to be in any way the agent of one's own death rather than its passive recipient, however strongly one might welcome it, was to incur the accusation of suicide. The latter was universally forbidden (except when a virgin killed herself to avoid submitting to rape, allowed by some authorities). This "passive" pattern is clear in the earliest of all postscriptural martyrdom accounts, that of Polycarp, bishop of Smyrna, written around 156, in which a certain Christian named Quintus spontaneously exposes himself to torture during a persecution and then makes a fool of himself by abandoning his faith, whereas Polycarp flees the persecution and, when discovered by the police, permits himself to be captured (*Martyrdom of Polycarp* 4–7). This is the model that has dominated throughout Christian history: Christians have not sought persecution but have, with a minimum of resistance, allowed themselves to fall into the hands of their persecutors. For example, in the case of someone such as Thomas More (1478–1533), who was eventually beheaded under Henry VIII, recourse to the law served as the resistance and took the place of actual flight.

Persecution as blessing is a strongly if not necessarily a uniquely Christian idea. Certainly, not all religions view suffering inflicted by others in this way. Most Jews especially seem highly resistant to viewing pogroms or the Holocaust as anything but an unmitigated tragedy – one that might even call into question the very existence of God and that must never be repeated. To be sure Christians have suffered nothing remotely resembling the Holocaust (although they too were victims of the concentration camps). The persecutions of Christians in antiquity were sporadic and far from universal despite the fact that they acquired mythic proportions in the Christian consciousness and helped substantially to shape the Christian identity even to the present day. Subsequent persecutions have been more violent and more systematic, especially in the 20th century, but nothing can compare with the eruption of terror and death against the Jews known as the Holocaust. It is hard to know what Christians would think of such a catastrophe if it were part of their own history. Nonetheless, communal memory of persecution, weakened though it might be, strongly suggests that Christians are not entirely repelled by the notion of it or at least that room exists for it in their spiritual and psychological makeup.

The esteem and fascination enjoyed by Christian martyrs and by the various circumstances of their martyrdom bears witness to the truth of this. In the first centuries of the Church's existence, the martyrs were the saints par excellence. It was hardly possible to achieve holiness, in the popular mind, without having suffered. The martyrs were believed to be endowed with virtue to a remarkable degree, especially fortitude, which they possessed in superhuman measure. The most cruel and most refined torments could not sway them from their determination not to renounce Christ and Christianity. Martyrologies, as the accounts of their tortures are known, delighted in dwelling on their sufferings and very frequently exaggerated them; this was both edifying and constitutive of a gripping tale. It is worth observing that martyrologies, often in extremely popular and fabulous forms, were as avidly pursued by Christian readers as any other genre of literature until into the 20th century. That the monastic, whose life offered fewer intrinsic possibilities for drama, should have succeeded in the fourth and fifth centuries to the mantle of the martyr is all the more noteworthy in the context of the martyr's unique image.

Whatever the reasons for the martyr's esteem might have been in the popular view, from the more narrowly theological perspective these reasons can be reduced to one: a profound personal relationship to Christ on the part of the martyr, manifested in the imitation of his suffering and death, for the torments of the martyr were nothing less than a conformation to the torments of Christ. If his suffering and death were the defining moment of Christ's earthly existence – a conclusion that is more than implicit throughout the New Testament – the Christian martyr touched more closely on that defining moment than anyone else and, in so doing, touched somehow on his essence. Only this can explain why martyrdom was the equivalent of baptism, which was itself understood to be a conformation to the suffering Christ. Thus, unbaptized persons who suffered and died for the sake of Christ were considered to have been baptized in their own blood. Similarly, baptized persons who had fallen into grave sin but who nonetheless offered their lives on behalf of Christ were forgiven their sins as if through a kind of "second baptism." This understanding of the connection between baptism and martyrdom, first aired in Tertullian's late second-century treatise *On Baptism*, is still valid in Christian theology today. The martyr's special relationship with Christ also explains an aberrant opinion that surfaced in the middle of the third century. Those who held it believed that the martyrs, who in this case were persons who had suffered but not been put to death, had the power to forgive sins. Although this opinion was not influential for long and soon disappeared, it was as plausible in its own way as the one that maintained that martyrs need not be baptized.

It has been noted that the persecutions of the first Christian centuries made a profound impression on the Christian consciousness. Without denying the truth of this observation, it is also correct to say that the Christian spirituality of the present century, as of the immediately preceding ones, has not been marked by any special awareness of martyrdom. It can no longer be stated that the saint par excellence is the martyr or that holiness is inconceivable without persecution. At least this seems to be the case in Western Europe and North America. The irony in this regard is that the 20th century has produced perhaps more martyrs than all the others combined, including such significant figures as Charles de Foucauld, Franz Jäggerstätter, Edith Stein, Maximilian Kolbe, Dietrich Bonhoeffer, Martin Luther King, Jr., Oscar Romero, and the four American churchwomen who died in El Salvador in 1980. Despite these and countless other 20th-century witnesses to the sanguinary opposition that the practice of Christianity is capable of arousing, persecution and martyrdom are no longer important elements, if they are elements at all, of Western spirituality. The implications for Western monasticism, which has been profoundly influenced by the culture that surrounds it, are clear. The spirituality of a persecuted Church and of its monasteries (e.g., in Egypt) presents a salutary contrast. Westerners, both monastics and nonmonastics, certainly are preoccupied with suffering, but it is personal suffering that concerns them – emotional and relational problems, physical illness, unemployment, and so on – and the vast market for the self-help literature that addresses these issues is evidence of this. However, whether such personal problems can be adequate substitutes for persecution and martyrdom is a question that must be posed. Thus, one of the important tasks facing Western Christian spirituality is the rediscovery of some sense of martyrdom's importance as the most profound form of the imitation of Christ. In turn this suggests the retrieval of the insight of the monastics of the fourth and fifth centuries who did not hesitate to use the rhetoric of martyrdom to describe their lives.

BONIFACE RAMSEY, O.P.

See also Asceticism: Christian Perspectives; Charism; Desert Fathers; Dissolution of Monasteries; Egypt; Hagiography: Eastern Christian; Hagiography: Western Christian; Hermits: Eastern Christian; Martyrs; Orthodox Monasticism: Slavic; Portugal; Russia: Recent Changes; Spirituality: Western Christian

Further Reading

Baumeister, Theofried, *Die Anfänge der Theologie des Martyriums*, Münster: Aschendorff, 1980
Baumeister, Theofried, *Genese und Entfaltung der altkirchlichen Theologie des Martyriums*, Bern and New York: Peter Lang, 1991
Metz, Johannes-Baptist, and Edward Schillebeeckx, editors, *Martyrdom Today*, Edinburgh: Clark, and New York: Seabury Press, 1983

Peter of Alcántara, St. 1499–1562

Spanish founder of Alcantarine Franciscans and advocate of the Counter-Reformation

Saint Peter of Alcántara founded the Alcantarine Franciscans, a branch of the Observants, which was part of the Discalced Franciscan movement of 16th-century Spain and a key factor in the renewal of the Roman Catholic Church during the Counter-Reformation. Peter was educated in Alcántara and Salamanca and by age 16 had become a Franciscan in a convent of Stricter Observance near Valencia de Alcántara. Ordained as a priest at 25, he held positions of authority within the many religious communities in which he spent his early years. Peter was convinced of the need for vigorous reform within the Catholic Church to combat the Protestant Reformation, and during his tenure as minister of St. Gabriel's province he drew up the Constitutions of Stricter Observance, which he presented at the Chapter of Plasencia in 1540. These constitutions were rejected on the basis that they were too severe. Determined to follow this stricter lifestyle himself, he retired to the mountains of Portugal, where other friars soon joined him in his ascetic life. Peter led an exceedingly austere life, eating and sleeping very little, and by 1554 he had established a new congregation based on this stricter way of life. With more convents following his example, Peter drew up statutes to formalize the new congregation.

Although its authorship has been disputed, the traditional Franciscan view is that the *Tratado de la oración y meditación* (c. 1541–1551; *Treatise on Prayer and Meditation*) is Peter's work. Judged as a masterpiece by many of his contemporaries, it has been translated into most European languages. Peter was also a counselor, spiritual adviser, and friend to St. Teresa of Avila (1515–1582). After first assuring her that her visions indeed came from God, he then supported Teresa's reform of her Carmelite Order, defending her desire for a stricter form of life and helping her found a reformed convent. His support of Teresa did not end with his death; Teresa admitted that he often appeared to her in visions to dispense sage advice.

The Alcantarines spread rapidly to other religious houses in Spain and Portugal as well as around the world: to Italy, Mexico, the East Indies, the Philippines, and Brazil. They disappeared as a separate order in 1897, when Pope Leo XIII (1878–1903) united the different branches of the Observant Franciscans. Peter died in 1562; he was beatified in 1622, canonized in 1669, and named patron of Brazil in 1826 and patron of Estremadura in 1962.

LEE TUNSTALL

See also Franciscans: General or Male; Latin America; Spain: History; Teresa of Avila, St.

Biography

After studying at Salamanca, Peter joined the Franciscans, being ordained in 1524 and serving the Observant branch of that Order within which he founded the new Alcantarine Franciscans. In 1560 the renowned ascetic met Teresa at Avila and counseled her about how to reform the Carmelites.

Major Works

Constitutions of Stricter Observance (for Discalced Franciscans), 1540
Tratado de la oración y meditación, c. 1541–1551; as *Treatise on Prayer and Meditation*, translated by Dominic Devas, 1926

Further Reading

Barrado, Arcángel, "Proceso de canonización de San Pedro de Alcántara: Introducción de la Causa, Proceso y Cartas recomendatorias," *Archivo Ibero-Americano* 29 (1969)
Butler, Alban, *Lives of the Saints*, edited by Donald Attwater and Herbert Thurston, volume 4, Montreal: Palm Publishers, 1956
"Estudios sobre San Pedro de Alcántara," *Archivo Ibero-Americano* 22 (1962)
Marchese, Francesco, *The Life of St. Peter of Alcantara*, 2 vols., London: Richardson, 1856
Sanz Valdivieso, Rafael, editor, *Vida y escritos de San Pedro de Alcántara*, Madrid: Biblioteca de autores cristianos, 1996

Pharmacology

Although pharmacology has a long and illustrious history, the Church's participation in the development of pharmaceutical science was almost nonexistent until after the period of the Diocletian persecution (303–313). This is not to say that the Church did not come to the aid of the suffering or that isolated monks were not adding to the storehouse of knowledge, but for the most part the Church was by necessity devoting its energy to preserving its existence. However, not long after the cessation of the persecution we find notable examples of the Church's involvement in medicine. We find the large hospital of St. Basil in Caesarea (370), the almshouses of the Roman Lady Fabiola in Rome and Ostia (400), and that of St. Samson adjoining the church at St. Sofia in Constantinople (c. 500). As the monastic movement flourished, so did the study of medicine, especially that of pharmacology. For the most part the study and practice of medicine followed that of Hippocrates (c. 430) and Aristotle (384–322 B.C.) or the Pergamum physician Galen (129–c. 200). Both schools emphasized dietetics and pharmaceutical botany. Aristotle's pupil Theophrastus (c. 371–c. 287 B.C.) cataloged the medicinal properties of some 550 plants ranging from Europe to India. It was Theophrastus who introduced the pharmaceutical doctrine of "signatures" ("if it looks like an adder's tongue, it must be good for snake bite") and the notion that the gods placed plants on earth for the sole use and benefit of humankind. The first century of the Christian era saw the production of the most influential pharmaceutical of antiquity, *De Materia Medica* (The Matter of Medicine). Written by the Greek physician Discorides, this volume discusses the medical properties of over 600 plants. Pliny the Younger's 37-volume Natural History provided much additional detailed herbal information. The most prolific medical writer of all, the physician Galen (130–200), added even more information regarding the pharmaceutical properties of plants and in doing so created an entirely new school of medicine.

Building on these references and acquiring along the way the pharmaceutical knowledge of native practitioners, the *infirmarers* of the monasteries contributed greatly to knowledge of the pharmaceutical properties of plants and later of minerals. How diligently the *infirmarers* went about their work is attested to by the vast wealth of manuscripts, many still unedited and untranslated, lying about in monastic, cathedral, and museum libraries throughout Europe. At St. Gall, Switzerland (c. 820), one of the primary tasks of the monks was to copy ancient herbals, especially Anglo-Saxon ones, and to re-create "pagan" healing formulas. One of those greatly influenced by the research at St. Gall's was the abbot of the nearby Abbey of Reichenau, Walafrid Strabo (c. 808–849), who produced in poetic form one of the first monastic herbals, *De cultura hortorum* (On the Cultivation of Gardens). In his *Hortulus* Walafrid describes the value of native medicinal plants and expounds his method of teaching medicine (including pharmacology) in monasteries. Three centuries later another Rhinelander, St. Hildegard of Bingen (1099–1179), wrote her *Physica*, containing a description of drugs from the "three kingdoms of nature." About the same time the bishop of Rennes, Marbodus of Angers (d. 1123), wrote of the curative properties of minerals in his *Lapidarius*.

If the practice in English monasteries is any indication, it appears that in the vocabulary of the monastic infirmary "pharmaceutical" generally came to refer to a remedy concocted from herbs or minerals to be taken internally. However, in some records the word is used in a wider sense to include herbal and mineral-derived ointments for the skin as well as solutions in which affected bodily parts were bathed. Records from Westminster Abbey (1305–1306) note that "medicines" included some powders, depilatory water, various syrups, licorice, and *calagogi*, probably intestinal remedies (Westminster Abbey Manuscript 193119). The value of these remedies is debatable. Many were clearly placebos, and some were sure to have debilitating effects on the monks. Because the practice of medicine was as much dietetic as therapeutic, the use of herbs had, if nothing else, an inherent nutritional value and did double duty as potherbs. Some were clearly effective and are still in use today. Herbs such as the aloes and rhubarbs are still being used as natural purgatives. The dandelion, which is rich in vitamins A and C, is a major ingredient of natural diuretics and astringents, and meadowsweet, or Bride's wort, is used as an ingredient of fungicides and fumigants, as a source of vanillin aldehyde and salicylic acid, and as the base of vermouth. Meadowsweet is one of the 50 herbs used in a cure-all called "Save" in Chaucer's (1342–1400) "Knight's Tale."

In 789 the Synod of Aachen decreed that each monastery and cathedral chapter should institute a school. According to the Capitulary of Charlemagne (768–814) at Diedenhofen in 806, medicine with a strong emphasis on pharmacology was being taught at almost every monastic school in the Western Church. However, such monastic schools were virtually nonexistent in the Eastern Church. It is only reasonable that in time the monastery school would give rise to the great universities of Europe. So it was that during the 13th century we find the rise of the first great monastically associated colleges of medicine, among which were the medical school at Bologna and its daughter school at Padua, which soon excelled its mother. In both these schools, as in others that were to follow, the study of pharmacology played a significant role. It was also during the 13th century that Emperor Frederick II (1212–1250) offered his protection to Arab art and science, and with this protection the Arabic medicinal influence began to make itself know in monastic medicine, especially in the area of pharmacology. One of the earliest proponents of Arab polypharmacy was Nicolaus Praepositus of Salerno (c. 1140), whose collection of compound pharmaceutical formulas, *Antidotarium* (Antidotes), became a model for later works and a textbook for pharmaceutical study. Toward the end of the 12th century, Matthaeus Platearius wrote a commentary on *Antidotarium* and a work about simple drugs, *Circa instans* (the work's name is taken from its first words, "Concerning urgent").

With these works and the schools that soon followed, monks ceased to be the primary healers within the Church, giving way to "physicians-in-ordinary." However, a few 13th-century *infirmarers* of note remained. One of these was the Dominican Albertus Magnus (Albert Count of Bollstädt, 1193–1280), whose works on plants contributed much to the knowledge of pharmacology. Although Albertus was an independent thinker whose most valuable contribution to medical science was to advocate an independent observation of nature, in some ways he built on the works of contemporaries, such as the encyclopedic works of the Franciscan Bartholomaeus Anglicus (c. 1260) and the natural history composed by the monks of the Monastery of Meinau on Lake Constance. In the 14th century the monk-physician-professor Galeazo, of a famous family of physicians, compiled a pharmacopoeia, *Santa Sophia*, which offered a fully independent observation in the field of botanical pharmacology. Each of these works in its own way influenced the future study of pharmacology, and along with the earlier works they form the basis of much of our modern use of herbs in naturalistic healing.

FRANK A. MILLS

See also Albertus Magnus, St.; Botany; Food: Christian Perspectives; Gardens: Christian Perspectives; Hildegard of Bingen, St.; Reichenau, Germany; Social Services: Western Christian; Walafrid Strabo

Further Reading

Editio princeps (Venice, 1471) of the *Antidotarium*, translated by D. Goltz, in *Mittelalterliche Pharmazie und Medizin dargestellt an Geschichte und Inhalt des Antidotarium Nicolai, mit einen Nachdruck der Druckfassung con 1471*, Stuttgart, 1976

Foster, Steven, *101 Medicinal Herbs: An Illustrated Guide*, Loveland, Colorado: Interweave Press, 1998

Harvey, Barbara, *Living and Dying in England, 1100–1540: The Monastic Experience*, Oxford: Clarendon Press, and New York: Oxford University Press, 1993

Hunt, Tony, *Popular Medicine in Thirteenth-Century England: Introduction and Texts*, Cambridge and Wolfeboro, New Hampshire: Brewer, 1990

Liber de simplici medicina dictus "Circus instans," in *Practica vel Breviarium Johannis Serapionis* (Lyons, 1525), fos. Ccxxiii-lii; translated by P. Dorveaux as *Le livre des simples médecines*, Paris: Société française de la médecine, 1913

Whiteman, Robin, and Rob Talbot, *Brother Cadfael's Herb Garden: An Illustrated Companion to Medieval Plants and Their Uses*, Boston: Little, Brown, 1996

Philokalia

The *Philokalia* ("the love of beauty") is a collection of 4th- to 15th-century Greek and Syriac ascetic and mystical texts on Hesychasm (stillness) and the Jesus Prayer, edited by Nikodemos of the Holy Mountain (c. 1749–1809) and Makarios Notaros of Corinth (1731–1805). All the texts were in Greek, with the exception of two Latin texts that had been translated into Greek in Byzantine times. The *Philokalia* is in the tradition of the collection of Origen's writings (also called the *Philokalia*, compiled by Basil the Great [c. 330–379] and Gregory of Nazianzus [329/30–389/90] in 358–359) but has more in common with the *Apophthegmata or Sayings of the Desert Fathers* of Egypt (fourth to fifth century).

The *Philokalia* was first published in Greek at Venice in 1782. In 1893 a second Greek edition was published at Athens and added Patriarch Kallistos' writings on prayer. A five-volume third edition was published between 1957 and 1963, also at Athens. In 1793 Paisy Velichkovksy (1722–1794) translated a selection of the texts into Church Slavic. Theophan the Recluse (1815–1894) published a greatly expanded Russian edition in five volumes from 1876 to 1890 titled *Dobrotolubiye*, and Ignatius Brianchininoff (1807–1867) also made a Russian translation, published in 1857. In 1946 Dumitru Staniloae (1903–1993) began a Romanian translation that was completed with the eighth volume in 1986. He added new biographical notes, full textual commentaries, and additional texts. The new texts are by Maximus the Confessor (c. 580–662), Symeon the New Theologian (949–1022), Gregory Palamas (c. 1296–1359), and a number of contemporary Romanian writers. G.E.H. Palmer, Philip Sherrard, and Kallistos Ware began a complete English translation in 1979. Palmer died in 1984 as the proofs for the third volume were being corrected, and the fourth volume appeared in 1995 under the editorship of Ware and Sherrard, the latter of whom died in 1995 just before its publication. The fifth and concluding volume has yet to be published. Earlier selections from the texts in English were compiled by E. Kadloubovsky and Palmer as *Writings from the Philokalia on Prayer of the Heart* (1951) and *Early Fathers from the Philokalia* (1954). These were translations made from Theophan's Russian translation rather than from the original Greek.

The *Philokalia* was compiled during a period in the 18th century when the Greek Orthodox world was under the rule of the Ottoman Turk Empire (*Turcocratia*). On one side the Greek Church had become entrenched in conservatism and self-preservation to the detriment of creative development; on the other side ideas of the Western Enlightenment were becoming increasingly current among educated Greeks. A group of monks on Mount Athos, the *Kollyvades* (a name derived from their insistence on strictly observing the rules of liturgical services, including eating boiled wheat, or *kollyva*, at memorial services), rallied to the call. They believed that the only true salvation for the Greek nation would be through a return to the authentic spiritual roots of Orthodox Church, which meant a return to the Fathers. At the same time these monks of Athos did not favor restrictive parochialism but rather were inflamed with a vision of the One, Holy, Catholic, and Apostolic Church. Most prominent among this group were Nicodemos of the Holy Mountain and Macarius of Corinth, both staunch proponents of Hesychasm. The *Philokalia* is the fruit of their joint labors.

The *Philokalia* is a deeply involving guidebook to the contemplative life (*theoria*). Its basic purpose is reflected in the subtitle of the 1782 edition: that through the love of the beautiful, "the intellect (*nous*) is purified, illumined, and made perfect." Thus, the emphasis of these texts is to lead one to the inner discipline of guarding the intellect and of achieving pure prayer, and ultimately to behold the vision of God. This constitutes the practice of Hesychasm. It is very important to understand that Hesychasm is not a world unto itself but is integrally connected to the sacramental and liturgical life of the Church. The writers of the texts and their audiences were steeped in the Orthodox monastic tradition as well as in church life. Thus, a basic condition assumed by the writers is not so much that one be a monk as that one be actively involved in the sacramental and liturgical life of the Orthodox Church. Only then can the individual fully participate in what the texts have to offer. Another basic requirement needed for participation in the Hesychastic way is to commit oneself to repentance. Rather than only to be sorry for one's sins, it means to have a change of mind (*metanoia*) involving radical conversion wherein one becomes fully centered on God.

According to Bishop Kallistos (Ware), the distinguishing characteristic of the texts is that monks wrote them but intended them for both monks and laity. The need for guidance by a spiritual father is continually emphasized. Spiritual life is always integrally connected with theological doctrine, especially Trinitarian and Christological thought. Internal consistency rather than external rules regulates the spiritual life. Some important concepts that reoccur are vigilance (*nepsis*), attentiveness (*procoche*), discrimination (*diakrisis*), dispassion (*apatheia*), stillness (*hesychia*), and the constant recollection of God through unceasing prayer, especially the Jesus Prayer ("Jesus Christ, Son of God, have mercy on me a sinner."). The writers are drawn mostly from the tradition of Evagrius Ponticus (346–399) and Maximus the Confessor (c. 580–662). Some of the other, better-known writers include John Cassian (c. 360–c. 435), Mark the Ascetic (fifth century), Nilos the Ascetic (fifth century), Symeon the New Theologian (949–1022), Gregory of Sinai (c. 1265–1346), and Gregory Palamas (c. 1296–1359). The collection omits many important Greek theologians, including the Cappadocian Fathers and Nicolas Cabasilas (Ware, "The Hesychast Renaissance," 1986).

The mind-heart dichotomy in contemplative prayer is an area of some confusion in the texts. The writings of Evagrius describe how God is known in contemplative prayer through the activity of the intellect or mind (*nous*). However, *nous* is not intended to mean exclusively the faculty of discursive reason but more the intuitive comprehension of spiritual truth. A second school of thought emphasizes the heart (*kardia*) as the center of prayer. Heart in this context refers more to a way of knowing than to any notion of affection or emotion. Especially the Macarian Homilies heal this rift by locating the intellect in the heart so that the heart is the conjunction of soul and body. Thus, for example, when the Jesus Prayer is referred to as the "prayer of the heart," one must understand *heart* in a comprehensive way that includes the whole person. The same is true for *nous*.

The *Philokalia* has become something of a literary classic in the Western world, largely as the result of the popularity of the anonymous *The Way of a Pilgrim*. However, the *Philokalia* is obviously much more than a literary text and much more than a work that one picks up and puts down at leisure. It is, in fact, the embodiment of a call to God, which is a soul-shattering event. This is why the work should be used carefully in conjunction with spiritual direction and, preferably, in the context of active participation in the sacramental and liturgical life of the Orthodox Church.

Michael D. Peterson

See also Cassian, John; Elders, Russian Monastic (Startsi); Evagrius Ponticus; Macarian Homilies; Mount Athos, Greece; Orthodox Monasticism; Paisy Velichkovsky; Palamas, Gregory, St.; Russia: History; Spirituality: Eastern Christian; Symeon the New Theologian, St.; Theology, Eastern Christian; Vision, Mystical: Eastern Christian

Further Reading

Bacovcin, Helen, translator, *The Way of a Pilgrim and The Pilgrim Continues His Way: A New Translation*, Garden City, New York: Image Books, 1978

Bobrinskoy, Boris, "Encounter of Traditions in Greece: St. Nicodemus of the Holy Mountain (1749–1809)," in *Christian Spirituality: Post-Reformation and Modern*, edited by Louis Dupré, Don E. Saliers, and John Meyendorff, New York: Crossroad, 1989

Kadloubovsky E., and G.E.H. Palmer, translators, *Early Fathers from the Philokalia: Together With Some of the Writings of St. Abba Dorotheus, St. Isaac of Syria, and St. Gregory Palmas*, London: Faber and Faber, 1954

Nikodemos of the Holy Mountain, and Makarios of Corinth, compilers, *The Philokalia: The Complete Text*, 4 vols., translated and edited by G.E.H. Palmer, Philip Sherrard, and Kallistos Ware, London: Faber and Faber, 1979–1995

Palmer, G.E.H., translator, *Writings from the Philokalia on Prayer of the Heart*, London: Faber and Faber, 1951; Boston: Faber and Faber, 1992

Scrima, Andre, "The Hesychastic Tradition: An Orthodox-Christian Way of Contemplation," in *Traditional Modes of Contemplation and Action: A Colloquium Held at Rothko Chapel, Houston, Texas*, edited by Yusuf Ibish and Peter Lamborn Wilson, Tehran: Imperial Iranian Academy of Philosophy, 1977

Sherrard, Philip, "The Revival of Hesychast Spirituality," in *Christian Spirituality: Post-Reformation and Modern*, edited by Louis Dupré, Don E. Saliers, and John Meyendorff, New York: Crossroad, 1989

Temple, Richard, "Silence of the Heart," *Parabola* 15:2 (1990)

Ware, Kallistos, "Ways of Prayer and Contemplation: I. Eastern," in *Christian Spirituality: Origins to the Twelfth Century*, edited by Bernard McGinn and John Meyendorff, New York: Crossroad, 1985; London: Routledge, 1986

Ware, Kallistos, "The Hesychast Renaissance," in *The Study of Spirituality*, edited by Cheslyn Jones, Geoffrey Wainwright, and Edward Yarnold, New York: Oxford University Press, and London: SPCK, 1986

Pilgrimages, Buddhist

The practice of pilgrimage is found in most of the world great religions, yet its study as a religious phenomenon is quite recent, especially in the context of Buddhism. For its analysis different approaches have been adopted, the major ones being sociological and anthropological. For a good summary of the state of affairs and a comprehensive bibliography on the subject, see Reader and Swanson's (1997) article on "Pilgrimage in the Japanese Religious Tradition."

Pilgrimage within Buddhism is often categorized as popular religion. The practices of going to sacred places, worshiping idols, or turning prayer wheels are often contrasted to the more sober practice of meditation, performed within the confines of monasteries or secluded places. Consequently, one may view the development of pilgrimages as tangential to the tradition founded by the Buddha and his closest disciples. It could be thought of as something that evolved to accommodate the spiritual needs of laypeople, leaving behind or ahead (depending on one's understanding of the development of Buddhism as a whole) the community of monks and nuns. This dichotomous view of Buddhism might be appropriate to some extent: one cannot deny, even today, the tendency to value the merits of one form of spiritual practice above others, thereby establishing a kind of hierarchy among spiritual seekers. However, such a view would disregard one of the most important characteristics of Buddhism, namely, its ability to convey the essence of its teachings in a variety of forms. The Buddha himself did not hesitate to praise the virtues of the true Brahmin or to encourage the practice of Hindu rituals for the sake of transmitting his liberating message.

It is often difficult to evaluate the impact of a spiritual practice. Very often one must accept the words of those who belong to the tradition that promotes it. Even if the insider's view is not taken as reliable, it nevertheless remains an interesting subject of investigation. Whatever the origins of a spiritual practice, it is fascinating to see how a religious tradition succeeded in raising it to the status of a full-fledged means of emancipation. For example, even if a practice clearly appeared as a manifestation of popular aspirations, it may, through the ingenuity and wisdom of those who adopted it, have become an expression of a very profound spiritual insight. Thus, the believer's testimony becomes an important point of reference, enabling us to see relationships with other practices that at first sight appear different.

Thus, the main concern of this article is twofold: first, to discuss the spiritual significance of pilgrimage and, more specifically, how this practice can be seen as a form of meditation and, second, to present the contribution of Buddhist communities and organizations in promoting this type of religious practice. Whereas the first aspect deals more with philosophical and religious considerations, the second allows us to describe some of the major Buddhist sites of pilgrimage and discuss their importance as religious and tourist centers.

Buddhist Pilgrimage: Origins and Spiritual Significance

According to the *Mahāparinibbāna Sutta* of the *Dīgha Nikāya*, the Buddha himself established the practice of pilgrimage:

> Ānanda, there are four places that the believer should visit with feelings of reverence. Which are they? "Here the Tathāgata was born" is the first (Lumbinī). "Here the Tathāgata became fully awakened" is the second (Bodh Gayā). "Here the Tathāgata set in motion the Wheel of Dhamma" is the third (Sārnāth). "Here the Tathāgata entered Parinirvāṇa" is the fourth (Kuśinagara). (*DN* II–140)

This practice was open to all categories of spiritual seekers: "And Ānanda, the faithful monks and nuns, male and female lay-followers will come to those places" (*DN* II–141). However, its fruits seemed not to be what all Buddhists should ultimately strive for, that is, *nirvāṇa*: "And whoever should die while making the pilgrimage to these sites with a heart established in faith will, at the breaking up of the body after death, be reborn in a realm of heavenly happiness" (*DN* II–141).

Historically speaking, little is known of the practice of pilgrimage after the death of the Buddha. The first accounts of this practice are from Aśoka's inscriptions. Aśoka was a Mauryan emperor who reigned about 100 years after the death of the Buddha. According to the legends this emperor carved inscriptions on pillars and rock slabs that were scattered on almost the entire sub-Indian peninsula. These inscriptions contain information about historical events related to his reign as well as moral precepts that ought to be followed by his subjects. For example, one learns from one such inscription carved on a pillar found at Lumbinī, the birthplace of the Buddha, that Aśoka came there as a pilgrim 20 years after his coronation. According to the *Aśokāvadāna* (Accounts of Aśoka), this emperor, after his conversion to Buddhism, asked the Buddhist master Upagupta to show him the places where the Buddha performed miracles or where he has just been present. Then Aśoka, accompanied by Upagupta, went on a grand pilgrimage throughout India for 256 days. At each site he ordered the construction of a stūpa (monument containing the Buddha's relics); at some places, such as Lumbinī, he had pillars erected. Thus, from the original four sites, which, according to tradition, were very early increased to eight to include Rājagṛha (where the Buddha tamed the maddened elephant Nālagiri), Srāvastī (the site of an event known as the Miracle of the Pairs), Vaiśālī (where monkeys offered the Buddha a gift of honey), and Sāṃkaśya (where the Buddha descended from the heavenly realms after teaching the Dharma to his mother), the number of places and locations where Buddhists could recollect the important events and deeds of the founder of their spiritual tradition multiplied.

In a different connection the idea of going back to the sources is a very important factor in the development of Buddhism. When the teachings of the Buddha spread beyond the limits of the Indian peninsula, the new converts always felt the need, for spiritual as well as political reasons, to travel to India either to get better training, to receive official accreditation, or simply to gather new scriptures. Such is the case of the Chinese pilgrims Fa-hsien (early fifth century), Hsüan-tsang, and I-ching (seventh century), to whom we owe most of our knowledge of Buddhism during the second half of the first millennium. Tibetans also made pilgrimages to India for the same reasons. In this regard one should not forget to count as pilgrimage sites, especially for the monks, the famous Buddhist universities of Nālandā and Vikramaśīla. When Buddhism became well established in China, that country became in turn a place of spiritual inspiration for the Japanese Buddhists.

With regard to the historical and spiritual dimensions of Buddhist pilgrimage, one may add the practice of representing in bas-reliefs, as seen at Bhārhut and Sāñcī, or in single portable icons, the major events of the Buddha's life. As pointed out by John Huntington, through icons the pilgrimage began to travel with the devotee rather than the devotee to the pilgrimage. The development of this iconography might then reveal something about the Buddhist attitude toward pilgrimage sites: these sites are ultimately sacred not because they are places where mythological events occurred, as a result of which they might be endowed with some kind of spiritual energy, but because they, like their symbolic representations, have the capacity to kindle awareness of various spiritual realities. In other words the site of Lumbinī is important not because *the Buddha* was born there but because there the Buddha *was born*. Here it is the idea of being born as a human being that ultimately matters, not the fact that it is the historical Buddha's birthplace.

The idea of being reborn as a human being is undoubtedly an important theme of Buddhist meditation. Buddhists view such an event, in contrast to the possibility of ending up as an animal or a hungry ghost, as a great opportunity and a unique juncture. Not to be wasted in doing futile tasks, it is a moment that should be dedicated as much as possible to the practice of Buddhist virtues. Countless passages in the inspirational literature of Buddhism can be cited as examples of this reflection/meditation. For example, Tsong kha pa, a Tibetan scholar of the 15th century, situated such a meditation within the first stages of a devotee's spiritual progression. As he explained, the devotee should first cultivate an attitude of renunciation by meditating on the rarity and value of a human rebirth. Then he or she meditates on karma and its possible destinies together with their inherent sufferings and spiritual opportunities. Through a series of such meditations, the devotee is brought to the next stage, which is the development of compassion, and ultimately to the realization of emptiness. Similarly, the place where the Buddha became enlightened (Bodh Gayā) might trigger a reflection/meditation on the possibility of one's own spiritual emancipation – this is the third Noble Truth. Sārnāth can remind us of the importance and the value of the Dharma (the teachings of the Buddha), and finally Kuśinagara, where the Buddha passed away or entered Parinirvāṇa, might become the occasion to contemplate one of the cardinal truths of Buddhism, namely, the impermanence of all things. Thus, each pilgrimage site, or a representation thereof, can serve as a source of spiritual inspiration, and visiting these sites with a feeling of reverence, as prescribed by the Buddha, is comparable if not identical to engaging in meditative practices in a monastery.

Viewed in this light the Buddhist practice of pilgrimage can be compared to more specific spiritual practices that evolved in the course of Buddhist history, especially the practice of *buddhānusmṛti*, which likely is known to all schools of Buddhism and consists of recollecting the special qualities and virtues of the Buddha. One of the fruits of this practice is, according to Buddhaghosa, a Buddhist commentator of the fifth century, to enhance mindfulness and understanding and to come to feel as if one were living in the Buddha's presence. In this regard it might be noteworthy to relate Piṅgiya's story, as told in the *Sutta Nipāta* of the Pāli Canon, likely one of the oldest extant Buddhist texts. Piṅgiya was asked why he would not spend all his time with the Buddha. He replied that it was not necessary because he could see the Buddha with his mind as clearly as with his eyes. As a result of this, Piṅgiya could experience the powers of confidence and joy and of intellect and awareness. (*SN* 1131–49)

To sum up this first part, the practice of pilgrimage, despite its popular or lay origins, is not to be viewed as an isolated practice within the structure of Buddhist spirituality. On the contrary it can be seen as an adaptation or an alternative, depending on one's point of view, to the most fundamental spiritual practice of Buddhism, namely, the cultivation of mindfulness. Thus, a visit to Buddhist pilgrimage sites can yield spiritual benefits that exceed the simple acquisition of merits. For this reason the maintenance of a pilgrimage site may be deemed to be as important as the construction of a monastery or even the careful copying of a sacred text.

Actual Buddhist Pilgrimage Sites in India

For many centuries most of the pilgrimage sites relating to the major events of the Buddha's life appeared to have been abandoned if not forgotten. Mainly because of the efforts of the 19th-century archaeologists, they were rediscovered and made known to us today. For example, such is the case of Lumbinī, where in 1896 a German archaeologist found a broken pillar bearing Aśoka's inscriptions that marked the site as the Buddha's birthplace. In discussing the spiritual significance of Buddhist pilgrimage, this article hinted that the development of iconography might have indirectly contributed to the falling into oblivion of the actual pilgrimage sites by favoring a shift of attention to symbolic representations. However, the main reason for their disappearance is the fact that Buddhism itself had, from the 12th century on, practically no devotees in India. Even today this historical reality makes it difficult to identify the sites that were visited by earlier pilgrims, such as Fa-hsien or Hsüan-tsang, as they were either totally wiped out by successive foreign invasions or taken over by other religious traditions. Thus, the sites that can be visited today are results of the efforts, on the one hand, of the newly established Buddhist communities that revitalized them as spiritual centers, and on the other, of the Indian government that transformed them into tourist destinations. Presented here are the cases of Bodh Gayā, the place of the Buddha's enlightenment, and Sārnāth, where the Buddha taught his first sermon. These places have been chosen because the contribution of the various Buddhist communities is probably the most visible here.

1. Bodh Gayā

The location of this pilgrimage site has never been doubted. It has been visited by Buddhist and Hindu pilgrims for over 2,000 years. Again owing to the accounts of the Chinese pilgrims Fa-hsien and Hsüan-tsang, we know some details about the development of this site. For example, Fa-hsien who visited it in 409, reported the presence of only three monasteries. Hsüan-tsang, who came to Bodh Gayā two centuries later, described a complex of many structures, the most important being the Mahābodhi Temple. During his time this temple was a splendid three-storied building standing 160 or 170 feet high. Today it is still the most impressive structure to be seen at Bodh Gayā. However, the Mahābodhi Temple is not the holiest place of this pilgrimage site; the most venerated spot is the Vajrāsana (Diamond-Throne), a carved stone seat between the wall of the temple and the Bodhi Tree marking just where the Buddha sat when he reached enlightenment. For the Buddhists this spot is the very center of the universe.

From Hsüan-tsang we also learned that in Bodh Gayā a Sri Lankan monastery was occupied by 1,000 monks of the Theravāda tradition. It is said that the Sri Lankan monks maintained a presence there through the end of the 13th century. These monks remained in Bodh Gayā despite the various invasions that occurred in this part of India from the beginning of the 11th century. Some of these invasions damaged the buildings of the site, including the Mahābodhi Temple, which was partly restored owing to the support of Burmese kings. However, with the continuing presence of Muslims, the presence of Buddhist monks at Bodh Gayā became impossible. We do not know when they left, but it is said that toward the end of the 16th century Hindu devotees resettled the site, which had long been deserted.

In 1812 the Mahābodhi Temple was in ruins. Bodh Gayā was no longer recognized as a Buddhist sacred site. It took the efforts of many individuals as well as Buddhist communities from Burma, Japan, and Sri Lanka to convince the English and later the Indian authorities to hand over the responsibilities of caring for the site to the Buddhists. This concerted effort led to the founding of the Mahābodhi Society in 1891 and finally to the official recognition of Bodh Gayā as a Buddhist site in 1949. Since 1953 Bodh Gayā has been developed as an international pilgrimage site owing to the Buddhists from Sri Lanka, Thailand, Burma, Tibet, Bhutan, and Japan who have established monasteries and temples within walking distance of the Mahābodhi compound. Today the site of the Buddha's enlightenment is visited by Buddhists and tourists from all over the world and functions as a place of inspiration and learning.

2. *Sārnāth*

The place where the Buddha gave his first teaching is located about six miles north of the city of Vārāṇasī (Benares), one of the most sacred places in India. Even before the Buddha's time, this city had already acquired a reputation among the spiritual seekers of ancient India. Thus, it was natural for the Buddha to start his teaching career there. After his death and the establishment of the first Buddhist communities, the city became important not only as a pilgrimage site but also as monastic center. Buddhism prospered at Sārnāth under the patronage of kings and wealthy laypeople who over the centuries had monasteries, temples, and shrines built and maintained up to the destructive invasions mentioned earlier.

Again owing to the Mahābodhi Society and the concerted efforts of Buddhist communities around the world, the site of Sārnāth has been restored. Archaeological excavations have revealed many artifacts witnessing the intense activity of the early Buddhist monastic orders that had established themselves there. One of its most important structures is the Dhamekh Stūpa, a solid, round tower 93 feet in diameter at its base and 128 feet high. According to archaeologists this stūpa might have been built prior to the reign of Aśoka.

Today Sārnāth, in addition to being a pilgrimage site, is an important religious center. Outside the boundaries of the site, one can find temples and educational institutions recently established by monks of the Tibetan and Burmese Buddhist traditions.

FRANCIS BRASSARD

See also Bodh Gayā, India; Buddhaghosa; Buddhism: Overview; China; Festivals, Buddhist; India: Sites; Kandy, Sri Lanka; Kyoto, Japan; Meditation: Buddhist Perspectives; Mount Hiei, Japan; Mount Kōya, Japan; Mountain Monasteries, Buddhist; Nagano, Japan; Pilgrims to India, Chinese; Shikoku, the Pilgrimage Island of Japan; Stūpa; Travelers: Buddhist

Further Reading

Bagri, S.C., *Buddhist Pilgrimages and Tours in India*, Noida: Trishul Publications, 1992

Huntington, John, "Pilgrimage as Image: The Cult of the Aṣṭamahāpratihārya, Part I," *Orientations* 18:4 (April 1987)

Lamotte, Etienne, *Histoire du Bouddhisme indien*, Louvain: Publications universitaires, 1958

McKay, Alex, editor, *Pilgrimage in Tibet*, Surrey, England: Curzon, 1998

Reader, Ian, and Paul L. Swanson, "Editor's Introduction: Pilgrimage in the Japanese Religious Tradition," *Japanese Journal of Religious Studies* (1997)

Tulku, Tarthang, editor, *Holy Places of the Buddha*, Berkeley, California: Dharma Publishing, 1994

Pilgrimages, Christian: Eastern Europe

Soon after they received Christianity, the peoples of Eastern Europe shared the common Christian aspiration to visit the holiest places of their faith. Those who had been baptized by the Greek Church traveled to Mount Athos, Constantinople, and the Holy Land, whereas those belonging to the Latin Church went mostly to Rome or Santiago de Compostela and also to Cologne and Aix-la-Chapelle (Aachen). Through the centuries these pilgrims (*palomniki*) have enriched Old Slavic literatures with many precious accounts. One of the very first is the travel book of Daniel, "abbot of the Russian land," who lived in Chernihiv (Ukraine) and tells us about his pilgrimage to Jerusalem in the years 1104 to 1107. Six centuries later a Kievan, Vasilii Grigorovich Barskii, peregrinated for 23 years, first across Poland, Hungary, Austria, and Italy and then all through the Greek islands to Egypt and Palestine (1723–1747), leaving us a vivid, personal testimony. Such accounts were kept for purposes of edification and also to dissuade other would-be wanderers by offering them readings that should quench their curiosity.

It is relatively more difficult to get a clear picture of pilgrimage customs in Eastern Europe itself. Some prominent national

Pilgrims visiting the Cathedral of the Dormition (Uspensky Cathedral), Holy Trinity–St. Sergius Monastery, Sergeyev Posad (Zagorsk), Russia, 16th century.
Photo courtesy of Robert E. Jones

or supranational centers are already well studied, but a complete mapping of local devotions is still a long way from having been completed. Naturally the divide between Eastern and Western Christianity makes itself strongly felt on this subject, and the Ottoman conquest of the Balkans disrupted many local pilgrimage traditions. Examples of the differences (as well as of certain similarities) between the Slavia Orthodoxa (i.e., the Orthodox Slavic world) and the other Eastern European nations, belonging to the tradition of the Latin Church, can be examined by comparing Kievan and imperial Russia on one side and Poland-Lithuania on the other.

Among the Eastern Slavs the main places of pilgrimages are famous monasteries where the tomb of the saint-founder is the focus of worship. The birthplace of monasticism in Kievan Russia (Rus'), the Kievan Cave monastery (founded c. 1051), always enjoyed a special devotion from the ruling elite (whether princes of the Rurikid dynasty, the Romanov family, or the Cossack atamans) and the commoners. Further West in Volhynia the Dormition monastery of Pochaev (founded in the 13th century) rose to prominence with abbot Job (Ioann Zhelezo, d. 1651), who was revered as a saint after his death. For a century (1713–1831) the abbey became a Uniate center, then it was forcibly returned to Orthodoxy by the Russian authorities and used as a base for the liquidation of the Uniate Church in Ukraine. In Russia the principal cenobitic foundations of the 14th to 15th century became pilgrimage sites. The most famous one was the Trinity St. Sergius monastery (in Sergeyev Posad, known under the Soviet period as Zagorsk, north of Moscow). As early as the mid–15th century, pilgrimages of commoners and visits by the grand prince of Moscow to the tomb of Sergius are documented, especially on the anniversary of Sergius' death (25 September 1392). Basil (Vasilii) II (1425–1462) swore peace with his cousins in the Trinity abbey-church in 1442 and was arrested by one of them, in the very same place, in 1446. Ivan the Terrible (1533–1584) turned the pilgrimage to the Trinity into a court ritual, and the first Romanov czars followed suit. During the Petersburg period the bond between the imperial dynasty and Sergius was kept tight, and the whole Russian population became familiar with the reputation of the abbey through oral tales and popular engravings. Foreigners were usually treated with a trip to "Troitza," where they could get a taste of the "ebullient" Russian piety. In 1892 the fifth-centenary pilgrimage to the Trinity drew a crowd estimated at one million, including the future czar Nicholas II. In the second half of the 19th century, the hermitage of Optina, where four successive "elders" (startsi) devoted themselves to spiritual guidance, was also a place of pilgrimage of sorts.

Besides the cult of holy monks, the Eastern Slav tradition venerates numerous wonder-working icons of the Mother of God, associated with the delivery from invasions or epidemics. They can be found in monasteries and in some parish churches. Old Russian religious literature is rich in short or elaborate "tales" (*povest'* or *skazanie*) celebrating the power of these icons. Among the most revered was the one kept in the monastery of Tikhvin (northeast of Novgorod), which began to be visited by the Russian sovereign under Grand Prince Basil III (1505–1533). Court pilgrimage to Tikhvin was still in fashion in the 18th century, although the icon left the future empress Catherine II (1762–1796) unimpressed. She wrote in her memoirs, "No one saw [the image] because it is so black, that one would not distinguish it from the board on which it is supposed to be painted."

During the 19th century and possibly earlier, some Russian subjects vowed to spend their life as pilgrims, traveling from one place to another. They commanded an instinctive respect in the population, but czarist police looked upon them with extreme suspicion and sometimes prevented them from circulating. They were called "wanderers"(*stranniki*), but the same term was used to designate an extremist fraction of the Old Believers, also known as the "runaways" (*beguny*), who refused altogether to acknowledge imperial authority. The prestige of pilgrims among the population is further attested by the popularity of a series of texts known as the *Genuine Tales of a Wanderer to His Spiritual Father*, published in Kazan in 1870 and 1881 and translated into several languages by the end of the 19th century. The book takes the form of a spiritual conversation between the two men, as the first, a young widower, describes his peregrinations from Ukraine to Irkust (Siberia), then back, and to Solovki on the White Sea.

In Poland the first centers of pilgrimage were the episcopal towns of Gniezno and Krakow. In Gniezno the remains of bishop-martyr Aldalbert-Wojcech (d. 997) were revered by Germans, Polish and Bohemian alike, at least until the 14th century. They were also coveted and robbed by Czech Prince Bretislav in

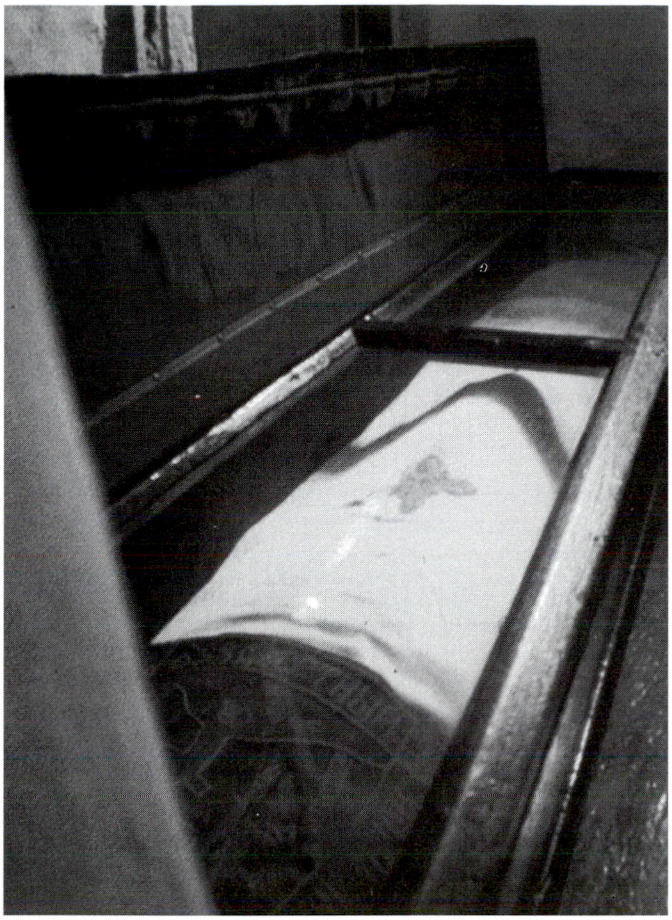

Body of Nestor, Monastery of the Caves (Petcherskaia Lavra), Kiev, Ukraine, 17th century. Nestor wrote the *Russian Primary Chronicle* (12th century).
Photo courtesy of Robert E. Jones

1038, although the Poles pretended that they had kept part of the relics. In Krakow Bishop Stanislas, assassinated in 1079 by order of King Boleslas, became an object of cult long before his official canonization (1254). By the 15th century 17 other new saints were revered in Krakow, most of them monks. This is the period when the monastery of Częstochowa, on Jasna Góra (near Katowice), started to be the main Polish pilgrimage site. The abbey had been founded in 1382 as a local outpost for the Hungarian order of the Hermits of St. Paul. Its popularity was due to a wonder-working icon of the Mother of God, attributed to the apostle Luke, and known as the "Black Madonna," whose cult very much resembles the Eastern Slavic ones. The monastery sustained many sieges in times of peril for Poland (in 1430, 1466, 1702, 1771, and 1793 but above all in 1655 against the Swedish army), and the icon became a special protector of Polish national identity. It attracted Hungarian, Silesian, and Moravian pilgrims as well. It was solemnly crowned in 1717, and copies were exposed in churches all across Poland. The Black Madonna was also celebrated in hymns, in printed records of miracles (as early as 1523), in guides printed for pilgrims, and even in a novel, *Potop* (1886; *The Flood*), by Nobel Prize winner Henryk Sienkiewicz. Even today the pilgrimage to Częstochowa draws crowds, and the leader of the trade union Solidarity, turned president of Poland, Lech Walesa, showed special devotion to the icon.

Meanwhile the diverse regional and ethnic components of the Polish-Lithuanian state (which existed under various forms of organization between 1385 and 1795) identified themselves with more specific pilgrimage sites. Populations of Silesia and the Dabrow basin favored Piekary. In the Kielce region there was a traditional cult of the reliquary of the Holy Cross, located in the monastery of the Benedictines on Mount Łysiec (Łysogory, or Świętokrzyskie Gory). Zebrzydow was for the people of Krakow, Podolia, and a few Silesians, and Wilno was for the Lithuanians, whereas Wejherowo drew the Cachoubs and Catholic Pomeranians (although they celebrated the pilgrimage at different dates). The three last sites were pilgrimages to a calvary, a modern form of devotion developed in imitation of the Sacro Monte pilgrimage near Turin, Italy, created in the second half of the 16th century. Zebrzydow was the oldest Polish example, but from the end of the 16th century many calvaries were erected in the country.

In Hungary, Bohemia, and on the Balkan peninsula, the first local Christian cults were devoted mainly to saint-princes. A tendency existed, especially in Hungary, to transform them into a cult of the whole ruling dynasty. In the 14th century Hungarian and Czech sovereigns also "exported" these cults to Aix-la-Chapelle, Cologne, Nürenberg, and Rome, where they founded altars or chapels and offered some remains of their holy ancestors. At the same time Charles IV, king of Bohemia (1347) and Roman emperor (1349), promoted a new center of the state cults in the castle of Karlstein (near Prague), where he assembled an immense collection of relics. Other, more popular places of pilgrimage were traditionally established in the vicinity of local economic centers, for example, the Valley of the Virgin near Pressburg (present-day Bratislava, Slovakia), Margit Island near Buda, and the chapel of St. Loup near Sopron (Hungary). Hungarian pilgrimages to holy springs can often be traced back to pagan traditions (as in the case of Jásd and Dénesfalva). At one and the same time, Mount Gerard (near Budapest) was supposed to be the place where the apostle of Hungary had suffered martyrdom and where witches held their Sabbath. Under Ottoman rule most of the Balkan princely sanctuaries lost their significance as pilgrimage sites to abbeys or episcopal towns. By holding the rank of patriarchate from 1394 to 1767, Ohrid (Achrida, Macedonia) became one of the main Orthodox centers in the region, but the most attractive place of pilgrimage for Balkanic Christians remained Mount Athos.

Finally Eastern Europe knew some "dissident" pilgrimage sites. During the Hussite crisis a community was established on so-called Mount Tabor (south of Prague) after Wenceslas IV, king of Bohemia (1363–1419), expelled the pro-Hussite Kelchpriester from Prague in the spring of 1419. Their partisans organized massive "pilgrimages to the mountain" (*pouty na hory*), and soon the Taborite faction, led by Jan Zizka, became one of the most radical against the official Church. It was subdued only by military action (1433–1434). In 19th-century Russia another irregular place of pilgrimage rose to prominence in

Nizhnii-Novgorod province: the Svetloe ozero, or ozero Svetloiar (Clear Lake). Around its banks came pilgrims from all the branches of Russian Orthodoxy for the feast of St. John the Baptist (24 June). They hoped to hear the bells of the "invisible town," supposed to have drowned miraculously in the lake, so as to avoid capture by the Tatars. At the same time they could enjoy the rare pleasure of open debate about faith between every sort of Old Believer and defender of the official Church. Spontaneous controversy, with endless quotations from Holy Scripture and dashes of self-made theology, furnished a fascinating spectacle for the people and the intelligentsia under the embarrassed scrutiny of the authority. The pilgrimage to Svetloe ozero knew its golden age between 1905 and 1918, when for a brief moment religious freedom was a reality in Russia. The novelist Mikhail Prishvin (1873–1954) captured that very moment in his book *U sten grada nevidimogo* (1909; *Under the Walls of the Invisible Town*). He recalls the description of the place made a few years earlier by Zinaida Hippius (1869–1945), who traveled there with her husband, Dmitrii Merezhkovskii (1866–1941), and notes the new self-confidence of the dissident believers. Like other religious demonstrations the pilgrimage to the Clear Lake was quickly suppressed by the Soviet regime.

PIERRE GONNEAU

See also Czech Republic; Częstochowa (Jasna Góra), Poland; Hungary; Mount Athos, Greece; Orthodox Monasticism: Slavic; Poland; Russia; Sergius of Radonezh, St.; Spirituality: Eastern Christian; Ukraine; Visual Arts, Eastern Christian: Painting

Further Reading

Bango, J.F., *Die Wallfahrt in Ungarn*, Vienna, 1978
Czarnowski, Stefan, "La culture religieuse des paysans polonais," *Archives de sciences sociales des religions* 65:1 (1988)
Majeska, George P., *Russian Travelers to Constantinople in the Fourteenth and Fifteenth Centuries*, Washington D.C.: Dumbarton Oaks Research Library and Collection, 1984
Müller, Klaus, *Itineraria rossica: Altrussische Reiseliteratur*, Leipzig: Reclam, 1991
Récits d'un pèlerin russe, Paris: Seuil, 1978
Seemann, Klaus-Dieter, *Die altrussische Wallfahrtsliteratur: Theorie und Geschichte eines literarischen Genres*, Munich: Fink, 1976
Stavrou, Theofanis G., and Peter R. Weisensel, *Russian Travelers to the Christian East from the Twelfth to the Twentieth Century*, Columbus, Ohio: Slavica, 1986
Wiesiolowski, Jacek, editor, *Pielgrzymki w kulturze średniowiecznej Europy*, Poznan: PTPN, 1993
Witkowska, Aleksandra, "The Cult of the Jasna Gora Sanctuary in the Form of Pilgrimages till the Middle of the 17th century," *Acta Poloniae historica* 61 (1990)

Pilgrimages, Christian: Near East

The Near East has played a key role in the history of both monasticism and pilgrimage. Christian monasticism made its earliest appearance toward the end of the third century in Egypt and Palestine. Pilgrimage to places in the Holy Land began after 324/25 and boomed considerably after Helena (d. c. 329), the mother of Constantine the Great (emperor 306–337), undertook a pilgrimage to Palestine in 326. Increasingly lay Christians as well as more famous holy figures displayed interest in visiting places where biblical events had occurred.

The supposed originator of community monasticism, Pachomius (c. 292–346), established a collective foundation in Tabennesis on the site of a deserted village beside the Upper Nile; the monastery incorporated a guest house where the rule required that visitors be housed. As monastic settlements grew in Egypt, Palestine, and Syria, they tended to include accommodation to provide for constant streams of pious travelers who often came from far away. In addition many memorial churches were built in parts of the Near East not to serve a specific community but to act as focal points for pilgrimage. Usually a staff of monks was attached to the church to serve the pilgrims, and a small monastery to house the staff was built nearby. At key pilgrimage sites monks and nuns produced and sold devotional materials while agriculture was developed to provide food for monks, priests, and pilgrims.

The fact that so many sacred figures came to settle in the Near East provided an added incentive for early followers of the faith to travel to the area. Such holy figures provided living proof of the present reality of miracles and demonstrated that the era of the apostles and the martyrs was not over. Antony the Great (c. 251–356), regarded by many as the father of monasticism, withdrew in the third century into the Natron valley northwest of Cairo and was followed by numerous other hermits. The growing number of sightseers that he attracted forced Anthony to withdraw to a ruined fortress on the edge of the desert where he lived in solitude for 20 years before becoming a teacher of other monks.

In the centuries following the foundation of Christianity, pilgrimage and monasticism can be seen to have reinforced each other in a number of ways. Pilgrim accounts as well as monastic settlements could, over time, endow the landscape of the Holy Land with powerfully charged significance. Thus, in the 380s the pilgrim Egeria refers to Carmel as the place where Elijah consecrated an altar to the Lord. Biblical episodes from Elijah's life that were not located specifically on Mount Carmel came subsequently to be placed there by monastic writers and pilgrims, and monasteries were founded over the centuries that encouraged pilgrims to come to the site. Egeria's account itself was picked up at the end of the seventh century by a monk called Valerius, who used it in a letter on the holy life addressed to his brethren in Spain and who presented Egeria's journey as a paradigm of spiritual virtue.

Monks in the Near East not only hosted pilgrims – and derived important income from them – but also relied on the influx of pious travelers to maintain their numbers. Both pilgrimage and monasticism catered for the ascetic ideals of the early faith, and often the decision to enter a cloister or settle in the wilderness of the Holy Land and its environs provided a way to make a pilgrimage permanent. It seems likely that pilgrims who became monks were motivated by seeing so many people from their own lands who had already decided to stay, for monasticism in some parts of the Near East (e.g., the Judaean desert) attracted followers from far distant parts of the world.

Many desert monks had experienced monastic life before arriving in the area, and they journeyed around the holy places for the express purpose of joining a monastery in the desert. Others were simply pilgrims who decided not to return home. Theodosius (423–529), who was born in the district of Caesarea, reached Jerusalem around 451 and went to the Judaean desert. His monastery, built over 20 years later on the southern bank of the Kidron Valley, became the largest in the Judaean desert, with an emphasis on social welfare expressed both in providing help for the elderly and infirm and in giving hospitality to pilgrims.

An important role for monks in the Near East, as elsewhere, has been that of guide to and guardian of holy places. According to Egeria's account of her visit to the Holy Land from 381 to 384, she was met in many places by monks and priests who lived on the site or in the vicinity. The monks pointed out sacred spots, at each of which a group might stop to read an appropriate passage from Scripture and to pray. Thus, they provided not only knowledge of the area but also liturgy, helping to turn travel through Palestine into a coherent religious experience. Egeria even talks of how monks themselves became one of the goals of her pilgrimage: the sight of holy, miracle-working monks of Syria was one of the highlights of her trip.

Despite the importance of the Near East as a place of pilgrimage, a physical journey to the Holy Land and associated sites was not always seen as an ideal part of monastic life. Leading reformers in the West, notably Bernard of Clairvaux (1090–1153), discouraged involvement in the Holy Land, as the monastic cloister was itself to be seen as a representation of Paradise. Pilgrimage to far-off lands could be regarded merely as a distraction from a stable, monastic vocation. Although a journey to the Holy Land could provide opportunities for salvation for the laity, such a function was perceived as unnecessary for regular clergy. Thus, in 1124 a proposed monastic pilgrimage to Jerusalem caused a crisis among Cistercians. When the abbot of Morimond set off for Jerusalem with some of his monks, Bernard accused him of deserting his flock (in fact the abbot died before reaching Jerusalem). In 1147 St. Bernard went so far as to write a letter to all Cistercian abbots, reminding them not to permit their monks to go to the Holy Land and recommending that monks who violated the prohibition be excommunicated.

The popularity of the Holy Land as a place of pilgrimage during the Middle Ages derived partly from its exceptional status as a living relic. In addition many pilgrims believed that the journey would allow them to break away from established, Benedictine forms of monasticism. A frequent aim was to found monastic communities that could reclaim an integrity evident among the earliest Christian monks. Many Latin (as well as Orthodox) monks consciously imitated their forebears who had settled in the Near East many centuries earlier. Thus, theological opposition to pilgrimage was largely ignored, and pilgrims from both Western Europe and the Byzantine world knew that they would find in Palestine monasteries associated with all of the major shrines: the Holy Sepulcher, the tomb of the Virgin, the grotto of the Nativity, Mount Tabor (the site of the Transfiguration), and so on.

Punctuating and often profoundly influenced pilgrimage practices as well as monastic life was the military and cultural influence of Islam. The holy cities of Palestine fell to the Muslims early in the seventh century, prompting a growth in the importance of Constantinople as an alternative destination for spiritual journeys. In 1071 Jerusalem was captured by the Seljuk Turks, who kept Christian pilgrims from worshiping at the holy sites. Such events, combined with the split between the Eastern and Western Churches that developed through the Middle Ages, meant that both Palestine and shrines in Western Europe became rather inaccessible to Orthodox pilgrims, who focused their attention instead on Constantinople as well as on the tombs of Orthodox saints in remote monastic settlements, such as Mount Athos or Meteora in Thessaly, Greece. Among Western Christians the threat from Islam helped launch the Crusades as part sacred journey, part military conquest. In 1095 believers in Europe were urged by Pope Urban II (1088–1099) to engage in an armed pilgrimage to rescue Jerusalem and the other holy places. Participants were offered indulgences, that is, remissions of the penance due for their sins.

A striking feature of the Crusades was the formation of military orders or societies of monk-knights (*Milites Christi*) who participated in the holy wars. Perhaps surprisingly an important figure in the encouragement of such orders was St. Bernard. Yet his emphasis fell not on the value of physical holy places per se, nor did he advocate that conventional monastic communities be reconstituted as fighting units. Rather he emphasized the spiritual benefits of crusading. He saw in the new militias the ideal means of salvation for Christians who showed no aptitude for traditional, physically inactive types of monastic life. In practice soldier-monks took vows of chastity and obedience; followed a form of community life, including fasts and vigils (with some dietary concessions to the needs of the military life); and assisted at the Divine Office. Battles and sieges were preceded and accompanied by prayer. The Knights of the Temple, the first to be constituted as a military order, were called into being partly to protect pilgrims from Muslim raiders. The Knights of St. John of Jerusalem began as a fraternity serving a hospice for poor and sick pilgrims in Jerusalem (Hospitallers) and then became a military organization from the 12th century. By 1180 the Order possessed 25 castles in Palestine.

Pilgrims, settlers, and soldiers continued to travel to the Near East during the Crusades, and a number of religious houses were set up to re-Christianize the area. However, in 1187 Jerusalem was reconquered for Islam by Saladin (1137–1193). The collapse of the Western presence in the 13th century led eventually to the dissolution of some of the military orders, notably the Templars in 1312. Nevertheless the image of the holy sites in Palestine remained potent in many parts of the world as a focus for spiritual meditation, even if most areas remained barred to Christian believers. Some holy sites, tended by monastic foundations, became the means through which pilgrims could gain a vicarious taste of the Holy Land. Thus, for example, Walsingham in England became a major shrine in the Middle Ages. Its founding myth told of how Jesus' house in Nazareth had been reconstructed in the local countryside, so that the associations of a holy place in Palestine were translated to a different, more accessible setting.

Walsingham itself has been undergoing a revival since the 20th century, although its monastic connections are now much reduced. Meanwhile in the Near East desert monasticism saw a resurgence in the 19th century. Indeed some of the customs and ways of life of the early monks have been maintained to this day. Pilgrimage to monasteries and associated Christian sites has rebounded, often under the impulse of tourism as well as of religious faith.

SIMON COLEMAN

See also Antony, St.; Bernard of Clairvaux, St.; Crusades; Desert Fathers; Egypt; Hospitality, Christian; Hospitallers (Knights of Malta since 1530); Israel/Palestine; Meteora, Thessaly, Greece; Mount Athos, Greece; Origins: Eastern Christian; Origins: Western Christian; Pachomius, St.; Spirituality: Eastern Christian; Templars

Further Reading

Chitty, Derwas J., *The Desert a City*, Oxford: Blackwell, 1966; Crestwood, New York: St. Vladimir's Seminary Press, 1966

Coleman, Simon, and John Elsner, *Pilgrimage: Sacred Travel and Sacred Space in the World Religions*, London: British Museum Press, 1995; as *Pilgrimage: Past and Present in the World's Religions*, Cambridge, Massachusetts: Harvard University Press, 1995

Hirschfeld, Yizhar, *The Judean Desert Monasteries in the Byzantine Period*, New Haven, Connecticut: Yale University Press, 1992

Hunt, E.D., *Holy Land Pilgrimage in the Later Roman Empire, A.D. 312–460*, Oxford: Clarendon Press, and New York: Oxford University Press, 1982

Jotischky, Andrew, *The Perfection of Solitude: Hermits and Monks in the Crusader States*, University Park: Pennsylvania State University Press, 1995

Lawrence, C.H., *Medieval Monasticism: Forms of Religious Life in Western Europe in the Middle Ages*, London and New York: Longman, 1984; 2nd edition, 1989

Milis, Ludovicus, *Angelic Monks and Earthly Men: Monasticism and Its Meaning to Medieval Society*, Woodbridge and Rochester, New York: Boydell Press, 1992

Sivan, H.S., "Pilgrimage, Monasticism, and the Emergence of Christian Palestine in the 4th Century," in *The Blessings of Pilgrimage*, edited by R. Ousterhout, Urbana: University of Illinois Press, 1990

Pilgrimages, Christian: Western Europe

Christian pilgrimage in Europe has been associated with monks and monastic establishments since early Christian times. Several shrines are dedicated to St. Benedict of Nursia, the sixth-century founder of Western monasticism, and numerous monasteries, old and new, are currently important as pilgrimage centers.

Pilgrimage, defined as the religiously motivated journey to a holy place, is an ancient and widespread type of voluntary travel. In many parts of the world, religiously sanctioned travel was a precursor to tourism, including various forms of a religious tourism that merges almost imperceptibly into pilgrimages of the present. Ancient pilgrim roads have often been converted into major thoroughfares for modern travelers, and these have long been principal routes of diffusion for techniques and ideas.

Pilgrimage shrines are special kinds of places that symbolize not only the relationship between humans and divinity but also sacral aspects of the human-environment relationship. Some shrines are located at monastic establishments, but many others are not. In a survey of 6,150 European pilgrimage places conducted between 1976 and 1988, I found 658 shrines located at monastic establishments (Nolan and Nolan, 1989). This represents slightly less than 11 percent of the shrines surveyed. Some kind of historical monastic association was indicated at an additional 266 shrines, suggesting that at least 15 percent of Europe's Christian pilgrimage shrines are related to the institution of monasticism. However, in this discussion I will use the term *monastic shrines* only for the 658 found at active monasteries and convents.

At some monastic shrines a monastery or convent existed before pilgrims began arriving. At others the monastic complex was established because pilgrims had already defined the place as the destination of their religiously inspired journeys. In either case symbiotic relationships often developed between monks and pilgrims. Monks or nuns can provide the infrastructure support needed by pilgrims as travelers. In turn pilgrims can bring prestige and economic support to a monastic establishment and its residents. Pilgrims also provide a communication channel for whatever message the monastic community might seek to spread among the faithful.

In some cases the pilgrimages and the offering traditions associated with them continue long after the monastic needs that they once served have disappeared. An example comes from the hilly regions of northern Portugal. Here modern pilgrims bring salt, wax, and eggs as offerings to district shrines marked by isolated country chapels at the sites of long-abandoned Benedictine monasteries. The monasteries were established during the 10th and 11th centuries by missionary monks who were attempting to restore Christianity in a region that had suffered during the eighth-century Muslim invasion of Iberia but had not been effectively occupied by followers of the Prophet Muhammed. These early medieval Benedictine establishments were agriculturally based and largely self-sufficient in their food needs. However, they were located some distance from the sea, so the monks would have needed salt. Wax was needed for candles that provided light after nightfall, and egg whites served as a binder for paints used in the illumination of manuscripts. Although none of these needs currently exist at the country shrine chapels, the tradition of offerings continues.

Nave and apse, Abbey Church of La Madeleine (Benedictine), Vézelay (Yonne), France, 12th century. From the 11th to the 14th century and after the supposed relics of Mary Magdalene attracted innumerable pilgrims.
Photo courtesy of Mary Schaefer

Obviously the relationship between pilgrimage destinations and monastic establishments in Europe is complex. Functioning monasteries make up only a small proportion of today's pilgrimage centers. Many monasteries are not pilgrimage shrines even though their historical or architectural significance might draw tourists or their residents may actively promote layman's retreats or spiritual encounter weekends. Thus, monastic shrines are a subset in Europe's contemporary pilgrimage field, and it is of some importance to know how they resemble or differ as a group from other shrines.

Subjects of Devotion

Nearly all pilgrimage shrines in Europe are centers of a special devotion focused on a particular holy person who is associated historically or symbolically with the pilgrimage center or with a relic or image venerated at the shrine. At 66 percent of European shrines in general, as well as at monastic shrines, the Virgin Mary, mother of Christ, is the primary subject of devotion. Christ-centered shrines represent 7.5 percent of all cases and are found in the same proportions at monastic shrines. Male and female saints make up the other subjects of devotion typically found at pilgrimage centers. Again no difference exists in these proportions between monastic shrines and shrines in general.

However, unusually high monastic associations do occur in the case of particular saints. For example, although monastic shrines account for only 11 percent of the shrines surveyed, half the 20 shrines dedicated to St. Francis of Assisi, the medieval founder of the Franciscan Order, are found at Franciscan monasteries. Many of these are located at places in Italy associated with significant events in the life of this charismatic 13th-century mystic. In the case of St. Benedict of Nursia, 28 percent of his shrines are located at Benedictine monasteries. Many of the others are found at the sites of former monasteries. Other saints whose shrines are especially likely to be found at monasteries are St. Mary Magdalene (19 percent), St. Michael the Archangel (18 percent), St. Roch (17 percent), and St. Anthony of Padua (16 percent). In contrast other popular saints with numerous pilgrimage centers are rarely if ever found as primary devotional subjects at monastic shrines. Examples include St. John the Baptist, St. Sebastian, and the Germanic cattle guardian St. Wendel.

Sacred Objects

From earliest times most Christian pilgrimages in Europe have focused on sacred objects that symbolize the holy person or persons honored at the shrine. Initially these cult objects were relics of various kinds, including the bodily remains of saints and objects associated with them. Especially powerful were relics of Christ's Passion, such as pieces of the True Cross, thorns from the Crown of Thorns, and earth from the Holy Land thought to be saturated with blood spilled during the Crucifixion. Images of holy persons, venerated in the East from early times, emerged as powerful cult objects in central and Western Europe toward the end of the first millennium A.D.

Cult objects in the form of relics and images give the place where they are enshrined a kind of sanctity that appears to be especially attractive as a focus for pilgrim devotions. Only 6 percent of Europe's pilgrimage shrines have no sacred object. Cult objects appear to be somewhat less critical for monastic shrines because 10 percent of these have no especially venerated image or relic to serve as a focus for pilgrim devotions. At these shrines devotional emphasis is usually placed on the mystique of the monastic complex or, occasionally, at a sacred water source within the complex.

Among the 90 percent of monastic shrines with cult objects, there are five venerated images for each cultus focused on a relic. However, relics of various kinds are more likely to be the principal cult object at monastic shrines than at shrines with no monastic association. Nineteen percent of the monastic shrines are focused on relics as compared with only 11 percent of other shrines. Relics of Christ's Passion tend to be concentrated at monastic shrines. These house 32 percent of all such relics described in the survey.

Cult Formation Stories

Most shrines have origin stories. Some of these stories are best considered as myths or legends, although accounts from shrines founded over the past few centuries are often historically documented. Regardless of the extent to which origin stories can be verified from the historical record, they serve as explanations for how and why the shrine was established. Typically they explain the association of a particular sacred place with a holy person and usually with a cult object symbolizing that person.

Origin stories told at monastic shrines fall into the same seven categories as those recorded from other shrines. However, the preponderance of one type of story over another is different (Table 1). Monastic shrines are much more likely than other shrines to be at significant sites, gaining their special sanctity from a relationship to events in the historical development of Christianity or in the lives of saints. This partly reflects the fact that many monastic shrines are quite old but also that they are frequently places associated with monks or nuns who became saints. They are also more likely than usual to have become pilgrimage centers after acquiring a sacred object from another place. To a considerable extent this results from a tradition of donating venerated images and relics to monastic establishments. Often the gift was made by a king, a powerful nobleman, or an important family. In addition noblewomen whose dowries included holy objects sometimes donated them to monasteries or convents. In still other cases established monasteries often provided important relics or images to new or struggling monasteries maintained by the same religious order.

Table 1: Types of Origin Stories

Shrine Story Type	% *Monastic Shrines*	% *Other Shrines*
Significant Site Shrines: Places related to the historical development of Christianity in a region or to events in the life of a saint.	30	14
Acquired Object Shrines: Cultus develops when a relic or an image is from another place and proves miraculous in its new setting.	19	14
Found Object Shrines: Cultus develops after an image or a relic is found, usually under strange circumstances.	13	14
Ex-Voto Shrines: Created as a thank offering for deliverance from catastrophe.	11	21
Spontaneous Miracle Shrines: Cultus develops as a result of a revelation of sacred power at the site other than through the finding of an object or an apparition.	10	15
Apparitional: Cultus develops as the result of a vision.	10	12
Devotional Shrines: Created as the result of individual or group devotion unrelated to miracles or unusual events.	7	5
Total	100	100

The only other type of cult formative story more commonly told at monastic shrines than at other shrines is of an individual or a group promoting a pilgrimage for purely devotional reasons. This is not an uncommon thing for members of a religious community to attempt, but development of an enduring pilgrimage cultus based on devotional promotion alone is rare. Unless a powerful cult object is acquired or discovered on site or the pilgrimage promoter achieves sainthood, devotional cults tend to fade with time.

The Temporal Dimension of Monastic Pilgrimage Foundings

Christian pilgrimage in Europe is rooted in the evolution of a religious tradition based on the life and teachings of Jesus Christ as interpreted by disciples and early evangelists and, as with any living religion, reinterpreted through the generations. Since at least the fifth century A.D., monastic establishments in Europe have been important in both the preservation and the reinterpretation of Christian traditions and appear to have been of major importance in the development of the region's pilgrimage ideals and circulation patterns.

The century of cult formation was recorded for 515 monastic shrines, or 78 percent of those identified in the survey (Table 2). Two thousand and ninety-three, or 38 percent, of the other shrines were dated by century. Table 3 indicates that monastic shrines are, on the average, somewhat older than other shrines for which dates were obtained. Very few monastic shrines were established before the fourth century A.D., but after that monastic cult formations increased. Slightly more than 25 percent of today's monastic shrines had become pilgrimage centers before the end of the 11th century.

The earliest European pilgrimage centers were established concurrently with the spread of the message of Christ's life, crucifixion, and resurrection throughout the Roman Empire during the first few centuries A.D. Tombs of early Christian martyrs provided the most important focus for European shrine establishment during the first four to five centuries after Christ.

In the early fourth century, Roman Emperor Constantine (306–337) decreed tolerance for the Christians. His mother, now known as St. Helen, made a pilgrimage to the Holy Land in

Table 2: Number of Monastic Shrines Founded by Century

Century of Pilgrimage Cult Formation	*Number of Monastic Shrines*
First, Second, and Third	2
Fourth	7
Fifth	7
Sixth	17
Seventh	11
Eighth	20
Ninth	20
Tenth	16
11th	32
12th	37
13th	47
14th	25
15th	46
16th	35
17th	85
18th	30
19th	26
20th	52

search of relics from the time of Christ, such as pieces of the True Cross, nails from the Crucifixion, and thorns from the Crown of Thorns. Many of these relics are said to have eventually found their ways into monastic shrines.

By the end of the fourth century, Christianity had become the official religion of the Roman Empire, and by the early fifth century the evolving belief system had spread beyond the confines of the disintegrating western Roman world to Ireland. Here, on Europe's Celtic fringe, shrines of the new religion were often superimposed on natural site features already considered to be sacred, and Celtic monasteries were established in ancient sacred places already visited by pilgrims.

Associations of men seeking a religious life were also developing on the Continent. Early in the sixth century, Benedict of Nursia retreated from worldly concerns to life of poverty, prayer, and hard work in the hilly region of Subiaco near Rome. Here, and later at Monte Cassino between Rome and Naples, he developed his Rule, which laid a foundation for the highly influential Benedictine Order. As Benedictine monasticism expanded some monasteries became centers of pilgrim devotion. Perhaps even more important for the development of Europe's medieval pilgrimage system was the Benedictine tradition of hospitality to wayfarers. This provided an important role in a travel infrastructure that eventually supported mass long-distance pilgrimage.

Table 3: Centuries of Pilgrimage Cult Formation

Centuries	*% Monastic Shrines*	*% Other Shrines*
First through seventh (1–699 A.D.)	9	5
Eighth through 11th (700–1099)	17	8
12th through 15th (1100–1499)	30	32
16th through 18th (1500–1799)	29	39
19th and 20th (1800–1988)	15	16
Total	100	100

During the seventh and eighth centuries, Christian pilgrimage traditions were affected by the expansion of Islam. Pilgrim access to the Holy Land was restricted as Muslims gained control of the Middle East, and Christian territory was reduced by Muslim occupation of North Africa and most of the Iberian Peninsula. However, even as many lands formerly Christian became Muslim, missionaries were taking Christianity to previously unconverted Germanic and Slavic peoples east of the Rhine and north of the Danube, often establishing monasteries and promoting pilgrimages as an inducement to conversion. Other missionaries were penetrating remote hinterlands where Europeans still clung to pagan beliefs. By the ninth century Christian pilgrimage centers were being reestablished in Iberia as the Christian reconquest of the peninsula moved southward. Throughout this period most shrines in the West focused on veneration of saints' relics as these cult objects were transferred north and west from Italy, the Holy Land, and Byzantium. Many of the recipients of these relics were monastic establishments.

In Europe the 11th century marked a major watershed in shrine establishment with the Truce of God movement, the Cluniac reform of Benedictine monasticism, a rapid increase in the proportion of shrines devoted to the Virgin Mary, and an increasing emphasis on images rather than relics as cult objects. A high medieval period from about 1100 to the close of the 14th century can be thought of as a golden age of Christian pilgrimage. During the early part of the period, when the Holy Land was in Christian hands, Jerusalem was relatively accessible to affluent or very highly motivated pilgrims. Large numbers of Europeans representing all social classes also trekked long distances to the tomb of St. James in Santiago de Compostela, Spain, to the shrine of St. Thomas Becket in Canterbury, England, to the shrine of the Three Kings in Cologne, Germany, and to Rome, where the first great Holy Year pilgrimage was proclaimed in 1300. Monastic establishments, some of which were pilgrimage centers in their own right, provided resting places and en route attractions for pilgrims journeying to the great shrines of medieval Christendom. This period also witnessed the development of numerous regional and district pilgrimage centers, some of them at monastic establishments and others promoted by monks from nearby monasteries. By this time a very substantial proportion of new pilgrimage cults were devoted to the Virgin Mary, and images were becoming more common than relics as cult objects.

New shrine establishments seem to have accelerated during the 15th and early 16th centuries. Most that have survived as pilgrimage sites down to the present are of merely district or regional importance and include a substantial number formed as the result of reported apparitions of the Virgin Mary and other holy personages. Shrine formations then experienced a precipitous decline all over Europe with the advent of the Protestant Reformation. Pilgrimage shrines along with monastic establishments, whether pilgrimage centers or not, were special targets for destruction in regions that became Protestant. However, the Catholic Reformation of the 16th through the 18th century saw the creation of many new pilgrimage places in southern and parts of central Europe. More of the currently visited pilgrimage centers were established during the 17th century than during any other single century before or since. This is the case for both monastic and nonmonastic shrines, although the data suggest that the Catholic Reformation centuries witnessed substantially lower proportions of monastic shrines than those not connected with monasteries. Except for a few regions, such as Hungary, which had recently been liberated from Ottoman Turkish control, the 18th century marked a period of decline in Christian cult formations and pilgrimage activity in general. This lull was followed in the 19th and 20th centuries by a renewed interest in pilgrimage and the rise of several great new Marian apparitional shrines, including the French shrine of Lourdes, the Irish pilgrimage center of Knock, Fatima in Portugal, and much more recently Medjugorje, Bosnia. Members of monastic orders have played crucial roles in the establishment of these great modern pilgrimage centers, although those mentioned cannot be considered monastic shrines per se. Other modern shrines, generally of district or regional importance, have developed at monasteries and convents. Some of the most notable examples are in England and some Germanic regions where monastic establishments have served as a leading edge in the reintroduction of Catholic practices in lands formerly Protestant by edict. During the past two centuries, the proportion of monastic and nonmonastic pilgrimage formations has been about the same.

Location and Site Features

Like other shrines, those found at monasteries and convents might be located in central cities, on the edge of cities and towns, in or near villages, or in the remote countryside. There is no particular tendency for monastic shrines to be more remote than other shrines, although some isolated hermitages, not counted here as monastic shrines, are tended by monks. In addition in some cases, as at Guadalupe in Spain, communities have grown up around monastic establishments that once were isolated.

Monastic shrines are, however, somewhat more likely to be located at pre-Christian holy places than are other shrines. Of the 259 shrines described as existing at places venerated before Christianity, 56, or 22 percent, were monastic establishments. Because early shrines are more likely to have pre-Christian associations than those established at later dates, this might reflect the older average age of monastic shrines. In some cases, as at Oropa in northern Italy, monks apparently sought to Christianize ancient holy sites by their presence.

Site features such as height, water, and grottoes are frequently found at monastic establishments. Twenty percent are on high places, and 14 percent feature some kind of sacred water source, such as a spring or well considered to have healing powers. Six percent boast natural caves or grottoes with especially sacred power. These shrines account for a quarter of all the holy caves and grottoes found in the survey. A few of Christian Europe's sacred stones, such as a rock outcropping thought to look like the Virgin Mary at Peña de Francia in Spain, are also found at monastic shrines.

Summary and Conclusions

In terms of the aggregate characteristics considered in this article, monastic shrines are not very different from other pilgrimage centers in modern Europe. Shrines located at monasteries and convents tend to be somewhat older on the average and are slightly more likely to be environmentally grounded in site features such as height, water, and/or grottoes. Cult formation stories tend to emphasize the historical importance of the place in the development of the Christian tradition, and monastic shrines house a relatively high proportion of important relics.

What is not immediately apparent in the statistical data presented in this article is the importance of monasteries as infrastructure in the development of long-distance pilgrimage routes and the role that members of religious orders have played in the establishment and maintenance of shrines located in places other than monastic establishments. In these and probably in other ways, the symbiotic relationship between monasticism and pilgrimage has much deeper roots than might be immediately apparent.

MARY LEE NOLAN

See also Exile, Western Christian; German Benedictine Reform, Medieval; Island Monasteries, Christian; Liturgy: Western Christian; Monastics and the World, Medieval; Mont-St.-Michel, France; Relics, Christian Monastic; Santiago de Compostela, Spain

Further Reading

Nolan, Mary Lee, and Sidney Nolan, *Christian Pilgrimage in Modern Western Europe*, Chapel Hill: University of North Carolina Press, 1989

Pilgrims to India, Chinese

The most common Chinese Buddhist narrative of the entry of Buddhism into China depicts Emperor Ming (r. A.D. 58–75) of the Han dynasty dreaming of a golden image that is later identified as the Buddha. The emperor sent a team of his envoys to "the West" to seek out and bring back textual sources and images of this miraculous golden man. From the earliest times and even today, Chinese have been acutely conscious of the fact that

Buddhism is a foreign religion and of the remoteness of the source of Buddhism in India or, more vaguely, "the West." In practical terms this distance meant that problems existed in acquiring and translating texts. Especially during the first 500 or 600 years of Buddhism in China, a strong sense of India as a source of Buddhist culture and texts as well as a site of pilgrimage to the homeland of Buddha was present. New translations of Sanskrit texts newly brought from India could overturn previously held views and lend legitimacy to their bearers.

Many Indians and central Asians went to China, working there to translate texts, for example, An Shigao (fl. 148–170) Lokaksema (fl. 167–186), and Kumārajīva (350–409). In turn China was a site of pilgrimage for many Korean and Japanese monks, few of whom felt the need to travel to India.

Later pilgrimage to India dwindled as Buddhism in India declined and as more indigenous or nativist forms of Buddhism developed in China (e.g., Chan). Although pilgrims existed in the 11th century, their impact was much less than that of the earlier pilgrims, and by the 13th century Muslim invaders had destroyed many Buddhist sites in India.

Faxian left China in 399 and spent six years in India. His motivation for this journey was to collect a complete set of vinaya (monastic discipline) texts. His pilgrimage included Jetavana, Lumbinī, Rājagṛha, Bodh Gayā, and Vārāṇasī. His route home included two years in Sri Lanka and then by sea (courtesy of a typhoon) to Sumatra and finally to China in 412. He wrote of his travels in his *Record of the Buddhist Countries* before his death in 418.

Yang Xuanzhi's *A Record of Buddhist Monasteries in Loyang* gives us an account of Song Yun and Hui-sheng on a pilgrimage to Udyana and Gandhāra (northwestern India) from around 516 to 523. They were commissioned by the empress dowager of the Wei dynasty to go in search of scriptures, and they returned with 170 titles. As they traveled they recorded some of the lore of each place they visited. Thus, pilgrimage records were of great interest to political rulers and merchants. Their accounts also emphasize the karmic connections that their physical presence established with the Buddha, as, for example, when they visited the very spot where Śākyamuni (in a previous lifetime) had saved the life of a dove or when they witnessed the teeth and hair of the Buddha. They also saw the "shadow" of the Buddha in a cave, later witnessed by Xuanzang.

The Buddhist monk Yijing (635–713) traveled to India in 671, returned to China in 695 after 24 years in India, and traveled through Southeast Asia on his return trip. Like Faxian he brought back corrections and additions to the vinayas.

The best-known pilgrim was Xuanzang (c. 596–664). Ordained at age 13 he decided early in life that he had learned all he could about the Buddha's teachings in China. Disobeying an imperial command to remain in China, he left China in 627 and arrived in India two years later. He studied at the Buddhist university Nālandā, in Bihar, North India. This enormous Buddhist university was founded in the fourth or fifth century and at that time was at its height. Xuanzang received the patronage of the powerful King Harsa. He studied especially the Yogācāra teachings, which he championed after he returned to China in 645 and founding the Faxiang ("Dharma-characteristics," or Chinese Yogācāra) lineage. His pilgrimage back to the founding sites of Buddhism was echoed by his conservatism in resisting new Tantric practices.

Five-storied pagoda containing the remains (*sari*) of the pilgrim Xuanzang, built in 669 (repaired in 828), southern outskirts of Xi'an (Changan), Shaanxi province, China.
Photo courtesy of Marylin M. Rhie

Xuanzang brought back not only doctrinal texts but also sacred objects and accounts of such objects in India. He saw a "bathing jug used by the Buddha," "a Buddha tooth, one inch long and eight or nine *fen* in breadth, of a yellowish white color, and it often issued an auspicious light. There was also a broom made of *kuśa* grass that had been used by the Buddha. . . . These three objects were always exhibited on festival days for the monks and laity to see and worship." He saw Buddha's parietal bone, which was used for divination. He also saw "a Buddha's eye relic, as large as an apple," and the Buddha's robe and staff.

Of course Xuanzang worshiped these objects. He carried home not only books but images and flower seeds as well. When he returned, huge processions were held for him and for the images he had brought back. The immediate and quite lavish imperial attention he received included installation in a large imperially funded monastery in the capital city. He wrote of his travels in his *DaTang xiyuji* (Record of West, during the Great Tang Dynasty).

The figure of Xuanzang was popularized as the hero of *Xiyouji* (Journey to the West), which in turn has been adapted for many folktales, children's books, and animated cartoons. Here his pilgrimage provides the plot structure for a sequence of entertaining episodes involving the monkey Sun Wukong and others. Their quest for the pinnacle of scriptural revelation ends with their receiving first a blank book and then – because they obviously are disappointed – a sūtra of mere words. By the time the *Xiyouji* was written, India had ceased to be considered a necessary and authoritative source of Buddhist revelation because of both the influence of Chan nativist ideology and the decline of Buddhist institutions in India.

ERIC REINDERS

See also Buddhist Schools/Traditions: China; China; Daoxuan (Tao-hsüan); Nālandā, India; Officials: Buddhist; Rules, Buddhist (Vinaya); Travelers: Buddhist

Further Reading

Fa-hsien (Faxian), *The Travels of Fa-hsien 399–414 A.D., or Records of the Buddhist Kingdoms*, translated by Herbert A. Giles, London: Trubner, 1877; reprint, London: Routledge and Kegan Paul, 1959

Hui-li, *A Biography of the Tripitaka Master of the Great Ci'en Monastery of the Great Tang Dynasty*, translated by Li Rongxi, Berkeley, California: Numata Center for Buddhist Translation and Research, 1995

I-ching (Yijing), *A Record of the Buddhist Religion as Practiced in India and the Malay Archepelago, A.D. 671–695*, translated by Junjiro Takakusu, Oxford: Clarendon Press, 1896; reprint, Delhi: Munshiram Manoharlal, 1966; New York: Paragon Book Gallery, 1970

Wriggins, Sally Hovey, *Xuanzang: A Buddhist Pilgrim on the Silk Road*, Boulder, Colorado: Westview Press, 1996

Wu, Ch'eng-en, *The Journey to the West*, translated by Anthony C. Yu, 4 vols., Chicago: University of Chicago Press, 1977–1983

Yang, Hsüan-chih (Yang Xuanzhi), *A Record of Buddhist Monasteries in Lo-yang*, translated by Yi-t'ung Wang, Princeton, New Jersey: Princeton University Press, 1984

Pirminius, St. d. c. 753

Christian missionary to Francia and founder of the Abbey of Reichenau

Pirminius was one of the most important missionaries independent of Boniface (c. 675–754) who operated in Francia (now southwestern Germany and Alsace) during the first half of the eighth century. His origins have long been a subject of dispute among scholars, and although it is impossible to decide whether he was an Irishman, a Frank, or a Visigoth, it seems more likely that he reached Francia from Visigothic Spain shortly after the Islamic conquest.

In Francia, Pirminius concentrated his missionary activity in the regions of Alemania, Rhaetia, and Alsace (as far north as Metz). He started his independent missionary career as a protégé of the Frankish *major domus* Charles Martel (714–741) and, with the support received from him and subsequently from numerous local aristocrats, founded several monasteries in the regions of his activities, most notably Reichenau (724), Murbach (728), and Hornbach (742), where his life ended around 753. These monasteries, together with their daughter foundations (e.g., Niederaltaich, Pfäfers, and Gengenbach), became important centers of religious and cultural activity during the Carolingian period.

The many monasteries that Pirminius and his followers founded in northeastern Francia followed the Rule of St. Benedict, and all were destined by their founders for a missionary role. However, Pirminius did not envisage this mission as work among pagans. The inhabitants of the areas in which he operated were already Christian, and no evidence exists to support the assertion that a significant lapse toward paganism had taken place in those regions. Thus, his target was scattered Christian communities and not, as is often thought, pagan tribes, and the zenith of his mission was to instruct, educate, and promote Christianity among the already Christianized population of the region.

To instruct his missionary monks and to facilitate their job among the people of the countryside, Pirminius composed a little handbook for them, the so-called *Scarapsus*, or *Dicta Pirminii* (Sayings of Pirminius). This handbook, written in the shape of a sermon, is modeled to a large extent on Martin of Braga's *De correctione rusticorum* (On the Correction of Peasants). It begins with a summary of biblical history from the Creation to Christ's resurrection and continues with an explanation of the Christian Creed and the Christian dogma, followed by a list of prohibited practices that he regarded as non-Christian. The *Scarapsus* as a whole offered straightforward, elementary teaching that was addressed to Christians who were already baptized and covered traditional themes in catechetical admonition. It is the moral life of the Christian community that Pirminius seeks to regulate, and the *Scarapsus* might well represent a common type of admonition widespread at the time among missionary monks.

Throughout the eighth and ninth centuries, Pirminius' *Scarapsus* enjoyed a fairly wide circulation among Carolingian churchmen and preachers, who esteemed it mainly for its definition of the Christian orthodoxy. Thus, Pirminius' *Scarapsus* was used by later Frankish authors and preachers above all to define clear-cut boundaries between what is Christian and what is not in an attempt to instill communal self-identity among the Christians themselves.

YITZHAK HEN

See also Boniface, St.; Missionaries: Christian

Biography
Little is known of the life of the founder of the Abbey of Reichenau.

Major Work
Dicta Pirminii (contains the oldest text of the Apostles' Creed in its present form)

Further Reading
Angenendt, Arnold, *Monachi Peregrini: Studien zu Pirmin und den monastischen Vorstellungen des frühen Mittelalters*, Munich: Fink, 1972
Angenendt, Arnold, "Pirmin und Bonifatius: Ihr Verhältnis zu Mönchtum, Bischofsamt und Adel," in *Mönchtum, Episkopat und Adel zur Gründungszeit des Klosters Reichenau*, edited by Arno Borst, Sigmaringen: Thorbecke, 1974
Engelmann, Ursmar, editor, *Der Heilige Pirmin und sein Pastoralbüchlein*, Sigmaringen: Thorbecke, 1976
Fletcher, Richard A., *The Conversion of Europe: From Paganism to Christianity 371–1386 A.D.*, London: HarperCollins, 1997; New York: Holt, 1998
Jecker, Gallus, *Die Heimat des Hl. Pirmin des Apostels der Alamannen*, Münster: Aschendorff, 1927
Löwe, H., "Pirmin, Willibrord und Bonifatius: Ihre Bedeutung für die Missionsgeschichte ihrer Zeit," in *La conversione al cristianesimo nell'Europa dell'alto Medioevo: 14–19 aprile 1966*, Spoleto: Centro italiano di studi sull'alto Medioevo, 1967
Prinz, Friedrich, *Frühes Mönchtum im Frankenreich: Kultur und Gesellschaft in Gallien, den Rheinlanden und Bayern am Beispiel der monastischen Entwicklung (4. bis 8. Jahrhundert)*, Munich: Oldenbourg, 1988
Wallace-Hadrill, J.M., *The Frankish Church*, Oxford: Clarendon Press, and New York: Oxford University Press, 1983

Plainchant

Throughout the history of Christianity, the observance of the liturgy has occupied a central role in religious life, and monasteries have played a leading role in the development of the repertoire of single-line melodies to which liturgical texts are sung, collectively called "plainchant" or simply "chant." The total comprises several thousand pieces in different genres. These have entered into practice in layers of accretion over the centuries and have been adapted into particularized observances in different regions and monastic orders (a phenomenon especially evident in the late Middle Ages, when the veneration of some of the saints was a matter of regional custom). The term *plain* is misleading in one sense; even though references to *cantus planus* are found in medieval writings, there is reason to think that this music was performed in a highly ornamented manner – in commenting in his *Confessions* on the liturgical music sung in Milan, Augustine (354–430) remarked that he was sometimes moved "more by the singing than that which is sung."

The repeated cycle (or *cursus*) of the 150 psalms forms the core of the chant repertoire in history and in function, and the earliest witness of it is St. Benedict (c. 480–c. 550) himself. The Rule of Benedict (itself based on the "Rule of the Master") sets out the schedule for the observance of the offices and requires monks to go through all the psalms every two weeks. These were sung to very simple melodic formulas and expanded to accommodate longer texts by a practice called recitation, the repetition of one note for several syllables of text. Each strophe of a psalm was sung with a formula (called the intonation) of a few notes ascending to the pitch of recitation, followed by the recitation itself with slight departures at internal phrase endings (the flex and the mediation), and a termination formula for the last six syllables. Because every psalm ended with the doxology, the last words of which are "in secula seculorum amen," the termination formula was sometimes called the "seculorum amen" or "euouae" (the vowels of those two words) and can be found labeled in this way in manuscript sources. Psalmodic recitation of a similar kind is found in many other musical cultures, including the sacred music of Judaism. Two explanations have been offered for the spread of psalmody: the practical reason that a singing voice carries the text more clearly and effectively than a spoken voice and the suggestion that musical formulas like these were held to have a mystical purpose, perhaps the invocation of the deity, a conception that can be found in religions that influenced early Christianity, such as Mithraism. Indeed some of the Old Testament prophets used music to assist them, whereas others wanted nothing to do with music.

The enlargement of the chant repertoire over time resulted from the development of the monastic liturgy. It consists of the ordinary (the texts and melodies performed once every two weeks), the proper of the time or day (pieces for specific feasts commemorating events in the life of Christ, except Christmas), the proper of the saints, and more recently the common (e.g., the group of pieces sung on all Marian feasts). The proper of the time follows the lunar calendar, so that, for example, Easter is celebrated on a different day each year. These feasts begin with the morning offices of the day. The proper of the saints follows the solar calendar and begins with the vespers of the feast the evening before. Thus, the celebration of Christmas, which is part of the proper of the saints, begins on the evening of 24 December each year. Because of its importance in the liturgy, it has also taken the office of vespers on 25 December (which should have belonged to the feast of St. Stephen) for itself as the second vespers of the feast of the birth of Christ. The liturgy for a given day is formed by singing the entire chant for the proper of that day or, where there is no proper for that feast, singing the relevant pieces from the common or, where there is no common, observing the ordinary for that day. The proper grew from a very sparse calendar of feasts in the Middle Ages to a full calendar with a proper feast for every day in the modern calendar, and the chant repertoire grew with it.

The second-oldest genre of chant is the antiphon, sung at the offices. The major offices of the day (vespers, matins, and lauds) have a substantial amount of music, as does the mass. Antiphons are short melodies sung before and after a psalm. In monasteries four antiphons were sung in each major office and in cathedrals three. The monastic observance of chant (and of antiphons in particular) might have been taken up in the cathedral first in the late fourth century, when Ambrose (c. 339–397), bishop of Milan, ordered the adherents of the orthodox party to occupy the opposition Arian Church. His biographer wrote that in order to keep up their morale, he had his followers sing a new kind of liturgical music.

There are thousands of antiphons, and this genre has been the subject of many studies, including attempts to sort out the layers of accretion and to understand the musical rationale of the repertoire. Despite attempts to demonstrate specific musical links between Judaic and Christian sacred music, it is clear that the music of the Western Church had its genesis in the West, not in Palestine. Three general explanations have been offered for the musical style of chant, and all of them have been tested in the repertoire of antiphons. A note-frequency model has been put forward to try to show that antiphons developed from the recitation of psalms to melodies based on succeeding chains of the musical interval of a third in a system of pentatonic or five-note scales (Egeland Hansen, 1979). Some scholars have argued on the contrary that the basis of the repertoire is centonic, made up of small melodic mosaics (Ferretti, 1938). The best elaborated and most widely studied theory is that the very large repertoire of chant arose from the elaboration of a small number (fewer than 100) of melodic themes that were adapted to new liturgical texts by recitation and ornamentation (Gevaert, 1895). The thematic model has the advantage that the musical relationships are in most cases self-evident, and it offers a credible explanation for the genesis and performance of the repertoire prior to the implementation of musical notation in the eighth century. A new text could have been set to music simply by adapting the theme of a piece with a similar text. In fact it has been observed that in many cases chants with the same melodic theme have common

Music stand with wood inlay, Basilica of Sant'Ambrogio (Benedictine 784–c. 1470 and then Cistercian until 1797), Milan, Italy, 15th century. Photo courtesy of the Editor

elements in their texts; in other words it seems plausible that a new text added to the repertoire would have been attracted to one of the melodic themes by a point of textual commonality. In the early centuries of chant, an antiphon was sung before the psalm, between each of the psalm verses, and after the psalm. For the sake of brevity, this practice changed to singing it once before the psalm and once after the last verse.

The system of eight musical modes was introduced in the West only in the eighth century, long after the repertoire had been well established. For this reason it is incorrect to imagine that mode, as theoretical construct or musical scale, played any part in the genesis of chant melodies. Antiphons and the psalms with which they were sung were matched musically in two ways. First, the intonation formula and pitch of recitation were chosen to suit the antiphon melody. For example, when the last note of the antiphon is D, the pitch of the recitation of the psalm is A. Second, the termination formula of a psalm was matched more specifically with the beginning of the antiphon with which it was sung. There were over 90 of these termination formulas in the Gregorian dialect of chant but only seven pitches on which psalmodic recitation could take place.

Theorists in the Middle Ages wrote that the termination formulas make a melodic link between the end of the psalm and the beginning of the accompanying antiphon but did not explain the connection. Two points concerning this "link" are clear in the antiphons of the Ambrosian (Milanese) dialect, which has been held to reflect versions of chant that are older than the written Gregorian sources. First, antiphons of the same melodic-thematic family tend to have the same termination formula. The Ambrosian repertoire is thematically more cohesive than the Gregorian; the entire body of antiphons can be grouped into only 14 melodic themes: five for antiphons that end on the note D, five for those ending on G, and two each for those ending on E and F. Second, it has been suggested that, if one allows for the possibility of accretion and ornamentation within antiphon melodies – in other words if one supposes that beginnings of antiphon melodies might be in effect melodic prefixes – the themes of Ambrosian antiphons begin with the notes of the termination formulas with which they are sung. In other words, just as the psalms are slightly ornamented recitation, the antiphons might have begun as elaborated versions of the termination formulas.

Other genres of chant are performed like antiphons (before and after the psalm): introits and communions (both proper movements of the mass) are performed just like antiphons. The same is true for some canticles, such as the Magnificat, which has its own antiphons. The other arrangement of melody and psalm is called responsorial and consists of a melody followed by a verse of the psalm, another performance of the melody and then the second verse of the psalm, and so on, ending with the last verse of the psalm. The gradual of the mass is performed in responsorial psalmody, as are alleluias and responds. There also are cases of direct psalmody. Tracts comprise more than one psalm put together and are sung without interruption. Finally there are also some genres of chant (which came into the repertoire late) that are independent from psalms. Sequences, tropes (interpolations and extrapolations to existing chants), and the ordinary movements of the mass are examples.

The expansion of the Frankish kingdom in the eighth century brought important developments to chant. Charlemagne (768–814) went to great lengths to standardize the observance of the liturgy throughout his territory. He sent to Rome for "books and singers," and it is at this time that musical notation was first widely implemented. Some of the French clerics found that they disagreed with some notes in the melodies imposed on them by the Roman singers, but Charlemagne charged them to adopt the Roman versions in every detail, explaining that, just as the water of a stream is more pure near the source, the Roman chant must be considered closer to its (divine) origin. As part of his program to promulgate the authority of the office of the pope (who had crowned him emperor), Charlemagne encouraged the legend that Gregorian chant had been composed by Pope Gregory the Great (who died in 604). He caused an icon to be painted of that pontiff, receiving the chant repertoire from the Holy Spirit in the form of the dove and writing it down. For this reason the version of chant adopted in the Frankish kingdom at this time has been called "Gregorian," and it is distinguished from other dialects, including the Ambrosian rite, the Sarum rite in England, the Mozarabic rite in Spain, so-called Old Roman (apparently the chant sung in the city of Rome itself but after the time of Charlemagne), and others. Following Charlemagne the Gregorian version rapidly came to dominate almost all of Europe, Milan being a notable exception.

Monasteries were very much involved in the musical notation of chant at this time. The earliest Western notation (with symbols possibly derived from punctuation signs) comes from the monastery of St. Gall (c. 550–c. 650), who founded that house when he fell ill while on a missionary voyage with St. Columba (c. 521–597). The Saint-Gall musical notation is not diastematic and thus does not indicate the exact pitches, but it does represent many nuances of performance and serves as a memory aid to someone who knows the chant already. It could not have replaced the practice of learning the music by rote, something that changed only in the tenth century with the theories of the Benedictine Guido of Arezzo (c. 992–1050), who developed a full system of notation on the musical staff, very close to modern musical notation. The theorist wrote that in this way singers could learn the repertoire in one year, something that had taken them ten years to do by rote.

Also in the eighth century, the eight-mode system was introduced in the West from Byzantium. It was employed as a method of classification for the purposes of correct performance. Byzantine chant has its own type of notation, a complicated chain system that relates each note to the next. The classification of chant into modes and termination formulas occupied many musicians in treatises and in books called tonaries, which contained the list of chants with each termination formula. These must have served as authorities for the correction of melodies in the service books (antiphoners for the offices and graduals for the mass). Some of the monastic orders undertook reforms of chant melodies to make the ranges of the pieces fit theoretical ideals. The Cistercian reform of chant was the most ambitious of these, although by no means the only one. The monk Berno of Reichenau wrote important treatises on music and also worked to revise melodies and the practice of the modes, using his own theoretical writings and a tonary.

From the ninth century, as part of the effort to reunify the Eastern and Western churches, the latter adopted the *missa graeca*, the five ordinary Greek ordinary movements (Kyrie, Gloria, Credo, Sanctus, and Agnus Dei), into its mass. These had special musical importance in the late Middle Ages and the Renaissance because they were the movements most often set polyphonically. In those same periods chant was employed in the tenor voice of polyphony to confer authority on the new repertoire.

Because the rhythm of chant was not specified in medieval notation, this aspect has long been a disputed aspect of performance. Some evidence exists that early chant was performed with a measurable (countable) rhythm, but that tradition was lost by the tenth century. Controversy has also arisen over the early transmission of chant and genesis of the melodies. Within the various dialects, the transmission of the early written sources is very stable, suggesting a careful passing down of detailed, specific melodies rather than the practice of oral reconstruction argued for by some authors.

PAUL A. MERKLEY

See also Gregory I (the Great), St.; Guéranger, Prosper; Hymnographers; Liturgical Movement 1830–1980; Liturgy: Western Christian; Music: Christian Perspectives; Office, Daily: Western Christian; Solesmes, France

Further Reading

Apel, Willi, *Gregorian Chant*, Bloomington: Indiana University Press, and London: Burns and Oates, 1958

Bailey, Terence, and Paul A. Merkley, *The Antiphons of the Ambrosian Office* (Musicological Studies, volume 50, number 1), Ottawa, Ontario: Institute of Mediaeval Music, 1989

Bailey, Terence, and Paul A. Merkley, *The Melodic Tradition of the Ambrosian Office-Antiphons* (Musicological Studies, volume 50, number 2), Ottawa, Ontario: Institute of Mediaeval Music, 1990

Egeland Hansen, Finn, *The Grammar of Gregorian Tonality: An Investigation Based on the Repertory in Codex H 159, Montpellier* (Studier og publikationer fra Musikvidenskabeligt Institut, Aarhus Universitet, 3), translated by Shirley Larsen, Copenhagen: Fog, 1979

Ferretti, Paolo, *Esthétique grégorienne, ou, Traité des formes musicales du chant grégorien*, translated by Armandus Agaësse, Paris: Société de Saint Jean l'Evangéliste, 1938

Gevaert, François Auguste, *La mélopée antique dans le chant de l'église latine*, Gand: Librairie Générale de Ad. Hoste, 1895; reprint, Osnabrück: Zeller, 1967

Hughes, Andrew, *Late Medieval Liturgical Offices: Resources for Electronic Research* (Subsidia Mediaevalia), Toronto: Pontifical Institute of Mediaeval Studies, 1994

Hughes, David, "Variants in Antiphon Families: Notation and Tradition," in *La musique et le rite sacré et profane: Actes du XIIIe Congrès de la Société Internationale de Musicologie, Strasbourg, 29 août–3 septembre 1982*, edited by Marc Honegger and Paul Prévost, volume 2, Strasbourg: Association des publications près les Universités de Strasbourg, 1986

McCann, Justin, editor and translator, *The Rule of Saint Benedict: In Latin and English* (Orchard Books), London: Burns and Oates, 1952

Poland

In 966 Prince Mieszko I (d. 992) was baptized, after which began a rapid evangelization of Poland, carried through by monks, among others. One abbey of nuns (in Poznań?) is attested in that period, as is a hermitage, later an abbey, in Międzyrzecz (1002–c. 1030), founded by a few monks, companions of St. Romuald (c. 950–1027), on the initiative of the Emperor Otto III (983–1002) and Prince Bolesław Chrobry (992–1025). The initiative's aim was to train missionaries to work among pagan Slavic tribes. In this period monks gathered around a prince and served at churches in principal towns as well as at cathedrals. Until the end of the 12th century, most bishops were selected from among monks. Of great importance was the mission of St. Adalbert of Prague, a monk and bishop, to the pagan Prussians, ending in his martyrdom and death in 997.

In the aftermath of destruction inflicted by wars, internal strife, and pagan reaction in the 1030s, from around 1040 the so-called mission of Aaron, a monk and the bishop of Kraków, began its work with the participation of Benedictine monks from abbeys in the Rhine and Meuse regions. Around 1050 to 1075 three Benedictine abbeys (Tyniec, Mogilno, and Lubiń) came into being and through the end of the 12th century seven more (the most important being Łysiec, Sieciechów, and Płock) were founded. From the 1130s on the abbeys of Augustinian Canons were established, the largest being in Trzemeszno and Czerwińsk.

In the 1140s the Polish elite came in contact with Bernard of Clairvaux (1090–1153), inviting him to come to Poland and to Christianize schismatic Ruthenia. Bernard did not come, but around 1050 the two earliest Cistercian abbeys were founded (Łekno and Jędrzejów). By the end of the 13th century, 25 Cistercian abbeys came into existence in the present territory of Poland. A very important role, especially in female monasticism, was played by the Premonstratensian Canons (called Norbertines in Poland), who from the end of the 12th century acquired more than a dozen monasteries (the most important of them in Wrocław, Brzesko-Hebdów, and Kraków-Zwierzyniec). From the end of the 12th to the beginning of the 15th century, a congregation of Canons Regular of Arrouaise worked in Silesia, with the principal abbey in Wrocław. In the second half of the 12th century, religious military orders first appeared in Poland, the most important of which was the Teutonic Order, invited in 1226 to fight the pagan Prussians. In the first decade it absorbed the Order of the Brothers of the Sword of Livonia and the Polish Order of Brothers of Dobrzyń, established by a Cistercian monk named Christian (d. 1244), a missionary in Prussia. Having conquered Prussia the Teutonic Knights built a powerful state that was secularized in the 16th century.

In 1163 Jaksa of Miechów (d. 1176) invited Augustinian Canons of the Holy Sepulchre of Jerusalem, known in Poland as "Miechowici" (from Miechów, which was their first and most important abbey). After the Order had been abolished in most of Europe from 1483 to 1489 until its secularization in 1819, Miechów was the Order's principal abbey, active in running hospitals and in ministry. In the 13th century came also the Order of the Holy Spirit of Saxia and the Order of the Red Star Knights of the Cross. In 1257 the Canons Regular of Penitence first appeared in Poland; they were called "marki," from St. Mark, patron saint of their church in Kraków. Formally abolished in the 14th century, this order remained active in Poland and Lithuania until 1832.

Already in 1222 the Dominicans were expanding to Poland (Poles were among the first brothers to come to Kraków), as were the Franciscans from the 1230s. By the end of the 13th century, these orders had established about 80 monasteries. Female orders were developing rapidly, owing to the foundations of nunneries of the Norbertines (e.g., Kraków-Zwierzyniec and Strzelno), Cistercians (e.g., Trzebnica), Benedictines (e.g., Staniątki), and the Poor Clares, Dominicans, and Magdalenes. Overall, between 1200 and 1300, the number of monasteries grew from about 60 to about 330.

Monasticism developed quickly under Kazimierz the Great (1333–1370) and Władysław Jagiełło (1385–1434). At that time new orders came to the kingdom of Poland: the Augustinian Hermits (c. 1340 in Kraków; earlier they had owned a few monasteries in Silesia and Pomerania) and the Carmelites (1390 in Kraków), Paulite Fathers (in Częstochowa), the Bridgettines (Gdańsk and Lublin), and the Benedictines using the Slavic liturgy, who at the end of the 14th century came from Prague to Oleśnica and Kraków. The abbey of the Augustinian Canons established in Kraków in 1405 formed the Polish congregation of Corpus Christi, which from the beginning of the 16th century was a part of the congregation of the Canons of the Lateran. A visit from St. John of Capistrano (1386–1456) and his sermons preached in Silesia and Kraków (1454) contributed to the enormous success of the Franciscan Observants (called Bernardines in Poland). The number of monasteries grew further to about 440 in 1400 and to about 470 in 1500: almost half of them were those of mendicant friars.

The 16th century brought a crisis of monasticism in Poland as well as the coming of the Reformation and secularization in Western Pomerania and Silesia. As a result, by 1600 the number of monasteries declined to about 300. However, the triumph of the Counter-Reformation changed this situation, largely because of the activity of Jesuits who came to Poland in 1564. In the 17th and 18th centuries, monasticism was on the rise in the entire Commonwealth of the Two Nations (Poland and the grand duchy of Lithuania). In 1700 there were approximately 800 monasteries and in 1772 more than 1,000 (with 14,500 monks and 3,211 nuns). The most important were the orders of Regular Clerks: the Jesuits, the Brothers Hospitallers of St. John de Deo from 1609, the Piarists from 1642, the Missionaries of St. Vincent à Paulo from 1651, the Theatines from 1664, the Oratorians (called Filipine Fathers in Poland) from 1668, the Institutum Clericorum Saecularium in Communi Viventium from 1683, and the Marians (Congregatio Clericorum Regularium Marianorum sub titulo Immaculatae Conceptionis BVM), which was founded in Poland in 1673. This was also a period of brisk development for the Dominicans, the Discalced Carmelites (from 1605), and the Franciscan orders, in particular the Observants and the Reformati (from 1607) and the Capuchins (from 1680). At that time the Camaldolese (from 1605) and the Carthusians first appeared in Poland, while the Benedictines and the Cistercians, despite commendatory abbots imposed on them, managed internal reforms and established national congregations. In eastern Poland, Uniate Basilian male and female abbeys and Greek Orthodox monasteries were flourishing as well. Religious orders were promoting an enormous growth in pilgrimage movement, especially devoted to the cult of the Passion of Christ and the cult of the Virgin Mary, notably in Częstochowa and in Kalwaria Zebrzydowska (the Franciscan Observants).

In female monasticism the most important role was played by the Benedictine nuns of the congregation of Chełmno, established at the end of the 16th century, and, among the new orders, by the Discalced Carmelite Sisters, the Order of the Holy Sacrament, the Sisters of Charity, and the Visitandines. In Poland new female orders were founded, and these still exist: Katarzynki (Congregatio Sororum Sanctae Catharinae Virginis et Martyris) in the 16th century and Prezentki (Congregatio Virginum a Praesentatione BMV) in the 17th century. Both are active in charity work and teaching.

Between 1772 and 1795 Poland lost its independence and was partitioned among three powers – Austria, Prussia, and Russia – all of whom suppressed religious orders. The process lasted for the longest time in the part of Poland under Russian rule (until 1864). Of the monasteries operating before 1772, only a few dozen survived until 1914, all in the part of Poland occupied by Austria. The absence of independent statehood and the anti-monastic policy of Russia and Prussia hindered monastic revival despite efforts of the Community of the Resurrection (a small but influential order established by Polish émigrés in Paris), among others. This situation improved by the late 19th century. New congregations were founded to work among the poor and underprivileged: Albertins (Congregatio Fratrum III Ordinis Sancti Francisci Pauperibus Serviendum), founded in 1888 by St. Albert Chmielowski (1845–1916), and Michalins (Congregatio Sancti Michaelis Archangeli), founded by Father Bronislaw Markiewicz (1842–1912). Certain new orders came to Poland (e.g., Salesians and Redemptorists). Female monasticism was growing, aided by the Capuchins headed by Father Honorat Koźmiński (1824–1916). In conspiracy against the czarist government, it assumed unconventional forms and was abolished by Polish bishops after 1905. At that time in Poland, female monasticism became, as it did elsewhere in Europe, the most dynamic part of the monastic movement.

When independent Poland was restored in 1918, the monastic movement could develop freely. Although World War II (1939–1945) caused substantial losses, monasticism recovered despite considerable difficulties in the era of the Communist government (1945–1989), which did not suppress monastic life. Since 1989 monasticism has been developing apace, especially the female monastic movement. Monks and nuns have come back to serving the society actively. In 1997 there were 59 male monasteries, 129 nunneries, and 24 secular institutes in Poland that were operating 1,000 institutions: sanctuaries, retreat houses, kindergartens, community centers, hospitals, almshouses, and orphanages.

Monasteries to Visit

Gdańsk: churches and monasteries of the Bridgettines, Cistercians in Oliwa, Dominicans, and Carmelites; Kraków: churches of the Albertins and Albertines, Franciscan Observants, Hospitallers, Dominicans, Order of the Holy Spirit of Saxia (Male and Female), Franciscans, Jesuits, Canons Regular, Capuchins, Carmelites and Carmelite Sisters, Poor Clares, Canons Regular of Penitence, Missionaries of St. Vincent à Paulo, Paulite Fathers (Skałka), Prezentki (Congregatio Virginum a Praesentatione BMV), Saletins (Missionarii Dominae Nostrae a la Salette), Congregatio Sororum Beatae Mariae Virginis a Misericordia, Sisters of Charity, Trinitarians, Ursulines, Visitandines, and Community of the Resurrection; in the outskirts of the city: the Benedictine Abbey at Tyniec, Cistercian Abbey at Mogiła, Camaldolese Abbey at Bielany, abbeys of the Norbertines and of Congregatio Sororum S. Felicis de Cantalicae Tertii Ordinis Regularis Sancti Francisci at Zwierzyniec, and Augustinian Hermits' Abbey at Kazimierz; Warsaw: churches of the Jesuits, Capuchins, Reformati, Trinitarians, and Visitandines; Wrocław: churches of the Augustinian Hermits, Franciscans, Franciscan Observans, Hospitallers, Canons Regular (in Piasek), Red Star Knights of the Cross, and the Benedictine abbeys at Legnickie Pole, Mogilno, and Święty Krzyż (now the Oblates Regular of St. Benedict); Benedictine Nuns in Chełmno, Sandomierz, and Sierpiec; the Franciscans Observants at Leżajsk, Alwernia, and Kalwaria Zebrzydowska; "Miechowici" (Augustinian Canons of the Holy Sepulchre of Jerusalem) in Miechów; the Cistercian abbeys at Lubiąż, Koprzywnica, Krzeszów, Ląd, Oliwa, Pelplin, Sulejów, and Wąchock; Cistercian Nuns in Trzebnica; Dominicans in Gildy, Lublin, and Sandomierz; Franciscans Conventuals in Kalwaria Pacławska, Niepokalanów, and Nowy Korczyn; Jesuits in Braniewo and Święta Lipka; Hospitallers in Łagów, Stargard, and Strzegom; Canons Regular in Czerwińsk; Discalced Carmelites in Czerna; Katarzynki (Congregatio Sororum Sanctae Catharinae Virginis et Martyris) in Orneta; Carthusians in Kartuzy near Gdańsk; Poor Clares in Stary Sącz; Marians (Congregatio Clericorum Regularium Marianorum sub titulo Immaculatae Conceptionis BVM) in Puszcza Mariańska; Norbertine Nuns in Strzelno and Żuków (now the Benedictine Nuns); and Oratorians in Gostyń-Głogówko.

Marek Derwich

See also Augustinian Canons; Augustinian Friars/Hermits; Benedictines; Carmelites; Carthusians; Cistercians; Częstochowa (Jasna Góra), Poland; Dominicans; Franciscans; Hospitallers (Knights of Malta since 1530); Pilgrimages, Christian: Eastern Europe; Premonstratensian Canons; Teutonic Order; Visitandines

Further Reading

Derwich, Marek, "Les bénédictins et la christianisation des campagnes en Pologne," in *La christianisation des campagnes: Actes du colloque du C.I.H.E.C. (25–27 août 1994)*, edited by Jean-Pierre Massaut and Marie-Élisabeth Henneau, volume 1, Brussels-Rome: Institut Historique Belge de Rome, 1996

Derwich, Marek, "Les communautés monastiques en Pologne au Moyen Âge: Bilan et perspectives," *Quaestiones Medii Aevi Novae* 2 (1997)

Derwich, Marek, "Les fondations et implantations de monastères bénédictins en Pologne jusqu'au début du XVIe siècle," in *Moines et monastères dans les sociétés de rite grec et latin*, edited by Jean-Loup Lemaître, Michel Dmitriev, and Pierre Gonneau, Geneva: Droz, 1996

Encyklopedia Katolicka (Catholic Encyclopedia), volumes 1–7, Lublin: TNKUL, 1973–1997

Kłoczowski, Jerzy, *Od pustelni do wspólnoty: Grupy zakonne w wielkich religiach swiata* (From Hermitage to Community: Monastic Groups in Major Religions of the World), Warsaw: Czytelnik, 1987

Kłoczowski, Jerzy, *La Pologne dans l'Église médiévale*, Aldershot and Brookfield, Vermont: Variorum, 1993

Kłoczowski, Jerzy, editor, *Histoire religieuse de la Pologne*, Paris: Centurion, 1987

Łoziński, Bogumił, *Leksykon zakonów w Polsce: Informator o życiu konsekrowanym* (Lexicon of Religious Orders in Poland: Handbook of the Consecrated Life), Warsaw: KAI, 1998

Majkowski, J., "Polonia," in *Dizionario degli istituti di perfezione*, edited by Guerino Pellicca and Giancarlo Rocca, volume 7, Rome: Edicioni Paolini, 1983

Maręcki, Józef, *Zakony męskie w Polsce* (Male Religious Order in Poland), Kraków: TAiWPN Universitas, 1997

Maręcki, Józef, *Zakony żeńskie w Polsce* (Female Religious Order in Poland), Kraków: TAiWPN Universitas, 1997

Poor Clares. *See* Clare of Assisi, St.; Franciscans: Female

Popes, Monastic. *See* Papacy: Monastic Popes

Portugal

Monastic orders in Portugal have undergone an extraordinary number of setbacks and renewals, especially since the mid–18th century. Located in the western part of the Iberian Peninsula, Portugal is bordered on the west and the south by the Atlantic Ocean and on the east and the north by Spain. Until its independence in the early 12th century, Portugal formed part of the Leonese kingdom and had already enjoyed a strong monastic presence under its Visigothic rulers between the fifth and eighth centuries. During the military struggles against Muslim occupiers in the following centuries, monasteries were founded or restored, becoming especially important in the repopulation efforts north of the Douro River.

By the 12th century the Benedictines had become the preeminent religious order in the north of Portugal, having amassed the most wealth and power. By the 1150s the reforming Cistercians arrived in Portugal and almost completely halted the Benedictine influence southward, even absorbing some Benedictine monasteries. The great Cistercian abbey of Alcobaça was founded by the first Portuguese ruler, Alfonso Henriques (1128–1185). The Augustinians and the Cluniacs were also on the scene at this time but were neither so powerful nor so wealthy. In the south the military orders of the Knights Templar, the Hospitallers, Calatrava, and Santiago were kept active fighting against the Muslims. In the 13th century the mendicant orders arrived and immediately found great favor with the Portuguese monarchs and the people, and this translated into wealth and power. Franciscans, Dominicans, and Poor Clares constructed some of the most well-known convents of the Gothic style. Early on the monarchs saw a problem in concentrating wealth and property in the hands of religious orders and forbade private purchase by clerics and donations to the Church by the mid–13th century. The 14th and 15th centuries saw the construction of larger, more elaborate monasteries and convents, the monastery of Batalha being the best example. It was built to honor the victory of John I (1385–1433) over the Castilian army in the battle of Aljubarrota. Begun in 1387 it was substantially completed by the mid–15th century.

During the Counter-Reformation many reforms were instituted, including the suppression of commanderies, the prohibition of friars and monks owning private property, and a renewed emphasis on obedience and discipline. Many smaller monasteries were combined or even eliminated, but instead of diminishing, the number of convents and monasteries actually increased: 166 new houses were established between 1550 and 1668. Orders new to Portugal, such as the Discalced Carmelites, the Carthusians, and the Franciscan Capuchins, as well as newly founded orders, such as the Theatines, the Order of St. Philip Neri, the English nuns of St. Saviour (Inglesinhas), and the Conceptionist nuns, arrived at this time as well, albeit not in significant numbers. The most important new order to enter Portugal during this time was the Jesuits. Being exemplary missionaries and educators, the Jesuits followed the Portuguese explorers to the colonies. They came close to monopolizing education, and their affluence and influence made them targets of attack from other religious orders. They were especially active in Brazil, where they built a virtual empire of sugar plantations and cattle ranches.

Known as the Age of Reason, the 18th century saw a rise in anticlerical sentiment. New religious orders appeared, such as the French Capuchins (Barbadinhos), Ursulines, and Discalced Paulists, but they had little influence and no lasting impact. Older orders also saw little growth. The Jesuits fell from power, having ignored the advances made in science and education, and were expelled from Portugal in 1759. After 1782 no new religious orders were instituted. Liberalism brought with it radical changes for religious orders: tithes and other revenue taxes were abolished, and state taxes were imposed on them. With the constitutions of 1822 and 1826, the power of the regular clergy was vastly curtailed. The Jesuits, who had been welcomed back into Portugal in 1829, were again expelled, and many monks, friars, and nuns suffered persecution during the ensuing civil war. In 1833 no further novitiates were allowed, condemning the orders to gradual extinction. The following year all monasteries were abolished and their male populations disbanded. Nuns' convents were not dissolved, but with no new novices their fate was sealed.

By the mid– to late 1800s, religious orders were again active in Portugal, albeit in an altered form. In 1901 religious orders could operate, provided that their mission was charitable or educational. Again the Jesuits made the strongest comeback and established a lay association, the Apostolado da Oração, that numbered about two million members by 1909. With the republican revolution of 1910, religious orders again were dispersed, but the action this time unleashed a popular reaction, and the harassment ended with Sidonio Pais' government in 1918. The revolution of 1926 helped stabilized church-state relations, and under the concordat with the Holy See of 1940, religious orders and associations were again recognized. In recent years, although many missionaries have returned to Europe from former Portuguese colonies, a renewal of overseas missionary activity has occurred, but this time with a spirit of collaboration and cooperation between different orders and missionaries of different nationalities.

Sites to Visit

Convent of Christ, Tomar, Santarém
Monastery of the Hieronymites (Jerónimos), Belém, Lisbon
Monastery of the Holy Cross (Santa Cruz) of Coimbra, Coimbra
Monastery of St. Mary of Victory (Battle Abbey), Batalha, Leira district
Royal Abbey of St. Mary of Alcobaça, Alcobaça, Leira district
St. Clare of Porto, Porto
St. Francis of Porto, Porto
St. Francis of Evora, Evora
St. Vincent of Fora, Lisbon

LEE TUNSTALL

See also Benedictines: General or Male; Capuchins; Cistercians: General or Male; Latin America; Spain: History; Warrior Monks: Christian

Further Reading

Almeida, Fortunato de, *História da Igreja em Portugal*, 6 vols., Coimbra: Imprensa académica, 1910–1926; Porto: Portucalense Editora, 1967–1972

Bernardes Branco, Manoel, *Historia das Ordens Monasticas em Portugal*, 3 vols., Lisbon: Tavares Cardoso and Irmão, 1888

Bishko, Charles, *Spanish and Portuguese Monastic History, 600–1300*, London: Variorum Reprints, 1984

Cocheril, Maur, *Études sur le Monachisme en Espagne et au Portugal*, Paris: Les Belles Lettres, and Lisbon: Bertrand, 1966

Confederação Nacional dos Institutos Religiosos, *Ordens Religiosas Masculinas em Portugal*, Lisbon, 1964

I Congreso International del Monacato Femenino en Espana, Portugal y América, 1492–1992, 2 vols., Leon: Ediciones Lancia, 1993

Matoso, J., "Os estudos sobre o monaquismo beneditino em Portugal," *Studia monastica* 1 (1959)

Rodrigues, Francisco, *História da Companhia de Jesus na Assistência de Portugal*, 6 vols., Porto: Apostolado da Imprensa, 1931–1944

Prayer: Buddhist Perspectives

Overview

The concept of "prayer" is problematic from both a theological and a linguistic perspective but especially when one attempts to apply it across cultural or theological boundaries. In the case of Buddhism, the problems of definition and normative discourse are compounded by a number of factors. First, in Western theological discourse the term *prayer* carries implicit judgments regarding the nature of religion itself (a relation to a personal deity, the primacy of the individual consciousness and interpersonal communication) or the transcendent object of religion (a creator god). In common usage, furthermore, the term *prayer* tends to bring with it preconceptions regarding the nature of language as a vehicle of propositional thought and conscious intention. It is fair to say that there is no *analytic or theological category* in Buddhism that corresponds exactly to the Western concept of prayer (even if we admit that the latter is at times vague and controversial). Nevertheless one can identify within the broad range of Buddhist activities several that correspond to many of the Western practices subsumed under the term *prayer*.

In using the term analytically or as a tool of comparison, one must keep in mind that isolated instances might have a very different meaning in their respective contexts; similarities of detail do not constitute systematic correspondences. In other words an assemblage of Buddhist-Christian or Buddhist-Islamic correspondences from a variety of periods, individuals, and cultures cannot be used to establish a commonality, much less a universal law of religious behavior.

Even when *prayer* is understood as a family of terms with permeable and blurred boundaries, the various types and forms of religious practice subsumed under the word play different roles in different religions. They are also judged differently by both theological elites and outside observers. For example, prayers of petition, so central to Western traditions (see, e.g.,

Karl Barth), are seen by Buddhist elites as secondary and perhaps of questionable value. As a result of this emphasis in the internal hierarchy of values within Buddhism, Western observers tend to assume, mistakenly, that there are no prayers of petition in Buddhism. It would be more accurate to say that petitional prayers are viewed with a certain suspicion by the monastic elites, especially those devoted to study and meditation, but that petitional rituals, including explicit appeals for assistance, are not unknown. Needless to say Western theology likewise sees petition as only one aspect of prayer, and an important component of Western ascetic and mystical theologies is the tendency to regard prayers of petition with caution if not suspicion.

One should add that petition in Buddhism tends to have the formal characteristics of a "sacrifice." That is, it is more common to engage in some sort of explicit or implicit barter – a gift made in expectation of some return – than it is to formulate a desire as a formal petition to a personal superhuman being. However, one must hasten to note that this is also true in many popular manifestations of petitional approaches to deity in Christianity (e.g., in Latin American Catholicism, where the concepts of *promesa* and *milagrito* are still very much alive).

If we ascribe to the term *prayer* some analytical value in the study of Buddhism, we can then separate it provisionally from meditation and attempt a definition distinct from that often suggested in the West (e.g., Louth, 1998), which presupposes two movements: petition and communion. From a descriptive and comparative point of view, it makes more sense to think of a category that will allow for the wide diversity of acts of prayer attested in the West as well as in Buddhism (praise, lament, confession, and so on). Thus, I would suggest that the term *prayer* be used to mean an intentional verbal act used as a way of interacting with a sacred presence. In these verbal acts – public or private, uttered or silent – the performer addresses a transcendent presence to effect a sacred transformation, express an attitude, or seek a desired outcome through language. With this definition in hand, one can study the common elements that tie together the wide variety of such intentional verbal acts that occur in Buddhism – monastic as well as lay. These include prayers of confession or contrition; of commitment (confession of faith and taking of vows); of praise, invocation, and evocation; of ritual welcoming and parting; of lament and longing; or of petition or thanksgiving. These types are often ignored in the literature, as are the great variety of literary and musical forms that accompany their presentation (litany, hymn, invocation, chant, song, and so on).

Buddhist Examples

The oldest Buddhist liturgy is arguably the *uposatha* (also, *upavasatha*), or fortnightly recitation of the monastic code. Although the ritual might appear in the abstract as little more than a review of behavioral rules, in practice the *uposatha* is also a public confession of faith, a public confirmation of commitment to a sacred community. Furthermore, in some of the oldest forms found in the literature and in modern practice, it also involves the invocation of buddhas and deities as well as the classical form of the Triple Refuge. The latter may be taken as the quintessential Buddhist prayer of commitment and surrender.

Additionally, in its classical form, the review of the code in the *uposatha* took a form similar to the "chapter of faults" of Western monasticism, a ritual form that allowed for the gradual introduction of more general prayers of confession and contrition. Eventually the ritual evolved into a variety of rituals of the vow. In Mahāyāna Buddhism, this aspect evolved into the ritual of the bodhisattva vow.

A special form of prayer that may be considered the quintessential Buddhist prayer is the "dedication of merit." Here the performer offers an object, sacrifices a desire or pleasure, or performs a ritual presuming that this act will guarantee some sort of spiritual return, "merit," or a certain amount of "positive karma." The performer then offers this resulting merit itself to some other purpose, preferably attaining enlightenment itself or helping other sentient beings or members of the performer's family. This notion of "merit transference," and the corresponding practice of ritual and prayer, was a singular development during the transition between early Buddhist schools and the Mahāyāna schools. However, in some form or another it has affected all subsequent Buddhist traditions.

This particular form of prayer bridged the gap between prayer as commitment to the rules of restraint and decorum of a religious community (the vows of the monastic code) and prayer as a promise or commitment to general ethical principles (the vow of the bodhisattva). The dedication of merit, furthermore, makes it possible to transform a general act of worship into a personalized sacrificial or petitional prayer because it is possible to direct the merit to specific goals or desires.

However, Buddhist prayer occurs in contexts that go well beyond the confines of both monastic ideals and theological definitions of merit transference. We have evidence, albeit scant and sporadic, that even as the monastic liturgies and the liturgy of the bodhisattva vow were developing, Buddhists engaged in acts of devotion that involved gestures and words of praise, invocation, and evocation. A ritual could include words of welcoming that paralleled common protocols for offering hospitality or for the salutation of royalty. Although rare in the Indian context, plaintive prayers are not unknown in eastern Asia, where in the contemporary setting we also find a variety of prayers of petition – many, but not all, in the classical form of the dedication of merit. Hymns of praise are common and often serve also as confessional prayers, as in the Japanese *wasan*.

Perhaps some of the confusion regarding Buddhist prayer stems from the overwhelming primacy of meditation, that is, of mental exercise or mental ritualization, over the more obvious aspects of the external ritual. However, ritual forms – performative and rhetorical – are always closely linked to meditation. This link is unusually explicit in the tantric tradition, especially in the type of ritual-meditation script known as *sādhana*. Late tantrism, in fact, will even argue that acts of ritual and prayer can occur internally or as visualizations as well as externally and visibly. In this context it is impossible to understand the mental exercise without understanding the ritual gesture.

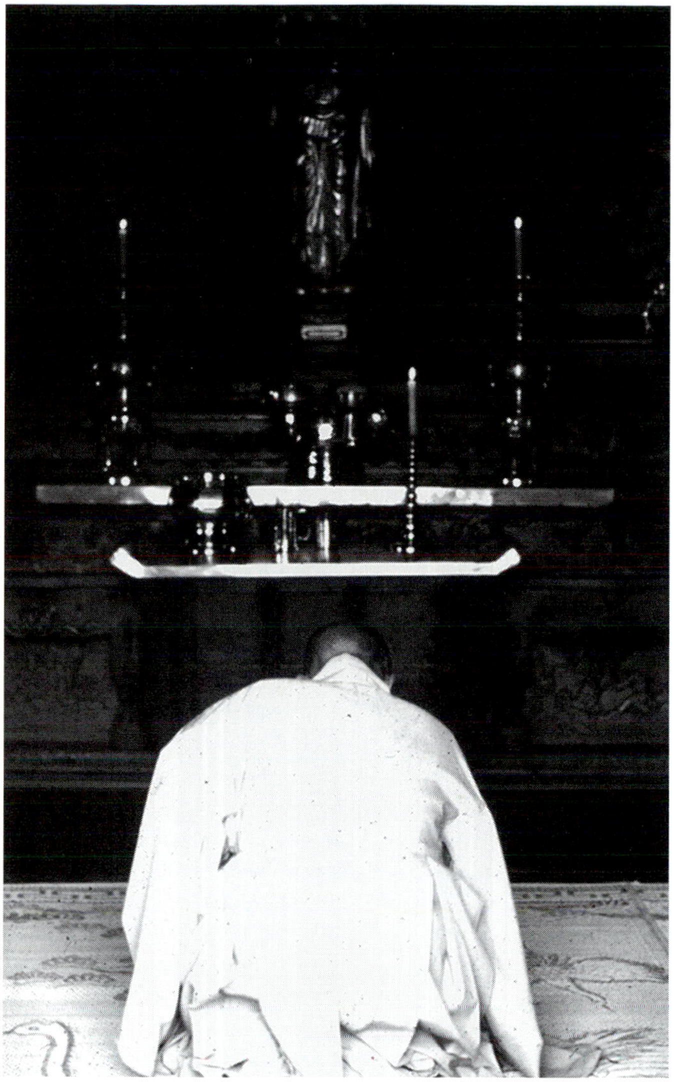

A Chinese monk praying in front of a buddha statue in a Chinese ceremony in India.
Photo courtesy of John Powers

Thus, Buddhist prayer in the broadest sense of the term occurs in a diverse range of settings and with a variety of contents and intentions. Additionally it occurs in a wide variety of forms – that is, the formal genres and the modes of utterance vary widely. Litanies and hymns are known in the earliest literature from India. These range from recitations of the names and epithets of buddhas to, in a later period, requests for help from bodhisattvas and deities, such as Avalokiteśvara and Tārā.

Invocations of different sorts are used to ward of evil or as indirect ways of petitioning (e.g., for health or better fortune). This form of prayer, known as "blessings" (*maṅgala*) or "protections" (*parittā*, *paritrāṇa*), occurs already in the canonical scriptures and is closely related to the classical *dhāraṇī* and the, perhaps more modern, *pirit*. In the *dhāraṇī* an invocation gradually shifts into a litany of rhythmic syllables that are mostly meaningless in the natural language but that are believed to somehow hold the true power of the invocation, the inner power of the deity herself or himself. In the *pirit* there is generally a greater proportion of meaningful statements of petition or invocation. Whether these forms are used as prayers of petition or protection, as invocation or praise, or even as elements of meditation or consecration, depends mainly on context, for the content of the prayer formula itself is ambiguous or simply nonreferential.

This is also true of other forms that may be distantly related (formally or psychologically, if not theologically) to the *dhāraṇī*, such as the recitation of names and mantras. In the first category one can begin with the Indian tradition of invoking the sacred names of bodhisattvas and deities. Also related genetically to this practice are several well-known Japanese practices of the invocation of sacred names: the invocation of the name of Amida, the *nenbutsu* (often written "*nembutsu*"), or the recitation of the sacred title of the *Lotus Sūtra* (*Myōhōrengekyō*). Contrary to what has sometimes been suggested, these forms of prayer, as well as all the others mentioned so far, are an integral part of monastic rituals and laicized church rituals, and they also form part of less formal or standardized forms of so-called popular prayer.

Finally, one cannot conclude a discussion of Buddhist prayer without mentioning another phenomenon on the margins of narrow definitions of prayer and closely related to the *dhāraṇī*, namely, the mantra. As in some of the other cases mentioned in this article, the mantra adapts itself to contexts that span the full social spectrum (from high monastic liturgy to informal and occasional use) and the full theological spectrum (from vehicle or embodiment of transcendent meaning to protective charm). The mantra is considerably shorter than the *dhāraṇī* and is more or less the equivalent of a phrase or short sentence in the natural language; it is composed of meaningful semantic elements combined with mystic syllables that have no transparent meaning in the natural language. For example, the famous mantra "Om mani padme hum" (*Oṃ maṇi padme huṃ*) is composed of two units with implied references (*maṇi*, "jewel," and *padma*, "lotus") and two elements that are not from the natural language; that is, they have no clear reference or meaning (*oṃ* and *huṃ*). Although Western observers have tried to give it a referential or natural meaning, even the two words taken from the natural language do not relate syntactically in any meaningful way within the mantra. Only context (usage or explanation) imbues this prayer formula with meaning.

And yet, within the tradition, it is this sort of statement that is considered to be the highest form of the religious verbal act. To paraphrase the classical folk etymology, a mantra embodies the essence of mind (*man-*) and is the means to protect body and mind (*-tra*). It is a sacred word that captures perfectly what the mind is and assures its spiritual health by transforming the mind, speech, and body of the performer into sacred reality.

Silent Prayer

Needless to say in Buddhism as in Christianity the verbal act is closely related to the idea of a nonverbal (or transcendentally verbal) communion or union with the sacred presence. The mantra and the *dhāraṇī* suggest that the language forms of prayer themselves push the verbal act beyond its function as conveyor of meaning or instrument. In the ritual act, as in poetry, language exhausts itself and touches silence in peculiar ways.

Whether one understands this meeting of utterance and silence as the foundation or the goal of the religious act or as merely an aspect of the verbal act, the two dimensions – prayer and silence – are closely related in practice as well as in theology. In fact one could argue that the most characteristic – although certainly not the most common – dimension of Buddhist prayer, especially in the monastic setting, is the Buddhist equivalent to the Western technical category of "orison." In the West orison is sometimes analyzed as composed of several degrees or modes, among which stand out a progression from oral prayer (including the act of reading, or *lectio*), through silent meditation, to the contemplation of divinity. An interesting Buddhist parallel has as its first level "hearing" (which in fact includes hearing, repeating or reciting, and memorizing and might involve the reading of sacred literature), "reflection" or "discursive meditation," and "nondiscursive realization" (i.e., "making real" the object of the discursive stage).

Because the subtleties of the latter system are discussed elsewhere in this encyclopedia, the present article has focused on other forms of "prayer." Suffice it to say that "nondiscursive realization" involves a process of internalization of or habituation to particular ways of looking at the world and the self. Yet this process of internalization takes many forms (often described in terms of "techniques of meditation") that range from a mental review of doctrinal concepts to the identification of the person (mind, speech, and body) of the meditator with a deity (so-called tantric practices).

Such meditations are usually framed in liturgical processes comprising other forms of Buddhist "prayer" presented here. However, as noted, Buddhist prayer in the broadest sense of the term occurs in a much broader range of settings. Thus, one should separate carefully attempts to describe the full range and the subcategories of Buddhist verbal acts from any attempt at defining what might be essential or what should be normative. The latter efforts, which fall under the purview of the theologian, have traditionally privileged silent prayer. Yet the importance of language as object and means suggests that perhaps there is more than one sense in which in Buddhism the verbal act is central. Perhaps there is a sense in which Buddhist prayer is "arguably the quintessential religious act" that it is taken to be in Christianity (Louth, 1998).

Luis O. Gómez

See also Deities, Buddhist; Dialogue, Intermonastic: Buddhist Perspectives; Dōgen; Hakuin; Lectio Divina; Liturgy: Buddhist; Mantras; Meditation: Buddhist Perspectives; Pure Land Buddhism; Repentance Rituals, Buddhist; Spirituality: Buddhist

Further Reading

Blofeld, John Eaton Calthorpe, *Mantras: Sacred Words of Power*, New York: Dutton, and London: Allen and Unwin, 1977

King, Sallie B., "Two Epistemological Models for the Interpretation of Mysticism," *Journal of the American Academy of Religion* 56:2 (1988)

Louth, Andrew, "Prière," in *Dictionnaire critique de théologie*, edited by Jean-Yves Lacoste, Paris: Presses Universitaires de France, 1998

Pe Maung Tin, U., *Buddhist Devotion and Meditation: An Objective Description and Study*, London: SPCK, 1964

Prayer: Christian Perspectives

Prayer in Christian monasticism has developed a variety of expressions, partly because of the many traditions within the broader division of Eastern and Western Christianity. However, the model for all is the pattern of prayer in the Gospels: (1) the prayer of Jesus, (2) Jesus' words to his disciples about prayer, (3) examples of supplication to Jesus himself, and (4) necessary qualities of prayer.

The Prayer of Jesus

Jesus sought solitude for prayer, going apart from his work to be alone with God, his father. Essential to monastic prayer, East and West, is withdrawal from the world. By 350 in the East, three distinct forms of monastic life were in existence, all marked by the belief that it is necessary to keep the Kingdom of God distinct from mundane interests: the eremitic, exemplified in St. Anthony of the Desert (250–356); the cenobitic, exemplified by St. Pachomius (c. 290–346) and set to rule by St. Basil (c. 329–379); and the semi-eremitic, characterized by smaller groups. By the sixth century in the West, St. Benedict (480–546) had founded Subiaco and Monte Cassino, and a rule of life was taking shape. The monastic tradition, rooted in the desire to attain as much of a Heavenly Kingdom on earth as possible, had been established.

The private prayer of monks and nuns involves striving for union with God and begging for their own and others' needs as well as the plea for strength and the outcry of suffering that Jesus modeled. Jesus prayed to his father in the presence of others, and likewise monastics practice what they consider a primary work: prayer and worship in common.

Jesus' Words to His Disciples about Prayer

Mount Athos and Monte Cassino can be taken as exemplary of the Eastern and Western traditions. Organized monastic life began on Mount Athos in northern Greece in 963. The peninsula became pan-Orthodox by the 11th century with monks from the Balkan peninsula and from northern Slavic countries, especially Russia, living there by the Rule of St. Basil or one derived from it. Prayer and worship are set between the two poles of the Eucharist and the Word of God, with emphasis on the interior spiritual disposition of the monk as a response to Christ's injunction to pray always. This interior life unfolds with the help of the starets (elder), or spiritual guide.

Monte Cassino in Italy was founded by St. Benedict around 529. It has undergone a number of destructions and reconstructions, the latest being in 1944, when it was destroyed by aerial bombardment, only to be rebuilt later by the Italian government. Benedictine monasticism furnished the paradigm for the other monastic orders in Western Christianity. Here as well prayer and worship are set between the two poles of the Eucharist and the Word of God, with emphasis on the Liturgy of the Hours as a response to the command to pray always.

Eastern monasticism makes use of the 150 Psalms of the Hebrew Scriptures, whereas Western monasticism is occupied with the interior life and personal spiritual direction. Nevertheless, in the literature of the two traditions a more personalist approach seems to characterize the Eastern and a more communitarian the Western.

Supplication to Jesus

The prayer of Christians has been modeled on the prayer of monastics. Its essence is union with God. However, for monks and nuns and other Christians in the East, the Jesus Prayer has been at the heart of prayer, whereas for monks and nuns and other Christians in the West, prayer before the Blessed Sacrament has been at the heart of prayer.

The aspect of prayer emphasized in Eastern writers – the inwardness of prayer – finds one of its best articulations in the writings of Theophan the Recluse (1815–1894). Prayer is a state of standing before God. Theophan says, "The principal thing is to stand with the mind in the heart before God, and to go on standing before Him unceasingly day and night, until the end of life." And again, "Inner prayer means standing with the mind in the heart before God, either simply living in His presence, or expressing supplication, thanksgiving, and glorification." For Theophan and others the human being is body, soul, and spirit. The body is matter made alive by the soul, but the spirit connects with the divine. The body acquires knowledge through the senses, the soul does so through the mind's reasoning, and the spirit does so by mystical insight passing beyond the intellect. The heart is the dwelling place of God – of his angels and saints – or else the dwelling of his adversaries. The heart is threefold: material, psychic, and above all joined to the spirit. It is the innermost, the hidden. Thus it is that to pray "with the mind in the heart" allows a person to "know God." The progress of inner prayer is travel into the deep places of the heart, a regress into the grace of Baptism. Such prayer abstains from images but not from feeling, which is experienced as spiritual light and warmth (see *The Art of Prayer*, edited by Timothy Ware, 1966).

The Jesus Prayer is the prayer of the heart par excellence for Eastern monasticism and for Orthodoxy in general. Its usual form is "Lord Jesus Christ, Son of God, have mercy on me," but it has several variations. The ascesis of the spiritual life requires the repetition of the Jesus Prayer so that it moves inward from the oral to the mental to the heart. It is intended to penetrate the whole person, becoming the heartbeat of the person, even coinciding with the physical heart's actual rhythm. The prayer has biblical foundations, and the name of Jesus was frequently invoked by the first Christians. Early monastics followed the practice of reciting short ejaculations, such as "Lord, have mercy," but Orthodox Christianity has given primary place to the formula of the Jesus Prayer.

In Western monasticism and in the Western spiritual tradition of prayer, by way of contrast, the first and pervasive form is prayer before the Blessed Sacrament. This also has biblical foundations. Christ told his disciples to do what he did at the Last Supper and to do it in remembrance of him. The Liturgy of the Word and the Liturgy of the Eucharist provide the source and summit of prayer in both the Eastern and the Western traditions. However, numerous saints of the Catholic Church have cultivated deep devotion to the Blessed Sacrament reserved in the tabernacles of churches, chapels, and oratories, whether monastic, conventual, or parochial. John Henry Newman (1801–1890) said that he never knew what worship was, "as an objective fact," until he became a Catholic (*The Letters and Diaries of John Henry Newman: XI: Littlemore to Rome, October 1845 to December 1846*, 1961). As a new convert he was in awe of dwelling under the same roof with Christ. He wrote,

> I am writing next room to the Chapel – it is such an incomprehensible blessing to have Christ in bodily presence in one's house, within one's walls, as swallows up all other privileges and destroys, or should destroy, every pain. To know that He is close by – to be able again and again through the day to go in to Him.

The Carmelite Thérèse of Lisieux (1873–1897) wrote, "Frequently, only silence can express my prayer; however, this divine Guest of the Tabernacle understands all" (*St. Therese of Lisieux: General Correspondence*, translated by John Clarke, 1988).

The monk or nun makes a brief or extended visit, speaking to Christ present, listening to him, being in silence before him. Then he or she carries into community the grace and love experienced in the private visit. Moreover, others might be present in the church, chapel, or oratory praying. There might also be a Holy Hour of adoration, an all-night adoration, a Benediction of the Most Blessed Sacrament, or a Eucharistic procession, all forms of praying before the Blessed Sacrament.

Qualities of Prayer

Monastic prayer is imbued with the great Christian virtue of charity. The holy man of the East, St. John of Kronstadt (1829–1908), says that the one who prays should try to feel with his heart the truth and power of his prayer. He should avoid overanxiety, doubt, and "diabolical dreaminess." He should not be "cold, sly, untrue, and double-faced" (John of Kronstadt, 1985). Saint John also says that the more emotional and ardent one's prayer, the humbler the one praying; the more inexpressive, the prouder. However, the real worth of prayer can be measured by the quality of our relations with others. John asks, Is our discourse with others about requests, about praise, about gratitude? When we do something for others, is it with warmth, from the heart, or is it done coldly, merely out of duty or courtesy?

Circle of Gerard David, Netherlandish, *Portrait of a Monk*, early 1500s, oil on wood, 36 x 30.4 cm. The Cleveland Museum of Art, 1999, bequest of John. L. Severance, 1942.632.
Photo courtesy of The Cleveland Museum of Art

Are we hypocritical or sincere? We will behave exactly the same way with God. Finally, John says, the greatest gift of prayer is peace of heart.

Saint Teresa of Avila (1515–1582) and St. John of the Cross (1542–1591) are two of the most distinguished writers on prayer in Western monasticism. Saint Teresa has much to say about humility and prayer. She tells the nuns in her monastery that if their prayer is dry and without consolation, they should derive humility from the experience. If humility is present, there will be peace and conformity. Sometimes dryness in prayer is due to imperfections in personal life. If acknowledged, this too can be beneficial for humility. Humility enables the prayer of thanksgiving. The fruit of prayer is not consolation but love of God and deeds done with greater truth and love (Teresa of Avila, 1979). Saint John of the Cross emphasizes faith, perfected by charity and the gifts of the Holy Spirit, as a means of union with God. He teaches, following St. Thomas Aquinas (c. 1225–1274), that the intellect in its natural capacity is incapable of attaining union with God. However, faith operates in the intellect, again according to St. Thomas. The intellect will see the essence of God in the beatific vision of heaven. On this earth the vision of the soul is by faith; its knowledge rests on belief. Thus, faith for St. John of the Cross provides the means to reach union with God, or prayer (Wojtyla, 1981).

What emerges in the contrast between authoritative spiritual writers in the Eastern and Western traditions is a difference in confidence regarding feeling, the heart, and spiritual sweetness. The East trusts the human heart elevated by God; the West trusts the will elevated by grace. If these contrasts are justified by observation of fact, they are even more justified when considered as two sides of the many-sided religion of Christianity. Monastic prayer, East and West, embodies Gospel prayer as this has evolved in the histories and traditions of Christianity.

MARY BERNARD CURRAN, O.P.

See also Basil the Great, St.; Benedict of Nursia, St.; Devotions, Western Christian; Elders, Russian Monastic (Startsi); Fasting: Western Christian; John of the Cross, St.; Monte Cassino, Italy; Mount Athos, Greece; Orthodox Monasticism: Slavic; Russia: Recent Changes; Seasons, Liturgical; Spirituality: Eastern Christian; Teresa of Avila, St.; Thérèse of Lisieux, St.; Thomas Aquinas, St.; Vision, Mystical: Eastern Christian

Further Reading

Bolshakoff, Sergius, and M. Basil Pennington, *In Search of True Wisdom: Visits to Eastern Spiritual Fathers*, Garden City, New York: Doubleday, 1979

John Cassian, The Conferences, translated and annotated by Boniface Ramsey, New York: Paulist Press, 1997

John of Kronstadt, *On Prayer*, Jordansville, New York: Holy Trinity Monastery, 1985

Prayer of the Heart: Writings from the Philokalia, translated and edited by G.E.W. Palmer, Philip Sherrard, and Kallistos Ware, Boston and London: Faber and Faber, 1992

Spidlik, Tomas, *The Spirituality of the Christian East: A Systematic Handbook*, translated by Anthony P. Gythiel, Kalamazoo, Michigan: Cistercian Publications, 1986

Teresa of Avila, *The Interior Castle*, translated with an introduction by Kieran Kavanaugh, New York: Paulist Press, 1979

Theofan, Saint, *Kindling the Divine Spark*, translated by Valentina V. Lyovin, Platina, California: St. Xenia Skete Press, 1994

Ware, Timothy, editor, *The Art of Prayer: An Orthodox Anthology*, London: Faber, 1966

Wojtyla, Karol, *Faith According to St. John of the Cross*, translated by Jordan Aumann, San Francisco: Ignatius Press, 1981

Premonstratensian Canons

The Premonstratensians are an international order of regular canons named after their first house at Prémontré in northern France. The Premonstratensians have also been known as the Canons Regular of Prémontré, Norbertines, and in England the White Canons, so called for their undyed habits.

The Order of Premonstratensian Canons was begun by St. Norbert of Xanten (c. 1080–1134). Born of noble parents near the present-day border of the Netherlands and Germany, the young Norbert was a worldly cleric first in the court of the archbishop of Cologne and then in the retinue of Emperor Henry V (1106–1125). After a religious conversion that began during a thunderstorm in 1115, Norbert was ordained a priest. When attempts to reform the clergy of his native Xanten met with hostility, Norbert abandoned his worldly goods and lucrative benefices; he journeyed to southern France, where Pope Gelasius II (1118–1119) authorized him to embark on a career as a wandering preacher. His preaching and teaching drew crowds of religious enthusiasts. Encouraged by Gelasius' successor, Calixtus II (1119–1124), and with the support of Bishop Bartholomew of Laon, in 1120 Norbert settled some of his followers in the quiet valley of Prémontré, about nine miles west of Laon. The Order began to take shape quickly. In 1121 Norbert founded a second house at Floreffe, in what is now southeastern Belgium, and others appeared within a few years. In 1126 Norbert, a missionary at heart, was elected archbishop of the See of Magdeburg, deep in still mainly pagan territory. From Magdeburg the Premonstratensian Order spread across central Europe before Norbert's death in 1134.

One facet of the economic and religious revival in Europe in the 11th and 12th centuries was the appearance of numerous communities of religious who called themselves canons. In this era, as an early 12th-century tract on various religious orders put it, canons lived in isolation from laymen, while other clergy lived close to or among men. These latter were often affiliated with churches or courts and were often worldly, as Norbert had been in his youth. Norbert's mature vision was for a community both contemplative and active, imitating the apostolic life in prayer and pastoral activity but functioning more away from men than among them. Moreover this life was to be open to all who wanted to join. Canons, nuns (later canonesses), and lay

Premonstratensian Abbey of Bellapais, Northern Cyprus, 14th century, sacked 1570. The view is from the gate tower north-northeast toward the cloisters and the refectory.
Photo courtesy of Chris Schabel

brothers and sisters joined together at Prémontré and other houses of the nascent order under the Rule of St. Augustine. The structure of clerics and laity living together later provided the model for the Dominicans and Franciscans. Divine service and care for the poor, the sick, and pilgrims in *xenodochia* (hospices) were equally important for the first Premonstratensians. Men and women lived in the same enclosure, with separate buildings for each gender and a common church. In 1126 Norbert obtained papal approval for the Order.

Not foreseeing a centralized order of houses, Norbert had continued his preaching mission rather than settle at Prémontré. The work of organization was carried out mainly by Hugh of Fosse, the first abbot of Prémontré, who preserved Norbert's ideals and their lived expression while regularizing houses of Prémontré and their organization. Hugh summoned the first Premonstratensian general chapter, which in 1128 assembled six superiors under Hugh, now the first abbot general of the Order. Three years later 18 houses of the Order existed, and when Hugh died in 1161 there were more than 100. By the middle of the 13th century, at least 500 Premonstratensian abbeys and priories stretched from Poland to Spain and from Norway and the British Isles to Palestine. Most of these were founded as colonies from established houses, but in some cases existing houses of canons or monks were incorporated.

Two changes characterized the evolution of the Order during its first century: exclusion of women and excellence in letters. The oldest extant account of Norbert and the Order, written around 1150, emphasized the preacher's mission to women, in explicit contrast with their exclusion from Cîteaux, the great Burgundian mother house of the Cistercian order of monks. "So if lord Norbert had done nothing else – disregarding for the moment conversion of men – but to attract so many women to divine service by his exhortation, would he not still be worthy of the highest praise?" However, starting around 1137, only a few years after Norbert died, the general chapter had mandated the physical separation of male and female communities. Some communities of sisters moved quickly and far from the male house; others did not relocate for decades and then moved only a short distance. Despite papal reminders to the canons of their continued material and spiritual obligations, the Order as a whole made little effort to perpetuate these communities of canonesses, and only a handful remained a century after the first separation decree. On the other hand, the Order of the 12th and 13th centuries was distinguished by an outstanding intellectual tradition. Its foremost writers include theologians Anselm of Hevelberg (d. 1158), Philip of Harvengt (c. 1100–1183), and Adam of Dryburgh (1127/40–c. 1213); the historian Burchard of Ursberg (before 1177–1231); and the poet Hermann Joseph of Steinfeld (d. 1241). Abbeys soon became training centers for clerics. Thus, the Premonstratensians made an important contribution to intellectual and educational life in the central Middle Ages.

The wealth of some Premonstratensian communities, their engagement with extraclaustral matters, and the canons' acquiescence to private wealth lead some historians to label the later Middle Ages a period of decline for the Order. Despite a period of reform in the wake of the Council of Trent (1545–1563), the political and religious dislocations in early modern Europe reduced the Order to a few communities by the early 19th century. Revival began in the Low Countries in the 1830s and included the foundation of missionary houses in the Americas, Africa, Asia, and Australia. Numerous communities of Premonstratensians still exist in Europe and abroad. In the United States the Premonstratensians are closely associated with Catholic secondary education.

Premonstratensian Abbey of Bellapais, Northern Cyprus, 14th century. A view from the cloister range to the lavabo, which is a Roman sarcophagus.
Photo courtesy of Chris Schabel

Premonstratensian Abbey of Bellapais, Northern Cyprus, 14th century. A view of the cloister walk terminating in a window into the chapter house.
Photo courtesy of Chris Schabel

BRUCE L. VENARDE

See also Double Houses, Western Christian; Fontevraud, France; France: History; Germany: Sites; Liturgy: Western Christian; Orders (Religious), Origin of; Poland

Further Reading

Note: the journal *Analecta Praemonstratensia* (January 1925–) publishes scholarship on the history of the order, and monographs appear regularly in the series Bibliotheca Analectorum Praemonstratensium.

Ardura, Bernard, *Abbayes, prieurés et monastères de l'ordre de Prémontré en France des origines à nos jours: Dictionnaire*

historique et bibliographique, Nancy: Presses universitaires de Nancy, 1993
Backmund, Norbert, *Monasticon Praemonstratense: Id est, Historia circariarum atque canoniarum candidi et canonici Ordinis Praemonstratensis*, 3 vols., Straubing: Cl. Attenkofersche Buchdruckerei, 1949–1956; reprint, Berlin: de Gruyter, 1983
Backmund, Norbert, *Geschichte des Prämonstratenserordens*, Grafenau: Morsak, 1986
Bulloch, James, *Adam of Dryburgh*, London: SPCK, 1958
Colvin, Howard M., *The White Canons in England*, Oxford: Clarendon Press, 1951
Erens, A., "Les soeurs dans l'ordre de Prémontré," *Analecta Praemonstratensia* 5 (1929)
Goovaerts, Léon, *Écrivains, artistes, et savants de l'Ordre de Prémontré: Dictionnaire bio-bibliographique*, 4 vols., Brussels: Société belge de librairie, 1899–1920
Kirkfleet, Cornelius J., *The White Canons of St. Norbert, a History of the Premonstratensian Order in the British Isles and America*, West De Pere, Wisconsin: St. Norbert Abbey, 1943
Petit, François, *La spiritualité des Prémontrés au XIIe et XIIIe siècles*, Paris: Vrin, 1947
Petit, François, *Norbert et l'origine des Prémontrés*, Paris: CERF, 1981

Prophethood, Japanese Buddhist

Buddhist monks are typed by Max Weber as "otherworldly mystics"; and in his scheme mystics are not expected to become "emissary prophets" who aim to change the world according to the will of God. However, such ideal types do not always cover the full range of possibilities, and within the wider spectrum of monastic expressions, Buddhist as well as Christian, there exist known trends toward more active world engagement. Shortly before Weber died in 1920, Anesaki Masaharu, who held the first Religionswissenschaft chair in Japan, condensed his study on Nichiren (1222–1282) into a shorter English work published by Harvard (1916) titled *Nichiren, the Buddhist Prophet*. Anesaki did not seem to know Weber's analysis of Buddhism or his comments on Nichiren's career. Thus, no exchange occurred on the usage of the terms *prophet* or *prophethood*. This article imagines that missed exchange by exploring the Buddhist premise that allowed Nichiren to become an "emissary" and a "mouthpiece" of the Buddha with a call to change Japan and the world. During World War II the mainline Nichiren temples supported Japan's war effort; that expresses Nichiren nationalism. The lay founder of the Soka Gakkai opposed the war; this is how the *Lotus Sūtra* might hold the nation in judgment.

The term operative in Anesaki's study is the Sanskrit *vyākarana* (assurance), rendered into English sometimes as "prophecy." It is derivative of one of the supernatural powers that came with the Buddha's enlightenment, namely, his omniscience or ability to recall all past lives and anticipate all future destinies of self and others. *Vyākarana* constitutes that "foretelling" with which the Buddha could positively "assure" a specific person or being about his or her future enlightened status. In one sense this equates with the crude reading of "prophecy" as "telling the future." The primary sense of the biblical prophet, or *nabi*, is that he is a "spokesman" for God. However, given the proper circumstance, as happened in the case of Nichiren, *vyākarana* as "personal assurance" may combine with *anuparidāna* (commission: the Buddha entrusting his disciples with a mission) to produce the same effect as biblical prophethood.

The first commission was given by the Buddha to the five ascetics who became his disciples. He told them to "go forth and teach likewise" his pathway to nirvāṇa. The original *Lotus Sūtra* (minus the later appended chapters) also ended with a commission: Go and spread the Lotus gospel – this good news that the Buddha is eternal and that everyone is welcomed into his presence and into the single vehicle of his Buddhayana. To underscore the last point, this Mahāyāna sūtra offers a generous amount of "assurances." The entire congregation that gathered around the Buddha – monk or lay, human or nonhuman – who heard the Buddha preach were assured of their future Buddhahood. Even Hīnayāna arhats will graduate into becoming Buddhas. In that regard the *Lotus Sūtra* planted one of the seeds for the notion of a "universal Buddha-nature" which came to fruition in the Mahāyāna *Nirvāṇa Sūtra*.

However, unlike that later philosophical dictum, assurances are, by their nature, always personal and specific. Like biblical revelation, assurance specifies this person's or those people's outcome in a future time and place. Such prophecy does not dissolve the temporal or spatial framework (however acosmic that framework might seem to us) into some generalized abstraction such as "all sentient beings have Buddha-nature." An important observation made by Taga Ryūgen in *Juki shisō no genryū to tenkai* (1974; On the Origin and Development of the Concept "Vyākarana") is precisely this: that as the specification of assured destinies matured in time into the doctrine of "universal Buddhahood" and as the *Nirvāṇa Sūtra* staked out that crisp, colorless doctrine, this sūtra thereby eliminated the need for the genre of *vyākarana* (assurance). That universal dictum delighted the Chan/Zen tradition. Chan/Zen espoused it. It also denied any historical degeneration of the dharma. In 13th-century Japan Nichiren condemned Zen, calling for a return to the all-inclusive Tendai school, and became the apocalyptic advocate of the *Lotus Sūtra*.

Anxiety about an end time emerges in the later chapters of the *Lotus Sūtra*. The text sprang from the once prosperous Mahāyāna center in northwestern India that faced renewed conflict, foreign invasion, and a Hindu revival around A.D. 300. To curb that decline of the dharma, this scripture urged a defense of the Lotus Dharma in an ardent hope for a revivified Ekayana (Single Vehicle). As participants in a millennial drama set on a cosmic stage, four heavenly hosts rose out of the four directions of the universe. Leading the army and ready to do battle in the East is the Bodhisattva Superior Conduct. All this appealed to Nichiren.

Nichiren was born into the midst of the so-called Kamakura Buddhist reformation in Japan. In the 13th century arose the new schools, beginning with the Pure Land sect, which broke away from the once "catholic" (all-inclusive, singular vehicle of the) Tendai school of the previous Heian era. Lamenting that historic schism, Nichiren, a steward of the Tendai tradition, took as his new name "Nichiren" (Sun + Lotus) from *Nihon* (Japan) and *Renge* (Lotus Blossom). He had been reading the *Lotus Sūtra* "with his flesh and blood," that is, as if it were addressed personally to him. He saw his own trial and tribulation foretold by the sūtra. With a radical Kierkegaardian ("truth is subjectivity") hermeneutics, he reviewed his past life and saw his having been rebutted by fellow Buddhists, his having been waylaid by enemies, and his near-death execution by the state all foretold in the *Lotus Sūtra*, in the career of the Bodhisattva Never Despise (i.e., always turning the other cheek), who under similar duress had remained the ever patient preacher. Nichiren saw himself in that figure; he *is* him. Then, on 20 December 1271, during his exile at Sado, he rose triumphant above his despair. He further realized that he was even more intensely the Bodhisattva Superior Conduct, the one destined to rise in the East (namely, Japan) during the last age to save Japan and the world. At that time the last age, or the millennium of the Degenerate Dharma, had been dated to commence in 1252. As Anesaki's title for his Japanese study would have it, Nichiren was a man with a mission destined to carry out the deeds or project of the Lotus Dharma.

That Buddhist monks could be "men on a mission" carrying a message more than "otherworldly mystical" is to be expected. Buddhist monks had long been actively involved in the world, and if Nichirenism has had a reputation of being the more militant wing of the Kamakura (counter) Reformation, that too is expected. He counted samurai warriors in his following, and in his single-minded devotion to the *Lotus Sūtra* he was not one to compromise. One Nichiren group openly refused any give-and-take with other Buddhist groups, but even that militant intolerance has its own history. The *Nirvāṇa Sūtra* arrived at the tolerant position of "all sentient beings have Buddha-nature" only toward the end. Faced with enemies of the dharma in northwestern India around 300, it had previously condemned certain evil people to eternal ignorance and even considered it permissible to kill them. In seeming violation of the Buddhist first principle of nonviolence, it called for an armed defense of the dharma. That led to the first "armed defense" of the city of Liangzhou (Liang-chou) in China in 439. Less noble might be the "monk-soldiers" of Heian Japan, a private army of the major temples given the nominal designation of monks. Through the *Lotus Sūtra* Nichiren espoused both utter humility as Bodhisattva Never Despise and superhuman confidence as Bodhisattva Superior Conduct, and in his writings he took care to keep the "I" of Nichiren apart. The "I" is so karma laden and sin ridden as to deserve all the misfortune he incurred. He refers to the flawless Bodhisattva Superior Conduct in the third person. To draw a Pauline parallel, that Bodhisattva is not him but the "Christ/Perfection in him." That Nichiren should believe the *Lotus Sūtra* to be talking to him and about him is not a mere subjective assumption. It accords with the narrative mode of the *Lotus Sūtra* itself. Whereas the Chan/Zen tradition justifies its claim to incontestable Truth by proclaiming a hidden, unbroken patriarchal transmission, the *Lotus Sūtra* needs no such myth. It opts for having the Words of the Buddha summon the auditor or reader into the presence of the Eternal Buddha, even now, at Vulture Peak. In its opening chapter the one who responded to the Buddha's Word (*Buddhavacana*) is Mañjuśrī, the guardian of Mahāyāna wisdom. He is transported, by way of memory, back to the first time when he heard that dharma preached. The Tiantai school in China was founded by Master Zhiyi when he met his master, Huisi. Their encounter transported both back, so the tradition insists, to their prior audience at Vulture Peak, where they received the *Lotus Sūtra* from the Buddha's "golden mouth," directly without mediation. Nichiren extended that notion to find his own prefiguration in the Bodhisattva Superior Conduct. Mount Minoru, where Nichiren spent his last years, becomes the transplanted Vulture Peak to his followers.

Ultimately the question is not whether "emissary prophethood" can exist in Buddhism. The question for any "man of mission" is, rather, What is the content, the world vision, of his call? For Nichiren there is only one world and one vision, whose egalitarian core is Buddhist but whose manifest values are East Asian. Today among his followers, Soka Gakkai boasts the third-largest party in the Japanese Parliament, the "clean" party of the Komeito. It champions time-honored values and a futuristic "Third Democracy" based on the principles of the *Lotus Sūtra*. More recently a falling out has occurred between the ordained heads of the Nichiren Shōshu (the small host temple) and the lay leadership of the Soka Gakkai, the massive, modern movement. Both claim to speak in the name of Nichiren's prophethood.

WHALEN LAI

See also Buddhist Schools/Traditions: Japan; Chan/Zen: Japan; Critiques of Buddhist Monasticism: Confucian; Disciples, Early Buddhist; Discourses (Sūtras): Mahāyāna; Governance: Buddhist Perspectives; Japan: History; Nation-Building and Japanese Buddhism; Rennyo; Warrior Monks: Buddhist

Further Reading

Anesaki, Masaharu, *Nichiren, the Buddhist Prophet*, Cambridge, Massachusetts: Harvard University Press, and London: Oxford University Press, 1916

Hurvitz, Leon, translator, *Scripture of the Lotus Blossom of the Fine Dharma*, New York: Columbia University Press, 1976

Lai, Whalen, "Why the Lotus Sūtra? On the Historical Significance of Tendai," *Japanese Journal of Religious Studies* 14:2:3 (1985)

Li, Huiren, "Some Notes on Mystical Militancy," *Insights* 2:2 (1977)

Weber, Max, *The Religion of India*, Glencoe, Illinois: Free Press, 1958

Wilson, Robert R., *Prophecy and Society in Ancient Israel*, Philadelphia: Fortress Press, 1980

Protestant Monasticism: Lutheran

Although the Lutheran Reformation leveled discouraging criticism against the monasticism of the late Middle Ages, neither Martin Luther (1483–1546) nor the confessional documents that emerged from his movement explicitly prohibited monastic life. In the event, however, in what became the Lutheran denomination, monastic life declined and disappeared and came to be viewed by most Lutherans as foreign to their tradition.

In more recent times the monastic impulse has reemerged, if somewhat tentatively, among Lutherans. The earliest sign of a new attitude were the deaconess communities organized in the mid–19th century by Pastor Theodor Fliedner (1800–1864) near Düsseldorf, Germany. Although these communities emphasized service and were not strictly monastic, common life and prayer prevailed. Enough parallels existed with Roman Catholic active orders for women that the participants were informally considered "Lutheran nuns."

Monastic life in explicit form has reappeared among Lutherans in the second half of the 20th century. In 1960 four theology students in Sweden made simple religious vows quietly but with the blessing of their bishop in the Lutheran State Church of Sweden. At first some interest existed in the Franciscan style of life, and for a time some of the brothers served in a very active pastoral ministry. However, by 1970 it was clear that the community had coalesced around the monastic Rule of St. Benedict. The brothers moved into an old country school building at their present location of Östanbäck near Sala. The building was dedicated as the Monastery of the Holy Cross and the Prophet Elijah by a Swedish bishop, and the community continues to function within the Lutheran Church of Sweden.

Father Caesarius Cavallin is the current superior of the community, which numbers ten, including those in junior vows. The full Benedictine *horarium* is maintained, including the daily celebration of Mass according to the official rite of the Church of Sweden. The offices are generally sung to the traditional tones, and much music from the Latin *Antiphonale Monasticum* has been adapted into Swedish. In addition to an active ministry to guests, the brothers are engaged in candle making, gardening, and most recently the raising of koi, an ornamental fish from Japan.

In Germany the Priory of St. Wigberti had its beginnings in 1967 when several Lutheran men began to live together guided by the Rule of St. Benedict and under the sympathetic eye of their local Lutheran bishop. Six years later the community moved to Werningshausen when one member was ordained and stationed there. Under the then existing East German government, the church building was slated to be torn down. The community set about rebuilding this church and its liturgical life, but not without arousing the suspicions of the state authorities. Since then it has done similar restoration work on 20 other churches in the region. In 1987 the constitution of the community was finally approved, and the Priory of St. Wigberti received official recognition within the German Lutheran Church. After extensive building and rebuilding, the community resides in a beautiful complex comprising the parish church of St. Wigberti, the monastic cloister, the guest house, and a small chapel.

Under the leadership of Pater Franz Schwarz, the monastic community has grown to ten members, including four Roman Catholics, and has been instrumental in the renewal of the Christian faith and life in Werningshausen and the surrounding region. A traditional daily schedule of prayer from morning to evening is kept, and the liturgical offices are prayed in a dignified fashion enhanced by music and the visual arts.

The community and local parish church gather for the Sunday Mass, which is well attended and is celebrated in a fullness of liturgical form not often seen among German Lutherans. In addition to parish ministry, in which all the monks are encouraged to participate, the time of the brothers is taken up with the care of guests, a communion wafer factory, a gift shop, and the upkeep of the buildings and grounds.

A third community is located in the United States. Saint Augustine's House actually pre-dates the others but also remains the smallest. Its founder, Father Arthur Carl Kreinheder, gave up a successful business career in midlife and moved to Sweden to study theology and to be ordained. He was briefly a novice of the Protestant Taizé community in France before returning to the United States. In 1956 he founded the Fellowship of St. Augustine to pray for and encourage the establishment of a Lutheran monastic community in the United States. His home, on 40 acres near Oxford, Michigan, became a retreat center for the Fellowship, and here he and two other men incorporated the Congregation of the Servants of Christ with a Benedictine rule of life. Since the death of the founder, there has been only one fully professed member, but responsibility for the life of the community is shared by many members of the Fellowship. With their participation and support, a recognizable monastic life is maintained with the traditional prayer offices and daily Mass.

A number of other communities at least loosely identified with the Lutheran tradition live a more or less monastic lifestyle, although not always derived from the Benedictine model. The Evangelical Sisterhood of Mary was founded after World War II near Darmstadt, Germany, and now has a number of daughter houses in various countries, including the United States. More recent are the Casteller Ring Community in Germany for women and, in Sweden, the Daughters of Mary, the Sisters of the Holy Spirit, the Sisters of Mary Magdalene, and several other foundations for women, including a Franciscan one and an Augustinian order for men.

Conferences of Lutheran bishops in both Sweden and Germany have issued statements appreciative of monastic life. Although no American Lutheran jurisdiction has made any comparable statement, the existence of monastic life among Lutherans is recognized and even welcomed by many influential U.S. Lutherans. Only time will tell whether monastic life will be able to sustain itself within the Lutheran ethos.

RICHARD G. HERBEL

See also Dissolution of Monasteries: Continental Europe; Luther, Martin; Reformation; Scandinavia; Taizé, France; Vadstena, Sweden

Further Reading

Biot, François, *The Rise of Protestant Monasticism*, translated by W.J. Kerrigan, Baltimore, Maryland: Helicon, 1963

Bloesch, Donald G., *Wellsprings of Renewal: Promise in Christian Communal Life*, Grand Rapids, Michigan: Eerdmans, 1974

Halkenhäuser, Johannes, *Kirche und Kommunität: Ein Beitrag zur Geschichte und zum Auftrag der kommunitären Bewegung in den Kirchen der Reformation*, Paderborn: Bonifatius-Druckerei, 1978
Weckman, George, *My Brothers' Place: An American Lutheran Monastery*, Lawrenceville, Virginia: Brunswick, 1992

Protestant Monasticism: Waldensian

Waldensianism was a heretical Christian sect launched by Valdes ("Waldo" and "Peter" are later additions to his name), a wealthy businessman who lived in Lyons, France, during the later 12th and early 13th century. Waldensian communities existed in France and Italy during Valdes' lifetime (the founder died sometime between 1205 and 1218) and spread to Germany and eastern Europe by the end of the 13th century. This article discusses the monasticism of the Waldensians from their 12th-century foundation until the late Middle Ages, when many Waldensian communities fused with the developing Protestant churches of the 16th century.

The foundation of Waldensian monasticism rested on three practices: embracing poverty, preaching the Christian Gospels openly and widely, and performing charitable works. Unlike conventional monasticism, which often demanded monks and nuns to be cloistered, Waldensian monasticism (especially in its later years) was performed in the world and in this sense anticipated later Protestant piety, which emphasized the importance of inner-worldly asceticism.

Beyond noting the shared values of poverty, preaching, and charity, few other generalizations can be made about Waldensian monasticism. Known variously as *barbi*, *fratres*, *Meister*, and *perfecti*, Waldensian brothers and sisters, who were often recruited from peasant and artisan families, owned nothing individually and rejected the communal wealth of monasteries. Some Waldensians were initiated into the brotherhood during a formal two- or three-year probation, during which they learned to read and write and were assigned to senior brothers who acted as spiritual mentors. Others believed that the act of embracing poverty itself was the equivalent of taking Holy Orders. Many Waldensian brothers and sisters begged for food and took shelter wherever they could. Others, however, lived a more stable existence, such as the sisters who inhabited houses in Montcuq and Beaucaire.

Although Waldensian monks and nuns rejected some of the practices of the Roman Church, they generally accepted its dogma. Indeed it appears that some brothers had among them learned men who adapted the traditions of the Roman Church to brothers of less learning. Some, however, departed from tradition and supported such practices as the rebaptism of adults and the hearing of confession by any Christian who had embraced apostolic poverty. Others rejected many if not all of the orthodox prayers, with the exception of the Lord's Prayer (which they emphasized). They also rejected the concept of purgatory and the power of the saints to intercede. Some, like the Donatists who had preceded them centuries earlier, maintained that the spiritual state of a brother or sister would affect the efficacy of the sacrament that he or she administered. Some argued that the Eucharist should be offered once a year, but others held that it should be made available daily. One of the most radical breaks that Waldensian monasticism made with the Roman Church was to accommodate women, who could not only hear confessions and be itinerant preachers but could also consecrate the Eucharist during the first century of the movement. However, the functions of Waldensian nuns became more restricted as of the late 13th century.

The organization of Waldensian brothers also varied from region to region. Some communities contained deacons, priests, and bishops and expected members to climb the ladder of hierarchical offices. Others, however, appear to have been modeled on a priesthood of all believers, a concept popular with many Protestants during the early modern period. Many communities met in chapters two or more times a year to discuss organizational and administrative matters. The threat of persecution during the later Middle Ages usually served to rigidify the hierarchy of the monastic communities, many of which lost their separate identities during the Protestant Reformation.

Dawn Marie Hayes

See also Anticlericalism: Christian Perspectives; Reformation

Further Reading

Audisio, Gabriel, *Les "Vaudois": Naissance, vie et mort d'une dissidence (XIIe–XVIe siècles)*, Turin: Meynier, 1989
Biller, Peter, "*Multum ieiunantes et se castigantes*: Medieval Waldensian Asceticism," *Studies in Church History* 22 (1985)
Cameron, Euan, *The Reformation of the Heretics: The Waldenses of the Alps, 1480–1580*, Oxford: Clarendon Press, and New York: Oxford University Press, 1984
Gonnet, Giovanni, and Amedeo Molnár, *Les Vaudois au Moyen Age*, Turin: Claudiana, 1974
Kaelber, Lutz, *Schools of Asceticism: Ideology and Organization in Medieval Religious Communities*, University Park: Pennsylvania State University Press, 1998
Kieckhefer, Richard, *The Repression of Heresy in Medieval Germany*, Philadelphia: University of Pennsylvania Press, and Liverpool: Liverpool University Press, 1979
Lambert, Malcolm, *Medieval Heresy: Popular Movements from the Gregorian Reform to the Reformation*, London: Arnold, 1977; 2nd edition, Oxford and Cambridge, Massachusetts: Blackwell, 1992
Leff, Gordon, *Heresy in the Later Middle Ages: The Relation of Heterodoxy to Dissent c. 1250–c. 1450*, volume 2, Manchester: Manchester University Press, and New York: Barnes and Noble, 1967
Marthaler, Berard, "Forerunners of the Franciscans: The Waldenses," *Franciscan Studies* 18 (1958)
Wakefield, Walter, *Heresy, Crusade and Inquisition in Southern France, 1100–1250*, Berkeley: University of California Press, and London: Allen and Unwin, 1974
Wakefield, Walter, and A.P. Evans, editors, *Heresies of the High Middle Ages*, London and New York: Columbia University Press, 1969

Pseudo-Dionysius. *See* Dionysius the Pseudo-Areopagite

Pure Land Buddhism

Buddhism began with an ancient Indian renunciant model defined by the myth of Śākyamuni. However, as the tradition began to diversify in the Mahāyāna movement, among the first variations was the Pure Land teaching, which was included in the earliest Mahāyāna literature in India (around A.D. 100; the central texts included the larger *Sukhāvatī-vyūha* and the smaller *Sukhāvatī-[amrta]vyūha* or *Amitābha-vyūha*). The object of Pure Land teaching was to obtain "rebirth" in a cosmological realm, called a Pure Land, by orienting oneself to the Amitābha Buddha, who governed it. This rebirth karmically transferred one's stream of consciousness to a special environment in which spiritual conditions for enlightenment were more auspicious, thus shifting transformative changes (which ideally might be undergone by a renunciant specialist in this world) to a future place and time where such transformation might be more accessible. Although the descriptions of the Pure Land famously featured many paradisac details, the ultimate aim was always the eventual attainment of Buddhist nirvāṇa, not the transitional rebirth itself.

The Pure Land mythos developed logically within the Mahāyāna movement (typically all of Indian Mahāyāna integrated emptiness philosophy, cosmology, meditation, a hierarchical ritual monastic system, and personal contact with concrete deities) and was an expression of ancient ideas about the vows of the bodhisattva. The distinctive character of the Pure Land mythos was the openness of the presupposed conditions needed to achieve transition to the Pure Land. In theory even beings who had not done well over their current lifetimes in attending to the Buddha could achieve rebirth with Amitābha if, for example, they directed their thoughts properly on their deathbeds and experienced a vision of Amitābha; even a single sincere thought might be sufficient. However, ordinarily Pure Land practices in India (and in Chinese monasteries) remained closely tied to visionary experience anyway, and most of the original management of Pure Land devotionalism occurred in the monastic context.

In India little is known about the concrete history of Pure Land after the emergence of the texts; it seems to have enjoyed

Longhuachansi temple, Shanghai, China, founded in the Tang dynasty as a Chan temple, now a Pure Land temple. Buildings date from the Qing dynasty (1644–1911).
Photo courtesy of Marylin M. Rhie

limited success. On the other hand in Tibet it was retained traditionally as one of the innumerable secondary strands of Tantrism.

The Pure Land mythos was carried into China at an early stage, and the main sūtras were translated within several centuries of their origination in India. Systematic practices appeared with the early monastic Lushan Huiyuan (Lu-shan Hui-yüan, 344–416), including visualization of the features of Amitābha and the Pure Land, cultivation of desire to be reborn in the Pure Land, and invocation of the name of Amitābha. Such traditions were later pervasive in Chinese (and Korean) monasteries and were practiced even by seminal figures such as the Tiantai (T'ien-t'ai) founder Zhiyi (Chih-i, 538–597). An important later addition to the canon was the *Guanjing* (*Kuan-ching*; Visualization sūtra), a text that probably originated in central Asia. The *Guanjing* described nine detailed levels of potential rebirth in the Pure Land.

Thus established, in contrast to India, Pure Land in China remained a permanent, standard aspect of the repertoire of monastic practice until the present. However, a decline in relative status occurred in the Tang period (618–907) because Pure Land tended to be subordinated to the claims of Chan lineages. This transition was marked by the Pure Land teacher Cimin (T'zu-min, 680–748), who engaged in polemics with Chan advocates, and beginning with Yanshou (Yen-shou, 904–975) the unification of Chinese schools under Chan rhetoric became normative. A notable later monastic figure with Pure Land interests was Zhuhong (Chu-hung, 1535–1615), who also promoted an official Buddhist movement for laymen that focused on practices of reciting the Buddha's name and the observance of precepts. A similar figure was Hanshan (Han-shan, 1546–1623).

Judging from records of traditional Chinese monastic life in the mid–20th century, Pure Land monastic routines emphasized extended recitations of the Buddha's name. Practitioners utilized special halls that stood in tandem with Chan meditation halls at most monasteries. Socially the Pure Land approach differed from that of Chan: it tried to attract laymen, was relatively gentle, was less hierarchical and formalistic, and was less gurucentric. Despite the Chan reputation of Chinese Buddhism, observers have suggested that in fact more monks put their hopes in rebirth in the Western paradise than in earthly success in pursuing the official Chan bodhisattva path.

Much of Pure Land tradition in China went beyond monasticism. The texts, especially the *Guanjing*, opened the way to nonmonastic approaches to Buddhism because certain descriptions of lower-level practices allowed rebirth to those of "inferior potential." The teachings of the handful of somewhat dissident early thinkers who emphasized this aspect of the Pure Land mythos, including Tanluan (T'an-luan, 476–542), Daochuo (Tao-ch'o, 562–645), Shandao (Shan-tao, 613–681), and Fazhao (Fa-chao, active c. 763–804), encouraged the highly significant lay Pure Land movements that flourished outside the official monastic system in the later imperial period (c. 1200–1900).

In Japan as in China, Pure Land was among the earliest aspects of Buddhism to be imported. As in China initially the Pure Land mythic forms and practices were embedded in the larger matrix of normal monasticism. It became common in the Nara period schools to study the Pure Land sūtras and to resort to Amitābha and the Pure Land as objects of meditation. Later Japanese monastics created variations, often featuring substantial use of pictorial arts. In Nara the monk Chikō (seventh century) created a style of Pure Land maṇḍala for visualization; other advocates included Yōkan (1032–1111) and Chinkai (1091–1152). In Shingon the monk Kakuban (1094–1143) creatively assimilated Pure Land teachings; Myōhen (1124–1224) organized recitation practice on Mount Kōya, the Shingon headquarters; and Kakukai (1142–1223) renewed their teachings. The Pure Land mythos also played a growing role in monastic Tendai. Pure Land was introduced at Mount Hiei, the Tendai headquarters, by Saichō's successor, Ennin (794–864) (who had visited China), and thereafter *jōgyō zammai* (perpetual chanting meditation with a Pure Land reference) was extensively practiced. Pure Land was renewed at Hiei by the reformist abbot Ryōgen (911–985).

As in China, Pure Land remained a permanent aspect of the repertoire of Japanese monastic practice until the present. However, unlike in China no relative decline in its overall status occurred. Indeed more than in China, Pure Land expanded beyond monasticism, and Japanese history witnessed the unique ascendancy of popularized forms of "lay" Pure Land thought. It was associated with figures on the borders of monasticism, such as Kūya (903–972), Genshin (942–1017), Ryōnin (1072–1132), and Ippen (1239–1289), along with Hōnen (1133–1212) and his disciples, including especially the radical Shinran (1173–1262). Shinran borrowed from the dissident Pure Land teachings in China and developed ideas that entirely undercut monastic claims for authority in Buddhism. Altogether these Japanese trends led to Pure Land's emergence as the demographically dominant mode of Buddhism in that country in the early modern period, but in nonmonastic forms.

Galen Amstutz

See also Anticlericalism: Buddhist Perspectives; Buddhist Schools/Traditions: China; Buddhist Schools/Traditions: Japan; Deities, Buddhist; Ennin; Hōnen; Initiation: Buddhist Perspectives; Kyoto, Japan; Mantras; Nembutsu; Rennyō; Saichō; Shinran; Spirituality: Buddhist; Tiantai/Tendai: Japan; Visual Arts, Buddhist: Japan; Wŏnhyo

Further Reading

Amstutz, Galen, "The Politics of Independent Pure Land in China," *Journal of Chinese Religions* 26 (1998)

Amstutz, Galen, "The Politics of Pure Land Buddhism in India," *Numen* 45 (1998)

Chappell, David W., "Chinese Buddhist Interpretations of the Pure Lands," in *Buddhist and Taoist Studies I*, edited by Michael Saso and David W. Chappell, Honolulu: Asian Studies Program, University of Hawaii, University of Hawaii Press, 1977

Chappell, David W., "From Dispute to Dual Cultivation: Pure Land Responses to Ch'an Critics," in *Traditions of Meditation in Chinese Buddhism*, edited by Peter N. Gregory, Honolulu: University of Hawaii Press, 1986

Gómez, Luis O., translator, *The Land of Bliss: The Paradise of the Buddha of Measureless Light: Sanskrit and Chinese Versions of the Sukhāvatīvyūha Sutras*, Honolulu: University of Hawaii Press, 1996

Hsu, Sung-peng, *A Buddhist Leader in Ming China*, University Park: Pennsylvania State University Press, 1978

Matsunaga, Alicia, and Daigan Matsunaga, *Foundation of Japanese Buddhism*, 2 vols., Los Angeles: Buddhist Books International, 1974

Okazaki, Jōji, *Pure Land Buddhist Painting*, Tokyo and New York: Kodansha International, 1977

Pas, Julian F., *Visions of Sukhāvatī: Shan-Tao's Commentary on the Kuan Wu-Liang Shou-Fo Ching*, Albany: State University of New York Press, 1995

Shih, Heng-ching, *The Syncretism of Ch'an and Pure Land Buddhism*, New York: Peter Lang, 1992

Tanaka, Kenneth K., *Dawn of Chinese Pure Land Buddhist Doctrine*, Albany: State University of New York Press, 1990

Welch, Holmes, *The Practice of Chinese Buddhism, 1900–1950*, Cambridge, Massachusetts: Harvard University Press, 1967

Yü, Chün-fang, *The Renewal of Buddhism in China: Chu-Hung and the Late Ming Synthesis*, New York: Columbia University Press, 1981

R

Rabanus Maurus c. 780–856

Benedictine scholar, abbot of Fulda, and Archbishop of Mainz

Rabanus (Hrabanus) Maurus was the most highly esteemed among the many monastic scholars and teachers of his generation in Carolingian Europe. He joined the community at Fulda as a child oblate and began his education there. Already demonstrating outstanding promise as a young monk, he was sent to study under Alcuin (c. 740–804) at least once around 802/03 at Tours and probably also in the 790s at Aachen. It was Alcuin who gave Rabanus the epithet Maurus, the name of St. Benedict of Nursia's favorite pupil, a good indication of the regard in which the Northumbrian master held him. Rabanus began his own pedagogic career on returning to Fulda from Tours. He became master of the cloister school in or before 819 and continued to teach even after elected abbot. His abilities are attested to by the sheer number of his students. In the 820s the population at Fulda reached over 600 monks, a figure never matched again in that monastery's history. In addition, top students from other monastic schools, such as Walafrid Strabo (c. 808–849) from Reichenau, were often sent to finish their studies with the master of Fulda.

The growth of the community was also a tribute to Rabanus' qualities as abbot. He added to the infrastructure of the monastery through building projects and the acquisition of numerous holy relics. Likewise, he looked to the spiritual welfare of the laity, erecting churches in as many as 30 rural villages in Fulda's domain. As abbot of a major monastery, he was by necessity involved in contemporary politics. Rabanus supported Emperor Louis the Pious (814–840) against his rebellious sons and after Louis' death backed the cause of the eldest son, Lothar I (840–855), against Lothar's brother Louis the German (843–876). When the latter succeeded in taking control over all territories east of the Rhine River, including Fulda, Rabanus had to resign as abbot and retire as teacher, withdrawing from the main monastery to one of its nearby dependencies. Eventually, Rabanus was reconciled with Louis the German, who saw to it that the most prominent scholar in the kingdom was made archbishop of Mainz. The former abbot ruled as an active reformer, presiding over three church councils during his nine years in office.

Rabanus remained a prodigious writer throughout his long life, from the completion around 810 of his first substantial composition – a devotional treatise of virtuoso complexity intertwining poetry, visual imagery, and prose in praise of the holy cross (*De laudibus sanctae crucis*; also known as *In honorem sanctae crucis*) – to theological tracts written in his last years as archbishop. Among his major works was a manual for priests (*De institutione clericorum*) to aid and instruct them in the performance of their office. Rabanus' literary output is comparable in scope to Bede's, and he provided some of the basic reference works on patristic knowledge and biblical exegesis used by European monks from the 9th to the 12th century. *De laudibus sanctae crucis* remained popular throughout the Middle Ages, and manuscript copies continued to be made into the early 1600s. Since he is known as the author of several poetic works, the Pentecost hymn "Veni creator spiritus" is also traditionally attributed to him.

SCOTT WELLS

See also Alcuin; Bede, St.; Fulda, Germany; Hymnographers; Monastics and the World, Medieval; Oblates; Scholars, Benedictine; Walafrid Strabo

Biography

Rabanus entered the abbey of Fulda as an oblate and went c. 800 to study under Alcuin at Tours. He served as master of the Fulda school in 818 and as abbot 818–842 before becoming Archbishop of Mainz 847–856. He was never formally canonized.

Major Works

De institutione clericorum
De rerum naturis, c. 842
De praedestinatione
Letters
Poems

Further Reading

Kottje, Raymund, "Hrabanus Maurus," in *Verfasserlexikon der deutschen Literatur des Mittelalters* 4:1, Berlin and New York: de Gruyter, 1982

Kottje, Raymund, and Harald Zimmermann, editors, *Hrabanus Maurus: Lehrer, Abt und Bischof*, Mainz, Germany: Akademie der Wissenschaften und der Literatur, 1982

Le Maître, Philippe, "Les Méthodes exégétiques de Raban Maur," in *Haut moyen âge: Culture, éducation et société: Études offerts à Pierre Riché*, Paris: Erasme, 1990
McCullough, John, "Introduction: Hrabanus Maurus," in *Rabani Mauri Martyrologium*, edited by John McCullough, Turnhout: Brepols, 1979
Perrin, Michel, "Quelques réflexions sur le *De laudibus sanctae crucis* de Raban Maur: De la codicologie à la théologie en passant par la poétique," *Revue des Etudes Latines* 67 (1989)
Schrimpf, Gangolf, editor, *Kloster Fulda in der Welt der Karolinger und Ottonen*, Frankfurt am Main: Knecht, 1996
Sears, Elizabeth, "Louis the Pious as *Miles Christi*: The Dedicatory Image in Hrabanus Maurus's *De laudibus sanctae crucis*," in *Charlemagne's Heir: New Perspectives on the Reign of Louis the Pious (814–840)*, edited by Peter Godman and Roger Collins, Oxford: Clarendon Press, 1990

Radegunde, St. c. 520–587

Frankish queen and founder of Monastery of the Holy Cross near Poitiers

Founder of the Holy Cross monastery in Poitiers, Radegunde was born in Erfurt in the royal family of Thuringia, daughter of Berthaire, granddaughter of king Berchtachar. In 531 the Franks, led by Clothar I, a son of Clovis (481–511), conquered the kingdom of Thuringia. Radegunde was captured and kept by Clothar in his palace in Athies (Vermandois). There she received education appropriate to her birth, and her faith was strengthened by reading the Bible and patristic commentaries. Prayer and caring for the poor became the goal of her life.

However, Clothar, in love with Radegunde and motivated by political reasons, decided to marry her. Notwithstanding Radegunde's protests and even her attempt to escape, the wedding ceremony took place in Soissons around 540. As the queen of the Franks, Radegunde continued her pious foundations and spent a lot of time praying and doing penance. For example, she would frequently leave the marital bed and spend several hours prostrated on the church's cold floor. Thus, at the court she was called a nun-queen (*Patrologia Latina* 88.500).

Around 555 Clothar, afraid of the separatist mood growing in Thuringia, had Radegunde's brother killed. This gave Radegunde an excuse to leave the royal court. In Noyon (Oise) she managed to convince the local bishop, St. Medard, to ordain her deaconess. Then she went on pilgrimage to the tomb of St. Martin in Tours. Having founded an almshouse on her estate in Saix (on the border of Touraine and Poitou), she lived there with her adopted daughter Agnes and a few companions, caring for the sick and poor.

Fearful of Clothar's plans to recover his wife, Radegunde decided to take refuge in a monastery. Around 561 she founded St. Marie Abbey in Poitiers. She refused the title of abbess (which went to Agnes instead) and asked only for a single cell. Radegunde's aim was to secure a degree of independence for her monastery. For this reason in 570 she paid a visit, accompanied by Agnes, to Arles (Bouches-du-Rhône). She wanted to meet St. Liliola (559–574), the abbess of St. John monastery, and especially to obtain the Rule of Caesarius of Arles (c. 470–542) written 50 years earlier for this abbey, governed at that time by his sister Caesaria. She acquired a copy of the Rule, making it possible to adopt the *Regula* of Caesarius at the monastery in Poitiers with the consent of the local bishop, Meroveus. Simultaneously Radegunde won approval for her action from the assembly of bishops presided over by Euphronius, bishop of Tours. The monastery was developing rapidly and at the time of Radegunde's death housed about 200 nuns.

The veneration of relics was a distinctive facet of Radegunde's spirituality. Owing to connections dating back to her life at the court, in 569 Radegunde was able to acquire from the Byzantine Emperor Justin II (565–578) a large fragment of the True Cross, which inspired Venantius Fortunatus (c. 530–c. 610) to write his famous *Vexilla Regis* and *Pange lingua gloriosa*. As a consequence the monastery changed its invocation to that of Holy Cross, and after Radegunde's death it became an important pilgrimage center.

Radegunde died on 13 August 587; obsequies were conducted by Meroveus, bishop of Poitiers, and by St. Gregory of Tours (538/39–594). She was buried in St. Mary's (later St. Radegunde's) church. The cult of Radegunde spread rapidly.

Marek Derwich

See also Benedictines: Female; Caesarius of Arles, St.; France: History; Holy Men/Holy Women: Christian Perspectives; Origins: Western Christian; Relics, Christian Monastic; Women's Monasteries: Western Christian

Biography

Daughter of a Thuringian prince, Radegunde was captured by invading Franks. She was Lothar I's Queen from c. 540 but fled his court after he murdered her brother c. 550. She was then ordained deaconess and soon founded a monastery outside Poitiers, adopting the rule of Caesarius of Arles. The Latin poet Venantius Fortunatus (c. 530–c. 610) settled in her community and later wrote her *Life*.

Further Reading

Radegunde' biographies were written by her contemporaries: her friend and confidant Venantius Fortunatus (*Vitas. Radegundis*, edited by B. Krusch in *Monumenta Germaniae Historica, Scriptores Rerum Merovingiarum* 2 [1888]; an English translation is available in *Sainted Women of the Dark Ages*, edited and translated by J.A. McNamara and others, 1992) and Baudonivie, her companion and later a nun herself (*Vita . . .*, ibidem).

Aigrain, René, *Sainte Radegonde*, Paris: Gabalda, 1918; Parthenay, France: Géhan, 1987
Brittain, F., *St. Radegund: Patroness of Jesus College*, Cambridge: Bowes and Bowes, 1925
Consolina, F.E., "Due agiografi per una regina," *Studi storici* (1988)
Gäbe, Sabine, "Radegundis," *Francia* 16 (1989)

Saint Radegunde enthroned, from the "Life of Saint Radegund," Ms. 250, fol. 43v, end of 11th century, Bibliothèque Municipale, Poitiers, France.
Photo courtesy of Giraudon/Art Resource, New York

Histoire de l'abbaye de Sainte-Croix de Poitiers: Quatorze siècles de vie monastique, Poitiers: Société des Antiquaires de l'Ouest, 1986

Leonardi, Claudio, "Fortunato e Baudonivia," in *Aus Kirche und Reich: Studien zu Theologie, Politik und Recht im Mittelalter: Festschrift für Friedrich Kempf*, Sigmaringen: Thorbecke, 1983

Merta, B., "Helena comparata regina – secunda Isabel," *Mitteilungen des Instituts für Österreichische Geschichtsforschung* 96 (1988)

Muschiol, Gisela, *Famula Dei: Zur Liturgie in merowingischen Frauenklöstern*, Münster in West: Aschendorff, 1994

Papa, C., "Radegonda e Boltilde," *Benedictina* 36 (1989)

Personnalité de sainte Radegonde: Conférences et homélies prononcées à Poitiers à l'occasion du XIVe centenaire de sa mort (587–1987), Poitiers: Comité du XIVe centenaire, 1988

Les religieuses dans le cloître et dans le monde des origines à nos jour: Actes du Deuxième colloque international du CERCOR, Poitiers, 29 septembre–2 octobre 1988, Saint-Étienne: Publications de l'Université de Saint-Étienne, 1994 (articles by Robert Favreau, Christian de Merindol, and Jean Verdon)

Schreibeltreiter, G., "Königstöchter im Kloster: Radegund (587) und die Nonnenaufstand von Poitiers (589)," *Mitteilungen des Instituts für Österreichische Geschichtsforschung* 87 (1979)

Rancé, Armand-Jean de 1626–1700

French scholar, Cistercian founder of the Trappists, and first abbot of La Trappe

Armand-Jean Le Bouthillier de Rancé is not an easy man to assess. Both during and after his life, he aroused extreme reactions, both of love and of loathing, and his penitential spirituality is little to modern taste.

Rancé was born in Paris on 9 January 1626 to an influential family (his godfather was Cardinal Richelieu), and from an early age he was destined for the church. Accordingly, he was in due course made a canon of Notre-Dame of Paris and commendatory superior of five benefices, among which was the abbey of La Trappe in Normandy, then an impoverished house in a state of decay.

The young Rancé was a precocious scholar – he published an edition and commentary on Anacreon at the age of 13 – and in 1642 took his M.A. at the University of Paris. He was ordained nine years later, but his ordination made little difference to the worldly life of the court that he had happily espoused. One of his intimate friends was Marie, duchess of Montbazon (1612–1657), an attractive socialite with a scandalous reputation, and little doubt exists that Rancé adored her. Whether they were lovers is unknown, but it was the unexpected death of the duchess from scarlet fever in 1657 that precipitated Rancé's dramatic conversion.

He left Paris and retired to his country home at Véretz, near Tours, to spend time in reading and reflection. After much heart searching, he became convinced of a calling to the monastic life and therefore abandoned his worldly ways, sold his property, resigned his benefices (keeping only La Trappe), and at age 37 became a novice at the Cistercian abbey of Perseigne on 13 June 1663.

After a difficult novitiate of one year, he was professed and entered La Trappe as its regular abbot on 14 July 1664. His next years were to be dedicated to the reform of the monastery, and although he based his ideas on the Rule of St. Benedict, he found the Rule insufficiently austere for his purposes. Therefore, he compiled a set of stricter regulations for use at La Trappe and instituted a program of severe asceticism. The most important statement of his principles was published in 1683 as *De la sainteté et des devoirs de la vie monastique*, in which we can clearly discern his fundamentally Augustinian spirituality and his conception that monasticism was essentially penitential.

For Rancé a monk was a guilty sinner whose sin had to be expiated by asceticism and humiliation. Intellectual pursuits were forbidden, and the keys to the spiritual life were continual prayer and hard manual labor. Yet this arduous austerity was combined with a deep charity, and although the views of Rancé provoked vigorous reaction elsewhere, his monks loved him, and he was much sought as a spiritual director. Under his administration the abbey became a populous community and much admired, but the formidable regimen took its toll. In 1695, his health broken by his exertions, Rancé abdicated as abbot. He died five years later, on 27 October 1700, in his 74th year.

David N. Bell

See also Asceticism: Christian Perspectives; Cistercians; Death: Christian Perspectives; La Trappe, France; Maurists; Scholars, Benedictine; Trappists

Biography

Rancé's life falls into two parts. Until 1657 he led a worldly Parisian life as a scholar-priest. The death of a lifelong friend, Madame de Montbazon, in 1657 caused him to embrace asceticism. He read the Desert Fathers and sold four of his five abbeys, retaining only the Cistercian house of La Trappe. He became abbot of La Trappe in 1664 and invited to the abbey fellow monks who wished to follow the Strict Observance. Orthodox in theology, he stressed penitence as the core of the monastic life.

Selected Works

Constitutions de l'abbaye de la Trappe, 1671

Requeste présentée au Roy, 1673

Lettre du R.P. abbé de la Trappe à un ecclésiastique, 1677

Relations de la mort de quelques religieux de l'abbaye de la Trappe, 1678 (and a number of enlarged editions)

De la sainteté et des devoirs de la vie monastique, 2 vols., 1683, reprinted in 1972; translated by "a Religious of the Abbey of Melleray" as *A Treatise on the Sanctity and on the Duties of the Monastic State*, 1830

Éclaircissemens de quelques difficultés que l'on a formées sur le livre de la sainteté, 1683

Les Instructions de Saint Dorothée, 1686

La Règle de Saint Benoist, nouvellement traduite et expliquée selon son véritable esprit, 2 vols., 1688
Carte de visite faite à l'abbaye de Notre-Dame des Clairets, 1690
Les reglemens de l'abbaye de Nostre-Dame de la Trappe, en forme de constitutions, 1690
Réponse au Traité des études monastiques, 1692
Instructions sur les principaux sujets de la piété et de la morale chrétienne, 1693
Conduite chrétienne, adressée à Madame de Guise, 1697
Maximes chrétiennes et morales, 2 vols., 1697–1698
Conférences ou Instructions sur les épitres et évangiles des dimanches et principales festes de l'année, 4 vols., 1698
Reglemens pour les Filles de la doctrine chrétienne de la Ville de Mortagne, 1698
Correspondance, edited by Alban J. Krailsheimer, 4 vols., 1993

Further Reading

Didio, Henri, *La querelle de Mabillon et de l'Abbe de Rancé*, Amiens: Rousseau-Leroy, 1892
Krailsheimer, Alban J., *Armand-Jean de Rancé, Abbot of La Trappe: His Influence in the Cloister and the World*, Oxford: Clarendon Press, 1974
Krailsheimer, Alban J., *The Letters of Armand-Jean de Rancé, Abbot and Reformer of La Trappe*, 2 vols., Kalamazoo, Michigan: Cistercian Publications, 1984
Krailsheimer, Alban J., *Rancé and the Trappist Legacy*, Kalamazoo, Michigan: Cistercian Publications, 1985
Tournoüer, Henri, *Bibliographie et iconographie de la Maison-Dieu Notre-Dame de La Trappe au diocèse de Séez, de A.-J. Le Bouthillier de Rancé . . . et en général de tous les religieux du même monastère*, 2 vols., Mortagne: Marchand et Gilles, 1894–1896

Recluses, Eastern Christian. *See* Hermits: Eastern Christian

Recluses, Western Christian

A recluse (also known as an anchorite) is a man or woman who accepts voluntary restriction to a small room. Reclusion was already an accepted ascetic practice among the fathers of the Egyptian desert, when, for example, Mark the Egyptian is credited with not leaving his cell for 30 years. The practice spread to Merovingian Francia by the time of Gregory of Tours (538/39–594), who tells of recluses enduring long fasts and wearing chains. There are early accounts of reclusion as a temporary penitential state, but in medieval Europe recluses would normally not leave their cell until death.

Although reclusion was a development parallel to that of monasticism rather than a purely monastic phenomenon, during the central Middle Ages (9th through 11th centuries) most recluses for which we have evidence were monastics or at least associated with monasteries. Grimlaicus, whose *Regula solitariorum* (Rule for Recluses) dates to sometime in the late ninth or early tenth century, assumes that recluses will be monks. However, in this period there were nearly equal numbers of male and female recluses. They were esteemed as the holy people par excellence of society, and many were venerated as saints, including Wiborada of St. Gall (d. 926), the first woman to be canonized by the papacy (1047).

The key to recluses' perceived sanctity was their lives of heroic asceticism. The conditions in which recluses lived had become considerably gentler by the 12th and 13th centuries, when Aelred of Rievaulx (1109–1167) and the author of the *Ancrene Riwle* describe a spartan but bearable regime in which the main asceticism is the fact of enclosure itself. However, in the central Middle Ages the ascetic practices of reclusion often exceeded the bounds of human endurance. At best it was a life of sensory deprivation, restricted to a small cell with one small window through which the recluse could receive food and other necessities. After a trial period of at least one year, the local bishop would come to shut up the recluse in his or her cell, sealing the door with his signet or in some cases walling it up and singing a requiem mass over the recluse who had been symbolically buried there. After that the recluse could never again leave. Some recluses prepared their own graves in their cells, and in several cases recluses refused to leave their cells even to save their own lives. Thus, it was a life of total dependence on others for basic physical needs, often made more difficult by becoming a recluse far from one's native land, as with the many Irish monks who became recluses on the Continent. In addition to all the trials associated with living in a dark and confined space, recluses in the central Middle Ages often practiced a grisly level of asceticism, freezing in the winter and suffering from a long list of illnesses, often encouraged by the recluses themselves, as when the recluse Sisu allowed herself to be eaten by worms, replacing those that fell from her decaying flesh, or when Wiborada wore an iron chain wrapped so tightly around her that it became permanently embedded in her flesh.

Reclusion became associated with monasticism in a variety of ways. Reclusion rose in popularity from the mid–ninth century, at a time when ecclesiastical authorities were turning against the unregulated life of hermits. Because reclusion is the most stable life imaginable, it could be monitored and thus was preferred for those seeking greater asceticism. Also, unlike eremitism, reclusion could be practiced by women as well as men. Because a monastic community could provide not only food but also spiritual guidance, enclosure at or near a monastery was the ideal arrangement and was advocated by several Church leaders. It seems clear that many monasteries regularly supported one or more recluses. Grimlaicus suggests that many of these recluses were members of the monastic community already, seeking a life of greater devotion. Because monastic life in the central Middle Ages was in general a well-regulated life of quite modest asceticism, many monks apparently wanted to prove their spiritual prowess with the greater strictness of the recluse's life.

Recluses rendered a substantial gift to the monastic community, as to society more generally. Their separation from the world was believed to forge a special link to God, and they served regularly as spiritual advisers, teachers, and prophets. Some recluses were even visited by bishops and emperors who sought their prayers and spiritual insights. For example, the Florentine monk-turned-recluse Teuzo not only advised Emperor Henry III (1039–1056) but also was a leading spokesman for ecclesiastical reform, invoking the wrath of Peter Damian (1007–1072) for his involvement in such worldly matters. However, in general the active role of recluses, owing to their physical solitude, was admired and encouraged. Sometimes when a recluse did not begin his or her career attached to a monastery, such a community grew up around the recluse's cell in response to reports of holiness. Thus, so many people came to a female recluse near Verdun in the early tenth century that she founded a nunnery for her disciples. Similarly, in the mid–11th century, Archbishop Poppo of Trier founded a monastery in honor of the city's most famous recluse, Simeon.

After the 11th century the position of recluses declined sharply in Europe. Partly this can be explained by the rapidly changing monastic life and spirituality of the time. Men who in earlier times might have become recluses gravitated instead to the new, more ascetic monastic orders, such as the Carthusians. Besides new ascetic options there was a new emphasis on symbolic rather than merely physical separation from the world, perhaps making reclusion seem less appropriate, at least for men. As reclusion increasingly became a women's spiritual practice, it lost in prestige, although as late as the 14th century recluses such as Dame Julian of Norwich (c. 1342–after 1416) were still noted spiritual advisers. A small number of monastic recluses can still be found today in both Roman Catholic and Anglican monasticism.

Phyllis G. Jestice

See also Aelred of Rievaulx, St.; Asceticism: Christian Perspectives; Benedictines: Female; Carthusians; Celtic Monasticism; Desert Fathers; Desert Mothers; England: History; Hermits: Western Christian; Holy Men/Holy Women: Christian Perspectives; Ireland: History; Solitude: Christian Perspectives

Further Reading

Aelred of Rievaulx, Saint, *La Vie de Recluse: La prière pastorale* (Sources Chrétiennes, 76), edited by Charles Dumont, Paris: Du Cerf, 1961

The Ancrene Riwle, translated by M.B. Salu, London: Burns and Oates, 1955; Notre Dame, Indiana: University of Notre Dame Press, 1956

Brown, Peter, "The Rise and Function of the Holy Man in Late Antiquity," in his *Society and the Holy in Late Antiquity*, Berkeley: University of California Press, and London: Faber and Faber, 1982

Gougaud, Louis, *Ermites et reclus: Études sur d'anciennes formes de vie religieuse* (Moines et monastères, number 5), Vienne: Abbaye Saint-Martin de Ligugé, 1928

Jestice, Phyllis G., *Wayward Monks and the Religious Revolution of the Eleventh Century* (Brill's Studies in Intellectual History, volume 76), New York: Brill, 1997

Mayr-Harting, H., "Functions of a Twelfth-Century Recluse," *History* 60 (1975)

Settimana internazionale di studio, *L'Eremitismo in Occidente nei Secoli XI e XII: Atti della seconda Settimana internazionale di studio, Mendola, 30 agosto–6 settembre 1962* (Publicazioni dell'Università cattolica del Sacro Cuore), Milan: Società editrice vita e pensiero, 1965

Warren, Ann K., *Anchorites and Their Patrons in Medieval England*, Berkeley: University of California Press, 1985

Reform, German Benedictine. *See* German Benedictine Reform, Medieval

Reform, Tenth-Century Anglo-Saxon Monastic

The English Church of the later tenth century saw a substantial reform movement, inspired in part by the Frankish liturgical and ecclesiastical reformation that had begun at the behest of Charlemagne (c. 742–814) in the early ninth century. However, during that same period of Continental reform Anglo-Saxon England had been ravaged by devastating raids and full-scale invasion at the hands of Danish pirates; nearly 100 years of these attacks had destroyed monasteries, burned libraries, and driven the men and women who in peacetime would have sought the cloister to concentrate their energies on subsistence and survival instead. Even after the peace treaty (c. 880–890) that marked an end to formal invasion and the establishing of the Danelaw (an agreed-on territory in which the Danes might live), sporadic raiding continued. Added to this was a tension among the regional kingdoms of Anglo-Saxon England that manifested itself in military encroachment by Wessex, ruled by the heirs of Alfred the Great (871–901), on the lands of Mercia and Northumbria. The educational system had been severely damaged with the destruction of the old monasteries, and although Alfred and his descendants attempted to reestablish monastic foundations and the schools that had been associated with them, it was not until the middle of the century, in the reign of Edgar, nicknamed "the Peaceful" (959–975), that a true reform could take place.

Dunstan of Canterbury

Dunstan (c. 909–988), was a Benedictine abbot (939–988), the archbishop of Canterbury (960–988), and a royal statesman, but he is renowned mainly as the moving spirit behind the Anglo-Saxon Benedictine reform of the mid–tenth century. Through his diligence and efforts, education and discipline within Benedictine practice again became the main concerns of the monastic houses that he helped reestablish throughout Anglo-Saxon England after a century and a half of invasion and political strife. Benedictinism had been firmly established in England with Wilfrid (fl. 660) when it replaced the Celtic practice that had laid the monastic foundation in the north; the renewal and subsequent endurance of English Benedictinism and the influence that it brought to bear on both Continental movements and Insular spirituality must be considered the legacy left by Dunstan and his two fellow reformers: Ethelwold and Oswald.

Dunstan was born near Glastonbury, and his first biographer asserts that he was connected to the royal family of Wessex that descended from Alfred the Great. His choice of monastic life over that of a life at court led to political machinations that caused considerable trouble for him because his abilities and perhaps his social rank saw him frequently in the role of adviser to the king despite his profession. In 939 King Edmund (939–946) granted Dunstan the rule of Glastonbury (then much decayed) and he spent about 15 years establishing it as a school of considerable reputation. In 955 a political reaction against Dunstan's influence at court sent him into exile in Ghent, where he came into contact with the monastic reforms taking place on the Continent. In 959 Dunstan was recalled to England by the new king, Edgar (959–975), who had him made first bishop of Worcester and London and then archbishop of Canterbury, a see that he held until his death on 19 May 988.

With the help of his friend and former pupil Ethelwold and of Oswald who had been influenced by similar Continental reform practice at Fleury, Dunstan undertook the great work of the reformation of Benedictinism within both new and refounded Anglo-Saxon monastic houses. These three reformers were responsible for both the synod and the document that resulted from it, the *Regularis Concordia,* around 972/73; this presented a code that was based on the Rule of St. Benedict (*Regula Sancti Benedicti*) and set out the detail of daily practice by which Benedictinism was to be carried out by the monks and nuns of England. Thus, although it is the descendant of traditional Benedictine custom, the *Regularis Concordia* is also uniquely English, involving the royal patronage of the king and queen at Winchester and unifying Anglo-Saxon England in its observance. It accomplished within liturgical and monastic practice what the heirs of Alfred had been working toward politically, with Wessex's focus on military dominance earlier in the century.

Immediately after his death in 988, Dunstan was revered as one of England's most popular saints. It is noteworthy that the greatest tenth-century interest in Dunstan's cult originated in centers other than Christ Church, Canterbury: this foundation had lost its monastic orientation most probably as a result of the Danish raids, and Dunstan tactfully did not try to alter its secular clerical practice or force it back toward Benedictinism while he was its archbishop. Although the Canterbury kalendars (liturgical calendars) had begun to make provision for Dunstan's feast day by the year 1000, earlier Winchester writers were crediting him with prophesies during his lifetime and miracles occurring at his tomb. A hagiographical account of his life by the anonymous scribe "B" (who was not a monk) was completed before 1000: this *Life* celebrates Dunstan's sanctity rather than his labors as a monastic reformer, and later writings based on it preserve the same focus. At some Continental monasteries, notably Ghent where he had once taken refuge in exile, Dunstan was honored as a confessor, as we find in the *Life* by Adelard, even before the close of the tenth century; by the 12th century he was esteemed not only on the Continent but in monastic centers in Ireland as well. Osbern of Christ Church, Canterbury, wrote an account of his life during the archepiscopate there (1070–1089) of Lanfranc, and the near contemporaries Eadmer (c. 1060–c. 1128, precentor of Christ Church) and William of Malmesbury (c. 1090–c. 1143, writing for the monks of Glastonbury) sought to correct Osbern's errors by writing their own accounts of Dunstan in the early 12th century. Finally, the Augustinian Friar Joannes Capgrave (John of Tynemouth) wrote yet another *Life of Dunstan* around 1468.

The great modern monastic historian David Knowles (1966) calls Dunstan "patron and father of the monks of medieval England," and in pre-Reformation centuries his example and inspiration gave guidance to those who followed after him in both abbacy and episcopacy. Thus, although Dunstan has been revered first and foremost as a Canterbury saint whose status was challenged only by that of Thomas à Becket (c. 1120–1170), modern Church historians now recognize that his role as a reformer and educator exerted an enormous impact on the future of English monasticism and learning. His sojourn on the Continent in the 950s placed him in contact with new ideas that he brought back to England with him. This cultural, aesthetic, and intellectual influence revitalized the production, artwork, and design of liturgical books and gave new impetus to education within the monastic houses of Anglo-Saxon England, and by a ripple effect in subsequent generations, the tenth-century reform in turn gave inspiration back to Continental monasticism. Without the revival of Benedictinism in England, no Stephen Harding (d. 1134) would have guided the development of Cîteaux a century after Dunstan's death.

Ethelwold of Winchester

Ethelwold (c. 904/05 or 909–984) was a reformer whose life was dedicated to education and hallmarked by zealous single-mindedness and an energetic determination that overrode all physical ailments. Like his fellow reformer and friend St. Dunstan, Ethelwold was an Englishman who had aristocratic connections; the two men might have met for the first time at the court of King Athelstan (924–939). Both became enthusiastic about the monastic activities then well under weigh on the Continent and were ordained to the priesthood by Ælfheah, bishop of Winchester, on the same day. When Dunstan received the rule of Glastonbury from King Edmund in 939, Ethelwold joined him there first as a pupil, receiving his monk's habit at Dunstan's hands, and thereafter as a co-worker. When he grew eager to travel to Fleury and learn directly about the reforms within Benedictinism there, the new king, Eadred (946–955), was advised by his mother to offer Ethelwold the small monastery of Abingdon, around 954, then badly in need of refoundation, so as to keep him in England. This ploy succeeded admirably, as Ethelwold rose to the occasion by taking on the abbacy of Abingdon, which he peopled with Glastonbury monks and made a fine center of education. He sent Osgar, one of his students, to Fleury instead. In 963, after Dunstan had returned to England and been installed as archbishop of Canterbury, he called on

Ethelwold to be bishop of Winchester, a post that he held until his death on 1 August 984.

Ethelwold placed the Fleury-trained Osgar in his stead at Abingdon and undertook major "renovation" at Winchester, the seat of the king's court in later Anglo-Saxon England. He was the first English bishop to establish a monastic cathedral through his efforts in the Old Minster, where, perhaps on King Edgar's direct orders, he unceremoniously expelled the clerics who peopled it, replacing them with his own Abingdon and Glastonbury monks. He insisted on monastic practice according to reformed Benedictinism at the New Minster and the Nunnaminster as well and chose new heads for each foundation who were sympathetic to his approach. Ethelwold undertook vast building projects that reordered the ecclesiastical structures of Winchester and at the same time oversaw the refoundation of monastic centers at Peterborough and Ely and a new foundation at Thorney between 964 and 971. In his efforts he was tireless, and in his standards he was absolute, implacable, and exacting.

A central and perhaps somewhat pragmatic project of Ethelwold's during his reorganization of Winchester was the culting of one of its ninth-century bishops, Swithun, who had been the adviser and spiritual guide to King Alfred's father, Æthelwulf (839–857), and died in 862. Until he attracted Ethelwold's attention, very little was known about Swithun, who lay buried outside the walls of his cathedral in relative obscurity, and no evidence whatsoever suggests that he was ever a professed monk. Ethelwold's expulsion of the secular clerics from the Old Minster had, not surprisingly, led to hostility between the priests and monks of Winchester. However, one can perhaps see Ethelwold's guiding hand in the closing of this rift through the rise of the cult of St. Swithun: according to his hagiographies, the saint appeared in a dream to one of the workmen engaged on Ethelwold's building projects, telling him to explain to the priest Eadsige that Bishop Ethelwold was to open his grave and bring his remains into the cathedral. The circumstances here are noteworthy: Eadsige was among the clerics whom Ethelwold had expelled from the Old Minster and as such was not on speaking terms with the bishop. Nonetheless, a reconciliation took place (with Eadsige bowing to the inevitable and becoming a monk) as a cult surrounding St. Swithun was established. On 15 July 971 his remains were translated (with a second elaborate translation ceremony shortly thereafter) to a new shrine near the High Altar of Winchester Cathedral, and almost immediately such miracles of healing occurred at this site that thousands of pilgrims flocked to Winchester.

The profit and publicity that this phenomenon created can hardly be exaggerated. It threw into enforced prominence the harmony insisted on by the bishop among the three Winchester monastic foundations and between both the clerical and the professed souls under his care. It also drew attention to the impressive revival of Benedictinism and the reestablishment of Winchester as a major center of monastic practice and education. Swithun as a secular cleric was now bestowing saintly approbation through his miracles for the work of Ethelwold in Winchester and for the ongoing Benedictine reform. Swithun's cult naturally gave rise to literary endeavors undertaken almost entirely by monastics. Lantfred of Fleury wrote the first Latin *Life of St. Swithun* in the 970s; before the century was over, a metrical reworking of this vita had been produced by the cantor Wulfstan, who then wrote a longer *Life* on the basis of new material as well. Ælfric of Eynsham used similar material for a shorter Latin vita, and then completed a vernacular *Life* in metrical prose during the early years of the 11th century. Swithun thus entered the kalendars of Anglo-Saxon England to become a patron saint of Winchester entirely as a result of Ethelwold's ambitious and determined revival of monasticism, although Swithun himself had never been a monk.

Ethelwold is best known for the role he played in writing texts that presented the liturgy and practice of Benedictinism in a form that the Anglo-Saxon monastic houses all over England could make their own. He translated the *Regula Sancti Benedicti* into English at the king's behest in exchange for a land grant to further his foundation activities, and after the *Regularis Concordia* synod his was the hand that drafted the document which outlined monastic practice as it should be carried out in England at that time. He is credited with having inaugurated an Office of the Virgin, an Office of Sts. Peter and Paul, and a supplementary Office for All Saints in Benedictine liturgical practice in England. We know too that the "Benedictional of Saint Ethelwold" (London, British Library Additional MS 49598) was commissioned by him, doubtless used by him during his lifetime, and that its makeup was probably of his own design and partial composition.

After his death Ethelwold was revered as a saint, and his cult grew up with the translation of his relics on 10 September 996. His monastic *familia* (community) included him in new liturgical devotions for Winchester, Old Minster, where he was invoked in hymn, trope, collect, and mass-prayer material. Two Latin *Lives* – the earlier by the cantor Wulfstan of Winchester, the later by his pupil Ælfric of Eynsham – appeared prior to 1006; thereafter, an account of Ethelwold's refoundation of Ely, known as the *Libellus Æthelwoldi* (Little Book of Ethelwold) drew on Wulfstan's life and was compiled anonymously at Ely itself in the early decades of the 12th century. The South English Legendary (composed in the West Midland dialect of Middle English during the second half of the 13th century) contains a *Life of Adelwolde* that once again looks back to the writings influenced by the reform period for its inspiration.

Many of the accounts from which we derive what we know of the tenth-century reform were set down by Ælfric, abbot of Eynsham (c. 955–c. 1020, although a case can be made for his birth having been as early as 940). He is the best known of all Anglo-Saxon monastic homilists and writers. He was trained at Winchester, Old Minster, in Ethelwold's own school, making him a second-generation witness to the process and effects of the reform, and, as noted earlier, he was one of Ethelwold's first biographers. In 987 he was sent as priest to Cerne Abbas at the request of its founder, the ealdorman Æthelmær, who was to be his patron for most of his life thereafter; in 1005 this Æthelmær founded a monastery at Evesham in Oxfordshire, where Ælfric took up the abbacy and held it until his death in the second decade of the 11th century.

Although a monk, Ælfric was an educational writer whose concerns extended to clerical issues as well. He wrote treatises on the Old and New Testaments and translated parts of the Bible but also wrote about the dangers of translation for the unwary. He compiled a Grammar and a Glossary and devised a Colloquy to provide his monastic students with a sound Latin vocabulary; in addition, he prepared a compilation from the Venerable Bede's work on astronomy and atmosphere known as *De Temporibus*. Ælfric wrote a series of pastoral and instructional letters in both Latin and Old English, but his reputation has come to rest on his Old English homilies and saints' lives: the first and second series of Catholic homilies each moves through the Temporale and Sanctorale of the Church year, creating two cycles of sermons for either parochial or monastic use, whereas his *Lives of Saints*, written in metrical prose, celebrates those heroes of the Church whom monks would venerate.

Oswald of Worcester and York

Oswald (c. 920–992), about ten years the junior of his two colleagues, was the third reformer who brought about the revival of Benedictinism and education in tenth-century Anglo-Saxon England. He is credited with having had the most agreeable personality of the three, being less obsessive than Dunstan, considerably less aggressive than Ethelwold, and on the whole possessed of a sociable, cheerful, and above all tactful turn of mind. He was the nephew of Oda ("the Good"), the archbishop of Canterbury who had also worn the habit of Fleury and adopted the Continental Benedictines' passion for relics and shrines by translating St. Wilfrid's remains from Ripon to Canterbury in 948. Unlike Dunstan and Ethelwold, who had connections with the English court families of Wessex, Oswald was of a financially well-to-do Danish family who had apparently come to England during the ninth-century invasions, settled in the Danelaw, and converted to Christianity only a generation or two earlier. His uncle Oda sponsored his monastic ambitions, first in fairly liberal practice in a small center at Winchester and thereafter, when Oswald desired a stricter rule, at Fleury. On Oda's death in 959, Oswald returned to England and went to York, where another Dane, his kinsman Osketel, was archbishop; Osketel drew Dunstan's attention to his promising protégé, and when Dunstan left the See of Worcester to become archbishop of Canterbury in around 960, he asked Oswald to take his place there.

Oswald's management of Worcester is typical of his remarkable personality. A larger cathedral building was needed, but Oswald took pains to preserve the beloved original church of St. Peter alongside his new "basilica" dedicated to St. Mary the Virgin. Worcester had never been a monastic foundation, but where Ethelwold would have insisted, Oswald merely suggested such an initiative by setting up a monastic school at some remove from Worcester, with stunning results. Benedictinism took root firmly and enthusiastically at the school in Westbury-on-Trym, and soon new foundations were needed to provide centers for Oswald's monks. Of the houses for which he made provision, the most famous were Ramsey (c. 970, dedicated 974), which was established with close contacts to Fleury, and Winchcombe (c. 972), which preserved a singular reputation for learning. By 977 Oswald's considerate handling of his episcopal seat had borne fruit, and Ramsey was providing monks for Worcester.

In 971 Dunstan had urged Edgar to appoint Oswald, likely because of his ability to work tactfully with the secular as well as the monastic, to the archbishopric of York on Osketel's death. However, the lack of a vibrant monastic tradition in the north caused Oswald to maintain his position in Worcester as well. He died in his own Cathedral of St. Mary during a liturgical celebration on the third Sunday of Lent, February 992, ever the most amenable and approachable of the three reformers.

It is generally believed that the earliest anonymous *Life of St. Oswald* was written by his own pupil, Byrhtferth of Ramsey; later *Lives* were prepared by the 12th-century Eadmer, precentor of Christ Church, Canterbury, and William of Malmesbury, each of whom had also written a *Life of Dunstan*. As with Ethelwold we find a Middle English *Life of St. Oswald*, and as with Dunstan's hagiography a *Life of St. Oswald* was written by Johannes Capgrave in the mid–15th century. Oswald was also celebrated as a saint within the monastic liturgy, as Latin hymns were composed in his honor for use in the *opus Dei*.

Sarah Larratt Keefer

See also Benedictines; England; Hagiography: Western Christian; Knowles, M. David; Lanfranc; Liturgy: Western Christian; Manuscript Production: Christian; Monte Cassino, Italy; Whitby, England

Further Reading

Æthelwold, *The Monastic Agreement of the Monks and Nuns of the English Nation*, edited by Thomas Symons, London and New York: Nelson, 1953

Brooks, Nicholas, and Catherine Cubitt, editors, *St. Oswald of Worcester: Life and Influence*, London and New York: Leicester University Press, 1996

Clemoes, Peter, "The Chronology of Ælfric's Work," in *The Anglo-Saxons: Studies in Some Aspects of Their History and Culture Presented to Bruce Dickins*, edited by Clemoes, London: Bowes and Bowes, 1959

Dales, Douglas S., *Dunstan: Saint and Statesman*, Cambridge: Lutterworth Press, 1988

Duckett, E.S., *Saint Dunstan of Canterbury: A Study of Monastic Reform in the Tenth Century*, New York: Norton, and London: Collins, 1955

Gameson, Richard, *The Role of Art in the Late Anglo-Saxon Church*, New York: Oxford University Press, 1995

Garmonsway, George N., translator, *The Anglo-Saxon Chronicle*, London: Dent, 1972

Gretsch, Mechthild, "Æthelwold's Translation of the *Regula Sancti Benedicti* and Its Latin Exemplar," *Anglo-Saxon England* 3 (1974)

Gretsch, Mechthild, editor, *Die regula Sancti Benedicti in England und ihre altenglische Übersetzung*, Munich: Fink, 1973

Knowles, David, *The Monastic Order in England*, Cambridge: Cambridge University Press, 1966; New York: Cambridge University Press, 1976

Kornexl, Lucia, editor, *Die Regularis Concordia und ihre altenglische Interlinearversion mid Einleitung und Kommentar*, Munich: Fink, 1993

Lapidge, M., and M. Winterbottom, editors, *Wulfstan of Winchester, The Life of St. Æthelwold*, Oxford: Clarendon Press, 1991
Needham, Gregory I., editor, *Lives of Three English Saints*, London: Methuen, and New York: Appleton-Century-Crofts, 1966
Parsons, David, editor, *Tenth Century Studies*, London: Phillimore, 1975
Ramsay, Nigel, et al., editors, *St. Dunstan: His Life, Times and Cult*, Woodbridge, England, and Rochester, New York: Boydell Press, 1992
Robinson, J. Armitage, *St. Oswald and the Church of Worcester*, London: Oxford University Press, 1919
Robinson, J. Armitage, *The Times of Saint Dunstan*, Oxford: Clarendon Press, 1923
Stenton, F.M., *Anglo-Saxon England*, 3rd edition, Oxford: Clarendon Press, 1971; reprint, 1998
Stubbs, William, editor, *Memorials of Saint Dunstan, Archbishop of Canterbury*, London: Longman, 1874
White, Louisa Caroline, *Ælfric: A New Study of His Life and Writings*, Boston: Lamson, Wolffee, 1898; reprint, Hampden, Connecticut: Archon, 1974
Wilcox, Jonathan, editor, *Ælfric's Prefaces*, Durham: Durham Medieval Texts, 1994
Winterbottom, Michael, editor, *Three Lives of English Saints*, Toronto: Pontifical Institute of Mediaeval Studies, 1972
Yorke, Barbara, editor, *Bishop Æthelwold: His Career and Influence*, Woodbridge, England, and Wolfeboro, New Hampshire: Boydell Press, 1988

Reformation

The Reformation of 16th- and 17th-century Europe brought with it a direct challenge to monasticism. Catholic and Protestants alike sought to reformulate the practices and principles of monastic life as it had developed over the course of the Middle Ages. Catholic reformers sought to restore original purposes and purity to monastic vocations, whereas Protestants argued that restoration of religion meant the abolishment of monastic institutions. Yet in each case reformers were forced to grapple with the role that monastic foundations played in their society and with how new and reformed monastic orders would meet the challenges of a world divided in its religious underpinnings. The histories of individual monastic foundations vary widely by order, by country, and by individual circumstances. It is fair to state, however, that no European house emerged from the Reformation untouched by the events of the 16th and 17th centuries.

Approaches to Monastic Institutions in Protestant Territories

1. Source of Converts

The Protestant Reformation owed a great deal of its early success to recruitment from monastic institutions. Not only was its most famous proponent, Martin Luther (1483–1546), an Augustinian friar, but many of its first converts and preachers were former monks and nuns. Luther actively encouraged both his fellow Augustinians and members of other orders to leave the cloister behind and carve out a new route to salvation and spiritual security.

Whereas monks often heard about the new religious ideas directly, nuns were more likely to read about them in letters and books smuggled into the convent and to discuss them with sympathetic chaplains. Their departure from the cloister, whether surreptitious or authorized, raised serious questions about their new role in society. Katherina von Bora (1499–1552) and Charlotte de Bourbon are well-known examples of nuns who fled the convent and eventually found new roles as the wives of reformers. Both entered the convent as teenagers and left secretly to join the Protestant movement. When Katherina von Bora and eight other sisters escaped from the convent at Nimschen, their families refused to receive them, and they were placed as teachers or with Protestant families or were married. In von Bora's case that meant marriage to a man 16 years her senior, Martin Luther. Charlotte de Bourbon took similar action, fleeing in her mid-20s the convent where she had lived for 13 years. Her French noble family also refused to be reconciled with her choice, and she eventually found refuge in Calvinist Heidelberg, where she assisted fellow refugees from France and later married William the Silent (1533–1584) of the Netherlands.

The radical wing of the Reformation also drew on religious orders for its leadership. Michael Sattler (c. 1490–1527) was a Benedictine monk before he joined the Anabaptists in the 1520s. Historians have argued over what influence his Benedictine background had on the development of the Schleitheim Confession (1527), but the recruitment of personnel from monasteries was a persistent feature of the early Reform movements. In the Anabaptist movement in Münster, monastic foundations played important, if divergent, roles. The nuns from the convents of St. Aegidius and Überwasser provided Bernd Rothmann (c. 1495–1535) with support early in his campaign, whereas the convent of Niesing rejected the radical Anabaptist message and escaped the city.

2. Dissolution of Monasteries and Convents and the Redistribution of Resources

In Protestant territories most monasteries and convents were dissolved or transformed into hospitals and schools. Their revenues were diverted to the state, with a percentage reserved for the functions previously carried out by religious institutions. On the Continent male monastic foundations were almost universally dissolved when they fell under Protestant control. Luther did not insist on the abandonment of monastic life but maintained that life in a cloister carried no assurance of salvation or merit. His followers were more adamant. Secular authorities called for the immediate dismantling of monastic orders, especially where important landholdings and revenues were at stake. Philipp of Hesse's agents offered monks the choice of becoming Lutherans or settling elsewhere. Approximately 60 percent of the revenues from their holdings went toward supporting hospitals, schools, and universities. The remaining income financed Philipp's court and administration.

In Württemberg monastic properties were used to support the duke's comprehensive educational plan that provided educated and loyal proponents of the Reform in the pulpit, the classroom, and the University of Tübingen. Whereas in the short term it was often former monks who filled these positions, in the long term it was the revenues and buildings of the old monasteries that supported the education of a new generation of Protestant leaders. The pattern of life for students in the monastery schools emphasized religious observances as well as a strong religious education in Latin. Students who went on to receive the duke's scholarships for the university (*Stift*) were expected to study Lutheran theology and to serve the duke throughout their careers.

Converted monastic resources supported many of the charitable services formerly provided by the Catholic Church and met new demands as well. Schools, libraries, homes for widows, and building sites for new housing all emerged from monastic properties. The monastic buildings of Nuremberg's *Egidienkirche* housed the new municipal secondary school (*Gymnasium*) founded on Melanchthon's recommendation in 1526. The Augustinian cloister in Wittenberg was given over to Luther to house his family, students, and guests.

The new charitable foundations often maintained many characteristics of monastic life, even though the theological foundations had changed. The hospital founded at Haina in Hesse required its patients to adopt a life of regular prayer, light work for the able-bodied, and instruction from the Bible and Luther's *Catechism*. In addition Haina maintained the monastic tradition of hospitality and almsgiving. Pilgrims and travelers could find one night's food and lodging there, whereas widows, orphans, and the poor could beg for food. Several of the former monks of Haina remained to help staff the hospital. Württemberg's new Protestant monastery schools called for a strict regime of prayer and biblical studies, interspersed with Latin, Greek, and choir practice. In addition the code of behavior for the boys was designed to develop the type of moral and ethical character appropriate for future preachers.

In Nuremberg the Reformation split the regular clergy. At a debate sponsored by the town council in 1525, representatives of the Augustinian and Benedictine houses argued for Luther's interpretation, whereas preachers from the Dominican, Franciscan, and Carmelite houses defended the Catholic position. Nonetheless all the male monastic foundations were dissolved in the succeeding months, with their possessions, including buildings, real estate, and rents, turned over to the city. The monks themselves either became members of the growing Lutheran clergy or accepted annuities from the city for their maintenance. The contention resulting from these acts continued for decades. The last remaining Dominicans were pensioned off in 1543, and the Franciscans followed suit in 1562. Nuns proved more difficult to resettle. Whereas the city was successful in forbidding any new professions, Protestant Nuremberg could not seize complete control of the convents (and their property) until the last of the sisters had died. In the case of the Dominican nuns, this phase lasted until 1596. The case in England was quite different. Although efforts were made to exclude individual convents from dissolution, English nuns were pensioned off at the same time as their male counterparts.

A variety of arguments have been forwarded to account for the greater durability of the convents on the Continent under the Reformation. Whereas former monks seem to have disappeared into the general population or to have taken up positions in the newly formed churches, there was no corresponding role for women in the Reformation. Despite the tremendous support given to the Reform by individual women, no organizational structure developed that could accommodate groups of unmarried women. Many examples of reformers can be found, including Luther, who expressed concern about what would happen to the women outside the cloister. As noted previously, attempts to return women to their families were not always successful, and these early experiences may have encouraged later reformers to be less zealous in their attempts to remove women from convents.

More recent scholarship has concentrated on the efforts of nuns and abbesses themselves to prevent their institutions from being dissolved. Wiesner (1992) has studied several free imperial abbeys and convents in central Germany that either were able to maintain their Catholic identity or accepted the Reformation and transformed themselves into Protestant institutions for women – despite the rejection of monasticism explicit in Protestant theology. The high social status and family connections of the abbesses and many of the convents' residents helped them resist political and sometimes military pressure to dissolve. Barker (1995) has argued that Caritas Pirckheimer, the abbess of the convent of St. Clare, used her humanist education to defend the nuns' position so effectively that Philip Melanchthon was persuaded to urge restraint in actions against all the Nuremberg convents.

Approaches to Monastic Institutions in Catholic Territories

1. Source of Reform and Spiritual Renewal

Historians have argued about whether the Catholic Reformation has its roots in reaction to Protestantism or in an independent spiritual revival. The growth of Catholic religious orders during the 16th and 17th centuries has been used as evidence for both sides of the issue. Donnelly (1995) has argued that the new orders did not specifically mention the fight against heresy as a part of their purpose and were not founded or especially strong in those areas of Europe where the main conflicts with Protestantism arose (Germany, the Netherlands, and Eastern Europe). He argues that the new orders were devoted to the mission of reviving Catholicism. Opposing views suggest that the emphasis of the Catholic Reform on just those elements of Catholicism that came under the greatest attack by the Protestants (including monastic life) points to a more reactive model.

Whatever the initial impetus, the 16th and 17th centuries were times of vigorous revival for Catholic religious orders. Old orders were reformed, new orders were founded, and new roles developed for eager participants. The Council of Trent

(1545–1563) called for the reform of religious orders under the strictest observance of their rule. Religious professions were limited to adults (over the age of 16) who had lived as a novice for at least one year. Appointments of abbots and abbesses were to be based on proven records of virtue and sanctity. The attractiveness of the new and reformed religious orders under these stricter guidelines is undeniable. Membership in all religious orders grew, and the sincerity of individual vocations shows in the pleas of Catholic families who tried to restrain their children from abandoning secular life.

The most important new orders that emerged during the Catholic Reformation started as reformed versions of older monastic orders. The Capuchins were part of a larger movement among Franciscan Observants who desired a more stringent interpretation of St. Francis' Rule. However, whereas the Reformed, the Discalced, and the Recollects remained under the Observant wing of the Franciscans, the Capuchins were recognized as an independent order in 1528, and their separation became complete in 1619. The Discalced Carmelites began as a reform movement. Saint Teresa of Avila (1515–1582) and St. John of the Cross (1542–1591) provided the spiritual leadership that inspired the establishment of convents and monasteries throughout Catholic Europe and achieved the independence of the Discalced Carmelites by the end of the 16th century.

Numerous smaller orders also developed at this time, including the creation of a new type of religious order, the clerks regular. These small orders (e.g., Theatines, Barnabites, and Piarists) had a variety of specific missions, including hospital work, education, and Church reform.

The earliest 16th-century efforts to reform monastic institutions in Catholic territories were scrutinized for possible heretical elements. The Italian Benedictine Congregation of Santa Guistina of Padua aimed for the middle ground between the theologies of the Protestant reformers and the Catholic reformers of Trent. Their reliance on Greek Patristic tradition, as developed by Don Luciano degli Ottoni, led to positions that were condemned as heretical by both the Council of Trent and John Calvin. Not all suspicions of Protestant tendencies were unfounded. The Spanish Jeronomite monastery of San Isidro del Campo outside Seville had powerful patrons and great wealth, but it was also a refuge for Protestants and a distribution center for Castillian New Testaments. The prior, several monks, and some nuns from the Jeronomite convent of Santa Paula fled from the Inquisition in the 1550s.

Reform moved at different paces, depending on the support received from the government. France did not initially accept the decrees of the Council of Trent and moved more slowly to reform monastic life. The importance of royal privilege in French Church appointments delayed responses to changing religious circumstances. Odet de Coligny, a leading Huguenot (French Protestant), became the titular abbot of Fleury in 1562. Income from the abbey was still being paid through an intermediary to Odet's brother, Gaspard de Coligny (1519–1572), a Huguenot military leader, as late as 1571.

The Council of Trent called for strict cloistering of women in religious orders. The Discalced Carmelites, under the leadership of a noted contemplative, fit into this model of female monasticism. Other new orders, however, struggled in their initial years to find a more active role for women religious. The Ursulines and the Visitandines are two examples of orders established in the 16th and 17th centuries whose initial impetus lay in providing a more active religious life for women. Both came under pressure to become fully cloistered, and both prospered under the stricter rule. There were, however, exceptions to this pattern. The Daughters of Charity worked in hospitals and schools and provided a host of services to the poor and received papal approval for their activities in the mid–17th century.

Overall historians have argued that the Reformation did little to enhance the status of women and much to limit their options. This conclusion is based in part on the closing of convents in Protestant territories, thereby removing the option for women to live in an independent female community, and on the failure of Protestantism to provide alternative roles for women in the structure of the new churches. In contrast the Catholic Reformation, although emphasizing the importance of the cloister and providing fewer freedoms in monastic life, nonetheless attracted generations of women into the reformed orders and inspired a whole range of other more secular devotional activities.

MARY JANE CHASE

See also Anglican Monasticism; Asceticism: Christian Perspectives; Augustinian Friars/Hermits; Critiques of Western Christian Monasticism; Dissolution of Monasteries; Images: Christian Perspectives; Monasticism, Definitions of: Christian Perspectives; Pilgrimages, Christian: Western Europe; Protestant Monasticism; Scandinavia; Switzerland; Vadstena, Sweden

Further Reading

Barker, Paula S. Datsko, "Caritas Pirckheimer: A Female Humanist Confronts the Reformation," *Sixteenth Century Journal* 26:2 (Summer 1995)

Collett, Barry, "A Benedictine Scholar and Greek Patristic Thought in Pre-Tridentine Italy: A Monastic Commentary of 1538 on Chrysostom," *Journal of Ecclesiastical History* 36:1 (January 1985)

Collett, Barry, *Italian Benedictine Scholars and the Reformation: The Congregation of Santa Giustina of Padua* (Oxford Historical Monographs), New York: Oxford University Press, and Oxford: Clarendon Press, 1985

DeMolen, Richard L., editor, *Religious Orders of the Catholic Reformation: In Honor of John C. Olin on His Seventy-Fifth Birthday*, New York: Fordham University Press, 1994

Dickens, A.G., *Late Monasticism and the Reformation*, London and Rio Grande, Ohio: Hambledon Press, 1994

Diefendorf, Barbara B., "Give Us Back Our Children: Patriarchal Authority and Parental Consent to Religious Vocations in Early Counter-Reformation France," *Journal of Modern History* 68 (June 1996)

Donnelly, John Patrick, "The New Religious Orders, 1517–1648," in *Handbook of European History, 1400–1600: Late Middle Ages, Renaissance, and*

Reformation, volume 2: *Visions, Programs and Outcomes*, edited by Thomas A. Brady, Heiko A. Oberman, and James D. Tracy, New York: Brill, 1995
Grieser, D. Jonathan, "A Tale of Two Convents: Nuns and Anabaptists in Münster, 1533–1535," *Sixteenth Century Journal* 26:1 (Spring 1995)
Harris, Barbara J., "A New Look at the Reformation: Aristocratic Women and Nunneries, 1450–1540," *Journal of British Studies* 32:2 (1993)
Martin, Dennis D., "Monks, Mendicants and Anabaptists: Michael Sattler and the Benedictines Reconsidered," *Mennonite Quarterly Review* 60:2 (1986)
Maué, Hermann, "Nuremberg's Cityscape and Architecture," in *Gothic and Renaissance Art in Nuremberg, 1300–1550*, New York: Metropolitan Museum of Art, 1986
Methuen, Charlotte, "Securing the Reformation through Education: The Duke's Scholarship System of Sixteenth-Century Württemberg," *Sixteenth Century Journal* 25 (Winter 1994)
Midelfort, H.C. Erik, "Protestant Monastery? A Reformation Hospital in Hesse," in *Reformation Principle and Practice: Essays in Honour of Arthur Geoffrey Dickens*, edited by Peter Newman Brooks, London: Scolar Press, 1980
Rapley, Elizabeth, *The Dévotes: Women and Church in Seventeenth-Century France* (McGill-Queen's Studies in the History of Religion, 4), Buffalo, New York: McGill-Queen's University Press, 1990
Snyder, C. Arnold, "Revolution and the Swiss Brethren: The Case of Michael Sattler," *Church History* 50 (1981)
Wiesner, Merry E., "Ideology Meets the Empire: Reformed Convents and the Reformation," in *Germania Illustrata: Essays on Early Modern Germany Presented to Gerald Strauss* (Sixteenth Century Essays and Studies, volume 18), edited by Andrew C. Fix and Susan C. Karant-Nunn, Kirksville, Missouri: Sixteenth Century Journal, 1992
Wiesner-Hanks, Merry, editor, *Convents Confront the Reformation: Catholic and Protestant Nuns in Germany* (Women of the Reformation, volume 1), translated by Wiesner-Hanks and Joan Skocir, Milwaukee, Wisconsin: Marquette University Press, 1996
Woodward, G.W.O., *The Dissolution of the Monasteries* (Blandford History Series: Problems of History), New York: Walker, and London: Blandford Press, 1966

Regulations: Buddhist Perspectives

The basic "regulations" of Buddhist monasticism consist of codes of detailed disciplinary rules enumerated first within the ancient *Prāṭimokṣa Sūtra* and then further embedded in the developed vinayas ("Books of Discipline") of the various and emergent schools of Indian Buddhism. All Buddhist codes of detailed monastic discipline are remarkably similar. There is almost complete unanimity in seven of the eight categories of regulations in whatever vinaya texts have survived to this day. However, in the seventh (and most minor) section of these recensions, the number of rules ranges in number from 218 in the Mahāsaṃghīka recension to 263 in the Sarvāstivāda. The variance is the result of the appendage of many minor observations having to do with correct apparel, diet, and possession of various requisites. Yet, despite similarity in detail and substance, what might appear to the outsider to be minor differences between various recensions actually sparked intense controversies between rival monastic communities throughout history. Indeed scholars have argued soundly that the rift that eventually resulted in the Mahāyāna/Hīnayāna divide within Buddhist tradition arose in arguments about disciplinary rules between the Mahāsaṃghīka and Sthaviravādin communities occurring in the fourth century B.C.

The centrality of monastic discipline to the collective life of the early *saṅgha* is reflected in the fact that communal recitation of the *Prāṭimokṣa Sūtra* by *bhikkhu*s within each monastic *sīmā* (boundary) on the new- and full-moon days of each month likely comprised the earliest formal ritual occasions regularly celebrated by the Buddhist order of monks. The purpose of this recitation was to generate conscious awareness of the vinaya rules as the vehicle through which the community defined and maintained itself. The sūtra seemed to have functioned as type of public charter or confession. Moreover within the early Pāli *nikāya*s of the *Suttapiṭaka* the Buddha is almost always made to say, when referring to his basic teaching: "this *dhamma* and this *vinaya*." The consistent yoking together of dhamma and vinaya signifies the fact that doctrine and practice were understood as integrally related to each other. Buddhist monastic regulations regarding behavior were cultically celebrated from the inception of the Buddhist community, functioning as a defining charter in relation to other religious communities. Moreover their significance needs to be understood in relation to the soteriology of the Buddha's teaching. Buddhist monastic regulations are not regarded as mundane but rather as affective expressions of the Buddha's teaching, or as theory put into practice. Indeed each rule is regarded as *Buddhavācāna*, the "word of the Buddha."

The initial sermon at Deer Park in Sārnāth, in which the Buddha preached the well-known Four Noble Truths and the Noble Eightfold Path, contains the heart of Buddhist thought: the unsatisfactory human condition of *dukkha* within the impermanent flux of saṃsāra results from actions influenced by ignorance and attachment and can be assuaged by cultivating wisdom (*paññā*), concentration (*samādhi*), and morality (*sīla*). These three cultivations are the basis for the Noble Eightfold Path leading to nirvāṇa (unconditioned experience and the transcendence of rebirth). Many scholars have understood *sīla* as the basis for the over 200 major and minor regulations of monastic discipline found in the Vinaya and *Prāṭimokṣa Sūtra*. At first glance this interpretation seems reasonable enough, for the concerns of *sīla*, especially as they are articulated within the first four cardinal behavioral precepts (not to kill, not to take what is not given, not to willingly lie or distort the truth, and not to engage in sex of any kind), can be directly or indirectly related to issues of regulation addressed in almost all the disciplinary rules. Many of the rules constitute a type of preventive defense, enabling the monk to uphold the major moral precepts noted previously. From this perspective the monastic regulations prescribed in the canonical Vinaya texts simply extend the more general moral and ethical imperative included within the Buddha's prescriptive path that leads to nirvāṇa.

However, the theoretical and spiritual basis of Buddhist monastic regulations is actually far more comprehensive in scope. The early Buddhist theory of action found within the Vinaya text itself relates more fully to the Buddha's dharma in general, not only to *sīla* specifically. The *Mahāvagga* (the first section of that part of the Pāli Theravāda Vinaya in which the institutional rites and regulations of the *saṅgha* are detailed) recounts the Buddha's enlightenment experience, his first public first sermon at Deer Park, and his initial conversions of monks and laity. In the text's numerous accounts of conversion, the pattern is always the same. Whenever encountering a prospective convert, the Buddha preaches an initial sermon, "a talk on giving, talk on moral habit, talk on heaven, he explained the vanity, depravity of pleasures of the senses, the advantage of renouncing them" (*Book of Discipline* 4.23; this stock phrase is repeated no less than eight times in the *Mahāvagga*). On hearing the sermon the listener takes refuge in the Buddha, dhamma, and *saṅgha* and becomes a lay adherent. The elements of this sermon embody the central aspects of religiosity to be cultivated in the lay life: positive karmic efficacy leading to a heavenly rebirth as a result of *dāna* (giving) and *sīla* (moral rectitude) and a warning to those who fail to reckon adequately with the problem of *taṇhā* (desire). However, if the Buddha discerns that his listener is capable of understanding truth of a more profound nature, he preaches a second sermon. The second sermon is the same as the famous Deer Park homily, consisting of the Four Noble Truths and the Noble Eightfold Path. When this second sermon has been preached, the listener gains "dharma-vision" or the "dharma-eye"; that is, he grasps what is known as "the principal doctrine of the Buddhas":

> When this is present, that comes to be;
> from the arising of this, that arises.
> When this is absent, that does not come to be;
> of the cessation of this, that ceases.

Thus, when the Buddha's listener attains dharma-vision, he responds positively to the Buddha's invitation to "go forth and wander for the welfare of the many," to become part of the collective *bhikkhusaṅgha*, and to live the life of religious discipline by observing the monastic regulations. Having understood dharma, the convert will now practice vinaya. With dharma-vision, that is, with an understanding of *paṭiccasamuppāda* ("the principal doctrine of the Buddhas," codependent arising, the conditioned and causal nature of existence), he understands that ego consciousness is based on the erroneous assumption that individuals are autonomous reified beings.

The logic of Buddhist monastic behavioral regulations rests on the "principal doctrine of the Buddhas," or *paṭiccasamuppāda*. When even desire or ignorance is present, suffering (*dukkha*) comes into being. When they are absent, *dukkha* ceases. When even dharma is realized, vinaya is practiced. Disciplined behavior, according to Buddhist monastic regulations, means acting without the kinds of ego-centered motivations or volitions that cause suffering for oneself and others in the world.

If one examines the monastic code of discipline in detail, one discovers the soteriological reasons that impelled the Buddha to promulgate such a detailed set of regulations. In each of the stories that lead up to the Buddha's pronouncements regarding which specific behavior is allowed and which is not, one can identify "wrongful states of mind" or unhealthy conditioning dispositions that the Buddha deems responsible for the monastic behavior called into question. In these stories and in illustrative case histories in the Vinaya corpus (the material that constitutes the casuistry of Buddhist monastic law), what inhibits sustained awareness of dharma-vision as well as behavioral realization of *paṭiccasamuppāda* is the presence of the *āsava*s ("mental sores") that ulcerate the mind. These *āsava*s are egocentric compulsions that include the well-known formulaic triad inimical to spiritual and mental health: passion or desire (*rāga*), hatred or ill will (*dosa*), and confusion or ignorance (*moha*). Attachment to any or all of these *āsava*s, especially when reinforced by *ahamkara* ("I-ness," or selfish conceit), is what poisons or distorts volition and generates immoral behavior involving killing, lying, stealing, or illicit sexual actions. Here it is significant to note that by *cetanā* (volition) the Buddha had defined the meaning of karma, or action. In his understanding of karma, it is the relationship between inward mental dispositions and outwardly expressive behavior that best illustrates the principal of cause and effect. The corollary to this understanding is this: actions performed with a will or volition unattached to or uninfluenced by the *āsava*s (passion, hatred, and delusion) will be actions expressive of dharma-vision (seeing reality as it is without self-impositions), for it is the quality of mind or nature of disposition that is willed into action through the agencies of body, speech, or thought. The Buddha understood the principal of cause and effect or *paṭiccasamuppāda* in just this way: the quality of mind gives rise to the quality of action. Thus, in a mind in which the harmful presence of the *āsava*s is absent, no harmful behavior will arise. Buddhist monastic regulations are then explicit indices of a mind in which there is a calmed, nongrasping, selfless disposition, a mind that has realized the wisdom intrinsic to the "principal doctrine of the Buddhas."

Thus, Buddhist monastic regulations involve more than extending the significance of *sīla* (morality) into a detailed regimen. They can be understood as integral to the soteriological quest of nirvāṇa ("extinction" or "blowing out"). Although ever reluctant to discuss the nature of nirvāṇa to any great extent, the Buddha does indeed equate the extinction of the *āsava*s with the realization of nirvāṇa in several early Pāli *nikāya* sources:

> O bhikkhus, what is the uncompounded? It is,
> O bhikkhus, the extinction desire [*rāga*],

the extinction of hatred [*dosa*], the extinction of illusion [*moha*].
(*Book of Kindred Sayings* 4.359; ibid., 177; *Book of Gradual Sayings* 4.251)

Whereas the Vinaya code of Buddhist monastic regulations was said to be formulated by the Buddha and cultically and juridically maintained by monks and nuns, another type of monastic regulation was established by kings and government authorities in Buddhist societies. In Theravāda southern and Southeast Asia, these were known as *katikāvata*s, or injunctions prescribed by kings in to check the *saṅgha* from become overly concerned with economic or political matters or to prevent the *saṅgha* from being manipulated by rival political forces. Similarly in eastern Asia, especially in medieval China, various authorities felt compelled periodically to prohibit the sale of "monk's certificates" that enabled individuals to escape from paying taxes or from participating in public service. In this vein it is interesting to note that even within Vinaya literature the laity are noted as playing an extremely important role in ensuring that monks keep to the rule and spirit of Buddhist monastic regulations. Thus, whereas the monks and nuns maintained discipline within their communities and grounded their understanding of the monastic regulations in relation to the religious quest, secular authorities intervened at times from the outside to make sure that monastic communities remained spiritually oriented and not politically motivated communities.

JOHN HOLT

See also Abbot: Buddhist; Buddhism: Overview; Discourses (Sūtras): Mahāyāna; Dōgen; Forest Masters; Hermits: Buddhist; Liturgy: Buddhist; Officials: Buddhist; Rules, Buddhist (Vinaya): Historical; Rules, Buddhist (Vinaya): Lineage; Saichō; Self-Immolation, Buddhist; Sexuality: Buddhist Perspectives; Ten-Precept Mothers as Theravādin Nuns

Further Reading

Dutt, Sukumar, *Buddhist Monks and Monasteries of India*, London: Allen and Unwin, 1962

Frauwallner, Erich, *The Earliest Vinaya and the Beginnings of Buddhist Literature*, Rome: Instituto per il Medio ed Estremo Oriente, 1956

Holt, John Clifford, *Discipline: The Canonical Buddhism of the Vinayapitaka*, Delhi: Motilal Banarsidass, 1981; Columbia, Missouri: South Asia Books, 1983; 2nd edition, Delhi: Motilal Banarsidass, 1995

Horner, I.B., translator, *The Book of the Discipline (Vinaya-Pitaka)*, 6 vols., London: Oxford University Press, 1938–1966

Pachow, W., *A Comparative Study of the Pratimoksa*, Santiniketan: Sino-Indian Cultural Society, 1955; reprint, Delhi: Motilal Banarsidass, 1997

Prebish, Charles S., and Janice J. Nattier, "Mahasamghika Origins: the Beginnings of Buddhist Sectarianism," *History of Religions* 16 (1977)

Wijayaratna, Mohan, *Buddhist Monastic Life*, translated by Claude Grangier and Steven Collins, Cambridge and New York: Cambridge University Press, 1990

Regulations: Christian Perspectives

Tradition

Christian monasticism is one of these phenomena in the history of our civilization that cannot function without constantly referring to its roots. They are, on the one hand (in common with the whole Church), the Bible (especially the New Testament) and the writings of the Church fathers and, on the other, literary and legislative works of fathers of monasticism. Their importance manifests itself in a monastic's everyday life (e.g., language, values, and perception of the world), especially during moments of crisis and transformation. An indispensable introduction to this literature is Jean Leclercq's *The Love of Learning and the Desire for God* (first French edition 1957).

One of the pivotal texts of monasticism is the *Life of St. Antony* (c. 251–356), Athanasius the Great (c. 295–373), bishop of Alexandria. It describes a heroic struggle against the weakness of the body fought to attain the absolute. In fact it can be said that Christian monasticism developed on the basis of this *Life*. It was translated into dozens of languages (Latin, Coptic, Ethiopian, Armenian, Georgian, and Old Church Slavonic), it could be found in every monastery, and it was known to all monks. A similarly important role was played by the second book of the *Dialogues* of Pope Gregory I (590–604), containing the *Life of Benedict of Nursia,* as well as by the writings of the Desert Fathers John Chrysostom, Gregory of Nyssa, John Cassian, Jerome, Bernard of Clairvaux, and many others.

Literary tradition exerted special influence in the earliest period of monasticism, even in Eastern Christian monasticism, in which monastic legislation has never been as rich as in Western monasticism. This article classifies types of regulations in both Western and Eastern Christian monasticism.

Normative Texts

From the inception of the cenobitic period, monastic life has been regulated by normative acts that set its rhythm, establish its position in society, regulate contacts of monks with the outside world, and so on. These are based on monastic and Church tradition as well as on canon and civil law. In this respect a fundamental difference separates Eastern Christian monasticism (discussed later) from Western monasticism.

1. Western Christian Monasticism

According to Jacques Dubois (*Les Ordres monastiques*, 1985), the history of the *ordo monasticus* is the history of "rules which gave way to the Rule of St. Benedict and then of Institutions evolving around the Rule which became unalterable." He distinguishes three groups of normative acts: (1) rules that describe the "spirit and main principles"; (2) customaries (*consuetudines*), which, although "not always written down, convey details pertaining to practice of everyday life"; and (3) "institutions" (statutes), that is, "canon, liturgic, and discipline directives gathered in collections called ordinances, customaries, constitutions, or declarations."

Monastic rules. These define general rules of monastic life, its spirit, and its main principles, which are specified in turn in other normative acts, especially in customaries and monastic statutes.

Monastic rules have evolved alongside the development of monastic life. Already in the earliest period of the cenobites, the need arose to put monastic life in order. From the end of the fourth century until the middle of the seventh, many rules of local importance functioned mainly in Western Europe. Only the most important can be mentioned here.

The earliest monastic rules came into being around 400; these include the Augustinian Rule (c. 395), the rule of Basil the Great (397), the rule of Pachomius (404), and the *Regula Quattuor Patrum* (400–410). In 427 the *Regula Patrum Secunda* and that of John Cassian emerged and around 500 the *Regula Macarii* (i.e., that of Porcarius, abbot of Lérins). The heyday of "local" rules was in the sixth century. Between 515 and 542 several rules were written, among them the *Regula Orientalis* (515–520), the rules of Caesarius of Arles for virgins (512–534) and for monks (534–542), the *Regula Magistri* (before 530), the *Regula Eugippi* (530–535), the *Regula Patrum Tertia* (535), a second version of the *Regula Quattuor Patrum* (535–540), the rule of Benedict of Nursia (530–555), and the *Regulae Aureliani* for virgins and monks (547–551). Among the rules written in the second half of the sixth century were the *Regula Tarnatensis*, the *Regula Ferrioli* (553–573), and the *Regula Pauli et Stephani*. The beginning of the seventh century brought the rule of Columban and the rule of Isidore of Seville (c. 640). The process of creating monastic rules drew to a conclusion in the second half of the seventh century when the *Regula Fructuosi* (c. 640), the *Regula communis* (665–680), and the *Regula concensoria* were written in Spain, and the *Regula Walberti* (629–770), the *Regula cuiusdam Patris*, and the rule for women attributed to Columban (and additions to his rules) emerged in Gaul. These rules were collected by Benedict of Aniane in his *Codex regularum* (*Patrologia Latina* 103.393–702) and thus became better known in the West. The most important of these rules were those of Pachomius, Basil the Great, and Benedict of Nursia as well as the Augustinian Rule.

In the seventh century mixed observances became popular. *Vita monastica* was understood at that time as *evangelica et apostolica traditio et regula sanctorum patrum*. In practical terms it was the founder or superior who decided what "tradition" or "rule" was to be followed in an abbey. It was within his discretion whether the new community adopted one of many already existing rules, adopted customs of a nearby abbey (frequently one in which they themselves had been monks), or created a new observance specifically for this community. The Rules of Columban and of Benedict of Nursia were frequently combined. These observances are referred to in scholarly literature as a "mixed rule" (*regula mixta*). They disseminated knowledge of the Rule of Benedict of Nursia and paved the way for its triumph in the eighth century.

In defense of doctrinal purity of monastic life, the Fourth Lateran Council (1215) recognized as only and universally applicable three rules existing at that time (those of Augustine, Basil, and Benedict), forbidding the creation of new ones. Nevertheless in 1223 the Rule of Francis of Assisi was approved. From that moment these four monastic rules have been the only standing rules in Western monasticism. Apart from them exist a number of monastic constitutions and statutes commonly called rules, the most important of which are rules of the Templars, Poor Clares, and Bridgettines.

Monastic customaries. This term is derived from the Latin *consuetudo* (customary). Monastic customaries specify, in written or oral form, details of everyday life in a monastic community.

The Benedictines have never formed a centralized order. Rather the basis of their development and organization has always been individual abbeys, each jealously guarding its autonomy and sometimes united in more or less centralized federations and confederations. Governed *sub Regula vel abbate* (Rule of St. Benedict 1.2), the life of these communities has been based on both the Rule of St. Benedict and more or less local monastic customaries, so-called *consuetudines*.

Monastic customaries deal in general with, for example, describing a particular way of life, taking meals, working, sleeping, or celebrating liturgy throughout the day and the year. They do not formulate the program of life or spiritual formation, as is the case with rules. In particular customaries define more accurately and adapt to everyday life (and to local customs and traditions) the general stipulations of the Rule of St. Benedict. Their importance was officially acknowledged at Carolingian synods in Aachen in 802 and 816–817.

Two main "literary" types can be distinguished, both rarely occurring in pure form. The *consuetudines* of the first type aim at regulating the material and organizational conditions of an abbey's functioning. They contain detailed regulations of monastic everyday life within the daily and yearly framework, frequently augmented by a roster of monastic officials and their responsibilities. The *consuetudines* of the second type deal with the liturgy, containing not only regulations pertaining to prescribed behavior during the liturgy but also those pertaining to the very course of *officium divinum*, with quotations of incipits of various liturgical forms. In historiography customaries of the first type are called *consuetudines* and those of the second *ordinaria*. A third type of monastic customaries, so-called *consuetudines mixtae*, unites the two types.

The basic stock of Benedictine (including Cluniac) customaries is published in *Corpus consuetudinum monasticarum* (curo pontifici Athenaei S. Anselmi de Urbe coeptum et sub praesidiis Instituti Herwegeniani continuatum moderante Kassio Hallinger O.S.B., Siegburg, Fr. Schmitt: 1963–1996, volumes 1–12, 14;

continued, see Pius Engelbert, "Bericht über den Stand des *Corpus Consuetudinum Monasticarum* (*CCM*)," *Studien und Mitteilungen zur Geschichte des Benediktinerordens und seiner Zweige* 102 [1991]). Kassius Hallinger lists also earlier editions and known manuscript accounts of *consuetudines* of the Benedictines and of other orders (*CCM*, volume 1, 1963, pp. LIX–LXXIV; "Consuetudines Benedictinae," "Consuetudines canonicorum reularium," in *Repertorium fontium historiae Medii Aevi*, volume 3, Rome: Istituto storico italiano per il medio evo, 1970, pp. 624–636).

Constitutions and monastic statutes. These are canonical, liturgical, and disciplinary directives gathered in collections called ordinances, customaries, constitutions, or declarations. They establish the framework and mark directions in which monasticism is to develop. One cannot understand the history of an order without understanding the type of "institutions" that govern it.

The names monastic "constitutions" and "statutes" are often used interchangeably, especially with respect to the period preceding the Council of Trent (1545–1563). Their exact meaning is as follows: (1) Monastic constitutions in orders established before the 16th century are collections of detailed norms regulating monastic life and organization, thus supplementing the rule. In orders established after the 16th century, especially in congregations originating in the 19th and 20th centuries as well as in associations of apostolic life, constitutions are fundamental law codes of each institute. (2) Statutes define monastic internal norms that supplement the rule or monastic constitutions. Depending on the entity to which they pertain, there are (a) general statutes for an entire order, (b) provincial statutes for a monastic province, and (c) special statutes for an institution run by the order (e.g., a school or university), for a specific group of monks (e.g., missionaries), or for specific types of activity (e.g., for running a kitchen or library). Statutes may be issued by the authorities of an order or by the state or Church authorities.

In practical terms the boundary is between *consuetudines* and ordinances regulating or reforming various regions of the abbey's activity, its dependencies, and offices. Statutes are referred to in sources in various ways (most often as *statuta* or *consuetudines*), and it is their narrower scope that distinguishes them from customaries. The latter deal with the abbey's everyday life in general, whereas the former are limited to certain issues. Thus, it is not surprising that many of the oldest documents of this kind were published in the *Corpus consuetudinem monasticarum* (volume 1.6–7).

The term *statutes* also applies to legislative acts issued by monarchs (especially by the Carolingians), popes, councils, and synods. Statutes often aim at reforming or codifying monastic regulations and customs and at defining the responsibilities of monastic authorities.

Recent changes. The new *Codex Iuris Canonici* of 1983 (canon 587) ordered every institute of consecrated life to have its own regulations to govern principles of monastic life in the form of either a rule or monastic constitutions. Thus, both these terms, in use for a long time, have acquired a new meaning. However, this evolution has been in progress since the 16th century.

In orders established after the 16th century, especially in congregations originating in the 19th and 20th centuries as well as in associations of apostolic life, it is constitutions rather than rules that provide the fundamental law codes of each institute. They are supplemented by (1) rules (in the plural), which are collections of regulations and detailed norms; (2) so-called "customaries," which are equivalents of *consuetudines* and contain a detailed list of customs and ways of a given monastic community; and (3) monastic *directoria*, which are collections of secondary monastic norms enacted by authorities of a given congregation or institute.

2. Eastern Christian Monasticism

Characteristic of Orthodox monasticism is the absence of monastic orders. Monastic life is based on free interpretation of the rules of Basil the Great (and of Pachomius). Orthodox monks have never called themselves Basilians; this is the name of various orders of the Byzantine rite in Catholic Europe. In Orthodox monasticism a crucial role has been played by monastic tradition and by the founders of a given abbey.

Apart from the *Life of St. Antony*, as well as the writings of the fathers of the Eastern Church and of the Desert Fathers, the so-called *patrikon*s play a tremendous role in the life of Eastern monks. *Patrikon*s are books of lives of ancient saints in Eastern Churches, originating from a particular monastic center. The best known are the Sinai *patrikon* (the so-called *Limanor*), the Egyptian *patrikon* (the so-called *Lawsaik*), and the Kiev *patrikon* (the so-called *Pieczerski*). A separate genre of *patrikon* are *apophthegmata* of fathers (i.e., collections of sayings of noted ascetics and monks) together with examples derived from their lives. The most important of these, arranged in alphabetic order, was written by an anonymous monk at the beginning of the sixth century (*Patrologia Graeca* 65.71–440). They were written in various languages, and a Latin thematic collection exists (*Patrologia Latina* 73.855–1024).

The so-called *typikon*s issued for particular monasteries by founders or on their initiative became widespread from the tenth century on. Their role was similar to that of customaries in Western monasticism. They governed the status and functioning of a monastery. Apart from general regulations concerning monastic life and the observance of monastic rules, *typikon*s contained regulations pertaining to everyday life, liturgy, administration, officials, election of *igumens'*, and material needs of a monastery. Frequently an inventory of monastic real estate and other belongings (a so-called *brébion*) was appended to the *typikon*.

The development of Orthodox monasticism was greatly influenced by certain statutes and monastic constitutions. Worthy of mention are the centralizing reforms conducted by Theodore of Stoudios (759–826) and those implemented by Joseph of Volokolamsk (1439–1515).

Because of the close ties between Orthodox monasticism and state authorities, state and Church legislation, especially that issued by Emperor Justinian (527–565) and by councils, has played a major role in the history of Orthodox monasticism.

MAREK DERWICH

See also Antony, St.; Augustinian Rule; Basil the Great, St.; Benedict of Aniane, St.; Benedict of Nursia, St.; Bernard of Clairvaux, St.; Bridgettines; Caesarius of Arles, St.; Cassian, John; Cluniacs; Columban, St.; Desert Fathers; France: History; Gregory I (the Great), St.; Gregory of Nyssa, St.; Isidore of Seville, St.; Lérins, France; Monasticism, Definitions of: Christian Perspectives; Monastics and the World, Medieval; Templars; Theodore of Stoudios, St.

Further Reading

Cygler, Florent, "Règles, coutumiers et statuts (Ve–XIIIe siècle): Brèves considérations historico-typologiques," in *La vie quotidienne des moines et chanoines réguliers au Moyen Âge et Temps modernes: Actes du Premier Colloque International du L.A.R.H.C.O.R., Wrocław-Książ, 30 novembre–4 décembre 1994*, edited by Marek Derwich, Wrocław: Institut d'Histoire de l'Université de Wroclaw, 1995

Cygler, Florent, "Ausformung und Kodifizierung des Ordensrechts vom 12. bis 14. Jahrhundert. Strukturelle Beobachtungen zu den Cisterziensern, Prämonstratensern, Kartäusern und Cluniazensern," in *"De ordine vitae": Zu Normvorstellungen, Organisationsformen und Schriftgebrauch im mittelalterlichen Ordenswesen*, edited by Gert Melville, Münster-Hamburg-London: LIT, 1996

de Vogüé, Adalbert, *Les règles monastiques anciennes (400–700)*, Turnhout, Belgium: Brepols, 1985

de Vogüé, Adalbert, *Histoire littéraire du mouvement monastique dans l'antiquité*, Première Partie: *Le monachisme latine*, volume 1: *De la mort d'Antoine à la fin du séjour de Jérôme à Rome (356–385)*; volume 2: *Le monachisme latin de l'Itinéraire d'Égérie à l'éloge funèbre de Népotien (384–396)*; volume 3: *Jérôme, Augustin et Rufin au tournant du siècle (391–405)*; volume 4: *Sulpice Sévère et Paulin de Nole (393–409): Jérôme, homéliste et traducteur des "Pachomiana"*; volume 5: *De l'épitaphe de saint Paule à la consécration de Démétriade (404–414)* (Patrimoines - Christianisme), Paris: Cerf, 1991–1998

Derwich, Marek, *Monastycyzm benedyktyński w średniowiecznej Europie i Polsce: Wybrane problemy* (Benedictine Monasticism in Medieval Europe and Poland), Wrocław: Wydawn. Uniwersytetu Wrocławskiego, 1998

Donat, Lin, "Les coutumiers monastiques: Une novelle enterprise et un territoire nouveau," *Revue Mabillon* 3 (1992)

Gallen, Joseph F., *Canon Law for Religious*, New York: Alba House, 1983

Handbuch des katholischen Kirchenrechts, edited by J. Listl, H. Müller, and H. Schmitz, Regensburg: Pustet, 1983

Hourlier, Jacques, *L'âge classique (1150–1378): Les religieux*, Paris: Cujas, 1973

Iogna-Prat, Dominique, "Coutumes et statuts clunisiens comme sources historiques (ca 990 –ca 1200)," *Revue Mabillon* 3 (1992)

Lemoine, Robert, *Le droit des religieux du Concile de Trente aux Instituts séculiers*, Bruges and Paris: Desclée, DeBrouwer, 1956

Melville, Gert, *Ordenstatuten und allgemeines Kirchenrecht: Eine Skizze zum 12./13. Jahrhundert*, in *Monumenta Iuris Canonici*, Series C, volume 10, hg. v. P. Landau, Città del Vaticano, 1998

Puzicha, Michale, editor, *Die Regeln der Väter: Vorbenediktinische lateinische Regeltradition*, Münsterschwarzach: Vier-Türme-Verlag, 1990

Reichenau

In 724 the wandering bishop Pirminius (d. c. 753) founded a monastery on Reichenau, an island in Lake Constance. Some dispute exists over whether Pirminius founded the cloister with the support of the duke of the Alemanni, who was seeking to preserve the area from Frankish control, or with the support of the Frankish leader Charles Martel (714–741), but in any event political factors were involved. By the second half of the eighth century, the monastery firmly supported the Carolingian dynasty, and the rise of Reichenau to a position of intellectual and cultural prominence in Western Europe coincided with the reign of Charlemagne (768–814). Abbot Waldo (786–806) was one of the most influential men at the court of Aachen. His successor, Haito (806–822/23), made Reichenau into a leading center of learning and spirituality, a position that it retained through the first half of the 11th century. The intercessory prayers of the monks at Reichenau were especially valued. Some 38,000 persons from over 50 different monastic communities in Germany, France, and Italy were entered into the monastery's confraternity book over the course of the Middle Ages, most of them before 1100. The cloister also won renown as a center for the production of illuminated manuscripts and for the composition of hagiographic texts.

The period of most intense activity occurred before 850. The community attained its largest population (about 134 monks), and the cloister school produced the most gifted poet and theologian in the monastery's history, Walafrid Strabo (c. 808–849). The famous "Plan of St. Gall," made at Reichenau, also dates from this era. A second blossoming occurred under Abbot Bern (1008–1048), a monk from Prüm who was imposed on the abbey by Emperor Henry II (1002–1024) to introduce some of the reforms developed during the tenth century at the monastery of Gorze. Bern succeeded in winning the support of the monks of Reichenau for the new customs and liturgical practices (despite the fact that he was not freely elected) and also oversaw an increase in scholarly production at the monastery. Hermann the Lame (d. 1054) was the chief among Reichenau's 11th-century scholars, writing works on history, musicology, and astronomy as well as on the measuring of time.

During the 1100s the monastery began a gradual decline, numbering ever fewer monks offering ever fewer prayers. Its days as a center of scholarship and artistic production were also largely over. One final attempt was made at reform by Abbot Friedrich von Wartenberg (1427–1453), who rebuilt the choir of the main abbey church and renewed the community's practice of offering intercessory prayer for those listed in its confraternity book. The community itself survived until 1757, when the monks were dispersed by the bishop of Constance. Reichenau was secularized in 1803, but the churches of the main abbey (the Mittelzell) and two of its dependencies (the Oberzell and the Niederzell) survive on the island. The churches incorporate architecture from as early as the ninth century as well as Ottonian and Romanesque frescos from the period when Reichenau was a leading center of manuscript painting.

SCOTT WELLS

See also Bobbio, Italy; Germany: History; Island Monasteries, Christian; Liturgy: Western Christian; Manuscript Production: Christian; Pharmacology; Pirminius, St.; Walafrid Strabo

Further Reading

Autenrieth, Johanne, Dieter Geuenich, and Karl Schmid, editors, *Das Verbrüderungsbuch der Abtei Reichenau*, Hannover: Hahnsche Buchhandlung, 1979

Berschin, Walter, *Eremus und Insula: St. Gallen und die Reichenau im Mittelalter, Modell einer lateinischen Literaturlandschaft*, Wiesbaden: Reichert, 1987

Beyerle, Konrad, editor, *Die Kultur der Abtei Reichenau Erinnerungsschrift zur zwölfhundertsten Wiederkehr des Gründungsjahres des Inselklosters, 724–1924*, Munich: Münchener Drucke, 1925

Borst, Arno, *Mönche am Bodensee: 610–1525*, Sigmaringen: Thorbecke, 1978

Klüppel, Theodor, *Reichenauer Hagiographie zwischen Walahfrid und Berno*, Sigmaringen: Thorbecke, 1980

Martin, Kurt, *Die ottonischen Wandbilder der St. Georgskirche Reichenau-Oberzell*, Konstanz: Thorbecke, 1961; 2nd edition, Sigmaringen: Thorbecke, 1975

Maurer, Helmut, editor, *Die Abtei Reichenau: Neue Beiträge zur Geschichte und Kultur des Inselklosters*, Sigmaringen: Thorbecke, 1974

Rappmann, Roland, and Alfons Zettler, with a contribution by Karl Schmid, *Die Reichenauer Mönchsgemeinschaft und ihr Totengedenken im frühen Mittelalter*, Sigmaringen: Thorbecke, 1998

Zettler, Alfons, *Die frühen Klosterbauten der Reichenau: Ausgrabungen, Schriftquellen, St. Gallen Klosterplan*, Sigmaringen: Thorbecke, 1988

Relics, Christian Monastic

The word *relics* comes from the Latin *reliquiae* (Greek, *leipsana*), which meant some object remaining as a memorial of a departed person. The veneration of relics has been linked to the history of human civilization and culture from its beginnings, not just to the Christian religion. It appears to be a primitive instinct to collect and give special importance to objects that were a part of, or that were touched by, an important personage in the culture.

The Roman Catholic Church summed up its teachings on the veneration of relics in the decree of the 25th Session (1563) of the Council of Trent (1545–1563), which states that bishops and pastors should teach their members that

> the holy bodies of holy martyrs and of others now living with Christ – which bodies were the living members of Christ and "the temple of the Holy Ghost" (I. Cor., vi, 19) and which are by Him to be raised to eternal life and to be glorified are to be venerated by the faithful, for through these [bodies] many benefits are bestowed by God on men, so that they who affirm that veneration and honour are not due to the relics of the saints, or that these and other sacred monuments are uselessly honoured by the faithful, and that places dedicated to the memories of the saints are in vain visited with the view of obtaining their aid – all such are wholly to be condemned, as the church has already long since condemned them, and also now condemns them . . . the visitation of relics must not be by any perverted into revellings and drunkeness . . . no new miracles are to be acknowledged or new relics recognized unless the bishop of the diocese has taken cognizance and approved thereof.

Acceptance of the possibility of miracles and of direct intervention by God in human affairs was and is an essential part of the mentality of nearly all religious cultures. In the culture of the early Christian religion, this mind-set was manifest through a number of circumstances. As old pagan holy places became Christian shrines, some physical manifestation of the new power needed to be installed. Also, because the early Church was persecuted and its leaders and followers executed by the Roman authorities, the presence of their remains imbued such martyrs with power for the faithful. Thus, the relics exemplified the power of the saint, which could be demonstrated in miracles of healing, and the shrine that held the relic became a point of contact between the present world and the divine. However, the decision that all altars were to have relics contained within them, mandated at the Second Council of Nicaea in 787, not only sanctioned the cult of relics but also generated a mass market in the finding, transporting, selling, trading, and even stealing of relics, creating a medieval "stock market" economy that affected the fortunes of monasteries, abbeys, cathedrals, towns, cities, regions, and even entire countries.

The city of Rome was undoubtedly the greatest source of martyrs' relics during the Middle Ages. It derived great advantages from its earlier associations as the capital of the Roman Empire, where many of the early heroes of the Church had suffered martyrdom. The benefit for Rome was that the Western Church came to regard the city as its capital, effectively boosting the bishop of Rome above other patriarchs of the Church and positioning him to become head bishop, or pope, of the entire Christian Church. The catacombs beneath Rome, which contained the remains of numerous Christian followers of the early Church, furnished relics from the fourth century on. The fact that Rome was also the site of the martyrdom of the two most

Relics of St. Ambrose, St. Gervase, and St. Protase, in the crypt beneath the High Altar, Basilica of Sant'Ambrogio (Benedictine 784–c. 1470 and then Cistercian until 1797), Milan, Italy. Among the oldest relics anywhere, these date from the late fourth century and the silver reliquary from 1897. Photo courtesy of the Editor

important Christian leaders, the apostles Peter and Paul, further enhanced the reputation and political opportunities of the bishop of Rome.

Early History

One of the earliest instances of the veneration of relics in the Christian Church can be found in a letter written by the inhabitants of Smyrna around A.D. 156 describing the death of St. Polycarp. After being burned at the stake, Polycarp's disciples tried to carry off his remains, but Jews urged the Roman officer to prevent them for fear that his disciples "would only abandon the Crucified One and begin to worship the man." However, the Smyrnaens "took up his bones, which are more valuable than precious stones and finer than refined gold, and laid them in a suitable place, where the Lord will permit us to gather ourselves together, as we are able, in gladness and joy, and to celebrate the birthday of his martyrdom." This type of remembrance is echoed in many other hagiographies and eyewitness accounts of martyrs and saints. In fact the date of martyrdom or death of a saint is recorded as the date of the celebration of the feast day in the Christian calendar.

Not only were the bones or remains of a saint or martyr subject to veneration, but so were any articles of clothing or personal possessions that had come into contact with the holy person. These types of items were known as secondary relics, and they often were accorded as much, if not more, adoration than primary relics, especially as the later medieval period coped with new monastic foundations and a limited supply of primary relics. The development of the cult of the Eucharist as the real body and blood of Christ in the seventh century helped meet the need for relics, as when the Council of Chelsea in 816 declared that the deposition of the consecrated host in a newly hallowed altar at its dedication was sufficient to sanctify it. Similarly the cult of the Virgin Mary was also supported by secondary relics.

After physical martyrdoms became rare, other forms of heroic virtue began to be recognized as indicating the holiness of

Crypt of the Carmelite church of Saint-Joseph-des-Carmes, Paris (17th century), containing relics of some of the 115 priests massacred on the site in September 1792. The relics were recovered in 1860.
Photo courtesy of the Editor

an individual, and the growth of a "spiritual martyrdom" began to develop. The austerities of early monastics and hermits highlighted one group of saints, but a good life was not in itself sufficient. Evidence that an individual had received divinely inspired visions, had shown prophetic gifts, or had unleashed posthumous miracles all combined to convince the faithful of the sanctity of an individual. In Christianity's first millennium sanctity was recognized, and cults were developed by the populace. However, during the High Middle Ages this procedure became the prerogative of the papacy.

The reputation of a locality's relics helped attract worshipers and their offerings, and thus the collecting of many kinds of relics, as well as the prestige of the names associated with the relics, became crucially important for monasteries and cathedrals. The attraction of a locality's relics to pilgrims could lead to that locality's being placed on a pilgrimage route, thus ensuring a continual stream of money and pilgrims into the economy. Probably the two most famous pilgrimage routes were those leading to Santiago de Compostela in Spain and Canterbury in England. The writing of hagiographies, or the lives of saints, also promoted a locality's relics by reaching a wider audience who would be moved by the life and miracles of those saints. Finally, for many monasteries and cathedrals, the theft of relics in order to transfer a saint's influence (and pilgrims) from one locality to another generated an interesting subculture in the religious monastic environment. The development of the *translatio* as a substantial hagiographic subgenre, along with vitae and *passiones*, resulted in more testimonies on the powers of certain relics. A translation of a saint's relics was an occasion of great celebration, symbolizing a transfer of power from one place to another. Church dedications, calendars, and liturgical and secular processions were closely connected to the translations of relics.

Ceremonies that accompanied relics held at a particular monastery often aid scholars today in identifying and dating ecclesiastical medieval manuscripts. The feast days, liturgies, and processions that accompanied the yearly cycle of the Church year were followed faithfully by both the rich and the poor. The insertion of feast days of particular saints into a locality's liturgical calendar often means that the presence of that saint's relics in the local monastery or cathedral is a definite possibility. The composition of a processional, or the high ranking of a particular feast day, are further indicators of a saint's importance in the local round of holidays and celebrations. Fairs, special indulgences, and the visitation of high-ranking clergy and pilgrims were all tied to the relics collected and housed locally. Two major feast days usually prompted a procession during which a church's relics were displayed to the public: the dedication day of the church and the Feast of Relics. When a church was dedicated, the relics to be housed there would be put on display in a tent outside the building the night before. This "wake" allowed the local populace to view their spiritual intercessors and protectors and permitted the saints to sanctify and hallow the new worship building. The date on which this was done became the Dedication Feast of that church, and both the Sarum and the Roman rites contain elaborate liturgies for this major feast. The Feast of Relics was the day on which the relics of all the saints and martyrs in a given church were displayed to the public through an elaborate procession around and inside the church. Elaborate inventories of relics still survive today from which the presiding ecclesiastic would read as the relics were paraded in front of the populace. In the Sarum rite the Feast of Relics was listed as a major double feast, just one rank below the feasts of Christmas and Easter, and was celebrated in the later medieval period on the Sunday after the Feast of the Translation of St. Thomas of Canterbury (7 July).

Elaborate and expensive units to house relics became a major yet necessary expenditure for many churches. These housings were called reliquaries, and they often became as important and famous as the relics they contained. Probably the most famous example is the reliquary containing the forearm of St. Foy in

France, which was made of solid gold in the shape of an actual human hand and forearm, encrusted with precious jewels, carvings, and illustrations of the life and miracles of the saint. These reliquaries were constructed not only to house the relic and to provide a pleasing, sometimes dazzling visual display to the populace but also to protect the relic both from theft and from the elements and to show the actual relic to the public. This often involved some type of glass housing that could be opened, so that locals and pilgrims might physically touch the relic and perhaps add another to the list of miracles chronicled in the saint's hagiography.

The Carolingian renaissance in the ninth century furthered the use of relics in both secular and ecclesiastical life, reinvoking the canon *Item placuit* of the Fifth Council of Carthage (401) that required all altars to contain relics. The swearing of oaths on relics was also encouraged. Finally, increases in the supply of relics north of the Alps began to provide the Christian populace with support and protection from the spiritual world at a time when national identity, central government, and fiscal planning were nonexistent. For monastic communities saints and their relics safeguarded order, organization, and sanity in a world of changing political landscapes, papal intrigues, and economic uncertainties. Saints and their relics functioned as fund-raisers, doctors, oath takers, blessers, protectors, and family members to the monastics and the local community. These roles became particularly important in post-Carolingian Europe. The monastery of Cluny was able to capitalize on this familial identity by establishing a network of sister monasteries all across Europe. Once monasteries were able to regularize incomes and budgets and incorporate agricultural improvements, relics were no longer called on as often as fund-raisers, but this did not lessen their importance. The rise of the cult of Christ in the form of the Eucharist and the cult of the Blessed Virgin Mary became the main focus of the latter Middle Ages, giving rise to the elevation of the host and a number of new feasts dedicated to it, especially the feast of Corpus Christi (proclaimed in 1264).

Bradford Lee Eden

See also Asceticism: Christian Perspectives; Body: Christian Perspectives; Brewing, Western Christian; Cluny, France; Death: Christian Perspectives; France: History; Hagiography: Western Christian; Martyrs: Western Christian; Pilgrimages, Christian: Western Europe; Rome, Italy; Santiago de Compostela, Spain; Visual Arts, Western Christian: Liturgical Furnishings

Further Reading

Brown, Peter, *The Cult of the Saints: Its Rise and Function in Latin Christianity* (Haskell Lectures on History of Religions, new series, number 2), Chicago: University of Chicago Press, and London: SCM Press, 1981

Geary, Patrick J., *Furta Sacra: Thefts of Relics in the Central Middle Ages*, Princeton, New Jersey: Princeton University Press, 1978; revised edition, 1990

Rollason, David W., *Saints and Relics in Anglo-Saxon England*, Cambridge, Massachusetts, and Oxford: Blackwell, 1989

Snoek, G.J.C., *Medieval Piety from Relics to the Eucharist: A Process of Mutual Interaction* (Studies in the History of Christian Thought, volume 63), New York: Brill, 1995

Rennyo 1415–1499

Japanese organizer of Pure Land Buddhism

Rennyo was the "middle founder" of the Jōdoshinshū (Shinshū) school of Japanese Buddhism. His shrewd transmission and adaptation of Shinran's teachings enabled the practical growth of the Shinshū institutions into the largest single Buddhist tradition in Japan.

Rennyo was born into a weak temple tradition, Honganji, which had inherited the ideas of Shinran but had not been especially successful. When he became head in 1457, he launched into recruitment for new members and attracted attention from trading and merchant communities in the Kyoto region. His methods included giving out scriptures, granting *nembutsu* (name of the Amida Buddha) inscriptions, making personal preaching appearances, and writing vernacular *ofumi* (pastoral letters).

His growing influence irritated the old monastic center on Mount Hiei, and in 1465 mercenaries descended from the mountain and destroyed Rennyo's headquarters at Ōtani, causing Rennyo to flee for safety. In 1471 he moved to a more northern site called Yoshizaki, from which he led an upwelling of religious enthusiasm that secured Honganji's political position. After 1475 he reestablished himself near Kyoto and supervised the building of a new headquarters at Yamashina. Giving up the role of head in 1489, he moved to a site that became the foundation of the future central Japanese merchant city of Ōsaka.

Rennyo's success was based on a synergy between his expressions of Shinran's doctrines and the evolution of medieval social politics and economics in Japan that was creating a profound realignment of power. The Shinshū idea of egalitarian fellowship provided a working ideal for a broad spectrum of people in a newly fluid society containing multiple levels. Rennyo emphasized the essential religious equality of members (especially the equivalent spiritual potential of women), the irrelevance of occupation, and the superstitious nature of pollution beliefs. He encouraged the networking of *kō* (local confraternal circles), the consolidation of villages around Shinshū religious practice, and the systematization of ritual. The *ofumi*, combining folksiness, story, and indoctrination, became the lingua franca of the later Shinshū tradition after they were collected in the 16th century. Rennyo's restatements of Shinran's teachings offered sophisticated semantic ambiguities that allowed the remarkable coexistence of elite and folk planes of interpretation in a unified community.

Rennyo's institutional policies were highly effective: married five times, he was the father of numerous children who were appointed and married throughout the growing temple network to reinforce organizational ties. He also re-enunciated a principle of separation between the *ōbō* (realm of civil governance) and *buppō* (Shin Buddhist religious life) that helped restrain the political rebelliousness of members. Such pragmatic policies were the key to the flourishing of Honganji between about 1500 and 1900 in Japan.

In a global comparative context, the relationship of Rennyo to monasticism was prominently subversive. More than any other single leader at any time or place in Buddhist history, his work enabled the practical flourishing of nonmonastic forms of spirituality.

GALEN AMSTUTZ

See also Buddhist Schools/Traditions: Japan; Japan; Mount Hiei, Japan; Nembutsu; Pure Land Buddhism

Biography

Active in and around Kyoto as an inheritor of Shinran's Pure Land Buddhism (Shinshū), Rennyo promoted alternatives to Buddhist monasticism. As head of the temple of Honganji, he attracted followers to such an extent that monks on Mount Hiei destroyed his center in 1465. Ten years later he returned to the Kyoto region, and in 1489 settled on the site that became the city of Ōsaka.

Major Works

See Rogers below for an English translation of Rennyo's letters.

Further Reading

Dobbins, James, *Jōdo Shinshū: Shin Buddhism in Medieval Japan*, Bloomington: Indiana University Press, 1989

Rogers, Minor, and Ann Rogers, *Rennyo: The Second Founder of Shin Buddhism: With a Translation of His Letters*, Berkeley, California: Asian Humanities Press, 1991

Weinstein, Stanley, "Rennyo and the Shinshū Revival," in *Japan in the Muromachi Age*, edited by John Whitney Hall and Takeshi Toyoda, Berkeley: University of California Press, 1977

Repentance Rituals, Buddhist

Repentance Rituals in Vinaya (Discipline), i.e., Theravāda

To achieve a Theravādin monastic community's complete purity, monastic discipline requires a repentance ritual. This ritual is performed in two ceremonies. One is the *Uposatha* ceremony, held every half month on full- and new-moon days with the recital of the *Paṭimōkkha* (discipline code). The other is the *Pavāraṇā* ceremony, which removes any offenses that *bhikkhus* (monks) and *bhikkhunīs* (nuns) committed with regard to the disciplinary code during the three-month-long *Vassa* (rainy season).

1. Uposatha *Ceremony*

The main function of the *Uposatha* ceremony is to preach the disciplinary rules. All the ordained *bhikkhus* and *bhikkhunīs* must participate. The ceremony cannot take place if even one of the *bhikkhus* or *bhikkhunīs* is absent for any reason other than illness.

Before the *Uposatha* ceremony is held, *bhikkhus* and *bhikkhunīs* must proclaim their purity, that is, perform the repentance ritual. The ritual generally is arranged one night before the ceremony. While a virtuous and learned *bhikkhu* presides over the repentance ritual and goes through the disciplinary rules one after another, *bhikkhus* or *bhikkhunīs* who have violated the disciplinary rules must recite their faults three times to confess thoroughly. At the same time vows must be taken. If some members remain silent, the learned, virtuous *bhikkhus* acknowledge their purity. Afterward the ritual violators receive punishment according to their different degrees of transgression. Once the entire repentance ritual is completed, the *bhikkhus* and *bhikkhunīs* are considered pure and thus able to participate in the *Uposatha* ceremony the next day.

During the *Uposatha* ceremony the main activity is expounding the monastic discipline code, *Paṭimōkkha*. The *Paṭimōkkha* will not be recited if any one in the crowd is not purified, including those who are ill and not able to participate. Even if a *bhikkhu* or *bhikkhunī* is prevented from attending because of his or her illness, he or she must make a declaration to another *bhikkhu* or *bhikkhunī* that he or she has not violated any rule of *Paṭimōkkha*.

The importance of reciting the *Paṭimōkkha* is further to ensure that absolutely no doubt exists in the minds of *bhikkhus* and *bhikkhunīs* regarding purity in body, speech, and mind in relation to each disciplinary rule.

2. Pavāranā *Ceremony*

The *Pavāraṇā* ceremony is held at the end of the three-months rainy season retreat. During the ceremony each *bhikkhu* and *bhikkhunī*, in order of seniority, pronounces their *Pavāraṇā* (self-restraint) before the *saṅgha* (community). In doing so they invite the *saṅgha* to charge them with any offenses they might have committed. Seniority is counted not according to age but according to years of ordination. While being criticized by members of the *saṅgha*, the accused must keep silent, regardless of the accuracy of the accusation. Final judgment is pronounced by the competent, learned, and virtuous *bhikkhus*. This ceremony provides an opportunity for participants to receive advice from others and for violators to repent in front of the assembly of gathered members. Once the repentance ritual has been performed and vows have been taken, the violators regain their purity. In addition their seniority increases by one year at this annual ritual.

Normally the *Pavāraṇā* seems to encourage *bhikkhus* to evaluate each other's conduct, and seniority is respected. However, not just anyone can accuse others. For example, a *bhikkhu* who has been ordained more than five years but does not possess enough knowledge about the disciplinary rules cannot prosecute others for disciplinary violations. Furthermore not even a senior *bhikkhunī* (nun) can disclose an offense of a *bhikkhu* (monk).

The procedure for determining the legitimacy of an accusation is clearly delineated by the Buddha. The accusing *bhikkhu* must explain his understanding of three points: what counts as a moral transgression, what counts as a transgression against the rules of conduct, and what counts as a transgression that constitutes heresy. If one has been guilty of an offense, then he or she is charged according to the rules made explicit within the *Suttavibhaṅga* section of the Vinaya.

Basically eight kinds of disciplinary rules are included in the *Suttavibhaṅga* section of the Vinaya as follows:

a. *Pārājikā*: *Bhikkhu*s or *bhikkhunī*s who commit the offense of having sex, stealing, killing (including urging others to kill or suicide), or proclaiming oneself the supreme spiritual leader shall be exiled from the *saṅgha* (monastic community) forever. Repentance is not accepted.

b. *Saṅghādisesā*: *Bhikkhu*s or *bhikkhunī*s who commit the offense of purposely leaking semen, touching women, being a matchmaker, illegitimately building a house, defaming the reputation of other *bhikkhu*s, fomenting discord, and ignoring advice are considered to have violated the rules. Violators shall be temporarily suspended and must stay out of the *saṅgha*. *Bhikkhu*s shall undergo a six-night *mānatta* discipline (probation) and then confess sin and repent in front of a group of *bhikkhu*s consisting of at least 20 persons; after that the *bhikkhu*-ship can be recovered. *Bhikkhunī*s, however, in the same case will receive heavier suspension. They will undergo a 15-night *mānatta* discipline and repent in front of *bhikkhu*s and *bhikkhunī*s with at least 40 persons.

c. *Nissaggiyā Pācittiyā*: *Bhikkhu*s or *bhikkhunī*s who commit the offense of owning excessive daily supplies or receiving and using improper clothing and bedding. The improper clothing and bedding shall be confiscated.

d. *Aniyatā*: *Bhikkhu*s who commit the offense of sitting in a private place with a woman. Violators shall be punished and repent for having violated *Pārājikā*, *Saṅghādisesā*, or *Nissaggiyā Pācittiyā* rules, depending on the different situations.

e. *Pācittiyā*: *Bhikkhu*s or *bhikkhunī*s who commit the offense of lying, shouting, staying in a room with a woman, excessive eating, drinking, killing animals, drinking water, having insects, or walking with a nonrelative *bhikkhu* or *bhikkhunī*.

f. *Paṭidesanīyā*: *Bhikkhu*s who commit the offense of receiving foods from nonrelative *bhikkhunī*s, taking food without invitation, or failing to warn almsgivers of the danger of one's residence.

g. *Sekhiyā*: *Bhikkhu*s or *bhikkhunī*s who commit any violation of regular discipline laws (mostly about clothing, eating, and teaching).

h. *Adhikaraṇa Samathā*: *Bhikkhu*s or *bhikkhunī*s who commit the offense of disputing with other *bhikkhu*s or *bhikkhunī*s.

Violators of different disciplinary rules repent in front of different numbers of virtuous *bhikkhu*s, according to the relative degree of the offenses. In the cases of violating *Nissaggiyā Pācittiyā*, *Pācittiyā*, or *Paṭidesanīyā*, violators shall repent in front of one *bhikkhu*, and in the *Sekhiyā* or *Adhikaraṇa Samathā* violators can repent in their own mind.

Mahāyāna Repentance Rituals

Basically early Buddhism emphasized repentance for transgressions of the disciplinary rules. In addition Mahāyāna Buddhism developed repentance rituals for eliminating all sins and evil deeds committed under delusion or ignorance in present, past, or future lives. The forms of the Mahāyāna ritual process involve praising of the buddhas and bodhisattvas, worshiping, and chanting sūtras in a group. The Mahāyāna repentance rituals focus more on repentance within one's self-nature; that is, as the *Bodhisattva Sīla Sūtra* (*Pusa Jiejing*) says, "our self-nature is intrinsically pure, and if we know our mind and realize what our nature is, all of us would attain buddha-hood."

The following Mahāyāna repentance rituals may not be directly designed for monastic practice but are performed by ordained *bhikkhu*s and *bhikkhunī*s in monasteries in which laypeople are also welcome to participate. For example, in Tibetan Buddhism there is *Bodhisattva's Confession of Downfalls*, and in Chinese Buddhism there are many, such as *Lotus Samādhi Confessional Ritual* (*Fahua Sanmei Chanfa*) made by Master Zhiyi (Chih-i, A.D. 538–597), the founder of the Tiantai (T'ien-tai) school. Some others are *Large Scale Confessional Ritual* (*Fangdeng Chanfa*), the *Golden Light Confessional Ritual* (*Jinguangming Chanfa*), and *Medicine Buddha Confessional Ritual* (*Yaoshi Chanfa*). In the seventh century Master Shandao (Shantao, A.D. 613–618), founder of the Pure Land school, invented the *Amitabha Confessional Ritual* (*Amituo Chanfa*). In the eighth century Master Zongmi (Tsung-mi, A.D. 780–841) of the Huayan (Hua-yen) school also established a set of confessional rituals for the Huayan school in his work *The Ritual of Practice and Realization at the Sanctuary of Complete Enlightenment Sūtra* (*Xianmi Yuantong Chengfo Xinyaoji*). Later Master Zhixuan (Chih-hsuan, A.D. 809–881) developed it into the *Compassion Water Confessional Ritual* (*Cibei Shuichan*). In Japanese Buddhism repentance rituals follow Chinese Buddhist tradition. In particular the Tendai school's *Lotus Samādhi Confessional Ritual* is widely performed at present.

Although the contents of the confessional sūtras mentioned above have no direct relation with the Vinaya, these repentance rituals are still being performed in monasteries. Gradually they become rituals for anyone who wishes to participate, whether for their own liberation or for dedication to the dead.

Repentance rituals enable practitioners to purify negative actions, including transgression of disciplinary rules and other forms of obscuration that prevent one from achieving realization on the path to enlightenment. Thus, repentance rituals provide consolation and reorientation in ways that produce behavioral uniformity and facilitate the achievement of a better rebirth or enlightenment.

Julianna Lipschutz

See also Liturgy: Buddhist; Prayer: Buddhist Perspectives; Sexuality: Buddhist Perspectives

Further Reading

Hirakawa, Akira, *Ritsuzō no Kenkyū* (A Study of the Vinayapiṭaka), Tokyo: Sankibō Busshorin, 1960

Hirakawa, Akira, *Bikuniritsu no Kenkyū* (A Study of the Bhikkhunī-vinaya), Tokyo: Shunjūsha, 1998

Holt, John C., *Discipline: The Canonical Buddhism of the Vinayapiṭaka*, Columbia, Missouri, and Delhi: South Asia Books, 1983

Jampa Gyatso, Geshe, *Everlasting Rain of Nectar: Purification Practice in Tibetan Buddhism*, edited by Joan Nicell, Boston: Wisdom, 1996

Kamata, Shigeo, *Chūgoku no Bukkyō Girei* (China's Buddhist Ceremonies), Tokyo: Tokyo Daigaku Tōyō Bunka Kenkyūjo, 1986

Kon-sprul Blo-gros-mtha-yas, *Buddhist Ethics*, translated by the International Translation Committee, Ithaca, New York: Snow Lion, 1998

Muller, Max F., editor, *The Sacred Books of the East*, volume 13, Oxford: Oxford University Press, 1881

Shi, Sheng-yan, *Jielüxüe Gangyao* (Essentials of the Disciplinary Code), Taibei: Dongchu Chubanshe, 1993

Wayman, Alex, "Purification of Sin in Buddhism by Vision and Confession," in *A Study of Kleśa*, edited by Genjun H. Sasaki, Tokyo: Shimizukōbundō, 1975

Yinshun, *Yüanshi Fojiao Shengdian Zhi Jicheng* (A Collection of the Original Buddhist Scriptures), Taibei: Zhengwen Chubanshe, 1988

Retreat, Christian

Retreat, in the Christian tradition, is a period of withdrawal from the ordinary round of life to devote oneself to prayer, ascetic practice, and the search for God. The roots of this practice can be traced back to the Old Testament and especially to Moses' solitary sojourn on Mount Horeb (Exod. 3:1–4:18). This brief episode, which seems to have lasted but a few hours, includes every element that we associate with Christian retreat: asceticism, in the demand that Moses remove his shoes "for the place on which you are standing is holy ground"; visions, in God's appearance as a burning bush; holy gifts, in the present of the holy rod and the promise of freedom for Israel; and revelation, in the unveiling of the Divine Name.

Inevitably, however, Christian retreat draws its main inspiration from the teaching and example of Jesus Christ. Jesus seemed to consider retreat an essential part of the religious life. He often ascended alone into the mountains to pray (Matt. 14:23, Luke 5:16) and exhorted his disciples to "come away by yourselves to a lonely place, and rest a while" (Mark 6:31). Immediately after his baptism and just before the declaration of his messianic mission, he entered his most famous retreat, a 40-day sojourn in the wilderness that involved fasting and struggling with demons (Matt. 4:1–11, Mark 1:12–13, Luke 4:1–13). The importance of this retreat for Christian tradition can scarcely be overstated, and eventually it was codified into the Church calendar under the impetus of the Councils of Nicaea (325) and Laodicaea (360) as the season of Lent, a 40-day period of fasting, prayer, and penance in preparation for Easter. Lent has been called, rightly, the retreat of the whole Church. Originally Lenten restrictions were harsh, including abstinence from meat and dairy products by all the faithful; in recent years, rules (at least in the Western churches) have been relaxed. Nonetheless the emphasis on metanoia – reawakening to the truths embodied in the life, death, and resurrection of Christ – remains.

A far more comprehensive form of retreat emerged in the first Christian centuries: permanent withdrawal from the world undertaken by monks and nuns, as hermits or in cenobitic communities. The prototypical monastic retreat is that of St. Antony of the Desert (c. 251–356), who fled to the Egyptian desert and secreted himself inside a ruined fortress for 20 years. According to St. Athanasius' biography of Antony, this retreat was a great success. Antony emerged from his cell as a fully realized Christian, wise and serene, given neither to anger nor uproar, a healer and comforter to many. Other Desert Fathers surpassed Antony in radical retreat if not in spiritual perfection, the most famous example being St. Symeon Stylites (c. 390–459), who spent a reported 49 years atop a 50-foot pillar in the Syrian desert. The cenobitic form of monastic retreat, founded by St. Pachomius (c. 290–346) and standardized by the great St. Benedict (c. 480–c. 550), tends to be much milder, seeking a middle way that encompasses prayer, scholarship, manual labor, ascetic discipline, and even recreation. Benedict's Rule makes much of Lent as a period of special retreat for monks – a retreat within a retreat, as it were; the Rule also emphasizes that visitors should be greeted with special respect and encouraged to join the brethren in prayer and reading, a practice that continues to this day in monastic guest houses, which have become one of the major loci for Christian retreats.

Little evidence exists of organized Christian retreat (apart from monastic life) in the Middle Ages, although the widespread practice of pilgrimage to saints' tombs and other holy locales often involved penance, fasting, prayer, and withdrawal from the world. Christian retreat received a tremendous boost in the 16th century through St. Ignatius of Loyola's Spiritual Exercises. Ignatius (c. 1491–1556) developed the rudiments of his exercises in 1522 while on retreat in Manresa, Catalonia, and continued to refine his system until it was finally approved by Pope Paul III (1534–1549) in 1548. The aim of the exercises is conquest of self, regulation of life, and discernment of one's true calling. The course is divided into four one-week sections conducted under the supervision of a spiritual director. The first week focuses on sin and redemption, the second on the life of Christ, the third on Christ's Passion, and the fourth on the Risen Lord. In addition instruction in discernment of spirits, prayer, charity, devotion, and examination of conscience play a large role. Although designed initially for use by Jesuits, Ignatius' exercises have proven so successful that they are now ubiquitous through the Catholic world, undertaken by laity as well as religious and clergy. The exercises have been recommended by numerous popes, most notably Pius XI (who proclaimed Ignatius patron of retreats in 1922) in his encyclical *Mens Nostra* of 1929. In this remarkable document Pius recalls the "unutterable consolations" that he himself enjoyed through the Spiritual Exercises; praises them for bringing maturity to the mind, firmness to the will, and restraint to the passions; and urges them on all as a "singular resource" for the salvation of souls. To this day the Spiritual Exercises remain the most widely used and beloved guide to organized Christian retreat.

Less intensive forms of Christian retreat also abound in modern times. Retreats can last one or a few days and can be undertaken with minimal or no spiritual direction. Elements of Eastern religious practice, especially in the form of mantra recitation or Zen meditation, might play a part. At the same time rigorous retreats remain in vogue. One influential modern movement with Catholic and Protestant branches, Cursillos de Cristiandad, founded in 1949 on Majorca, involves a three-day intensive retreat focused on basic Christian doctrine. In recent decades a variety of retreat centers, including inns, conference centers, and even summer camps, has proliferated throughout the Christian world, as has the practice of laymen and -women making retreats for a few days or a week in a monastic community. Another striking new development is the concept of retreat "in the moment," pausing for a minute in the midst of one's daily activities to turn to God, a technique that has much in common with the "practice of the presence of God" taught by the 17th-century French Carmelite Brother Lawrence of the Resurrection (c. 1614–1691). All this great ferment of innovative activity, along with the continuing popularity of the Spiritual Exercises, suggests that the 21st century promises to be the golden era of Christian retreat.

PHILIP ZALESKI

See also Antony, St.; Benedict of Nursia, St.; Biblical Figures and Practices; Carmelites; Desert Fathers; Pachomius, St.; Seasons, Liturgical: Eastern Christian; Spirituality: Eastern Christian; Stylites

Further Reading

Athanasius, Saint, *The Life of Antony and the Letter to Marcellinus*, translated and with an introduction by Robert C. Gregg, New York: Paulist Press, and London: SPCK, 1980

Benedict, Saint, *RB 1980: The Rule of St. Benedict in English*, edited by Timothy Fry, Collegeville, Minnesota: Liturgical Press, 1981

Ignatius of Loyola, *Personal Writings*, translated and with an introduction and notes by Joseph A. Munitiz and Philip Endean, London and New York: Penguin, 1996

Pius XI, Pope, "Mens Nostra," in *The Papal Encyclicals*, volume 3, edited by Claudia Carlen, Ann Arbor, Michigan: Pierian Press, 1990

Waddell, Helen, editor, *The Desert Fathers: Translations from the Latin*, New York: Holt, and London, Constable, 1932

Riepp, Benedicta (Sybilla) 1825–1862

Bavarian founder of U.S. Benedictine monasteries for women

Benedictine monasticism among women in North America represents a unique chapter in the long history of cenobitic monasticism in the West. It has its roots in the aftermath of the French Revolution (1789–1815) and the German secularization (1803–1830), during a period of revival in the history of the Benedictine Order initiated by King Ludwig I (1825–1848) of Bavaria.

The Bavarian tradition of Benedictine women in North America owes its origin to Benedicta (Sybilla) Riepp. She was born in Waal, Bavaria, on 28 June 1825. In 1844 she entered the Benedictine monastery of St. Walburg in Eichstätt, Bavaria, where she subsequently professed her monastic vows in 1846. During the eight years she lived at St. Walburg, she taught in the girls' school of Eichstätt and served as mistress of novices until her departure for North America.

Imbued with the missionary zeal so characteristic of the post-secularization Catholic revival in Bavaria, Riepp volunteered to go to the United States when the request came to Prioress Edwarda Schnitzer in Eichstätt to send nuns to teach the children of the German immigrants who had settled in Pennsylvania. Riepp and her companions arrived in the wilderness clearing of St. Marys, Pennsylvania, on 22 July 1852 and established there the first monastery of Benedictine women in North America. The six years she spent as superior there were plagued with physical hardship and misunderstandings between herself and local churchmen, most notably Abbot Boniface Wimmer (1809–1887) of St. Vincent Abbey in Latrobe, Pennsylvania. She resisted his interference in the internal matters of the fledgling community as well as his efforts to thwart her authority in her role as the legitimate superior of the earliest monasteries of Benedictine women in North America. Nonetheless, her leadership during those years resulted in the establishment of three new monasteries in Erie, Pennsylvania (1856); Newark, New Jersey (1857); and St. Cloud, Minnesota (1857).

In 1857 Riepp returned to Europe, confident that her superiors in Eichstätt and Rome could help her resolve the controversial issues surrounding the threatened autonomy of the newly established communities in the United States. She and her companion were not favorably received in Eichstätt and were prevented from traveling to Rome, where she was prepared to present her case before Pope Pius IX (1846–1878).

Broken in spirit and failing in health, Riepp returned to the United States in 1858 and was shut out of the monasteries that she had founded in the East. Ostracism had been the price of her efforts to resolve the issues that were threatening the autonomy of the newly established monasteries of women in the United States. On the invitation of Prioress Willibalda Scherbauer in St. Cloud, Minnesota, Riepp took up residence there in the spring of 1858, until she died of tuberculosis on 15 March 1862. In 1884 her remains were transferred from St. Cloud to the cemetery of the Sisters of the Order of St. Benedict, St. Joseph, Minnesota, which has become a pilgrimage site for Benedictine women nationwide.

The only extant writings of Riepp are 15 letters that she wrote between 1852 and 1861. These letters reveal the conviction that her Benedictine vocation was privileged and graced, that gratitude was the only appropriate response to the providential workings of God, and that the goal of Benedictine life was the search for God in unity and mutual love.

Today, nearly 150 years later, the legacy of Mother Benedicta Riepp is evidenced in three major federations of Benedictine women in North America, totaling about 4,150 members. The history of American Benedictine women represents the evolution of a new form of life according to the sixth-century Rule of St. Benedict. The process of transplanting the female tradition of Benedictine life from Eichstätt, Bavaria, to North America necessitated some fundamental innovations that clearly reshaped the way of life embraced by Benedictine women in North America. Among the changes were a modified form of enclosure, an adapted schedule for praying the Divine Office, the incorporation of external apostolic works, and the custom of members living away from the main monastery in branch houses. At the same time that the process of adaptation took into account the realities of a new time and place in American history, at another level the European monastic tradition of life continued essentially the same as it had for 1,400 years, characterized by its steady rhythm of prayer, work, and communal interaction.

EPHREM (RITA) HOLLERMANN, O.S.B.

See also Germany: History; Schools and Universities, Benedictine; United States: Western Christian; Wimmer, Boniface; Women's Monasteries: Western Christian

Biography

Born in Bavaria, Benedicta entered the monastery of St. Walburg in Eichstätt 1844–1852. In the latter year she volunteered to go to the United States, where she founded in the wilderness at St. Marys, Pennsylvania, the first Benedictine women's house in North America. Disagreements afflicted her for five years, during which three new monasteries were founded. After a year in Europe in 1857–1858, she settled in the Benedictine house at St. Cloud, Minnesota, where she died of tuberculosis in 1862.

Major Works

Fifteen letters are published in Incarnata Girgen's *Behind the Beginnings*, 1981

Further Reading

Baska, Mary Regina, *The Benedictine Congregation of St. Scholastica: Its Foundation and Development (1852–1930)*, Washington, D.C.: Catholic University of America, 1935

Drey, Emmanuel, *Die Abtei St. Walburg, 1035–1935: 900 Jahre in Wort und Bild*, Eichstätt, Bavaria: St. Walburg Abbey, 1934

Girgen, Incarnata, *Behind the Beginnings: Benedictine Women in America*, Saint Joseph, Minnesota: Saint Benedict's Convent, 1981

Hollermann, Ephrem, *The Reshaping of a Tradition: American Benedictine Women, 1852–1881*, Saint Joseph, Minnesota: Sisters of the Order of Saint Benedict, 1994

Mathäser,Willibald, "König Ludwig I von Bayern und die Gründung der Ersten Bayerischen Benediktinerabtei in Nordamerika," *Studien und Mitteilungen* 35 (1926)

Ronneburger, Rasso, "Mother Benedicta Riepp, O.S.B., 1825–1862, Klostergründerin in den USA," in *Lebensbilder aus dem Bayerischen Schwaben*, Memmingen, Germany: Konrad, 1997

Robe. *See* Clothing

Romania

History

The Christian gospel was brought north of the Danube to ancient Dacia (now Romania) by Roman colonists in the second and third centuries. Tradition associates St. Andrew with Scythia Minor in the southeast, where the diocesan seat of Tomis, present-day Constanţa, is recorded in 369; some of its bishops participated in the great ecumenical councils. The Roman Christian legacy includes not only archaeological remains but also Latin terms for doctrine and worship, for Romania is the only Orthodox country with a romance language. Many believers suffered for Christ under Diocletian (284–305) and Julian the Apostate (361–363) and again under the Goths; Christian life was disrupted about the year 600 by the great Avaro-Slavic migration.

By around 360 both eremitic and cenobitic monasticism existed in this region bounded today by Ukraine on the north and east, Moldova also to the east, Bulgaria on the south, and Serbia and Hungary on the west and northwest. The apostle of the Dacians, Nicetas of Remesiana (d. c. 415), founded several monastic communities. Saint John Cassian (c. 360–after 430) came from this region. Little is known of Romanian monasticism in the first millennium. Small cliff-chapels in the Carpathian Mountains witness to solitaries who imitated the Desert Fathers and Mothers.

Early in the second millennium, Byzantine monasteries existed at Cenad and Maidan. Followers of St. Cyril (826–869) and St. Methodius (c. 815–885) introduced Slavic as the language of the Byzantine liturgy into the principalities of Wallachia (independent in 1330) and Moldavia (independent from 1359);

Secul Monastery, Romania, early 17th century, outer gateway to the monastery complex.
Photo courtesy of Mary Schaefer

it was also the court language. Mount Athos inspired monasticism. Nicodemus (d. 1406) came from Serbia to take up the life of an ascetic on Mount Athos, then founded the monastery of Vodiţa in Wallachia (1369) and Tismana (1375–1378), with attached villages and Romany families, tithing, and fishing rights; the latter's location countered Hungarian Catholic expansion. In Moldavia followers of Nicodemus along with Serbian monks fleeing Turkish expansion established monasteries closely connected to the local ruler. Only Neamţ (the oldest monastery-fortress) and Bistriţa, Moldoviţa, and Probota had priests as abbots. Moldoviţa, an important economic center, controlled the road to Transylvania. Putna was erected by Stephen the Great (1457–1504) as a fortress against Turks and Tatars. Another of Stephen's foundations, the church of St. George at Voroneţ (1488) with its sky-blue walls in a sylvan setting, is a masterpiece of mural painting. Every inch of wall, outside and inside, was covered (1547) with scenes ranging from the Garden of Paradise to the Final Judgment. Women's monasteries are first known at Horodnic in the north (1439; moved to Putna in 1490) and at Iţcani (1463). Suceava, a metropolitanate from 1401, was the site of the first public hospital (1619), sponsored by Putna Monastery.

The region was prey to continuing Turkish and Tatar invasions. In the 15th and 16th centuries, Wallachia, Moldavia, and Transylvania fell to Turkish rule. The Ottoman rulers accepted the monasteries as institutions useful for maintaining culture and order. Larger monasteries were fortified; the main church was located within an inner quadrangle framed by high walls (Neamţ, Secul, and Suceviţa). Liturgical use of the Romanian vernacular dates from around 1560.

Transylvania came under Catholic influence after it was annexed to the Habsburg Empire in 1687. Latin Benedictines were found there, whereas Cistercians from Pontigny, Premonstratensians (60 monasteries), Dominicans, Franciscans, and the orders of knights had been established in the 12th and 13th centuries. In 1698 a synod at Alba Julia effected a union between Rome and many Romanian Orthodox in Transylvania, leading to the formation of the Romanian Greek Catholic Church.

The most enduring reform of Orthodox monasticism was the work of Paisy Velichkovsky (1722–1794). Ukrainian-born, he left theological studies in Kiev in search of a spiritual guide, first in Romania from 1742 to 1746 and then at Mount Athos. He returned north to settle with 63 monks at Dragomirna. They translated patristic texts into Romanian and Slavonic. War drove his community to Secul, where he became abbot of a community of 300 monks and hermits, then to nearby Neamţ with 700 monks and a library of 500 manuscripts and 1,100 volumes. The Paisian reform of rule and offices and its teaching of the Jesus Prayer remained influential into the 19th century.

Important Changes in Church and State

In 1863 the goods and properties of monasteries were secularized. Prince Alexandru Cuza proclaimed the autocephaly of the Romanian Orthodox Church (1864); in 1885 the ecumenical patriarch Joachim IV acknowledged it. In 1948 the Vatican Concordat of 1929 was annulled by the communist government, which then officially dissolved the Greek Catholic Church, handing all its property over either to the state or to the Romanian Orthodox Church. In 1949 the religious orders and congregations of the Roman Catholic Church were suppressed. Many Catholics were imprisoned until the general amnesty of 1964.

Educational institutions affiliated with recognized churches were closed except seminaries training ministers of worship. In 1953 an Orthodox synod reorganized monastic life. Three grades of monasteries (monastery, *metochio* or dependency, and the *skit* or hermitage) were established; admission standards, leadership status, and conciliar structures of governance were determined; and prayer, work, education, and discipline were regularized. A library and museum, health care, security, and hospitality were required.

The Romanian Orthodox Church existed alongside the Ceauseşcu regime until the latter fell in December 1989. Of the population of 21 million people, 86 percent remain Orthodox, making it the most robust of the Christian churches in Eastern Europe, although its coexistence with communism led to charges of collaboration and internal tensions. In 1990 the Roman and Greek Catholic Churches were officially recognized, but the reclaiming of Greek Catholic Church properties resulted in clashes with the Orthodox. Although the right to private ownership was returned to peasants on the land, uncertainties regarding large monastic holdings continued.

Characteristics of Romanian Monasticism

Since the 14th century men and women have followed the same Basilian rule and wear an identical habit. The principle of complete autonomy for a monastery is maintained. The office of

Secul Monastery, Romania, early 17th century, inner quadrangle with the church on the right.
Photo courtesy of Mary Schaefer

Suceviţa Monastery, Romania, 16th century, wall with elevated enclosed walkway.
Photo courtesy of Mary Schaefer

abbess or abbot is undertaken for life. Each monastic center may have attached to it dependencies and one or more *skits* or *colibe* (huts). Three forms of vowed life – cenobitic, idiorhythmic, and solitary (eremitical) – may exist in the same monastery. Every day involves the traditional rhythms of liturgical prayer and contemplation, work, and ascetic practices.

The numbers of monastics continue to increase. In early 1996 more than 4,000 nuns and 2,000 monks resided in 380 monasteries. Nuns now maintain a number of historic foundations, including Moldoviţa, Suceviţa, and Voroneţ. Romanian nuns are noted for their practice of the ancient ascetic postures of private and liturgical prayer: *proskynesis* (a profound bow, with one hand touching the ground), *gonyklisia* (dropping down on both hands and knees), the "little" *mătania* (a low bow), and "great" *mătania* (*gonyklisia* with the forehead touching the ground). Such prostrations might be repeated very rapidly hundreds of times in the four directions. Recalling Turkish prohibitions against the ringing of bells, a wooden plank, the *semantron*, is beaten rhythmically to call to liturgy.

Agriculturally self-supporting, larger monasteries are centers of literary and artistic culture. There may be on-site schools, or student monastics may attend village schools, seminaries (of which 33 existed in 1995), or theological institutes (14). Since the 1950s theological training has been taken together by men and women. Translation, editing and printing of books (especially biblical and patristic) in a number of languages, and arts and crafts (weaving, tapestry, and icon painting) may contribute to the monastery's income; museums educate visitors in culture and heritage.

An outstanding feature is closeness to nature. This "nature mysticism" is rooted in the eremitic tradition of solitaries, both women and men, living in the wilderness of Transylvania and northern Moldavia. It is seen in the siting of monasteries and the painted walls of the Bukovina monastic churches. The establishment, especially in the 16th century, of "dedicated" monasteries (daughter houses attached to Mount Athos, Mount Sinai, Constantinople, or Jerusalem) encouraged communication with those Orthodox centers. Some monasteries have been participating in ecumenical initiatives, building bridges between East and West.

The church year begins in September with the feast of the Nativity of Mary. The Nativity of the Lord is celebrated from 25 December to 6 January, the feast of Theophany or Baptism of Christ in the Jordan. The sixth of August, the Transfiguration, is the feast of the monasteries. On that day the nuns of Suceviţa Monastery in Bukovina province host a fish feast that tempers the fast leading up to 15 August, the Dormition of the Virgin and the feast of the Christian people.

The Painted Churches of Bukovina

The monasteries of northern Moldavia allow a pilgrim to experience the life and rhythms of monasticism as lived in the undivided churches of the first millennium. The monastic enclosure is entered through an elaborate gateway like those giving entrance to each house of a peasant village. An outdoor altar flanked by a large cross accommodates pilgrimages. The church consists of two or three small rooms and a porch; its exterior walls might be painted with intricate biblical and historical subjects or rows of iconic saints. These 16th-century paintings, executed with vegetable and mineral dyes, have for the most part withstood the ravages of weather. At Moldoviţa the nuns inhabit a veritable museum of 16th-century folk art. Voroneţ, reopened in its green valley in 1991 by seven nuns from Moldoviţa, is a retreat center.

On the slopes of the Carpathian ridge known as the Romanian Athos, Varatec, a monastic village led by its stăreţa, Mother Nazaria Nita Natalia, includes three cenobitia (each with its church), 160 small dwellings for three to five nuns living idiorhythmically, and a large farm with extensive grazing lands and forests. Peasant homes are nearby. Varatec welcomes ecclesiastical dignitaries, writers, ecumenical groups, and schoolchildren. Agapia (founded in 1642–1647), about two miles distant, has murals painted by Nicolae Grigorescu (1858–1861). Home to 450 nuns (1992), Agapia has been a center for Scripture study under its abbess Mother Eustachia Ciucanu (d. 1992). In 1975 Agapia hosted the first international meeting of Orthodox women. Across the mountain ridge at the isolated renewal center of Sihastria, 60 contemplative monks welcome retreatants. On the mountain separating the women's and men's monasteries is the hermitage of Sihla, where St. Theodora of Sihla (b. c. 1650) lived in a cave and was fed by birds.

A Day in the Life of Varatec Monastery

Varatec was founded in 1781–1785 by Mother Olimpiada as part of the Paisian reform. Her solitary life had attracted disciples who built the original hermitage with their own hands and income from their dowries. As daughter of a village priest, Olimpiada was accustomed to chanting the liturgy rather than relying on a male cantor. At Varatec sister-acolytes trim the huge oil lamps, take part in the Great Entrance, and assist behind the iconostasis.

The weekday schedule is as follows. Those living in the cenobium rise at 5:00 a.m. The Akathist hymn to the Virgin is chanted standing in cell or church from 5:30 to 6:30. Holy

Suceviţa Monastery, Romania, 16th century, quadrangle showing (from the left) main gate with nuns, 15-foot-high walls, monastery, church porch. Photo courtesy of Mary Schaefer

Retreat center, Sihastria, Romania, 20th century.
Photo courtesy of Mary Schaefer

Liturgy and service for the dead is from 6:30 to 8:30 and breakfast from 9:00 to 9:30. Work is done until dinner at 1:00 p.m. Work between 1:30 and 3:00 p.m. is followed by vespers. Free time, for reading and tea, is from 4:00 to 5:00. Work or courses for the novices (5:00 to 6:30) is followed by supper. Matins (music lessons for the novices) is from 7:00 until 9:00 p.m. An hour of private prayer in the cell leads to sleep until midnight and private prayers. The Sunday schedule is more relaxed. In the idiorhythmic sectors of the monastery, nuns living three to five in a house pray the hours in common. Many sisters work on the farm; at harvest time all assist.

Monastics confess every Friday, with communion every three weeks on Saturday except for the elders, who communicate weekly. Practice of more frequent communion is encouraged by the monks of Sihastria. Non-Orthodox are offered the *antidoron* (blessed bread). The Jesus Prayer with many hundreds of *mătanii* is the prayer of choice; a few monasteries recite all 150 Psalms daily. Observance of the Orthodox fast from meat, fish, eggs, milk, or cheese during the lengthy periods prescribed by the Church calendar is the chief ascetic practice.

Sites

Numerous monasteries plus smaller dependencies, many in the context of peasant culture, are found in four monastic regions.

1. Bukovina: the painted churches of Arbore, Humor, Voroneţ, Moldoviţa, and Suceviţa are unique; Putna and Dragomirna.
2. The Romanian Athos: Varatec, Agapia, Neamţ, Secul, and Sihastria (derived from the Greek *hesychast*, "hermit," or seeker of interior and exterior peace as the foundation for perfect prayer). Sihastria is completely contemplative. All these are situated on the northern slopes of Mount Stinişoarei; additional monasteries (Bistriţa and Horaiţa) are found on its southern flanks.
3. Transylvania, noted for hermits: Rīmeţi, a nunnery founded 1214, is the most important Orthodox center in the region; Nicula (1552) is a center for icons painted on glass; Prislop (nuns, founded 14th century).
4. Bucharest region: Cernica, Pasarea (nuns noted for chant), Tigăneşti (nuns who do tapestry work), Antim, Caldarusani, Snagov, and Plumbuita.

Mary M. Schaefer, with Silvia Chitimia and Ronald G. Roberson

See also Basil the Great, St.; Bulgaria; Fasting: Eastern Christian; Hungary; Libraries: Eastern Christian; Meteora, Thessaly, Greece; Mount Athos, Greece; Mount Sinai, Egypt; Orthodox

Monasticism; Paisy Velichkovsky; Russia: History; Serbia; Theology, Eastern Christian

Further Reading

Bouyer, Louis, *Orthodox Spirituality and Protestant and Anglican Spirituality*, London: Burns and Oates, and New York: Desclee, 1969
Cassiana, Mother, *Come, Follow Me: Orthodox Monasticism in Moldavia*, Minneapolis, Minnesota: Life and Light, 1991
Christophora, Mother, "Pilgrimage to Romania," *Life Transfigured* 26:1 (1994); 26:2; 26:3; and 27:1 (1995)
Dragut, Vasile, *Die Wandmalerei in der Moldau im 15. und 16. Jahrhundert*, Bucharest: Meridiane, 1983
Dumitru-Snagov, I., "Romania," in *Dizionario degli Istituti di Perfezione* 7 (1983)
Ionescu, Ion, *Inceputurile creştinismului românesc Daco-Roman* (The Beginnings of Daco-Romanian Christianity), Bucharest: Ed. Universitătii Bucureşti, 1998
Joanta, Seraphim, *Romania: Its Hesychast Tradition and Culture*, Wildwood, California: St. Zenia Skete Press, 1992
Pacurariu, Mircea, *Istoria Bisericii Ortodoxe Române* (The History of the Romanian Orthodox Church), Chisinau: Stiinta, 1993
Roberson, Ronald G., "The Romanian Orthodox Church," *The Catholic World* (September–October 1989)
Roberson, Ronald G., "The Profile of Eastern Monasticism Today," *Melita Theologica* 3 (1994)
Schaefer, Mary M., "Between East and West: Women Monastics in Romania," *Sisters Today* (May 1995)
Špidlík, Tomás, "Monachesimo e Religiosità Popolare in Romania," *Civiltà Cattolica* 138 (1987)
Vlasie, Mihai, *Drumuri spre Mănăstiri* (The Ways to the Monasteries), Bucharest: Ed. Uranus, 1992

Rome and the Papacy

The capital of Italy and Latium lies about 65 feet above sea level on the banks of the Tiber in the Campagna di Roma. This is the most highly populated and largest city in Italy (municipality covering about 935 square miles), a historical and cultural center of extraordinary importance, and the capital of the Roman Catholic Church.

Founded by the Latin peoples around the eighth century B.C. (tradition dates it to 753) near the Isola Tiberina, perhaps on the Palatine Hill, it was at first a monarchy until Tarquinius Superbus, the last king, was expelled and it became a republic (509 B.C.). In the fourth and third centuries B.C., it went to war with its neighbors (e.g., Latins, Etruscans, Aequi, Volsci, Sabini, Samnites, and Umbrians) for supremacy over the area and the whole of south-central Italy until in 264 B.C. it gained control of the peninsula. The Punic Wars (264–146) and the Macedonian Wars (215–168) marked the first great Roman conquests and prepared Rome for rule over the lands then known. After the battle of Actium (31 B.C.), when Anthony was defeated by Octavian, the latter took the title of emperor, opening the greatest period in Roman history, marked by conquest but also by enormous urban development of the city. Rome began to decline in the third century A.D. (under the Severi dynasty): the western Roman Empire (divided from the eastern empire) fell in A.D. 476 to Odoacer, king of the Heruli. After an initial period of decadence linked to the Greek-Gothic War (535–553) and frequent battles with the Lombards, the city gradually reorganized under papal guidance, and, after the arrival of the Franks and the creation of the patrimony of St. Peter (the early nucleus of the Papal States), the popes succeeded in combining temporal and spiritual power. Subsequently Rome was always subject to the power of the papacy, alternating darker periods, such as the exile of the Pontiff to Avignon (1305–1370) and the Western Schism (1378–1414), with others of great urban, artistic, and cultural development, most important the Renaissance, associated mainly with Pope Julius II (1503–1513). After the Napoleonic period (1798–1799 and 1809–1815), the town was the scene of Risorgimento turmoil, such as the proclamation of the Roman Republic in 1848, championed by Mazzini, and the attempt on it by Garibaldi, thwarted at Mentana in 1867. Rome was finally united with the kingdom of Italy in 1870, the year that marked the end of the Papal States. In 1929, under the Lateran Treaty, the Vatican city-state was created within the city's perimeter, its sole sovereign being the pope.

Ancient Rome reached its greatest urban expansion (perhaps a million inhabitants) in the third century A.D., surrounded by the Aurelian walls, which still define the city's historical center. After the fall of the empire, Rome had a rapidly declining population, reduced to a few tens of thousands of inhabitants. In successive centuries development was marked by important construction work, especially in the 16th and 17th centuries, still within its ancient boundaries. Only when Rome became capital of Italy (1871) did it begin to grow rapidly, spreading beyond the central area at the start of the 20th century. Expansion was often haphazard and motivated by speculation, leading to the construction of working-class suburbs (the so-called borgate), lacking in essential services, while administrative offices and company headquarters were concentrated in the city center.

In view of the importance and the size of Rome, one can mention only those important monuments that are of extraordinary archaeological, cultural, and artistic value. Old Roman remains include the Colosseum (first century A.D.), the Roman Forum, the Imperial Forum, Trajan's Column (A.D. 113), the Column of Marcus Aurelius (A.D. 193), the Arch of Titus (first century A.D.), the Arch of Constantine (A.D. 315), the Basilica of Massenzio (A.D. 312), the Pantheon (first to second century A.D., housing the tombs of the kings of Italy and Raphael), the Baths of Caracalla (A.D. 217), and the evocative ancient Appian Way. Civil buildings include Palazzo del Museo Capitolino (16th century), Palazzo dei Conservatori (16th century), Palazzo Venezia (15th century), Palazzo della Cancelleria (15th century), Palazzo Farnese (16th century), Palazzo Barberini (17th century, baroque), and the Villa della Farnesina (Renaissance). Places of special beauty are Parco di Villa Borghese, Piazza Navona in baroque style, the steps of Trinità dei Monti with Piazza di Spagna, and the Campidoglio. There are numerous artistic fountains, the most famous being the Fontana di Trevi (18th century) and the Fontana di Fiumi (17th century). There are also countless reli-

Interior of Dominican Church of Santa Maria sopra Minerva, Rome, Italy, 13th century.
Photo courtesy of Chris Schabel

gious buildings: the proto-Christian churches of St. Constanza, St. Giovanni in Laterano, St. Maria Maggiore, St. Sabina, St. Paolo fuori le Mura, and St. Pietro in Vincoli (housing the famous *Moses* by Michelangelo) and the Renaissance St. Maria del Popolo (frescoes by Raphael and Caravaggio).

However, Rome is thought of mainly as the center of the Roman Catholic Church. The Basilica of St. Peter, built at the start of the fourth century, was rebuilt by Pope Julius II at the beginning of the 16th century under the direction of Bramante. Michelangelo added the famous cupola, and the basilica was completed in 1589. Ornate and majestic, it houses some remarkable masterpieces, such as Michelangelo's famous *Pietà*, the monument of Clement XIII (1758–1769) by Canova, and Bernini's funeral monument for Urban VIII (1623–1644), the altar canopy of which is about 95 feet high. Outside stretches the monumental Piazza St. Pietro (St. Peter's Square), a Bernini masterpiece, with its majestic colonnade of 284 columns topped by 140 statues.

Monasticism in Rome

Early monasticism in Rome was strongly influenced by the Rule of St. Benedict, compiled in the early sixth century. Pope Gregory I (590–604), in his *Dialogues*, commented on the lucidity and discretion of this Rule. However, the development and rise of the papacy was the most important influence on Christianity from the Middle Ages to the present. For Rome the prominent role that the papacy has played in its history ranks alongside its imperial conquest history. The authority of the pope as bishop of Rome, the collective authority of the pope and the cardinals, the bureaucracy of the Western Church headed by the pope, or even the Western Church as a whole had very different connotations in varying circumstances and time periods. The primacy of the bishop of Rome, although claimed early in the Western Church's history, did not effectively translate into reality until the ecclesiastical revolution of the 11th century.

The term *Apostolic see* (*sedes apostolica*) appeared in the late fourth century, and by 422 Boniface I (418–422) claimed primacy in the Church. As the Christian Church developed, five cities stood as preeminent sites: Alexandria, Antioch, Jerusalem,

Cypresswood doors (fifth century), church of Santa Sabina (Dominican), Rome, Italy. A wooden panel on the doors contains what may be the earliest sculpture of the Crucifixion.
Photo courtesy of Mary Schaefer

Constantinople, and Rome; however, only one lay outside the eastern empire. This "pentarchy" remained important until the seventh century, when the rise of Islam either destroyed or captured three of these centers, leaving only Rome and Constantinople vying for dominance. The importance of holiness in the early Church being associated with relics and sanctified places, and especially Rome's association as the city of St. Peter's and St. Paul's martyrdom, essentially assisted Rome in becoming the preeminent bishopric.

As the spiritual power of the papacy grew, its political influence was also developing. The most influential early pope was Gregory I, known as "the Great" (590–604), a monastic whose name is linked to a number of important reforms, especially the reform of music and liturgy that bears his name: Gregorian chant. Uneasy relations between the papacy and the emperor in Constantinople were frequent during the Middle Ages. The last imperial visit to Rome was in 663. Theological disputes were common between the Eastern and Western Churches, such as the Monophysitism and monotheletism controversies as well as the Iconclast issue in the eighth century.

Determination of the date of Easter according to the Roman rather than the Celtic tradition, as well as appeals from Gaul to settle disputes between churches and church authorities, helped Rome consolidate both ecclesiastical and political power in the West during the seventh and eighth centuries. Threats from barbarians and political struggles in the Italian peninsula kept the papacy busy in these centuries as well. An alliance with Frankish Gaul and the Carolingians in 751 eventually led to the crowning of Charlemagne as Holy Roman emperor on Christmas Day A.D. 800. This connection with the Frankish royal house led to more political support for the papacy and assisted in the papacy's eventual break with the Byzantine Empire and the Eastern Church. Charlemagne (768–814) promulgated and standardized liturgical practice in favor of the Roman rite throughout his entire empire. However, the papacy discovered that imperial control over papal elections resulted from the mutual collaboration.

With the crumbling of Frankish imperial power at the end of the ninth century, the feuds of Roman noble families once again prevailed on papal politics. The family of Theophylact in the tenth century led to a generation of popes controlled by Roman intrigue. The rise of the German emperors led to a number of popes whose powers were limited and controlled by the imperial court into the 11th century. A new sense of direction and reform began under Leo IX (1049–1054) in a movement that attacked simony and clerical marriage, and eventually papal election was able to free itself from both imperial control and Roman politics to move toward a monarchical authority revered throughout Christendom.

With the call for the First Crusade by Urban II (1088–1099) at the Council of Clermont in November 1095 and the new monastic orders of the Carthusians and Cistercians in the early 12th century, the papacy found a renewed presence and power in the Western world. The rise of the friars in the 13th century assisted in the evangelical and intellectual activities of the papacy in Rome as well. With Innocent III (1198–1216) as pope, both imperial and local Roman politics were finally subsumed under the growing spiritual authority of the papacy. Increasing influence over appointments to high positions in the Church helped bring more of Christendom under the control of the pope. The Fourth Lateran Council in 1215 consolidated papal authority, and the primacy of the Roman See was affirmed.

Almost as soon as the Roman See confirmed its primacy over all of Western Christendom, the fortunes of the papacy were reversed. The decline was due mainly to a collapse of temporal power and political direction. In the late 13th century papal elections became protracted battles, often leaving the papacy vacant for extended periods of time. The powerful Roman families once again asserted control on papal elections, and imperial interests also took advantage of the weakness. As a result a credibility gap between actual papal power and theoretical claims to authority developed in spiritual and political matters.

The move of the papal court to Avignon in France in the early 14th century assisted the papacy in regaining some authority. From 1309 to 1377 Avignon was the seat of the papacy. Avignon was geographically better located than Rome and was more accessible to the large numbers of people who sought favors, and the area was less turbulent than the Roman peninsula. The Great Schism of 1378 between French and Roman factions resulted in often two or three popes in power at the same time. The election of Martin V (1417–1431) in 1417 reunified the Church, and he was able to restore much of the prestige and power of the papacy. Rome as the center of both the Roman Empire and the Roman Catholic Church in the ancient and medieval worlds set the stage for its continued influence into the modern era.

BRADFORD LEE EDEN

See also Abbot Primate, Benedictine; Gregory I (the Great), St.; Gregory VII; Jerusalem, Israel; Liturgy: Western Christian; Martyrs: Western Christian; Pilgrimages, Christian: Western Europe; Plainchant; Relics, Christian Monastic

Further Reading

Brown, Peter, *Authority and the Sacred: Aspects of the Christianisation of the Roman World*, Cambridge and New York: Cambridge University Press, 1995

Dyson, Stephen L., *Community and Society in Roman Italy*, Baltimore, Maryland: Johns Hopkins University Press, 1991

MacMullen, Ramsay, *Christianity and Paganism in the Fourth to Eighth Centuries*, New Haven, Connecticut: Yale University Press, 1997

Rahner, Hugo, and Leo Donald Davis, *Church and State in Early Christianity*, San Francisco: Ignatius Press, 1992

Woodward, Christopher, *Rome*, Manchester and New York: Manchester University Press, 1995

Royal Patrons, Christian. *See* Patrons, Christian: Royal

Rule of St. Benedict. *See* Benedict of Nursia, St.; Regulations: Christian Perspectives

Rules, Buddhist (Vinaya): Historical

Buddhist monastic law (vinaya) is the sum total of rules of conduct for Buddhist monks (Sanskrit, *bhikṣu*; Pāli, *bhikkhu*) and nuns (Sanskrit, *bhikṣuṇī*; Pāli, *bhikkhunī*) as codified in the canonical "Book of Discipline," the Vinaya-Piṭaka. Obviously drawing on pre-Buddhist material, this text contains the oldest Indian legal code. It is, by its nature, case law; that is, the rules were formulated with reference to a specific incident of misconduct.

In regard to Buddhist monastic law, it is important to point out that the subject is far from being monolithic: nothing like *the* Buddhist monastic law exists, just as nothing like *the* Buddhist order does. During the long history of Buddhism, many schools developed and split up into a large number of subgroups, many of which have (or had) their own Vinaya tradition.

Only a small fraction of this wealth of textual tradition has been edited and translated into Western languages. A large number of relevant texts must be considered lost, whereas others survived only in Chinese or Tibetan translations. For example, the Vinaya of the Mūlasarvāstivāda school is preserved partly in Sanskrit and partly in a Chinese translation, whereas the complete text has come down to us only in the Tibetan translation. Our knowledge of these various strains of tradition and their mutual relations is still too sketchy for a comprehensive survey. Thus, it seems advisable to confine this article to the – preferably self-contained – tradition of one school. The canonical texts of the Theravāda school, handed down in Pāli, a Middle Indo-Aryan language, provide the most promising basis for such a venture, not least so because they are generally available in reliable editions as well as translations into Western languages.

The Vinaya lays down general rules of conduct for monks and nuns and regulates the social relations between the members of the order as well as their dealing with the world outside the Buddhist order, especially the laity. In giving detailed rules for the occasional and regular legal procedures of the monastic community and explicating rights and duties, the text covers a wide range of topics, including food, clothing, furnishings, buildings, and medicament.

The Buddhist community (*saṅgha*), in the broad sense of the term, consists of seven classes, namely, monks, nuns, female "probationers" (Sanskrit, *śikṣamāṇā*; Pāli, *sikkhamānā*), male novices (Sanskrit, *śrāmaṇera*; Pāli, *sāmaṇera*), female novices (Sanskrit, *śrāmaṇerikā*; Pāli, *sāmaṇerī*), and laypeople of both sexes (Sanskrit, Pāli, *upāsaka*, *upāsikā*). In a narrower sense *saṅgha* designates the community of monks or nuns who received full ordination (*upasampadā*) in a legally valid ceremony (Pāli, *upasampadākamma*; Sanskrit, *upasaṃpadākarman*) executed by the order. Only members of this latter *saṅgha* are subject to Buddhist monastic law as codified in the Vinaya. With few exceptions membership of the Buddhist order is open to all. A male applicant must be at least 20 years of age and in good health, he must not be in debt or persecuted for an offense against secular law, and his parents must give their permission. In addition female applicants must be fertile but not pregnant or giving suck. Moreover they must complete two years of studentship before they can attain full ordination.

Buddhist tradition states unanimously that the Buddha himself proclaimed the rules for monks and nuns. However, modern research has shown that large portions of the Vinayas of the various schools were most probably formulated and integrated into the monastic discipline only after the demise of the Buddha.

Before his death the Buddha explicitly refused to appoint a successor to the position of leader of the monastic community. Instead he told the monks that his teaching (Sanskrit, *dharma*; Pāli, *dhamma*) and discipline constituted the highest authority. However, at that time no authoritative collection of his words existed because he had preached his sermons and laid down the rules of conduct to differing audiences on various occasions. According to tradition, one year after the death of the Buddha the so-called "first council" was convened to compile an authoritative canon of teachings and monastic rules. However, the corpus brought together during this "first council" was not accepted by all. For example, the Theravāda Vinaya tells the story of the monk Purana who wanted to follow only those teachings that he himself had heard from the Buddha.

As Buddhism spread over the different regions of India, the texts collected during this "first council" were transmitted orally in various Middle Indo-Aryan dialects (later Sanskrit was also used). After some time new texts or rules and new interpretations of old rules were incorporated. This process took different courses in various regions. One factor that contributed considerably to this diverse development is that Buddhist monks and nuns are not allowed to earn their livelihood. They always have to live dependently on the laity, which supplies them with their necessities (food, clothing, and lodging). As far as possible the monks and nuns should be free from worldly bonds and obligations so that they can concentrate on their spiritual development. However, in the beginning Buddhism was one of many religious communities that all came into existence at the same time – the Buddhist monks and nuns were only one of many groups of ascetics courting the laity's favor. Thus, it was very important to show consideration for the sensivities and irritabilities of the laity, even if the conduct concerned was not directly connected with Buddhist teachings and concepts. Many deviations in the various Buddhist disciplines are based on the adjustment to local habits, as could be shown by the comparison of minutiae in the Vinayas of the Mūlasarvāstivāda and the Theravāda school.

The split-up of local communities also led to the formation of various Vinaya schools. In this context *saṅgha* is defined as a local community of fully ordained monks or nuns that is defined by a "boundary" (*sīmā*) that was fixed by them. This definition is relevant mainly with regard to legal aspects because only local communities consisting of at least four monks or nuns were authorized to handle legal procedures (Sanskrit, *karman*; Pāli, *kamma*) of the community.

Already in the canonical texts, we find the report of a "split-up of the order" (*saṃghabheda*) caused by differing opinions regarding monastic discipline. In the Vinaya, Saṃghabheda is consistently presented as a serious disturbance of monastic life. The reason most commonly mentioned for the formation of new Buddhist schools are such bipartitions of a local community of at least nine monks or nuns, resulting in the formation of two separate orders.

The temporary expulsion of monks and nuns in consequence of misconduct most probably led to the formation of new schools as well. A monk or nun remained expelled (Sanskrit, *utkṣipta*; Pāli, *ukkhitta*) from the community until he or she confessed his or her irregularity. However, if he or she found enough other monks or nuns sharing his or her opinion, they could form a separate order with its own Vinaya tradition.

The use of different languages also contributed to the diversification of Vinaya traditions, especially with regard to legal procedures of the order. These are strongly ritualized acts that aim to uphold the rules of the *saṅgha* and secure a peaceful living. Legal procedures are performed regularly at fixed dates during the year or whenever a call for action arises. In any case the procedure and the correct wording of the formulas is of utmost importance: if any deviation occurs, the procedure is considered legally invalid. Consequently monks using different languages for their tradition could not perform these acts together. The diversification of Vinaya schools is evident in later legal texts, such as collections of "formulas" (Sanskrit, *karmavācanā*; Pāli, *kammavācā*) for the legal procedures.

Thus, the early formation of different Buddhist schools most likely resulted from the lack of an authority, from the orality of tradition in different languages up to the fourth or fifth century A.D., from the wide geographical spread of the Buddhist community, and from the division of local communities due to disagreements on Vinaya matters.

The term for these old schools, which share one discipline but at the same time might have diverse traditions of teaching, is *nikāya*, or "Vinaya school." According to tradition most of them came into existence during the second and third centuries after the Buddha's death. Each monk or nun is a member of that *nikāya* that bestowed full ordination on him or her. Only the legal tradition of this school is authoritative for him or her. Only members of the same legal tradition can perform legal procedures of the community together. Moreover one cannot perform a legal procedure together with monks or nuns whose integrity is doubtful, as the legal act itself is then considered invalid.

In this sense a partition of Buddhist communities is hardly reversible. The teacher-pupil succession of the monks or nuns always has to be traced back to the Buddha himself. Only a full ordination performed by correctly ordained monks or nuns is valid, and another precondition for a valid ordination is a faultless ordination procedure. In Theravāda countries a monk can be ordained in a second ordination line if uncertainty exists about the validity of his ordination tradition or if a traveling monk visits a local community of another ordination tradition that doubts the validity of his ordination. Thus, the monk is authorized to perform legal procedures in two different Buddhist schools.

In all Buddhist traditions the "Book of Discipline" is the first part of the canon. The Theravāda Vinaya-Piṭaka begins with the *suttavibhaṅga* section. Embedded into an old commentary, it contains the "formula of confession," the *pātimokkha* (Sanskrit, *prātimokṣa*), which most likely is the oldest part of the text. This list of rules is recited collectively by the *saṅgha* every other week on the so-called Uposatha day.

The "formulas of confession" for monks (Sanskrit, *bhikṣuprātimokṣa*; Pāli, *bhikkhupātimokkha*; Theravāda: 227 rules) and nuns (Sanskrit, *bhikṣuṇīprātimokṣa*; Pāli, *bhikkhunīpātimokkha*; Theravāda: 311 rules) are given in two separate chapters. Those rules common to monks and nuns are listed only in the monks' section.

The *pātimokkha* is divided into seven categories arranged according to the seriousness of the offense. Within the seven chapters the rules are not arranged uniformly.

The first category of offenses (*pārājika*; Theravāda: four monks' rules, eight nuns' rules) is visited with the permanent, lifelong expulsion of the transgressor. He or she can never attain full ordination again. Pārājika 1 prescribes celibacy and thus forms the basis for all further prescriptions regulating sexuality in this and other categories. Its importance is underlined by the fact that it is the first rule listed in the Vinaya. Two of the Pārājika rules deal with matters that are illegal in worldly law as well: taking things that are not given (theft) and the murder of human beings. Pārājika 4 prohibits the public exaggeration of one's spiritual abilities. Two of the additional four nuns' Pārājika rules deal with sexual misconduct, one forbids the concealment of a Pārājika transgression of another nun, and one prohibits the adherence to a monk who is temporarily suspended.

The second category (Pāli, *saṃghādisesa*; Sanskrit, *saṃghāvaśeṣa* /*saṃghātiśeṣa*; Theravāda: 13 monks' rules, 17 nuns' rules) is punished with the temporary (Theravāda: monks, 6 days; nuns, 14 days) expulsion of the culprit. This expulsion, as well as the subsequent restoration, is effected by a legal procedure of the monastic community. In addition the duration of the expulsion for monks depends on whether and, if so, how long they concealed their offense. Some of the Saṃghādisesas are considered an offense immediately after the misconduct occured, and some are considered an offense only after three fruitless admonitions. Five of the monks' Saṃghādisesa rules deal with sexual misbehavior (e.g., "intentional emission of semen" is forbidden). Two Saṃghādisesa rules prohibit the unfounded accusation of another monk, and two relate to a "split-up of the order" (*saṃghabheda*). Many of the nuns' Saṃghādisesa rules deal with quarrelsome behavior toward other nuns. One states that a nun may not live or set on tour without an accompanying nun.

The Aniyata section consists of two rules exclusively applicable to monks (nuns: no rules); the consequence varies from permanent expulsion to simple confession, depending on the nature of the offense.

The Nissaggiya-Pācittiya category (Sanskrit, *naiḥsargika*; Theravāda: 30 rules for monks and nuns) is subdivided into groups of ten and deals with objects acquired or used in an inappropriate manner. The respective items must be handed over to another monk or nun or to the *saṅgha*. The rules deal with the set of three (monks) or five (nuns) robes (*cīvara*), with a mat for sitting (*nisīdana*), with the material used for this mat, and with the alms bowl (Pāli, *patta*; Sanskrit, *pātra*) and its size and material. However, in most cases the handing over is not permanent but rather a symbolical act: later the item is given back to the offender. Two rules concern transactions of gold and silver. If a monk or nun accepts or spends money, it is not given back to him or her later but remains with the *saṅgha*. In this category only the requisites of monks or nuns that are the items acquired during monkhood are concerned because only these belongings, not the private property of their (former) worldly life, can be affected by the jurisdiction of the *saṅgha*.

The most voluminous category of offenses is Pācittiya (Sanskrit, *pātayanika*; *prāyaścittika*, or *prāyaścittīya*; Theravāda: 92 monks' rules, 166 nuns' rules), which is again subdivided into groups of ten. A Pācittiya offense is extinguished by confession. The rules in this chapter are not uniform at all. Conscious lying; insulting; gossiping; too close contact with the laity (especially with women); boasting; lack of consideration toward others; disrespect (especially toward the Buddha and his teaching); quarrelsomeness; and injury of animals, plants, or other living beings are prohibited. Furthermore this chapter contains rules concerning bathing, robes (color and size), furniture and other items, quality and quantity of food and drink (no alcohol), the proper time for eating (before noon), entertainment, and relations to nuns and other ascetics. Some deal with the daily almsround, some with invitations by the laity, and some with the regular exhortation of nuns (date, circumstances, place, and authorization). The additional Pācittiyas for nuns are sex specific (e.g., prescribing a special cloth for menstruation), prohibit household work and similar activities, deal with clothes, and define the relation of nuns and monks.

The next category, Pāṭidesaniya (Sanskrit, *pratideśanīya*; Theravāda: four monks' rules, eight nuns' rules), deals mainly with the almsround and the food that may be accepted. Relevant offenses are expiated by a simple confession.

The Sekhiya rules (Sanskrit, *śaikṣa*; Theravāda: 75 rules for monks and nuns) lay down the general "code of conduct," the transgression of which remains without consequences. In this chapter one finds, for example, instructions how to enter a house or village, how to dress properly, how to take meals, how to preach the Buddhist doctrine, and how to use toilets. For example, monks and nuns should not smack their lips while eating, should not urinate while standing, and should not make unnecessary noise. In the Vinayas of the various schools, this category deviates very much in the number of rules as well as in their contents. Thus, it is most likely a later addition to the Vibhaṅga.

The last chapter of the Suttavibhaṅga, Adhikaraṇasamatha (Sanskrit, *adhikaraṇaśamatha*; Theravāda: seven items for monks and nuns), briefly refers to the different possibilities of settling "cases" or "legal questions" (*adhikaraṇa*) within the order. This chapter is not recited during the Uposatha day, and the Adhikaraṇasamatha are described extensively in another part of the Theravāda Vinaya (Cullavagga 4).

The Theravāda Vinaya has 22 more chapters (*khandhaka*; chapters 1–10: Mahāvagga; chapters 11–22: Cullavagga; Sanskrit, *skandhaka* or *vinayavastu*) containing the unnumbered rules of the Vinaya.

They list mainly "formulas" and rules for most of the legal procedures of the community, namely, for the procedure of admission (higher and lower ordination), for the observance of *uposatha* (the occasion to confess offenses) every other week, for the residence during the rainy season, for the "ceremony of invitation" (i.e., an invitation to produce evidence of others' offenses they witnessed, heard of, or merely suspect) (Pāli, *pavāraṇā*; Sanskrit, *pravāraṇā*), for the time for the laity to hand over presents to the order at the end of the rainy season, for suspension and rehabilitation, for restrictions during the probationer period after having committed an offense, for imposing and revoking certain punishments, for various procedures of settling legal questions in the order, and so on. Many terms used here are highly technical.

These chapters also regulate daily life and deal with food (e.g., fish or meat may be consumed only if the animal was not killed on the monk's or nun's behalf), requisites (e.g., belt, razor, needle, water strainer, staff, and toothpick), diseases, lodging for the retreat during the rainy season (three to four months, from Asadha to Karttika), property, and general conduct and special rules for nuns. Furthermore prescriptions for the conduct of the teacher toward his pupil and vice versa are given.

The Parivāra section of the Theravāda Vinaya gives a systematic survey of law. Therein the different rules and formulas of the Suttavibhaṅga and Khandhakas are arranged according to varying principles. The Parivāra is an appendix or directory to Suttavibhaṅga and Khandhakas and cannot be understood without the preceding parts of the Vinaya.

As stated at the beginning, this short introduction into Buddhist monastic law is based on the canonical texts of the Theravāda school. It should be kept in mind that this is only one tradition of many. Despite their common roots, these traditions can differ considerably.

Ute Hüsken

See also Asceticism: Buddhist Perspectives; Buddhism: Overview; Buddhist Schools/Traditions: South Asia; Burma (Myanmar); Clothing: Buddhist Perspectives; Councils, Buddhist; Daoism: Influence on Buddhism; Discourses (Sūtras): Mahāyāna; Economics: Buddhist; Food: Buddhist Perspectives; Initiation: Buddhist Perspectives; Jain Monasticism and Buddhist Monasticism; Mahāpajāpatī Gotamī; Novices, Theravādin Rituals for; Origins: Comparative Perspectives; Regulations: Buddhist Perspectives; Repentance Rituals, Buddhist; Saichō; Sexuality: Buddhist Perspectives; Women's Monasteries: Buddhist

Further Reading

Dhirasekara, Jotiya, *Buddhist Monastic Discipline: A Study of Its Origin and Development in Relation to the Sutta and Vinaya Pitakas*, Colombo: Ministry of Higher Education, 1982

Frauwallner, Erich, *The Earliest Vinaya and the Beginnings of Buddhist Literature*, Rome: Is. M.E.O., 1956

Hecker, Hellmuth, "Allgemeine Rechtsgrundsätze in der buddhistischen Ordensverfassung (Vinaya)," *Verfassung und Recht in Übersee* 10:1 (1977)

Hinüber, Oskar von, "Das buddhistische Recht und die Phonetik des Pāli: Ein Abschnitt aus der Samantapāsādikā über die Vermeidung von Aussprachefehlern in *kammavācās*," *Studien zur Indologie und Iranistik* 2:13–14 (1987)

Hinüber, Oskar von, *Das Pātimokkhasutta der Theravādin*, Studien zur Literatur des Theravāda-Buddhismus 2, Mainz, 1999

Jampa Tsedroen, Bhikṣuṇī, *A Brief Survey of the Vinaya: Its Origin, Transmission and Arrangement from the Tibetan Point of View with Comparisons to the Theravāda and Dharmagupta Traditions*, Hamburg, 1992

Kieffer-Pülz, Petra, *Die Sīmā: Vorschriften zur Regelung der buddhistischen Gemeindegrenze in älteren buddhistischen Texten*, Berlin: Reimer, 1992

Nolot, Édith, "Studies in Vinaya Technical Terms, I–III," *Journal of the Pali Text Society* 22 (1996)

Pachow, W., *A Comparative Study of the Prātimokṣa on the Basis of Its Chinese, Tibetan, Sanskrit and Pāli Versions*, Santiniketan: Sino-Indian Cultural Society, 1955

The Pāṭimokkha: 227 Fundamental Rules of a Bhikkhu, translated by Thera Ñāṇamoli, Bangkok: Social Science Association Press of Thailand, 1966

Prebish, Charles S., *A Survey of Vinaya Literature*, Taipei: Jin Luen Publishing House, 1994

Upasak, Chandrika Singh, *Dictionary of Early Buddhist Monastic Terms Based on Pali Literature*, Varanasi: Bharati Prakashan, 1975

Wachirayanawarorot, Prince, King of Siam, *The Entrance to the Vinaya, Vinayamukha*, 3 vols., Bangkok: Mahamakutarajavidyalaya, 1969, 1973, 1983

Wijayaratna, Mohan, *Le Moine Bouddhiste: Selon les textes du Theravāda*, Paris: Editions du Cerf, 1983; as *Buddhist Monastic Life: According to the Texts of the Theravāda Tradition*, Cambridge and New York: Cambridge University Press, 1990

Wijayaratna, Mohan, *Les Moniales Bouddhistes: Naissance et Développement du Monachisme Féminin*, Paris: Éditions du Cerf, 1991

Yuyama, Akira, *Systematische Übersicht über die buddhistische Sanskrit-Literatur/A Systematic Survey of Buddhist Sanskrit Literature*, part 1: Vinaya texts, Wiesbaden: Steiner, 1979

Rules, Buddhist (Vinaya): Lineage

Lineage (Pāli, *theraparampara*; literally, "elders one after the other") is the Buddhist equivalent of apostolic succession. Each Buddhist monk should be able to recite a list of names that trace his ordination lineage back to the Buddha. The first few names are standard boilerplate as given in the fifth-century vinaya commentary (Sp vi 57): the Buddha ordained Upali, who ordained Dasaka, who ordained Sonaka, and so on. The last ten or so names are most significant. These differ from monk to monk and will be understood by other monks as signifying either certain idiosyncrasies of practice or a propensity to a certain specialization. (As Jesuits specialize in education, so some Buddhist lineages tended to specialize in meditation, vinaya, or scholarship.) The middle of the lineage list can safely be forgotten. The Pāli commentary instructs monks, "If one is not able to know the names of teachers in the whole series completely, one ought at least to know one or two names." This supports Mendelson's (1975) observation that monastic lineages might not always record the sober truth: anthropologists commonly describe similar manipulations of genealogical lineages for ideological purposes. All Buddhist monks are descendants of the Buddha, but distant cousins – for example, Korean and Sinhalese monks – have different practices. The question of which different practices should be tolerated and which anathematized is discussed through the language of lineage. A monk's status among fellow monks depends on his answer to two questions: How many rainy seasons have you spent in the order? and What is your lineage? The first question determines seniority, whereas the second determines vinaya practice.

A monk follows the tradition of vinaya observance into which he was ordained. As a 12th-century Pāli subcommentary puts it, "Lineage is a matter of knowing how one's forebears interpreted the canon" (Vmv 106). By choosing an ordination master, one can choose how strict a reading of the vinaya to be bound by. The canon says explicitly that new austerities can be added to the vinaya only by way of ordination lineage. If Upasena declares that he will ordain only those monks who undergo the extra austerity of wearing rag robes, then his lineage is bound by their promise "Lord, my preceptor is one who wears rag-robes, therefore I am also one who wears rag-robes" (V iii 230). So much is true of Buddhist monasticism in general. To look deeper into the phenomenon of lineage, we must examine it within a specific culture. Burma is especially rich in chronicle, pamphlet, and newspaper accounts of lineage rivalries. Recent research by Mendelson (1975), Ferguson (1975), Schober (1989), and others supplies a fairly detailed view of how Burmese lineages have evolved over the last four centuries. The rest of this article concentrates on lineage in Burma.

The last king of Burma described the connection between lineage and vinaya in a beautifully apposite simile. In Than Tun's summarized translation,

> The king wants to do all he could to make the Buddha's Religion prosper. *Pariyatti* (scripture) is like the embankment, *Pa.tipa.ti* (the order of monks) the water and *Pa.tivedha* (enlightenment) the lotus. In *Pa.tipa.ti* the vinaya is the most important part. (Royal Order, 22 June 1882)

The simile is based on upper Burma's irrigation systems, wherein dams in the foothills tap the mountain streams to irrigate the dry plains below. By enunciating Scripture the Buddha built a dam that turned a valley between the foothills into a reservoir full of merit-making monks. Only in such a reservoir can the lotus of enlightenment grow. *Pa.tipa.ti* means "order, succession," and therefore suggests the practice of a lineage. Thus the final sentence could be read as "Vinaya is the most important element in monastic lineage." Let us consider two aspects of the interaction between lineage and vinaya. First, a functional aspect: lineage was called into being by the need to bring vinaya disputes to a resolution. Second, a literary aspect: lineage has produced its own genre of vinaya text that can be called *lineage cases*.

Lawyers rely on the resolution of a case to generate its legal meaning. Because vinaya disputes cannot be authoritatively resolved, the vinaya is not, in this sense, a legal system. Buddhism cannot have a final court of appeal, because any hierarchy requires violence for its support. An important function of lineage is to provide an alternative method for bringing disputes to a resolution. The canonical vinaya applies to all monks: whether they live together in monasteries or alone as hermits, they must follow the first half of the vinaya, the 227 rules of the *Pātimokkha* that define how a monk should behave. The second half, the 20 speech acts of the *Kammavācā*, tells monks how to unite to perform acts (e.g., ordination and expulsion) that they could not achieve alone. The *Kammavācā*s define a unit of monastic government and lay down the administrative procedures by which it can make and enforce collective decisions. Because the vinaya shows no preference between the monastery and the hermitage, the unit of monastic government is the *sīmā* (parish boundary), which combines both. Twice a month hermits and monastery dwellers living within the *sīmā* join in a ceremonial recital of the *pātimokkha*, thus reaffirming their commitment to the life of a monk. These are generally the meetings at which *kammavācā*s (collective acts of governance) take place. Such acts are valid only if the specified formal requirements are followed and if the entire *sīmā* community is present. As the fifth-century commentary cheerfully notes, one can get a *kammavācā* wrong in three ways but right in only one: only the formal act of a united *sīmā* counts as valid.

Any *kammavācā* can be impugned on these three grounds. How were such arguments deployed, given that no court of appeal existed that could force a *sīmā* to reconsider its act? Suppose that the *sīmā* has just expelled a monk called Ananda. Ananda can argue that the act was void on any number of grounds. He can claim that one syllable in the formula of expulsion was mispronounced or that Sariputta (a monk living within the *sīmā*) was not present at the expulsion or that Revata (who was present) is not a valid monk. If the *sīmā* reject his challenge, he must leave the neighborhood, but the dispute is not thereby resolved: Ananda remains convinced that he is still a monk and will try to convince monks elsewhere that this is the case. If the *sīmā* accept his challenge and reinstate him, Revata, who doubts the decision, must himself leave the neighborhood: Ananda's presence would invalidate all future formal acts that the *sīmā* purports to make. If Ananda or Revata can persuade three other colleagues to leave with him, they can form their own *sīmā* community, which will become a new lineage when they ordain their first postulants. They must be prepared to rebut any suspicion of their credentials by repeating the details of the vinaya dispute that led to the split and explaining why their interpretation of vinaya was correct. Each lineage must preserve details of the dispute that gave birth to it. These details form the new lineage's charter. They resolve the original dispute by making it the foundation stone of a new *sīmā*. The new *sīmā*'s rhetorical claim is as follows: Because we found ourselves living among shameless monks who misinterpreted the vinaya, we drew ourselves aside and founded this well-disciplined community.

Once the details of Ananda's attempted expulsion have been written down, the manuscript joins the other vinaya texts in that monastery's book chest. It is a lineage-specific text: monks in Ananda's lineage have every reason to copy it, whereas monks in other lineages have no interest in it at all. This is the lineage-case genre in its purest form. The mechanics of monastic education ensure that the manuscript will contain other material. Burmese vinaya experts acquired their skills in their 20s by attaching themselves to a vinaya master. Manuscripts were generally handed down and recopied within the lineage. A senior pupil inherits his teacher's library and would often circulate fair copies of some of his teacher's writings. In Burmese such posthumous collections are known as *Winipyatton* (Vinaya Precedents). Their title in Pāli usually includes the word *vinicchaya* (judgments, rulings, or precedents.) All three are used for pedagogical purposes: the vinaya master will have notes of his *judgments* in actual vinaya disputes, notes of hypothetical *rulings* in class discussion of moot points, and notes of *precedents* that he took down at his own teacher's dictation. In its wider sense the lineage case genre includes all this material. Consider, for example, the elite lineage that includes the First, Second, and Third Maungdaung *sayadaws*. The Third Maungdaung (1815–1868) made a Pāli translation of the *Sasana lankara sadan* (Chronicle of Religion) composed by the First Maungdaung (1753–1833). These 19th-century monastic chronicles explain everything in terms of lineage, but they are not lineage casebooks as such. Third Maungdaung also edited and enlarged two works by the Second Maungdaung (1801–1866). One of these was a treatise on Pāli orthography, the other a lineage-case collection (*Vivada vinicchaya kyan*). Here we see linguistic and legal knowledge snowballing as the lineage recopies its manuscripts. Conversely, splits in the lineage affect the authority of lineage-case works. Consider, for example, the Thilon *sayadaw*'s *Winipyatton*. Thilon (1786–1860) was eminence grise to King Mindon (1853–1878). He stimulated, but stayed aloof from, the great lineage split of the 1850s:

> [The Thilon *sayadaw*] was the teacher of the Thingaza and the Shwegyin sayadaws, the latter of whom founded the Shwegyin or Sulagandhi Sect (as opposed to the Thudhamma or Mahagandhi Sect). The Thingaza sayadaw was also highly venerated, and in his day was head of the Mahagandhi. But the monks of *both* sects look up to the decisions of the Thilon sayadaw given in his *Winipyatton*. (*Shwe Ton v Tun Lin*, Lower Burma Reports, 1918, volume 9, pages 229, 252, *per* Maung Kin, J.)

After the split Shwegyin produced lineage casebooks of his own, which those in Thingaza's lineage disdained to read. However, both lineages treat a lineage casebook written just before the split took place as authoritative.

Is it only in Burma that lineage determines the choice of vinaya texts? Pāli literature written between the 5th and the 14th centuries shows some hints of a similar development. Analysts of the three earliest Pāli vinaya subcommentaries have suspected that they might draw on different collections of vinaya text held by separate lineages. Bollée (1969), noting that the two Sri Lankan works cite different texts, suggests that Vajirabuddhi and Sariputta belonged to different sects. Bapat (1967) examines a passage in Mahakassapa of South India's work that violently attacks Sariputta of Sri Lanka's work for promoting a "heretical view . . . eradicated by the great Elder Buddhapiya." Mahakassapa emphasizes that "the great elders have already condemned such views and those who held such views were banished." Possibly this is a regional dispute between South Indian and Sri Lankan monks, but Sri Lankan forest monks are recorded as consulting the South Indian work. More likely, then, is a lineage explanation: Mahakassapa is a lineage descendant of Buddhapiya and the other great elders, whereas Sariputta is not. The great Pāli commentary compiled in fifth-century Sri Lanka contains a few judgments by named monks. One of them tells of three generations of vinaya master. In the youngest generation Mahapaduma spent 18 years learning from his master, whereas Mahasumma spent only nine (Sp vii 43). The story implies that, when fellow pupils of a famous teacher disagree, we should listen to the student who stayed longer with his teacher.

ANDREW HUXLEY

See also Buddhism: Overview; Burma (Myanmar); Hermits: Buddhist; Master and Pupil: Buddhist Perspectives; Regulations: Buddhist Perspectives; Rules, Buddhist (Vinaya): Historical; Tibetan Lineages

Further Reading

Bapat, P.V., "Vimati-vinodani, a Vinaya Commentary, and Kundalkesi-vatthu, a Tamil Poem," *Journal of Indian History* 45 (1967)

Bollée, W.B., "Die Stellung der Vinaya-tikas in der Pali Literatur," in *XVII Deutscher Orientalistentag vom 21. bis 27. Juli 1968 in Würzburg, Vorträge*, Wiesbaden: Franz Steiner, 1969

Ferguson, John P., "The Symbolic Dimensions of the Burmese Sangha," Ph.D. Diss., Cornell University, 1975

Lingat, Robert, "Vinaya et droit laïque: Études sur les conflits de la loi religieuse et de la loi laïque dans l'Indochine hinayiste," *Bulletin de l'École Française de l'Extrême-Orient* 37 (1937)

Mendelson, E.M., *Sangha and State in Burma: A Study of Monastic Sectarianism and Leadership*, edited by John P. Ferguson, Ithaca, New York: Cornell University Press, 1975

Schober, Juliane S., "Paths to Enlightenment: Theravada Buddhism in Upper Burma," Ph.D. Diss., University of Illinois, 1989

Rules, Buddhist (Vinaya): Monks

Soon after having attained enlightenment, Buddha went to the Deer Park in Benares. It was to the five companions who in earlier days had stayed with him during the six years he devoted himself to the most severe austerities that he preached for the first time. These five earlier companions became the first monks. In this way an order of monks (*bhikṣusaṃgha*/*bhikkhusaṃgha*) came into being. Initially, Buddha himself called on candidates to join the Buddhist order, using the simple words "Welcome, monk," by which newcomers were admitted into the order and were immediately considered to be fully ordained monks. With the growth of the Buddhist community, Buddha allowed the monks to carry out an ordination ceremony during which the candidate recited the formula of the triple refuge: "I take refuge in Buddha, in the doctrine, and in the community." In this way the candidate went forth into the homeless state and at the same time received the ordination. Later Buddha stipulated that a clear distinction should be made between the going forth (*pravrajyā*/*pabbajjā*) and the ordination (*upasaṃpadā*/*upasampadā*): only after having gone through these two stages could a candidate become a monk (*bhikṣu*/*bhikkhu*) and be entitled to all the rights and the duties of the order of monks.

Most of the vinayas give a minimum age to go forth. However, they do not agree on the exact age: some say it is 12, others say it should be 15. Exceptions might be allowed. The novice (*śrāmaṇera*/*sāmaṇera*) has to pay attention especially to ten rules: (1) he may not kill; (2) he may not steal; (3) he may not have an unchaste behavior; (4) he may not lie; (5) he may not drink alcohol; (6) he may not wear flowers or perfume; (7) he may not sing, dance, or make music or go to see singing, dancing, and music; (8) he may not use a high, large, or big bed; (9) he may not eat at an improper time (i.e., after noon); and (10) he may not possess gold, silver, or valuables. A novice does not participate in the ceremonies or in the formal acts carried out by the order. At the age of 20, a novice can receive the ordination and become a full member of the Buddhist order. The full members (the monks) assume total responsibility for the order. Leading functions are assigned by an assembly of monks. A hierarchy is based only on seniority, reckoned from the date of the ordination.

Initially, monks had no fixed residence. They traveled around in the lay world. Nevertheless, during three, sometimes four, months of the rainy season, they went into retreat and stayed in one place. In this way monasteries (*vihāra*) came into being. Soon many monks began to stay in the same residence year-round, and monasteries gained importance. Still the rain retreat remained an important period in the organization of the order.

The life of Buddhist monks is regulated by many rules and ceremonies. The most important ceremonies are the *Poshadha* ([*U*]*poṣadha*/*Uposatha*), the Invitation (*Pravāraṇā*/*Pavāraṇā*), and the *Kathina* (*Kaṭhina*). The *Poshadha* ceremony, held every two weeks, is an essential ceremony in the communal life of monks. The term *poshadha* is related to the vedic term *upavasatha*, which refers to the day of fasting preceding the sacrifice on the days of the new and the full moon. *Upavasatha* is derived from the verb *upa-vas* (to remain with), which can be interpreted as "the gods remain with the person who will make a sacrifice the next day." The tradition of observing days of fasting has been adopted by the Buddhist lay community. The number of days increased: the Buddhist laypeople observed four *poshadha* days every month. Also in the order of monks, *poshadha* days were introduced. In the order the main significance of the *poshadha* days shifted to the recitation of the set of precepts to be observed (*prātimokṣa/pātimokkha*). It was further stipulated that this recitation should take place every two weeks. Apart from reminding the participants of the precepts, the recitation confirms the unity of the monks. During the ceremony the monks are asked whether they have violated one of the precepts. If they have, they should confess it. Soon, however, the questioning of the monks became only a ceremonial act, as a violation had to be confessed before the start of the actual ceremony.

The Invitation, or *Pravarana*, ceremony is carried out at the end of the rain retreat. During this ceremony every monk invites his fellow monks to point out his wrongs, if any, whether seen, or heard, or suspected. The inviting monk further declares that he is ready to confess any violation pointed out. Soon, however, violations were confessed not during but before the ceremony. The Invitation ceremony has an important symbolic function. Before the start of a new period of peregrinations, at least in theory, the order is declared "pure" (i.e., free from violations). The Invitation ceremony is followed by a period of one month, during which the lay community traditionally offers many gifts, especially robes and robe material, to the order. This period can be extended to a maximum of five months if a *Kathina* ceremony is carried out. The *Kathina* ceremony is the official start of the *kathina* period. The meaning of the term *kathina*, which refers to a cotton cloth used during the *Kathina* ceremony, still is not clear. During this period the monks enjoy five privileges that differ slightly from vinaya to vinaya but generally are as follows: (1) a monk can have an extra robe, i.e. more than the three robes a monk is entitled to in normal times: an inner robe (*antarvāsa/antaravāsaka*), an upper robe (*uttarāsaṅga*), and an outer cloak (*saṃghāṭī*); (2) a monk can pass the night without being in the possession of the three required robes; (3) monks can eat in a group, away from the order; (4) a monk can eat in one place and then again in another place; and (5) a monk can always enter a village without informing the other monks. All these privileges constitute temporary relaxations of some precepts of the order.

Every residence belongs to an autonomous district (*sīmā*) that normally encloses the whole monastery and an area around the monastery. These districts are strictly determined and may not overlap. All the ceremonies and the formal procedures must be carried out within the district. To have a legally valid decision, all the monks present in the district must take part in the procedures. As the number of monks increased and the monasteries became larger, this practice could no longer be always sustained. Therefore, on certain occasions a small *sima* was determined in the larger, original *sima*. In this small *sima* only a group of monks carries out a procedure while the remaining monks continue to do their daily tasks. Conflicts must be avoided as much as possible. If they do arise, the vinaya prescribes detailed rules to settle them.

In the course of time, monks acquired an important status in society. In principle monks are concerned with Buddhism and essentially study the path to enlightenment. In practice religious and social affairs sometimes have become intermingled so that monks play a significant social role.

Ann Heirman

See also Disciples, Early Buddhist; Regulations: Buddhist Perspectives; Saṅgha

Further Reading

Bechert, Heinz, and Richard Gombrich, editors, *The World of Buddhism, Buddhist Monks and Nuns in Society and Culture*, London: Thames and Hudson, and New York: Facts on File, 1984

Chung, Jin-il, *Die Pravāraṇā in den kanonischen Vinaya-Texten der Mūlasarvāstivādin und der Sarvāstivādin*, Göttingen: Vandenhoeck and Ruprecht, 1998

Dutt, Sukumar, *Early Buddhist Monachism*, London and New York: Kegan Paul, Trench, Trübner, and Dutton, 1924; reprint, Delhi, India: Munshiram Manoharlal, 1984

Dutt, Sukumar, *Buddhist Monks and Monasteries of India: Their History and Their Contribution to Indian Culture*, London: Allen and Unwin, 1962

Hirakawa, Akira, *Ritsuzō no Kenkyū*, Tokyo: Sankibō Busshorin, 1966

Horner, Isaline Blew, *The Book of the Discipline (Vinaya-Piṭaka)*, 6 vols., London: Pali Text Society, 1938–1966

Hu-von Hinüber, Haiyan, *Das Poṣadhavastu: Vorschriften für die buddhistische Beichtfeier im Vinaya der Mūlasarvāstivādins*, Reinbek: Inge Wezler, 1994

Kieffer-Pülz, Petra, *Die Sīmā: Vorschriften zur Regelung der Buddhistischen Gemeindegrenze in älteren Buddhistischen Texten*, Berlin: Reimer, 1992

Shih, Robert, *Biographies des moines éminents: Kao Seng Tchouan de Houei-kiao*, Louvain: Institut Orientaliste, 1968

von Hinüber, Oscar, "Buddhist Law According to the Theravāda-Vinaya: A Survey of Theory and Practice," *Journal of the International Association of Buddhist Studies* 18:1 (1995)

Wijayaratna, Môhan, *Buddhist Monastic Life According to the Texts of the Theravāda Tradition*, translated by Claude Grangier and Steven Collins, Cambridge and New York: Cambridge University Press, 1996

Rules, Buddhist (Vinaya): Nuns

In the Buddhist community two orders can be distinguished: a monk's order (*bhikṣusaṃgha/bhikkhusaṃgha*) and a nun's order (*bhikṣuṇīsaṃgha/bhikkhunīsaṃgha*). When Buddha permitted women to go forth, the monk's order was already well organized. In the beginning the nun's order likely copied the organizational pattern of the monk's order, and both orders further developed in the same general direction. The status of these two orders is not equal: the nun's order relies on the monk's order in several ways. This dependency is laid down in the eight fundamental rules (outlined here) to be followed by the nuns (*bhikṣuṇī/bhikkhunī*) in their relation with the monks (*bhikṣu/bhikkhu*). The fact that a woman has to be ordained both in the nun's order and in the monk's order is of fundamental importance. It implies that the monks always control the admission of new members into the nun's order.

In addition, some regulations hold only for the nun's order. Whereas a man must go through two compulsory stages (the going forth [*pravrajyā/pabbajjā*] and the ordination [*upasaṃpadā/upasampadā*]) to become a monk, for a woman a probationary period between the going forth and the ordination has been added. First, a girl must go into the homeless state. She becomes a novice (*śrāmaṇerī/sāmaṇerī*). As a novice she must pay special attention to ten rules: (1) she may not kill; (2) she may not steal; (3) she may not have an unchaste behavior; (4) she may not lie; (5) she may not drink alcohol; (6) she may not wear flowers or perfume; (7) she may not sing, dance, or make music, or go to see singing, dancing, and music; (8) she may not use a high, large, or big bed; (9) she may not eat at an improper time (i.e., after noon); and (10) she may not possess gold, silver, or valuables. When she is 18 years old, she can become a probationer (*śikṣamānā/sikkhamānā*). During her probationary period some rules deserve particular attention. These rules differ from vinaya to vinaya. The six rules of the Pāli vinaya and of the vinaya of the Dharmaguptakas are probably the oldest ones. The first four of these six rules coincide with the first four *parajika* (*pārājika*) precepts for monks and nuns, a violation of which leads to a lifetime exclusion from the order: the four rules prohibit (1) sexual intercourse, (2) stealing (anything with a value of five coins or more), (3) taking human life, and (4) lying about one's spiritual achievements. The other two rules require (5) that a probationer may not eat at an improper time (i.e., after noon) and (6) that she may not drink alcohol. The *Dharmaguptakavinaya* adds that a probationer who violates one of the first four rules (the *parajika* precepts) must be excluded permanently from the nun's order; for a probationer who violates one of the two other rules or who violates a rule closely linked to a *parajika* precept, the probationary period must be extended.

At first sight it seems that a novice must follow more rules than a probationer. Moreover, if we compare the ten rules imposed on a novice with the six rules for probationers, we see that these six rules coincide with six of the ten rules for novices. Thus, the question arises whether at first a woman candidate must follow ten rules and later only six. Possibly, the vinaya of the Dharmaguptakas gives a clue to a solution. From this vinaya we can deduce that both a novice and a probationer must observe all the rules of the order of nuns. The vinaya also says that a novice must pay special attention to ten rules, a probationer to six. Because all these rules for novices and probationers belong to the set of rules for nuns, it implies that the number of rules to be observed by a novice and by a probationer does not differ. However, it is noteworthy that the structure used to formulate the ten rules of the novice and the six rules of the probationer differs substantially. The structure of the ten rules for novices resembles that of rules for lay followers, who must observe the first five of these rules at all times, the first eight on special occasions, and all ten rarely. The structure of the six rules for probationers resembles the one for nuns. The *Dharmaguptakavinaya* further informs us that identical disciplinary measures are to be taken against a novice and against a probationer who violates one of the rules for nuns. In addition, for a probationer the probationary period can be extended.

Finally, it is interesting to note that all formal acts and ceremonies carried out by the nun's order can be done only by the nuns themselves; neither novices nor probationers can participate. Thus, the difference between a novice and a probationer appears to be only formal. This can also be deduced from the way in which the novice and the probationer are admitted into the order: the admission ceremony of a probationer – by means of a formal act consisting of a motion, three propositions, and a conclusion (*jñapticaturtha karman/ñatticatutthakamma*) – is much more elaborate than the procedure for the going forth of a novice, for which no formal act is required. Thus, we can conclude that because the rights and the duties of novices and of probationers are the same, no essential difference exists between the position of novice and that of probationer except, probably, in terms of social rank in the order, given the importance attached to the admission ceremony of a probationer. Finally, at the age of 20, after two years of study as a probationer, a woman can receive ordination and become a nun. An exception is allowed for married women: they can become probationers at the age of ten and can receive ordination when they are only 12 years old.

As was the case with the monk's order, rules for the nun's order were not formed in a day. For example, the probationary period is clearly the result of a gradual development. It was introduced only after the order of nuns already had existed for some time. Nevertheless, once introduced this probationary

A Korean nun protesting an attempt by the head of the Chogye Order to stand for a third term, at Chogye-sa Monastery, Seoul, South Korea. Photo courtesy of John Powers

period rapidly became a necessary condition to become a nun. The creation itself of the order of nuns did not lack for difficulties. According to the vinayas the idea of an order of nuns arose when Mahaprajapati Gautami (Mahāpajāpatī Gotamī), Buddha's stepmother, together with 500 Shakya (Śākya) women, asked Buddha for permission to go forth and become a nun. At first Buddha refused. Nevertheless, Mahaprajapati did not acquiesce. Having cut off her hair and wearing a monk's robe, she later went to see Buddha again and, together with the 500 Shakya women, wept outside the monastery where he was staying. When the disciple Ananda (Ānanda) saw the women, he decided to help them convince Buddha. At first Buddha refused again. However, when Ananda asked him whether women have the capacities to become an arhat, he answered in the affirmative and thus conceded that women can attain the same goal as men. After Ananda again asked him to allow the women to go forth, he finally agreed to it, provided that the women accepted eight fundamental rules (*garudhamma/gurudharma*) that make the nun's order depend on the monk's order. This attitude of Buddha is said to correspond to conditions in the lay community, where women clearly depend on men.

The eight fundamental rules for nuns differ slightly from vinaya to vinaya. The following is limited to the most essential differences:

1) Although a nun may have been ordained for 100 years, she must rise up from her seat when she sees a newly ordained monk, then pay obeisance to him, and offer him a place to sit.
2) A nun may not reproach a monk by asserting that he has disregarded morality, right views, or right behavior.
3) A nun may not punish a monk or prevent him from joining in the ceremonies of the order. A nun may not admonish a monk, whereas a monk may admonish a nun.
   Or: the nuns should ask for the date of the *Poshadha* (*[U]poṣadha/Uposatha*) ceremony, held every two weeks, during which the precepts are recited; they should also ask the monks for instruction.
   Or: the nuns should ask the monks for instruction in the three jewels (*sūtra /sutta*, *vinaya*, and *abhidharma/ abhidhamma*).
   Or: a nun may not receive gifts before these gifts have been presented to a monk.
4) After a woman as a probationer has been trained in the six rules for two years, the ordination ceremony must be carried out in both orders (i.e., first in the nun's order and next in the monk's order).
5) When a nun commits a *sanghavashesha* (*saṃghāvaśeṣa/ saṃghādisesa*) offense – one that leads to a temporary suspension from the order – she must undergo the *manatva* (*mānatva/mānatta*) penance (which involves paying a kind of ceremonial homage to the order) in both orders (i.e., in both the nun's and the monk's order) during half a month.
6) Every two weeks the nuns must ask the monks for instruction (in the eight fundamental rules, or vinaya).
   or: a nun may not address a monk (to ask questions).
7) The nuns cannot spend the rain retreat in a place where no monks are present.
8) At the end of the rain retreat, the nuns must carry out the Invitation (*Pravāraṇā/Pavāraṇā*) ceremony – during which every monk (nun) invites his (her) fellow monks (nuns) to point out his (her) wrongs, if any, whether seen, or heard, or suspected – in the monk's order as well.

As far as Mahaprajapati Gautami and the 500 Shakya women are concerned, their acceptance of these rules carried the same value as an ordination. However, some of these rules cannot have been applied to the first Buddhist nuns, as at the moment when Mahaprajapati accepted the rules no nun's order yet existed. Several rules came into force only after the establishment of this order. Although Buddha thus agreed to the creation of a nun's order, he was concerned about this new situation and predicted that, because of this, the doctrine would last only for 500 years. This statement is seen mostly as a warning of the risks involved in the creation of a nun's order. Presumably, Buddha was worried about a possibly negative reaction of the lay community.

This is how the order of nuns came into existence. However, in the Theravāda (Theravāda) countries the order has died out. Because ordinations of new nuns must be carried out in both the nun's and the monk's order and because no Theravāda nuns are in existence, the order of nuns cannot be restored. When exactly the order died out cannot yet be said with certainty, but it might have been in the fifth century A.D. In China the first nun (Zhu Jingjian) was ordained in the middle of the fourth century. However, the fact that this ordination, in the absence of an order of nuns in China, could not take place before a twofold community (monks and nuns) led to a discussion of whether this ordination was valid. This discussion continued until, around 433, when a large group of nuns was reordained, this time in the presence of an order of nuns (represented by nuns of Sri Lanka). This ordination might have been based on the rules of the *Dharmaguptakavinaya*. Until today this vinaya is still practiced in China, Korea, and Vietnam. The Tibetan tradition has no full ordination for women.

ANN HEIRMAN

See also Gender Studies: Buddhist Perspectives; Labdron, Machig; Mahāpajāpatī Gotamī; Regulations: Buddhist Perspectives; Saṅgha; Ten-Precept Mothers as Theravādin Nuns

Further Reading

Hirakawa, Akira, in collaboration with Zenno Ikuno and Paul Groner, *Monastic Discipline for the Buddhist Nuns: An English Translation of the Chinese Text of the Mahāsāṃghika-Bhikṣuṇī-Vinaya*, Patna: Kashi Prasad Jayaswal Research Institute, 1982

Horner, Isaline Blew, *Women under Primitive Buddhism: Laywomen and Almswomen*, New York: Dutton, 1930

Hüsken, Ute, *Die Vorschriften für die buddhistische Nonnengemeinde im Vinaya-Piṭaka der Theravādin*, Berlin: Reimer, 1997
Nolot, Edith, *Règles de discipline des nonnes bouddhistes, le bhikṣuṇīvinaya de l'école Mahāsāṃghika-Lokottaravādin*, Paris: Collège de France, 1991
Paul, Diana, *Women in Buddhism: Images of the Feminine in Mahāyāna Tradition*, Berkeley, California: Asian Humanities Press, 1979
Tsai, Kathryn Ann, *Lives of the Nuns: Biographies of Chinese Buddhist Nuns from the Fourth to the Sixth Centuries*, Honolulu: University of Hawaii Press, 1994
Waldschmidt, Ernst, *Bruchstücke des Bhikṣuṇī-Prātimokṣa der Sarvāstivādins, mit einer Darstellung der Überlieferung des Bhikṣuṇī-Prātimokṣa in den verschiedenen Schulen*, Leipzig: Deutsche Morgenländische Gesellschaft, 1926
Wijayaratna, Môhan, *Les moniales bouddhistes, naissance et développement du monachisme féminin*, Paris: Éditions du Cerf, 1991

Rules, Christian. *See* Governance: Christian Perspectives; Regulations: Christian Perspectives

Russia: History

The monastic tradition of medieval Muscovy and modern Russia traces its origins to the Kyivan Caves Monastery in the 11th-century principality of Kyivan Rus' and its two outstanding figures, St. Anthony and St. Theodosius. After repeated sackings by the Tatars in the 13th century, Kyiv was reduced to virtually total ruin, and the Metropolitan See of Kyiv was moved northward to Vladimir and then, in the early 14th century, to Moscow.

In the latter part of the 14th century, monasticism in Muscovy took a significant new turn with the emergence of a movement of hermit monks (*pustinniki*). Breaking with the preceding cenobitic tradition of Theodosius and possibly drawing on contemporary Hesychast trends at Mount Athos, it began to cover the northern territory with a network of hermitages (*skiti*). Small communities of several monks, they became the source of an intense spiritual renewal. The movement produced a significant heritage of hagiography and iconography.

The central figure of the new, Slavic "desert fathers" was St. Sergius of Radonezh (1314–1392). After a sojourn at the monastery in Khotkovo, Sergius took up the solitary life in a forest near Radonezh. Combining manual labor with prayer and scripture reading and a sanctified coexistence with wild animals not unlike that of St. Francis of Assisi (1181/82–1226), he achieved a special sense of unity with all creation. Eventually other monks joined him, and a community was formed, for which Sergius adapted the Rule of the Stoudios Monastery. Ordained a priest he became *hegumen* of the new monastery of the Holy Trinity.

Outer wall, Monastery of the Caves, near Pskov, Russia, 16th century.
Photo courtesy of Robert E. Jones

The community grew, and so did its wealth, but Sergius managed to maintain austerity for himself and the others. Rather than accept a nomination as metropolitan of Moscow, Sergius endeared himself to the people by sending two monks to pray at the battlefield at Kulikovo, where the forces of Dimitri Donskoi won a key battle against the Mongols (1380).

In the next two centuries, the pattern set by the Lavra of the Holy Trinity would be repeated many times. A solitary monk would leave the world, only to be joined by others; the hermitage would grow into a full-fledged monastery, sponsoring cultural and philanthropic activities: hospices, libraries, iconography, and agriculture. Yet again a disciple would leave the monastery in order to establish another hermitage, which would become the seed of a new monastic community. This rapid growth of monasticism generated great creativity in theological reflection and religious art – manifested in the churches in Vladimir and Suzdal, the icons of Rublev and Theophan the Greek and monastic liturgical chant.

In the middle of the 16th century, Russian monasticism endured a confrontation between two opposing views of the monastic, and indeed the Christian, life. The individualism of Nilus of Sora's mystical way stood in sharp contrast to a sometimes authoritarian collectivism within the theocratic ideal of Joseph of Volokolamsk.

In Nilus of Sora (1433–1508), a previously little-known current of Russian Hesychasm acquired an eloquent representative. In his *skit* the spiritual life was centered on a specific form of

Two Churches, Holy Trinity–St. Sergius Monastery, Sergeyev Posad (Zagorsk), Russia, 16th century.
Photo courtesy of Robert E. Jones

prayer – the constant invocation of the name of Jesus – and on uncompromising opposition to the inordinate accumulation of wealth. At a synod in Moscow in 1503, Nilus vigorously attacked a proposal to enrich the monasteries. In his view their spiritual integrity was challenged whenever they came into possession of villages, but it was nourished whenever they upheld the principles of solitude and living from the fruits of their labor. However, Nilus was no match for the political clout of the influential *hegumen* Joseph of Volokolamsk, whose side won the day at the synod. Persecuted after Nilus' death, his followers retreated northward, where they continued to live according to his teachings.

The Josephist stream took the reins of Russian monasticism, imposing what some have interpreted as a shift toward legalism and cold ritualism. However, Joseph's vision was not without its own elements of authenticity. The well-to-do monastery's food was regularly distributed to the poor. The monks had no possessions of their own, and their austere lives were truly laborious. Under Joseph's leadership a new breed of monks and bishops emerged; they won respect from others through a particular blend of ascetic rigor and paternalism. Upholding Muscovite patriotism and the theocratic rule of the czar and also forging the myth of Moscow as the "Third Rome," they played a significant role in shaping spiritual and political consciousness.

The 18th century is generally regarded as a period of decline in Russian monasticism. Peter the Great (1689–1725) considered monks as opponents of his policy of Westernization, although for reasons of state interest he founded the Lavra of St. Alexander Nevski on the outskirts of his new capital city. During the subsequent reign of Catherine II (1762–1796), monastic properties were nationalized, abbots were taken into the civil service, and many monks were forcibly enlisted into the armed forces.

In the midst of these ordeals, seeds were sown for monastic renewal in the next century. The return to mystical, charismatic monasticism can be traced to the Ukrainian starets, Paisy Velichkovsky (1722–1794). Enrolled at the Kyivan Academy, Paisy eventually left the school and, after extensive travels to monasteries throughout Ukraine, Poland, and Bessarabia, settled at Mount Athos, where he was tonsured as a monk. Reading extensively, he was inspired by ascetic and mystical writings, including those of Nilus of Sora. A number of like-minded Moldavian monks joined him and took steps to organize a mode of life according to Nilus' teaching. Together with Paisy they established a monastic community in Moldavia. A strong adherent of the Jesus Prayer in the Russian and Athonite Hesychast tradition, Paisy balanced the cenobitic life with liturgical prayer. Under his guidance the community pursued a regulated lifestyle of manual or intellectual labor and common or private prayer adjusted in relation to personal and seasonal rhythms. Paisy restored the ancient function of the "spiritual father" and extended this ministry to monks and visitors alike. Despite a voluminous correspondence and a treatise on spiritual prayer, Paisy is perhaps best remembered for his Slavonic translation of the Greek Philokalia, an extensive anthology of mystical works published in Venice in 1782. In the Slavonic translation (Dobrotolubie, Moscow, 1793–), Russian monastic spirituality received a new lease on life.

This spiritual renewal first came out into the open with the prophetic figure of Seraphim of Sarov (1759–1833), a proponent of life in the Holy Spirit. At the end of a life of prayer and complete reclusion, Seraphim received masses of people who began to flock to the monastery at Sarov. His esoteric teaching centered on the need to become attuned to the indwelling of the Spirit in the human soul.

Also in the 19th century, the startsi of the hermitage at Optina exerted an influence that permeated the social fabric of Russia: Leonid (1768–1841), a monk of peasant origin, ministered especially to the poor, and Makarius (1788–1860), an erudite contemplative, spread the teachings of Paisy and published a biography of the starets; Ambrose (1812–1891), the "starets of the active life," took an ardent interest in all forms of human endeavor. By the end of the 19th century, many Russian writers and philosophers had visited Optina: Gogol, Dostoevsky, Soloviev, Tolstoi, and others. The starets tradition produced a number of outstanding theologians (Filaret of Moscow and Archimandrite Theodore Bukharev) and missionaries (Herman of Alaska, Nicholas of Japan, and Innocent of Moscow). Inspired by the ancient figure of the spiritual father, the starets was a monk who renounced all ties to the world in order to devote his entire life to progress toward divine peace. His radical separation included also the charism of dedicated service to others as a spiritual father. Originally a principle binding an experienced monk with a novice, spiritual fatherhood was later extended to some laypeople. In modern Russia great masses of people turned to the starets for his advice and benediction. As a broadly based social phenomenon, the starets tradition was thus a potent vehicle for a concrete and very personal witness to the salvific light of love and hope in the gospel message.

Although Russian women's monasteries flourished from the period of Muscovy onward, few records remain. Our knowledge of their silent apostolate is limited to their work in the social sphere (assistance to unwed girls and to widows), to accounts of aristocratic founders (Anna Kachinskaia), and to personalities such as Iuliana Lazarevskaia and Princess Evdokia Urusova. The startsi supported women's monasticism: Seraphim of Sarov maintained close ties with the sisters at Diveevo, while Ambrose

Former refectory (Trapeznaia), now a church, Holy Trinity–St. Sergius Monastery, Sergeyev Posad (Zagorsk), Russia, 16th century.
Photo courtesy of Robert E. Jones

Tomb of Tsar Boris Godunov (1598–1605), Holy Trinity–St. Sergius Monastery, Sergeyev Posad (Zagorsk), Russia, 17th century.
Photo courtesy of Robert E. Jones

of Optina was a spiritual father to the sisters at Chamordino. On the eve of the Revolution (1917), women's monasticism in Russia was numerically and qualitatively strong. After the Revolution women's monasteries generally fared better in the emigration than their male counterparts.

The Soviet regime's persecution of religion was especially thorough with regard to monasticism. By 1920, of 1,105 monasteries of the former Russian Empire, only 352 remained. By 1929 all had been closed. Monks in the thousands are believed to have died in the gulag, whereas many others were dispersed. After World War II, the Soviet Union occupied a number of territories, notably western Ukraine, with 104 monastic institutions. Here too antireligious policies ensured a steady decline: 90 monasteries and convents operated in the 1950s. By 1961 their number was down to 40 and in 1977 to 16. Of these only one was in the Russian republic (the Holy Trinity Monastery at Zagorsk).

A few exceptions to the overall decline under Soviet rule provided continuity and hope for the future. For a time Holy Trinity Monastery at Zagorsk was the only monastery on the territory of the former Russian Empire that was permitted to reopen and function. With a community of around 100 monks in the 1980s, the monastery became a popular pilgrimage center. Accessible to tourists even then, it benefited from working relations with the nearby seminary and academy. The Monastery of the Caves in Pechory near Pskov was the only Russian Orthodox monastery never to have been closed. Because of a change in political administration in 1918, the monastery found itself within the territory of the newly formed republic of Estonia. With a community estimated at between 60 and 100 monks, the monastery was also a popular pilgrimage center. The Danilov Monastery (13th century), the oldest in Moscow, was returned to the patriarchate in 1983 in order to permit restoration and rebuilding of the entire monastery complex. Targeted for completion in 1988, the project included plans for a new patriarchal residence, accommodations for departments of the Holy Synod, and a conference hall. As for the starets tradition, little is known about its fate in the Soviet era, although the ministry of Archmandrite Tavrion (Batozsky, 1898–1978) has been noted. Despite some 27 years of exile in Siberian labor camps, he carried on his spiritual ministry in various corners of the Soviet Union. Appointed confessor to the Transfiguration Hermitage at the convent in Riga in 1968, he was renowned as an exceptionally inspiring preacher and holy man, drawing pilgrimages in the tens of thousands.

Subsequent developments in post-Soviet Russia have seen an unprecedented revival of religious life in general and of monasticism in particular. The rapid and multifaceted processes of change have opened up unexpected opportunities for the future of monasticism and many new challenges, including the question of the place of traditional monastic values in a postmodern world. Thus far monasticism in Russia appears to have resisted the kinds of revisions that have been made by monastics in the West. Time will tell whether rootedness in the spiritual heritage of Russia will become an increasingly characteristic feature of this monasticism or whether creative ways will be found to remain attentive to and serve the spiritual needs of the world. No doubt as with so many other East European communities, the Russian monasteries of the Western diaspora can and will be counted on for many forms of support.

ANDRII S. KRAWCHUK

See also Archaeology: Russia; Architecture: Eastern Christian Monasteries; Bulgaria; Elders, Russian Monastic (Startsi); Hagiography: Eastern Christian; Isaac the Syrian (Isaac of Nineveh), St.; Kiev (Kyiv), Ukraine; Libraries: Eastern Christian; Maximus the Greek, St.; Mount Athos, Greece; Nilus of Sora, St.; Orthodox Monasticism: Slavic; Paisy Velichkovsky; Philokalia; Pilgrimages, Christian: Eastern Europe; Seasons, Liturgical: Eastern Christian; Seraphim of Sarov, St.; Sergius of Radonezh, St.; Theology, Eastern Christian; Ukraine; Visual Arts, Eastern Christian: Painting; Women's Monasteries: Eastern Christian

Further Reading

Behr-Sigel, Élizabeth, "Le monachisme russe," in *La Russie: Histoire des mouvements spirituels* (Dictionnaire de spiritualité, 14), edited by Gerhard Podskalsky, Paris: Beauchesne, 1990

Denisov, L.I., *Pravoslavnye Monastyri Rossiiskoi imperii*, Moscow: Stupina, 1908

Ellis, Jane, "Monasticism," in her *The Russian Orthodox Church: A Contemporary History* (Keston Book, number 22), Bloomington: Indiana University Press, and London: Croom Helm, 1986

Fedotov, George P., *The Russian Religious Mind*, volume 2: *The Middle Ages; The Thirteenth to the Fifteenth Centuries*, edited by John Meyendorff, Cambridge, Massachusetts: Harvard University Press, 1966

Florovsky, Georges, *Ways of Russian Theology* (Collected Works of Georges Florovsky, volume 5), Belmont, Massachusetts: Nordland, 1979

The Life of Paisij Velychkovs'kyj (Harvard Library of Early Ukrainian Literature, volume 4), translated by Jeffrey Featherstone, introduced by Anthony-Emil N. Tachaios, Cambridge, Massachusetts: Harvard University Press for the Ukrainian Research Institute of Harvard University, 1989

Spidlík, Tomás, *I Grandi Mistici Russi*, Rome: Città Nuova Editrice, 1977; 2nd edition, 1983

Russia: Recent Changes

Monasteries have always played a crucial role in the history of the Russian Orthodox Church. Throughout many centuries they have been centers of spiritual life and enlightenment for people. Miracle-working icons and shrines located in monasteries have attracted thousands of pilgrims. After the revolution of 1917, all Russian monasteries were closed, and many were completely destroyed. After World War II some were reopened, but their life was kept under strict control by the Communist state. In the mid-1980s the Russian Orthodox Church had 18 monasteries (most of them outside the Russian Federation).

Social and political changes of the late 1980s exerted a direct impact on the religious situation in general and on Orthodox monastic life in particular. The state began to return monastery buildings to the Church. The number of monasteries has grown steadily and by the end of the 20th century hovers around 500. In Moscow alone four monasteries and four convents have been reopened.

An average of ten monks or nuns live in each Russian monastery. The immense task of restoration of monastic life falls on their shoulders. It is monks and nuns who rebuild churches and houses that had been reduced to ruins, and it is monks and nuns who paint icons and frescoes, who organize a monastery's economy, and who receive hundreds and even thousands of pilgrims. Daily church services, usually quite long, are also conducted by monks and nuns.

Restoration of monastic life cannot proceed without serious problems. Many of the monastery buildings that are now being returned to the Church were previously used as prisons, military barracks, orphanages, warehouses, or vegetable stores. Returning these buildings to their proper condition is not an easy task. In most cases monks themselves have to raise money without any support from the state. The famous Solovetsky monastery on the White Sea serves as a good example. During the Soviet era the vast territory of the monastery was used as a prison where thousands of prisoners, including monks, priests, and bishops, faced death. When the monastic property was returned to the Church, it was in wretched condition, and monks began to restore it with the help of countless volunteers and pilgrims. After a decade of hard work, the process of restoration is still far from complete.

In better condition are monasteries that the Soviets used as museums: the state took care of their maintenance. However, when these monasteries are returned to the Church, problems often arise on the part of museum authorities who are unwilling to give property back to its legitimate owners.

In many monasteries ancient church art is being restored: the Znamenny chant is being sung at church services, and icons are being painted according to old Russian or Byzantine patterns. The most famous among contemporary icon painters is Archimandrite Zinon (Teodor), formerly a monk of Pskov-Caves monastery, who now lives in solitude in the Pskov district.

Several monasteries and convents run printing houses where religious literature is being published. In particular the publishing house of the Novospassky monastery in Moscow has published a six-volume collection of the Acts of the Local Council of 1917–1918 that had long been a rarity. The Zachatyevsky convent in Moscow has produced dozens of books, among them the Russian translation of newly discovered texts of St. Isaac the

Tourists in 1986 at Holy Trinity–St. Sergius Monastery, Sergeyev Posad (Zagorsk), 16th century.
Photo courtesy of Robert E. Jones

Syrian (d. c. 700). Some monasteries and convents publish periodicals and newspapers.

Many monasteries and convents are involved in social and charity work. Monastic communities often minister to hospitals, orphanages, and prisons. In particular the monks of the famous Holy Trinity–St. Sergius Lavra regularly visit the local prison, talk to its inhabitants, and perform sacraments. The Varnavinsky monastery in Vladimir diocese has close links with the local military garrison, whose soldiers help restore the monastery. Some monasteries provide shelter and food for the homeless and beggars.

A close connection exists between monasteries and theological schools of the Russian Orthodox Church. At many theological schools the executive positions – those of rector, pro-rector, and inspector – are held by monks. There are also quite a few monks among teaching staff. Moreover some of the seminaries are situated near monasteries. The students have an opportunity to seek spiritual guidance from monks, to attend monastic divine services, and to experience directly the age-old tradition of Orthodox monasticism. Some of the students themselves take monastic vows on graduation from a seminary or an academy.

A characteristic trait of many contemporary Russian monasteries is the youthfulness of their inhabitants. Even abbots are often chosen from among monks who are still in their 20s. During the last decade of the 20th century, Russian monasticism in general became visibly younger. Positive by itself, this phenomenon in some cases can have negative repercussions. In particular some newly opened monasteries have no experienced spiritual directors able to guide the spiritual health of the younger brotherhood. Occasionally vows are taken by immature people, sometimes even teenagers, who subsequently realize that monasticism is not their real vocation. The number of people who have left monasticism and returned to the world markedly increased in the 1990s.

Because experienced spiritual directors, or startsi (elders), can by no means be found in every monastery, those monasteries where startsi live become centers of pilgrimage: thousands of people come for spiritual counseling. Most famous and respected among contemporary spiritual directors are Archimandrite Kirill (Pavlov) of the Holy Trinity–St. Sergius Lavra and Archimandrite Ioann (Krestyankin) of the Pskov-Caves Monastery. Their authority among believers is extraordinarily high.

The main task of monks has always been prayer. A monk prays not only for himself but also for his neighbor and for the whole world. Living outside the world a monk does not forget his fellow humans but in the silence of his cell prays for them. A 20th-century Russian ascetic, St. Silouan of Mount Athos, says, "A monk is someone who prays for the whole world, who weeps for the whole world; and in this lies his main work. . . . Thanks to monks, prayer continues unceasing on earth, and the whole world profits. . . . Perhaps you will say that nowadays there are no monks like that, who would pray for the whole world; but I tell you that when there are no men of prayer on the earth, the world will come to an end."

HILARION ALFEYEV

See also Archaeology: Russia; Isaac the Syrian (Isaac of Nineveh), St.; Libraries: Eastern Christian; Moscow, Russia; Mount Athos, Greece; Orthodox Monasticism: Slavic; Russia: History; Social Services: Eastern Christian; Ukraine

Further Reading

Ellis, Jane, *The Russian Orthodox Church: A Contemporary History*, Bloomington: Indiana University Press, and London: Croom Helm, 1986

Ellis, Jane, *The Russian Orthodox Church: Triumphalism and Defensiveness*, London: Macmillan, and New York: St. Martin's Press, 1996

Pile, Emily, "Prospects for a Third Wave of Russian Monasticism," *Report on the USSR* 1:31 (1989)

Steeves, Paul D., editor, *The Modern Encyclopedia of Religions in Russia and the Soviet Union*, 7 vols., Gulf Breeze, Florida: Academic International Press, 1988–

Tretyakov, Andrei, "Siberian Convent," *Frontier* (November/December 1991)

Russia: Sites

In Russia proper, which before the Tatar invasion of 1237–1240 was the northeastern part of the old Kievan Rus, two stages of monastic development can be distinguished. Before the second half of the 14th century, Russian monasticism followed the Kievan model: abbeys were located in the vicinity of big cities, sometimes even within their walls, and they were founded by princes and princesses, bishops, or aristocratic families. The cenobitic rule, introduced in the famous Kievan Caves monastery (established c. 1051–1074, as an exception, by monks themselves), was largely mitigated or ignored: monks and nuns of higher extraction kept personal belongings with them and sometimes took an active part in the administration of their family estates. Although a few foundations might have been endowed with villages, fiscal privileges, and judicial immunities (as early as the 12th century in Novgorod), monastic landowning as a whole was not significant.

In the second half of the 14th and during the 15th century, following the example of St. Sergius of Radonezh (c. 1322–1392), a new generation of founders transformed Russian monastic life. They were monks who took the initiative of creating new abbeys "in the desert," far away from the cities. It appears that they often benefited from the support of a prince or a bishop and that the place they chose was not quite as isolated as it seems in the Vita cliché. Indeed the movement of foundations accompanied a colonization effort, around Moscow itself and to the north, following some of the main waterways (the Sheksna, Kostroma, Vychegda, and Northern Dvina basins). More than 150 new monasteries appeared between 1350 and 1400, and in the first half of the 15th century monasticism reached the White Sea with the foundation of the Solovki abbey. These monasteries were novel for another reason. Following again the example of Sergius' Trinity abbey (c. 1356), they adopted a strict cenobitic rule that imbued them with a strong sense of community. During a time of distress (both plague and dynastic war for the Muscovite throne were raging in the first half of the 15th century), they received much landed property that they often increased by an active purchasing policy. They also managed to get considerable fiscal and judicial privileges. The way in which the cult of the saint-founder developed into a local or even national devotion was also crucial for the fortune of each abbey. The Trinity St. Sergius and the Dormition St. Cyrill were major actors in Russian economic life already in the second half of the 15th century; this in turn contributed to their moral and even political authority. One cannot help comparing them with Cluny or Cîteaux for their agricultural, commercial, and even "industrial" role (as in the exploitation of salt and fisheries). Notice the chronological gap: Russia actually experienced its "monastic golden age" during the time of Western Europe's Renaissance and the Reformation. In addition in the 16th century, by building impressive stone (brick) compounds, major Russian abbeys acquired new, ambiguous purposes. A monastery such as the Trinity St. Sergius was at once a pilgrimage site, a treasury of Russian art and agriculture, a strategic fortress, and a state prison for disgraced bishops or boyars.

Monastic property reached unprecedented size in Russia between the late Middle Ages and the 18th century. It has been overestimated (at up to a third of the Russian soil in the 16th century, according to English Protestant observers, hostile to Church wealth), but it must have represented between at least a fifth and a fourth of the landed property in central Russia around 1551. At that time the Stoglav (Hundred Chapters) council forbade any more acquisitions, and this ban was confirmed many times, but in vain. The Russian state took effective steps toward controlling ecclesiastic wealth only in 1649, when it published a new code, the *Sobornoe Ulozhenie* (Assembly's Establishment). It inaugurated a "monastic bureau" in charge of ecclesiastical lands until 1676 and again from 1700 to 1721. This was followed by the bureaucratization of the Church under Peter the Great (1689–1725) (complete with measures against "superfluous" monks) and by the full secularization of ecclesiastical property in 1764 under Catherine the Great (1762–1796). By that time the empress had ordered the closure of 411 men's monasteries and 52 nunneries, representing more than half the existing regular communities.

Cathedral of the Dormition, Monastery of the Caves, near Pskov, Russia, 15th century. This monastery survived Communist rule unscathed. Photo courtesy of Robert E. Jones

Meanwhile for about two centuries, between 1666 and 1855, the most vivid monastic culture in Russia was that of the Old Believers, who resisted the ecclesiastical reforms initiated by Patriarch Nikon (1652–1658). Condemned as schismatics (*raskol'niki*) and persecuted, they took "to the desert" and created large brotherhoods in the north (along the Vyg River near Olonets), around Irgiz (northeast of Saratov), in the Kerzhenets region (north of Nizhnii-Novgorod), and near the Polish border (Starodub'e). These communities endured much hardship, for the authorities denied them the status of abbeys. Finally most of them were done away with by order of Emperor Nicholas I (1825–1855). Roughly at the same time, monastic spirituality experienced a certain revival within the official Church. Its symbol is the hermitage of Optina (Kaluga region, southwest of Moscow), where members of the Slavophile intelligentsia met the charismatic figure of the holy starets, popularized by

Fortified wall, Holy Trinity–St. Sergius Monastery, Sergeyev Posad (Zagorsk), Russia, 16th century.
Photo courtesy of Robert E. Jones

Dostoevsky's novel *Brat'ia Karamazovy* (1880; *The Brothers Karamazov*).

The atheist campaigns, launched in 1920 by the Bolshevik regime, brought the enforced closure of all the monastic communities in Russia. By that time some important archaeological and historical studies were being conducted on the sites and gave a promising start to Soviet history of arts and architecture, but the essential goal was total liquidation of religious culture. As a consequence even the "preserved" museum sites suffered severe degradation. Between 1946 and 1988 the Soviet government returned some buildings to monastic life while keeping it under strict control. Under Perestroika and after the collapse of the Soviet Union, the state has ostentatiously given many monasteries back to the Church. Satisfactory compromises are yet to be found between the patrimonial and the religious vocation of the famous ones.

Monasteries to Visit

Despite the Bolshevik destruction, monasteries corresponding to the various types described can be seen in Russia and are among the finest architectural landmarks of the country. Their historic treasures (archives) and artistic treasures (icons, books, and embroideries) have often been seized, sometimes as early as the 18th century, so that most of them reside in the main libraries and museums of St. Petersburg and Moscow. Still some local collections are quite rich.

One of the oldest Novgorodian monasteries, St. George's (Iur'ev monastyr'), was founded on the left bank of the Volkhov River in 1119. Its abbey-church dates back to that time and keeps fragments of frescoes. Ivan the Terrible (1533–1584) took with him the venerated icons of the Savior and of St. George when he devastated Novgorod during the "emergency rule" known as the *oprichnina* period (1570). They can be seen in Moscow's Dormition cathedral. Near Pskov, the Caves monastery of Pechory, dedicated to the Dormition (Pskovo-Pecherskii Sviato-Uspenskii, founded c. 1450), shows impressive fortifications of the 16th century. Indeed it had strategic importance during the Time of Troubles (1598–1613).

The major cenobitic abbey "in the desert" is Trinity–St. Sergius, located about 50 miles north of Moscow. Founded around 1342, in the 15th century it was already one of the largest ecclesiastic landowners in Russia. In 1764 it possessed 106,500 "souls." By that time it had been promoted to the rank of *lavra* (1744), an honorific title that it shared only with the Kievan Caves monastery and, later, St. Alexander Nevskii's abbey in St. Petersburg and the Dormition monastery of Pochaev (Volhynia). This favor was due to the popularity of the Trinity's founder, St. Sergius of Radonezh, who was considered the protector of the Muscovite dynasty and of the Russian nation. The monastery played a vital patriotic role by resisting the siege of Polish troops between September 1608 and January 1610 at a time when the Russian state seemed on the verge of collapse. The

Domenico Trezzini, courtyard, Alexander Nevskii Lavra, St. Petersburg, Russia, 18th century. Fyodor Dostoevsky and Pyotr Tchaikovsky are buried at this monastery.
Photo courtesy of Robert E. Jones

Trinity abbey-church was built between 1422 and 1427. On this occasion the monk Andrei Rublev painted his masterpiece, the Trinity icon, now on display in Tretiakov Gallery (Moscow). The monastic compound covers a very large area, with buildings dating from the 15th to the 19th century, including the Moscow Theological Academy, which was transferred there in 1814.

Another famous cenobitic abbey is the Dormition St. Cyrill near Beloozero (the White Lake, 275 miles north of Moscow), founded in 1397 by Cyrill (d. 1427), a follower of Sergius' example. This abbey became quite wealthy but still managed to keep a reputation for austerity. In its vicinity other communities sprouted, such as St. Therapont (founded by a companion of Cyrill), famous for splendid frescoes in the Nativity of the Virgin abbey-church, painted in 1502–1503 by the monk Denis. There were also little hermitages (*skity*, *pustyni*), such as the one founded by Nilus of Sora (1433–1508), a revered ascetic and religious moralist.

Further north the Transfiguration of the Savior on Solovki Island in the White Sea was founded around 1459. The Solovki community became the main landlord of the White Sea region (Pomor'e) and developed a strong identity, sometimes proving rebellious toward Muscovite authority. It venerated its founders, Savvatios (d. c. 1462) and Zosima (d. 1478), and also Abbot Philip (Kolychev), who was chosen as metropolitan of the Russian Church (1566–1568). He was soon deposed and assassinated by order of Ivan the Terrible. In 1657 the elders of Solovki refused the new reformed liturgy of Patriarch Nikon. They did not budge even after a Church council (1666–1667) confirmed these reforms. In 1668 Czar Alexis (1645–1676) ordered Solovki to be taken by force, but it took almost eight years of siege to break its resistance, and the capture of the abbey-fortress was followed by a massacre. Then and only then did it revert to "normality." In 1920 Solovki became the first camp of political prisoners of the Bolshevik regime, the first island of the Gulag Archipelago.

The monastery of the Resurrection or New-Jerusalem (Voskresenskii Novoierusalimskii) was founded by Patriarch Nikon, and its abbey-church was built as a replica of the Holy Sepulchre (1658–1685). It is located near Istra, southwest of Moscow. In it were collected many important manuscripts, such as the so-called Resurrection Chronicle, a major historiographical achievement of the mid–16th century.

In St. Petersburg, Peter the Great started to build a monastery as early as 1710. It was dedicated to St. Alexander Nevskii

(1236–1263), who as prince of Novgorod had defeated a Swedish army in 1240. At the time Peter was engaged in a long-lasting war against Sweden. By 1764 the abbey possessed 25,000 souls. It was elevated to the rank of *lavra* in 1797. During the 19th century its cemetery was a favorite place of burial for Russian artists. The other famous monastery of St. Petersburg is the Smolnyi Resurrection Convent. In 1764 an institution for young noble girls was established there, and this became the purveyor of lady companions for the imperial court. The actual building of the institution was reconstructed by G. Quarenghi in 1806–1808. During the Russian Revolution of October 1917, Lenin established his headquarters there. The sites of the Old Believers communities are mostly in ruins, but a vivid picture of the Kerzhenets region around 1840 can be found in the novel *V lesakh* (*In the Forests*) by P.I. Mel'nikov-Pechersky.

PIERRE GONNEAU

See also Archaeology: Russia; Elders, Russian Monastic (Startsi); Kiev (Kyiv), Ukraine; Lavra; Moscow, Russia; Nilus of Sora, St.; Pilgrimages, Christian: Eastern Europe; Ukraine

Further Reading

Budovnits, Isaak U., *Monastyri na Rusi i bor'ba s nimi krest'ian v XIV–XVI velkakh: Po "zhitiiam sviatykh"* (Monasteries in Russia and the Struggle of Peasants Against Them in 14th–16th centuries, According to the Vitae), Moscow: Nauka, 1966

Crummey, Robert O., *The Old Believers and the World of Antichrist: The Vyg Community and the Russian State, 1694–1855*, Madison: University of Wisconsin Press, 1970

Gonneau, Pierre, *La Maison de la Sainte Trinité: Un grand monastère russe du Moyen-âge tardif, 1345–1533*, Paris: Klincksieck, 1993

Lemaître, J.-L., M. Dmitriev, and P. Gonneau, editors, *Moines et monastères dans les sociétés de rite grec et latin*, Geneva: Droz, and Paris: Champion, 1996

Smolitsch, Igor, *Russisches Mönchtum: Entstehung und Wesen, 998–1917*, Würzburg: Augustinus-Verlag, 1953

Zverinskii, V.V., *Material dlia istoriko-topograficheskogo issledovaniia o pravoslavnykh monastyriakh v Rossiiskoi imperii s bibliograficheskim ukazatelem* (Material for a Historico-Topographical Study of the Orthodox Monasteries in the Russian Empire, with a Bibliographical Index), 3 vols., St. Petersburg, 1892

S

Sabas, St. 439–532

Palestinian Christian monk and founder of the Lavra of Mar Saba in Palestine

According to the detailed and reliable *Life of Sabas* (a Cappadocian by birth) by Cyril of Scythopolis (d. c. 525), composed not long after his death, Sabas, after enduring many privations as a solitary and a disciple of Euthymius "the Great" (377–473) in the Judaean wilderness, was joined in 483 by "many of the scattered anchorites and grazers," some from distant lands. For these he discovered a spring and established a *lavra* in the terrible canyon of Wadi Kedron, roughly halfway between Jerusalem and the Dead Sea. In due course he organized at least six other *lavra*s, each functioning as a weekend koinobion from which the brethren dispersed to spend the weekdays in their individual hermitages. In 490 Sabas reluctantly accepted priestly ordination (then rare for monks), and two years later the Patriarch of Jerusalem made him archimandrite ("chief of the fold") responsible for all the monks of Palestine who were not living in koinobia.

Of all Sabas' monastic foundations, it is the *lavra* still bearing his name, Mar Saba, that is most famous. The Lavra of Mar Saba is the last of the ancient monasteries of the Holy Land still surviving as a functioning community. The monks there (who recently regained the physical relics of their founder) still observe the oral tradition of the monastic rule (*typikon*) Sabas bequeathed to them, and still proudly tell the story of their foundation. Today the importance of Mar Saba lies chiefly in its past glory, for it was one of the intellectual and spiritual centers of the Christian East, its extreme isolation notwithstanding. Over the centuries it functioned both as pilgrimage center and as a disseminator of ideals and ideas, monastic and secular. This was particularly true before the rise of Islam when Jerusalem was still more truly the center of the church than any other city and Mar Saba was very much the spiritual and intellectual powerhouse of Jerusalem. Thus, for instance, the liturgical influence of Mar Saba on the early evolution of the Byzantine rite via Jerusalem is clearly discernible. That *lavra*'s predominant role in the sixth-century fight against "Origenism" is a further example of its influential position. Under Muslim domination, Mar Saba pioneered the work of interpreting the Christian tradition in the language of the conqueror (Arabic), thereby probably assuring the survival of Christianity in the conquered lands. Here Cyril of Scythopolis composed his *Lives of the Monks of Palestine* (including St. Sabas'). But most famous of all the significant scholars who worked at Mar Saba is John of Damascus/ibn Mansour (c. 655–c. 750), who, in addition to his better known accomplishment of pioneering what became the Orthodox position concerning the icons, composed some outstanding examples of the Eastern church's amazingly rich hymnography. In *The Fount of Knowledge* he provided the first serious analysis of Islam from a Christian point of view.

JOHN WORTLEY

See also Hagiography: Eastern Christian; Hermits: Eastern Christian; Israel/Palestine; Jerusalem, Israel; Lavra; Libraries: Eastern Christian; Pilgrimages, Christian: Near East

Biography

Born in Cappadocia, Sabas lived as a hermit and monastic in various places before founding the Great Lavra at Mar Saba, Palestine. Known as Wadi en-Nar, his foundation attracted others and is still extant. He was ordained in 490 and appointed superior of all hermits in Palestine in 492. In 530 he traveled to Constantinople to vindicate Palestinian Christians in the eyes of Emperor Justinian. Sabas was a steadfast if irascible upholder of Orthodoxy.

Further Reading

Price, R.M., translator, *Lives of the Monks of Palestine* by Cyril of Scythopolis, with an introduction and notes by John Binns, Kalamazoo, Michigan: Cistercian Publications, 1991

Sacred Topography, Buddhist. *See* Topography, Sacred (Buddhist)

Saichō 767–822

Founder of Tendai Buddhism in Japan

Saichō, known posthumously as Dengyō Daishi, was the founder of Tendai (Chinese, Tiantai/T'ien-t'ai) Buddhism in Japan. After a brief pilgrimage to China in the early ninth century, he returned to Japan to establish the great temple complex on Mount Hiei, northeast of Kyoto, centered around the temple called Enryakuji. Saichō is especially important for his innovations concerning monastic regulations and discipline and for his advocacy of an independent Tendai ordination system, known as the bodhisattva precepts (*bosatsukai*).

Saichō was born in Ōmi province. It is said that his father was a fervent Buddhist. Saichō entered a provincial temple to study Buddhism in 780 at age 13. Five years later he received full ordination at the Tōdaiji ordination platform (*kaidan*). In Saichō's day the Tōdaiji *kaidan* was the only place where one could legally receive full ordination, a regulation tied to government control of the priesthood that Saichō would himself later challenge.

Soon after he was ordained, for reasons that are not entirely clear, Saichō retired to Mount Hiei from 785 to 797 to carry out a religious life of solitude and contemplation. There he studied Buddhist thought and practice, becoming absorbed with Tendai teachings, which were little known in Japan at that time. Tendai is based on the *Lotus Sūtra* – the "One Vehicle" teaching – and the Chinese Tendai founder Zhiyi/Chih-i's explication of these ideas in his *Mohezhiguan* (*Mo-ho chih-kuan*; Japanese, *Maka shikan*, "Great Calming and Contemplation"). Saichō came to view the *Lotus Sūtra* as the ultimate teaching of the Buddha – all other teachings were provisional to the profound truth of the *Lotus Sūtra*. Saichō adopted the Tendai system of classification of the Buddha's teachings, which places the *Lotus Sūtra* at the top of the system as the One Vehicle teaching leading to Buddhahood.

In 794 Saichō's contemplative life on Mount Hiei was forever altered because of the transfer of the capital to Kyoto – a means of diminishing the power of the Nara monastic institutions, which exerted great influence on the imperial court. Mount Hiei was only a short distance to the northeast of the new capital, a location that had geomantic significance. It was believed that evil spirits and other ills came from the northeast, and thus Saichō's fledgling mountain monastery held an important position as insurance against such threats. In 797 Saichō was honored with an appointment as one of ten priests assigned to the imperial court, affording him significantly more extensive exposure to the larger aristocratic and Buddhist world. In 798 he inaugurated an annual series of lectures on the *Lotus Sūtra* for which he earned a reputation as a gifted monk. Subsequent invitations to lecture provided Saichō with the opportunity to promote Tendai doctrine, which he deemed superior to Hossō and other Nara Buddhist school teachings. Through connections made as a result of these activities, Saichō was able to request that two students be sent to China to further study Tendai doctrine. One of those selected was Saichō himself.

In 804 Saichō journeyed to China to deepen his understanding of Buddhist thought and practice, especially Tendai doctrine, through study with Chinese Buddhist masters and to bring back to Japan accurately copied Tendai texts. He spent time at Mount Tiantai/Tien-t'ai – the center of the Chinese Tendai tradition originally established by Zhiyi – and was exposed to an eclectic array of both esoteric and exoteric texts and practices. Significantly he gained broad exposure to esoteric teachings and received initiation into esoteric rituals. He was also instructed on the Mahāyāna bodhisattva precepts.

In Saichō's time the bodhisattva precepts had already become established as a set of vows taken by both monastics and laity to bolster their resolve to faithfully practice the Mahāyāna teachings. Although regarded as secondary precepts that were never intended to replace the full ordination – known as the Four-Part Precepts (Chinese, *sifenlu/ssu fen lü*; Japanese, *shibunritsu*) – for initiation into the monastic life, Saichō later innovated on the bodhisattva precepts and attempted to make them central to ordination rites. That Saichō was involved with monastic rules and precepts used for ordination is not surprising, given his aspirations to ordain monks directly into the Tendai school rather than relying on the authority of the monastic precepts that had traditionally been transmitted at the Tōdaiji ordination platform. For Saichō changes in monastic initiation procedures would advance Tendai's development outside of government restrictions or the supervision of the Nara schools. The struggle over the precepts consumed much of Saichō's life, but he did not secure permission to use the bodhisattva precepts on Mount Hiei as the sole ordination ritual during his lifetime. However, shortly after Saichō's death permission was received from the court, and the bodhisattva precepts replaced the traditional monastic precepts.

On his return to Japan in 805, Saichō carried with him an extensive collection of sūtras and commentaries, both exoteric and esoteric, that became the focus of study and practice at the Enryakuji temple. However, Saichō's monastic aspirations became complicated by issues of imperial patronage. For example, when Saichō returned from Japan, Emperor Kammu (781–806) was very sick. In hopes of effecting a cure, Saichō was called to the imperial palace to recite sūtras and perform esoteric rituals – common strategies for combating disease in the Heian period. Although Saichō supported the study of esoteric Buddhism, his primary interest was in the One Vehicle teaching of the *Lotus Sūtra* and its Tendai interpretations. Firm beliefs then developing among the aristocracy and imperial court concerning the efficacy of esoteric rituals to resolve a variety of crises likely inspired Saichō's use of such rituals to treat Kammu's illness. Here the seeds were sown for the development of Tendai esoteric practice, or Taimitsu.

In 805, Saichō obtained permission – perhaps as a reward for his efforts on Emperor Kammu's behalf – for the Tendai school to receive its first two officially sanctioned ordinands from among the official monastic quota system then in effect. This system was meant to regulate the number of monastics who could be ordained as a way of controlling the power of the monastic community. Of the two annual ordinands, one was to study esoteric practices – the so-called Esoteric Course (*shanagō*), focusing on the study of the Daibirushanakyō (Sanskrit, *Mahāvairocana-sūtra*) – whereas the other was to study exoteric practices, specifically the Tendai meditation practices described in Zhiyi's *Mohezhiguan* and thus known as the Meditation Course (*shikangō*). The allocation of two yearly ordinands signaled the formal acknowledgment of Tendai as a separate Buddhist school. Yet despite the advances achieved in 805, many of Saichō's hopes for rapid acknowledgment of his new school were compromised on the death of his patron, Kammu, in 806.

After Kammu's death, Saichō continued to study esoteric teachings. However, Kūkai (774–836), founder of the Japanese Shingon (esoteric) school, had sojourned to China at the same time as Saichō expressly to study esoteric Buddhism. Kūkai developed an understanding of esoteric practices far deeper than the brief initiation into Shingon that Saichō obtained during his short stay in China. By borrowing esoteric texts and sending Tendai monks to Kūkai for training, Saichō attempted to shore up his deficiencies in esoteric doctrine and ritual. In the end Saichō and Kūkai developed an antagonistic relationship, at least partly because Kūkai began to refuse Saichō's requests to borrow esoteric texts – saying that Saichō could not understand their profundity without further knowledge of esoteric practice – and because some of Saichō's disciples left him permanently to become Kūkai's disciples. It was only with Saichō's later disciples that a Tendai tradition of esoteric practices came to dominate Kūkai's own Shingon esoteric school. Despite Saichō's fitful relationship to Shingon, he continued to promote a combination of exoteric and esoteric teachings, although he regarded esoteric practices as largely supplementary to a primary focus on the *Lotus Sūtra* and other exoteric texts.

Saichō's achievements were twofold: he defended his new denomination against its detractors, especially those attacks originating with Hossō and other traditional Nara schools, and he worked to secure new monastic regulations to be applied to Tendai. Initially Saichō had studied the doctrines of the Hossō school, which taught, in part, that the potential for anyone to attain Buddhahood depended on individual abilities, and that attainment of Buddhahood was an impossibility for the most wicked people. Tendai teachings offered a significant alternative view: all sentient beings have the innate potential to become enlightened in their present lifetime. Even plants and trees, it was said, had the Buddha nature and thus could attain Buddhahood.

Saichō, in defense of Tendai, debated monks from other Buddhist denominations. A series of doctrinal debates with Tokuitsu, a Hossō monk, is among the most famous. The Saichō-Tokuitsu debates concerned such issues as how to classify Buddhist teachings (a problem also central to Zhiyi's Tendai system), the nature of Tendai doctrine, and, most especially, the issue of whether all people had the potential for obtaining Buddhahood – as Tendai claimed – or whether there were those too evil to attain Buddhahood – as Hossō claimed. Saichō contended that because all sentient beings possess the Buddha nature, no one is denied the possibility for Buddhahood. Tokuitsu argued that some sentient beings do not possess the Buddha nature at all and thus have no possibility of gaining Buddhahood.

Saichō's greatest accomplishment was his reworking of the rules that had hitherto governed monastic practice in Japanese Buddhism. In 818 Saichō produced the Regulations for the Annual Quota Students of the Tendai Lotus Sect (*Tendai hokkeshū nenbun gakushō shiki*). This work expressed Saichō's desire to do away with the 250 precepts – that he and all other Tōdaiji-ordained monks had received – which were the basis of the Four-Part Precepts. In place of this traditional ordination regulation, Saichō favored a new, independent one based on the *Brahma Net Sūtra* (*Bonmōkyō*). The *Bonmōkyō* lists ten major precepts that Saichō believed articulated the needs of Mahāyāna monastics far better than the older regulations – the Hīnayāna precepts – which he saw as based on ideals that no longer fit the conditions of his day.

Saichō utilized the *Bonmōkyō* in his doctrinal justifications for implementing new precepts to replace the older Tōdaiji regulations. The older Nara Buddhist schools, especially Hossō, argued against his revisions on the basis that the traditional ordination was for monastics, whereas Saichō's regulations were for lay practitioners and thus were secondary to the primary precepts. Whatever the doctrinal grounds for changes in monastic regulations, it is clear that Saichō's attempt to inaugurate a new ordination platform had political implications because of the threat posed to the power to ordain traditionally reserved for Nara institutions exclusively. At stake was the issue of authority over ordination and monastic regulations. In short Saichō wanted autonomy for his ordination, which in turn would earn autonomy for Tendai. Still he needed imperial permission for this autonomy. Saichō wrote three major petitions asking for permission to use the bodhisattva precepts as the basis for the ordination of Tendai monks. His petitions sought to gain official approval for his plan to replace the traditional Hīnayāna precepts with the bodhisattva precepts as the basis for ordaining monastics into the order. These petitions articulated Saichō's position and defended it against his detractors. Seven days after his death, word finally came from the imperial court that Saichō's petition for an independent ordination platform had been granted. This meant that the monks assigned through the annual quota system could be ordained on Mount Hiei. The result was the increasing independence of all sects from government control.

In the end Saichō's legacy was significant. He set in motion a thriving monastic community with its own monastic rules, a community that was to produce some of the most important monks in Japanese Buddhist history. Monks who studied at Mount Hiei included those associated with the founding of Pure Land, Zen, and Nichiren Buddhist traditions.

William E. Deal

See also Buddhist Schools/Traditions: Japan; Esoteric Buddhism in China and Japan; Japan: History; Kūkai; Mount Hiei, Japan; Mountain Monasteries, Buddhist; Nation-Building and Japanese Buddhism; Pure Land Buddhism; Tiantai/Tendai: Japan

Biography

The introducer of Tiantai/Tendai into Japan, Saichō withdrew to a hut on Mount Hiei near Kyoto shortly before Emperor Kammu (d. 806) moved the capital of Japan there in 784 and became Saichō's protector. In 804–805 Saichō studied Tiantai in China and returned to disseminate it in Japan. His earlier friendship with Kūkai degenerated into a rivalry. The flourishing of Mount Hiei as the center of Tendai is owing to Saichō and his pupils Enchin and Ennin.

Major Works

Shugo-kokkai-shō (Treatise on the Protection of the State)
Hokke-shūku (Superlative Passages of the Lotus Sūtra)
Kenkai-ron (Treatise on the Precepts); a brief excerpt of the *Kenkai-ron* is translated in *Sources of Japanese Buddhism*, volume 1, edited by Ryusaku Tsunoda et al., 1964

Further Reading

Groner, Paul, *Saichō: The Establishment of the Japanese Tendai School* (Berkeley Buddhist Studies Series, 7), Berkeley: Center for South and Southeast Asian Studies, University of California at Berkeley, Institute of Buddhist Studies, 1984
Sonoda, Kōyū, "Saichō (767–822)," in *Shapers of Japanese Buddhism*, edited by Yūsen Kashiwahara and Kōyū Sonoda, Tokyo: Kōsei, 1994
Waka, Shirato, "Inherent Enlightenment and Saicho's Acceptance of the Bodhisattva Precepts," *Japanese Journal of Religious Studies* 14:2–3 (1987)
Weinstein, Stanley, "The Beginnings of Esoteric Buddhism in Japan: The Neglected Tendai Tradition," *Journal of Asian Studies* 34:1 (1974)

St. Gallen, Switzerland

Saint Gallen, once a Benedictine monastery but now a city, is located on the southern shore of Lake Constance. For more than 1,100 years, it was one of the most important abbeys in Western Europe. Its location put it near the center of medieval communications: within easy reach along the Rhine to French and German lands and through the passes to northern Italy. Unwavering interest in learning, the diffusion of books, and the liturgy made it a transmission point between north and south of the Alps.

Although named after an Irish hermit, Gall (Latin, *Gallus*), the monastery was not founded by him. Gall had been a monk with Columban (d. 615) in Luxeuil and was one of the group that followed him into present-day Switzerland. However, when in 612 Columban desired to go south, ending up in Bobbio in the Apennines, Gall and some others left him and built hermit's cells near the present St. Gallen. These hermits do not appear to have survived as a group down to the time of the later monastery, but evidently they made some impact on the surrounding population. Gall's relics were preserved in a special church and became the focus of a cult. It was to this church that the priest Othmar (c. 689–759) was appointed in the early eighth century, and he founded the monastery in 719. However, two curious links exist between these Irish hermits and the new monastery. First, Othmar adopted the rule of Columban to govern the monastery, and, second, a library catalog (Stiftsbibliothek 728) of around 885 records "the books written in Irish script" (i.e., then difficult to read). Othmar's monastery grew, and its location ensured it strategic importance during that most constricted period of Latin culture. This can be seen from the fact that it was at royal prompting that the monastery introduced the Rule of St. Benedict in 749. During the following 100 years, it performed its greatest service to Western Christianity by serving as a key center in the Carolingian revival of culture. Its library was crucial to the ninth-century flowering of Latin theology. The so-called Plan of St. Gall (c. 820), presenting a paradigmatic monastery, was drawn elsewhere but resides at the library of St. Gallen.

The tenth century saw the destruction of the abbey by the Hungarians, but a revival occurred under Notker (971–975), whose building of an abbey wall resulted in the development of the town. Increasingly over the centuries the abbey grew as landowner and became ever more involved in German imperial politics. The next major monastic reform came in the 1440s with a decision to follow the observance of Subiaco; at this time the abbey also became affiliated to the Swiss Confederation. When the town opted for the reformers in 1527, the abbey was closed for five years. In 1532 the monks returned, and during its last centuries the abbey flourished again as a center both of Benedictinism and of theological study and publishing. In 1756 building of the present rococo church began, and the library was enlarged, but the French Revolution brought its end: the monastery was secularized in 1798. The church is now the city's cathedral, and its library (over 30,000 manuscripts and printed works) is owned by the Canton, although it is still called the "Stiftsbibliothek" (convent library).

THOMAS O'LOUGHLIN

See also Bobbio, Italy; Brewing, Western Christian; Columban, St.; Dissolution of Monasteries: Contiental Europe; Hymnographers; Manuscript Production: Christian; Switzerland; Visual Arts, Western Christian: Sculpture

Further Reading

Anderes, Bernhard, *The Abbey of St. Gall: The Ancient Ecclesiastical Precinct*, St. Gallen: Kulturpflege des Kantons St. Gallen, 1990
Duft, Johannes, *The Abbey Library of Saint Gall*, St. Gallen: Verlag am Klosterhof, 1985
King, James C., and Werner Vogler, editors, *The Culture of the Abbey of St Gall: An Overview*, Stuttgart and Zürich: Belser, 1991

St. Riquier, France

The patron saint Richarius, whose name has become attached to both church and township, is reputed to have founded a monastery at a place then called Centula (20 miles northwest of Amiens) and a small cell elsewhere on the estate, where he died around 645. Soon afterward his remains were translated to Centula itself, where Angilbert (c. 750–814), one of Charlemagne's courtiers, reestablished the monastery in 790. With royal support a major church was built, drawing its building materials from as far afield as Rome, with a dual dedication to Our Savior and St. Richarius. Rebuilding programs in the 10th and 11th centuries included the addition of a then fashionable outer crypt at the east end. At the end of the 11th century, a total reconstruction was undertaken, followed by a further campaign in the 13th. In 1475 a fire, one of a number to afflict the church, damaged the west tower; in the period between the fire and 1536, the nave and side aisles, the radiating chapels at the east end, and possibly the tower itself were rebuilt. Finally, in the second half of the 17th century the Maurist Order took over the monastery and constructed two blocks of conventual buildings, which were rebuilt after yet another fire in 1719. With the suppression of the Maurists in 1790, St. Riquier was secularized.

Despite the lack of any significant remains from the Carolingian and Romanesque periods, St. Riquier is a site of major importance for the understanding of monastic architecture and liturgy in the early Middle Ages. The reason for this is the survival of extensive, mainly secondhand documentary evidence, notably, Hariulf's *Chronicon Centulense*, completed in 1088 and updated by 1105. This included a supposed autograph description by Angilbert, who is also credited with a liturgical customal preserved in the Vatican library. Together these describe the monastic liturgy and the altars, relics, and other furnishings in the church, although it is not entirely clear whether they refer to the Carolingian or the later pre-Romanesque church. Nevertheless, they give considerable insight into liturgical practices at the end of the 11th century. These practices include the use of the great western complex (westwork), which functioned to some extent as a separate unit independent of the main church, and the liturgical involvement of minor churches on the site. Dedicated to St. Mary and St. Benedict, the lesser churches were linked to the principal church and to each other by galleries on two stories.

No trace of these chapels exists above ground, although their location has been established; excavation has revealed St. Mary's as a small polygonal building with a western porch, and topographical research has shown that the area enclosed by the galleries was about six hectares in size. Because of later building it is difficult for the modern visitor to appreciate the huge extent of the early monastic complex. The church is accessible at all normal times, but the visible remains of the early building are confined to some plain walling that is visible in a passage on the south side of the church. Displayed in the church are the skull of St. Richarius and chests with other relics; a small site museum is open at irregular hours. The Maurist buildings can be viewed externally but are of little architectural interest.

David Parsons

See also Architecture: Western Christian Monasteries; France; Liturgy: Western Christian; Maurists

Further Reading

Heitz, Carol, *L'Architecture religieuse carolingienne*, Paris: Picard, 1980

Parsons, David, "The Pre-Romanesque Church of St-Riquier: The Documentary Evidence," *Journal of the British Archaeological Association* 130 (1977)

Parsons, David, "Saint-Riquier Abbey," in *The Dictionary of Art*, volume 27, edited by Jane Turner, New York: Grove, 1996

Rabe, Susan A., *Faith, Art and Politics at Saint-Riquier: The Symbolic Vision of Angilbert*, Philadelphia: University of Pennsylvania Press, 1993

Saints, Italian Benedictine

Because Benedict of Nursia (c. 480–c. 550) is the "father of Western monasticism" and the author of the Benedictine Rule, it might be assumed that Benedictine saints are the holy men and women who lived under that Rule. In Italy, however, Benedict himself was also a local saint, the preeminent image of personal ascetic sanctity from the 7th through the 12th century. Even Francis of Assisi (1181/82–1226), who eventually eclipsed him, was still modeled after Benedict in several details. Thus, in Italy "Benedictine saints" are not only saints affiliated with Benedictine communities but also saints who imitated Benedict.

Is there any disjunction between the two? Not according to Pope Gregory I (590–604), who established the hagiographic image of Benedict in Book II of his *Dialogues*. Gregory claims, "Anyone who wishes to know more about Benedict's life and character can discover in his *Rule* exactly what he was like as an abbot, for his life could not have differed from his teaching" (*Dialogues* II xxxvi). However, abbot was only Benedict's final role. Gregory actually tells the story of a young scholar, scandalized by Rome, who left the world to become a hidden hermit. Because he was clothed in rough skins, shepherds mistook him for a wild animal. Once he had been recognized as a holy man, he exhibited prophetic deeds of power, but his administrative career was nearly cut short when, after he had been recruited to supervise a dozen monasteries, his monks tried to murder him. Only with the foundation of Monte Cassino did his career begin to conform to the monastic stability of the Rule.

In early medieval Italy it is not easy to trace the exact influence either of Benedict the legislator or Benedict the person. A relative hagiographic "dark age" lies between the *Dialogues* written by Gregory I and the *Dialogues* that Abbot Desiderius of Monte Cassino (d. 1087, as Pope Victor III) wrote in their image. However, by the 11th century Benedictine saints had come to dominate Italy.

The most common type is an *alter Benedictus*, a person who recapitulates Benedict's career as a world-rejecting hermit, ascetic wanderer, and charismatic monastic founder and rule giver, often in charge of many monasteries. Such individuals are remembered not only because they conformed to a dominant ideal of Italian spirituality but also because the communities they created were able to maintain their cults. Although not all their varied congregations are classified by historians today as "Benedictine," it was Benedict himself who provided the model by which the sanctity of such founders was perceived. Among the *altri Benedicti* is Romuald of Ravenna (c. 950–1027), later acclaimed as the founder of the Camaldolese Order, who was described by his hagiographer Peter Damian (1007–1072) not only as a reincarnation of the Desert Fathers but also as an itinerant monastic founder modeled after Benedict. The hagiography of

Dominic of Sora (d. 1032) is filled with explicit Benedictine echoes, and his actual career offers an eerie parallel to Benedict's in that it features a similar life journey from north to south, rule over a dozen rural Benedictine monasteries (some in the same regions where Benedict had worked), and the final foundation of a major monastery on the edge of Campania. John Gualbert (d. 1073), after he had established himself as a Benedictine hermit near Florence, founded the Vallombrosans. John of Matera (d. 1139) founded the hermetic congregation of Pulsano, and his friend William of Vercelli (d. 1142) founded the congregation of Montevergine, distinguished for its austere white-robed hermits. William of Malavalle (d. 1157) produced the *Guglielmiti*, the Order of the Hermits of St. William. Joachim of Fiore (d. 1202), who wrote a commentary on Benedict's life, seems to have been inspired by him when he founded the Florensians. Sylvester Guzzolini (d. 1267) founded the Silvestrines. Bernardo Tolomei (d. 1348) of Siena, who died ministering to victims of the plague, was the hermit founder of Monte Oliveto and of the *Congregazione olivetana*. The importance of Benedict as a model should not be underestimated: Pietro of Morrone (d. 1296), who captured the hopes of Italy and of all Europe as the "angel pope" Celestine V (1294), reached that eminence because, as the charismatic leader of his hermit monks, he had been a typical model of this type of Benedictine sanctity.

Not all the Benedictine abbots who founded and reformed monasteries were distinguished hermits. More cenobitic careers were exhibited by Peter (d. soon after 1022) of San Pietro in Perugia and by Adelmarius of Monte Cassino (d. early 11th century), a monk of Monte Cassino who moved through various offices and ultimately restored Beneventan monasteries, which were, according to his hagiographer, "too many to be named." The first four abbots of Cava – Alferius, Leo, Peter, and Simon – received solid biographies and later cult. Benedictus (d. 1091) Junior (II), abbot of Chiusa, was commemorated in a vita written by his pupil William. Lidanus of Sezze (d. 1118), a former Monte Cassino oblate, was made the abbot of a house located on properties that his family had donated to St. Benedict. Walter of Servigliano (d. c. 1340), monk and abbot of the Benedictine monastery of Servigliano in the Diocese of Fermo, received an early cult, although little biographical commemoration. Andrew "di Paolo" (d. 1344), born at Assisi, founded the Umbrian congregation of Corpus Christi under the Benedictine Rule.

What of Benedictines who were not abbots? Some companions of Benedict, mentioned in Gregory's *Dialogues*, went on to be commemorated in their own elaborate cults. Placidus, thanks to a Sicilian connection, had his cause advanced by partisans of Monte Cassino's claims in Sicily, such as Peter the Deacon (d. 1159). From Carolingian times on, Maurus was publicized by the monks of St.-Maur at Glannfeuil in France, who saw him as the agent by which Benedict's relics were moved north. Benedict's sister Scholastica (c. 480–c. 543) became a model for Benedictine nuns. Although these companions themselves are ultimately portrayed as monastic leaders, their original roles as disciples allow their hagiographies to present them as models of Benedictine obedience.

Benedictine hermits were also commemorated. There were those who became affiliated with important monasteries, such as Palumbus (d. c. 1115), a wandering hermit at Subiaco; Galganus (d. 1181) at Monte Siepi, finally associated with the *Guglielmiti*; and Placidus of Abruzzi (d. 1248), who at the end of his life submitted his incipient monastery to the Cistercian house of Casanova. Some Benedictine hermit saints had special distinctions, such as Bononius of Lucedio (d. 1026), who had been living in the Egyptian desert until he was recruited to run an Italian monastery, and Theobald of Provence (d. 1066), a French nobleman who became a hermit in northern Italy. Some were hermit preachers, such as Adelbert of Casuria (d. after 1047), Peter of Trevi (c. 11th century); and Alan (d. 1313), an Austrian who died as a recluse at Sassovivo near Foligno.

Benedictine nuns, from Scholastica onward, elicited parallel albeit less numerous commemorations. Abbesses, especially those nobly born, were remembered, including three at Padua: Beatrice I d'Este (d. 1226), Beatrice II d'Este (d. 1262), and Juliana Collalto (d. 1262), associated with Beatrice I but, after her death, with Venice, where she founded her own monastery. Exalted birth, even without high office, might still be remembered, as in the case of Filippa Guidoni (d. before 1327), a noble nun in an early house of the "Santuccie," a Benedictine congregation whose actual founder was a man, Santuccia Terebotti of Gubbio. Umilità da Faenza (d. 1310) was a recluse who helped develop a feminine branch of the Congregation of Vallombrosa. Other recluses included Chelidonia (d. 1152), a hermitess near Subiaco who took the Benedictine habit in the basilica of St. Scholastica; Rosalia of Palermo (fl. 12th century), a hermitess on Monte Pellegrino known through an early modern legend; and Sperandea (d. 1276), a hermitess and penitential preacher near Gubbio, who finished her days as abbess of the convent of St. Michael near Cingolo in the Marches.

Some abbots and monks were honored as saints for reasons not inherently Benedictine. The monk Hildebrand became Pope Gregory VII (1073–1085), and Abbot Desiderius of Monte Cassino became Pope Victor III (1086–1087). Some became sainted bishops, as did Octavian, a monk of San Pietro in Ciel d'Oro of Pavia, who became bishop of Savona (1123–1132), and Boniface, a scion of the counts of Valperga, a monk of Fruttuaria who ended his days in charge of the Diocese of Aosta (1219–1243). Some were remembered because they suffered persecution, such as abbot Peter III of Subiaco (d. c. 1003), who ended his days in the prison of a local count; Peter II (d. 1208), who ruled Cava during a time of political turbulence unusual even for southern Italy; and Arnold of Santa Giustina in Padua (d. 1255), imprisoned because of his hostility to Emperor Frederick II (1215–1250) and his Ghibelline followers.

In the modern era, as in the later Middle Ages, Benedictine saints were eclipsed to some extent by the saints of newer religious orders. Benedictine nuns did have a mystical efflorescence during the Counter-Reformation: among those who received ecclesiastical honors are Giovanna Maria Bonomo, a nun at San Gerlamo at Bassano (d. 1670), and Maria Crocifissa Tomasi (d. 1699), from the family of the princes of Lampedusa and dukes of Palma, whose family monastery she entered. This tradition has produced more contemporary saints and *beatae*, including Maria Adeodata Pisani (d. 1855) and Maria Fortunata Viti (d. 1922). The causes of some modern Benedictine bishops and cardinals are being advanced, including Marianno Falcinelli Antoniacci (1806–1874), Giuseppe Benedetto Dusmet (1818–1894), Michelangelo Celesia (1814–1904), and Guglielmo Sanfelice (1834–1897), monks whose careers were disrupted to a greater or lesser extent by the suppression of religious houses during Italian unification.

Altogether there are literally hundreds of Italian Benedictine saints. Their cults are often local, poorly documented, and of uncertain status. There is no comprehensive list, which ought not to be surprising given the lack of consensus about what constitutes either "Italian," "Benedictine," or, in this context, "saint." To get some impression of the material, one could research the geographic origins of the Benedictine saints listed in Alfons Zimmermann's *Kalendarium Benedictinum* (Zimmermann indexes by city but not by country). Another approach would be to look at the presently available volumes of the series *Monasticon Italiae*, which include much hagiographic data in an attempt to document Italian monasteries region by region. The *Bibliotheca Sanctorum*, the great hagiographic encyclopedia available only in an Italian version, remains the best place to begin investigating individual saints.

JOHN HOWE

See also Benedict of Nursia, St.; Benedictines; Gregory I (the Great), St.; Gualbert, John, St.; Joachim of Fiore; Monte Cassino, Italy; Subiaco, Italy

Further Reading

Bibliotheca Sanctorum, 13 vols., Rome: Istituto Giovanni XXIII nella Pontificia Università Lateranense, 1961–1970

Cowdrey, H.E.J., *The Age of Abbot Desiderius: Montecassino, the Papacy, and the Normans in the Eleventh and Early Twelfth Centuries*, Oxford: Clarendon Press, 1983

De Vogüé, Adalbert, "Benoît, modèle de la vie spirituelle d'après le deuxième livre des *Dialogues* de saint Grégoire," *Collectanea Cisterciensia* 38 (1976)

Farnedi, Guistino, and Giovanni Spinelli, editors, *Settecento monastico italiano: Atti del I Convegno di studi storici sull'Italia Benedettina, Cesena, 9–12 settembre 1986* (Italia Benedettina, 9), Cesena: Badia S. Maria del Monte, 1990

Feller, Laurent, "Saintété, gestion du patrimoine et réforme monastique: Le *Vie* de saint Aldemar de Bucchianico," *Médiévales* 15 (1988)

Herde, Peter, *Cölestin V. (1294): Peter vom Morrone, Der Engelpapst: mit einem Urkundenanhang und Edition zweier Viten* (Päpste und Papsttum, 16), Stuttgart: Hiersemann, 1981

Howe, John, *Church Reform and Social Change in Eleventh-Century Italy: Dominic of Sora and His Patrons* (The Middle Ages), Philadelphia: University of Pennsylvania Press, 1997

Lunardi, G., "Benedettine, Monache," in *Dizionario degli istituti di perfezione*, volume 1, edited by Guerrino Pelliccia and Giancarlo Rocca, Rome: Edizioni Paoline, 1974

Mancone, Ambrogio, Jean Leclercq, Giorgio Picasso, and E. Zaramella, "Benedettini," in *Dizionario degli istituti di perfezione*, volume 1, edited by Guerrino Pelliccia and Giancarlo Rocca, Rome: Edizioni Paoline, 1974

Monasticon Italiae (Pubblicazioni del Centro storico benedettino italiano), 3 vols., Cesena: Badia di Santa Maria del Monte, 1981–

Penco, Gregorio, *Storia del monachesimo in Italia dalle origini alla fine del Medioevo* (Tempi e figure, 31), Rome: Edizioni Paoline, 1961; reprint, Milan: Jaca Book, 1983

Penco, Gregorio, "San Benedetto nel ricordo del Medio Evo monastico," *Benedictina* 16 (1969); reprinted in his *Medioevo monastico* (Studia Anselmiana, 96), Rome: Edizioni Abbazia S. Paolo, 1988

Philippart, Guy, editor, *Hagiographies: Histoire internationale de la littérature hagiographique latine et vernaculaire en Occident des origines à 1500=International History of the Latin and Vernacular Hagiographical Literature in the West from Its Origins to 1550* (Corpus Christianorum), 2 vols., Turnhout: Brepols, 1994–1996

Phipps, Colin, "Romuald – Model Hermit: Eremitical Theory in Saint Peter Damian's *Vita Beati Romualdi*," in *Monks, Hermits, and the Ascetic Tradition: Papers Read at the 1984 Summer Meeting and the 1985 Winter Meeting of the Ecclesiastical History Society* (Studies in Church History, 22), edited by W.J. Sheils, Oxford: Blackwell, 1985

Trolese, Francesco G., editor, *Il monachesimo italiano dalle riforme illuministiche all'unità nazionale (1768–1870): Atti del II Convegno di studi storici sull'Italia benedettina, Abbazia di Rodengo (Brescia) 6–9 settembre, 1989* (Italia benedettina, 11), Cesena: Badia di Santa Maria del Monte, 1992

Trolese, Francesco G., editor, *Il monachesimo in Italia tra Vaticano I e Vaticano II: Atti del III Convegno di studi storici sull'Italia benedettina, Badia di Cava dei Tirreni (Salerno), 3–5 settembre 1992* (Italia benedettina, 15), Cesena: Badia di Santa Maria del Monte, 1995

Wessley, Stephen, "*Bonum Est Benedicto Mutare Locum:* The Role of the *Life of St. Benedict* in Joachim of Fiore's Monastic Reform," *Revue bénédictine* 90 (1980)

Zimmermann, Alfons M., compiler, *Kalendarium Benedictinum: Die Heiligen und Seligen des Benediktinerordens und seiner zweige*, 4 vols., Metten: Abtei Metten, 1933–1938

Sakya. *See* Tibetan Lineages: Sakya

Sakya Pandita (Sapen) 1182–1251

Tibetan Buddhist philosopher, translator, and promoter of Indian Buddhism in Tibet

Sakya Pandita Künga Gyeltsen (Sa-skya Paṇḍita Kun-dga'-rgyal-mtshan), or Sapen, is "one of the most influential figures in the transmission of Indian Buddhist religion and learning to Tibet

. . . a savant who is counted among the very greatest Tibetan scholars of all time . . . one of the key figures in the religious, political and scholarly history of Tibet" (David Jackson, 1987). Sapen was one of the "Five Great" founders of the Buddhist monastery of Sakya in Tibet and the sixth abbot of the Abbatial See. He began his formal education in early childhood, mastering the numerous Tantric texts and rituals transmitted in his tradition: general Mahāyāna teachings, medicine and calligraphy, drawing, painting, and astrology. From 1200 to 1216 Sapen pursued further philosophical and doctrinal studies with various Tibetan and Indian masters in the main fields of traditional Buddhist scholarship, that is, Mādhyamaka (the Middle Way), Abhidharma (higher dharma), Prajñāpāramitā (perfection of wisdom), and above all Pramāṇa (logic-epistemology), in which he excelled. In addition he translated several Sanskrit classics, most importantly Dharmakīrti's *Pramāṇavārttikālaṁkāra* (The Ornament Which Is a Commentary on [Dignāga's] "Compendium on Valid Cognition").

In 1216 Sapen became Sakya Trizin (throne holder), a great religious master, scholar, writer, and teacher in Ü and Tsang (dBus and gTsang). In 1244 he set out for the court of one Mongol prince, Köden, where he stayed until his death in 1251 as the religious teacher of that prince, who in turn conceded him temporal authority over central Tibet.

Sapen's lasting impact on later monastics can be seen from the many commentaries and other literary output that his writings inspired and provoked. For more than seven centuries, intersectarian doctrinal disputes and discussions of his philosophical and hermeneutical views, his motifs, and his scholarly methods have continued among Tibetan Buddhist monastics within both the Sakya tradition and other schools. Lately modern Western scholars also have engaged in debating, interpreting, translating, and editing more than 40 of Sapen's works (e.g., David Jackson, Leonard W.J. van der Kuijp, Roger Jackson, J.D. Schoening, and R.M. Davidson).

Around 1219 Sapen composed his pivotal work on logic-epistemology (*pramāṇa*), *Tshad ma rigs pa'i gter* (Treasury of the Knowledge of Valid Cognition), in which he tried to establish in Tibet the authentic tradition of the Indian Buddhist philosophers Dignāga and Dharmakīrti. Up to around 1967, no fewer than 24 Tibetan scholars have written commentaries on this work, among them such luminaries as the Sakya scholars Rongtön (Rong-ston, 1367–1449), Gorampa (Go-rams-pa, 1429–1489), and Shakya Chogden (Śākya-mchog-ldan, 1428–1507) and the Nyingma (rNying-ma) scholar Mipam (Mi-pham, 1846–1912).

Sapen's great doctrinal polemic, *sDom pa gsum gyi rab tu dbye ba* (Differentiation of the Three Vows), unleashed such prolonged controversy that to the present at least 28 Tibetan masters as well as several Western scholars have written extensively on this work. Among his commentators, critics, and followers are the previously mentioned scholars as well as Lowo Khenchen (Glo-bo mkhan-chen, 1456–1532) and Ngawang Chödrak (Ngag-dbang-chos-grags, 1572–1641). In *sDom pa gsum gyi rab tu dbye ba*, as in all his major works, Sapen applied rational and critical methods to defend genuine doctrines of Indian Buddhism against what he considered inauthentic or erroneous practices of some Tibetan schools and their masters.

For example, by the early 1200s an antirational and antischolastic soteriology had developed in connection with Gampopa's (sGam-po-pa, 1079–1153) theory of the Great Seal (Phyag-chen) and the ancient Tibetan tradition of the Great Perfection (rDzogs-chen). The issue pivoted around the doctrine of the White Self-Sufficient or Singly Efficacious Remedy (dkar po chig thub). Its adherents, such as Zhang Tshal-pa, advocated an instantaneous, all-at-once enlightenment through the single factor of direct insight. Sapen, whose great concern was the establishment and transmission of the pure Buddhist doctrine in Tibet, emphasized the primacy of authentic Indian sūtras, śāstras, and tantras (i.e., teachings of the Buddha, commentarial literature, and precepts for meditational and ritual practice, respectively), which taught the need for multiple factors for reaching enlightenment.

In addition to his five major works, Sapen wrote a hundred or so works on various subjects, such as logic-epistemology, theory and practice of Mahāyāna, Sanskrit language arts, Tantric practice, and music. He composed commentaries, liturgies, epistles, shorter letters, and a biography. To date his major works continue to be part of the curriculum at Tibetan academic institutions.

SIGRID PIETSCH

See also Buddhist Schools/Traditions: Tibet; Gampopa; Mahāyāna; Scholastics, Buddhist; Tibet: History; Tibetan Lineages: Sakya

Biography

One of the "Five Great" founders of the Buddhist monastery of Sakya in Tibet, Sakya Pandita, or Sapen, studied with both Indian and Tibetan masters. He translated a number of works from Sanskrit into Tibetan. His treatises on Indian Buddhist philosophy stimulated dozens of commentaries on his work. From 1244 to 1251 he lived at the court of the Mongol Prince Köden, who granted him rule over central Tibet.

Major Works

Thub pa'i dgongs pa rab tu gsal ba (Elucidating the Intention of the Sage)

Sa-skya legs bshad, as *Ordinary Wisdom: Sakya Pandita's Treasury of Good Advice*, translated by John T. Davenport and Sallie D. Davenport, 2000

sDom pa gsum gyi rab tu dbye ba (Differentiation of the Three Vows)

Tshad ma rigs pa'i gter (Treasury of the Knowledge of Valid Cognition)

mKhas pa rnams 'jug pa'i sgo (The Entrance Gate for the Wise)

These five principal works are to be found in their original Tibetan in *Sa skya pa'i bka' 'bum*, volume 5, 1968.

Further Reading

Broido, Michael, "Sa-skya Paṇḍita, The White Panacea and the Hva-shang Doctrine," *The Journal of the International Association of Buddhist Studies* 10 (1987)

Jackson, David, "Commentaries on the Writings of Sa-skya Paṇḍita: A Bibliographical Sketch," *Tibet Journal* 8:3 (1983)
Jackson, David, "The Entrance Gate for the Wise (Section III): Sa-skya Pandita on Indian and Tibetan Traditions of Pramâna and Philosophical Debate," *Wiener Studien zur Tibetologie und Buddhismuskunde* 17 (1987)
Jackson, David, "Sa-skya Paṇḍita the 'Polemicist': Ancient Debates and Modern Interpretations," *The Journal of the International Association of Buddhist Studies* 13:2 (1990)
Jackson, David, "Birds in the Egg and Newborn Lion Cubs: Metaphors for the Potentialities and Limitations of 'All-at-once' Enlightenment," in *Tibetan Studies: Proceedings of the 5th Seminar of the International Association for Tibetan Studies, Narita 1989,* 2 vols., Narita-shi, Chiba-ken, Japan: Naritasan Shinshoji, 1992
Jackson, David, *Enlightenment by a Single Means*, Vienna: Verlag der Österreichischen Akademie der Wissenschaften, 1994
Jackson, Roger, "Sa skya paṇḍita's Account of the bSam yas Debate: History as Polemic," *The Journal of the International Association of Buddhist Studies* 5 (1982)
Kuijp, Leonard W.J. van der, "On the Sources for Sa-skya Paṇḍita's Notes on the bSam-yas Debate," *The Journal of the International Association of Buddhist Studies* 9 (1986)

Śākyamuni Buddha. *See* Buddha (Śākyamuni)

Saṅgha

Historical Overview

The origins of the Buddhist monastic community, the *saṅgha*, may be traced to northeastern India during the sixth to fourth centuries B.C. At that time India witnessed a great deal of social change as well as intellectual and religious fervor. Among the religious virtuosi who emerged during this period of efflorescence was a young man who came to be called Gautama Buddha, the person credited by the Buddhist tradition with establishing the basic patterns of practice intrinsic to the *saṅgha*.

Overcome by encounters with suffering, Gautama renounced his princely life to become a wandering mendicant. Frustrated in his attempts to learn from other mendicants, he embarked on a solitary quest for understanding into the true nature of life and the suffering inherent in it. Later Buddhists believed that Gautama's quest culminated in extraordinary insight. He became a Buddha, or "awakened one."

According to tradition the Buddha discerned that all existence, including all sentient life, is constituted by composite entities that are subject to a virtually endless cycle of dissolution and reconstitution, of death and rebirth. He realized that desire – especially the desire for self-preservation – is the primary force that drives this cycle. He knew that entrapment in this cycle can be overcome by the mindful practice of a "middle path" that avoids the extremes of self-indulgence on the one hand and an overly austere lifestyle on the other. Gautama Buddha preached this message in a multitude of forms over the 50 or so years that followed his enlightenment up to his death. This basic message shaped the earliest ethos of the *saṅgha*.

The ethos of the early monastic community was preserved, at first orally and later in written form, in the Vinaya-piṭaka, or "Basket of Discipline." This basket contained the various regulations for the monastic community, including the *prātimokṣa*, a list of codes of conduct (see the following discussion). The Vinaya and subsequent Vinaya literature (commentaries, handbooks, and so on) have remained essential to the legal and liturgical constitution of the *saṅgha* and its self-identification with the life and teachings of the Buddha.

Since its beginnings under the guidance of the Buddha, the *saṅgha* has sustained the historical development of the Buddhist tradition. Although modest in its beginnings, the *saṅgha* eventually grew in size to consist of major institutional bodies responsible for the preservation of the purported teachings and practices of the Buddha, the ordination of novices and monks, and the performance of various kinds of rituals intended to safeguard the lay members of the Buddhist community.

A significant contribution of the *saṅgha* was its role in the transmission of Buddhism to lands beyond the Indian context. This transmission began in a serious way with the reign of the Indian monarch Aśoka (r. c. 270–230 B.C.), remembered by later Buddhists as a *Dharmarāja*, or righteous king. Although it is not absolutely clear from the historical evidence that Aśoka was personally a Buddhist, he nonetheless provided major support for the Buddhist cause. Among other actions Aśoka sent Buddhist monastic emissaries to areas beyond his realm. From his reign onward such traveling monks played a crucial role in the flowering of Buddhism as a pan-Asian religious tradition as well as in the rise of distinctive cultural forms of the tradition.

The high-water mark of Buddhism as a pan-Asian religious tradition (fourth to sixth century A.D.) witnessed the interregional passage of monks along both land and sea trade routes. The encompassing character of the Buddhist tradition eventually broke down, but acculturation to local customs in each of the areas to which Buddhism spread spurred major innovations in monastic life and practice. In many areas – including China, Japan, Korea, Tibet, Thailand, Sri Lanka, Burma, Vietnam, Cambodia, and Laos – Buddhist monastic traditions developed their own distinctive character.

A case in point is the growth of Buddhist liturgies for the dead in medieval China. Confucian opponents of the Buddhist cause maintained that monastic renunciation of the household life removed children, especially sons, from the responsibilities required by filial piety and ancestor worship. In response to their Confucian opponents, Buddhists, including Buddhist monks, engaged in a number of apologetic activities. Among these activities were the reformulation of stories about Mu-lien, a disciple of the Buddha, which provided an ideological foundation for Buddhist monks to perform liturgies for the dead. Such liturgies were intended to demonstrate that monastic life need not oppose more traditional Chinese values. In fact the liturgies were meant to emphasize the convergence of the activities of monks with such distinctively Chinese values.

Two developments were central to the long-term success that the Buddhist *saṅgha* achieved in both its pan-Asian and its cultural dimensions. First, although the tradition of wandering monks remained a vital component of monastic practice, many monks decided to forgo it in favor of living in permanent residences. This development, which probably began during the lifetime of the Buddha, was facilitated by large-scale gift giving (*dāna*) from lay patrons, such as kings and wealthy merchants. Such gifts promoted the growth of monasteries and temples as centers of missionary work, scriptural study, philosophical speculation, artistic innovation, and retreat. By around the fifth century A.D., large-scale monastic centers appeared on the scene, and in many cases they excelled as sites of learning, attracting scholars from various regions across the Buddhist world.

A second development important for the *saṅgha*'s long-term success was the emergence a broad but increasingly important distinction between the ethos of monastic and lay life. Ideally the *saṅgha* was the communal body that most authentically interpreted and exemplified the Buddha's message. It was a repository of the Buddha's continuing presence in the world and, therefore, mediated that presence. This point is underscored by the fact that the *saṅgha* was and is perceived as one of the three refuges in Buddhism, the other two refuges being the Buddha and the dharma (the Buddha's teachings). On their part the laity took increasing responsibility for, among other things, the material care of the monastic community. (It is both interesting and important to acknowledge that one of the broad areas of overlap between monastic and lay life has concerned the cultic activities surrounding relics of the Buddha and other Buddhist saints.)

These two developments greatly altered the ways in which Buddhist sociopolitical order was conceived as well as the role of monks within it. The king or ruler was to be the ideal lay patron, supported in his endeavors by lay subordinates, while monks, performing protective rituals on behalf of the state, also acted as advisers to the throne. In this regard the Aśokan paradigm has proved absolutely essential to many later Buddhist monks and kings, especially those of a Theravāda-based orientation. The contemporary situation in Burma (Myanmar) provides an example of this long-standing political tradition. Myanmar's political elite have quite consciously drawn on models of kingship and polity related to the Aśokan scheme, and many monks have acted on their behalf.

Other distinctive visions of Buddhist polity and its relationship to monastic life have occurred throughout the Buddhist world. In the 17th century, for example, Tibetan Buddhists successfully established a theocracy under the guidance of monks – known as the Dalai Lamas – who were upheld as successive incarnations of the bodhisattva Avalokiteśvara (a bodhisattva is a type of spiritually advanced being). Tang dynasty China witnessed a vision of Buddhist polity in which an esoteric Buddhist master (the *ācārya*) was represented as a "world conqueror" and "world renouncer" who also served as a spiritual adviser to the sage-king who himself was considered to be a bodhisattva-on-the-path.

Organization and Practices

Initially comprised of a few devout disciples, the *saṅgha* grew considerably even before the Buddha's death. From an early time it probably consisted of both monks (*bhikṣus*) and nuns (*bhikṣuṇīs*). Later tradition records that the Buddha at first resisted admitting women into the monastic order. Sustained petition from one of his leading disciples is thought to have led the Buddha to allow women entry, but only provided that they rank as subordinate to monks, even the most junior. The official order of Buddhist nuns died out in the Theravāda world of southern and Southeast Asia sometime during the latter half of first millennium A.D. However, orders of nuns have continued to exist in the Mahāyāna and esoteric traditions of eastern Asia and Tibet.

The purported relationship between early monks and nuns notwithstanding, evidence in the Vinaya literature suggests that the early *saṅgha* was founded along democratic and antiauthoritarian lines. Strictly speaking, of course, the Buddha was regarded as the most important authority for the *saṅgha* while he was alive. However, after his death, no individual monk held supreme authority over the *saṅgha*. In fact the early literature states that the Buddha left explicit instructions to his disciples to be governed solely by the dharma. Questions and issues were to be decided communally by vote, with consent for a given idea or solution signaled by silence. Further, seniority in the *saṅgha* was determined only by the number of years in robes.

The antiauthoritarian and democratic emphasis of the early Buddhist community was strained by the demands of large-scale settled monastic life. Such demands often resulted in formal divisions of labor and rigid administrative hierarchies that placed a great deal of power in the hands of officials. For example, it was and is not uncommon for abbots – throughout the Buddhist world – to direct the activities of the *saṅgha*.

The early *saṅgha* also obeyed two types of injunctions that encoded the parameters of interaction with the laity. One type of injunction encouraged the members of the *saṅgha* to wander in the world for the "benefit of the many." They were to preach sermons to those who would listen, debate with those who wished, and collect alms from those who wanted to offer them. In these capacities the monks were to act as "fields of merit" (*puṇyakṣetra*) for the laity by providing them an opportunity to cultivate states of mind and stores of karma conducive to positive retribution in this life and the next. In short, monks were to afford the laity an occasion to generate religious merit.

Different Buddhists understood the dynamics of this generation of merit in different ways. On the one hand it was believed that certain monks possessed a great deal of merit that they could to transfer to others. In many Buddhist contexts this encouraged an emphasis on giving gifts to monks of high regard. On the other hand Buddhists have emphasized the notion that gift giving to monks provides an opportunity for the gift giver to calm his or her own mind – an important prerequisite for the generation of merit for and by oneself.

A second type of injunction for the early *saṅgha* focused on abstinence from personal engagement in the mundane affairs of the world, such as politics, the acquisition of wealth, killing (even of insects whenever possible), sexual activity, and so on. It was argued that such abstinence, augmented by ardent striving on the middle path, could lead to religious attainment.

The middle path itself consisted of three basic components: the cultivation of wisdom (*prājñā*), ethical conduct (*śīla*), and mental concentration (*samādhi*). This path was also identified as the noble eightfold path because wisdom consisted of two factors (right understanding and right thought), ethical conduct three factors (right speech, right action, and right livelihood), and mental concentration three factors (right effort, right mindfulness, and right concentration).

When taken together the two types of injunctions for monastic life highlight the fact that the ideal activity of the early Buddhist monk consisted of begging, wandering, and preaching, all the while practicing poverty, meditation, nonviolence, and sexual abstinence as well as making deliberate efforts to avoid and/or resolve communal conflict. In short, the early monastic was to be a living embodiment of the Buddha's dharma. (Literary images of the schismatic monk Devadatta, a cousin of the Buddha, suggest that this ideal was not always realized.)

The ideal for the early Buddhist monk clearly influenced later monastic practice, but not without significant reinterpretation. Some esoteric traditions of Tibet and Japan have permitted – as part of a carefully enacted ritual program – violations of traditional prohibitions against sexual activity. Clerical marriage has been practiced in places ranging from medieval Sri Lanka to contemporary Korea. Vows of poverty tended to become moribund in many if not most monastic contexts, especially because of lay giving, and Buddhist warrior monks became a feature of medieval Japanese political life.

For the early Buddhist monastic community, the practice of the middle path entailed a lifestyle that alternated between a period of wandering and a period of temporary settlement during the southern Asian rainy season (from July to August). Both periods involved begging for alms and other requisites as well as study under the guidance of the Buddha, or, after his death, under the tutelage of senior or more knowledgeable monks. It is interesting to note in this regard that the word for Buddhist monk, *bhikṣu*, can be literally translated as "beggar." The Buddhist monk was to accept his position as a religious seeker indebted to others for the tools (food, religious knowledge, lodging, and, if the occasion warranted it, protection from physical harm) that would allow him to strive for his own salvation.

To facilitate proper practice of the middle path and to provide the means to cope with problems of a rapidly expanding monastic body, the Buddha is said to have instituted a series of codes (vinayas) for the regulation of monastic life. The codes governed the monastic community in both its wandering and its settled phases.

The codes, as well as the preeminent position accorded to them within monastic life, persisted as a hallmark of the early *saṅgha*. Following the Buddha's death the early community continued to alternate between periods of wandering and temporary settlement. However, during the latter of the two phases, these early monks would affirm their solidarity and commitment to the Buddhist path through a recitation of the *prātimokṣa*. The precise content of the earliest *prātimokṣa* is debatable, but it probably consisted of basic rules laid down by the Buddha pertaining to discipline. The recitation of the *prātimokṣa* took place during a communal ceremony (*poṣadha*), a ceremony in which the laity might have also participated.

The *prātimokṣa* was eventually preserved as part of the canonical literature dealing with the *vinaya* (discipline) of the *saṅgha*. Historical evidence suggests that from the first century B.C. onward, such literature became increasingly prominent in the pan-Asian spread of Buddhism.

The specific number of rules in the *prātimokṣa* sections of the various Buddhist canons has differed. The Chinese canon contains 250 rules for monks, the Tibetan canon 253, and the Pali canon 227. Typically more rules were listed for nuns than for monks. Despite these differences across texts and gender, the rules as a whole remain fundamentally the same in terms of their ethical and practical content. They identify the major infractions – sexual intercourse, murder, theft, and boasting about one's magical powers – that warrant expulsion from the *saṅgha*. They also specify less severe transgressions that require other forms of expiation. Recitation of the *prātimokṣa* during the *poṣadha* ceremony every other week (around the full and new moons) remains important in many settled monastic contexts.

Recitation of the *prātimokṣa* and the sense of communal identity it fostered have been complemented and enhanced by other monastic activities. Traditionally, full ordinations of monks were required to take place within officially established legal boundaries (*sīmā*s) to which the monastic community performing the rite consented. (In the case of the ordination of women, both monks and nuns were required to participate.) Ordination patterns have changed from school to school, but monastics of the three major branches of Buddhism that persist today – Theravāda, Mahāyāna, and esoteric (Vajrayāna) – have maintained various degrees of inclusiveness and exclusiveness relative to their ordination procedures.

Likewise the preservation of certain types of Buddhist literature (including but not limited to Vinaya literature) has been central to the identity of different monastic groups and their religious goals. Theravāda monks have tended to focus their energies on a relatively conservative transmission of texts related to the teachings of Gautama Buddha. These texts also communicated a more or less conservative religious goal, the attainment of the state of an arahant, a fully perfected saint. A monk who strove to be an arahant was required to engage in the solitary meditative quest laid down by the Buddha.

Mahāyāna monks played an important role in developing a new kind of text attributed to Gautama Buddha. These texts recorded sermons supposedly preached by the Buddha to special audiences comprised of his most adept disciples. Such new Mahāyāna texts affirmed a new religious goal, that of the bodhisattva. The bodhisattva was a being who cultivated a great deal of merit and power. However, out of compassion for the world, he or she intentionally retained a small measure of defilement that would keep him or her bound within the cycle of death and rebirth. In this way the bodhisattva – an exemplar for both monastic and lay practice – could use his or her power and insight to work unceasingly for the salvation of all beings.

Monks of the esoteric tradition preserved yet other types of texts that emphasized meditative techniques and ritual practices believed to be capable of generating tremendous amounts of spiritual insight and magical power. Many of these texts have been preserved in a form that makes them extremely difficult to understand. This manner of preservation led to the development of a relationship – important in most Buddhist monastic traditions – between a disciple and his or her more spiritually adept mentor. Personal guidance by a living esoteric master, often perceived as a "living Buddha," was a prerequisite for any possible achievement of spiritual advancement along the path to enlightenment.

Remarks on Recent History

The past 400 to 500 years have witnessed a great deal of social, political, and economic change on a global scale. This change has involved, among other developments, the spread of modernity, the rise and fall of colonial rule, and the expansion of Buddhism to the West. In many cases such change has prompted Buddhist monks and their lay supporters to adapt the ethos of monastic life to new kinds of social and cultural expectations. Contemporary movements aiming to "purify" Buddhist teachings in light of so-called modern, rational ideals have encouraged new types of social engagement, including participation in national politics and organization on an international level. Even so, throughout all these developments, attempts have been made to preserve a distinctive character of Buddhist monastic life – a character rooted in the activities and teachings first explored by the early Buddhist *saṅgha* itself.

JASON A. CARBINE

See also Bodhisattva; Buddha (Śākyamuni); Burma (Myanmar); Death Rituals, Buddhist; Disciples, Early Buddhist; Missionaries: Buddhist; Patrons, Buddhist; Rules, Buddhist (Vinaya)

Further Reading

Collins, Steven, *Selfless Persons: Imagery and Thought in Theravada Buddhism*, Cambridge: Cambridge University Press, 1982

Collins, Steven, *Nirvana and Other Buddhist Felicities: Utopias of the Pali Imaginaire*, Cambridge: Cambridge University Press, 1998

Faure, Bernard, *Visions of Power: Imagining Medieval Japanese Buddhism*, translated by Phyllis Brooks, Princeton, New Jersey: Princeton University Press, 1996

Gunawardana, R.A.L.H., *Robe and Plough: Monasticism and Economic Interest in Early Medieval Sri Lanka*, Tucson: University of Arizona Press, 1979

Havnevik, Hanna, *Tibetan Buddhist Nuns: History, Cultural Norms, and Social Reality*, Oslo: Norwegian University Press, 1989

Holt, John Clifford, *Discipline: The Canonical Buddhism of the Vinayapitaka*, Delhi: Motilal Banarsidass, 1981

Kieschnick, John, *The Eminent Monk: Buddhist Ideals in Medieval Chinese Hagiography*, Honolulu: University of Hawaii Press, 1997

Orzech, Charles D., *Politics and Transcendent Wisdom: The Scripture for Humane Kings in the Creation of Chinese Buddhism*, University Park: Pennsylvania State University Press, 1998

Prebish, Charles S., *Buddhist Monastic Discipline: The Sanskrit Pratimoksa Sutras of the Mahasamghikas and Mulasarvastivadins*, University Park: Pennsylvania State University Press, 1975

Ray, Reginald A., *Buddhist Saints in India: A Study in Buddhist Values and Orientations*, New York: Oxford University Press, 1994

Schopen, Gregory, *Bones, Stones, and Buddhist Monks: Collected Papers on the Archeology, Epigraphy, and Texts of Monastic Buddhism in India*, Honolulu: University of Hawaii Press, 1997

Silber, Ilana Friedrich, *Virtuosity, Charisma, and Social Order: A Comparative Sociological Study of Monasticism in Theravada Buddhism and Medieval Catholicism*, Cambridge: Cambridge University Press, 1995

Wijayaratna, Mohan, *Buddhist Monastic Life: According to the Texts of the Theravada Tradition*, translated by Claude Grangier and Steven Collins, Cambridge: Cambridge University Press, 1990

Santiago de Compostela, Spain

Santiago de Compostela (Iago = James in Spanish) is located in the northwestern corner of Spain in the department of La Coruña in Galicia. Compostela is said to be the burial site of the Apostle James the Greater, martyred A.D. 44 in Jerusalem. His body was believed to have been transported in a stone boat to the present hamlet of Padrón on the Atlantic coast a few miles from Compostela. Following numerous miracles attributed to the intervention of the saint, the region came to be regarded as sacred. Around 1095 the ancient see of Iria was transferred to Compostela, which became the center of the national and Christian movement against the Muslim rulers of the country. James' shrine evolved into the third most prestigious pilgrimage site in Christendom, ranking behind only Rome and Jerusalem.

A famous guide that was compiled around 1140 by an anonymous French cleric details four routes through France and Spain by which one might have reached Compostela. It also describes field conditions encountered along the way (including the effects of rural water pollution) and the appearance of the Cathedral of Santiago de Compostela with its sculptured portals. The medieval pilgrim using this guide several generations later would have encountered a walled Compostela of considerable importance with seven gates, a Romanesque cathedral, and a number of other parish churches and monastic establishments. The latter included the Abbey of St. Pedro de Fora (no longer extant), the Monastery of St. Martín Pinario, and St. Pedro de Antealtares (now rebuilt and rededicated as St. Pelayo de Antealtares). Pilgrims unable to lodge at these monastic establishments might have stayed at a large pilgrims' hospice that formerly stood opposite the north transept portal of the cathedral.

The scallop shell is the badge of the Compostela pilgrim. The pilgrimage to Santiago de Compostela continued throughout the period after the Middle Ages as a relative trickle that, in recent years, has swollen to a torrent. This increase can be attributed to many factors: a recent focus on the logistics of this pilgrimage by the Council of Europe, increased worldwide interest in pilgrimages of all kinds, a papal visit, a plethora of telecommunications and publications about aspects of the Compostela pilgrimage, and a recent concentration of Holy Years (ones in which St. James' Day, 25 July, falls on a Sunday). The normal interval between Holy Years is 6, 5, or 11 years. The most recent were 1993 and 1999; will the next be 2004?

Present-day visitors to Compostela find the central, old part of the city preserved as a historic district of arcaded streets and 17th- and 18th-century stone buildings. The cathedral, still very much its centerpiece, now has an elegant 18th-century Baroque overcoat surrounding a Romanesque core. The interior is a beautiful example of the "Pilgrimage Road" type of basilica, with barrel-vaulted nave, transept and choir surrounded by half-barrel-vaulted galleries, groin-vaulted aisles, ambulatory, and radiating chapels – a plan that accommodates simultaneously large numbers of visitors and regular services at the main altar.

Annie Shaver-Crandell

See also Pilgrimages, Christian: Western Europe; Relics, Christian Monastic; Spain: History

Further Reading

Conant, Kenneth John, *The Early Architectural History of the Cathedral of Santiago de Compostela*, Cambridge, Massachusetts: Harvard University Press; annotated translation into Gallegan and Castilian as *Arquitectura románica da Catedral de Santiago de Compostela*, translated by J.G. Beramendi, Santiago de Compostela: Colexio Oficial de Arquitectos de Galica, 1983 (this work includes Serafín Moralejo Álvarez's "Notas para unha revisión de K.J. Conant")

López Alsina, F., "La sede compostelana y la Catedral de Santiago de Compostela en la Edad Media," in *La Catedral de Santiago de Compostela*, Loracha (La Coruña): Xuntanza Editorial, 1993

López Ferreiro, Antonio, *Historia de la Santa A.M. Iglesia de Santiago de Compostela*, 12 vols., Santiago de Compostela: Facsimilar, 1983

Moralejo, Serafín, "The Codex Calixtinus as an Art-Historical Source," in *The Codex Calixtinus and the Shrine of St. James*, edited by John Williams and Alison Stones, Tübingen: Narr, 1992

Passini, Jean, *El Camino de Santiago: Itinerario y núcleos de población*, Madrid: MOPT, 1993

Santiago, Camino de Europa: Culto y Cultura en la Peregrinación a Compostela: Monasterio de San Martín Pinario, Santiago de Compostela, 1993, Santiago de Compostela, 1993 (exhibition catalogue)

Shaver-Crandell, Annie, and Paula Gerson, with the assistance of Alison Stones, *The Pilgrim's Guide to Santiago de Compostela: A Gazetteer*, London: Harvey Miller, 1995

Sapen. *See* Sakya Pandita (Sapen)

Savonarola, Girolamo 1452–1498

Italian Dominican friar, prophetic preacher, and political agitator, eventually excommunicated

Girolamo Savonarola was born in Ferrara, Italy, into a merchant family. As a youth he studied Latin, scholastic theology, medicine, and the humanistic disciplines. In 1475 he entered a Dominican house in Bologna and was later transferred to St. Marco in Florence.

From 1482 to 1490 Savonarola established himself as a preacher and champion of the poor in Florence and other cities. Recalled to Florence in 1490, he became increasingly critical of the government (1478–1492) of Lorenzo dei Medici and the citizens' avarice and materialism. Although his preaching style was considered crude and outdated, he was friends with well-known humanists. He terrorized many in Florence with his prophecies of the coming of a second Charlemagne and a new Cyrus who would purge the city and Italy of vice. When in 1494 the scourge of God did in fact arrive in the person of King Charles VIII (1483–1498) of France, the Signoria sent Savonarola to dissuade Charles from attacking Florence. The fall of the Medici and the departure of the French from the city greatly added to the Friar's prestige, enabling him to promote a Venetian-style republic, a reduction in public entertainments, programs for the poor, and an alliance with the French king.

No figure in Florentine history has perhaps ever been so revered as Savonarola was during the years 1494–1498. Despite resistance from pro-Medicean and other families, he influenced the city's foreign and domestic policies. He tried but failed to establish a monastery outside Florence that would serve as a prototype of moral reform for his Dominican order, for the city, and for the Church universal. The friars of the monastery of St. Marco became renowned for their austerity and piety. After 1494 Savonarola toned down his theme of a degenerate Florence about to be punished for its sins; now he emphasized the city as the new Jerusalem that would usher in the millennium and the conversion of the Jews and Turks. The commune's turn to repentance and faith would bring it fame and prosperity; the rest of Italy would soon follow its example. A number of factors – Florence's internal divisions, fear of external attack and of the return of the Medici, Savonarola's popularity, and the Piagnoni faction ("weepers," named after those who wept during his sermons) – permitted the friar to exercise power behind the political scenes.

In 1497–1498 Savonarola's prestige suffered because of economic setbacks for Florence, failure to recover Pisa, and Milan's intrigues as well as hostility from Franciscans and the secular clergy. Aristocratic resentment also existed regarding popular participation in government, and more anti-Savonarolan members now belonged to the Signoria. Impatient with the friar's attacks on immorality in the Vatican and with Florence's refusal to join the league against France, the Borgia Pope Alexander VI (1492–1503) excommunicated him and threatened to impose an interdict on the city. The farcical collapse of an ordeal by fire that was intended to prove the friar's sanctity emboldened his enemies to capture, torture, and burn him at the stake as a false prophet. This occurred on 23 May 1498 in the Piazza della Signoria.

In his sermons and writings, Savonarola utilized at least four monastic and semi-monastic themes: (1) the monastery as a model for moral reform for secular communities and for the Church at large, (2) the monastery as an anticipation of the heavenly Jerusalem, (3) the return to a simple way of life without material refinement and secular learning, and (4) the centrality of prayer and the life of the suffering Christ. He also evoked prophecy drawn from Joachim of Fiore (c. 1135–1202). Savonarola sought to marshal the resources of the community for the common good and to stamp out greed and sexual misconduct. He emphasized the spiritual dimension of the sacraments and liturgical expression of the faith, obedience to Christ alone, and a Christian society based on love and cooperation. He saw the lay community as an elect nation and tended to place personal sanctity above the concept of ecclesiastical office. He believed that God occasionally sent a prophet, a liminal monk-like figure, to restore the true Church.

For half a century after Savonarola, the Piagnoni continued to advocate his agenda of republican government, apocalyptic prophecy, mystical speculation, sumptuary laws, concern for the poor, reform of civic and ecclesiastical institutions, and the moral imperative for Christians to improve society. Savonarola's genius was to synthesize certain monastic traditions of loving community and apocalyptic prophecy with Florence's heritage of republicanism, civic pride (expressed in public liturgical and secular festivals and processions), territorial integrity, and cultural supremacy.

THOMAS RENNA

See also Dominicans: General or Male; Florence, Italy; Joachim of Fiore; Sexuality: Christian Perspectives

Biography

Born and raised in Ferrara, Italy, Savonarola entered the Dominican order in Bologna in 1475. From 1482 to 1487 and again from 1490 he was lector at San Marco, Florence, where he became Prior in 1491. A fiery preacher, he launched a new Congregation in 1493, calling for moral reform and siding with the invading French king Charles VIII in 1494–1495. A three-year conflict with Pope Alexander VI ended in Savonarola's excommunication in 1497 and condemnation to hanging by Florentines in 1498.

Major Work

Triumphus Crucis, 1497

Further Reading

Erlanger, Rachel, *The Unarmed Prophet: Savonarola in Florence*, New York: McGraw-Hill, 1988
Guicciardini, Francesco, *The History of Italy*, translated by Sidney Alexander, New York: Macmillan, 1969
Macey, Patrick, *Bonfire Songs: Savonarola's Musical Legacy*, Oxford: Clarendon Press, 1998
Polizzotto, Lorenzo, *The Elect Nation: The Savonarolan Movement in Florence 1494–1545*, Oxford: Clarendon Press, and New York: Oxford University Press, 1994
Ridolfi, Roberto, *The Life of Girolamo Savonarola*, translated by Cecil Grayson, London: Routledge and Kegan Paul, 1959
Weinstein, Donald, *Savonarola and Florence: Prophecy and Patriotism in the Renaissance*, Princeton, New Jersey: Princeton University Press, 1970

Scandinavia

Monastic impulses reached Scandinavia through the first missionaries. Saint Ansgar (801–865), the founder of Christianity in Denmark and Sweden and first archbishop of Hamburg-Bremen, was a monk from Corvey. Some Anglo-Saxon missionaries of the 11th century had a monastic background, for example, Abbot David of Munktorp (d. 1060), Sweden.

However, the earliest monastic community we are certain of in Denmark is the Benedictine Cathedral Chapter, Odense, Funen, founded around 1095 by King Erik Ejegod (1095–1104) to receive monks from Evesham, England, for the cult of the martyr king St. Cnut (d. 1086). The existing buildings on the site show the original setting around the cathedral, itself the monks' church. Another royal foundation is the remarkable church of Veng north of Skanderborg, Jutland, built at the latest around 1125. This Benedictine abbey ceased to exist around 1165, when Cistercians took over the site, only to abandon it. In the decades around 1100, bishops founded Our Lady's nunnery in Roskilde, Sjælland, and St. Peter's nunnery in Lund, Scania, each with its still existing church. (The province of Scania/Skane, today Swedish, was Danish during the Middle Ages.)

The well-preserved Augustinian church of Holy Cross, Dalby, Scania, where the 12th-century *Dalby Book* was written, has an early crypt from around 1060. Already before 1088 monks were at Our Lady's in Ringsted, Sjælland, richly endowed in 1135 by King Eric II and thereafter magnificently transformed into the sanctuary of King Valdemar the Great's (1157–1182) father, Cnut Lavard, who was canonized 1170. This is truly a royal sanctuary.

In Norway foundations have been excavated of the royal abbey on the island of Nidarholm near Trondheim from around 1100. Ruins on the stormy island of Selja between Bergen and Trondheim indicate a St. Alban's abbey also from around 1100 with a pilgrimage cave.

Sweden's first monastery was Vreta, founded around 1100 by King Inge and Queen Helena. Its present church contains proof of beautiful Cistercian architecture from around 1200.

Abbey church (Cistercian), Esroem, Denmark.
Photo courtesy of Chris Schabel

Some early monasteries in Denmark promoted by bishops left no visible traces above ground: St. Michael's, Slesvig (today Schleswig), Germany; Seem near Ribe; All Saints, Lund, Scania; and Our Lady's, Randers, Jutland. In 1135 Lady Bodil and her sons made a foundation in Næstved, Sjælland, where St. Peter's church was given to Benedictine monks. They later moved to a site "in the forest," Skovkloster, today the boarding school of Herlufsholm. In Bergen, Norway, Munkeliv was founded for Benedictine monks around 1110. For a short period around 1200, a Benedictine Cathedral Chapter existed in Uppsala, Sweden, for the cult of its patron, St. Eric (d. 1160).

Several remaining churches witness to the life of Danish Benedictine nuns: the Romanesque brick church of Dalum, Funen, from around 1200, with the convent buildings indicated on the ground, and Bosjökloster, Scania, impressively situated between the two largest lakes of that province, surrounded by myth and legend. Northern Jutland preserves the full site of three Benedictine nunneries, each transformed into church with manor house: Oxholm, Dronninglund, and, near Viborg, Ørslevkloster, today a spiritual refuge with guest rooms. The churches of Stubber and Gudum, Jutland, still stand.

Benedictine history continued in Denmark through the Middle Ages. In the upper part of the Gudenå River basin, Jutland, Benedictine monks lived in Voer and nuns in Ring. The Randers monks moved to Essenbæk around 1150. The church in Halskov, Lolland, was taken over by monks from Ringsted who settled there around 1300 and adapted it to their needs.

The splendid wave of Cistercian inspiration at the time of Bernard of Clairvaux (1090–1153) had a deep impact, not least because of his devotee, Eskil (1137–1177), archbishop of Lund and a compelling prelate. As ecclesiastical head of the church in all Scandinavia, Eskil inspired two kings to support the Cistercians: in Sweden, Sverker (d. 1156), who in 1143 founded Alvastra on his own family property at the foot of the hill of Omberg near Lake Vättern, Östergötland, and in Denmark, Valdemar the Great (d. 1182), who in 1157 founded Vitskøl on the bay of Limfjorden in northern Jutland. Impressive ruins of church and convent buildings testify to the Cistercian monastic life that flourished in these two abbeys for more than 400 years. Some ruins also remain of Danish Øm near Skanderborg with its abbey museum and of Esrum, Sjælland, also with a museum opened quite recently. Some Danish Cistercian abbey churches became Lutheran parish churches and were thereby preserved: the famous Sorø, Sjælland, home of the noble family of the Hvide, today a boarding school; Brahetrolleborg, Funen, with church and monastic quadrangle; and Løgum, southern Jutland,

West range and church facade, Carmelite monastery, Helsingør, Zeeland, Denmark, second half of the 15th century.
Photo courtesy of Chris Schabel

an impressive Cistercian church with an excellent chapter house preserved. Brick is the building material in all three cases. Nothing is left above ground of the Danish abbeys of Herrevad, Scania, or its daughter foundation in Tvis, western Jutland.

In Norway the ruins of Lyse (1146) in a valley south of Bergen, of Hovedøya (1147) on an island in Oslo Bay, and of Tautra (1207) on an island outside Trondheim testify to Cistercian life. In Sweden the ruins of Roma (1164) on the island of Gotland and those of the nunnery of Gudhem, Västergötland, still remain.

In Sweden, besides Vreta, Cistercian Varnhem in Västergötland is the best example of a monastic layout. Its church enjoyed generous support from the noble family of the De La Gardie long after the Reformation. Uniquely isolated and built in stone is Nydala, Småland, Sweden, founded in 1143, as was Alvastra. Julita, Södermanland, Sweden, is a manor house today. Of the Cistercian nunneries in Sweden, Skokloster near Uppsala is most worth mentioning. Cistercian nuns also resided in well-preserved Riseberga and in Askaby.

The great monastic movement of the 12th century comprised Augustinian (Austin) Canons as well. Saint William of Æbelholt, Sjælland, who died in 1203 after many decades of monastic leadership in Denmark (canonized in 1224), was a French canon of St. Geneviève in Paris. He made Æbelholt famous for medical treatment, as seen by excavations of the cemetery. As they did in Dalby, Scania, Austin Canons resided in Grinderslev and Vestervig, northwestern Jutland, as testified by grand monastic churches. The Augustinian Cathedral Chapter in Viborg, Jutland, played a leading role in monastic observance among the Austin Canons in Denmark. Their community life might have begun in the church of Asmild across the lake, where they were replaced by nuns. In 12th-century Norway monasteries for Austin Canons, some of whom were inspired by the abbey of St. Victor in Paris, were founded for the pastoral and administrative support of the bishops of Trondheim, Bergen, and Stavanger. In the 1260s those of Stavanger moved to Utstein on the island of Mosterøy, Norway's best-preserved monastic site. Even Iceland had Austin Canons sharing the religious and literary heritage of the island.

A branch of Austin Canons, the Premonstratensians, served as Cathedral Chapter of Børglum and had a nuns' convent in Vrejlev, both in northern Jutland. Among this Order's abbeys in Scania, Bäckaskog from the 13th century, now a manor house, is well preserved, except the church, which has been cut through to provide an entrance porch. Its canons came from Vä with its 12th-century church, an early royal foundation. Övedskloster is a manor house, but nothing is left of Tommarp in southeastern Scania, founded around 1150, once the Order's most important cultural center for the easternmost tip of medieval Denmark. In Lund the foundations of the Order's first abbey church, St. Drotten (Christchurch), can be seen in a museum below street level. The excavated remains of the Order's circular church in Tønsberg, Norway, dedicated to Norway's patron, St. Olav (d. 1030), and part of convent buildings can be visited.

From 1280 the Order of the Hospitallers of St. John served the church of St. Hans, Odense, Funen. The Reformation king refashioned the convent and hospital buildings into a castle that is still in use. In Dueholm, Mors, northern Jutland, the local museum has acquired what is left of the convent buildings. The leading Hospitallers' convent lay in Antvorskov outside Slagelse, Sjælland, later rebuilt into a royal castle but today in ruins. The churches of the Hospitallers in Eskilstuna and Stockholm, Sweden, were torn down during the Reformation.

The number of convents grew rapidly after the arrival of the mendicants from around 1230. Scandinavia's best-preserved

South aisle of church, Carmelite monastery, Helsingør, Zeeland, Denmark, second half of the 15th century. The chalk painting on the ceiling is a Danish specialty.
Photo courtesy of Chris Schabel

Cloister garth, Carmelite monastery, Helsingør, Zeeland, Denmark, second half of the 15th century.
Photo courtesy of Chris Schabel

Dominican churches are St. Katarina in Ribe, Denmark, and Our Lady's in Sigtuna, Sweden. Convent life was introduced into present-day Finland by the Dominicans, who had their convent in Turku/Åbo and deeply influenced religious life in the Cathedral and all Finland.

Preaching and Franciscan piety spread, as can be seen in Ystad, Scania, and in remarkable churches: the present cathedral in Bergen, Norway; Riddarholmskyrkan in Stockholm, Sweden, the mausoleum of Swedish kings; Arboga, Sweden, with rich Franciscan paintings; and Horsens in Jutland, with carved wooden choir stalls displaying the special saints of the Order. Convent buildings alone are preserved in Odense, Funen, and some other places.

The waves of new piety in the 15th century brought Carmelites to Denmark. Their spacious church and convent buildings can be seen in Elsinore/Helsingør. Paintings from their monastic period are extant in the church of Sæby, northern Jutland. The Order of the Holy Spirit built several monasteries of which that in Fåborg, Funen, still exists as parish church of the town. Antonites arrived in Præstø, Sjælland. A cultural renewal took place in the old abbeys, where the *Rhyme Chronicle* and other historical works were written.

However, the most remarkable feature of Scandinavian monastic history is the foundation of a new religious order, the Bridgettines (the Order of the Holy Savior) by St. Birgitta, a Swedish noble lady (1303–1373, canonized 1391). Its first house was Vadstena, founded in Birgitta's lifetime. Erik the Pomeranian (1397–1438), king of the three Scandinavian kingdoms, wanted to provide each of his two other kingdoms with an abbey of this Order, so he founded Maribo, Lolland, Denmark, in 1416, today the cathedral of Maribo, and handed over Munkeliv, Bergen, Norway, to the Bridgettines. High nobility of Jutland founded Mariager around 1445, a section of which is a parish church today. In Finland, Naantali/Nådendal was founded around 1450, the pride of medieval Finland and likewise a parish church today. Spiritual and intellectual renewal and the new devotions of the 15th century were greatly favored by this new Order through its libraries and the preaching of its priests.

The mendicant orders were the first to be attacked in the Reformation upheavals. In 1536, when King Christian III (1534–1559) transformed the Catholic Church in Denmark and Norway into a Lutheran state church, urban monasteries were soon dissolved and emptied. Rural monasteries were allowed to exist but could not accept novices; as the last monks and nuns died, the property went into secular hands. In Sweden only Vadstena and Nådendal managed to survive into the 1590s. In 1595 all exercises of Catholic cult and all monasteries were prohibited by law.

The ban on monasticism was formally lifted in Denmark by the law of religious freedom in 1849, but not until 1936 was a convent of Benedictine nuns established, from 1942 in Åsebakken, Copenhagen. In 1960 Cistercian nuns bought the castle of Sostrup, Jutland, where they became an abbey in 1999. Since 1947 Carmelite nuns have a convent in Iceland, and in 1990 they initiated a convent in Tromsø, Norway.

In Sweden the ban on monasteries was lifted in 1951, and the first Catholic convent became that of Carmelite nuns in Glumslöv, Scania, followed by Bridgettine sisters in Vadstena, who took up monastic rule in 1963, and by Carmelite fathers in Norraby, Scania, in 1973. In 1983 the Lutheran "Sisters of Jesus' Mother Mary" under Magda Wollter (d. 1968) converted to the Catholic Church; in 1991 they established the abbey of Mariavall, Scania. Meanwhile the Lutheran "Daughters of Mary" under Paulina Norrman (d. 1985) built convents in Vallby, Vadstena, Kollund/Denmark, and Naantali/Finland. In 1988 the Vadstena community became Catholic, and in 1997 they moved to their new "Abbey of the Sacred Heart," Borghamn.

TORE NYBERG

See also Augustinian Canons; Bridgettines; Carmelites; Dominicans; Franciscans; Hospitallers (Knights of Malta since 1530); Premonstratensian Canons; Protestant Monasticism: Lutheran; Reformation; Vadstena, Sweden; Victorines

Further Reading

Cinthio, Erik, editor, *Skånska kloster* (Skånes Hembygdsförbunds Årsbok 1987/88), Lund: Skanes Hembygdsförbund, 1989

Daugaard, J.B., *Om de danske Klostre i Middelalderen* (On the Danish Monasteries in the Middle Ages), Copenhagen: Seidelin, 1830

Foreningen til Norske Fortidsminnesmerkers Bevaring, Arbok 141, 1987, Oslo, 1987 (Year Book [141, 1987] of the Association for Maintenance of Historical Artifacts in Norway; the entire volume is devoted to monasticism in Norway)

France, James, *The Cistercians in Scandinavia* (Cistercian Studies Series 131), Kalamazoo, Michigan: Cistercian Publications, 1992

Gallén, Jarl, *La Province de Dacie de l'ordre des Frères Prêcheurs (I: Historie Générale jusqu'au Grand Schisme)* (The Dominican Province of Dacia, I: General History until the Great Schism), Helsingfors: Söderström, 1946

Karlsson, Jan O.M., "Klostren i det medeltida Sverige" (The Monasteries in Medieval Sweden), *hikuin* 20 (1993)

Lange, Christian C.A., *De Norske Klostres Historie i Middelalderen* (History of the Norwegian Monasteries in the Middle Ages), 2nd edition, Christiania: Tönsbergs, 1856

McGuire, Brian Patrick, *The Cistercians in Denmark: Their Attitudes, Roles, and Functions in Medieval Society* (Cistercian Studies Series 35), Kalamazoo, Michigan: Cistercian Publications, 1982

Nyberg, Tore, *Monasticism in North-Western Europe, 800–1200*, London: Ashgate, 2000

Ortved, Edward, *Cistercieordenen og dens Klostre i Norden, I: Cistercieordenen Overhovedet* (The Cistercians and their Monasteries in Scandinavia, I: General History), Copenhagen: J.H. Schultz, 1927; *II: Sveriges Klostre* (II: The Swedish Monasteries), Copenhagen: J.H. Schultz, 1933

Vellev, Jens, editor, "Danske klostre: Arkæologiske undersøgelser 1972–1996" (Danish Monasteries: Archaeological research 1972–1996), *hikuin* 23 (1996)

Scholars, Benedictine

Scholarship, especially in the modern critical sense, is not essential to Benedictine life but can easily emerge within it because an unfailing monastic practice has been the reading, studying, and meditating on the Scriptures. Pachomian tradition had already insisted on the necessity of learning how to read, and Cassiodorus (484–580) wrote two treatises on study and learning. The pattern of life stipulated by the Rule of St. Benedict (RB) establishes an environment that not only conduces to serious study and research but also supports and stimulates it. The monastic routine and daily *horarium* lend themselves to the possibility of scholarly activity, legislating the quiet hours of reading and reflecting necessary for any prolonged research. The RB not only provides leisure time, but also inculcates attitudes of critical judgment and healthy self-suspicion that aid the Benedictine who engages in scholarly work.

The Benedictine *horarium* schedules for the monk at least two to three hours of reading each day, both privately and publicly. Serious texts provide the basis of such reading: biblical commentaries, theological treatises, liturgical and patristic volumes, historical works, and devotional literature. The RB also provides for periods of discussion or disputation when presuppositions can be challenged and defended (cf. RB 42 *collatio*). It takes for granted a collection of books to be used for liturgy, common reading, and private reading. Good libraries are part of monastic patrimony.

The RB proposes to establish a "school of the Lord's service" (cf. RB Prol. 45). The precise meaning of the term *schola* has occasioned much discussion and dispute. Although it is not quite equivalent to our modern notion of school, the term can be used as the basis for considering the scholarly activities among Benedictines. In root meaning *schola* refers to leisure or to freedom. One is free to pursue activities that transcend mere survival. One is free to study, to read, to reflect, and to write. In the RB this notion of leisure is probably better expressed by the locution *vacare lectioni*: to enjoy a holiday with a book in hand! No Benedictine is coerced to do scholarly work, nor is one even explicitly encouraged to do so by the RB. Nevertheless a monk's involvement with serious texts occasionally blossoms into authentic scholarship, a result, as it were, of a "monastic schooling"!

In a short essay it is impossible to note all recognized Benedictine scholars, and, moreover, what one age or period would deem to be true scholarly activity, another age might not. Only in more recent times can a canon be established to determine what constitutes scholarship. Nevertheless as one looks at 1,500 years of Benedictine history, one can discern in almost every period men and women of outstanding intellectual merit: curious, critical, cautious, yet creative.

In a broad or extended sense, the sixth-century author of the RB could be considered a scholar, as he was evidently well acquainted with the earlier literary monastic traditions of the East and the West. Source criticism reveals the finished RB to be a distillation and synthesis of biblical, liturgical, patristic, and canonical positions melded into a new and harmonious whole.

Not much is known for certain about the early diffusion of the RB or about the monasteries that adopted it as a single norm for life. Historical evidence exists that the RB was known in England in the early eighth century, as witnessed by the oldest extant manuscript (Oxford: Hatton 48). The Venerable Bede (c. 672–735), monk of Wearmouth-Jarrow, should be considered in Benedictine tradition, as he set the canons of monastic scholarship for later generations. He wrote biblical commentaries that depended heavily on earlier Fathers but is famous above all for his historical works.

On the Continent the rise of the Carolingian dynasty exerted a lasting influence on any future scholarly direction taken by Benedictine tradition. The imposition of a Roman rule on a newly united Europe demanded established texts and authoritative interpretations. Charlemagne, king of the Franks (768–814) and Holy Roman emperor (800), grasped the importance of an educated clergy in bringing about reform and unity and insisted that schools be established in monasteries and at cathedrals. The resulting system of learning was both the cause and the result of what has come to be called the Carolingian Renaissance. Under the influence of Paul the Deacon (c. 730–799), Lombard monk of Monte Cassino, and of Alcuin of York (c. 735–804), a Palace school was established at Aachen. The initial group of scholars and students came from every part of the kingdom, from Ireland to Visigothic Spain and from the Atlantic to the Rhine-Danube border. It is impossible to catalog the names of all those who participated in the movement. Many of them were Benedictines, such as Hilduin of St. Denis (c. 775–859) and Smaragdus of St.-Mihiel (c. 760–825).

Alcuin was from York, and although not a monk until late in life when he was appointed lay abbot of St. Martin at Tours, he was the guiding force in the Carolingian Renaissance, writing in the fields of liturgy, scripture, grammar, and theology. One of his favorite pupils at Tours was Rabanus Maurus (c. 776–856), a monk from Fulda who became head of the school there, then abbot, and eventually archbishop of Mainz. Rabanus was a man of extraordinary learning and scholarship, competent in various fields. His biblical commentaries show both fidelity to tradition and imaginative creativity. He is a theologian, a liturgist, a mathematician, and a brilliant figurative poet. One of Rabanus' pupils was Walafrid Strabo (809–849), future abbot of Reichenau. Another pupil was Lupus of Ferrières (805–862), whom some call the first great Western humanist and encyclopedist. His great love for the classics merits him the title of a true Renaissance man. These four Benedictine scholars together span the geographical area from Tours to Fulda to Reichenau to Ferrières and the period from 800 to 860.

Such monastic scholars were able to blossom because of both the solid scholarly tradition established in monastery schools and the collection and preservation of manuscripts that made famous the libraries at Fulda, Reichenau, Corbie, St. Gall, St. Denis, Fleury, Luxeuil, Lorsch, St.-Riquier, and elsewhere.

The scholarly tone and impulse of the Carolingian Renaissance diminished along with the breakup of the empire that resulted from the invasion of the Norsemen. However, a new impulse came to be identified with such Norman abbeys as Bec and Fécamp. Lanfranc (c. 1005–1089) and Anselm (c. 1033–1109), future archbishops of Canterbury, can be considered important pre-Scholastics. Anselm is famous for the dictum *credo ut intelligam*. For him faith and reason worked hand in hand and could be distinguished but not separated. To some extent he already anticipated Abelard (1079–1142), who died a Cluniac monk. Abelard also distinguished between faith and reason but seemed to make faith subservient to reason, thus earning the wrath of Bernard of Clairvaux (1090–1153).

Scholasticism sharpened the distinction between faith and reason, ultimately contributing to their disjunction and opposition. From this disjunction would stem the divorce between philosophy and the sacred sciences that has dominated the West from the late Middle Ages to the present. The dichotomy would become more pronounced as science rather than wisdom became the norm for scholarship in the Enlightenment. After Anselm of

Tomb (16th century) of St. Bede in the westernmost chapel (14th century) of Durham Cathedral, Durham, England.
Photo courtesy of the Editor

Bec no Benedictine ranks among the great recognized philosophers in the West. That does not mean that monks did not study philosophy, but by and large they earned recognition as scholars in the fields of scripture, patristics, theology, canon law, and history rather than in philosophy and occasionally in genetics, physics, and medicine, in which faith and reason need not come into direct conflict. It is clear that a monk cannot sidestep his faith when doing scholarly activity.

Hildegard of Bingen (1098–1179) has a rightful place among Benedictine scholars of the 12th century. A contemporary of Abelard, Heloise, and Bernard of Clairvaux, she is known for her music and poetry. Her visions, dictated in *Scivias* (1141–1151), reveal her knowledge of Scripture, the Fathers, and liturgical texts. She is recognized also as a medical physician.

Throughout the period of Scholasticism and humanism as well as the Renaissance, few Benedictine scholars emerge that are worthy of special notice. One reason for this is that with the rise of the friars and the universities, scholarly hegemony passed to other religious orders. Moreover, as became evident with the Reformation, faith and reason were seen to be diverging. Eventually piety and scholarship, like faith and reason, would appear to be in conflict.

In later Benedictine tradition pride of place in scholarship indisputably belongs to the scholars and community of the French Maurists. A result and product of humanism and the Renaissance, the Congregation of St. Maur was the French descendant of the Congregation of St. Vannes centered at Verdun in Lorraine. Both benefited from the reforming decrees of the Council of Trent (1545–1563). The 17th century was a golden age of scholarship when the French monasteries produced a generation of highly educated men who while full of curiosity appreciated the history and literature of the past. For almost two centuries the Maurists set the tone for scholarly activity in the post-Tridentine Counter-Reformation as well as in the salons of Enlightenment France. Guidance given by the members of this Congregation has left a lasting impression on subsequent history. Ever since, monks in essence are considered to be learned.

The Maurists treated intellectual activity and production as part of the monastic mission, and the Congregation expressly admitted this aspect of its vocation. This does not mean that every individual member/monk was a scholar, but the energies, resources, and talents of all were channeled toward this goal. It would be futile to attempt to recount the dynamic development within the Congregation from its beginning around 1600 to its suppression in 1789. Dom David Knowles distinguishes four periods during this arc of time, each having its own physiognomy. The second period (1665–1707) is the "age of Mabillon." Jean Mabillon (1632–1707) is unique even among the other extraordinary scholars who were Maurists, such as Luc d'Achery (1609–1685), Edmond Martène (1659–1739), and Bernard Montfaucon (1655–1741).

The fact that learned work was becoming the distinguishing employment for monks came under severe criticism from within the Benedictine monastic tradition. An outspoken critic of Mabillon was his contemporary Armand-Jean de Rancé (1626–1700), the reforming abbot of the Cistercian abbey of La Trappe who taught that monks must banish intellectual activity. This dispute was but a new manifestation of the constant and lingering tension between piety and intellectual endeavors that seems to be coterminous with monasticism. It is analogous to the fundamental tension between faith and reason, but the polarization and exclusion of one or the other of these dimensions usually leads to distortion.

The French Revolution and subsequent Napoleonic suppression of the majority of Benedictine monasteries diminished all scholarly activity. However, in the period of "rebirth" the newly formed Congregations of Solesmes and Beuron, alongside such ancient abbeys as Monte Cassino and Einsiedeln, resumed the role of pathfinders in the areas of historical criticism, liturgy, patristics, paleography, and Church music.

The 19th-century revival of Benedictine monasticism took place in the context of Romanticism, liberal theology, and critical historiography. Interest was renewed in authentic historical texts and critical editing of them. The musical paleography school at Solesmes sought to reestablish the ancient chants of the Latin Rites: Roman, Mozarabic, and Milanese. Monks from both Solesmes and Beuron became undisputed authorities in patristic and liturgical texts. Encyclopedias and dictionaries, such as the *Dictionnaire d' archéologie chrétienne et de liturgie* (1903–1953), were products of Benedictine scholars sometimes working almost single-handedly, as did for instance Henri Leclercq (1869–1945).

For at least a century, modern methods of study have been applied in monastic research just as in patristic studies generally. A type of critical scholarship that employs scientific historical and literary methods has expanded the horizon and understanding of Benedictine tradition. In this way Benedictines too have been shaped by the intellectual revolutions of the modern period, including the scientific revolution of the 16th and 17th centuries and the revolution in historical method that was the great achievement of the 19th century.

In patristic scholarship special mention should be made of Dom Germain Morin (1861–1946), monk of Maredsous. His familiarity with Caesarius of Arles (c. 470–542) enabled him to reestablish the authorship of sermons that for years had been attributed to St. Augustine. Morin, along with confreres at Maredsous, such as Usmer Berlière (1861–1932), supplied the backbone of the *Revue Bénédictine*. In more recent times the Abbey of Steenbrugge has guided the publication of Corpus Christianorum: Series Latina (CCL) and Corpus Christianorum: Continuatio Mediaevalis (CCLM), a series of critical patristic and medieval texts that acts as a corrective to Migne's *Patrologiae*, which in turn had utilized the Maurist editions.

Many monastic texts have been critically established by Benedictine monks. Scholars such as Cunibert Mohlberg (1878–1963), monk of Maria Laach, are recognized for their work on ancient liturgical texts. In biblical criticism the monks of San Gerolamo in Rome have established the critical text of the Vulgate, whereas monks at Beuron have been working on the *Itala* or *Vetus Latina*.

Today the areas of special interest for monastic scholars remain the fields of the Bible, the Fathers, liturgy, and history. In the past half century, a "school of theology" has emerged at St. Anselmo in Rome. It can be traced from Anselm Stolz (1900–1942), monk of Gerleve, through Cyprian Vagaggini (1909–1999), monk of Camaldoli. This serious and scholarly theological endeavor shows itself dependent on and faithful to the biblical-patristic-liturgical-historical core of Benedictine spirituality and academic interests.

For monastics, scholarly endeavors are not mere academic pastimes. Scholarship belongs to the lifeblood of monastic life. Not every monk must be a scholar, but without the contribution of Benedictine scholars monastic life could quickly become insipid and dull.

AMBROSE G. WATHEN

See also Abelard, Peter; Alcuin; Anselm, St.; Bede, St.; Benedict of Nursia, St.; Bernard of Clairvaux, St.; Cassiodorus; Education of Christian Monastics; France: History; Fulda, Germany; Guéranger, Prosper; Hildegard of Bingen, St.; Historiography, Recent; Knowles, M. David; Lanfranc; Leclercq, Jean; Libraries: Western Christian; Maurists; Rabanus Maurus; Rancé, Armand-Jean de; Rome, Italy; Solesmes, France; Trappists; Visual Arts, Western Christian: Book Arts before the Renaissance; Walafrid Strabo

Further Reading

Duckett, Eleanor Shipley, *Carolingian Portraits: A Study in the Ninth Century*, Ann Arbor: University of Michigan Press, 1962

Knowles, David, "The Maurists," in *Great Historical Enterprises: Problems in Monastic History*, London and New York: Nelson, 1962

Kristeller, Paul Oskar, "The Contribution of Religious Orders to Renaissance Thought and Learning," *The American Benedictine Review* 21 (1970)

Laistner, M.L.W., *Thought and Letters in Western Europe, A.D. 500 to 900*, London: Methuen, and New York: MacVeagh, 1931

Leclercq, Jean, *The Love of Learning and the Desire for God*, New York: Fordham University Press, 1961; London: SPCK, 1978

Schmitz, Philibert, *Histoire de l'Ordre de Saint-Benoît*, volumes 2 and 5, Éditions de Maredsous, 1948

Sullivan, Thomas, *Benedictine Monks at the University of Paris, A.D. 1229–1500: A Biographical Register*, London and New York: E.J. Brill, 1995

Scholastics, Buddhist

In modern discourse Scholasticism is often deemed irrelevant, being caricatured as focusing on questions such as "How many angels can dance on the head of a pin?" This article will show, with a Buddhist example, how that might not be such an unreasonable query after all.

The Buddha taught the dharma in the sūtra basket of the canon. Commentaries thereon constitute the third basket, called the abhidharma, or "advanced teaching." That systematization of the dharma grew after King Aśoka (third century B.C.) helped to support learning. Like Constantine, Aśoka hated internal dissension and pushed for doctrinal uniformity, so we are told by the Pāli records that label its tradition, Theravāda, the Aśokan orthodoxy. However, the story is not that simple. Unlike that southern path where Buddhaghosa (fifth century) became the singular commentarial authority, the north knew many more sectarian groups giving rise to more disagreements and more fine-tuning of the scholarly opinions.

At its core abhidharma denies the reality of self (*ātman*) but affirms the reality of the parts (dharmas). In insisting that these latter elements are each logically discrete or "real in itself," it promotes a form of rational realism. One hair-splitting school was Sarvāstivāda, which held the extreme position that "everything exists"; that is, everything conceivable must conceivably be. Another school, Prajñaptivāda, conceded that "everything is mere name." Its conceptualism stops short of saying "everything is unreal" or "is of the mind only." In addition, Mahāyāna rose with the Emptiness Sūtras, which were systematized later into the Emptiness philosophy. It undercut Hīnayānist realism by declaring everything to be empty and that saṃsāra and nirvāṇa are "not two." This emptiness or nonduality is nondiscursive; it can be only intuited. However, that radical anti-intellectualism prompted a reaction within Mahāyāna called Yogācāra. This idealist school declared everything to be mental "representation only." The final intellectual development in Indian Buddhism is Buddhist logic. Two Scholastic topics are discussed here.

On the Size of Angels

In seeking a rational account of all possible realities, Vasubandhu's *Abhidharmakośa* (fourth or fifth century A.D.) might hold a key to "How many angels can dance on the head of a pin?" That question grants angels some minimal substantiality. Within the Great Chain of Being, where God on top as pure spirit is omnipresent and matter at the bottom has fixity of location and dimension, angels fall somewhere in between. However, high above dense matter, they fall short of God. Thus, conceivably they might have enough infinitesimal substance as to take up a determinably tiny amount of space, such as a fraction of a pinhead. Dividing the total area of that with that tiny angelic dimension would yield a logical count (not that such a question was ever posed in the *Summa theologica*).

Now it seems that in the *Abhidharmakośa* the assumption is the exact reverse. The higher the gods are in the various Buddhist heavens, the more bloated in size they become. They balloon up like heated gas. This is because, as Buddhism subscribes to "no soul," nothing is just "pure spirit." Thus, the realist solution to calculating a god's status is to grant him a rational decrease in material density. The higher and less dense the god, the more space he takes up – the reverse of those dancing angels. Actual calculations of cubic volume are provided by Vasubandhu. All such measuring of gods and angels might of course appear ridiculous to us moderns, but there are Whiteheadians who, as modern "natural theologians," can still so speculate on the "size of God"!

On Spiritual Ladders

Both the Christian and the Buddhist scheme treated here presuppose some form of a Great Chain of Being (or Non-Being in the Buddhist case), which helped underwrite a medieval socio-spiritual hierarchy. Here is design for the Church from Dionysius the Pseudo-Areopagite:

Heavenly Hierarchy
1. Seraphim
Cherubim
Thrones
2. Dominions
Powers
Authorities
3. Principalities
Archangels
Angels

Ecclesiastical Hierarchy
4. Bishops
Priests
Deacons
5. Monks
Baptized Christians
Cathechums

The following is the Buddhist scheme of the Three Realms: 3. of Desires, 2. of Form, and 1. of Formlessness, arranged in descending order. Take note of the gods in 2., the realm of form:

1. Realm of Formlessness
Neither perception nor non-perception
Nothing at all
Infinite space
Infinite consciousness

2. Realm of Form
Pure abodes
Splendid gods
Radiant gods
Creator gods

3. Realm of Desires
Six classes of heavenly beings
Men
Angry spirits
Animals
Hungry ghosts
Eight levels of hells

In the West the Great Chain of Being provides the foundation for the three medieval ladders of speculation, of contemplation, and of works. The overall structure is created by scholarly reason, coordinated with mystical practice, and sustained by self-effort. Although divided according to the labors of the philosopher, the mystic, and the laity, the trio – of mind, soul, and body – should ideally work as one. The Great Chain of Being had lent support to sacramentalism and sacrodotalism by considering universals to be real. When since the 14th century the Nominalists disputed the objective reality of those universals, they also put issues of faith outside the reach of reason. When Luther condemned the idea of "salvation by works," he doomed all three ascending scales. When he insisted on "faith alone," he endorsed the irrational will of God. The Buddhist Far East witnessed a similar bout with Scholastic reason before the "waning of the Middle Ages" also brought that down. Buddhist scholastics in China went beyond the Indian systems described earlier. They added a triune (three-one Ekayāna) schema derived from the *Lotus Sūtra* and a totalistic ("one is all; all is one") schema derived from the *Wreath Sūtra*. However, then they overextended those neat numerical correlations. But even if we take the Indian canonical count of 52 stages in the bodhisattvic ascent to Buddhahood, we can grant how it makes sense on paper and how it synthesized prior spiritual ladders. But do we really need to climb all 52 flights of stairs to be fully enlightened? Why not one less or one more? Or, does any of that really matter? Like the number of angels or the size of gods, this game of numbers can grow tiresome or become irrelevant, and it did. Zen opted for an all-or-nothing "sudden enlightenment"; Pure Land gambled on a "leap of faith" in the dark; and the neo-Confucians would return the spiritual world to a more classical and more naturalistic proportion.

WHALEN LAI

See also Arhat; Buddhaghosa; Buddhist Schools/Traditions: China; Buddhist Schools/Traditions: South Asia; China; Dao-xuan (Tao-hsüan); Dionysius the Pseudo-Areopagite; Examinations, Theravādin; Forest Masters; Liturgy: Buddhist; Master and Pupil: Buddhist Perspectives; Sakya Pandita (Sapen); Tibetan Lineages: Sakya; Wŏnhyo

Further Reading

Carre, Meyrick Heath, *Realists and Nominalists*, London and New York: Oxford University Press, 1946
Leff, Gordon, *William of Ockham: The Metamorphosis of Scholastic Discourse*, Manchester: University of Manchester Press, and Totowa, New Jersey: Rowman and Littlefield, 1975
Lovejoy, Arthur O., *The Great Chain of Being*, Cambridge, Massachusetts: Harvard University Press, 1936
Nygren, Anders, *Agape and Eros*, 2 vols., London: Society for Promoting Christian Knowledge, and New York: Macmillan, 1932–1939; reprint, New York: Harper and Row, 1969
Tatz, Mark, and Jody Kent, *Rebirth, the Tibetan Game of Liberation*, Garden City, New York: Anchor Press, 1977; London: Rider, 1978
Vasubandhu, *L'Abhidharmakośa*, 6 vols., translated by La Vallée Poussin, Paris: Guethner, 1923–1931

Schools and Universities, Benedictine

The celebration of the sesquimillennium of the birth of Benedict of Nursia (c. 480–c. 550) in 1980 had monastic communities worldwide participate in programs designed to examine the Benedictine charism and its expression in the modern world. The Rule for Monks left by the "Father of Western Monasticism" has been interpreted in so many different ways that the conventual life might range from the strictly contemplative to the "mixed," which joins apostolic work, such as teaching, nursing the sick, or parish ministry, to the monastic life.

In late February and early March 1981, some 65 monastic men and women and others interested in issues concerning Benedictine education gathered at the Abbey of Maredsous in Belgium to examine both the historical antecedents and the contemporary expressions of Benedictine educational activities. The list of participants and the character of their schools show that Benedictine men and women in the contemporary world participate in elementary, secondary, and higher education activities. The list of schools worldwide indicates that Benedictine men and women engage in educational activities as diverse as conducting a small program within the enclosure (the *scuola interna*) to running a nationally accredited university offering bachelors, masters, and doctoral degrees.

Because Benedictines lack a central government structure such as in found in religious orders having a general superior (usually residing in Rome), the 15 centuries between Benedict's Monte Cassino and the contemporary world have found Benedictine men and women involved in educational ventures that rise and fall. Insistence on local autonomy of each monastery would seem to prevent any "saving action" by an overseeing body.

From the very beginning at Benedict's Monte Cassino (c. 520), there is evidence that educational activities were part of the daily schedule within the monastic enclosure. Contemporary histories of education allude to the part played for centuries by monastic and cathedral schools. In most cases monastic schools were designed for the religious training and general education of students who intended to live a monastic or clerical life.

In any discussion of Benedictine schools, a distinction should be made between Benedictine scholars and Benedictine education. Benedictine scholars are men and women who have contributed significantly as individuals to the advancement of scholarship by teaching, writing, and research. In rare cases some of these scholars were also associated with specific institutional structures.

One interesting case is the foundation in the mid–17th century of the University of Salzburg, which was thronged with Benedictine monks who developed a center for scholarship. At another point in history, the general chapter of the English Benedictine Congregation appointed monks to take degrees at Oxford and Cambridge and remain there as scholars. A contemporary residue of this is St. Benet's at Oxford with its "master" Dom Henry Wansbrough, a monk of Ampleforth Abbey in England. As a contemporary pontifical institute in Rome (authorized to confer degrees in the name of the Catholic Church), the International University of St. Anselmo on the Aventine depends on an international faculty of philosophical, theological, and liturgical scholars to educate Benedictine and other students in the sacred sciences.

Most monastic schools in the Middle Ages enrolled a small group of students who were instructed by monastics. They had mastered the necessary disciplines of study as a result of being taught by older members of the community. In many monasteries there developed a "genealogy of the masters," a list of "who taught whom," analogous to Buddhist lineages.

Children generally entered a monastic school at age six or seven, much as a contemporary child might begin elementary school today. With books being copied by hand, early education focused on reading and writing along with extensive memorization of texts. Materials would be read aloud, the principal text being the Bible. Gradually "secular" authors were added, albeit with an emphasis on the Latin language. The programs differed little, whether the students were boys in a men's monastery or girls in a women's monastery.

Hastings Rashdall claims that "the period which intervenes between the time of Charles the Great and the eleventh century

"Mathematical Tower," used as an observatory, Kremsmünster Abbey (Benedictine), Upper Austria, 1748–1759. Founded in 777 by Tassilo III, Duke of Bavaria, Stift Kremsmünster has operated a secondary school (Gymnasium) since 1549.
Photo courtesy of the Austrian National Tourist Office

has been called the Benedictine age." Scholars were found in individual monasteries, but the latter were not numerous, nor did they create large centers of learning similar to that of the major universities. In 1754 the monk-scholar Oliver Legipont published an extensive four-volume work developed by Magnoald Ziegelbauer (d. 1750). He attempted to trace all Benedictine educational activities from their beginnings to his own day. Ziegelbauer lists schools, libraries, and individual scholars with extensive descriptions.

Over the centuries frequent debates took place over how monks and nuns should balance the work of the schools with the monastic life. In some cases ecclesiastical authorities issued decrees forbidding the running of an "external school," that is, one in which the students were not child oblates and were not being prepared to become professed monks or nuns. History is filled with arguments relative to the role of both monastic schools and lives of scholarship for monk. The Benedictine Jean Mabillon's (1632–1707) controversy with the Trappist founder Armand-Jean le Bouthillier de Rancé (1626–1700) on the question of whether learning is compatible with the monastic life has fascinated scholars for some time!

Commenting on the development of education over time, Charles Homer Haskins declared that "a great teacher like Socrates gave no diplomas." When Benedict, according to the account of Gregory the Great (590–604), went to Rome as a young man, he did not encounter a well-structured and administered institution. A "dialogue" would take place between masters and students, and much later the Trivium and Quadrivium would provide an exposure to the "seven liberal arts."

Chapter 59 of Benedict's Rule for Monks describes how laypeople offered their sons to the monastery. This practice was neither new nor unique to Benedict, having appeared earlier among pagans, Jews, and early Christians. The concept of "child oblation" could be found in fourth-century monastic foundations in Syria, Egypt, and Palestine. In all these cases the children received an exceptional education, some continuing to live the monastic life until they reached the age stipulated for a valid monastic profession, whereas others would leave for secular pursuits, such as medicine and law.

Can this broad-brush view of Benedictine involvement in education help explain the role of Benedictine men and women teachers in the contemporary world? Monastic history recognizes that at some point secular sovereigns began to view monasteries and their properties as sources of wealth for themselves. In the Habsburg Empire Maria Theresa (1740–1780) as well as Emperor Joseph II (1780–1790) seized monasteries and curbed normal growth through the reception of new members. With the French Revolution more abbeys closed, and monasteries and churches were plundered and destroyed. In most cases monastic men and women were scattered and had to engage in various secular occupations simply to survive.

Around 1810 a gradual program of restoration began, beginning first in Germany with the support of King Ludwig I (1825–1848) of Bavaria. In 1830 the monastery of Metten was reestablished, with many of its first monks coming from former suppressed monasteries and from the diocesan clergy as well. This abbey is key in understanding the ways in which Benedictines became reinvolved in schools and universities. The modern Benedictine school breathes a "missionary" spirit regardless of the area of the mission.

In 1846 Boniface Wimmer (1809–1887), a former diocesan priest and now monk of Metten, left Bavaria, supported by the king, to follow Germans immigrating to the United States. Out of a desire to "preserve the faith," he and a group of nonclerical monks and some students with a missionary spirit founded St. Vincent Abbey in Latrobe, Pennsylvania. Any apostolic work that supported the evangelizing mission was permissible: teaching (grade school, high school, college, or seminary), parochial work, publishing of religious reading materials, preaching retreats, and conducting parish missions were all deemed to be legitimate. Naturally with this regimen the traditional monastic day of following the hours of the Divine Office, doing meditative reading of the Scriptures, and performing other tasks prescribed

Josef Kornhausel, Assembly Hall (Aula), Schottenstift (Benedictine), Vienna, Austria, 1826–1832. Here since 1807 Benedictines have conducted a secondary school (the Schottengymnasium), which became a favorite of the Austrian aristocracy.
Photo courtesy of the Austrian National Tourist Office

by the Rule were "squeezed together" in such a way that a school day could be conducted. In Wimmer's own lifetime eight independent Benedictine monasteries were founded in the United States, most of these engaged in educational activities.

Abbot Wimmer secured the help of Benedictine women from the Abbey of St. Walburga in Eichstätt to join the missionary activity. Originally cloistered contemplative nuns, they faced such demands on the new frontier that eventually they were reformed as modern apostolic religious, engaging in teaching, nursing, and other such activities.

In the same way the Abbeys of Engelberg and Einsiedeln along with Benedictine women in Switzerland established American communities. Within this tradition seminary programs, rather than the purely "secular" programs found in colleges and universities, dominated.

In other countries the story is the same. For example, with the restoration of the English Benedictine Congregation, "colleges" (preparatory schools for university study) were established in most monasteries, including three in the United States. The German missionary-oriented Congregation of St. Ottilien established schools in Africa and Asia. Other monastic communities, through missionary work, established schools in Central and South America as well as in Canada.

In some respects Benedictine men and women educators today resemble religious of modern apostolic congregations, such as the Christian Brothers or the Sisters of Mercy. At the same time any meeting of monastic men and women will always reflect a desire to return to the "balance" of life as visualized in St. Benedict's Rule. The Rule is recognized as a basis for an educational structure that serves the contemporary world well.

One might doubt whether the contemporary Benedictine education venture is truly a "monastic school" in the original sense of that phrase. With declining numbers of monastic teachers and the employment of lay teachers in Benedictine-sponsored schools, a student does not experience the personal involvement and care that would have been present in Benedict's time. Nonetheless monastic men and women, as was evident by the papers given at the Maredsous conference, continue to see a unique contribution that can be made when monastics are educators. One speaker at this conference, Dominic Milroy of Ampleforth College, suggested that Benedictines "have access to a wisdom which is not rigid. And with our human style, developed over many centuries, in particular ways and in different places, we have established points of reference for human society which have run right through the very cultural, social, industrial, academic, and intellectual changes to which the Benedictines have contributed in the past." Many Benedictine men and women educators look to a future where they can continue to influence, as Father Milroy said, with "a freedom which has brought serenity without rigidity, openness without flabbiness, or being loose at the edges, so we can draw from our faith at a time when this great flux robs society, even when it has faith, of its serenity."

DAVID TURNER, O.S.B.

See also Benedict of Nursia, St.; Benedictines: General or Male; Contemporary Issues: Western Christian; Education of Christian Monastics; Knowles, M. David; Leclercq, Jean; Libraries: Western Christian; Maurists; Oblates; Scholars, Benedictine; Spain: History

Further Reading

Colloque de Pédagogie bénédictine, *Bénédictini Vivendi Praeceptores: Les Bénédictins Pédagogues Hier Aujourd'hui Demain*, Actes de Colloque de Pédagogie bénédictine, Maredsous, 27 fevrier–1er mars 1981, Denée, Belgium: Maredsous, 1981

Haskins, Charles Homer, *The Rise of Universities*, New York: Holt, 1923; Ithaca, New York: Cornell University Press, 1957

Leclercq, Jean, *The Love of Learning and the Desire for God: A Study of Monastic Culture*, New York: Fordham University Press, 1961; 2nd edition, London: SPCK, 1978; 3rd edition, New York: Fordham University Press, 1982

Quinn, Patricia, *Better Than the Sons of Kings: Boys and Monks in the Early Middle Ages*, New York: Peter Lang, 1989

Rashdall, Hastings, *The Universities of Europe in the Middle Ages*, 3 vols., Oxford: Clarendon Press, 1895; New York: Oxford University Press, 1942; special edition, Oxford and New York: Oxford University Press, 1997

Riche, Pierre, *Éducation et culture dans l'Occident Barbare, Vie–VIIIe siècles*, Paris: Seuil, 1962; as *Education and Culture in the Barbarian West, Sixth Through Eighth Centuries*, Columbia: University of South Carolina Press, 1976

Ziegelbauer, Magnoald, *Historia Rei Literariae Ordinis S. Benedicti*, 4 vols., Augsburg: Martin Veith, 1754

Schools, Buddhist. *See* Buddhist Schools/Traditions

Schutz, Roger 1915–

Swiss founder of Taizé community and advocate of Christian ecumenism

Roger Louis Schutz-Marsauche was born in the Swiss Juras, the second son of nine children of a Swiss pastor. He was deeply influenced by his French maternal grandmother, who as a widow during World War I suffered the results of divided Christians killing one another. He knew that, as a Protestant, she had taken the risk of a move toward reconciliation by attending Catholic services. While a student Roger boarded with a Catholic family. During university studies at Lausanne, he became president of the Christian Student Association and founded his Grand Communauté, a group that met for retreats, reflection, and communal prayer. A Reformed Protestant, he increasingly questions the divisions among Christians and did not experience a vocation as pastor. Rather he planned to be a writer and a farmer. At the age of 25, in 1940, near the beginning of World War II, he traveled to Taizé near Cluny, where he purchased some property and buildings. Taizé was close to the line that divided France; until 1942, when his refuge was raided, he offered refuge to those escaping Nazi rule, especially Jews, and thereafter found safety in Geneva until the end of 1944. In Geneva the Grand Communauté continued, meeting for monastic prayer three times a day. In 1941 he had drafted his concept of a monastic community, essentially *oraret laborea ut regnet*: to pray and to work for the reign of Christ. He returned to Taizé with Brother Roger as prior in 1944 accompanied by three of the members of the Grand Communauté, and in 1949 the first seven brothers professed lifetime monastic commitments: celibacy, acceptance of the ministry of the prior, and community of material and spiritual goods. In 1953 they received a short rule, based on his earlier draft, that came to be known as the *Sources of Taizé*. The brothers were to support themselves with secular jobs and "never resign thyself to the scandal of the separation of Christians." Since the mid-1950s small communities of brothers from Taizé have lived among the poor in North and South America, Asia, and Africa. The first Catholics entered the community in 1969. Taizé has continued to grow as an ecumenical community of men – there are about 100 brothers from 30 countries and from every continent – Anglicans, Protestants, and Catholics. Brother Roger attended every session of the Second Vatican Council (1962–1965) and has brought his case for ecumenism to Canterbury, Constantinople, and Geneva as well as to Rome. At Taizé the ecumenical nature of the community declares its mission: Taizé seeks to be both a realization and a symbol of reconciliation. The community lives in trust of this mission and accepts neither gifts nor inheritances but rather supports itself solely by the work of the brothers. The ministry at Taizé is expressly one of ecumenical reconciliation, and weekly retreats for young people attract thousands annually. On a recent Good Friday, the Passion of Jesus was read in eight languages to 8,000 pilgrims of many denominations who later chanted "Ubi caritas, est amor,

Deus ibi est" ("Where charity and love are, God is"), a chant identified worldwide with Taizé. The monks of Taizé routinely hold "The Listening," where pilgrims have the opportunity to discuss personal problems privately with one of the monks. In addition Taizé organizes "pilgrimages of trust," mainly for young people, in cities around the world. The rule was revised in 1990 to *No Greater Love: Sources of Taizé*, which states, "The boldness involved in not ensuring any capital for ourselves, without fear of possible poverty, is a source of incalculable strength. . . . Ecumenism fosters illusory hopes when it puts off reconciliation till later. It comes to a standstill, becomes fossilized even, when it accepts the creation of parallel paths on which the vital energies of forgiveness are wasted."

PHYLLIS ZAGANO

See also Anglican Monasticism; France: History; Switzerland; Taizé, France

Biography

Brother Roger Schutz is world-renowned as the Swiss Protestant founder and prior of the ecumenical monastery at Taizé in Burgundy, France. In 1949 seven brothers professed a lifetime commitment, in 1969 Roman Catholics joined the community, and recently Taizé has excelled at attracting thousands of youth on pilgrimages.

Major Works

This Day Belongs to God, translated by J.C. Dickinson, 1961
Unity: Man's Tomorrow (*L'Unite: Espérance de vie*), 1962
The Power of the Provisional (*Dynamique du provisoire*), 1969
Afire with Love: Meditations on Peace and Unity, translated by Emily Chisholm and the Taizé community, 1981
Meditations on the Way of the Cross, with Mother Teresa of Calcutta, 1987

Further Reading

Brico, Rex, *Taizé: Brother Roger and His Community*, London: Collins, 1978
Spink, Kathryn, *A Universal Heart: The Life and Vision of Brother Roger of Taizé*, San Francisco: Harper and Row, 1986

Scotland

Early Christianity in Scotland was mainly monastic in its ethos and organization. In the sixth century, Gaelic-speaking Christian *Scoti* from Ireland extended their dominion to form the kingdom of Dalriada in western Scotland. This Celtic Christianity, although agreeing with the Continental and Roman Church in essentials, was uncentralized, with authority vested not in bishops with territorial dioceses but in abbots possessing an extended sphere of influence, termed their *paruchia*. Indeed, even bishops were subject to abbots who were not themselves bishops. These Scotic monks had also retained much of the individualistic and rigorously ascetic character of the early desert monasticism.

The story of the Celtic Church in Scotland is centered on the towering figure of St. Columba and the monastery he founded around 563 in Iona and on the conversion of Pictland through the mission that he initiated. Eventually, Iona's *paruchia* not only covered all of northern Scotland but extended throughout eastern Scotland and into Northumbria as well. Monastic foundations were made, for example, in Tiree (Hebrides) and Deer (Aberdeenshire), and episcopal centers, such as Old Melrose (Borders) and Whithorn (Galloway), became monasteries.

Monastic fervor did not remain at its initial high level, and in the late eighth century reformed communities of Céli Dé (Culdees) came into being. However, many of these developed into groups of secular priests living in community. In fact, monasticism merged gradually with the clerical church system and the patriarchical structure of society. The office of abbot became hereditary, passing from father to son. Only in Iona, and perhaps also at Turriff (Aberdeenshire), did a fully monastic structure survive, although individual hermits and small, isolated groups of monks continued to exist. In the ninth century, too, Viking raids interrupted life in Iona, and part of Columba's relics and the hegemony were transferred to Dunkeld (Perthshire), from where leadership in the Scottish Church passed to St. Andrews.

Iona's penetration into Northumbria brought the Celtic Church into conflict with the missionary Church in England, leading to the decision at Whitby in 664 in favor of Roman observance. To a large extent, this eroded the isolation of the Celtic Church as Roman influences thereafter grew stronger, although centuries would elapse before the old system finally crumbled away. In the mid–11th century, the process was greatly stimulated by St. Margaret, wife of King Malcolm III (both d. 1093). She also brought in three Benedictine monks to Dunfermline, a small but influential step.

This was a period of remarkable monastic fervor and expansion on the Continent. The new orders came into Scotland very soon and, once there, expanded rapidly, especially in the reign of Margaret's son David I (1124–1153), whose foundations "must rank as the most remarkable . . . of any monarch of the age" (Dom David Knowles, preface to Cowan and Easson, 1957). However, the Celtic heritage was not suddenly abandoned. Many of the hallowed places were chosen for the new foundations. For example, Culdees, at St. Andrews, remained alongside the new Canons Regular; elsewhere (e.g., at Monymusk), Culdees adopted the Rule of St. Augustine and became Black Canons. Benedictines settled at Coldingham (which had been a "double monastery") and later in Iona, Cistercians at Melrose and Deer, and White Canons at Whithorn.

The first new order was the Tironensians, who arrived in 1113, settled eventually at Kelso, and then made other foundations at Kilwinning, Arbroath, and Lindores. Soon, however, the connection with Tiron was severed. Cistercians came to Melrose in 1136 and expanded rapidly until they had 11 abbeys: Melrose and Newbattle in the southeast; Dundrennan, Sweetheart, and Glenluce in the southwest; Culross, Balmerino, and Coupar Angus in Fife and Tayside; Deer and Kinloss in the northeast;

Chapter house entrance, Dryburgh Abbey (Premonstratensian), near Melrose, Scotland, 12th century. Sir Walter Scott and Field Marshal Sir Douglas Haig are both buried inside the ruins of the abbey.
Photo courtesy of Chris Schabel

and Saddle in Argyll. Cluniacs founded houses at Paisley and Crossraguel, and from 1230 to 1231 three Valliscaulian priories were founded. The only charterhouse was established at Perth in the 1420s. Augustinian Black Canons founded a score of houses of varying size and status, the most important being Cambuskenneth, Holyrood, Jedburgh, St. Andrews, and Scone. Dryburgh and Whithorn were the principal monasteries among the six of the Premonstratensian White Canons.

Such an assembly of monasteries was unique in Europe. The strongest were not the Black Monks and Cluniacs (for the initiative now lay with the new orders) but rather Cistercians and Black Canons. White Canons were relatively strong, as were monks originating from Tiron. The Valliscaulian houses were the only ones of the Order outside France, and, most unusually, the two cathedral priories were not Benedictine: St. Andrews and Whithorn were held by Black and White Canons, respectively. Even more unusual, both Cluniac houses became abbeys.

The monasteries enjoyed great prestige: St. Andrews was the primatial see; Holyrood, Dunfermline, and Scone were linked to royal palaces; kings were crowned at Scone; royal persons were buried in Dunfermline and other monasteries; and parliament was held at Cambuskenneth. Arbroath was known for the declaration of Scottish independence and Paisley for its connection with the patriots William Wallace and Robert the Bruce. Many monasteries were places of pilgrimage with notable relics of saints, the most celebrated being Whithorn (St. Ninian), Dunfermline (St. Margaret), St. Andrews (St. Andrew), and Arbroath (St. Thomas à Becket).

Abbots often held the most important offices in the country, such as chancellor or treasurer. In the late Middle Ages, as the provision of monastic superiors by Rome became the norm, it was increasingly common in Scotland to appoint secular clerics who then made their profession; this was followed by the appointment of commendators, that is, monastic superiors who were not monks. This late and mild form of commendation was ironically deprived of its worst effects by a monastic abuse, namely the system of "portions" whereby each monk was legally entitled to a personal stipend.

Cloister, Inchmahome Priory (Augustinian Canons), on an island in the Lake of Menteith, Scotland, 13th century. Photo courtesy of Chris Schabel

The 13th century saw other orders entering Scotland (figures are less exact than for monks). The double order of Gilbertines came for a short time, as did Friars of the Sack; Augustinian friars had at least a presence. Dominicans arrived perhaps as early as 1230 and had 16 houses, most of which survived to the Reformation. In 1481 a separate Scottish province that accepted the reformed observance was formed. It had priories in the university cities of Aberdeen, Glasgow, and St. Andrews and as far north as Inverness. Franciscans came at almost the same time and had eight houses, which became a separate province; a reformed branch of the Order then arrived in 1463 and founded nine houses. The two branches separated, the earlier friars being known as Conventuals to distinguish them from the reformed Observants. Friars' communities were not large, but the Reformed Franciscans and Dominicans were influential. Carmelite friars had ten houses, all of which survived. Trinitarians had eight, of which four survived.

The nunneries played no important role. The largest group, seven in all, were Cistercian, but most perhaps had originally been Benedictine. The only remaining Benedictine house was suppressed in 1389. Augustinian canonesses had two houses, in Iona and Perth, the latter being suppressed in the 1430s. Of the later orders, Franciscans had two houses and Dominicans only one, which was founded in 1517 at Sciennes (a corruption of *Siena*) near Edinburgh and enjoyed a reputation for austere observance.

The Reformation Parliament in August 1560 established Protestantism as the official religion but left the monasteries in being, although public choir office and the acceptance of new novices were no longer possible. The religious were not deprived of their livelihood. Some resisted the change, notably Gilbert Brown, abbot of Sweetheart, who kept Catholicism alive in Galloway for some decades. Others served in the Reformed Church, and a few, especially the Carthusians, went abroad to continue their religious lives.

Scottish monasticism did not, however, disappear. By the end of the 11th century, Celtic monks on the Continent observed the Rule of St. Benedict, and their activity was confined to the German lands. The abbey of St. James at Regensburg (Ratisbon) became the mother house of ten monasteries that recruited from Ireland and were known as the *Monasteria Scotorum*, or *Schottenklöster* (monasteries of the Scots). The meaning of *Scot* changed and came to signify an inhabitant of present-day Scotland, but the Irish monks held to the traditional term, resulting in 1515 in these Scotic monasteries being taken over by monks from Scotland. It was a troubled time, but eventually Scots

Church interior, Benedictine monastery, Dunfermline, Fife, Scotland, 12th century. The Norman romanesque columns have chevron decorations.
Photo courtesy of Chris Schabel

Benedictines were in peaceful possession of three houses in Germany: at Ratisbon, Würzburg, and Erfurt. During the 17th and 18th centuries, they recruited from Scotland and played a dual role, taking part in the religious and academic life of Germany and conducting a missionary apostolate in Scotland.

The Scots suffered greatly during the wars of religion in the 17th century but recovered under Placid Fleming, abbot of Ratisbon from 1672 to 1720. He founded a seminary for Scots boys at Ratisbon to provide recruits for the monastery and thus missionary priests, and the monks took an oath to help their Church in Scotland. Monks at Erfurt, which became a dependent priory of Ratisbon, held professorships in Erfurt university and gained reputations as philosophers and scientists. Ratisbon monks in the late 18th century were known as scientists and were influential in the Academy movement, and the Würzburg Scots played a full part in the life of Catholic Franconia. There was also a continuous presence of monks on the Scottish mission. To a man, the Scots monks supported the Jacobite cause; indeed, some were active in it. When the antireligious laws put an end to monastic life in most of northern Europe, the Würzburg house was secularized in 1803 and that at Erfurt in 1819. The Ratisbon abbey was crippled by the legislation. Although it was allowed to reopen its seminary and accept novices in 1820, it never recovered, and in 1862 it was finally suppressed.

However, once again that was not the end. In 1878 the English Benedictine Congregation founded a monastery at Ft. Augustus (Inverness-shire) to continue both the Scottish Ratisbon abbey and the English abbey at Lamspringe (near Hanover), whose community had returned to England. From 1882 to 1910, Ft. Augustus was directly subject to the Holy See. It became the mother house of two abbeys in the United States: St. Anselm's in Washington, D.C., and St. Gregory's in Portsmouth, Rhode Island. In 1946 Cistercians from Roscrea founded Nunraw (East Lothian), and in 1948 Benedictines from Prinknash took over the former Benedictine priory of Pluscarden (Moray). All three monasteries are abbeys.

Premonstratensians were in Galloway from 1889 to 1896 and have had a house in the southwest since 1957. Friars have returned in greater numbers, the first being Franciscans, coming to Glasgow in 1868 and then to Edinburgh in 1926 and Dundee in 1933. Dominicans have been in Edinburgh since 1931 and in Glasgow since 1965. Augustinians arrived in Dundee in 1948 and extended their work to Edinburgh. Capuchins were in

Augustinian Canons' house, Inchcolm Island, Fife, Scotland, 12th century. This island monastery was known as the "Iona of East Scotland."
Photo courtesy of Chris Schabel

Abbey of St. Mary (Premonstratensian), Dryburgh, Berwickshire, Scotland, 12th century.
Photo courtesy of Chris Schabel

Uddingston (Lanarkshire) from 1949 to 1980. Servites have been in Dundee since 1950 and were in Glasgow from 1974 to 1988. Carmelites are the most recent arrivals, coming to Glasgow in 1978, followed by the Discalced branch in 1988. Apart from the Dominican apostolate in the universities, most friars have worked in urban parishes, and this makes dates for foundations only approximate.

Not many women's communities could be described as monastic. Benedictines of the Blessed Sacrament came to Dumfries in 1884, moved to Largs (Ayrshire) in 1988, and were replaced by Tyburn nuns in 1992. Benedictine nuns were at Ft. Augustus from 1892 to 1920. Poor Clares had a short-lived foundation in Dunblane (Perthshire) from 1884 to 1885, came to Edinburgh in 1895 (moving outside the city in 1992), and have been in Hamilton (Lanarkshire) since 1953. Carmelites are the most numerous, with houses lasting varying amounts of time and six still existing. Dominican nuns of the Rosary were in Glasgow from 1948 to 1987.

Monasteries to be visited are Ft. Augustus, a converted Hanoverian fortress on the shore of Loch Ness (although a closing mass was celebrated at Ft. Augustus in December 1998, the closure is not yet definitive); Pluscarden, the only medieval monastery in Britain or Ireland presently inhabited by monks; and Nunraw, on a hillside looking over the Firth of Forth. Iona is now fully restored and has a thriving ecumenical apostolate. Paisley abbey church is still in use for Protestant worship. Inchcolm, being on an island in the Forth, is the best preserved of the unused monasteries, and the ruins of Melrose are still impressive.

MARK DILWORTH O.S.B.

See also Architecture: Western Christian Monasteries; Dissolution of Monasteries: Scotland; Iona, Scotland; Lanfranc

Further Reading

Cameron, Nigel M. de S., editor, *Dictionary of Scottish Church History and Theology*, Edinburgh: T. and T. Clark, and Downers Grove, Illinois: InterVarsity Press, 1993

The Catholic Directory for Scotland (annual), various places, 1829–

Cowan, Ian B., and David E. Easson, *Medieval Religious Houses: Scotland*, London and New York: Longman, 1957; 2nd edition, 1976

Dilworth, Mark, *The Scots in Franconia: A Century of Monastic Life*, Edinburgh: Scottish Academic Press, and Totowa, New Jersey: Rowman and Littlefield, 1974

Dilworth, Mark, "Religious Orders in Scotland, 1878–1978," *Innes Review* 29:1 (1978); reprinted in *Modern Scottish Catholicism, 1878–1978*, edited by David McRoberts, Glasgow: Burns, 1979
Dilworth, Mark, *Scottish Monasteries in the Late Middle Ages*, Edinburgh: Edinburgh University Press, 1995

Sculpture, Christian. *See* Visual Arts, Western Christian: Sculpture

Seasons, Liturgical: Eastern Christian

The purpose of the liturgy, to praise God and offer all of creation to the healing of the divine light, provides the foundation for parish and monastery alike. However, a distinction exists between what is emphasized in the parish and what is emphasized in the monastery. As this article will show, the ethos of the liturgy varies considerably between these two forms of church life.

In the monastic life the intent of festal services is to use the movement of the seasons of the liturgical year – the temporal ground and character of these services – as a pathway for the eternal to deepen in the mind and heart of the monastic. Parishes draw from the cycle of liturgical feast days the meaning of the celebration in the life of Christ and the life of the Theotokos (Virgin Mary) and bind this meaning to the experience and struggles of parishioners. The emphasis is on the journey of sanctification through daily struggles. Given the high regard of the Christian East for the grace-bearing character of creation, it is not uncommon to find churches adorned with foliage, fruits, and flowers appropriate to the liturgical seasons. The natural seasons themselves represent a kind of icon of God's grace. Time and creation are central to the church's liturgical drama, which is a way of helping the faithful to claim God's grace in their lives in this world, that is, to claim the incarnation in the midst of time. In parishes the ethos of the festal season in parishes emphasizes the created world, whereas in monasteries the emphasis falls on a claiming of the eternal through detachment from the play of time.

The explicitly monastic intent of the liturgical services is to teach the art of prayer as a way of emptying and guarding the mind and heart so that one is open to the experience of eternity. The festal cycle calls monastics to contemplate the temporal with detachment and to do so as a pathway opening to the eternal. For example, the Feast of Transfiguration is a Thanksgiving service in the parish as well as in the monastery. In the parish customarily the first fruits of the harvest are brought for blessing to the church, and the church is transformed into a garden of creation. However, in the monastery this feast is intended to encourage the monastic to contemplate the heavenly kingdom, to relate the feast of the Transfiguration to the transfiguration of the "inner person" by divine grace. In the monasteries each of the major feast days is seen as a theophany of the eternal.

When the whole cycle of services animates the monastic life, it becomes clear that each weekly cycle of services is itself a type of Holy Week and culminates in Pascha, the Sunday liturgy. Each week binds together both the first day of creation and the Eighth Day, the day-spring of the eternal. On Wednesday and Friday the betrayal and crucifixion of Christ are commemorated; on Saturday there is the great memorial service because it was (and is) on this day that Christ descended into Hades and gave the gospel to the departed. Layered into this primary set of motifs are the historical cycles of memorials. Monday commemorates the angelic powers, Tuesday commemorates St. John the Forerunner and all the holy prophets, and on Thursday the holy hierarchies and teachers of the tradition are contemplated. On Saturday, along with Christ's burial, the holy martyrs throughout time are remembered in the liturgy. On Wednesday and Friday the cross itself as the Tree of Life and fountain of salvation, of healing, is layered into this historical cycle.

Many liturgical feasts are associated with monasteries and the lives of monastics. Whereas a parish or household might hold special festivities associated with saints such as Nicholas of Myra (d. c. 343) or Spyridon (d. c. 348), monasteries focus their attention on saints who were great monastics. They include St. Antony the Great (c. 251–356), St. Pachomius (c. 290–346), St. Theodosios the Coenobiarch (423–529), St. Sabas the Sanctified (439–532), St. Pambo of the Desert (d. 393), St. Macarius the Great (c. 300–c. 390), Dorotheus of Gaza (c. 506–c. 560), St. Sisoes (d. c. 380), Sts. Varson (d. 563) and John the Prophet (d. c. 575), St. Euthemios of Palestine (d. 473), St. Seraphim of Sarov (1759–1833), St. Herman of Alaska (1756–1837), and John "Smirrenikov," the Aleut Elder (d. 1829).

On the feast day of a great monastic saint, a special blessing of loaves, wine, and oil is added to the vesper service. The canon for the matins service takes its theme from the feast for the saint in order to proclaim the spiritual aspects of the saint's life and the grace it teaches the faithful. The life of the saint is also read in the refectory (Trapeze) during mealtime, a specific part of monastic liturgical life. Divine services guide the mind in order to safeguard it during the daily movement of life. They form part of the cultivation of emotional and mental detachment, *apatheia*, a dispassionate stance in the face of the world's preoccupations.

Monasteries also find a place in the liturgical life of the larger church communities in which they reside. Laypeople come to monasteries for a service, on retreat, or on pilgrimage to shed the demands and requirement of daily life and benefit from the monastic *askesis* (training or discipline) as part of their growth in the spiritual life. In the monastery they find a radically different point of view toward the ultimate values in life, glimpse their own experience from this distinct perspective, and cultivate the art of prayer. For example, the larger community attached to Holy Trinity monastery in Jordanville, New York, gathers at the monastery for the feast of the founder, St. Job of Pochaev. At the Monastery of All Saints of North America, in Dewdney, British

Columbia, Canada, the monastery feast day is associated with the icon of the Theotokos, Joy of Canada. The day is shaped around a procession with the icon, liturgy, and a community feast in the monastery grounds.

The liturgical calendar of the Orthodox Church also commemorates several monasteries, most notably All Saints of the Kievan Caves and All Saints of Mount Athos. During Great Lent, Saturday of the Holy Ascetics commemorates all the saints who struggled on the monastic path.

David J. Goa

See also Hesychasm; Liturgy: Eastern Christian; Martyrs: Eastern Christian; Office, Daily: Eastern Christian; Spirituality: Eastern Christian

Further Reading

Day, Peter D., *The Liturgical Dictionary of Eastern Christianity*, Collegeville, Minnesota: Liturgical Press, and Tunbridge Wells, Kent: Burns and Oates, 1993

Patrinacos, Nicon D., *A Dictionary of Greek Orthodoxy: Lexicon Hellenikes Orthodoxias*, Pleasantville, New York: Hellenic Heritage, 1984

Seasons, Liturgical: Western Christian

Presuppositions

A description of the shape and character of liturgical seasons requires an appreciation of what the liturgy itself is, of what it celebrates and how it does so, and of how monastics experience it. Succinctly put, the sacred liturgy is that ensemble of words and actions done by and for the church in order that it might experience again and again "the work of our redemption" (from the prayer over the gifts, Evening Mass of the Lord's Supper, Holy Thursday) derived from the actualization of Christ's paschal (Easter) mystery. In her book *The Coming of God* (1982) concerning the Advent-Christmas liturgical cycle and its spiritual meaning, especially for monastics like herself, Maria Boulding asserts simply and poignantly that "all liturgy is paschal." This underscores how every act of Christian liturgy derives from Christ's obedient life, betrayal, agony, suffering, death, resurrection, and ascension – mysteries that, taken together, constitute "the paschal mystery." When the church gathers to pray liturgically, it commemorates these events not in the sense that it repeats or simply recalls them but rather in the sense that it experiences them as happening still in our time, for our sakes and for our salvation, until the Lord comes again in glory. The sense of time that is operative here is not historical in the sense of a chronological looking back. Rather it is an act of memory here and now that recalls Christ's unique sacrificial death and resurrection so that it is experienced as salvific in the present as believers yearn for its fulfillment in God's kingdom in eternity. Thus, through liturgical memorial the church experiences the fullness of Christ's incarnation, paschal suffering, and exaltation in such a way that our very human lives are drawn into his dying and rising. Every act of liturgy is a new act of redemption whereby the present church is sanctified and redeemed through Christ. Thus the value of the memorial acclamation during the Eucharistic prayer:

> Dying you destroyed our death
> Rising you restored our life.
> Lord Jesus come in glory.

The purpose of liturgical prayer during the liturgical seasons is to allow the church to enter ever more fully and deeply into Christ's paschal mystery and thereby to be transformed by it.

The celebration of annual seasons in the liturgical calendar (i.e., Advent-Christmas-Epiphany and Lent-Easter) derives from the annual repetition of the seasons in nature and the cosmic phenomena of solstice and equinox, darkness and light, specifically at Christmas (when the sun grows stronger) and Easter (its date established from the phases of the moon). This computation is apparent in the northern hemisphere (e.g., the term *Lent* means "spring" in Old English), and the fact that the same dating applies in the southern hemisphere adds an important emphasis. That is, although in the southern hemisphere the sun is brightest at Christmas, and Easter comes when the people are facing toward winter, these cosmic phenomena point to the essential paradox that all liturgy is also eschatological and incomplete. Liturgy celebrates hopefulness in the midst of what has yet to be fulfilled.

Lent-Easter

The historical evolution of the season of Lent-Easter derived from three impulses: (1) penitential preparation before the celebration of initiation of new converts to the Christian faith, (2) a desire to identify with Christ's fasting in the desert for 40 days before beginning his public ministry (e.g., Matt. 4:1–13), and (3) concern to deepen one's conversion to Christ by linking fasting, prayer, and almsgiving (Matt. 6:1–18, which Gospel is proclaimed on Ash Wednesday, the first day of Lent). The fast before the celebration of the Easter triduum (Holy Thursday, Good Friday, and Easter vigil) was especially severe so that the new converts' senses would not be dulled by overindulgence and they could thus be attentive and attuned to what they were experiencing through the sacramental liturgy of water baptism, anointing with chrism, and sharing the Eucharist.

The traditional Gospels for the five Sundays of Lent exemplify the themes of the season: temptation; transfiguration (on the first and second Sundays) and Johannine Gospels applied to baptism (third to fifth Sundays), that is, Samaritan woman (John 4); the man born blind (John 9); and the raising of Lazarus (John 11). In other contemporary lectionaries (e.g., Roman Catholic), on these Sundays in alternate years texts about identifying with Christ's paschal dying and rising are proclaimed (i.e., John 2:13–35, about three days in the tomb; John 3:14–21, about Moses and the serpent in the desert; and John 12:20–33, about the grain of wheat having to die in order to rise). There are also texts about reconciliation (i.e., Luke 13:1–9, about the necessity for repentance; Luke 15:1–3, 11–25, the parables of the lost sheep, the lost coin, and the prodigal son; and John 8:1–11, about the woman taken in adultery). The celebration of Easter is the center of the Lent-Easter season with the following 50 days termed "the great Sunday" leading to the celebration of Ascension (Jesus' return to his Father) and Pentecost (the sending of the Spirit) 40 and 50 days later, respectively.

Given the fact that Christian monks are already baptized, their liturgical observances at this time of year emphasize the renewal of their vows of baptism (done annually at the Easter vigil), enhanced by the overturning of expectations through the paradox of masters serving those in their care (superiors washing the feet of the members of the community on Holy Thursday in light of that night's Gospel, John 13). The Rule of St. Benedict (chap. 49) notes that Lent should be a time when monks redouble what should be their daily application of ascetic practices. Saint Benedict (c. 480–c. 550) states that "the life of monk ought to be a continual Lent. Since few, however, have the strength for this, we urge the entire community to keep its manner of life most pure" in this season (verses 1 and 2). The recommended Lenten practices are "prayer with tears, . . . reading . . . compunction of heart and self-denial" (verse 4) as well as denying oneself "some food, drink, sleep, needless talking and idle jesting" (verse 7).

Advent-Christmas

These weeks liturgically commemorate the themes of Christ's second coming (at the beginning of Advent), the events leading to Christ's incarnation (17 through 24 December), the event of Christ's birth among us as the Word made flesh (thus the traditional Gospel for Christmas Day, John 1:1–14), his manifestation to all nations (e.g., the visit of the Magi), and the inauguration of his public ministry (i.e., feast of the Baptism of the Lord, the Sunday after Epiphany). The term *Advent* is from the Latin *adventus*, meaning "coming" or "arrival"; the Greeks had two equivalents for this term: *epiphaneia*, meaning "manifestation" (thus the name for the Epiphany feast), and *parousia*, meaning the final coming of Christ at the end of time (to bring time to an end).

Historically, in some parts of Gaul when baptisms occurred on Epiphany (6 January), the Advent season was a six-week season of penitential preparation for initiation comparable to Lent. Advent here was called "St. Martin's Lent," beginning around the feast of St. Martin of Tours, 11 November, thus the veracity of the commonly repeated phrase "Advent is Lent in the winter." At Rome such was not the case, and its four-week duration there eventually became universal. So did its themes of restrained and quiet joy leading to exuberant festivity at Christmas as the commemoration of the incarnate Word among us in human flesh and our becoming divinized through and in him, thus the opening prayer for Christmas from the time of Leo the Great (440–461) that acknowledges how at this feast we celebrate our becoming divine through Christ, who became human for us. Again because Christian monks were already baptized, the liturgical and communal observances dealt more with penitential practices in preparation for the exuberant festivity of Christmas itself and not because of sacramental initiation. Thus, special fasts and deprivations were customarily practiced, but not to the same extent as in Lent. Special emphasis on *lectio divina* in imitation of the Virgin Mary would be common; she who pondered the holy word of the Scriptures gave birth to him who is the Word made flesh.

In addition to the understanding that Christmas coincided with the return of the sun (winter solstice on 21 December), another theory has been proposed to trace the origins of this season. Termed "the computation theory" by church historian Louis Duchesne (1843–1922), 25 December was chosen to commemorate the birth of Jesus in the flesh because it came nine months after the feast of the Annunciation, 25 March, when Mary received word that she would bear the Son of God (see Luke 1:26–38). Furthermore in some ancient sources 25 March was also the date on which the church commemorated Christ's death, which commemoration would underscore how "all liturgy is paschal," even that commemorating the incarnation, thus the appropriate comment in the Christmas prayer that this feast celebrates "the beginning of our redemption" (prayer over the gifts, vigil of Christmas).

Kevin W. Irwin

See also Devotions, Western Christian; Fasting: Western Christian; Lectio Divina; Liturgical Movement 1830–1980; Liturgy: Western Christian; Office, Daily: Western Christian; Prayer: Christian Perspectives

Further Reading

Adam, Adolf, *The Liturgical Year*, New York: Pueblo, 1981

Boulding, Maria, *The Coming of God*, Collegeville, Minnesota: Liturgical Press, 1982; London: SPCK, 1983; new edition, 1994

Daniélou, Jean, *The Bible and Liturgy*, Notre Dame, Indiana: University of Notre Dame Press, and London: Dartman, 1956

Days of the Lord, volume 1: *Advent-Christmas-Epiphany*, volume 2: *Lent*, and volume 3: *Easter Triduum-Easter*, translated by G. LaNave, D. Molloy, and M. Beaumont, Collegeville, Minnesota: Liturgical Press, 1991–1993

Irwin, Kevin W., *A Guide to Eucharist and Hours*, volume 1: *Advent-Christmas*, volume 2: *Lent*, and volume 3: *Easter*, New York: Pueblo, 1986–1991

Lectionary for Mass, Chicago: Liturgy Training, 1998

Martimort, A.G., *The Church at Prayer*, volume 4: *Liturgy and Time*, translated by Matthew O'Connell, New York: Herder and Herder, 1968; new edition, Collegeville, Minnesota: Liturgical Press, 1991

Order of Prayer in the Liturgy of the Hours, Mahwah, New Jersey: Paulist Press, 1998

Roll, Susan, *Toward the Origins of Christmas*, Kampen, Netherlands: Kok Pharos, 1995

Sacramentary for Mass, New York: Catholic Books, 1985
Talley, Thomas, *The Origins of the Liturgical Year*, New York: Pueblo, 1986; 2nd edition, Collegeville, Minnesota: Liturgical Press, 1991

Self-Immolation, Buddhist

To immolate means to sacrifice, especially in the religious sense of a sacrificial offering. In recent years the term *self-immolation* has come to be understood popularly as referring more narrowly to self-sacrifice by burning.

Buddhist self-immolation became known worldwide with the public self-immolation of the venerable Vietnamese monk Thích Quang Duc, who burned himself to death on 11 June 1963 at a downtown crossroads in Saigon, South Vietnam. This act ushered in a great wave of Vietnamese self-immolations on the part of monks, nuns, and laypersons.

The practice of self-immolation is long established in eastern Asia, justified for Mahāyāna Buddhists mainly by the *Lotus Sūtra*. In chapter 23 of this scripture, "The Former Affairs of the Bodhisattva Medicine King," this bodhisattva, also known as "Seen with Joy by All Living Beings," burns his body as a devotional offering to the Buddha until it is entirely consumed by fire. The Buddha praises this act as the supreme gift, the highest offering to the Buddha. Other texts, such as the *Jātaka*s, told tales of bodhisattvas who sacrificed their bodies and lives for the welfare of others; these played a lesser justifying role.

In a classic study Jan Yun-hua argues that Indian Buddhists took these stories as imaginative hyperbole and did not consider them (or any other text) justification for self-immolation. The vinaya prohibited any form of self-destruction, and public opinion condemned the rare religiously motivated suicide. However, the Chinese took the *Lotus Sūtra* literally and did act on it, burning their bodies or killing themselves by other means. Chinese monastic biographies highly praised those who immolated themselves, provided that their motivation was pure, that is, based on the desire to imitate the bodhisattvas, to express one's devotion to the Buddha, or both. Chinese biographers also esteemed the self-mastery that these acts presupposed. Such approval spread from China to the rest of eastern Asia.

Originally justified as acts of devotionalism, acts of self-immolation (whether by burning or otherwise) soon came to be motivated as well by a desire to protect the Buddha dharma, to protest the persecution of the Buddhist religion, or both. The earliest known case of politically motivated self-immolation is a group of eight Chinese monks who fasted to death in 574 in protest of imperial persecution of Buddhism.

The self-immolation of Thích Quang Duc was a response to the repression of the Buddhist religion by the Diem regime of South Vietnam (which strongly favored Catholicism) and to the death and misery caused by the war. Thus, its motivation was in the mainstream of ancient tradition and was well understood by the South Vietnamese people, who widely responded to it with respect and awe as a profoundly sacred act. This act, captured in a famous photograph, ignited the Buddhist antiwar movement in Vietnam, profoundly shook and bewildered the American public, and made the Buddhist act of self-immolation by burning known throughout the world. It might be noted that in this photograph Thích Quang Duc is surrounded by a dense circle of robed monks and nuns as he burns. Many hold their hands palm to palm in witness of a holy act. Certainly no one tries to stop him. Thus, the act of an individual is also a group act, and the moral responsibility for the act is shared by the group.

The justification by the *Lotus Sūtra* notwithstanding, the ethical status of self-immolation for a Buddhist monastic is a controversial issue, given that suicide is regarded in Buddhism as a grave misdeed with severe negative karmic consequences and is expressly forbidden for monastics by the vinaya. In the Theravāda tradition, which does not accept the *Lotus Sūtra*, self-immolation is not accepted for these reasons.

However, Mahāyāna thinking is rather different and more complex. Mahāyāna thinkers point out that the moral and karmic nature of an act is determined mainly by the motivation behind the act. When a person sacrifices him- or herself for the sake of others or for the sake of the Buddhist religion, the motivation is altruistic and thus good. In this sense, they argue, self-immolation is not suicide because suicide is an act motivated by the selfish consideration of personally escaping pain, sorrow, or suffering. An act motivated by altruism should not be regarded as suicide, nor should it be understood to have negative karmic consequences. Yet Mahāyāna thinkers are aware that negative aspects to self-immolation exist: it is a violent act and does break the precepts. The solution, as stated in such texts as the *Bodhisattvabhūmi*, is as follows: first, it is acknowledged that negative karmic consequences will accrue to the self-immolator for the violence of the self-destruction and for breaking the precepts; but, second, the fact that the self-immolator willingly accepts these negative karmic consequences and the suffering they will entail in a future life is regarded as a second level of altruism because accepting the negative karma is a further self-sacrifice for the sake of others (in addition to the primary self-sacrifice of giving up one's life); thus, third, this second level of altruistic motivation finally cancels out the negative karma that would otherwise have accrued, and the self-immolator not only accrues no negative karma but earns much merit as well.

An informal and unscientific survey of Theravāda and Mahāyāna monastics regarding their attitudes toward Buddhist self-immolation was made by this author in late 1997. About half the Theravāda monastics regarded this act as forbidden for Theravāda monastics but acceptable for Mahāyāna monastics, as it was in line with their principles; the other half regarded self-immolation as immoral and contrary to the teachings of the Buddha for anyone. A minority expressed admiration for Buddhist self-immolators, seeing their acts as great examples of selflessness and love; one expressly identified self-immolation as *dāna-paramitā*, the perfection of giving, as demonstrated in the *Jātaka*s.

Many of the Mahāyāna monastics approved of self-immolation, provided that the motivation is that of a bodhisattva: one who has utterly forgotten himself and acts purely out of love and compassion for others. All were prepared to recognize the heroic selflessness and exalted loving compassion implicit in the act. Some remained troubled by the violence of the act. The Dalai Lama has publicly discouraged self-immolation as incompatible with the nonviolence that is essential to Buddhism in his view. Thus, monastic views on self-immolation are generally aligned with but do not exactly follow the Theravāda-Mahāyāna division.

The global attention given the Vietnamese Buddhists' self-immolations has resulted in a proliferation of incidents of self-sacrifice by burning. Some of these incidents fit the pattern of motivation broadly accepted by the Mahāyāna, and some do not. In some cases non-Buddhists have adopted self-burning as a tactic. In April 1998 a former Tibetan monk burned himself to death in protest of Chinese rule of Tibet. In December 1998 a Korean monk poured gasoline over himself and threatened to set himself on fire as South Korean police raided a Buddhist temple to end a violent dispute over control of the Chogye Order. In the 1980s young Indian men burned themselves to death in protest of the Indian government's preferential treatment of the scheduled castes. Many other cases could be cited.

Even in the Mahāyāna view, self-immolation by burning is not an act that should be undertaken by anyone except a person who has eliminated all vestiges of self-concern. It is a sacred act that aspires to express the core values of Mahāyāna spirituality at their highest level of development. The fact that since the war in Vietnam its use has degenerated to a "tactic" used by political activists for a great variety of partisan purposes, some of them clearly out of line with Buddhist principles, might be a matter of concern for the monastic leadership in coming years.

Sallie B. King

See also Body: Buddhist Perspectives; China; Death: Buddhist Perspectives; Hermits: Buddhist; Holy Men/Holy Women: Buddhist Perspectives; Mahāyāna; Nhát Hanh, Thích; Peace Movements, Buddhist; Persecution: Buddhist Perspectives; Rules, Buddhist (Vinaya): Historical; Vietnam

Further Reading

Hurvitz, Leon, translator, *Scripture of the Lotus Blossom of the Fine Dharma*, New York: Columbia University Press, 1976

Jan, Yun-hua, "Buddhist Self-Immolation in Medieval China," *History of Religions* 4 (1964–1965)

King, Sallie B., "They Who Burned Themselves for Peace: Quaker and Buddhist Self-Immolators during the Vietnam War," *Buddhist-Christian Studies* 20 (2000)

Nhát Hanh, Thích, *Vietnam: Lotus in a Sea of Fire*, New York: Hill and Wang, and London: SCM Press, 1967

Self-Mutilation, Christian

The Old Testament forbade self-mutilation to Jews, not least to counter certain pagan practices, such as that of the prophets of Baal who, in their contest with Elijah, slashed themselves in a trance state (1 Kings 18:29). Eunuchs were prohibited from becoming members of the Israelite community (Deut. 23:2). Israelites were not to gash themselves in grieving (Lev. 19:28) for the reason given in Deuteronomy 14:21: "For you are a people sacred to the Lord, your God, who has chosen you from all nations on the face of the earth to be a people peculiarly his own"(yet see Jer. 4:5). The human body was respected as the work of the Creator. Yet it was recognized that the body sometimes provides the occasion of sin, and thus circumcision was commanded for all Israelite males (Gen. 17:10–11; Lev. 12:3) but not genital cutting for females. Circumcision was given a spiritual explanation (Exod. 5:24–26; Lev. 26:41; Deut. 10:16, 30:6; Jer. 4:4) as indicating submission to God and commitment to the Covenant.

This ambiguity troubled early Christian ascetics who practiced fasting and other forms of "mortification" of physical desires in order to free themselves for obedience to the commandments and openness to spiritual realities. What proved especially confusing were the words of Jesus himself:

> You have heard that it was said: You shall not commit adultery. But I say to you, everyone who looks at a woman with lust has already committed adultery with her in his heart. If your right eye causes you to sin, tear it out and throw it away. It is better to for you to lose one of your members than to have your whole body thrown into Gehenna. And if your right hand causes you to sin, cut it off and throw it away. It is better for you to lose one of your members than to have your whole body go into Gehenna. (Matt. 5:27–30)

That this admonition was taken seriously is evident from St. Paul's words: "No I drive my body and train it, for fear that, after having preached to others, I myself shall be disqualified" (l Cor. 9:27). Thus, physical asceticism was seen as entirely Christian but could be understood too literally. The great biblical exegete and future martyr Origen (c. 185–c. 254) castrated himself lest he be tempted to sin with his young students.

The Church, to be sure, vigorously rejected Origen's example. Although it permitted many kinds of physical discipline, it recalled also the advice of Paul to Timothy: "Train yourself for devotion, for while physical training is of limited value, devotion is valuable in every respect, it holds a promise of life both for the present and for the future (1 Tim. 4:8). The many severe and sometimes bizarre practices of the Desert Fathers led to caution by spiritual guides so as to prevent excesses. Yet from the fifth century scourging as a punishment for monks who seriously break the rule is often mentioned. However, it seems that it was not until the time of St. Peter Damian (1007–1072), who wrote a treatise on the subject, that self-flagellation became a common monastic practice. When taken up by later religious orders, this practice was justified by the words of St. Paul already quoted about disciplining his body. The key verb has a very general sense and what is now translated "I drive" was then translated "scourge." Many saints, including St. Dominic (c. 1172–1221) in the 13th century and St. Ignatius (c. 1491–1556) in the 16th, practiced self-flagellation "unto blood." And provision for flagellation was sometimes included in compline, the bedtime liturgy.

Physical discipline served both an ascetic and a symbolic purpose. Pain, especially to the sense of touch, like fasting to the sense of taste, was thought to curb excessive desires for pleasure. Today we would say that such discipline was a negative sensory conditioning of biological appetite that when uncontrolled by reason not only could lead to sin but also could distract from prayer.

The notion that the ability to endure pain shows remarkable spiritual domination of the material body no doubt also played some role in this thinking, as it seems to do in the practices of some yogis in Hinduism. However, Christian asceticism rejects such display as contrary to humility, according to Jesus' condemnation of hypocrites who "neglect their appearance, so that they may appear to others to be fasting" (Matt. 6:16). The Buddha, having spent some years in severe asceticism, also decided that it was of little benefit to his spiritual quest. Certainly self-mutilation does not harmonize with the strong emphasis on nonviolence in Buddhism.

For Christians physical pain was seen also as a symbolic way of identifying with the Crucified. As late as the 19th century, Henri Lacordaire (1802–1861), the restorer of the Dominican Order in France, used to have himself beaten and hung on a cross before preaching at Notre Dame in Paris. He explained that by temperament he was so cerebral and emotionally cold that he found it difficult to be eloquent in his preaching without first experiencing the Cross!

It was always recognized that such discipline should not be allowed permanently to injure bodily integrity or health. Yet serious abuses that today would be seen as indications not of curbing illicit pleasure but rather of sadism and masochism no doubt occurred. Certain fanatical practices of Flagellants are still found in New Mexico and crop up elsewhere in syncretistic cults. Today spiritual directors are generally reluctant to permit physical discipline of this type, but used moderately it still can have a place in Christian asceticism and might be assigned by confessors as a penance. Nevertheless spiritual directors should be aware that self-mutilation can be a symptom of depressive or schizophrenic psychosis or else of autism.

Some charismatics report that they have observed and delivered (i.e. liberated) through prayer persons suffering what they believe to be possession in which self-mutilation was a symptom. They point to the case in Mark 5:5 of the Gerasene demoniac: "Night and day among the tombs and on the hillsides he was always crying out, and bruising himself with stones" before Jesus cast out his demons into the swine.

One can wonder where to draw the line between self-mutilation and various forms of cosmetic alteration of the body, such as tattooing, deliberate scarification, breast implants and reductions, and various forms of piercing. The purpose of these is not injury to the body but to enhance its beauty and sensuousness. On the contrary in the monastic tradition, emphasis falls on simplicity of life, and the religious habit has been intended both to symbolize the vowed state and to remove the possibility of calling special attention to bodily attributes. In any case respect for the human body as a "temple of the Holy Spirit" (1 Cor. 6:19) must remain a guiding principle in all such matters.

BENEDICT M. ASHLEY, O.P.

See also Asceticism: Christian Perspectives; Buddha (Śākyamuni); Damian, Peter, St.; Desert Fathers; Devotions, Western Christian; Dominic, St.; Fasting: Western Christian

Further Reading

Arintero, Juan G., *The Mystical Evolution in the Development and Vitality of the Church*, 2 vols., translated by Jordan Aumann, St. Louis: Herder, 1951

Bailly, Paul, "La 'discipline' dans les instituts religieux," in *Dictionnaire de Spiritualité ascétique et mystique: Doctrine et histoire*, volume 5, Paris: Beauchesne, 1964

Constable, Giles, *Medieval Monasticism: A Select Bibliography*, Toronto and Buffalo, New York: University of Toronto Press, 1976

de Guibert, J., "Ascètique (Théologie Ascètique)," in *Dictionnaire de Spiritualité ascétique et mystique: Doctrine et histoire*, volume 1, Paris: Beauchesne, 1937

Favazza, Armando R., *Bodies Under Siege: Self-Mutilation and Body Modification in Culture and Psychiatry*, 2nd edition, Baltimore, Maryland: Johns Hopkins University Press, 1996 (this is the best book on the psychological aspects of self injury)

Frank, H. Suso, editor, *Askese und Mönchtum in der alten Kirche*, Darmstadt: Wissenschaftliche 'Buchgesellschaft, 1975

Leclercq, Jean, "'Disciplina' and 'Disciplina au sens de flagellation'," in *Dictionnaire de Spiritualité ascétique et mystique: Doctrine et histoire*, volume 3, Paris: Beauchesne, 1957

Royo Marín, Antonio, and Jordan Aumann, *The Theology of Christian Perfection*, Dubuque, Iowa: Priory Press, 1962

Vogüé, Adalbert, editor, *Saint Colomban: Règles et penitentiels monastiques*, Bégrolles-en-Mauges: Abbaye de Bellefontaine, 1989

Note: St. Peter Damian's *De laude flagellorum* (in *Patrologia Latina*, edited by Migne, volume 145, pages 674–686) is the classic source for monastic practices of self-flagellation.

Seraphim of Sarov, St. 1759–1833

Russian Orthodox monk, hermit, and revered spiritual father

Seraphim was born Prokhor Moshnin on 19 July 1759 at Kursk in southern Russia near the Ukraine. Known for his piety as a child, by the age of 18 he had decided to become a monk. He received the blessing of Dositheus, recluse of the Kiev Caves, to go to Sarov. Prokhor then applied to Sarov Monastery in the heavily forested Arzamas district of Tambov province, about 350 miles northeast of Kursk and about 250 miles east of Moscow. On 20 November 1778 he was admitted there as a novice under the spiritual guidance of Fr. Joseph, the monastery's treasurer. He was not granted permission from the Holy Synod to become a monk for 15 years, during which time he lived the ordinary life of the community. In 1780 he contracted dropsy, an illness that lasted three years until he was healed through a vision of the Mother of God (*Theotokos*). On 13 August 1786, at the age of 27, he was tonsured monk and given the name Seraphim. The same year he became a deacon. A religious (but not monastic) community of devout women was founded in 1788 in the nearby village of Diveyevo, and the leadership of the community passed to Pakhomius, the abbot of Sarov, and to Seraphim. A convent would eventually evolve out of this religious community and become very dear to Seraphim. On 2 September 1793, at the age of 34, he was ordained priest, and on 21 November of the following year he was given permission to withdraw from the monastery to enter eremitical life following the ancient Rule of St. Pachomius of Egypt. He retired to a hut in the forest about four miles from Sarov, where he practiced unceasing prayer, fasted, and tended a small garden and beehives. On Sundays he returned to Sarov to receive Holy Communion. His fasting became ever more stringent. In the beginning he ate bread brought from the monastery, supplemented with vegetables from his garden; then he ate only vegetables; finally, for a three-year period, he ate only grass. He received a few visitors at first as well as companions who wanted to share his ascetic way of life. His friend Timon of Nadeev Monastery was among the visitors. Few were able to remain with him for long because of his extreme austerity.

In 1796 Seraphim was tendered the abbacy of Alatuir Monastery and later of Krasnoslobodsk Monastery. He refused both offers. From 1802 to 1804, over a period of 1,000 days, he prayed the Publican's prayer of Luke 18:13 ("God, be merciful to me, a sinner") while kneeling and standing in the Stylite tradition on stones. On 12 September 1804 his solitary life in the forest came to a brutal end when he was beaten by robbers. Although left for dead he managed to revive and reach Sarov, where it was determined that his wounds were so serious that he would not recover. At this time Seraphim received another miraculous vision of the Theotokos that restored him to life. However, his injuries left him physically bent and enfeebled. Even so he returned to his hut after five months of recuperation at the monastery. When the robbers were finally caught, Seraphim forgave them and had them pardoned. In 1806 he was elected abbot of Sarov but declined the position. So that he would not to come into conflict with the new abbot, Seraphim removed to a forest hermitage about one mile from the monastery where for three years he lived in complete silence and isolation. In August 1810 he was required by the abbot and monastic council to return to the monastery, where he retired to a cell in strict seclusion as a recluse. He never left his cell and never received visitors. This period of Seraphim's life lasted until 1813 and included an experience of heavenly rapture lasting five days and five nights.

From 1813 on Seraphim began to receive visitors and to take an active role in the spiritual guidance of the women of the religious community in Diveyevo, seven miles from Sarov. In 1821 his connection with the community led to rumors, and as a consequence Seraphim was examined by Bishop Jonas of Tambov, who declared him innocent. In 1824 he received a vision from the Theotokos instructing him to form and spiritually direct a religious community of nuns within the preexisting community at Diveyevo. These nuns would support themselves by working a mill established by Seraphim. These "miller women" nuns were required to be virgins. On 25 November 1825 he returned to the nearby hermitage. He stayed in the hut by day, practicing hesychastic prayer, working in the forest and the garden, and receiving visitors. He returned to his cell at night and on holy days. He took one meal a day and slept little. On Sundays and feast days, he was brought Communion in his cell by the celebrant, clergy, monks, and people in solemn procession. However, this procedure provoked animosity, and Seraphim was required to receive in church.

On 24 March 1831 he received his 12th and final vision from the Theotokos. In it she told him, "Soon, my dear one, you shall be with us." From this date on he began seriously preparing for his imminent death. Seraphim became extremely popular as a spiritual father (starets). It was not uncommon for him to attract as many as 5,000 people on a feast day and an inordinate number on ordinary days. He was entirely selfless in his care for these people, and his prescience about their needs was uncanny. He proffered the term "my joy" when he addressed them. He always recommended spiritual direction (*starchestvo*) to monks and laity who were in spiritual need and also cured many of their diseases. One of these was the young nobleman Nicholas Alexandrovich Motovilov, who was brought to Seraphim on 7 September 1831, the eve of the Feast of the Birth of the Theotokos. Motovilov suffered from an incurable form of rheumatism so severe that he had to be carried. On 9 September, after several meetings, Seraphim asked him whether he believed in Christ, in the Theotokos, and in the healing power of Christ. When Motovilov said yes, the saint replied that he was already cured, and the young man was able to walk away. This event was recorded by Motovilov, together with the even more astonishing event from November 1831 of the transfiguration of St. Seraphim. During an interview about the spiritual life that took place near the saint's hut, Motovilov asked him, "How can one know the presence of the Holy Spirit?" at which point Seraphim began to glow as bright as the sun. When Motovilov showed signs of fear, Seraphim comforted him. In effect Seraphim became a living manifestation of the Holy Spirit. This is the second recorded instance of the saint's transfiguration. The first occurred when he recounted to Ivan Tikhonovich the vision of heaven that he had received during his five-night, five-day rapture from the 1810–1815 period of reclusion.

In 1832 Seraphim again fell under suspicion for his relationship with the Sisters of Diveyevo. In August, Bishop Arsenius of Tambov came to examine him, and once again Seraphim was pronounced innocent of the charges. Remarkably, as recently as the 1990s rumors existed of a secret tunnel that connected Sarov with Diveyevo, although archaeological evidence has discredited the rumors. In this year the saint began to prepare for his death, often meditating before his coffin at the entrance of his cell. On 1 January 1833 he received Holy Communion in the infirmary chapel, bidding the community, "Be saved, be courageous and watchful. Today crowns are ready for us." On the following day he was found dead in a prayerful kneeling position before the icon of the Theotokos. On 19 July 1903, 70 years after his death, he was canonized by the Russian Church. His feast day is 2 January.

In March 1927 Bolsheviks removed the saint's relics from Sarov and put them on display in the Museum of Godlessness in Moscow. For years the relics were lost, until December 1990, when they were rediscovered in the Museum of Atheism in Leningrad. For almost six months they were kept in the Patriarchal Cathedral of the Epiphany in Moscow as the object of intense rejoicing and veneration. From 23 July to 1 August 1991, they were taken in procession from Moscow to the newly reopened convent at Diveyevo. The monastery at Sarov was no longer an option because in the late 1940s the town and its monastery became Arzamas-16, the center of Joseph Stalin's effort to develop the atom bomb for the Soviet Union. As of 1996 only Sarov's small chapel, which had recently served as a grocery store, had been restored. The monastery's restoration is in the offing.

MICHAEL D. PETERSON

See also Elders, Russian Monastic (Startsi); Hermits: Eastern Christian; Kiev (Kyiv), Ukraine; Nilus of Sora, St.; Orthodox Monasticism: Slavic; Russia: History; Stylites

Biography

Born the son of a builder in Kursk, Seraphim joined the monastery at Sarov at age 19. From 1794 to 1825 he lived as a hermit, first in the forest (where for a period of 1,000 days he knelt on a high rock) and after 1810 in a cell. From 1825 to 1833 he opened his cell in order to serve as spiritual director to visitors from all over Russia. He epitomizes the monastic elder (starets).

Further Reading

Bolshakoff, Sergius, *Russian Mystics*, Kalamazoo, Michigan: Cistercian Publications, 1977

Cavarnos, Constantine, and Mary-Barbara Zeldin, *St. Seraphim of Sarov: Widely Beloved Mystic, Healer, Comforter, and Spiritual Guide: An Account of His Life, Character and Message, Together with a Very Edifying Conversation with His Disciple Motovilov on the Acquisition of the Grace of the Holy Spirit, and the Saint's Spiritual Counsels*, Belmont, Massachusetts: Institute for Byzantine and Modern Greek Studies, 1980

de Beausobre, Iulia, *Flame in the Snow: A Life of St. Serafim of Sarov*, preface by Donald Nicholl, Springfield, Illinois: Templegate, 1996

Dobbie-Bateman, A.F., "St. Seraphim of Sarov," in *A Treasury of Russian Spirituality*, edited by G.F. Fedotov, New York: Harper and Row, 1950; London: Sheed and Ward, 1952

Evdokimov, Paul, "Saint Seraphim: An Icon of Orthodox Spirituality," *Ecumenical Review* 15:3 (April 1963)

Moore, Lazarus, *St. Seraphim of Sarov: A Spiritual Biography*, Blanco, Texas: New Sarov Press, 1994

Zander, Valentine, *St. Seraphim of Sarov*, translated by Sister Gabriel Anne, introduction by Fr. Boris Bobrinskoy, London: SPCK, and Crestwood, New York: St. Vladimir's Seminary Press, 1975

Serbia

According to Constantine VII Porphyrogenitus (913–959), the Serbs – a Slavic tribe that had penetrated into the Balkans in the seventh century – were first converted to Christianity during the reign of the Byzantine Emperor Heraclius (610–641). With the permission of the Byzantine emperor, the Serbs inhabited the lands that stretched from the Sava River, including the Dinaric range, to the hinterland of the late Roman coastal towns of southern Dalmatia (far to the southwest of what we now think of as the center of Serbia). However, the first conversion was rather unsuccessful, and a second, between 867 and 874, was undertaken with more success during the reign of Basil I (867–886). Modern historiography agrees that the first missionaries arrived from Rome and only later from Byzantium at the time when disciples of Methodius (c. 815–885) were active in the Balkans. Methodius was, together with Constantine, a native of Thessaloniki and the first missionary (863) among the Slavs to

The 12th-century Studenica monastery, near Kraljevo, Serbia, aerial view.
Photo courtesy of Gojko Subotic

preach in the Slavic language. The first Christian names (Stephen = Stefan, Peter = Petar) appeared among the Serbs at the end of the ninth century. Serbian Church terminology contains both Latin and Greek words, reflecting the twofold origin.

In the ninth and tenth centuries, the archbishop of Split and the metropolitan of Durres were responsible for the hinterland of the coastal towns of Dalmatia. Some northern lands were possibly subject to the Diocese of Pannonia under the jurisdiction of the Roman Church or to the bishoprics of Belgrade (878) and Braničevo (879), both subject to the Bulgarian Church.

St. Peter's rotunda (near modern Novi Pazar), one of the oldest sacred buildings built by the Serbs, dates from the late ninth century and later became the Bishopric of Ras. In the 11th century the Serbian lands were divided between the Archbishopric of Ohrid (Patriarchate of Constantinople) and the Archbishopric of Bar (Roman Church), to which the coastal hinterlands were subjected. The 12th century was the turning point, and Serbian lands were united under the grand *župan* Stefan Nemanja (1168–1196), founder of the Nemanjid dynasty (1168–1371). His son, Rastko, became a monk Sava (St. Sava) at Mount Athos and in 1219 the first archbishop of the independent Serbian Church. Sava was the most important personality and architect of both Church legislation and monastic life in Serbia. Under him the Serbian Church acquired its independence from Byzantium and has been a part of the Orthodox Christian community ever since. However, Latin bishoprics in the coastal areas remained active. An archbishop was installed in the Žica monastery, and ten bishoprics existed in Serbia in the 13th century, as did both male and female monasteries and anchoritic abodes. The 13th-century St. Peter of Koriša is the only Serbian medieval hermit included among the saints.

Two monasteries founded by Stefan Nemanja, Studenica (1183) and Chilandari on Mount Athos (1198) became the most important monastic centers. Sava wrote the monastic rules (*tipik*) for Chilandari (1199) and Studenica (1208). Life in the monasteries was of the coenobitic type. A few laurae existed in

Saint Sava and St. Simeon-Nemanja, the Studenica monastery, King's Church, near Kraljevo, Serbia, fresco 14th century. Photo courtesy of Svetlana Popovic

The Studenica monastery, near Kraljevo, Serbia, 12th century.
Photo courtesy of Svetlana Popović

which the coenobitic monastery acted as the core, and several anchoritic cells were outside the monastery (e.g., Studenica, Chilandari, and Mileševa). The monastery of Studenica became the prototype for the monastic life and building program.

The architectural specialty of Serbian monasteries was the circular plan of the enclosure. The church was placed centrally and oriented toward the east. Monastery buildings were located along the circular enclosure wall. The refectory, for communal meals and commemorations, was often built in the western part of the monastery, facing the main church portal. The main entrance to the monastery was usually located to the west of the church. The monastery had residences for the superior and church dignitaries, monks' cells, workshops, stores, a communal kitchen, library, infirmary, and so on. Outside the enclosure monasteries possessed vast estates. The church interior was decorated with frescoes, and the rite performed was Orthodox (Byzantine). Architectural styles were of both provenances (Romanesque and Byzantine). The ranking of monasteries descended from independent foundations of the ruling dynasty, through archepiscopal (later patriarchal) and episcopal monasteries, to private foundations of the secular and church nobility. No monastic "orders" existed as in the West, and each monastery had a superior (*iguman*), steward (*ikonom*), sacristan (*eklisijarh*), and other lower officials. The size of the monasteries varied between 10 and 80 monks.

Archbishop Nikodim introduced the Sabaitic liturgical *Tipik* in 1319, and the Serbian patriarchate was proclaimed in the monastery of the Holy Apostles in Peć (modern Kosovo) in 1346. Under Archbishop Danilo II (1324–1337), a great number of monasteries were built. A complex of churches was added to the Church of the Holy Apostles in Peć; the famous monastery of Dečani in Kosovo was built from 1327 to 1348.

After the fall of the Serbian state to the Ottoman Turks (1459), monasteries continued their life in different circumstances. During the reinstatement of the Patriarchate at Peć (1557–1766), whose jurisdiction covered the vast territory from Pannonia in the north to Macedonia and from Dalmatia and eastern Croatia to western Bulgaria, monastic life revived. Later, however, it was almost completely abandoned because of Ottoman persecution. A number of monasteries were converted into mosques, and in 1594 venerated relics of St. Sava were burned on a pyre. Important monastic centers in the 16th century included the colony in Ovčar and Kablar Gorge on the Morava River (central Serbia), monasteries at Fruška Gora

The Patriarchate of Peć, Kosovo, 13th–14th century.
Photo courtesy of Slobodan Curcic

(in Vojvodina), Papraća (Bosnia), Krka (Croatia), and so on. In the process of liberation in the 19th century, the Turks (the *hatišerif* of 1830) permitted churches and monasteries to be reopened and the installation of bells, which had been prohibited since the 15th century. Monasteries flourished again until after World War II. In socialist Yugoslavia the postwar period was a difficult time for monastic life and the Church in general. However, in the 1980s monastic life began to flourish again in several monasteries (e.g., Mesić, Ljubostinja, Crna Reka, and Dečani).

SVETLANA POPOVIĆ

See also Archaeology: Near East; Architecture: Eastern Christian Monasteries; Istanbul, Turkey; Lavra; Libraries: Eastern Christian; Mount Athos, Greece; Orthodox Monasticism

Further Reading

Ćirkovic, Sima, "Pravoslavna crkva u srpskoj državi," in his *Rabotnici, Vojnici, Duhovnici: Društva srednjovekovnog Balkana*, Belgrade: Equilibrium, 1997

Constantine VII Porphyrogenitus, *De administrando imperio*, edited by Gyula Moravcsik, translated by Romilly J.H. Jenkins, Washington D.C.: Dumbarton Oaks Center for Byzantine Studies, 1967

Ćorović, Vladimir, editor, *Spisi svetoga Save i Stevana Prvovenčanoga*, Belgrade: Drž. štamp. Kralj. Jugoslavije, 1939

Domentijan, Hieromonach, *Život svetoga Simeuna i svetoga Save*, edited by Djura Daničić, Belgrade, 1865

Kalić, Jovanka, "Crkvene prilike u srpskim zemljama do stvaranja arhiepiskopije 1219. godine," in *Medjunarodni naučni skup Sava Nemanjić – sveti Sava: Istorija i predanje: Decembar 1976*, edited by Vojislav Djurić, Belgrade: Srpska akademija nauka i umetnosti, 1979

Marković, Vasilije, *Pravoslavno monaštvo i manastiri u srednjevekovnoj Srbiji*, Sremski Karlovci: Srpska manastirska štamp., 1920

Popović, Svetlana, *Krst u krugu: Arhitektura manastira u srednjovekovnoj Srbiji*, Belgrade: Prosveta; Republički zavod za zaštitu spomenika kulture, 1994

Popović, Danica, "The Cult of St. Petar of Koriša: Stages of Development and Patterns," *Balcanica* 28 (1997)

Radojičić, Djordje Sp., "La date de la conversion des Serbes," *Byzantion* 22 (1952)
Slijepčević, Djoko, *Istorija srpske pravoslavne crkve*, 2 vols., Diseldorpf: Ostrug, 1978

Sergius of Radonezh, St. c. 1314–1392

Russian Orthodox monk, reformer, and pivotal supporter of the prince of Moscow

Sergius of Radonezh was the guiding spirit of a new "desert" monasticism that turned Russian monasticism in a different direction from that of the earlier Kievan urban monasteries. As the most important monastic figure of 14th-century Russia, he influenced most of the monks of his period. Much is known of his life owing to a contemporary *Life* (a rarity for 14th-century Russia) composed by his disciple Epiphanius the Wise, a monk at the Trinity Monastery.

Sergius, born in the territory of Rostov, was the son of a Rostov boyar, Cyril. At his baptism he was named Bartholomew. Cyril and many of his countrymen migrated from Rostov to Radonezh, a small town in the territory of Moscow. Sergius, an adolescent at this time, thus became a Muscovite, which is significant for his later work as spiritual guide and political helper to the prince of Moscow.

From his youth Sergius desired monasticism and, unlike his two brothers, did not marry. Before his parents died, they were tonsured as monks, as was his eldest brother Stephen, then a widower. Sergius went off to become a monk, but instead of joining his brother in his monastery, he persuaded him to leave his monastery and go with him into a "desert" place. They roamed through vast forests before they found a place to stay, some 10 miles from Radonezh, where they cut wood to build a small chapel and a cabin. The chapel was consecrated in the name of the Holy Trinity in remembrance of a miracle that took place before Sergius' birth when his mother, Mary, felt him move three times in her at the most solemn moments of the Divine Liturgy. Because neither brother was ordained, the Divine Liturgy was celebrated only when a priest came visiting. The most frequent visitor was Abbot Metrophanes, who tonsured Bartholomew and gave him the name Sergius at the age of 23.

Stephen could not endure the difficulties of the solitude and moved to a monastery in Moscow, leaving Sergius alone in his wilderness. Sergius worked daily in difficult manual labor, often as a carpenter. These "works of St. Sergius" became deeply imprinted in the memory of the Russian people and in their iconography.

After a few years some monks began to gather around him. He tried to turn them away but had no success. They built huts for themselves and began to live according to Sergius' way of life. At the time of the death of Metrophanes, the brethren, who were then 12, insisted that Sergius assume the abbacy and the priesthood. Gradually, over some 15 years, the monks felled and burned the surrounding woods for fields and built farms and villages, thus beginning the prosperity of the Trinity Monastery. Sergius, however, lived in complete poverty.

Painted gateway, Holy Trinity–St. Sergius Monastery, Sergeyev Posad (Zagorsk), Russia, 18th century.
Photo courtesy of Robert E. Jones

About 1355 Sergius received a directive from the patriarch of Constantinople stating the necessity of introducing communal life among his monks. Sergius consulted Metropolitan Alexis and accepted a cenobitic rule for his brethren. The only Greek rule that was known and used in Russia was that of the Studion of Constantinople, and this was introduced into the monastery. The rule abolished private property and appointed many monastic officers to have orderly administration. Monks who secretly disagreed left the monastery. At one point even Sergius left, and he and a number of monks began to create a new monastery. Eventually he was invited back.

During Sergius' lifetime some of his disciples were appointed heads of newly founded monasteries in the city of Moscow and surrounding towns, and the Trinity Monastery became a center of monastic influence throughout a vast area. Much of this initiative came not from Sergius but from Alexis and the princes of the Moscow dynasty, who used Holy Trinity as a seedbed for new monastic foundations.

The importance of Sergius in the destiny of the young Muscovite state was one of the reasons that Muscovy and, afterward, all of Russia venerated him as its heavenly patron. This period

Cathedral of the Dormition (Uspensky Cathedral), Holy Trinity–St. Sergius Monastery, Sergeyev Posad, Russia, 16th century. The tomb of St. Sergius is inside the cathedral.
Photo courtesy of Robert E. Jones

saw a struggle for power led by the Moscow princes. In this national conflict Sergius stood on the side of Moscow; he visited the city, was godfather to the sons of Prince Dmitri Donskoi (1359–1389), and even undertook political missions.

The second half of the 14th century saw considerable changes in the political life of northeastern Russia, which gained more independence from the Golden Horde. When Prince Dmitri refused to pay the regular tribute, the Horde ruler launched a campaign against the Rus, moving large military forces toward the frontiers in the summer of 1380. Moscow was the center of the struggle, and the main forces of the country united around it. Before the battle, Prince Dmitri went to the Trinity Monastery to ask Sergius for his blessing. Sergius blessed and encouraged him and prophesied a victory. His spiritual role in the battle of Kulikovo Field on the upper Don was seen as ensuring the first successful attempt of the Russians to resist the Tatars. This battle started the final all-Russian period of struggle for liberation from the Tatars and established Moscow's authority as the political and military center of Russia. It also strengthened the influence of Sergius and his monastery.

Toward the end of his life, Sergius was offered the metropolitan see at a time when Alexis, an old man concerned with the nomination of a successor, and Prince Dmitri wanted a Russian, not a Greek, in the See of Moscow. Sergius refused. He died in 1392 and in 1442 was declared a saint of the Russian Church.

After Sergius' death, during a Tatar raid in 1408 that failed to conquer Moscow, the Tatars discovered the Trinity Monastery on their retreat and razed it. The monastery was rebuilt by Sergius' disciple and successor, Nikon. The earliest stone construction of the monastery, built between 1422 and 1423 under Nikon, was the Trinity Cathedral, which was built at the expense of Prince Yuri of Zvenigorod, the son of Dmitri Donskoi, to praise Sergius and his great services to the country. The remains of Sergius were brought here from the wooden Trinity Church, where they remain to this day. To paint the iconostasis and the frescos of the cathedral, Nikon invited two outstanding icon painters: Andrei Rublev and Daniil Chorny. It was for the Trinity Cathedral that Rublev created his icon *The Trinity*.

Tsar Ivan the Terrible (1533–1584) favored the Trinity Monastery, having given rich contributions to it and many works of art. During his time the five-domed Cathedral of the Dormition was added, having been finished in 1585. Ivan created a united system of defensive fortifications around Moscow with a ring of powerful fortresses, one of which was the Trinity Monastery, whose new stone walls were fortified with powerful towers. In the 17th century the monastery became a major landowner, with the peasant lands belonging to it more numerous than those belonging to the tsar's family and the patriarch. It is said that Russia had three powers: the tsar, the patriarch, and the head of the Monastery of the Trinity.

In 1744, according to a special edict of the tsar, the monastery was honored with the title of *lavra* and called the Monastery of the Trinity and St. Sergius. The great flow of pilgrims promoted a rich market in the village of Sergeyev Posad.

After the revolution in 1917, special decrees protected the buildings and contents of the then closed monastery, which was made into a museum. After World War II, with the return of many of the monastery's riches that had been evacuated, specialists in restoration began training in a school that was created there in 1945. The monastery was also reopened and the Moscow Theological Academy established there. Since 1969 Zagorsk, the name given the town after the revolution, became a tourist center and was included in the list of "Golden Ring" towns around Moscow. In 1991 some 700,000 pilgrims and tourists from Russia and abroad came to visit the monastery. Since then, the original name has been returned to that of the surrounding town, Sergeyev Posad.

DAVID PAUL HESTER

See also Elders, Russian Monastic (Startsi); Istanbul, Turkey; Kiev (Kyiv), Ukraine; Lavra; Moscow, Russia; Nilus of Sora, St.; Orthodox Monasticism; Russia: History

Biography

Born Bartholomew at Rostov but raised in Radonezh, he established a forest hermitage in what is now Sergeyev Posad (previously known as Zagorsk) outside Moscow. There he founded the Monastery of the Holy Trinity, which inspired some 30 others in his lifetime. As priest and later abbot, he inspired resistance to the Tatars, particularly that by Prince Dmitri in 1380. Sergius is venerated as the "Builder of Russia." His monastery is now known as "Holy Trinity–St. Sergius."

Further Reading

Fedotov, George P., *A Treasury of Russian Spirituality*, New York: Sheed and Ward, 1948; London: Sheed and Ward, 1950 (a shortened English translation of the *Life of St. Sergius*)

Fedotov, George P., *The Russian Religious Mind*, volume 2: *The Middle Ages: The Thirteenth to the Fifteenth Centuries*, Cambridge, Massachusetts: Harvard University Press, 1966

Meyendorff, John, *Byzantium and the Rise of Russia: A Study of Byzantine Russian Relations in the Fourteenth Century*, Cambridge and New York: Cambridge University Press, 1981

Milosevic, Desanka, *Der goldene Ring: Das Christentum Russlands*, Freiburg: Herder, 1982

Zernov, Nicholas, *St. Sergius – Builder of Russia*, London and New York: Macmillan, 1939

Zernov, Nicholas, *The Russians and Their Church*, London and New York: Macmillan, 1945

Zagorskii Muzei Zapovednik, Moscow, 1991

Servites

The Order of Friar Servants of Mary or Servites emerged in the 13th century during an age of intense Marian piety and of mendicant religious orders. Unlike in most orders there is no one founder of the Servites. Usually this role is assigned to the Seven Founders: Bonifilius, John Bonagiunta, Gerard Sostegni, Bartholomew Amidei, Benedict dell' Antella, Ricoverus Uguccione, and Alexis Falconieri (canonized in 1888). However, recent scholarship points out that only Bonifilius and Alexis can be documented and that the last names assigned to the founders are unreliable. Tradition dates the foundation of the Order to 1233, when devout Florentine laymen withdrew from the city to lead a life inspired by the example of the early Church. Some of them were supposed to have settled at last at Monte Senario, whereas others dwelt in Cafaggio. However, the earliest secure date for the Servites is 1245 to 1247.

This new community, under Dominican influence, adopted the Rule of St. Augustine, with their own additional customs and enactments, and these friars began wearing a distinctive black habit. They assumed the name Servants of Mary, and both the bishop of Florence and the papacy extended protection to the Servites. A life of strict poverty was embraced. The Order was approved by Pope Alexander IV (1254–1261) in 1256. A more definite legislative framework was provided during the generalate of Philip Benizi (1267–1285). The Servites were suppressed by the Second Council of Lyons (1274) in an attempt to restrain the proliferation of new orders, but Benizi secured the continuation of the Order by moderating the emphasis on strict poverty. Benedict XI (1303–1304), a Dominican, granted final approval to the Servites in 1304.

The Servites soon had a small network of priories, mostly in Italy with a few in Germany. By the end of the 13th century, about 40 priories existed in the provinces of Tuscany, Umbria, and Romagna. Further expansion into Lombardy was resisted at first by the friars of Tuscany, but it succeeded through the efforts of Peter of Todi (general from 1314 to 1344). Servite houses used the Roman liturgy with minor differences, prescribing special veneration of Mary, and they began to acquire works of art for their churches. Emphasis was placed on the spiritual and corporal works of mercy rather than on preaching or study. (The Florentine orphanage of the Holy Innocents, designed by Filippo Brunelleschi [1377–1446], is attached to a Servite church, SS. Annunziata.) Only in 1318 would a general chapter issue rules for studies. A house of studies in Paris eventually was eclipsed by houses attached to the Italian universities. Women were attracted to the Servite movement. Some became nuns, whereas others became tertiaries, known as Mantellate for their long veil. Their foundation is attributed to St. Juliana Falconieri (1270–1341), who received her habit from Philip Benizi in 1284.

Like most mendicant orders the Servites faced a divisive period in the 15th century. Conventuals, committed to the status quo, were confronted with a challenge by observants eager to reform the Order and reattain primitive austerity. Eventually a Congregation of the Observance was established within the Order. This movement produced a phase of renewed growth, witnessed by the foundation of new convents. Monte Senario, ten miles north of Florence, became the site of an eremitic wing of the Order and lasted to the late 18th century. Attending this movement were the expansion of the Servites into France in the late 15th century and an increase in the number of Servite nuns and tertiaries.

This observant movement was not uniformly successful in reforming the Servites. In the Tridentine era there were scandals involving either irregular conduct or suspect theological opinions. The Order formulated and reformulated its constitutions, the edition of 1588 applying to the Order the decrees of the Council of Trent (1545–1563). Efforts were made to spread the Order to the Iberian Peninsula, the greatest success being obtained in Catalonia and Valencia. Nonetheless the Servites nearly had died out in Spain by middle of the 19th century because of government hostility. (In the 20th century the Servites reestablished themselves in Spain and Portugal.) The French branch survived the wars of religion in the 16th century, only to be suppressed by the crown in 1770. New growth was experienced in Germany and Austria in the 17th century, but the hostility of Emperor Joseph II (1780–1790) destroyed the Bohemian province while weakening other branches of the Order. The Servites became zealous proponents of the cult of the Sorrows of Mary, leading to authorization of the celebration of the feast of Our Lady of Sorrows in 1668. Servite savants, especially Paolo Sarpi (1552–1623) of Venice, are noted for their historical scholarship.

Following the French Revolution and the Napoleonic period, which saw many religious houses suppressed and their possessions confiscated, the Servites experienced new growth. They undertook missionary labors, especially in Aden and the Philippines. In 1864 the foundation was laid for an English province of the Servite Order. In 1870 the first Servites were sent to the United States, led by Father Austin Morini. They worked first in Wisconsin and later in Illinois. Until 1901 the Servites in North America were supervised by a vicar-general. Steps were taken thereafter to found a full province, a status attained in 1909. A second province, based in Colorado, was founded in 1952 by separation from the existing grouping, but it was reunited with its parent community in 1998. By 1964 Servites were active in Latin America, Africa, and Australia. They continue to pursue charitable endeavors, including in hospitals, but some Servites run schools and colleges. Monte Senario still is regarded as the mother house, but the generalate resides in Rome together with a theological faculty. Numerous groups of Servite sisters exist, active in both the Eastern and the Western Hemisphere. Servite tertiaries also continue their ministries. The cult of Our Lady of Sorrows continues to be propagated through Servite shrines. Devotion to St. Peregrine Laziosi is tied to ministry to sufferers from cancer, AIDS, and other life-threatening diseases.

Thomas M. Izbicki

See also Augustinian Rule; Florence, Italy; Social Services: Western Christian

Further Reading

Benassi, Vincenzo, *A Short History of the Servite Order*, Rome: General Secretariat for the Servite Missions, 1987

Dal Pino, Franco Andrea, *Brothers and Servants: The Seven Holy Founders of the Servite Order*, Berwyn, Illinois: Eastern Province of Servites, 1978

Morini, Austin, *The Foundation of the Order of Servants of Mary in the United States of America (1870–1883)* (Scrinium Historiale, 19), Rome: Edizioni Marianum, 1993

Origins and Early Saints of the Order of Servants of Mary: Writings of the Fourteenth and Fifteenth Centuries, Chicago: Friar Servants of Mary, 1984

Related Web Site

http://www.servite.org/index.htm (Order of the Friar Servants of Mary)

Sexuality: Buddhist Perspectives

Buddhism promotes monasticism, and almost by definition monks and nuns are required to be celibate. In such a context what could there to be say about the perspective of Buddhist monasticism on sexuality, except that it is forbidden? However, even celibate monastics are sexual beings whose female and male organs and desires remain intact. Although they ought not to engage in sexual activity, they have perspectives on sexuality. Why is sexual activity so strictly prohibited? Are some specific sexual acts more problematic than others? How should male and female monastics interact? What happens when infractions occur – when, despite prohibitions against sexual activity, monastics do engage in sex? The answers to all these questions are grounded in Buddhist attitudes toward sexuality per se apart from monastic rules. However, Buddhist perspectives on sexuality are not monolithic. Newer perspectives have developed in later forms of Buddhism, and the definitions of acceptable sexual activity vary from one Buddhist country to another.

Contemporary commentators are careful to distinguish between sex and gender, although the boundary between these two is often blurred even in the most careful discussions. In simplest terms *sex* is a biological term and *gender* a cultural term. *Gender* refers to the self-image, behaviors, and limitations that one experiences as a result of having male or female biological sex. In keeping with that distinction, this article focuses on sexual norms and behaviors, discussing gender only in limited fashion when there is direct spillover from ideas about sexuality into Buddhist concepts about gender.

Because Western attitudes about sexuality are deeply (although often unconsciously) ingrained into westerners, it is crucial not to project those attitudes onto Buddhist perspectives on sexuality. Sex is forbidden to both Christian and Buddhist monastics, but the reasons for the prohibition might not be the same. Christian texts, especially from the formative period of the Church fathers, often give the impression that sex is to be avoided because it is "bad." Sex is avoided for moral reasons. Read superficially by people who have imbibed (even if they do not accept) Christian views about sex, Buddhist texts can often give the same impression.

However, for Buddhism the fundamental issue is not morality. Sex is not necessarily "bad"; rather it is distracting and promotes attachment. The most basic Buddhist perspective on sexuality is embedded in the worldview of early Indian Buddhism. Conventional life is filled with suffering; suffering is caused by *tṛṣṇa* (craving), which is ultimately rooted in ignorance about *anātman* (egolessness). Having given in to craving, one engages in sex or, ignorant of egolessness, one seeks self-perpetuation through the perpetuation of a family lineage. Because desire or craving (*tṛṣṇa*) is almost inevitably a concomitant of sexual activity, it entangles one in saṃsāra (cyclic existence), thus trapping the individual in repeated rebirths – an undesirable fate. Sex easily distracts one from the calm equanimity that cuts the root of saṃsāra. Furthermore sex produces additional entanglements in the form of family responsibilities toward the children that result from sex. These only increase one's entanglement in saṃsāra at the same time as they limit one's time for the spiritual disciplines that bring liberation from saṃsāra. Freedom is found only by renouncing desire and overcoming ignorance, not by self-perpetuation in any form. The monastic lifestyle is said to be infinitely superior to the householder lifestyle, with its active sexuality, for accomplishing that state of mind.

That sexuality involves not primarily a moral issue but a practical issue of how best to attain enlightenment is further demonstrated by the fact that Buddhist moral principles do not elaborate on proper sexual conduct for laypeople. Avoiding sexual misconduct is a lay precept found in all forms of Buddhism, but what that means is rarely spelled out in great detail. Instead lay Buddhist sexual norms usually follow the norms of the culture and vary widely. In contemporary times that has meant that Buddhists usually do not forbid birth control and sometimes allow homosexuality and abortion. Japanese Buddhist rituals surrounding abortion and stillbirth are the most famous example of the way in which lay Buddhist sexual morality can accommodate practices that many religions forbid.

The situation is quite different regarding monastic sexual regulations, which are strict and spelled out in great detail. The greatest sexual misdeed, heterosexual intercourse (with any species, not only humans), merits expulsion from the monastic order. Intercourse is defined as involving penetration, "even as much as a sesame seed," of any of the three (two for men) sexual orifices. However, some later commentaries state that if no pleasure is felt, the monk or nun is not guilty. For nuns touching the body of another person between the shoulders and the knees or meeting alone with a man are equally grave offenses. However, homosexual intercourse, especially between monks, does not elicit much comment. Nuns are subject to extra rules that keep them from any intimate contact with another woman. They cannot undress in a woman's presence, be massaged by a woman, or sit on a woman's bed. Nuns are never to sleep two to a bed unless one of them is sick. Finally, autoeroticism is a moderately serious offense for both monks and nuns. Again the rules for nuns are more detailed than those for monks and include, for example, prohibiting nuns from bathing facing flowing water!

Male-dominated cultures that value monasticism often exhibit some misogyny, and Buddhism is no exception. Most of the monastic literature was written by men and reflects their difficulties with maintaining their own celibacy. Irrationally they blame women for these difficulties; many an early monastic text disparages women and warns monks to have nothing to do with them. Practices of meditating in the cremation ground while watching a female corpse decompose were recommended to curb monks' sexual desires. Monastic literature contains few parallels for women. Nevertheless the authors of the monastic codes subscribed to ancient Indian beliefs that women have more sexual desires than men but are less capable of controlling them. This explains why nuns are subject to stricter rules.

These perspectives and rules remain intact to the present day. However, in Mahāyāna and Vajrayāna forms of Buddhism, other perspectives on sexuality also developed and coexist with these early norms.

Mahāyāna Buddhism collapsed the dualities prevalent in early Buddhist thought, including the duality between proper and improper conduct, claiming that both are "empty" (*śūnya*). Mahāyāna discipline tends to emphasize mental attitudes over actions, thus interiorizing discipline. The person who is truly free is not the person who must avoid some acts and pursue others, for that still involves subtle attachment. Rather the truly free person is one who can engage in any act without being attached to it, without developing aversion or clinging to the act. Thus, something that might appear externally to be improper might be undertaken with a pure, detached attitude. Conversely keeping all the rules without the proper mental attitude does not bring liberation. However this new ethic does not mean that Mahāyāna condones or encourages behaviors that are improper by the standards of conventional morality. It means only that defining proper conduct is not as simple as it might appear to be to those who rely on a precisely spelled out code.

To express this new understanding of proper conduct, a new code of discipline, the bodhisattva precepts, developed in China, especially in the Chan (Japanese, Zen) school. Eventually they became the main code of discipline in Japan. This code of discipline is much simpler than the ancient Indian code and does not impose such harsh penalties for infractions. Sexual misconduct is still a major offense and for monastics still means heterosexual intercourse. However, expulsion from the monastic order is no longer the consequence of such sexual misconduct. Instead repentance by the offender is sufficient to restore him or her to good standing in the order. Perhaps in part because of the prominence of this code in Japan, male homosexuality became quite common in Japanese monasteries, and Japan eventually became the only Buddhist culture to largely do away with celibacy for its monastics. (Again the rules are stricter for women than men; eventually monks could legally marry, but nuns usually could not.)

The form of Buddhism most famous for its alternative understanding of sexuality is Vajrayāna Buddhism, in which sexual symbolism is common and many of the greatest practitioners take consorts as part of their spiritual discipline. Vajrayāna Buddhism's reversal of conventional norms regarding sexuality stems not only from the Mahāyāna understanding that freedom means not being bound by conventional rules but also from the uniquely Vajrayāna concept of transmutation. According to this concept, the *kleśa*s (defilements) themselves change or transmute into wisdom when their energy is properly unlocked by an advanced practitioner. Thus, they are not necessarily to be avoided but are to be properly experienced. Obviously this practice is not simple or easy, so it is quite restricted and hedged with warnings about its danger. It is simply a mistake to imagine that every practitioner of Tibetan Vajrayāna Buddhism, whether in Tibet or in the West, engages in the kind of sexual rituals that one can read about in books on Tantra.

However, sexual symbolism is prominent in Vajrayāna Buddhism. The *yab-yum* (father-mother) icon of a couple in sexual embrace is common in art and ritual. For Vajrayāna Buddhists the focus is not on the sexual imagery itself but on its meaning. This icon means many things, but all its meanings turn on nonduality. Nonduality does not obliterate difference and blend everything into one, as does monism; rather differences cohere in the larger whole. The *yab-yum* icon expresses nonduality perfectly, for it is both two (the two partners) and one (the one couple) at the same time. The masculine and feminine principles each carry with them a long string of symbolic associations, and the *yab-yum* icon expresses their inseparability. The most important of these dyadic unities is wisdom and compassion. The male element is associated with compassion, the female with wisdom. Both are necessary to and inseparable in enlightenment. An enlightened being who is wise but unkind is as impossible as an enlightened being who is compassionate but foolish. The primary Tantric ritual implements, the bell and the vajra scepter, also share in these associations. The feminine bell is held in the left hand and the masculine scepter in the right hand. These instruments are inseparable; they are always used together, just as one always has two hands. These sexual symbolisms are quite well known to Vajrayāna Buddhists, both monastics and laypeople. Thus, rather than banishing all thoughts of sexuality, monastic practitioners contemplate the secret, liberating symbolism of sexuality.

However, the practice of such contemplative practices does not mean that monastics routinely engage in literal, physical sexual rituals. The practice of living with a consort who is one's spiritual partner in esoteric sexual meditations and rituals is relatively common in Vajrayāna Buddhism but is more typical of practitioners known as yogis and yoginis than monastics. These practitioners, who include many of the greatest figures in Vajrayāna Buddhism, regard themselves as neither monastic nor lay. They often live outside conventional society and keep no conventional rules, whether of the monastery or the lay community. Tibetan hagiography is replete with stories about these adepts.

In the contemporary world Buddhism faces new challenges about its perspectives on sexuality. Although celibacy remains the norm for monastics, new issues and controversies cannot be completely avoided by them, not least because they often are asked questions about sexual practices by their students. In North America questions about homosexuality frequently surface. Some lay Buddhist precepts about sexuality do forbid having sex "in the wrong orifice." Although this rule was intended for heterosexual sex, it is easily extended to homosexuality. However, no consensus exists that this rule should be applied to homosexuals or even that it is relevant for heterosexuals. Other questions concerning birth control and abortion are also frequent. Again the advice varies from one teacher to another.

In the 1980s and 1990s, the Buddhist world was rocked by a series of sexual scandals, many of which involved Asian (male) Buddhist teachers in North America who were having secret sexual relationships with their students. In a few cases monastics have been accused of having such relationships. In many other cases they are drawn into arguments about and repercussions from these scandals because controversies regarding teacher-student sexual relationships have become entangled with the much larger question of the teacher-student relationship and the role of gurus. In Western Buddhism this issue will not be settled easily.

RITA M. GROSS

See also Body: Buddhist Perspectives; Celibacy: Buddhist; Deities, Buddhist; Hygiene: Buddhist Perspectives; Rules, Buddhist (Vinaya): Historical; Tibetan Lineages: Nyingma

Further Reading

Cabezon, Jose Ignacio, editor, *Buddhism, Sexuality and Gender*, Albany: State University of New York Press, 1992

Faure, Bernard, *The Red Thread: Buddhist Approaches to Sexuality*, Princeton, New Jersey: Princeton University Press, 1998

Gross, Rita M., "Helping the Iron Bird Fly: Western Buddhists and Issues of Authority," in her *Soaring and Settling: Buddhist Perspectives on Contemporary Social and Religious Issues*, New York: Continuum, 1998

Leyland, Winston, editor, *Queer Dharma: Voices of Gay Buddhists*, San Francisco: Gay Sunshine Press, 1998

Shaw, Miranda, *Passionate Enlightenment: Women in Tantric Buddhism*, Princeton, New Jersey: Princeton University Press, 1994

Snellgrove, David, *Indo-Tibetan Buddhism: Indian Buddhists and Their Tibetan Successors*, volume 1, London: Serindia, and Boston: Shambhala, 1987

Sexuality: Christian Perspectives

The most substantial discussion of sexuality in the Bible comes in the seventh chapter of the First Letter to the Corinthians, where St. Paul attempts to restrain the enthusiasm of his

Corinthian converts for sexual renunciation. The most striking feature of the discussion is the way in which Paul accepts most of the assumptions of his addressees: he agrees that a special period of devotion to prayer requires sexual abstinence, that (in the context of the Christian indifference to a merely earthly future) procreation is no longer worth mentioning, and that the married state is incompatible with single-minded service of the Lord. All Paul leaves himself as a defense of marriage is that "it is better to marry than burn" – that marriage might be necessary as an outlet for those sexual passions that would otherwise lead to fornication or adultery. It was all too easy for later ascetic writers, such as St. Jerome (c. 345–420), to argue that Paul did not want people to marry.

The second century saw a determined attempt by the "encratite" ("continent") movement to impose sexual renunciation on all the baptized. Although the attempt was defeated, it led to a general acceptance of a two-tier Christianity in which full, single-minded commitment to the Gospel was felt to be virtually impossible within marriage. A virgin, male or female, was believed to reinstate the life of human beings before the Fall, to be the true follower of the prophets and the apostles (who were now assumed, unhistorically, to have been celibate), and to anticipate the age to come through a pattern of life similar to that of the angels. Christ had taught that no marriage exists in heaven (Luke 20:35), presumably because the cessation of mortality makes procreation unnecessary: in this context the theme of realized eschatology – that Christians already participate in the life to come – provided a stimulus to sexual renunciation that early Christian seekers after perfection found impossible to resist.

However, this did not exclude a positive message to married couples. Through lifelong fidelity to each other and a firm rejection of extramarital sex, they could express the purity and inviolability of the Church as the bride of Christ. As Origen (c. 185–c. 254) rightly insisted, because marriage is a symbol of the union between Christ and his Church and because respect for the symbol follows from respect for what it symbolizes, not even an ascetic has the right to denigrate marriage. Christian marriage was less opposed to Christian asceticism than allied with it in embodying that purity that distinguished Christian virtue from pagan excess. The exceptional sexual discipline of the Christians, married and celibate alike, was made to bear the full weight of expressing and safeguarding the holiness of the Church as the "enclosed garden" of Scripture, now that the fuller and more balanced requirements of the Jewish law were no longer felt to be incumbent.

An important development in late antique and medieval Christianity was the linking of sexuality to the liturgical calendar. Married couples were required to abstain from sexual relations on holy days, immediately before them, and during the seasons of fasting. It has been estimated that the number of nights left for procreation was inadequate to sustain the size of the population. Like full observance of the fasting laws, these restrictions were not and could not be imposed, but they added to the sense that sexual self-discipline was a central element in Christian culture, an essential mechanism by which Christian values could extend into the private lives of the laity.

However, the teaching of St. Paul that sexual self-discipline must not be carried to extremes was not forgotten. Against the almost hysterical propaganda of certain champions of the ascetic movement, St. Augustine (354–430) argued forcibly that for most people marital sex is necessary as a remedy for concupiscence, that is, as the only outlet for sexual desire free of grave sin. Augustine believed that the resistance to rational control of the sexual drives and of the physiological facts of erection, orgasm, and parturition was the consequence of the Fall and therefore an inescapable fact of the human condition. Most humans are incapable of sexual renunciation and so need to marry. Within marriage sexual desire can be channeled into procreation but cannot be eradicated. If it remains true that sex for pleasure is a sin even within marriage, this behavior is so inevitable as to become venial. Within the restrictive context of the Pauline inheritance and the ascetic movement, Augustine did what he could to assert that God has made us sexual beings who cannot be required to practice abstinence or to take no pleasure in sex.

Independently of Augustine, similar ideas developed in Eastern Christendom. In the world of traditional Slavic Christianity (900–1700), the sexual drive was regarded as the work of Satan rather than part of the creation of God; the father of a child was called, in contrast to the godfather, the "father in sin"; but at the same time it was thought unrealistic to expect anyone apart from a monk or nun to live chastely. Even homosexuality and lesbianism were treated indulgently, in contrast to the revulsion and often savage penalties to which they were subjected in Western Christendom.

Therefore, in practice the failure to attribute any positive value to sexuality served less to deter people from marriage than to divide life into two areas, the sacred and the sexual (or, more broadly, the biological), which, although both subject to Christian law, could not, without pollution and profanation, intermix. Medieval culture, which frankly accepted the division of life into the sacred and the profane, lived happily with this divorce. The more earnest Christianity of the early modern period, which aimed at a complete Christianization of life, could not be so easily satisfied. An attempt was made to reduce the gap by intensifying the demand for sexual purity in the Christian law, but this only intensified the conviction that sexuality itself was unregenerate.

Not until the 18th and 19th centuries was the divide decisively breached, as a result of a new emphasis on mutual affection between husband and wife and the acceptance that this affection would find expression and reinforcement in their sexual relations. Marital intercourse was elevated from being a remedy for concupiscence, which perilously appeased what it was trying to restrain, to being seen as a participation in the love of God. Emanuel Swedenborg (1688–1772), in *The Delights of Wisdom Concerning Conjugial Love* (1768), was typical of this new attitude in distinguishing sharply between three sexual drives: first, the natural unfocussed sexual drive as it exists, for example, in adolescents; second, a perverted drive toward sinful sexual relations; and third, the physical love between spouses that arises from a spiritual bond between them, a bond that in turn flows from the love between Christ and his Church. Earlier

Christian tradition had viewed marital intercourse as simply the satisfaction within marriage of a sexual drive that in itself merely seeks pleasure and could be satisfied just as effectively (although less permissibly) in fornication or adultery. Against this it was now insisted that desire within marriage is a new and distinct drive of spiritual origin. Marital sex is spiritualized, whereas sex outside marriage is condemned with a new virulence. A more balanced view is expressed in the rite of marriage in the 1928 *Anglican Prayer Book*, which gives as one of the ends of marriage "that the natural instincts and affections, implanted by God, should be hallowed and directed aright"; this recognizes the essential identity between the sexual drive outside marriage and that within it while adding that this drive is transformed and sanctified within marriage through serving the other two ends of marriage: procreation and mutual comfort between husband and wife. Current Catholic moral theology would go beyond even this in insisting that the natural sexual drive is from the first oriented by the Creator toward the sacrament of marriage. We have moved a long way from the doctrine of Augustine, who saw the sexual drive as a corrupted impulse that in itself seeks only pleasure, that remains tainted even within Christian marriage, and that is directed toward marriage and procreation only when dominated by the rational will.

This new theology of sexuality is firmly entrenched in the modern Church. It serves two important ends at the same time. On the one hand it preserves the traditional Christian hostility toward promiscuity and hedonism in opposition to the allurements of a permissive society. On the other it elevates the dignity of marriage and procreation at a time when the very survival of Christianity depends on the strength of the Christian family, now that the culture of society as a whole is substantially de-Christianized. Therefore, we can expect that this new theology, so positive toward marriage and marital sex and so condemnatory of sex outside marriage, will continue to constitute Christian teaching in the third millennium.

This theology is open to criticism on several fronts. First, the heavy emphasis on the wonders of Christian marriage places an increasing psychological burden on the unmarried. Celibacy and virginity have been deprived of their traditional kudos as states of life higher than marriage; it is scarcely surprising that there now exists a serious shortage of religious and priestly vocations. Meanwhile, in the context of the high valuation of sexuality that this new theology of marriage encourages, the insistence on sexual abstinence outside marriage imposes too heavy a burden on the unmarried who have no vocation to celibacy – on those who cannot find a suitable spouse, on the divorced who respect the traditional ban on remarriage, and on homosexuals. This is accentuated by the Church's failure to convince the faithful of the teaching of *Humanae Vitae* (1968), with its condemnation of contraception and encouragement of sexual self-discipline within marriage; in practice, sex within marriage is allowed a completely free rein, making the Church's insistence that the unmarried be totally chaste appear unrealistic and discriminatory.

However, a more fundamental point needs to be made. The main drawback in official Church teaching on sexuality is that it addresses the wrong question, namely: in what circumstances is sexual intercourse permissible under the Christian law? This question is too narrowly moralistic and ignores the autonomy of post-Enlightenment society, where people demand the right to make their own moral decisions. The real question that needs to be addressed is a different one. Under the influence of Freud, modern society has come to see sexuality as central to personal identity; as a "permissive" society of free individuals in pursuit of happiness, it looks to the satisfaction of the sexual drive (in its broadest sense, including the emotions and the subconscious as well as the body) as an essential part of self-fulfilment. Therefore, the question that arises is the relation between the sexual drive and human orientation toward God. A dualistic anthropology that sunders the sexual drive from spiritual aspiration and sets the two in opposition no longer carries conviction.

A spirituality that will do justice to the sexual drive will insist that sexuality is oriented toward the perfecting of the person in self-transcendence, normally through a union with another human being that enables the individual to attain wholeness and often at the same time to participate in the creative power of God as the source of new life. As such sexuality is both fulfilled in marriage (and in other stable sexual relationships) and frustrated by it because marital union is neither physically nor spiritually complete and because procreation leads immediately to mere repetition, as one generation succeeds another, rather than to the new creation promised by the Gospel. This must be acknowledged if justice is to be done to the long Christian tradition that encourages the renunciation of marriage. However, the dignity of marriage is reestablished by its sacramental character: all the sacraments prefigure the perfecting of the recipient rather than accomplish it. A properly Christian spirituality of sexuality will teach us to recognize our sexuality as essential for our orientation toward God, and it will at the same time restore our freedom to marry, to enter into a different form of sexual union, or to embrace the celibate life, as all these options point us toward an ultimate union with God as the only relationship in which the drives of human nature can be totally satisfied.

RICHARD M. PRICE

See also Asceticism: Christian Perspectives; Gender Studies: Christian Perspectives; Jerome, St.; Spirituality: Western Christian; Transvestite Saints

Further Reading

Brown, Peter, *The Body and Society: Men, Women and Sexual Renunciation in Early Christianity*, New York: Columbia University Press, 1988

Brundage, James A., *Law, Sex, and Christian Society in Medieval Europe*, Chicago: University of Chicago Press, 1987

Cahill, Lisa Sowle, *Sex, Gender and Christian Ethics*, Cambridge and New York: Cambridge University Press, 1996

Countryman, L. William, *Dirt, Greed and Sex: Sexual Ethics in the New Testament and Their Implications for Today*, Philadelphia: Fortress Press, 1988
Levin, Eve, *Sex and Society in the World of the Orthodox Slavs, 900–1700*, Ithaca, New York: Cornell University Press, 1989
Thatcher, Adrian, and Elizabeth Stuart, editors, *Christian Perspectives on Sexuality and Gender*, Leominster: Gracewing, and Grand Rapids, Michigan: Eerdmans, 1996
Theology and Sexuality: The Journal of the Institute for the Study of Christianity and Sexuality, Sheffield: Sheffield Academic Press, 1994–
Timmerman, Joan H., *Sexuality and Spiritual Growth*, New York: Crossroad, 1992

Shaolin, China

Shaolin Si, Monastery of the Forest of Shao(shi), is located at the foot of Mount Shaoshi in the Song Massif, about 43 miles southeast of Luoyang, an occasional Chinese capital. Founded in 496 by Emperor Xiaowen of the Tabgatch Turk Wei dynasty (386–535) for the Indian monk Buddhabhadra, who was famed for meditation, scripture translations, and paintings, the monastery was state funded, enabling Buddhabhadra to escape the bustle of the new capital, Luoyang. Under his leadership Shaolin became a major center for translation, scholarship, and meditation, attracting his pupils Daofang, Huiguang (468–537), and Sengchou (480–560) and the Indian translators Bodhiruci (d. 535) and Ratnamati. This ended temporarily when the monastery was abolished by Emperor Wu of Northern Zhou in 577 as part of his anti-Buddhist policy. In 580 his son Emperor Jing and the de facto ruler, Yang Jian, fervent Buddhists, restored the monastery under the name Zhihu (Yearning for Father). Two eminent monks, the scholar Huiyuan (523–592) and the Vinaya master Hongzun (529–608), were installed there. When Yang Jian founded the Sui dynasty in 581, the name Shaolin was restored, and an estate of over 500 hectares at Baigu, about 16 miles to the northeast, was granted in perpetuity to the monastery. The Sui soon collapsed, and in defending their wealth from peasant rebels the entire monastery, except for a sacred stūpa, was burnt down. In 620 the monks attacked a warlord who was contesting control over North China and occupying their Baigu estate and handed him over to Li Shimin (598–649), the future emperor Taizong, a founder of the Tang dynasty. Li Shimin rewarded the 13 leading monks and granted Shaolin over 200 hectares. Leading Vinaya and Chan masters came to live there, and it was visited by the succeeding emperors and empresses. In 704 the pilgrim and Vinaya master Yijing (635–713) and others were invited to establish a precepts platform there. However, when Emperor Xuanzong decreed in 722 the confiscation of surplus monastic lands, the monks appealed, and in 728 an inscription by Pei Cui was erected to reinforce their official exemption from the decree and record the history of Shaolin, including its legendary association with Bodhidharma.

The monastery survived intact through the Tang and Song dynasties, maintaining extensive estates, numerous buildings on ten hectares, and up to 2,000 monks. It was known as the "first monastery of the empire," and many Chan monks were residents. Later the monastery declined, and it was reduced to ashes in the Mongol conquest. Chan Master Deren began rebuilding around 1236, but the great restorer was the Caodong Chan monk Fuyu (1203–1275), who was ordered by the future Yuan emperor, Khubilai (1260–1294), to reconstruct Shaolin. Thereafter, the Shaolin abbots were from the Caodong branch of Chan. Many were imperial appointees, for Shaolin controlled up to 72 subordinate monasteries and large estates in the region. However, much of Shaolin was destroyed by the anti-Yuan Red Kerchief rebels in the 1350s.

After the inauguration of the Ming dynasty, Shaolin was gradually restored, and subsequently it was repeatedly repaired and augmented. Eight Ming princes became Shaolin monks, who thus defended the Ming against peasant insurgents, but by the 1640s, the early Qing dynasty, the monastery was in ruins. Rebuilding commenced in 1684, and several Manchu emperors visited and made donations. By the early Republican period (1912–1949), Shaolin had declined, and in 1928 much of it was destroyed by a warlord.

The monastery itself rises in seven terraces from the entrance gate. Burned down were the main buildings of terraces 2 to 4, the Hall of Heavenly Kings, the Great Buddha Hall, the Dharma Hall, the halls of the Sixth Patriarch and Kinnara, and the Drum and Bell towers (which dated to the Yuan). Several have been recently reconstructed; only the stonework and the bell cast in 1204 are original. Note that the placement of a hall of the patriarchs with a statue of Bodhidharma at the center was imitated by all other Chan monasteries. Surviving the conflagration were the abbot's quarters of 1336 on terrace 6, the Hall of the Thousand Buddhas/Vairocana Pavilion built in 1588, and the halls of Dizang (Kṣitigarbha) and Guanyin (Avalokiteśvara) on terrace 7. Guanyin Hall contains murals of the monks "boxing." Beyond the monastery walls are the Hermitage of the First Patriarch (Bodhidharma) of 1125, since rebuilt and originally a separate monastery, and nearby the Grotto of Bodhidharma, a natural limestone cave with a Ming period stone arch entrance. Further distant is the Hermitage of the Second Patriarch (Huike), behind which is a brick stūpa dated 696. The "forest of stūpas" just outside the walls is a graveyard surrounded by trees, containing various stūpas, the earliest dated 791 and the most recent 1803. The monastery entrance path is lined by excellent stelae, some inscribed by prominent literati. Some have been removed to Xi'an.

Shaolin is famed as the "precinct of the first patriarch," Bodhidharma as the "founder" of Chan. It is likely that Faru (638–689) or his Chan circle invented the legends of Bodhidharma at Shaolin meditating, being poisoned by rivals and teaching Huike after this supplicant cut off his own arm. By the time Pei Cui wrote, this association had become part of the monastery's official history and was literally built on, with the construction of hermitages and the "discovery" of the grotto. It was even sanctioned by emperors. As Chan became the dominant order of Buddhism during the Song dynasty, Shaolin became a major pilgrimage destination. However, tourists now flock there

The "Forest of Pagodas" at the Shaolin Si, Songshan, Honan province, China.
Photo courtesy of Marylin M. Rhie

because of the current popularity of *gongfu* (martial arts) in Chinese movies, novels, and records of folktales that attribute *gongfu*'s inception to Bodhidharma and its development, especially in *chuanfa* (boxing), to Shaolin monks. Excluding the conflicting presumptions of "secret transmissions," the Shaolin tradition was that early in the Northern Song dynasty (960–1127) the monk Fuju recorded the best of China's martial arts and that around the start of the 13th century this was transmitted to Chan Master Jueyuan, who left ten instructions. Evidence of Shaolin martial exploits appear in official records of the suppression of peasant insurgents in the 1460s and Japanese pirates in the 1550s. These arts disappeared because of the suspicions of the Manchu rulers and the advent of modern warfare, which forced Shaolin to hire mercenaries in the 1920s. Since the 1980s government sponsorship has revived the martial arts there, and they are now heavily commercialized.

Shaolin has evolved from being a center of scholarship and meditation like other major monasteries into a monastery unique for its associations with the legendary beginnings of Chan and later with the martial arts, both of these being invented traditions. In addition the martial arts monks even claimed that they were exempted from the dietary and other prohibitions required of all other Chinese monks.

John Jorgensen

See also Buddhist Schools/Traditions: China; China

Further Reading

Demiéville, Paul, "Le bouddhisme et la guerre," in *Choix d'Études Bouddhiques*, edited by J.W. de Jong, Leiden: Brill, 1973

Faure, Bernard, "Relics and Flesh Bodies: The Creation of Ch'an Pilgrimage Sites," in *Pilgrims and Sacred Sites in China*, edited by Susan Naquin and Chün-fang Yü, Berkeley: University of California Press, 1992

Pak, Tonggi, "Kagwŏn Sŏnsa ŭi Sorim muye sipkyeyul e kwanhan sogo," *Han'guk Pulgyohak* 9 (December 1984)

Pelliot, Paul, "Notes sur quelques artistes des Six Dynasties et des T'ang," *T'oung Pao* 22 (1923)

Tokiwa, Daijō, *Shina Bukkyō shiseki tōsaki*, Tokyo: Shina Bukkyō shiseki tōsaki kankōkai, 1938; reprint, Tokyo: Kokusho kankōkai, 1972

Tonami, Mamoru, *The Shaolin Monastery Stele on Mount Song*, translated and annotated by Penelope A. Herbert,

Kyoto: Istituto Italiano di Cultura, Scuola di studi sull'Asia orientale, 1990
Wang, Hongjun, *Tales of the Shaolin Monastery*, collected and edited by Wang Hongjun, translated by J. Lonsdale, Hong Kong: Joint, 1988
Washio, Junkyō, editor, *Bodaidaruma Sūzan shiseki taikan*, Tokyo: Bodaidaruma Sūzan shiseki taikan kankōkai, 1932
Zhao, Baojun, *Shaolin Si*, Shanghai: Shanghai Renmin chubanshe, 1982

Shenoute of Atripe c. 350–c. 466

Egyptian Christian monastic exemplar and theologian

Shenoute (Shenudi or Sinuthi) was born around 350 as a peasant's son in a village of the Thebaid. By 371 at the latest, he had entered the monastery of his uncle Pgol near Akhmim in Upper Egypt. When Pgol died around 385, Shenoute took over the leadership and made the site into an important monastic center. The numbers of ascetics greatly expanded, and figures have been given to suggest that 2,200 monks and 1,800 nuns resided in this early example of a double monastery. Shenoute's rule was severe. He practiced a regime of floggings and imprisonments even for slight faults. In this he offers a contrast with the more humane rule of Pachomius (c. 290–346). Shenoute imposed, for the first time in Christian history, a written promise of obedience on his monks. This became the basis of the formal "profession" of monastics that was soon to have universal application. In its original context it probably demonstrates the depth of authority problems in the local area and the extent to which his own life was an active and apologetically focused one. Shenoute often made heavy demands on the allegiance of his extended "family" in the form of quasi-military raiding parties, pressing the Christian cause on hostile or resistant pagan villagers. In his *Life* written by his immediate successor, Besa, it is often not clear whether the hostility Shenoute stirred up against himself came only from pagan quarters or whether certain Christians also made known their objections to his style of righteous violence. By inciting his monks to actively deconstruct Egyptian religious shrines, Shenoute extended the power of the Alexandrian bishops with whose imperially backed policies he was associated.

Shenoute became involved in the theological controversies of the day, attacking Origenism in the desert and advocating a highly realist view of the Eucharistic presence. His divine Christology allowed no correspondence with the subtleties of the Antiochene theologians then being advanced on the international front. In 431 he was asked by Cyril of Alexandria (d. 444) to accompany him to Ephesus, and he was probably among those who lobbied Emperor Theodosius II (408–450) in Constantinople in the aftermath of the council. The lobbying tactics included street riots. He was also invited to the Council of Chalcedon (451) but was prevented by illness from attending.

Shenoute is portrayed in several texts interacting with local governors and assisting in the refugee problems created by attacking tribes of the Blemmi nomads. He emerges as a strong local political leader, someone whom both imperial and ecclesiastical powers wished to have associated with them. In almost all the texts, he is very closely identified with Egyptian magic. Apologetically orientated, the texts wish to present him as a foe of magical practices, but to the modern reader he seems to have been fighting fire with fire. In addition to his hagiographic depiction as a great thaumaturge, evidence shows that he seems to have advocated a spirituality of ecstatic vision: he "sees" heavenly visitors – a theme that runs through in a less dramatic form other aspects of the Egyptian desert literature, such as the *Life of John Climacus* (c. 570–c. 649) – and ultimately is himself "seen" by his disciples as a heavenly agent, in particular in the guise of the prophet Elijah. This biblical archetype of the wonder-working prophet who was jealous for the honor of his God and thus attacked the priests of Baal undoubtedly is behind much of Shenoute's hagiography and likely behind most of his own understanding of the monastic state and his own place within it.

As a monastic organizer Shenoute allowed older monks to live apart from the central foundation as hermits. He reinforced what was a growing pattern for the close association of cenobitic and eremitic life in Egypt, with the latter standing as an advanced stage for senior monks in a community. All his surviving writings have come from the scriptorium of the White Monastery on the Nile but are now scattered among 20 modern libraries and still await a complete edition.

JOHN MCGUCKIN

See also Climacus, John, St.; Desert Fathers; Egypt; Hermits: Eastern Christian; Origins: Eastern Christian; Pachomius, St.; Women's Monasteries: Eastern Christian

Biography

Son of a peasant in the Thebaid desert, by 371 Shenoute had entered the monastery of his uncle Pgol near Akhmim. He took over the monastery's leadership c. 385. His double house attracted several thousand members, all of whom were required to make a written promise of obedience. Known for his severity, Shenoute aided the bishops of Alexandria in the Christological controversies up to the Council of Chalcedon (451).

Major Work

Opera (not yet fully edited)

Further Reading

Besa, Abbot of Athripe, *The Life of Shenoute*, translated by D.N. Bell, Kalamazoo, Michigan: Cistercian Publications, 1983
Frandsen, P., *Studies in Honour of J.J. Polotsky*, East Gloucester, Massachusetts, 1981
Grillmeier, Alois, *Christ in Christian Tradition*, volume 2, London: Mowbray, and Louisville, Kentucky: Westminster John Knox, 1995
Guillaume, A., "Copte," in *Dictionnaire de Spiritualité, ascétique et mystique: Doctrine et histoire*, volume 2, Paris: Beauchesne, 1953

Limbi, J., "The State of Research on the Career of Shenoute of Atripe," in *The Roots of Egyptian Christianity*, edited by B.A. Pearson and J.E. Goehring, Philadelphia: Fortress Press, 1986
McGuckin, John A., *St. Cyril of Alexandria: The Christological Controversy*, Leiden and New York: Brill, 1994
Young, D.W., "The Milieu of Nag Hammadi: Some Historical Considerations," *Vigiliae Christianae* 24 (1970)

Shenxiu (Shen-hsiu) c. 606–706

Chinese Chan master

The Chan master Shenxiu was a descendant of the Li family of Bianzhou (in the present-day Weishi district in Henan province). Having enjoyed a traditional education in the Chinese classics, he became a Buddhist monk in 625. He spent most of his life in the Tiangong Monastery in Luoyang (present-day Henan province). At age 50 he moved to the Shuangfengshan Monastery in Qizhou (present-day Hubei province), where Hongren (602–674), the fifth patriarch of Chan, resided. Having studied for six years under Hongren, he was invited by Empress Wu Zetian of the Zhou dynasty (690–705) to the Tiangong Monastery in Luoyang in 700. Here he was highly honored, and lay followers are reported to have come from remote places to listen to his lectures. Shenxiu died in Luoyang in 706. His most important disciples were Puji (651–739) and Yifu (658–736). His disciples propagated his doctrine under imperial patronage.

Chan can be seen as the apex of a process of Sinicization of Indian Buddhism that started with Dao'an and Huiyuan. This growth and maturation of Chan can be explained by the fact that exactly at the moment when traditional Chinese culture dominated Tang China, Chinese Buddhist monasteries were cut off from the great monastic centers of India and Central Asia because of the revival of Hinduism and a reinforced Islam. In these circumstances Chinese Buddhist monasteries had to rely solely on themselves. Chinese Buddhism responded by advancing a typical Sinicization of Indian Buddhism that provided far-reaching parallels with the tradition of philosophic Daoism. Thus, Chan likely is the most "Chinese" of all Buddhist schools, and it is the only school that continued to flourish after the major persecution of Buddhists in 845. That Chan contemplation does not make use of external attributes surely was instrumental for its further growth after the persecution.

According to the genealogy of Chan patriarchs that was accepted until the beginning of the eighth century, Shenxiu is the sixth patriarch (succeeding Bodhidharma, the first patriarch of Chan in China, who is thought to have entered China in 520; Bodhidharma's disciple Huike; and Sengcan, Daoxin, and Hongren). In 734 Shenhui (670–762), a monk of the south, attacked Shenxiu's concept of gradual enlightenment and favored the concept of another of Hongren's disciples, Huineng (638–713), who advocated the theory of sudden enlightenment. This made Shenhui further claim that Huineng, not Shenxiu, should be regarded as the sixth patriarch. This incident was only the apogee of a debate that already existed during the lifetime of Hongren himself. From this moment on, the Northern Chan school (Shenxiu) and the Southern Chan school (Huineng) were differentiated. In 745 Shenhui was invited to Luoyang, where he enjoyed great prestige, and this further stirred up the debate. Eventually, the Southern school became the dominant one and was considered orthodox.

Beginning in the second half of the eighth century, the Chinese government, in great need of financial resources, started selling monkshood certificates. Shenhui took advantage of this policy to help the government raise funds, thus enlarging the Buddhist community and re-enforcing his position and that of his Southern Chan school.

Bart Dessein

See also Bodhidharma; Chan/Zen: China; China

Biography

This Chan master of the Northern tradition in China lived mostly at the Shuangfengshan Monastery in Qizhou before spending his final five years in Luoyang. As rival of the legendary Huineng, Shenxiu embodied the Northern tradition of gradual enlightenment. He consolidated Chinese assimilation of the Indian "insight" Buddhism whose transmission legend ascribes to Bodhidharma.

Major Work

Guanxin lun (Treatise on the Contemplation of Mind)

Further Reading

Dumoulin, Heinrich, *Zen, Geschichte und Gestalt*, Bern: Francke, 1959; as *A History of Zen Buddhism*, translated by Paul Peachey, Boston: Beacon Press, and London: Faber and Faber, 1963
Chang, Chen-chi, *The Practice of Zen*, Westport, Connecticut: Greenwood Press, 1978
Ch'en, Kenneth, *Buddhism in China: A Historical Survey*, Princeton, New Jersey: Princeton University Press, 1964
Fung, Yu-lan, *A History of Chinese Philosophy*, 2 vols., Princeton, New Jersey: Princeton University Press, and London: Allen and Unwin, 1952
Hu, Shih, "Ch'an Buddhism in China: Its History and Methods," *Philosophy East and West* 3 (1953)
Gernet, Jacques, *Le monde Chinois*, Paris: Collin, 1972; as *A History of Chinese Civilization*, Cambridge and New York: Cambridge University Press, 1985
Zhongguo Dabaike Quanshu - Zongjiao, Beijing: Zhongguo Dabaike Quanshu Chubanshe, 1982
Zhongguo Fojiao, 4 vols., Shanghai: Dongfang Chuban Zhongxin, 1980

Shikoku, the Pilgrimage Island of Japan

Shikoku is best known for a pilgrimage of 88 sacred places, a thousand-mile clockwise circumambulation of the island. From the Seto Inland Sea southward to the Pacific Ocean, from caves in sheer mountain cliffs to city streets, the 88 temples hold historical significance and abundant treasures, and the offerings of pilgrims support many priests. Reflecting the mainly funerary function of Japanese Buddhism today, resident priests can be seen smoking cigarettes and watching television, before traveling by motorbike to perform services. In some monasteries priests are themselves pilgrims in search of what Shikoku represents, for the pilgrimage of Shikoku symbolically recapitulates the career of Japan's great saint, Kūkai or Kōbō Daishi (774–835), from birth to enlightenment.

The pilgrimage of Shikoku became popular long after Kūkai's time, in the Edo period, when restrictions on travel were lifted. Kōya Hijiri, or wandering holy men from Mount Kōya, headquarters of Kūkai's Shingon sect, were instrumental in magnifying the image of Kūkai as a savior whose homeland was sacred. They descended the mountain south of Kyoto and Nara, then crossed over to Shikoku so regularly that the first of 88 temples was changed from Kūkai's birthplace of Zentsūji in present-day Kagawa prefecture to Tokushima prefecture near where the Kōya holy men disembarked. Mount Kōya is sometimes added to comprise a more complete pilgrimage including Kūkai's chosen resting place.

A gripping tale of reincarnation central to the pilgrimage of Shikoku was told by Kōya holy men wandering the countryside. Emon Saburō was a rich man who spurned the repeated plea of a mendicant priest until his sons died off one by one for a week. He went around and around Shikoku Island until he finally turned counterclockwise to catch up with that monk, who turned out to be the great saint Kūkai. His dying wish was to be reborn as lord of the province to do the utmost good for the common people. Soon afterward a son was born to the Daimyō with one hand that would not open until priests were summoned to pray. The tiny hand, when it was finally opened, revealed a stone that read "I am Emon Saburō reborn." This gripping chronicle of Ishiteji (Stone-Hand Temple) in Matsuyama, Ehime prefecture, implicitly warned the public to bestow hospitality on pilgrims. It was a self-serving subtext inasmuch as such mistreatment as the sons' dying would not have been condoned by the historical Kūkai. Nonetheless, with such vivid tales conveying the idea that St. Kūkai was present on the path, the celebrated pilgrimage of Shikoku gave new impetus to the faith, supporting the institutionalized monasticism of the Shingon sect through medieval strife to the present.

Bird's-eye view of Ishiteji (Stone-Hand Temple), number 51 on the Pilgrimage of Shikoku, which claims to have the stone that Emon Saburō was holding when he was reincarnated.
Photo courtesy of Steve McCarty

In accord with the ecumenism or syncretism practiced by Kūkai himself, the 88 designated sacred places include other Buddhist sects as well as Shingon. For although Kūkai espoused the critical classification of Buddhist doctrines, he accepted all schools previous to esotericism as suitable for particular stages in the mind's development. Moreover, although Kūkai's aristocratic Saeki clan, related to Ōtomo courtiers, had been among the first outside the main island to embrace Buddhism, Kūkai allowed them to maintain their piety also for Shintō. Even after the forced separation of Shintō from Buddhism with the Meiji Restoration, Shintō shrines still tend to adjoin Shingon temples, all oriented to a sacred mountain, harking back to indigenous animism.

Since Shingon also needed to adapt to the popularity of devotional trends such as Pure Land Amidism to survive, pluralism without a sense of contradiction has gradually come to characterize Japanese religion.

Commemorating Kūkai's birthplace, Zentsūji Temple has a long and relatively well-documented history. Zentsūji has remained the gathering place for Buddhism on Shikoku Island, a monastery as well as a mecca for pilgrims with faith in Kūkai (Kōbō Daishi Shinkō). Buddhism entered Japan formally around 538, and at the Zentsūji site, which Kūkai ostensibly completed in 813, an earlier temple with Hōryūji-style roof tiles has recently been discovered to date from the Hakuho period (645–710). Around Zentsūji is an unusual cluster of temples dedicated to the Medicine Buddha Yakushi-nyorai. This might be because a disease was spreading in the late seventh century and a Yakushi image was made by an ancestor of Enchin, Kūkai's independent-minded nephew. Many of Kūkai's relatives were instrumental in developing Shingon monastic institutions. However, among those later designated Daishi (Great Teacher), Kūkai being the supreme example, Enchin studied longer in China but then headed a branch of the Tendai sect. Because the Tendai patriarch Saichō (767–822), having sailed to China with Kūkai, returned earlier and reached the emperor as sole administrator of the esoteric rites then popular with Tang dynasty courtiers, Kūkai suffered fallow years on returning before gaining the imperial recognition necessary to establish the Shingon sect. Kūkai had tried to transcend rivalry with Tendai but came to tire of Saichō's dependency on esoteric scriptures and expertise brought back by Kūkai. Thus, for Enchin to join Tendai where he could head an independent branch seems to stem from his own desire for autonomy. Yet in the small town of Zentsūji today, Enchin and the temple at his birthplace have ended up being overshadowed after all.

Zentsūji Temple has played a role of regional headquarters, spawning a town at its gates (*monzen-machi*). It administered branch temples and later a medieval fiefdom. Priests of the monastery itself have received little historical notice compared to eminent pilgrims there, such as Hōnen (1133–1212), who wrote in the Kamakura period that all Pure Land Buddhas would befriend pilgrims to Zentsūji. Saigyō came from Mount Kōya, staying at Zentsūji in 1183 and writing the *Sangashū* based on his pilgrimage to Shikoku. Dōhan was commissioned from Mount Kōya to teach at Zentsūji from 1243 to 1249, and his *Nankai Rurō Ki* includes an inventory of the original temple. From 1278 to 1288 Emperor Go-Uda sponsored repairs, and in 1331 Abbot Yūhan, native to Zentsūji, supervised repairs, including the Golden Hall and the nearly 164-foot-high five-story Great Pagoda. In 1344 the Muromachi period Shōgun Ashikaga Takauji had Yūhan build a stone pagoda as a consolatium for his violent rule. However, in 1558 and again in 1575, Zentsūji served as a fortress in clan warfare and was burned down. Today Abbot Hasuo Zenryū presides over a large monastery with about 200 employees, and his writings view the historical Kūkai as sufficient to his faith.

Today in urbanized and secularized Japan, Shikoku maintains a tenuous balance with tradition, nature, and religiosity. Three colossal bridge systems by way of Seto Inland Sea islets, including a train line, connect Shikoku with the main island of Japan. Thus, the problem of accessibility is mainly the language barrier. Yet most recently it has become possible through the Internet both to plan an itinerary and to find bilingual assistance, as each locality publishes English-language Web sites with e-mail links.

STEVE MCCARTY

See also Esoteric Buddhism in China and Japan; Hōnen; Kūkai; Mount Kōya, Japan; Nara, Japan; Pure Land Buddhism; Syncretism in Japan, Buddhist; Tiantai/Tendai: Japan

Further Reading

Hasuo, Zenryū, *Ningen Kōbō Daishi*, Takamatsu, Japan: Sohonzan Zentsūji, 1984
Hasuo, Zenryū, editor, *Kōbō Daishi Kūkai: Kinenhi konryū kinen*, Takamatsu, Japan: Do Kankoki, 1982
Hasuo, Zenryū, and Kazuyuki Mizobuchi, *Kōbō Daishi to Shikoku Reijō*, Takamatsu, Japan: Bikōsha, 1976
Inui, Sentaro, *Kōbō Daishi tanjōchi no kenkyū*, Zentsūji, Japan: Daihonzan Zentsūji Goonki Jimukyoku, 1936
Kajiwara, Aisui, editor, *Kokon Sanuki Meisho Zue*, Tokyo: Rekishi Toshosha, 1976
McCarty, Steve, "Kūkai, Saigyō, Dōhan and Hōnen in Zentsūji," *Kagawa Junior College Journal* 13 (1985)
Nakao, Takashi, *Shikoku, Kyūshu no Koji*, Tokyo: Shūeisha, 1985
Shikoku, Shimbunsha, *Kagawa-ken Daihyakkajiten*, Takamatsu, Japan: Shikoku Shimbunsha Shuppan, 1984
Takemoto, Akiko, and Steve McCarty, *Shikoku Bilingual Guidebook*, Takamatsu, Japan: Bikōsha, 1993
Zentsūji-shi, Kikakuka, *Zentsūji-shi Shi*, Takamatsu, Japan: Shin-Nihon Insatsu, 1977

Related Web Sites

http://www.kagawa-jc.ac.jp/~steve_mc/shikoku/ (Multilingual Guide to the Pilgrimage Island of Japan, 1999)
http://www.kagawa-jc.ac.jp/~steve_mc/ejdiver.html (Legend of the Woman Diver, 1998)
http://asiandoc.lib.ohio-state.edu/v1n1/dbs/globalshikoku.html ("The Global Shikoku Internet Project," *Asian Database Online Community Electronic Newsletter* 1:1 [March 1998])
http://asiandoc.lib.ohio-state.edu/v1n2/dbs/Gshikoku.html ("Multilingual Initiatives from Southwestern Japan: Global Shikoku Internet Project Update," *Asian Database Online Community Electronic Newsletter* 1:2 [June 1998])

Shinran 1173–1262

Japanese advocate of Pure Land Buddhism

A Japanese Mahāyāna Buddhist teacher and a radical revisionist who rejected special claims for traditional monastic authority, Shinran has been the most prominent representative of such "protestant" views in Buddhist history, which is otherwise strongly dominated by the renunciant mythos. Shinran's ideas became the basis for the several Shin sect branches (Jōdoshinshū, abbreviated as Shinshū), mainly the Honganji institutions, which together have constituted the largest single integrated religious tradition in Japan.

Shinran's is one of the best-known Japanese religious biographies. Born in an aristocratic family in Kyoto, at the age of eight he was placed in the Tendai monastery on Mount Hiei. During his training he developed an encyclopedic acquaintance with primary scriptural sources. In 1201 he left to become a follower of the controversial Pure Land teacher Hōnen. Entangled in a scandal surrounding the Hōnen group in 1207, he was exiled to the remote Echigo district, an event that removed him entirely from centers of traditional social and intellectual power in Japan and exposed him to the rising energies of the outlying regions. Despite the lifting of the exile order in 1211, Shinran elected not to return to the capital but instead headed for the provinces north of modern Tokyo. Gathering a network of followers, he gradually formulated a text called the *Kyōgyōshinshō*, an anthology of scriptural quotations including his own embedded commentaries. This became his central doctrinal statement. About 1235, possibly for political reasons, Shinran moved back to the capital at Kyoto. During the remaining third of his life, he finalized his views and wrote works in a variety of genres in both classical Chinese and Heian vernacular Japanese.

Shinran's teaching was a conceptual and linguistic reformulation of the earlier Pure Land mythos, based on a "leap" notion of authority. Its key points were enlightenment as *ekō*, Buddhist practice as *akuninshōki* awareness, and the institutional transcendence of the lay-monk polarity in the *hisō hizoku* principle.

The *ekō* (transfer of merit; Sanskrit, *parināma*[*nā*]) concept was essential. Shinran's conception was that enlightenment had to happen in the final analysis by itself, by some process coming, as it were, from "outside" the ego. *Ekō* referred to the transformation involving absolute *shinjin* (yielding or entrusting) toward the deity of the Amida Buddha, which symbolized perfect enlightenment. Amida independently had a certain dynamic energy, or a "working," to effect enlightenment in human minds. The process did not ultimately require monasticism, meditation, texts, other Buddhist deities, or any ritual practices understood as able to cause enlightenment intentionally; such miscellaneous practices were lumped together under the classification of *jiriki* (self-power). In this context Shinran redefined the traditional Pure Land practice of *nembutsu* (vocal recitation of the name of Buddha) as merely an expression of thanksgiving that the Amida Buddha was constantly active.

Although his undermining of monastic authority was unconventional, Shinran's ideas were otherwise a restatement of certain traditional Buddhist problems, especially the necessary spontaneity of the "leap" to religious transformation. The notion of "reliance on an external deity" was also traditional.

Having marginalized many of the normal monastic approaches, religious practice for Shinran consisted instead of the recognition of the give-and-take of the states of suffering and liberation in everyday life, that is, the push and pull of human ignorance and Amida's light. This was *akuninshōki* awareness. The *akunin* (evil person) – virtually everyone, according to Shinran's special definition – was inherently the *shōki* (true object) of the activity of the Amida. However, instead of depending on precepts, visualization, and meditation in the usual sense, this awareness relied on critical introspective study of the processes of the ego in everyday life. Observation resulted in eventual recognition of the interaction between the evil produced by the ego and the good produced by the intervention of the Buddha (from "outside" as it were) into the ordinary consciousness.

Shinran's ideas culminated institutionally in the denial of the meaningfulness of the monk-lay categories in the experience of enlightenment. This was the *hisō hizoku* (neither monk nor lay) principle. Traditional Buddhism often conceded that enlightenment involved a "leap" whose exact karmic preconditions were not precisely knowable but had generally accepted the authority of mythic models of monasticism or of charismatic teachers and lineages. Instead Shinran pushed to the limit the idea that no person or lineage could mediate the working of the Buddha in another. The teaching could still be embodied in a community of followers and in a mundane teaching leadership but not a monastic community and not a monastic leadership. The working principle rather became *dōbō* (equal followership) among persons linked by commitment to the *ekō* teachings.

Shinran's teaching lineage (the Honganji temple network) began to be consolidated by his grandson Kakunyo (1270–1351), but it was only under the Honganji headship of Rennyo (1415–1499), in conjunction with major political and social changes accompanying civil war and economic growth in Japan, that Shinshū really flourished. Membership continued to grow into the 19th century, at the peak including about a third of the Japanese population. Shinran's teachings led to a stylistic shift in the presentation of Buddhism toward a simplification of ritual, text, and iconography. However, Shinshū shared most features of Buddhist religious culture with the older monastic schools, including philosophy, ritual, the arts, and a practical moral seriousness.

Shinran's doctrines are the subject of huge literature in both premodern and modern Japanese and of a broad spectrum of spiritual reflection. His teachings might be rated as one of the very most important variants of Buddhism, for Japan currently has the world's second-largest economy, has been the only non-Western country to fully compete with the Euro-American sphere, and has possessed in Shinshū a democratic religious culture that helped paved the way for its rapid modernization. However, Shinran's thought has remained relatively unattractive to non-Japanese. The reasons for this lack of interest include factors such as Western orientalism, the appeal of the exotic (including monasticism), the marginalization of Shinshū in the standard historiography of Japan, and damaging Shinshū involvements with the vagaries of 20th-century Japanese politics. Fundamentally, however, Shinran's radically "protestant" questions about religious authority apparently have been interpreted as irrelevant to the purposes of the modern world outside Japan.

GALEN AMSTUTZ

See also Animals, Attitude toward: Buddhist Perspectives; Buddhist Schools/Traditions: Japan; Nembutsu; Pure Land Buddhism; Rennyo

Biography

Born in Kyoto, Shinran became a Tendai monk on Mount Hiei at age nine, and 20 years later became a disciple of Hōnen in Kyoto. After Hōnen's exile in 1207, Shinran left monastic life. He modified Hōnen's conceptions of reliance on Amida Buddha and on the calling of his name (the nembutsu) as a way to guarantee salvation in Amida's Golden Land of the West. Even more completely than Hōnen and other Pure Land teachers, Shinran subverted the distinction between monastics and laypersons who seek enlightenment.

Major Works

The Collected Works of Shinran, 2 vols., translated and with introductions by Dennis Hirota et al., 1997

Further Reading

Amstutz, Galen, "Shinran and Authority in Buddhism," *Eastern Buddhist* 30:1 (1997)

Bloom, Alfred, *Shinran's Gospel of Pure Grace*, Tucson: University of Arizona Press, 1965

Dobbins, James C., *Jōdō Shinshū: Shin Buddhism in Medieval Japan*, Bloomington: Indiana University Press, 1989

Keel, Hee-sung, *Understanding Shinran: A Dialogical Approach*, Fremont, California: Asian Humanities Press, 1995

Kikumura, Norihiko, *Shinran: His Life and Thought*, Los Angeles: Nembutsu Press, 1972

Matsunaga, Daigan, and Alicia Matsunaga, *Foundation of Japanese Buddhism*, 2 vols., Los Angeles: Buddhist Books International, 1974

Takahatake, Takamichi, *Young Man Shinran: A Reappraisal of Shinran's Life*, Waterloo, Ontario: Wilfred Laurier University Press for Canadian Corporation for Studies in Religion, 1987

Ueda, Yoshifumi, and Dennis Hirota, *Shinran: An Introduction to His Thought*, Kyoto: Hongwanji International Center, 1989

Siam. *See* Thailand

Siddhartha Gautama. *See* Buddha (Śākyamuni)

Slavic Monasticism. *See* Orthodox Monasticism: Slavic

Social Services: Buddhist

Buddhists are impressed less by the faith than by the good works of the Christian missions. Buddhists have been quick to emulate the efforts of the YMCA, church schools, or free clinics and hospitals. However, modernity has obscured the fact that at one time Buddhists and Christians observed nearly the same set of "corporal works of charity," namely, to feed the hungry, clothe the naked, nurse the sick, and bury the dead. The one exception might be the visit of condemned men in prisons. Whereas Christian priests go to hear confessions, administer the last rites, and mediate the prospect of God's forgiveness, Buddhist monks do this less frequently.

Such Christian and Buddhist acts of charity ran contrary to ancient norms, for in taking care of the poor and the needy the early Church ran afoul of the Roman authorities, who regarded this as a monopoly of the city or state. The same rule existed in China, where it was also improper for a subject to usurp prerogatives of the king. Thus, when a disciple of Confucius, an office-holder, wanted to care for the dispossessed on his own initiative, the master prudently asked him to desist. However, as Buddhism and Christianity have come to embrace all humankind as one family or one body, a higher law of love and compassion to follow now exists. Love thy neighbor once meant helping anyone in need (the word *karuṇā*, for "compassion," is a near synonym of *agape*), and universal suffrage and merit transference now exist in the new economy of salvation/enlightenment. When a man gives a coat to a beggar, the ghost of the man's uncle might appear in a dream, wearing that coat against some hellish snow, and thank his nephew for that simple act of kindness. An *exemplum* told by clerics to encourage the laity to observe open-handed charity, it underscores the new morality, namely, that no man is an island.

Like its Christian counterpart Buddhist mendicancy furthered this call to aid the poor. Poverty was no virtue in classical society. Now the monks are the "blessed poor." In body and soul they exemplify a pure life and as such became a prime merit field through which lay people can acquire merit. This benefits regular beggars who now go about reminding people to "do good." In Chinese they "call people to change their karmic conditions." Unlike modern, secular notions of charity as a one-way street in which the haves give to the have-nots, the medieval ritual of giving and receiving requires both parties to thank one another with bowed heads. The donor thanks the mendicant, sacred or secular, for the opportunity to acquire merit, and the recipient says a prayer and wills that merit prayer be transferred to the donor. In Christianity the beggar who still says "Bless you, sir" is abbreviating "May God bless you for your kind deed, sire." In China this translates into the proverbial chant of "homage to Amitābha Buddha," the merit of which the chanter now wishes on his benefactor. This religious exchange informed much of the medieval sense of economic justice. At a time when social inequality was taken for granted, it was the duty of the *potente* to aid the *paupere*. To neglect such basic courtesy invites karmic retribution. Gypsies had been hanged as witches on the related premise or rumor that, when refused a pittance, a woman had uttered a curse instead of a prayer against the would-be benefactor.

On this matter of giving, Buddhism ran up against a doctrinal hurdle of its own making. Christ had taught that whatever a man does for one of them (the poor) so much has been done for Him. In Buddhism one also gives to a beggar in memory of the *saṅgha* and the Buddha. However, a basic principle in Theravāda ethics is that one acquires more merit in giving to a monk than to a beggar because a monk can do so much more good. In other words merit is calculated not only by the goodness of the intention but also by the measure of the result. A monk of course would not think of depriving the beggar of his food. Monks have refused food at times of famine so that others might live. Nevertheless the sad irony is that the same rule would deem higher a gift to the Buddha, who, being purer still, brings to the donor even more merit. A situation arose whereby the Buddha attracts gifts at or around his reliquary, and because those gifts were earmarked for his use only, no one – not even monks or beggars – can touch them. In response to that dilemma, a Chinese Mahāyāna apocryphal text from the early sixth century called itself the scripture "To Aid the Widowed and the Orphaned." It reversed the Hīnayāna ethics of purity: better it is to aid the poor and the needy in the "field of compassion" than to shower still more gold and silver on the well-endowed Three Jewels in the "field of reverence."

The term "the field of compassion" was soon adopted to describe free hospice care in the temples. "Compassion ward" became the term for hospitals in medieval China and Japan. In the Christian West hospitals also grew out of clinics set up to take care of pilgrims who had fallen sick. In China monasteries had sickrooms for their own sick and aging members. The monastic dispensary had also benefited from the transmission of Indian medical knowledge. A number of early foreign monks were famous healers, and itinerants often offered such cures on the side, but the Hīnayāna monastic code warns against monks plying medicine as a trade. It took a rewrite by Mahāyāna preceptory texts to endorse the medical arts as a means of benevolence. However, such individual minstering to the sick aside, the record suggests that actual clinics set up to help the sick were created by lay sponsors. Princes, kings, and queens had the resources to emulate the model of King Aśoka – the first to set up free hospitals. Around A.D. 701–704, Empress Wu sponsored such free hospital care in the "compassion wards" of the state-run temples. By 717 a Confucian minister objected. He recalled the classical judgment of Confucius (cited previously) and reminded the new emperor that Buddhist temples had no business running such charities. The system was demolished during the persecution of Buddhism in 845, when these state-supported clinics were moved out from under temple supervision. Many of monastic charities were taken over by the state in the Song period (960–1279). The temples on their own took in many abandoned children and did so more willingly before the neo-Confucian ideologues decried the practice. By the Ming dynasty (1368–1644), many of these charities had fallen into the laps of private philanthropists among the local elite.

Burying the unclaimed dead, previously a duty of the state, also became a free offering from the Buddhist institution. Monks would perform masses for the war dead regardless of friend or foe, Chinese or barbarian. Some monks would even go out to collect old bones and exposed skeletons to grant them proper burial. That was before cremation, the Buddhist norm in India, became the Buddhist practice in China. The task of disposing the remains became much more affordable with cremation. When the neo-Confucians restored the classical norm of burials in coffins and criticized the Buddhists for their barbaric practice of cremation, many large cities in China were left with unclaimed corpses because the living could not afford to bury the dead. Unmourned, these dead became vengeful spirits and hungry ghosts who haunted the conscience of the living. This in turn required large-scale Buddhist ritual appeasement and feeding.

WHALEN LAI

See also Aśoka; Buddhadāsa; Critiques of Buddhist Monasticism: Confucian; Death: Buddhist Perspectives; Death Rituals, Buddhist; Economics: Buddhist; Food: Buddhist Perspectives; Forest Masters; Governance: Buddhist Perspectives; Hygiene: Buddhist Perspectives; Intercession for the Dead, Buddhist; Medicine, Buddhist; Virtues, Buddhist

Further Reading

Demiéville, Paul, *Buddhism and Healing: Demiéville's Article "Byo" from Hobogirin*, translated by Mark Tatz, Lanham, Maryland: University Press of America, 1985

Lai, Whalen, "Chinese Buddhist and Christian Charities: A Historical Comparison," *Buddhist-Christian Studies* 12 (1992)

Schmitt, Jean Claude, *Ghosts in the Middle Ages, the Living and the Dead in Medieval Society*, Chicago: University of Chicago Press, 1998

Social Services: Eastern Christian

An understanding of charity and monasticism in the Byzantine era (330–1453) requires examining many factors, including the religious climate, Christian ethics and eschatological expectations, social circumstances, and the Church's social obligations.

Christian monasticism has its origin in New Testament teachings and began as a lay movement by individuals who sought to put New Testament teachings into practice. Achieving moral perfection and eternal salvation were the major motives. It was based on the teaching of Jesus Christ, who said, "If you would be perfect, go, sell what you possess and give to the poor, and you will have treasure in heaven; and come follow me" (Matt. 19:21).

Although some Christians had taken this admonition seriously and had renounced the world, it was the example and teachings of St. Antony (251–356) that launched monasticism. Although Antony's form of monasticism was eremitic (individuals living in the deserts or in tombs), his contemporary Pachomius (c. 293–346) introduced the cenobitic, or communal, form of monasticism.

However, throughout the Byzantine era it was the rules and teachings of Basil the Great (329/30–379) that guided the ideal of monks as individuals and shaped monasticism as an institution. Basil harmonized the eremitic and the cenobitic principles of Antony and Pachomius and structured a system of moderation, emphasizing the need for monasticism to come under the aegis of the Church. He made monasticism an institution of the organized Church, accenting the need to imitate the enthusiasm, unity, harmony, and activity of the Apostolic and the early Church fathers, including the study of Scriptures and applied charity.

In addition to the teachings of Basil and his followers, the religious climate of the Byzantine era was conducive to the growth of monasticism. Its notions that perfect life cannot be achieved in a worldly environment and that earthly life is a *propaideia* (a preparation) for eternal life made monasticism popular among all classes of people. The eschatological and ethical teachings of the Church were ever present in the life of the monks. The Church's social obligations, as they were emphasized by leading Church fathers, such as Gregory of Nazianzus (329/30–389/90), Basil the Great, and John Chrysostom (c. 347–407), contributed to the development of a social consciousness that made both individual monks and entire monastic communities devoted to the practice of charity.

Charity, from the Latin *caritas* and its cognate the Greek *charis* (love, expecting nothing in return), was perceived as a divine commandment. Monastic charity evolved in full agreement with both the cultural Hellenic climate and the Christian teachings about charity (a synonym for the Greek terms *agape* and *philanthropia*, "love for the human being"). In its ancient Hellenic content, charity was the command of the divinities, the *Charites*, the source of happiness and joy of life on earth. Philanthropic activity received its inspiration from the example of Prometheus, who, because of his "great philanthropy" for the human race, brought light, life, and happiness into this world. A very similar principle was emphasized by St. Paul, who wrote that it was because of his *philanthropia* for humankind that the *Logos* (God) assumed humanity to save the human (Titus 3:4).

Throughout the Byzantine era charity was expressed by individual monks but also through organized monastic communities. In imitation of Antony and Basil, a future monk would first distribute his possessions to the poor, orphans, widows, and philanthropic institutions. A hermit such as Eulogios of Alexandria might take a lantern and walk around the streets of Alexandria to find homeless strangers and offer them a place to sleep. Other individual monks served as advisers and educators, and the physicians among them would seek out lepers and other ill people to help them. The monk Telemachos left the Egyptian desert and moved to Rome, where he sacrificed his life to abolish the gladiatorial fights. Lives of saints especially provide much information about charity distributed from person to person.

We know much more about monastic charity from *Typika*, or the charters of monasteries. The latter abounded in the cities; as many as 280 existed in Constantinople and vicinity and nearly 1,000 throughout the Byzantine Empire. Some monastic communities had as few as eight to ten monks, and others, such as the Studios monastery in Constantinople, had hundreds.

Monasteries away from a major city, such as the monastery of St. Catherine in the desert of Sinai, supplied bread and other goods to as many as 600 travelers, pilgrims, and local Bedouins daily. Those in cities offered refuge to those in need: beggars, orphans, the elderly, strangers, and poor visitors to the city. Remote monasteries functioned as an oasis for strangers and travelers.

In addition to charity from the monastic community to the needy, monasteries maintained philanthropic institutions, such as hospitals, *gerokomeia* (homes for the aged), *xenodocheia* (homes for strangers or travelers), and even *xenotapheia*, or cemeteries for the burial of travelers and pilgrims who happened to become sick and die on their way.

Frequently, the initiative for the establishment of an institution was taken by the *hegoumenos* (abbot), and the means were provided by a wealthy individual or the imperial court. For example, the hospital of St. Sabas monastery in Palestine was the work of Sabas and his community, but the money came from Emperor Justinian's treasury. Monastic *Typika*, although similar in spirit and composition, reveal also the diversity of Byzantine monasticism's nature, functions, and aims. Whereas some emphasized a complete divorce from the secular world and concentrated on a life of *theoria* – contemplation, prayer, and a liturgical life – others saw themselves as an integral part of the organized Church, with a sense of mission in society, whether as educators, physicians, counselors, or social workers delivering works of charity. For example, the *kanonismoi*, or the rules of the Mount Sinai monastery (one of the oldest in the Byzantine Empire), reflecting the content of an original *Typikon*, reveals the social consciousness of monasticism.

In one of its articles we read, "The sacred monastery of Sinai has a double purpose for its existence. First the moral perfection of its members, to the extent that it is possible, through the practice of '. . . the great commandment you shall love the lord your God with all your heart . . .'" The second purpose of the monastery's existence is love in action toward fellow human beings, not only from person to person but also through the establishment of educational and vocational schools, the foundation of homes for the poor (*ptochokomeia*), orphanages, *xenones* (hospices), and other kinds of charitable institutions.

The distribution of free meals, clothes, and medications to the poor, the sick, and the outcasts of society – all were among the social obligations of monasteries. Furthermore, monks were expected not only to participate in communal work for their own good and that of the needy but also to pursue intellectual work. Monks composed liturgical hymns, delivered homilies, wrote biographies and chronographies, served as itinerant preachers (such as St. Nikon *o Metanoeite*), and often took up the task of defending the poor before civil authorities.

Whereas some monasteries failed in their mission and instead of becoming champions of the poor became their exploiters, others played a major role in the economy of a province by employing many peasants and laborers from the area. Frequently, we find admonitions that monks should possess the virtues of prudence, logic, wisdom, justice, courage, understanding, meekness (*aorgesia*), love for the poor, and hospitality – all the products of faith and love for Christ. It was not uncommon to find monastic teachings that declared, "love in practice, or working on behalf of the needy is to a far greater degree superior to prayer," as St. Athanasios Philanthropenos, the *hegoumenos* of the Mamas monastery, advised in his *Typikon* (composed in 1158).

Never uniform and monolithic, mainstream Byzantine monasticism possessed a vigorous social conscience that was expressed in charities from person to person and through organized philanthropic establishments.

DEMETRIOS J. CONSTANTELOS

See also Antony, St.; Basil the Great, St.; Egypt; Israel/Palestine; Istanbul, Turkey; Mount Sinai, Egypt; Orthodox Monasticism: Byzantine; Russia: History; Russia: Recent Changes

Further Reading

Note: No monastic *Typika* of the Byzantine era have been translated into English. The second and third sources listed below provide some basic information and bibliographical references to the Greek sources.

Charanis, P., "The Monk as an Element of Byzantine Society," in *Dumbarton Oaks Papers: Number 25*, Washington, D.C.: Dumbarton Oaks Research Library and Collection, 1971

Constantelos, Demetrios J., *Byzantine Philanthropy and Social Welfare*, New Brunswick, New Jersey: Rutgers University Press, 1968; revised edition, New Rochelle, New York: Carantzas, 1991

Constantelos, Demetrios J., *Poverty, Society, and Philanthropy in the Late Mediaeval Greek World*, New Rochelle, New York: Carantzas, 1992
Hussey, J.M., "Byzantine Monasticism," in *The Cambridge Medieval History*, volume 4: *The Byzantine Empire*, part 2 edited by J.M. Hussey, D.M. Nicol, and G. Cowan, Cambridge: Cambridge University Press, 1967

Social Services: Western Christian

For some 1,500 years Christian monastic establishments have provided to local populations a variety of social services that range from commonsense advice to spiritual comfort. Before the modern age of state-sponsored aid, monasteries were the major providers of welfare and poor relief for the medieval world; today monastic orders continue to supply a wide range of social services for the needy.

Christian monastic involvement in social services is but one part of the Christian ideal of relieving the sufferings of the involuntary poor and needy, and over the ages those monastic orders that do not retreat completely from outside involvement have played an active role in furnishing social services to local communities. One of the primary roles of the monastic orders was, and remains, dealing physical aid (as well spiritual comfort) to the needy. The 12th-century monastic reformers placed great emphasis on relieving the needs of the local poor and ill: "It was an established custom . . . held almost as law, to receive everyone in the hospice, to nourish the needy, to restore the poor, to clothe the naked, to bury the dead, and to carry out other works of mercy and piety" (Constable, 1996). This type of social welfare has taken many forms over the centuries, but monastic orders have involved themselves mainly (and historically) with charity (the giving of alms), education (establishing schools), and health care (establishing hospitals and using the herbs and herbal knowledge gained from a monastic herb garden to cure the sick). In addition, monks and nuns provided care for the dying, funerals for paupers, husbands or good homes for penitent prostitutes (French convents did especially good work in this area right through the medieval period into the 20th century), and even some forms of rudimentary craft training. Monastic orders also built guest houses or accommodation for travelers and pilgrims.

In the medieval world "social service" was a far broader concept than it is now. Social services not only involved various forms of tangible charity but also meant spiritual care and advice. For many communities their local monastic establishment provided an island of spirituality and peace in a world of darkness and despair. During the Dark Ages (A.D. 600–1000) in particular, monasteries became places of comfort and refuge, although they were just as often a target of plunder by invaders. A monastery was a place where, in a threatening world, the prayers of the monks could guarantee aid and comfort to those who merited it. For the medieval monastic house, salvation was as much a social service as was charity, health care, and education, although this article concentrates on the more tangible instances of social service.

Passage to the infirmary, Cistercian Abbey at Maulbronn, Baden-Württemberg, Germany, 13th century.
Photo courtesy of Chris Schabel

It was a rare monastery that did not distribute some form of alms, and both female and male monastic orders participated in alleviating the suffering of the poor in their immediate areas. The almoner of a monastic house was usually in charge of distributing alms, although, depending on the monastic house, the chamberer, the sacrist, and the prior's cellarer might play a role. The almoner might also visit the sick and needy in those communities outside the monastic establishment. Generally the almoner provided alms on a daily basis, perhaps scraps of food left over from the monastic table. These might prove minimal during the various fasts during the religious year. Monasteries also supplied charity on an occasional basis, perhaps when a member of the order died (a monk's clothes might go to the poor a few weeks after his death) or on the anniversary of the death of the order's founder. Monks or nuns might also hand out alms on sundry festival or holy days throughout the year; Maundy Thursday was often a day of almsgiving by the nuns of medieval northern England. Sometimes charity to the poor might consist of food: again Easter was a notable time for such giving. Then medieval nuns of Redlingfield handed out beef, bread, and herring to the poor. Monastic orders also furnished clothing. The nuns of Longchamps, a religious house established by Isabella, the only sister of Louis IX (1226–1270) of France, educated and maintained poor girls, wove and made clothes for the poor, and distributed the rest of their disposable income in alms. In medieval times the amount of monastic annual revenue devoted to social services varied from between 1 percent and almost 20 percent of a house's annual income. If a particular monastic establishment was located close to other religious houses or to a city where guilds and other organizations also participated in caring for the needy, it might spend a significantly smaller percentage of its yearly revenue on social services than would a religious house that was the only source of poor relief in its area.

Notwithstanding the very good work that monastic orders did in providing for the poor and needy, by the 12th century considerable unrest existed around Christian Europe about possible (or even documented) abuses of this system. In the late 12th century, Gerald of Wales accused some monastic orders of eating luxurious and excessive meals on the excuse that this would produce more leftovers to hand out as alms. Criticisms grew ever more virulent by the 14th and 15th centuries, aided by the widespread Lollard and Hussite movements. Some political authorities accused monasteries of pocketing alms for the needy themselves or of feeding the daily scraps meant for the poor to the order's pet dogs instead. For example, the local bishop instructed the nuns at the small religious houses of Arden and Esholt in England to dispose of their dogs and return to giving the local poor their food scraps. However, generally it appeared that it was male rather than female monastic orders that were more at fault in diverting alms meant for the poor into their own coffers.

As well as alms, medieval monastic orders supplied essential health services in their localities many centuries before states became involved in the provision of health services. Medieval aid and advice took place on several levels. First, monasteries, especially during the Dark Ages and early medieval period, were some of the only repositories of medical knowledge and manuscripts. Second, every monastery or convent had an herb garden that furnished medicines not only for the members of the order and its lay servants but also for the local community. Finally, monastic houses established infirmaries that treated members of the monastic community and the local sick not to mention the outcast sick, such as lepers.

Because of the emphasis on the care of the sick by monastic orders, the monastery garden was an important part of the medieval religious establishment. The gardens grew food for the monks and their guests and provided herbs and medicines for the sick. Most monasteries had an infirmary (often very large) for the poor and ill that needed a constant supply of herbs and

Infirmary, Cistercian Abbey at Ourscamp, Aisne, France, c. 1230. Photo courtesy of Chris Schabel

medicines. These medicines were often very potent, and the poisonous narcotics, such as mandrake, hemlock, henbane, and the opium poppy, were generally kept under lock and key. Other nonmedicinal herbs went into the leftover scraps that the almoner distributed to the poor each day.

Medieval monastic gardens not only grew food and medicinal herbs but were also vital in agricultural innovations. Monastic horticulture made important contributions to the development of agricultural techniques, such as soil enrichment, marling, land reclamation, and systems of drainage. Monastic gardeners often were responsible for introducing new strains of crops, aided the development of competent orchard and vineyard management, and, through their collation and transcription of manuscripts disseminated botanical and medical knowledge widely. The Cistercians and Benedictines and, to a lesser extent, the Augustinian Canons were at the forefront of agricultural and gardening innovations.

From the Dark Ages monastic orders were particularly active in the care of lepers, whom few other people would (literally) touch. The hospitaller order of St. Lazarus, originally active in the Holy Lands, established lazar hospitals under royal patronage close to Paris and Orleans in the 12th century. Louis VII (1137–1180) of France, anxious to cater for leprous women, established a female monastic house at La Saussaie to care for female lepers: this house flourished under the patronage of both French and English kings. Leper houses and monastic orders to care for them were established across Western Europe under royal patronage throughout medieval times. Although guilds and eventually the state took over the care of the sick, monastic orders have continued to be active worldwide in providing health care to those who need it.

Traditionally, Christian monastic orders have played an important part in education. Many monastic orders were heavily involved in teaching and scholarship in Europe's major medieval universities. However, in premodern times it is doubtful whether monastic efforts at education were widely effective; only a tiny percentage of any population attended a university, most people did not need to be literate, and the guild schools of towns undoubtedly played a larger role in educating the children of craftsmen. Nevertheless, the disruption caused to monastic education during the Reformation was keenly felt. When the monasteries were dissolved in England in the mid-1530s, one of the complaints made by local communities was that the education of local children had suffered badly. In the 18th century the essayist and topographer Francis Blomefield claimed that Norfolk society had suffered a great loss during the dissolution because until then the Convent of Carrow had educated and boarded local children.

Monastic houses, whether monasteries or convents, were not the only orders that provided social services in the premodern world. The mendicant orders, especially the Franciscans, did the poor and outcast of Europe a great service with their ministrations. They offered sympathy and spiritual comfort, medical aid, and occasionally some basic education. They acted as parish priests if a local community was without a resident cleric, performing marriages, baptisms, and burials and hearing confessions. The friars provided as much a spiritual service as a social service: if an isolated community had no parish priest, often the only spiritual comfort they received was from the occasional Franciscan or Dominican who wandered their way.

Finally, and briefly, a monastic order supplied a number of social services to a local community that are not immediately apparent. In isolated regions a monastery's chapel might also function as a parish church. The monastery's bells marked the major rhythms of premodern life: the hours of the day, the festivals and holy days, and local tidings of either grief or joy. Work in the field revolved about the bells of the local monastery. Monks and nuns also aided the passage of souls from this world into the next. They recorded, registered, and executed wills for the dying; acted as witnesses at the deathbed; and in the absence of a parish priest might take the last confession and execute the last rites. Members of the religious house often took part in the funeral services and would continue to say prayers for the departed.

Since the middle of the Dark Ages, the Christian monastic communities have played a vital role in providing various forms of social services to the poor and needy in almost all countries of the world. Perhaps their role can be effectively summed up with Francis Bacon's words in his essay "Of Love": "There is in man's nature a secret inclination and motion towards love of others, which, if it be not spent upon some one or a few, doth naturally spread itself towards many, and maketh men become humane and charitable; as it is seen sometime in friars."

SARA WARNEKE

See also Agriculture, Western Christian; Antonians; Beghards; Beguines; Benedictines: Female; Economics: Christian; England: History; France: History; Gardens: Christian Perspectives; Monastics and the World, Medieval; Officials: Western Christian; Patronage, Christian: Royal; Pharmacology; Travelers: Western Christian

Further Reading

Aveling, J.C.H., *The Jesuits*, London: Blond and Briggs, 1981; New York: Stein and Day, 1982

Burton, Jane, *Monastic and Religious Orders in Britain, 1000–1300*, Cambridge and New York: Cambridge University Press, 1994

Constable, Giles, *The Reformation of the Twelfth Century*, Cambridge and New York: Cambridge University Press, 1996

Landsberg, Sylvia, *The Medieval Garden*, London: British Museum Press, 1995; New York: Thames and Hudson, 1996

Olivia, Marilyn, *The Convent and the Community in Late Medieval England*, Woodbridge, Suffolk, and Rochester, New York: Boydell Press, 1998

Zarnecki, George, *The Monastic Achievement*, London: Thames and Hudson, and New York: McGraw-Hill, 1972

Related Web Site

http://www.op.org/opwest/dmf1.html (Missionaries in Action: The Dominican Mission Foundation)

Solesmes, France

This French abbey was responsible for a revival of scholarship and interest in Gregorian chant during the 19th century. The Benedictine monastery of St. Solesmes was founded in 1010 by Geoffrey, seigneur of Sablé in the Department of Sarthe in France. It was established as a priory dependent of the Abbey of St.-Pierre de la Couture at Le Mans. Solesmes was twice pillaged and once destroyed by fire during the Hundred Years' War (1337–1453). Its early history was basically uneventful until the end of the 15th century, when the church was rebuilt from a basilica form into a Latin cross form. A number of restoration efforts were accomplished in the early 16th century, especially on the library, sacristy, and cloisters. Two famous groups of statuary, known as the "Saints of Solesmes," were also sculpted at this time. One group represents various episodes of the Dolors of Our Lady and the other the entombment of Jesus. These groups of statues were almost destroyed by the Huguenots and other Iconoclasts but were saved by barricades constructed by the monks. The last regular prior of Solesmes, Jean Bougler (1505–1556), was followed by a series of commendatory priors until 1664, when the monastery was absorbed by the Congregation of St. Maur. In 1722 every building associated with the monastery, except for the church, was entirely rebuilt. In 1791 the monastery was suppressed along with other French monasteries, and the buildings passed into private hands for the next 40 years.

Prosper Guéranger, a 27-year-old priest, bought the property in 1831. Having grown up in the neighborhood of the monastery, Guéranger wanted to restore Solesmes back into a functional monastic community. With five other zealous priests, he took possession of the restored Benedictine community in 1833. Pope Gregory XVI (1831–1846) raised Solesmes to the rank of abbey in 1837, named Guéranger its first abbot, and formally established Solesmes as the mother house of the new "Congregation of France" and Guéranger as superior-general of the Order. Nine daughter houses were established by Solesmes in the mid– to late 19th century: Ligugé (1853), Marseilles (1865), Silos in Spain (1880), Glanfeuil (1892), Fontanelle (1893), Paris (1893), Farnborough (1895), Wisque (1895), and Kergonan (1897). Solesmes itself was dissolved by the French government no less than four times: in 1880, 1882, 1883, and 1903. Each time locals in the neighborhood assisted the monks in reentering the abbey. After the final expulsion the monks established themselves on the Isle of Wight, where they built a completely new abbey at Quarr on former monastic property.

Solesmes has achieved a worldwide reputation in the area of monastic and liturgical studies. The foundation for this erudition was laid by Guéranger himself as well as those who followed him, including Jean-Baptiste Pitra (1812–1889), who in 1863 became a cardinal and librarian at the Vatican; Joseph Pothier (1835–1923); Marius Férotin (1855–1914); Jean-Martial Besse(1861–1920); Fernand Cabrol (1855–1937); Henri Leclercq (1869–1945); Henri Quentin (1872–1935); and André Mocquereau (1849–1930). What Solesmes is best known for is the restoration of the Gregorian chant of the Catholic Church. At a time when liturgical and chant scholarship was unsound and numerous performance and observance techniques for chant were competing, Guéranger revived the principle of the accent and rhythm of plainsong. He resuscitated sound liturgical traditions in France by examining, classifying, and comparing the various chant manuscripts in existence. Where manuscripts of different places and periods agreed on a text or chant version, Guéranger argued that this was the correct text or chant melody. Paul Jausions (1834–1870) and Pothier assisted Guéranger in these studies. Pothier published a number of important works in the area of chant restoration, especially *Les Mélodies Grégoriennes* in 1880 and the *Liber Gradualis* in 1883. The Solesmes Imprimerie, an important appanage of the abbey, printed many of these seminal chant books and research compilations. However, the entire plant was confiscated by the French government at the suppression, and since then all Solesmes scholarship has been published by Desclée of Tournai.

The earlier Solesmes editions were defective because of the absence of previous competent research, the insufficiency of many selected manuscripts, and the desire to be conciliatory between the Reims-Cambrai and the Ratisbon chant editions available at that time. However, Solesmes scholarship served its purpose of stimulating further chant research and a return to the manuscripts themselves as the source for correct chant transcription. André Mocquereau followed the pioneering work of Pothier through the publication of the *Paléographie Musicale* series and his personal training of the Solesmes *Schola*. Photographic reproductions of various manuscripts from all the principal libraries of Europe were examined and compared and variants of the chant melodies classified according to date, school or church of origin, influences, and other intrinsic qualities. Numerous criteria were developed by the Solesmes chant scholars in deciding which chant variants were the most nearly universal or correct versions. If insufficient evidence existed, preference was given to the Roman version, if that one survived.

The publication of the *Liber Gradualis* in 1883 by Pothier and the beginning volumes of *Paléographie Musicale* in 1889 by Mocquereau were recognized by the Holy See, which wanted to prepare an edition of the official chants that would satisfy everyone's wishes and needs. With the ascension of Pius X (1903–1914) as pope in August 1903 and the publication of his *Motu Proprio* on the reform of sacred music in November 1903, a reform commission of ten members and ten consultants under the chairmanship of Pothier was appointed in 1904. The research of Mocquereau and other Solesmes scholars led them to produce the *Kyriale*, the popular repertory of chants sung by the congregation. Unfortunately a tremendous number of variants exist in the manuscripts. The commission split into two factions: the first supported the "legitimate" or scientific approach, and the second preferred the "living" or popular tradition. In addition musicologist Peter Wagner wanted to retain variables of the German "dialect" in the final edition. Finally, when collaboration became impossible, Pothier edited almost all the books entirely by himself. The *Liber Usualis* appeared in 1903, the

Graduale in 1908, the *Antiphonale* in 1912, a new *Ordo Cantus Missae* in 1972, and the *Graduale Romanum* in 1974.

BRADFORD LEE EDEN

See also Beuron, Germany; Dissolution of Monasteries: Continental Europe; France: History; Guéranger, Prosper; Liturgical Movement 1830–1980; Liturgy: Western Christian; Maurists; Music: Christian Perspectives; Plainchant; Spain: History; Wolter, Maurus

Further Reading

"Abbey of St. Solesmes," *New Catholic Encyclopedia*, Internet version

Bergeron, Katherine, *Decadent Enchantments: The Revival of Gregorian Chant at Solesmes*, Berkeley: University of California Press, 1998

Cardine, Eugene, *Beginning Studies in Gregorian Chant*, translated and edited by William Tortolano, Chicago: GIA, 1988

Cardine, Eugene, *An Overview of Gregorian Chant* (volume 16 of Études Grégoriennes), Orleans, Massachusetts: Paraclete Press, 1992

Encyclopédie des musiques sacrées, 3 vols., Paris: Labergerie, 1968–1971

Hourlier, Jacques, *Reflections on the Spirituality of Gregorian Chant*, Orleans, Massachusetts: Paraclete Press, 1995

Solitude: Buddhist Perspectives

The importance of retreat in Buddhism cannot be overstated. For the monastic and layperson alike, the ability to withdraw from the world and spend time in contemplation and in rebalancing the body and mind is of primary importance. It is an unusual practitioner who fails, at least once during his or her lifetime, to undertake some kind of retreat.

Most practitioners choose, at least at first, to withdraw in company with other people. In the West as in the East, monasteries hold sessions or retreat weekends, and certain Tibetan traditions provide an opportunity for the traditional three-year, three-month, and three-day retreats. Alongside these traditional group retreats, the practice of solitude is also considered valuable; interestingly, however, many teachers advise against solitary retreat until one has completed at least one group retreat. For example, Akong Rinpoché of Kagyü Samyé Ling in Scotland describes the group retreat as being like a bag full of rocks, rubbing against one another until the sharp edges have been softened away. Only when one has softened is one truly ready for the experience of solitude.

From the Buddhist point of view, we alone are responsible for the state of our body and mind: if we react inappropriately to some external event, whatever that might be, we create suffering for ourselves. By taking ourselves away into what Christian mystics might refer to as the desert, we are forced into an encounter with the ground of being, the very face that we had before we were born. There are no others with whom we might share this experience – no one with whom we can share the joy, relieve the boredom, or quiet the (existential or literal) terror that we feel in our hearts.

Traditionally, most Buddhist monastics, like their Christian counterparts, have dwelt within their monasteries, withdrawing into solitude only after they have completed many years within the community. However, some free spirits, for whatever reason, choose to go off and live alone in the wilderness (whether a literal or metaphorical wilderness) for days, months, or even years. In Tibet and Mongolia especially, the practice of solitude has been popular and highly influential, probably because of the geography of those countries: the great Kagyü lama Kalu Rinpoché (1906–1989) spent 13 years, from the age of 25, wandering the mountains of eastern Tibet and undertaking yogic practices; the practitioners of the *gcod* ("cutting-off" or "activity" ritual, depending on which reading you favor) lineage spend their lives wandering from cemetery to cemetery, living off what food they can find and wearing robes made from the clothes of the dead; some people choose to undertake the bardo (or "dark") retreat, spending 49 days in total darkness, seeking to (re)create the period between incarnations. The list goes on: 108-day solitary retreats in Japan and Korea, Buddhist and Daoist monks living their meditation far into the mountains and forests of China, and westerners flocking to sit in the wildernesses of India during the 1960s. Many are drawn to solitude, and some never come back.

Another, more timely approach to solitude is to recognize it as being one of the things that make us human. That is, as people first and only later as monastics or laypeople, we are, by nature, alone and constantly in need of realizing this fact. Each of us is responsible for his or her actions and reactions, and no one else can be blamed for our sadness, and no one else can be loved for our joy: we are obliged to recognize our aloneness.

As for meditating on such an understanding, Zen master Shunryū Suzuki says, "When you do something, you should burn yourself completely, like a good bonfire, leaving no trace of yourself" (Suzuki, 1970). This is similar in tone to certain Carthusian authors: in the same way as they suggest that silence is the most complete way of opening to God, so Suzuki suggests the dissolution of the self, as if in a fire. For the solitary practitioner, whether wandering the mountains of Asia or sitting in a room in a busy metropolis, it is this total self-immolation, this bearing silent witness to the reality of the here and now, that is decisive.

This brings us to another aspect of solitude, one that is growing in importance in today's crazy and city-centered world. Whereas Buddhism was earlier based more commonly in the countryside or in small towns and villages, today, with the spread of the teachings to the West, practitioners of all types are more likely to be found in the cities. So again we need to redefine solitude in existential terms. As Buddhism spreads throughout the West, an existential depth of solitude, of aloneness, will gradually become more necessary.

Gautama Buddha was himself rooted in solitude. As an ascetic, he lived within meditation, and as a teacher he embodied nonattachment, which points toward our selfness, our individuality, as much as toward our interconnectedness.

After all, the very act of sitting in meditation is an act of separation. Alone with our bodies (our actions and reactions), we watch our minds roam abroad and seek anywhere but where we are. Our attempt to escape the nowness of meditation illustrates how much we want to communicate and lose ourselves within the world. Even as a monk (especially as one perhaps), one vacillates between a desire to sit alone, to be me in my essence, and the opposing desire to leave one's place and go walking in a town or a forest, to go talk with people, to consume food or media, or to consort with the Other. Such a tension shows the uses of solitary practice, for it shows how aloneness focuses the mind on meditation and on what is felt to be most important. If, as Buddhists suppose, they are endlessly becoming the silent witness within the turning world, they occupy the center of their maṇḍala, gradually being Buddha and slowly assisting others to open their eyes.

SIMON WICKHAM-SMITH

See also Buddhism: Overview; Buddhism: Western; Hakuin; Hermits: Buddhist; Meditation: Buddhist Perspectives; Mountain Monasteries, Buddhist; Prayer: Buddhist Perspectives

Further Reading

Friedman, Lenore, and Susan Ichi Su Moon, editors, *Being Bodies: Buddhist Women on the Paradox of Embodiment*, Boston: Shambhala, 1997

Ryōkan, *One Robe, One Bowl: The Zen Poetry of Ryōkan*, New York: Weatherhill, 1977

Suzuki, Shunryū, *Zen Mind, Beginner's Mind*, New York: Weatherhill, 1970

Solitude: Christian Perspectives

Solitude has long been associated with Christianity and monasticism. Most significantly it holds a prominent position within the mystical tradition of Western spirituality as it has been understood since the advent of monasticism. Even before the monastic movements of the Middle Ages, the concept of solitude has been central to Christianity.

Within both the Old and the New Testament, there are many images of solitude and isolation, such as Moses' solitary journey to receive the law of God, Daniel's isolation and solitude in fulfillment of the Lord's will, David's isolation and solitary contemplation of God in the Psalms, and, most notably for Christianity, the solitary figure of Christ facing the will and judgment of God. As part of the Christian obligation to follow Christ's example, Christians have for centuries sought solitude and isolation as a means of attaining holiness. The earliest Christian hermits in the African desert were following this model of spiritual contemplation and devotion. This was followed by the growth of communities of religious "hermits," that is, religious communities, monasteries, and anchor holds. The vast growth of religious communities in the Middle Ages is not tied exclusively to the desire of individual Christians to live a life modeled after the life of Christ. Social, economic, personal, and emotional reasons existed for many people to enter the religious life of isolation. Whatever the reasons, the product was a monastic society that touched every Christian nation in the medieval world and that continues today as an integral part of Christian life.

The life of a member of a religious community has not changed much since the early Church. In most orders some ceremony in which the penitent "dies" symbolically to the world is required. In medieval Europe the death mass would be said for anyone entering the life of an anchorite or anchoress, perhaps the most isolated experience of Christian devotion of any time. Once within the walls of the monastery, the monk or nun would give up any association with a previous life, which often included abandoning children and sometimes spouses. The solitary life of the monastic world was very important if the religious person was to achieve fulfillment of any kind – this is as true outside of Christianity as within it. Hindus pursue *vidya*, or a "true knowledge of things," and disciples of Buddha follow his dharma, through which they pursue truth, knowledge, and liberation (Marquette, 1949, 1965). In Christianity the journey from an earthly life to a spiritual union with God, sometimes called the *via mystica*, is characterized by three steps: the *via purgativa*, the *via illuminativa*, and the *via contemplativa*. In the *via purgativa* the penitent separates herself from all thoughts and activities of daily life, eradicating passions and urges as much as possible. Many reached this first stage through isolation, fasting, or other sensual deprivation. In the *via illuminativa* the penitent loses any sense of human connection or discourse. Concentrating on the image of Christ crucified or on some other spiritual icon, the penitent begins to feel a sense of enlightenment and liberation from the source of her concentration. In the *via contemplativa* the spiritual journey reached its goal: direct communication with the presence of the Divine. The penitent might hear a voice, see a vision, or feel a sensory change or stimulation – this transcendent, mystical moment can take many forms. In whatever way it is experienced, the main ingredient for successful accomplishment of the *via mystica* or, indeed, for any other longed-for union with the Divine is solitude. The mystic or nun or priest must be quite alone in order for the powerful spiritual experience to unfold.

The uses and extremes of solitude in Christianity vary depending on the period in which the Christian lived and the area in which he or she resided. For example, different degrees of isolation and solitude prevailed in most medieval European countries. A woman could live as an anchoress (a hermit whose shack bordered a church or cathedral), as a nun living in a community of other religious women, or as a beguine living in the secular world and doing good deeds for her community. None of these types of women were more or less highly privileged, although a rule, the *Ancrene Wisse*, was compiled for anchoresses in England in the 12th century. However she chose to live her life – within the secular world or locked away from it – she would certainly have placed a high degree of value on solitude and

Exterior, reconstructed cell, Mount Grace Priory (Carthusian), North Yorkshire, England, 15th century.
Photo courtesy of Chris Schabel

Cross on La Penna, La Verna (Tuscany), Italy. Near here St. Francis received the stigmata in September 1224.
Photo courtesy of Mary Schaefer

isolation as part of her daily routine. An anchoress, for example, would have had daily contact with a maid (if she came from a wealthy background) and frequent contact with a priest (mainly for Mass and confession). She was sometimes allowed a pet but was otherwise completely isolated. Although there was a small window onto the outside world, it was covered by a heavy black cloth that was always kept in place. The opposite wall would often contain a small hole for the anchoress to view the Mass, but it would not have been big enough for anyone to view her or for her to see much of the world around her.

This death to the world that was experienced by religious men and women in the Middle Ages seems extreme by today's standards, but it was crucial to the medieval understanding of devotion and spirituality. If we are to be fully devoted to Christ, we must allow all the cares of human life to melt away. If the presence of anchoresses and of a good deal else of the monastic world has gradually diminished over the last 1,000 years, desire for solitude and contemplation has remained a powerful and meaningful element of life for the Christian of any era.

SUSANNAH MARY CHEWNING

See also Claustration (Cloister), Rules of; Hermits: Eastern Christian; Hermits: Western Christian; Initiation: Christian Perspectives; Monastics and the World, Medieval; Origins: Comparative Perspectives; Recluses, Western Christian; Spirituality: Eastern Christian; Vision, Mystical: Western Christian

Further Reading

Constable, Giles, *Monks, Hermits, and Crusaders in Medieval Europe* (Variorum Reprint, CS273), London: Variorum Reprints, 1988

Marquette, Jacques de, *Introduction to Comparative Mysticism*, New York: Philosophical Library, 1949; 2nd edition, Bombay: Bharatiya Vidya Bhavan, 1965

Warren, Ann K., *Anchorites and Their Patrons in Medieval England*, Berkeley: University of California Press, 1985

Watson, Nicholas, and Anne Savage, *Anchoritic Spirituality: Ancrene Wisse and Associated Works* (Classics of Western Spirituality), New York: Paulist Press, 1991

Sŏn. *See* Chan/Zen: Korea; Korea: History

Spain: History

The earliest monastic ideas and institutions in Spain appear in the late fourth century. The acts of the Council of Zaragoza (c. 380) forbade consecrated virgins from taking the veil before the age of 40. Similar regulations feature in the acts of the First Council of Toledo (c. 397). There follows a period of over a century for which no conciliar legislation has survived, but it is likely that the fifth century saw the spread of monastic teaching and institutions, especially in northeastern Spain, which was strongly influenced by developments in southern Gaul. The main inspirations were the writings of John Cassian (c. 360–after 430) and the influential example set by the island monastery of Lérins. A second and slightly later source of monastic influence was that of the African Church, especially in southern Spain in the course of the sixth century.

Evidence for early monastic life in the Iberian Peninsula becomes more substantial in the sixth century. The earliest Spanish conciliar decree referring specifically to monks comes in the acts of the Council of Tarragona (516). This presupposes the existence of properly constituted monasteries, functioning under the authority of their own abbots. Significantly the bishops of the province of Tarraconensis stipulated that monks should follow the regulations laid down in the canonical decrees of the Gallic Church, which was still leading the way in the West in the development and expansion of monasticism.

No names or sites of the earliest monasteries in Spain are known, nor is it possible to say whether they were located mainly in towns or in the countryside. The first named monastic founder in Spain is the mid-sixth-century hermit Donatus, a refugee from Africa. He, like other African monks who came to Spain in this period, might have been escaping from Emperor Justinian's (527–565) attempt to crush opposition to his religious policies in the so-called Three Chapters controversy. Donatus' monastery of Servitanum was located in the region of Valencia on the Mediterranean coast, but the site has never been identified. The claim made by Ildefonsus, bishop of Toledo (657–667), that Donatus was the first to introduce a written rule of monastic life into Spain does not mean that monasteries had not existed in the peninsula before his time. After the conversion of the Visigoths from Arianism to Catholicism, formalized at the Third Council of Toledo in 589, in which Donatus' successor Eutropius is said to have played a leading part, monasteries proliferated in Spain. The names, although not the precise locations of several of them, are known. Especially important was Agali near Toledo. In the seventh century four of the abbots of Agali (Helladius, Justus, Eugenius, and Ildefonsus) were chosen by successive kings to become metropolitan bishops of Toledo and de facto primates of the Visigothic Church.

Caves and other sites associated with hermits of the Visigothic period, most of whose names are now lost, continued to be venerated in the period following the fall of the kingdom to the Arabs in 711. Although in theory the Christians in al-Andalus, those parts of Spain under Muslim rule, were forbidden to build new churches, mid-ninth-century literary texts indicate that this prohibition was not enforced, even in Córdoba, the capital of the Umayyad amirate. Several monasteries were founded in the vicinity of the city, especially in the mountains to the north, and several of these were closely involved in the Voluntary Martyr Movement of the late 840s and 850s. Consequently, several of them were destroyed by Amir Muḥammad I (852–886), and restrictions on Christians were thereafter more rigorously enforced. This, and the growth of political turmoil inside al-Andalus, led to the migration of individual monks and whole monastic communities to the Christian-ruled kingdoms of northern Spain.

Here, under royal and aristocratic patronage, they built new monasteries, mainly on estates donated to them in the frontier regions of Castille and León. Other such houses came into being in Galicia and Catalonia. Surviving churches built by these so-called Mozarabic communities display strong traces of the architectural and decorative traditions of the Arabized south. The monks also brought with them aspects of the learning and of the liturgy of the Church of the Visigothic period that had either died out or made only limited impact on the newer Christian kingdoms of northern Spain. In some cases these monasteries became centers of learning that attracted scholars even from beyond the Pyrenees. The best-known example is that of Ripoll in Catalonia, founded by Count Wifred the Hairy of Barcelona (d. 897), which housed one of the foremost schools of poetic and scientific study in Western Europe in the late tenth century. Among those who came here to study at this time was the Frankish scholar Gerbert of Aurillac, the future Pope Sylvester II (999–1003).

In general the period of the flowering of the Mozarabic monasteries proved short-lived, partly because their cultural and artistic traditions were at variance with the new movements in monastic reform that began to develop in western Francia and Lotharingia from the tenth century on and that are associated not least, although not exclusively, with the great monastery of Cluny and its growing family. These reforming ideals first made themselves felt in the early 12th century in Catalonia, where they were welcomed by Oliba (d. 1046), a member of the comital house of Barcelona, abbot of Cuxa and Ripoll, and bishop of Vic (1017–1046). Under his influence interest in monastic revival grew in the kingdom of Navarre, which, under king Sancho III the Great (1004–1035), briefly dominated the Christian realms of northern Spain. Around 1025 Sancho persuaded Abbot Odilo of Cluny to send some monks to reinvigorate the Aragonese monastery of San Juan de la Peña. Other houses, such as Leire and Albelda in Navarre and Oña in Castille, which had come under Navarrese control in 1018, might have been similarly affected. The king himself became a lay member of the community of Cluny, but after his death Cluniac influence in Navarre and Castille lapsed.

The sons of Sancho III inherited different parts of his realm. The most powerful of them proved to be Fernando I of León-Castille (1037–1065), who from 1055 on renewed his dynasty's links with Cluny after nearly two decades of neglect. Fernando, like his father, became a lay *socius*, and from the mid-1050s paid a fixed annual grant to the great Burgundian monastery of 1,000 gold coins (*maravadis*). This was doubled by his son, Alfonso VI (1072–1109), and this regular contribution, funded from the tribute (*parías*) now given to him annually by the Muslim rulers of al-Andalus, paid for the rebuilding of Cluny.

Despite Fernando I's personal interest, no Spanish monastery became a dependency of Cluny before 1072. San Isidoro de las Dueñas was the first, and by 1079 it had been joined by the Castillian house of San Zoilo de Carrión and Santa María de Nájera in western Navarre. Following Alfonso VI's conquest of the Muslim kingdom of Toledo in 1085, Cluniac monks received several of the bishoprics that were then restored or created. In particular Bernard, abbot of Sahagún since 1180, was given the primatial see of Toledo.

However, this sudden expansion into central Spain undermined the financial links between León-Castille and Cluny, as the apparent Christian threat to the survival of the remaining Muslim states led their rulers to appeal for aid to the Berber Almoravids, who defeated Alfonso in battle in 1086 and then rapidly overran al-Andalus. The loss of the *parías* meant that Alfonso was unable to maintain the same level of contribution to Cluny after 1095. By the time of his grandson, Alfonso VII (1126–1157), this had reduced itself to 200 gold *maravedis* a year. Although in his reign Cluny also acquired control of a number of other important Spanish monasteries, including Sahagún (1132), which had hitherto resisted formal absorption by Cluny, its influence and institutional holdings in the peninsula thereafter declined sharply.

While León had felt the strongest Cluniac influences, the Cistercians made their presence felt more widely. Under the patronage of Alfonso VII, their first colonizing ventures, directed from the house of L'Escale-Dieu in Gascony, saw the foundation of the monasteries of Fitero (1140), Monsalud (1141), Sacramenia (1142), Huerta (1144), Veruela (1146), La Oliva (1150), and Bugedo (1172). The influence of the most famous French Cistercian house, Clairvaux, made itself felt principally in Catalonia, where the main colonizing activity came from its southern French foundations of Grandselve and Fontfroide. The latter house was responsible for the establishment of Poblet (1149), which in turn became the mother house to four more Cistercian monasteries in Catalonia, including La Real in Mallorca (1236). Grandselve founded Santes Creus (1150) and Moruela (1158). From the start the counts of Barcelona, who in 1163 also became kings of Aragón, especially patronized Poblet and Santes Creus, both of which were made burial places for the Aragonese monarchs and the sites of royal palaces.

In general the tide of Cistercian expansion in Spain came to an end in the late 13th century. Surprisingly, although a total of 58 Cistercian houses were established in Spain, only three of these were in the south, which was being rapidly conquered by León-Castille and Aragón from the 1220s on. However, two distinctively Hispanic Cistercian institutions played important roles in this process of "Reconquista." The military orders of Calatrava (founded in 1158) and of Alcántara (1158), whose knightly members lived under monastic vows, both came to be incorporated into the Cistercian Order under the authority of the abbey of Morimond in 1187 and 1221, respectively. Both orders had their own rules, which in the case of Calatrava was that of Cîteaux, and were under the immediate authority of their own chapters, grand priors (who were normally monks of Morimond), and grand masters. Both orders were placed under direct royal control in 1489, and the office of grand master was in both cases annexed permanently by the crown in 1523.

In the 15th century the Spanish Cistercian houses benefited from a major program of reform and secured independence from the mainly French Cistercian general chapter. This was largely the work of Martín Vargas, a monk of Piedra who acquired his reforming ideas during a visit to Italy in 1425. In 1427 he received papal approval to found a new house at Montesión near Toledo with 11 companions. Seven other houses rapidly accepted his reformed rule, and despite Vargas' excommunication by the general chapter, Pope Eugenius IV (1431–1447) approved the establishment of a Cistercian Chapter of Castille in 1437. By 1532 this had expanded to 25 houses, and by 1559 all the Spanish Cistercian monasteries had placed themselves under its authority. It also established Cistercian colleges in the universities of Salamanca (1504) and Alcalá de Henares (1534).

Saint Domingo de Guzmán or Dominic (1171–1221) was born at Caleruega in Castille, and although the order that he founded in 1215 was first centered on Toulouse, it spread itself widely and rapidly across all parts of Spain, as did that of the Franciscans. However, the history of both orders in the peninsula has been surprisingly little studied other than as regards a movement of reform among the Dominicans that developed in Castille in the mid–15th century. Rather more attention has been devoted to the mainly Iberian Jeronimite Order, which was recognized by Pope Gregory XI (1370–1378) in 1373. Founded in the monastery of Lupiana (province of Guadalajara) in 1370 by Pedro Fernández Pecha, it adopted the Rule of St. Augustine. By 1415, the date of its first general chapter, the Order had incorporated 25 houses. This rose to 50 by the time of the exclaustration of 1836. In the 16th century in particular, the Jeronimites enjoyed powerful patronage. Charles V (ruled Spain as Charles I [1516–1556]) retired to the Jeronimite house at Yuste in 1556, and in 1563 his son Philip II (1556–1598) entrusted them with his planned palace-monastery of El Escorial (completed in 1584), which also became the Habsburg and Bourbon royal burial place.

Unquestionably the most famous movement of monastic reform in Spain in the 16th century is that of the Discalced (meaning "shoeless") Carmelites, begun in 1555 by St. Teresa of Avila (1515–1582). She reacted against the lack of ascetic rigor in the lifestyle of the Carmelite convent of the Encarnación in Avila and in 1562 was permitted to found a new house of her own in the town following a much more severe rule. Despite initial strong opposition and with the assistance of the Carmelite monk St. John of the Cross (1542–1591), her reform spread and by the 17th century had become highly patronized, with the Discalced Carmelite house in Madrid serving as the place of retirement for the widowed ladies of the royal house. From here Marianna of Austria ruled the Spanish Empire for most of the period from 1665 to 1675.

In the period of the Napoleonic Wars, several Spanish monasteries, including the important Catalan house of Montserrat, were damaged or looted by the French, but they were generally spared the large-scale destruction that had accompanied the Revolution in France. However, the close association between the Church and the highly conservative Bourbon monarchy, following the restoration of Fernando VII (d. 1833) in 1812, made the monasteries a target for Liberal reaction, especially following the outbreak of the Carlist Rebellion in 1833. Monks were attacked and murdered in Madrid in 1834. In 1836 the Liberal government decreed the closure and expropriation by the state of the monasteries. Many were demolished, and several were sacked by the local populace. Major libraries, such as that of Ripoll, and works of art were destroyed. Although finally reversed in 1880, the exclaustration severely weakened Spanish monasticism. Purely Spanish orders, such as the Jeronimites, were never revived, and many once important monastic houses were not reoccupied. Others, such as Silos, which was recolonized by Benedictine monks from Solesmes in France, depended on external support for their initially slow recovery. The radical anticlericalism of the Republican period (1931–1939) and the widespread clerical support for the Nationalist rising in 1936 led to further attacks on monks and monasteries during the Spanish Civil War (1936–1939) and yet further destruction of the artistic and intellectual heritage of Spanish monasticism. Not least of these losses was that of the remarkable 12th-century frescoes in the chapter house of the convent of Sigena.

ROGER COLLINS

See also Architecture: Western Christian Monasteries; Carmelites; Cistercians: General or Male; Cluny, Abbots of; Cluny, France; Dominic, St.; Dominicans: General or Male; Isidore of Seville, St.; John of the Cross, St.; Lérins, France; Mercedarians; Origins: Western Christian; Peter of Alcántara, St.; Santiago de Compostela, Spain; Servites; Teresa of Avila, St.; Warrior Monks: Christian

Further Reading

Beltrán de Heredia, V., "The Beginnings of Dominican Reform in Castile," in *Spain in the Fifteenth Century, 1369–1516: Essays and Extracts by Historians of Spain* (Stratum Series), edited by John Roger Loxdale Highfield, London: Macmillan, and New York: Harper and Row, 1972

Bishko, Charles Julian, "The Cluniac Priories of Galicia and Portugal: Their Acquisition and Administration, 1075–1230," *Studia Monastica* 7 (1965)

Bishko, Charles Julian, "Fernando I y los orígenes de la alianza castellano-leonesa con Cluny," *Cuadernos de la Historia de España* 47:8 (1968); also in his *Studies in Medieval Spanish Frontier History* (Variorum Reprint, CS124), London: Variorum Reprints, 1980

Cocheril, M., "L'implantation des abbayes cisterciennes dans la Péninsule Ibérique," *Anuario de Estudios Medievales* 1 (1964)

Linage Conde, Antonio, *Los orígenes del monacato benedictino en la Península Ibérica* (Colección Fuentes y estudios de historia leonesa, numbers 9–11), 3 vols., León: Centro de Estudios e Investigación San Isidoro, Consejo Superior de Investigaciónes Científicas, 1973

Mundó, Ansacari M., "Monastic Movements in the East Pyrenees," in *Cluniac Monasticism in the Central Middle Ages* (Readings in European History), edited by Noreen Hunt, London: Macmillan, and Hamden, Connecticut: Archon Books, 1971

O'Callaghan, Joseph F., *The Spanish Military Order of Calatrava and Its Affiliates* (Collected Studies, CS37), London: Variorum Reprints, 1975

Mahābodhi temple, Bodh Gayā, Bihar, India.
Photo courtesy of John C. Huntington, the Huntington Archive

Gate of the Xiantongsi with view of the pagoda of the Tayuansi, Wutai-shan, Shanxi province, China, both Ming dynasty (1368–1644).
Photo courtesy of Marylin M. Rhie

Wenshu (Mañjuśrī) hall at the top of Pusading, Wutai-shan, Shanxi province, China, Ming dynasty (1368–1644).
Photo courtesy of Marylin M. Rhie

Bronze Pagoda built in 1610 of the Ming dynasty at the Xiantongsi, Wutai-shan, Shanxi province, China.
Photo courtesy of Marylin M. Rhie

Lamayuru Monastery (Kagyü lineage), Ladakh.
Photo courtesy of John Powers

Statue of Buddha delivering his first sermon, Deer Park, Sārnāth, India.
Photo courtesy of John Powers

Śākyamuni Buddha in a rock carving in a cave grotto near Kyŏngju, South Korea, eighth–ninth century. This is the most visited religious spot in Korea.
Photo courtesy of John Powers

A monumental statue of Maitreya in Tikse Monastery, Ladakh.
Photo courtesy of John Powers

A group of statues with Vajradhara in the middle, Hemis Monastery (Kagyü lineage), Ladakh.
Photo courtesy of John Powers

A statue of the 1,000-armed Avalokiteśvara, Hemis Monastery (Kagyü lineage), Ladakh.
Photo courtesy of John Powers

Gyuto monk chanting, wearing the characteristic yellow hat.
Photo courtesy of John Powers

Monk performing 'cham dance at Phyang Monastery, Ladakh.
Photo courtesy of John Powers

Indian Paṇḍit Gāyadhāra, Guru of Sakya Order, Central Regions, Tibet, probably Tsang, second half of 16th century, thangka, water-based pigments on cotton, 31 × 26 inches. The Zimmerman Family Collection, in Rhie and Thurman, *Wisdom and Compassion* (1991). Photo courtesy of John Bigelow Taylor

Vajradhara, thangka, cotton support with opaque mineral pigments in water-based (collagen) binder, 23.25 × 32.75 inches, indeterminate region, c. 16th century. The Rezk Collection of Tibetan Art, Southern Alleghenies Museum of Art, #: 94.003.
Photo courtesy of John C. Huntington, the Huntington Archive

Ekadasamukha ("11-Headed") Avalokiteśvara in Potalaka Paradise thangka, cotton support with opaque mineral pigments in water-based (collagen) binder, 26 × 39.5 inches, painted area only Central Tibet, c. 18th or 19th century, indeterminate style. The Rezk Collection of Tibetan Art, Southern Alleghenies Museum of Art. Photo courtesy of John C. Huntington, the Huntington Archive

Tsong Kalpa and the Gelukpa Refuge Tree, Eastern Tibet or Central Regions, late 18th to early 19th century, thangka, water-based pigments on linen, 53 × 37 7/8 inches. Mead Art Museum, Amherst College, Gift of Mrs. George L. Hamilton (1952.25). Photo courtesy of John Bigelow Taylor

Parinirvāṇa Buddha, Gal Vihāra, Poḷonnaruva, Sri Lanka, colossal stone relief (length 14.12 meters), reign of Parākramabāhu I (A.D. 1153–1186). Photo courtesy of Marylin M. Rhie

Detail of the colossal standing Buddha (about 25 meters in height) in Cave 18, Yungang cave temples, near Tatong, Shanxi province, China, c. A.D. 460s, Northern Wei dynasty.
Photo courtesy of Marylin M. Rhie

Standing Buddha, Yangpy'ŏng-dong, Koch'ang-gun, Koch'ang-up, Kyŏngsang-namdo, South Korea, c. mid–tenth century, later Paekche or early Koryŏ dynasty, granite, 3.7 meters in height.
Photo courtesy of Marylin M. Rhie

Hermitage frequented by St. Francis and his earliest followers, Eremo delle Carceri, near Assisi, Italy. The buildings date from the 15th century.
Photo courtesy of Mary Schaefer

Chapel of Santa Maria della Carceri (converted from a grotto), Eremo delle Carceri, near Assisi, Italy, with 16th-century fresco. St. Francis and his followers dwelt here on retreat.
Photo courtesy of Mary Schaefer

Woodland altar in front of a rockface, Eremo delle Carceri, near Assisi, Italy. This mountainside was a favorite retreat of St. Francis and his followers.
Photo courtesy of Mary Schaefer

Monastery of the Deposition of the Robe (Rizhepolozhenie Monastery), Suzdal, opened 1688.
Photo courtesy of Robert E. Jones

Cathedral of the Dormition (Uspensky Cathedral), Holy Trinity–St. Sergius Monastery, Sergeyev Posad (Zagorsk), 16th century.
Photo courtesy of Robert E. Jones

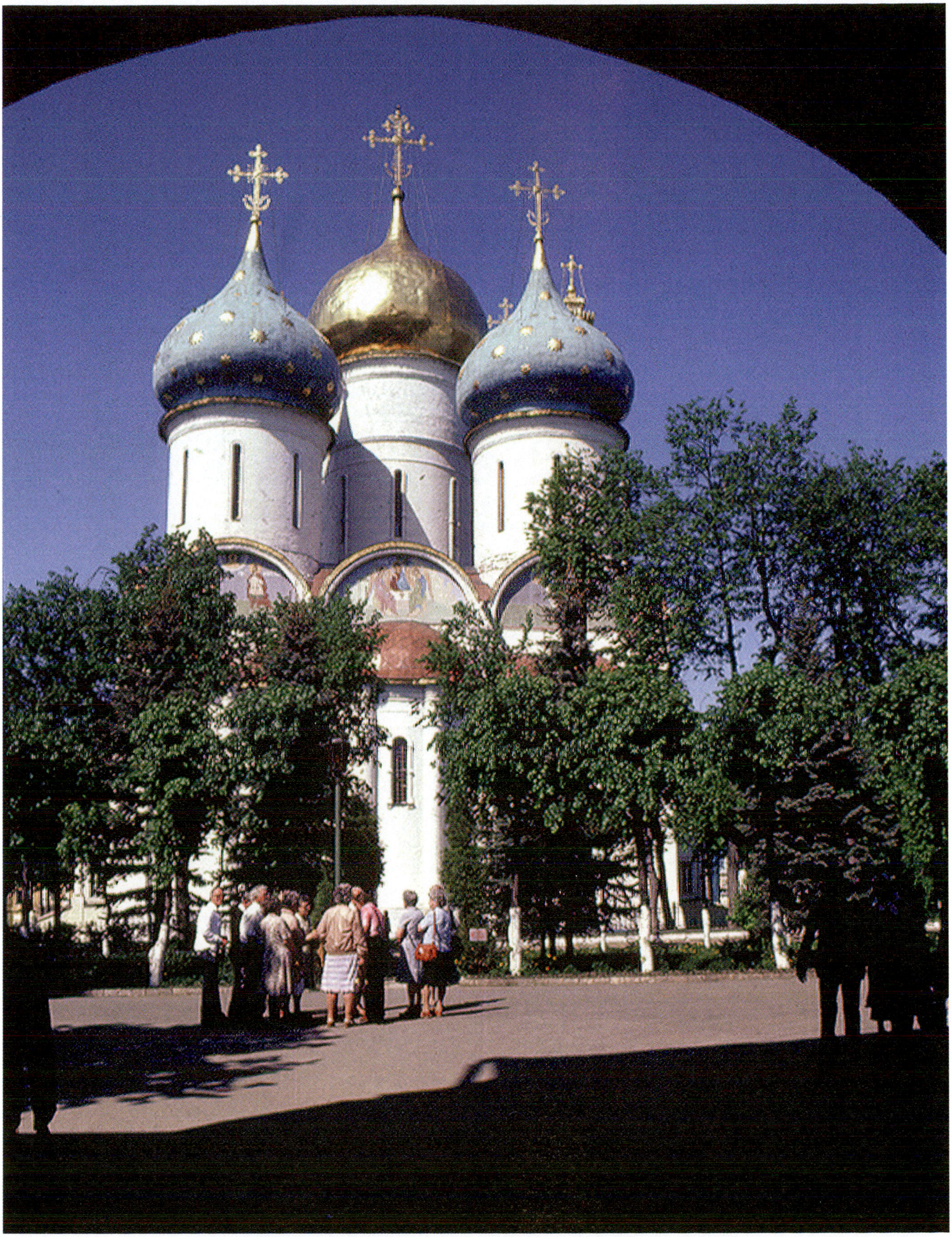

Domenico Trezzini, Alexander Nevskii Lavra, St. Petersburg, 18th century.
Photo courtesy of Robert E. Jones

Round Tower and High Cross, Monasterboice (County Louth), Ireland, 10th to 11th century.
Photo courtesy of Mary Schaefer

High Cross and Church, Monasterboice (County Louth), Ireland, 10th to 11th century.
Photo courtesy of Mary Schaefer

Temple Dowling (Teampull Dooling) with High Cross, Clonmacnois (County Offaly), Ireland, 10th century, rebuilt 14th century.
Photo courtesy of Mary Schaefer

Temple Dowling (Teampull Dooling) with High Cross, Clonmacnois (County Offaly), Ireland, 10th century, rebuilt 14th century.
Photo courtesy of Mary Schaefer

Fountains Abbey (Cistercian), 12th century.
Photo courtesy of Chris Schabel

Rievaulx Abbey (Cistercian). Nave in foreground c. 1180; choir in back c. 1225.
Photo courtesy of Chris Schabel

Ruins in North Yorkshire, England

Byland Abbey (Cistercian), 13th century. The rounded stairway leads into the church from the cloister.
Photo courtesy of Chris Schabel

Fountains Abbey (Cistercian), choir and Chapel of the Nine Altars (c. 1210–1240).
Photo courtesy of Chris Schabel

East range and south transept, Kirkstall Abbey (Cistercian), Leeds, South Yorkshire, 12th century.
Photo courtesy of Chris Schabel

Choir, St. Mary's Abbey (Benedictine), York, 13th century.
Photo courtesy of Chris Schabel

East end of church, Guisborough Priory (Augustinian Canons), 12th–14th century.
Photo courtesy of Chris Schabel

RUINS IN YORKSHIRE, ENGLAND

Doorway of the refectory, Kirkham Priory (Augustinian Canons), North Yorkshire, 12th century.
Photo courtesy of Chris Schabel

Orlandis, José, *Estudios sobre instituciones monásticas medievales*, Pamplona: Universidad de Navarra, 1971
Pérez de Urbel, Justo, *Los monjes españoles en la Edad Media*, 2 vols., Madrid: Ediciones ancla, 1933; 2nd edition, 1945

Spain: Sites

None of the monasteries of the late Roman and Visigothic periods in Spain named in the literary sources has left material remains, but the impression that they were few in number is contradicted by the growing number of discoveries of cave churches datable to this period. The greatest concentrations of these, almost certainly eremitic sites, have been found in Alava, but individual examples have been discovered as far south as the province of Málaga.

In some cases archaeological excavations have revealed the presence of small churches or chapels forming part of the structure of some late Roman aristocratic villas. Although none of these is documented, they probably represent Spanish examples of the house-monasteries that developed in North Africa, Rome, and southern Gaul in the fifth and sixth centuries. The best-preserved example of such a building in the Iberian Peninsula is that of the Villa Fortunatus at Fraga (province of Lérida). This fourth-century villa had a church constructed out of its principal dining room in the early fifth century. By the middle of the sixth century, the residential sectors of the villa had been abandoned and only the church continued in use.

Excavations in the 1980s have verified the monastic origin of the seventh-century church of Santa María de Melque near Toledo. This site is especially important in that, in addition to the well-preserved church, the excavators were able to detect and study the foundations of other buildings within an enclosure wall, parts of which remain visible.

None of the numerous monasteries in al-Andalus that survived or were built after the Arab conquest has survived, with the possible exception of a small church partly carved out of the rock and built over a cave near the El Chorro Dam (province of Málaga). Far more numerous are the sites in the north associated with the Mozarabs. Among the best preserved of the monasteries founded by these communities of culturally Arabicized monks fleeing from the south in the later ninth and tenth centuries is San Miguel de Escalada. Excavations here have revealed the previous presence on the site of a villa that seems to have developed into a monastery in the early Visigothic period. Other Mozarabic monastic churches worthy of attention include Santo Tomás de las Ollas (in Villafranca del Bierzo), Santiago de Peñalba, and San Cebrian de Mazote. There is also a small Mozarabic chapel within the walls of the great Galician monastery of Celanova.

A number of early medieval, non-Mozarabic monasteries have also survived in the Asturias and in Catalonia. The former are represented by the largely tenth-century churches of Santa María de Bendones, San Pedro de Nora, and San Salvador de Valdedíos (adjacent to a relatively well preserved Cistercian monastery of 1218). In Catalonia, Ripoll (founded 888 and with a church dating to 1035 but badly damaged in 1835) has been well restored, as has the monastery of San Pere de Rodhes (or San Pedro de Roda) of 1022. Like Ripoll, San Joan de les Abadesses was founded by Count Wifred the Hairy (d. 897) of Barcelona in 887. It is now represented by a church consecrated in 1150 and a 14th- to 15th-century cloister.

In Aragón the monastery of San Juan de la Peña, which was founded in the mid–ninth century and brought under Cluniac influence in the time of Sancho the Great (1004–1035), remains impressive. Few other Cluniac sites have survived so well, although some remains exist of the once very important monastery of San Facundo at Sahagún. From the same period comes the well-preserved abbey of Santo Domingo de Silos in Castille, which was founded in the early tenth century but entirely rebuilt in the abbacy of its St. Dominic (1041–1073), not to be confused with the founder of the Dominican Order. It retains a cloister full of the finest Spanish Romanesque stone carving.

Cistercian foundations began in Castille in the 1140s. In some cases Cistercian monks were introduced into existing monasteries, such as Carracedo in the Bierzo, founded by King Vermudo II the Gouty around 991. This has a relatively well preserved church and chapter house of 12th-century date, the foundations of two cloisters, and the remains of a royal palace. Other monasteries were built specially for the Cistercians by the king or other lay patrons. One of the best preserved of these is Santa María de Huerta on the eastern edge of the province of Soria. This was founded around 1144 on a different site, which was abandoned in favor of the present one in 1162. Work on the church began in 1179, and the cloister is 13th century, with an upper story being added in 1547. Owing to generous Aragonese royal patronage, the two principal Cistercian houses in Catalonia, Santes Creus (1150) and Poblet (1149), are among the finest surviving examples of later medieval monastic architecture.

The indigenous military orders of Alcántara, Calatrava, and Santiago, as well as the two international orders of the Templars and the Hospitallers, have left numerous traces of themselves throughout Spain in the numerous castles that they held. The monastic dimension to life in a military order is usually difficult to detect in such sites, but the castle of Calatrava la Nueva, headquarters from 1217 of the Order of Calatrava, is a remarkable exception. Here not only have impressive remains of a powerfully defended castle survived, but so too have many of the monastic buildings at its heart. These include the church, cloister, chapter house, kitchen and refectory, library, parlor, and knights' dormitories. The keep of the castle contains the master's quarters and the site of the Order's principal archive. Most of these structures date to the 13th century, but the cloister and refectory were reconstructed in the late 15th century.

Dominican and Franciscan friaries are to be found widely in Spain, with one or more in most major towns, but several are still occupied by friars and in general have been little studied. Because of the their urban locations and continuity in use, many of them have been substantially rebuilt at various times. A good, although late, example is the Dominican house of San Estebán in

Salamanca, founded in 1256. The present church dates to 1524 and the cloister from the following decade.

The indigenous, although now defunct, Jeronimite Order is well represented not only by the royal sites of Yuste (founded in 1404, with a church of 1508) in Extremadura and El Escorial (built 1563–1584) but also by the shrine of Nuestra Señora de Guadalupe (14th to 16th centuries) and the church of San Jeronimo (1505) near the Prado in Madrid.

Avila provides the best examples of accessible Discalced Carmelite houses, other than for the Descalzas Reales in Madrid. The latter preserves the cells, the habits, and even the gold funerary crowns of several of its numerous royal abbesses and nuns as well as the 16th- to 17th-century church and conventual buildings. Saint Teresa's first foundation, the convent of San José in her hometown of Avila, was rebuilt in 1615. The convent that she first entered, La Encarnación, which was built in 1479, still stands outside the city, and within the walls there is the 17th-century convent of Santa Teresa, which was erected on the site of her birth.

ROGER COLLINS

See also Archaeology: Western Europe; Architecture: Western Christian Monasteries; Carmelites; Cistercians: General or Male; Cluny, Abbots of; Cluny, France; Dominic, St.; Dominicans: General or Male; Isidore of Seville, St.; John of the Cross, St.; Lérins, France; Mercedarians; Origins: Western Christian; Peter of Alcántara, St.; Santiago de Compostela, Spain; Servites; Teresa of Avila, St.; Warrior Monks: Christian

Further Reading

Collins, Roger, *Oxford Archaeological Guide to Spain*, Oxford: Oxford University Press, 1998

Romanò, Cesare, *Abteien und Klöster in Europa*, Milan: Mondadori, 1997

Spiritual Direction, Christian

Saint Antony established the central position and the characteristics of spiritual direction during the first stage of monasticism, when he sought "the gift of honey" from those living "the disciplined life." Athanasius (c. 296–373) tells us in his *Vita* of Antony (c. 251–356) that "he obeyed all those whom he visited in his eagerness to learn" and that after seeking their advice Antony "would think these things over and strive to imitate the good points of each of them." After Antony mastered the life others came and asked "the holy Antony to provide some guidelines for their way of life." For the rest of Antony's life, he "advised others who came to him," each "according to what wounds he found" within each individual but reminding all that God "judges not from outward appearance but according to the secrets of the mind" (see "Life of St. Antony by Athanasius," in *Early Christian Lives*, 1998).

These characteristics – the necessity of spiritual direction, the personal experience of directors, individualized direction, obedience to directors, and emphasis on inner thoughts – are developed more thoroughly by those who followed Antony. Women served readily as directors: Amma Syncletica (fourth century) warned directors that "it is dangerous for anyone to teach who has not first been trained in the 'practical' life. For if someone who owns a ruined house receives guests there, he does them harm," whereas Amma Theodora provided a list of necessary qualities for directors: the director "ought to be a stranger to the desires for domination, vainglory, and pride; one should not be able to fool him by flattery, nor blind him by gifts, nor conquer him by the stomach, nor dominate him by anger; but he should be patient, gentle and humble" (*Sayings of the Desert Fathers*, 1975). Desert direction was preoccupied with human passions and with the need for the director to share insight into the human condition with anyone who sought such knowledge. Following this pioneering effort to probe the depths of the human psyche, the role of the spiritual director was recognized in a more public and explicit way, and a deeper consciousness of sin was realized by those who followed the monastic life. Evagrius Ponticus (346–399) did much to promote the importance of both a sense of sin and spiritual direction, and it is interesting to note that his own director was Melanie the Elder (d. c. 410). This fact brings to the forefront a final characteristic of early monastic direction: its universality. It was by and for both women and men. In the East the seventh-century monk Martyrios tells us that his spiritual directors were his mother and Shirin, a woman whom all monastic abbots of his time considered to be their spiritual director, and in the West we have the testimony of Venantus Fortunatus (c. 530–c. 610) and Gregory of Tours (538/39–594) concerning the spiritual direction of Radegunde (c. 518–587); both are typical examples of how common and acceptable women directors were. This inclusiveness was not peculiar to monasticism, for the first spiritual director to the gentiles in the New Testament is the Samaritan woman in John 4:4–42, but no other institution did more to promote genderless accessibility to the ministry of spiritual direction or its accessibility.

Most of the monastic rules adopted during the early Middle Ages contained reference to the necessity of direction and assigned the role to the abbot or abbess. However, the Rule of St. Benedict is concerned much less with personal, individualized direction than desert monasticism had been. Instead, it directs members to the Bible and to written works for guidance (*RB 1980*, 1981). Medieval Benedictine direction emphasized reading, sermons, and example as a means of guidance for the whole community. During the central Middle Ages, written spiritual direction became popular, as witnessed by the epistolary literature of Peter Damian (1007–1072), Hildegard of Bingen (1098–1179), Anselm (1033–1109), and Hadewijch (dates unknown). Hildegard's *The Book of the Rewards of Life*, Hadewijch's poems, Gertrude the Great's (1256–c. 1302) *Herald of Divine Love*, and Angela of Foligno's (c. 1248–1309) *Book* establish a new genre of literature during this same period: that of spiritual guidance. The most famous of these manuals is *Imitation of Christ* (c. 1418), in which the text actually becomes the director, as it advises the reader in the proper approach to God. However, written direction is not to supplant individualized direction completely, for other authors within the monastic family, especially Catherine of Siena (c. 1347–1380), returned more consciously to the desert tradition and its emphasis on personal direction.

Increasingly during the late medieval period, people turned to confessors for direction, and this new confessor-director was in part responsible for ushering in a golden age of direction. Even with the popularity of this composite figure, direction was far from restricted to men. Indeed direction received a powerful impetus with the analysis of the spiritual life by Teresa of Avila (1515–1582) and her disciple John of the Cross (1542–1591). Teresa advocated the necessity of direction and the presence of discernment, experience, and learning within the director. Ignatius Loyola's *Spiritual Exercises* (1541) echoed these sentiments, and Jesuits soon became the most sought after spiritual directors in post-Reformation monasteries. During the 17th century Francis de Sales (1567–1622) and Jane Frances de Chantal (1572–1641) developed and popularized the new methods and approaches of spiritual direction among the laity, thus ending the near monopoly that monks and nuns had held on giving and receiving spiritual direction. Like desert direction Salesian direction emphasized the personal spiritual experience of the director and individualized direction but in addition encouraged spiritual friendships between directors and directees as an essential element of spiritual direction. Eventually, the main tenets of Salesian direction were adopted within monastic circles as well.

Personal spiritual direction did not receive much attention among the reformers, although in the post-Reformation world Anglicans, such as William Law, George Herbert, and Jeremy Taylor, focused on it. Puritans and Quakers also emphasized the need for direction, as did John Wesley and the Methodists of the 18th century. All considered it only among the laity, as monasticism was not a viable institution within their churches. Thus, monastic spiritual direction remained almost wholly identified with Roman Catholicism into the 20th century with a few notable exceptions, such as the ecumenical monastic community of Taizé.

PATRICIA RANFT

See also Antony, St.; Desert Fathers; Desert Mothers; Hildegard of Bingen, St.; Meditation: Christian Perspectives; Origins: Comparative Perspectives; Radegunde, St.; Reformation; Taizé, France; Teresa of Avila, St.

Further Reading

Ashley, Benedict, "St. Catherine of Siena's Principles of Spiritual Direction," *Spirituality Today* 33 (1981)
Corbishley, Thomas, translator, *Spiritual Exercises of Saint Ignatius*, Wheathampstead, England: Clarke, 1979
François de Sales, *Oeuvres*, edited by Andre Ravier, Paris: Gallimard, 1969
Fry, Timothy, editor, *RB 1980: Rule of St. Benedict in Latin and English with Notes*, Collegeville, Minnesota: Liturgical Press, 1981
Gertrude of Heltfa, *Les exercices: Oeuvres spirituelles*, Paris: Sources Chrétiennes, 1967
Giallanza, Joel, "Spiritual Direction According to St. Teresa of Avila," *Contemplative Review* 12 (Summer 1979)
Hildegard of Bingen, *The Book of the Rewards of Life*, translated by Bruce W. Hozeski, New York: Garland, 1994
Lachance, Paul, translator, *Angela of Foligno: Complete Works*, New York: Paulist Press, 1993
"Life of St. Antony by Athanasius," in *Early Christian Lives*, London and New York: Penguin, 1998
Peers, E. Allison, translator, *Complete Works of St. Teresa*, 3 vols., London: Sheed and Ward, 1957; New York: Sheed and Ward, 1963
Ranft, Patricia, *A Woman's Way: The Forgotten History of Women Spiritual Directors*, New York: St. Martin's Press, 2000
Rivet, M.M., *Influence of the Spanish Mystics on the Works of Saint Francis de Sales*, Washington, D.C.: Catholic University of America Press, 1941
Thibert, P.M., translator, *Francis de Sales, Jane de Chantal: Letters of Spiritual Direction*, New York: Paulist Press, 1988
Thomas a Kempis, *The Imitation of Christ*, edited by Harold C. Gardiner, Garden City, New York: Doubleday, 1955
Tracey, Wesley, "John Wesley, Spiritual Director: Spiritual Guidance in Wesley's Letters," *Wesleyan Theological Journal* 23 (Spring-Fall 1988)
Ward, Benedicta, "Traditions of Spiritual Direction: Spiritual Direction in the Desert Fathers," *The Way* 24 (1984)
Ward, Benedicta, translator, *Sayings of the Desert Fathers*, London: Mowbray, and Kalamazoo, Michigan: Cistercian Publications, 1975

Spirituality: Buddhist

The word *spirituality* has become fashionable in contemporary discourse about religion, theology, and psychology. The concept is relatively modern and may refer to the "contemplative life," or to religious feelings and attitudes understood as private aspirations transcending the presumed limitations of cultural or historical circumstances. The latter conception of contextless spirituality has been the object of much criticism by historians and theologians alike. The notion appears to run counter to everything that cultural criticism has stood for in the last two centuries, and yet the notion seems to respond to a fundamental need or aspiration of human beings in the late modern or postmodern age. It expresses an eminently contemporary sense of what it means to be religious: that religious life finds its full expression primarily in the individual conscience and through a process of self-transformation. This feeling, so prevalent at the end of the 20th century, is often presumed to have been present also in the Buddhist tradition.

However, when applied concretely to the historical contexts of Buddhist religious life and ideals, *spirituality* refers to two dimensions of Buddhist practice that may in fact stand in tension. On the one hand the term seems to be used to characterize life in the monastery as an "inner life" – presumably a life "of the spirit" – abstracting from varying degrees all that is social, economic, or political in the monastic life yet idealizing life in community. On the other hand, the term refers to the modern notion of religion as a private matter, as an inner or psychological transformation. In the latter sense religion is seen as a source of inspiration or a guide in a journey of self-discovery.

The application of these two meanings of the term *spirituality* to Buddhism is to a certain extent justified, but not without serious problems of history and method. Traditionally Buddhism has set up meditation as the highest ideal of the monastic life and as the ultimate source of the religion. The Buddha's own practice of meditation is, after all, seen as the primary source for both the authority and the value of the tradition. Thus, one could argue that life in the cenobium exists for the sake of a radical transformation in the inner self and that the paragon of such transformation, the Buddha's own experience, was an individual or private event achieved in solitude. However, it is important to understand that our interpretation of the Buddhist ideal may be colored by our eagerness to associate a modern, psychologized, and vague notion of a "life of the spirit" or the mind with the mythical ideals of a classical tradition. Without this awareness one risks overlooking the degree to which Buddhism has been grounded throughout its history in institutional forms and traditional systems of practice and orthodoxy. The rhetoric of solitude and isolation makes sense only against the backdrop of those institutional and doctrinal constraints.

Historically Buddhism has presented tendencies that parallel some of the ideals and idealizations subsumed under the term *spirituality* in contemporary usage. At least at the normative level, the Buddhist tradition emphasizes the interiority of religious experience, deeming the mind and the will to be the defining centers of human growth and ethical effort. Thus, Buddhism often presents itself as a sort of psychological religious ideal.

Furthermore, from an early period in its formation, Buddhism posited, at least in theory, the inner journey of self-discovery as the paradigmatic religious quest. However, we must qualify these dominant themes in the Buddhist view of the religious in a number of ways. Doing so might help us understand some of the limitations of the concept of the spiritual, or of religion as "spirituality."

Monks making *tormas* in Tikse Monastery, Ladakh. *Tormas* are made from butter and *tsampa* (ground barley flour), molded into shape, and then painted. They are destroyed after the ceremony for which they were made.
Photo courtesy of John Powers

A monk circumambulating the main shrine while turning prayer wheels at Lamayuru, Ladakh. Photo courtesy of John Powers

First, although Buddhism makes a distinction between body and spirit, the dichotomy is, so to speak, made along a different cleavage line. There is no rhetoric of "matter" versus "spirit." The body is treated in a variety of ways that range from its condemnation as impure and the source of evil to its glorification as a vehicle for transformation or as embodiment of enlightenment. Even when condemned it is not so much the body as matter that is the problem but the body as desire, and thus, ultimately, the problem with the body is in fact the mind. Mind is all-important, but by the same token mind is the problem. Mind is the locus of salvation (or, rather, liberation), but it is also the locus of spiritual blindness and bondage. Or, we may say, that release can only occur in the place where bondage occurs. This means that in a view that may be called characteristically or dominantly Buddhist, the body is no more of a problem than is the mind. Accordingly, to speak of Buddhist spirituality in a strictly etymological sense might be a mistake, and to speak of the spirit as the key to liberation may be misleading.

Second, as already implied, in some Buddhist traditions, especially the so-called tantric schools, body, speech, and mind are all aspects of the one ground of awakening. These three aspects are discovered or actualized through a combined ritual-meditational process called a "realization" (*sādhana*). One may speak of a life of the spirit, but only as part of a life of transformation that includes the discovery of a true body, speech, and mind. The realization of these "three mysteries" is tantamount to an identification with the Buddha. One may then speak of spirituality in such a context as a process of self-discovery, but the process is as much ritual born as it is contemplative, and as such it is defined or constrained by traditional imagery and myth in which individual preference and conscience play only a minor role.

Third, some of the radical historical shifts that have helped to define contemporary notions of spirituality – namely, secularization and modernity – have only recently begun to touch Buddhism. In the West religion has been under a constant pressure to adopt a primarily lay modality for at least 500 years. For most of Buddhist history, the tendency to laicize the religion has been only the flip side of the tendency to monachize the lay life. That is, lay religious life was often modeled on monastic life, and lay virtue followed a pattern of ascetic ideals.

However, to present a fair and nuanced picture of the historical complexities of Buddhism, some notable exceptions must be mentioned. For example, the tantric tradition, despite its most common manifestations as monastic ritual or high-court liturgy, has a number of features that may reflect its probable origins among wandering ascetics and local shamans. Its monastic forms encounter parallel or competing lay and eremitic traditions in India, Nepal, and Tibet. However, these traditions of lay or unaffiliated tantric yogis, priests, and thaumaturges vary in the extent to which they are compatible with our notion of spirituality as inner quest.

Also of note is the general tendency within Japanese Buddhism since the late 13th century toward an erosion of monastic institutions in favor of a lay priesthood. The most dramatic form, and the historical origin of this tendency, is found among the Pure Land tradition of the Shinshū denominations. Not only does their concept of priesthood parallel Western notions of the lay minister, but social and ecclesiastical practice is also connected to a concept of spirituality that is eminently modern. Here the religious quest is envisioned as an encounter between an individual conscience and a higher power, albeit a power that is sometimes conceived as solely an inner presence.

Japanese Zen Buddhism also developed a lay priesthood and in recent times has developed a stronger rhetoric of lay spirituality. However, this rhetoric has roots going back to Chinese Buddhism in the Tang dynasty and appears also in Japan during the Edo period – represented by figures such as Bankei (1622–1693) and Suzuki Shōsan (1579–1655). The Zen traditions also have a long history of a doctrine and practice of inner experience (what has been called, with a certain degree of justified skepticism, a "rhetoric of immediacy"). An especially strong emphasis on the uniqueness of an inner, individual, or private experience appears in the Sambōkyōdan, a Zen movement that has met with special success in the United States, where it exists as an almost exclusively lay movement.

Another case of a rediscovery of a long tradition of immediacy and interiority is the Insight Meditation movement (also called the Vipassanā movement). It originated in Burma in the early 20th century under various teachers of meditation – notably Ledi Sayadaw (1856–1923) and Sayagyi U Ba Khin (1889–1971) – and emphasizes individual experience through meditation and accessibility to lay practitioners. A variety of methods of meditation has been taught by various representatives of this tradition, but they tend to emphasize the practice of mindfulness (sustained awareness of the present moment, especially of bodily and mental states). This was the focus of Ledi Sayadaw's teachings and is believed by the tradition to have been the method used by the Buddha himself.

Our fourth qualification concerns the very notion of the primacy of experience. Experience, especially understood as an authoritative, nonmediated contact with sacred reality, is indeed an important concept in Buddhism. The popular assumption that individual, unmediated experience is the central goal of the practice of meditation is confirmed by many classical scriptural and scholastic texts of Buddhism. However, the tradition is well aware that this unmediated experience, if it is to occur, must be guided by or grounded in a number of preparatory practices that can hardly be called unmediated or nondiscursive. These include various conceptions of the structure of the spiritual path that dictate the proper order and hierarchy of a variety of experiences. One could mention, for example, the division of the Eightfold Path into moral behavior, wisdom, and mental concentration or the division of wisdom according to the method by which it is produced, namely, into learning, reflection, and self-cultivation.

This last point is closely connected with a fifth necessary qualification: the inner quest is almost invariably framed by life in a monastic community – or at the very least by the teachings of a monastic teacher. For most Buddhists the monastery and the monastic community, with their traditions and rules, embody the life of the spirit. What is more crucial, seldom do Buddhist question the importance of the regimented life of the monastery. Even an inspired seeker of individual awakening like Zen Master Dōgen (1200–1253) praises the value of monastic ritual, monastic vestments, and so on. It is fair to say that for the Buddhist tradition the constraints of institution and tradition are central to the quest of the spirit. In the end "the spirit" has to be reconceptualized in a way that might be at odds with modern ideas of individual freedom and autonomy or of a totally spontaneous inner life.

Finally, and as a sixth qualification, Buddhist notions of no-self (sometimes misconstrued as simple "selflessness") imply in some traditions a blurring, if not a disappearance, of the separation between self and others. Although such notions lead to edifying reflections on the unity of all living things, they also can imply that the very notion of an autonomous inner life is not only suspect but also, in fact, illusory. At least in Asia today, no-self is often taken to have social implications: no self, or loss of self, also means subjection to the community. This is perhaps the one aspect of Buddhist spirituality that is most problematic to Western observers and practitioners.

These qualifications are not only of interest in a summary review of Buddhist notions of spirituality; they suggest also some of the fault lines in this important (and otherwise worthy) aspiration of modern religiosity. One must wonder whether these qualifications do not reveal precisely the problems that we would face if we could engage in dialogue with premodern practitioners of Western spirituality.

Luis O. Gómez

See also Asceticism: Buddhist Perspectives; Buddha (Śākyamuni); Dōgen; Hagiography: Buddhist Perspectives; Holy Men/Holy Women; Buddhist Perspectives; Intercession for the Dead, Buddhist; Laicization of Spirituality: Buddhist Perspectives; Liturgy: Buddhist; Master and Pupil: Buddhist Perspectives; Meditation: Buddhist Perspectives; Mount Meru; Mountain Monasteries, Buddhist; Prayer: Buddhist Perspectives; Scholastics, Buddhist; Stūpa; Worship Space: Buddhist Perspectives

Further Reading

Cupitt, Don, *Mysticism after Modernity* (Religion and Modernity), Malden, Massachusetts: Blackwell, 1998

Gyatso, Janet, "Healing Burns with Fire: The Facilitations of Experience in Tibetan Buddhism," *Journal of the American Academy of Religion* 67:1 (1999)

Haskel, Peter, translator, *Bankei Zen: Translations from the Record of Bankei*, edited by Yoshito Hakeda, foreword by Mary Farkas, New York: Grove Press, 1984
King, Winston L., *Theravāda Meditation: The Buddhist Transformation of Yoga*, University Park: Pennsylvania State University Press, 1980
King, Winston L., *Death Was His Kōan: The Samurai-Zen of Suzuki Shōsan* (Nanzan Studies in Religion and Culture), Berkeley, California: Asian Humanities Press, 1986
Kornfield, Jack, *Living Buddhist Masters*, Santa Cruz, California: Unity Press, 1977
Sharf, Robert H., "Buddhist Modernism and the Rhetoric of Meditative Experience," *Numen* 42 (1995)
Sharf, Robert H., "Sanbōkyōdan: Zen and the Way of the New Religions," *Japanese Journal of Religious Studies* 22:3–4 (1995)
Springsted, Eric O., editor, *Spirituality and Theology: Essays in Honor of Diogenes Allen*, Louisville, Kentucky: Westminster John Knox Press, 1998
Trainor, Kevin, *Relics, Ritual, and Representation in Buddhism: Rematerializing the Sri Lankan Theravada Tradition* (Cambridge Studies in Religious Traditions, 10), Cambridge and New York: Cambridge University Press, 1997

Spirituality: Eastern Christian

Introductory Remarks: The Need for a New Approach to Eastern Christian Spirituality

Spirituality is a recent and ticklish word. Broadly speaking it seems in a Christian context usually to denote the attitudes and practices of piety and is often, although not inevitably, considered in relative isolation from theology proper. In a Western Christian setting, one may speak of spiritualities in the plural, a point to which this article will return in its conclusion. However, when such an approach is taken to the Christian East, serious problems and distortions arise. The enormously influential article written 65 years ago by Father Irenée Hausherr, "The Main Currents of Eastern Christian Spirituality," is a case in point. Hausherr's taxonomy of Eastern spirituality amounted in sum to projection onto early and Byzantine-era monastic writers of the categories to which he was accustomed from the medieval and postmedieval Counter-Reformation West: "intellective" versus "affective" mysticisms, spiritualities featuring sober obedience, or Neoplatonist ecstasies, or the peculiarly poisonous (for Hausherr) combination of the first, second, and fourth of these earlier "schools" in the 14th-century Byzantine Hesychasts. Because Hausherr's categorizations are reflected in virtually every major study or compendium of Eastern Christian spirituality to have been published since his article appeared, endless confusion and misapprehension has ensued.

The latter fact makes the assignment confronting this article daunting: the sketch of a new approach to Eastern Christian spirituality that must try to do justice at once to recent advances in scholarship and to the thrust and continuity of the Eastern tradition itself. The word "sketch" must be emphasized, for what follows can be no more than the barest outline, offered in the hope that succeeding and more extensive studies will appear in future. Just over two millennia cannot be treated otherwise in the space of a few thousand words. Saying *over* two millennia is to assert the thesis that the present article seeks to present: that Eastern Christian asceticism and monasticism – that is, Eastern spirituality – arose out of an original matrix in the pre-Christian era of Second Temple Judaism. As Ernst Käsemann remarked some decades ago, Jewish apocalyptic literature is "the mother of all Christian theology." The same holds for that theology as expressed in praxis, which is to say in spirituality.

Scripture, Asceticism, and Transfiguration in Second Temple Jewish Apocalyptic and Early Christianity

Asceticism does not feature prominently in the Hebrew books of the Old Testament, save in the temporary celibacy imposed by holy war (e.g., 2 Sam. 11:10–11), preparation for theophany (Exod. 19:15; cf. 34:28 on fasting), and, related to the latter, service in the Temple (Lev. 15:2–15) or in the fasts, tears, and sackcloth that are the tangible expressions of repentance (e.g., Jon. 3:6 ff.). However, in the so-called intertestamental, or Second Temple, era and especially in the two centuries before and after the birth of Christ, one finds testimony to traditions that would carry on both in Rabbinic literature and, in Christianity, through the New Testament period to the fourth-century emergence and self-definition of Christian monasticism as the East has known the latter ever since. The precise lines of this continuity have yet to be charted in any single study, but virtually all the raw materials are present for such a work in existing scholarly editions of primary texts and the accompanying secondary literature. Briefly the apocalypses that feature an ascent or "heavenly journey," to use the phrase of John Collins and other recent scholars of the apocalyptic genre, and that appear as early as around 200 B.C. with *1 Enoch* display certain common features, including the following: (1) a preparatory ascetic praxis involving fasting, mourning, constant prayer, often at least temporary celibacy, and prostrations; (2) the ascent to the heavenly palace or temple and therein to the throne of God; (3) initiation into the mysteries of heaven and creation; and (4) the acquisition of, or transformation into, angelic status by virtue of which (5) the visionary becomes a concelebrant of the liturgy of heaven and (6) is accorded a vision of the divine Glory in order (7) to return to earth bearing a unique authority and message concerning the things of God. To employ a phrase from later Byzantine monastic literature, the apocalyptic seer becomes an "earthly angel and heavenly man," initiate and initiator, the priest of the heavenly mysteries.

This is the original model for the sainted elder, the *geron* or starets, of Eastern Christian literature, from Athanasius of Alexandria's portrait of the "father of monks" in *The Life of Antony* to Dostoyevsky's Starets Zossima in *The Brothers Karamazov* (1879–1880). In both the fourth-century biography of Antony and in the 19th-century literary creation of Zossima, the Eastern Christian soteriological doctrine of *theosis*, deification, is fully present and, indeed, understood as incarnate. Here, in other words, is Eastern Christian doctrine and spirituality made visible, its paradigm and embodiment. Here is both the perennial theme of Eastern teaching and the key to its extraordinary continuity: the human being as called on to be transfigured, to become him- or herself the revelation of the Glory of God, the presence of Immanuel, theophany.

The Gospel of the Risen Jesus compelled a certain parting of the ways with Christianity's Jewish matrix, but it would be wrong to exaggerate the extent of that rupture. The lines of continuity and discontinuity appear perhaps most clearly in the scriptural idea of the "temple." In biblical Israel the temple is the locus of the divine presence, the *kevod YHWH*, or "Glory of God," whose fiery manifestation appeared to Moses atop Sinai (Exod. 24, 33–34) and that took up residence with Israel first in the tabernacle (Exod. 40) and then in Solomon's temple (1 Kings 8). In the apocalyptic literature just mentioned, it is the heavenly or original temple and place of God that becomes the primary focus of attention, although not necessarily with prejudice to its earthly copy. When the temple is destroyed by the Roman legions in A.D. 70, Judaism carries on, looking first of all for God's Presence (*Shekinah*) with Israel in the holy books of the Torah as in a sort of portable temple (cf. Sirach 24), second in the gathering of Israel for worship in the synagogue, and third in the person of the sage or rabbi himself. In the New Testament and nascent Christianity, there is an analogous and parallel development. The great difference is the person of the Lord Jesus, who replaces temple and Torah as the primary "place" of the divine presence. He is himself the Glory or *Shekinah* who has "tabernacled among us" (John 1:14). His divinity is manifested at once on the mountaintops of Tabor at the Transfiguration, and of Golgotha, at the Crucifixion, which become in turn the twin poles around which Eastern spirituality will revolve: suffering and splendor, humbling unto death and transfiguration, ascetic mortification and the *visio dei luminis*. Second, the worship of the assembly of the Church also becomes the temple (e.g., Eph. 2:20–22), the place of the Risen One's presence and, with Him, of the heavenly Zion (Heb. 12:18–24). Third, temple is also applied to the Christian him- or herself (1 Cor. 6:19–20), who is called at once to share in the Cross and to be "transfigured from glory to glory" (2 Cor. 3:18), to see within his or her heart the light of the Glory of God in the face of Christ (2 Cor. 4:6). To borrow from a mid-fourth-century Syrian Christian ascetic work, the *Liber Graduum*, already in the New Testament one finds the adumbration of "three churches": "the church on high," that is, heaven and the heavenly liturgy around the throne of Christ God; "the church on earth," with its clergy and sacraments; and "the little church" of the heart or soul. Yet in each "church" it is the same glorified Christ Who is made present by the action of the Spirit.

Between the New Testament era and the fourth century, pre-Nicene Christianity glorifies as heroes and exemplars of the Faith both the martyr and the ascetic, for example, in the second century *Shepherd of Hermas*, where martyrs and virgins stand, respectively, at the right and left hand of Christ enthroned. Ignatius of Antioch (d. c. 115) and Polycaryp of Smyrna (d. c. 165), together with Stephen in the Acts of the Apostles, are exemplary martyrdoms, where the martyr is transformed and becomes himself the locus of theophany, thus Stephen's face "like the face of an angel" (Acts 6:15) and his vision of the heavenly throne (7:55–56) or Ignatius' suggested and Polycarp's explicit assimilation to the Eucharistic offering and presence. The asceticovisionary continuum is especially pronounced in the second-century *Ascension of Isaiah* and *Gospel of Thomas*, with the latter providing the first literary attestation of the word "monk" (*monachos*) for the Christian ascetic, and the same basic line continues in both the second- and the third-century Apocryphal Acts of the Apostles and – albeit in strange and twisted ways – in much of the literature of Gnosticism and of early Manichaeanism as well. In all these documents motifs from pre-Christian apocalyptic literature are to the fore, and one should also take into account the fact that the older Jewish works, too, appear to have been continuously copied, read, and interpolated by Christian readers who, after the fourth century, were doubtless primarily monks. The Old Testament Pseudepigrapha, featured in the contemporary edition compiled recently by J.H. Charlesworth, would not have been preserved without this constant Christian interest, which extends well into medieval times and even beyond.

In Alexandria of the late second and third centuries, another layer is added to the Jewish-based asceticomystical tradition. This is the vast literature of pagan Greek philosophy, in particular of Platonism and Stoicism, with their attention to, and elaborate vocabulary for, charting the training of the soul and the latter's struggle with the passions. In the persons of Clement (c. 150–c. 215) and Origen (c. 185–c. 254) of Alexandria, this vocabulary enters permanently into the Greek Christian bloodstream. Clement's portrait of the "Christian Gnostic" and Origen's of the perfected teacher are at once responses to the heretical Gnosticism that flourished in Alexandria and to the ancient traditions of apocalyptic ascent and vision, which Origen in particular is anxious to internalize and frame within the vocabulary of philosophical discourse. The latter's treatise *On Prayer* is especially important and influential in this regard, relocating as it does the ascent, transformation, and *visio dei gloriae* of apocalyptic literature to the "inner man" of the soul.

The Fourth Century: Emergence of the Imperial Church, the Ecumenical Councils, and Monasticism

The conversion of the Emperor Constantine (306–337) to Christianity is the first great watershed of the fourth century. The Ecumenical or, more accurately, Imperial Councils of Nicaea (325) and Constantinople (381) are a direct result. The Creed that emerges from the councils seals Christianity's commitment to the philosophical lexicon of Greek antiquity with its consecration of the term *homoousios* (consubstantial) in application to the Second Person of the Trinity, a development that, in its turn, stimulates the furthering of Clement's and Origen's efforts to articulate the inner life of the Christian in accordance with the same vocabulary. This project is clearly at work in the two most

Secul Women's Monastery, Romania, early 17th century. Outdoor altar and cross.
Photo courtesy of Mary Schaefer

important episcopal spokesmen for and to the nascent monastic movement: Athanasius of Alexandria (c. 296–373) and Basil of Caesarea in Cappadocia (c. 330–379). The former's *Life of Antony* and the latter's Longer and Shorter Rules (collections of his correspondence with ascetic communities in Cappadocia) exercise great influence in their overall efforts to keep the monks within the communion of the imperial church, focused on community and mutual charity, observant of the Church's common worship, and subordinate to the bishop's authority. Basil had in fact little use for solitaries of Antony's type, but in this regard his judgment would not prevail. The hermit has remained a constant presence in Eastern spirituality, rare but never absent, and often celebrated.

The endeavors of these two Church fathers also reflected Christianity's new place in the Roman Empire. In parallel to the secular magistrates, the bishops, too, were accorded local authority and backed by imperial power. The, as it were, "ingathering" of the ascetics under the episcopal pallium is part of this process. Likewise, the bishop's – and, by extension, the village priest's – altar becomes the focal point of the city or town. Here, and especially in the capital, is the birthplace of the imperial liturgy, embellished with the etiquette of the court and all the wealth and sophistication of the empire's resources, which would later achieve definitive form in the rite of "the Great Church of Christ," *Hagia Sophia*, in Constantinople. Perhaps no polarity in Eastern Christian spirituality is more striking and more apparently contradictory than that of the hermit's stark poverty and simplicity on the one hand and the gorgeous splendor of the late Byzantine liturgy, dripping gold and conducted in the presence of mosaics and murals fabricated with all the expense and subtlety available to a millennial civilization on the other. Yet neither the hermit nor the episcopal celebrant would at all accept this as a paradox, let alone a contradiction. The former would – and does – understand the magnificence of the earthly church's liturgy as a mirror both of the angels' worship in the heavenly temple before the throne of God and of the divine presence within the purified heart. The bishop and, perhaps even more so, the devout laity see in their turn the Kingdom of God reflected equally in the glory of the Church's common worship and in the hallowed ascetic elder, the *geron* or starets, bright and fragrant already with presence of the world to come.

The first conscious coordination between the liturgies of heaven, earth, and the heart can be found in the ascetic literature of, especially, fourth-century Christian Syria and Mesopotamia. Three writers are of particular note here: Ephrem Syrus (c. 306–373) and the anonymous authors of the *Book of Steps* (*Liber Graduum*) in the mid-fourth century and of the *Macarian Homilies* (c. 360–390). The first two wrote exclusively in Syriac, so it is the third who was destined to have a profound influence on the Greek-speaking, Christian tradition. The hierarchies of Dionysius the Pseudo-Areopagite, just over a century later, are based in great part on the linkage that the Macarian homilist wishes to establish between the liturgies of heaven, earth, and the soul. The Church's worship becomes for "Macarius" the model or paradigm of the inner life, its shaping icon, given us by God in Christ in order to conform the soul to the "shape" of heaven and enable it thus to encounter within itself the light of glory and presence of the angels. The *Homilies* effect a remarkable and powerful synthesis between the Alexandrian spiritualism of an Origen and the Jewish-based asceticomystical traditions rooted in apocalyptic literature, which were especially prominent in the early Syrian Church. Overall, however, "Macarius" is at one with Origen's effort to focus on the "inner man" in order to discover the divine Presence within the soul. This is in turn linked at once with baptismal grace, planted by the Holy Spirit within the soul as a kind of seed and with fidelity to the Trinitarian teaching of Nicaea-Constantinople – a synthesis that makes the author of the *Homilies* one of the two most important monastic writers of the fourth century and thereafter.

The other one is Evagrius Ponticus (346–399), who spent his last 12 years in the hermitages of the Cells, between Nitrea and Scete in the Egyptian desert. Unlike "Macarius," who was much involved in the formation and direction of monastic communities in Roman Mesopotamia, Evagrius was a hermit, although himself continually busy with monastic correspondence. In the course of replying to questions concerning the life of solitude and even occasionally of life in monastic community, he produced a significant and vastly influential body of work that included *scholia* on several books of the scriptures, the treatise *On Prayer*, a trilogy of works, the *Praktikos*, *To the Monks*, and the *Gnostic Chapters*, together with more than 60 extant letters. His favored mode of composition featured "centuries," groups of usually 100 or more short sayings or aphorisms, a style adapted from biblical Wisdom literature and Cynic diatribe and intended to be pondered slowly in the quiet of a hermitage. By means of these collections of sayings, he in fact elaborated a system, a precise map of spiritual progress, beginning with the struggle against the passions and cultivation of the virtues in order to arrive at dispassion, *apatheia*, a term of Stoic provenance that at Evagrius' hands signifies less a negative passionlessness than it does the freedom to begin to love as God loves, selflessly and without sentimentality, and so to assist in the work of divine Providence. This is the stage covered by the *Praktikos*. The second level, set out in *To the Monks*, is the knowledge of created being, seen now truly for the first time through the liberation of *apatheia* and cooperation with the saving love of God. Third and last, the subject of *On Prayer* and the *Gnostic Centuries* is what he calls "theology," the vision of God or, in his own language, the intellect's reception as vessel and throne of the "light of the Holy Trinity." Here he employs especially an interiorized reading of the theophany of Exodus 24. It is the sanctified intellect that is called to become the inner "mountain of the knowledge of God," the temple and altar of the Trinity, Sinai within.

Evagrius thus sounds the exact same note of the interiorization of the journey to heaven as does the Macarian homilist, especially in the first of the latter's *Fifty Spiritual Homilies*, where, instead of Sinai, it is Ezekiel's vision of the *merkavah*, or chariot throne of God, that is read as a type of the Christian soul. Both men are substantially identical in the way they understand the goal of Christian life and the role of prayer and ascesis and often recall (Evagrius most deliberately) Origen before them. Both are faithful adherents of Nicene Trinitarianism and faithful at the same time to the ancient currents of transformation going back to apocalyptic literature. Both, thirdly, represent at once in their writings and in their own persons, exemplars of the ascetic holy man, the spiritual father or illumined elder, the "man of God."

The latter is a figure perhaps best known, aside from the *Life of Antony*, in the collections of sayings coming primarily from the monastic center of Scete in fourth- and fifth-century Egypt: the *Verba seniorum* or *Apophthegmata patrum*. The earliest of these collections is the one assembled by Evagrius himself at the end of the *Praktikos*, whereas the final forms, the "alphabetical" and "systematic," or "topical," collections, were edited in their present form sometime in early sixth-century Palestine, perhaps at Gaza. These sayings comprise words of advice addressed to disciples and inquirers and handed down by oral tradition, brief accounts of the practices of the elders, and occasional short narratives. All are intended to edify and instruct. The basic message, if one may so summarize collections that were never intended as continuous or systematic presentations, is an emphasis on sobriety, manual labor, meditation on the Scriptures, obedience to one's elder, and warnings directed especially against anger, judging others, and too ready a disposition to trust in one's own visions. The emphasis on transformation is thus muted, treated cautiously, although it is never absent. The place, Scete, appears thereafter (and even within these sayings) often as a kind of ideal, and its pattern of monastic life, rather on the basis of village life with the monks living in separate cells or huts and gathering once a week in a central church, reappears persistently in Eastern monasticism: in the sixth-century *lavras* of Palestine, in the Transvolgan forests of Nilus of Sora in 15th-century Russia and Optina in the 19th, in the *sketes* of Mount Athos from the 16th century to the present, and in the woods of Romanian Moldavia in the 17th and 18th centuries, to cite a few notable examples. Likewise the origins of Scete in a group of ascetics choosing to live in the vicinity of the Macarius the Egyptian (c. 300–c. 390) (Evagrius' spiritual father), who had been the first to settle that dreadful desert in the 330s, became itself a pattern for the origin of monastic communities. This is precisely what would occur with Sabas (439–532) in Palestine, Benedict in Italy, Sergius of Radonezh in 14th-century Muscovy, Païsy Velichkovsky in late 18th-century Moldavia, and indeed in the beginnings of several communities in the contemporary, 20th-century revival of monasticism on Mount Athos: a sainted ascetic lives alone, disciples come to him, the elder sees the need for a common rule of life, and, more often than not, a common-life monastery, cenobium, emerges at the end of the process.

Another example of this pattern is the founder of cenobitic monasticism himself, Pachomius of Upper Egypt (c. 290–346), in the 320s and 330s. The earlier scholarly portrait of him as a kind of ascetic drill sergeant, rigidly subordinating his monks to the exigencies of his rule, has been shown by the recent work of Phillip Rousseau and others to be quite false. He was instead an elder, *geron*, compelled by the increase of disciples wishing to live with him and under his direction to provide for them. The solution he arrived at, which later tradition ascribed to direct heavenly inspiration, was the cenobium. Yet, and this is what deserves underlining, the latter was first of all never intended to take precedence over the inner life of the monks but rather was designed precisely to facilitate that growth while providing a certain security for the necessities of life: food, shelter, clothing, and the monks' regular "feeding" on Scriptures and common worship. Second, the rule of Pachomius' establishments was always fundamentally the example of his own life and practice. His presence as exemplar, guide, and illumined father shines through all the works of the Pachomian Koinonia. Third, it was he and, after his death, his presence as continuing in his successors that drew recruits to his monasteries. They came, to borrow a phrase from Bishop Kallistos Ware, "less for the abbey than for the abba," in whom the presence of the risen Christ and gift of the Spirit were sought and perceived.

It is this last element that is largely missing from St. Basil's Rules and yet that time and again is repeated in Eastern monasticism. Any account of the latter that credits Basil exclusively for the rule of later Byzantine establishments is thus fundamentally incomplete. The great Cappadocian Father did contribute essential elements to the later tradition of the common life in his emphasis on charity, community, and especially the latter as rooted in the picture of the earliest Church in the Acts of the Apostles, and these elements would reappear consistently in the later rules of Mar Saba in Palestine and the Studion in Constantinople and thence of the Great Lavra on Mount Athos and subsequently of the first monasteries in Kievan Rus'. However, one thing that he could not eliminate, if indeed it ever occurred to him to try, was the charismatic office of the inspired elder, with its ancestry in the transfigured seer of the ancient apocalypses. The latter has never disappeared from Eastern monastic spirituality but instead has reappeared, time and again, with singular force in the creation of new foundations or in the renewal of existing communities. To lose sight of this phenomenon is to overlook perhaps the single most fundamental thread tying together and in fact comprising the unity and continuity of Eastern spirituality.

From the Fifth Century to the Present: Icons and the Jesus Prayer

By the end of the fourth century, the main lines of Eastern Christian spirituality and theology are set in the forms they possess to the present day. These include the following: (1) the trinitarian confession of the Nicene-Constantinopolitan Creed; (2) deification offered through the Word of God become man; (3) this participation in divinity as embodied in every generation by the saints, "the men (and women) of God"; (4) the interiorization of the heavenly journey and transformation of apocalyptic; and (5) the mutual reflection of the deified soul and the Church's liturgy, with both of them mirroring the liturgy of heaven and with the earthly worship understood as mediating heaven to the "inner man" and thus as forming the latter for the inhabitation of Christ in the Spirit. The whole is marked by the continual interplay and mutual affirmation of the realms of dogmatic theology, of sacraments and liturgy, and of the asceticomystical tradition. All three are seen as expressions of a single whole, which is again summed up in the person of the saint who reflects Christ and is made possible by Christ.

Likewise by the end of the fourth century, the main expression of this spirituality, namely, monasticism, has taken on the forms – hermit, monastic village, and cenobium – that it would use to the present. Evagrius' precisions and vocabulary, together with the rich scriptural imagery of the *Macarian Homilies*, enter permanently into and shape the self-expression of Eastern monasticism. In the centuries that follow to the end of Byzantium in 1453, these lines continue unbroken. They are lent further expression and a certain sharpening in their lexicon by the Christological controversies of the fifth through seventh centuries – for example, in a Maximus Confessor (c. 580–662), in the more developed articulation between the liturgies of heaven, earth, and the soul in a Dionysius the Pseudo-Areopagite (c. 500), in the stages of the Christian life in grace that one finds in John Climacus' *Ladder of Divine Ascent* (seventh century), or in the fiery and highly personal witness to the Gospel of personal transfiguration carried on by Symeon the New Theologian (949–1022) – but in each case these writers are lending their particular voices to a single common stream that, as the case of Isaac the Syrian (d. c. 700) indicates, was shared across the apparent divide of formal schisms over Christology.

However, two later controversies are of interest, as they were waged mainly by Byzantine monks. The first was the conflict over imperial iconoclasm (730–843), and the second was the Hesychast controversy of later Byzantium (1330s to 1340s). The icon in design, theory, and practice is again a kind of distillate expression of the three realms – dogma, liturgy, and spirituality – noted previously. As the monks John of Damascus (c. 655–c. 750) and Theodore of Stoudios (759–826) pointed out in their treatises in defense of the sacred images, the icon is first of all a testimony to the truth of the Incarnation and of the change that the latter has effected in the relations between God and humanity. If in the Decalogue and especially in Deuteronomy 4:12 ("You saw no form in the fire") God is the invisible One, then, says John, in the Incarnation He has put on "the form of a servant" (Phil. 2:7) and has done so permanently. He has thus become visible and therefore can be depicted. It is, adds Theodore in an echo of the vocabulary of the Christological controversies, the very Person (*hypostasis*) of the Incarnate Word whom one encounters in His icon. Not to depict Him in images, both men argue, is in fact to deny the Incarnation itself, as it is the latter that has made matter, the material creation, a vehicle of the divine presence. This is, John adds, the very basis of the Church's life in the sacraments.

The last remark highlights the second and liturgical aspect of the icon, which finds its home first and foremost in the Church's public worship and then, as the extension of that worship, in the home, monastic cell, workshop, or wayside shrine. It serves as a constant reminder of and window into heaven, carrying within itself, precisely as a sacramental object, the presence of the heavenly liturgy and the intercession of the saints around the throne of Christ. With the note of the saints, the "friends of God" in John of Damascus' phrase, one arrives at the third aspect of the icon: its distinctive artistic form as intended exactly to underline the note of transfiguration that is at the heart of Eastern spirituality. The reversed perspective, elongation of the figure depicted, lack of *chiaroscuro*, and diminishment of its sensory organs – nose, mouth, and ears – save for the eyes, which are enlarged as gazing on God, together with the golden background, all come out of the spiritual tradition. The light in particular no longer falls *on* the figure from outside but rather streams out *from within* it and surrounds it. This is the light or glory of the divine presence in which the saint stands and that he or she also carries within as indwelling grace – thus the icon as depiction at once of the eschatological transformation of soul and body and of the mystical experience available in the present life.

It was exactly over the availability of that experience, the *visio dei luminis*, that the last great debate of the Byzantine era was fought, the Hesychast controversy of the 1330s and 1340s, and where monks were once again at the center of things. The claim of certain hermits on Mount Athos that by virtue of their constant repetition of the Jesus Prayer ("Lord Jesus Christ, have mercy on me a sinner") and of the visitation of grace they had been vouchsafed a vision of the "uncreated light" of the Transfiguration on Mount Tabor led one Byzantine court theologian,

Barlaam the Calabrian, to question both the monks' sanity and their orthodoxy. The reply to Barlaam on behalf of the "holy Hesychasts" was taken up by Gregory Palamas (1296–1359), whose argument constituted a kind of extended assembly and summary of the lines of tradition sketched in this article. Palamas insisted on the reality of deification as an immanent and not merely eschatological possibility. Likewise the divine light is rooted in the Old Testament tradition of the Glory of God and now, through the advent and gift of the Incarnate Word, is an inner presence and experience to which the entire literature of Christianity, beginning with the New Testament itself and continuing unbroken especially in the monastic tradition, bears constant witness. The Orthodox Church agreed with Gregory's analysis and declared his teaching that of the universal Church at councils held in Constantinople in 1341, 1347, and 1351.

The Jesus Prayer itself constitutes an example of this continuity. It is first of all rooted in the ancient theology of God's "Name" and "Glory" originating in the Old Testament and applied to Christ in the New (cf. Phil, 2:6–11, John 17). The repetition of the Name as means of access to the divine Glory is, second, witnessed to in early apocalyptic literature (e.g., *Apocalypse of Abraham* 17–18), and might conceivably lie behind St. Paul's exhortation "to pray without ceasing" (1 Thess. 5:17). Third, although the breathing exercises associated with the prayer have usually been ascribed to Sufi influence or compared with the Hindu mantra, and although it is true that explicit directions of this sort appear for the first time only in later, 13th-century texts, one can find an earlier parallel in the exercises of Jewish *merkavah* mystics in late antiquity, and one can point as well to Diadochus of Photiki's fifth-century recommendation to join one's breath to the name of Jesus and to John Climacus' similar advice in the seventh century. In short the origins of the practice as well as of the theology of the Jesus Prayer might well be sited in the same traditions of apocalyptic literature as underlie the rest of Eastern spirituality. In any case it is a fact that the cultivation of this prayer has remained a key to the practice and understanding of that spirituality to the present day. Like the icon the Jesus prayer is itself a kind of distillate of the Eastern tradition. Everything about the latter is in a sense contained within it. This is evident in the understanding of the prayer's importance that is on prominent display in subsequent Church history, from the spread of Byzantine Hesychasm throughout the Orthodox world – for example, to Bulgaria in Euthymius of Trnovo and to Russia in perhaps the person of Sergius of Radonezh (c. 1314–1392) and certainly of Nilus of Sora (1433–1508) – and its continued reappearance in the renewals of monastic spirituality led in the 18th century by Païsy Velichkovsky (1722–1794) among the Slavs and Romanians and by Nicodemus of the Holy Mountain (c. 1749–1809) among the Greeks or in the renewals on Mount Athos, as well as in Romania and Serbia, that are under way in those places today.

An Anecdote and Concluding Remarks

Some 50 years ago a successful young pharmacist in Cairo sold off his business, gave the proceeds to the poor, and retired to a cave in the desert. There three books in particular informed his prayer and meditation: the Scriptures in Arabic translation, the Kadloubovsky-Palmer translation of *Early Fathers from the Philokalia*, and Wensinck's English rendering of Isaac the Syrian's *Spiritual Discourses*. Young men heard of the hermit and came to live as his disciples in the neighborhood of his cave. A few years later the group moved to the largely abandoned monastery of St. Macarius in Scete, where they continue to be the most important moving force in the contemporary renewal of Coptic monasticism.

This story of Fr. Matthew the Poor has its precise analogues in some of the accounts of the contemporary Athonite renewal, for example, about the figure of Joseph the Hesychast (d. 1959) or the current abbot of the monastery of Simonos Petras, Fr. Aemilianos. What is peculiarly striking and illustrative of the essential unity of Eastern Christian spirituality in the story of Fr. Matthew is the fact that he, a "Monophysite" Copt, found his primary inspiration in the writings of both ancient Chalcedonian monks (the *Philokalia*) and of a seventh-century "Nestorian" saint (Isaac). None of these three great divisions of Eastern Christianity has been in communion with each other for more than 1,500 years, yet each – as this anecdote makes clear – continues to speak the same spiritual "language." From Murmansk to Addis Ababa and from the Ionian islands to the Aleutians, across the gap of centuries covering huge cultural and demographic changes, Eastern Christianity remains fundamentally one in spirit, if not always consciously so. This essential unity has survived the schisms of the fifth-century Christological controversies; the rise of Islam; the slaughters of Genghis Khan, Tamerlane, the last Ottomans, and Bolshevik rule; and the overwhelming recent dominance of Western European culture and institutions. It is, in sum, the single most powerful witness to the thesis of this article, which is that there are not different "schools" or "currents" of spirituality in Eastern Christianity but rather a single great stream deriving from Christianity's origins and surviving to the present among the monks to whom Eastern believers continue to look as exemplars of their faith.

When one then turns to look at Western Christianity, the difference is unmistakable. Whereas Western Europe (and its later extensions in the Americas) offers a history that, after the conversion of the Norsemen, presents a single, relatively smooth, and increasingly triumphant growth into world dominance, in contrast to the nearly uninterrupted dislocations and catastrophes of the Christian East, the inward story is very different. From especially the High Middle Ages through the late medieval to the Reformation, Counter-Reformation, Enlightenment, Romantic, Victorian, and modern periods, one finds a never ending efflorescence of different spiritualities, from the growth of the medieval orders to the ever more manifold expressions of Protestantism. One may, of course, view this difference positively, instanced in the dynamism of Western Christian creativity and its lively embrace of change and progress against Eastern intellectual decrepitude and stagnation, or negatively, instanced in Eastern fidelity to Christian origins in opposition to a West that has lost its way. Both approaches certainly had their advocates in the

20th century. What one cannot overlook and should not obscure with distorting projections of one's own world onto the other, as in the involuntary case of Hausherr, is the fact of this difference and its importance. Whether for purposes of simple understanding, of ecumenical rapprochement, or of preparing "deep background" for the analysis of contemporary politics and culture, there can be no genuine perception without some appreciation of this contrast.

HIEROMONK ALEXANDER GOLITZIN

See also Liturgy: Eastern Christian; Orthodox Monasticism; Seasons, Liturgical: Eastern Christian; Theodore of Stoudios, St.; Theology, Eastern Christian; Vision, Mystical: Eastern Christian; Visual Arts, Eastern Christian: Painting

Further Reading

1. Introduction: Some Standard Works on Eastern Spirituality

Bouyer, Louis, *The Spirituality of the New Testament and the Fathers* (A History of Christian Spirituality, volume 1), London: Burns and Oates, 1960; New York: Seabury Press, 1963; reprint, London: Burns and Oates, and New York: Seabury Press, 1982

Bouyer, Louis, *Orthodox Spirituality and Protestant and Anglican Spirituality* (A History of Christian Spirituality, volume 3), translated by M.P. Ryan, London: Burns and Oates, and New York: Seabury Press, 1969; reprint, 1982

Clément, Olivier, *The Roots of Christian Mysticism: Text and Commentary*, translated by T. Berkeley, London: New City Press, 1993; 2nd edition, 1994; New York: New City Press, 1995

Dupré, Louis, Don E. Saliers, and John Meyendorff, editors, *Christian Spirituality: Post-Reformation and Modern* (World Spirituality, volume 18), New York: Crossroad, 1989

Gillet, Lev (A Monk of the Eastern Church), *Orthodox Spirituality: An Outline of the Orthodox Ascetical and Mystical Tradition*, London: SPCK, and New York: Macmillan, 1945; 2nd edition, London: SPCK, and Crestwood, New York: St. Vladimir's Seminary Press, 1978

Hausherr, Irenée, "Les grands courants de la spiritualité orientale," *Orientalia christiana periodica* 1 (1935)

McGinn, Bernard, John Meyendorff, and Jean Leclercq, editors, *Christian Spirituality: Origins to the Twelfth Century* (World Spirituality, volume 16), New York: Crossroad, 1985; London: Routledge and Kegan Paul, 1986

McGinn, Bernard, Jill Raitt, and John Meyendorff, editors, *Christian Spirituality: High Middle Ages and Reformation* (World Spirituality, volume 17), New York: Crossroad, and London: Routledge and Kegan Paul, 1987

Prokurat, Michael, Alexander Golitzin, and Michael Peterson, *Historical Dictionary of the Orthodox Church* (Religion, Philosophies, and Movements, number 9), Lanham, Maryland: Scarecrow Press, 1996

Sofronii, Archimandrite, *On Prayer*, translated by Rosemary Edmounds, Essex: Stavropegic Monastery of St. John the Baptist, 1996; Crestwood, New York: St. Vladimir's Seminary, 1998

Spidlík, Tomás, *The Spirituality of the Christian East: A Systematic Handbook* (Cistercian Studies Series, number 79), translated by Anthony Gythiel, Kalamazoo, Michigan: Cistercian Publications, 1986

Vlachos, Hierotheos, *Orthodox Psychotherapy: The Science of the Fathers*, translated by Esther Williams, Levadeia, Greece: Birth of the Theotokos Monastery, 1994

Ware, Kallistos, *The Orthodox Way*, London: Mowbray, and Crestwood, New York: St. Vladimir's Orthodox Theological Seminary, 1979; revised edition, Crestwood, New York: St. Vladimir's Seminary Press, 1995

2. Scripture, Asceticism/Mysticism, Jewish Apocalyptic, and Early Christianity

Bible with Deuterocanonical Books

Cameron, Ron, and Arthur J. Dewey, editors, *The Cologne Mani Codex (P. Colon. inv. nr. 4780): Concerning the Origin of His Body* (Texts and Translations, 15), Missoula, Montana: Scholars Press, 1979

Chadwick, Henry, and John Ernest Leonard Oulton, translators and editors, *Alexandrian Christianity: Selected Translations of Clement and Origen with Introduction and Notes* (Library of Christian Classics, volume 2), London: SCM Press, and Philadelphia: Westminster Press, 1954

Charlesworth, James H., *The Old Testament Pseudepigrapha*, 2 vols., Garden City, New York: Doubleday, and London: Darton, Longman and Todd, 1983–1985

Colson, F.H., and G.H. Whitaker, translators, *Philo, with an English Translation* (Loeb Classical Library), 10 vols., London: Heinemann, and New York: Putnam, 1929–1962

Lightfoot, Joseph Barber, editor, *The Apostolic Fathers* (Ancient and Modern Library of Theological Literature), 2 vols., London: Griffith, Farran, Okeden and Welsh, 1881–1989; New York: Macmillan, 1889–1990

Origen, *Origen* (Classics of Western Spirituality), translated and introduced by Rowan A. Greer, New York: Paulist Press, 1979

Robinson, James M., editor, *The Nag Hammadi Library in English*, New York: Harper and Row, 1977; 4th revised edition, New York: Brill, 1996

Schneemelcher, Wilhelm, editor, *New Testament Apocrypha*, translated by R. McL. Wilson, 2 vols., Philadelphia: Westminster Press, and London: SCM Press, 1963–1966; revised edition, Cambridge: Clarke, and Louisville, Kentucky: Westminster/Knox Press, 1991–1992

Vermes, Geza, translator and editor, *The Dead Sea Scrolls in English*, Baltimore, Maryland: Penguin Books, 1962; Harmondsworth, Middlesex: Penguin Books, 1968; 4th edition, Sheffield, South Yorkshire: Sheffield Academic Press, and Baltimore, Maryland: Penguin Books, 1995

Wimbush, Vincent L., editor, *Ascetic Behavior in Greco-Roman Antiquity: A Sourcebook* (Studies in Antiquity and Christianity), Minneapolis, Minnesota: Fortress Press, 1990

3. The Fourth Century: The Imperial Church and the Emergence of Monasticism

Ammonas, *The Letters of Ammonas: Successor of Saint Anthony* (Fairacres Publication), translated by Derwas Chitty, revised and introduced by Sebastian Brock, Oxford: SLG Press, 1979

Antony, *The Letters of St. Antony: Monasticism and the Making of a Saint* (Studies in Antiquity and Christianity), edited and translated by Samuel Rubensen, Minneapolis, Minnesota: Fortress Press, 1995
Aphrahat, "The Liber Graduum," in *The Syriac Fathers on Prayer and the Spiritual Life* (Cistercian Studies Series, number 101), translated by Sebastian Brock, Kalamazoo, Michigan: Cistercian Publications, 1987
Athanasius, Saint, Patriarch of Alexandria, *The Life of Antony and the Letter to Marcellinus* (Classics of Western Spirituality), translated by Robert C. Gregg, New York: Paulist Press, and London: SPCK, 1980
Basil, Saint, Bishop of Caesarea, *Ascetical Works* (Fathers of the Church, volume 9), translated by Monica Wagner, Washington, D.C.: Catholic University of America Press, 1950
Basil, Saint, Bishop of Caesarea, *On the Holy Spirit*, translated by David Anderson, Crestwood, New York: St. Vladimir's Seminary Press, 1980
Ephraem, Syrus, Saint, *Ephrem the Syrian: Hymns* (Classics of Western Spirituality), translated by Kathleen McVey, New York: Paulist Press, 1989
Ephraem, Syrus, Saint, *Hymns on Paradise*, translated by Sebastian Brock, Crestwood, New York: St. Vladimir's Seminary Press, 1990
Evagrius Ponticus, *Les six centuries des "Kephalaia Gnostica"* (Patrologia Orientalis, 28), edited and translated by Antoine Guillaumont, Paris: Firmin-Didot, 1958
Evagrius Ponticus, *The Praktikos: Chapters on Prayer* (Cistercian Studies Series, number 4), edited by John E. Bamberger, Spencer, Massachusetts: Cistercian Publications, 1970
Gregory of Nyssa, Saint, *From Glory to Glory: Texts from Gregory of Nyssa's Mystical Writings*, edited by Jean Daniélou, translated by Herbert Musurillo, New York: Scribner, 1961; London: Murray, 1962
The Lives of the Desert Fathers (Cistercian Studies Series, number 34), translated by Norman Russell, Kalamazoo, Michigan: Cistercian Publications, and London: Mowbray, 1980
Pachomius, *Pachomian Koinonia* (Cistercian Studies Series, 45–47), edited and translated by Armand Veilleux, 3 vols., Kalamazoo, Michigan: Cistercian Publications, 1980–1982
Palladius, Bishop of Aspuna, *Palladius: The Lausiac History* (Ancient Christian Writers, 34), translated by Robert T. Meyer, New York: Paulist Press, 1964
Pseudo-Macarius, *The Fifty Spiritual Homilies; and, the Great Letter* (Classics of Western Spirituality), translated by George Maloney, New York: Paulist Press, 1992
Theodoret, Bishop of Cyrrhus, *A History of the Monks of Syria* (Cistercian Studies Series, number 88), translated by R.M. Price, Kalamazoo, Michigan: Cistercian Publications, 1985
Ward, Benedicta, *The Sayings of the Desert Fathers: The Alphabetical Collection* (Cistercian Studies Series, number 59), London: Mowbray, and Kalamazoo, Michigan: Cistercian Publications, 1975; revised edition, London: Mowbray, 1981; Kalamazoo, Michigan: Cistercian Publications, 1984
Yarnold, Edward, translator and editor, *The Awe-Inspiring Rites of Initiation: Baptismal Homilies of the Fourth Century*, Slough, Berkshire: St. Paul, 1972

4. Fifth Century to the Present: Icons, Hesychasts, and the Jesus Prayer

Byzantine Era

Cabasilas, Nicolaus, *A Commentary on the Divine Liturgy*, translated by J.M. Hussey and P.A. McNulty, London: SPCK, 1960; Crestwood, New York: St. Vladimir's Seminary Press, 1977
Cabasilas, Nicolaus, *The Life in Christ*, translated by Carmino J. deCatanzaro, Crestwood, New York: St. Vladimir's Seminary Press, 1974; London: Janus, 1995
Climacus, John, Saint, *The Ladder of Divine Ascent* (Classics of the Contemplative Life), translated by Colm Liubheid and Norman Russell, introduced by Kallistos Ware, London: Faber and Faber, and New York: Harper, 1959; revised edition, Boston: Holy Transfiguration Monastery, 1978
Cyril of Scythopolis, *Lives of the Monks of Palestine* (Cistercian Studies Series, number 114), translated by R.M. Price, annotated by John Binns, Kalamazoo, Michigan: Cistercian Publications, 1991
Dorotheos, Archimandrite of Gaza, *Dorotheos of Gaza: Discourses and Sayings* (Cistercian Studies Series), translated by Eric P. Wheeler, Kalamazoo, Michigan: Cistercian Publications, 1977
Germanus I, Saint, Patriarch of Constantinople, *On the Divine Liturgy*, translated and introduced by Paul Meyendorff, Crestwood, New York: St. Vladimir's Seminary Press, 1984
Gregory, Sinaites, Saint, *Saint Gregory the Sinaite: Discourse on the Transfiguration*, edited, translated, and introduced by David Balfour, Athens, 1982; San Bernardino, California: Borgo Press, 1985
Holy Women of the Syrian Orient (The Transformation of the Classical Heritage, 13), translated and introduced by Susan A. Harvey and Sebastian P. Brock, Berkeley: University of California Press, 1987; updated edition, 1998
Isaac, Bishop of Nineveh, *The Ascetical Homilies of Saint Isaac the Syrian*, translated and introduced by Dana Miller, Boston: Holy Transfiguration Monastery, 1984
Jacob of Serug, *On the Mother of God*, translated by Mary Hansbury, Crestwood, New York: St. Vladimir's Seminary Press, 1998
John of Damascus, Saint, *On the Divine Images: Three Apologies against Those Who Attack the Divine Images*, translated by David Anderson, Crestwood, New York: St. Vladimir's Seminary Press, 1980; 2nd edition, 1994
Lang, David Marshall, editor and translator, *Lives and Legends of the Georgian Saints* (Ethical and Religious Classics of East and West, number 15), London: Allen and Unwin, and New York: Macmillan, 1956; 2nd edition, London: Mowbray, and Crestwood, New York: St. Vladimir's Seminary Press, 1976
Maximus, Confessor, Saint, *Selected Writings* (Classics of Western Spirituality), translated with notes by George C. Berthold, New York: Paulist Press, 1985
Maximus, Confessor, Saint, *Maximus the Confessor* (Early Church Fathers), translated and introduced by Andrew Louth, London and New York: Routledge, 1996
Moschus, John, *The Spiritual Meadow* (Cistercian Studies Series, number 139), translated by John Wortley, Kalamazoo, Michigan: Cistercian Publications, 1992

Palamas, Gregory, Saint, *The Triads* (Classics of Western Spirituality), selected with notes and introduction by John Meyendorff, translated by Nicholas Gendle, New York: Paulist Press, and London: SPCK, 1983
Palamas, Gregory, Saint, *The One Hundred and Fifty Chapters* (Studies and Texts, 83), edited, translated, and introduced by Robert E. Sinkiewicz, Toronto: Pontifical Institute of Mediaeval Studies, 1988
Paul, Bishop of Monemvasia, *The Spiritually Beneficial Tales of Paul, Bishop of Monembasia and of Other Authors* (Cistercian Studies Series, number 159), translated with notes and introduction by John Wortley, Kalamazoo, Michigan: Cistercian Publications, 1996
Saints Barsanuphius and John: Questions and Answers, edited and translated by Derwas Chitty, Blanco, Texas: New Sarov Press, 1966
Simeon Stylites, *The Lives of Simeon Stylites* (Cistercian Studies Series, number 112), translated and introduced by Robert Doran, Kalamazoo, Michigan: Cistercian Publications, 1992
Stéthatos, Nicétas, *Vie de Syméon le Nouveau Théologien (949–1022): Un grand mystique Byzantin* (Orientalia Christiana, number 45), edited, translated, and introduced by Irénée Hausherr, Rome: Pont. institutum orientalium studiorum, 1928
Symeon, Archbishop of Thessalonike, *Treatise on Prayer: An Explanation of the Services Conducted in the Orthodox Church* (Archbishop Lakovos Library of Ecclesiastical and Historical Sources, number 9), translated by Harry Simmons, Brookline, Massachusetts: Hellenic College Press, 1984
Symeon, the New Theologian, Saint, *On the Mystical Life: The Ethical Discourses*, 3 vols., translated by Alexander Golitzin, Crestwood, New York: St. Vladimir's Seminary Press, 1995–1997
Theodore of Stoudios, Saint, *On the Holy Icons*, translated by Catharine Roth, Crestwood, New York: St. Vladimir's Seminary Press, 1981
Theoleptos, Metropolitan of Philadelphia, *The Life and Letters of Theoleptos of Philadelphia* (Archbishop Lakovos Library of Ecclesiastical and Historical Sources, number 20), translated and introduced by Angela C. Hero, Brookline, Massachusetts: Hellenic College Press, 1994

Some 18th- and 19th-Century Sources

Holy Women of Russia: The Lives of Five Orthodox Women Offer Spiritual Guidance for Today, translated by Brenda Meehan-Waters, San Francisco: HarperSanFrancisco, 1993
John of Kronstadt, Saint, *Spiritual Counsels of Father John of Kronstadt: Select Passages from "My Life in Christ,"* selected and translated by W. Jardine Grisbrooke, Cambridge: Clarke, 1966; Crestwood, New York: St. Vladimir's Seminary Press, 1981
Nicodemus the Hagiorite, Saint, *A Handbook of Spiritual Counsel* (Classics of Western Spirituality), translated by Peter Chamberas, introduced by George Bebis, New York: Paulist Press, 1989
Païsy Velichkovsky, *Blessed Paisius Velichkovsky*, volume 1: *The Life and Ascetic Labors of Our Father, Elder Paisius, Archimandrite of the Holy Moldavian Monasteries of Niamets and Sekoul, Optina Version, by Schema-Monk Metrophanes*, Platina, California: Saint Herman of Alaska Brotherhood, 1976
Scupoli, Lorenzo, *Unseen Warfare, Being the Spiritual Combat and Path to Paradise as Edited by Nicodemus of the Holy Mountain and Revised by Theophan the Recluse*, translated by E. Kadloubovsky and G.E.H. Palmer, introduced by H.A. Hodges, London: Faber and Faber, 1952

Spirituality: Western Christian

In general terms spirituality encompasses the manifold ways in which humans participate in the animating spirit of life and express their relationship to it, to themselves, to other persons and beings, and to the deepest sources of meaning, value, and purpose that motivate their lives. In terms of Christian faith and life, these relationships and meanings are constituted with particular reference to Jesus Christ, to the God whose kingdom he proclaimed, and to the Holy Spirit present in the world and in the Christian community.

Western Christian spiritualities developed within larger contexts that also formed the matrix for the evolution of monastic spiritualities. This article describes the general features of those contexts and traces the major developments of Western monastic spiritualities down to 1500 in relationship to them. In doing so it will identify several recurring themes that emerge from the ongoing interaction of Christian faith with human history and culture.

Contexts

The life and ministry, death, and resurrection of Jesus, which are the foundation of Christian faith and the touchstone of all forms of Christian spirituality, occurred within the dual contexts of Palestinian Judaism and the political and cultural world of the Roman Empire. The movement that gathered around Jesus during his lifetime and the communities that formed after his death and resurrection reflect the legacies of both contexts. The early Christian communities were shaped by what they appropriated from Judaism and the Greco-Roman world as well as by what they left behind or rejected from each.

From Judaism the earliest Christians brought forward the writings of the Law and the Prophets (their only scriptures for several generations), the expectation of God's coming reign, and patterns of prayer and ritual that profoundly influenced Christian practice even when significantly modified in form and content. The fall of the Temple in A.D. 70 during the first Jewish revolt and the destruction of Jerusalem during the second revolt in 135 combined with the rapidly expanding Gentile mission to impart an overwhelmingly Gentile cast to Christianity from the second century on.

From the political and cultural world of the Roman Empire Christianity absorbed large portions of the philosophical heritage of Hellenism while rejecting its religious expressions. Despite conflicts with political authorities and the civil religion of the empire that led to persecution and martyrdom in the early centuries, Christianity had taken on many of the structures of imperial administration and the rituals of the imperial court by the end of the fourth century. The experience of martyrdom and the inherent rejection of Roman culture that it represents deeply affected Christians' sense of identity. At the same time the efforts of Christian apologists to bring about an end to persecution through persuasion and information about who Christians are, what they believe, and how they live opened the way for a more positive engagement with culture and the expression of Christian faith in the philosophical language of Stoicism and Platonism that was common to much of the educated Roman world.

Traditions of asceticism and communal or monastic living found in Judaism and among philosophical schools and sects also form part of the background for early Christian spiritualities without necessarily directly influencing their development. The instinct to withdraw from ordinary life, whether to prepare for an apocalyptic end of days or to clarify the mind for the contemplation of truth, is an ancient one. It manifests itself in the history of Christianity in ascetic and monastic spiritualities that take on distinctive features in different geographic and linguistic regions (mainly West or East, Latin or Greek, Coptic, and Syriac) and in different historical eras.

Patterns

Already present in this formative period are some common themes in the development of Christian spiritualities in general and monastic spiritualities in particular that appear or recur across changing cultural and historical contexts. Chief among them is the interaction with culture itself and the degree of appropriation and assimilation or distancing and opposition characteristic of each period or place. Another is the way in which the charism of a founding figure or moment is institutionalized and then reappropriated through subsequent movements of renewal or reform. Equally important is the emergence of new forms and expressions of spirituality in response to critical changes in the social, political, and cultural context and the challenges that these present to established patterns of praxis and meaning.

Rather than attempting to summarize the history of Western Christian spiritualities or its monastic expressions, this article looks at some key instances up to 1500 of foundation, transition, renovation, and innovation. Such an examination serves to reveal deeper currents of interaction with the historical and cultural context and also suggests ways of understanding later developments.

Foundations: 100–600

Two moments in this formative period are of particular importance: the transition from a period of persecution and martyrdom to one of asceticism and monasticism as the Roman Empire became increasingly Christian and then as the empire gradually disintegrated in the face of major disruptions in its western portion caused by the movements of Germanic peoples across its frontiers. Until the end of persecution with the Edict of Milan in 313, the experience of martyrdom as public witness to one's faith in Jesus Christ and as a way to imitate or follow him in his suffering and death had profoundly shaped Christian attitudes toward political power and ultimate values as well as to personal suffering and death. The influences of martyrdom continued to affect Christian spirituality even as some of its motivations and meanings were transposed into the rapidly expanding practice of asceticism, regarded by many as the "new martyrdom."

Although the roots of Christian asceticism reached back to the second century or even earlier, it flourished in the changed climate associated with Emperor Constantine (306–337). Following or imitating Jesus by means of bodily discipline, sexual renunciation, almsgiving, prayer, and study of the Scriptures became an alternative to and critique of the new political and religious arrangements that were making Christianity at home in the Roman Empire, more at ease with classical culture, and rapidly aligning it with imperial power. Ascetic life attracted individuals and communities of laypeople, many of them from the lower classes, in the deserts of Egypt, Syria, and Palestine, where the solitary Antony (c. 251–356) also instructed groups of monks and Pachomius (c. 290–346) founded some of the first monastic communities and provided them with rules. It was also practiced in the urban homes of wealthy women in cities such as Rome (Paula, Marcella, Melania, and others; Jerome and Rufinus were among their spiritual directors) and in the provincial estates of aristocratic men and women elsewhere in the empire. Augustine retreated to a friend's nearby estate after his baptism in Milan and Paulinus of Nola and his wife to their estate, where they lived in poverty and chastity.

Teachers and founders of asceticism and monasticism in the West learned extensively from the experience of the Desert Fathers (and some Desert Mothers) in the East. With the financial patronage of Paula, Jerome (c. 345–420) established a double monastery in Bethlehem while Rufinus (c. 345–411) did the same on the Mount of Olives with the help of Melania's fortune. Their letters to friends and families back in Rome and the reports of their visitors did much to spread ascetic fervor in the West. The disruptions and uncertainties caused by the migrations and military expeditions of Gothic peoples into the western empire also encouraged those with means to flee the cities and centers of "civilization" and take up lives of asceticism in its outlying and temporarily safer regions.

John Cassian (c. 360–after 430), who had lived in a Bethlehem monastery for a time and then among the monks of Egypt for about 15 years, founded two monasteries in Marseilles (after c. 410). He systematized the sayings and teachings of the Desert Fathers and made them available to the Latin-speaking world in his *Conferences*, while also providing an organizational basis for Western monasticism in his *Institutes*. It is through Cassian that the teachings of Evagrius Ponticus (346–399) on the eight principal thoughts (*logismoi*) or vices (gluttony, impurity, avarice, sadness, anger, acedia, vainglory, and pride) come into Western spirituality, later to be transformed by Gregory the Great into the seven deadly sins. Sometime in the mid-fifth century, an anonymous monastic teacher (thought by some scholars to be Cassian) wrote the *Rule of the Master*, a lengthy work that likely influenced Benedict of Nursia (c. 480–c. 550) when he composed his own Rule around 529 or later. The Rule of Benedict (RB) was moderate, sensible, and practical, a "little rule for beginners" (RB 73) living in community and seeking to return to God by the "labor of obedience" (RB, Pref.). It established a life of prayer (*opus Dei*, the monastic office), work, and study in a stable environment under the direction of an abbot responsible for the care and salvation of the brothers in his charge. Monasteries following Benedict's Rule unwittingly became centers of stability in the rapidly changing world. By the end of the sixth century, Pope Gregory I (590–604) would look to these centers to provide missionaries to the "barbarians" now peopling much of the former western empire.

Transitions: 600–900

Notwithstanding Benedict's emphasis on stability, monks following his Rule were at the forefront of the missionary enterprise in the centuries of transition from the world of late antiquity to the formation of Western Christendom. Monastic discipline and a strong dose of miracle working contributed significantly to the reevangelization of the eastern part of the British Isles from which, in the eighth century, British and Celtic monks would launch missions to the northern and eastern frontiers of Europe. In both waves of missionary activity, the establishment of communities of monks and nuns served as the nucleus of newly founded local churches.

Undertaken in obedience to the directive of Gregory the Great in 596, the mission of Augustine of Canterbury (d. 604/9) and his fellow monks succeeded in converting King Ethelbert of Kent and brought a Roman-oriented Christianity and Benedictine monasticism to the Angles and Saxons. The stage was set for further Romanization of the remaining British and some Celtic bishops in the farther reaches of the isles at the Synod of Whitby in 664. English monks led by Willibrord (658–739) would evangelize the Frisians along the North Sea and, under Boniface (c. 680–754), the peoples of the German frontier. As part of his missionary strategy, Boniface asked the nun Leoba to leave her monastery in England in order to establish a women's community at Bischofsheim (near Mainz). Boniface also played a key role in a series of councils that met to reform the Frankish Church during the 740s.

Christianity in Ireland had developed independently of both Britain and Rome from at least the time of Patrick (c. 389–461) if not earlier. Centered around kinship groups and monasteries whose abbots were more influential than bishops, Celtic Christianity evolved a distinctive spirituality and followed ecclesiastical customs and usages (e.g., calculating the date of Easter or the style of monastic tonsure) that differed from those of Rome and Gaul. Celtic monasticism was more akin to that of the Egyptian desert than to Benedict's and its asceticism harsher; it produced its own rules for communal life. As the monastic practice of private confession of sins was extended to the laity, handbooks of sins and their penalties were compiled for the guidance of confessors. These Irish Penitentials (the earliest consists of canons attributed to St. Patrick and dates to the fifth century) exerted considerable influence on later Western spirituality and moral theology, especially in the prominence given to matters of sin, guilt, penance, and its substitutes (pilgrimages, private masses, and eventually provision and procuring of indulgences).

Irish monks had their share of missionary zeal and undertook missions at their own initiative: Columba (c. 521–597) journeyed to Scotland to establish the monastery of Iona in 563. From there Columbanus (d. 615) and companions set out to evangelize the eastern Franks around 590, establishing monasteries at Luxeuil and later at Bobbio in northern Italy. The monk Aidan (d. 651) left Iona to evangelize Northumbria, where he founded the monastery of Lindisfarne and was succeeded by the famed Cuthbert (c. 636–687). Moved by a spirit similar to these missionary monks, wayfaring saints and scholars (as represented by the *Voyage of St. Brendan*) were another hallmark of Celtic Christianity in this period.

The monasteries of Ireland, Scotland, and England, as well as those of the later Frankish kingdom and the empire of Charlemagne, were centers of study as well as of prayer and mission. For their own use in *lectio divina*, the reflective reading of the Scriptures and the writings of the earlier Latin fathers, many monasteries produced copies of these texts in their scriptoria, thus preserving substantial portions of the heritage of the patristic church. Works of classical antiquity were often copied as well. Lives of saints and martyrs were composed and existing vitae copied; recent ecclesiastical and secular history was recorded, as in Bede's *History of the English Church and People* (written in 731). Monastic copyists created brilliantly illuminated manuscripts, such as the Book of Kells and the Lindisfarne Gospels, which offer windows onto the imaginative world of the times.

Along with the scriptoria, monastic schools served to transmit the culture of the ancient world, both Christian and classical, while educating their own monks and boys from the surrounding areas. Valuing the learning that he himself lacked and viewing the monastic schools as a means of raising the educational level of his kingdom, Charlemagne (sole king of the Franks from 771, emperor from 800 to 814) invited the English monk Alcuin (c. 740–804) to his court in 781, where he took intermittent charge of the "palace school" and set in motion the intellectual revival of the Carolingian renaissance. As Jean Leclercq put it, the "love of learning" was intimately connected to the "desire for God." Aided by Charlemagne's approbation, the Rule of Benedict came to dominate in the Frankish lands and elsewhere in the West.

As new kingdoms emerged from the remains of the western Roman Empire, a new, agriculturally based economy developed in which political power was tied to the holding of land. Because churches and monasteries supported themselves from the produce of their lands, bishops and abbots were an integral part of the feudal hierarchy of lordship, vassalage, obligation, and protection. The long struggle over real and apparent lay control of ecclesiastical institutions had its origins in the structures of feudalism, within which bishops or abbots were invested with the signs of their office by secular lords to whom they owed political

Discalced Carmelite nun in tune with nature.
Photo courtesy of Jim Young

allegiance. In addition to their secular power and responsibilities, monasteries and churches could draw on the spiritual power that resided in their prayers and masses and especially in their relic collections and their proximity to and control over the shrines of saints and martyrs. Legitimate translations of relics, as well as thefts and even fabrications, remained a profitable enterprise throughout the Middle Ages.

Renovations: 900–1200

In 910 Duke William of Aquitane endowed the monastery of Cluny, a new foundation that was to be free of lay control in perpetuity and to follow the Rule of Benedict without interference. Under a series of powerful and long-lived abbots in its first century of existence, Cluny and its daughter houses (either founded from Cluny or brought into association with it) became one of the driving forces for monastic renewal. Another current of reforming activity arose from the monastery of Gorze in Germany at nearly the same time. Both movements fed into the papally directed reforms of the 11th century that sought to eliminate simony (the sale of ecclesiastical office) and promote clerical celibacy.

In part because of its success and the reach of its daughter houses, Cluny grew prosperous from the gifts and bequests of wealthy donors. By the 12th century its abbots were among the most powerful men in Europe, its liturgy was splendid, and its treasury of artwork and precious metals was magnificent. Founded to counter the assimilation of monasticism and feudal culture, Cluny itself became ripe for reform. Peter the Venerable (abbot from 1122 to 1156) labored from within to simplify the liturgy and customs of Cluny and to reduce its dependence on the diminishing stream of benefactions by living within the income generated by its landholdings.

About the same time another movement of Benedictine renewal was taking form at the new monastery of Cîteaux. Founded in 1098 by monks dissatisfied with the pace of Cluniac reform and led by Robert of Molesme (c. 1027–1111), its first abbot, Cîteaux intended to follow the Rule of Benedict to the letter and observe strict simplicity of life at the margins of forest and cultivated land. The Cistercian experiment was languishing when the young Bernard (1090–1153, later of Clairvaux) and nearly 30 companions entered the community in 1112. The infusion of new blood reinvigorated Cîteaux and led to the foundation of Clairvaux by Bernard in 1115, from which, as abbot, he became a dominant force in shaping Cistercian spirituality while also playing a major role in all the significant ecclesiastical events of the day. New foundations appeared rapidly (68 from Clairvaux alone) until, by 1200, there were more than 500 Cistercian houses in Europe, and the number continued to increase throughout the 13th century. Unforeseen by Robert and unwelcomed by Bernard, communities of Cistercian women appeared almost spontaneously and persisted steadfastly in following the customs of Cîteaux.

Often regarded as "the last of the Fathers," Bernard stands at the apogee of the theological and spiritual traditions that Western Christianity inherited from the early Church, especially through Augustine, Gregory the Great, and centuries of Benedictine experience. His sermons on the *Song of Songs* delineate a mystical union of Christ the Bridegroom with the soul of the beloved (monk or nun), his treatise *On Loving God* offers a more theoretical analysis of the movement from fear of the Lord to perfect love, and *The Steps of Humility and Pride* describes the descent into pride, the inverse experience of the ladder of humility so central to the Rule of Benedict (chap. 7). Through hundreds of letters, numerous sermons, and other treatises, Bernard's voice was heard throughout the Western Church, not least of all in his preaching of the Second Crusade (1145–1149).

Monasticism in the Benedictine tradition afforded at least some women the opportunity for education and literary activity, most notable among them Hildegard of Bingen (1098–1179). Abbess of a small community of women following the Rule of Benedict at Disibodenburg on the Rhine, Hildegard became known throughout Germany and beyond for her prophetic visions, about whose orthodoxy she consulted Bernard and for which she received the approbation of Pope Eugenius III (1145–1153). Her extensive writings include visionary and moral treatises (*Scivias* and *Book of Life's Rewards*), medical and scientific works, hymns, antiphons and liturgical poetry (*Symphonia*), and a large repertoire of liturgical music. In the 13th century Cistercian nuns were among the leading representatives of the intense mysticism that was rapidly gaining currency among both religious and laywomen. The monastery of Helfta was especially noteworthy in this respect, being the home of Gertrude the Great (1256–1301) and Mechthild of Hackeborn (1240–1298) as well as a refuge for the beguine visionary Mechthild of Magdeburg (c. 1208–c. 1282) in the last years of her life.

The Cistercians' desire to remove themselves from the centers of civilization and cultivate a life of monastic solitude and hard work in the wilderness led them, inadvertently, to the growing edges of agricultural society. Their productivity and spare lifestyle generated more income than they could use. Their spirituality attracted not only members but benefactors. Combined with the prominence of Bernard, these factors soon brought the Cistercians back into the mainstream of church life and involvement in politics and culture. The "success" of both the Cluniac and Cistercian reforms led ultimately to their reintegration into Western society even as the agriculturally based world that supported such monasticism was being eclipsed by the expansion of commerce and the growth of towns and cities that followed the Crusades (the first in 1095, the fourth and, in practical terms, the last in 1204).

The demographic shift to the cities was accompanied by a shift in the centers of theological activity from the monastic schools to the newly forming universities. These transitions created a new set of pastoral needs in face of the growing numbers of urban poor and engendered new emphases in spirituality that moved away from monastic withdrawal and stability to embrace a more itinerant evangelicalism. At the same time the character of theology was transformed as the contemplative approach of *lectio divina* and the thought world of Augustinian neo-Platonism yielded ground to the analytical and systematic methods of Scholastic theology informed by the newly translated works of Aristotle.

Innovations: 1200–1500

Most of the responses to the changing context of Western Christianity in the High Middle Ages occurred outside the confines of the monastic world strictly understood. What one historian has termed an "evangelical awakening" had developed among laypeople during the 12th century, generating popular movements that sought to preach the gospel through the simplicity of lives dedicated to following Jesus in his poverty and humility. A kind of popular and practical mysticism arose as well and continued to thrive during the next centuries. Many of these movements ran afoul of ecclesiastical authority. Energized and cautioned by such movements, new religious orders developed in the cities and towns, notably among the cathedral and other clergy, who lived communally as Canons Regular and followed a Rule (such as that of St. Augustine). The most striking innovation was the emergence of the mendicant orders of friars associated with Francis of Assisi (c. 1181/82–1226) and Dominic de Guzman (c. 1170–1221). The Franciscans, Dominicans, and somewhat later the Carmelites and Augustinian Friars embodied the evangelical ideals of poverty and preaching in the new urban centers and in missions to the Holy Land and elsewhere. Initially they owned no property and had no permanent institutions, but within a century they had been drawn into the theological world of the universities as well as into the mainstream of urban church life, with all that this required by way of permanence and possessions. These orders, too, would develop distinctive spiritualities and go through cycles of renewal and reform similar to those experienced by the monastic orders.

It is beyond the scope of this article to follow these developments among the mendicants, their so-called second orders of women, and the various "third orders" of laity, not to mention the more loosely structured confraternities and pious societies that arose during this period. Contemporaneous movements such as the beguines and beghards or the Brethren of the Common Life are also outside the purview of monastic spirituality as such.

The widely varied circumstances of the Reformation in Continental Europe and England make it impossible here to recount the fates of monastic communities in the 16th century or to detail the slow processes of recovery, sometimes centuries long, in countries where monasteries were dissolved or destroyed and the spiritualities of late medieval Catholicism were rejected in favor of new expressions of Christian faith in keeping with the religious, social, and political changes of the times – so, too, for the expansion of monastic communities and the missionary spiritualities that carried them into the New World of the European explorers and conquerors or the challenges posed by the Enlightenment and by the destruction and rebuilding that followed the French Revolution. However, the patterns and problems of monastic development, adaptation, and inculturation outlined here pertain to each of these historical contexts as well as to the increasingly global and pluralistic contexts of the 20th century, as do the resources of monastic spiritualities that continue to be appropriated from this heritage and fashioned anew.

FRANCINE CARDMAN

See also Asceticism: Christian Perspectives; Bernard of Clairvaux, St.; Cassian, John; Celibacy: Christian; Celtic Monasticism; Charism; Cluny, Abbots of; Devotions, Western Christian; Dialogue, Intermonastic: Christian Perspectives; Liturgy: Western Christian; Martyrs: Western Christian; Mystics, German Monastic: Female; Origins: Comparative Perspectives; Penitential Books; Relics, Christian Monastic; Seasons, Liturgical: Western Christian

Further Reading

Benedict, Saint, *RB 1980: The Rule of St. Benedict in Latin and English with Notes*, edited by Timothy Fry, Collegeville, Minnesota: Liturgical Press, 1981

Bernard, of Clairvaux, Saint, *On the Song of Songs* (Cistercian Fathers Series, numbers 4, 7, 31, 40), translated by Kilian Walsh and Irene Edmonds, 4 vols., Spencer, Massachusetts: Cistercian Publications, 1971–1980

Bernard, of Clairvaux, Saint, *Treatises II* (Cistercian Fathers Series, number 13), Washington, D.C.: Cistercian Publications, 1974

Bynum, Caroline Walker, *Jesus as Mother: Studies in the Spirituality of the High Middle Ages* (Publications of the Center for Medieval and Renaissance Studies, 16), Berkeley: University of California Press, 1982

Cassian, John, *John Cassian: The Conferences* (Ancient Christian Writers, number 57), translated by Boniface Ramsey, New York: Paulist Press, 1997

Hildegard, Saint, *Symphonia: A Critical Edition of the "Symphonia armonie celestium revelationum" ("Symphony of the Harmony of Celestial Revelations")*, with introduction, translations, and commentary by Barbara Newman, Ithaca, New York: Cornell University Press, 1988; 2nd edition, 1998

Hildegard of Bingen, Scivias, translated by Mother Columba Hart and Jane Bishop, New York: Paulist Press, 1990

Jones, Cheslyn, Geoffrey Wainwright, and Edward Yarnold, editors, *The Study of Spirituality*, New York: Oxford University Press, and London: SPCK, 1986

Leclercq, Jean, *The Love of Learning and the Desire for God: A Study of Monastic Culture*, translated by Catharine Misrahi, New York: Fordham University Press, 1961; 2nd edition, London: SPCK, 1978; 3rd edition, New York: Fordham University Press, 1982

McGinn, Bernard, John Meyendorff, and Jean Leclercq, editors, *Christian Spirituality: Origins to the Twelfth Century* (World Spirituality, volume 16), New York: Crossroad, 1985; London: Routledge and Kegan Paul, 1986

Ranft, Patricia, *Women and Spiritual Equality in Christian Tradition*, New York: St. Martin's Press, 1996

Sri Lanka: History

Buddhist monasticism, which began in India in the fifth century B.C., took root in Anurādhapura during the reign of King Dēvānāmpiyatissa (c. 250–210 B.C.) with the arrival of Emperor Aśoka's son Arhat Mahinda. While the first Buddhist missionaries arrived in Mihintale, Buddhism spread to other parts of Sri Lanka from Anurādhapura. Over 13 centuries Anurādhapura remained as Sri Lanka's capital and became the home for three prominent Buddhist monastic centers: Mahāvihāra, Abhayagiri, and Jētavana.

Mahāvihāra was the earliest monastic establishment in Anurādhapura. Although Mahāvihāra's dominant position was weakened at certain periods, it flourished as the center for spreading Theravāda Buddhist doctrine and monastic practices. The main religious sites in the capital were Thūpārāma, Ruvanvälisāya, and Śrī Mahābōdhi.

In the history of Sri Lankan monasticism, four important scholastic achievements are the following: (1) Because Sri Lankan monastics had recognized the threats to oral transmission and its vulnerability as a means of preservation, they wrote down the *Buddhavacana* (word of the Buddha) on palm leaves to preserve it from possible variation and corruption as early as the first century B.C. at Alu Vihāra, Mātale. This early, cautious step was crucial for other pioneering achievements. (2) In the fifth century Buddhaghosa Thera arrived in Mahāvihāra and living there composed Pāli commentaries (*aṭṭhakathā*) on the basis of Sinhala sources. Whereas Buddhaghosa's magnum opus, the *Visuddhimagga*, established a solid foundation for Theravāda interpretation of Buddhism, his successors – Buddhadatta and Dhammapāla – continued the commentarial project and enhanced the Theravāda position. These scholastic activities were crucial in reaffirming the unquestioned authority attached to Mahāvihāra as a custodian of the pristine teachings of the Buddha. (3) With the guidance of Mahākassapa Thera of Poḷonnaruva, his pupils composed subcommentaries (*ṭīkā*) to the Pāli commentaries in the 13th century, marking another milestone in Theravāda scholasticism and interpretations. (4) In the 13th century cosmopolitan Buddhism took an "inward" orientation and gave birth to a localized form of "vernacular" Buddhism based on a vast corpus of vernacular literature written in Sinhala. This *baṇakathā* literature played an important role in the history of Theravāda monasticism in later centuries.

Mahāvihāra monasticism faced a severe challenge for the first time when King Vaṭṭagāmaṇi Abhaya (c. 89–77 B.C.) constructed Abhayagiri Vihāra. Initial petty disputes between these two fraternities intensified, resulting later in the devastation of the most prestigious Mahāvihāra by King Mahāsena (c. A.D. 274–301). After destroying Mahāvihāra he built Jētavana Vihāra within the Mahāvihāra boundary. Although Mahāvihāra was reconstructed later, it never assumed a preeminent position until the unification of the three monastic fraternities by King Parākramabāhu I (1153–1186).

Whereas Mahāvihāra was faithful in preserving the Buddha's words as found in the Pāli Canon, the latter two fraternities were more liberal in their approach to the Buddha's teachings. Both Abhayagiri and Jētavana fraternities were ready to embrace foreign influences, including Mahāyāna religious ideas and Tantric popular practices, to create a more appealing cosmopolitan and popular devotional religiosity. Recent archaeological excavations at Abhayagiri and Jētavana demonstrate their tolerant and syncretic approach in incorporating Mahāyāna sūtras, such as the *Pañcaviṃsatisāhaśrikā Prajñāpāramitā Sūtra* and the *Kāśyapaparivarta*, Tantric mantras and *dhāraṇī*s, and atypical square-shaped terraced architectural features in constructing stūpas.

Several important monastic centers, such as Ālāhena Piriveṇa and Jētavana monastery, emerged in the medieval capital Poḷonnaruva (1055–1235). While the eight *āyatana*s, which had formal affiliations with the previous three fraternities, became prominent in monastic life, Mahāvihāra moved to Poḷonnaruva, from which its prestige extended to Southeast Asia and its power gradually ascended. Since the second century B.C., Sri Lankan monastic institutions had accumulated wealth and monastic property that brought new developments in the life of the *saṅgha* and in their relationships with laity. The loss of monastic wealth and the political instability caused by foreign invasions had weakened the *saṅgha*, but now monastic rivalry gradually disappeared, generating a tolerant attitude toward each other. Whereas Mahāvihāra was able to maintain its scholarly standards and monastic practices because of its strong hold within the indigenous tradition, Abhayagiri faced difficulties in maintaining its international contacts and in receiving inspiration from abroad. These problems increased when Indian Buddhism weakened and the Coḷa invasion (981 and 1017) caused difficulties in traveling abroad. When Māgha (1215–1236) invaded Sri Lanka, the political turmoil eroded the *saṅgha*'s fortunes.

Kandy, the capital for seven kings of the Kandyan kingdom from 1592 to 1815, became the home for Malvatta and Asgiriya, two major branches of the Siyam Nikāya (founded 1753), the largest of the three existing Buddhist monastic fraternities. The other two are Amarapura (founded 1803) and Rāmañña (founded 1864).

For Theravāda monasticism the valid higher ordination (*upasampadā*) tradition is crucial. When enough monks were no longer found within Sri Lanka to perform the higher ordination, several kings attempted to revive it. In the Poḷonnaruva period King Vijayabāhu I (1055–1110) invited monks from Aramana, Burma. In the Kandyan period King Vimaladharmasūrya I (1591–1604) invited Burmese monks to Kandy to initiate the long-lapsed higher ordination rites. Again when Buddhist practices declined sharply, giving birth to the institution of Ganinnānse (a group of half lay and half monastic practitioners), King Kīrti Śrī Rājasinha (1747–1782) invited Upāli Thera with a retinue of Buddhist monks from Siam to perform higher ordination rites for the revivalist Saṅgharāja Välivita Saraṇaṅkara (1698–1777) and other members of the Silvat Samāgama in May 1753.

At present, the monks of Malvatta and Asgiriya take turns in rotation in attending Gautama Buddha's Tooth Relic. It took on unusual symbolic and political importance in Sri Lanka since its arrival during the reign of King Sirimeghavaṇṇa (c. 301–328), functioning as a sacred object that legitimizes one's right to kingship. With Daḷadā Māligāwa and many historic temples around it, Kandy has become Sri Lanka's preeminent Buddhist monastic site.

MAHINDA DEEGALLE

See also Anurādhapura, Sri Lanka; Asceticism: Buddhist Perspectives; Critiques of Buddhist Monasticism: Indo-Tibetan; Death Rituals, Buddhist; Kandy, Sri Lanka; Mahāpajāpatī Gotamī; Monasticism, Definitions of: Buddhist Perspectives; Patrons, Buddhist: India; Pilgrims to India, Chinese; Stūpa; Ten-Precept Mothers as Theravādin Nuns; Theravādin Monks, Modern Western; Virtues, Buddhist

Further Reading

Adikaram, E.W., *Early History of Buddhism in Ceylon*, Migoda, Sri Lanka: Puswella, 1946

Deegalle, Mahinda, "*Baṇa*: Buddhist Preaching in Sri Lanka (Special Focus on the Two-Pulpit Tradition)," Ph.D. Diss., University of Chicago, 1995

Deegalle, Mahinda, "A Bibliography on Sinhala Buddhism," *Journal of Buddhist Ethics* 4 (1997)

Dewaraja, L.S., *The Kandyan Kingdom of Sri Lanka 1707–1782*, Colombo, Sri Lanka: Lake House Investments, 1988

Dharmadasa, K.N.O., "The *Ganinnānse*: A Peculiar Development of the *Saṅgha* in Eighteenth Century Sri Lanka," in *Studies in Buddhism and Culture*, Tokyo: Sankibo Busshorin, 1991

Gunawardana, R.A.L.H., *Robe and Plough: Monasticism and Economic Interest in Early Medieval Sri Lanka*, Tucson: University of Arizona Press, 1979

Hettiaratchi, S.B., and T.G. Kulatunge, *Abhayagiriya*, Colombo, Sri Lanka: Madhyama Saṃskṛtika Aramudala, 1992

Hinüber, Oskar von, "Sieben Goldblätter einer Pañcaviṃsatisāhaśrikā Prajñāpāramitā aus Anurādhapura," *Nachrichten der Akademie der Wissenschaften in Göttingen: Philologisch-Historische Klasse* 7 (1984)

Holt, John Clifford, *The Religious World of Kīrtī Śrī: Buddhism, Art, and Politics in Medieval Sri Lanka*, New York: Oxford University Press, 1996

Ilangasinha, H.B.M., *Buddhism in Medieval Sri Lanka*, Delhi: Sri Satguru, 1992

Jayasuriya, M.H.F, "A Fragmentary Sri Lankan Recension of the Pañcaviṃsatisāhaśrikā Prajñāpāramitā Sūtra," *Sri Lanka Journal of Buddhist Studies* 2 (1988)

Liyanagamage, Amaradasa, *The Decline of Poḷonnaruwa and the Rise of Dambadeṇiya, circa 1180–1270 A.D.*, Colombo, Sri Lanka: Department of Cultural Affairs, 1968

Malalgoda, Kitsiri, *Buddhism in Sinhalese Society 1750–1900: A Study of Religious Revival and Change*, Berkeley: University of California Press, 1976

Mudiyanse, Nandasena, *Mahāyāna Monuments in Ceylon*, Colombo, Sri Lanka: Gunasena, 1967

Panabokke, Gunaratne, *History of the Buddhist Saṅgha in India and Sri Lanka*, Colombo, Sri Lanka: Postgraduate Institute of Pali and Buddhist Studies, University of Kelaniya, 1993

Paranavitana, Senarat, and Cyril W. Nicholas, *A Concise History of Ceylon: From the Earliest Times to the Arrival of the Portuguese*, Colombo: Ceylon University Press, 1961

Prematilleke, Leelananda, and Roland Silva, "A Buddhist Monastery Type of Ancient Ceylon Showing Mahāyānist Influence," *Artibus Asiae* 30:1 (1968)

Rahula, Walpola, *History of Buddhism in Ceylon: The Anurādhapura Period 3rd Century BC – 10th Century A.D.*, Colombo, Sri Lanka: Gunasena, 1956

Seneviratne, H.L., *Rituals of the Kandyan State*, Cambridge and New York: Cambridge University Press, 1978

Silva, K.M. de, *A History of Sri Lanka*, London: Hurst, and Berkeley: University of California Press, 1981

Sirisena, W.M., *Sri Lanka and South-East Asia: Political, Religious and Cultural Relations from A.D. c. 1000 to c. 1500*, Leiden: Brill, 1978

Vacissara, Kotagama, *Saraṇaṅkara Saṅgharāja Samaya*, Colombo, Sri Lanka: Y. Don Advin saha Samāgama, 1960

Sri Lanka: Recent Changes

As a small nation in southern Asia, Sri Lanka has played a crucial role in the development and preservation of Theravāda Buddhist monasticism. Since Sri Lanka's Independence from England in 1948, Theravāda monasticism has undergone many changes. The monastics of the three major *nikayā*s – Siyam (founded 1753), Amarapura (founded 1803), and Rāmañña (founded 1864) – have struggled with modernization and increasing secularization. Some monastics, albeit definitely not the majority, have increasingly involved themselves in politics. During the late 1980s with the rise of militant Janatā Vimukti Peramuṇa, a number of young monks have actively joined the left-wing politics of JVP and continue to pose a serious threat to the peaceful survival of Buddhist monasticism.

Another significant change has occurred in education. In addition to the University of Ceylon, two Buddhist monastic schools – Vidyōdaya (founded 1873) and Vidyālaṅkāra (founded 1875) – were elevated to the status of national universities in 1959. In 1966 Buddhaśrāvaka Dharmapīṭhaya at Anurādhapura was established exclusively for traditional Buddhist studies. In 1981 Buddhist and Pali University of Sri Lanka was established for renewing and carrying out Buddhist studies within a monastic atmosphere. In the 1980s Śāriputra Vidyāpīṭhaya at Niṭṭambuva was established to train young monastics as schoolteachers. All these developments exerted a positive impact on the educational standards and vocational capabilities of the monastics. As a result the number of monks who work as professional teachers in government and monastic schools has increased. The negative impact is that some monks alienated themselves from their temples as well as from traditional monastic routine, teachers, and lay devotees. The ever expanding educational and vocational opportunities combined with changing circumstances have challenged monastic values, routine, and lifestyle.

Although some monastics have been secularized through education, others have assumed more socially productive roles as social workers. Earlier with Sarvōdaya (founded 1958) many young monks learned to engage in social welfare. At present increasingly more monks have recognized their social responsibility and try to do whatever they can to elevate the standard of living in the communities in which they live.

When weaknesses arose in established Buddhist monastic institutions, laypeople responded in two ways. Some became self-ordained and tried to follow the ideals depicted in the canon. Others attempted to be exemplary laymen by following the "monastic ideal" and proclaimed themselves to be the "persons who are committed in reviving the discipline" (*vinayavardhana*). These lay responses demonstrate signs of renewal within established Theravāda.

Sri Lanka is witnessing a mounting concern about the status of Buddhist women. Recently more have advocated reestablishing higher ordination rites for "ten-precept mothers" (*dasa sil mātā*). In general ethnic turmoil (between Sinhalese and Tamils) has threatened the renewal of Buddhist values among both monastics and laity. As political activism rises and the potential of monastics as peacekeepers declines, it will be fascinating to see how Theravāda monasticism responds to challenging social conditions.

MAHINDA DEEGALLE

See also Anurādhapura, Sri Lanka; Kandy, Sri Lanka; Ten-Precept Mothers as Theravādin Nuns

Further Reading

Amunugama, Sarath, "Buddhaputra and Bhūmiputra?: Dilemmas of Modern Sinhala Buddhist Monks in Relation to Ethnic and Political Conflict," *Religion* 21 (1991)

Bartholomeusz, Tessa J., *Women Under the Bo Tree: Buddhist Nuns in Sri Lanka*, Cambridge and New York: Cambridge University Press, 1994

Bond, George, *The Buddhist Revival in Sri Lanka: Religious Tradition, Reinterpretation and Response*, Columbia: University of South Carolina Press, 1988

de Silva, Chandra R., "The Plurality of Buddhist Fundamentalism: An Inquiry into Views among Buddhist Monks in Sri Lanka," in *Buddhist Fundamentalism and Minority Identities in Sri Lanka*, edited by Tessa J. Bartholomeusz and Chandra R. de Silva, Albany: State University of New York Press, 1998

Deegalle, Mahinda, "Buddhism in a 'Value' Changing World: The Case of Modern Sri Lanka," paper read at *The Basis of Values in a Time of Change*, at the University of Peradeniya, Sri Lanka, 6–8 January 1997

Gombrich, Richard F., and Gananath Obeyesekere, *Buddhism Transformed: Religious Change in Sri Lanka*, Princeton, New Jersey: Princeton University Press, 1988

Kemper, Steven, "Buddhism Without Bhikkhus," in *Religion and Legitimation of Power in Sri Lanka*, edited by Bardwell L. Smith, Chambersburg, Pennsylvania: ANIMA Books, 1978

Rahula, Walpola, *The Heritage of the Bhikkhu: A Short History of the Bhikkhu in the Educational, Cultural, Social, and Political Life*, New York: Grove Press, 1974

Tambiah, Stanley Jeyaraja, *Buddhism Betrayed?: Religion, Politics, and Violence in Sri Lanka*, Chicago: University of Chicago Press, 1992

Sri Lanka: Sites

Buddhist monastic sites for both monks and nuns, ancient and contemporary, are scattered throughout Sri Lanka and range in character from simple village temples and remote forest hermitages to major monastic complexes for monks in Kandy at the Asgiriya and Malvatta Nikayās, which still house hundreds of *bhikkhu*s and *sāmaṇera*s (novices).

For 13 centuries (third century B.C. through tenth century A.D.), the major centers of monasticism were located in Anurādhapura during a period of spectacular civilizational growth. The *Mahāvaṃsa*, a historical chronicle of the *saṅgha* dating to the fifth century A.D. and written from the Mahāvihāra fraternity's Theravāda perspective, purports that the great Indian emperor Aśoka's missionary son, Mahinda, and his daughter, Saṅghamittā, established the *bhikkhu* and the *bhikkhunīsaṅgha*s in Anurādhapura. They acted under the converted king Dēvānāmpiya Tissa in the third century B.C., at which time Dēvānāmpiya Tissa consecrated the capital by plowing a *sīmā* (sacred boundary) around the city's perimeter. From the staggering amount of archaeological remains still extant in Anurādhapura, it is clear that a flourishing hydraulic-based civilization supported a massive monastic community of monks and nuns in north-central Sri Lanka. The fifth-century Chinese pilgrim Fa Hsien reports that 3,000 monks resided at the Mahāvihāra fraternity in Anurādhapura and another 2,000 at nearby Mihintale. In addition 5,000 monks inhabited the doctrinally eclectic Abhayagiriya monastery in Anurādhapura. The Jētavana monastery in Anurādhapura and the Tissamahārāma monastery in the southeast of the country must have also housed substantial numbers of monks. In all Fa Hsien reports the presence of 60,000 monks on the island. The enormous still extant stūpas (structures second in size only to the Egyptian pyramids of those times) that were constructed within the confines of these monasteries bear contemporary physical witness to the prosperity of these communities.

The authoritative writings on philosophy and practice by the fifth-century Anurādhapura monastic commentator Buddhaghosa, especially his *Visuddhimagga* ("Path of Purity") and *Vimuttimagga* ("Path of Freedom"), present the definitively orthodox Theravāda monastic perspective on dhamma (the Buddha's teaching) and vinaya (monastic discipline) to this day. A medieval literary tradition reified in devotional songs and late medieval Kandyan temple paintings ascribes 16 sacred places for Buddhists to venerate in Sri Lanka. Five of these are in Anurādhapura: Śrī Mahābodhi (the Bodhi Tree brought to the island by Saṅghamittā), Abhayagiriya stūpa, Jētavana stūpa, Ruvanvälisāya stūpa, Mirasaväti stūpa, and Thūpārāma, the last three belonging to the Mahāvihāra Theravāda fraternity with a sixth, Sīlacetiya (also Mahāvihāra), located in nearby Mihintale. From at least the sixth century until the tenth, the identities of monastic communities throughout the island were determined by administrative affiliations with either the Mahāvihāra, Abhayagiriya, or Jētavana fraternities in Anurādhapura. Among other outstanding extensive monastic archaeological sites dating to the Anurādhapura period are Sīgiriya (25 miles south-southeast of Anurādhapura), Riṭigala (a secluded forest hermitage 19 miles east-southeast of Anurādhapura), Mädirigiriya (38 miles east-southeast of Anurādhapura), Magul Mahā Vihāra (9 miles west-southwest of Pottuvil on the southeastern coast), Tiriyāya (19 miles north of Trincomalee on the eastern coast), Buduruvegala (6 miles southwest of Wellawaya in the south-central region), and Maligawila (9 miles southwest of Buttala in the south-central region), the latter four clearly of Mahāyāna orientation. All these sites can be visited today.

During the 11th through the 13th century, the Poḷonnaruva period, when the *saṅgha* was finally unified under the Theravāda banner by Parākramabāhu I, the Ālāhena Piriveṇa (monastic school of higher studies) in the center of the capital might have housed as many as 10,000 monks during its peak. The remains of Dim̆bulāgala, a forest hermitage on a mountainside about 9 miles the southeast of Poḷonnaruva, indicate the presence of a contemporaneous thriving community of *vanavāsī* (forest-dwelling) monks.

Trivanka Image Hall with standing Buddha image, Poḷonnaruva, Sri Lanka, reign of Parākramabāhu I (A.D. 1153–1186).
Photo courtesy of Marylin M. Rhie

In modern Sri Lanka the locales of the *bhikkhu* monastic community represent an interesting phenomenon. Kandy, the last of the traditional Sri Lankan royal cities, remains the nominal orthodox hub of Buddhist monasticism with its Asgiriya and Malvatta Nikāyas, the central monasteries for the Siyam Nikāya, which claims descent from the Anurādhapura and Poḷonnaruva Mahāvihāra. The Amarapura and Rāmañña Nikāyas, Theravāda orders established in the 19th century by low-country non-*goyigama* (rice-growing) caste monastics, have no analogous centers of their own. The Rāmañña is especially strong and has major temples in Galle on the southwestern coast. Vajirārāma Vihāraya in the Bambalapitiye neighborhood of Colombo about 3 miles south of Colombo Fort is a major temple and monastic complex for the Amarapura. Substantial monasteries can also be found at other major temples in the Colombo area, such as Kälaniya, Belanvila, and Hunapitiya. Numbers of *dasa sil mātā*s ("ten-precept-holding" nuns) are found especially at Biyagama (just northeast of Colombo) at the Upasika Ārāmaya supported by the Vihāra Mahā Devi Sammitiya and in many *ārāmaya*s located in Kandy, Kataragama, and Anurādhapura. Following the transformation of the Colombo area *bhikkhu piriveṇa*s at Vidyōdya (Kälaniya) and Vidyālaṅkāra (Sri Jayawardenepura) into national universities in the 1960s, many monks are now educated and continue to teach in Sri Lanka's university system. In apparent reaction against this, a new Buddhist monastic university, exclusively for the religious higher education of Theravāda monks, has been recently established in Anurādhapura.

Monasteries Easily Visited

1. Ancient and medieval: Abhayagiriya, Mahāvihāra, Jētavana, and the Mihintale complexes, all in or near Anurādhapura; Alahena Piriveṇa and Diṁbulāgala in Poḷonnaruva; and Mädirigiriya, Tiriyāya, Tissamahārāma, Buduruvegala, and Maligawila.
2. Contemporary: Asgiriya and Malvatta Rājamahāvihārayas in Kandy; Vajirārāma, Belanvila, and Kälaniya Vihārayas in Colombo; and Upasika Ārāmaya in Biyagama.
3. Forest hermitages: see Carrithers (1983).

JOHN HOLT

See also Anurādhapura, Sri Lanka; Aśoka; Kandy, Sri Lanka; Pilgrims to India, Chinese; Ten-Precept Mothers as Theravādin Nuns; Theravādin Monks, Modern Western

Further Reading

Bandaranayake, Senake, *Sinhalese Monastic Architecture: The Viharas of Anuradhapura*, Leiden: E.J. Brill, 1974
Bartholomeusz, Tessa J., *Women Under the Bo Tree: Buddhist Nuns in Sri Lanka*, Cambridge and New York: Cambridge University Press, 1994
Carrithers, Michael, *The Forest Monks of Sri Lanka: An Anthropological and Historical Study*, Delhi: Oxford University Press, 1983
Gunawardana, R.A.L.H., *Robe and Plough: Monasticism and Economic Interest in Early Medieval Sri Lanka*, Tucson: University of Arizona Press for the Association for Asian Studies, 1979
Mudiyanse, Nandasena, *Mahayana Monuments in Ceylon*, Colombo: Gunasena, 1967
Rahula, Walpola, *History of Buddhism in Ceylon: The Anuradhapura Period, 3rd Century B.C.–10th Century A.D.*, Colombo: Gunasena, 1956; 3rd edition, Dehiwala, Sri Lanka: Buddhist Cultural Center, 1993

Startsi. *See* Elders, Russian Monastic (Startsi)

Stephen of Perm, St. c. 1340–1396

Russian Orthodox monk, missionary to the Zyrians, and first bishop of Perm

Stephen of Perm is known in the Eastern Church as the sainted apostle to the Zyrians, and his feast day is celebrated on 26 April every year. A peaceful and educated missionary, he converted the indigenous population of northern Russia from shamanism to Orthodox Christianity. He created the Zyrian (or Permian) alphabet, established a literary language, and translated large portions of the Bible and the religious services. After becoming the first bishop of Perm, he attempted to create a national Zyrian church and founded schools and seminaries to train native clergy. Although Stephen's intellectual legacy was largely obliterated in succeeding centuries, the style and goals of his mission deeply affected later Russian Christian missions to shamanistic cultures, not least of which was the Russian mission to Alaska.

Stephen was the son of a cathedral cleric in the city of Velikiy Ustyug in the North Dvina River region, south of Arkhangelsk. The region was populated by native western Permians or Zyrians (also Zyryans or Komi), with a minority of Russians, and at that time was in the process of transferring from the political sphere of Novgorod to Muscovy. Even as a boy Stephen may have recognized his calling to become a missionary to the shamanistic Zyrian population, whose language he spoke. He early mastered the reading and writing of Russian, became a lector in the church, and exhausted the "wisdom" of the literary repository of the city. Although the young Stephen displayed few ascetic gifts, he journeyed to the monastery of St. Gregory the Theologian in Rostov, northeast of Moscow, and was tonsured a monk. This monastery was known for its "many books."

While in Rostov Stephen continued his intellectual and spiritual growth. He learned Greek – one of the few in the north who did – and devoted himself to the study of Holy Scripture. He befriended Epiphanius "the Wise," who was the biographer of St. Sergius of Radonezh (c. 1314–1392) and who later became Stephen's biographer as well. Epiphanius wrote about Stephen as one would about a close friend and included long conversations and theological discourses justifying the missionary's apostolic work among the Zyrians. Stephen also met and became friends with Sergius of Radonezh, as Rostov was not far from Sergius' retreat in Sergeyev Posod (Zagorsk), although he did not become Sergius' disciple, nor did he share his contemplative nature.

Around 1370 Stephen began inventing an alphabet for the Permian language without Russifying it. The "Trilingual Heresy" still held some sway in Byzantine and Russian circles, that is, the notion that the language of prayer must reflect Hebrew, Greek, or Latin roots, as these languages were inscribed on the cross of Jesus. (Put simply, Church Slavic and the Cyrillic alphabet took most of their letters from Greek and Hebrew.) In contrast to the precept, Stephen chose portions of the Permian alphabet from local runes or line designs borrowed from indigenous carvings and embroidery without using Cyrillic characters. After creating a written language and acting with the blessing of

Muscovite authorities, he proceeded to translate the Divine Liturgy and a large portion of the Holy Scriptures into Zyrian. These included the Gospels, the Psalter, the daily and weekly cycle of services, and those parts of the Old Testament that were used liturgically. In 1378 Stephen set out for the Permian land to preach the Gospel with a few clerics and no military support from Muscovy because of the latter's notoriety for violence among the Zyrians. His alphabet and translations became the primers and required reading for the newly baptized. When Stephen was elevated to the episcopacy in 1383, he ordained his disciples to clerical ranks and taught them to write books in their native language.

The Zyrians (Komi) constitute one of two parts of the Permyak branch of the Finno-Ugric populations of central Russia. In the ninth century the Permians divided into Komi and Udmurts. Komi had come into contact with Christianity possibly as early as the 12th century, as they were trading partners with Novgorod. Today the Zyrians continue to live between the upper Western Dvina River, Kama, and Pechora, a large region west of the northern Urals toward Arkhangelsk. In 1979, according to a Soviet census, the Komi numbered over 325,000 (Hoppál, 1987).

In the opinion of Epiphanius, Stephen's apostolic witness to the population was as magnificent as were his literary achievements. He destroyed the shrines of the Finnish polytheists with ax and fire, preaching all the while. Although the people did not like him and would have preferred to get rid of him, they did not because of their meekness. Stephen was an avid preacher, aggressive toward idols but not combative toward persons. The natives recognized this and even complained, "He has a bad habit of not starting a fight." Slowly they were won over, mainly by his preaching and personal example – for the Bible, even in their own language, could not speak forcefully to the unconverted who did not recognize its authority.

Another potent factor in the conversion of the Permians was the Divine Liturgy. Stephen built the first church in the main settlement at Ust-Vim and adorned it with iconography, wooden architectural ornamentation, and liturgical accoutrements. The Zyrians were attracted to both the ritual and the beauty of the small edifice. In addition Stephen engaged the Permian *volxv*, the tribal chief and shaman, in a series of moral and physical contests reminiscent of the Old Testament prophets combating the Baalists but without resorting to violence. The contests crowned Stephen's apostolic ministry with success, and Ust-Vim became his new episcopal see. Again as bishop Stephen promoted indigenous Zyrians into clerical ranks and promulgated the reading and writing of books in the native script. He maintained ties mainly with Moscow but also with Novgorod and once in a time of agricultural failure bought food for his people from the Russians. Only one literary work survives him, an item written against the Strigolniki – a dualistic heretical sect like the Cathari or Bogomils. He died on a trip to Moscow in 1396 and was buried there.

The *Vita* by Epiphanius, written shortly after Stephen's death and from which much of the information in this article was taken, does not exist today in a critical edition despite its many remarkable hagiographic and literary features, such as "word weaving." It concludes with *threnoi*, or formal lamentations in three voices – the lament of the Zyrian people, their church, and of Epiphanius himself – lamentations at the loss of their chief pastor. The *threnos* is an ancient Byzantine and Slavic poetic genre lauding epic heroes. It resembles the Eastern Church's liturgical lamentation in three voices before the tomb of Jesus on Holy Friday. (The same may well be based on the genre in the biblical Book of Lamentations.) The *threnos* genre is also familiar from Slavic folklore and can be heard used today in provincial funeral orations. In death Stephen's Permian legacy was brief, historically speaking. Within 200 years all the Finnish tribes in Russian territory, including the Zyrians, were Russified. The Zyrians were not strong enough to preserve the distinctive national identity of their own church established earlier by Stephen. Whatever effort they made to do so was undermined by Moscow.

MICHAEL PROKURAT

See also Moscow, Russia; Russia: History; Sergius of Radonezh, St.

Biography

Coming from northern Russia, near Arkhangelsk, Stephen became a monk near Rostov, not far from the monastery of Sergius of Radonezh. Stephen undertook to evangelize the Zyrians, a Finno-Ugric people, converting them from shamanism. He devised an alphabet for their language, into which he translated much of the Bible and the liturgy. Eventually he became bishop of Perm.

Major Work

"On Strigolniki," in *Pamyatniki drevne-russkago kanonicheskago prava, I* (Monuments of Old Russian Canonical Law, I), edited by A.S. Pavlov, St. Petersburg, 1880

Further Reading

Epiphanius the Wise, *Zhitie sv. Stefana episkopa permskago* (The Life of St. Stephen Bishop of Perm), edited by V. Druzhinin, St. Petersburg: Izd. Arkheograficheskoi Kommissii, 1897; reprint, with an introduction by Dmitrij Čiževski, The Hague and Paris: Mouton, 1959

Fedotov, G.P., *The Russian Religious Mind*, volume 2: *The Middle Ages, 13th to the 15th Centuries*, edited by John Meyendorff, Cambridge, Massachusetts: Harvard University Press, 1966

Goldblatt, Harvey, "On the Place of the Cyrillo-Methodian Tradition in Epiphanius's *Life of St. Stephen of Perm*," in *California Slavic Studies XVI: Christianity and the Eastern Slavs*, edited by Boris Gasparov and Olga Raevsky-Hughes, Berkeley: University of California Press, 1993

Hoppál, Mihály, "Finno-Ugric Religions," in *The Encyclopedia of Religion*, volume 5, edited by Mircea Eliade, New York and London: Macmillan, 1987

Klyuchevski, V., *Drevnerusskiya zhitiya sviatykh kak istoricheski istochnik* (The Old Russian Lives of the Saints as a Historical Source), Moscow, 1871; reprint, The Hague-Paris: Mouton, 1968

Lytkin, Vasilii I., *Drevnepermskii iazyk* (The Old Permian Language), Moscow: Izd-vo Akademii Nauk SSSR, 1952
Meyendorff, John, *Byzantium and the Rise of Russia*, Cambridge and New York: Cambridge University Press, 1981; Crestwood, New York: St. Vladimir's Seminary Press, 1989
Obolensky, Dimitri, *Byzantium and the Slavs*, Crestwood, New York: St. Vladimir's Seminary Press, 1994

Stūpa

In Buddhism certain sacred places are vivified with the living presence of the Buddha. Such places are invested with spiritual potency through relics – physical and symbolic reminders of the teacher (Fig. 1). Relics of the Buddha were of three types: *śarīraka*, or "bodily," relics (pieces of bone, teeth, and hair); *paribhogaka* relics, or objects that the Buddha had used (his begging bowl and throne); and *uddeśaka* relics, or symbolic reminders of the Buddha (images, texts, and other allusions to the Buddha that are neither related to his body nor came into direct contact with him). From the earliest of times, such relics were enclosed and enshrined in a structure known as a stūpa. Essentially a stūpa serves as a reminder of the Buddha and communicates the essence of Buddhist teachings. Thus, it embodies the absolute totality of Buddhism.

Historical Background

The authorization for building a stūpa (or reliquary mound) to commemorate the Buddha's remains is found in the *Mahāparinirvāṇasūtra*. In this text the dying Buddha Śākyamuni states that, in the manner similar to commemorating a king, his own cremated remains should be encased in a stūpa (Maurice Walshe, translator, *The Long Discourses of the Buddha: A Translation of the Dīgha Nikāya* [1995], pp. 264–265). No clear evidence of pre-Buddhist "royal" stūpas has been found. The text further asserts that it is not for the mendicants to concern themselves with such matters but that it is the responsibility of the laity to establish and pay homage to the stūpas.

Fig. 1: Bone relics of Buddha Śākyamuni, from the Priprawa site in Northern Bihar, National Museum, New Delhi.
Photo courtesy of John C. Huntington, the Huntington Archive, copyright 1984

After Śākyamuni's death there was a serious conflict between eight powerful clans over who had the right to obtain the teacher's relics. Each ruler sought to attain the relics that would legitimize him as king and elevate the position of his territory. An important Brahmin priest named Droṇa, literally "measure[ing vessel]," was finally brought in to settle the prolonged dispute. He suggested that the relics be divided into eight portions, one for each of the competing clans, and that each then builds a stūpa in memory of the Buddha. Droṇa's proposal was accepted and the relics, divided into eight portions, were each enshrined in eight stūpas. These came to be known as the eight Mahācaityas, or "Great Sacred Locales," of Buddhism.

In time stūpa building escalated with increased royal patronage. According to the *Aśokāvadana*, Aśoka, the great Mauryan emperor, converted to Buddhism and had seven of the eight Mahācaityas opened and the relics within redistributed throughout his vast empire. The text notes that the emperor erected 84,000 stūpas encasing the redistributed relics. According to legend the emperor had 84,000 stūpas built in a single night. The actual number of stūpas that the emperor had built is unknown. The number, 84,000, is simply a standard Indic reference to a large but nonspecific number. The relics were distributed to far-reaching Mauryan provinces, such as the Swat valley in Pakistan, Amaravati in Andhra Pradesh, Sāñcī in central India, and other sites where stūpa remains from Aśokan times have been excavated by modern archaeologists.

The Stūpa

Visually stūpas vary greatly in size, material, and form. They range from enormous structures in stone and wood (Fig. 2); to small reliquaries made of precious metal, crystal, and so on used as devotional objects in shrines; to tiny clay objects made by the millions as votive offerings. Moreover specific geographic locations throughout the Buddhist world have distinct styles of stūpa, and in each area the structure might be known by a different name. For example, in southern Asia in general, the stūpa began as a hemispherical mound placed on a low platform. Over time this structure increased in verticality, resulting in a tower-like edifice. Whereas the structure is called a stūpa in India, Nepal, Pakistan, Afghanistan, and Bangladesh, it is specifically referred to as a *dāgoba* in Sri Lanka. In the trans-Himalayan regions, a stūpa maintains the southern Asian format with few minor differences. However, in Tibet the structure is specifically known as *chorten*, or "Dharma receptacle." In Thailand the structure is referred to as *chedi*, the Thai pronunciation of the word *caitya*. In eastern Asia the form of the structure is altered significantly into the pagoda, a multistory (2 to 13 levels), tower-like monument. They are referred to as *ta* in China and as *tō* in Japan, the pronunciation of the common character for the word "tower" in both languages. However, regardless of differences in form, the stūpa, throughout the Buddhist world, carries com-

Fig. 2: The Great Stūpa at Sāñcī, India, c. 250 B.C.E. through fifth century C.E. The stūpa is of Aśokan origin; however, the main form and the gates are primarily Śuṅga period, second to first century B.C.E.
Photo courtesy of John C. Huntington, the Huntington Archive, copyright 1984

mon symbolic significance, frequently communicated through its structural components.

Structural Components of a Stūpa and Their Symbolism

As one of the most profound symbols in Buddhism, the stūpa can be interpreted on several levels. On one level it is inherently the presence of the Buddha. Second, it is a direct representation of Mount Meru, or Buddhist world system. Third, it is the meditative definition of a practitioner's path toward enlightenment. These notions are communicated through the various structural components of a stūpa.

Five primary components form the basis of all stūpas throughout the Buddhist world. They are the *aṇḍa*, literally "egg," or the hemispherical dome of the stūpa; the base on which the dome rests; the *yaṣṭi*, or the central shaft; the *harmikā*, or fence-like railing, enclosing the *yaṣṭi* above the dome; and the *chattra*, or "umbrella" (or *bhūmi*, "stage" or "ground"), that surmounts the stūpa structure (Fig. 3).

The *aṇḍa*, or dome, is the main element of all stūpas. It is within this hemispherical dome that the relics are placed. With time the low hemispherical dome was increased in verticality and enriched with sculptural representations.

The *aṇḍa* sits on a base or "drum," generally circular in early stūpas. In some notably early stūpas, such as the one at Gum Bahal at Śankhu in Nepal, the base is altogether omitted. As is common in Indic art, the base serves to elevate the stūpa above ground level, thereby increasing its sanctity. The base is also regarded as Mount Meru, thereby implying that the stūpa, itself Mount Meru, is located at the pinnacle of the mountain. Such

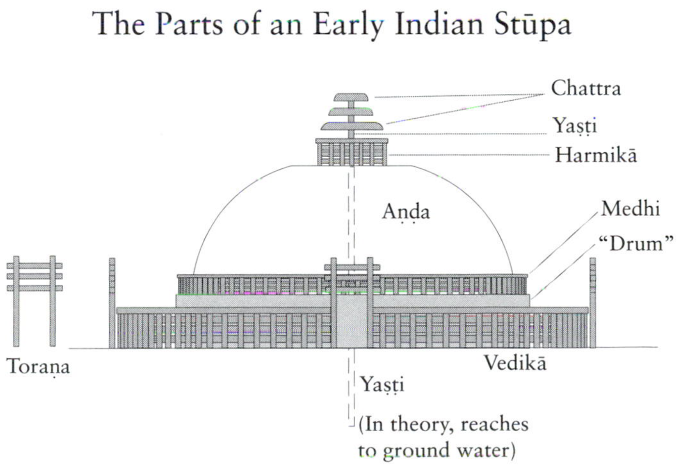

Fig. 3: Diagram of the basic stūpa with terminology.
Drawing courtesy of John C. Huntington, the Huntington Archive, copyright 1999

redundancy in Mount Meru symbolism is common in Buddhist iconography and underscores the fundamental nature of the concept of the mountain in Buddhist methodology.

The *yaṣṭi*, or pillar, runs through the center of the stūpa and is the true axis of the monument. In the *Atharvaveda*, a Vedic apocryphon dating to about 1200 to 1000 B.C., an axial pillar (called a *skambha* in this text) is described as rising from the subterranean waters below and extending into the highest of heavens (William Dwight Whitney, translator, *Atharva Veda Saṁhitā* [1962], volume 2, p. 594, verse 35). The text also states that the *skambha* serves to separate the earth from the heavens, thereby providing space for worldly existence. It is the axis of the world around which all phenomena become manifest. The notion of the *skambha* is communicated through the *yaṣṭi* in stūpa symbolism. Running through the center of the monument, the *yaṣṭi* is the world axis around which all Buddhist existence revolves. It is the absolute immutable core and seat of Buddhist enlightenment. Thus, the *yaṣṭi* is conceptually identical to the vertical axis that runs through the center of Mount Meru, located at the heart-mind of every sentient being.

Fig. 4: Remains of a stūpa in the small stūpa court between the *vihāra* and the *caitya* hall at Bhājā, Maharashtra, India, c. late second or early first century B.C.E.
Photo courtesy of John C. Huntington, the Huntington Archive, copyright 1970

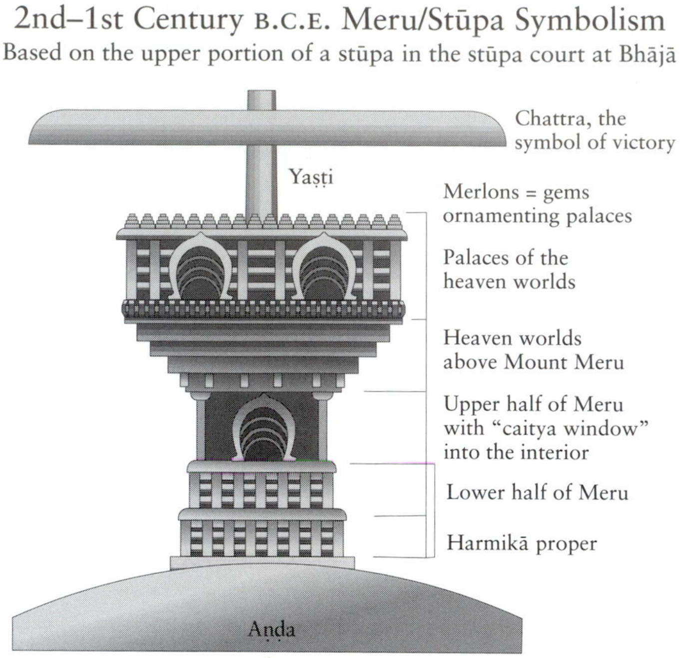

Fig. 5: Drawing of the details of the superstructure of the stūpa in Fig. 4.
Drawing courtesy of John C. Huntington, the Huntington Archive, copyright 1999

The *yaṣṭi* rises through the drum base, through the *aṇḍa*, and emerges from the top of the dome. This point on the dome is frequently marked by a fence-like structure known as a *harmikā*. Similar fence-like structures are known as markers of sacred or holy space from as early as the Indus Valley civilization (2300–1750 B.C.). Thus, the *harmikā* marks out sacred space above the dome, around the central axis of the stūpa. As discussed previously, the *yaṣṭi* is identical to the vertical axis at the core of Mount Meru, thereby demonstrating that the stūpa is also identical to the Buddhist world system. Within this context the *harmikā* serves to mark the sacred space represented by the heaven worlds atop Mount Meru.

Frequently a cantilevered structure with a series of merlons along the upper rim was added to the simple square-like *harmikā* (Figs. 4 and 5). Such *harmikā* were probably initially made of wood and served as prototypes for stūpas made of stone and other material in later years. This particular type of *harmikā* is not discussed in any literary source or inscription. However, they had become ubiquitous in art and architecture by the second century B.C. Throughout the Buddhist world merlons appear as markers of transcendence. Thus, the cantilevered structure appears to be a further elaboration of the heaven worlds above

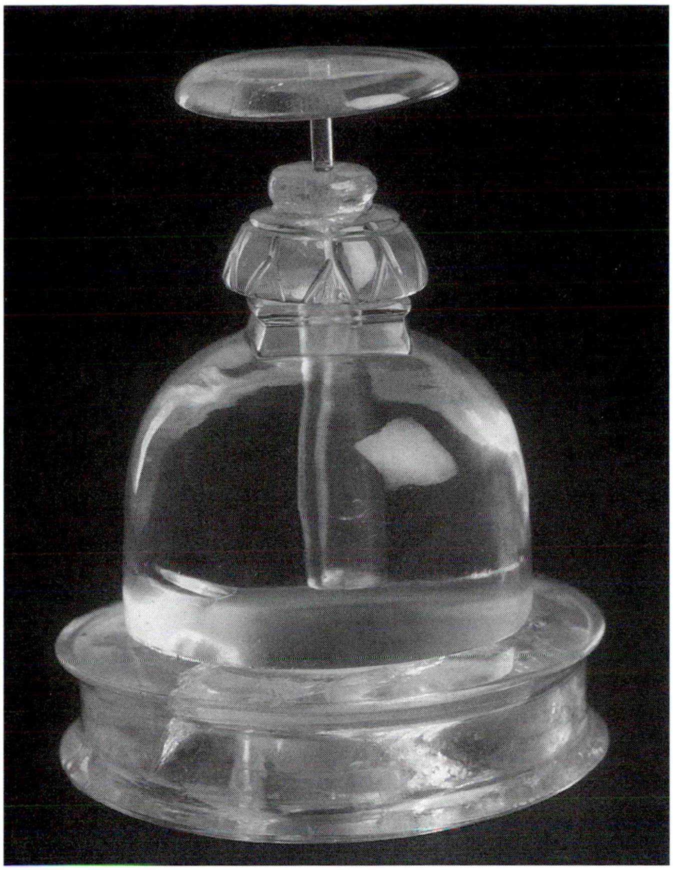

Fig. 6: Relic container in the form of a miniature stūpa from Bhojpur Stūpa II, Bhopal area of Madhya Pradesh, India. Mauryan period, presumably from the Aśokan redistribution of the relics of Śākyamuni Buddha. Victoria and Albert Museum, London, museum photograph. Photo courtesy of John C. Huntington, the Huntington Archive

Mount Meru, in particular a reference to the more ethereal realms.

In all stūpas the *yaṣṭi* supports one or more horizontal disks at the top. Depending on the context these disks are known either as *chattra*, or "umbrella(s)," or as *bhūmi*s, or "stages" or "grounds." The *chattra* are usually honorific umbrellas signifying the stature of the attainment by Śākyamuni. The number of *chattra* varies greatly, especially in early stūpas. They range from one, as seen on a Maurya-period crystal reliquary from Bhojpur Stūpa II in the Bhopal area (Fig. 6), to great numbers, as seen in the relief panels from Amaravati (Fig. 7).

As noted previously the stūpa communicates the soteriological methodology of Buddhism. Specifically three concepts describing the final attainment were developed and communicated through the structural components of a stūpa. The first, underlying concept is that of the *bodhipākṣa*, or the 37 wings of enlightenment (Edward Conze, editor and translator, *The Large Sūtra on Perfect Wisdom* [1975], pp. 151–156).

The *bodhipākṣa* are the 37 progressing attainments in the enlightenment process that, in stūpa iconography, are represented by the various components from the base to the top of the *harmikā* (Fig. 8). The 37 wings of enlightenment (*bodhipākṣa*) are as follows:

(First step): Four applications of mindfulness
1. (01) mindfulness of body
2. (02) mindfulness of feelings
3. (03) mindfulness of thought
4. (04) mindfulness of dharmas

(Second step): Four right efforts
1. (05) future nonproduction of evil dharmas
2. (06) forsake past production of evil dharmas
3. (07) bring about the future production of good dharmas
4. (08) concentrate on the past production of good dharmas

Fig. 7: Stūpa slab relief from Amaravati, Andhra Pradesh, c. second century C.E., British Museum, London. The billowing, cloud-like formation of *chattra* above the stūpa is yet to be satisfactorily explained; however, this type of representation is the extreme of the multiplication of the *chattra* convention.
Photo courtesy of John C. Huntington, the Huntington Archive, copyright 1992

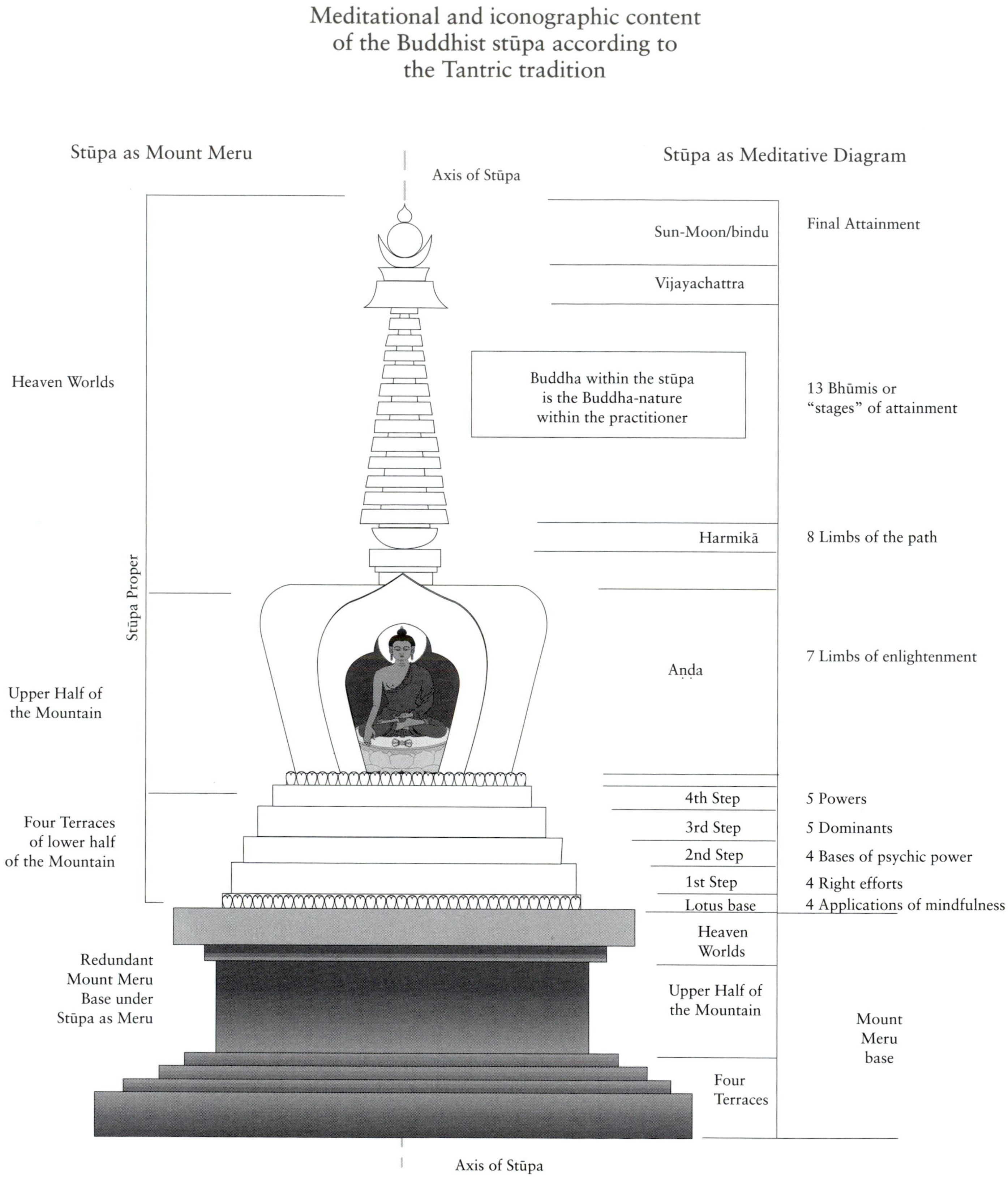

Fig. 8: Diagram of the meditational relationships of the *bodhipākṣa* to the components of a stūpa. Based on the Tibetan tradition. Drawing courtesy of John C. Huntington, the Huntington Archive, copyright 1999

(Third step): Four bases of psychic power
1. (09) desire-to-do (faith)
2. (10) vigor
3. (11) thought
4. (12) exploration

(Fourth step): Five dominants
1. (13) desire-to-do (faith)
2. (14) vigor
3. (15) mindfulness
4. (16) concentration
5. (17) wisdom

Fig. 9: Left: a relic casket, of stucco and gemstones, in the form of a stūpa from Taxila, Pakistan, c. sixth century, Taxila Museum. The top is missing, although fragments suggest the basic convention. Right: Bronze stūpa from Swat valley, c. eighth century, Peshawar Museum, Peshawar, Pakistan. This stūpa illustrates undamaged convention. Photo courtesy of John C. Huntington, the Huntington Archive

Fig. 10: North (main) entrance to Phra Pathom Chedi, Nakhon Pathom, Thailand, 19th- and 20th-century recontructions. Photo courtesy of John C. Huntington, the Huntington Archive, copyright 1992

(Base of *aṇḍa*): Five powers
1. (18) desire-to-do (faith)
2. (19) vigor
3. (20) mindfulness
4. (21) concentration
5. (22) wisdom

(*aṇḍa*): Seven limbs of enlightenment
1. (23) mindfulness
2. (24) investigation into the dharma
3. (25) vigor
4. (26) joyous zest
5. (27) tranquility
6. (28) concentration
7. (29) even-mindedness

(*harmikā*): Eight limbs of the path
1. (30) right views
2. (31) right intentions
3. (32) right speech
4. (33) right conduct
5. (34) right livelihood
6. (35) right effort
7. (36) right mindfulness
8. (37) right concentration

While the *bodhipākṣa* symbolism continued, a second concept, evident especially in Sri Lanka, Burma, and Thailand, was layered into stūpa iconography. This was the notion of the ten *jñānaṁ*, or "insights," of the final attainments of the arhat, the perfected being in Theravāda Buddhism. In stūpas this notion is communicated through ten layers, arranged in the form of a conical spire, above the *harmikā*.

Finally, an additional interpretation was included into stūpa iconography. As early as the sixth century in Taxila and especially popular within the Tantric context, the number of *chattra* on the stūpas increased to 13 and were referred to as *bhūmi* (Fig. 9). The first ten *bhūmi*s denoted the *daśabhūmika*, or the ten stages that a bodhisattva achieves on his path to realization. The final three *bhūmi*s are the qualities of a Buddha's mind. In Tantric stūpas generally, a single *chattra* topped the 13 *bhūmi*s and signified the exalted status of the Buddha's attainment. Above the *chattra* was a configuration comprising a crescent moon, a sun disk, and a *bindu*, or flame-like finial. This surmounting configuration denotes the final enlightened stage and the absolute realization of *śūnyatā*.

Monasteries and Stūpas

Monasteries and stūpas have had a parallel development throughout the history of Buddhism. Monastic sites all over the Buddhist world usually have at least one stūpa in their premises. The stūpa might be the very reason for the existence of the monastery, or it might simply be one of many devotional objects within the monastic site. To cite but a few examples, Phra

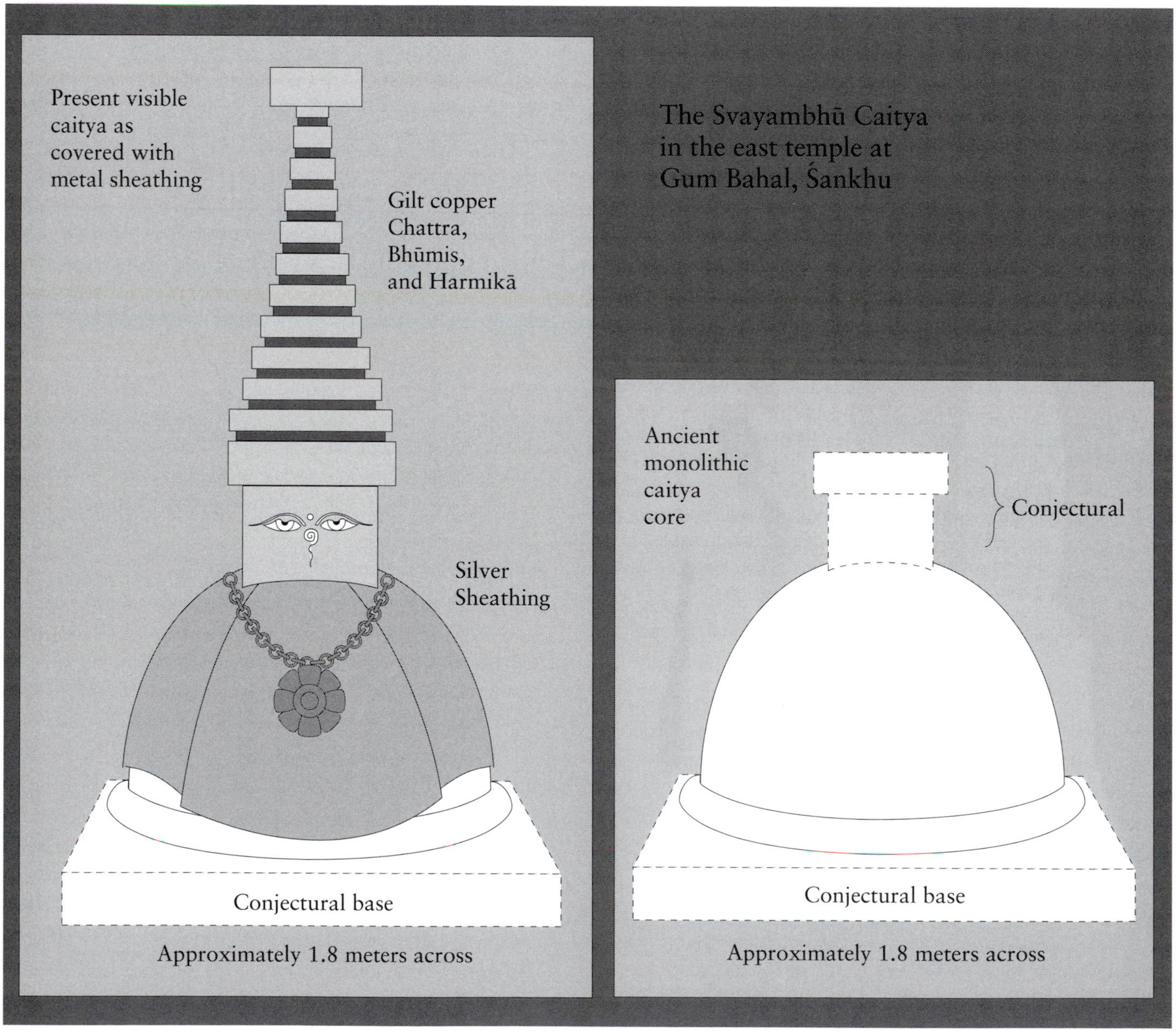

Fig. 11: The Svayambhu Stūpa at Gum Bahal, near Śankhu, Kathmandu Valley, Nepal, c. fourth century B.C.E. Drawing courtesy of John C. Huntington, the Huntington Archive, copyright 1996

Fig. 12: The Svayambhū Mahācaitya at Gosingu Parvat Mahāvihāra (Svayambhunāth), Kathmandu, Nepal, various dates from antiquity to recent. Photo courtesy of John C. Huntington, the Huntington Archive, copyright 1994

Pathom Chedi in Nakhon Pathom, Thailand, is reputed to be the largest stūpa in the world (Fig. 10). However, the monasteries associated with this monument are modest in size. In Nepal's Kathmandu Valley are two early stūpas of major importance to the history of the stūpa as well as to its association with monasteries. These are a small stūpa at Gum Bahal (*Bahal* is the Newari pronunciation of the Sanskrit term *vihāra*, or monastery) near the town of Śankhu (Fig. 11) and the *mahāstūpa* known as Svayambhū Mahācaitya near the city of Kathmandu (Fig. 12).

At Gum Bahal the rock-cut stūpa is an extremely low hemispheric mound indicating an early date. The stūpa presently functions as the lineage deity of the local Buddhist *saṅgha*. The site is also home to what is probably the oldest monastery in Nepal. Some of its caves are in the form of simple rock-cut square chambers, undoubtedly used as monastic shelters. The existence of the stūpa, as well as the early rock-cut monastic dwellings at the site, attests to the interdependency of the two structures from the earliest of times.

Svayambhū Mahācaitya, also an early low hemispheric stūpa, is known to have been refurbished several times throughout history. Today the stūpa's profile appears to date approximately to the Licchavi period (c. sixth century A.D.). The stūpa is presently associated with the community of monks or, more appropriately, Tantric ritual specialists known as Buddhācaryas. Svayambhū Mahācaitya is the primordial source and the ontological basis of the whole of Newar Buddhism. Through a surrogate stūpa located in every *bahal* and *bahi* (two types of monasteries in the Kathmandu Valley), the Mahācaitya vivifies each monastery.

Two monasteries of the Buddhācaryas are located at the site of Svayambhū: the Gosingu Parvat Samhyeng Mahāvihāra and the Svayambhū Bahi. Further, the importance of the Mahācaitya is underscored by the two Tibetan monasteries, Svayambhū Gumba and Karmarāja Mahāvihāra, also established at the site.

Regardless of the size or importance of the stūpa at a monastic site, it is ubiquitously present. To varying extents it is the focus of devotion at a monastery. As such the stūpa fosters a symbiotic existence between the members of the laity and the monastic community throughout the Buddhist world, the very basis of Buddhist methodology.

In addition specialized forms of stūpas developed in various parts of the Buddhist world. For example, a particular type of stūpa, known as *kii chorten* in Tibet, is a hallow structure that allows a devotee to walk through a passage in the base and see the inside of the monument. Within the core of the monument are representations of the Buddhas presiding over their respective paradises. Standing at the center of the *kii chorten*, the devotee sees his or her own Buddha nature, defined by the Buddhas in the paradises. As such the devotee is literally in the core of Mount Meru itself, located in the very heart-mind of the viewer.

Whether a small reliquary or a massive stone monument and regardless of its form or configuration, geographic distinctions, or regional alterations based on local traditions, the stūpa is a perpetual reminder of the Buddha Śākyamuni and his teachings. The structure embodies the actual presence of the Buddha and is a reiteration of his compassion as manifested through his teachings. In essence the stūpa is a road map and a guide to one's own enlightenment in the form of Mount Meru, through the realization of the 37 wings of enlightenment and through the awareness of the potential of Buddhahood within the heart-mind of every being.

JOHN C. HUNTINGTON

See also Architecture: Buddhist Monasteries in Southern Asia; Aśoka; Cave Temples and Monasteries in India and China; Images: Buddhist Perspectives; Mount Meru; Mountain Monasteries, Buddhist; Nepal: History; Spirituality: Buddhist; Temple, Buddhist; Vajrayāna Buddhism in Nepal; Visual Arts: Buddhist; Worship Space: Buddhist Perspectives

Further Reading

Benisti, Mireille, *Contribution à l'étude du stupa bouddhique indien: Les stupa mineurs de Bodh-Gaya et de Ratnagiri*, Paris: École française, 1981

Govinda, Lama Anagarika, *Psycho-Cosmic Symbolism of the Buddhist Stupa*, Emeryville, California: Dharma, 1976

Pant, Sushila, *The Origin and Development of Stupa Architecture in India*, Varanasi: Bharata Manisha, 1976

Paranavitana, Senarat, *The Stupa in Ceylon*, Colombo: Memoirs of the Archaeological Survey of Ceylon, Government Press, 1946; reprint, 1980

Snodgrass, Adrian, *The Symbolism of the Stupa*, Ithaca, New York: Southeast Asia Program, Cornell University, 1985

Tucci, Giuseppe, *Stupa: Art, Architectonics and Symbolism*, edited by Lokesh Chandra, translated by Uma Marina Vesci, New Delhi, Aditya Prakashan, 1988

Stylites

A form of asceticism that developed in northern Syria in the fourth century was the "open-air" life of a hermit who had no cell or cave but exposed himself to the elements. Maro (after whom the Maronite Church was later named) was supposed to have initiated this practice. A peculiar variety of this mode of life was invented by Symeon "Stylites" (c. 390–459), who spent the last 37 years of his life on a column (Greek, *stulos*) situated on a hilltop on the limestone ridge east of Antioch. The column was gradually extended until it attained a height of over 50 feet. Its capital pro-

Apse in the northeast corner of the octagonal crossing, Church of St. Symeon Stylites, near Aleppo, Syria, late fifth century.
Photo courtesy of Chris Schabel

View from the west transept through the crossing to the south nave, Church of St. Symeon Stylites, near Aleppo, Syria, late fifth century. Photo courtesy of Chris Schabel

vided a reasonably broad platform that Symeon never left. Devoting most of his time to prayer with arms stretched out, he would devote about three hours per day to addressing the crowds of pilgrims or speaking to individual visitors (who could ascend the column on a ladder). He ate and slept extremely little; most probably, like later stylites, he slept standing, leaning against some form of balustrade. Symeon offered no explanation of this strange form of life; the monks who shepherded pilgrims asserted that it was akin to the symbolic actions of the Old Testament prophets and intended to draw attention to the holy man's message. A visitor who asked Symeon whether he was an angel uncovered the real significance of the column: it suspended the stylite between heaven and earth, standing erect in ceaseless prayer, a mediator who conveyed to God the prayers of ordinary mortals and brought down to them divine guidance and blessing. Symeon's apostolate extended from guiding emperors on points of doctrine to laying down interest rates for the local farmers.

Later stylites were numerous. The most famous were St. Daniel and St. Symeon the Younger. Beginning in 460 Daniel (409–493) lived on a column in Constantinople from which he briefly descended in 475 in a dramatic and successful gesture of protest against the ecclesiastical policy of the usurper Basiliscus. Symeon the Younger (521–592) became a stylite near Antioch at the almost incredible age of seven. Although mainly a Byzantine phenomenon, stylites spread beyond the empire into regions with a Byzantine culture, such as Georgia and Russia, and are recorded as late as the 19th century. Easily the most famous later "stylite" (although admittedly in an extended sense of the word) was St. Seraphim of Sarov (1759–1833), who for several years stood or knelt either on a huge rock in the forest or on a stone in his cell.

Some of St. Symeon's monastic contemporaries accused him of attention-seeking and urged him to descend from his column and to practice humility. It must be admitted that stylites did not seek to remain unknown. However, spirituality that remains hidden and unperceived lacks social impact. For many centuries the stylite posture of praying erect at a distance above the earth exerted a deep impression on Eastern Christianity as an unforgettable symbol of the essence of prayer and of mediation between human beings and God.

RICHARD M. PRICE

See also Asceticism: Christian Perspectives; Hagiography: Eastern Christian; Hermits: Eastern Christian; Istanbul, Turkey; Maronites; Missionaries: Christian; Origins: Eastern Christian; Orthodox Monasticism: Byzantine; Seraphim of Sarov, St.; Syria

Further Reading

Bibliotheca Sanctorum, volume 11, columns 1116–1157, Rome: Città Nuova Editrice, 1968

Delehaye, Hippolyte, *Les Saints Stylites*, Brussels: Société des bollandistes, 1923

Doran, Robert, *The Lives of Symeon Stylites*, Kalamazoo, Michigan: Cistercian Publications, 1992

Lietzmann, Hans, "Das Leben des heiligen Symeon Stylites," *Texte und Untersuchungen* 32:4 (1908)

Peña, Ignacio, *The Amazing Life of the Syrian Monks in the 4th–6th Centuries*, Milan: Franciscan Printing Press, 1992

Subiaco, Italy

At Subiaco, 40 miles east of Rome, Benedict of Nursia first found refuge (c. 500) in a cave (the *Sacro Speco*) overlooking the Aniene River and then established a monastic community. His monastery eventually attracted a dozen daughter houses. When the founder removed to Monte Cassino, monastic life continued at Subiaco under his disciples and their successors. A Saracen incursion in the ninth century did considerable damage, but the popes oversaw the rebuilding of the monasteries. However, observance eventually became concentrated at St. Scolastica, seat of the abbot, and at St. Benedetto, site of the *Sacro Speco*, each having a monastic compound. Although the abbots continued to be elected by the monks, they became heads of a small territorial state. This secular role could distract from religious observance and frequently vexed the population of the region. The monastery also became exempt from visitation by any ecclesiastical authority except the pope himself. Thus, local customs and liturgical practices became firmly rooted. In 1276 the papacy began to nominate the abbots. The Avignon period (1309–1377) saw an internationalization of the monastery that drew members from as far away as Germany and received non-Italian abbots named by the popes. After the Great Schism (1378–1417), Rome began to name commendatory abbots, usually curial cardinals. One of these was the Spanish Dominican theologian Juan de Torquemada (1388–1468), who promoted stricter monastic observance and restored the community's buildings. During his abbacy two German printers established the first press in Italy at the monastery, where they prepared several editions before moving on to Rome. (His nephew was the famous Dominican inquisitor Tomás Torquemada.)

The Subiaco observance found few followers in Italy, but it became rooted north of the Alps. However, Subiaco itself was in-

**Monastery of St. Benedict, Subiaco, Italy, 12th–13th century.
Photo courtesy of the Editor**

Scala Santa with frescoes (14th century), Monastery of St. Benedict, Subiaco, Italy.
Photo courtesy of the Editor

corporated into the Cassinese congregation of Benedictines, formerly that of St. Giustina, Padua, in 1516. This act produced a long struggle with the German monks; moreover, the commendatory abbots, frequently members of the Roman Colonna clan, retained their rights. Eventually, Subiaco became an *abbatia nullius* (territorial abbey), separate from any see but visited by its commendatory; however, it lost its temporal jurisdiction to the papal state. The 17th century found monastic observance and numbers of monks in decline, but this trend was reversed during the 18th. French penetration into central Italy after the Revolution disrupted religious life, and the Napoleonic regime temporarily suppressed the monastery at Subiaco. Unhappily, the Napoleonic administrator sold off both property rights and many volumes from the library. After Napoleon fell, monastic life was reestablished on the site. The monastery was not prosperous, nor were monks numerous for a time, but the *Sacro Speco* became a site of renewed pilgrimage activity. In 1847 Pius IX (1846–1878) assumed the commendatory abbacy, and then that practice vanished with the Risorgimento. The community also endured another brief period of suppression beginning in 1874, and St. Benedetto briefly had its own abbot, but the house was reunited with St. Scolastica. The abbacy also was united for a time with the office of abbot general in the Cassinese congregation. Despite earthquake and war, monastic life has continued at St. Scolastica and St. Benedetto down to the present time.

THOMAS M. IZBICKI

See also Abbeys, Territorial; Benedict of Nursia, St.; Benedictines; Dominicans

Further Reading

Allodi, Leone, *Inventario dei manoscritti della biblioteca di Subiaco*, Forlì: Casa Editrice Luigi Bordandini, 1891
Carosi, G.P., *I monasteri di Subiaco*, Subiaco, 1987
Egidi, Paolo, et al., *I monasteri di Subiaco*, 2 vols., Rome: Ministero della publica istruzione, 1904
Izbicki, T.M., "Medieval Legal Texts in the Manuscripts of S. Scolastica, Subiaco," *Bulletin of Medieval Canon Law* 18 (1988)
Salmon, Pierre, *The Abbot in Monastic Tradition*, translated by C. Lavoie, Washington, D.C.: Consortium Press, 1972
Schuster, Iidefonso, *Saint Benedict and His Times*, translated by G.J. Roettger, St. Louis, Missouri, and London: Herder, 1951

Suger c. 1081–1151

French Benedictine abbot of St.-Denis and initiator of Gothic architecture

Suger lived at the convergence of two competing monastic ideals, and his achievement was to accommodate the newer while remaining true to the older. The monastery of St.-Denis, to which Suger was pledged as an oblate at the age of ten, observed rather casually Benedictine practices inherited from the reformers of the Carolingian era. By the time that Suger became its abbot in 1122, new and far more stringent cloistered orders such as the Cistercians and the Carthusians were winning favor across Europe.

If St.-Denis' spiritual life seemed antiquated, its politics were not. The monastery boasted royal tombs dating back to the Merovingian era, and it actively cultivated a close relationship with France's rising Capetian dynasty. To the abbots strong royal government offered the best hope for restraining France's rapacious feudal nobility.

The abbot of St.-Denis needed a powerful royal ally. The disorder that attended the disintegration of the Carolingian monarchy had weakened the monastery's hold on valuable properties and burdened its monks with much secular business. Young Suger had received an adequate classical education and wielded literary gifts, but it was not scholarship that launched his career; rather, it was his promise as a man of affairs that won him the favor of his abbot, his king, Louis VI (1108–1137), and the monastic brethren who in 1122 chose him to be their leader.

When Suger took charge at St.-Denis, both Peter Abelard (1079–1142/43) and Bernard of Clairvaux (1090–1153) had harsh things to say about him and his house. However, their words need to be read in context. Abelard had taken the cowl at St.-Denis in 1117–1118 following the collapse of his teaching career, but his precipitous flight to the cloister was an act of desperation that he regretted, and he soon became involved in a bitter fight to win release from his vows. Bernard's complaint was

Transept of Basilica of St.-Denis, 13th century.
Photo courtesy of Caroline Rose/CNMHS

that the monks of St.-Denis were so deeply involved in secular affairs that their cloister resembled more a bustling court than a peaceful house of prayer. Suger's genius lay in his ability to respond to these criticisms without causing dissent within his community and without departing dramatically from St.-Denis' traditional Benedictine spirituality.

At the start of his career, Suger made a name for himself by defeating nobles who were preying on St.-Denis' endowments and by representing his abbot and his king on major diplomatic missions. Under Abbot Adam's lax supervision, this ambitious young monk might have indulged a personal taste for what the reformers of his generation regarded as unseemly display. However, Suger was astute enough to sense that standards were changing, and he adjusted appropriately. True to the Benedictine way, he avoided extremes and won praise for maintaining himself in a state that was neither luxurious nor so mean as to degrade the dignity of his office. He seems also, in his senior years, seriously to have regretted the violence to which he had once resorted to protect his abbey's lands. The mature Suger's victories were won by diplomacy and marked him as a man of peace.

Suger's moderation enabled him to reform St.-Denis without inciting the resistance that such programs often spawned. He won over his monks by promising a fair exchange: greater security and more comfortable working conditions came in exchange for additional duties and tighter discipline. Well before Suger's day Benedictines had come to the conclusion that the work required of them was the *opus Dei* in the choir, not labor in the fields. Although Suger believed this, he also believed in maximizing productivity. He laid on his monks an additional daily mass, new weekly offices, and obligations to observe a growing number of royal anniversaries. Suger astutely intuited that a reputation for modest living and spiritual vitality comprised a house's strongest claim to endowments and worldly influence. Saint-Denis was reformed so successfully that the pope commissioned its abbot to reinvigorate other communities.

For Suger, moderate austerity in the diet and housing of monks did not entail poverty in their working environment. Many of the newer religious orders (e.g., the Cistercians) were hostile to the arts, viewing the contemplation of physical beauty as a distraction from spiritual goals. Suger, however, clung to the old Benedictine belief that the service of God deserved the very best that human worshipers could provide. He argued passionately that visual displays were not prideful indulgences but rather a legitimate means for conveying the transcendent reality of God. In this he followed the lead of Neoplatonic theologians, chief among whom was reputed to be St. Denis himself. The *Celestial Hierarchy* of Dionysius (i.e., St. Denis) the Pseudo-Areopagite, in the translation of the late Carolingian scholar John Scotus Eriugena (c. 810–c. 877), enjoyed a revival through the works of Suger's contemporaries, the Victorines. Their conviction that meditation on the perfections of material things helped the mind climb toward the true light of God was for Suger not only an article of faith but a fact of human experience. The proof that Suger offered constitutes the achievement for which he is best remembered.

When Suger's involvement at the French court diminished after the death of Louis VI in 1137, the abbot threw his energies into rebuilding the church at St.-Denis. He strove to create a sanctuary that would compel respect as the central shrine of the emerging French nation, but his higher ambition was to build a church uniquely fit for Christian worship. What he envisioned was not the kind of cerebral, stripped-down building for which Bernard's Cistercians became known; instead, he wanted a lavish structure that would rival the glories of Cluny, the Benedictines' greatest church. Suger avidly stockpiled gold and gems and sought out exotic vessels to furnish his altars, but the glory of his new church was not its ornament alone but rather the originality of its design. Suger's architects created the prototype for the Gothic style that soon swept Europe and continues to this day to shape conceptions of religious architecture. As befitted the saint to whom it was dedicated – Dionysius, the champion of the Neoplatonic strategy of seeking God by progressing from the contemplation of material things to pure enlightenment – Suger's intricately vaulted "glass house" illumined celebrations of the Christian mysteries with the mystery of light.

A. Daniel Frankforter

See also Abelard, Peter; Architecture: Western Christian Monasteries; Bernard of Clairvaux, St.; Cistercians; Dionysius the Pseudo-Areopagite; France; Heloise; Victorines

Biography

Suger entered the abbey of St.-Denis c. 1091, where his fellow students included the future King Henry VI (1108–1137). Elected Abbot of St.-Denis in 1122, he served the king as ambassador and wrote his *Life*. Suger's plans for the new church at St.-Denis (consecrated in 1144) entitled Suger to be considered an initiator of Gothic architecture, particularly in the use of stained glass.

Major Works

Vita Ludovici Grosi
Libellus de Consecratione Ecclesiae S. Dionysii
Liber de rebus in Administratione sua gestis

Further Reading

Aubert, Marcel, *Suger*, Paris: Fontenelle, 1950
Cartellieri, Otto, *Abt Suger von Saint-Denis 1081–1151*, Berlin: Ebering, 1898
Crosby, Sumner McKnight, *The Royal Abbey of Saint-Denis in the Time of Abbot Suger (1122–1151)*, New York: Metropolitan Museum of Art, 1981
Crosby, Sumner McKnight, *The Royal Abbey of Saint-Denis from Its Beginning to the Death of Suger, 475–1151: Album Drawings*, New Haven, Connecticut: Yale University Press, 1987
Gerson, Paula Lieber, editor, *Abbot Suger and Saint-Denis*, New York: Metropolitan Museum of Art, 1986
Grant, Lindy, *Abbot Suger of St.-Denis: Church and State in Early Twelfth-Century France*, London and New York: Longman, 1998
Panofsky, Erwin, *Gothic Architecture and Scholasticism*, Latrobe, Pennsylvania: Archabbey Press, 1951; London: Meridian Books, 1957

Rudolph, Conrad, *Artistic Change at St.-Denis: Abbot Suger's Program and the Early Twelfth-Century Controversy over Art*, Princeton, New Jersey: Princeton University Press, 1990
Simson, Otto von, *The Gothic Cathedral: Origins of Gothic Architecture and the Medieval Concept of Order*, London: Routledge and Kegan Paul, and New York: Pantheon Books, 1956; reprint, Princeton, New Jersey: Princeton University Press, 1988
Spiegel, Gabrielle, *The Chronicle Tradition of Saint-Denis: A Survey*, Brookline, Massachusetts: Classical Folia Editions, 1978
Suger, *Abbot Suger on the Abbey Church of St.-Denis and Its Art Treasures*, translated by Erwin Panofsky, Princeton, New Jersey: Princeton University Press, 1946

Sūtras. *See* Discourses (Sūtras): Mahāyāna

Suttas. *See* Discourses (Suttas): Theravāda

Suzuki, Daisetz Teitaro 1870–1966

Japanese Buddhist scholar and popularizer of Zen in the West

Daisetz Teitaro Suzuki, Buddhist scholar, prolific author, and itinerant lecturer, remains the single most important figure in the popularization of Zen in the 20th century. Suzuki produced over 30 volumes on Buddhism and Zen in English and an even greater oeuvre in his native Japanese. Translations of his work into Korean, Chinese, and other Asian languages have contributed to a resurgence of popular interest in Zen throughout eastern Asia as well.

Suzuki was born in Kanazawa (Ishikawa prefecture) in 1870, the son of a physician who died when Suzuki was five. Although nominally a Rinzai Zen Buddhist through family affiliation, Suzuki's serious interest in Buddhism did not emerge until he came under the influence of his high school mathematics teacher, Hōjō Tokiyuki (1858–1929), a lay Zen practitioner. In 1891 Suzuki, then fluent in English, began study of philosophy at Tokyo Imperial University and soon thereafter began lay Zen practice at Engakuji, a Zen monastery in nearby Kamakura.

Suzuki's Zen teachers at Engakuji were Imagita Kōsen (1816–1892) and, following Kōsen's death, Shaku Sōen (1859–1919). (It was Sōen who gave Suzuki the name Daisetz, meaning "great simplicity.") Both masters were active in the revival of Zen following the government-sanctioned persecution of Buddhism in the 1870s. As progressives they joined other Buddhist leaders in an attempt to broaden Buddhism's appeal by encouraging lay participation in Buddhist practice, promoting the secular education of the priesthood, and advocating an ecumenical attitude toward other schools of Buddhism. This new spirit would dominate Suzuki's own understanding of Zen thought and practice.

Sōen traveled to Chicago in 1893 to attend the World Parliament of Religions, where he befriended Paul Carus (1852–1919), editor of Open Court Press and exponent of the Religion of Science. Following his return Sōen, at Suzuki's behest, arranged for Suzuki to study with Carus in La Salle, Illinois. Suzuki went on to spend 11 years in La Salle, during which time he was exposed to a broad cross section of contemporary Western religious thought and new religious movements.

Suzuki returned to Japan in 1909 and two years later married the American Beatrice Lane (1878–1938), with whom he had a son. Suzuki soon began to publish widely on Mahāyāna Buddhism and Zen in both English and Japanese while earning a living through a series of college lectureships in English. During this time Suzuki was involved in the Theosophical movement and was instrumental in introducing the writings of Swedenborg to the Japanese. In 1921 he was appointed professor of Buddhist philosophy at Ōtani University in Kyoto, where he continued his Buddhist research and launched the journal *Eastern Buddhist*.

Following World War II, Suzuki resumed his travels to Europe and the United States, sometimes for extended periods. He was a popular lecturer, speaking at college campuses around the world, and from 1951 to 1957 he held a series of professorships at Columbia University. His written work and quietly charismatic personality made a significant impact not only on those with an interest in religion but also on artists, writers, and philosophers.

Suzuki made substantial and lasting contributions to Buddhist scholarship. For example, his three-volume study of the *Laṅkāvatāra Sūtra*, published in the 1930s, remains the most comprehensive work on the subject. However, much of his writing was intended for a popular audience and shows the distinct influence of Western religious thinkers popular in his day, including Paul Carus and William James. At the same time a decidedly nationalist streak existed in Suzuki's oeuvre: works such as *Zen and Japanese Culture* and *Japanese Spirituality* unapologetically tout the unique spiritual gifts of the Japanese and the sublime affinity between Zen and the martial culture of medieval Japan.

Because he was a layman writing for a lay audience, it is not surprising that Suzuki's approach to Zen should deemphasize the role of traditional Buddhist monasticism. Although Suzuki celebrated the lives of famous Zen patriarchs and described the rigors of Zen monastic training, he regarded the traditional monastic emphasis on ritual, liturgy, and obedience as ancillary to Zen proper. For Suzuki true Zen is nothing more or less than satori, which he understood as pure experience, an idea culled in part from William James and mediated through the writings of the Japanese philosopher (and Suzuki's lifelong friend) Nishida Kitarō (1870–1945).

Although Suzuki was instrumental in the introduction of Zen to the West, his influence in Japan was tempered by the fact that he never ordained as a monk, nor did he ever receive formal sanction (*inka*) from a Zen master. Many Japanese monks found Suzuki's Zen too "intellectual." Nevertheless Suzuki's approach to Zen rendered it accessible to lay parishioners and commensurate with the contingencies of modern life, and as such it helped establish the credibility of Zen among religious leaders and intellectuals in Japan and the rest of the world.

ROBERT H. SHARF

See also Buddhism: Western; Buddhist Schools/Traditions: Japan; Chan/Zen: Japan; Critiques of Buddhist Monasticism: Japanese; Eisai (Yosai); Japan: History; Kōan; Laicization of Spirituality: Buddhist Perspectives; United States: Buddhist; Zen, Arts of; Zen and the West

Biography

A Zen Buddhist layman, Suzuki studied with the Zen masters Imagita Kōsen and Shaku Sōen in Kamakura before coming to the United States. From 1897 to 1908 he worked under Paul Carus, editor of Open Court Press, in La Salle, Illinois. In 1921 he was appointed Professor of Buddhist Studies at Ōtano University, Kyoto, and during the 1950s he held a series of visiting professorships at Columbia University in New York. A prolific translator and scholar, the Japanese nativist did much to disseminate Zen ideas in the West, although his approach had relatively limited impact on the Japanese Zen monastic establishment.

Major Works

Outlines of Mahayana Buddhism, 1907
An Introduction to Zen Buddhism, 1934
Nihonteki reisei, 1944; as *Japanese Spirituality*, translated by Norman Waddell, 1972
Essays in Zen Buddhism: First Series, 1949
Essays in Zen Buddhism: Second Series, 1953
Essays in Zen Buddhism: Third Series, 1953
Zen and Japanese Culture, revised edition, 1959
Suzuki Daisetz zenshū (Collected Works of Suzuki Daisetz Teitaro), 33 vols., 1968–1971

Further Reading

Abe, Masao, editor, *A Zen Life: D.T. Suzuki Remembered*, New York: Weatherhill, 1986
Sharf, Robert H., "The Zen of Japanese Nationalism," in *Curators of the Buddha: The Study of Buddhism Under Colonialism*, edited by Donald S. Lopez, Jr., Chicago: University of Chicago Press, 1995
Suzuki, Daisetz Teitaro, *Zen Buddhism and Its Influence on Japanese Culture* (Ataka Buddhist Library), Kyoto: Eastern Buddhist Society, 1938; revised as *Zen and Japanese Culture* (Bollingen Series, 64), New York: Pantheon Books, and London: Routledge and Kegan Paul, 1959

Sweden. *See* Scandinavia

Switzerland

As early as the third century during Roman rule, Arian, Roman, and Byzantine Christianity gradually arrived in Helvetia (Switzerland), mainly by way of Gaulish and Italian merchants, artisans, slaves, and Roman soldiers. The earliest extant Christian historical evidence that we have are two monograms of Christ: the first found on a fibula at a tomb in Basel, dating to the mid–fourth century, and the second on the inscription of Pontius Asclepiodotus, dating from 377. Dating to around 390 is the oldest Christian church excavated so far, a chapel built over the tomb of the Theban martyrs by Bishop Theodore of Octodurus. Theodore was known to have attended the synod at Agaunum (381) convened by St. Ambrose (c. 339–397). Because Geneva was the capital of an administrative district, the city must have had a bishop in attendance, although the earliest bishop of record is Isaac (c. 400). The same should also be true for Chur, although we do not have any record of a bishop before 451. Traces of Christianity become more abundant during the fifth century. From archaeological research it is evident that most of the Roman strongholds contained small Christian chapels dating to at least this period, if not earlier.

With the increasing barbarian invasions of the late fourth century, two mutually hostile peoples moved into Helvetia: the Burgundians from the west and the Alamanni from the north. After 400 the Roman general Aetius allowed the Burgundians to settle in the west as a buffer against new Germanic incursions. The Burgundians, mostly Arian Christians, quickly took to Latin culture, allowing Catholicism to gain a tenuous foothold in the region. Their king, Sigismund (d. 524), converted to Catholicism and in 515 restored the monastery of St. Maurice at Agaune, which had been devastated during the earlier barbarian invasions. However, the earliest identifiable monastery in Helvetia is from mid-fifth-century Romainmôtier: the Abbey of St. Maurice.

The pagan Alamanni presented a different picture, that is, a much less peaceful one. The Franks under Clovis (481–511) stopped the Alamanni's advance around 496; nevertheless over a period of time the Alamanni slowly infiltrated to the Saane in central Helvetia. As the Alamanni moved southward, they avoided the Roman strongholds, allowing Christianity to survive tenuously in the region and the episcopal see at Vindonissa to stand. However, in time the Alamanni moved into northern Vaud and in 587 sacked the monastery of Romainmôtier, yet the region of Churrhaetia withstood the advancing Alamanni, permitting Christianity to remain intact. From the sixth to the eighth century, both the bishopric and the government of Churrhaetia were in the hands of the powerful Churrhaetian Victoridae family.

The main legacy of the Alamanni incursions into Helvetia was three distinct political units – Burgundy, Alamannia, and Churrhaetia – which continued to exist even after the Franks incorporated them into their empire – keeping their status to some extent even into the Carolingian dynasty. From the sixth to the ninth century, Irish and Frankish monks ministered in pagan Alamannia, seeking to convert it for a second time to Christianity.

Church of the Cordeliers (Franciscan), Fribourg, Switzerland, 13th century.
Photo courtesy of Mary Schaefer

Very little reliable information is available about the missionary efforts of these monks. Other than the historical evidence of St. Gall (628), no real proof exists for the work of the Irish *Fridolin* before the ninth century. That Christianity regained a foothold at all was due mainly to the presence of Frankish settlers and the work of the monasteries established by the Irish St. Columban (d. 615) and his disciples. From the mother house at Luxeuil and the daughter houses of Moutier, Grandval, St. Ursanne, and Vermes in Jura came monks bent on evangelizing Alamannia. Of their work St. Gallen became the most important monastery in the eastern portion of the country and, eventually for a time, one of the most important centers of learning throughout Europe. Another center of Christianity was St. Pirminius' abbey on the isle of Reichenau (c. 724). A daughter house at Pfäfers was founded shortly thereafter. In the eighth century the monastery of Disentis was founded in Lucerne. The eighth century also saw the coming of the Benedictines, with the establishment of the Abbey of Einsiedeln in 934. The turn of the tenth century saw a dense network of monasteries spread throughout Alamannia. Early in the seventh century, Constance, the sixth of the historic dioceses, was created, becoming the center of Christianity in Alamannia.

Throughout the Middle Ages the diocesan structure saw only a few minor changes. By 1033 the three regions, following brief periods of independence, found themselves in the German Empire. In the mid–tenth century, the Cluniac reformed entered Switzerland. Queen Bertha founded the Cluniac monastery of Payerne in 962. Romainmôtier joined the monastic federation and experienced new growth as part of the Cluniac reform. All Saints in Schaffhausen received the Customs of Cluny in 1079 from the German reform monastery of Hirsau, and two new monasteries were founded according to the custom: Muri in 1027 and Engleberg in 1120.

The Cistercians entered Switzerland in 1123, when Bernard of Clairvaux (1090–1153) sent 12 monks to Bonmont near Nyon. In 1138 monks from Cherlieu founded Hauterive, who in turn founded Kappel on the Elbe in 1183. The later monasteries of St. Urban (1190) and Wettingen (1227) became pan-European centers of Cistercian life. In the 13th century several of the mendicant orders established houses. In 1231 the Franciscans established their first house in Basel and by 1269 had houses in Zurich, Schaffhausen, Bern, Geneva, Fribourg, Lausanne, and Lucerne. The Poor Clares followed in 1235 at Paradies and the Dominicans in 1286 at Zurich. The double monastery of

Königsfelden was founded in 1310 by the consort of the daughter of the slain Emperor Albert I (1298–1308).

The *Eidgenossenschaft* (Swiss League) period introduced no significant changes for the monastic foundations. During the Western Schism (1378–1418), the ecclesiastical authorities adhered initially to the Roman pope and then to the Pisan pope. With the coming of the Reformation, attention was at first directed toward reform within the Catholic structure. It was not until Zwingli took over the Swiss Reformation that reform became anti-Catholic, resulting in the wholesale destruction of images and in 1524 the dissolution of monasteries. In 1525 the celebration of the Mass was forbidden.

The Counter-Reformation, left entirely in the hands of the laity, fared poorly until the intervention of Charles Borromeo (1538–1584), the archbishop of Milan. The visit of the "Protector of Catholic Switzerland" in 1570 proved to be a turning point for Swiss Catholicism. Borromeo sent the Jesuits into Switzerland to implement the Tridentine reform. He also encouraged the entry of the Capuchin Franciscans, who established their first Swiss monastery at Altdorf in 1581, followed quickly by a number of others. The two wars of the religion (1656–1712) left Switzerland divided into two confessional camps that remained hostile until the coming of the Enlightenment, when "enlightened" Catholics and Protestants began to cooperate.

The Act of Mediation imposed by Napoleon I (1803) restored the old confederation and saw the rebuilding of the monasteries, reversing the destruction wrought by the anti-Christian, anti-ecclesiastical Helvetic Constitution (1798–1802). Under that constitution more than 130 monasteries were dissolved. The act imposed state controls on the Church and its monasteries, but only the Abbey of St. Gallen remained repressed. However, during a disastrous civil religious war brought about by the Catholic cantons' refusal to adhere to the Baden Articles (1834), the Catholics were soundly defeated, and all monasteries were once again dissolved (1847). The new constitution supported the newly formed Christian Catholic Church against the Roman Church, expelled all Jesuits from the country, and forbade any new monastic foundations as well as the restoration of dissolved foundations. Despite the restrictions Benedictines, Capuchins, Augustinian Canons, and secular priests stepped in to fill the vacuum left by the withdrawal of the Jesuits, and two new orders for women were founded.

Today, as a result of these political upheavals, Catholic Switzerland is divided into five dioceses and one administrative district. Two exempt abbeys also exist: St. Maurice with five parishes and Einsiedeln. The Catholic Church has recovered its prestige and along with its monasteries is an officially recognized Church (*Landeskirchen*), entitled to a church levy administered by the government. About 1,500 religious priests and about 9,500 religious women reside in a number of religious houses.

Sites to Visit

St. Gallen: Abbey of St. Gallen, abbey library, cathedral
The Convent of St. Gallen, a UNESCO trust property
Einsiedeln: Benedictine Abbey of Maria Einsiedeln
Payerne: Abbey of Payerne and abbey church
Romainmôtier: Abbey of St. Pierre and St. Paul

FRANK A. MILLS

See also Cistercians; Cluniacs; Columban, St.; Germany: History; Pirminius, St.; Reformation; Reichenau; St. Gallen, Switzerland; William of Hirsau

Further Reading

Barth, H., *Bibliographie der Schweizer Geschichte . . . bis Ende 1912*, 3 vols., Basel: Basler Buch- und Antiquariatshandlung, vormals A. Geering, 1914–1915
Braunfels, Wolfgang, *Abendländische Klosterbaukunst*, Koln: DuMont Schauberg, 1969; 4th edition, 1980; as *Monasteries of Western Europe: The Architecture of the Orders,* London: Thames and Hudson, 1972; 3rd edition, Princeton, New Jersey: Princeton University Press, 1973; reprint, London: Thames and Hudson, 1993
Horn, Walter W., and Ernest Born, *The Plan of St. Gall: A Study of the Architecture and Economy of and Life in a Paradigmatic Carolingian Monastery*, 3 vols., Berkeley: University of California Press, 1979–1982 (contains the garden plans found in the monastery of St. Gall library, Stiftsbibliothek, Ms. 1092)
Johnston, Pamela, and R.W. Scribner, *The Reformation in Germany and Switzerland*, Cambridge: Cambridge University Press, 1994
Ozment, Steven E., *Reformation in the Cities: The Appeal of Protestantism to Sixteenth-Century Germany and Switzerland*, New Haven, Connecticut: Yale University Press, 1975

Related Web Sites

http://lamar.colostate.edu (Draft Notes: 5. Monastic Order and Urban Gathering Spaces; monastery plan of St. Gall; includes plan for a monastery [not built], Switzerland, 830)
http://sgi3.dvl.utk.edu (St. Gall Architecture: Time Period 816–817, Carolingian Type Monastery; contains views of the monastery along with other examples of this style, related maps and diagrams, and related images and buildings of same decade)
http://www.kath.ch/einsiedeln (Abbey of Einsiedeln)

Symeon the New Theologian, St.

c. 949–1022

Byzantine Orthodox monk, priest, abbot, and influential theologian

Symeon was born around 949. While living in Constantinople at the age of about 20, he came under the influence of a spiritual father, Symeon Eulabes ("pious"), a lay monk of the Stoudios monastery in Constantinople, then perhaps the most famous in the Byzantine Empire. One night he had a vision in which all he could see was light. As time passed he became forgetful of what he had seen, but in 977 he abandoned a secular life to enter the monastery himself. However, such was his zeal that relations with the other monks became difficult, and before long he moved to the nearby monastery of St. Mamas, where he was ordained within a few years and became *hegoumen* (abbot). There he delivered to his monks the addresses that constitute his earliest surviving works, but again problems arose. Some of the monks rebelled, perhaps because Symeon attempted to reproduce with them the close relationship that he had enjoyed with his own spiritual father, and his attempt to give liturgical expression to the cult of the now dead Symeon Eulabes by the painting of an icon caused controversy. In 1005 he resigned his office and in 1009 was banished from Constantinople. Later he was rehabilitated and, in what might have been an attempt by the ecclesiastical establishment to win him over, he was offered episcopal consecration. Nevertheless he declined to return to Constantinople and died in 1022.

In many ways Symeon was a typical representative of the Byzantine monastic tradition. His own practice, as well as his writings, made much of the role of a spiritual father in mediating between God and his disciple. To such a person, the very sight of whom was like looking at Christ, total obedience was due. His thinking about God is resolutely Trinitarian, and his emphasis on the unknowability of an utterly transcendent Deity (who can appropriately be described with reference to what he is not) places him firmly within the tradition of Byzantine apophatic (negative) theology, which Dionysios the Pseudo-Areopagite had developed. Yet Symeon insists on the knowledge of God that is to be had by believers, especially in the form of light, and on the need for the experience (*aisthesis*) of his presence to be a matter of conscious awareness. For Symeon religion was largely a matter of experience, and he had no hesitation in making his own public. His experience of God often found expression in tears; he felt that it was possible to take Communion daily, being in tears on each occasion. No one, he taught, can be united to God without being consciously aware of this; we can tell that Christ is being formed within us with the same assurance that a woman, feeling a child move within her, knows that she is pregnant. Using precise terminology he held that one should move away from the passions (*pathoi*) to a state of dispassion (*apatheia*) and be detached (*aprospathein*) while being aware of the possibility of compassion (*sumpatheia*) being inspired by demons. Yet such union was only the beginning. Although Symeon felt that by the operation of their own disposition and grace believers would be deified (*theosis*), perfection would never be attained: growth toward an end that has no end can cease no more than the ungraspable can be grasped.

Symeon's practice and teaching aroused controversy in his own day, and aspects of it might seem problematic now. The essential role that he assigned to a believer's conscious experience of God might seem to make religion depend on subjective individual feeling. Such teaching could tend to lessen the value of the sacraments, and indeed Symeon held that not all who are baptized receive Christ; the water and oil used at baptism symbolize the tears and the interior action of the Holy Spirit, which come with one's second, spiritual baptism, and for Symeon the Spirit plays an important part in monastic and Christian life. Indeed he taught that those who are aware of possessing God have no need to read the Bible, having as their companion the one who inspired the authors of the Bible. Aware that accounts of early monks did not emphasize a personal relationship with God to the extent that he did, he suggested that the texts describing them merely told of their external practices. As for priests, ordination did not equip them to be spiritual directors; rather, holiness and personal experience were needed. His thought also displays a coolness toward family and friends; although this is in keeping with aspects of the monastic tradition, it also reflects a tendency toward isolation, which can be seen in other aspects of contemporary Byzantine society.

Symeon's ideas found little resonance in the immediately following generations but became influential in later Orthodox monasticism, especially as they formed part of the tradition from which Hesychasm later emerged. Although no evidence exists that he had been an exponent of the Jesus Prayer despite the addition of some words in the *Philokalia* that make it seem that he was, his emphasis on the apprehension of God by means of light and of a conscious awareness of the presence of God enjoyed by believers made him congenial to this strand of Eastern monasticism, as represented especially by St. Gregory Palamas (c. 1296–1359). Moreover, his advocacy of the role of the spiritual father and, by implication, his deemphasis of the ordained hierarchy remain features of Orthodoxy to the present day. Saint Nicodemos of the Holy Mountain and St. Macarius Notaras of Corinth presented some of his work in their compendium of monastic wisdom, the *Philokalia* (1782; subsequent important translation into Russian), and a recent edition with a translation into French and the appearance of translations into English point to an upsurge of contemporary interest.

JOHN MOORHEAD

See also Dionysius the Pseudo-Areopagite; Hesychasm; Istanbul, Turkey; Nilus of Sora, St.; Orthodox Monasticism: Byzantine; Palamas, Gregory, St.; Philokalia; Spiritual Direction, Christian; Spirituality: Eastern Christian; Theology, Eastern Christian; Vision, Mystical: Eastern Christian

Biography

After working in the Byzantine imperial bureaucracy, in 977 Symeon joined the monastery at Stoudios and then that of St. Mamas, both in Constantinople. He became priest and abbot. His mystical treatises aroused opposition, which caused him to be deposed as abbot in 1005. In 1009 he went briefly into exile in Asia Minor and remained in retirement thereafter. His writings earned him the title "the New Theologian."

Major Works

Hymns of Divine Love, edited by J. Koder, J. Paramelle, and L. Neyrand, translated by G.A. Maloney, 1975
Symeon the New Theologian: The Discourses, edited by B. Krivochénie, translated by C. de Catanzaro, 1980
Symeon, the New Theologian: The Practical and Theological Chapters: And the Three Theological Discourses, edited by J. Darrouzès and L. Neyrand, translated by P. McGuckin, 1982
Catecheses
Kephalaia

Further Reading

Darrouzès, J., editor, *Traités théologiques et éthiques*, 2 vols., Paris: Éditions du Cerf, 1966–1967

Maloney, George A., *The Mystic of Fire and Light: St. Symeon the New Theologian*, Denville, New Jersey: Dimension Books, 1975

Spidlík, Tomás, "Syméon le nouveau théologien," *Dictionnaire de spiritualité, ascétique et mystique: Doctrine et histoire*, volume 14, Paris: Beauchesne, 1990

Syncretism in Japan, Buddhist

Bewildering archaeological discoveries, combined with layers of lore from many religions, have been associated with the Elephant's Head Mountain Range (Zōzuzankei) on Shikoku Island, remote from familiar political and religious centers. No one has put all the puzzle pieces together in a comparative Asian perspective and with reference to religious syncretism of the Heian period in Japan. Reconstructing the "lost chord" from oblivion leads to the conclusion that premodern Japanese viewed the whole Zōzuzankei as a sacred area. Like certain other East Asian spaces, it culminates in a syncretic maṇḍala of mountains representing and uniting the religious cultures of India, China, and Japan. Japanese people have tended to live on the plains, perceiving the mountains and the sea beyond their purview as the abode of the sacred. On these mountains emerged examples of religious syncretism, often in the guise of triads.

Bird's-eye view of Kotohira Shrine on Mount Kompira, in Kagawa Prefecture on the island of Shikoku.
Photo courtesy of Steve McCarty

Today at the foot of the Zōzuzankei in tiny Kagawa prefecture are two small but famous religious towns (*monzen-machi*) that grew from the gates of a major Shintō shrine and a major Buddhist temple. Kotohira Shrine, called Kompira-san after its mountain, houses many Shintō priests, whereas Zentsūji Temple is a large Shingon monastery commemorating the birthplace of Kūkai (774–835), one of Japan's greatest religious figures. He studied in the Tang dynasty capital of Chang-an at a peak of Chinese civilization, just as it was drawing inspiration from the last flowering of Buddhism in India. Kūkai thus helped turn the dawning Heian period into a golden age for Japan.

The depth as well as breadth of religious phenomena concentrated in the space of a few miles is revealed in some of the archaeological discoveries. Nearby in the Seto Inland Sea, which was formed when land dropped down about 10,000 years ago, an Old Stone Age mammoth ivory doll has been found. Similarly, on Mount Elephant's Head (Zōzuzan, a Buddhist name for Mount Kompira) and near Kūkai's birthplace in Zentsūji, traces of Old Stone Age culture have been discovered along with New Stone Age culture of the Jōmon period. Although Mount Elephant's Head is now miles inland, seashells have been found near the summit, indicating that the Zōzuzankei formed the coastline a few millennia ago. Before any ritual bronze bells (*dōtaku*) of the Yayoi period that transformed ancient Japan were found in Kyūshū nearest to the Asian mainland, over a dozen have been found around Kotohira and Zentsūji. Flat bronze swords (*dōken*) found in Zentsūji constitute the most ever found in Japan. Around the Kotohira Shrine was found a 2,000-year-old bronze bell, now a designated national treasure in the Tokyo National Museum, depicting a building similar in proportions to those of the Grand Shrine of Izumo on the Sea of Japan. Then archaeologists were stunned by the finding of a Yayoi period ritual bell on the mountain where Kūkai as a child was believed to have met the Buddha. Tumuli of the following Kofun period number over 400 in Zentsūji, decorated with boats to carry the departed to the afterworld of the sea. Kompira-san is thought to have been a seafaring capital of ancient Japan, worshiping a sea god (*kami*). Such sites could be termed proto-Shintō, reflecting the fact that Shintōism was late to institutionalize in response to Buddhism. In Zentsūji some Kofun period tumuli have been turned into Shintō shrines as conduits to the *kami* (*shintai*), uniting ancestors with gods over millennia. Moreover, evidently an indigenous animism viewed a mountain such as Mount Kompira (or Zōzuzan, Elephant's Head Mountain) as itself the body of a god (*shintaizan*; cf. *shintai*, "the conduit to a god").

Into this congeries entered Heian esoteric Buddhism, reinforcing the deeper stratum of mountain worship by associating each temple with a mountain. A religious pluralism based on

An architectural remnant of Buddhist-Shintō syncretism on Daisen mountain, Japan. Photo courtesy of David Moore

assimilation reconciled the many Asian religious influences then current with the ex post facto theory (*honji suijaku setsu*) that all their representative divinities emanated from original Buddhas. Bureaucratic restrictions on the number of monks that could be ordained had led to spontaneous forms of Japanese Buddhism that favored mountain asceticism (especially Shugendō). It has been shown in connection with Mount Kumano and Mount Hiei that the sacred space outdoors was organized into a maṇḍala of Buddhist-Shintō syncretism that the ritual practitioner could traverse.

Similarly at Mount Kompira, by affinity of name with its sea god, the Buddhist guardian Kumbhīra, originally a Hindu crocodile god of the Ganges River, was said to have flown to Japan and became Kompira. He was accompanied by Elephant's Head Mountain near Bodh Gayā, which figures in the hagiography of the Buddha. Mount Kompira does resemble an elephant's head, although not as much as in conventionalized views by Hiroshige and other artists. Given the animism of mountain worship, various divinities could be perceived in Hindu fashion as riders on their mounts. Beyond being a crocodile god, suitable to protect seafarers, Kompira was elevated to a Great Incarnation of the Buddha (*daigongen*). Anthropomorphic iconography exists of Kompira Daigongen riding the mountain in the form of a white elephant – a creature associated with the Buddha and serving also as the mount of the ancient Hindu god Indra. In time the Shintō-Buddhist hybrid Kompira Daigongen became identified with the Shintō *kami* of Mount Kompira, Ō-Kuni-Nushi-no-Mikoto, one of the founding gods of Japan who was vaguely associated with crocodiles in the White Hare of Inaba myth in the Kojiki. A component from Chinese culture was later assimilated with the identification of the Buddhist and Shintō divinities atop Mount Kompira with Daikokuten in the guise of one of the Seven Gods of Good Fortune. In iconography he carries a bag like the *kami* Ō-Kuni-Nushi, with "Daikoku" a double pun on the Chinese characters for "Ō-Kuni."

Two more triads can be documented. The second on Mount Kompira is an Eastern Pure Land Triad of the Medicine Buddha Yakushi Nyorai as ruler, Kompira Daigongen as delegate, and Fugen Bosatsu as attendant. Here Fugen (Sanskrit, Samantabhadra Bodhisattva) rides a white elephant in iconography and has been closely associated with the Shingon Buddhist temple on Mount Kompira. Near the opposite and lower end of the Zōzuzan mountain range is a little-known temple with the prefix Mount Lion. Monju (Mañjuśrī Bodhisattva) has been viewed as riding Mount Lion, whereas Fugen rides Mount Elephant, just as they are portrayed in Buddhist iconography. Finally, between these two mountains are the Five Peaks, associated with those noted in pre–Han dynasty Daoism. They are also seen as the Five Wisdom Buddhas central to esoteric Buddhist maṇḍalas and especially carved inside the Great Pagoda of Zentsūji. Among the temples on Mount Five Peaks, two stand out: Mandaraji, where Kūkai dedicated the dual maṇḍalas that he brought back from China, and Shusshakaji, literally the "temple where the Buddha appeared" to Kūkai. Thus, in a process of what can be called iconographic association, the whole Elephant's Head Mountain Range might have been perceived esoterically as a Buddha Triad (*Shaka sanzon*) arranged in the customary fashion with lion-riding Mañjuśrī to the left and elephant-riding Samantabhadra to the right. Practitioners could enter such a complex as though it were a gigantic maṇḍala. Few sites anywhere embody such an overlay of religious traditions.

STEVE MCCARTY

See also Buddhism: Inculturation; Buddhist Schools/Traditions: Japan; Critiques of Buddhist Monasticism: Japanese; Deities, Buddhist; Japan: History; Kūkai; Shikoku, the Pilgrimage Island of Japan; Visual Arts, Buddhist: Japan

Further Reading

Grapard, Allan, "Flying Mountains and Walkers of Emptiness: Toward a Definition of Sacred Space in Japanese Religions," *History of Religions* 21:3 (1982)
Gyō, Shosei, *Kompira Sankei Meisho Zue*, Tokyo: Rekishi Zushosha, 1969
Kageyama, Haruki, *Shintaizan*, Tokyo: Gakugeisha, 1971
Kageyama, Haruki, *Miyamandara*, Kyoto: Sogeisha, 1978
Kajiwara, Aisui, editor, *Kokon Sanuki Meisho Zue*, Tokyo: Rekishi Toshosha, 1976
Kotooka, Mitsushige, *Kotohira-gu*, Tokyo: Gakugeisha, 1970
Matsunaga, Alicia, *The Buddhist Philosophy of Assimilation: The Historical Development of the Honji Suijaku Theory*, Tokyo: Sophia University, and Rutland, Vermont: Tuttle, 1969
Sawa, Ryūken, *Mikkyō Jiten: Zen*, Kyoto: Hōzōkan, 1975
Tobias, Michael, and Harold Drasdo, *The Mountain Spirit*, Woodstock, New York: Overlook Press, 1979; London: Gollancz, 1980

Syria

Syria was a satrapy of the Persian Empire when it was conquered and brought into the Hellenistic sphere by Alexander the Great (d. c. 323 B.C.). Seized by Seleucus some years after the death of Alexander, it remained under Seleucid control for about a century. After considerable disintegration of the Seleucid Empire and a brief annexation by Armenian King Tigran, a large part of the Middle East was conquered by Pompey (65–62 B.C.), and thus Syria became a Roman province. Septimius Severus (193–211) later divided it into two provinces: Syria Coele and Syria Phoenice. The extent of these provinces was roughly the equivalent of modern Syria, Lebanon, Jordan, and parts of Iraq.

Traditionally the apostle Thomas and his disciple Addai were the first missionaries to bring the Good News of Christianity to Syrian soil. According to the fifth- or sixth-century document *The Teaching of Addai*, King Abgar of Syria heard about the preaching and miraculous healings of Jesus in Palestine and wrote to him asking him to come to heal him and to preach to his people. Jesus responded that after he rose from the dead he would send one of his disciples. Thomas came to Syria but sent his disciple Addai to preach there while he himself went on to India. The importance of this tradition is not so much the attempt to connect the Syrian Church to an apostle but rather its witness to the very ascetic beginnings of Christianity in Syria. The *Gospel of Thomas*, the *Acts of Thomas*, and other early works associated with Tatian (c. 160) and others show a very marked preference for virginity with a correspondingly dismissive attitude toward marriage.

Unfortunately little source material exists by which to reconstruct a plausible scenario concerning these beginnings. Still much debated are theories concerning whether the beginnings of Syrian monasticism were offshoots of such contemporary movements as Palestinian Jewish Christianity, the Essene movement, Encratism, or Manichaeism or whether they were entirely independent developments. Debate also concerns the precise extent of the influences that these groups might have exerted. The motives behind monastic development are no less debated. Although these questions are much discussed and the solutions to them still far from certain, scholars now seem generally to agree that Syrian monasticism was an autochthonous growth, influenced at certain points by these groups.

Although details concerning its origins are difficult to unearth, monasticism quickly became a dominant movement in the Syrian Church, and Syria soon rivaled the more famous Egypt in monastic prowess. Whereas Egypt received the designation "cradle of monasticism," Syria quickly gained fame and notoriety for the stark and severe lifestyle of many of its ascetics, a fame so widespread that it has overshadowed other developments of Syrian monasticism in contemporary sources as well as in a number of modern studies. Another factor for this sometimes monolithic view is that the same vocabulary was used throughout the different phases and historical periods of Syrian monasticism. The terminology remained rather constant, whereas the lifestyle of those so designated changed radically over the first few centuries of monastic development in Syria. Consequently, later developments are read back into the early sources. Although it was the extreme asceticism of the fifth- and sixth-century hermits that gained such renown for Syria, one can actually distinguish four fundamental types of monastic lifestyles: (1) the protomonastic ascetic and the "sons and daughters of the covenant"; (2) the hermit; (3) the stylite, the most peculiar yet most uniquely Syrian monastic figure; and (4) the cenobite.

The protomonastic asceticism is known mainly from two early figures: Aphrahat, the "Persian Sage," and Ephrem (c. 306–373), the "Harp of the Holy Spirit," who is also the greatest figure of the Syrian Church. They called themselves and others like them *îhîdayê*. Although this term would later be appropriated by the

Exterior of west "transept," Church of St. Symeon Stylites, near Aleppo, Syria, late fifth century.
Photo courtesy of Chris Schabel

monastic movement, these two figures witness to a radical commitment to Christ, manifested by a personal, if not public, renunciation of marriage. Although the term was later translated as "solitaries," in this protomonastic usage the word contains a multifold meaning: "single ones" or simply "celibates" but also "single-minded" or "of single purpose." However, the term finds its source and most specific usage in the person of Jesus Christ who was the *îhîdayâ* (for "Only-begotten"; cf. John 1:14, 18; 3:16, 18; 1 John 4:9). Aphrahat perhaps states it most succinctly when he says, "These things are suitable for the *îhîdayê* who take up the heavenly yoke and become disciples of Christ. For in this way it befits the disciples of Christ to be like unto Christ their master, and the *îhîdayâ* will give joy to the *îhîdayê*." This Christlikeness is the essence of the Christian life for Aphrahat and Ephrem. Although these *îhîdayê* lived a solitary life, it was clearly within a church community, and in this sense they resembled the *virgines subintroductae* known from other sources. Aphrahat and Ephrem were certainly *îhîdayê* in this sense, as were Jacob and Abraham, two bishops whom Ephrem served in fourth-century Nisibis. Those with a penchant for a more penitential lifestyle were also known as *abîlê* ("mourners").

According to a panegyrical hymn composed by Jacob of Sarug, Ephrem's own vocation involved writing hymns, many of which survive, for choirs of the "daughters of the covenant." These "sons and daughters of the covenant" led a lifestyle very similar to that of the *îhîdayê* (for Aphrahat they were clearly identical), although this lifestyle involved something even more radical. At baptism a public, liturgical oath was taken that resembled the Israelite call to holy war (cf. Judges 7:4–8 and Deut. 20:1–9). If any doubt arose as to whether to take this oath, the potential "warrior" was to return home. Because the word stems from the same Syriac stem, *qwm*, some have argued that the term should be translated as "sons of the resurrection"; although overtones of this word are not inappropriate, the word seems more properly to refer to a covenant, and the language suggests a covenant, or pact, of marriage with God. In addition to love for virginity, Aphrahat exhorts them to continence in speech, attire, possessions, and respect for one another, all of which presuppose involvement in an active social atmosphere. According to the Rules of Rabbula, the bishop of Edessa in the early fifth century, the "sons and daughters of the covenant" were encouraged to live in groups, separated by gender and normally attached in some way to a church; to observe poverty under the supervision of a priest; and to memorize the Psalms.

With regard to the solitary lifestyle that developed from these early celibates, we have numerous witnesses, as the Syrian hermits were renowned throughout the Christian world for their superhuman feats of asceticism and their utter and complete renunciation of everything to do with the flesh: shelter, cooked food, and even hygiene. In addition to appropriating the titles already mentioned, these were called variously "hermits," "desert-dwellers," "mountaineers," and "recluses." A work of Theodoret of Cyrrhus (c. 393–c. 460), *The History of the Monks of Syria*, is by far our best source of information concerning some of the persons involved and various characteristics of this phase of Syrian monasticism. According to this history two distinct types of solitaries existed: the "open-air" solitaries, who had no shelter, and those who confined themselves within a small dwelling and had no outside contact. A number of early Syriac poems depict, from the inside, the unique characteristics of this Syrian asceticism. These texts describe solitary life in all its starkness. This life was one of complete suffering and renunciation. The ascetic was to own no clothing, to live a life of squalid filth devoid of all hygiene, and to find shelter among the rocks and clefts in the mountains. If the solitary were to leave this mountain dwelling or even to consider doing so, he would become just like a wild beast who had been skinned or like a bird who had its feathers plucked. His diet was to be that of the wild animals, his only companions, grazing on leaves and roots in the hope of soon eating from the tree (or table) of life. For this reason these ascetics were known in Greek tradition as *boskoi* ("grazers"). Renunciation of this world's goods was to be so complete that those who followed this life were to crucify their bodies in this life in the hope of gaining the eternal blessings promised by God. Incessant prayer, fasting, vigils, mourning, and penance constituted their only earthly treasures.

Along with these extreme types of solitaries must also be placed the stylites. Although striving for the same sort of ascetic renunciation as the hermits, they found their own niche by ascending pillars or columns of varying heights and living on a platform placed atop them. Symeon the Elder (c. 390–459), the earliest and most famous of the stylites, occupied successively three columns, the first 6 cubits in height, the second 22 cubits, and the third 37 cubits, for a total of nearly 40 years. The life of the stylite attracted a great number of followers, and sources witness to their existence even into the 12th century. The stylites were known not only for their extraordinary ascetic feats, sitting motionless for years and enduring the elements and disease, but even more for their great intermediary powers between the poor and the Church on the one hand and the political authorities on the other. A number of monasteries were built with a prominent tower in the corner for a solitary dwelling, suggests a development of, or at least some sort of relation to, the early stylites.

Little information about the earliest period of cenobitic monasticism in Syria has survived, and much of this information is late, legendary, and unreliable. According to tradition, as found in such works as the *Book of Chastity*, it was a Mar Awgin, a disciple of the great Egyptian cenobite Pachomius (c. 290–346), who came from Egypt and set up the first Syrian cenobitic monastery on Mount Izla, just outside of Nisibis. It has now been demonstrated that the legend of Mar Awgin does not occur in any source earlier than the tenth century. This anachronistic picture reflects an effort in the Syrian Church to align itself with the greater Byzantine Church, to the detriment of its own native traditions. Although these traditions can clearly be shown to be late, no sources survive that provide any clear picture of the beginnings of cenobitic monasticism in Syria. It is very likely that cenobitic monasticism in Syria developed from the hermetic lifestyle. When novices would apprentice themselves to an elder, more experienced monk, they would set up lodgings around him. Eventually this became a single lodging and developed into the semi-communal form of Syrian cenobitism. Fully cenobitic monasteries probably did not develop in Syria before the fifth century. What is clear is that this lifestyle established itself so rapidly that by the sixth century several hundred monasteries already existed in Syria. Theodoret makes the hyperbolic claim that the monasteries in Syria of the mid–fifth century were so numerous that if one tried to count them he would despair; however, Peña (1992) estimates that during the heyday of Syrian monasticism, Syrian monks constituted nearly 5 percent of the total population. Today nearly 60 inhabited villages that are still known by the prefix "Deir" survive; this prefix clearly designates an ancient site known by the presence of a monastery. The growth of the monasteries during the time of great increase in Syria's economic prosperity drew many hermits from the mountains into the outlying areas around cities and villages, causing a significant rift between newer and older generations of monks. Large monasteries were the exception in Syriac monasticism, the average monastery holding an average of 20 monks. Cenobitic monasteries flourished all over Syria and became the centers of the educative process, mainly for monks themselves but also for those who sought an education. Large one-room buildings often built near the monasteries were very likely used as school rooms and dormitories and also as infirmaries and meeting rooms. Few monasteries are now functioning in present-day Syria, but some significant archaeological research has been done on what remains.

Edward G. Mathews, Jr.

See also Archaeology: Near East; Asceticism: Christian Perspectives; Desert Mothers; Egypt; Hagiography: Eastern Christian; Hermits: Eastern Christian; Israel/Palestine; Origins: Eastern Christian; Pachomius, St.; Stylites; Women's Monasteries: Eastern Christian

Further Reading

Beck, Edmund, "Asketentum und Mönchtum bei Ephräm," in *Il monachesimo orientale, Atti del Convegno di Studi orientale*, Rome: Pontifical Oriental Institute, 1958

Brock, Sebastian P., *The Luminous Eye: The Spiritual World Vision of St. Ephrem*, 2nd edition, Kalamazoo, Michigan: Cistercian Publications, 1992

Brown, Peter, "The Rise and Function of the Holy Man in Late Antiquity," *Journal of Roman Studies* 61 (1971)

Canivet, Pierre, *Le monachisme Syrien selon Théodoret de Cyr*, Paris: Beauchesne, 1977

Delehaye, Hippolyte, *Les saints stylites*, Brussels: Société des bollandistes, 1923

Festugière, André-Jean, *Antioche païenne et chrétienne: Libanius, Chrysostome et les moines de Syrie*, Paris: Éditions de Boccard, 1959
Harvey, Susan Ashbrook, *Asceticism and Society in Crisis: John of Ephesus and The Lives of the Eastern Saints*, Berkeley: University of California Press, 1990
Murray, Robert, "The Exhortation to Candidates for Ascetical Vows at Baptism in the Ancient Syriac Church," *New Testament Studies* 21 (1974–1975)
Nedungatt, George, "The Covenanters of the Early Syriac-Speaking Church," *Orientalia Christiana Periodica* 39 (1973)
Palmer, Andrew, *Monk and Mason on the Tigris Frontier: The Early History of Tur 'Abdin*, Cambridge and New York: Cambridge University Press, 1990
Peña, Ignacio, *The Amazing Life of the Syrian Monks: In the 4th–6th Centuries*, Milan: Franciscan Printing Press, 1992
Peña, Ignacio, Pascal Castellana, and Romuald Fernandez, *Les Stylites Syriens*, Milan: Franciscan Printing Press, 1975
Peña, Ignacio, Pascal Castellana, and Romuald Fernandez, *Les Reclus Syriens*, Jerusalem: Franciscan Printing Press, 1980
Peña, Ignacio, Pascal Castellana, and Romuald Fernandez, *Les Cénobites Syriens*, Jerusalem: Franciscan Printing Press, 1983
Vööbus, Arthur, *History of Asceticism in the Syrian Orient*, 3 vols., Louvain: Secrétariat du CorpusSCO, 1958, 1960, 1988

T

T'ai-hsü. *See* Taixu

Taiwan

Overview

The existence of Chinese Buddhist monasteries and convents can be documented only from the massive migration of Chinese expatriates who fled to the island after the failure of a military attempt to restore the fallen Ming dynasty in 1662. The so-called Southern Ming court continued to rule Taiwan until the Qing dynasty took control of the island in 1683. After that the history of the monastic establishment falls into three periods related to the subsequent three changes in the political regime: the period of Qing dynasty rule (1683–1895), the period of the Japanese colonial government (1895–1945), and the period of Chinese Nationalist Party rule (1945 to present).

The Southern Ming/Qing Dynasty Period

Although records are scarce, Chinese and Japanese scholars agree that Buddhism, as it existed during this time, was of low quality. Taiwan was seen as a land of typhoons, plagues, and headhunting native peoples and so did not attract the elite of Chinese society. Many of the "monks" of this period were Ming dynasty loyalists who fled to the island in clerical disguise, and the few legitimate monks and nuns who resided in Taiwan were largely illiterate and ignorant of Buddhist teachings. Documents attest that those few whose names have come down as having earned the respect of the populace were known for non-Buddhist accomplishments, such as rainmaking, painting, composing poetry, and playing *go*. As for the rest, they functioned as temple caretakers and funeral specialists and did not engage in teaching, meditation, or other Buddhist practices.

The first known monk to migrate from the mainland to Taiwan was the Venerable Canche, who arrived in 1675. A military staff commander named Chen Yonghua had built a Buddhist temple called the Dragon Lake Grotto (Longhu Yan) and invited Canche to come as abbot. After his arrival Canche went on to found the Blue Cloud Temple (Biyun Si) on Fire Mountain (Huoshan) near the present-day town of Chiayi.

As the Qing period progressed and the island became more settled, many more temples were founded, especially in the city of Tainan, the capital. The most notable of these early monasteries include the Bamboo Stream Temple (Zhuxi Si, 1664), the Ocean Assembly Temple (Haihui Si, 1680), the Dharma-Flower Temple (Fahua Si, 1683), the Amitābha Temple (Mituo Si, date unknown), the Taipei Dragon Mountain Temple (Longshan Si, 1738), the Surpassing Peak Temple (Chaofeng Si, registered 1763), and the Great Immortal Temple (Daxian Si, date unknown) founded by one of Venerable Canche's disciples. The various gazetteers of Taiwan also list several tens of smaller temples, grottoes, and pavilions. Despite this apparently vigorous temple-building activity, it is doubtful that very many of the monks and nuns who inhabited them had received any more than a novice's ordination, as no ordaining monastery existed in Taiwan during this entire period, and records of those who journeyed across the Taiwan Strait to receive the full precepts on the mainland are scarce.

The Japanese Colonial Period

In 1895 the Chinese government ceded the island of Taiwan to Japan as one of the terms of defeat in the Sino-Japanese War. As Japanese troops arrived to pacify the island, they brought with them military chaplains, many of whom were Buddhist. These chaplains were eager to establish mission stations to propagate Japanese Buddhism among the native population, but funding from the home temples was low, and statistics show that only a very small percentage of the Han Chinese population ever became members of Japanese Buddhist lineages. In fact a Japanese government survey of 1941 revealed that the largest Japanese Buddhist school, the Jōdo Shinshū Honganji sect, had 21,204 Japanese devotees and only 5,184 Chinese devotees.

One of the most remarkable features of the Japanese period is the local Buddhist establishment's effort to retain its Chinese flavor and traditions. Most notably the Japanese period saw the founding of the first facilities for transmitting the full monastic precepts in Taiwan. Four temples came to the fore as "ordination platforms": the Lingquan (Spring of the Spirit) Chan Temple in Keelung, the Lingyun (Soaring Cloud) Chan Temple on Guanyin Mountain, the Fayun (Dharma Cloud) Chan Temple near Miaoli, and the Chaofeng (Surpassing the Peak) Temple in Kaohsiung County. All the founders and revivers of these temples received full monastic ordination at the Yongquan (Surging Spring) Temple on Gushan (Drum Mountain) in Fuzhou and then transmitted their tonsure lineages to Taiwan through their own ordination ceremonies. Thus, they created the four great "ancestral lineages" that defined and organized Buddhism during this period as ordinands from one or the other of these temples went and founded temples of their own.

In addition to keeping Chinese ordination lineages alive under the Japanese government, Chinese Buddhists sought to distance themselves from Japanese Buddhist practices, which they felt to be corrupt. Japanese monks ate meat, married, and drank wine, and the Chinese Buddhists wanted to stay clear of these infractions. However, at the same time small groups of Chinese Buddhist monks, such as Lin Qiuwu and his circle, studied Marxism and advocated relaxing monastic discipline to strengthen solidarity with ordinary working people while at the same time continuing to resist full assimilation into Japanese society.

However, even as Chinese Buddhism attempted to keep its own distinctive identity under the Japanese, it still had to accommodate to the government in some fashion; thus, monastic and lay Buddhists joined to form a series of islandwide Buddhist organizations to act as liaisons with the government. The largest of these, founded in 1922 by the Japanese official Marui Keijiro, was called the South Seas Buddhist Association, which operated until the end of the occupation in 1945.

These organizations were significant in that their membership also included members of *zhaijiao*, the so-called vegetarian religion. This represented a form of lay-based Buddhism that generally stood apart from the monastic form and refused to be dominated by it. Such groups had existed for centuries on the mainland and were often held in contempt by the monastic establishment and in suspicion by the government. Their participation in the Buddhist organizations in Taiwan marks the only time that these groups had ever cooperated with mainstream monastic Buddhism in Chinese history. This cooperation dissolved with the return of Taiwan to China at the end of World War II.

The Chinese Nationalist Government Period (1945 to present)
The end of World War II saw the return of Taiwan to China and the evacuation of all Japanese citizens. The newly arrived Chinese Nationalist government proved corrupt, and within two years there was an islandwide uprising against it known as the "2/28 Incident," which the Nationalists ruthlessly crushed. Two years later, in 1949, the mainland fell to the Communists, and the Nationalist government fled to Taiwan, hoping to use it as a springboard to retake the mainland.

All these events conspired to keep the political and economic situation in turmoil, and Buddhist monks and nuns had a very difficult time keeping their temples and monasteries viable. Because of the fear of Communist spies, a few Buddhist monks who had fled from the mainland, such as the Venerable Cihang (1895–1954), were even imprisoned on charges of vagrancy. At the height of the crisis, temples were loath to take in refugee monks, many of whom thus experienced difficult times.

Opening ceremony at the Nan Tien Temple, Woolongong, New South Wales, Australia, 1997. The temple of the Taiwanese Fo Kuang Shan Order shows five celestial buddhas.
Photo courtesy of John Powers

A few monks of national standing also arrived with the influx of mainland refugees. These monks, such as the Zhangjia Living Buddha (1891–1957) and the Venerables Baisheng (1904–1989), Wuming (1912–), and Yinshun (1906–), among others, were well known for their leadership in the newly revived Buddhist Association of the Republic of China (BAROC) and came to Taiwan for reasons that paralleled those of the Nationalist government: to use Taiwan as a base of operations until the defeat of the Communist regime enabled them to return home to rebuild Buddhism.

The BAROC acted as a liaison between the Buddhist monastic establishment and the government in several areas. For example, the government expected it to certify clergy who wanted to travel abroad and to help in framing laws dealing with religious life on the island. In other areas the BAROC confronted the government whenever religious interests were threatened. Two notable controversies in which the BAROC played a crucial role were the failure of the government to return many confiscated Japanese-era temples to religious use and the government's obstruction of efforts to establish a Buddhist university. Finally, the BAROC took charge of registering all clergy and all temples and took over the task of organizing and administering the ordination of new clergy once a year.

Because the Republic of China's laws on civic organizations allowed only one organization to fill any one niche in society, the BAROC maintained its hegemony in these areas until the late 1980s, after which several government decisions weakened it and left the field open for other Buddhist organizations to take on some of these tasks. In 1989 the government no longer dealt with Buddhist monks and nuns as a special category of citizen but registered them under their lay names as ordinary citizens. Thus, the BAROC was no longer needed to certify their status for the purpose of foreign travel or study abroad. That same year a new law on civic organizations took effect that abolished the "one niche, one organization" rule and opened the way for competition.

In the ensuing period, called by some scholars the "period of pluralization," other Buddhist organizations have taken root. Some grew out of preexisting groups, most notably, Fo Kuang Shan and the Buddhist Compassion Relief Tzu Chi Association. For example, Fo Kuang Shan has begun holding ordination sessions of its own since the laws were liberalized.

Recent Changes

Buddhism in Taiwan has undergone many changes during the last few decades as the island has shifted from an agrarian, village-based society to a modern industrial, urban-based economy. Four especially prominent developments are the increasing prominence of nuns, declining numbers of monastic ordinations relative to the total population, efforts to adapt Buddhism to modern life, and new economic realities. Each development is discussed here.

Increasing prominence of nuns. Throughout history monks have dominated over nuns numerically in Chinese Buddhism. In imperial times ordination brought with it exemption from taxes and corvée labor and the requirement of passing an examination, factors that favored men over women because men had more economic interests at stake and greater access to education.

On the other hand, in Taiwan since the 1950s the number of nuns has increased relative to the numbers of monks so that the ratio is now almost three to one. Between 1953 and 1986 the BAROC ordained 2,030 men and 6,006 women. One effect of this imbalance is that nuns have come to be regarded as the equals of the monks, and in some quarters they are even more highly regarded. The reason for this is that, with more women than men seeking ordination, women are much more likely to be eliminated or given longer periods of testing. This has raised the overall quality of the nuns' order.

At the same time several factors have come into play that militate against men seeking ordination. Families are now smaller, meaning that no "extra sons" can be given to the Buddhist order. With only one or two sons per family, the pressure is very great to marry and have children to carry on the family sacrifices and lineage. Also, because the government has ceased to grant Buddhist monks any extra privileges or exemptions, no economic incentive exists to seek ordination.

Declining numbers of monastic ordinations. These developments must be seen against a backdrop of a steadily decreasing number of ordinations overall. Between 1949 and 1989, when the population of Taiwan rose from 7.5 million to over 20 million, the numbers of new ordinands each year, especially men, did not keep pace. Many observers understand this phenomenon to be of a piece with the increasingly prominent role of the laity within the Buddhist world at large. With higher levels of education and leisure time, one need not be ordained in order to read, study, chant scriptures, and meditate; thus, with so much familial resistance to overcome, fewer people seek the monastic life.

Efforts to adapt Buddhism to modern life. The ethical content of Buddhism in Taiwan has undergone much change in recent decades. Traditionally, Chinese lay Buddhists have undertaken three rituals. In the first, the Three Refuges, they formally commit themselves to the Buddhist path. In the second they receive the Five Lay Precepts (not to kill, steal, engage in sexual misconduct, lie, or drink intoxicants). In the third they may elect to receive the so-called Lay Bodhisattva Precepts, which commits them to obedience to the clergy and practices of compassion for all living beings. Monastic Buddhists have further undertaken the many rules of the *Vinaya in Four Parts* and the monastic Bodhisattva Precepts.

Recently, some organizations, such as Fo Kuang Shan and the Buddhist Compassion Relief Tzu Chi Association, have propounded new precepts that followers formally undertake. In the case of Fo Kuang Shan, the focus is on monastics, and the founder, the Venerable Xingyun (1927–), has put forth his vision of Fo Kuang Buddhism in several lectures and books in which he regularizes and rationalizes many aspects of monastic life: a series of "ranks" that monks and nuns pass through, standardized monastic garb, prohibitions on private fund-raising and the taking of disciples, and so on. In the religious dimension Xingyun seeks to turn the attention of his monks and nuns away from otherworldly concerns, such as performing rituals for the dead and seeking rebirth in the Western Pure Land, so that they can concentrate their efforts on benefiting living beings in this world. They goal, he says, is to build a Pure Land on Earth.

Likewise, the Buddhist Compassion Relief Tzu Chi Association, under its charismatic founder and leader, the Venerable Zhengyan (1937–), seeks to train its followers to be of assistance within the present world. As an association composed almost entirely of laypeople, the focus is not on monastic practices and concerns but on social action. In her writings the Venerable Zhengyan interprets the traditional six perfections of Mahāyāna Buddhist practice through the lens of social welfare work. Seeking also to strengthen public morality, she adds five more precepts to the traditional five listed previously: members are to give up smoking, give up chewing betel nut, give up gambling (including video games and the stock market), look after their family lives, and buckle their seat belts (or wear helmets when riding motorcycles).

Efforts such as these to direct Buddhism away from traditional, otherworldly concerns are not unique to these two organizations. Individual temples, such as the Nongchan Temple in the northern Taipei suburb of Peitou and the Faguang Temple in downtown Taipei, are two of many that have given up using disposable chopsticks and bowls out of a concern for the environment. In this context as well, the slogan is "to build a Pure Land on Earth."

New economic realities. Finally, Buddhist monasticism in Taiwan has changed in response to many developments in the economic sphere. In traditional China, monasteries supported themselves by seeking donations and providing services in addition to which a few very large monasteries earned significant income from agricultural rentals. In Taiwan a few temples owned enough land to make significant money from renting farmlands, but decades of Japanese government confiscation and Nationalist land reform programs have effectively ended this means of self-support. Buddhism in Taiwan has also followed trends that began on the mainland in the early 20th century and reacted against an excessive dependence on funeral services for support.

Many temples in modern Taiwan seek to build bases of lay support in a more systematic, less overtly commercial way. They might organize their core constituency into a lay organization, such as the Dharmapala organization that helps support Dharma Drum Mountain. They might help found college and technical school Buddhist fellowships and lead retreats for Chan meditation or for Buddha recitation. Some of the larger temples in urban areas also have publishing concerns. However, the most universal means of raising money is to hold dharma meetings (*fa hui*), in which laypeople come to hear sūtras recited, see the ceremony of releasing living beings (*fang sheng*), or witness a ritual for the Release of the Burning Mouths (*yujia yankou*). Those who contribute to these events share in the merit, which they typically dedicate to their relatives both living and dead.

Monasteries to Visit

Because the history of Buddhism in Taiwan goes back no more than 330 years, no ancient Buddhist sites exist such as one can find in mainland China. To see the oldest temples, the visitor should go to Tainan, the first capital city, where one can visit the Kai-yuan Temple (successor to the Haihui Temple) and the other temples listed in the section "The Southern Ming/Qing Dynasty Period." Many visitors also go to Taipei to see the Lung Shan (Longshan) Temple, which dates from 1738.

For those who want to see modern Buddhism in Taiwan, Fo Kuang Shan, in the countryside outside of Kaohsiung, has been a popular stop, but lately it has closed its gates to pilgrims, although it might still be willing to admit small numbers of visitors with advance notice. While in the area one can also see the temples on and around Da Kang Mountain, notably the Chaofeng Temple, which is under restoration.

Around Taipei the Shan Tao (Shandao) Temple near the railroad station serves as a temple, library, and headquarters for the BAROC. The Fa Kuang (Faguang) Temple is the home of the Fa Kuang Buddhist Studies Institute, and the visitor can find a wealth of information about Taiwan Buddhism. Just north of Taipei, in the suburb of Peitou, is the Nong Ch'an (Nongchan) Temple, whose abbot, the Venerable Dr. Shengyan, is also the director of the nearby Chung Hwa Buddhist Studies Institute. From these places one can arrange a trip to see Dharma Drum Mountain.

For quiet retreats almost any temple will permit the visitor to stay the night for a small donation and a willingness to participate in the liturgical life. Many visitors favor Lion's Head Mountain near Hsin Chu as a picturesque site that houses several small, beautiful temples in a quiet mountain setting.

Charles B. Jones

See also Buddhist Schools/Traditions: China; Chan/Zen: China; Chan/Zen: Japan; China; Laicization of Spirituality: Buddhist Perspectives; Pure Land Buddhism

Further Reading

Jones, Charles B., *Buddhism in Taiwan: Religion and the State 1660–1990*, Honolulu: University of Hawaii Press, 1999

Taixu (T'ai-hsü) 1889–1947

Chinese Buddhist monk and reformer

Taixu, whose family name was Lü and whose first name was Gansen, was a native of Chongde in Zhejiang province. He left his home to become a religious mendicant in 1904. After first having stayed in a temple in Suzhou (Jiangsu province), he received full ordination from Jichan in the Tiantong Temple in Ningbo (Zhejiang province), still in 1904. Taixu was especially active in reviving Buddhism in the social confusion that characterized the end of the Qing dynasty (1644–1911) as well as in promoting a movement to internationalize Buddhism. When he died in 1947 in the Jade Buddha Temple in Shanghai, he had obtained control over the Zhongguo Fojiao Xiehui (Chinese Buddhist Association) that during the Republican period had succeeded in becoming the representative organization for all Buddhists in China.

Taixu headed a small group of progressives who advocated the idea that Buddhist monasteries had to be economically self-supporting, an opinion that refers back to the Tang ideal of Huaihai (720–814). This group of progressives claimed that the only way for Buddhist monasteries to survive in the modern world was to become more engaged in social affairs. Accordingly, they urged Buddhist monasteries to socially engage themselves without, however, also engaging themselves politically. Thus, Taixu and his followers claimed that social engagement had always been a high ideal of Mahāyāna Buddhism and that social engagement would again make the religion attractive to the youth. This situation is reminiscent of Ming times (1368–1644), during which the presence of secret societies in Buddhist monasteries explains why, in 1368, an official institution – the Shanshi Yuan (Buddhist Worthies Department) – was established to supervise the Buddhist monasteries. This institution stipulated that monks who had committed some crime against a nonmonk were to be judged according to secular law. As in Ming times, the task was to cleanse the community of all commercializing and superstition that had gained root in the Buddhist monasteries; it was to be remembered that, also in the past, noninterference with worldly matters had been a condition for gaining the support of the laity. Still this demand met with some resistance among monks who feared that social engagement would endanger the concept of noninterference with worldly affairs and thus would contradict their religious vow and obstruct their religious aim.

Taixu's guidelines sought to make monasteries centers of spiritual power for humankind and sought to close the gap between the Buddhist faith and practical life. With this aim Taixu proclaimed in 1915 the reorganization of the Saṃgha system. The movement of innovative Buddhism was especially strong in Wuhan. The curriculum that monks studied here was practical and included the study of current social questions. This sought to make monks alert and able to meet the needs of the new China. In the Republican period (1911–1949), Taixu's actions led to an increasing number of layfollowers who accepted the five vows for laypeople. In this way Taixu ordained more than 400 people of the Right Faith Buddhist Society in Hankou in 1929.

Taixu's engagement in reviving Buddhism made him follow Jichan to a provincial meeting on the education of monks in Jiangsu province in 1909. He was present also at another provincial meeting held in 1911 in Guangzhou. In 1912 Taixu established the Zhongguo Fojiao Xiejinhui (Chinese Society for Promoting Buddhism) with some of his fellow monks. Later this assembly was included in the Zhonghua Fojiao Zonghui (General Organization of Chinese Buddhism). Equally in 1912 he established the Buddhist Study Association of Wuchang. In 1927 he became president of the Buddhist Study Association of Minnan in Xiamen. In 1931 he established the Han-Zang Jiaoli Yuan (Sino-Tibet Institute for Instruction) in Chongqing and in 1943 the Zhongguo Zongjiaotu Lianyihui (Chinese Friendship Association of Religious Followers). After the victory over Japan, he was made responsible of the Zhongguo Fojiao Zhengli Weiyuanhui (Chinese Buddhist Rule Commission).

For republican China Taixu eagerly made use of the innovative medium of periodical publications. In this way he became editor-in-chief of the *Fojiao Yuebao* (Buddhist Monthly), in which articles in favor of the "movement for revitalizing Buddhism" were published. With Zhang Taiyan he published the *Jueshe Congkan* (Collection of the Association for Awakenment), the periodical of the Jueshe (Association for Awakenment). This periodical evolved into the monthly *Haichao Yin* (Sound of the Tide of the Sea), which published Taixu's lectures.

Among his international appearances he presided over a delegation of Buddhists in a meeting of Buddhists of East Asia held in Tokyo in 1925. While there, he examined the situation of Japanese Buddhism. In 1928 he established the Zhongguo Foxue Hui (Chinese Buddhist Study Association) in Nanjing. Members of this association visited England, France, Germany, Belgium, and the United States to proclaim Buddhism. These visits led to the establishment of the Buddhist World Study Center in Paris. This study center was the starting point for many Chinese monks before they went to Europe and the United States to proclaim the doctrine. For reviving esoteric Buddhism, Taixu sent one of his ablest students to Japan to study the esoteric school. Thus, it can be claimed that after people such as Huiyuan had made Buddhism acceptable to all strata of Chinese society, Buddhism gained an international dimension.

After Taixu's death and still in his spirit, the World Fellowship of Buddhists (founded in 1950) took up contacts with foreign Buddhists as its main mission, exchanging delegations and holding international congresses every two to three years.

Juzan (1908–1984), who met Taixu for the first time in 1918 and who studied under him in the South Fujian Seminar, became Taixu's most important disciple. He became the vice president of the Chinese Buddhist Association and the leading reformer of Buddhism during the Republican period.

BART DESSEIN

See also Buddhism: Western; China; Laicization of Spirituality: Buddhist Perspectives

Biography

This Buddhist reformer in post-imperial China was ordained in 1904 and thereafter established literally dozens of organizations for revitalizing Chinese Buddhism. In 1929 he became leader of the Chinese Buddhist Association, which attracted millions of members in Republican China. Taixu renewed monasticism and revived scholarship, particularly through the Wuchang Buddhist Institute.

Major Works

The Reorganization of the Buddhist Community, 1915
Collected Works, 64 vols.

Further Reading

Chan, Wing-tsit, *Religious Trends in Modern China*, New York: Columbia University Press, 1953
Fo-hang, "Zhongguo Fojiao de Xianzhuang," *Haichao Yin* 15:10 (1934)

Reichelt, Karl, *Truth and Tradition in Chinese Buddhism: A Study of Chinese Mahayana Buddhism*, Shanghai: Commercial Press, 1927; reprint, New York: Paragon Reprint Books, 1968
Tsukamoto, Zenryū, "Chūka Minkoku no Bukkyō," *Tōyōgaku Ronsō* (February 1952)
Welch, Holmes, *The Practice of Chinese Buddhism 1900–1950*, Cambridge, Massachusetts: Harvard University Press, and London: Oxford University Press, 1967
Welch, Holmes, *Buddhism Under Mao*, Cambridge, Massachusetts: Harvard University Press, 1972
Zhongguo Dabaike Quanshu - Zongjiao, Beijing: Zhongguo Dabaike Quanshu Chubanshe, 1988

Taizé, France

Six miles north of the medieval monastic center of Cluny in east-central France, the small Burgundian village of Taizé is home to one of the 20th century's new monastic communities that takes its name from the same village. The Taizé community was founded in 1949, and initially it had the appearance of a small and humble response to the divisions and general horror of World War II. However, it grew to be one of Europe's most important monastic experiments, enjoying wide international recognition and impact.

Roger Schutz-Marsauche (1915–), a Swiss theology student, originally traveled to Taizé in 1940 at the age of 25, and for two years his home was used to hide political and Jewish war refugees. Discovery by the Gestapo forced him to flee Taizé for his native Switzerland in 1942, but he returned with three friends in 1944 with the intention of living a communal life of prayer, reconciliation, and service according to monastic tradition. In 1949 seven brothers made monastic commitments of chastity, community of goods, and obedience to the prior, and in 1952 Brother Roger wrote a new rule for the community while functioning as its first prior.

The Rule of Taizé, written during a long retreat, was a short text in the tradition of the Rule of Benedict, and like the ancient model of Western monasticism its genius lay in its short and simple instructions, which focused on the essentials for living a common life in the contemporary context.

In the early years of the community, some of the brothers worked in nearby factories, with local farmers, and in other modest occupations or crafts. The brothers embraced the unusual economic policy of never building any capital reserve from year to year. Animated by what Brother Roger's writings describe as the "dynamic of the provisional," the community lived from its own work, made no investments, accepted no contributions for itself, and spent any extra money left at the end of each year mainly on charities.

Together with this radical simplicity, what distinguished this modest effort at the time was the fact that all the initial brothers were Protestant, making Taizé one of the first Protestant monastic experiments since the Reformation. However, from its inception the theme of Christian reconciliation was central to the community, and desire to act as a catalyst for Christian unity was one of its primary goals. Twenty years after its founding, in 1969, the first Roman Catholic brother joined the community, an event made possible largely by the new spirit of openness after the Second Vatican Council (1962–1965). Taizé, which Pope John XXIII (1958–1963) called "that little springtime" in the Church, subsequently acquired a central place in the ecumenical movement that gained momentum in the 1960s and 1970s. The community's church, built in part with funds given by a German group promoting reconciliation after the war, is named the Church of Reconciliation.

Besides the example of Catholics and Protestants sharing a common life together, Taizé also contributed to the theological work of the ecumenical movement through the work of one of the first brothers, Max Thurian (1921–). A working theologian for the World Council of Churches in the 1970s and 1980s, he was instrumental in helping to forge the common sacramental agreement among Roman Catholic, Orthodox, and Protestant communions known as the *Baptism, Eucharist and Ministry* document. It remains one of the most significant theological accomplishments of the ecumenical movement.

As its reputation grew in the 1960s, Taizé began to attract growing numbers of visitors and became an increasingly popular place of pilgrimage, especially for young people from throughout Europe. Hundreds of thousands of people traveled to Taizé in the following decades to spend a week taking part in the daily prayer of the community. On a liturgical level the distinctive music and style of prayer developed in Taizé constituted a popular renewal of the traditional monastic office and an important contribution to late 20th-century Christian worship. The prayer combined a traditional recitation of the Psalter, readings from Scripture, long periods of silent reflection, the presence of many Orthodox icons, and a distinctive chant of simple prayers that were easily learned. In addition to the daily prayer in Taizé, annual prayer meetings in European capital cities during the Christmas season routinely drew thousands of people for a week of prayer and discussions. Among the more famous visitors to Taizé were Mother Teresa, Pope John Paul II, the archbishop of Canterbury, and President François Mitterand, who frequently stopped at Taizé for prayer while visiting a family home in nearby Cluny.

Unlike most other monastic communities, the brothers of Taizé chose not to found new communities. Seeking a more direct link with the poor, small groups of brothers have lived outside of Taizé in impoverished areas, such as Hell's Kitchen in New York City and various parts of Africa, Asia, and Latin America, but without the intention of establishing a permanent presence or new communities. At the same time the community itself became more international in composition throughout the 1970s and 1980s. By 1999 more than 20 countries from around the world were represented among the 100 brothers of the community.

As with many monastic communities before it, the impact of the Taizé community on late 20th-century Christianity resulted in part from the animating spirit and charisma of its founder, commonly known as Brother Roger. The author of numerous spiritual memoirs, he co-authored two spiritual reflections with Mother Teresa (1910–1997), a longtime friend. His writings place special emphasis on simplicity, trust, faith, charity, solidarity with the poor, and spontaneity. As a small example of the practical implications of this spirit, Brother Roger adopted an Indian orphan during a visit with Mother Teresa in India in the late 1970s. She was raised in the home of his sister in the village of Taizé and was frequently at his side during the common prayer. Brother Roger has been awarded the Templeton prize for contributions to religion.

THOMAS DANDELET

See also Cluny, France; France: Sites; Protestant Monasticism: Lutheran; Schutz, Roger

Further Reading

Gonzalez-Balado, J.L., *The Story of Taizé*, New York: Seabury Press, and London: Mowbray, 1981
Schutz, Roger, *Parable of Community*, London: Mowbray, 1980; New York: Seabury Press, 1981
Schutz, Roger, *His Love Is a Fire*, Collegeville, Minnesota: Liturgical Press, 1990
Schutz, Roger, *The Taizé Experience*, London: Mowbray, and Collegeville, Minnesota: Liturgical Press, 1990
Schutz, Roger, *No Greater Love*, Collegeville, Minnesota: Liturgical Press, and Poole, England: Mowbray, 1991

Related Web Site

http://www.taizé.fr

Tao-hsüan. *See* Daoxuan

Taoism. *See* Daoism: Influence on Buddhism

Taungpila Sayadaw 1578–1651

Burmese Buddhist monk and authority on vinaya

The Taungpila Sayadaw was the most prominent Burmese monk of the 17th century. His Pāli vinaya manual *Vinayalankara tika* is generally regarded as having near canonical status.

He was born into a family of local officials at Salin in south-central Burma. Recognizing his great skill in Burmese and Pāli literature, his teachers sent him for advanced instruction to the city of Prome. Here he became a novice (as Munindaghosa) and was fully ordained (as Upali) in 1598. In 1608 King Anaukpetlun of Ava (1605–1628) conquered Prome. Taungpila, by now the city's leading young monk, was carried back to Ava with the booty. He settled in the university monasteries of the Sagaing Hills opposite Ava. As Taungpila's reputation as a lecturer and scholar increased, the king drew him deeper into court politics. King Thalun (1629–1648) recognized Taungpila as his chief monk.

The year A.D. 1638 was Burmese Era 1000. Taungpila and Thalun responded to the millennial fervor by organizing an expedition to the foothills of the Western Range to "rediscover" and rebuild the Golden Footprints of the Buddha shrine at Makula. The *Chronicle of the Golden Footprints* describes what transpired: by reciting an Abidhamma text, Taungpila attracted the attention of some powerful spirits who helped him accomplish his mission. Reciting the text again in celebration, he found himself talking to an aged spirit who had personally known the Buddha. This spirit encouraged Taungpila to declare his confident intention to achieve enlightenment. This Act of Truth was endorsed by supernatural portents: thereafter he was regarded as a bodhisatta. Following his triumphal return to Thalun's capital, he retired from public duties for a life of secluded meditation in the Taungpila monastery beyond the Sagaing Hills.

For members of Burma's mainstream monastic lineages, Taungpila's work holds great authority. His popular translations of Jataka stories and Abidhamma meditation texts are still in print. He coauthored the *Maharajathat*, the most innovative and one of the three most important texts of Burmese law. His *Lokavidu* and his *Notes on the Intercalendrical Month* deal with astronomy and the calendar: in 1811 King Badon ordered that Taungpila's calculations alone should determine the calendar. Most important of his works is the *Vinayalankara tika*, which takes the form of a subcommentary on a vinaya manual written in 13th-century Sri Lanka. Its content offers distinctively Burmese solutions to problems at the interface between lay and monastic law. In 1918 its quasi-canonical status was endorsed by the chief monk and by the leading lay Pāli scholar of the day.

However, for the minority reform lineages Taungpila gives off a whiff of brimstone. Suspicious of his close engagement in politics, they urge the merits of his contemporary, the Shwe-U-Myin sayadaw, who held himself above worldly involvement. Dismissing Taungpila's ordination lineage as provincial, they explain that he was the reincarnation of a 16th-century monk from an older and grander lineage. Critical of his Burmese school of vinaya interpretation, they prefer to follow only those works composed in Sri Lanka or India.

ANDREW HUXLEY

See also Bodhisattva; Burma (Myanmar); Rules, Buddhist (Vinaya): Lineage; Sri Lanka

Biography

During the first half of the 17th century, Taungpila became Burma's leading monk. He was favored by two successive kings, Anaukpetlun of Ava (1605–1628) and Thalun (1629–1648), in whose capital city of Ava he lived until he retired to the neighboring hills. His writings on monastic regulations (vinaya) remain authoritative.

Major Works

Vinayalankara tika
Maharajathat (coauthored)
Lokavidu
Manosara Shwe Myin dhammathat

Further Reading

Bechert, H., Khin Khin Su, Tin Tin Myint, and Heinz Braun, *Burmese Manuscripts*, 3 vols., Wiesbaden and Stuttgart: Steiner, 1979, 1985, 1996

Duroiselle, C., "Notes sur la Géographie Apocryphe de la Birmanie," *Bulletin de l'École Française de l'Extrême-Orient* 5 (1905)

Okudaira, R., "The Role of Kaingza Manuraja," *Ajia Afurika Gengo Bunka Kenkyu* 27 (1984)

Pannasami, *The History of the Buddha's Religion: Sasanavamsa*, translated by B.C. Law, London: Luzac, 1952

Templars

The Order of the Temple was founded around 1119 in Jerusalem by a group of arms bearers, led by Hugh of Payns, a knight from Champagne in France, and Godfrey of St.-Omer, a knight of Artois. The territories that were conquered during the First Crusade (1095–1099) and since then by Latin Christians from Western Europe were suffering frequent attack from their Muslim neighbors, and it was vital to protect Christian pilgrims on the road to the holy places. The new order was created to meet these needs.

Sources agree that the knights who became the first Templars initially came to the Holy Land for pious purposes but decided to remain and devote their lives to God. However, the sources disagree over whether the initiative for the formation of a group of warriors who would follow a religious lifestyle while combating Muslim aggressors lay with Patriarch Warmund of Jerusalem or with the knights themselves. In Western Europe it was relatively common for knights to form confraternities, bound together by oaths, in support of a righteous cause; possibly the Order of the Temple began as such a confraternity and was taken up by the patriarch and developed into a permanent religious order. King Baldwin II of Jerusalem gave the new group a base in his palace in the al-Aqsa mosque, which the Latin Christians called "the Temple of Solomon." Thus, the new group became "the Order of the Temple," or "Templars."

In January 1129 at the Council of Troyes, the Order of the Temple received official approval from the Church, and its religious rule was established and approved. This was firmly based on the Rule of St. Benedict, amended to allow for the exigencies of life on military campaign. From the 1130s the Templars became responsible for the defense of castles in the Latin East, were actively involved in the Iberian *Reconquista*, and went on to play a leading role in every crusading expedition to the Holy Land.

The Templars' headquarters remained in the East, supported by a network of houses in Europe. In Europe their lifestyle was indistinguishable from that of monks. Regarded in Europe as indispensable to the crusading cause, they received property and privileges from both ecclesiastical and lay donors and attracted many recruits, mainly men from the poorer knightly and nonknightly classes and (despite an official prohibition) a number of women. The Templars' involvement in transferring money and goods from Western Europe to the East led to their lending and transferring money for kings and merchants. The order's larger houses became important banking centers, and some brothers became royal almoners or treasurers.

Although the concept of winning merit through fighting in God's cause was not new, initially some Church authorities and even the Templars themselves were uncertain whether a fighting order could be the equal of a contemplative order. Letters survive from churchmen to the Templars, encouraging them in their vocation and reassuring them that it was a meritorious form of service for Christ. In particular, Bernard (1090–1153), abbot of Clairvaux, writing "In Praise of the New Knighthood," declared that the brothers were both monks and knights. By the end of the 12th century, doubts had faded. In fact, the Templars' vocation was so obviously essential to the defense of Christendom that further military orders were founded, notably the Hospitallers and the Teutonic order. When, during the trial of the Templars, King Philip IV (1285–1314) of France suggested to

Templar church, Scotland, 13th century.
Photo courtesy of Chris Schabel

View from the southwest of Temple Chapel, Laon, France.
Photo courtesy of Foto Marburg/Art Resource, New York

the masters of theology at the University of Paris that the Order of the Temple was not a valid religious order, the masters disagreed.

Successive popes took the order under papal protection, with the concomitant exemption from the jurisdiction of diocesan bishops; its main privileges and exemptions were set out by Pope Innocent II (1130–1143) in 1139 in the bull *Omne Datum Optimum*. Such exemptions often caused friction between the order and bishops at the local level but apparently did not undermine the bishops' fundamental belief in the value of the order.

The Templars' active involvement in military operations in the Holy Land did not end with the final destruction of the Latin kingdom of Jerusalem in 1291. They at once began plans for a new crusade but found little active assistance in the West. Some criticized the Templars for their involvement in the political problems of the kingdom of Jerusalem and their rivalry with the Hospitallers. Proposals to unify the military orders to form a single, more efficient order were opposed by the master of the Temple, James of Molay (d. 1314), who argued that the orders operated more effectively as independent units.

In October 1307 all the Templars in France were arrested on charges that varied from the obscene to the bizarre. Following interrogation and torture most of those arrested admitted at least some of the charges, although a few denied everything, and some died under torture. Pope Clement V (1305–1314) then intervened and ordered that all Templars be arrested and interrogated. Most other rulers of Europe were reluctant to arrest the Templars, as they valued their services and did not want their properties to pass to the Hospitallers, as the pope intended. Following a lengthy and inconclusive trial, the pope declared at

Templar church, Famagusta, Cyprus, c. 1300.
Photo courtesy of Chris Schabel

the Council of Vienne in 1312 that because the Templars' reputation had been irredeemably damaged (although they had not been found guilty), he would dissolve the order by papal provision. The brothers were sent to other religious houses, and most of their property was given to the Hospitallers to support crusading expeditions in the East. However, in the Iberian Peninsula, where there was an active crusading front, the Templars' property in Portugal and Valencia was used to found the new military orders of Christ and of Montesa.

The motives behind King Philip IV's attack on the Templars remain a matter of debate, but in view of his perennial financial problems, it seems most likely that the king hoped to obtain some financial gain. It is clear that up to the time of the trial, the Templars continued to enjoy a good reputation; although they were criticized for greed and pride, they were criticized no more than other religious orders, and contemporary literature depicted them as faithful and self-sacrificing knights of Christ. The charges of 1307 were not based on earlier criticism. It appears that the ministers of Philip IV made skillful use of propaganda to bring about the destruction of the Templars, who held considerable properties in France and had become vulnerable because of failing in their vocation to defend the Christian territories in the Holy Land.

HELEN J. NICHOLSON

See also Architecture: Western Christian Monasteries; Benedict of Nursia, St.; Bernard of Clairvaux, St.; Crusades; Germany: Sites; Hospitallers (Knights of Malta since 1530); Israel/Palestine; Pilgrimages, Christian: Near East; Spain: History; Warrior Monks: Christian

Further Reading

Barber, Malcolm, *The Trial of the Templars*, Cambridge and New York: Cambridge University Press, 1978

Barber, Malcolm, *The New Knighthood: A History of the Order of the Temple*, Cambridge and New York: Cambridge University Press, 1994

Barber, Malcolm, *Crusaders and Heretics, 12th–14th Centuries*, Aldershot, Hampshire, and Brookfield, Vermont: Variorum, 1995

Barber, Malcolm, editor, *The Military Orders: Fighting for the Faith and Caring for the Sick*, Aldershot, Hampshire, and Brookfield, Vermont: Variorum, 1994

Bulst-Thiele, Marie Luise, *Sacrae domus militiae Templi Hierosolymitani magistri: Untersuchungen zur Geschichte des Templerordens 1118/9–1314*, Göttingen: Vandenhoeck und Ruprecht, 1974

Forey, Alan, *The Military Orders: From the Twelfth to the Early Fourteenth Centuries*, London: Macmillan Education, and Toronto and Buffalo, New York: University of Toronto Press, 1992

Forey, Alan, *Military Orders and Crusades*, Aldershot, Hampshire, and Brookfield, Vermont: Variorum, 1994

Luttrell, Anthony, "The Earliest Templars," in *Autour de la Première Croisade: Actes du Colloque de la Society for the Study of the Crusades and the Latin East: Clermont-Ferrand, 22–25 juin 1995*, edited by Michel Balard, Paris: Publications de la Sorbonne, 1996

Nicholson, Helen, *Templars, Hospitallers and Teutonic Knights: Images of the Military Orders, 1128–1291*, Leicester: Leicester University Press, and New York: St. Martin's Press, 1993

Nicholson, Helen, editor, *The Military Orders*, volume 2: *Welfare and Warfare*, Aldershot, Hampshire, and Brookfield, Vermont: Ashgate, 1998

Selwood, Dominic, *Knights of the Cloister*, Woodbridge: Boydell Brewer, 1999

Temple, Buddhist

Asian Buddhists use a variety of terms – *vihāra* (Pāli), *pansala* (Sinhala), *tera* (Japanese), *wat* (Thai) – to identify a place of Buddhist worship as conveyed by the English term *temple*. A Buddhist temple is a place dedicated for religious devotion – a place of worship as well as a place for a variety of religious ceremonies that bring together the community in harmony. In the case of Buddhist temple, although the conception of divine presence is somewhat foreign, Buddhist temples enshrine sacred objects that demand reverence and respect from the pious devotees.

In the early stages of Buddhist monasticism in India, a temple was a simple building for temporary residence; such temporary buildings made out of straw were called *paṇṇasālā* (straw hut).

During the three months of rainy season (*vassāna*), itinerant monastics used such temporary huts for their lodgings. With the rapid growth of members and patrons, increasingly more luxurious buildings were gradually added to monasteries as permanent residences.

A modern Sri Lankan Theravāda temple contains several buildings for a variety of religious purposes: (1) a shrine room for the Buddha; (2) a stūpa enshrining Buddha's corporeal relics; (3) a Bodhi tree, which symbolizes Gautama Buddha's awakening under the Bodhi Tree at Bodh Gayā; (4) monks' lodgings; (5) a preaching hall for religious functions, such as reciting sūtras, giving sermons, and communal gathering; (6) a bell tower to announce auspicious occasions; (7) a *sīma* for performing ecclesiastical acts; (8) a refectory; (9) a Sunday school for educating the youth; (10) a library housing scriptures; and (11) a monastic school. Although each and every Buddhist temple might not possess all these items, even the smallest includes at least a few.

The abbot is the head; under his guidance and training, young novices and *bhikkhus* live in the temple. Because temples and their serving communities are small, often temples do not accommodate more than three or four resident monastics. A young boy or an adult living within the temple assists the resident monks in their daily activities.

On the full-moon days and other special occasions, devotees gather in the temple for worship. To facilitate such gatherings, the temple ground is kept spacious. The daily routine of monks includes work related to the proper maintenance of the buildings and of their surroundings. Cleanliness is a disciplinary requirement, as a clean and quiet environment is considered conducive to meditation and contemplative life. Describing monastic life the 13th-century Buddhist writer Dharmasēna Thera wrote, "As roosters forage for food all day and only curl up at dusk, at the end of the day, the monk Mahākāla swept the yard early, collected water, bathed, cleaned and cooled his body, worshipped at the Bō tree, paid his respects to the senior monks, sat, walked, and spent the night in meditation." The daily Buddhist monastic routine is highly regulated. The monastics get up early and clean the temple compounds. It is a typical scene in Sri Lanka that the young and the old alike sweep the temple compounds at the dawn and dusk. They take only two meals – breakfast and lunch – and spend evenings only with soft drinks. In the mornings and evenings, the abbot and his pupils gather in the shrine room for daily worship. They offer flowers and incense to the Buddha, recite Pāli verses (*gāthā*) and daily protections (*vatapirit*), practice meditation, and give short religious instructions if an audience is present. Depending on the place, time, and circumstances, such worship services often end with a short meditation either on the practice of cultivating loving-kindness (*mettā*) or on the cultivation of mindfulness of inhaling and exhaling of breath (*ānāpānasati*).

In Sri Lanka each Buddhist household is traditionally assigned to the village temple. A village that provides monastic requisites is called *godurugama*. The lay community supplies the four requisites – clothing, food, lodging, and medicine – for the monastics. The interdependent relationship that exists between the temple and the village community is very important. Whereas the temple and its monastics depend on the village community for material sustenance, each village more or less relies on the monastics and the temple whenever they need guidance in spiritual matters and instruction at times of crisis. Small village temples that are scattered around the country often function as community centers that provide spiritual guidance as well as educational facilities.

In other Buddhist societies religious systems similar to *godurugama* seem to have existed. In Japan during the Muromachi period (1333–1568), with the rapid popularity of Pure Land, Zen, and Nichiren schools among the masses, monastics established intimate connections with their devotees through a network of *danka* (parishioners) by performing funeral rituals and memorial services. In 1639 with the adoption of national seclusion policy and the prohibition of Christianity, the Tokugawa Shogunate (1603–1867) formalized the temple-*danka* relationship by decreeing that all Japanese must register with a local temple.

Traditionally, Buddhist monks were the educators in Sri Lanka. During the colonial period, although temple education was disrupted and monks' role as educators came under severe attack, they were able to maintain a low profile as educators. In the 20th century monastics have resumed their educational roles. Although most temples function as *dhamma* schools on Sundays, a significant number of monastics teach in public and monastic schools, delivering religious and secular education. The educational role of Buddhist monastics is not peculiar to Sri Lanka, as monks in other Theravāda countries have performed similar roles. Even in Mahāyāna countries (e.g., in Japan), traditional education took place in temple schools (*terakoya*). In the Tokugawa period, schools were established in Japanese Buddhist temples for elementary education.

An important religious duty of a Buddhist monastic is to give religious instruction. Buddhist monastics preach *baṇa* for two purposes: to guide the listeners on righteous living and to enable them to acquire merit (*puñña*). In addition to the traditional roles of teaching and giving religious instruction, modern Sri Lankan monks have assumed new roles in performing a variety of social welfare activities.

MAHINDA DEEGALLE

See also Buddhist Schools/Traditions: Japan; Chan/Zen: Japan; Discourses (Suttas): Theravāda; Economics: Buddhist; Japan: History; Kyoto, Japan; Mount Meru; Nara, Japan; Rules, Buddhist (Vinaya); Sri Lanka; Stūpa; Topography, Sacred (Buddhist); Visual Arts, Buddhist; Worship Space: Buddhist Perspectives

Further Reading

Deegalle, Mahinda, "Buddhist Preaching and Sinhala Religious Rhetoric: Medieval Buddhist Methods to Popularize Theravāda," *Numen* 44 (1997)

Deegalle, Mahinda, "Marathon Preachers: The Two-Pulpit Tradition in Sri Lanka," *Asiatische Studien: Études Asiatiques* 52:1 (1998)

Dharmasēna Thera, *Jewels of the Doctrine: Stories of the Saddharma Ratnāvaliya*, translated by Ranjini Obeyesekere, Albany: State University of New York Press, 1991

Gunawardana, R.A.L.H., *Robe and Plough: Monasticism and Economic Interest in Early Medieval Sri Lanka*, Tucson: University of Arizona Press, 1979

Murakami, Shigeyoshi, "Temples," in *Kodansha Encyclopedia of Japan*, volume 8, edited by Gen Itasaka et al., Tokyo: Kodansha, 1983

Wells, Kenneth Elmer, *Thai Buddhism: Its Rites and Activities*, Bangkok: Bangkok Times Press, 1939; New York: AMS Press, 1960 (see pages 26–135)

Tendai. *See* Tiantai/Tendai: Japan

Ten-Precept Mothers as Theravādin Nuns

Ten-Precept Mothers are referred to as *dasa sil mātās*/*dasa sil māniyo*s or *sil mātās*/*sil māniyo*s (precept mothers) in Sri Lanka. They are female monastics of the Theravāda Buddhist tradition who observe the ten precepts on a relatively permanent basis. These precepts involve undertaking the precept to abstain from (1) destroying the life of beings; (2) taking things not given; (3) engaging in sexual activity; (4) uttering false speech; (5) taking intoxicants; (6) taking food at inappropriate times; (7) engaging in dancing, singing, music, and seeing shows; (8) wearing flowers, perfumes, cosmetics, finery, and adornments; (9) using high and luxurious seats; and (10) accepting gold and silver.

*Dasa sil mātā*s do not have the full ordination (*upasampadā*) of a fully ordained woman (*bhikkhunī*) in the Buddhist tradition. The ten-precept ordination might be either a lay (*gihi*) or a renunciant (*pävidi*) ordination. The former involves reciting each of the ten precepts separately; breaking one of these precepts does not involve an infringement of the others. Laity may choose to take the ten precepts on a temporary basis. Most *sil mātā*s today have the *gihi* ordination. The *pävidi* ordination, which is comparable to the novice ordination of a Buddhist monk, involves the recitation of the ten precepts as one rule. Consequently the infringement of any one precept involves an infraction of all ten precepts. Although much of the scholarly literature refers to both the *dasa sil mātā*s and the *bhikkhunī*s as "nuns," this nomenclature is problematic because, unlike the Buddhist *bhikkhunī*s, "nuns" in the Catholic tradition have never received full ordination.

Flag of the *sil mātā*s, introduced in 1986.
Photo courtesy of Nirmala S. Salgado

The first hermitage for female ten-precept holders, known as the Saṃghamittā Upāsikārāmaya (Saṃghamittā hermitage for pious laywomen), was established in 1898 in Colombo, Sri Lanka, by Anagārika Dharmapāla (1864–1933) and organized by Madame de Souza Canverro, an American-born Catholic convert to Buddhism. The Saṃghamittā Upāsikārāmaya was influenced by the views of both the Theosophical Society and Catholicism. The success of this *upāsikārāmaya* was short-lived. Many *dasa sil mātā*s today trace their lineages back to Sister Sudharmachari, a Sri Lankan–born *sil mātā*. Known as Catherine de Alwis before her ordination, she was originally an Anglican convert to Buddhism. She received her ten-precept ordination in Burma and on returning to Sri Lanka helped establish and organize the Sudharma Upāsikārāmaya in Katukale, Kandy. Also known as the Lady Blake Upāsikārāmaya, it opened in 1907 and continues to function as a hermitage for *sil mātā*s to this day.

In the early years Sri Lankan ten-precept mothers shaved their heads, wore white robes and blouses, and were referred to as pious laywomen (*upāsikā*s) or pious ten-precept laywomen (*dasa sil upāsikā*s). Later they began to wear white blouses under the saffron robes. Today they wear saffron blouses and robes and are rarely referred to as *upāsikā*s. About 2,500 to 3,000 *sil mātā*s exist in Sri Lanka today. The majority of *dasa sil mātā*s are strict vegetarians and live either alone or in small communities of up to about 15 monastics. Although all follow the ten precepts, the various communities in which they live are diverse and loosely organized and often interpret their ascetic vocation in different ways.

A *bhikkhunī* lineage that was specifically associated with Theravāda Buddhists was unheard of in Sri Lanka after about the tenth century. Debates concerning the revival of the lineage have been especially controversial in Sri Lanka since the 1950s. Some argue against the possibility of this revival, maintaining that because Theravāda *bhikkhunī*s must participate at an *upasampadā* ceremony for women, their absence precludes this possibility. Others have made a case for the participation of Mahāyāna *bhikkhunī*s in an *upasampadā* ceremony for Theravāda women.

On 8 December 1996 the Mahāyāna monastics of the Korean World Buddhist Saṃgha Council sponsored the *upasampadā* of ten *dasa sil mātā*s from Sri Lanka in Sarnath, India. In July 1997 the first successful *bhikkhunī* training center for *sil mātā*s was inaugurated in Sri Lanka by the Sri Lanka Bhikkhunī Re-Awakening Organization (Bhikshuṇī Shāsanābhivṛddhi Samvidānaya), and 26 *sil mātā*s who were ordained as novices (*sāmanerī*s) began a six-month training period there. Some of them received

Sāmanerīs training for the *Bhikkhunī* Ordination at the Rangiri Dambulla Training Center, Dambulla, Sri Lanka. Photo courtesy of Nirmala S. Salgado

the *upasampadā* in Bodh Gayā, India, from Theravāda *bhikkhunīs*, who had been ordained in Sarnath. After returning to Sri Lanka and amidst considerable controversy, they conferred the *upasampadā* on *dasa sil mātās* in Dambulla in March 1998. Subsequent *upasampadā* ceremonies held in Sri Lanka in 1998 have brought the number of *bhikkhunīs* to about 100. International attempts to confer the *upasampadā* on *sil mātās* from Sri Lanka include those associated with the Mahabodhi Society, the Bhikshuṇī Foundation, and Sakyadhītā International.

In the 1980s the Sri Lankan government initiated attempts to educate and organize the *sil mātās* nationally in an endeavor to unify them. Regional educational centers and associations were formed. The National Sil Mata Organization (Sil Mātā Jātika Maṇḍalaya) was established in 1986 and began holding annual conventions in commemoration of Uduwap Pōya, the December full-moon day associated with the arrival of the first *bhikkhunī*, Saṃghamittā, to Lanka in the third century B.C. The national unity of the *sil mātās* is now symbolized in a *sil mātā* flag. In December 1990 the Sri Lankan government declared Uduwap Pōya National Women's Day.

Because the *sil mātās* do not constitute a "field of merit," unlike the fully ordained community of monastics (*saṃgha*), donations given to them are generally not considered to be as meritorious as those given to the *saṃgha*. Lacking the full ordination and technically considered laity despite their monastic vocation, the *sil mātās* are still denied privileges that fully ordained monks (*bhikkhus*) enjoy. The *dasa sil mātās* continue to seek state privileges that recognize and support their monastic vocation.

The closest equivalents to the *dasa sil mātās* of Sri Lanka in other Theravāda Buddhist countries are the *māē chī* of Thailand, the *thilá shin* of Burma, and the *don chī* of Cambodia. The *thilá shin* and the *don chī* may observe either eight or ten precepts, whereas the *māē chī* generally observe no more than eight. Like the *dasa sil mātās* of Sri Lanka, these female monastics lead celibate lives in religious communities, yet their religious and social status remains distinct from that of members of the *saṃgha*.

NIRMALA S. SALGADO

See also Bodh Gayā, India; Burma (Myanmar); Dharmapāla, Anagārika; Gender Studies: Buddhist Perspectives; Holy Men/Holy Women: Buddhist Perspectives; Mahāpajāpatī Gotamī; Regulations: Buddhist Perspectives; Rules, Buddhist (Vinaya): Historical; Sri Lanka: Sites; Thailand; Women's Monasteries: Buddhist

Further Reading

Bartholomeusz, Tessa J., *Women Under the Bō Tree: Buddhist Nuns in Sri Lanka*, Cambridge and New York: Cambridge University Press, 1994

Bloss, Lowell, "The Female Renunciants of Sri Lanka: The Dasasil mattawa," *Journal of the International Association of Buddhist Studies* 10:1 (1987)

Kabilsingh, Chatsumarn, *Thai Women in Buddhism*, Berkeley, California: Parallax Press, 1991

Kawanami, H., "The Religious Standing of Burmese Buddhist Nuns (thilá-shin): The Ten Precepts and Religious Respect Words," *Journal of the International Association of Buddhist Studies* 13:1 (1990)

Keyes, Charles F., "Mother or Mistress but Never a Monk: Buddhist Notions of Female Gender in Rural Thailand," *American Ethnologist* 3:2 (1984)

Salgado, Nirmala S., "Ways of Knowing and Transmitting Religious Knowledge: Case Studies of Theravāda Buddhist Nuns," *Journal of the International Association of Buddhist Studies* 19:1 (1996)

Salgado, Nirmala S., "Sickness, Healing and Religious Vocation: Alternative Choices at a Theravada Buddhist Nunnery," *Ethnology* 36:3 (1997)

Salgado, Nirmala S., "Buddhist Nuns, Nationalist Ideals and Revivalist Discourse," *Nēthrā* 2:2 (1998)

Thamel, Cleophas, "The Religious Woman in a Buddhist Society: The Case of the Dasa-Sil Maniyo in Sri Lanka," *Dialogue* 11:1–3 (1984)

Van Esterik, Penny, "Laywomen in Theravada Buddhism," in *Women of Southeast Asia*, DeKalb, Illinois: Northern Illinois University Center for Southeast Asian Studies, 1982

Teresa of Avila, St. 1515–1582

Spanish Carmelite nun, mystic, monastic reformer, and author

One of the most important religious writers, mystics, and Catholic monastic reformers of 16th-century Europe, Teresa of Avila was both a product and a shaper of the deeply religious culture and pervasive formal religious institutions of 16th-century Spain. As she recounted in her famous spiritual autobiography, *The Book of Her Life* (1565), it was already as a young girl that she and her brother, inspired by examples found in books of saint's lives, dreamed of seeking martyrdom in the Holy Land or at least of living the life of the desert hermits. Eventually these traditional monastic metaphors of martyrdom and the desert played a strong role in defining the life that Teresa chose when she entered the Carmelite Order in 1535 at the age of 20.

The granddaughter of a *converso* (i.e., a Jewish convert to Christianity) family and daughter of the nobles Alonso Sánchez de Cepeda and Beatrice de Ahumada, Teresa was taught to read and write at home at a young age and briefly lived in a school for girls at the Augustinian convent of Our Lady of Grace (1531), where she first began contemplating a formal religious life. However, poor health that was to haunt her all her life cut short her time with the Augustinians, and four years later, in 1535, she entered the Carmelite house of the Incarnation in Avila, one of only 11 Carmelite monasteries for women in Spain at the time. She formally took the habit of the order in 1536 and made her final vows in 1537.

The following two decades were marked by more illness, including a three-year period shortly after her final vows when she was bedridden. Recent scholars have speculated that she might have suffered from epilepsy or some other disease. It was the gradual emergence and description of spiritual experiences in her 40s that brought on her both suspicion and encouragement from her religious superiors and confessors. The list of men who served in this capacity during her life included well-known churchmen, such as the Dominicans García de Toledo and Pedro Ibáñez, the Jesuit St. Francis Borja (eventual general of the Jesuit Order), and the Franciscan St. Peter of Alcántara (1499–1562). Perhaps the most important of these was St. Peter, under whose spiritual direction she was encouraged to write an account of her experiences that resulted in her spiritual autobiography, or *Life* (1565), a work widely regarded as one of the classics of Christian spiritual writing as well as one of the first women's autobiographies to appear in early modern Europe.

The distinctive spirituality that emerged in the *Life* of Teresa was marked by interior prayer that went through various stages of increasing intensity. In one sense the spiritual development of Teresa between 1557 and 1565 and the experiences she recounted about those years provided a rough blueprint for her understanding of spiritual development in general. Indeed her account became a guide for the spiritual formation and goals of future generations of Carmelites and is now seen as one of the most lucid evocations of 16th-century Catholic mysticism.

This spiritual evolution began with what she described as her real conversion in 1557. It was prompted by a reading of St. Augustine's *Confessions* and meditation in front of a statue of the wounded Christ (*Life*, chap. 9). Over the next months Teresa described a growing sense of the presence of God that began with increased compunction, or tears in prayer, and eventually progressed through various degrees of interior prayer and recollection to what she described as the divine gifts of rapture and union (*Life*, chaps. 19 and 20).

Among the early spiritual experiences recounted in the *Life*, perhaps the most important for the future of the Carmelite Order in Spain and elsewhere was St. Teresa's discernment in 1557 that she was being called by God to live according to a strict, or reformed, interpretation of the Carmelite rule. Her interpretation was characterized by a strictly cloistered life and a generally more extreme asceticism that required, among other things, not wearing shoes. This gave Teresa's new branch of Carmelites their additional name, discalced, or barefoot. From Teresa's perspective her reforms were founded on a return to the primitive life of the early Carmelites who followed the Rule of St. Albert.

However, rather than simply embracing old forms she eventually transformed them by renewing their discipline and vigor while also providing an example of female leadership and intellectual productivity that transcended that of any of her medieval predecessors. In this she embodied an apparent paradox because, as the founder of the reformed, Discalced Carmelites she in fact imposed a more strict, cloistered life on the women of her Order. The contradiction of such an active, vocal, and well-traveled woman advocating stability and the cloister was not lost on some contemporary detractors, such as the papal nuncio Philip Sega, who described her as

> a troublesome, restless, disobedient, and stubborn female, who under the guise of devotion invented bad doctrines, running around outside the cloister against the order of the Tridentine Council and prelates, instructing like a teacher in defiance of what St. Paul taught, who ordered women not to teach. (Francisco de Santa María, 1644–1655)

This opinion did not prevail in large measure because of Teresa's extraordinary success at founding new houses of Discalced Carmelites that made her one of the most well known and admired religious figures in late 16th-century Iberia. In 1562 she founded the convent of St. Joseph's in Avila, the first house to live according to the primitive rule of the Order (*Life*, chap. 30). In 1567 she received permission from the Italian general of the order, Giovanni Battista Rossi, to found other houses of reformed Carmelite friars and nuns. Over the next 15 years, she became responsible for establishing 15 new houses of Discalced Carmelite monasteries for friars and 17 convents for nuns. She recounted the history of this work in her book simply titled *Foundations*.

Together with institution building Teresa's impressive corpus of spiritual writings also served to increase her reputation. In addition to her autobiography, she also wrote *The Interior Castle*, *The Way of Perfection*, and *Meditations on the Song of Songs* (*Collected Works*, volume 2). Masterpieces of spiritual reflection and foundations for Carmelite contemplative life during the following centuries, all these texts furthered Teresa's reputation and spread her influence far beyond her own Order. In these writings and in her voluminous correspondence with princes, prelates, and fellow religious, Teresa proved herself a product of the Christian humanist culture of high Renaissance Spain, if not of the formal university system. Like her friend and male Carmelite counterpart St. John of the Cross (1542–1591) and mystic contemporary and Augustinian hermit Fray Luis de León (1527/28–1591), she produced poetic reflections on scripture and prayers that displayed a sophisticated mastery of spiritual metaphor and more generally of the Castilian language.

The combination of her power as a writer and success as a founder of new Carmelite houses made Teresa in her own lifetime a famous holy woman throughout the Spanish Empire. Immediately after her death a forceful campaign for her canonization began. The testimony contained in the proceedings for her canonization included letters from two Spanish kings, Philip II (1556–1598) and Philip III (1598–1621); Philip III's wife, Queen Margarita; and Don Juan de Henestrosa, the secretary for the kingdom of Castile. Henestrosa summed up the sentiment of many when he wrote,

> Teresa of Jesus . . . in a space of thirty years, through her labor and holiness, founded in Spain, and in the Indies, and in Italy a great number of convents of male and female religious that with her holy life and doctrine have been, and are, a great influence for reforming the customs of the lands in which they reside. (Vatican Secret Archive, Riti, Ms. 3156, unfoliated)

Furthered by the testimony of major prelates from throughout the Spanish Empire – including the archbishops or bishops of Toledo, Valentia, Burgos, Zaragoza, Valladolid, Salamanca, Cordoba, Segovia, Tarragona, Palencia, Barcelona, Granada, Santiago de Compostela, and Mexico – Teresa was canonized in 1622 by Pope Gregory XV (1621–1623). At the same time she quickly became a favorite subject of Baroque artists: Gianlorenzo Bernini's sculpture of *St. Teresa in Ecstasy* (1646) in the church of Santa Maria della Vittoria in Rome is one of the best known and most admired pieces of 17th-century art.

The impact of Teresa's writings and new foundations on the history of Spanish monasticism generally and of Carmelite monasticism specifically is hard to overestimate. In Iberia convents or monasteries were founded in most of the major cities of the peninsula, including Seville, Granada, Vallodolid, Salamanca, Toledo, Alcalá de Henares, Segovia, Burgos, Lisbon, Alba de Tormes, Avila, and Medina de Campo. Moreover in many older foundations, such as the convent of the Incarnation in Avila, where Teresa had first taken vows, her reforms were eventually imposed. In short for Carmelites throughout the far-flung Spanish Empire, St. Teresa's interpretation of Carmelite monasticism became the dominant form, and Discalced convents flourished throughout Catholic Europe and the New World.

Moreover in succeeding centuries Carmelites following the Teresian reforms established themselves around the world as one of the strongest religious orders of the Catholic Reformation. For Discalced Carmelites the charism of St. Teresa continued to supply the animating spirit of their monastic life. It was a constant point of reference for numerous Carmelite nuns who became famous for piety in their own right, including the 19th-century nun St. Thérèse of Lisieux (1873–1897), the Spanish Teresa of the Infant Jesus (1909–1936), the Chilean Teresa of the Andes (1900–1920), the French Elizabeth of the Trinity (1880–1906), and the German St. Edith Stein (1891–1942).

Through her more institutional writings as well, Teresa remained a dominant figure and influence in the shape of Carmelite life up to the present day. More specifically Teresa's *Primitive Constitutions* and *The Way of Perfection*, together with the *Constitutions of Alcalá*, provided the institutional structure that was to be the foundation of the Discalced Carmelites.

The importance of this "spiritual patrimony" was put in high relief in the 20th century during the period of general ecclesiastical reform following the Second Vatican Council (1962–1965).

In the case of the Discalced Carmelites nuns, various parts of the Church hierarchy, including Pope John Paul II (1978–) and the male superior general of the Order, attempted in 1977 to impose a new constitution entitled *Declaration for the Updating of the "Primitive" Constitutions of the Discalced Nuns of the Order of the Blessed Virgin Mary of Mount Carmel in Accordance with the Directives of the Second Vatican Council.*

This document was met with strong opposition by a substantial minority of Carmelite houses led by convents in Spain. They took the name of the Association of United Carmels and opposed the new *Declaration* precisely because it was seen to go against the spirit of Teresa's original constitution. Of 753 Carmelite convents surveyed in 1982, 147 opposed it on these grounds. Eventually this group produced an alternative version of a new constitution simply called the *1990 Constitutions*. Reflecting the split between this more traditional group and other Carmelite houses, of the 869 female Carmelite monasteries worldwide in 1992, 125 chose the more conservative *1990 Constitutions*, with 59 of those located in Spain. The rest chose a 1991 revision of the *Declarations* titled the *1991 Constitutions* (Kuenstler, 1997).

In fact, the traditionalists chose to suppress one of the fundamental principles of Teresa's original ideas for her Order, namely, that both male and female houses should be united under a male superior general. From the traditionalist perspective this allowed their female houses to follow the spirit of Teresa more closely and also left them free from the influence and control of friars who were perceived as wanting to pursue the reforms of the Second Vatican Council too vigorously. Clearly St. Teresa's influence on modern Carmelites has remained strong well into the present century, but ironically by the 1970s the issue of what constituted the true legacy of Teresa had become a point of contention and division.

THOMAS DANDELET

See also Carmelites; Humanism, Christian; John of the Cross, St.; Spain; Spirituality: Western Christian; Thérèse of Lisieux, St.

Biography

Born near Avila into a noble Spanish family of *converso* (i.e. Jewish) descent, Teresa studied at the Augustinian convent before entering the Carmelite monastery of Vil in 1535. Her *Life* (1565) narrates bouts of illness over many years as she gradually entered the path of contemplation. St. Peter of Alcántara helped her in 1560, as later did St. John of the Cross. From 1567 she worked against strong opposition to establish houses of reformed ("Discalced," i.e. unshod) Carmelites throughout Spain. Her works, which were written in Spanish and published mostly shortly after her death, have inspired contemplatives ever since.

Major Works

The Book of Her Life, 1565
Meditations on the Song of Songs, 1566–1567, 1574
Foundations, 1574–1582
The Interior Castle, 1588
The Way of Perfection, 1588

The best recent edition of St. Teresa's works in the original language is *Obras completas de s. Teresa de Jesús*, 2nd edition, edited by Efrén de la Madre de Dios and Otger Steggink, 1967. The best English translation and edition of St. Teresa's works now available is *The Collected Works of St. Teresa of Avila*, 3 vols., edited and translated by Kieran Kavanaugh and Otilio Rodriguez, 1976

Further Reading

The most important early biographies of St. Teresa include the first by one of her confessors, Francisco de Ribera, *La vida de la m. Teresa de Jesús*, Salamanca, 1590. See also Diego de Yepes, *Vida, virtudes y milagros de la b. virgen santa Teresa*, Madrid: Sánchez, 1615, and Antonio de la Encarnacion, *Vida y milagros de la esclarecida i seráfica virgen santa Teresa*, Salamanca, 1614.

For perhaps one of the best 20th-century biographies see Silverio de St. Teresa, *Vida de s. Teresa*, 5 vols., Burgos: Tipografia Burgalesa (El Monte Carmelo), 1935–1938.

For an important early history of the reforms see Francisco de Santa María, *Reforma de los descalzos de Nuestra Señora del Carmen de la primitiva observancia, hecha por Santa Teresa de Jesús*, Madrid, 1644–1655.

For the best recent study of Teresa's reforms in their social context see Jodi Bilinkoff, *The Avila of St. Teresa*, Ithaca, New York: Cornell University Press, 1989, and Otger Steggink and Efrén de la Madre de Dios, *Santa Teresa y su tiempo*, Salamanca: Universidad Pontificia de Salamanca, 1982.

For the contemporary Carmelite situation see the collection of essays *Contemporary Carmelite Women*, London: The Way, 1997, especially Kate Kuenstler, "The Fractured Face of Carmel."

Territorial Abbeys. *See* Abbeys, Territorial

Teutonic Order

The Teutonic Order (usually, *hospitale sancte Marie Theutonicorum Jerosolimitanum*, the Hospital of St. Mary of the Germans of Jerusalem, or *der orden des Dûschen huses*, the order of the German house, in the sources) was one of the three major knightly or military orders that originated and evolved during the 12th and 13th centuries. The Templars and the Hospitallers are the other major orders.

The military orders were "true orders" of the Roman Church that were governed by regulations similar to those governing monks, generally variants of the Benedictine or Augustinian Rules. For most purposes technically they were answerable only to the pope. They did have some feudal responsibilities to lay and other clerical entities as dictated by circumstances of place and time. Large numbers of knights became monks but often dwelt in military fortifications rather than monasteries. The members of most orders took vows of poverty, chastity, and obedience.

Origins of the Teutonic Order

According to tradition, early in the 12th century a wealthy German couple built a hospital in Jerusalem at their own expense to care for poor and sick pilgrims who spoke German. The hospital and an accompanying chapel were dedicated to the Virgin Mary. This story is similar to traditions concerning the origins of the Hospital of St. John of Jerusalem founded by Amalfitans. The German hospital apparently was affiliated with the Hospital of St. John, at least in the observance of the Rule of St. Augustine. After Saladin's conquest of Jerusalem in 1187, no records of the German hospital there exist, nor does any indication that the German hospital ever had a military mission.

During the siege of Acre during the Third Crusade (probably 1190), Germans from Lübeck and Bremen established a field hospital for German soldiers, reportedly using ships' sails as cover from the elements. Duke Frederick of Swabia placed his chaplain Conrad in charge of the hospital and soon transformed the organization into a religious order responsible to the local Latin bishop. Although some scholars question its authenticity, Pope Clement III (1187–1191) apparently approved the Order on 6 February 1191. The Order was taken under Pope Celestine III's (1191–1198) protection on 21 December 1196 with the name Hospital of St. Mary of the Germans in Jerusalem. Possibly the name is the only connection with the earlier German hospital, although some argue a more direct relationship.

A ceremony purportedly held on 5 March 1198 altered the Order's raison d'être. The patriarch of Jerusalem, the king of Jerusalem, the head of the crusading army, and the masters of the Templars and the Hospital of St. John attended the celebration establishing the Teutonic Knights as a military order. A bull by Pope Innocent III (1198–1216) dated 19 February 1199 confirmed the event and specified that the Order would care for the sick according to the rule of the Hospitallers. It would conduct its other business by following the Templar rule and would wear the Temple's distinctive white cloak. Its black cross would differentiate the Teutonic Order from the Temple.

Internal Structure

During the first 20 years of its existence, the institutional structure of the Order developed and stabilized. The Teutonic Order followed the lead of the Templars and Hospitallers by creating a system of provinces. Unlike monastic orders, which were composed of independent abbeys, the Teutonic Knights had a hierarchical chain of command with commanderies (house, or *Kommende*) at the lowest level. Provinces or bailiwicks (*Ballei* or *Komturei*) were parts of "countries" that composed the Order as a whole. Its first independent rule was adopted in 1264.

The officials governing the Teutonic Order at the various levels were commander (*Komtur*, or preceptor) at the local level,

Tomb of Grand Master Konrad von Thüringen of the Teutonic Order, St. Elizabeth, Marburg, Germany, 13th century.
Photo courtesy of Foto Marburg/Art Resource, New York

province commander (*Landkomtur*), national commander (*Landmeister*), and grand master (*Hochmeister*, or magister). The highest leadership positions (including grand master, grand commander [*Grosskomtur*], marshal [*Ordensmarschall*], draper or quartermaster [*Trapier*], hospitaller [*Spittler*], and treasurer [*Tressler*]) were elected by the general chapter.

Membership of this mostly German-speaking order was composed of various distinct classes: knights, priests, and other brothers (lay brothers, sisters, and "familiars"). A large number of people supported the professed members of the Order, ranging from auxiliary knights to slaves. The highest ranking were secular knights, serving gratis. Originally Turcopoles (Greek for "son of Turk") likely were lightly armed, half-breed cavalry whose name pertained to Turkish mercenaries employed in the Byzantine army. Later the term was adopted by the military orders. Also present were attendants, called squires (*knechte*), and sergeants-at-arms. Footsoldiers were usually coerced from the local peasantry. Sister-aids (*halpswesteren*) were employed as domestics, as were *halpbrûderen*, who took religious vows. Married and single lay domestics also were employed by the Order. Artisans and laborers (e.g., gardeners, carpenters, and masons) worked for charity or wages. Many serfs and slaves were owned by the Order.

Nave of the Church of the Teutonic Knights (Deutscher Orden), Vienna, Austria.
Photo courtesy of Chris Schabel

Rapid Expansion

From the outset the possessions and wealth of the Teutonic Order grew astoundingly fast, and its numbers skyrocketed, especially under Grand Master Hermann von Salza (c. 1210–1239). Von Salza was successful in gaining many favors for the Order because he was a confidante of both German Emperor Frederick II (1212–1250) and the popes. His immediate successors also did well. Between 1215 and 1300 one or more commanderies were founded each year, usually through gifts.

The Teutonic Order was invited into Greece (1209), Hungary (1211), Prussia (1226), and Spain (1254?) by secular rulers to perform military duties on their behalf. In the Peloponnesus the Frankish prince of Achaia provided fiefs near Kalamata for the Teutonic Knights in return for military service; traces exist of the Order's continuous service there until 1500. Hungarian King Andrew II (1205–1235) expelled the Order in 1225 when it had become strong and might have threatened his rule. The conquest of Prussia began in 1230 (after the Order's grand master was named prince of the Holy Roman Empire and the pope gave the Knights almost carte blanche privileges) and lasted until 1283.

In addition to the Holy Land and other "theaters of war," the Order's members could be found elsewhere in the Mediterranean and Western Europe: Armenia, Cyprus, Sicily, Apulia, Lombardy, Spain, France, Alsace, Austria, Bohemia, the Lowlands, Germany, and Livonia. Only in the frontier areas (the Holy Land, Armenia, Greece, Hungary, Prussia, Spain, and Livonia) was military service required of members.

By 1221 the German Order was given the same privileges as the Templars and Hospitallers by Pope Honorius III (1216–1227). Both senior orders fought the autonomy of the Teutonic Order until about 1240. The German Order might never quite have equaled in wealth and possessions the other two military orders, both of which were more than 80 years older, but it became the only other order to rival them in international influence and activity.

The Baltic

After the crusaders were defeated at Acre in 1291, the Teutonic Order moved its headquarters to Venice, a longtime ally. In 1309, when the construction of an almost impregnable castle had been completed, the Order moved again, this time to Marienburg in Prussia. Here the Order had subdued the pagan inhabitants and established a theocratic form of government.

The position of the Knights in the Baltic region had been strengthened in 1237 when a knightly order in Livonia, the Brothers of the Sword (*Schwertbrüder*), joined the Teutonic Order. The history of the German Knights in Prussia and Livonia is one of almost perpetual revolts, uprisings, raids, conquests, victories, and defeats. Many secular knights from Western Europe (e.g., Chaucer's knight in *The Canterbury Tales*) would go to the Baltic to help the Order in "crusading activities" for a season or more. The grand master's prizes and feasting for heroic knights became legendary and remind one of various aspects of King Arthur's Knights of the Round Table.

During the 14th century the Order founded dozens of towns and about 2,000 villages in Prussia. Indicative of the organizational skills of the Order, an intricate network of signal towers was established at about seven-mile intervals. Some scholars credit the Order with the first characteristics of a modern "state" in medieval Europe. The Order was also successful in trade. As a major participant in the Hanseatic League, it provided Western Europe with some of its cheapest grain.

The nations of Poland and Lithuania, perennial enemies of the Order, grew stronger in the late 14th and early 15th centuries. The conversion of the pagan Lithuanians to Christianity facilitated a union of these traditional rival peoples. In 1410 at Tannenberg the Order was crushed in a battle against a coalition led by these powers. The result was a bankrupting of the Order and a significant reduction in its military and political capabilities.

In 1457 the unconquered fortress at Marienburg (Polish, Malbork) was abandoned to the Poles, and the Order's capital was moved to Königsberg. In 1467 the whole of western Prussia was ceded to Poland, and the eastern part acknowledged the suzerainty of the king of Poland.

1525 to 1797

Martin Luther's (1483–1546) Reformation affected the Teutonic Order significantly. In 1525 Grand Master Albrecht von Brandenburg converted to the Lutheran faith. He then was enfeoffed by the Polish king as duke of Prussia. As a medieval, crusading entity, the German Order essentially ended at this time. In 1526 the Teutonic Order's master of the German lands was given the title Administrator of the Grandmastery in Prussia and Master in German and Romance Countries. Mergentheim (Baden-Württemberg) became the main seat of the Order.

A great deal of confusion arose in Germany in the aftermath of the Reformation, its resulting wars, and the political changes. The bailiwicks of Saxony, Messe, and Thuringia became Protestant until Napoleonic times. The office of *Landkomtur* alternated among Lutheran, Reformed, and Catholic leaders in the 16th and 17th centuries, which became known as the "triconfessional period." The bailiwick of Utrecht was Calvinist until modern times. A new rule was adopted in 1606 in an attempt to accommodate the Order to these changes.

From time to time the Order still participated militarily in European affairs. In 1683 some 1,000 troops were raised to help the Austrians against the Turks. After 1696 a regiment of the Grand and German Master existed, but the numbers and wealth of the Order dwindled. Little other military activity is recorded. Emphasis fell on building secular palaces. Priests focused on pastoral work and administrative duties that accompanied that responsibility.

The French Revolution and After

As the anticlerical French government expanded its political control in the 1790s, the Order lost its commanderies in Belgium and those west of the Rhine (1797). Many east of the Rhine were lost in 1805. In 1809 Napoleon dissolved the Order in all countries under his dominion, leaving only the properties in the Austrian Empire. The Order was, once again, exclusively Roman Catholic.

Even in Austria the Order had to exist secretly for a number of years until 1839, when Austrian Emperor Ferdinand I (1835–1848) reconstituted the Order as the Order of the Teutonic Knights (*Deutscher Ritterorden*) with leadership coming from the Habsburg family. The mission fulfilled by the Order was mainly that of caring for wounded soldiers. In 1866 the Honorable Knights of the Teutonic Order was founded. Knights were required to provide annual contributions for hospitals. The *Marianer des Deutschen Ordens*, for women, was created in 1871. In 1914 some 1,500 sponsors from the Austrian nobility supported the caregiving efforts of the Order. During World War I the Order housed about 3,000 wounded soldiers in their facilities.

In 1923 masters of the Order were allowed to come from among the clerics rather than the "knighthood" for the first time. Under National Socialist rule, the Order was dissolved in Austria in 1938 and in Czechoslovakia in 1939. The leaders of the Third Reich distorted the history of the Teutonic Order.

After World War II the Order began anew in Germany. Its possessions in Austria were returned. Communist governments confiscated the Order's holdings in Czechoslovakia and Yugoslavia and imprisoned large numbers of its priests, sisters, and *familiaren* (lay members). In the late 1940s many fled to the Federal Republic of Germany to found new enterprises of the Order at abandoned church sites.

In Italy the Order had changed little. Support for the caretaking and missionary Order now occurs in Germany, Austria, Italy, Belgium, Israel, North and Central America, and even former Communist territory. A prime example of the latter is the building in only two years of a new convent (consecrated in August 1993) in a small Slovakian town, Topolcany. The Order has resumed pastoral work in Slovenia and the Czech Republic.

The Order's headquarters, treasury, archives, and Church of Saint Elizabeth are now located in the Deutsch-Ordens-Haus in Vienna, Austria. As of 1996 the Order had about 1,050 members (90 brothers, priests and lay brothers; 280 sisters; and 680 lay members, including seven honorary knights). The grand master is Abbot Dr. Arnold Othmar Wieland, O.T. The archivist is Father Dr. Bernhard Demel.

ERHARD P. OPSAHL

See also Augustinian Rule; Crusades; Dissolution of Monasteries: Continental Europe; Germany: History; Hospitallers (Knights of Malta since 1530); Israel/Palestine; Jerusalem, Israel; Poland; Reformation; Social Services: Western Christian; Templars; Warrior Monks: Christian

Further Reading

Barber, Malcolm, *The Military Orders: Fighting for the Faith and Caring for the Sick*, Aldershot, Hampshire, and Brookfield, Vermont: Variorum, 1994 (Part III is dedicated to the Teutonic Knights)

Johnson, Edgar N., "The German Crusade on the Baltic," in *A History of the Crusades*, volume 3: *The Fourteenth and*

Fifteenth Centuries, edited by Harry Hazard, Madison: University of Wisconsin Press, 1975
Sterns, Indrikis, "The Teutonic Knights in the Crusader States," in *A History of the Crusades*, volume 5: *The Impact of the Crusades on the Near East*, Madison: University of Wisconsin Press, 1985
Tumler, Marian, *Der Deutsche Orden im Werden, Wachsen und Wirken bis 1400 mit einem Abriss der Geschichte des Ordens von 1400 bis zur neuesten Zeit*, Vienna: Panorama, 1954
Urban, William, *The Baltic Crusade*, Chicago: Lithuanian Research and Studies Center, 1994

Related Web Site
http//:www.dtorden.or.at (Web Site of the Teutonic Order)

Thailand

Thai monasticism derives essentially from two sources: the Theravāda tradition of India and Sri Lanka and the local customs that have shaped its history since it first reached Southeast Asia in the first and second centuries A.D. The oldest and largest Buddhist site in Thailand at Nakhon Pathom dates from the sixth century, but evidence exists of Buddhist activity in the region before then.

Chedi (stūpa), Phra Boromathat, Chaiya, Thailand, eighth century, recently restored.
Photo courtesy of John C. Huntington, the Huntington Archive

The Indian emperor of the Maurya dynasty, Aśoka, lived and reigned during the second half of the third century B.C., and it is his application of the Buddha's teaching that has most decisively stamped the subsequent development of Buddhist monasticism in Southeast Asia. Drawing on a common stock of Indo-Aryan politico-moral ideals (in part Buddhist), Aśoka came to view himself as the supreme vehicle for the flow of the eternal dharma (universal law). He saw himself as the *cakravartin*, or turner of the wheel of cosmic law.

Such an exalted view of kingship was bound to have implications for the primitive communities that were emerging as settled monasticism began to replace an earlier period of mendicancy. In his Rock Edict at Bhabra, Aśoka pays tribute to the Buddha, the dharma, and the *saṅgha* (monastic community), adding, "But it is proper for me to enumerate the texts which express the true *dharma* and which may make it everlasting." These texts, which bear Aśoka's imprint, began to take shape in India and were completed as the Pāli Canon in Sri Lanka by the end of the first century B.C.

Buddhism declined in India soon after Aśoka's death, but in Sri Lanka as well as in the regions beyond the northern Himalayas and in Southeast Asia it underwent a variety of transformations, each with implications for particular monastic communities. The notion of the king as bodhisattva, or future cosmic liberator, absent in Aśoka's inscriptions, became part of Thai and Burmese soteriology. From the Indianized Mon and Khmer kingdoms came the cult of the king as *devarāja* (god-king), the influence of brahmins in addition to monks at court ritual, and a cosmology modeled on the parallelism between the suprahuman macrocosmos and the human microcosmos. Not to be overlooked were a variety of animistic beliefs and practices that continue to influence the contemporary *saṅgha*.

The monastic community in early Buddhism was organized under a teacher, even though the Buddha himself appointed no successor and appeared to advocate a form of democracy: "Be ye a refuge to yourselves. . . . Look not for refuge to any one besides yourselves." A set of regulations, which was codified into the Pātimokkha, was recited bimonthly, procedures were adopted for resolving disputes, special rules were generated for corporate life during the rainy season when monks may not travel without the express permission of the abbot, and an annual assembly took place during which the monks confessed their sins. Initiation required at least ten monks, an *upāydhyāya* (ordainer), and an *ācārya* (elder teacher). It is clear from a discussion between Aśoka and a novice recorded in the Mahavamsa that both men and women could be ordained at that time. The same account records that Aśoka, at least on that special day, permitted a representative of the *saṅgha* to sit on his throne.

The Thai kingdom of Sukhodaya lasted from the early 12th century (when the oldest extant monument from this period has been dated, part of a monastery known as the Sala Devaraksa)

Chedi (stūpa), Wat Mahathat, Nakhon Si Thammarat, Thailand, 13th century.
Photo courtesy of John C. Huntington, the Huntington Archive

to 1350, when the locus of power moved south to Ayutthaya. This kingdom suffered defeat at the hands of the Burmese on two occasions and lasted until 1767, after which the twin cities of Thonburi and Bangkok became the national capital. During this period the various kings saw themselves as protectors of the *saṅgha* against external enemies but rarely interfered in internal monastic affairs.

Tambiah has characterized the Thai polity as "galactic," in that the king's domain in his capital city was replicated in more or less independent regional centers whose governors were appointed by the king. During the 19th and 20th centuries, this galactic polity has become increasingly replaced by a "radial" one in which the capital acts as a magnet for the entire country. Paralleling the process whereby young and able people migrate to the metropolis in search of jobs, monks utilize elaborate monastic networks to move from poor, rural areas, where educational opportunities are scarce, to the larger cities, where standards are much higher. Such monks usually remain in the *saṅgha* for many years, either disrobing in their 30s or continuing into old age. However, it is also quite common for the sons of the well-off urban classes to ordain for a few weeks; such short-term ordinations are effectively a rite of passage to adulthood and usually occur in the rainy season, known as *phansā* (Lent).

The kings of the Bangkok period, which ran from about the end of the 18th century until the present day, are known collectively as the Chakri dynasty, and several of them made significant monastic reforms. Prince Mongkut, who became King Rama IV (1851–1868), had ordained as a monk in 1824, and thus it is not surprising that he made a number of major changes to the *saṅgha*. Dissatisfied with the way of life of the forest-dwelling monks, he insisted that primacy be given to learning rather than to meditation (*vipassanā*) or ascetic practices. He inspired and led the movement known as *dhammayuttika* – a term that means "those adhering to the law" (i.e., scripture). *Dhammayuttika* monks wear their robes across both shoulders and generally observe the letter of the monastic Vinaya rules more closely than unreformed *maha nikai* monks.

The architecture of many of the magnificent Bangkok *wat*s (temples or monasteries) belongs to the period of the Chakri kings. The types of buildings found in *wat*s include the *bot*, the hall for the ordination of monks; the *vihāra*, where preaching takes place; the stūpa, where religious relics are housed; the *sala*, or rest house; a library; a gallery; and a belfry. The *bot* and *vihāra*, practically identical in form, are rectangular buildings with tiered, pitched roofs of colored tile; solid white limed walls; and rows of columns outside the walls to support the roofs. The Wat

Phra Chettuphon (popularly known as the Wat Pho) is probably the finest temple from the early Chakri dynasty; it was built on the site of an older *wat* from the Ayutthaya period. The library contains a large collection of medical books, and statues represent various ethnic groups, each with what was considered an appropriate appellation. Thus, the Dutch figure represents "a seafaring nationality, strong and unshakable in their faith of Jesus Christ, who they believe created the world." Other important temples are the Wat Bovorniwes, which houses Mahamakut University, and the Wat Mahathat, which contains Mahachulalongkorn University (both for monks).

King Chulalongkorn (Rama V, 1868–1910) continued Mongkut's policies for promoting education and in 1898 entrusted the monks with a national program of primary education. In 1902 he passed the first of three *saṅgha* acts, which set out the obligation of monks to obey three types of laws: the laws of the land, the Vinaya, and custom. The act set out the duties of various monastic authorities and standardized *saṅgha* administration. Following the replacement of absolute by constitutional monarchy in 1932, the second *saṅgha* act of 1941 was a move in the direction of ecclesiastical democracy, whereas the third of 1963 reflected the authoritarian policies of Prime Minister Sarit. It concentrated power in the supreme patriarch and replaced the various *saṅgha* committees with a single (and ineffective) council of elders.

North niche, Phra Pathom Chedi (stūpa), Nakhon Pathom, Thailand, 19th century.
Photo courtesy of John C. Huntington, the Huntington Archive

Notwithstanding the control that the Thai secular authorities exercise over the Buddhist *saṅgha*, much variety exists among its members and among different monastic communities. We have noted the *dhammayuttika* breakaway movement from the older (and much larger) *maha nikai*. Many monks from both *nikai* have been strongly influenced by the late Buddhadāsa (known as Putatāt in Thai, 1906–1993), who reinterpreted cardinal Buddhist doctrines to give them a this-worldly emphasis. In turn this has stimulated ecclesiastical missionary and community development programs ranging from politically motivated attempts to propagate Buddhism among tribal groups in the north to highly sophisticated courses to train monks as paramedics. The latter project was the brainchild of Dr. Prawase Wasi, a distinguished hematologist, who has also been instrumental in persuading some monasteries to act as hospices for people with AIDS. Such activities are legitimated from a Buddhist perspective by appeal to expositions by distinguished monks, such as Phra Rajavaramuni, Phra Paññānanda, and Phra Payom Kallayano, a student of Buddhadāsa, who spices his sermons with street-level slang and is very popular with young Thais.

Extreme politically rightist Buddhism is represented by Phra Kittiwuddho, director of Chittapawan College near Bangkok, who has been accused of everything from gunrunning to illegally importing Volvo cars. Leftist monks must air their views carefully; they tend to be associated with Sulak Sivaraksa, social critic and a distinguished Buddhist scholar.

Maha Bua and Achan Mun are well-known teachers of meditation, and Phra Bodhirak leads the black-robed Santi Aśoke reformist group of monks (which ordains women as well as men). Some monks practice astrology, palmistry, and spirit exorcisms. Other groups, such as Samnak Paw Sawan (the abode of heavenly fathers) and Hooppha Sawan (the religious land), claim to be Buddhist but are not accepted as such by the *saṅgha* authorities.

Although historical evidence exists that women were once ordained in Thailand, the practice has died out. A few Thai women have been fully ordained in Taiwan. However, an increasing number of women are being initiated as lay nuns and live in communities similar and often adjacent to regular monasteries. They are known as *mae chii*.

Mae chii resemble nuns in various religious traditions in some respects, although in others they differ quite considerably. *Mae* means "mother," and *chii* or *ji* in Thai can refer to Buddhist monks, certain non-Buddhists (e.g., Jains), and to Buddhist women who shave their heads and wear white robes.

During the Buddha's lifetime there emerged both fully ordained women *bhikkhunī* and women who led lives very much like *mae chii*. In Thailand no evidence exists for the existence of *bhikkhunī* during the reign of King Ramkhamhaeng (1283–1317), meaning that they likely had died out by then. The *bhikkhunī* Order has never been revived in Thailand, but evidence exists for the reappearance of *mae chii* from the 17th century on.

No precedent exists in the Pāli Canon for *mae chii* initiation, but the requirements for membership are fairly similar to those for a monk. An aspirant must be a woman, must not be or become pregnant, must exhibit good behavior, must enjoy good health, must be free from debt, must be free from habit-forming drugs, must not be absconding from home or a government job, must not have a criminal record, must not suffer from infectious disease, must not be too old to perform religious duties, must not be lame, and must have permission to become a *mae chii* from her parents or husband.

These requirements have been standardized by the Nun Institute of Thailand, which has its headquarters at the Wat Bovorniwes in Bangkok. The institute also regulates the rules for initiation into membership, which cannot strictly be described as ordination because *mae chii* are laywomen. A woman who fulfills the qualifications for initiation goes to a *wat* and makes her request to the abbot. If this is granted, she will be put under the care of an abbot or senior *mae chii*.

The *mae chii* ceremony itself is conducted by four monks and several *mae chii* and thus imitates full *bhikkhunī* ordination in that both male and female orders are involved. During the ceremony the aspirant is told that meditation is her highest religious duty and is reminded of the Three Refuges of Buddhism: the Buddha, the dharma and the *saṅgha*. She is also given eight precepts; these include the five followed by all lay Buddhists prohibiting harm to any living being, stealing, sexual misconduct, lies and insults, and the taking of intoxicants (which cloud the mind and thus inhibit meditation) plus three more. These additional precepts require one to abstain from untimely eating (which means having the last meal of the day at noon); to abstain from dancing, singing, music, garlands, scents, and all kinds of embellishments; and to avoid sleeping on a high or luxurious bed. These eight precepts governing the conduct of a *mae chii* should not be confused with the *Gurudhamma*, the eight stipulations made by the Buddha before he would permit women's full ordination as *bhikkhunī*.

After initiation *mae chii* reside in monastic communities attached to *wat*s, each having its own head *mae chii*. These communities might be quite small, consisting of half a dozen members, and are usually called institutes by English-speaking *mae chii*. Certain communities, such as the one at the Wat Paknam Phasi Charoen in Thonburi, might contain up to 300 *mae chii* at any time.

Community development activities on the part of monks (and, increasingly, *mae chii*) are an important feature of the contemporary Thai *saṅgha*. Not only do they deter some of the most talented monks from disrobing to take up lay occupations (which can be done without social disapproval), but the public at large appears to be generally in favor. However, the notion of "appropriate" behavior on the part of a monk has its roots in Thailand in King Mongkut's strict reforms, which were based on rigid adherence to the letter of the Vinaya.

The rules governing the conduct of a monk are very strict and are based on the Pātimokkha, which consists of 227 very specific injunctions. Thus, for example, a monk may not cut down a tree or dig the earth because such actions might destroy life forms. However, these strictures do not apply to a novice, and the Pātimokkha rules do not encompass travel in vehicles that are capable of destroying all kinds of primitive and even less primitive life forms.

Monks approach these problems fairly sensitively, but it is easier for them if some overriding Buddhist justification exists for indulging in behavior that breaks certain rules. Thus, for example, Phra Chamrun, abbot of the Wat Tham Krabok in Saraburi, has discovered an herbal medicine that, if used in a therapeutic community based on his monastery, is highly successful in curing heroin and opium addicts. However, many of these addicts are teenagers, and it would hardly seem reasonable to treat only young men and not the women. Thus, the monks are obliged to do many things that bring them into what, according to the Pātimokkha, is an inappropriate amount of contact with women. From time to time they must also operate a sauna bath, clear up laypeople's vomit, and pursue absconders – for their own ultimate good, of course. The important point to note is that all these breaches of rules are acceptable because the Buddha clearly opposed the use of intoxicants, and thus the monastic rules can be set aside. It is important to appreciate this because some visitors to Thailand in search of what they regard as pure Buddhism are inclined to regard such innovative activities as an aberration. They are not; rather, they represent an important phase in the contemporary expression of Thai monasticism and are accompanied by novel reinterpretations of cardinal Buddhist doctrines of the kind associated with Buddhadāsa and other scholar monks.

Monasteries to Visit
Sala Devaraksa, Sukhodaya
Wat Phra Chettuphon (popularly known as the Wat Pho), Bangkok
Wat Bovorniwes, Bangkok
Wat Mahathat, Bangkok
Wat Paknam Phasi Charoen, Thonburi
Wat Tham Krabok, Saraburi

David L. Gosling

See also Bangkok, Thailand; Buddhadāsa; Gestures, Buddhist; Forest Masters; Libraries: Buddhist; Liturgy: Buddhist; Mongkut; Mun, Ajahn; Novices, Theravādin Rituals for; Rules, Buddhist (Vinaya): Historical; Sri Lanka; Women's Monasteries: Buddhist

Further Reading

Gerson, Ruth, *Traditional Festivals in Thailand*, New York and Kuala Lumpur: Oxford University Press, 1996
Gosling, David L., "Visions of Salvation: A Thai Buddhist Experience of Ecumenism," *Modern Asian Studies* 26:1 (1992)

Kabilsingh, Chatsumarn, *Thai Women in Buddhism*, Berkeley, California: Parallax Press, 1991
Queen, Christopher S., and Sallie B. King, editors, *Engaged Buddhism: Buddhist Liberation Movements in Asia*, Albany: State University of New York Press, 1996
Sivaraksa, Sulak, editor, *Radical Conservatism: Buddhism in the Contemporary World*, Bangkok: Sathirakoses-Nagapradipa Foundation, 1990
Tambiah, Stanley J., *World Conqueror and World Renouncer*, Cambridge and New York: Cambridge University Press, 1976

Theodore of Stoudios, St. c. 759–826

Byzantine Orthodox abbot, monastic reformer, and political combatant

A pivotal figure in Eastern Christian religious history, Theodore of Stoudios is remembered mainly both as an uncompromising political force within the official Church and imperial court and as a successful abbot, monastic founder, and reformer. His impact in both ecclesiastical and monastic spheres was dramatic in a public career that spanned three decades (c. 795–826).

Because of his involvement in ecclesiastical affairs, Theodore is sometimes called the last of the Greek Fathers. This judgment reflects his theological contributions and his political activism during two major conflicts within the Church: the so-called Moechian, or Adultery, Affair (795–797 and 808–811) and the second phase of the Iconoclastic Controversy (815–843). In both conflicts Theodore took the controversial step of soliciting papal support, a testimony to his independent bent of mind, pragmatism, and rather uncommon ecclesiological ideas. It is noteworthy that his connections with Greek monks in Rome facilitated negotiations with the popes.

In the monastic world, Theodore was the most dynamic leader and reformer of his generation. After serving for some years as abbot of the small, family-owned monastery of the Sakkoudion, in 798 he accepted an invitation from the ruling empress Irene (797–802) to refound the Stoudios Monastery in Constantinople. Under Theodore's tutelage the Stoudios soon became the premier institution of its day, attracting hundreds of monks and ultimately standing at the head of a federation of monasteries operated under Stoudite supervision. A reformed cenobitic way of life in the spirit of St. Basil (c. 330–379) and other early Eastern monastic fathers became the hallmark of Stoudite life. A renowned scriptorium was established, as was a school for the young. An extensive building program was also undertaken, including the redecoration of an existing early Christian basilica dedicated to St. John the Baptist. Remarkably, the integrity of the Stoudios and its federation of monasteries remained largely intact despite persecutions that disrupted monastic life there in the course of the Moechian and Iconoclast conflicts. The fact that Stoudite monks weathered these prolonged political storms is a testimony to the personal charisma of Theodore himself, the success of his monastic reforms, and the support that he and his monastery enjoyed from those outside its walls.

After Theodore's death the Stoudios remained for centuries a large and influential monastery in Constantinople. Its influence proved equally great outside the capital, owing not least to the prestige attached to Theodore's monastic rule. This rule, consisting of several of the abbot's oral and written precepts assembled after his death, subsequently enjoyed wide dissemination both within the empire and abroad. For example, within the empire Athanasius the Great (c. 920–1003) adapted it for use in his foundation (963) of the Great Lavra Monastery on Mount Athos. Outside Byzantium the Stoudite rule figured in the foundation charters of monasteries from Sicily and southern Italy to the Balkan and Slavic worlds.

The success of Stoudite reforms under Theodore and the broad influence of the monastery and its rule in later times invite comparison with the Benedictine movement in the West. However, consistent with Eastern Christian traditions the Stoudios was never recognized as an official monastic order.

PETER HATLIE

See also Basil the Great, St.; Hagiography: Eastern Christian; Hermits: Eastern Christian; Humanism, Christian; Hymnographers; Iconoclasm (Controversy); Italo-Greek Monasticism; Libraries: Eastern Christian; Office, Daily: Eastern Christian; Orthodox Monasticism; Seraphim of Sarov, St.; Spirituality: Eastern Christian; Theology, Eastern Christian

Biography

Nephew of a renowned abbot, St. Plato, at the monastery of Sakkoudion, Theodore entered the monastic life c. 780. Ordained in 787, he became abbot of Sakkoudion in 794. Banished for a time because of his opposition to an imperial marriage, in 798 Theodore and his monks took over the moribund monastery of Stoudios in Constantinople. He was skilled in monastic organizing and rule-making. Banished again in 809 and in 815 (during the renewed Iconoclastic Controversy), Theodore never returned to Stoudios, which his zeal had erected into a model for subsequent generations.

Major Works

The Small Catechesis
The Great Catechesis
Epigrams
Letters
Orations

Further Reading

Dobroklinskii, Alexander P., *Prepodobnii. Feodor', Ispovednik' i Igumen' Studiskii*, volume 1, Odessa, 1913
Frazee, Charles, "St. Theodore of Studios and Ninth Century Monasticism in Constantinople," *Studia Monastica* 23:1 (1981)
Gardner, Alice, *Theodore of Studium, His Life and Times*, London: Arnold, 1905; reprint, New York: Franklin Reprints, 1974
Hatlie, Peter, "The Politics of Salvation: Theodore of Stoudios on Martyrdom (*Martyrion*) and Speaking Out (*Parrhesia*),"

in *Dumbarton Oaks Papers: Number Fifty*, Washington, D.C.: Dumbarton Oaks Research Library and Collection, 1996
Hauscherr, Irénée, "Saint Théodore Studite: L'homme et l'ascète (après ses catéchèses)," *Orientalia Christiana* 6:1 (1926)
Henry, Patrick, III, "Theodore of Studios: Byzantine Churchman," Ph.D. Diss., Yale University, 1968
Karlin-Hayter, Patricia, "A Byzantine Politician Monk: St. Theodore Studite," *Jahrbuch der Österreichischen Byzantinistik* 44 (1994)
Leroy, Julien, "La réforme studite," in *Il monachesimo orientale*, Rome: Pont. Institutum Orientalium Studiorum, 1958
Leroy, Julien, *Studitisches Mönchtum: Spiritualität und Lebensform*, Graz, Vienna, Cologne: Styria, 1969
Leroy, Julien, "L'influence de Saint Basile sur le réforme studite d'après les catéchèses," *Irenikon* 52:4 (1979)
Patlagean, Evelyne, "Les Stoudites, l'empereur et Rome: Figure byzantine d'un monachisme réformateur," in *Bisanzio, Roma e l'Italia nell' alto medioevo, 3–9 aprile 1986*, volume 1, Spoleto: Presso la sede del centro, 1988
Pratsch, Thomas, *Theodoros Studites (759–825) – zwischen Dogma und Pragma*, Frankfurt and Berlin: Peter Lang, 1998

Theodosius of Kiev, St. d. 1074

Ukranian Orthodox founder of the Monastery of the Caves and champion of cenobitic monasticism

Theodosius, saint, spiritual director, founder, and *hegumen* (abbot) of the Monastery of the Caves near Kiev in Pechersk (Kievo-Pecherskaya Lavra), established cenobitic monasticism in Kievan Russ and ranks as a precursor to later Slavic monasticism. The Slavic and especially Russian Orthodox spiritual tradition of emulating the poverty and humiliation of Christ, the so-called kenotic Christ (from the Greek *kenosis*), was first practiced by Theodosius. He inaugurated the tradition of spiritual director, or "elder" (Russian, *starets*; Greek, *geron*). Previously Pechersk had been the home of the solitary priest Hilarion, whom Grand Prince Yaroslav had selected as the first native metropolitan of Kiev around 1051. Monks had lived earlier near Kiev, but their style and quality of life remains unknown.

Theodosius came from a wealthy family in which at a young age he demonstrated a propensity for religious life. Although this claim is typical of Eastern Christian hagiography, in this case historians judge it to be both literally and factually true. As a child he was known to dress humbly, work in the fields, and bake church bread, and accordingly, out of aristocratic embarrassment, his mother disciplined him for it. For escapades such as leaving on a pilgrimage to the Holy Land without telling her, she punished him severely. Later in life the two became reconciled, and his mother entered a convent so as to pursue monasticism and to be near her son.

As a young man Theodosius continued to feel strongly drawn to a religious vocation. He made the rounds of extant monasteries but was not admitted to orders, reportedly because of his self-inflicted poverty. The monasteries of that day appear to have received many professions from, and to have been clientele of, the nobility, who treated the property as their own assets. This rejection later led him, as monastery abbot, to accept all who applied for religious life in his monastery – even those who repeatedly left and returned.

After some searching Theodosius became the disciple of Anthony, a saintly eremite trained on Mount Athos and known for having brought traditional monastic eremitic practice to Kievan Russ. Because no vita of Anthony (d. 1072) has survived, Theodosius' *Life* constitutes the first monastic hagiography for Slavs in Russ. His *Vita*, written by Nestor the Chronicler within 20 years of Theodosius' death, is documented by living witnesses whom Nestor names. Nestor incorporates literary characteristics from classical Palestinian and Byzantine hagiography, but the work itself is fresh and original.

From his childhood throughout his tenure as monastery abbot, Theodosius displayed a spiritual disposition that spurned wealth to provide charity and spiritual direction to the poor and the powerful alike. He taught obedience by example, taking quite literally the saying of Jesus that he who would be first should serve all others. Although he was known for kindness, gentleness, and not anger, he was assertive when it came to community obedience: everything was done only after a blessing (i.e., permission) was granted; a monk's accumulated excess food and clothing would be burned on discovery; and community charity came before any ascetic quest for personal salvation.

Community life in the monastery was facilitated by the Rule of the Monastery of Stoudios, similar to that of St. Basil, which Theodosius had requested from a friend in Constantinople. This proven Rule, known from the iconodule theologian St. Theodore of Stoudios (759–826), provided the groundwork for cenobitic monasticism and shaped the style of monasticism practiced for centuries in Ukraine, Russia, and elsewhere. Nonetheless Theodosius' personal stamp of self-sacrificing humility and identification with the poor remained a typically Slavic spiritual trait, celebrated in folklore and by the literary giants of 19th-century Russia (e.g., Dostoevsky). Theodosius personally supervised the construction of an above-ground church and a hostel for visitors. Hospitality was extended to the sick and the hungry, among others. Two successive grand princes of Kiev, Iziaslav and Sviatoslav, sought Theodosius' blessing and spiritual direction in matters of state and for personal needs.

Life in the monastery affected the social conscience and political events transpiring in Kiev and beyond. In imitation of the *lavra*, monasteries proliferated in Kievan Russ, located in and near towns according to the Stoudite model. Lives of about 30 early monks of Pechersk have been preserved, including *Paterik Kievo-Pecherskago Monastyria* (1911; *The Paterik of the Kievan Caves Monastery*), along with a few of Theodosius' sermons. Theodosius himself was canonized formally in 1108, and his cultus is recognized in both the Eastern and the Western Church. The current abbot of the Monastery of the Caves is Bishop Paul of Veschorod.

MICHAEL PROKURAT

See also Hagiography: Eastern Christian; Kiev (Kyiv), Ukraine

Biography

The founder of the Monastery of the Caves near Kiev, Ukraine, Theodosius introduced cenobitic monasticism to Kievan Russ. His life is known from his *Vita* by Nestor the Chronicler, who records Theodosius' indebtedness for his customs to the Monastery of Stoudios in Constantinople. Theodosius' personal humility exemplified what became known as the kenotic (self-emptying) ideal of Slavic monasticism.

Major Works

"Sermons," in *Trudy Otdela drevnerusskoy literatury* (Works of the Department of Old Russian Literature), volume 5, 1934

Further Reading

Cross, S.H., and O.P. Sherbowitz-Wetzor, *The Russian Primary Chronicle, Laurentian Text*, Cambridge, Massachusetts, Harvard University Press, 1953
Fedotov, G.P., *Kievan Christianity, The Tenth to the Thirteenth Centuries*, volume 1: *The Russian Religious Mind*, New York: Harper, 1946
Fennell, John, and Anthony Stokes, *Early Russian Literature*, London: Faber and Faber, and Berkeley: University of California Press, 1974
Florovsky, Georges, *Ways of Russian Theology*, edited by Richard S. Haugh, translated by Robert L. Nichols, Belmont, Massachusetts: Nordland, 1979
Grunwald, Constantin de, *Saints of Russia*, translated by Roger Capel, London: Hutchinson of London, 1960
Lilienfeld, Fairy von, "The Spirituality of the Early Kievan Caves Monastery," in *Christianity and the Eastern Slavs*, edited by Boris Gasparov and Olga Raevsky-Hughes, Berkeley: University of California Press, 1993
Smolitsch, Igor, *Russisches Mönchtum: Entstehung, Entwicklung und Wesen, 988–1917* (Russian Monasticism: Origin, Development and Life, 988–1917), Amsterdam: Hakkert, 1978

Theology, Eastern Christian

Introduction and Definitions

This article provides an overview of the historical development of Eastern Christian theology from the perspective of monasticism. Special attention is given to patristic and Byzantine sources and to their later reception in the Greek and Slavonic traditions. Authors, traditions, and schools of thought that are not directly embedded within a monastic context do not enter into this survey.

Eastern Christian theology is intimately connected with monasticism and the ascetic life on which its character and vitality have traditionally hinged. Theology and "spirituality" (a word unknown in the East) are not understood as separate disciplines or activities but together constitute the realization of spiritual knowledge in both mind and body. Perhaps more than any other Christian tradition, Eastern Christian theology is a deeply ascetic theology and unfolds in conjunction with the bodily performance of ascetic and ritual practices that seek to engage, convert, and transform the self at the basic level of will and desire. The theological life of conversion and transfiguration is appropriated and expressed through prayer and contemplation; through the reading of Scripture; through liturgy, hymnology, and iconography; and through spoken and written theological discourse. Thus, the locus of theology is an ecclesial life of prayer and holiness, of repentance and superabundant grace. In the words of one ascetic theologian, "You are a theologian when you truly pray; and when you truly pray, you are a theologian" (Evagrius Ponticus, *On Prayer*, chap. 60).

Theology as an ascetic and contemplative endeavor is a recurring theme among the Cappadocian Fathers Basil of Caesarea, Gregory of Nyssa, and Gregory of Nazianzus. Drawing on the imagery of the Sinai narrative (Exod. 19:3–25), Basil (c. 330–379) called on his hearers to "ascend the unapproachable heights of theology" (*On Isaiah*, chap. 2; *Patrologia Graeca* 30.237C), although his brother Gregory of Nyssa (c. 330–395) warned that the "mountain of theology is steep and difficult to climb, and most people scarcely reach its base" (*Life of Moses*, chap. 158). Gregory of Nazianzus (329/30–389/90) similarly argued that "theology is not for everyone, being no cheap or effortless pursuit. Nor is it for every occasion, or every audience; neither are all of its aspects open to inquiry . . . it is not for all men, but only for those who have been tested and found a sound footing in study, and, more importantly, have undergone purification of body and soul" (*Oration* 27.3; see also Basil, *Long Rules*, chap. 33). To this he immediately added, "I am not maintaining that we ought not to be mindful of God at all times . . . it is more important that we should remember God than that we should breathe: indeed, if one may say so, we should do nothing else besides" (*Oration* 27.4). Gregory returns to this theme, noting that true theology involves personal purification: "Advance by your conduct; through purity acquire the pure. Do you wish to become a theologian, and to be worthy of the divinity? Keep the commandments . . . for deeds are the foundation of contemplation" (*Oration* 20.12; *Patrologia Graeca* 35.1380CD). The end result of such theologizing is to "become like God, and to be mingled with the unmingled divine light" (*Oration* 21.2; *Patrologia Graeca* 35.1084C).

In this light three writers alone have been granted the exceptional title of "Theologian": (1) John the Theologian, the mystic seer of the Divine Logos and the author of the Fourth Gospel (c. 90–100); (2) Gregory the Theologian (of Nazianzus), an ascetic bishop and Trinitarian visionary; and (3) Symeon the New Theologian (c. 949–1022), a monk of Byzantium and a proponent of the radically transformative power of the Holy Spirit. These sainted theologians exemplify the notion that theology is inseparable from lived religious experience. As theologians they struggled to live theology with their minds and bodies, to write theology with the material of their own life; in their very being, hidden and unknown, each *became* theology.

Origins through Late Antiquity (First to Seventh Century)

Eastern Christian theology emerged from the religious and cultural crucible of late antiquity, a transitional period that marked a dramatic shift from antiquity to the Middle Ages. The earliest theological formulations (after those of the New Testament) appear in the records of martyrdom, often in the form of a final confession of faith. The harrowing moment of death was conceptually assimilated to the Eucharistic liturgy, and in the arenas of the Greco-Roman world the martyrs rendered present the spectacle of Christ's sacrificial death on Golgotha. The experience of martyrdom, understood as the climax of Christomimetic union with God, was internalized by the early anchorites who sought a similar union with God through the daily death of asceticism and the martyrdom of virginity (see *Life of Antony*, chaps. 19, 89; John Climacus, *Ladder of Divine Ascent*, chap. 6).

Interweaving the symbolic vocabularies of martyrdom and asceticism began with Clement of Alexandria (c. 150–c. 215) with further embroiderings by Origen (c. 185–254) and Gregory of Nyssa, masters of the spiritual life and the fountainheads of much subsequent theological thinking and debate. For Clement martyrdom is directly linked to spiritual knowledge (*gnosis*) achieved in the conduct of life. Like martyrdom asceticism was the perfect concord of theory and practice (*Stromateis*, chap. 4). Origen likewise speaks of the "martyrdom that is in secret" (*Exhortation to Martyrdom*, chap. 21), while Gregory of Nyssa describes the dying body of his ascetic sister Macrina (c. 327–380) as the relic of a martyr radiant with eschatological glory (*Life of Macrina*). By the fourth century the death and martyrdom of the self was a drama that could be enacted in the arena of a Cappadocian cloister.

Central to both monastic life and early doctrinal debate was the contemplative study of Scripture, biblical exegesis being the principal mode of spiritual pedagogy and theological method. Such exegesis uncovered the presence of Christ in Scripture by a hermeneutical move from "letter to spirit" (see 2 Cor. 3:6), a process that mirrored the ascent of the soul from carnal attachments to divine dispassion and love. Origen plotted this ascent across the books of Solomon's trilogy (i.e., Proverbs, Ecclesiastes, and Song of Songs) as a threefold progression culminating in the soul's union with the heavenly Bridegroom (*Commentary on the Song of Songs*). Origen called the final stage *theoria*, or "contemplation," although his disciple Evagrius Ponticus called it *theologia*, which for him signified mystical union with the Holy Trinity (*To the Monks*, chaps. 135–136; *Commentary on Proverbs* 22.20). For both the myth (later condemned) of the soul's recurring fall from union with God, followed by its arduous return heavenward, provided an objective theological basis for the ebb and flow of the spiritual life by projecting it onto the backdrop of cosmology and eschatology (Origen, *On First Principles* 1.4).

The Period of the Seven Ecumenical Councils (325–787)

The Seven Ecumenical Councils, whose definitions remain normative for the theology of the East, were influenced and in some cases directly provoked by the concerns and disputes of monastic thinkers. Antony the Great (c. 251–356), the traditional "father of monasticism," is said to have strongly resisted the heresy of Arianism during the Council of Nicaea (325) (*Life of Antony*, chap. 70). In addition Antony's *Life*, written by Athanasius of Alexandria (c. 296–373) and the model for all subsequent monastic lives, embodied the author's attempt to convey orthodox Christological and soteriological beliefs through the concrete vehicle of an exemplary life. The Second Ecumenical Council (Constantinople, 381) canonized the theology of the Cappadocian Fathers, whose theological apophaticism was based on a dynamic perception of God discovered in the experience of prayer and contemplation. The Third Council (Ephesus, 431) enjoyed the overwhelming (and at times violent) support of the monks of Egypt and Constantinople, who conspired to bring about the downfall of the patriarch Nestorius (c. 381–451). The notorious "Robber Council" (or *Latrocinium*, Ephesus, 449) was triggered by the Constantinopolitan abbot Eutyches (c. 370–454), and the influence of monastic leaders at the ensuing Fourth Council of Chalcedon (451) is amply documented (see H. Bacht, in *Das Konzil von Chalkedon*, 1951–1954, pp. 193–314). A feud among the monasteries of Palestine concerning the nature of the spiritual life (as described in the works of Origen and Evagrius) set the stage for much of the work conducted by the Fifth Council (Constantinople, 552). The Sixth Ecumenical Council (Constantinople, 681) validated the Christology of Maximus the Confessor (c. 580–662), whose nuanced understanding of the obedience of Jesus' human will to the Father clearly owes something to his experience as a spiritual director of monks. The Seventh Council of 787, which affirmed the creation and veneration of sacred images, was a victory for the iconophile monks (some of whom suffered martyrdom) and was followed by a vigorous revival and reorganization of monastic life. The two most influential proponents of the theology of the icon, John of Damascus (c. 675–749) and Theodore of Stoudios (759–826), were both monastic leaders, the former having written a *summa* of Christian dogma, *The Fountain of Knowledge*, which was read widely throughout the West as well as in the Near East and in Slavic lands.

The Byzantine Period (9th to 15th Century)

After the final liquidation of Iconoclasm in 843, it seemed that the theological controversies of earlier centuries had finally ended, and a sense of closure was brought to the basic lines of doctrine as well as to traditional forms of piety and worship. Following the post-iconoclastic triumph of the monastic party, fixed definitions of religious orthodoxy increasingly proscribed more liberal and speculative modes of thinking. For example, dialogue with the Latin West was marked by highly politicized debates over the procession of the Holy Spirit (the *filioque* controversy) and over differences in liturgical practices. The trial of the Neoplatonic philosopher John Italos (c. 1025–1082) and the public burning of Basil the Bogomil (c. 1111; see Anna Komnena, *Alexiad* 15.10) are two extreme, although admittedly rare, examples of violent internal repression, as was the burning of anti-Latin monks during the tenure of the pro-Western patriarch John Bekkos (1275–1282).

Theological decadence and empty religious formalism were challenged by Symeon the New Theologian, a Constantinopolitan monk who repristinated the practice of theology as a mystagogical illumination eventuating in a conscious experience of God. "What more unclean thing can there be," he asked, "than an arrogant man who tries to teach the things of the Spirit without the Spirit" (*First Theological Discourse*)? The Athonite monk and later archbishop of Thessaloniki Gregory Palamas (1347–1359) similarly emphasized the immediate experience of God, available to all the baptized, as the real basis and criterion of true theology. To the rationalist theologians who criticized his lack of philosophical strictness, Palamas answered that true theology is "not found in theories and arguments, but is manifested by works and by life . . . every theory, it is said, contradicts another theory, but what theory can contradict life" (*Triads* 1.3.13)? As a contemplative theologian Palamas sought to provide a theological foundation for the paradoxical presence and absence of God in prayer: God was fully present in his eternal uncreated energies (*energeiai*) (i.e., divine immanence) while remaining totally inaccessible and unknowable in his essence (*ousia*) (i.e., divine transcendence). The work of Palamas was continued by monastic theologians such as Joseph Bryennios (1350–1432) and Mark Eugenikus (1392–1444), the latter hailed in the East as the "Pillar of Orthodoxy" for his rejection of specious union with Rome at the Council of Ferrara-Florence (1438–1439).

Throughout the 14th and 15th centuries, the Byzantine Empire was reduced to a second-rate political and economic power, a situation that might not have seemed promising for the study and practice of theology. However, the final years of the empire were characterized by an extraordinary revival of cultural life in general and of theological and ecclesiastical activity in particular. Contemporary innovations in ritual, iconography, and church architecture rank among the finest artistic achievements of the entire Byzantine period. Theological literature (much of it still unedited) was produced in great abundance, ranging from the polemical and the dogmatic to the hagiographic, ascetic, and mystical. At the same time, a pro-Latin school emerged in Constantinople, devoting itself to the translation and study of seminal works by Western thinkers such as Augustine (354–430), Anselm (c. 1033–1109), and Thomas Aquinas (c. 1225–1274). It is impossible to know where this intellectual ferment might have taken the theological tradition of the East, as the entire project was prematurely cut short.

Early Modern Period to the Present

The Byzantine Empire came to a violent end at the hands of the Ottoman Turks in May 1453, beginning a long period of subjugation and decline for the Greek-speaking East (see S. Runciman, *The Great Church in Captivity*, 1968). One figure of note from this period is Nikodemos the Hagiorite (c. 1749–1809), a monk of Mount Athos and compiler of the *Philokalia* (Venice, 1782), a collection of ascetic and mystical works dating from the 4th to the 15th century. Since the establishment of a modern Greek state in 1821, or perhaps because of it, cultural assimilation to Western Europe has (until recently) prevented Greek theologians from fully expressing their Orthodox ethos.

However, the Byzantine theological tradition survived in Russia, where it was applied and developed with tremendous vitality, especially in the areas of spirituality, iconology, eschatology, and speculative theology, including theosophy and sophiology. These developments came to fruition in the later 19th and early 20th centuries, when Russian philosophers and theologians entered into substantive conversation with German idealism through the works of Hegel (1770–1831), Schelling (1775–1854), and the Lutheran mystic Jakob Böhme (1575–1624). Pioneering work in this area was done by Ivan Kireevsky (1806–1856) and Vladimir Solovyov (1853–1900), although neither was deeply influenced by monasticism. The movement was redirected by Pavel Florensky (1882–1937), a polymath priest with advanced degrees in mathematics, science, and theology. Florensky synthesized the realms of philosophy, poetry, aesthetics, linguistics, and physics largely under the inspiration of the monastic elder Isidore (d. 1908), a hermit living on the outskirts of Moscow. Florensky also maintained contacts with other celebrated Russian elders, and to these figures he was indebted for his theology of spiritual friendship and for his metaphysical conception of personhood and love. Theology again merged with martyrdom when Florensky was executed in 1937 by the Soviet authorities. Like its Byzantine predecessor the Russian religious renaissance was also prematurely terminated, this time by the Bolshevik Revolution of 1917, in which tens of thousands of ecclesiastical and academic persons were murdered, along with millions of the faithful.

With the mid-20th-century revival of monastic life among the monasteries of Mount Athos (Greece) and elsewhere, the traditional conjunction of theology and asceticism has again returned to the center of Eastern Christian theology. Directly involved in this renewal is the Athonite Abbot Vasileios (Gondikakis), whose essay titled *Hymn of Entry: Liturgy and Life in the Orthodox Church* (1984) articulates a fresh and compelling view of theology based on the insights and resources of the monastic life. One can also point to the work of the lay theologian Panayiotis Nellas, *Deification in Christ: The Nature of the Human Person* (1987), which, as the author notes, was largely written in the libraries of Mount Athos and stems from the same context of renewal. The ascetical and theological discourses of Archimandrite Aemilianos, abbot of the Monastery of Simonopetra, also on Athos, are now appearing in their original Greek and in English translation (*Authentic Seal* [*Teachings and Discourses*, volume 1], 1995). Archimandrite Aemilianos' commitment to the practice of living theology has been furthered by his charismatic disciple Archimandrite Dionysios, who has established vibrant monasteries and convents throughout Greece and abroad in which the majority of nuns and monks, in addition to their rich devotional and liturgical lives, have either completed or are currently engaged in advanced theological studies.

Also working within a monastic-inspired tradition was Dumitru Staniloae (1903–1993), one of the greatest Orthodox theologians of the 20th century who spent five years in a Communist concentration camp. Staniloae's arrest and imprisonment interrupted his work on the ten-volume Romanian edition of the

Philokalia, which he later resumed and completed in 1981, having inserted additional works by Maximus the Confessor, who occupies the whole of volumes 3 and 4. Staniloae called for a "concrete theology, a theology of experience," along with a "new asceticism" that would be incarnate and world affirming. Staniloae's major theological work, *The Experience of God*, was published in Romanian in 1978, and an English translation of volume 1 appeared in 1994.

Russia, too, has recently returned to the theological scene, and in both the East and the West, there are promising signs of renewed interest in traditional forms of Orthodox theology, spirituality, and monasticism.

NICHOLAS P. CONSTAS

See also Asceticism: Christian Perspectives; Gregory of Nazianzus, St.; Gregory of Nyssa, St.; John of Damascus, St.; Macrina, St.; Martyrs: Eastern Christian; Palamas, Gregory, St.; Spirituality: Eastern Christian; Symeon the New Theologian, St.; Theodore of Stoudios, St.; Vision, Mystical: Eastern Christian

Further Reading

Bacht, H., "Die Rolle des orientalischen Mönchtums in den kirchen-politischen Auseinandersetuzungen um Chalkedon (431–519)," in *Das Konzil von Chalkedon: Geschichte und Gegenwart*, edited by Alois Grillmeier and Heinrich Bacht, 3 vols., Würzburg: Echter-Verlag, 1951–1954

Blowers, Paul M., *Exegesis and Spiritual Pedagogy in Maximus the Confessor: An Investigation of the Quaestiones ad Thalassium* (Christianity and Judaism in Antiquity, volume 7), Notre Dame, Indiana: University of Notre Dame Press, 1991

Burton-Christie, Douglas, *The Word in the Desert: Scripture and the Quest for Holiness in Early Christian Monasticism*, New York: Oxford University Press, 1993

Chrestou, P., "Neohellenic Theology at the Crossroads," *Greek Orthodox Theological Review* (1983)

Davis, Leo Donald, *The First Seven Ecumenical Councils (325–787): Their History and Theology* (Theology and Life Series, 21), Wilmington, Delaware: Glazier, 1987

Florovsky, Georges, "The Ascetic Ideal and the New Testament," in his *The Byzantine Ascetic and Spiritual Fathers* (Collected Works of Georges Florovsky, volume 10), Belmont, Massachusetts: Büchervertriebsanstalt, 1987

Golitzin, A., "Liturgy and Mysticism: The Experience of God in Eastern Orthodox Christianity," *Pro Ecclesia* 8:2 (1998)

Hussey, J.M., *The Orthodox Church in the Byzantine Empire* (Oxford History of the Christian Church), Oxford: Clarendon Press, 1986

Kazhdan, A.P., editor, *The Oxford Dictionary of Byzantium*, 3 vols., New York: Oxford University Press, 1991

Louth, Andrew, *The Origins of the Christian Mystical Tradition from Plato to Denys*, New York: Oxford University Press, and Oxford: Clarendon Press, 1981

Louth, Andrew, *Maximus the Confessor* (Early Church Fathers), London and New York: Routledge, 1996

Maloney, George A., *A History of Orthodox Theology since 1453*, Belmont, Massachusetts: Nordland, 1976

Meyendorff, John, *Byzantine Theology: Historical Trends and Doctrinal Themes*, New York: Fordham University Press, 1974; London: Mowbray, 1975; 2nd edition, New York: Fordham University Press, 1979

Nichols, Aidan, *Light from the East: Authors and Themes in Orthodox Theology*, London: Sheed and Ward, 1995

Norris, Frederick W., *Faith Gives Fullness to Reasoning: The Five Theological Orations of Gregory Nazianzen* (Supplements to Vigiliae Christianae, volume 13), New York: Brill, 1990

Palmer, G.E.H., Philip Sherrard, and Kallistos Ware, editors, *The Philokalia: The Complete Text*, 4 vols., London and Boston: Faber and Faber, 1979–1995

Pietarinen, Rauno, *A Bibliography of Major Orthodox Periodicals in English*, Joensuu: Joensuun Yliopiston, 1987

Prokurat, Michael, et al., editors, *Historical Dictionary of the Orthodox Church* (Religion, Philosophies, and Movements, number 9), Lanham, Maryland: Scarecrow Press, 1996

Schmemann, A., "Russian Theology: 1920–1972: An Introductory Survey," *SVTQ* (1972)

Slesinski, Robert, *Pavel Florensky: A Metaphysics of Love*, Crestwood, New York: St. Vladimir's Seminary Press, 1984

Staniloae, Dumitru, *The Experience of God*, Brookline, Massachusetts: Holy Cross Orthodox Press, 1994

Tsirpanlis, Constantine, *Introduction to Eastern Patristic Thought and Orthodox Theology* (Theology and Life Series, volume 30), Collegeville, Minnesota: Liturgical Press, 1991

Vassiliades, P., "Greek Theology in the Making," *SVTQ* (1991)

Yannaras, C., "Theology in Present-Day Greece," *SVTQ* (1972)

Theology, Western Christian: Augustinian Friars/Hermits

Although the Order of the Hermits of St. Augustine was established formally in 1256, (decades after the Franciscans and Dominicans) and long retained its eremitical roots, it soon assumed a place in education along with the two older mendicant orders and the Carmelites. Like these orders it created a pyramidal educational structure with its main *studia generalia* alongside the universities. In keeping with the Order's Italian focus, most significant medieval Augustinian masters of theology were Italians and often had some of their early theological training in Italian *studia* before ending up in Paris or, to a lesser extent, Oxford. They were to make notable innovations.

The history of the Order's theology revolves around Giles of Rome (c. 1245–1316), Gregory of Rimini (c. 1300–1358), and Martin Luther (1483–1546). Giles studied theology at Paris around 1270, likely under Thomas Aquinas (c. 1225–1274), whom Giles followed closely in his early works. Giles, the Order's first regent master of theology at Paris from 1285 to 1291, was made the official doctor of the Order in 1287. Thus, at the beginning of its entry into theology, the Order imposed a standard on its members, and Giles dominated the Augustinians' theology for decades. However, in later years Giles moved away from the Aristotelian-Thomist line and toward that of St. Augustine, especially on the subject of grace. Subsequent Parisian Augustinians expressed their "Aegidianism" (Aegidius = Giles) in various ways, some preferring Thomism and others Augustine. Among the more influential of the latter group were Gerard of Siena (fl. 1320s) and Thomas of Strasbourg (fl. 1330s).

Popular as some of these theologians were, usually they were also conservative. James of Viterbo (c. 1288) and Michael of Massa (c. 1330) are examples of more daring Augustinian Hermits. By Michael's time the attacks on Aquinas by Henry of Ghent (fl. 1285) and the Franciscans John Duns Scotus (c. 1265–1308) and Peter Auriol (c. 1280–1322) called for a more independent response, and it is interesting that on the question of divine foreknowledge, Michael chose to follow another Franciscan, Francis of Marchia (fl. 1320). With Gerard and Thomas of Strasbourg representing the older, more Dominican-oriented school and Michael the newer, Franciscan-influenced group, the relative importance of the Order in Parisian theology was rising during the late 1320s and 1330s. Gregory of Rimini can be seen as the culmination of this development.

Gregory was arguably the most important theologian between Auriol and William of Ockham (c. 1285–1347) and the Reformation. He studied arts at Paris in the 1320s and taught at various schools of the Augustinian order in Italy during the 1330s before returning to Paris, where he lectured on Peter Lombard's *Sentences* from 1343 to 1344. Gregory absorbed both the current theological debates at Paris and new developments in theology at Oxford, which had experienced a golden age following Ockham's stay there. Initially, it was through Gregory that future generations of Parisian theologians encountered the new English thought. Gregory also introduced a new type of doctrinal "Augustinianism," coupling a fresh and more extensive reading of Augustine's works with the adoption of an extreme Augustinian doctrine of grace, justification, and predestination. This position has been called "double predestination" or "double particular election" because Gregory held that God actively wills both the salvation of the elect and the damnation of the reprobate, without any instigating cause on the part of either the elect or the reprobate. On this issue and others, Gregory became the leader of doctrinal Augustinianism into the 16th century.

Gregory has also been seen as a key figure in the development of a "historico-critical" method in theology, a foretaste in part of modern scholarly methods. In particular, an attempt was made to establish reliable texts of Augustine and to separate authentic works from the pseudo-Augustinian corpus. Gregory's commentary on the *Sentences* was sometimes mined for Augustinian quotations. Moreover, works were now cited in the text down to the smallest detail. In the Augustinian order this historico-critical tendency reached its zenith in the theological works of John Hiltalingen of Basel (fl. 1365). In John's *Sentences* commentary one finds citations as detailed as this: "I argue at greater length against this in my *Responses*, question four, conclusion one, corollary one."

Gregory had a great impact inside and outside his Order, and even major figures, such as Pierre d'Ailly (1350/51–1420), paraphrased or even copied sections of his *Sentences* commentary. More generally, after 1360 a special "symbiotic" relationship existed with the Cistercians, who from the middle of the century adhered to the doctrines of one or more of the Augustinians, such as Alphonsus Vargas of Toledo, Hugolino of Orvieto, or the only Oxford Augustinian whose theological works survive, namely, John Klenkok (c. 1310–1374). The more conservative Thomas of Strasbourg retained some influence as the main representative of the *via antiqua*. Hugolino of Orvieto (c. 1380–1457) followed Gregory's lead in developing a new, radically anti-Pelagian version of the *via moderna*: the *schola Augustiniana moderna*. Its views, which John Calvin later adopted, have been summarized as follows:

> (1) A strict epistemological "nominalism" or "terminism." (2) A voluntarist, as opposed to intellectualist, understanding of the *ratio meriti* [nature of merit]. (3) The extensive use of the writings of Augustine, particularly his anti-Pelagian works. (4) A strongly pessimistic view of original sin, with the Fall being identified as a watershed in the economy of salvation. (5) A strong emphasis upon the priority of God in justification, linked to a doctrine of special grace. (6) A radical doctrine of absolute double predestination. (McGrath, 1987)

Considerable doctrinal latitude and even conflict within the Order was evident in the later 14th and 15th centuries, and by the early 16th century *Aegidistae* and *Gregoriistae* schools of thought were in existence. In the Reformation, Martin Luther, who entered the Augustinian convent at Erfurt in 1505, appears not to have had direct contact with the *schola Augustiniana moderna* before 1519, but he did share many of its views by way of the *via moderna*, which was called the *via Gregorii* at Wittenberg, where he studied and taught from 1508. Later, however, John Calvin adopted all six points of the *schola Augustiniana moderna*, perhaps taken directly from Gregory's then-printed *Sentences* commentary. Thus, the theology of Augustinian Friars/Hermits exerted influence for centuries to come.

CHRIS SCHABEL

See also Augustinian Friars/Hermits; Augustinian Rule; Luther, Martin

Further Reading

Courtenay, William J., *Schools and Scholars in Fourteenth-Century England*, Princeton, New Jersey: Princeton University Press, 1987

Grassi, Onorato, "L'agostinismo trecentesco," in *Storia della teologia nel Medioevo III: La teologia della scuole*, edited by Giulio d'Onofrio, Casale Monferrato: Piemme, 1996

Halverson, James, *Peter Aureol on Predestination: A Challenge to Late Medieval Thought*, Leiden and Boston: Brill, 1998

McGrath, Alister, *The Intellectual Origins of the European Reformation*, Oxford and New York: Blackwell, 1987

Oberman, Heiko, editor, *Gregor von Rimini: Werk und Wirkung bis zur Reformation*, Berlin and New York: de Gruyter, 1981

Schabel, Chris, "Questions on Future Contingents by Michael of Massa, OESA," *Augustiniana* 48 (1998)

Trapp, Damasus, "Augustinian Theology of the 14th Century: Notes on Editions, Marginalia, Opinions and Book-Lore," *Augustiniana* 6 (1956)
Zumkeller, Adolar, "Die Augustinerschule des Mittelalters: Vertreter und philosophisch-theologische Lehre," *Analecta Augustiniana* 27 (1964)

Theology, Western Christian: Benedictine

Because the purpose of this article is to describe the kind of theology that has typically been produced within the ambit of Benedictine monasticism, it is important to note first certain factors within this form of monastic life that especially influenced Benedictine theology. The first factor is that the sixth-century Rule of St. Benedict did not mandate some new kind of religious life in the Church but simply handed on a tradition that was already in place, although with some modifications that Benedict deemed appropriate for the monks of his day. That earlier tradition was essentially "a wisdom tradition," in other words, a tradition in which a particular way of living the Christian life was passed down by the word and example of wise elders from generation to generation. Such a tradition has, almost by definition, a deep respect for the past and a certain suspicion about what seems novel. Correspondingly, monasticism has also had a strong emphasis on humility; Benedict's appropriation of this ideal is evident in the fact that chapter 7 of his Rule, "On Humility," is the longest chapter of all. These factors – emphasis on lived practice, reverence for the past, and humility – are characteristic marks of Benedictine theology through the centuries. A few of the most important Western monastic theologians are singled out here to illustrate one or more of these traits.

Pope St. Gregory the Great (590–604), author of the earliest *Life of Benedict*, lived as a monk for some years in Rome before being called to serve the Church first as a deacon in that city, then as nuncio in Constantinople, and finally as pope. Whether he followed the Benedictine Rule during his monastic years cannot be ascertained, but it was common in that era for monasteries to make use of several written rules simultaneously. However, Gregory, who as pope frequently expressed a yearning to return to the cloister, was a very influential monastic theologian in the West. Like many authors of the early and High Middle Ages, he mainly wrote commentaries on parts of the Bible. Especially noteworthy are his *Moralia* on the Book of Job. These "moral books" (*Libri morales*) served for centuries as a basic treatise of moral and ascetical theology and did more than any of Gregory's other writings to establish his doctrinal authority.

No Western monastic author rivaled Gregory in influence for the next four centuries, but some significant theologians carried on the kind of theology that he had practiced. Bede the Venerable (c. 673–735) is best known as the early historian of the Church in England, but he also composed many scriptural commentaries that were characterized by the kind of allegorical and moral interpretations found in early fathers of the Church, whom Bede frequently cites. At the French abbey of Corbie, Paschasius Radbertus (c. 790–860) composed a treatise on the Eucharist that is considered the first scientific monograph on that sacrament, marred though the work is by overemphasis on the identity between the historical and the Eucharistic body of Christ. Across the Rhine, Abbot Rupert of Deutz (c. 1075–1129) followed the example of many of his monastic predecessors by writing commentaries on Scripture, some of which have titles showing an interest in central themes of Christian theology, for example, *On the Trinity and Its Work* and *The Glory and Honor of the Son of Man*. A short passage from his commentary on the Book of Revelation reflects the emphasis of humility so common in monastic theology:

> This knowledge does not come from an outer, as if foreign, document; it comes from an inner and personal experience. As for those who are puffed up with learning, let them increase their knowledge – or at least what they think is knowledge – as much as they will, as much as they can; they will never acquire that particular comprehension. (*In Apoc.* 2.2).

The monastic theologians discussed thus far – and many others too numerous to mention – were mainly commentators on Scripture, and in large part the commentaries they penned were compilations drawn from the writings of Church fathers, such as Ambrose, Jerome, and Augustine. To be sure, the monks did make some use of philosophical categories and methodology (i.e., the discipline then commonly known as dialectics), but philosophical (or "scholastic") argumentation was not a prominent part of their work. Quite different in this regard was the work of St. Anselm of Canterbury (c. 1033–1109), who had been a teacher and abbot at the Norman monastery of Bec before being called in 1093 to head the Church in England. Anselm broke the mold of monastic theology as it had been known up that time by making fuller use of philosophy in an attempt to attain deeper understanding of the mysteries of the Christian faith (in accordance with his description of theology as "faith seeking understanding" [*fides quaerens intellectum*]). At times this development has led historians of medieval thought to call Anselm "the founder of Scholasticism," but this appellation must not obscure the fact that he retained to a significant degree the devotional tenor that had marked earlier monastic theology. For example, Anselm's *Proslogion* contains a severely philosophical argument for the existence of God, but it begins and ends with prayerful phrases of a most heartfelt kind: "Come now, Lord my God, teach my heart where and how to seek You, where and how to find You" (chap. 1), and "O God, I pray, let me know and love You, so that I may rejoice in You. And if I cannot in this life [do so] fully, let me advance day by day until the point of fullness comes" (chap. 26).

A generation or two later, the scholastic method had gone much further in the work of Peter Abelard (1079–1142/43), whose search for clarity via the tools of dialectics appeared arrogant and dangerous in the eyes of monks such as William of St.

Thierry (1075/80–1148) and his good friend St. Bernard of Clairvaux (1090–1153). The Psalm verse "I do not occupy myself with things too great and too marvelous for me" (Ps. 131:1) was applied by Bernard to all those who "have contented themselves with the learning that puffs up" (*On the Song of Songs* 85.9.7). Bernard's own approach, whether in his sermons on the *Song of Songs* or his many other treatises, was once described by him in the following words: "We search in a worthier manner, we discover with greater facility through prayer than through disputation" (*On Consideration* 5.32). Bernard, the most influential monk of the reformed branch of the Benedictines known as Cistercians, has often been criticized for the vigor with which he pursued Abelard and eventually got him condemned by an ecclesiastical council. Nevertheless, the kind of monastic theology that Bernard unhesitatingly preferred does have a lasting place within Christianity. M.-D. Chenu (1895–1990), who as a Dominican theologian would have no personal interest in defending a non-Scholastic approach to theology, concisely sums up the nature and importance of monastic theology in the following passage, which includes a reference to the quarrel that Bernard had with Abelard's rationalism:

> The continuing presence of the text of the Scriptures, the absolute value of faith for its own sake with its accompanying silent adoration; the perception of mystery which, despite its excesses, was legitimately championed by St. Bernard against Abelard's extravagant attacks; the contempt for dialectics the moment it becomes self-complacent; . . . the inferiority of the "theologian" who is nothing more than a professor: all these are permanently valid, and the *schola Christi*, which the monastery truly is, is their essential and enduring expression. ("Culture et théologie à Jumièges après l'ère féodale," quoted in Leclercq, 1961)

During Bernard's lifetime and into the 13th century, a number of Benedictine and Cistercian nuns began to make their mark in theology. One of the first of these was even a correspondent of Bernard's, the Benedictine abbess Hildegard of Bingen (1098–1179). Her theology, full of biblical references and often expressed in the genre of reflections on her visions, breathes a cosmic scope that has found numerous admirers in our own day. Whereas Hildegard wrote in Latin, the Cistercian visionary Beatrice of Nazareth (1200–1268) was one of the earliest representatives of the new vernacular theology. Her *Seven Manners of Loving*, written in Middle Dutch, presents the drama of the soul's encounter with God as culminating at a point at which the soul "will be united with her Bridegroom and will become one spirit with him in inseparable faithfulness and eternal love." One finds in this language a reflection of earlier monastic commentaries on the *Song of Songs*, including that of St. Bernard.

This era of an emerging vernacular theology likewise saw the rise of the cathedral schools and universities. The growing importance of the Scholastic method as practiced in these institutions led to a corresponding decline in the influence of monastic theology on Western culture as a whole. Monks with academic promise were sometimes sent to study at the universities, but the stereotype of "the learned Benedictine" comes mainly from the cloistered labors of scholars such as Luc d'Achery (1609–1683), Jean Mabillon (1632–1707), and other members of the Congregation of St. Maur in the 17th century. Although their work was mainly historical or paleographical, the outstanding theological syntheses to be found in their prefaces to the works of the Fathers reveal these Maurists to have been genuine theologians as well. In that same century the foundation of a Benedictine university at Salzburg was largely responsible for a renaissance of theological studies in the German-speaking parts of Europe.

In the past hundred years, another central feature of traditional Benedictine life – the liturgy – has helped bring some Western monastic authors to theological preeminence. Odo Casel (1886–1948), of the abbey of Maria Laach in the Rhineland, founded the important journal *Jahrbuch für Liturgiewissenschaft* in 1921 and served as its editor for 15 years. He was also a pioneer in combating what he judged to be an impoverished, overly moralistic idea of the Christian religion. Casel's theological writings brought out the meaning of the liturgy as a celebration of the mysteries of Christ and the Church, showing how the liturgical rites truly make present Christ's work of salvation. Some of his theses, especially those that saw the ancient Hellenistic mystery cults as a kind of preparation for Christ, understandably encountered opposition, but his main thesis – that the mystery of Christ, his saving action, is carried on and made actual through the "mysteries" of the Church's worship – is considered by many scholars to be an enduring contribution to liturgical theology.

Another liturgical theologian of note – and one who has been critical of many aspects of Casel's thought – is the Italian Benedictine Cyprian Vagaggini (1909–1999), who was for many years a professor at the Benedictine athenaeum of St. Anselmo in Rome. His major work, *Theological Dimensions of the Liturgy*, is an exhaustive, systematic study that concludes with a lengthy section on spiritual and pastoral aspects of the liturgy. Today, professors at the Liturgical Institute at St. Anselmo carry on Vagaggini's work of liturgical scholarship in their teaching and research, as do Benedictines in many other parts of the world. In the United States, an important center for such work is St. John's Abbey in Minnesota, where Virgil Michel (1890–1938), the founder of the American liturgical movement, was once a monk and where the prominent journal of liturgical theology, *Worship*, is published. Other leading liturgical theologians in the United States are Mary Collins, a sister of Mt. St. Scholastica Priory in Kansas who taught for many years at the Catholic University of America, and Aidan Kavanagh, a monk of St. Meinrad Archabbey in Indiana and a longtime professor of liturgics at the Yale University Divinity School. Kavanagh's book *On Liturgical Theology* is one of the best introductions to the subject, while his other publications enter more deeply into questions of ritual, sacraments, and liturgical history. As would be expected, other Benedictines carry on the work of biblical theology that was highlighted in the first part of this article, prime examples being the Americans Irene Nowell and Demetrius Dumm.

JAMES A. WISEMAN, O.S.B.

See also Abelard, Peter; Anselm, St.; Bede, St.; Benedict of Nursia, St.; Benedictines; Bernard of Clairvaux, St.; Casel, Odo; Gregory I (the Great), St.; Liturgical Movement 1830–1980; Liturgists, German Monastic; Maurists; Scholars, Benedictine

Further Reading

Casel, Odo, *The Mystery of Christian Worship and Other Writings*, Westminster, Maryland: Newman Press, 1962

Gilson, Etienne, *The Mystical Theology of Saint Bernard*, translated by A.H.C. Downes, London and New York: Sheed and Ward, 1940; Kalamazoo, Michigan: Cistercian Publications, 1990

Kavanagh, Aidan, *On Liturgical Theology*, New York: Pueblo, 1984

Leclercq, Jean, *The Love of Learning and the Desire for God: A Study of Monastic Culture*, translated by Catharine Misrahi, New York: Fordham University Press, 1961; London: SPCK, 1978

Saint Bernard théologien: Actes du Congrès de Dijon, 15–19 septembre 1953, Rome: Editions Cistercienses, 1955

Schmitz, Philibert, *Histoire de l'Ordre de Saint-Benoît*, 7 vols., Liège, Belgium, Éditions de Maredsous, 1948–1956

Southern, R.W., *Saint Anselm: A Portrait in a Landscape*, Cambridge and New York: Cambridge University Press, 1990

Vagaggini, Cypriano, *Theological Dimensions of the Liturgy: A General Treatise on the Theology of the Liturgy*, translated from the fourth Italian edition by Leonard J. Doyle and W.A. Jurgens, Collegeville, Minnesota: Liturgical Press, 1976

Theology, Western Christian: Carmelite

The first Carmelites on Mount Carmel were a community of lay hermits for whom education was not a critical issue. As they migrated to Europe in the middle decades of the 13th century and took their place alongside the other mendicant orders, studies became essential to their identity and mission. By the second half of the 13th century, the Order, like the Franciscans and Augustinian Friars, was rapidly clericalizing to permit the friars to preach and to administer the sacraments both for the spiritual good of their neighbors and for their own financial survival. Clerical ministry demanded a more focused approach to theological education, and by the end of the 13th century, the Carmelites took their places in the university alongside the other mendicants.

The earliest extent constitutions of the Carmelite order date from 1281 and mandated the establishment of several *studia generale*, including one at Paris, the preeminent theological faculty of the time. It is difficult to reconstruct the status of studies in the Order before those constitutions, but because the Carmelites had established themselves in cities that were known as centers of learning (e.g., Paris, Cologne, and Cambridge), it can be presumed that although they likely were not able to set up their own *studia* before the end of the 13th century, they had elected to be in academic environments. However, Gerard of Bologna, the first Carmelite to attain the doctorate in theology, completed his degree as late as 1295.

Carmelites never attained the theological prominence of the Dominicans, Franciscans, or Augustinians. They came to the universities after the great apex of scholasticism, and in theology they were more followers than innovators. Throughout their history Carmelites have shown proficiency more for mystical theology than for scholastic thought. A very important mystical text that pre-dates the Carmelite commitment to university education is the *Ignea Sagitta*, a treatise written in 1270 by Nicholas the Frenchman, prior general of the Order. On the surface this treatise is Nicholas' lament that his Order has abandoned its contemplative focus for the busy life of the mendicant friar. However, beneath the somewhat dyspeptic tone is a magnificent treatise on the spiritual life. Many themes that would become central in Carmelite spirituality, such as the purification of the heart, can be found in this early document. Nicholas' writing style betrays his own education, and the work is rich in allusions to sacred scripture, liturgical sources, canon law, monastic authors, and classical authors.

Gerard of Bologna (d. 1317), Guy Terreni (d. 1342), and Sibert deBeka were three Carmelites who studied in Paris in the late 13th and early 14th centuries. They tended to the extreme Aristotelian thought of Godfrey de Fontaines. Terreni's *Summa de heresibus* was still in use in the 17th century. Terreni was consulted by Pope John XXII (1316–1334) in the papal condemnation of the Spiritual Franciscans; deBeka was consulted by the same pope in his condemnation of the *Defensor Pacis* of Marsilius of Padua (c. 1275–1342). deBeka also served on a commission of mendicants that condemned the works of Meister Eckhart (c. 1260–c. 1328).

John Baconthorpe (d. 1348), Carmel's most important scholastic thinker, studied at Oxford and Paris. His writings present more a critique and synthesis of an array of other scholastic thinkers than original thought. His commentary on the sentences was reprinted as late as 1754. Baconthorpe, like many other Carmelite theologians, invested much of his talent in developing Mariological themes.

English Carmelites achieved some theological prominence in the Wycliffite controversies of the 14th century. John Cunningham (d. 1399), confessor to John of Gaunt; Richard Maidstone (d. 1396); Peter Stokes; and Stephen Patrington were all Wycliffite controversialists. However, the most prominent Carmelite in this controversy was Thomas Netter of Walden, who publicly upbraided King Henry V (1413–1422) for his slackness in protecting Catholic orthodoxy. Henry took Netter as his confessor and also used him on diplomatic errands. He attended the Council of Constance in 1415 as the king's representative.

Carmel provided a constant stream of minor theological figures through the 15th century. Arnold Bostius, a Belgian Carmelite, achieved some preeminence with his defense of the doctrine of the Immaculate Conception against Dominican antagonists and was also noted for his humanist literary style.

Carmelites played minor though not insignificant roles in the 16th-century reformations. Sebastian Crayes and Nicholas Baechem of Egmond were among the antagonists of Erasmus (1466/69–1536). Eberhard Billick of Cologne preached against the abuses that had led to the Lutheran Reformation, especially clerical ignorance. Billick was one of the theologians who represented the archbishop of the Colloquy of Worms. Paulus Helie of Copenhagen was another Carmelite who was critical of the Church in its need to reform but anxious to defend it against Protestantism. On the other side, Peter Laurentsen and Francis Wormordsen took roles in the evangelical leadership in Denmark. John Byrd, provincial of England, and John Bale, the playwright, were two English Carmelites who embraced the Henrician Reformation, although neither can be said to have taken any serious theological role in it. Several Continental Carmelites wrote in defense of Henry's marital cause, including James Calco, who was instrumental in persuading the University of Paris to support Henry's petition. Several Carmelites served as theologians for the Council of Trent (1545–1563), including Antonio Marinari and Vincenzio deLeone.

At the University of Salamanca, the Discalced Carmelite Antonio of the Mother of God (d. 1637) began a monumental treatise titled the *Cursus Theologicus*, which was completed by Domingo de Santa Teresa and Juan de la Anunciación. *Cursus Theologiae Moralis* was published by the Discalced Carmelites at Salamanca between 1665 and 1724 to treat moral questions that had been deliberately omitted from the *Cursus Theologicus*.

Historically, Carmel's forte had never been systematic theology, and it was the Catholic Reformation that stimulated Carmel's unique gifts in mystical theology to come to the fore. Sixteenth-century Spain saw the emergence of two of the preeminent Catholic mystical theolgians: Teresa of Avila (1515–1582) and John of the Cross (1542–1591). Between them, these two collaborators organized and defined the Carmelite school of mystical theology. Drawing on the medieval Carmelite heritage found in the primitive rule and the 14th-century treatise *The Institute of the First Monks* and combining that heritage with the insights of the 15th-century Devotio Moderna and influenced, at least in part, by the methodology of Ignatius Loyola (1491–1556), these Carmelites created a rich body of spiritual literature that is more widely read today than it was even in the 16th and 17th centuries. Subsequent Carmelite writers, including Thérèse of Lisieux (1873–1897) and Edith Stein (1891–1942), drew on and continued the theological tradition established by John and Teresa. Since her recent canonization, the work of Edith Stein is drawing considerable attention from philosophers and theologians. Teresa of Avila, John of the Cross, and Thérèse of Lisieux have all been named Doctor of the Church in recognition for the importance of their teaching. The Carmelite mystical theology is finding an avid contemporary audience both within and beyond Catholicism. Themes and images – such as the "dark night of the soul" and the dwelling of God at the center of the soul, first developed by Teresa of Avila and John of the Cross in their mystical theology – are being revisited by contemporary thinkers in several disciplines, including systematic theology.

Intellectually as well as economically and numerically, both observances of Carmel were seriously damaged by the Reformation and the wars of religion. The French Revolution and the secularist governments of the 18th and 19th centuries all but finished off the Order. It was a time of survival and one not conducive to intellectual vitality. However, the 20th century saw a theological revival in the Order. Bartolome Xiberta, a Catalan, played an important role as a theological peritus at the Second Vatican Council and was especially important in developments regarding the sacrament of reconciliation (penance). A number of American Carmelites – Ernest Larkin, Eamon Carroll, and Christian Ceroke – and the distinguished Old Testament scholar Roland Murphy have taught at Catholic University of America and on other Catholic and Protestant theological faculties. Internationally, Carmelites teach on several of the pontifical faculties in Rome and on theological faculties in Nijmegan, Dublin, Melbourne, and several other cities.

Patrick Thomas McMahon, O.Carm.

See also Biblical Figures and Practices; Carmelites; Dominicans; Franciscans; John of the Cross, St.; Teresa of Avila, St.; Thérèse of Lisieux, St.

Further Reading

Egan, Keith, "The Carmelites Turn to Cambridge," in *In the Land of Carmel: Essays in Honor of Joachim Smet, O. Carm.*, edited by Egan and Paul Chandler, Rome: Institutum Carmelitanum, 1991

Lickteig, Franz-Bernard, "The German Carmelites at the Medieval Universities," Ph.D. Diss., Catholic University of America, 1977; Rome: Institutum Carmelitanum, 1981

Smet, Joachim, *Cloistered Carmel: A Brief History of the Carmelite Nuns*, Rome: Institutum Carmelitanum, 1986

Welch, John, *The Carmelite Way: An Ancient Path for Today's Pilgrim*, New York: Paulist Press, and Leominster: Gracewing, 1996

Theology, Western Christian: Dominican

Founded in 1216 by Dominic Guzman (1170–1221), the Order of Preachers was given the apostolic mission of preaching the gospel for the salvation of souls. In one sense, then, the theology of the Dominicans ranges as widely as Christian theology itself. However, the historical moment of the Order's foundation, as well as the lifestyle developed for it by Dominic, mean that Dominican theology shows distinctive emphases.

The Order was founded as part of the Church's response to Albigensianism. Dominic incorporated into his new form of religious life certain values, notably poverty and democracy, which were being promoted by those with whom he differed theologically. Although poverty became more closely associated with Francis of Assisi (1181/82–1226), it was just as important for Dominic. Dominican democracy has proved to be a remarkably resilient system of government that has guided Dominicans in their life together and in their intellectual and missionary work.

Dominican theology is pursued within a shared life, centered on the Word of God in liturgical prayer and preaching. The manual work of monasticism is replaced by study, monastic stability by missionary mobility. The largely rural setting of monasteries supported a certain rhythm and style of life and a certain approach to contemplation. The friars undertook a new thing, seeking to combine monastic and canonical traditions – choral office, silence, common life, and poverty – with the demands of apostolic ministry in the towns. The priority in this undertaking is clear from the Order's ancient custom of dispensation from the practices of conventual life wherever study or preaching require it.

The emergence of the friars illustrates how pastoral demands from outside stimulated developments within monastic tradition. Contemplation of God and of God's ways remains central to Dominican life but with two distinctive emphases: contemplation is undertaken now with a view to preaching, and it is understood to include intellectual study of the mysteries of faith.

It was said that Dominic spoke only to God or about God, and Dominican life itself is "theological." His successor, Jordan of Saxony (d. 1237), writing to the whole Order in May 1233, says,

> we say a lot, we do a lot, we endure a tremendous lot, which would make us so much richer in virtue, so much more fruitful in merit, if only charity abounded in our hearts, directing and ordering everything towards our proper goal, which is God. (Tugwell, 1982)

Dominican theology sought to continue the engagement with intellectual life and ideas encouraged by Dominic. The earliest literary productions of the Dominicans were manuals for preachers and confessors. The extraordinary and abiding influence of Thomas Aquinas (c. 1225–1274) might lead some to conclude that Dominican theology is, for all practical purposes, equivalent to his. That would be too simple. At the same time, in the words of Damian Byrne, late Master of the Order,

> it was the genius of Thomas Aquinas to carry forward Dominic's fundamental orientation and to broaden the basis of theological education in the Order through his study of Aristotelian philosophy, which enabled him to give an intellectual foundation to the theology of the goodness of creation and the rejection of dualism. (*Letter on the Role of Study in the Order*, 29 May 1991)

This fundamental orientation means that Dominican theology is "Creator-centered," focused on God while valuing the created order as a gift of God's mercy. The conviction that "Grace does not replace nature but brings it to perfection" is a distinctive Thomistic and Dominican principle. Thus, the natural, even secular, order enjoys its own integrity and meaning while being radically dependent on God for all it is, has, and does. God is found nowhere in this world because God is everywhere in this world, present to each least thing as the giver of its being, the most radical perfection in things. The distortions introduced to creation and its history through the sins of humanity find a remedy in Jesus Christ, the way by which human beings in fact return to God.

Albert the Great (c. 1200–1280) stands at the head of a German Dominican school, which includes Henry Suso (c. 1295–1366), John Tauler (c. 1300–1361), and above all Meister Eckhart (c. 1260–c. 1327). Their work brings together earlier philosophical and theological ideas in a way that was quite different to that of Thomas.

Greatest of the Dominican women is Catherine of Siena (1347–1380), whose life and writings show a distinctive Dominican weighting of spiritual concerns, theological understanding, pastoral care, and political involvement.

The missionary work of the Order also helped to shape Dominican theology. This took an evangelical, even apocalyptic, turn with Vincent Ferrer (1350–1419) and Girolamo Savonarola (1452–1498). Dominicans were involved in theological reflection on the issues raised by colonization. Bartolomé de las Casas (1484–1566) was an exemplary preacher of justice in the Americas, and Francisco de Vitoria (1483–1546) played Thomas to his Dominic by providing intellectual foundations for what de las Casas knew instinctively. The heir not only to Thomas' teaching about natural law but also to Dominic's approach to government, Vitoria is one of the founders of international law.

Cajetan (1469–1534) was a faithful commentator on St. Thomas and an independent thinker during the first decades of the Reformation. Catherine de Ricci (1522–1590) witnesses to the continuing fruitfulness of Dominican mysticism. Henri-Dominique Lacordaire (1802–1861) worked tirelessly to keep the Church and the Order in contact with the emerging modern world of the 19th century.

In the 20th century Dominican theology was further developed by many members of the Order, notably Marie-Dominique Chenu (1895–1990), Yves Congar (1904–1995), and Edward Schillebeeckx (b. 1914). Their work was guided by the distinctive concerns of the Order's tradition: truth, whether theological, philosophical or historical; the grace of God in creation and in Jesus Christ; and interpreting the presence of God for God's people. Late 20th-century interest in spirituality and the prophetic preaching of justice has helped the Order reappropriate earlier resources, both pastoral and intellectual.

Dominican theology encompasses renowned individuals, distinctive themes, and a unique context for theological work. It flourishes within a contemplative tradition for which the pursuit of truth is central. The Order of Preachers has been home to a Christian humanist tradition, just as it has supported a strongly evangelical and missionary one. It is an ecclesial family whose theological concerns have been as broad as those of the Church but that, like all families, has a unique history and a particular style.

VIVIAN BOLAND, O.P.

See also Albertus Magnus, St.; Dominic, St.; Dominicans; Eckhart, Meister; Savonarola, Girolamo; Spirituality: Western Christian; Thomas Aquinas, St.

Further Reading
Bedouelle, Guy, *In the Image of Saint Dominic: Nine Portraits of Dominican Life*, translated by Sister Mary Thomas Noble and W. Becket Soule, San Francisco: Ignatius Press, 1994
Faculty of Aquinas Institute of Theology, *In the Company of Preachers*, Collegeville, Minnesota: Liturgical Press, 1993
Hinnebusch, William A., *The Dominicans: A Short History*, New York: Alba House, 1975; Dublin: Dominican Publications, 1985
Tugwell, Simon, *The Way of the Preacher*, London: Darton, Longman and Todd, and Springfield, Illinois: Templegate, 1979
Tugwell, Simon, *Early Dominicans: Selected Writings*, New York: Paulist Press, and London: SPCK, 1982
Tugwell, Simon, *Albert and Thomas: Selected Writings*, New York: Paulist Press, 1988
Vicaire, M.H., *Saint Dominic and His Times*, translated by Kathleen Pond, Green Bay, Wisconsin: Alt Publishing Company, and London: Darton, Longman, and Todd, 1964
Woods, Richard, *Mysticism and Prophecy: The Dominican Tradition*, London: Darton, Longman and Todd, and Maryknoll, New York: Orbis Books, 1998

Theology, Western Christian: Franciscan

With its beginnings early in the 13th century, a recognizable Franciscan theological tradition developed over the next centuries and came to play a dominant role in later medieval and early modern university thought. Many of the fundamental tenets that characterize Franciscan theology (e.g., Christocentrism, Mary's Immaculate Conception, an emanation trinitarian theology, divine voluntarism, and apostolic poverty) were developed by Franciscans in the late 13th and early 14th centuries, often in conscious opposition to the Thomistic theology generally defended by Dominicans.

Historical Development

Franciscan efforts to attain theological education for members of their Order came very soon after the foundation of the Order itself. By 1219 members of the Order had reached Paris, and soon thereafter they began theological studies there; by 1224 they were in Oxford. The convents that were erected in these two great centers of theological training became in time the apex of a large and complex system of Franciscan education, all directed toward the goal, originally borrowed from the Dominicans, of creating theologically trained preachers and defenders of the faith.

The Oxford Franciscan convent soon established strong ties with the bishop of Lincoln, Robert Grosseteste (c. 1170–1253), one of the outstanding intellectuals of the 13th century, although not himself a Franciscan. However, it was at Paris, with Alexander of Hales (c. 1186–1245), a regent master in theology before he became a Franciscan in 1236–1237, that the Order got its first chair of theology and could begin to produce its own masters of theology. This was the foundation of a true Franciscan theological tradition in which a core set of theological tendencies and positions were not only handed down from master to pupil but also discussed and developed. Hales was a noted theologian in his own right, and in his works we see an early version of many of the theological tendencies that would come to characterize Franciscan thought. These tendencies were woven into a compelling system by Hales' student, Bonaventure (c. 1217–1274), whose role in the Order's theology is just one facet of his immense impact on the Franciscan Order as a whole: with Bonaventure Franciscan theology was set on firm ground. This is not to say that the Order's theology had no room to grow: in the later 13th century it was developed considerably – and increasingly in opposition to Dominican theological ideas – by, among others, John Peckham (c. 1225–1292, archbishop of Canterbury from 1278 to 1292) and Matthew of Aquasparta (c. 1234/40–1302, minister-general of the Franciscan Order from 1287 to 1289 and cardinal from 1288 to 1302). That the Franciscan theological current was not limited to members of the Order is shown most clearly by the Parisian secular theologian Henry of Ghent (d. 1293), whose theological positions and dispositions fit neatly into the Franciscan theological tradition and who made significant contributions to the tradition in his own right.

Much of the Franciscan John Duns Scotus' (c. 1265–1308) theological system is in fact a reaction to or a development of Henry of Ghent's. Scotus' position in the Franciscan theological tradition is central: if Bonaventure laid the groundwork for Franciscan theology, Scotus gave it the form in which it would come to influence the thought of the rest of the Middle Ages and even the early modern period. Scotus came from Scotland and studied first at the Franciscan convent in Oxford and later at Paris, where he became a master of theology in 1305. Although his thought fits into the general current of Franciscan theology stemming from Alexander of Hales and Bonaventure, Scotus repackaged it, offering both terminological and conceptual changes. Most important Scotus fashioned a cogent theological system that had as its foundation a sophisticated and elaborate philosophy.

Scotus' impact was immediate and wide ranging: it would be difficult to find a medieval scholar writing after Scotus who was not influenced by him in some way, and this influence can be seen in nearly every facet of theology and philosophy. Although he was generally criticized by Dominican theologians, a spectrum of reactions to Scotus existed among Franciscans. This spectrum ranged from an uncritical endorsement of Scotus' theology (e.g., Peter of Aquila [d. 1361] and to a lesser extent Francis of Mayronnes [fl. 1320]) to a critical reception of Scotus' views by highly independent scholars who became very influential in their own right. Included among the latter group are the most creative and significant Franciscan theologians of the 14th century: the Parisians Peter Auriol (c. 1280–1322) and Francis of Marchia (d. after 1344) and the Englishmen William of Ockham (c. 1285–1347) and Adam Wodeham (d. 1358). Most Franciscan theologians of the 14th century fell somewhere in between these two groups, offering critique of Scotus in some matters but accepting and often defending his positions on many others.

In the later years of the 14th century and into the 15th, Franciscan theology and theologians are not as prominent as before. One notable Franciscan theologian of this later period is Peter of Candia (c. 1339–1410), who was elected Pope Alexander V at the Council of Pisa in 1409. Peter tended to approach theological problems by presenting a history of the scholastic solutions given to those problems without offering any definitive solutions himself. This theological procedure reflects the fact that the complexity and multitude of earlier theological positions made it difficult for later Franciscan theologians (and theologians in general) to make room for their own position.

A further manifestation of this is that competing schools of thought dominate Franciscan theology of the 15th century. Thus, one of the participants in a late 15th-century dialogue devoted to considering the revival of Peter Auriol's views on future contingents at the University of Louvain (1465–1475) – supposed to represent an actual discussion in which, among others, the protector of the Franciscan Order, Cardinal Bessarion (1403–1472), and the Franciscan Francesco della Rovere (1414–1484; served as Pope Sixtus IV from 1471 to 1484) took part – mentions three distinct Scotistic schools: Mayronnists, Bonetists (named after Nicholas Bonet, O.F.M., d. 1343), and "true" Scotists. Thus, while Bonaventure remained influential, the great theological master in this period among the Franciscans was Scotus, and this is indicated by the fact that although the Roman Catholic Church made Bonaventure one of its teaching doctors in 1588, the Franciscan Order made Scotus its teaching doctor in 1593. Recent studies indicate that much of early modern scholasticism was Scotistic in nature.

Central Theological Positions

Although it is impossible to make airtight generalizations about a theological tradition as rich as the Franciscan, several broad positions are nearly ubiquitous among theologians in the Order.

At its foundations Franciscan theology is characterized by a conception, descended ultimately from Neoplatonism, of God as the self-diffusing good. God is overflowing goodness and love, and on account of this he voluntarily creates and gives to creation, and especially to mankind, his only begotten son, Christ. Thus, Franciscan theology, like Franciscan spirituality as a whole, is basically Christocentric. Although it is true that the incarnation was the way that God chose to redeem fallen mankind, Christ was not sent primarily to redeem. The incarnation took place because God in his overflowing goodness willed to give his Son to the world as an expression of his love; the incarnation's effects as redress for original sin were strictly subordinate to this end.

In line with the centrality of Christ in their theology, the Franciscans developed and staunchly defended one of the most influential doctrines of medieval Latin scholasticism: Mary's Immaculate Conception. It was unacceptable to Franciscans that the Mother of God should share in the original sin that marred all other members of the human race. Whereas earlier theologians, including Thomas Aquinas (c. 1225–1274), had made Mary the least sinful of creatures, lacking original sin from birth, they had denied that Mary was sinless, since this would seem to obviate the need for the incarnation itself. The Franciscan tack was to push Mary's sinlessness back to her conception: she was conceived sinless. Although John Duns Scotus was not the first Franciscan to defend this theory, he did it with such philosophical sophistication and persuasiveness that it earned him the honorific title Doctor Marianus. After Scotus' death, other Franciscans, including Peter Auriol and the Oxford theologian Robert Cowton (fl. 1310), defended Mary's Immaculate Conception, and during the 14th century this became the accepted opinion for nearly all theologians outside the Dominican Order (which largely followed Aquinas on this question). After centuries of often bitter arguing over the issue between Franciscans (and others) and Dominicans – quarrels in which the pope sometimes had to take a hand – Mary's Immaculate Conception became an official doctrine of the Roman Catholic Church in 1854.

A further consequence of the Franciscan conception of God as overflowing goodness is manifested in the Order's trinitarian theology, which is characterized by a reliance on emanations, that is, the putting into being or origination of one of the divine persons by another. This emanation trinitarian theology was developed in opposition to Dominican trinitarian theology, which was based on relation. For the Franciscans broadly speaking, the divine persons are distinct because, although they are the very same divine essence, they are that same essence in three fundamentally different ways, namely, the ways that they emanate. Specifically the Father is unemanated (he comes from no other), the Son is emanated as a Word or Concept by intellectual emanation from the Father, and the Holy Spirit is emanated as Love by Father and Son. Thus, because the unemanated Father is full of goodness, he emanates, or gives being to, the Son; because Father and Son are the same divine essence emanated in fundamentally different ways, they are distinct from each other and yet are both God. Mutatis mutandis, the same applies to the Holy Spirit's emanation and distinction from the Father and the Son. A continuous development in Franciscan trinitarian thought can be traced from the later 13th century, when, among others, Henry of Ghent and Matthew of Aquasparta elaborated Bonaventure's ideas, to a reformulation of those ideas with Scotus and further critique of Scotus' reformulation at the hands of, for example, Peter Auriol and William of Ockham.

A final characteristic of Franciscan theology is its emphasis on divine voluntarism. Franciscans tended to hold that the created will was a more noble faculty than the created intellect, and they emphasized the fact that the dictates of the intellect did not bind the will to a particular course of action; in effect the intellect did not have causal priority over the will. This was a general feature of Franciscan scholastic thought, and it certainly colors their moral theory. It also colors their view of God. God was first and foremost for Franciscans a being who wills: it was not what God knew to be right or true but what he chose to be right or true that was emphasized. This applied, for example, to both creation and the incarnation, which God willed out of his overflowing goodness from all eternity without any necessity. Divine voluntarism is also a general element of Franciscan theories on predestination and God's knowledge of future contingent events; a prominent example is Scotus' notion of contingency in the world, a notion that is ultimately rooted in the divine will: the universe is not necessitated, because the divine will is in no way necessitated.

Although it by no means characterizes Franciscan theology as a whole, mention should be made of specifically Franciscan ideas on apostolic poverty and ecclesiology. In the later 13th and early 14th centuries, a group of Franciscans, the so-called Spiritual Franciscans, adhered strictly to Francis' own desire for absolute poverty, arguing further that Christ himself and his Apostles had owned nothing. This view was accepted as a valid one in 1279 by Pope Nicholas III (1277–1280) in the bull *Exiit qui seminat*. Because of its radical overtones, later popes progressively tried to downplay the importance of this view, culminating in Pope John XXII's (1316–1334) condemnation of it in his bull of 1323, *Cum inter nonnullos*. Theologians among the Spiritual Franciscans, most significantly William of Ockham, argued against these measures by claiming that a later pope could not reverse an earlier papal decision on a matter of faith or morals because such decisions are infallible. This is a remote origin of the modern notion of papal infallibility.

RUSSELL L. FRIEDMAN

See also Bonaventure, St.; Francis of Assisi, St.; Franciscans: General or Male; Thomas Aquinas, St.

Further Reading

Brown, Stephen F., "Peter of Candia's Hundred Year 'History' of the Theologian's Role," *Medieval Philosophy and Theology* 1 (1991)

Catto, J.I., "Theology after Wycliffism," in *The History of the University of Oxford*, volume 2: *Late Medieval Oxford*, Oxford: Clarendon Press, and New York: Oxford University Press, 1992

Courtenay, William J., *Schools and Scholars in Fourteenth Century England*, Princeton, New Jersey: Princeton University Press, 1987

Courtenay, William J., *Capacity and Volition: A History of the Distinction of Absolute and Ordained Power*, Bergamo: Lubrina, 1990

Friedman, Russell L., "Divergent Traditions in Later-Medieval Trinitarian Theology: Relations, Emanations, and the Use of Philosophical Psychology, 1250–1325," *Studia Theologica* 53 (1999)

Halverson, James L., *Peter Aureol on Predestination: A Challenge to Late Medieval Thought*, Leiden and Boston: Brill, 1998

Schabel, Christopher D., "Peter de Rivo and the Quarrel over Future Contingents at Louvain: New Evidence and New Perspectives," *Documenti e studi sulla tradizione filosofica medievale* 6 (1995) and 7 (1996)

Tierney, Brian, *Origins of Papal Infallibility, 1150–1350*, Leiden: Brill, 1972; 2nd edition, Leiden and New York: Brill, 1988

Wolter, A.B., editor, *John Duns Scotus: Four Questions on Mary*, Santa Barbara, California: Old Mission Santa Barbara, 1988

Theravāda. *See* Discourses (Suttas): Theravāda; Rules, Buddhist (Vinaya): Historical; Sri Lanka: History

Theravādin Monks, Modern Western

Ananda Metteyya (1872–1923)

Although literary evidence exists that Bactrian Greeks entered the Buddhist order in post-Aśokan India, the first Western monk to gain a public profile appeared only in modern times. This was Bhikkhu Ananda Metteyya, born in London in 1872 with the name Allan Bennett.

A sensitive young man trained as a chemist, Bennett had developed an early interest in spiritualism that gradually evolved into an attraction to Buddhism, Hinduism, and yoga. He even joined the esoteric Hermetic Order of the Golden Dawn and befriended the controversial occultist Aleister Crowley. Afflicted by asthma since childhood, in 1900 he traveled to Sri Lanka (then the British colony of Ceylon) in the hope that the tropical climate would be more congenial to his health. Here, through deep exposure to Buddhism, he felt more and more acutely an intense calling toward the life of renunciation. For uncertain reasons he chose to become a monk in Burma rather than Sri Lanka, taking novice ordination (*pabbajjā*) there in 1901 and higher ordination (*upasampadā*) six months later with the name Ananda Metteyya.

Soon after his ordination a plan began to crystallize in Ananda Metteyya's mind of bringing Buddhism to the West as a living faith. To prepare for his mission he established a Buddhist society with an international membership and published a journal *Buddhism* for which he wrote prolifically. The mission was launched in 1908, when he arrived in England for six months to sow the seeds of Western Buddhism. Although the response was mixed, Ananda Metteyya still hoped to launch a second mission two years later. However, back in Burma his health steadily declined, and in 1914 he disrobed and returned to England as a layman.

Despite poor health and poverty, Bennett continued to write and speak on the Dhamma until shortly before his death in 1923, a few months after his 50th birthday. Although his dream did not materialize during his own lifetime, the hope that he inspired gradually took root and came to fruition over half a century later with the emergence of a Western *saṅgha* based on English soil.

Nyanatiloka (1878–1957)

The German-born Nyanatiloka was the first known *bhikkhu* from Continental Europe. Born Anton W.F. Gueth in 1878 at

Wiesbaden and trained as a classical musician, he developed an interest in Buddhism while studying at conservatories in Frankfurt and Paris. By 1902 his interest had turned into an irresistible compulsion to travel to Asia and embrace the monastic life. He came first to Sri Lanka but proceeded to Burma, where he received novice ordination in 1903 and higher ordination the next year.

In 1905 he returned to Sri Lanka and embarked on the project that was to occupy him throughout his monastic career: the translation of Buddhist texts from Pāli into German (and later English). He also started to attract European pupils who entered the order under his guidance. In keeping with his own temperament, as a teacher he placed strong emphasis on the study of Pāli and orthodox Theravāda doctrine, in both of which his knowledge was extensive.

In 1910 Nyanatiloka left for Europe, hoping to set up a Buddhist monastery in Switzerland. The plan did not succeed, and in 1911 he returned to Sri Lanka. That same year his dream of a Western monastery was fulfilled, although in a different way than he had envisaged. One of his pupils discovered a vacant island in a lagoon in southern Sri Lanka, at Dodanduwa, and here Nyanatiloka established a base for Western monks named Island Hermitage. From 1911 to the present, Island Hermitage has been an important monastic center in Sri Lanka where many Western monks have received their initial training.

During the two world wars, Nyanatiloka and his German pupils underwent difficult ordeals, including years of detention in British internment camps. After World War I they were forbidden to reenter Lanka (a British colony), and Nyanatiloka himself had to teach in Japan until 1926. During World War II they were detained for six years in Dehra Dun (northern India), where conditions were more tolerable.

When permitted to reenter Lanka in 1946, Nyanatiloka again took up residence at Island Hermitage, but in 1951, for health reasons, he shifted to the cool hill town of Kandy, where he established Forest Hermitage, which since then has been continuously occupied by Western monks. When he died in 1957, as a token of respect the Sri Lankan government accorded him a state funeral, attended by the prime minister and the German ambassador.

Although living for many years under difficult conditions, Nyanatiloka was an immensely productive worker, turning out German translations of many important Pāli texts and three classics (in both German and English): *The Word of the Buddha*, *The Buddha's Path to Deliverance*, and *Buddhist Dictionary*.

Nyanaponika (1901–1994)

The most distinguished of Nyanatiloka's many German pupils and his literary heir was born Siegmund Feniger, of Jewish parentage, in Hanau in 1901. He became a convinced Buddhist before his 20th year solely by reading books on Buddhism and later came under the influence of the works of Nyanatiloka. In 1936 he left Germany for Sri Lanka, where he joined Nyanatiloka's monastic community at Island Hermitage. During World War II Nyanaponika too was detained in internment camps along with his teacher and returned with him to Sri Lanka in 1946. In 1952 he followed his teacher to Forest Hermitage, where he was based until his death in 1994.

Nyanaponika's most significant achievement in his life as a monk was the founding, in 1958, of the Buddhist Publication Society in Kandy, which he served as longtime editor and president. Under his guidance the society became a leading publisher of Theravāda Buddhist literature in English with a global readership. Nyanaponika also translated Buddhist texts into German and English. His original work, *The Heart of Buddhist Meditation*, introduced Buddhist insight meditation to the West and inspired many to take up the practice.

After the War

In 1948 Osbert Moore and Harold Musson, two British war veterans, came to Sri Lanka seeking a deeper knowledge of Buddhism. The next year they took ordination at Island Hermitage, respectively, as Ñāṇamoli and Ñāṇavira. Ñāṇamoli quickly mastered Pāli and became an accomplished scholar and translator. In his 11 years in the *saṅgha*, he translated into lucid English some of the most difficult texts of Theravāda Buddhism, including the voluminous *Visuddhimagga*. In 1960, on one of his rare outings from Island Hermitage, he died of heart failure at the age of 55, a great loss to Buddhist scholarship.

In the 1960s and 1970s, partly because of fallout from the "flower power" generation and partly to work in the U.S. Peace Corps, a large influx of young Westerners came to Buddhist Asia in search of the "wisdom of the East." A surprising number joined the *saṅgha*. Most lacked the firm determination of their predecessors, so the turnover rate was high, but a few weathered the storms of doubt and distraction and either found a congenial vocation in Asia or returned to the West to transplant Buddhist monasticism there.

The most successful of the latter is the American-born Ajahn Sumedho (b. 1934, Robert Jackman), a disciple of the Thai master Ajahn Chah. Sumedho settled in England in 1977 and, under the auspices of the English Sangha Trust, established the Cittaviveka Monastery in Sussex and the Amaravati Monastery near London. His network includes branches in Switzerland, Italy, New Zealand, and the United States, with affiliates in Australia and Thailand. Its community also includes Western nuns. In 1991 Thanissaro Bhikkhu (Geoffrey DeGraff), an American trained for 14 years in Thailand, established the Metta Forest Monastery in southern California, which continues the Thai forest tradition on American soil. Several senior Asian monks resident in the United States have also attracted Western pupils into the *saṅgha*, most notably Henepola Gunaratana (of the Bhavana Society in West Virginia) and U Silananda (of the Dhammananda Vihara near San Francisco).

Theravāda monasticism is still in its infancy in the West, and its future is hard to predict. Given the Western trend toward a lay-oriented expression of Buddhism, Theravāda monasticism is unlikely to play the same central role in the West that it plays in

Asia. However, by providing anchorage in the oldest Buddhist tradition and by maintaining the discipline laid down by the Buddha himself, its contribution might well be an important one.

BHIKKHU BODHI

See also Buddhism: Western; Holy Men in Power (Hierocrats), Buddhist; Sri Lanka: History; Ten-Precept Mothers as Theravādin Nuns

Further Reading

Batchelor, Stephen, *The Awakening of the West: The Encounter of Buddhism and Western Culture*, Berkeley, California: Parallax Press, and London: Aquarian, 1994

Bodhi, Bhikkhu, editor, *Nyanaponika: A Farewell Tribute*, Kandy: Buddhist Publication Society, 1995

Harris, Elizabeth J., *Ananda Metteyya: The First British Emissary of Buddhism*, Kandy, Sri Lanka: Buddhist Publication Society, 1998

Nyanaponika Thera, "Nyanatiloka Mahāthera: His Life and Work," in *Nyanatiloka Centenary Volume*, edited by Nyanaponika Thera, Kandy, Sri Lanka: Buddhist Publication Society, 1978

Peiris, William, *The Western Contribution to Buddhism*, Delhi: Motilal Banarsidass, 1973

Thérèse of Lisieux, St. 1873–1897

French Carmelite nun and inventor of the "Little Way"

Marie-Françoise-Thérèse was born at Alençon, France, to Azélie (Zélie) Guérin and Louis Martin on 2 January 1873, the last of nine children and youngest of the four daughters who survived into adulthood. The five surviving daughters entered religious life. Pauline, Marie, Thérèse, and Céline, in that order, became nuns at the Discalced Carmelite monastery in Lisieux. After previous attempts Léonie became a nun in the Visitation convent at Caen. Zélie Martin died of breast cancer when Thérèse was four years old. This death and the loss of two of her elder sisters to religious life bred an overly sensitive child who received little formal education. After persistent efforts and special permission, Thérèse became a Carmelite nun at Lisieux in April 1888 at the age of 15. There she became known as Sister Thérèse of the Child Jesus and of the Holy Face.

Plaster effigy of Thérèse of Lisieux, Church of Santa Teresa del Gesù Bambino (Carmelite), Parma, Italy, 20th century.
Photo courtesy of the Editor

Life-sized replica of St. Thérèse's cell, located in the museum of the Basilique Ste-Thérèse, Lisieux, France.
Photo courtesy of the Editor

During her short life in the monastery, Thérèse's understanding of the spiritual life was honored when she was appointed in 1893 as a mentor to the novices. Thérèse developed an approach to holiness known as her "little way" or "the way of spiritual childhood," which she developed from her intuitive grasp of Scripture. This little way consisted in developing absolute trust in God as one performed the ordinary tasks of life with loving faithfulness. Besides the Scriptures Thérèse's main resource was John of the Cross (1542–1591), for whom she had a direct and unerring understanding. Toward the end of her life, Thérèse endured an absence of sensible faith. She died from tuberculosis on 30 September 1897 at age 24.

By September 1898, 2,000 copies of *L'Histoire d'une Âme* (*Story of a Soul*) were printed. This document was an edited version of the reflections on her life that Thérèse had written in three portions at the request of others in the monastery. This autobiography has achieved a phenomenal impact and won unbelievable success as a publication. By 1925, 400,000 copies of *Story of a Soul* had been published in French. Since that time this book has attained an immense readership in many languages. The English version is its publisher's ongoing best-seller. Thérèse's other writings include her poetry, plays, and correspondence.

In the face of intense devotion to this young woman, popularly known as the Little Flower, the Catholic Church, with uncommon haste, recognized her among its saints. Pope Pius XI (1922–1939) beatified her in 1923 and canonized her in 1925, and in 1997 Pope John Paul II declared her the third woman

Facade, Basilique Ste-Thérèse, Lisieux, France, 1929–1954.
Photo courtesy of the Editor

Doctor of the Church. In 1914 Pius X (1903–1914) called her "the greatest saint of modern times."

A tendency existed among devotees to trivialize her spirituality, but the 1990s has seen a return to a more authentic understanding of her teaching. She has exercised significant impact on many modern figures, such as Thomas Merton (1915–1968) and Dorothy Day (1897–1980). She was named the principal patroness of the missions along with St. Francis Xavier (1506–1552) and secondary patroness of France along with her heroine, Joan of Arc.

KEITH J. EGAN

See also Carmelites: Female; John of the Cross, St.; Merton, Thomas; Spirituality: Western Christian; Teresa of Avila, St.

Biography

Daughter of a watchmaker in Alençon, Thérèse entered the Carmelite monastery of Lisieux in 1888 at age 15. She served as assistant novice mistress from 1893. She died of tuberculosis in 1897. Her autobiography was circulated to all Carmelite houses, and its ensuing popularity led to her canonization in 1925. Known as the "Little Flower," she exemplifies the ideal of achieving sanctity through performing ordinary actions with love.

Major Work

L'Histoire d'une Âme, translated as *Autobiography of a Saint*, 1958; as *Story of a Soul*, 1976 (new edition, 1997)

Further Reading

Day, Dorothy, *Thérèse: A Life of Thérèse of Lisieux*, Springfield, Illinois: Templegate, 1987
Descouvement, Pierre, and Helmuth Nils Loose, *Thérèse and Lisieux*, translated by Salvatore Sciurba, Grand Rapids, Michigan: Eerdmans, and Dublin: Veritas, 1996
Gaucher, Guy, *The Story of a Life: St. Thérèse of Lisieux*, translated by Anne Marie Brennan, San Francisco: Harper and Row, 1987
Gaucher, Guy, *The Passion of St. Thérèse of Lisieux*, translated by Anne Marie Brennan, New York: Crossroad, 1990
Görres, Ida, *The Hidden Face: A Study of St. Thérèse of Lisieux*, London: Burns and Oates, and New York: Pantheon, 1959

Meester, Conrad de, editor, *Saint Thérèse of Lisieux: Her Life, Times, and Teaching*, Washington, D.C.: Institute of Carmelite Studies, 1997

Thích Nhát Hanh. *See* Nhát Hanh, Thích

Thomas Aquinas, St. 1224/25–1274

Dominican friar, philosopher, theologian, and founder of Thomism

Thomas Aquinas was born at Roccasecca in the kingdom of the Two Sicilies of a noble family. For a time he was an oblate at Monte Cassino before study in Naples. In Naples, Thomas became acquainted with the Dominicans, entering the Order of Preachers around 1244. His family, which had grand plans for the young scholar, had him held in custody for a time, but Thomas finally was permitted to join the priory at Naples. (Stories about this captivity and "escape" would proliferate in later legends.) The friars decided to send Thomas to the University of Paris, far from his kin, where he studied under Albertus Magnus (1245–1248), another of the great Dominican intellectuals. From 1248 to 1252 he was Albert's assistant and disciple at the Dominican convent in Cologne, then returned to teach at Paris from 1252 to 1256. By 1256 Thomas was regent master in Paris, commenting on the Bible. By 1259 Paris was seething with tensions between the friars and the secular masters over both doctrinal and institutional issues, especially the inability of the latter to control the academic activities of the former through the masters' corporation (*universitas*). Heated polemics by secular masters led Thomas to reply in his *Contra Impugnantes Dei Cultum et Religionem* (c. 1259), defending the mendicants' type of religious life.

By the end of 1259 Thomas had been sent back to Italy. By 1261 he was residing in Orvieto as conventual lector. The friars was consulted frequently even by the pope. One of his commitments in this period was the composition of an office for the feast of Corpus Christi, and the hymns of that office have remained widely known. From 1265 to 1268 Thomas resided in Rome, where he began writing his monumental *Summa Theologiae*, which employed Aristotelean categories of thought in the study of the mysteries of the faith. Then the friar was sent back to Paris for an unprecedented second term as regent master.

During the 1260s and 1270s Paris was a hotbed of controversy. Mendicants and seculars still disputed the validity of the friars' unusual combination of poverty and pastoral ministry (preaching and hearing confessions). Other strife focused on the use of Aristotle's works, especially in the study of theology. (This issue often is identified with the influence of the commentaries of the Arabic philosopher Averroes on young intellectuals.) This also involved tension between the Dominicans and the Franciscans, many of the latter becoming Thomas' fiercest foes. Despite involvement in these debates, Thomas continued lecturing on Scripture and engaging in the expected disputations. He also began composing commentaries on the works of Aristotle.

In 1272 Thomas returned to Naples, where he was to found a new center of studies. However, late during the following year, he seems to have undergone a period of withdrawal from his previous scholarly activities. Then, early in 1274, he was called away to participate in the Second Council of Lyons. On his way, while staying at the monastery of Fossanova, he was taken ill, dying on 7 March. An ugly confrontation ensued between monks and friars over his body because Thomas had come to be regarded as a potential canonized saint. However, canonization would not occur until 18 July 1323 during the pontificate of John XXII (1316–1334).

However, neither death nor canonization would end the debate surrounding Thomas, who came to be known as the Angelic Doctor. Controversies continued to be waged concerning the authenticity of his theological legacy. Franciscan doctors wrote *Correctors* to underline his mistakes, the Dominicans replying with corrections of the correctors. This might have spurred some of Thomas' disciples to complete such works, in-

Interior of Abbey Church at Fossanova, Lazio, Italy, late 12th century. Photo courtesy of Chris Schabel

Abbey Church (Cistercian) at Fossanova, near Priverno, Lazio, Italy, late 12th century. Thomas Aquinas died in the pilgrims' hostel (Foresteria) here, which was then converted into a chapel.
Photo courtesy of Chris Schabel

cluding the *Summa*, which their master had not finished before his death. They also began to agitate for official recognition of Thomas' teaching by the order. The general chapters soon began to issue decrees punishing Dominicans who treated his doctrines in an unseemly manner and to promote their defense against unjustified criticism. One important Dominican author, Durandus of St. Pourcain (c. 1275–1334), would be censured for dissenting from the Angelic Doctor's opinions.

Later friars would not dissent so boldly, but controversy still could erupt. Most notably, early in the 16th century, Cajetan (Thomas of Gaeta, 1469–1534), master general of the order and then a cardinal, would be strongly criticized by other Dominicans for departing from Thomas' meaning in the exposition of his works, especially in a monumental commentary on the *Summa*. This controversy also expressed ongoing tension between the Conventual wing of the order, to which Cajetan belonged, and the Observants, who wanted to see the mendicant life led with greater purity.

However, a different development deserves mention. Thomas' cult became more important during the 15th century. His feast was celebrated in Rome with greater pomp, and eminent preachers were engaged to grace the occasion. One, Lorenzo Valla (c. 1406–1457), managed to create controversy by describing the Angelic Doctor as playing the cymbals in the celestial orchestra. Thomas also became a subject for religious art, including depictions by Fra Angelico and Filippino Lippi. One motif shows him seated on his magisterial chair with a refuted Averroes weeping at his feet.

Thomas' *Summa* did not always hold a central place in medieval theological study; most often it was employed by other Dominicans, following the dictates of the order. However, its sections dealing with virtues and vices were widely used by friars engaged in preaching, teaching, and the hearing of confessions, and during the 16th century it was made the centerpiece of theological teaching by Francisco de Vitoria (1483–1546) and his school, many of them his fellow Dominicans, at the University of Salamanca. As such, it was widely quoted in controversies over Spain's role in the New World, including that on the humanity of the indigenous peoples and their natural rights. These teachings often were used to support the efforts of Dominicans laboring in the New World in support of their missionary labors. Pope Pius V named Thomas a doctor of the Church in 1567. Eventually, in

1880, Pope Leo XIII (1878–1903) would declare him the patron of all Catholic schools.

Thomas M. Izbicki

See also Albertus Magnus, St.; Dominicans; Humanism, Christian; Hymnographers; John of Damascus, St.; Liturgy: Western Christian; Theology, Western Christian: Dominican; Theology, Western Christian: Franciscan

Biography

Son of an aristocratic family near Aquino (Kingdom of Naples), Thomas was given as a child to the Benedictine Abbey of Monte Cassino but left for the University of Naples in 1239. Here he joined the Dominicans. His family confined him for two years (1244–1246) before he was allowed to be a friar. At Paris and at Cologne he studied with Albertus Magnus. While teaching at St. Jacques in Paris, he began the *Summa contra Gentiles*. From 1259 he served as *lector* in Dominican houses. As director of the Dominican center at Santa Sabina, Rome, he began the *Summa Theologiae*. From 1268 to 1272 he taught in Paris before returning to Naples. He died at the Cistercian Abbey of Fossanova on his way to the Second Council of Lyons.

Major Works

De Ente et Essentia
Summa contra Gentiles
Summa Theologiae

Further Reading

Colledge, E., "The Legend of St. Thomas Aquinas," in *St. Thomas Aquinas 1274–1974*, volume 1, Toronto: Pontifical Institute of Mediaeval Studies, 1974

Davis, Brian, *The Thought of Thomas Aquinas*, Oxford and New York: Clarendon Press, 1992

Douie, Decima, *The Conflict Between the Seculars and the Mendicants at the University of Paris in the Thirteenth Century*, London: Aquin Press, 1954

O'Malley, John W., "Some Renaissance Panegyrics of Aquinas," in *Rome and the Renaissance: Studies in Culture and Religion*, London: Variorum Reprints, 1981

O'Meara, Thomas F., *Thomas Aquinas Theologian*, Notre Dame, Indiana: University of Notre Dame Press, 1997

Tavuzzi, M., *Prierias: The Life and Works of Silvestro Mazzolini da Prierio, 1456–1527*, Durham, North Carolina: Duke University Press, 1997

Torrell, Jean-Paul, *Saint Thomas Aquinas*, volume 1: *The Person and His Work*, translated by Robert Royal, Washington, D.C.: Catholic University of America Press, 1996

Tugwell, Simon, translator, *Albert and Thomas: Selected Writings*, New York: Paulist Press, 1988

Tiantai/Tendai: China

The Tiantai (Tien-tai) school of Chinese Buddhism takes its name from Mount Tiantai (Heavenly Terrace), located in Zhejiang province in southeastern China. According to Tiantai accounts, such as the *Fozu tongji* (Record of the Lineage of the Buddhas and Patriarchs), Tiantai history is a patriarchal lineage starting with the Buddha. Such patriarchal lineages are common among eastern Asian schools of Buddhism and seek to establish a direct link between the Buddha and the traditions of later masters. In the case of Tiantai, that lineage starts with the Buddha, then progresses to China through the first Chinese patriarch, Huiwen.

Huiwen (fl. Mid–Sixth Century)

Beyond accounts claiming that Huiwen was a meditation master whose insight was "pure and refined," little is known about him. The real difficulty for Tiantai histories is the chronological gap between the Indian Buddhist Nagarjuna (Nāgārjuna) and Huiwen. Tiantai historians bridged that gap by claiming that Huiwen "saw Nagarjuna's mind" when he achieved enlightenment.

Huisi (515–577)

According to later hagiographies Huisi entered a Buddhist monastery at 14 and achieved enlightenment at 19. He soon developed a reputation as an expert in meditation, met Huiwen, and studied a form of meditation based on the "Triple Truth" of Nagarjuna. Huisi's ideas were controversial and generated severe criticism in some areas. One account says that he was twice poisoned by monks who were angry over his teachings. Despite these problems Huisi eventually made his way to southern China, where he met and taught a young Zhiyi.

Zhiyi (538–597)

Tiantai traces almost all its core teachings to Zhiyi, who appropriately is considered the actual founder of this school. He wrote very little himself but lectured extensively while his eventual successor, Guanding (561–632), recorded the lectures. Three of his works are central to the school's philosophy and practice. The *Miaofa lianhua jing xuanyi* (Profound Import of the Lotus Sūtra) is a survey of Buddhist teachings that focuses on the *Lotus Sūtra*. The *Miaofa lianhua jing wenzhu* (Textual Commentary on the Lotus Sūtra) establishes the fourfold exegetical method that would become a standard Tiantai device. Finally, the *Mohe zhiguan* (*The Great Calming and Contemplation*) establishes the ritual forms of meditation that became a standard part of Tiantai practice.

Guanding (561–632)

Guanding was Zhiyi's permanent attendant during the last 15 years of his life. He succeeded Zhiyi as abbot and, as mentioned previously, was responsible for recording his master's lectures. He also provided the tradition with two extensive commentaries on the *Mahāparinirvāna Sūtra* (Sūtra on the Buddhas Supreme Nirvāṇa) and secured imperial patronage for the monastery on Mount Tiantai.

Zhanran (711–782)

Zhanran studied Tiantai doctrines for 20 years as a layman before taking full ordination in 748. He earned the title Master of Commentaries by writing extensively on Zhiyi's works during a time when the tradition was in decline. Because only Zhanran's line left any substantial literary tradition and his students subsequently ended up at all major Tiantai regional centers, the later tradition claims that he "clarified the orthodox line" and traces most of its doctrines and practices back through him. Zhanran also influenced the transmission of Tiantai to Japan as the Japanese monk Saichō (767–822), founder of Japanese "Tendai" Buddhism, arrived in China shortly after Zhanran's revival and studied under two of his leading followers: Daosui and Xingman.

Zhili (960–1028)

Following the death of his mother when he was six, Zhili's father sent him to live at a local monastery. He was ordained at 14 and started studying Tiantai when he was 19. After mastering Tiantai doctrines he devoted his life to religious instruction and produced a prodigious number of accomplishments. He wrote numerous commentaries, was the impetus behind the construction of scores of monasteries and Buddhist images, oversaw the printing of Tiantai literature, and, perhaps most important, championed the "Home-Mountain" side of the "Home-Mountain/Off-Mountain" debates discussed here.

The dominant feature of this traditional account is its emphasis on a linear sequence of patriarchs and masters who pass down "orthodoxy." Certainly one key component of that "orthodoxy" shared by the different Tiantai movements was Zhiyi's notion of the "Threefold Truth." The Threefold Truth, a doctrine that Tiantai derived from Nagarjuna's famous *Mūlamadhyamaka-kārikā* (*Treatise on the Middle Way*), holds that all phenomena reflect a threefold nature. First, because all phenomena lack an independent nature, they are fundamentally "empty." Second, because they are empty of a self-nature, they interdependently come to exist "provisionally" as distinct phenomena. Third, the interdependency between the "emptiness" and the "provisional" existence of phenomena is called the "middle truth." On the basis of these notions, Tiantai thinkers advocated the mutual identity of the whole and its parts. Of course the movement's explanation of these and other ideas varied from master to master and from institution to institution, but the basic concepts were held in common.

In addition to shared doctrines, Tiantai institutions also shared certain structural similarities. By the tenth century the state was classifying monasteries as "teaching" or "meditation" monasteries. The distinction came to denote Chan (meditation) and Tiantai (teaching) institutions. Nevertheless actual differences between institutions were fairly small, and the two types were more alike than different.

Structurally the monasteries were generally laid out on a north-south axis with the central halls and abbot's quarters at the north end. The western half was devoted to quarters and practice halls for those monks who were actually engaged in day-to-day training. The eastern half contained offices and officer's quarters for those involved in the day-to-day operation of the facility. The one feature of Tiantai institutions that differed from Chan monasteries was a special area set aside for practice of the Tiantai "Four Samādhis" meditation.

Day-to-day activities within the monasteries varied between the two sections. Activities of the western half centered around dawn and evening discourses, debates on texts, and two periods of seated meditation. This routine was broken by bimonthly services led by the abbot and more intensive summer and fall training periods. The eastern half's day focused on the requirements of running and maintaining the facility. For example, cooking duties were handled by this section of the monasteries. Although generally engaged in different activities during the day, occupants of the two halves would come together regularly for special services.

Classification and status within the institutional hierarchy centered on the individual's relationship with the abbot. Postulants, day laborers, and laity in residence occupied the lowest rung of the hierarchical ladder. Among fully ordained monks seniority was determined by date of ordination, monastic rank, and, perhaps most important, the monk's relationship to the abbot. Those fully ordained monks who were in residence but not students of the abbot stood relatively lower (distinguished guests excepted of course) than those monks who were the abbot's students. Among the latter group some of the most promising would be designated the abbot's "Dharma heirs." Such a designation signified officially that the follower stood in the master's line of succession, having demonstrated mastery of doctrine, texts, teaching ability, and meditative insight. In general these characteristics were shared by all Tiantai institutions of the period.

Although the previously mentioned individuals, doctrines, and institutional structures undoubtedly played an important role in this school's history, it is now evident that the tradition was much more diffuse than the traditional accounts suggest. For example, it appears that the school itself did not consider the notion of a central doctrinal and patriarchal lineage a reality before the Song dynasty. Even the idea that Mount Tiantai is the geographic center of the school was not without its dissenters. Furthermore, it has been maintained by the guardians of the traditional patriarchal view (and by many modern interpreters utilizing that view) that this school considers the *Lotus Sūtra* the highest form of the Buddha's teachings. No doubt this stems in part from Zhiyi's commentaries on that text, but, perhaps more important, it stems also from the later tradition's acceptance and establishment of Zhiyi as center stream in the patriarchal tradition. Although it is difficult to determine precisely because the extant textual tradition is a product of that view, it is nevertheless clear that some Tiantai masters also emphasized ideas from sources such as tathagatagarbha (*tathāgatagarbha*), Huayan, vijnanavada (*vijñānavāda*), Chan, and Pure Land texts. Even the traditional view acknowledges this diversity with its accounts of the Home-Mountain/Off-Mountain debates.

The so-called Home-Mountain/Off-Mountain split of the Song dynasty was actually a series of debates precipitated by Zhanran's revival of Tiantai fortunes. In fact the designation "Home-Mountain/Off-Mountain" is normative and reflects the eventual outcome of those debates. The early phase of this long-running disagreement started with a dispute over which version of a treatise dealing with the *Suvarnaprabhāsa Sūtra* (Sūtra of the Golden Light) was the one composed by Zhiyi. Eventually the debate evolved to include a number of points concerning the ontological and soteriological status of ritual.

The "Off-Mountain" side was first championed by Ciguang Wuen (912–986) and upheld by his successors. They maintained that Zhiyi's and Zhanran's writings should be interpreted by employing works such as the *Shūrangama Sūtra* (Sūtra on Heroic Virtue), *Awakening of Faith*, and Huayan treatises by masters Chengguan (738–839) and Zongmi (780–841). This side of the debate tended to emphasize tathagatagarbha thought and Chan notions of "sudden" insight. They interpreted Zhiyi's notion of a "single moment of thought" as manifesting the undifferentiated Thusness that is the nature of all things. In Chan-like fashion, because they considered such a "thought-moment" a complete and authentic insight, achieving moment-to-moment awareness became the goal of practice. Once the aspirant achieved insight, his primary task was to incorporate that awareness into daily activities. Accordingly adherents of this view tended to place a greater emphasis on meditation while downgrading the significance of ritual. Some even argued not only that monastic ritual does not provide such insight but also that it is worthless without it.

In contrast the "Home-Mountain" view was championed by Zhili and maintained the effectiveness of monastic ritual itself as both a means to produce enlightenment and an activity that reflects the enlightened state of mind. Claiming that the "Off-Mountain" proponents either misunderstood or ignored Zhiyi's writings on ritual, this side justified its view with Tiantai notions of the mutual identity of the whole (undifferentiated Thusness) and its parts (individual phenomena). On this basis they claimed that ritual, as a particular expression of the Thusness, fully and completely expresses Thusness as well as any specific "thought-moment." This movement emphasized the Buddha nature inherent in all phenomena, and thus ritual, ritual texts, and other forms of practice beyond meditation were generally given greater attention in their monasteries.

These points illustrate a diversity within the Tiantai tradition that has often been overlooked or deemphasized in the traditional lineage histories. Recent studies suggest that rather than considering this a school with a clearly delineated line of masters associated with a relatively fixed and common body of texts, it is probably more accurate to think of it as a "movement" of like-minded although fairly loosely affiliated individuals who happen to share an interest in many, but by no means all, of the same texts, doctrines, institutional structures, and practices.

DIRCK VORENKAMP

See also Buddhist Schools/Traditions: China; China; Ennin; Saichō; Taiwan

Further Reading

Andō, Toshio, *Tendai shisō-shi*, Kyoto: Hōzōkan, 1959

Andō, Toshio, *Tendai-gaku: konpon shisō to sono tenkai*, Kyoto: Heirakuji Shoten, 1968

Chappell, David, *Tien-tai Buddhism: An Outline of the Fourfold Teachings*, Honolulu, Hawaii: Daiichi-Shobō, 1983

Donner, Neal, and Daniel B. Stevenson, *The Great Calming and Contemplation: A Study and Annotated Translation of the First Chapter of Chih-i's Mo-ho chih-kuan* (Classics in East Asian Buddhism), Honolulu: University of Hawaii Press, 1993

Stevenson, Daniel, "The Tien-tai Four Forms of Samadhi and Late North-South Dynasties, Sui, and Early Tang Buddhist Devotionalism," Ph.D. Diss., Columbia University, 1987

Swanson, Paul, *Foundations of Tien-tai Philosophy: The Flowering of the Two Truths Theory in Chinese Buddhism* (Nanzan Studies in Religion and Culture), Berkeley, California: Asian Humanities Press, 1989

Tiantai/Tendai: Japan

The term *Tendai* is the Japanese word for the Buddhist school known in Chinese as Tiantai/T'ien-t'ai (Heavenly Terrace), named after Mount Tiantai in southeastern China, where the school was centered. Development of the Tiantai tradition in China – and subsequently the Tendai tradition in Japan – was shaped mainly by the ideas of the Chinese monk Zhiyi (Chih-i, 531–597), who systematized Tiantai doctrine and practice on the basis of his understanding of the *Lotus Sūtra* (Sanskrit, *Saddharma-puṇḍarīka-sūtra*; Chinese, *Fa-hua Ching*; Japanese, *Hokekyō*). In the early ninth century this tradition was inaugurated in Japan by the Japanese monk Saichō (known posthumously as Dengyō Daishi, 767–822), who founded the Enryakuji temple on Mount Hiei as the center of Japanese Tendai.

Tendai thought – both Chinese and Japanese – is detailed and complex. Arguably the most distinctive aspect of Tendai doctrine is the organization of the entirety of Buddhist teachings under the framework of the *Lotus Sūtra* – specifically its pronouncement that the apparent multitude and diversity of the Buddha's teachings are but expedient devices (*hōben*) intended to lead sentient beings to the ultimate truth. This system ranks the myriad Buddhist sūtras into a hierarchy, asserting the superiority of the *Lotus Sūtra* above all other scriptures while acknowledging the expedient value of other Buddhist teachings.

This inclusive nature of Tendai thought is also expressed in the idea of universal salvation. All sentient beings contain the source of enlightenment, or the Buddha nature (*busshō*), as part of their nature. According to Tendai thought the distinction between enlightenment and delusion is a matter of perspective and not an ontological reality. By extension birth and death, good and bad, and other seemingly dualistic concepts are really parts of the same reality and not separate categories. In part Tendai monastic practice was meant to lead one to an experiential realization of these ideas.

As he attempted to adapt and apply Zhiyi's ideas to a Japanese context, Saichō set the early direction for Tendai. Although he based Japanese Tendai on Zhiyi's interpretations, Saichō's nine-month experience as a student in China ultimately led him to incorporate Pure Land, esoteric, and other Buddhist ideas into his version of Tendai. Thus, Japanese Tendai monastics meditated, recited the Buddha's name (*nembutsu*), performed esoteric rituals, and took vows to follow monastic regulations and to uphold monastic precepts.

Saichō gained official recognition for Tendai in 805, when permission was obtained for the first time for the Tendai school to receive two officially sanctioned ordinands from among the monastic quota system then in effect. Monks chosen through this system engaged in one of two courses of study: the Meditation Course (*shikangō*) focused study on exoteric practices, specifically the Tendai meditation practices described in Zhiyi's *Mohezhiguan* (*Mo-ho chih-kuan*; Japanese, *Maka shikan*, "Great Calming and Contemplation"), and the Esoteric Course (*shanagō*) centered on the study of the Daibirushanakyō (Sanskrit, *Mahāvairocana-sūtra*).

Saichō also endeavored to create an independent Mahāyāna ordination platform that would free Tendai from the control and scrutiny of the imperial court and the established Nara Buddhist schools. The contention surrounding the issue of the ordination platform was in part a struggle about control of who could be ordained but was also a debate over the substance of monastic practice and the question of its ultimate goal.

After Saichō internal debates arose within Tendai over the future direction of the school. Saichō's successor and third abbot of Enryakuji, the priest Ennin (known posthumously as Jikaku Daishi, 794–864), promoted esoteric practices within Tendai (Taimitsu, or Tendai esotericism), thereby gaining increased patronage from aristocrats who viewed esoteric rituals not as much as aids to their own personal enlightenment as powerful antidotes to such real-world problems as the loss of health, status, and prosperity. Ennin also contributed to the development of Pure Land ritual traditions within Tendai through the introduction of meditation practices focusing on the physical attributes of Amida Buddha. By the mid-Heian period (late tenth century), these practices moved Tendai away from esoteric practices and toward an exoteric practice that blended Pure Land eschatology with *Lotus Sūtra* ritual practice. In this view salvation was conceived in terms of birth in the Pure Land of Amida Buddha. The means to that goal involved the five practices of upholding, reading, chanting, preaching, and copying the *Lotus Sūtra*; the recitation of Amida Buddha's name (*nembutsu*); or some combination of these two ritual components. It was believed that the merit accrued by such ritual acts eventually gained one entrance into the Pure Land.

The promotion of Pure Land aspirations within the structure of Tendai thought and practice was especially influenced by the Tendai monk Genshin (942–1017), whose famous *Ōjōyōshū* (The Teachings Essential for Birth [in the Pure Land]) vividly depicts the vicissitudes of hell and the pleasures of paradise – that is, the Pure Land. Although Genshin saw himself as firmly within the Tendai school, his ideas were later adapted by Pure Land practitioners who founded separate schools on ideas, such as the *nembutsu* recitation practice, discussed in Genshin's famous treatise.

Tendai, despite its widely inclusive practices, was nevertheless subject to internal disputes over issues of doctrine and lineage that eventually led to sectarian splits, such as the one that occurred in the late tenth century over the issue of succession of Tendai abbots. Tendai also confronted a crisis in 1571, when Oda Nobunaga (1534–1582) destroyed most the Enryakuji complex on Mount Hiei out of fear of Tendai's religious power and political influence.

Tendai had a significant impact on the development of Japanese Buddhism through innovations in practice and doctrine. Tendai's eclectic blend of meditation traditions, Pure Land practices, esoteric rituals, and a concern for monastic regulations was at least partly responsible for producing monks who later went on to found some of Japanese Buddhism's most important movements, such as Zen, Pure Land, and Nichiren schools. Famous Kamakura Buddhists, such as Hōnen (1133–1212), Shinran (1173–1262), Nichiren (1222–1282), and Dōgen (1200–1253), all originally trained on Mount Hiei. Today Tendai remains a vital Japanese Buddhist monastic tradition, although it has been eclipsed in numbers of lay adherents by such schools as Pure Land and Nichiren.

William E. Deal

See also Asceticism: Buddhist Perspectives; Buddhist Schools/Traditions: Japan; Eisai (Yosai); Ennin; Esoteric Buddhism in China and Japan; Hermits: Buddhist; Japan: History; Marathon Monks; Mount Hiei, Japan; Mountain Monasteries, Buddhist; Nation-Building and Japanese Buddhism; Pure Land Buddhism; Saichō; Shinran

Further Reading

Groner, Paul, *Saichō: The Establishment of the Japanese Tendai School* (Berkeley Buddhist Studies Series, 7), Berkeley: Center for South and Southeast Asian Studies, University of California at Berkeley, Institute of Buddhist Studies, 1984

McMullin, Neil, *Buddhism and the State in Sixteenth-Century Japan*, Princeton, New Jersey: Princeton University Press, 1984

McMullin, Neil, "The Sanmon-Jimon Schism in the Tendai School of Buddhism: A Preliminary Analysis," *Journal of the International Association of Buddhist Studies* 7:1 (1984)

Petzold, Bruno, *Tendai Buddhism*, Yokohama: International Buddhist Exchange Center, 1979

Ui Hakuju, "A Study of Japanese Tendai Buddhism," in *Philosophical Studies of Japan*, volume 1, Tokyo: Japan Society for the Promotion of Science, 1959

Weinstein, Stanley, "The Beginnings of Esoteric Buddhism in Japan: The Neglected Tendai Tradition," *Journal of Asian Studies* 34:1 (1974)

Tibet: History

Bordered by the world's highest mountains and by vast wastelands, the Tibetan plateau was for centuries one of the most inaccessible places on earth. This remote region developed and preserved a rich monastic and cultural heritage that remained remarkably stable for centuries. Traditional chronicles assert that during Tibet's prehistory the buddha Avalokiteśvara gradually prepared its people for the introduction of Buddhism. The process reached its culmination during the reign of King Songsen Gampo (Srong btsan sgam po, c. 618–650), who embarked on a successful program of conquest, eventually creating a vast empire whose capital was located in the Yarlung Valley in central Tibet. As part of his military efforts, he married a number of wives in order to forge alliances or to cement friendly relations.

Two of these wives – a Chinese princess and a Nepalese princess – are portrayed in Tibetan histories as physical emanations of the buddhas Tārā and Bhṛkuṭī, while the king is said to have been an incarnation of Avalokiteśvara. This story, however, only developed centuries after the death of the king, and contemporary records give no indication that he was interested in Buddhism (nor do they even mention his Nepalese wife). In dynastic records Songsen Gampo is said to have been buried in the traditional manner for Tibetan kings, and there is no indication that any Buddhist ceremonies were performed at his death, nor is there any mention of Buddhism in contemporary literary sources.

It is not until the following century, during the reign of King Trisong Detsen (Khri srong lDe btsan, c. 740–798) that Buddhism is mentioned in official documents. The king reportedly worked to promote Buddhism in Tibet, and he is portrayed in later histories as an incarnation of the buddha Mañjuśrī and as the second of the three great "Religions Kings" (*chos rgyal*). These chronicles report that during his reign he invited the Indian scholar-monk Śāntirakṣita to Tibet, but that the latter's mission was derailed by human and demonic forces inimical to Buddhism and supportive of the indigenous religion of Bön (Bon). Before departing, Śāntirakṣita advised the king to invite Padmasambhava, a yogic adept with the power to quell Tibet's demons.

Upon his arrival in Tibet, countless demons massed against Padmasambhava, but he subdued them with magic spells and gestures, until they all offered up their "life force" to him. In exchange for sparing their lives, Padmasambhava bound them to oaths ensuring that they would henceforth protect the dharma (Buddhist doctrine and practice). Later histories recount that Trisong Detsen, Śāntirakṣita, and Padmasambhava then established the first monastery in Tibet at Samye (bSam yas), southeast of Lhasa on the banks of the Brahmaputra river. A group of Tibetans referred to as the "Seven Probationers" were ordained as Tibet's first monks.

During the reign of Relpachen (Ral pa can, r. 815–838, the third "religious king"), Buddhism experienced rapid growth as a result of royal patronage, but the king's largesse engendered fierce opposition, and he was assassinated. His elder brother Lang Darma (gLang dar ma) succeeded him as king, but he reversed the policies of royal patronage for Buddhism, which forced some monasteries to close and led many monks and nuns to return to lay life. Lang Darma's actions aroused opposition from Buddhists, and he was assassinated by a Buddhist monk in 842. In traditional histories the assassination is said to be a "liberation" rather than a murder, prompted by the monk's compassionate concern for the king, whose evil deeds were creating negative karma and dooming him to future suffering in hell.

Following Lang Darma's death, the Yarlung dynasty collapsed and Tibet entered an interregnum period during which no one had sufficient power to rule the country. The period of the three "Religious Kings" is known to Tibetans as the "first dissemination" (*snga dar*) of Buddhism, and, although the fortunes of Buddhism waned during the interregnum period, many of the achievements of the first dissemination remained intact, most notably translations of Buddhist texts, which had been sponsored by the kings.

During the interregnum, Buddhism went underground. Deprived of the funding necessary to maintain large-scale monastic establishments, Buddhism was still practiced in scattered communities consisting mostly of nonmonastic practitioners of tantric Buddhism (a Mahāyāna offshoot of Buddhism based on texts called tantras that employs symbolism and visualization, as well as sexual yogas). When Buddhism was later restored in the "second dissemination" (*phyi dar*), these tantrics were often at odds with members of the monastic establishment, many of whom viewed the tantrics' activities (which included ritual sexual activities, ingestion of substances forbidden in Buddhist monastic codes, and even animal sacrifices) with some suspicion.

The second dissemination was initiated by the kings of Guge (Gu ge) in western Tibet, who had remained Buddhists during the interregnum. These kings invited the Indian scholar-monk Atiśa (982–1054) to propagate the dharma in Tibet. Traditional sources report that he arrived in 1042, and his mission proved to be decisive in establishing the character of later Tibetan Buddhism. His teachings and practices combined elements of both tantric and non-tantric Indian Buddhism, two strands that had entered Tibet through different routes and had often been at odds with each other. Atiśa presented a vision of the path which combined both strands in an integrated system of practice, and this model later became predominant in Tibet. Together with his disciple Dromdön ('Brom ston, 1008–1064), Atiśa founded the Kadampa (bKa' gdams pa, "Bound by Instruction") order, which emphasized study of the entire range of Buddhist topics and strict adherence to the Buddhist monastic code (vinaya).

Although the Kadampa failed to attract a large number of followers, it exerted a major influence on the development of Tibetan Buddhist monasticism. During the 14th century it was absorbed into a new order, the Gelukpa (dGe lugs pa, "System of Virtue"), founded by Tsong Khapa (Tsong kha pa bLo bzangs grags pa, 1357–1419), who, like Atiśa, urged his followers to study intensively and to strictly adhere to the vinaya.

At the same time that Atiśa was establishing his school in central Tibet, a very different form of Buddhism was being introduced from Bihar and Bengal. The teachers of this strand of Buddhism were often charismatic and iconoclastic figures who rejected the rules and restrictions of Buddhist monasticism, claiming that their practices conferred magical powers on adepts and provided a path to buddhahood that was far more rapid and effective than the slower gradual path advocated by such mainstream figures as Atiśa. One of these teachers, the tantric master Marpa (Mar pa, 1012–1097), traveled to Bihar, where he received tantric empowerments and teachings from the Indian yogin Nāropa. Marpa's most famous disciple was the hermit Milarepa (Mi la ras pa, 1052–1135), whose biography highlights the tensions between the charismatic tantric tradition and the monastic establishment.

The tradition of Marpa and Milarepa was later named "Kagyupa" (bKa' rgyud pa, "Instructional Lineage"); unlike the scholastic orders (the Sakyapa and Gelukpa, discussed below), it placed particular emphasis on the direct mind-to-mind transmission of teachings from master to disciple. Interestingly, this tradition, which had been founded by lay tantric yogins, eventually developed a monastic tradition of its own, a process initiated by Milarepa's disciple Gampopa (sGam po pa, 1079–1153).

The 11th and 12th centuries, a time of great vitality in Tibetan Buddhism, saw the establishment of several branches of the Kagyupa and of another major order, the Sakyapa. Founded by Gönchok Gyelpo (dKon mchog rgyal po, 1034–1102) in 1073, the school took its name from the site of its first monastery at a place called Sakya ("Gray Earth") in the province of Tsang (gTsang). Gönchok Gyelpo belonged to the powerful Khön ('Khon) family, which still controls the order today. Succession generally passes between uncles and nephews of different branches of the family. The Sakyapas rose to prominence in the 13th century, when Sakya Pandita (Sa skya Pandita, 1182–1251) met the Mongol ruler Ködän Khan in 1244. His visit to the Mongol court was intended as a formal surrender of Tibet to the Mongols, but Tibetan and Mongol histories indicate that Ködän was so impressed by Sakya Pandita that he converted to Buddhism and later worked to propagate it among the Mongols. He declared that Tibet was to become a part of the Mongol empire, but that it would be administered by Sakya Pandita and his successors. When Mongol power waned in the following centuries, however, so did the fortunes of the Sakyapa.

The next order to emerge in Tibet was the Gelukpa, which, like the Sakyapa, rose to power as a result of Mongol backing. By the 14th century, succession by reincarnation had become widespread within Tibet; upon the death of a renowned teacher it was common that his (and less commonly her) successor would be identified as a child whose birth roughly coincided with the death of his predecessor. These reincarnate lamas were referred to as *tülku* (*sprul sku*, "emanation bodies"), and they were invested with the authority and property of their predecessors. The practice of recognizing *tülku*s began with the Gyelwa Karmapa (rGyalba kar ma pa) line of the Kagyupa order, but the Gelukpa reincarnation series named "Dalai Lamas" eventually rose to preeminence.

This rise occurred when the fifth Dalai Lama, Ngawang Losang Gyatso (Ngag dbang rgya mtsho, 1617–1682) was installed as ruler of Tibet by Gushri Khan, leader of the Qoshot branch of the Mongols. (The links between the Dalai Lamas and the Mongols were particularly strong because the fourth Dalai Lama had been the grandson of the Mongol ruler Altan Khan.) With Mongol backing, the fifth Dalai Lama became ruler over most of the Tibetan plateau. In the following centuries the Gelukpa order grew to become the largest and most powerful of the four Tibetan Buddhist lineages, and the Dalai Lamas acted as heads of state until the 14th Dalai Lama Tenzin Gyatso (bsTan 'dzin rgya mtsho, 1935–) fled to India in 1959.

While the Sakyapa, Kagyupa, and Gelukpa (collectively referred to as the "New Schools" because they favor the translations of Buddhist texts prepared during the second dissemination) were constantly involved in political maneuvering – and even occasional internecine warfare – the fourth order of Tibetan Buddhism, the Nyingmapa (rNying ma pa, "Old School," so called because it favors the translations of texts prepared during the first dissemination), remained largely aloof from such intrigues. Although the Nyingmapa established a number of large monasteries, much of its lineage was comprised of religious practitioners – both monastics and lay tantrics – in small hermitages and isolated monasteries.

After the orders had been formed and their major reincarnational lineages established, Tibetan Buddhism entered a period in which little changed, either doctrinally or institutionally. This period came to an end in the 1950s when a newly resurgent China invaded and annexed Tibet beginning in 1951. By 1959 China had gained control over the entire Tibetan plateau; soon after its power was consolidated China initiated a program of Marxist restructuring of Tibetan society, even though Chinese authorities initially promised that Tibet's religion and culture would not be affected by the occupation. This reached its peak during the Cultural Revolution in the 1960s and 1970s, when fanatical Red Guards marauded through Tibet, destroying religious structures and killing and torturing monks and nuns. Of the more than 7,000 monasteries and temples that existed in Tibet prior to the invasion, by the early 1970s only a handful remained.

Since the invasion and annexation of Tibet, Chinese policy toward religion has gone through periods of persecution and relative tolerance. At present organizations monitoring human rights report that religious freedom is virtually nonexistent in occupied Tibet and that the monasteries that are allowed to operate are under strict government control, with spies reporting "nonpatriotic" monks to the government. The religious lives of monks who remain in Tibet are also severely curtailed, and monks who have escaped report that they are not allowed to study their religion (although they are encouraged to perform ceremonies for the benefit of tourists). As a result the tradition is being reduced to a hollow shell: while the surface elements of the tradition are being preserved, the depth of understanding that came from decades of study in pre-invasion Tibet is being denied the monks, who must spend much of their time memorizing Marxist theory.

Some 80,000 Tibetans followed the Dalai Lama into exile in India. Many of these were monks and nuns who soon began rebuilding their monastic institutions. In Dharamsala, seat of the Tibetan exile government, several small monasteries and a nunnery have been built. In south India, Nepal, and in the Indian Himalayan states of Ladakh and Sikkim many others have been reconstructed, and the traditional curricula reinstated. The future of Tibetan Buddhist monasticism, however, is still uncertain. Young monks and nuns are entering the monastic life, the major *tülku*s are recognized and trained in the liturgical and scholastic traditions of their orders, and the support of the Tibetan community remains strong. But this is a small refugee community, and in its homeland Tibetan Buddhism is systematically being suppressed. The next few decades may very well prove decisive, but it is impossible at present to predict what the future of Tibetan monasticism will be.

C. John Powers

See also Critiques of Buddhist Monasticism: Indo-Tibetan; Dalai Lama (Tenzin Gyatso); Deities, Buddhist; Gampopa; Labdron, Machig; Ladakh, India; Meditation: Buddhist Perspectives; Missionaries: Buddhist; Nepal: History; Padmasambhava; Peace Movements, Buddhist; Persecution: Buddhist Perspectives; Sakya Pandita (Sapen); Tibetan Lineages; Vajrayāna Buddhism in Nepal

Further Reading

Cabezón, José Ignacio, *Buddhism and Language: A Study of Indo-Tibetan Scholasticism*, Albany: State University of New York Press, 1994

Dudjom Rinpoche, *The Nyingma School of Tibetan Buddhism: Its Fundamentals and History*, 2 vols., Boston: Wisdom Publications, 1991

Goldstein, Melvyn, *A History of Modern Tibet, 1913–1951: The Demise of the Lamaist State*, Berkeley: University of California Press, 1989

Gyaltsen, Khenpo Könchog, *The Great Kagyu Masters: The Golden Lineage Treasury*, Ithaca, New York: Snow Lion, 1990

Haarh, Erik, *The Yar-lun Dynasty*, Copenhagen: Gad, 1969

Havnevik, Hanna, *Tibetan Buddhist Nuns: History, Cultural Norms, and Social Reality*, Oslo: Norwegian University Press, 1989

Karmay, Samten, *The Great Perfection (rDzogs Chen): A Philosophical and Meditative Teaching of Tibetan Buddhism*, Leiden and New York: E.J. Brill, 1988

Lopez, Donald S., editor, *Religions of Tibet in Practice*, Princeton, New Jersey: Princeton University Press, 1997

Powers, John, *Introduction to Tibetan Buddhism*, Ithaca, New York: Snow Lion, 1995

Willis, Janice D., *Enlightened Beings: Life Stories from the Ganden Oral Tradition*, Boston: Wisdom Publications, 1995

Tibet: Sites

Although it developed in a sparsely populated region, Tibetan Buddhism has influenced the cultures of a vast area that includes: Tibet's central provinces Ü (dBu) and Tsang (gTsang); Kham (Khams) and Amdo (A mdo) in the east; the western Tibetan plateau; much of present-day Mongolia; large portions of Central Asia; smaller areas of present-day Russia and parts of several republics of the former Soviet Union; much of the Himalayan region of northern India, including Ladakh (La dwags), Zanskar (Zangs dkar), and Sikkim, and the neighboring countries of Nepal and Bhutan. Throughout this region, Tibetan Buddhist religious sites abound. Prior to the Chinese invasion and annexation of Tibet in the 1950s, it is estimated that there were more than 7,000 monasteries, temples, hermitages, and other religious structures in Tibet alone. All but a handful were destroyed by Chinese forces during the 1960s and 1970s, but in recent decades many of these have been rebuilt. In addition, there are thousands of monastic institutions in other parts of the Tibetan cultural area, as well as a number of Tibetan Buddhist monasteries and centers that have been established in Europe and North America.

Many of the largest and most historically important monastic sites and temples are located in the region of Lhasa, the capital of Tibet and the holiest city of Tibetan Buddhism. Among these, the Potala, widely regarded as the most impressive example of traditional Tibetan architecture, is probably the best known. The Potala, which sits on a hill overlooking the city, was built as the residence of the Dalai Lamas, but it also served as the seat of the Tibetan government and housed Namgyal (rNam rgyal), the personal monastery of the Dalai Lamas. Plans for the palace were drafted in 1645 on the orders of the fifth Dalai Lama, Ngawang Losang Gyatso (Ngag dbang blo bzang rgya mtsho, 1617–1682), who died before it was completed. Fearing that an announcement of the Dalai Lama's death might halt construction, his regent managed to conceal the death for 12 years by telling the Tibetan government that the Dalai Lama was in a long retreat and could not be disturbed.

Within Lhasa there are a number of other important monastic sites, including two nunneries, Tsamkhung (mTshams gur) and Druptop Lhakhang (Grub thob lha khang). Tsamkhung, the larger of the two, is a Gelukpa (dGe lugs pa) nunnery that was originally built in the 15th century and greatly expanded by Pabongkha Rinpoche (Pha bong kha Rin po che, 1878–1941). Although it was looted during the Cultural Revolution, Tsamkhung has been mostly restored and today houses approximately 80 nuns.

Just outside Lhasa are Ganden (dGa' ldan), Drebung ('Bras spungs), and Sera (Se ra), the three major monasteries of the Gelukpa order. Together these monastic universities housed more than 20,000 residents prior to the Chinese invasion, attracting monks from all over the Tibetan cultural area. Today, these monastic universities have only a few hundred monks each, yet they remain impressive examples of traditional Tibetan architecture. Ganden was heavily damaged by Chinese mortar attacks during the invasion in the 1950s, but today much of it has been rebuilt. Monks who have escaped from Tibet report that, although monasteries are allowed to remain open, the religious lives of residents are severely curtailed; in particular, residents are prevented from undertaking the rigorous study that, prior to the Chinese invasion, was the cornerstone of Tibetan monastic life, particularly in the Gelukpa monasteries. Ganden, Drebung, and Sera all have been rebuilt in southern India, where they have again become flourishing centers of monastic learning, although with far fewer monks in residence than during their pre-invasion heyday. (It is estimated that approximately 15 percent of the adult male population of Tibet were monks prior to the 1950s, but young Tibetan refugees are entering monasteries in far smaller numbers today).

Tibet's first monastery, Samye (bSam yas), is located to the southeast of Lhasa. Built in the eighth century by king Trisong Detsen (Khri srong lDe btsan, c. 740–798), the central buildings and surrounding monuments are laid out in a maṇḍala pattern that reflects traditional Buddhist cosmology. When Buddhism became the state religion, Samye was designated as the chapel of the ruling kings. Between the eighth and tenth centuries Samye played a major role in the establishment of Buddhism in Tibet, but it fell into disrepair after the fall of the dynasty. In the 15th century it was taken over by the hierarchs of the Sakyapa (Sa skya pa) order. The complex has suffered from a number of disasters such as fires, and was mostly destroyed by Chinese Red Guards in the 1960s (despite being declared a protected cultural site by the Chinese government), during which time statues and other artwork were looted and most of the important stūpas and several buildings were destroyed, along with the roof of the main chapel. Some old buildings are still standing today, but the whole complex lies in a general state of disrepair.

In the Drachi (Grwa phyi) Valley south of Lhasa there are a number of historically important monastic sites, including the Sakyapa monastery Tsongdu Tsokpa (Tshong 'dus tshogs pa) and Mindroling (sMin grol gling), the latter one of the two largest monasteries of the Nyingmapa (rNying ma pa) order (the other is the nearby Dorje Drak [rDo rje grags] monastery). The present site of Mindroling was constructed primarily under the guidance of Terdak Lingpa (gTer bdag gling pa, 1646–1714), who greatly expanded on an early chapel built in the tenth century. Although it was looted during the Cultural Revolution and several buildings were destroyed, parts of the original monastery remain today, and others have been rebuilt.

Tsurpu (mTshur phu), the main seat of the Karma Kagyupa (Karma bKa' rgyud pa) order lies in the upper Tölung (sTod lung) Valley northwest of Lhasa. During the 15th and 16th centuries this order became the dominant power in Tibet owing to patronage from the Ming and Yüan rulers of China. With the aid of the king of Tsang, the Karma Kagyupa hierarchs were the main obstacle in the ascension of the Dalai Lamas to supreme power, and, when the fifth Dalai Lama gained control of the country with Mongol help in the 17th century, the Karma Kagyupa order suffered a decline in fortunes. The monastery was badly damaged during the 1960s but much of it has been rebuilt, and today it houses the 17th Karmapa, one of the most important reincarnate lamas (*sprul sku*) of Tibetan Buddhism.

During the time when the Sakyapa hierarchs ruled Tibet (late 13th and 14th centuries), Sakya Monastery, the main seat of the order, became a huge monastic complex. At one time it contained more than 40 chapels and monastic buildings in two areas, one on each side of the Trum River. Prior to the Cultural Revolution, Sakya Monastery was one of Tibet's largest monastic institutions, surpassed only by Ganden, Drebung, and Sera. At present, most of the complex on the northern bank of the river lies in ruins, but a number of impressive buildings remain in the southern complex. Today the headquarters of the Sakya order is the rebuilt Sakya Monastery in Dehradun, India.

To the east of Sakya lies the city of Shigatse (gZhis dkar rtse), in which is located Tashilhünpo (bKra shis lhun po) Monastery, seat of the Panchen Lamas. Founded in 1447 by Tsong Khapa's nephew and disciple Gendün Drup (dGe 'dun grub, 1391–1474, later designated the first Dalai Lama), it was greatly expanded by the fourth Panchen Lama, Losang Chökyi Gyeltsen (bLo bzang chos kyi rgyal mtshan, 1570–1662). In 1642 Losang Chökyi Gyeltsen was given the title of "Panchen" (Great Scholar) by the fifth Dalai Lama, and his three previous reincarnations were retrospectively given the same title. The Panchen Lamas are believed by Tibetan Buddhists to be physical emanations of the buddha Amitābha, and several have been among the most influential scholars of the Gelukpa order.

The tenth Panchen Lama was the most senior Buddhist leader to remain in Tibet following the Chinese invasion, and, because he cooperated with the Chinese, Tashilhünpo was one of the few monastic sites that avoided destruction during the Cultural Revolution. The Panchen Lama eventually broke with the Chinese government, however, and publicly criticized its social and religious policies. He subsequently spent a number of years in prison or under house arrest.

Tashilhünpo is currently the center of a controversy concerning the recognition of the 11th Panchen Lama. In 1996 the Dalai Lama designated a boy named Gendün Chökyi Nyima (dGe 'dun chos kyi nyi ma) as the 11th Panchen Lama, but non-Buddhist Chinese officials declared his choice "illegal and invalid" and installed their own candidate, who is the son of Chinese Communist Party cadres. The abbot of Tashilhünpo was sentenced to a long prison term for passing information concerning the search for the reincarnation to the Dalai Lama, and more than 100 monks from the monastery were either imprisoned or expelled. The monastery effectively is run by the Chinese government, and monks are closely watched by soldiers stationed within the complex.

For those wishing to see traditional Tibetan monastic lifestyles, architecture, and art, the best place to do so is the Indian Himalayan region, as well as Bhutan and Tibetan-speaking areas of Nepal. These areas were spared the depredations of the Chinese invasion that decimated the monasteries and monastics in Tibet, and they preserve an ancient monastic culture as well as some impressive religious art. The Tibetan plateau is mostly arid and barren, with little vegetation, but inside Buddhist monasteries one is confronted by a profusion of color and symbolism. The doorways to monasteries are often extremely ornate, and the inside walls are commonly covered with murals. Richly colored brocades and painted scrolls called *thangka*s hang from the ceilings, and even beams and benches are often decorated with religious designs.

Some of the most impressive monasteries may be found in Ladakh and Zanskar. The oldest monastery in this region is Lamayuru (g.Yung drung dgon pa), about a three-hour ride from the capital of Leh. Local legend has it that the site was

A classic Tibetan monastery just outside Leh, Ladakh.
Photo courtesy of John Powers

selected by Nāropa (c. 956–1040), who magically drained a lake to make way for its construction. Situated on a steep hill and surrounded by high peaks, Lamayuru is a Drukpa Kagyupa ('Brug pa bka' rgyud pa) monastery housing several hundred monks. Also of note is the nearby Alchi (A lci) Monastery, which is best known for its ornate wall murals.

During the tourist season (May–September), a steady stream of visitors arrives at Ladakh's monasteries to see the artwork and to view the lives of the monks. Most monasteries charge a fee for entry; the money is used to support monks, restore walls and artwork, establish new buildings, buy books, and so on. Other monasteries of note in Ladakh and Zanskar include Phyang (Phyi dbang), a small Kagyupa monastery near Leh; Stok (Stog), just outside of Leh, which contains some excellent religious art; Hemis (He mis), a Drukpa Kagyupa monastery; Rizong (Ri rdzong), a Gelukpa monastery that boasts a commanding view of the Brahmaputra river and a spectacular statue of Maitreya (the future buddha); and Likir (Li kyir), a small and isolated Gelukpa monastery that is mainly devoted to meditation.

The most famous monastery in Bhutan is Daktsang, a hermitage perched on the side of a cliff. Daktsang was gutted by fire in 1998 but is currently being rebuilt. The most impressive monastery in the neighboring state of Sikkim is Rumtek (Rum btegs), built according to the instructions of the 16th Gyelwa Karmapa, Rangjung Rigpe Dorje (rGyalba Karma pa Rang 'byung rigs pa'i rdo rje, 1924–1981).

After the flight of the Dalai Lama and more than 80,000 other Tibetans to India in 1959, the Indian government allowed many of the refugees to settle in the former British hill station of Dharamsala in the northern state of Himachal Pradesh. Several small monasteries have been built in and around Dharamsala, as well as a large nunnery named Gedün Chöling (dGe ldan chos gling). Situated below Gedün Chöling is Nechung Monastery, the seat of the state oracle, who is consulted about important religious and secular matters. The medium is a monk who goes into a trance, during which he utters often cryptic messages in a high-pitched voice.

Dharamsala is also the home of the Dalai Lama and site of his main residence, next to which is Namgyal Monastery, formerly housed in the Potala. Nearby is the School of Buddhist Dialectics (mTshan nyid slob grwa), a monastic educational center that specializes in the traditional Gelukpa scholastic curriculum. Other Tibetan Buddhist monasteries and training centers are scattered throughout India, and a number have also been built in Nepal. The southern Indian state of Karnataka is home to several important monastic complexes, including the major Gelukpa monasteries. Tibetans in exile have demonstrated remarkable resilience in reestablishing their traditional monastic culture, despite the difficulties involved in escaping to a new country and beginning with only those items they could carry with them. While Tibetan monasticism has managed to rebuild its major centers and train new generations of monks, Buddhism in Tibet is being eradicated by Chinese authorities, who see it as antithetical to their goal of remaking Tibet into a patriotic part of the "motherland." For now, however, Tibetan Buddhism still flourishes in exile, thanks to the Tibetan exile community's commitment to keeping the tradition alive.

Monasteries to Visit

The most accessible traditional Tibetan Buddhist monasteries are all located in the Indian Himalayas and Nepal, including a number of old and well-preserved sites in Ladakh: Alchi, Lamayuru, Stog, Hemis, Phyang, Rizong, and Likir. All are accessible by road and located within a few hours of Leh. Rumtek in Sikkim is another major monastic complex in the Himalayan region, and a number of important monasteries have been built in the southern Indian state of Karnataka. A number of small monasteries may be visited in Dharamsala, including Nechung (seat of the state oracle) and the Gedün Chöling nunnery. In Tibet many important monastic sites are located in restricted areas forbidden to tourists (although designations change frequently and capriciously). The monastic complexes in the Lhasa area (such as the Potala, Ganden, Drebung, Sera, and Tsamkhung) are generally accessible to foreigners.

C. John Powers

See also Critiques of Buddhist Monasticism: Indo-Tibetan; Dalai Lama (Tenzin Gyatso); Deities, Buddhist; Gampopa; Labdron, Machig; Ladakh, India; Meditation: Buddhist Perspectives; Missionaries: Buddhist; Nepal: History; Padmasambhava; Peace Movements, Buddhist; Persecution: Buddhist Perspectives; Sakya Pandita (Sapen); Tibetan Lineages; Vajrayāna Buddhism in Nepal

Further Reading

Batchelor, Stephen, *The Tibet Guide*, London: Wisdom Publications, 1987

Chan, Victor, *Tibet Handbook: A Pilgrimage Guide*, Chico, California: Moon Publications, 1994

Chogay Trichen Rinpoche (Thubten Legshay Gyatsho), *Gateway to the Temple: Manual of Tibetan Monastic Customs, Art, Building, and Celebrations*, translated by David Paul Jackson, Kathmandu: Ratna Pustak Bhandar, 1979

Dowman, Keith, *The Power-Places of Central Tibet: The Pilgrim's Guide*, London: Routledge, 1988

Francke, A.H., *Antiquities of Indian Tibet*, Part 2: *The Chronicles of Ladakh and Minor Chronicles*, Calcutta: Archeological Survey of India, 1926; reprint, New Delhi: S. Chand and Co., 1972

Grimshaw, Anna, *Servants of the Buddha: Winter in a Himalayan Convent*, London: Open Letters, 1992

Gyatso, Tenzin (Dalai Lama XIV), *The World of Tibetan Buddhism: An Overview of Its Philosophy and Practice*, Boston: Wisdom Publications, 1995

Petech, Luciano, editor, *Guide to the Holy Places of Central Tibet*, Rome: Istituto italiano per il medio ed estremo oriente, 1958

Tucci, Giuseppe, *The Temples of Western Tibet and Their Artistic Symbolism*, New Delhi: Aditya Prakashan, 1989

von Fürer-Haimendorf, Christoph, *The Renaissance of Tibetan Civilization*, Oracle, Arizona: Synergetic Press, 1990

Tibetan Lineages: Gelukpa

Among the various Buddhist schools that developed in Tibet, the Gelukpa (dGe-lugs-pa), or "Way of Virtue" Order – founded by the scholar-monk Je Tsongkhapa (rJe Tsong-kha-pa, 1357–1419) in 1409 – is most closely associated with a strongly "clerical" approach to Buddhism, emphasizing rigorous monasticism and a highly structured scholastic and philosophical training over the more "shamanic" forms of Buddhism found within other schools, such as the "unreformed" Nyingmapa (see Samuel, 1993). Indeed many Western commentators have seen Tsongkhapa as a kind of Luther figure, railing against the prevailing overdependence on Tantrism and especially sexual yoga in the Buddhist traditions of 15th-century Tibet.

In reality, although the Gelukpa certainly regard celibacy as an essential criterion for ecclesiastical authority, and Tsongkhapa himself saw the practice of certain ritual traditions (e.g. actual rather than symbolic sexual yoga) as easily misunderstood and thus inappropriate to the vast majority of Mahāyāna Buddhists, the founding of the Gelukpa Order in no way represented a rejection of tantra per se. Rather Tsongkhapa sought a systematic synthesis of the tantric and sutric forms of Mahāyāna Buddhism that Tibet had inherited from its Indian predecessors, practiced within the context of the celibate monasticism followed by the Gelukpa's forerunners, the Kadampa (bKa'-dams-pa) Order.

Studying under teachers from both Sakya and Kagyud traditions of Tibetan Buddhism, Tsongkhapa received a vast range of teachings and tantric empowerments, which traditions he sought to rejuvenate and systematize, filtering out those elements that were not either (1) original sūtras and tantras spoken by the Buddha, (2) the treatises (*śāstras*) of the Indian masters, or (3) the works of early Tibetan translators such as Marpa and Atiśa. This led to a range of key treatises on Buddhist understanding and method, especially Tsongkhapa's massive *Lam-rim Chen-mo* and *Ngag-rim Chen-mo* texts, whose core teachings cover, respectively, the non-tantric preliminary disciplines (e.g., meditations on renunciation, compassion, and emptiness, to be mastered in advance of tantric training) and the correct performance of tantric rites and meditations.

Principles of Gelukpa Lineage

This attempt to fix the canonicity of Buddhist traditions implied a relatively exclusive concentration on the New or Sarmapa (gSar-ma-pa) tantric lineages that arrived during the second dissemination of Buddhism to Tibet in the 11th century and a rejection of the older, first-dissemination tantras favored by the Nyingmapa (Mayer, 1996) as well as the principle of subsequent "revealed" truths, such as the so-called hidden treasure (gTer-ma) traditions. It also sought to unify the two dominant views of the ultimate origins of Buddhist teachings – those that saw the Mahāyāna sūtras as originating principally in Śākyamuni's discourses on the Vulture Peak and those that saw the tantras as being promulgated by Śākyamuni's "shamanic" alter ego, the tantric Buddha Vajradhara – by seeing them as historically unified within a single biography. Thus, rather than rejecting the shamanic tendencies within existing Tibetan Buddhism in favor of the clerical, the Gelukpa united these two within a single view and program of religious disciplines.

Amid this process key elements of Vajrayāna Buddhism were maintained, especially guru devotion and the cognate notion that unbroken lineages of teachings and teachers mark the basis of religious legitimacy. Within Tibetan culture, lineage (brgyud) has three dimensions: genealogical inheritance (e.g., between father and son), teaching lineage (between teacher and student), and lineages of regularly reincarnating officeholders, an institution first introduced in the 12th century within the Kagyud Karmapa school. In the case of teaching lineages, a distinction is drawn between simple instruction and actual lineage: as with many religious systems, a teacher may *instruct* many thousands of students in a particular tradition but will actually *pass the lineage* to only one or two. In many such cases teaching lineages followed the line of genealogical inheritance either directly or, in the case of celibate orders such as the Gelukpa, indirectly, from brother to brother or from uncle to nephew. However, as the Gelukpa order expanded, such intimate ties gave way to more bureaucratically generated ones; nonetheless, whether celibate or not, and no matter how such relations began, religious (and most especially tantric) tutelage maintained a strong metaphorical quality of kinship.

Moreover spiritual tutelage was organized around three kinds of "transmission": *lung* (lung), or textual transmission through recitation by the teacher; *tr'id* (khrid), or formal teaching and explanation; and *wang* (dbang), or tantric empowerment. In the structure of religious training within the Gelukpa, *lung* is seen very much as the beginning of the process, often being regarded as a formal "permission" for students to begin learning to recite particular texts for themselves. However, *understanding* a text or recitation comes through *tr'id*, the commentarial analysis of the text by the teacher. Finally, *wang* is tantric in nature, ritually conferring the "seeds" of the mental, verbal, and physical qualities of a particular tutelary Buddha (yi-dam) on a student, acting as the ritual basis for the subsequent embodiment of such qualities in the future.

In each case real spiritual and scholastic understanding (sgrub-pa) is seen as replicating the realizations of the spiritual guide, or *lama* (bla-ma): tantric realizations especially are seen as impossible without the blessings of the *lama*, who – being the source of the Buddhist doctrine – should be thought of by his disciples as a Buddha and specifically as the Buddha Vajradhara (rdo-rje chang), especially within the context of tantric ritual. Within the Gelukpa Order such guru devotion is most commonly manifested in the recitation of the First Panchen Lama's *Offerings to the Spiritual Guide* (bLa-ma mChod-pa) prayer, in which the student's "root guru" (rTsa-ba'i bLa-ma, a student's main tantric guru) is visualized as the Buddha Vajradhara, manifest in the form of Tsongkhapa.

However, guru devotion and teaching lineage are not altogether the same thing. Unlike the practice of early Tibetan virtuosi, such as Milarepa and Marpa, the religious life of Gelukpa monks is not wholly dominated by a single guru from whom all is learned. Although an emphasis usually is placed on one particular teacher as representing a student's root guru, the monastic

The late KhenSur Yeshe Thubten, former abbot of Loseling, a college of Drebung monastery. KhenSur Yeshe Thubten was one of the great Gelukpa masters of the 20th century.
Photo courtesy of John Powers

environment of the Gelukpa meant that monks received training from a variety of teachers specializing in different traditions. Moreover, although many teaching traditions begin as "whispered" lineages that are passed orally from lineage holder to lineage holder, they are often written and systematized at a certain point, thus becoming more widely available.

Although the Gelukpa Order (especially in the centuries following their political ascendancy under the Fifth Dalai Lama [1618–1682]) was relatively bureaucratic in structure, it maintained a considerable internal diversity of religious traditions. Particular monastic communities tended to follow the spiritual emphases of their incumbent incarnates, which, although maintaining a core "curriculum," often concentrated on divergent elements of the Gelukpa synthesis, such as debating skills, monastic discipline, or certain corpuses of tantric ritual. Similarly, although some Gelukpa lamas, such as the late-18th-century writer Sumpa Khenpo (Sum-pa mKhan-po), extolled the virtues of an orthodox and exclusive core of Gelukpa tradition, others, such as the Fifth Dalai Lama, sought teachings from a wide range of non-Gelukpa sources. This diversity makes it impossible to give a comprehensive picture of Gelukpa lineages as a whole; however, it is possible to sketch out some of their more prominent features.

Foundation Lineages

Tsongkhapa's particular canonical and philosophical emphases led to the acknowledgment of several prior lineages of Buddhist teaching and practice to which subsequent generations of Gelukpa see themselves as heirs (for these, see Pabonkha Rinpoche, 1991, 1993). Initially the two primary lineages of the Mahāyāna derived from Śākyamuni Buddha: the Lineage of Profound View, which emphasized teachings on the philosophy of emptiness, and passed to the bodhisattva Mañjuśrī and then to Nagarjuna, Chandrakirti, and Vidyakokila the elder; and the Lineage of Extensive Deeds, which emphasized compassion and meritorious acts, and passed from the bodhisattva Maitreya to Asaṅga, Vasubandhu, and Vimuktisena and on to Ratnasena and Suvarnadvipa. These two lineages were unified with Atiśa (982–1054), the founder of the Kadampa Order in Tibet, who passed them on to Dromtonpa (brom-ston-pa, 1005–1064).

Within the Kadampa Order these were in turn split into three lineages, one to each of Dromtonpa's disciples: the Lam-Rim lineage, from Gampopa and Neuzurpa to Namkha Gyaltsen; the Instruction lineage, from Chen Ngawa and Tsultrimbar and on again to Namkha Gyaltsen; and the Classical lineage, from Potowa (1031–1106) to Sharawa (1070–1141) and on to Choekyab Zangpo. Choekyab Zangpo and Namkha Gyaltsen in turn passed these lineages on to Tsongkhapa, who unified them. Moreover from Atiśa, Drom-ton-pa, and Potowa passed the whispered lineage of the "Mind Training" (bLo-sbyong) teachings on *bodhicitta*, the compassionate mind of enlightenment, which were initially committed to text as the *Seven Point Mind Training* by Geshe Chekawa (1101–1175) and later systematized in *The Rays of the Sun* by Tsongkhapa's own disciple, Horton Namkaphel. In the Consecrated lineage of the specific tantras, Tsongkhapa also recognized those lineages that surrounded Marpa the Translator (Mar-pa, 1012–1096), including Vajradhara, Tilopa, Nāropa, Ḍombhipa, and Atiśa, although wide divergences exist within the Order as to this "composite" lineage's precise constituents and order.

As with all orders of Tibetan Buddhism, the Gelukpa tantric lineages are highly diverse, containing much that is standard to all forms of Tibetan Buddhism (such as the worship of Avalokiteśvara and Tārā). They mainly follow Tsongkhapa's own spiritual concentrations and systematizations. In terms of tantric systems, the Gelukpas largely adhere to Bu-ston's 14th-century systematization of New Tantras into the four classes of *kriya* (bya-ba, "action tantra"), *carya* (sbyod-ba, "performance"), *yoga* (rNal-'byor, "yoga"), and finally the complex and sophisticated *anuttarayoga* (rNal-'byor-bLa-na-med-pa, "highest yoga") tantras. These last *anuttarayoga* disciplines are further divided into "generation-stage" (sKyed-rim) and "completion-stage" (rDzogs-rim) yogas. Of the *anuttarayoga* generation-stage tantras, most Gelukpa monasteries concentrate on the so-called *Sangde Jigsum* (gSang-bde 'Jigs gSum, the three "Fearsome Systems of Secret Bliss"), that is, those tantras centered on the Buddha *Vajrabhairava* (rDo-rje-'Jigs-byet, often seen as preeminent), *Guhyasamaja* (gSang-ba'i Dus-pa), and *Cakrasamvara* (bDe-mChog). The *Kalacakra* ('Dus-'khor) and *Hevajra* (Kye-ba rDo-rje) tantric lineages are also of crucial importance to the Gelukpas. Of the completion-stage tantras, perhaps the best known is the lineage founded on Tsongkhapa's version of the Six Yogas of Nāropa (Naro'i Chos-Drug; see Mullin, 1996).

Principal Teaching Lineages

The synthesizing of these various traditions into programs of religious teachings produced at the core of the Gelukpa several dominant teaching lineages. Most substantial among these was the

Gyuto monks performing in 1998 at the Royal Albert Hall, Canberra, Australia.
Photo courtesy of John Powers

Mahāmudrā oral tradition – a combined training in the *Sangde Jigsum* and the Six Yogas, taught at Ganden, the founding monastery of the Gelukpa. The Ganden oral tradition (dGa'-ldan bKa'-rgyud) derived directly from Tsongkhapa's work, although its lineage precedes him into a mythic past, passing through the Buddha Vajradhara (rDo-rje 'Chang), the bodhisattva Mañjuśrī ('Phags-pa 'Jam-dpal), Je Tsongkhapa, Tokden Jampel Gyatso (rTogs-ldan 'Jam-dpal rGya-mtsho, 1356–1428), Khe Drub-je (mKhas-grub rJe, 1385–1438), Baso Choskyi Gyaltsen (Ba-so Chos-kyi-rGyal-mtshan, 1402–1473), Drubchen Choskyi Dorje (Grub-chen Chos-kyi-rDo-rJe), Gyalwa Ensapa (rGyal-ba dbEn-sa-pa, 1505–1566), Kedrup Sanggye Yeshe (mKhas-grub Sangs-rgyas Ye-shes, 1525–1591), Panchen Losang Chos-kyi-Gyaltsen (Panchen bLo-bZang Chos-kyi-rGyal-mtshan, 1570–1662), and Dorje Dzinpa Konchok Gyaltsen (rDo-rje 'Dzin-pa dKon-mchog rGyal-mTshan, 1612–1687). Also central to this lineage were teachings such as the *Kadam Emanation Scripture*, centering on Vajrayāna Mahāmudrā, and various *sādhana*s to Mañjuśrī, the Bodhisattva of Wisdom; in particular this lineage (often called the "Ensapa father and son" lineage) contained teachings on the *Lama Chodpa*, or "Offerings to the Spiritual Guide" tradition, which was finally committed to writing by the First Panchen Lama (see the previous discussion).

The Ganden oral tradition's conclusion at the end of the 15th century marks not the breaking of the lineage but rather the point at which many of the individual teaching lineages constituting the tradition began to diverge, as the Gelukpa Order itself expanded far beyond its beginnings in central Tibet. Thus, the Fifth Dalai Lama wrote two influential versions of the *Lam-rim* teachings titled "The Stages of the Path in Mañjuśrī's Own Words" (Lam-rim 'Jams-dpal Zhal-lung), which became the basis of the so-called southern and central lineages of these teachings. At the same time many of the previously oral traditions, previously shared among a few select individuals, were committed to writing and in some cases widely printed.

The importance of the Ganden oral tradition for the Gelukpa can be seen in the fact that almost all its members maintained key relations either as student or, more important, as tutor and guru to the Dalai Lamas, the highest incarnates of the Gelukpa Order. Indeed in many respects the previous list represents the heart of many of the principal teaching lineages within the Gelukpa Order, largely because of its position at the center of Gelukpa power. However, other lineages, even of the *Kadam Emanation Scripture*, did exist: Tsongkhapa also passed the scripture on to Je Sherab Sengge of Se (rJe Shes-rabs Seng-ge), but this time with an emphasis on the non-tantric *Ganden Lhagyama* (dGa'-ldan Lha rGya-ma, the "Hundred Deities of the Joyful Land") form of guru worship, thus founding the so-called Segyu whispered lineage.

Principal Incarnate Lineages

Although the continuity of teachings is of crucial importance to any Buddhist religious community, the emphasis on the Buddhist dharma as a *realized* rather than as a primarily written doctrine implied an equal emphasis on the continuity of realized teachers as the center of an order's institutional existence. Within Tibetan Buddhist orders this often involved the possibility of highly realized teachers being reborn again and again to carry the torch of the teachings.

The Gelukpa's adoption of lineages of reincarnating hierarchs such as the Dalai Lamas was perhaps inevitable given the institution's political convenience for the maintenance of monastic authority in the Buddhist context: while circumventing direct genealogical inheritance, religious authority could be maintained with relative ease over the long term within a well-structured religious bureaucracy. The Dalai Lamas themselves are seen as deriving not from the rebirth of Tsongkhapa – who is seen to have attained enlightenment immediately following his death and thus not to have returned to saṃsāra – but from his principal disciple, Gedun Drup (dGe-'dun-grub, 1391–1474), the "throne holder" (khri-pa) of Ganden monastery from 1431 to 1438 and founder and first abbot of Tashilhunpo monastery in Shigatse.

Historically the title of Dalai Lama was itself applied retroactively after being bequeathed to Gedun Drup's second reincarnation, Sonam Gyatso (bSod-rNams rGya-mTsho, 1543–1588; the "Third" Dalai Lama), by Altan Khan, chieftain of the Tumed Mongols, with whom he had developed powerful political and religious links. These links were consolidated following Sonam Gyatso's death, when his rebirth, Yonten Gyatso (1589–1617; the Fourth Dalai Lama), was found among Altan Khan's kin. The combined weight of these links came to the fore during the reign of the Fifth Dalai Lama, Lobzang Gyatso (bLo-bzang rGya-mtsho, 1617–1682), a consummate political and religious leader who used his unique relations with the Mongol leadership to institute centralized rule from Lhasa, creating for the first time a greater Tibetan state. The so-called Great Fifth also saw to the building of the now-famous Potala Palace over the ruins of the palace of Srongtsen Gampo (who had been Tibet's first "religion king" [T. chos-rgyal]) and consolidated the growing tradition that the Dalai Lamas, like Srongtsen Gampo himself, were manifestations of Tibet's own patron deity Chenresig. However, subsequent Dalai Lamas have rarely proven as influential: the sixth, Tsangyang Gyamtsho (Tshang-dbyang rGya-mtsho, 1683–1706), was a noted poet and womanizer who refused to take full ordination to the monkhood and died in exile; subsequent Dalai Lamas either failed to reach their political majority or lived quietly under the firmer hand of a series of powerful regents. This unfortunate trend was turned around by the Thirteenth Dalai Lama, who, like his present successor, sought to modernize the Tibetan polity, often against great resistance.

Also of crucial importance within the Gelukpa Order was the lineage of the Panchen Lamas, owners and abbots of Tashilhunpo monastery and its vast attendant estates since the departure of Gedun Drup's reincarnation to Lhasa. Recognized by the Fifth Dalai Lama as both the reincarnation of his four predecessors and a manifestation of the Buddha Amitābha ('Od-pag-med), the Panchen and Dalai Lamas form a traditional symbolic link (Chenresig being a form of Amitābha) that is often described as being like "father and son." However, their relationships with one another and with the centers of political power in traditional Tibet have made the question of their succession a delicate and hugely sensitive one. The right of the Dalai Lama to choose a new Panchen Lama and, in a lesser way, the right of the Panchen Lama to "recognize" a new Dalai Lama have placed the relationship between the two lineages at center stage in the ongoing battle between the Tibetan government-in-exile and the Chinese government in the decades following the Chinese invasion of Tibet.

Although these and the hundreds of other incarnate lineages in the Gelukpa Order maintain huge symbolic prestige, none of them is the actual head of the Order itself. This duty lies with the Ganden Tri-pa (dGa'-ldan Khri-pa), the throne holder of Ganden monastery and direct *bureaucratic* successor of Tsongkhapa and Gedun Drup. Ganden throne holders are chosen from the select ranks of those ordinary, non-incarnate monks who have, through perseverance and study, attained the highest scholastic rank of *geshe lharampa* (dge-bshes lha-rams-pa). Being high Buddhist scholars and tantric yogins themselves, they hold the post of throne holder for seven years and are entitled, following the mold of Gedun Drup, to institute an incarnate lineage of their own following their deaths.

MARTIN A. MILLS

See also Abbot: Buddhist; Asaṅga; Bön Monasticism; Buddhist Schools/Traditions: Tibet; Dalai Lama (Tenzin Gyatso); Ladakh, India; Lhasa, Tibet; Liturgy: Buddhist; Master and Pupil: Buddhist Perspectives; Milarepa; Scholastics, Buddhist; United States: Buddhist

Further Reading

Mayer, Robert, *A Scripture of the Ancient Tantra Collection: The Phur-pa bcu-gnyis*, Edinburgh: Kiscadale, 1996

Mullin, Glenn H., *Tsongkhapa's Six Yogas of Naropa*, Ithaca, New York: Snow Lion, 1996

Pabonkha Rinpoche, *Liberation in the Palm of Your Hand: A Concise Discourse on the Stages of the Path to Enlightenment*, Boston: Wisdom, 1991; revised edition, 1993

Samuel, Geoffrey, *Civilized Shamans: Buddhism in Tibetan Societies*, Washington, D.C.: Smithsonian Institution Press, 1993

Tibetan Lineages: Kagyü

One of several possible translations of the term *Kagyü* (bKa' brgyud) is "the lineage/continuity of the [Buddha's] word." Thus, this name emphasizes that the Kagyü tradition traces its origin back to the primordial Buddha Vajradhara and the historical Buddha Śākyamuni. The teachings have been passed on in an uninterrupted succession through the Indian mahāsiddha Tilopa (Ti-lo-pa, 988–1069) and his main disciple Nāropa (Naro-pa, 1016–1100) to the Tibetan translator Marpa (Mar-pa lotsā-ba, 1012–1097), to the great yogi Milarepa (rJe-btsun Mi-la ras-pa, 1040–1123) and on to Dagpo Lhaje Gampopa (Dwags-po Lha-rje sGam-po-pa, 1079–1153), the founder of the Dagpo Kagyü tradition (Dwags po bka' brgyud) within the Marpa Kagyü.

The Dagpo Kagyü tradition gave rise to four "major" and eight "minor" schools, four of which survive to the present day. One of the most important among them, the Karma Kagyü, is referred to as "major" in that it originated from Gampopa himself: it was founded by Gampopa's direct disciple, the first Karmapa Düsum Kyenpa (Karma-pa Dus-gsum-mkhyen-pa, 1110–1193). The three others are the Drikung ('Bri gung) Kagyü, the Taglung (sTag lung) Kagyü, and the Drukpa ('Brug pa) Kagyü, all of which were founded in the 12th century by later generations of masters.

Gampopa founded the monastery of Dagla Gampo (Dwags lha sgam po), his disciple Pagmodru (Phag-mo-gru, 1110–1170) established Densateel (gDan sa mthil), and Düsum Kyenpa founded, among other monastic centers, Karma Densa (Karma gdan sa) in 1147 and Tsurphu (mTshur phu) as the main seat of the Black Hat Karmapas in 1185. Tsurphu was destroyed by the Chinese during the Cultural Revolution in the 1960s, but it has been mostly restored.

After the Chinese takeover in 1959, the lineages of the Kagyü tradition reestablished their monasteries in exile: the Drikung Kagyü lineage is presently headed by the 37th successor to the abbatial see, Drikung Kyabgon Che Tsang (b. 1946), who resides in his monastery in Ladakh. The Taglung Kagyü lineage reestablished their monastery in Sikkim, with Shabdrung Rinpoche as their head. The present head of the Drukpa Kagyü lineage is the Twelfth Drukchen Rinpoche, who resides in Darjeeling, India. The Karma Kagyü lineage made Rumtek in Sikkim the place of its main monastic center and university. As to their head, the Karmapa, there is currently a schism among the followers of this lineage: since the 1990s, two successors are claiming to be the true incarnation of the Sixteenth Karmapa, Rangjung Rigpe Dorje, who passed away in 1981. One of them, Ugyen Trinley Dorje (b. 1985), was enthroned in the original main monastery in central Tibet, Tsurphu, with the favorable consent of the Chinese government. In early January 2000 he fled secretly to India. The other one, Trinley Thaye Dorje (b. 1983), is presently residing in Delhi, India, in the Karmapa International Buddhist Institute.

Furthermore, refugees from Tibet as well as Western Buddhists have founded Kagyü monasteries, practice centers, and retreat sites all over the world, in North and South America, Europe, Australia, Asia, and Africa. Among these the Karma Kagyü lineage is the most successful.

The Karma Kagyü lineage was the first to introduce the tulku (sprul sku) system to Tibetan monasticism: Through the discovery and identification of the reincarnations of the order's previously deceased head lamas, their hierarchy has continued in an uninterrupted succession up to the present day. Since the recognition of the second Karmapa, Karma Pakshi (1204–1283), the tulku system has been adopted by other Tibetan monastic lineages as well, thus ensuring the continuity of the order as a religious and political institution. During the times of interim, appointed "lineage holders" are in charge of the order's affairs and responsible for the transmission of the teachings. These lineage holders are tulkus in their own right, such as the incarnation lineages of Jamgön Kongtrül ('Jam-mgon Kong-sprul), Tai Situ (T'ai Si-tu), and others.

Among the incarnations of the Karmapa were several great scholars, teachers, artists, ascetics, and poets. The third Karmapa Rangjung Dorje (Rang-byung-rdo-rje, 1284–1339), for example, composed several important philosophical works, some of which are still read and taught in monastic institutions. He managed to bring about a synthesis of the Mahamudra (mahāmudrā) system of his own order and the Dzogchen (rDzogs chen) doctrine of the Nyingma tradition (rNying ma). He and the two incarnations following him were teachers of the emperor of China. The eighth Karmapa Mikyö Dorje (Mi-bskyod-rdo-rje, 1507–1554) wrote extensively on Buddhist philosophy, whereas the ninth Karmapa Wangchug Dorje (dBang-phyug-rdo-rje, 1556–1603) composed basic meditation texts of his tradition.

The Seventh, the Eighth, and the Fourteenth Karmapas were great artists as well as teachers of art, and some of their disciples became renowned masters of the tradition in their own right. They also composed or compiled manuals and treatises on maṇḍala representation, iconometry, and so on, one of which has in recent years been used in the art department of the Tibetan school in Derge. Kagyüpa paintings can be classified into a number of distinctive styles and periods, ranging from the 12th century to the present. The Karma Kagyü tradition of Khams in eastern Tibet, for example, created a style of painting and sculpture known as Karma Gadry (sGar-bris). An outstanding figure is the great scholar and artist Situ Panchen Chökyi Jungnay (Situ Paṇ-chen Chos-kyi-'byung-gnas, 1700–1774), a high incarnated lama and founder of the great monastery of Palpung (dPal-spungs), which is an important Kagyü center in Kham. Quite a few scroll paintings (*thangkas*), sculptures, and various other types of sacred images depicting the Karma Kagyüpa lineage masters, the tantric deities of the tradition, their maṇḍalas,

Two young Karma Kagyüpa monks at a public ceremony at Phyang Monastery, Ladakh, India. Photo courtesy of John Powers

Mahamudra lineage masters, and so on have survived. They are now scattered mainly in Western countries.

The Karma Kagyü tradition was very supportive of the nonsectarian Rime (ris-med) movement of eastern Tibet (Kham). The first of the incarnation lineage of the Jamgön Kongtrüls, Jamgön Kongtrül Lodrö Tahyay ('Jam-mgon Kong-sprul Blo-gros-mtha'-yas, 1813–1899), played an important role in this effort to overcome sectarian bias through creating an attitude of tolerance and teaching mutual acceptance among the various traditions of Tibetan monasticism. His personal background might have influenced him: he grew up in a family of Bönpos (Bon po, or practitioner of Bön, the Tibetan religion that existed before the introduction of Buddhism to Tibet); he received his first monastic ordination from the Nyingma tradition and later a second one from the Kagyü Order. He was a principal student of the nonsectarian Sakya lama-scholar Jamyang Khyentse Wangpo ('Jam-dbyangs-mkhyen-brtse-dbang-po, 1811–1892) and also of the Twelfth Tai Situpa, Pema Nyinje Wangpo (T'ai Si-tu Padma-nyin-byed-dbang-po, 1774–1853), the head lama of Palpung (dPal- spungs) monastery. Jamgön Kongtrül Lodrö Tahyay's collected works are divided into five collections, the *Five Great Treasuries* (*mDzod chen lnga*). Among these *The Store of Knowledge* (*Shes bya mdzod*) is an encyclopedia covering the whole range of knowledge from cosmology, sciences, and philosophy up to the history of Buddhist lineages and practices in Tibet. *The Mantra Store of the Lineages of Transmitted Precepts* (*bKa' brgyud sngags mdzod*) is a collection of esoteric teachings and practices from the Nyingma and Kagyü Orders. *The Store of Instructions* (*gDams ngag mdzod*) comprises the most important instructions of all the different lineages of Tibetan Buddhism.

Until the Chinese takeover of Tibet in 1959, the political and religious structures in Tibet were characterized by the fact that the abbots or head lamas of the most important monastic lineages also held the secular power. Monastic establishments struggling for political power, as well as power politics invading the realm of religion, was a common occurrence in the unique and complex religio-cultural phenomenon of Tibetan monastic culture. Similar to the practice of the Sakya (Sa skya), for example, the Pagmodru (Phag mo gru) head lamas came from the local ruling family, thus combining religious and secular power. Subsequently both these orders have been involved in political struggles: owing to patronage from the Mongolian rulers, the Sakya Order ascended to power in the 13th century, leading to increasing intersectarian rivalries and warfare, until Sakya lost its power to the Pagmo Drupa (Phag-mo-gru-pa) Tai Situ Jangchub Gyeltsen (T'ai-si-tu Byang-chub rgyal-mtshan, 1302–c. 1364) in the 1350s. He was the first Pagmo Drupa to combine spiritual and worldly leadership, and he in turn had to face constant rebellion and intrigue himself. Because of patronage from the ruling Ming and Yüan dynasties in China, the Kagyü Order held religious and secular power in Tibet in the 15th and 16th centuries; it declined, however, when the Geluk (dGe lugs) Order became the supreme political force with the help of the Mongols in the 17th century.

Gampopa successfully combined the monasticism of the then-established Kadampa Order (bKa' gdams pa) with the solitary lifestyle of the tantric yogin: a three-year, three-month, and three-day solitary retreat, for example, is common practice among the followers of the Kagyü tradition. Thus, Gampopa founded an order where the monastic environment also left room for extensive esoteric tantric practice.

Accordingly a threefold system determines the lives of the followers of this tradition, the Kagyüpas: monastic discipline, meditative practice, and the study of philosophical systems and texts. The Kagyü tradition places the greatest emphasis on the guru-disciple relationship and on meditation practice, claiming that through these two aspects of practice, enlightenment and liberation are possible in one single lifetime. Thus, the role of intellectual study is not of the same importance as it is, for example, in the Geluk Order, but this does not mean that it is neglected. In his autobiography Tai Situ Jangchub Gyeltsen asserts that the reason why he founded the great monastery of Tsaydang (rTse thang) in 1351 was "to introduce book learning to the monks of the area, who were apparently solely involved in tantric ritual practice and meditation" (Kuip, 1991).

On the one hand the monastic curriculum includes the traditional fields of knowledge that are shared by all the major monastic traditions of Tibetan Buddhism: the Perfection of Wisdom (Prajñāparamitā), the Middle Way (Madhyamaka), Epistemology or Valid Cognition (Pramāṇa), Monastic Law or Discipline (Vinaya), and Higher Doctrine (Abhidharma). Thus, scholastic learning includes all the general Mahāyāna teachings, such as the Two Truths and the Bodhisattva path as propounded by both Indian and Tibetan authors.

On the other hand the Kagyü tradition considers the tantric practices and meditation techniques of Mahamudra (Tibetan, Phyag rgya chen po, "great seal") and "The Six Yogas of Nāropa" (Nā ro chos drug) the essence of all Buddhist teachings, which is a unique feature of this order.

In some respect Mahamudra is similar to the Dzogchen (the great perfection or completeness) path of the Nyingma and Bön traditions: it is not scholarly book learning but, rather, spontaneous nonconceptual awareness that leads the practitioner to instantaneous enlightenment involving a personal experience and direct realization of the nature of the mind, which is voidness and pure luminosity. It is the actualization of the potential for Buddhahood that is inherent in each and every sentient being.

The "Six Yogas of Nāropa" are meditative practices: (1) generation of "inner heat" (*gtum mo*), (2) experience of the "illusory body" (*sgyu lus*), (3) "dream state" (*rmi lam*), (4) perception of "clear light" (*'od gsal*), (5) "intermediate state" (*bar do*), and (6) "transference of consciousness" (*'pho ba*). For the generation of "inner heat," the yogin works with channels, currents, and centers of energy in his or her own body (Sanskrit, *nadi*, *prana*, and *cakra*, respectively) until he or she experiences directly the clear nature of the mind. The mastery of this first yoga is the basis for the successful practice of the other five, the ultimate goal being full comprehension of the luminous nature of the mind and direct perception of the true nature of all phenomena, which is voidness and nonself. Thus, this practice is a means of attaining enlightenment.

Similar to the other monastic traditions of Tibetan Buddhism, a guru with enlightened qualities to guide the practitioner on his or her path to enlightenment is crucial to the student's success. The direct transmission of instructions, empowerment, and initiation through a guru endowed with spiritual authority is a precondition for the student who wants to engage in tantric practice.

The Kagyü system of tantric theory and practice is mainly based on the Cakrasaṁvara Tantra and the Guhyasamāja Tantra. The deities that this tradition associates its tantric practices with are, among others, Avalokiteśvara, Mañjuśrī, Vajrapāṇi, Green Tārā, and Heruka Cakrasaṁvara.

SIGRID PIETSCH

See also Abbot: Buddhist; Bön Monasticism; Buddhist Schools/Traditions: Tibet; Deities, Buddhist; Gampopa; Hermits: Buddhist; Ladakh, India; Milarepa; Tibetan Lineages: Nyingma; United States: Buddhist

Further Reading

Chang, Garma Chen-chi, *The Hundred Thousand Songs of Milarepa,* 2 vols, Boulder, Colorado: Shambala, 1989

Douglas, Nik, and Meryl White, *Karmapa: The Black Hat Lama of Tibet,* London: Luzac, 1976

Dowman, Keith, *Masters of Mahamudra: Songs and Histories of the Eighty-Four Buddhist Siddhas*, Albany: State University of New York Press, 1986

Guenther, Herbert V., *The Jewel Ornament of Liberation by sGam-po-pa,* London: Rider, 1963; reprint, Berkeley, California: Shambala, 1971; Boulder, Colorado: Prajna Press, 1981

Guenther, Herbert V., *The Life and Teaching of Nāropa,* Oxford: Clarendon Press, 1963

Gyaltsen, Khenpo Könchog, *The Great Kagyu Masters: The Golden Lineage Treasury,* Ithaca, New York: Snow Lion, 1990

Jackson, David Paul, *A History of Tibetan Painting*, Vienna: Verlag der Österreichischen Akademie der Wissenschaften, 1996

Kuip, Leonard W.J. van der, "On the Life and Political Career of Ta'i-si-tu Byang-chub rgyal-mtshan," in *Tibetan History and Language: Studies Dedicated to Uray Geza on His Seventieth Birthday*, edited by Ernst Steinkellner, Vienna: Wiener Studien zur Tibetologie und Buddhismuskunde, Heft 26. Arbeitskreis fuer tibetische und buddhistische Studien, 1991

Lhalungpa, Lobsang P., *The Life of Milarepa: A New Translation from the Tibetan,* Boston: Shambala, 1977

Mullin, Glenn H., editor and translator, *Readings on the Six Yogas of Naropa*, Ithaca, New York: Snow Lion, 1997

Petech, Luciano, "The 'Bri gung pa Sect in Western Tibet and Ladakh," in *Proceedings of the Csoma de Körös Memorial Symposium Held at Matrafüred, Hungary, 24–30 September 1976* (Bibliotheca Orientalis Hungarica, volume 23), Budapest: Akademiai Kiado, 1978

Powers, John, *Introduction to Tibetan Buddhism,* Ithaca, New York: Snow Lion, 1995

Richardson, Hugh E., "The Karma-pa Sect: A Historical Note," in *Journal of the Royal Asiatic Society* (1958)

Shakabpa, Tsepon W.D., *Tibet: A Political History,* New Haven, Connecticut: Yale University Press, 1967; reprint, New York: Potala, 1984

Snellgrove, David L., and Hugh E. Richardson, *A Cultural History of Tibet,* London: Weidenfeld and Nicolson, 1968; Boulder: Prajna Press, 1980

Stewart, Jampa Mackenzie, *The Life of Gampopa*, Ithaca, New York: Snow Lion, 1995

Tucci, Guiseppe, *The Religions of Tibet,* London: Routledge and Kegan Paul, and Berkeley: University of California Press, 1980

Tibetan Lineages: Nyingma

The term *Nyingma* or (ancient) is a blanket designation assigned retrospectively to the original schools of Tibetan Buddhism transplanted from India to Tibet during the seventh and eighth centuries. The foundation of this school is traditionally ascribed to three important eighth-century figures: Padmasambhava (c. eighth to ninth century), Śāntarakṣita (c. eighth century), and King Trisong Detsen (khri srong lde brtsan, 742–c. 797). These three are credited with the founding of Samye (bsam yas) monastery near Lhasa, the country's first Buddhist monastic institution. It was under their auspices that the seven original Tibetan Buddhist monks, known as the "Seven Who Were Tested" (mi sad bdun), were ordained. Moreover Śāntarakṣita, the abbot of the important Indian monastery of Nālandā, established the Sarvāstivāda ordination lineage in Tibet that continues to the present day in all Tibetan sectarian traditions. Thus, although the most famous of these three, Padmasambhava, is generally portrayed as a lay Buddhist ritual specialist, the tradition he helped establish was deeply concerned with promoting Buddhist monasticism in Tibet. Nevertheless the Nyingma school was never a purely monastic tradition and from its very inception possessed a strong lay orientation.

Initially, the term *Nyingma* was not used to designate the earliest forms of Buddhism in Tibet, as they were not "ancient" in relation to any more recent type of Buddhism. These older traditions felt the need to refer to themselves as the "Nyingma" school only after a series of significant events. First, Buddhism experienced a period of persecution during the reign of the King Lang Darma (glang dar ma, r. 838–842). Following Lang Darma's assassination there ensued a period of political chaos. Finally, a major renaissance of institutional Buddhism took place in the tenth century following these "dark ages," known as the "later diffusion" (*phyi dar*) of Buddhism. The resurgence of interest in Buddhism and especially in monastic Buddhism made the need to affirm the venerability and prestige of the traditions of the "earlier diffusion" (*snga dar*) even more crucial to their adherents.

A pivotal figure in the later diffusion was Yeshe Ö (ye shes 'od, c. 10th to 11th century), the king of Purang (pu hrangs) in western Tibet. Between the ninth and tenth centuries, no strong institutional foundation existed for the regulation of religious activities in Tibet. Instead there had been a tendency for individuals and groups to devise their own ethical norms for Tantric practice. Yeshe Ö was greatly concerned with the authenticity of the Tantric teachings in general and was especially critical of what he perceived to be the moral license taken by its followers. He issued a famous ordinance (*bka' shog*) attacking Tantric teachings central to the as-yet-unnamed Nyingma tradition in which he specifically criticized the practices of "union" (*'byor ba*) and "liberation" (*sgrol ba*), both prominent features of *The Secret Essence Tantra* (*guhyagrabhatantra, gsang ba'i snying po'i rgyud*), which was widely venerated in Nyingma circles. "Union" is generally interpreted to refer to Tantric practices involving sexual union, whereas "liberation" is taken to refer to the practice of animal and even human sacrifice. Thus, because the Nyingma tradition had always possessed a strong lay (i.e., noncelibate) component, and because Tantric sexual rites lent themselves well to what their detractors viewed as degenerate forms of Buddhism, its followers increasingly found themselves under attack.

This critique of tantra was accompanied by a shift in Tibetan religious discourse away from cultic activities to safer matters, such as dialogues of the Buddha (known as sūtras) as well as academic discussions of epistemology, ontology, and so on. This turn from exotic Tantric practices to staid philosophical reflections was also reflected in the rise of the large monastic institutions affiliated with the "Sarma" (gsar ma), or "modern" schools. It is fair to surmise that such philosophical discourse was more compatible with the interests of celibate monks than were ruminations on the spiritual efficacy of unorthodox sexual practices. Similarly it is not surprising that Nyingma followers felt a greater affinity for the highly sexualized discourse of tantra than for abstruse philosophical inquiry, as they were mainly members of patrilineal lay traditions, whereas Nyingma monks were more likely to be involved with meditation and ritual than with scholastic pursuits.

However, this is not to say that the boundary between these two in the Nyingma and Sarma traditions was hard and fast. For example, Atiśa (982–1054) and other prominent figures in the second diffusion of Buddhism in Tibet indeed were interested in tantra but sought to downplay the ethical ambiguities inherent in the literal interpretation of many of its practices, emphasizing instead their symbolic nature. On the other hand Nyingma figures, such as Rongzom Chökyi Zangpo (rong zom chos kyi bzang po, 1012–1131), wrote extensively on the topics of logic and epistemology favored by followers of the Sarma schools.

Nyingma monastic traditions were largely inactive during the reemergence of Buddhism between the 10th and 14th centuries. Instead lay followers of the school concentrated on the newly emerging genre of religious literature known as "treasure texts," or Terma (*gter ma*). Tradition holds that Padmasambhava and other prominent figures from the period of the early diffusion concealed these texts to be later discovered by "treasure revealers" called "Tertons" (*gter ston*). The majority of these texts are clearly apocryphal and Tantric in character and thus were largely unacknowledged by proponents of the modern traditions. Moreover by the 14th century Budön (bu ston, 1290–1364) and others began to create canons of "authentic" Buddhist scriptures, pointedly omitting these "treasures" as well as many of the texts transmitted during the earlier period of translation (*snga 'gyur*) and revered by followers of the Nyingma tradition. This led the Nyingmapas to collate their own scriptural canon, *The Collected Tantras of the Ancients* (*rnying ma'i rgyud 'bum*), as a means to reestablish their credibility and prestige.

It was in the fertile 14th century that Longchen Rabjampa (klong chen rab 'byams pa, 1308–1363), perhaps the most remarkable exponent of Nyingma monasticism, was born. Longchenpa (as he is popularly known) successfully synthesized the intellectual concerns of both the Nyingma and the Sarma traditions. Not only did he systematize the arcane Tantric topics specifically associated with the Nyingma school, but he studied the modern schools' tantras as well. In addition he spent several years studying scholastic topics popular with scholar-monks of the modern schools at Tibet's preeminent institution for the study of logic and epistemology, Sangphu Neutok (gsang phu sne'u thog). Longchenpa is generally regarded as an exemplary monastic figure, an unusual description for prominent Nyingma figures at that time. In fact he was considered an expert in monastic discipline (vinaya, *'dul ba*), and several of his works harshly criticize the lax moral standards (including inappropriate sexual behavior) of monks in his day. Thus, Longchenpa represented a synthesis of many diverse trends in Tibetan religious life in the pivotal 14th century and symbolized a new, reinvigorated Nyingma monasticism.

However, as highly regarded as Longchenpa was, he too experienced difficulties in keeping his monastic vows. During his approximately ten-year sojourn in Bhutan, he is said to have had two children with a nun who was also his disciple. Traditionally this is explained as being the result of Longchenpa being a monk externally while being a Tantric yogin internally. Nevertheless he was evidently embarrassed by this apparent incongruity, as he did not publicly acknowledge paternity until forced to do so and is said to have lived in celibacy for the remainder of his life.

This case raises interesting questions regarding the standards of acceptable monastic conduct in Tibetan Buddhism. In valorizing a figure such as Longchenpa as an exemplary monk, the Nyingma tradition finds itself in the uncomfortable position of having to explain or defend his seemingly contradictory behavior. Followers of the Geluk (dge lugs) school of Tibetan Buddhism, which was founded on the principles of ethical and monastic reform, criticized the Nyingma tradition for precisely this inconsistency. The essence of the dispute is the way in which the different traditions interpret the hierarchy of moral conduct. All schools of Tibetan Buddhism posit three main categories of vows (*sdom gsum*) that must be observed by spiritual aspirants: (1) vows of individual liberation, (2) vows of altruism, and (3) esoteric Tantric vows. The first set pertains to an individual's pursuit of liberation or nirvāṇa and is composed largely of series of prohibitions; all monastic vows fall into this category. Higher on the spiritual hierarchy is what are popularly known as the "bodhisattva vows," whereby one vows to become enlightened for the sake of others. At the highest spiritual level are the arcane vows that relate to esoteric Tantric practices, said to achieve the same results as the bodhisattva vows but in a much shorter time.

However, different schools interpret the relationship between these vows differently. For example, the Geluk school holds that each class of vows exists as a separate entity and so must be observed discretely. Thus, even if the higher vows require one to participate in certain activities prohibited by the lower vows, one must make every attempt to observe both, as one is bound by both and each set has its own logic and integrity. For example, the founder of the Geluk school, Lozang Drakpa (blo bzang grags pa, 1357–1419), is said to have forgone the Tantric requirement of taking a physical sexual partner because he wished to uphold his monastic vow of celibacy. On the other hand the Nyingma interpretation is that although all three of these classes of vows may differ conceptually, they ultimately are a single entity. The result of this interpretation is that all three sets of vows are seen as being a continuum, with the higher vows always superseding the lower ones. Thus, it is more important to observe the Tantric precepts regardless of whether they appear to contradict the lower vows of individual liberation, even for a monk. This divergence of interpretations might partially explain the use in the Tibetan region of Dingri of the generic terms *monk* (*grwa pa*) and *nun* (*a ni*) – usually reserved for celibate religious anchorites – to refer to married lamas of the Nyingma Order and their spouses.

Unlike the Sarma schools' more institutional forms of monasticism, Nyingma institutions had been comprised largely of small monasteries and hermitages up until the 17th to 18th century. It was during this period that the six most important monastic centers of the Nyingma tradition (other than Samye) – Kathok (ka' thog), Dorje Drak (rdo rje brag), Mindrol Ling (smin grol gling), Palyul (dpal yul), Dzok Chen (rdzogs chen), and Shechen (zhe chen) – were first established. This revival of Nyingma monasticism was a reflection of a growing ecumenical or "nonsectarian" (*ris med*) movement and was very much a reaction against the Geluk domination of religious discourse in Tibet. This movement represented in part the attempts of the Nyingma, Kagyü (bka' brgyud), and Sakya (sa skya) schools to establish their own traditions of monastic discipline and scholarship. However, important Nyingma monastic figures, such as Dodrupchen Jikmay Tenpay Nyima (rdo grub chen 'jigs med bstan pa'i nyi ma, 1865–1926), were deeply influenced by Gelukpa monastic education and scholasticism.

Since the Chinese takeover of Tibet in 1959, thousands of young men and women have fled to India and Nepal in search of a traditional monastic education. In the early 1960s the Indian government donated large parcels of land called "Lama camps" for the resettlement of Tibetan refugees. Many of the major Tibetan monasteries have reestablished their institutions and curriculum in these camps and elsewhere. Among the Nyingma monasteries successfully transplanted to Nepal and India are the Shechen, Dzok Chen, Mindrol Ling, and Palyul monasteries. Of these the Palyul monastery, located near Mysore, has experienced the greatest development. At present there are about 1,500 young monks in its main monastery, with over 100 advanced students studying in its traditional college (*bshad grwa*). The level of education and scholarship at this institute is so highly regarded that it attracts students from across the Tibetan cultural region, including Nepal, Sikkim, and Bhutan, all traditional Nyingma strongholds. Perhaps because of cultural pressures, the college has chosen to adopt certain scholastic practices more common to the monastic curriculum of the modern schools, such as the use of formalized philosophical debate; this practice has been heretofore almost entirely unheard of in Nyingma monasteries. H.H. Penor Rinpoche, head of the Palyul monastery and of the Nyingma lineage as a whole, is a fully ordained monk. It is a point of pride with the monks at Palyul monastery that their standards of monastic discipline are as strict as or stricter than those of any other Tibetan monastic community in exile. Since the 1980s a similar, albeit smaller, revival has been taking place as well in Nyingma monasteries in Tibet itself, mainly in the eastern provinces of Kham and Amdo.

Thus, Nyingma (rnying ma) monasticism is a highly problematic topic for a variety of reasons. First, no significant tradition of Nyingma monasticism seems to have existed before the 17th century. Second, the Nyingma tradition in general places greater emphasis on meditation and ritual – activities generally associated with lay clerics – than it does on the scholastic topics usually pursued in Tibetan monastic settings. Finally, the Nyingma tradition has never emphasized monasticism, specifically celibacy, to the same extent as other Tibetan Buddhist sects; indeed the Nyingma conception of monasticism appears to differ considerably from that of its rivals. Thus, Nyingmapas have been the objects of criticism for their interpretations of Buddhist monasticism for hundreds of years, and they have responded with polemical treatises or renewed attempts to establish stricter monastic standards. Despite its history and divergent interpretations of certain central issues, Nyingma monasticism remains a robust and flourishing tradition throughout Asia.

Gregory A. Hillis

See also Buddhist Schools/Traditions: Tibet; Hermits: Buddhist; Kathmandu Valley, Nepal; Lhasa, Tibet; Liturgy: Buddhist; Nalanda, India; Nepal: History; Padmasambhava; Tibet: History; United States: Buddhist

Further Reading

Aris, Michael, *Hidden Treasures and Secret Lives: A Study of Pemalingpa (1450–1521) and the Sixth Dalai Lama (1683–1706)*, Delhi: Motilal Banarsidass, 1988; London and New York: Kegan Paul, 1989

Aziz, Barbara N., *Tibetan Frontier Families*, New Delhi: Vikas, and Durham, North Carolina: Carolina Academic Press, 1978

Dudjom, Rinpoche ('jigs bral ye shes rdo rje), *The Nyingma School of Tibetan Buddhism*, 2 vols., translated and edited by Gyurme Dorje and Matthew Kapstein, London: Wisdom, 1987

Karmay, Samten G., "The Ordinance of lHa Bla-ma Ye-shes-'od," in *Tibetan Studies in Honour of Hugh Richardson*, edited by Michael Aris and Aung San Suu Kyi, Warminster, United Kingdom, and Forest Grove, Oregon: Aris and Phillips, 1980

Kon-sprul Blo-gros-mthai'-yas, *Buddhist Ethics*, Ithaca, New York: Snow Lion, 1998

Samuel, Geoffrey, *Civilized Shamans: Buddhism in Tibetan Societies*, Washington, D.C.: Smithsonian Institution Press, 1993

Snellgrove, David, and Hugh Richardson, *A Cultural History of Tibet*, New York: Praeger, and London: Wiedenfeld and Nicolson, 1968; revised edition, Boulder, Colorado: Prajñā Press, 1980

Tshe-rin Bla-ma' Jam-dpal-bzan-po, Rmugs-sans, *A Garland of Immortal Wish-fulfilling Trees*, translated by Sangye Khandro, Ithaca, New York: Snow Lion, 1988

Tucci, Giuseppe, *Die Religionen Tibets und der Mongolei*, Stuttgart: Kohlhammer, 1970; as *The Religions of Tibet*, Berkeley: University of California Press, and London: Routledge and Kegan Paul, 1980

Tulku, Tarthang, et al., *Masters of the Nyingma Lineage*, Emeryville, California: Dharma, 1995

Related Web Sites

http://www.palyul.org (Palyul Monastery in South India)
http://www.nyingma.org/ (International Nyingma Institutes)
http://shechen.12pt.com/ (Shechen Monastery in Nepal)

Tibetan Lineages: Sakya

The Sakya (Sa-skya) religious tradition is named after the temple founded by Khön Gönchog Gyelpo ('Khon dKon-mchog-rgyal-po, 1034–1102) in 1073 at a "place of pale earth," Sakya, in western Tibet. The Sakya lineage is rooted in, has developed within, and has exercised enormous influence on what is a unique and complex religiocultural phenomenon: Tibetan Buddhist monastic culture.

Sakya developed into a great monastic center with two major institutions: the North Monastery, for the study and practice of the Tantrayāna, and the South Monastery (Lha-khang chen-mo), for the study and practice of the Sūtrayāna. The former is no longer extant, but the latter still houses the greatest religious library in Tibet.

In traditional Sakya accounts the origin of the lineage is traced back to mythological times as an uninterrupted hereditary lineage of the Khön clan, the prince-abbots of Sakya. Their male descendants are considered to be emanations of great bodhisattvas (saintly beings). Among the early abbots of Sakya are the "Five Hierarchs" (Sa-skya gong-ma lnga), who were outstanding in their scholarship, spiritual accomplishments, and Tantric realization: Sachen Künga Nyingpo (Sa-chen Kun-dga'-snying-po, 1092–1158), Lobpön Sönam Tsemo (Slob-dpon bSod-nams-rtse-mo, 1142–1182), Jetsün Dagpa Gyeltsen (rJe-btsun Grags-pa-rgyal-mtshan, 1147–1216), Sakya Pandita Künga Gyeltsen (Sa-skya Paṇḍita Kun-dga'-rgyal-mtshan, 1182–1251), and Chögyel Pagpa (Chos-rgyal 'Phags-pa Blo-gros-rgyal-mtshan, 1235–1280). To the present their collected works, the *Sakya Kambum* (Sa-skya bka'-'bum), have directly or indirectly influenced Buddhist scholars of all schools and monastic lineages and shaped the political, religious, philosophical, and sociocultural development of Tibetan Buddhist monasticism.

Among the famous abbots, scholars, and teachers of the tradition are Lama Dampa Sönam Gyeltsen (Bla-ma dam-pa bSod-nams-rgyal-mtshan, 1312–1375), Rongtön (Rong-ston Shes-bya-kun-rig, 1367–1449), Gorampa (Go-bo rab-'byams-pa bSod-nams-seng-ge, 1429–1489), Shakya Chogden (Śākya-mchog-ldan, 1428–1507), and many others.

Until 1959 the political and religious structures in Tibet were characterized by the fact that the abbots or head lamas of the most important monastic lineages also held secular power, a fact that made Tibet a theocratic state. In the 1260s, when the Mongols were the dominant power in Asia, the Mongolian ruler Kubilai Khan and the Sakya abbot Pagpa established the relationship of "patron and priest" (*yon mchod*). While accepting Mongolian authority over Tibet, Pagpa acted as the spiritual preceptor (*mchod gnas*) to the Khan, who in turn made him the religious and spiritual ruler of Tibet. Thus, the Sakya lamas' rise to power and decline was connected with that of their overlords: with the waning supremacy of the Mongols, Sakya faced increasing intersectarian rivalries and warfare and eventually lost power to the Pagmo Drupa (Phag-mo-gru-pa) Jangchub Gyeltsen (Byang-chub rgyal-mtshan) in the 1350s.

In Tibetan monastic lineages the main institution of a lineage, the mother monastery, fostered numerous subsidiary institutions (daughter monasteries). In the Sakya tradition dozens, if not hundreds, of branch monasteries were founded, such as Ngor, Nalendra, Dar Drongmoche, and many others. Accordingly, subsects developed: the traditions of Ngor and Tsar (Tshar), Dzongpa (rDzong-pa), Gongkarba (Gong-dkar-ba), and Nalendra. Among these the Ngor school was the most prominent subdivision, famous as a great center of Tantric learning and renowned for outstanding scholars. The monastery Ngor Evam Chöden (Ngor E-waṁ-chos-ldan) was founded in 1429 by Ngorchen Künga Zangpo (Ngor-chen Kun-dga'-bzang-po, 1382–1456). It quickly developed into an influential head monastery in its own right, with numerous branch monasteries mainly in the eastern province of Kham (Khams) and in Ngari (Nga'-ris) in the far west of Tibet. Since the 1960s both refugees from Tibet and Western Buddhists have founded Sakya monasteries all over the world, in the United States, Europe, Asia, and Australia. The Forty-First Sakya Trizin resides in Rajpur, India.

The Sakya doctrine is Madhyamaka (the Middle Way), offering a symbiosis of two kinds of spiritual practices: that of the Sūtrayāna, or Parāmitāyāna, and that of the Tantrayāna, which is also called Mantrayāna or Vajrayāna. In the Sakya tradition the two strands of scholastic scholarship and esoteric Tantric practice are complementary. Sakya masters are famous for contributing to textual transmission of sūtras and śāstras as well as tantras, together with their explanations, commentaries, and empowerments. They were outstanding scholastic writers as well as accomplished masters of meditational and Tantric practice.

Tantric practice involves visualization and generation of meditational deities and their maṇḍalas, secret yogas, recitation of mantras, and other practices that are forbidden to be taught publicly to the uninitiated. The transmission lineage for the Tantric tradition of Sakya is traced back to the Indian Mahāsiddha Virūpa (c. eighth or ninth century). From this Tantric master the Sakya *Lamdre* system (the Path with Its Fruit) was handed down through empowerment and secret oral instructions in an uninterrupted succession from master to disciple. Texts and practices of this distinct esoteric doctrine are based on the *Hevajratantra*, which was brought from India to Tibet by Drogmi ('Brog-mi) Lotsāwa (993–1074/87). He translated that tantra from Sanskrit and passed its explanations on to his disciple Khön Gönchog Gyelpo.

In connection with the Lamdre tradition, remarkable works of art were created. For example, Ngorchen commissioned a set of 45 maṇḍalas of the Vajrāvalī cycle, which was one of the main collections of Tantric teachings that he himself had received. Other Sakya masters wrote highly influential treatises, such as meditational manuals, biographies of great Lamdre masters, Lamdre chronicles, instructions on esoteric meditation practices of Hevajra *sādhana*s (*sgrub-thabs*, or tantric rituals for visualizing or "generating" deities, their respective maṇḍalas, and so on), commentaries on the Hevajra tantra, liturgies for initiation rites and rituals, and exegeses of Virūpa's basic text.

The nonsectarian scholar Jamyang Khyentse Wangpo ('Jam-dbyangs-mkhyen-brtse-dbang-po, 1811–1892) compiled various Sakya and non-Sakya *sādhana*s in a collection called *Drubtab Küntü* (Grub-thabs kun-btus), which comprises 139 maṇḍalas associated with various Tantric deities. His student Loter Wangpo (Blo-gter-dbang-po, 1847–c. 1914) brought together 32 volumes of the *Gyüde Küntü* (rGyud-sde kun-btus), which is an eclectic collection of secret teachings on tantra. Recently a book showing 123 maṇḍalas of various deities of this collection has been published in the West. Loter Wangpo also compiled the *Lamdre Lobshe* (Lam 'bras slob bshad), the "uncommon Lamdre teachings," and the *Lamdre Tsogshe* (Lam 'bras tshogs bshad), the "common Lamdre teachings" of the Sakya tradition. In this way the transmission of the main Sakya esoteric tradition has been kept alive to the present.

The Sakya tradition is renowned for its many notable scholars, and its monasteries were among the most distinguished seats of scholastic learning. Since the 15th century the standard curriculum for Sakya monks comprises the study of the "Eighteen Famous Topics" in six fields of knowledge, concentrating on great Indian classics and their interpretation by Sakya Paṇḍita, as follows:

1. The Way of the Perfections (Pāramitā), which focuses on the *Five Dharmas of Maitreya*: *Ornament for Clear Realization* (*Abhisamayālaṁkāra*), *Ornament for the Mahāyānasūtras* (*Mahāyānasūtrālaṁkāra*), *Differentiation between the Middle and the Extremes* (*Madhyāntavibhāga*), *Differentiation of Phenomena and the Essence of Phenomena* (*Dharmadharmatāvibhāga*), *Sublime Continuum of the Great Vehicle* (*Mahāyānottaratantraśāstra*), and Shāntideva's *Entrance to the Bodhisattva's Way of Life* (*Bodhisattvacaryāvatāra*).

2. Epistemology (Pramāṇa), which focuses on Dignāga's *Compendium on Valid Cognition* (*Pramāṇasamuccaya*), Dharmakīrti's *Commentary on Dignāga's Compendium on Valid Cognition* (*Pramāṇavārttika*), and Sakya Paṇḍita's pivotal work that is based on it, *Treasury of the Knowledge of Valid Cognition* (*Tshad ma rigs pa'i gter*).

3. Monastic Law (Vinaya), which focuses on two sūtras: the *Sūtra of Individual Liberation* (*Pratimokṣasūtra*) and the *Sūtra on Monastic Discipline* (*Vinayasūtra*).

4. Higher Doctrine (Abhidharma), which focuses on Vasubandhu's *Treasury of Abhidharma* (*Abhidharmakośa*) and Asaṅga's *Compendium of Higher Doctrine* (*Abhidharmasamuccaya*).

5. The Middle Way (Madhyamaka), which focuses on Nāgārjuna's *Root Verses on the Middle Way* (*Mūlamadhyamakakārikā*), Candrakīrti's *Entry into the Middle Way* (*Madhyamakāvatāra*), and Āryadeva's *Four Hundred* (*Catuḥśataka*).

6. Discrimination of the Three Vows (*Trisaṁvaraprabheda*), which focuses on Sakya Paṇḍita's *Differentiation of the Three Vows* (*sDom gsum rab dbye*).

Mainly in the 14th and 15th centuries, Sakya masters had students from different traditions, such as the Gelukpa (dGe-lugs-pa), Kagyüpa (bKa'-brgyud-pa), and Nyingmapa (rNying-ma-pa). Many of them became abbots, great scholars, and teachers themselves, including Tsongkhapa, Karmapa Düsum Kyenpa (Dus-gsum-khyen-pa), and the great Longchenpa (Klong-chen rab-'byams-pa).

SIGRID PIETSCH

See also Abbot: Buddhist; Buddhist Schools/Traditions: Tibet; Ladakh, India; Libraries: Buddhist; Sakya Paṇḍita (Sapen); Scholastics, Buddhist; Tibet; United States: Buddhist

Further Reading

Dagyab, Loden Sherab, "Die Sādhanas der Sammlung rGyud-sde Kun-btus," in *Ikonographie und Symbolik des Tibetischen Buddhismus*, edited by Klaus Sagaster, Part F, Wiesbaden: Otto Harrassowitz, 1991

Davidson, Ronald M., "Preliminary Studies on Hevajra's Abhisamaya and the Lam-'bras Tshogs-bshad," in *Tibetan Buddhism: Reason and Revelation*, edited by Steven D.

Goodman and Ronald M. Davidson, Albany: State University of New York Press, 1992
Jackson, David Paul, *The Entrance Gate for the Wise (Section III): Sa-skya Paṇḍita on Indian and Tibetan Traditions of Pramāṇa and Philosophical Debate*, 2 vols., Vienna: Arbeitskreis für Tibetische und Buddhistische Studien, Universität Wien, 1987
Jackson, David Paul, "Sources on the Chronology and Succession of the Abbots of Ngor E-waṁ-chos-ldan," *Berliner Indologische Studien* 4/5 (1989)
Jackson, David Paul, *The Early Abbots of 'Phan-po Nalendra: The Vicissitudes of a Great Tibetan Monastery in the 15th Century*, Vienna: Arbeitskreis für Tibetische und Buddhistische Studien Universität Wien, 1989
Powers, John, *Introduction to Tibetan Buddhism*, Ithaca, New York: Snow Lion, 1995
Schoening, Jeffrey D., "The Religious Structures at Sa-skya," in *Reflections on Tibetan Culture: Essays in Memory of Turrell V. Wylie*, edited by Lawrence Epstein and Richard Sherburne, Lewiston, New York: Edwin Mellen Press, 1990
Shakabpa, W.D., *Tibet, A Political History*, New Haven, Connecticut: Yale University Press, 1967; New York: Potala Publications, 1984
Snellgrove, David L., and Hugh E. Richardson, *A Cultural History of Tibet*, New York: Praeger and London: Weidenfeld and Nicolson, 1968; revised edition, Boulder, Colorado: Prajna Press, 1980
Thub-bstan-legs-bshad-rgya-mtsho, Bco-brgyad Khri-chen XVIII, *The History of the Sakya Tradition*, translated by David Stott, Bristol: Ganesha, 1983
Tucci, Giuseppe, *Die Religionen Tibets und der Mongolei*, Stuttgart: Kohlhammer, 1970; as *The Religions of Tibet*, translated by G. Samuel, London: Routledge and Kegan Paul, and Berkeley: University of California Press, 1980

Timekeeping: Buddhist Perspectives

Buddhists typically do not pay much attention to the passage of time. Because Buddhism aims at releasing oneself from the cycle of births and rebirths (*saṃsāra*), time as part of the physical world does not play a large role. Buddhist monasteries, especially ones in the Theravāda tradition, reflect this attitude. Timekeeping in general is quite lax. It functions as a means to keep the monks' daily routine more or less regular and does not become, as in a typical Christian monastery, part of a rigid routine prescribing life. In Buddhism monks live in a monastery so that each one can practice the Dharma (teachings) according to his own path. Because Theravāda Buddhism teaches that the way toward *nibbāna*, or release from *saṃsāra*, is possible only through individual effort, monasteries exist only to serve each monk's individual purpose.

This emphasis on the individual is reflected in monastic timekeeping. In a typical Theravāda Buddhist monastery, monks wake up a few hours before dawn, around 4:00 to 4:30 a.m. Then they sweep their living quarters and gather for a short, early morning prayer at around 5:00. The monks go for an almsround in the village or the city neighborhood at 6:00 and return to the monastery by 8:00. Especially in Thailand monks gather for formal morning prayer exactly at 8:00 a.m. and then enjoy free time for about two hours. Most spend their time in their living quarters; some do their personal chores around the temple. At 11:00 a.m. the monks gather for the main meal of the day. The Vinaya states that monks cannot eat anything after "noon," which is defined as the time when the shadow cast by a straight pole is exactly the length of two finger joints. In the afternoon the monks do their serious activities, which consist mostly of teaching, studying, or meditating. No rules are prescribed for what the monks must do during this time. However, in Thailand all the monks have to gather for a third time for evening prayer at 6:00 p.m. Both the morning and the evening prayer last about an hour. After evening prayer all are free to themselves, and by 9:00 p.m. they all go to bed. This routine prevails throughout the Theravāda Buddhist world, that is, in Thailand, Laos, Cambodia, Burma, and Sri Lanka. Moreover, in Thailand the prayers at 8:00 a.m. and 6:00 p.m. have become national institutions. All monasteries in the kingdom are required by the Ecclesiastical Council, the supreme governing body of Thai Buddhism, to hold them precisely at the times prescribed. All government agencies and all schools are required by the government to raise the national flag exactly at 8:00 a.m. and to lower it at 6:00 p.m. All radio and television stations in the country are required to broadcast the national anthem live from the central government station exactly at these times to accompany the nationwide ceremonies. This way of ensuring accurate timekeeping throughout the kingdom is universally practiced.

The method used to keep time varies according to the technology available. In the Buddha's time the sun was used to tell the time of day and the moon for counting days of the calendar. In fact the Vinaya rule concerning the time after which monks may not eat is the only one that mentions a definite point of time in a day. Another rule states that monks may not enter a house of a layperson at "night," which is defined as the time when it is so dark that one cannot read the lines on one's hands. However, today monasteries use mechanical or electrical clocks and watches. In addition, the Vinaya also requires that each monastery appoint one monk who is responsible for keeping and watching the calendar. This is a very important activity because the monks are required to assemble for the *pāṭimōkkha*, a large gathering of monks in which the rules are recited and transgressors confess their wrongdoings to the assembly. The Vinaya states that the *pāṭimōkkha* must be held every full-moon and new-moon day. The calendar keeper must determine and announce such days in advance and tell everyone accordingly. Because monks from many monasteries in one area often convene together for the *pāṭimōkkha*, unanimity must be reached among the calendars used. Today, to be sure, modern calendars containing both Western (solar) and lunar systems are widely available and are ubiquitous in monasteries.

One can see striking differences between Buddhist and Christian monasteries. Stanley Tambiah, in *The Buddhist Saints of the Forest and the Cult of Amulets* (1984), reports that a westerner

Interior of the Jungyang-sa Monastery, South Korea. The bell is used to mark the beginning and end of teaching and meditation sessions. The wooden gong is used in most ceremonies.
Photo courtesy of John Powers

who had experienced a Christian monastery and later was ordained in the Theravāda tradition told him that Christian monasteries are much more rigid and structured. A Christian monastery is bounded by walls. On the other hand a typical Theravāda monastery is a place where people and animals come and go more or less as they wish. Whereas the Christian monastery has more rules, the Theravāda one allows more freedom to individual monks to pursue their own interests. A Christian monastery thinks of itself far more as a collective unit than does a Theravāda one. Finally, the Theravāda monastery does not exalt physical work to the extent that its Christian counterpart does. Physical work is performed only when necessary. In fact monks are not allowed to perform hard physical labor. A Theravāda monastery does not and cannot sustain itself as an economic unit. The monks need laypeople to feed them and provide clothing, medicine, and physical labor for constructing new compounds and anything else. Laypeople gain merit from such acts, whereas monks are expected to maintain their quest for *nibbāna* and to teach the laypeople how to get rid of sufferings. On the other hand Christian monasteries often became wealthy corporations for which the monks themselves performed the economic work. Christian monasteries employed the ancient Roman solar-based calendar, which is used today. The lunar calendar used in the Theravāda world – a system based on the waxing and waning of the moon – reflects the need of the monks to assemble every full-moon and new-moon day, as prescribed by the Buddha himself.

SORAJ HONGLADAROM

See also Chan/Zen: Japan; Festivals, Buddhist; Nepal: Sites; Rules, Buddhist (Vinaya); Thailand

Further Reading

Buddhism in Thai Life, Bangkok: National Identity Board, Office of the Prime Minister, 1981

Lester, Robert C., *Theravada Buddhism in Southeast Asia*, Ann Arbor: University of Michigan Press, 1973

Na Rangsri, Sunthorn, *Putthapratyaa Chaak Phra Traipidok* (Buddhist Philosophy from the Tripiṭaka), Bangkok: Chulalongkorn University Press, 1998

Piker, Steven, *Buddhism and Modernization in Contemporary Thailand*, Leiden: Brill, 1973

Smith, Bardwell L., editor, *Religion and Legitimation of Power in Thailand, Laos, and Burma*, Chambersburg, Pennsylvania: ANIMA Books, 1978

Spiro, Melford E., *Buddhism and Society and Its Burmese Vicissitudes*, New York: Harper and Row, 1970; London: Allen and Unwin, 1971

Swearer, Donald, *Buddhism and Society in Southeast Asia*, Chambersburg, Pennsylvania: ANIMA Books, 1981

Tambiah, Stanley Jeyaraja, *World Conqueror and World Renouncer: A Study of Buddhism and Polity in Thailand Against a Historical Background*, Cambridge and New York: Cambridge University Press, 1976

Tambiah, Stanley Jeyaraja, *The Buddhist Saints of the Forest and the Cult of Amulets*, Cambridge and New York: Cambridge University Press, 1984

Wijayaratna, Môhan, *Buddhist Monastic Life According to the Texts of the Theravada Tradition*, translated by Claude Grangier and Steven Collins, Cambridge and New York: Cambridge University Press, 1990

Timekeeping: Christian Perspectives

Learned people in the Middle Ages considered time to be a sacred element of life that would unfold only between the Creation and the Last Things. Starting from the Creation and proceeding through the Old and New Testaments up to the present, time would eventually end with Christ's second advent (Doomsday), at which point it would give way to eternity.

Christian linear time seeks meaning and perfection above all in the future. Recursive, or cyclical, time devotes similar concentration to contemplating the past, hoping to discover in it the meaning and perfection of a Golden Age that has been lost. The doctrinal certainty that Christ will come again and that beyond this world and time lie eternal reward or punishment has always made future expectation more powerful for Christianity than contemplation of the past. However, Christian concern with the past ought not to be overlooked. Yet Christian belief is founded on truly new and unique events, such as the Creation, the Incarnation, and the Last Judgment. Linear time's orientation toward the future – its yearning for the *telos* (goal) and another world beyond it – is the most important difference between Christianity's linear concept of time and older, recursive, or cyclical, notions.

The most influential source ideas about linear timekeeping is St. Augustine's *De civitate Dei* (412–426), in which he replaced the Neoplatonic "*anakuklosis*" (endlessly revolving time) with the Christian element of "*providentia*," that is, God's provident involvement in evolving history. Augustine (354–430) was also one of the first Christian authors who divided world history into six ages (*sex aetates*), followed by a seventh age (the age of sabbatical peace) and finally, after the Last Judgment, by a perpetual eighth age (the end without end). The influence of this schema during the Middle Ages can hardly be overestimated. A different division of time and world history is proposed by the Old Testament Book of Daniel and is known as the theory of the Four Empires. This theory was reinterpreted by Hippolytus of Rome (c. 170–c. 236), who held the Roman Empire to be the final era after which the world would end. This notion helps explain why Carolingian and Ottonian emperors emphasized the almost divine importance of the *translatio imperii*, that is, the continuation of the Roman Empire into their era. They legitimated themselves by claiming to be the true successors to the Roman emperors. In this way the continuity of Daniel's Fourth Empire would be assured and the end of the world postponed.

Augustine's teleological orientation of world history is, to be sure, the most significant Christian contribution to Western ideas about historical time, yet Christian liturgy was based mainly on repetition. The Divine Office, a daily rotating pattern of prayer, incorporated the routine of the canonical hours. The public ringing of bells to call clerics to prayer at specified hours was the chief means by which any person in the medieval West measured time. Even laymen organized their lives around the canonical hours, at least insofar as these were announced publicly by the ringing bells. Regulating the measure of time provided the Church with a means to establish permanent social order, a keystone for medieval society. The liturgical year also exemplifies an obvious expression of repetitive timekeeping. In the ecclesiastical calendar, certain feasts are assigned to fixed days according to the solar year of 12 months. Other feasts are assigned to Sundays or to seasons of the liturgical year; thus, they are moveable (i.e., not assigned to fixed dates), although they recur every year. Moreover the fixed feasts were not identical in all countries or dioceses. The calendar varies not only from year to year but also from place to place within any single year.

A classic problem for liturgical observance concerned dating the feast of Easter. Disputes raged over both the accuracy and the authority of its calculation, two elements inextricably joined in medieval thought. Easter is to be held on the first Sunday after the first full moon (lunar argument) after the vernal equinox (solar argument). Thus, it became necessary to reconcile the solar calendar of ancient Rome with the lunar calendar of the Jews. Reconciling the requirements of fixed and moveable feasts led to lunisolar Easter tables that repeated not annually but after long intervals, providing a partial repetition after 19 years and a full repetition only after 532 years.

Easter tables were devised not to chronicle the past but to chart the future, essentially as forecasts of the great moveable feasts. Only afterward did the tables supply a framework for analistic records of the past. Easter tables then came to preserve past, present, and future together not only in a linear form but also in the 532-year cycle, the *annus magnus*.

Another example of Christian timekeeping occurs in the introduction of the notion of the Christian era by a sixth-century Scythian monk, Dionysius Exiguus (d. after 550). As a *magister* in Rome he was asked to calculate the correct date of Easter for the following year (A.D. 526). Because of his acquaintance with a more accurate Alexandrian Easter table, Dionysius Exiguus could solve the problem posed. Simultaneously he created a new Easter table that could be seen as a continuation of this Alexandrian cycle. In his table Dionysius Exiguus introduced one crucial change. He preferred to count the years not from the imperial coronation of Diocletian (284), as was the custom in Alexandria and the East, but rather from the Incarnation of the Lord (*ab incarnatione Domini*). Thus, he did not designate the first year of his Easter table as the 248th year of the Diocletian era but instead wrote "the 532th year since the Incarnation of the Lord." Because of this innovation Dionysius Exiguus can be considered the founder of the notion of a Christian era. He did not clearly specify either the reasons or the calculations by which he equated the year 248 *anno Diocletiani* with the year 532 *anno Domini*.

Medieval authors such as Abbo of Fleury (d. 1004), Heriger of Lobbes (d. 1007), Marianus Scottus (d. 1082), Gerland of Besançon (d. after 1094), Sigebert of Gembloux (d. 1112), and Heimo of Bamberg (d. 1139) contested, by drawing on the Gospels (*secundum Evangelii veritatem*), the computational accuracy of the start of the Christian era and made their own corrections. Ranging from inaugural dates of 33 B.C. (Heimo) to A.D. 8 (Heriger), each of the reasonings reveals the unique and original mind of a medieval intellectual. Modern research as well has proven that Dionysius' reckoning was incorrect. Although most scholars agree that Christ was born sometime between 12 and 7 B.C., they too are unable to present convincing arguments for their dates.

Despite its linear aspects the liturgical *cursus* (cycle) is based on recurring natural and astronomical (solar and lunar) phenomena. Thus, line and *cursus* are different models of Christian time structure, with one never entirely excluding the other. Both are integral to Western medieval thought on timekeeping.

PETER VERBIST

See also Biblical Figures and Practices; Liturgy: Eastern Christian; Liturgy: Western Christian; Music: Christian Perspectives; Whitby, England

Further Reading

Borst, Arno, *The Ordering of Time: From the Ancient Computus to the Modern Computer*, Cambridge: Polity Press, and Chicago: University of Chicago Press, 1993

Ducos, Joëlle, and Claude Thomasset, *Le temps qu'il fait au Moyen Âge: Phénomènes atmosphériques dans la littérature, la pensée scientifique et religieuse*, Paris: Presses de l'Université de Paris-Sorbonne, 1998
Ehlert, Trude, *Zeitkonzeptionen, Zeiterfahrung, Zeitmessung: Stationen ihres Wandels vom Mittelalter bis zur Moderne*, Paderborn: Schöningh, 1997
Higgins, Anne, "Medieval Notions on the Structure of Time," *Journal of Medieval and Renaissance Studies* 19:2 (1989)
Jones, Charles W., "The Development of the Latin Ecclesiastical Calendar," *The Mediaeval Academy of America* 41 (1943)
Ribémont, Bernard, editor, *Le temps, sa mesure et sa perception au Moyen Âge: Actes*, Cannes: Paradigme, 1992
Spazi, tempi, misure e percorsi nell'Europa del bassomedievo: Atti del XXXII Convegno storico internazionale, Todi, 8–11 ottobre 1995, Spoleto: Centro italiano di studi sul basso medioevo, 1996
Stevens, Wesley M., *Cycles of Time and Scientific Learning in Medieval Europe*, Aldershot, Hampshire, and Brookfield, Vermont: Variorum, 1995
Whitrow, Gerald J., *Time in History: The Evolution of Our General Awareness of Time and Temporal Perspective*, Oxford and New York: Oxford University Press, 1988

Topography, Sacred (Buddhist)

Analysis of directions and layouts – for example, the four cardinal points and the architecture of a temple – can reveal some fine points about a religious tradition's uses of space. Thus, the four stations of the Buddha's life are associated with the four directions: he left home in the east, was enlightened in the south, began teaching in the west, and passed away in the north. To this day Buddhist pilgrims make a symbolic round, touring the four sacred city sites in a clockwise direction. Legends also align the cardinal points with the Four Sights that the young Śākyamuni encountered. On an outing from his pleasure garden, he saw an old man in the east, a sick man in the south, a corpse in the west, and a wandering ascetic in the north. This does not make a perfect fit. He did not encounter the "pain of (child)birth" in the east, but instead the north, normally associated with death, now marks the beginning of a new calling that ended in his final nirvāṇa (extinction). Thus, he broke the cycle, and there will be no further rebirth for him.

In early Mahāyāna the Pure Lands in the east arose first and belonged to the Buddha Akṣobhya, the Immovable. Like the young prince leaving home in the east to become a mendicant, this "happy field" in the east is rather ascetic. The truly luxuriant paradise belonged to Amitābha/Amitāyus in the west. The direction of sunset is normally deemed secondary to the direction of sunrise, but west being where the Buddha first taught, it could anticipate the compassion of this Buddha of Eternal Light/Life. Eternal light and life being attributes of the Zoroastrian deity Ahura Mazda, some scholars believe that the cult of the western Pure Land might actually have a Persian origin.

Concerning the evolution of the Buddhist temple called *saṅghārama*, two hypotheses are put forth about its evolution: either it grew from the *vihāra* cloister or it grew from the stūpa reliquary. The cloister belongs to the *saṅgha* just as the stūpa does to the Buddha. These two of the three Jewels were at an early point discrete and distinct, and the distinction between monk and lay is just as clear:

monk	nirvāṇa	wisdom	withdrawn cloisters
lay	saṃsāra	karma	the world outside

Ideally these two domains were kept separate. The stūpa of the Buddha initially stood on its own. In the next stage the two lines of development began to merge. The *lena* monastery took in the stūpa, whereas the stūpa grew into a *caitya* complex with lodgings for monks. Admired by both monk and lay, the Buddha had opened up in the temple a "transcendental" space where both monk and lay could commingle. In the mature temple we see that final integration. For a clearer picture we turn to the layout of the Tōdaiji (temple) in Nara (simplified in the diagram), where Japan has preserved this oldest of Chinese temple plans. China had created the longitudinal layout of the temple ground when an architect, around A.D. 500, borrowed that grand "processional" design from the imperial palace. With this design we can catch the logic of the placement more easily than we could with the often open, seemingly haphazard temple layout in Theravāda countries. China has the temple facing south so that the monastic cloisters at the back face toward the north:

		North	
A	monk	cloister off limits	nirvāṇa pure
B	buddha	image hall/pagoda open to the public	
C	laity	secular market food and sex	saṃsāra polluted
		South	

Areas A and B make up the temple proper. It is traditionally enclosed by a low wall. Once inside the main, southern gate, no secular buying and selling is permitted. Area C outside the gate is the opposite of area A. This area outside the main gate (*monzen*) often grew into a market town (*machi*), called a *monzenmachi* in Japan. It resembles a *Marktplatz* (market square) in Germany. It often harbors the sinful pleasures denied to the cloistered monks, that is, hostels with good food, warm baths, and female companions. Impious as that conjunction might appear, it not only reflects medieval religio-economic developments but might also echo a central tenet of Mahāyāna which says that "saṃsāra is nirvāṇa, nirvāṇa is saṃsāra." Thus, sacred topography comes to encapsulate ideology.

That is because area B is suspended between the nirvāṇa of the monk in A and the saṃsāra of the marketplace in C. Area B is the Buddha arena, which the early *vihāra* cloister did not have.

This is where the Buddha relic (in the stūpa, which is now called a pagoda) and the Buddha image (a later addition now housed in the Buddha hall) are found. On public display they attract both monk and laity. The nirvāṇic monks in the cloister are drawn out into this atrium where as monk-clerics ("priests") they serve the lay visitor and pilgrim. The laymen are drawn in from the "dusty world" outside the temple gate, but they are not allowed to intrude into the cloisters (marked usually "out of bounds"). They choose to flock around the Buddha relic and icons – where the temple priests know to put "donation boxes" for the temple's upkeep. This mingling of monk and laity in this liminal ground amounts to a blessed fusion of nirvāṇa and saṃsāra. Being "between and betwixt" it is the theater for the Mahāyāna bodhisattva, who while abiding in saṃsāra as if it were nirvāṇa can "move freely at will."

This commingling of sacred and profane that Mahāyāna idealized remained present as a possibility in Theravāda, whose large temples have their share of cloisters, pagodas, and image halls as well as a market nearby. The difference is that Theravāda, protective of the sanctity of the cloisters, would not accommodate its teaching to popular devotion to the Buddha. However, the process does not end there. As noted previously, outside the temple gate lies the truly secular world of meat, wine, and sex. There too flourish local gods and demons, shamans, and magicians, whom the early or purist Buddhist tradition repudiated. Their incorporation into the dharma is the final move and mark of Vajrayāna (esoteric Buddhism). Thus, the evolution of Buddhism is literally "laid out" in a line of progression from A to C. A is purist Theravāda with its nirvāṇic ideal, B is liberal or liminal Mahāyāna embracing the betwixt-and-between, and C is radical Vajrayāna acculturating all.

WHALEN LAI

See also Architecture: Buddhist Monasteries in Southern Asia; Architecture: Structural Monasteries in East Asia; Buddha (Śākyamuni); Buddhist Schools/Traditions: Japan; Esoteric Buddhism in China and Japan; Images: Buddhist Perspectives; Kyoto, Japan; Liturgy: Buddhist; Maṇḍala; Mountain Monasteries, Buddhist; Nara, Japan; Pilgrimages, Buddhist; Stūpa; Temple, Buddhist; Visual Arts, Buddhist: Nepal

Further Reading

Dutt, Sukumar, *Buddhist Monks and Monasteries in India: Their History and Contribution to Indian Culture*, London: Allen and Unwin, 1962

Hirakawa, Akira, "The Rise of Mahāyāna and Its Relationship to the Stūpa," in *Memoirs of the Research Department of the Toyo Bunko*, volume 38, Tokyo: Toyo Bunko, 1963

Nagao, Gadjin, "The Architectural Tradition in Buddhist Monasticism," in *Studies in History of Buddhism*, edited by A.K. Narain, New Delhi: B.R. Pub., 1980

Prip-Moller, J., *Chinese Buddhist Monasteries*, Copenhagen: G.E.C. Gad, and London: Oxford University Press, 1937

Schopen, Gregory, "Mahāyāna in Indian Inscriptions," *Indo-Iranian Journal* 21 (1979)

Shizutani, Masao, *Shōki Daijō Bukkyō seiritsu katei* (The Founding and Development of Early Mahāyāna), Kyoto: Hyakkaen, 1974

Welch, Holmes, *The Practice of Chinese Buddhism 1900–1950*, Cambridge, Massachusetts: Harvard University Press, 1967

Transvestite Saints

Cults of female transvestite saints signal key aspects of the early medieval Church's attitude toward women and their supposed inferiority. These cults were attached exclusively to female cross-dressing saints: there is no celebration of saintly male transvestites. They were at their most popular up to around A.D. 900, after which other forms of female sanctity began to dominate. The cults flourished in the eastern Mediterranean and Asia Minor, but their fame was even more widespread. The saints' exploits were admired by monastic communities in the Christian West. Spain provided the example of the bearded and probably nonexistent Wilgefortis. Stories reached beyond mainland Europe into England and Ireland. The legendary Eugenia was lauded by the Anglo-Saxon Aldhelm (c. 640–709) and in the Old Irish martyrology *Félire Óengusso*. All this occurred despite the fact that Deuteronomy 22:5 explicitly forbids both male and female transvestism.

Thecla, of Iconium in Asia Minor, is the earliest recorded transvestite saint. She proved something of a trendsetter, and her cult center at Seleucia was a place of devotion. Whatever might be said about her doubtful historicity, Thecla was imagined to be the convert and preaching companion of the apostle Paul. Her deeds were first celebrated in the late-second-century *Acts of Paul and Thecla*. It has been argued that the anonymous author of this most influential text might have been an upper-class educated woman, for Thecla is presented as being able to preach and baptize like men. The evidence is not especially convincing. Indeed Tertullian (c. 160–c. 230) stated that the author was a literate priest. Of course it must be remembered that he was writing in response to those women who claimed leading roles in the Christian community on the strength of Thecla's example.

Thecla exemplifies a woman who is spiritually transformed by God, a transformation that is physically signaled by her adoption of male clothing. Significantly Thecla assumes a male haircut and male clothing only after her dramatic baptism in the amphitheater. It has been argued that Thecla takes up the masculine identity of the Christian believer. Here the key text is Paul's Letter to the Galatians 3:27–28, which asserts that there is no male or female and that all believers are one in Christ. Commentators on this passage expressed this ideal in masculine terms. Women of notable holiness were imagined as attaining spiritual manhood by Ambrose of Milan (339–397) and Jerome (342–420). Earlier still this notion seems to have inspired one of the visions of the historical martyr Vibia Perpetua (d. 203). Gnostic sects speculated along similar lines and readily employed language that describes female transformation into perfect maleness. The implications of saintly female cross-dressing do not seem to have been regarded in the hostile light that was reserved for male transvestism with the attendant danger of men masquerading as women in female religious communities. After all female transvestism served the symbolic function of asserting the oneness of the Christian believer. This oneness was male. However, a man dressing as a woman was suspected of having dubious motives, usually of a sexual nature.

Thecla's career was read in different ways, and the tales of other transvestite saints came to diverge from it. On one level Thecla's example was taken literally. For example, Jerome criticized those women who cut their hair short in male fashion and dressed as men. These same practices were condemned by the Council of Gangra in 348 and by the *Codex Theodosianus*. Male commentators preferred to concentrate on the symbolic nature of Thecla's transformation and on her virginity. In the latter sense she was admired by Jerome and became an object of devotion for Gregory of Nyssa (c. 330–c. 395) and Gregory of Nazianzus (329/30–389/90).

Other factors played a role as well. Legends localized in the Egyptian desert of Scetis suggest that a male monastic audience became dominant from the sixth century, if not earlier. The deserts of Egypt were supposedly the refuge of the legendary transvestite virgin saints Anastasia, Theodora, Athanasia, Pelagia, and Marina, among others. Of this group Pelagia was the most influential. The earliest form of her tale, recorded by John Chrysostom (c. 347–407), tells how an unnamed prostitute in Antioch repents and adopts a male monastic habit. A number of women are imagined to have used similar strategies, although few had formerly been as sinful as Pelagia. It has been suggested that an entire literary cycle had come into being by the sixth century that concentrated on a woman, disguised as a monk, who lived undetected in a male monastic community. Some of these disguised women suffer false accusations of paternity in silence. In all cases they seem to have expiated their female sinfulness by adopting a male level of asceticism. Such women tend to remain in situ in their chosen monastery. They do not wander from place to place and preach in the manner of Thecla.

Gradually female transvestite saints came to embody less of an ideal. Most important, perhaps, the loss of Syria, Egypt, and eventually large parts of Asia Minor to Islam from the seventh century on meant that the Christian communities that had originally fostered the female transvestite saints became obscure. Furthermore, although the image of the transvestite saint was popular in the West, the practice was never properly transplanted there. The counterexamples of Abbess Radegunde (518–587) or Hilda (614–680) seemed more relevant. Brigit, the Irish virgin saint, abbess, and bishop who supposedly flourished in the fourth and fifth centuries, is more in the mold of the Eastern transvestites. Like Thecla she adopts a male preaching role, although her ninth-century hagiographer never describes her as having taken up male dress along with her episcopacy. The historical Joan of Arc (1412–1431) could also be considered a successor. However, Joan's cross-dressing, which was the ostensible cause of her execution, was very different. She adopted male clothing for a male military role. She was not inspired by ideals of divine androgyny or female-to-male spiritual transformation that marked the transvestite saint.

Elva Johnston

See also Asceticism: Christian Perspectives; Body: Christian Perspectives; Brigit, St.; Desert Fathers; Egypt; Hagiography: Eastern Christian; Hermits: Eastern Christian; Hilda, St.; Radegunde, St.; Sexuality: Christian Perspectives; Syria

Further Reading

Albrecht, Ruth, *Das Leben der heiligen Makrina auf dem Hintergrund der Thekla-Traditionen: Studien zu dem Ursprüngen des weiblichen Mönchtums im 4. Jahrhundert in Kleinasien* (Forschungen zur Kirchen- und Dogmengeschichte, 38), Göttingen: Vandenhoeck and Ruprecht, 1986

Anson, John, "The Female Transvestite in Early Monasticism," *Viator* 5 (1974)

Bullough, Vern L., "Transvestites in the Middle Ages," *American Journal of Sociology* 79 (1974)

Cooper, Kate, *The Virgin and the Bride: Idealized Womanhood in Late Antiquity*, Cambridge, Massachusetts: Harvard University Press, 1996

Dagron, Gilbert, *Vie et miracles de Sainte Thècle: texte grec, traduction et commentaire* (Subsidia Hagiographica, 62), Brussels: Société des Bollandistes, 1978

Davies, Stevan L., *The Revolt of the Widows: The Social World of the Apocryphal Acts*, Carbondale: Southern Illinois University Press, and London: Feffer and Simons, 1980

Delcourt, Marie, *Hermaphrodite: Myths and Rites of the Bisexual Figure in Classical Antiquity*, translated by J. Nicholson, London: Studio Books, 1961

Patlagean, Evelyne, "L'histoire de la femme déguisée en moine et l'évolution de la sainteté feminine à Byzance," *Studi Medievali* 3:17 (1976)

Trappists

The designation "Trappist" can be misleading, for not all Cistercians are Trappists, many so-called Trappists have little patience with the old traditions of La Trappe, and Trappists of today are not the Trappists of yesterday.

The story begins in 1098 with the foundation of Cîteaux and the intention of Robert of Molesme (c. 1027–1111) to live a life based strictly on the Rule of St. Benedict. The austere asceticism of the early Cistercians was well known, but it was inevitable that over the years accommodations would be made to changing times and circumstances. Some of these accommodations were justified, some less so, and by the late Middle Ages it is not difficult to find examples of laxity and negligence.

The situation was exacerbated by a series of natural and political disasters – famine, plague, war, and especially the system of commendatory abbots – and by the end of the 16th century most French abbeys had fallen into disrepair and disrepute. The situation gave rise to a number of vigorous attempts at reform, the most important of which was that instituted at La Trappe west of Chartres by Armand-Jean de Rancé (1626–1700).

Those who supported reform sought a return to the ideals of the early years of the Order and focused especially on its original vegetarianism. The Rule of St. Benedict, the fundamental document of the Cistercian Order, permits meat only to the sick, but by the 16th and 17th centuries the prohibition was rarely observed. The reformers – the "Abstinents" – regarded this meat eating as a symbol of all decadence, utterly rejected it, and (with papal approval) formed themselves into a congregation known as the Congregation of St. Bernard of the Strict Observance. However, they were not unopposed, and those who disagreed with them saw meat eating simply as an accommodation to changing times and regarded the Strict Observance as a collection of deluded enthusiasts.

The schism was so acrimonious that Pope Alexander VII (1655–1667) was called to intervene, and in 1664 he invited representatives of both parties to Rome to put their cases to a commission of cardinals. Two years later Alexander promulgated the bull *In suprema*, which recognized two Cistercian observances, common and strict, the main difference between them being that the former would eat meat three times a week (except during Lent and Advent) and the latter would not.

Meanwhile, Rancé, who had been in Rome in 1664 defending the Abstinents, had established his own rule at La Trappe: a rule more severe than that either of the early Cistercians or of the Abstinents. His monks were forbidden not only meat but also fish, eggs, cheese, and butter. The austerity of the house – the seclusion, the silence, the fasts, the intensity of the *opus Dei*, and the hard manual labor – became a matter of such wide renown that "Strict Observance" and "Trappist" came to be used (incorrectly) as synonyms.

For all its severity, the regimen at La Trappe attracted numerous postulants, and by the time of the Revolution the community was flourishing. However, in 1791, when the abbey was about to be suppressed, the last novice-master, Dom Augustin de Lestrange (1754–1827), left the abbey with a group of 22 religious and fled to Switzerland. There, on 1 June 1791, he reestablished the Strict Observance at La Val-Sainte in the canton of Fribourg and imposed on his monks an even stricter regimen than that of La Trappe. There was no heating, the monks slept on the floor, their food was bread and boiled vegetables, their drink was water, and apart from six or seven hours of sleep, the entire day was spent in either hard manual labor or the *opus Dei* in church.

Nevertheless, this extreme asceticism attracted an extraordinary number of vocations, and in 1794 Pope Pius VI (1775–1799) recognized La Val-Sainte as an abbey and named the observance the Congregation of Trappists. Two years later Lestrange founded the first convent of Trappistines, the female branch of the congregation, at Sembrancher in the Bas-Valais, although Cistercian nuns trace their ultimate origin to the 12th-century abbey of Tart, near Dijon.

Thus, from this small and dedicated community, the Strict Observance was refounded. Groups of monks were sent out by Lestrange, and slowly, with many difficulties and after remarkable adventures, the Order crept back into other parts of Europe, although the real expansion took place only after the defeat of Napoleon in 1814.

Hyacinthe Rigaud, *Armand-Jean le Bouthillier de Rancé*, 17th century. Photo courtesy of Abbaye de La Trappe

The history of the Order in the 19th century was marked by internal dissension. Some houses continued to follow the regimen of Lestrange, some found that regimen too severe and idiosyncratic and returned to the principles of Rancé, and elsewhere some were obliged by the state to modify their rule and take on certain pastoral duties. Thus, by the middle of the 19th century three observances existed within the Strict Observance, and it was not until 1892 that the three were united by Pope Leo XIII (1878–1903) as the Reformed Cistercians of Our Lady of La Trappe. Six years later mention of La Trappe was dropped from the title, and in 1902 Leo officially renamed the order the Order of Reformed Cistercians, or the Strict Observance. It is now called the Cistercian Order of the Strict Observance: *Ordo Cisterciensis Strictioris Observantiae*, or O.C.S.O.

Legrand, *Dom Augustin de Lestrange*, 18th century.
Photo courtesy of Abbaye de La Trappe

The practices of the O.C.S.O. were further modified after the Second Vatican Council (1962–1965). The Rule of St. Benedict was reaffirmed as the fundamental guide to monastic life, but the extreme asceticism of Rancé, and especially of Lestrange, was moderated. The monastic day is still divided between the *opus Dei*, manual labor, *lectio divina*, and study, but the monks and nuns eat fish, eggs, and dairy products, and although silence remains the norm, it may be broken when required by the circumstances. Sign language is no longer used. The earlier penitential spirituality has given way to an emphasis on inward transformation, but the simplicity and charity that were so important to Rancé himself remain at the heart of the Cistercian way.

David N. Bell

See also Asceticism: Christian Perspectives; Cistercians; France: History; La Trappe, France; Maurists; Origins: Comparative Perspectives; Patrons, Christian: Lay; Rancé, Armand-Jean de

Further Reading

Bianco, Frank, *Voices of Silence: Lives of the Trappists Today*, New York: Paragon House, 1991
Commission pour l'histoire de l'Ordre de Cîteaux, under the direction of Jean de la Croix Bouton, *Les Moniales cisterciennes*, 4 vols., Grignan, France: Abbaye N.D. d'Aiguebelle, 1986–1989
Downey, Michael, *Trappist: Living in the Land of Desire*, New York: Paulist Press, 1997
Gaillardin, Casimir, *Les Trappistes; ou, l'Ordre de Cîteaux au XIXe siècle: Histoire de la Trappe depuis sa fondation jusqu'à nos jours, 1140–1844*, 2 vols., Paris: Comptoir des imprimeurs-unis, 1844
Kervingant, Marie de la Trinité, *Des moniales face à la Révolution française: Aux origines des Cisterciennes-Trappistines*, Paris: Beauchesne, 1989
Krailsheimer, Alban J., *Armand-Jean de Rancé, Abbot of La Trappe: His Influence in the Cloister and the World*, Oxford: Clarendon Press, 1974
Krailsheimer, Alban J., *Rancé and the Trappist Legacy*, Kalamazoo, Michigan: Cistercian Publications, 1985
Lekai, Louis J., *The Rise of the Cistercian Strict Observance in Seventeenth Century France*, Washington, D.C.: Catholic University of America Press, 1968
Lekai, Louis J., *The Cistercians: Ideals and Reality*, Kent, Ohio: Kent State University Press, 1977
Lelóczky, Julius D., *Constitutiones et acta capitulorum strictioris observantiae ordinis cisterciensis (1624–1687)*, Rome: Editiones Cistercienses, 1967
Louf, André, *The Cistercian Way*, translated by Nivard Kinsella, Kalamazoo, Michigan: Cistercian Publications, 1983
Réformes et continuité dans l'Ordre de Cîteaux: De l'étroite observance à la stricte observance: Actes du colloque Journées d'histoire monastique, Saint-Mihiel, 2–3 octobre 1992, Brecht: Cîteaux: Commentarii cistercienses, 1995
Zakar, Polycarpe, *Histoire de la stricte observance de l'Ordre cistercien depuis ses débuts jusqu'au généralat du cardinal de Richelieu (1606–1635)*, Rome: Editiones Cistercienses, 1966

Travelers: Buddhist

The Buddhist ideal of the homeless, wandering monk began with the historical Buddha's "Great Renunciation" of the worldly life of a homeowner and his departure onto the path of a peripatetic religious mendicant (*śramaṇa*). After his enlightenment the Buddha spent many years traveling by foot through the kingdoms of Maghada and Kośala (in present-day Nepal and northern India), visiting places such as the Deer Park near Benares, Bodh Gayā, and Rajagṛha. Such a lifestyle was characteristic for religious ascetics at that time, who roamed the forests and towns of the Indian cultural sphere begging for their food and seeking to accomplish spiritual goals. The initial ordination of a Buddhist monastic is traditionally known as "going forth [into homelessness]" (*pravrajyā*), an act that is ritually reenacted by monks and nuns to this day. This homeless ideal is celebrated throughout early literature, as seen in *The Fruits of the Homeless Life Scripture* (*Sāmaññaphala Sutta*). Apart from three months of rainy season retreat (*varṣāvasana*), during which such travel was virtually impossible, the Buddha and his disciples traveled constantly, carrying only the traditional eight requisites (*aṣṭapariṣkāra*, i.e., robes, a begging bowl, a belt, a razor, a needle, a strainer, a staff, and a toothpick) and sleeping in the open air. At the time of his passing away, the Buddha instructed his disciples to continue their travels, declaring, "Let not two of you go in one and the same direction." As time moved on, the homeless, wandering lifestyle of Buddhist monks and nuns became superseded by the establishment of permanent residences (*vihāra*s), although many continue the tradition of wandering to the present day, such as the forest dwellers (*āranyaka*s) living in Sri Lanka.

The spread of Buddhism from its Indian homeland was due largely to the mobility of Buddhist monastics, who journeyed by land and sea to spread their teachings, retrieve scriptures, visit pilgrimage sites and Buddhist universities, or attend formalized assemblies. Traveling independently, in groups, or together with merchant caravans, they brought their tradition as far west as Greece and Egypt, north to Mongolia, south to Sri Lanka and Indonesia, and east to the island of Japan. Some of the earliest archaeological evidence, such as Rock Edict XIII and the inscription found in Kandahar (Afghanistan), suggest that the first great wave of international Buddhist travelers were missionaries of Mauryan Emperor Aśoka (r. 272–231 B.C.), who sent hundreds of monks in all directions from his kingdom to spread the teachings of the Buddha. Many nations attribute the arrival of Buddhism in their land to these Aśokan missionaries. For example, the Buddhists of Sri Lanka claim that Buddhism was brought to their island by the monk Mahinda, the son of Aśoka, who established the Buddhist order there after successfully converting its king, Devānaṃpiya Tissa. Legends of Thailand also tell of Aśoka's missionaries bringing Buddhism to their land, and those of Burma attribute the introduction of Buddhism in their land to the arrival of his monks Soṇa and Uttara in Suvaṇṇabhūmi.

Many of the most famous Buddhist travelers are those who are renowned for having first brought Buddhism or a particular sect of Buddhism into a new region. After Aśoka's missionary endeavors, Buddhist monks continued to make their presence felt in central Asia, moving on the winding Silk Road throughout places such as Kashmir, Khotan, Kuchā, and Parthia (in India, Pakistan, Afghanistan, and Iran). This great merchant highway, the artery of travel linking China to Rome on which Marco Polo made his famous journey in the 13th century, comprised a primary pathway for the movement of Buddhist monastics during the early spread of Buddhism. At Kashgar in central Asia, the Silk Road split into two major routes that lay on the northern and southern borders of the Taklamakan, Tarim, and Lop deserts, rejoining near the Chinese border towns of Dunhuang and Anxi. Although Buddhism was probably brought into China by monks from central Asian locations spread along the Silk Road, Chinese legends describe the earliest harbingers of the Buddhist faith as Indian Buddhist masters who were invited to China by Han Emperor Ming (r. 58–75). The Chinese Buddhist monk Shundao is credited with bringing Buddhism to the north Korean Koguryŏ kingdom in 372 at the command of Chinese Qin King Fu Jian. In 384 the Serindian monk Maranant'a brought Buddhism to the southwest Paekche kingdom, followed by the arrival of the Koguryŏ monk Mukhoja in the southeast Silla Empire in 424, although Buddhism was not officially recognized in Silla until 527. Buddhism was introduced to Japan in 552 when Korean Paekche King Syŏng-myŏng sent an envoy with Buddhist images and scriptures to the Japanese imperial court. Under the advocacy of Prince Shōtoku (573–622), often recognized as the founder of Buddhism in Japan, Korean monks and nuns, such as Shōtoku's own teacher, the Koguryŏ monk Hyeja, were provided a warm welcome on the islands.

Paralleling the movement of Buddhism through central Asia to these eastern Asian countries, Buddhist monastics from India traveled along the southern border of the Himalayas, spreading their tradition to the Southeast Asian countries now known as Burma, Thailand, Cambodia, and Laos and converging with the Chinese cultural sphere in Vietnam. Buddhism is said to have entered Indonesia in the fifth century on the conversion of the Javanese king by the Indian missionary monk Guṇavarman. Because of its relative isolation on the "roof of the world," Tibet was one of the latest Asian countries to feel the impact of the Buddhist tradition. Tibetans trace the presence of Buddhism in their country to the reign of King Songsen Gampo (616–650), who established contact with neighboring Buddhist regions such as central Asia, China, and Nepal after conquering nearby areas along the Silk Road. During the eighth century Buddhism was officially recognized in Tibet on the arrival of the monk Śāntarakṣita from Nālandā University in India and the Tantric master Padmasambhava from Uddiyana, Kashmir (Pakistan), both of whom came to Tibet at the invitation of King Trisong Detsen (740–798). Until modern times a primary route of travel between India and Tibet stretched through Nepal by way of Kriyong.

Of the many Buddhists who traveled throughout southern Asia during historical times, some visited Sri Lanka, such as the Theravāda scholar and translator Buddhaghosa, who journeyed from Magadha to the island during the fifth century, where he composed the important Theravāda text *The Path of Purification* (*Visuddhimagga*). His successor, Buddhadatta, known as The Commentator, came to Sri Lanka from Uragapura in southern India. Groups of Burmese monks are also known to have frequented the island, especially between the 12th and 14th centuries, aiming to receive higher ordination and retrieve copies of the Pāli scriptures. Other well-known travelers began their journeys from this island, such as the group of Sri Lankan nuns who arrived in China in 434. Āryadeva, the famous disciple of Nāgārjuna (c. 150–250), is believed to have come to India from the island of Sri Lanka during the third century. A number of Sri Lankans are also reputed to have made journeys to the islands of

Indonesia. A professor from Nālandā University named Dharmapala is said to have visited Suvarṇa-dvīpa (Indonesia) in the seventh century, and there are legends that the renowned Indian scholar Atiśa (982–1054) also visited Indonesia at one point. In 1042 Atiśa traveled to Tibet, where he founded the Kadampa sect and made a tremendous impact on the course of Tibetan Buddhist history. Monastic travel in Southeast Asia was often, as elsewhere, influenced by political relations among kingdoms. For example, a number of Theravāda monks from Thaton in Thailand were captured by Burmese King Anawrahta in 1057 and brought back to his capital at Pagan together with a copy of the Pāli Canon.

China was a frequent destination for Buddhist monks from all directions and an inevitable way station for those traveling between central, southern, and eastern Asian countries. Some of the earliest recorded visitors to China were translators and precedent-setters, such as the Parthian monk An Shigao, who, after settling in the northern Chinese city of Luoyang around 148, translated a number of Buddhist texts on meditation. The first known Mahāyāna Buddhist missionary was Lokakṣema, who headed a translation project in Luoyang from 168 to 188. The Kuchean monk Fotudeng (232–348), who arrived in northern China around 310, served as a court adviser for the later Zhao dynasty and is credited with officially establishing the order of Buddhist nuns in China. The Kuchean monk Kumārajīva (344–413), who arrived in the Chinese capital of Chang'an in 401, headed a prolific translation team whose renditions of scriptures are still treasured by Chinese Buddhists today. Buddhabhadra (359–429), who journeyed from Kashmir to China in 409, first worked with Kumārajīva in Chang'an before traveling south to Lushan and then Jiangang, where he translated *The Flower Garland Scripture* (*Avataṃsaka Sūtra*). Another famous translator, Paramārtha (499–569), traveled from northern India to China by way of Southeast Asia, arriving in southern China in 546 and eventually settling in Canton. Bodhidharma, the first patriarch of Chinese Chan (Zen) Buddhism, arrived from the west in Luoyang sometime between 516 and 526.

The legacy of the wandering monastic also took root in Korea and Japan, where some of the most celebrated historical characters traveled extensively throughout their own countries and beyond. Since the seventh century, hosts of Korean monks visited China, such as Yuan Ts'o (613–683), Yuan Hiao (617–670), and Yi Siang (625–702), whereas some traveled east to Japan, such as Gyōgi (668–749). The Japanese monk Kūkai (774–835) sailed to China in 804 and returned to Japan in 806 to found the Japanese Shingon sect. Similarly Saichō (767–822) founded the Japanese Tendai school after studying in China, and his disciple Ennin (794–864) subsequently traveled throughout the mainland from 838 to 847. The diary that Ennin kept during his expedition is still considered an important source of information on China at that time. Another Tendai monk, Eisai (1141–1215), journeyed to China in 1168 and returned again in 1187 with the intention of tracing Buddhism to India. Although this plan fell through and his travels were restricted to China, he succeeded in returning to Japan in 1191 to initiate the school of Rinzai Zen, the first Japanese school of Zen. Soon thereafter his disciple Dōgen (1200–1253) left for China in 1223, returning to Japan in 1227 with the Sōtō Zen sect.

Notwithstanding Tibet's landscape of plateaus and Himalayan mountains, Buddhist monastics demonstrated a surprising fluidity of movement throughout the region. This mobility is exemplified in the international debate recorded to have taken place in Samye monastery near the capital city of Lhasa in 792. The two sides, headed by Kamalaśīla from India and Heshang Moheyan from China, argued at length over the issue of sudden versus gradual enlightenment, resulting in the victory of the gradualist Kamalaśīla. During the tenth century a number of Tibetan monks were sent to India to retrieve added knowledge of Buddhism. Two of these monks, Rinchen Sangpo and Lekbe Sherap, returned to Tibet in 978, bringing with them many texts and Indian scholars who produced what is known as the Second Dissemination of Buddhism in Tibet. During the 11th century Marpa (1012–1097), founder of the Kagyü sect, traveled to India three times and studied at Nālandā University with Nāropa. By the 16th century, following the Mongol invasion of Tibet, the close political and religious ties between Tibetans and Mongolians resulted in a strong presence of Tibetan monastics throughout the Mongolian Empire. During the early 20th century, the French adventurer Alexandra David-Neel (1868–1969) and the Japanese Zen monk Kawaguchi Ekai made well-known journeys to the Tibetan plateau and outlying areas, leaving behind fascinating accounts of their experiences among Tibetan communities.

Since the development of rapid transportation in recent centuries, Buddhism has become a global phenomenon, as monastic and lay practitioners have visited literally every region of the earth. Today Buddhist monks and nuns travel by airplane, train, ship, and automobile, founding Buddhist centers in places far from Asia, such as the Americas and Australia. Although fewer practitioners adhere to the ideal of the homeless, wandering monk prevalent during the historical Buddha's lifetime, this legacy continues to be an important constituent of the modern lifestyle of Buddhist monastics.

TALINE GOORJIAN

See also Aśoka; Buddha (Śākyamuni); Buddhism: Overview; Buddhist Schools/Traditions: China; Buddhist Schools/Traditions: Japan; Festivals, Buddhist; Forest Masters; Korea; Padmasambhava; Pilgrims to India, Chinese; Sri Lanka; Tibet

Further Reading

Batchelor, Stephen, *The Awakening of the West: The Encounter of Buddhism and Western Culture*, Berkeley: Parallax Press, 1994; as *The Awakening of the West: The Encounter of Buddhism and Western Culture, 542 BC–1992*, London: Aquarium, 1994

Berry, Scott, *A Stranger in Tibet: The Adventures of a Wandering Zen Monk*, Tokyo and New York: Kodansha International, 1989

Carrithers, Michael, *The Forest Monks of Sri Lanka: An Anthropological and Historical Study*, Delhi: Oxford University Press, 1983

Ennin, *Ennin's Diary*, translated by E.O. Reischauer, New York: Ronald Press, 1955
Fields, Rick, *How Swans Came to the Lake: A Narrative History of Buddhism in America*, Boulder, Colorado, and New York: Shambala, 1981
Foster, Barbara M., and Michael Foster, *Forbidden Journey: The Life of Alexandra David-Neel*, San Francisco: Harper and Row, 1987
Lancaster, Lewis R., and C.S. Yu, editors, *Introduction of Buddhism to Korea: New Cultural Patterns*, Berkeley, California: Asian Humanities Press, 1989
Prebish, Charles S., *Historical Dictionary of Buddhism*, Metuchen, New Jersey, and London: Scarecrow Press, 1993
Von Hinüber, Oskar, "Expansion to the North: Afghanistan and Central Asia," in *The World of Buddhism: Buddhist Monks and Nuns in Society and Culture*, edited by Heinz Bechert and Richard Gombrich, London: Thames and Hudson, and New York: Facts on File, 1984
Zurcher, Erik, *Buddhism: Its Origin and Spread in Words, Maps, and Pictures*, New York: St. Martin's Press, and London: Routledge and Kegan Paul, 1962

Travelers: Western Christian

One of the great emphases of Christianity is care for those less fortunate, whether the sick, the poor, or the desperate. In the premodern era this included care of travelers: one of medieval Christianity's good works was to feed and bed itinerants. From the Dark Ages (A.D. 600–1000) to the early modern period, when hostels and inns began to assume the care of travelers, monastic orders played a vital role in housing travelers. Although we tend to think of the medieval period as a time when people largely stayed at home, bound to the soil, in fact large numbers of people frequented the roads. Interrupted only during times of outright war, each year hundreds of thousands of pilgrims roamed Europe's roadways to scores of shrines, even to the Holy Land itself. Scores of people other than pilgrims traveled on the roads: merchants, soldiers, peddlers, journeymen, friars, students, criminals, lepers, and, by the early modern period, hundreds of thousands of the desperately poor and homeless. In an age of few inns, virtually no private accommodation, and no state welfare or hostel establishments, it fell to the Church and especially the monasteries and convents of Europe to provide free shelter and food for these travelers.

The monastic role in caring for travelers began in the Dark Ages. Initially monasteries were havens of peace in a world made chaotic with sundry invasions, but as the invasions lessened during the middle Dark Ages and the numbers of pilgrims and traders once more increased, monasteries became more involved in furnishing travelers with food and shelter. Charlemagne (768–814) was especially concerned for the safety of travelers and caused houses to be built across France and Italy so that travelers could receive free food and lodging for a night or two. A reduction in the amount of road traffic occurred during the Viking invasions, but by the 11th century pilgrimage was well on its way to becoming the great tourist industry of the medieval age. Many monastic houses were built to cater to the needs of the pilgrim trade; Sumption (1975) argues that the revival in mass pilgrimage from the 11th century was largely responsible for the monastic revival in southern France.

Monasteries along the main pilgrimage routes established large guest houses, and all monastic houses had at least a small dormitory for passers-by. In smaller establishments the almoner generally took charge of the monastery's guest dormitories in addition to his duties in distributing alms to the poor, but monasteries with large guest houses catering for wealthier visitors had a hosteler supervising the care of guests. The wealthier monastic houses operated two separate residences for itinerants and guests: one for the wealthy and another for the poor. These two residences often would be divided into dormitories for men and women. Guest houses could be very large, depending on the wealth and importance of the monastic house itself. At Cluny the guest house measured 135 feet by 30 feet; the male dormitory had 40 straw mattresses and 40 individual latrines, and the female dormitory had 30 mattresses and a similar number of individual latrines. The refectory, situated between the two dormitories, was lavish, with table linens and a large staff on hand to cater for the needs of the guests, the most important of whom could count on a extravagant welcome from the abbot and monks (Ariès and Duby, 1988).

Although the monasteries' major role in caring for travelers was to supply food and lodging, monasteries also played a vital role in providing information. Monks undoubtedly informed travelers of local conditions (e.g., the state of the road ahead, brigands, and any military activity in the area) and in some cases were able to furnish maps or itineraries. The monks of St. Martial in Limoges kept a detailed topographical map of the Holy Lands, and other monasteries supplied itineraries of travel routes. All this would have provided much-needed support (if not always accurate information) for pilgrims and travelers generally. Some monastic houses also kept extensive stables so that travelers could swap their weary horses.

Monastic houses not only catered to passing pilgrims: the monasteries themselves became destinations. The pilgrimage trade was too important and too wealthy for a monastic house to content itself with providing lodging for itinerants. During the medieval craze for saints and relics, monastic houses acquired whatever they could to make themselves destinations for pilgrims. Relics were bought (newly established monastic houses provided an eager buyers for relic merchants), obtained, or dug up in vegetable patches. Once the magical prowess of the relic had been substantiated by several miracles, monks controlled access to the relic, generally permitting only the wealthy to view or touch the holy shrine. Although relics were of mainly religious import, some monastic establishments preferred more secular inducements to attract the curious wealthy. In 1191, with considerable royal support, the monks at Glastonbury claimed to have found the tomb of King Arthur and Queen Guinevere. For several years thereafter the abbot of Glastonbury produced Arthur's shinbone – twice the size of an ordinary man's – to impress

Billboard in Poitiers advertising the wall paintings (11th and 13th centuries) of the former Abbey Church of St.-Savin, Gironde, France. Photo courtesy of the Editor

visitors. Once a monastic church had become a site of pilgrimage, the monks not only catered for the lodging and feeding of pilgrims but also sold mementos of the particular saint whose relic they held and even practiced their medical arts on the sick who came.

Although monastic orders catered to the needs of travelers, particularly pilgrims, monastics also became travelers themselves. Many medieval monks spent most of their lives on the road (especially the Franciscans, Dominicans, Carmelites, and Augustinians), and the annual numbers of monks and friars wandering the roads of Europe numbered in the tens of thousands (although many of these would have been "false" clerics, i.e., criminals who donned a habit to escape secular justice). Monastic homelessness was a recognized form of life in medieval Europe; monks and friars were found on pilgrimages, on crusades, or just wandering, sometimes earning respect and their keep as they catered to the religious needs of isolated communities and sometimes earning condemnation if they were too demanding of food and shelter.

By their nature some of the medieval mendicant orders spent a great deal of time on the road. The early Franciscans, forbidden to own property and possessing only the most basic of clothing, wandered about Europe and begged for their sustenance and shelter: "The brothers . . . shall go confidently to beg alms like pilgrims and strangers in this world, serving our Lord in poverty and humility." The Franciscans were to give utmost sympathy to the outcasts they met: lepers, criminals, the poor, and the needy. Moreover the Franciscans wandered well beyond the European landmass in their efforts to convert pagan peoples. Many went to the Middle East to attempt a conversion of the Islamic peoples (St. Francis among them); others traveled to the Far East partly as adventurers and partly as diplomats on behalf of the papacy. Although some friars endured great hardship, others patently enjoyed their wanderings. Depending on the largesse of the communities through which they passed, they received as much good food and wine as they could consume and spent a good deal of their time singing jolly songs as they wandered along.

These friars often provided invaluable services to local communities. If no local priest was present – as often happened in mountainous or more isolated regions – an itinerant friar would perform the accumulated baptisms, marriages, and burials of a community; corpses would have been buried with a pole stuck out of the ground so that, once the pole was removed, the friar could pour holy water down the hole. One Franciscan, St. Bernardino, traveled with a veritable procession of penitents, a choir of boys, several priests who could hear the accumulated confessions of the priestless, and a notary to record the subsequent reconciliations. Sometimes these wandering friars caused considerable resentment among local clergy, who felt that the friars were trying to usurp their position within society. Visiting friars also brought news of the outside world and, more often than not, collected news and information for their masters: wandering friars made excellent spies. Dominican friars often had a more sinister purpose in traveling to isolated communities: their task was to ferret out heresy for the Holy Church and, it was hoped, to reclaim the souls of heretics before the Inquisition would be needed.

The peculiar freedoms of traveling monks and friars meant that the system was open to abuse by the less worthy. Although many folk welcomed the appearance of a friar in their community, especially if they lacked a parish priest, others deplored the appearance of wandering monks and friars. By the 13th and 14th centuries, lay populations openly resented the Dominican and Franciscans as itinerant beggars who demanded that people put them up and feed them. The ploughman poems, a genre of popular medieval verse that voiced social complaint, often ridiculed the demands of the various friars wandering by:

> Then come the grey friars and make their moan,
> And call for money our souls to save;
> Then come the white friars and begin to groan,
> Wheat or barley they fain would have;
> Then commeth the friars Augustine and beginneth to crave,
> Corn or cheese, for they have not enough,
> Then commeth the black friars . . .
>
> (*God Spede the Plough*, late 15th century)

Some friars posed as pardoners, selling indulgences. Indeed the Church tried to prevent monks from becoming itinerant beggars. In 1380 the bishop of Exeter drove out of his diocese a Dominican friar who extorted money from simple folk by "feigned falsehoods" (Rowling, 1971), and in 1386 the Council of Salzburg labeled them "false prophets" who led astray the hearts of their listeners. Such measures did little to deter the tens of thousands of less than holy friars begging and extorting financial gain from the devout. Although many true friars abused their holy privileges, in defense of the mendicant orders it must be pointed out that a significant number of these wandering "friars" were laymen (often criminals) seeking an easy path to bed and board by preying on the devout.

Criticism of the Church spread during the late 14th century throughout the 15th century, culminating in the Reformation of the 16th century. After the Reformation the role of the monastic and mendicant orders in travel and in the care of travelers changed dramatically. In Protestant countries pilgrimages ceased, and monastic orders were dissolved: both pilgrims and wandering friars disappeared from the roadways of central, northern, and western Europe. However, monastic orders still played a part in travel, if a slightly sinister role as seen through Protestant eyes. Within Europe the mendicant orders, as well the Jesuits, acted as border inspectors and heresy hunters, trying to detect the passage of Protestants through their territories and waylaying them and trying to win them back to the Catholic faith. If the effort failed, the unfortunate Protestant was handed over to the Inquisition.

The role of monastic orders in caring for travelers or resorting to the life of the road itself has diminished in the modern world. In underdeveloped countries monastic houses still care for travelers, especially refugees, and for pilgrims. However, in the developed Western world, where tourism has replaced pilgrimage, hotels, motels, and a variety of secular hostels cater to the needs of the travel-weary, and the helpful monk has been replaced by the local information center.

SARA WARNEKE

See also Cluny, France; Dominicans; Francis of Assisi, St.; Franciscans; Heretics, Christian; Pilgrimages, Christian; Reformation; Relics, Christian Monastic; Social Services: Western Christian

Further Reading

Ariès, Phillipe, and Georges Duby, *A History of Private Life: Revelations of the Medieval World*, Cambridge, Massachusetts: Belknap Press, 1988

Rowling, Marjorie, *Everyday Life of Medieval Travellers*, New York: Putnam, and London: Batsford, 1971

Sumption, Jonathan, *Pilgrimage: An Image of Mediaeval Religion*, London: Faber and Faber, and Totowa, New Jersey: Rowman and Littlefield, 1975

Warneke, Sara, *Images of the Educational Traveller in Early Modern England*, Leiden and New York: Brill, 1995

Trinitarians (Mathurins)

The Trinitarians, the Order of the Most Holy Trinity and of Captives (*Ordo Sanctae Trinitatis et Captivorum*), was founded in northern France in the last decade of the 12th century by John of Matha (d. 1213) and a group of companions. The main sources for the early history of the order are letters of Pope Innocent III (1198–1216), the *Historia Occidentalis* of James of Vitry, and a few references in various chronicles. In addition, an early 13th-century mosaic – the work of the Cosmati, depicting Christ with two captives, one a Christian and the other a Moor – above the portal of San Tommaso in Formis in Rome is based on a vision of the founder. No early history of the order exists, nor does a vita of St. John of Matha. The earliest document of the order is its rule, promulgated by Pope Innocent III in his letter of 17 December 1198, on the recommendation of Odo de Sully, bishop of Paris and the abbot of St. Victor. The order is also known as the Mathurins from the name of its foundation in Paris.

The Trinitarian rule, like others of this period, draws on a variety of sources, including the rule of the Knights Hospitaller of St. John and, very likely, the contemporary confraternity tradition. It is also related to the rule of the Ospedale di Sancto Spirito in Rome, promulgated about his time. One of its distinctive features, the division of most of its income into thirds – one for the ransom of captives, one for good works, and one for the needs of the community – seems to derive from a provision of the Hospitaller rule. A prohibition against keeping money on deposit that appeared in the 1198 version of the rule was removed when the rule was confirmed by Pope Honorius III (1216–1227) in 1217. The habit of the Order consists of a white tunic with belt; a white scapular with a distinctive cross, the horizontal arm of which is blue and the vertical red; and a black choir cape marked with the same cross on the left side. In accordance with the rule, the Order followed the Victorine liturgy.

Among the early patrons of the order were Countess Margaret of Burgundy, who gave the Trinitarians their first house in Cerfroid (Dep. de l'Aisne). Within a few years they had some 50 houses, including those in Paris and Rome and in important seaports, such as Barcelona and Genoa. From their inception, they were involved in two major works: the ransoming of captives from the Muslims and the care of the sick and poor in hospitals. The work of the order was closely related to the Crusades but extended to all who were taken captive by Muslims, whether in the East, North Africa, or Spain. The provision of the rule dividing the income of the order into thirds proved burdensome and put a severe strain on the ability of the Order to carry out its ordinary activities.

From an early period, the Trinitarians were grouped with other mendicant orders, such as the Dominicans, the Franciscans, and the Augustinians. In their administrative organization, they were quite similar to these orders. The head of the Order was referred to as minister general. The heads of local houses were referred to as ministers of the House of the Holy Trinity. All churches of the Order were to be named in honor of the Holy Trinity. Women were affiliated with the Order as early as the 13th century. They worked with the male Trinitarians in caring for the sick and poor. The 20th century saw an effort to unify the various Trinitarian congregations of women.

As with other religious orders, the Trinitarians were influenced by the various movements of reform in the 15th and 16th centuries that emphasized a return to the primitive observance of the rule. The reform of the Order worked substantial changes. One group of 16th-century reformed Trinitarians went on in 1766 to form the Canons Regular of the Most Holy Trinity, following the rule of St. Augustine. They ceased to exist toward the end of the 19th century. A more permanent reform, the Discalced Trinitarians, was initiated in 1597 in Spain by Blessed John Baptist of the Conception, and it was this reform that has survived in the modern order. By the end of the 16th century, more than 150 houses were formed, the largest number being in France. The Trinitarians were also active in England and Scotland prior to the Reformation.

The redemption of captives continued to be the most characteristic work of the order, even into the 18th century. The printing in 1582 of a discourse on the liberation of captives from the Turks and Berbers gave rise to a literary genre that narrated voyages of redemption. Among the most famous of those ransomed was Miguel de Cervantes (1547–1616) in 1580. In the 18th century, the minister general of the order aided the United States in ransoming captive sailors from the Barbary pirates. Perhaps as many as 140,000 captives were ransomed by the order. In the 20th century, the order devoted itself to missionary activity in Madagascar, work in parishes and hospitals, and education. The largest numbers of Trinitarians are found in the Spanish and Italian provinces, followed by the United States and Canada.

James M. Powell

See also Crusades; Hospitallers (Knights of Malta since 1530); Social Services: Western Christian

Further Reading

Brodman, James, *Ransoming Captives in Crusader Spain: The Order of Merced on the Christian-Islamic Frontier*, Philadelphia: University of Pennsylvania Press, 1986

Cipollone, Giulio, *Il mosaico di San Tommaso in Formis a Roma*, Rome: Ordinis Trinitatis Institutum Historicum, 1984

Cipollone, Giulio, "La famiglia Trinitaria (1198–1998)," in *Dizionario degli Istituti di Perfezione*, volume 9, edited by Giancarlo Rocca, Rome: Paoline, 1997

Gross, Joseph J., "Trinitarier, -innen," in *Lexikon des Mittelalters*, volume 8, Munich: LexMa, 1997

Gross, Joseph J., editor, *The Trinitarians' Rule of Life: Texts of the Six Principal Editions*, Rome: Trinitarian Historical Institute, 1983

Walsh, A.T., "Trinitarians," in *New Catholic Encyclopedia*, volume 14, Washington D.C.: Catholic University of America Press, 1967

Turkey. *See* Cappadocia, Turkey; Istanbul, Turkey

U

Ukraine

The Eastern Christianity shared by Russians, Ukrainians, and Belarussians traces its origins to the late tenth-century Varangian principality of Kyivan Rus', present-day Ukraine. According to tradition, the shore of the Dnipro River, which flows through Kyiv, was the scene of a baptism of aristocratic masses at the suggestion of Grand Prince Volodymyr. Christianity having been adopted from Byzantium (c. 988), the subsequent influx of Greek bishops and their monastic assistants inspired the local folk to follow their example. Others were attracted to Mount Athos, probably to the monastery of Khylourgou. It is possibly from here that Antony returned to his native Rus' (c. 1051–1052), where he founded the Monastery of the Kyivan Caves. Although some records mention earlier monasteries in Kyiv, the rapid growth and dominance of the Kyivan Caves Monastery gave it a privileged place within the story of Ukrainian monasticism.

Settling in a cave previously used by Ilarion, who became metropolitan, Antony embarked on a rigorous spiritual life of solitude, prayer, manual labor, and a rudimentary diet of bread and water. His way of life began to attract others, and when their number reached some 12 or 15, Antony appointed Varlaam as superior and retired to a cave beyond the limits of the community. Varlaam was succeeded by Theodosius (d. 1074), whose *Vita*, recorded by the chronicler Nestor in the Kyivan Caves *Paterikon*, is the only full-length treatment of its kind that has survived from the Princely period of Kyivan Rus'. A disciple of Antony's almost from the very beginning, Theodosius became superior (c. 1062), serving in that capacity for some 12 years and seeing the monastic community grow to 100 monks. According to the *Vita*, Theodosius' pious disposition and his inclination toward poverty, along with a fervent desire to imitate Christ, were the key ingredients of his spiritual vision. Having come to Kyiv, Theodosius was rebuffed by aristocratically sponsored communities but then met Antony, who had him tonsured and later ordained. As superior Theodosius continued to inspire those in his charge with exemplary prayer, charity, humility, and courage in the face of injustice. In 1091, 17 years after Theodosius' death, the monks of the Caves Monastery transferred his relics into the monastery, an implicit canonization. Another 17 years later the feast and cult of Theodosius, "the founder of the common life," was officially recognized throughout the entire Church of Kyivan Rus'.

The two founders of the Kyivan Caves Monastery are sometimes said to have represented two poles between which the monastic tradition of Kyivan Christianity would evolve: a reclusive rupture with the world coupled with an asceticism of the desert (Antony) and the cenobitic, communitarian variant of evangelical spirituality (Theodosius). It was under the latter's hegumenate that the community of the Kyivan Caves moved into closer contact with the world, evolving a social and relational model of life that maintained its commitment to prayer. This shift has also been interpreted as a move away from an emphasis on individual achievement in spiritual combat toward a gentle embrace of the spirit of poverty for the sake of one's neighbor and toward a more compassionate style of leadership and discipline – "maternal" in the words of the chronicles. Theodosian monasticism took on specific social responsibilities, ministering to the sick, the poor, and prisoners. The philanthropic thrust of the move toward the people had cultural implications as well: scholarship at the Kyivan Caves went beyond the copying of ancient manuscripts to the composition of the first chronicles of the people of Rus', with their nascent sense of a distinctive identity; hagiographers recorded accounts of the lives of local bearers of the holy (Borys, Hlib, and Theodosius). A distinctive iconography emerged. The pastoral work of the monastery was extended to all; princes and paupers alike were welcomed. The monastery became a place of reconciliation between foes and of treaties signed by warring princes. By opting for openness to the world, Theodosian spirituality was centered on orienting one's whole life toward the evangelical teaching of the Beatitudes. His legacy may be expressed as a linkage between voluntary participation in the suffering of the kenotic, humiliated Christ and practical expression of this ideal within an all-embracing humility and poverty of spirit.

Theodosius instituted a monastic rule at the Caves Monastery based on the Studite *typikon*, or rule (Slavic, *ustav*). Inspired by Theodore of Stoudios (c. 759–826), a leading Byzantine monk at the Stoudios monastery in Constantinople, the actual *typikon* was elaborated two centuries later by the patriarch of Constantinople Alexius the Studite (1025–1043) and became one of several monastic rules later adopted by Byzantine monasteries.

Monastery of the Caves (Petcherskaia Lavra), Kiev, Ukraine, 17th century.
Photo courtesy of Robert E. Jones

The Kyivan Caves Monastery had an impact on the spread of monasticism elsewhere. Its monks founded other monasteries: the Klov monastery in Kyiv and that in Tmutorokan' were established by Stephen and Nikon, respectively. Others became *hegumens*: Varlaam at St. Demetrius in Kyiv and Simon in Vladimir. In addition, *hegumens* at the Caves Monastery and elsewhere were routinely favored for appointment as bishops.

The earliest Kyivan monasteries played a significant role in social and cultural life. The Primary Chronicle was edited at the Kyivan Caves and the Vydubytsky monasteries. Many other chronicles and manuscripts were also compiled in monasteries. Such work advanced education and scholarship and also provided support for developments in printing, liturgical chant, and religious art, from graphic art and icons to architecture. Monks were known for evangelization and pastoral work outside the monastery walls. Some of this work involved direct parish assignments, a natural extension of the ancient practice of ministering to pious folk who turned to the monastery for spiritual direction and consolation.

The first monasteries of Rus' were established by endowments of land from *ktytors*, or wealthy secular founders. Following a pattern that existed in Byzantium, Prince Yaroslav the Wise (1019–1054) and his son Iziaslav were the first such founders in Kyivan Rus'. In return the *ktytor* was granted a burial place for the family, usually in the monastery church, and with the assurance of constant prayer on their behalf. In addition the founder often reserved the right to screen new candidates to the monastery and to appoint the superior. Despite occasional abuses (e.g., deathbed monastic professions and coercive tonsures), the overall thrust of Kyivan monastic spirituality was such that its influence extended far beyond the monastery. Inspiring the faithful with an ideal of perfection, the monks of Rus' enjoyed high esteem within society.

The Mongol (Tatar) invasions in the 13th and 14th centuries destroyed most of the monasteries of Kyivan Rus' and dispersed the communities. As a result, except for the few monasteries that survived or that were subsequently restored, the historical continuity of monasticism was ruptured. Among the monasteries that, along with the Kyivan Caves, were spared from devastation were several in western Ukraine: St. Daniel's in Uhriv, St. Michael's in Volodymyr Volyns'ky, and another in Polonne. Others were located in the area of Polotsk, today within Belarus.

Second in size and historical importance only to the Caves Monastery in Kyiv and the only other senior monastery in Ukraine designated as a *lavra*, is the Pochaiv (Dormition) Monastery in Volhynia. It may have been founded by monks who fled from the Caves Monastery as the Mongols invaded in 1240. In the 17th century the monastery flourished under the 50-year leadership of Hegumen Yov Zalizo (1551–1651), who instituted a Studite rule there. Legend has it that the monastery was saved from attack by Turks and Tatars in 1675 by an apparition of the Theotokos. In 1713 the monastery joined the Unia, and by 1730 the Basilian Order had established a respectable theological press there. In 1831 the czar returned the monastery to the Russian Orthodox Church. In the early 20th century, under Archbishop Antonii Khrapovitskii, the monastery became a popular pilgrimage center that attracted tens of thousands of people, especially on the feasts of the Dormition (28 August) and of St. Yov Zalizo (10 September). After World War II western Volhynia was incorporated into the Ukrainian SSR, and, as elsewhere in Ukraine during the Soviet period, monastic life here was subjected to systematic repression. In the period from 1939 to 1970, the community of monks dropped from 200 to 12. An attempt to shut the monastery down in 1964 was met with effective resistance both locally and internationally. Today the awe-inspiring architecture and the natural setting of the complex, with its vast (6,000 capacity) 18th-century rococo cathedral, attract pilgrims and growing numbers of tourists. It is a functioning unit of the Moscow patriarchate.

The 15th-century annexation of Ukrainian territories by Lithuania and then Poland brought about an expansion of monastic life. By 1500, 44 monasteries existed in Galicia alone. The further development of monasticism in the 16th and 17th centuries was actively promoted by enlightened metropolitans of Kyiv (in particular Yov Boretsky, Isaia Kopynsky, and Petro Mohyla) and by Cossacks such as Bohdan Khmelnytsky and Ivan Mazepa, who ordered that many ancient monasteries be restored and new ones founded.

In this period the Kyivan Caves Monastery became a stronghold of Orthodox resistance to Catholicism. In 1631 Archimandrite Petro Mohyla established a school of philosophy and theology at the Kyivan Caves. However, the ecclesiastical center of Orthodoxy had moved northward to Moscow, setting the stage for a major shift of religious affiliation. The Union of Brest (1596) brought a significant portion of the Ukrainian Orthodox Church into communion with Rome. Most of the monasteries in Right-Bank Ukraine as well as those in Belarus accepted this Unia, or union, and reformed their way of life to form a new monastic order, the Order of St. Basil the Great. By the 18th century this Greco-Catholic order comprised some 150 monasteries in the Ukrainian territories of Poland.

Another important center of Orthodoxy after the Union of Brest was the Maniavskyi Skyt (founded 1611–1612), today in the Ivano-Frankivs'k region. Its founder, Yov Kniahynytsky, tonsured at Mount Athos, was a staunch supporter of Orthodoxy who collaborated with the Rus' monk of Mount Athos Ivan Vyshensky as well as with Zachariah Kopystensky (d. 1627), a Kyivan Caves archimandrite known for his *Palinodiia* (a defense of Orthodoxy criticizing a treatise by Uniate Hegumen Lev Krevza of Vilnius). When other monks joined Kniahynytsky at Maniava, the hermitage was granted *stauropegion* status, or autonomy, by Patriarch Timothy II of Constantinople. The *skyt* thus managed to remain Orthodox, without subjection to Moscow, while the surrounding area joined with Rome. An important cultural center that inspired literature and art and that at its height housed 240 monks, this fortified monastery in a picturesque valley of the Gorgany Mountains was closed by Joseph II of Austria in 1785. In recent years it has been thoroughly renovated.

Dating likewise from the early 17th century is the fortified monastery of St. Nicholas at Krekhiv, in the Zhovkva region, which united with Rome in the early 18th century. The site of a Basilian novitiate from 1902, the monastery was dismantled by the Soviets. Thoroughly restored in 1997 the monastery is again a fully functioning Basilian monastery and a very popular pilgrimage center.

The tide turned in the second half of the 18th century. Monasteries in the western territories, located within Habsburg Austria after the partitions of Poland, were deprived of landholdings and closed as a result of the reforms of Joseph II (1780–1790). The same patterns affected monastic life in Transcarpathia and Bukovyna as well. However, key Eastern-rite Basilian centers remained in Zhovkva and Mukachiv, whereas those at Lavriv, Drohobych, Buchach, and the St. Onuphrius Monastery in L'viv were noted for their educational work and commitment to scholarship and library development.

In Left-Bank Ukraine, which was gradually incorporated into the Russian Empire from the 1770s on, Roman Catholic monasteries were either closed or required to join the Orthodox Church. Subsequent imperial policies deprived all monasteries of their self-sufficiency, and by order of Catherine II (1762–1796) all their assets were confiscated (1786). In 1908 the nine Ukrainian *gubernias* of the Russian Empire held 67 men's and 43 women's monasteries.

The 19th century saw the introduction of some significant changes in Ukrainian monasticism. It was during this century that archimandrites, formerly appointed for life, were henceforth elected only for a term. In addition the ancient and uninterrupted practice of selecting Ukrainian bishops exclusively from monastic ranks was terminated. Both of these innovations remain in effect today.

In the wake of the Russian Revolution, Soviet persecution of religion practically put an end to monasticism in the Ukrainian gubernias of the former Russian Empire. A systematic repression began as monastic holdings were nationalized (1918) and monasteries liquidated. By 1920, of 1,105 monasteries, most of them in the eastern territory of Ukraine, only 352 remained. By 1929 all had been closed. Monks by the thousands are believed to have died in the gulag, and many others were dispersed.

From 1944 on the Soviet Union occupied formerly Austrian regions of western Ukraine, where some 100 to 150 monastic institutions were located. Here too, antireligious policies produced a steady decline: from 39 monasteries and convents still operating in the Ukrainian SSR in 1954, the number declined to seven in 1970. In 1985 two of the six men's monasteries operating as such in the Soviet Union were located in Ukraine: both were monasteries of the Dormition, in Pochaiv and in Odessa. Of the ten women's monasteries in the Soviet Union, seven were in Ukraine: two in Kyiv, another two in the Transcarpathian region, and one each in Rivne, Odessa, and Cherkassy regions.

Among the outstanding monks who made lasting contributions were figures from the period of the Union of Brest (1596): Greek Catholic Metropolitan of Kyiv Yosyf Rutsky (1574–1637) and Polotsk Archbishop Yosafat Kuntsevych (1580–1623, martyred for the Unia), who collaborated in instituting far-reaching educational and monastic reforms, and Meletii Smotrytsky (1577–1633), who wrote classic theological tracts in defense of Orthodoxy before himself joining the Unia (1627). Other monks from Ukraine exerted a greater impact in other countries – Stefan Yavors'kyi (1658–1722) and Teofan Prokopovych (1681–1736) in Russia and Paisy Velichkovsky (1722–1794) at Mount Athos as well as in Moldavia and the wider Slavic world.

The Eastern-rite Ukrainian orders of men – Basilian, Studite, and Redemptorist – took root in Rome and throughout the western diaspora largely as the result of two processes in the late 19th and 20th centuries: the massive migration and spiritual needs of Ukrainians abroad and the persecution of religion in Ukraine after the Soviet takeover.

The process of religious change in the former Soviet Union has included the dramatic revival of monasticism. In 1997, 172 monasteries existed in Ukraine: 90 Orthodox (Moscow patriarchate, 75 [including both *lavras*]; Kyiv patriarchate, 15; Autocephalous, 1), 79 Catholic (Greek Catholic, 55; Roman Catholic, 24), and two monasteries of the Old Believers. In monasticism as in other sectors of religious life, there are indications that the rapidity and intensity of the post-Soviet religious revival has tapered off, whether as a natural process or because institutions of education and formation, stretched to the limit, have imposed greater selectivity in admissions. Faced with a range of organizational and canonical questions, monasticism in Ukraine is seeking a clearly defined place within the context of post-Soviet modernity. No doubt the practical answers that will be worked out and the common life that emerges will reflect a creative interpretation of the traditional sources of Kyivan monastic spirituality.

ANDRII S. KRAWCHUK

See also Archaeology: Near East; Archaeology: Russia; Architecture: Eastern Christian Monasteries; Bulgaria; Hagiography: Eastern Christian; Kiev (Kyiv), Ukraine; Libraries: Eastern Christian; Mount Athos, Greece; Orthodox Monasticism; Pilgrimages, Christian: Eastern Europe; Russia: History; Theodore of Stoudios, St.; Theodosius of Kiev, St.

Further Reading

Denisov, L.I., *Pravoslavnye Monastyri Rossiiskoi imperii*, Moscow: Stupina, 1908

Ellis, Jane, "Monasticism," in her *The Russian Orthodox Church: A Contemporary History* (Keston Book, number 22), Bloomington: Indiana University Press, and London: Croom Helm, 1986

Frick, David A., *Meletij Smotryc'kyj* (Harvard Series in Ukrainian Studies), Cambridge, Massachusetts: Harvard University Press, 1995

Goetz, Leopold, *Kievo-Pecherskii monastyr. Das Kiever Höhlenkloster als Kulturzentrum des vormongolischen Russlands*, Passau: Waldbauersche Buchhandlung, 1904

Janin, R., "Le monachisme byzantin au Moyen Âge," *Revue des études byzantines* 22 (1964)

Korovytsky, I., and I. Patrylo, "Monasticism," in *Encyclopedia of Ukraine*, volume 3, edited by Danylo Husar Struk, Toronto: University of Toronto Press, 1993

Libackyj, Anfir, *The Ancient Monasteries of Kiev Rus'*, New York: Vantage Press, 1978

The Life of Paisij Velyckovs'kyj (Harvard Library of Early Ukrainian Literature, English Translations: volume 4), translated by Jeffrey Featherstone, introduced by Anthony-Emil N. Tachaios, Cambridge, Massachusetts: Harvard University Press for the Ukrainian Research Institute of Harvard University, 1989

The Paterik of the Kievan Caves Monastery (Harvard Library of Early Ukrainian Literature, English Translations: volume 1), translated by Muriel Heppell, Cambridge, Massachusetts: Harvard University Press for the Ukrainian Research Institute of Harvard University, 1989

Senyk, Sophia, *Women's Monasteries in Ukraine and Belorussia to the Period of Suppressions* (Orientalia Christiana Analecta, 222), Rome: Pont. Institutum Studiorum Orientalium, 1983

Senyk, Sophia, "Monasticism," in her *A History of the Church in Ukraine, Volume 1: To the End of the Thirteenth Century* (Orientalia Christiana Analecta, 243), Rome: Pontificio Istituto Orientale, 1993

Vavryk, Mykhailo, *Narys rozvytku i stanu Vasyliians'koho Chyna: XVII–XX st.: topohrafichno-statystychna rozvidka* (Zapysky ChSVV, seriia 2, sektsiia 1), Rome: Basiliani, 1979

Vavryk, Mykhailo, "Monasteries," in *Encyclopedia of Ukraine*, volume 3, edited by Danylo Husar Struk, Toronto: University of Toronto Press, 1993

United States: Buddhist

Two general types of Buddhist groups can be detected in the history of Buddhism in the United States. The first group is made up of Asian-Buddhist immigrants and their descendants. The second group consists of Euro-Americans whose attraction to Buddhism has been one of an intellectual and spiritual nature. The former has been a part, however small, of the American fabric since the first Asian immigrants came to the United States. The latter group began to develop around the turn of the 20th century, influenced by Buddhist monks who came to the West to promote their teachings.

In 1893 the World's Parliament of Religions in Chicago welcomed two Buddhist monks. In the years following, many Buddhist missionaries made their way to the United States to serve the interest that the conference had sparked. During World War II many American soldiers stationed in Japan became interested in Buddhism. During these years and on through the 1950s, American fascination with Buddhism proliferated. The Chinese invasion of Tibet during the 1950s and the subsequent occupation of the Tibetan plateau compelled many Tibetan refugees to flee their homeland. Many eventually made their way to the United States, bringing with them Buddhist monastic culture. Throughout the latter half of the 20th century, numerous schools of Buddhism launched themselves onto the American religious scene.

Zen Buddhism is represented in the United States by both the Rinzai and the Sōtō lineage through the many Zen centers and monasteries that are found across the nation, especially in California. Zen monasteries are the most numerous of the Buddhist monastic institutions in the United States. The earliest of them was the Zen Mountain Center at Tassajara Hot Springs, California. The Japanese Zen Buddhist layman Daisetz Teitaro Suzuki (1870–1966) did much to fan interest in Zen thought.

The Zen Mountain Monastery, located in Mount Tremper, New York, is an extremely influential institution with many affiliates throughout the Northeast. It is one of many American Zen communities founded by the influential Zen master Taizan Maezumi Rōshi, who transmitted his teachings to 12 successors, one of which, John Daido Loori, is the abbot of the monastery.

The Diamond Hill Monastery in the small town of Cumberland, Rhode Island, on the grounds of the Providence Zen Center is also part of a network of Buddhist institutions, a Korean Zen school known as the Kwan Um Zen school. Founded by Seung Sahn, the first Korean master to live and teach in the West, the Kwan Um school tends to emphasize social action over spiritual liberation. The Diamond Hill Monastery and the Providence Zen Center serve as the headquarters for the school, which consists of institutions throughout the United States.

The Dharma Realm Buddhist Association resulted from yet another union of a multitude of Buddhist centers and monasteries in the United States. In 1962 the Venerable Master Hsüan Hua came to America from Hong Kong to take over leadership of the Sino-American Buddhist Association. At the time the association was made up mainly of Chinese-Americans; however, through Master Hsüan Hua's charismatic lectures and teachings many Westerners became a part of Dharma Realm, the organization he founded. In 1972 Hua conducted the first ordination ceremony in the West at his Gold Mountain Monastery in San Francisco, California. From that time until his death in 1995, Hua ordained more than 200 people from all around the world. One especially important feature of Hua's Buddhism was his ability to bring together Buddhists from both the Mahāyāna and the Theravāda tradition. He actively encouraged dialogue and congenial relations between the distinct Buddhist communities.

According to current estimates between 400 and 650 Theravāda monks now live in the United States. Most of these are Asian nationals who were brought from their homelands to serve immigrant temples. Reports indicate an extreme lack of interest in the monastic life on the part of second-generation Asian immigrants. Moreover non-Asians do not seem to be as attracted to Theravāda schools as strongly they are to their Zen and Tibetan counterparts. For these reasons American Theravāda Buddhism has had difficulty in establishing a dynamic monastic community.

A few Theravāda monastic communities do exist. Among these is the Bhavana Society, located in Highview, West Virginia, on 42 acres of secluded forest. There eight monks and two nuns, along with lay Buddhists and visitors, practice Vipassanā (insight meditation). Seven of the ten monastics in residence are westerners in token of the society's aim to divest Theravāda Buddhism of some of its cultural trappings so that it may thrive in a Western setting.

Tibetan Buddhism is the most recent of the Buddhist schools to be imported to the United States. In 1955 Geshe Wangyal settled in New Jersey and set up the first Tibetan monastery on American soil: the Lamaist Buddhist Monastery of America. This monastery was associated with the Gelukpa (dGe lugs pa) Order of Tibetan Buddhism, the Order headed by the Dalai Lama. The three Tibetan Buddhist Orders of Gelukpa, Sakyapa (Sa skya pa), and Nyingmapa (rNying ma pa) were represented by 1970 when Chögyam Trungpa Rinpoche (1939–1987) arrived in the United States, bringing with him the fourth: Kagyupa (bKa' rgyud pa). Trungpa Rinpoche set up many communities that now function under the auspices of Shambhala International.

Probably the most important of the Tibetan monasteries in the United States is Namgyal (Rnam rgyal), located in Ithaca, New York. Namgyal was started in 1992 by the Dalai Lama as a North American seat of the charter monastery in Dharamsala, India. Namgyal, like many other American Tibetan monasteries, is inhabited solely by Tibetan refugees. Some westerners have been ordained as Tibetan monks and nuns, but not in significant numbers.

Although many Buddhist monasteries in the United States appear to be mere transplants of their Asian counterparts, it is important to highlight a key "innovation" of the American form. In the United States monasteries do not serve mainly as training facilities for monks and nuns but rather as centers for Buddhist learning and practice by monastics as well as laypeople; and even to speak of "monastics" in the American Buddhist context is problematic because to be a monk or a nun in the United States is not necessarily a full-time endeavor. Many Buddhists live as lay followers for most of the time, spending various durations utilizing the facilities of the monasteries. Given the pluralistic nature of our age, the opportunity to be a part-time monastic is specifically American.

Monasteries to Visit

Almost all the monasteries in the United States are open to visitors. Many are available for retreats and extended visits. Monasteries to be visited in the United States include the following: Zen Mountain Monastery (Mount Tremper, New York), Diamond Hill (Cumberland, Rhode Island), Sagely City of Ten Thousand Buddhas (Talmage, California), Bhavana Society (Highview, West Virginia), Dagom Gaden Tensung Ling (Bloomington, Indiana), Jizo-An (Cinnamonson, New Jersey), Abhayagiri (Redwood Valley, California), Dharma Vijaya Buddhist Vihara (Los Angeles, California), Namgyal (Ithaca, New York), and Sunnataram Forest Monastery (Escondido, California).

DEVRA JAFFE

See also Buddhism: Western; Chan/Zen; Dalai Lama (Tenzin Gyatso); Dharamsala, India (Tibetan); Intermonastic Dialogue; Missionaries: Buddhist; Sexuality: Buddhist Perspectives; Suzuki, Daisetz Teitaro; Tibetan Lineages; Zen and the West

Further Reading

Batchelor, Stephen, *The Awakening of the West: The Encounter of Buddhism and Western Culture*, Berkeley, California: Parallax Press, and London: Aquarian, 1994

Buddhism in America: Proceedings of the First Buddhism in America Conference, Rutland, Vermont: Charles E. Tuttle, 1998

Fields, Rick, *How the Swans Came to the Lake: A Narrative History of Buddhism in America*, Boulder, Colorado, and New York: Shambhala, 1981; 3rd edition, Boston: Shambhala, 1992

Kashima, Tetsuden, *Buddhism in America: The Social Organization of an Ethnic Religious Tradition*, Westport, Connecticut: Greenwood Press, 1977

Layman, Emma McCloy, *Buddhism in America*, Chicago: Nelson-Hall, 1976

Morreale, Don, editor, *Buddhist America: Centers, Retreats, Practices*, Santa Fe, New Mexico, and New York: John Muir, 1988

Prebish, Charles, *American Buddhism*, North Scituate, Massachusetts: Duxbury Press, 1979

Prebish, Charles, and Kenneth Tanaka, editors, *The Faces of Buddhism in America*, Berkeley: University of California Press, 1998

Tweed, Thomas, *The American Encounter with Buddhism, 1844–1912: Victorian Culture and the Limits of Dissent*, Bloomington: Indiana University Press, 1992

United States: Western Christian

At the beginnings of the European settlement of the United States, Christian monasticism was passing through a great crisis. The Protestant movement, radical cultural changes, civil revolutions, and nationalism had taken a heavy toll. With the preaching, service, and missionary emphases in the religion of the times, monastic communities tended to be dismissed as isolated, irrational, and irrelevant by many "modern" people both inside and outside the Church. Beginning with the suppression of English religious by Henry VIII (1509–1547) in the 16th century and continuing through the hostility of the French Revolution into the late 18th century, many governments considered religious as foreign operatives for the papal realm, a useless burden on society, or a presence "inimical to the state."

The number of monastics worldwide was very small. In most areas of Europe and South America, either monasteries were suppressed or the residents were allowed to remain together but in dire conditions with no new members admitted. However, in the mid-1800s public sentiment and that of government authorities began to ease. Part of the interest in monasticism was cultural, being a revival of appreciation for the part that monastics had played in the history of Europe. Monasteries began to be restored; new members came to them with a particular desire to reclaim the grand medieval heritage of the arts and scholarship. In Bavaria the Benedictine Boniface Wimmer (1809–1887) launched a campaign to get others to do for the new country of the United States what the Anglo-Saxon missionaries had done to establish Christianity in Germany.

Immigration from continental Europe to the United States had begun in earnest by the mid–19th century. Without clergy and teachers who understood their language and customs, many immigrants would not have continued in their faith. Missionary enthusiasm represented only part of the appeal of monastic migrations from Europe. In countries that had at least once before attempted to eradicate religious life, monastics found it good insurance to have establishments in another country to which to flee if necessary.

From 1846 until the Civil War, small groups of Benedictine men and women, assisted initially by the generous interest of King Ludwig I (1825–1848) of Bavaria's foreign mission society, traveled first to Latrobe and St. Marys, Pennsylvania, from the monasteries of Metten and Eichstätt. From there they radiated throughout the country, moving west as the frontier did, and established themselves in many places in the eastern and southern United States. About the same time monks from Einsiedeln in Switzerland came to St. Meinrad, Indiana, to be followed later by other Swiss Benedictine men and women from Engelberg and Maria Rickenbach, settling first near Maryville, Missouri (Conception). At the end of the 19th century, they also spread across the Midwest and into the new western territories. Fueled especially by the missionary zeal of Martin Marty of St. Meinrad's, they established an early and lasting presence among Native Americans.

It had been centuries since Benedictines had been missionaries to any part of Europe, and many things had altered in their lifestyle since then. As religious life diversified over time, Benedictines had become more identified with the enclosed contem-

Baroque window, San Jose y San Miguel de Aguayo Convent (Franciscan), San Antonio, Texas, 1720.
Photo courtesy of Chris Schabel

Nave of First Abbey Church, Saint John's Abbey, Collegeville, Minnesota.
Photo courtesy of Saint John's Abbey Archives

plative life than with the active ministries of such later groups as the Jesuits or the apostolic communities of sisters. Many of the first Benedictines to arrive in the United States came with the idea that they would establish monasteries like their European homes, centers to which people would come for liturgy and education rather than places from which missionaries go forth to perform active ministries.

Upon arriving they found conditions primitive and needs great. In Europe contemplative religious had to rely for their sustenance on dowries or other family assets that members could provide or on the generosity of benefactors and royal patrons. The United States was considered by the Catholic Church as a mission country needing all resources to be devoted to the utilitarian. Within a few years after the arrival of the Benedictines, the bishops declared at the Second Council of Baltimore (1866) that they would allow no more contemplative religious in solemn vows (i.e., cloistered) to establish themselves there, making exceptions only for some communities of Visitation nuns already present. Thus, the Benedictines were "freed" to take a more active role in missionary efforts.

The monastics themselves became more aware of the needs around them. Ordained members began to minister to parishes farther from their monasteries. As they did so they pleaded for nuns who would take up the education of the children. Small satellite communities that did active works while still trying to keep up the monastic Liturgy of the Hours began to spring up in areas farther removed from the monasteries. Soon they were caught in the tension of trying to be both active and contemplative. This was especially difficult for nuns, who, once they had left their enclosures, were technically considered by many to be no longer monastic and thus no longer permitted many monastic practices and canonical privileges. They were threatened with having to form apostolic governance structures with a single novitiate and single general superior. They were told by spiritual

Facade of San Xavier del Bac, Arizona, 1797. The earlier Jesuit foundation was taken over by Franciscans during the 18th century. Photo courtesy of Chris Schabel

directors that they should no longer pray the Divine Office, and they were placed under bishops who had no understanding or appreciation of their lifestyle. Men fared somewhat better canonically but often lost their sense of community and monastic identity, trying to live alone or in small groups and to function within a diocesan system while maintaining their own authority structures and customs.

Appreciation for the many needs around them and for the active ethos of American culture served also to unleash a new sense of what it meant to be monastic and how this might best be carried out in the world in which these men and women found themselves. The growth of a North American monastic identity has been a long and complex process and remains distinctive as compared to the traditional European model. With the help of Benedictine men who understood the importance of monastic tradition, women were able eventually to get autonomy for their monasteries. Despite not being enclosed, they were recognized as having the right to separate governance and other concessions, distinguishing them from apostolic orders of sisters. The men, who had always had freedom to leave the enclosure for pastoral duties, found themselves more apostolically oriented than most of the world's other Benedictines. Eventually this missionary emphasis would repeat itself in bringing monastic life to Latin America.

Today the more than 100 Benedictine communities tend, for the most part, to continue a monastic tradition that is a mixture of active and contemplative. In keeping with their history, they tended to locate in rural rather than urban areas and maintain some agricultural rootedness. During the 20th century many communities grew to over 100 members, and some have substantially more than that. They built vast complexes of buildings for seminaries, colleges, boarding schools, publishing enterprises, and health care facilities. Some became centers of education and culture for the people surrounding them. Although a large number of these ministries still flourish, changing demographics have brought about changes in demands. Where many built boarding schools for country children or minor seminaries for very young priesthood candidates, today some of these houses are using their facilities to welcome small children, the elderly, the homeless, and the abused.

More recently many communities have been making great efforts to explore and reclaim their own unique heritage. Some are curtailing the number of members serving as pastors or living at great distances from the monastery. Women are making special efforts to use language that reflects their charism, for example, in making sure that their houses are called monasteries rather than convents. From liturgical reform to higher education for women, from peace and justice movements to innovative ecological practices, they have provided versatile leadership in the cultural development of their country. Yet they have also continued to invest energy in their prayer and common vowed life, providing models for meaningful worship and caring community.

For purposes of mutual support and accountability, most monasteries in the United States have associated with one another in congregations. The majority of men's communities belong to either the American-Cassinese or the Swiss-American Congregation. The three major groupings of women use the term "federation" to avoid confusion with the modern congregations of apostolic sisters. These are the Federations of St. Scholastica, St. Gertrude, and St. Benedict. A congregation of Benedictine Sisters of Perpetual Adoration leads a life without external ministries and encourages movement of sisters between the different houses of the congregation. In addition several monasteries belong to international congregations, such as the English, Ottilien Missionary, and Olivetan; a few remain unaffiliated.

Although Benedictines constitute the majority, other types of Catholic monastic communities exist in the United States as well. Because the strictly contemplative life was at first impractical and discouraged, Cistercians faced an even more difficult struggle. The first foundations at Gethsemani, Kentucky, and Dubuque, Iowa, also experimented with educational ministry. Eventually they were able to abandon these works and to lead a more traditionally Cistercian life. Not until well into the 20th century did the Catholic Church in the United States begin to value and accept contemplative communities. Now more than 20 Cistercian communities of men or women exist in the United

Facade, Holy Spirit Convent (Franciscan), Goliad, Texas, 1722.
Photo courtesy of Chris Schabel

States. Although not totally and strictly enclosed, they do not engage in external ministries of service but devote themselves to prayer, contemplation, manual labor, and the provision of spiritual resources to retreatants and other guests. Most monasteries in the United States are of the reformed Cistercian observance, commonly known as Trappist.

In addition to these are a variety of other monastic groups, including Camaldolese hermits, Carthusians, and several monastic communities of the Anglican tradition. Recently a tremendous upsurge of interest has taken place in the Rule of St. Benedict and other aspects of monastic spirituality among persons not permanently committed to the monastic way of life. Some communities invite others to live with them for short periods of time to acquaint themselves with the spirituality and to experience its gifts. The ancient Benedictine tradition of having oblates is also enjoying a revival. Oblates are laymen and laywomen of any denomination of Christian faith who associate themselves with a monastic community. They remain in their own homes and vocations but commit themselves through a public ritual of profession to incorporate Benedictine values into their prayer and their lifestyle. A large number of recent books and the proliferation of retreat centers at monasteries have introduced countless Americans, especially non-Catholics, to monastic spirituality and its practices. In addition intentional communities of laypersons or families model their life together along monastic lines.

Although traditional monasticism in the United States is experiencing declining numbers – something to be expected in a time of multiplying social options as well as secularization and a culture that encourages mobility and impermanence in many ways – many signs of promise are evident. An increasing number of younger people are expressing interest in the lifestyle. Openness of liturgies to the public and the use of facilities for retreats and social welfare activities have introduced people of diverse faiths or of no religious affiliation to the contemplative life. Monastics themselves are studying more about their unique history and charism and affirming the distinctions between themselves and either the more ministry-oriented or the very strictly enclosed religious communities. A way of life that is rooted in the earliest centuries of Christianity seems destined to survive and thrive, adapting itself to the culture and needs of the United States and, at the same time, modeling values of contemplation, peace, harmony, stability, and balance in challenge to that culture.

Judith Sutera, O.S.B.

Bell tower, San Juan de Capestrano Convent (Franciscan), San Antonio, Texas, 1731.
Photo courtesy of Chris Schabel

See also Charism; Congregations, Benedictine; Collegeville, Minnesota; Contemporary Issues: Western Christian; Dissolution of Monasteries; Exile, Western Christian; Gethsemani, Kentucky; Keating, Thomas; McInerney, Michael Joseph Vincent; Merton, Thomas; Reformation; Regulations: Christian Perspectives; Riepp, Benedicta (Sybilla); Schools and Universities, Benedictine; Servites

Further Reading

Chittister, Joan, et al., *Climb Along the Cutting Edge: An Analysis of Change in Religious Life*, New York: Paulist Press, 1977

Dowling, Dolores, *In Your Midst: The Story of the Benedictine Sisters of Perpetual Adoration*, St. Louis, Missouri: The Printery, 1988

Fracchia, Charles, *Living Together Alone: The New American Monasticism*, San Francisco: Harper and Row, 1979

Girgen, M. Incarnata, *Behind the Beginnings: Benedictine Women in America*, Saint Joseph, Minnesota: St. Benedict's Convent, 1981

Hollerman, Ephrem (Rita), *The Reshaping of A Tradition: American Benedictine Women, 1852–1881*, Saint Joseph, Minnesota: Sisters of the Order of St. Benedict, 1994

Kleber, Albert, *History of St. Meinrad Archabbey, 1854–1954*, St. Meinrad, Indiana: Grail, 1954

Klimisch, Jane, *Women Gathering: The Story of the Benedictine Federation of St. Gertrude*, Toronto: Peregrina, 1993

Malone, Edward, *A History of the First Century of Conception Colony, Abbey and Schools*, Omaha, Nebraska: Interstate Printing, 1971

Merton, Thomas, *The Waters of Silence*, Dublin: Clonmore and Reynolds, 1950; as *The Waters of Siloe*, Garden City, New York: Garden City Books, 1951

Oetgen, Jerome, *An American Abbot: Boniface Wimmer, O.S.B., 1809–1887*, 2nd edition, Washington, D.C.: Catholic University Press, 1997

Pecklers, Keith F., *The Unread Vision – The Liturgical Movement in the United States of America: 1926–1955*, Collegeville, Minnesota: Liturgical Press, 1998

Rippinger, Joel, *The Benedictine Order in the United States*, Collegeville, Minnesota: Liturgical Press, 1990

Sutera, Judith, *True Daughters: Monastic Identity and American Benedictine Women's History*, Atchison, Kansas: Benedictine College Press, 1987

V

Vadstena, Sweden

Descending from the noble Swedish Bjälbo family, King Valdemar (1266–1275) built *Vat-sten* (the stone house on the water) on the eastern shore of Lake Vättern for the administration of his estates. At the age of three, his grandnephew Magnus Eriksson became king in 1319. In the 1330s the visionary noble lady St. Birgitta (Bridget, c. 1303–1373), serving at the court, became aware of the oppression of the people and the moral corruption emanating from the palace. Christ showed her how the palace was to be transformed into a convent for 60 nuns, adjacent buildings along the shore into a residence for 25 priests and male religious, and between the two a huge monastic church with three aisles where the lay community could attend services and receive divine grace and religious education. As a widow (1344) she convinced the king and the queen of the divine origin of her vision. By a will of 1 May 1346, the royal couple donated Vadstena palace with estates to Birgitta for the establishment of the monastery. Her vision and the royal donation became her guide for the rest of her life, which from 1350 she spent in Rome, traveling to pilgrimage sites in Italy and the Holy Land. On 5 August 1370, Pope Urban V (1362–1370) granted permission for the construction of two monasteries in Vadstena, one for nuns and one for priests, both to follow the Rule of St. Augustine. In 1369 Birgitta had sent her confidant Johan Petersson to Vadstena to inaugurate construction work, which implied lowering the walls of the palace (Birgitta viewed the high elevation of the walls as an expression of pride), and to refashion the upper floor into a dormitory for 60 nuns. After her death in Rome on 23 July 1373, her bodily remains were brought to Vadstena, and both pilgrimages and vocations to monastic life ensued. In 1384 the comprehensive monastery was inaugurated, and all applicants were consecrated. The monastery was now led by an abbess, with one convent for nuns and one for priests, as authorized by Pope Urban VI in 1378. On 7 October 1391, Birgitta was canonized in Rome by Pope Boniface IX (1389–1404).

After the blue sandstone church dedicated to Our Lady had been consecrated in 1430, the monastic complex made an impression of spiritual sublimity on every visitor. Many accounts from Vadstena as well as from daughter houses witness to the feelings of awe and heavenly presence that filled the visitors when the nuns sang their divine praise from the gallery without being seen from the church floor or when the priests gathered unseen beyond the high altar in the western end of the church, performing their hours of chanted Divine Office alternating with the nuns and celebrating daily High Mass. The two eastern entrance porches for the public were called "Doors of the Forgiving of Sins," whereas the door by which the priests entered their choir in the western end of the church was called "The Porch of Reconciliation" and one entrance for the nuns in the northern wall of the church "The Porch of Grace and Glory." On each side of the entrance porches was a house where visitors could speak to monks (south) or nuns (north). The priests were famous for sermons (which lasted for hours) not only in the church but also in the open from a pulpit above the entrance. Numerous volumes of sermons now repose in the University Library of Uppsala. Each convent had a fruit garden; some walls surrounding the enclosed areas still exist.

The priests' convent was dissolved by Lutheran King Gustav Vasa (1523–1560) in 1546. The church became Vadstena's parish church, and the last nuns had to leave Sweden in 1595. The convent buildings were used first as a home for former soldiers and then as a mental hospital. In the 1950s century-old memories of St. Birgitta and the efforts of the Birgittastiftelsen and others led to a decision to restore the complex of remaining buildings to some of their original cultural and spiritual uses. Only then was it discovered that the nuns' main convent building was identical with the old palace, which was thought to have perished during construction work in the 1370s. The 13th-century palace as well as the monastic rooms were restored, and parts of the convent buildings have been transformed into a guest house. During the Reformation the relics of St. Birgitta had been merged with other saints' relics, but nontheless they are still in the medieval relic chest now standing in the west choir, an object of intense devotion.

Remarkable personalities made Vadstena keep its role as a spiritual center, even during the Protestant age. The historian Johannes Messenius (1579–1636) grew up in Vadstena and became a professor in Uppsala, but because of the ban against Catholics, he spent 19 years in prison. The renewal started with the convert Erik Ihrfors (1846–1929), who lived in Vadstena in a monk's dress, reminding every visitor of the monastic past of the place. In 1935 Catholic Bridgettine Sisters, led by Maria Elisabeth Hesselblad (1870–1957), opened a guest house in Vadstena

Cloister and palace, Vadstena, Sweden, 15th century.
Photo courtesy of Andreas Lindblom

that in 1963 was transformed into a convent, today an abbey. Vicars of the Lutheran Church as well as the Swedish High Church Societas Sanctae Birgittae promoted Vadstena's reputation as a center of church renewal. Lutheran "Daughters of Mary" opened a convent in Vadstena in 1963, the members of which converted to the Catholic Church in 1983 and later established an abbey in neighboring Borghamn. Most remarkably the ecumenical rapprochement of the Roman Catholic Church and the Swedish Lutheran Church has manifested itself in the most striking way in Vadstena by ecumenical and pontifical services, especially in the presence of the Lutheran bishop Bertil Gärtner and the Catholic bishop Hubertus Brandenburg (resigned 1998) and even during Pope John Paul II's visit to Vadstena in 1989.

Vadstena's place in Swedish consciousness is that of the nation's and indeed all Scandinavia's mother sanctuary, devoted to Mary, the Mother of God, and her representative, St. Birgitta.

TORE NYBERG

See also Augustinian Rule; Bridgettines; Double Houses, Western Christian; Pilgrimages, Christian: Western Europe; Reformation; Scandinavia

Further Reading

Anderson, Iwar, *Vadstena gård och kloster* (Vadstena Palace and Monastery), 2 vols., Stockholm: Almqvist and Wiksell, 1972
Hogg, James, editor, *Studies in St. Birgitta and the Brigittine Order*, volumes 1 and 2 (Analecta Cartusiana 35:19), Salzburg, Austria: Institut fur Anglistik und Amerikanistik, Universitat Salzburg, and Lewiston, New York: Edwin Mellen Press, 1993
Höjer, Torvald, *Studier i Vadstena klosters och birgittinordens historia intill midten af 1400–talet* (Studies in the History of Vadstena Abbey and of the Birgittine Order until the Middle of the 15th Century), Uppsala: Almqvist and Wiksell, 1905
Lindblom, Andreas, *Birgittas gyllene skrin* (The Golden Shrine of Birgitta), Antikvariska serien 10, Stockholm: Almqvist and Wiksell, 1963
Lindblom, Andreas, *Kult och konst i Vadstena kloster* (Cult and Art in Vadstena Abbey), Antikvariska serien 14, Stockholm: Almqvist and Wiksell, 1965
Lindblom, Andreas, *Vadstena klosters öden* (The Story of Vadstena Abbey), Finspång: Finspångs Bokhandel, 1973

Vajrayāna Buddhism in Nepal

Vajrayāna, or Tantric, Buddhism is practiced among the Newar community in Nepal. Newar Buddhism flourishes in a small yet culturally diverse area of the Kathmandu Valley, where it has shared the religious environment with the Hindu practices for at least 2,000 years. Today Newar Buddhism represents the last remaining legacy of Indian Buddhism that is actively practiced within a southern Asian cultural context.

Nepal's historical connections with Indian Buddhism have been strong since the 11th to 12th century, when Tantric teachers of the Pāla period from northeastern India migrated to the Kathmandu Valley after the monastic centers in India were destroyed by the Muslim invasions. From this period onward the Kathmandu Valley became an important entrepôt for cultural exchanges between the northern and northeastern regions of India and the Tibetan plateau. Early epigraphic evidence of Buddhism in Nepal begins only in the Licchavi period (fourth to ninth century), but oral history indicates that Buddhism was already present at a much earlier date. Tradition recalls the visit of King Aśoka of the Maurya dynasty in the third century A.D. The Indian king is said to have married his daughter Cārumatī to a Nepali prince and formally established Buddhism in the valley. The four "Aśoka" stūpas in Patan are used as evidence of Aśoka's visit. The cosmogonic myth of the Newar Buddhists in fact traces the origins of Buddhism in the valley even earlier, to the period of the Mānuṣi Buddhas preceding Śākyamuni. As narrated in the *Svayambhū Purāṇa*, one of the most important religious text of the Newar Buddhists, the narrative begins with the visits of the seven Mānuṣi Buddhas, including Śākyamuni, to the valley, which was at that time a great lake. In the contemporary tradition the narrative serves as the mythological history of Buddhism for the Newars as well as a doctrinal basis within which the local practices are validated in the larger ideologies of Mahāyāna and Vajrayāna Buddhism.

Newar Buddhism has developed several unique features not found in other Buddhist communities in Asia. It has an intricate social organization of a highly structured, caste-stratified Buddhist community of married monks where entrance into the Buddhist faith is based on patrilineal descent. Newar Buddhism does not have an institution of permanent celibacy, but, rather, two caste groups, the Vajrācārya and the Sakya, constitute the monastic community (*saṅgha*). Both castes undergo monastic ordinations, and as married householders upholding Tantric path, they also undertake the highly esoteric initiations (*dīkṣā*) not accessible to other members of the Buddhist community. The Vajrācārya and Sakya castes receive monastic ordination as a passage-rite ceremony in early childhood, and their ritual status as a monk is repeatedly affirmed through their membership in monasteries (*bāhā* or *bahī*). As a caste group they are also referred to as *bande*, *bare*, or *bandyeju*, whose etymological root is related to the Sanskrit term *vande* or *vandana*, meaning "those who are worthy of respect" (i.e., Buddhist monks).

They are the highest caste groups in the Newar Buddhist community, yet their primary status is that of a monk. Within the caste group there is an implied hierarchy in that the Vajrācārya, by virtue of his title as "*vajra* master," holds the position of power as Tantric priest and ritual specialist. The Sakya's foremost identity is that of a monk. Historically the Sakya castes of the valley consider themselves descendants of Śākyamuni's clan of the Sakyas of Kapilāvastu, who migrated into the valley at a very early date. Recalling this honored heritage they are also formally called *Śākyavaṃsa* (descendants of the Sakya lineage) or *Sakyabhikṣu* (Sakya monk).

In contemporary Newar Buddhism the Vajrācārya priest is the teacher, or guru, of the community, as the individual who performs the rituals into highest Tantric teachings. As the *Vajrācārya* (Teacher of the Adamantine [Path]) of the Vajrayāna tradition, he is addressed as *gubhāju* (respected guru), a term which refers to his role as the initiating teacher. In this context Vajrācārya fulfills the ideals of the Tantric *siddha* of the Vajrayāna path. As an archetype of the *siddha* and Tantric priest, the Vajra master possesses the powers and qualifications to invoke, control, and summon deities for the benefit of sentient beings. In his social and ritual roles, the Vajrācārya's dual identity as Tantric *siddha* and priest is always at play; he, therefore, defines the path of the Vajrayāna tradition. The Vajrācārya embodies the ideal of the esoteric and dangerous adamantine path and empowers and directs the rest of the Buddhist community to function in a Vajrayāna framework.

The Buddhist rituals of the monastic community consist of three categories of rituals: *bare-chuegu* (making of the monk), *ācā luegu* (making of the Vajra master), and *dīkṣā*, or Tantric empowerment to Cakrasaṁvara. The initiation rituals of the Vajrācāryas and Sakya performed at the *bāhā*s reinforce their roles as Buddhist monks. Monastic initiations of the two castes are performed as life-cycle rituals in the Buddhist monasteries found throughout the valley. Initiation in a monastery gives the male members of the community the right and duty to serve as the guardian priest of the principal deity of the monastery for a week, two weeks, or a month. The length of their service on this rotational basis depends on the number of *saṅgha* members of the particular monastery. As monks they have the right to serve in the governing body of elders, who are responsible for the ritual functions related to the monastery. The second mandatory life-cycle ritual (*ācā luegu*) confers on the Vajrācārya his ritual status as Tantric priest through the five empowerments. Subsequent higher initiations (*dīkṣā*) provide esoteric empowerments of Cakrasaṁvara and Vajravārāhī, although other Heruka deities of the Highest Yoga class (Anuttara Yoga) Tantras, such as Hevajra/Nairātmā and Yogaṁvara/Jñānaḍākinī, are equally significant.

In its own terms Newar Buddhism is said to consist of three hierarchical levels, encompassing the methodologies of Śrāvakayāna, Mahāyāna, and Vajrayāna Buddhism. Śrāvakayāna is the monastic level, in which celibate monkhood remains fundamental to Newar Buddhist ideology. Mahāyāna serves as the Buddhist householder practice, whereas the Vajrayāna or esoteric Tantric tradition remains the highest and most powerful of the three soteriological methodologies. The hierarchy of the Three Ways integrates the apparently opposed ideals of celibacy and restraint of monkhood on the one hand and the full participation in worldly activities as a householder on the other. This ideological framework is also reflected in the rituals, pantheon, and iconographic schema of the Newar Buddhist monasteries.

DINA BANGDEL

See also Celibacy: Buddhist; Deities, Buddhist; Initiation: Buddhist Perspectives; Kathmandu Valley, Nepal; Maṇḍala; Nepal; Topography, Sacred (Buddhist); Visual Arts, Buddhist: Nepal; Worship Space: Buddhist Perspectives

Further Reading

Allen, Michael, "Buddhism without Monks: Vajrayāna Religion of the Newars of the Kathmandu Valley," *South Asia* 2:1–14 (1973)

Gellner, David N., *Monk, Householder, and Tantric Priest: Newar Buddhism and Its Hierarchy of Ritual* (Cambridge Studies in Social and Cultural Anthropology, 84), Cambridge and New York: Cambridge University Press, 1992

Lienhard, Siegfried, "Nepal: The Survival of Indian Buddhism in a Himalayan Kingdom," in *The World of Buddhism: Buddhist Monks and Nuns in Society and Culture*, edited by Heinz Bechert and Richard Gombrich, New York: Facts on File, and London: Thames and Hudson, 1984

Locke, John K., *Buddhist Monasteries of Nepal: A Survey of the Bahas and Bahis of the Kathmandu Valley*, Kathmandu: Sahayogi Press, 1985

Locke, John K., "Features of Newar Buddhism," in *The Buddhist Heritage: Papers Delivered at the Symposium of the Same Name Convened at the School of Oriental and African Studies, University of London, November 1985* (Buddhica Britannica, Series Continua, 1), edited by Tadeusz Skorupski, Tring: Institute of Buddhist Studies, 1989

Slusser, Mary S., *Nepal Mandala: A Cultural Study of the Kathmandu Valley*, 2 vols., Princeton, New Jersey: Princeton University Press, 1980

Vajrayāna Buddhism in Tibet. *See* Buddhist Schools/Traditions: Tibet

Vallombrosans

The early history of the Vallombrosans – today a small Benedictine congregation in northern central Italy – was of particular significance for the development of Christian monasticism in the West in terms of both its community structure and its evolving constitutional arrangements.

Their founder, St. John Gualbert (c. 995–1073), canonized 1193, was a monk at the Bendictine monastery of St. Miniato in Florence when he learned that his abbot had bought his way into office. Appalled by this blatant simony (an abuse then prevalent in parts of the Western Church), Gualbert denounced both his superior and the bishop of Florence and left St. Miniato in outrage. After some years of wandering, in 1036 (the first definite date in his life) he settled with two companions on the wooded slopes of Monte Secchieta, 22 miles east of Florence. There, the following year, he was given some land on which to construct a monastery (Vallombrosa).

Gualbert's intention was now to live according to the full rigor of the Rule of St. Benedict (as he understood it). He was suspicious of clerical ordination and insisted that his monks observe a strict regime of poverty, simplicity, and silence. Intent on contemplative prayer, they were to keep their distance from heavy manual labor, and from all external activity and administration. The latter tasks were to be carried out by a separate class of *conversi* (lay brothers), who would wear a different habit and have a briefer prayer schedule. This innovation is seen as a forerunner of the Cistercian use of *conversi* and thus heralds a far-reaching change in organized religious life.

Gualbert also sought to be part of the movement within the Church that opposed simony and advocated clerical celibacy. In fact, because other monasteries were soon attracted by his policies (and new foundations followed), the Vallombrosans were to become one of the principal instruments of the papal reform policy in Italy.

At the time of the founder's death in 1073, only eight monasteries existed in the Vallombrosan observance. However, soon afterward expansion began into Umbria, and in the first half of the 12th century – mainly through the activities of St. Bernard degli Uberti (d. 1133), abbot of Vallombrosa, cardinal legate of Pope Paschal II (1099–1118), and later bishop of Parma – numerous houses were founded in Lombardy, especially around Milan. Monasteries existed also in Sardinia and Emilia-Romagna, as did one in France. By the mid–12th century, a total of 53 houses were affiliated with Vallombrosa. A century later, 79 abbeys, 29 priories, 9 monasteries of nuns, and 17 *ospedali* (for the poor and pilgrims) were in existence.

At first the various houses were linked not juridically but simply by a bond of charity and (uniform) observance (*vinculum caritatis et consuetudinis*). The way in which this initially loose association developed over time into a separate and highly structured religious order is another reason that the Vallombrosans have a significance in monastic history greater than themselves, for the process was to be repeated again and again in subsequent centuries.

In a bull of April 1090, Pope Urban II (1088–1099) granted apostolic protection (or exemption from diocesan jurisdiction) to the Vallombrosan monasteries and spoke of the abbot of Vallombrosa as exercising a general vigilance over the other houses. He was to be elected not only by the monks of Vallombrosa itself but also by a *conventus abbatum* that, although originally neither a consultative nor a legislative body, gradually took on the character of a general chapter. (Somewhat in contradiction to this, in the early decades signs of an embryonic filiation system were evident as well.)

However, by the early 12th century, the abbot of Vallombrosa was referred to as abbot major (*abbas maior*), and his powers began to be juridically defined. No abbot was to be elected in any of the other monasteries without his knowledge and approval. No novices were to be admitted without his permission, and he was empowered to transfer monks to other houses when he judged it necessary. From 1139 on monastic profession was made, in effect, not to the individual monastery but to the congregation as a whole, which, by the first half of the 13th century, began to be referred to as the Order of Vallombrosa (*ordo Vallisumbrosae*). Official visitators were appointed, and a monk procurator was sent to live in Rome to represent Vallombrosan interests before the Papal Curia. From 1258 definitors were also elected to legislate during the general chapters.

However, by the early 15th century, the Vallombrosans were suffering the same decline and malaise that afflicted Italian monasticism generally, especially because commendatory abbots had been imposed on many of the monasteries. Successive popes, beginning in 1432 with Eugenius IV (1431–1447), encouraged a renewal movement along the lines of the new, reform congregation of St. Giustina of Padua. This eventually led to a schism among the Vallombrosan houses, but finally, in 1485, the reform group won an almost total victory. Although the abbot of Vallombrosa was now declared to be, ex officio, abbot general (for life) of the newly named Congregation of St. Maria of Vallombrosa, all the traditional Vallombrosan structures were swept aside. In their place stood a "modern," centralized congregation on the St. Giustina model, with power firmly in the hands of an annual general chapter that appointed all abbots and transferred monks as the need arose. By 1543 the post of abbot general had been reduced to a triennial office and was no longer necessarily linked to the abbacy of Vallombrosa at all.

It is significant perhaps that the outstanding Vallombrosans of the 17th and 18th centuries were not abbots general or influential spiritual writers but a series of distinguished botanists – Francesco Maratti (1697–1777) being the most celebrated – whose research, publications, and university teaching were renowned throughout Italy and beyond. However, for the congregation as a whole, this same period witnessed its increasing subjection to the grand dukes of Tuscany (first the Medici, then the Habsburgs). In March 1662, partly as an attempt to weaken this control, Pope Alexander VII (1655–1667) forced through a union of the Vallombrosans with another small Benedictine order in central Italy, the Sylvestrines. The latter, concentrated in the Marches (within papal territory), were less

Neri di Bicci, *St. John Gualberto and Ecclesiastics*, S. Pancrazio, Florence, Italy, 15th century.
Photo courtesy of Alinari/Art Resource, New York

numerous (134 monks compared to 273) and much less wealthy than the Vallombrosans, who regarded them with disdain, because they sometimes taught in public schools (judged to be a slight on monastic status). This predictably unhappy marriage was dissolved in October 1667 after Alexander's death.

However, a century later, following the papal suppression of the Jesuits (1773), it was, ironically, the Vallombrosans with whom Grand Duke Leopold I (1765–1790) of Tuscany sought to replace the Jesuits as a teaching order. Between 1770 and 1786 a series of small Vallombrosan houses were closed and their revenues allocated to colleges where the monks were to teach. However, even more dramatic changes were imminent. With the advance of the French revolutionary armies into northern Italy in 1792, the remaining Vallombrosan monasteries in Lombardy were suppressed, as were two in Emilia-Romagna. The final coup de grace came in 1810 with a decree of Napoleon's that suppressed all the monasteries in Tuscany (and later the one in Rome) and expelled the monks.

Numerically, the Vallombrosans have never recovered from this catastrophe. At the time the congregation comprised about 200 monks (123 of them priests). When a decade later three monasteries in Tuscany (Vallombrosa itself, St. Maria at Montenero, and St. Trinità in Florence) and St. Prassede in Rome had been reopened, only 70 or so (including 48 priests) returned to once more take up the monastic life. During the 1860s, after the second round of suppressions in Italy, the monks were once more rendered homeless, except for the few who could stay on as rectors of churches. Vallombrosa itself now became the headquarters of the national forestry institute.

With the new constitutions of May 1922, the post of abbot general was once more united with that of abbot of Vallombrosa, and finally, in 1949, both he and the novitiate (for a time removed to France) were able to return to the mother house. (This, as a national monument with buildings dating largely from the 15th and 17th centuries, remains the property of the state.) In the same year a mission was begun in Brazil. In 1995 this community (near São Paolo) numbered about eight monks, whereas in Italy only 53 Vallombrosans were distributed across seven monasteries (two of them abbeys). More recently a small foundation has commenced in India in the southern state of Kerala. (In 1966 the Vallombrosans became part of the international Benedictine Confederation.)

From the first half of the 12th century, monasteries of nuns were also affiliated with Vallombrosa, following the same observance and usages and recognizing the preeminent position of the abbot major. However, in the 17th century these communities began to move into the jurisdiction of the local bishops. Today four of them remain with a total population of less than 60 nuns, the largest community being that of St. Umiltà at Faenza, founded by the saint herself in 1266. However, these convents have no juridical link with the monks or even among themselves because each has its own constitutions. The only common bond is the Vallombrosan calendar and liturgy.

TERENCE KAVENAGH

See also Benedictines: General or Male; Florence, Italy; Gregory VII; Gualbert, John, St.; Monastics and the World, Medieval

Further Reading

Giustarini, Luca Bernardo, "'Lotta per una stanza': Le vicissitudini della congregazione vallombrosana nei secoli XIX–XX," in *Il monachesimo in Italia tra Vaticano I e Vaticano II*, edited by F.G. Trolese, Cesena: Centro Storico Benedettino Italiano, 1995

Meade, Denis, "From Turmoil to Solidarity: the Emergence of the Vallombrosan Monastic Congregation," *American Benedictine Review* 19:1 (1968)

Paoli, Ugo, *L' unione delle congregazioni Vallombrosana e Silvestrina (1662–1667)*, Fabriano: Montisfani, 1975

Spinelli, G., and G. Rossi, editors, *Alle origini di Vallombrosa: Giovanni Gualberto nella società dell 'XI secolo*, Milan: Jaca, 1984

Vasaturo, N., "L'espansione della congregazione vallombrosana fino alla metà del secolo XII," *Rivista di storia della Chiesa in Italia* 16 (1962)

Vasaturo, N., *Acta Capitulorum Generalium Congregationis Vallis Umbrosae I. Institutiones Abbatum (1095–1310)*, Rome: Edizioni di Storia e Letteratura, 1985 (note that the "General Preface" to this volume is in English and is a survey, by Denis Meade, of Vallombrosan constitutional history until 1485)

Vasaturo, R.N., "I Vallombrosani nella società italiana dei secoli XI e XII," edited by G. Monzio Compagnoni, *Archivio Vallombrosano* 2 (1995)

Vasaturo, R.N., "Vallombrosa, Vallombrosane, Vallombrosani," in *Dizionario degli Istituti di Perfezione*, volume 9, edited by Giancarlo Rocca, Rome: Paoline, 1997

Vasaturo, R.N., et al., *Vallombrosa nel IX centenario della morte del fondatore Giovanni Gualberto 12 luglio 1073*, Florence: Giorgi e Gambi, 1973

Vegetarianism. *See* Animals, Attitude toward; Food

Velichkovsky, Paisy. *See* Paisy Velichkovsky

Victorines

In 1108 William of Champeaux (c. 1070–1121), archdeacon of Paris and teacher at Notre-Dame, resigned his offices and retired with some students to a place called St. Victor on the left bank of the Seine River. Unlike other converted clerics he continued to teach and to live on the edge of the city. Those two characteristics were the defining characteristics of this community of canons regular. In 1113 William was elected bishop of Châlons. He seems to have taken the occasion to prevail on King Louis VI (1108–1137) to endow St. Victor generously.

The monastery of St. Victor prospered under William's successor as abbot, Gilduin (d. 1155). Recruits from many nations joined the community. Its teaching offices were filled with a number of brilliant scholars. Hugh of St. Victor (d. 1141), a German, laid the foundations for a Victorine tradition in theology that combined fidelity to the monastic and poetic theology of the early Church with openness to the methods and questions of the newly emerging theology of the schools with its emphasis on order, logic, and argument. He wrote a number of introductory works, including a guide to reading (*Didascalicon*), biblical exegesis, treatises, and a synthesis of theology called *De sacramentis*. Adam of St. Victor (d. 1143) was a poet and composer associated both with Notre Dame and with St. Victor. Achard of St. Victor (d. 1170/71), an Englishman who was both teacher and abbot before becoming bishop of Avranches, has left behind some highly developed sermons and sermon-treatises on the spiritual life as well as several philosophically oriented treatises. Richard (d. 1173), a Scot, wrote sermons and sermon helps, treatises on the spiritual life and mysticism, and biblical exegesis. Andrew (d. 1175), an Englishman, pioneered literal exegesis of the Bible. Little is known of the biographies of these Victorine canons; apparently, it was not a Victorine custom to write about oneself.

The monastery experienced grave difficulties under Abbot Ernis, who was deposed in 1172. His successors for the next 50 years were worthy men, but the academic life of the community began to decline. However, the canons continued to minister to the students of the schools as confessors and spiritual directors, and two of them, Robert of Flamesbury (c. 1208–1213) and Peter of Poitiers (after 1215), wrote guides for confessors in the early 13th century. The last great intellectual figure of the medieval abbey was Thomas Gallus (d. 1246), founder and abbot of the Abbey of St. Andrew in Vercelli. Thomas of St. Victor, as he was also called, was a student of Pseudo-Dionysius' works and had considerable influence on the early Franciscans.

The lifestyle at St. Victor was regulated by the *Liber ordinis*, a customary based on Cluniac and other monastic sources. This customary likely goes back to the Abbot Gilduin. Oddly, it makes no mention of teaching or schools but rather legislates regarding the officials, the daily order and discipline, and liturgy. It refers to dependencies of the abbey, of which a number existed (e.g., Puiseaux and Amplonville). The *Liber ordinis* seems to have been one of the bonds that tied together the fragile Order of St. Victor, which included houses in France (e.g., St. Euvert at Orléans and Eu), England (e.g., Wigmore and Bristol), Ireland (e.g., Thomascourt in Dublin, Waterford, and Bridgetown), and Scandinavia. The ties between these other communities and St. Victor appear never to have been very strong, although it seems that all communities were to have been represented at the annual general chapters held at St. Victor. Many other communities borrowed from the *Liber ordinis* without becoming members of the Victorine Congregation, including the Trinitarians and the Canons Regular of Windesheim. In effect the Congregation of St. Victor ceased to exist with the bull of Benedict XII (1334–1342), *Ad decorem Ecclesiae* (1339).

Monasteries of Victorine canonesses existed by the end of the 12th century. The most noteworthy of these was Prémy, near Cambrai, a foundation of Cantimpré, a double monastery affiliated to St. Victor in 1180. Prémy was the source of a number of houses of Victorine canonesses (e.g., Waasmunster, Roesbrugge, Nieuclooster, and Le Quesnoy). Some preexisting monasteries of canonesses also joined St. Victor. Most of these have disappeared, but some survive either as members of the Order of the Holy Sepulcher or as Victorine houses.

During the 15th century the monastery of St. Victor was diminished in size and fervor. Toward the end of the century, John Mombaer, a Canon Regular of Windesheim, suggested that a new congregation of canons regular be formed with the Abbey of St. Victor as leader. A meeting in 1501 sought to carry out his suggestion. Saint Victor petitioned to join the resultant federation in 1513, and in 1515 the name of the group was changed to the Congregation of St. Victor. During the 16th century other monasteries joined the Congregation, but the wars of religion and the practice of installing lay abbots *in commendam* undermined the bonds between the abbeys. Saint Victor received a commendatory abbot in 1543 and thereafter was directed by a prior-vicar.

In 1622 Cardinal François de La Rochefoucauld (1558–1643) undertook the reform of the Benedictines and the Augustinian canons of France. He wanted to end the system of benefices and recall all the canons regular to their cloisters. The Victorines objected. They wanted to keep their priories and saw no incompatibility between their parochial ministry and their canonial vocation. Because the Victorines were adamant, St. Geneviève in Paris was made head of the new French Congregation of Canons Regular. The existing Congregation of St. Victor was dissolved.

Jean de Thoulouse was elected prior-vicar of the monastery in 1636. He was a vigorous defender of the independence of St. Victor and to that end compiled a vast historical study of the community. However, although the monastery managed to resist assimilation into the French Congregation, it did not prosper. The terms of the priors were limited to three years, and recruitment was restricted to the upper classes. Simon Gourdan (1646–1729) was a saintly religious, but he could not convince his fellow canons to follow his example. In 1790, at the time of the secularization, 21 canons resided in the community. One, Jean Charles Maria Bernard, died in a massacre and was beatified in 1926.

HUGH FEISS, O.S.B.

See also Canons Regular, Origins of; Cluny, France; Dionysius the Pseudo-Areopagite; Double Houses, Western Christian; Education of Christian Monastics; France: History; Hymnographers

Further Reading

Achard of St. Victor, *Works*, translated by Hugh Feiss, Kalamazoo, Michigan: Cistercian Publications, 2000

Adam de Saint-Victor, *Quatorze proses du XIIe siècle à la louange de Marie*, edited by Bernadette Jollès, Turnhout: Brepols, 1994

Berndt, Rainer, *André de Saint-Victor ([d.] 1175) Exégète et théologien*, Paris: Brepols, 1991
Bonnard, F., *Histoire de l'abbaye royale et de l'ordre des chanoines réguliers de Saint-Victor de Paris*, 2 vols., Paris, 1904–1907
Châtillon, Jean, *Théologie, spiritualité et métaphysique dans l'oeuvre oratoire d'Achard de Saint-Victor*, Paris: Vrin, 1969
Châtillon, Jean, "Canonici Regolari di San Vittore," *Dizionario degli Istituti di Perfezione* 2 (1973)
Châtillon, Jean, "Richard de Saint-Victor," *Dictionnaire de Spiritualité, ascetique et mystique: Doctrine et histoire*, volume 13, Paris: Beauchesne, 1987
Hugh of St. Victor, *Opera*, Migne, *Patrologia Latina*, Paris, 1844–1864
Hugh of St. Victor, *Didascalicon of Hugh of St. Victor: A Medieval Guide to the Arts*, edited by Jerome Taylor, New York and London: Columbia University Press, 1961
Liber ordinis Sancti Victoris Parisiensis, Turnhout: Brepols, 1984
Longère, Jean, editor, *L'abbaye parisienne de Saint-Victor au Moyen Âge: Communications présentées au XIIIe Colloque d'Humanisme médiéval de Paris (1986–1988)*, Paris: Brepols, 1991
Richard of St. Victor, *Opera*, Migne, *Patrologia Latina* 196 (also 177, *Sermones centum*), Paris, 1844–1864
Richard of St. Victor, *The Twelve Patriarchs: The Mystical Ark: Book Three of the Trinity*, translated by Grover A. Zinn, New York: Paulist Press, and London: SPCK, 1979

Vienna, Austria

Seen from the standpoint of history, the capital of Austria is not a center of ancient monasticism, as the earliest convents of this country were founded in Salzburg. However, in Vienna, a metropolis of about 1.7 million inhabitants today, numerous churches survive that belonged originally to a monastery as well as a few belonging originally to a nunnery, most of them founded in the late Middle Ages. Vienna itself goes back to a Roman camp and *municipium* named Vindobona, but after the fall of the Roman Empire it seems to have been abandoned. An unimportant small settlement in the early Middle Ages, it did not become the site of any monastery. This changed only in the 12th century, and from the late Middle Ages onward, when Vienna evolved into the center of the Holy Roman (Habsburg) Empire, it could boast of an impressive number of monastic sites. Yet the more visible structures of monasticism that have lasted to the present were founded in the 17th and 18th centuries, when, in the course of the Counter-Reformation, both new orders were called into the city and many monastic churches and convents of the established ones could be rebuilt. Compared with other cities it is a remarkable feature of sacred topography that all remaining monastic sites of some importance belong to a male order; although more female convents existed at the end of the Middle Ages, many of them perished later or never became important.

The first Viennese monastery was founded when Babenberg Duke Heinrich II (1141–1177) chose Vienna as his residence. Here he established both a palatinate and, in 1155, a convent, the monks of which were taken from Regensburg and were Irish-Scottish Benedictines. This is the Schottenkloster, whose members until 1418 invariably had to come from Ireland or Scotland, and from 1418 until today has been inhabited by Benedictines from Germany. The Romanesque church was completely transformed into a heavy baroque one by Italian architects between 1638 and 1648, and the other buildings date from 1827 to 1832. In the museum an important late Gothic reredos from the former main altar, painted from 1469 to 1475, shows a view of late medieval Vienna. In the secondary school (f. 1807), the elite of the city's upper class has been educated.

According to tradition the history of the mendicant orders in Vienna begins around 1224 (1230?), when Duke Leopold VI (1198–1230) bade the followers of St. Francis to settle between the Schottenkloster and his new castle outside the city walls. The mighty Minoritenkirche dates mainly from the 14th century, but since it served the Protestants from 1559 to 1620, the old fur-

East end of the Franciscan Church (Minoritenkirche), Vienna, Austria, 14th century.
Photo courtesy of Chris Schabel

Imperial crypt (Kaisergruft), Kapuzinerkirche (Capuchin), Vienna, Austria, early 17th century. The crypt holds sarcophagi of Habsburg emperors and archdukes.
Photo courtesy of the Austrian National Tourist Office

nishings have been lost. About a year after the Franciscans, the Dominicans founded a convent; their church represents the Roman baroque of the 17th century. The Augustinian friars' convent was transferred from the suburbs to the city's center in 1327, and the church erected then is still in existence. From 1634 on its services were frequented especially by the emperor and his court. After the friars had died out in 1838, the church was committed to secular clerics until 1951, when it was given back to the Order. The Carmelites came in 1360; their church, Zu den 9 Chören der Engel, was given to the Jesuits under Petrus Canisius in 1554, and the building impressively dominates an open square and dates mainly from the 17th century.

Among the military orders the Teutonic Knights and the Knights Hospitallers have made their presence felt in Vienna. The Teutonic Knights, settling around 1200, became the head of the Ballei Österreich. The Hoch- und Deutschmeister, Austria's most famous traditional military band, originated in the troops furnished by this commendatory. The church dates mainly from 1720 to 1722, nonetheless reviving Gothic forms. The Knights Hospitallers, called "Johanniter" or "Malteser," began to build their hospital around 1210; the small church dates from the second quarter of the 14th century.

The Counter-Reformation led to the installation of new orders. Mention should be made of the Piarists (f. 1716), whose church is an excellent example of Austrian baroque, having been designed on an oval ground plan by Lukas von Hildebrandt and frescoed by Franz Maulpertsch. Also an important monument of the 17th and 18th centuries is the Universitätskirche, which was served by the Jesuits. However, the best-known monastery of Vienna is that of the Capuchins, endowed in 1618 by Empress Anna. The church is architecturally unimportant, but the vault beneath it, the Kapuzinergruft, attracts many visitors, being the Habsburgs' mausoleum. Here 138 metal sarcophagi of this dynasty are housed, among them the tomb of Maria Theresia and that of Franz Joseph II. Other monasteries of less historical and artistic importance are those of the Barmherzige Brüder (late 17th century) and the Paulaners (f. 1627) and the nunnery of the Elisabethinnen (early 18th century).

Peter Dinzelbacher

South flank of the Minoritenkirche, Vienna, Austria, 14th century. Photo courtesy of Chris Schabel

See also Austria; Benedictines; Germany; Melk, Austria

Further Reading

Perger, Richard, and Walter Brauneis, *Die mittelalterlichen Kirchen und Klöster Wiens*, Vienna: Zsolnay, 1977

Stoklaska, Anneliese, "Zur Entstehung der Ältesten Wiener Frauenkloster," Ph.D. Diss., Vienna, 1986

Vietnam

Introduction of Buddhism in Vietnam

Visits by Indian Buddhist monastics and merchants beginning at the end of the second century effected an unobtrusive introduction of Buddhism into Vietnam. These Buddhists used the maritime passage from India to indianized islands to extend their activities into China. While visiting Vietnam they often had to wait several months for a favorable monsoon. During these sojourns they practiced their faith and brought Buddhism to Vietnam, which was being invaded by China at this time. The names of the four initial propagators of Buddhism are preserved: Mārajīvaka, Kālaruci, Kang Senh-huei, and Meou-tseu.

Around 189 Mārajīvaka, an Indian monastic traveler, reached Luy Lâu (near Hanoi), capital of Giao-Châu, as the Chinese called annexed Vietnam. There he performed miracles: cures, walking on rivers, and domination of tigers.

Kālaruci (or Kalyanaruci), an Indoscythian, stayed in Giao-Châu a long time. Between 255 and 257 he undertook to translate the *Saddharma-samādhi* sūtra.

Meou-tseu (or Meou Po; Vietnamese, Mâu-tủ or Mâu Bác) was a young Chinese Daoist, born between 165 and 170, who took refuge from wars in Giao-Châu around 189 and subsequently converted to Buddhism. He wrote the *Lý-hoặc-luận* to defend Buddhism against Chinese Daoists and Confucianists in Giao-Châu. His book shows the existence of a large community of Vietnamese monastics from long before his arrival. This community followed Indian monastic rules and possessed a number of sūtras (some already translated into Chinese), including the Forty-Four Chapters. The *saṅgha* included Indian, Middle Eastern, and Vietnamese monks.

Kang Senh-huei (Vietnamese, Khuổng-Tăng-Hội) was born in Giao-Châu of Sogdian parents and became a monk at age ten following their death. Having mastered the Tripiṭaka in Sanskrit and Chinese, he taught Buddhism and translated 14 sūtras into Chinese. Around 255 he continued his mission in China, converting the king of the Wu dynasty as well as building stūpas and pagodas. He died in China in 280.

Buddhism encountered no resistance in Giao-Châu. Suffering under Chinese domination, the Vietnamese people welcomed the Buddha's teaching of compassion and tolerance. Moreover Buddhism did not contradict the age-old beliefs of the Vietnamese, nor did the Chinese try to stop its spread. Some Daoists, such as Meou Po, became Buddhists. Between the third and fourth centuries, Buddhism in Giao-Châu followed Indian practices. Pagodas, monasteries, and about 20 *chaitya*s (assembly halls) were built in the capital Luy Lâu to house "more than 500 religious who recited 15 scrolls of texts." Nevertheless Buddhist practice was limited to teaching and reciting sūtras. A few learned monks undertook translations using rudimentary technical terms borrowed from Chinese Daoism. They did not have time to refine their translations.

Implantation of Buddhism in Giao-Châu (Chinese-Ruled Vietnam, 268–939)

After three centuries of Buddhism in Giao-Châu, the religion expanded with the arrival of masters of Chan or Dhyāna (Vietnamese, Thiên) meditation. Three masters founded three different schools: Vinītaruci (arrived 580), Vô-Ngôn-Thông (arrived 820), and Thảo-Dường (arrived 1069).

Vinītaruci (Vietnamese, Tỳ-Ni-Da-Lủu-Chi) was a brahmin from South India who had visited China in 562. In 574 Emperor Wudi of the Sui dynasty oppressed Buddhism, forcing the third patriarch of Chinese Chan, Seng-Tsan, to flee to Hunan, where he met Vinītaruci and adopted him as a disciple. On his journey to the South, Vinītaruci stopped in Kủang-Tcheou to translate the *Gaya-sirsa* sūtra, a Mahāyāna work on enlightenment. In 580 he arrived in Giao-Châu and settled in the Pháp-Vân pagoda at Luy Lâu to translate the *Mahāyāna-vaipulya-dhāraṇī* sūtra. In 594 he died as first patriarch of his school, having transmitted to his favorite disciple, Pháp-Hiên, the teaching of Seng-Tsan. Pháp-Hiên constructed the Chúng-Thiên Pagoda at Bắc-Ninh, where he taught the doctrine of Vinītaruci to more than 300 disciples.

The Dhyāna school of Vinītaruci followed in its essentials Indian tradition, even though the master had received the Seal of the Heart from a Chinese master. Methods of reaching *samādhi* gradually would lead ultimately to enlightenment. Once achieved, enlightenment imparted six supernatural powers associated with Vajrayāna. The school of Vinītaruci lasted from 580 to 1213 through 19 generations of monastics. Certain masters became famous for supernatural powers, including Vạn-Hạnh, Tu-Dạo-Hạnh, and Minh-Không.

The second Chan (Thiên) school in Giao-Châu was founded by Dhyāna master Vô-Ngôn-Thông, a Chinese born at Kủang-Tcheou. In 820 he came to Giao-Châu and settled at the Kiên-Sơ Pagoda to practice the method of wall-facing meditation, which he transmitted to his successor, Cảm-Thành. This method practiced the tradition of Huineng, which seeks sudden enlightenment, in contrast to the gradual method taught by Vinītaruci. A first the doctrine of Vô-Ngôn-Thông had no esoteric element, but later a mystical element emerged, especially in the 10th and 11th generations. This school lasted 13 generations, from 820 until the 13th century. In its ranks are a number of remarkable monks: Master Khuông-Viêt, Master Thủờng-Chiêu, Emperor Lý Thai-tôn, Master Thông-Biên (a Buddhist historian), Master Biên-Tài, Master Không-Lộ, and Master Hiện-Quang (founder of the Chan school Yên-Tủ).

At the time of the Champa conquest in 1069, led by Vietnamese King Lý Thánh-Tông, among the prisoners of war was a Chinese monk on mission. The vast learning of this monk, Thảo-Dủờng, astonished the Vietnamese king, who granted him the country's highest religious title, Quôc-sủ (Religious Master of the State), and founded the Chan school of Thảo-Dủờng in his honor. Lasting six generations from 1069 to 1210, this third Chan school remained confined to the royal court. Among its 19 members were three kings and three high mandarins, including King Lý Thánh-Tông (1054–1071), King Lý Anh-Tôn (1138–1175), and King Lý Cao-Tôn (1175–1210). This school preached harmony between Buddhism and Confucianism and later spread among mandarins and literati. The use of poetry and of poetic images to illustrate Buddhist themes was characteristic of this school and influenced the other schools of Chan.

Spread of Buddhism

In 1007 Lê-Ngọa-Triêu, king from the Lê dynasty of Vietnam, sent a delegation to the imperial Song court to request a copy of the Chinese Tripiṭaka published in 983 by the emperor of China, Tông-Thái-Tô. By 1098 Vietnam possessed four copies of this same edition requested at different dates. The arrival of the Tripiṭaka awakened a vast movement of reading the sūtras, unleashed by the nobility and then spread among the people. Such reading prompted remarkable progress among Buddhists not only in writing interpretations and commentaries on the sūtras but also in composing literary works on Buddhist themes. Art of Buddhist inspiration enjoyed an unprecedented flowering. The majority of the most beautiful pagodas were built during this period.

At the beginning of the 11th century, most Buddhist currents were present in Vietnam: Theravāda, Mahāyāna, Dhyāna, Pure Land, and Mysticism. Although differing in their practices, these currents did not contradict one another in doctrine. Gradually they developed into more fully structured schools whose members were better trained and more adept at teaching dharma. Schools of meditation drew their followers from the upper classes of mandarins and literati. By way of contrast most of the people were attracted by Pure Land Buddhism (Vietnamese, Tịnh-Dộ). However, these Buddhist currents were not the sole beliefs in the country, for already present were Confucianism and Daoism. A process of mutual assimilation and a spirit of tolerance treated all beliefs without discrimination.

The 13th century was marked by a tendency to fuse all schools of meditation, beginning with Master Thuởng-Chiêu and ending with King Trân Thái-Tôn, of the Trân dynasty. The Chan (Thiên) school was known as the Trúc-Lâm Yên-Tủ school. Hiện-Quang, a Vietnamese monk, disciple of Master Trí-Thông and Master Pháp-Gíởi, combined the teachings of the Chan schools of Vô-Ngôn-Thông and of Vinītaruci. He founded the fourth Chan school, Yên-Tủ, which fused the doctrines of these two schools.

Five Chan Schools of Meditation

Having repelled the two final Mongol invasions, King Trân Nhân-Tông abdicated, was ordained in the Chan school Yên-Tủ in 1299, and soon became its sixth patriarch. Later he changed the name of this Chan school to Trúc-Lâm Yên-Tủ and became the first patriarch of this new school, which fused all previous Vietnamese Chan schools. The study of sacred texts was furthered through the use of more subtle translations. The most rarefied themes were studied and explicated by monks and laypeople, such as Prince Tuệ-Trung Thuởng-Sì, King Trân Thái-Tông, and King Trân Nhân-Tông. Poetry was devised to express the indescribability of *śūnyatā* (emptiness). At an advanced age, King Trân Nhân-Tông traveled through the country to urge his people to practice the Ten Meritorious Acts, each of which stipulates an act to avoid and an act to perform:

1. Do not kill. Instead protect life.
2. Do not steal. Instead make gifts of charity.
3. Do not commit illegal sexual acts. Instead protect women.
4. Do not lie. Instead respect truth.
5. Do not speak duplicitously. Instead speak in order to reconcile.
6. Do not speak crudely. Instead speak with politeness.
7. Do not speak trivia. Instead speak only if necessary.

8. Do not become enslaved to sexual desires. Instead lead a healthy and holy life.
9. Do not give way to anger. Instead practice compassion.
10. Do not harbor false thoughts. Instead follow Correct Thinking.

Practice of the Ten Meritorious Acts brings rebirth on the level of the deities. The king wanted to make this practice the moral foundation of social and spiritual values.

When the Manchus invaded China, many Chinese, including Buddhist monks, fled to Vietnam. Among them the monk Nguyên-Thìêu (1648–1728), a grand master of the Chan school of Lin-chi in China, founded the Chan school of Lâm-Tê in Vietnam.

Between 1573 and 1599 the Chinese Chan master Nhât-Cú Tri-Giáo of the Tào-Dông school in China introduced to North Vietnam yet another Chinese school of meditation. Descendants of this school still function in the pagodas of Hòa-Giai, Hàm-Long, and Trán-Qûôc at Hanoi.

During the same period in North Vietnam, the Chan school of Liên-Tông was founded by the Chan master Nhủ-Trủng Lân-Giác. The school lasted six generations.

Modern Times

After the liberation of the country from China in 939 by Ngo Quyen, Buddhism flourished under the Vietnamese dynasties of the Lý and the Trân (from 1010 to 1400). During this period kings and princesses became monks and nuns. However, with the rise of Confucianism, Buddhism was criticized by a number of Confucian intellectuals and mandarins who objected to the waste of energy and national resources. Periods of royal repression forced monastics to return to lay life as pagodas were destroyed. However, whenever the country suffered natural cataclysms, the kings sought help from the monks to "correct their mistakes." During droughts the king had brought to him the statue of Pháp-Vân, known for its power of bringing rain.

After the French conquered Vietnam in the 1880s, they favored Roman Catholicism over the country's local traditions. The only religion acknowledged as such by France was Christianity. Other religions were recognized merely as private associations.

During the 1920s and 1930s, two popular movements had a more or less close link with Buddhism and remain very active today. The first was founded by Lê Văn Chiêu in 1925 in South Vietnam under the name of Cao-Dài (Vietnamese, Dạo Cao-Dài). This syncretist religion asserts the unique origin of the three great Eastern religions: Buddhism, Confucianism, and Daoism. Its syncretism embraces popular beliefs, Christianity, and a cult of international figures, such as Winston Churchill, Sun Yat-Sen, Napoleon, and Victor Hugo. It believes in a supreme being, creator of the universe, and at one time it held under command its own armed troops.

The second movement was called "Buddhism of Hòa-Hảo" (Vietnamese, Phát-Gíao Hòa-Hảo). It is a Buddhist sect connected to the cult of heaven and the cult of ancestors as well as to traditional beliefs. It even includes elements of Confucianism and Daoism. Founded in 1947 by Huỳnh Phú Sô in the village of Hòa-Hảo in the province of Châu-Dôc in South Vietnam, it conducted warfare against both the French and the Vietnamese Communists.

Since April 30, 1975, Vietnam has lived entirely under a Communist regime. Civil rights are restricted. Pagodas have been locked and placed under guard. All the heads of the Unified Vietnamese Buddhist Church (Gíao-Hôi Phât-Giáo Việt-Nam Thông-Nhút), which was founded in 1964, were put in prison, notwithstanding their earlier collaboration with the Communists, and the church was abolished. This period of hardship lasted until 1987 and ceased with the fall of the Soviet Union. A policy of renewal (*dôi-mỏi*) by the government seeks to attract international investors. As a result, the surviving pagodas have been repaired and reopened to the public. Other pagodas have been built at state expense, but secret police oversee their religious activities. The masses take advantage of this politico-economic opening to return to the pagodas that their ancestors had built and protected even at the cost of their lives. In 1999, 12 years after the end of the period of austerity (1975–1987), certain Buddhist leaders and prisoners of conscience were freed, under international pressure, along with 5,000 other prisoners in an amnesty. The monks Huyên-Quang, Quảng-Dô, and Trí-Siêu and the famous doctor Nguyễn Dan-Qûe were among them. The oddity is that numerous Communist officials and soldiers, all of them nonbelievers, take advantage of the popular resurgence of Buddhism to come to prostrate themselves before the Buddha in ceremonies of repentance.

Many luckier Vietnamese escaped this regime by fleeing their country at the risk of their lives. This Vietnamese diaspora comprises more than two million people, of whom the majority are Buddhists. Monastics have been active in restoring Buddhism abroad by founding religious organizations. In 1984 in Montreal, Master Thích Tâm-Châu, a monk renowned for his activities during the 1960s and former president of the Unified Vietnamese Buddhist Church, founded the World Vietnamese Buddhist Order (Giáo-Hội Phật-Giáo Việt Nam Trên Thê-Gíởi), a grouping of more than 30 pagodas scattered across the United States, Canada, Europe, and Australia. Most of these pagodas are in the tradition of Pure Land or the Double Way of Meditation and Pure Land (Thiên-Tịnh Song-Tu). A few years later under the leadership of Master Thích Hộ-Giác, regional offices of the Overseas Unified Vietnamese Buddhist Church opened in various North American, European, and Australian cities. These two groupings support their development and functioning of Buddhist organizations and of Vietnamese pagodas outside the country. They contribute as well to the struggle waged by the Vietnamese diaspora for religious freedom and the rights of man in Vietnam. Based in France since 1970, Master Thích Huyên-Vi founded the Buddhist Cultural Association Linh-Sỏn and leads a movement in several countries of study and practice of both meditation and Pure Land. Another resident of France in his Làng-Hông (Plum) village, Master Thích Nhát Hạnh (1926–) engages in the practice and teaching of different techniques of meditation, ranging from control of breathing in the *Ānāpānasati*-sūtra to Daoist tantras. Through lectures and books he enjoys remarkable success among young Vietnamese intellectuals, not to mention among French and American Buddhists.

VŨ VĂN THÁI

See also Buddhist Schools/Traditions: China; Chan/Zen: China; Chan/Zen: Vietnam; China; Daoism: Influence on Buddhism; Discourses (Sūtras): Mahāyāna; Esoteric Buddhism in China and Japan; Nhát Hanh, Thích; Peace Movements, Buddhist; Persecution: Buddhist Perspectives; Pure Land Buddhism; Self-Immolation, Buddhist

Further Reading

Boisvert, Mathieu, editor, *Un Monde de Religions: Tome I. Les Traditions de l'Inde*, Sainte-Foy: Presses de l'Université du Québec, 1997

Minh-tuệ, Thích, *Luộc-sử Phật Gíao Việt Nam*, Ho Chi Minh City: Thanh hoi Phat giao TP. Ho Chi Minh, 1993

Nguyễn, Lang, *Việt Nam Phật Giáo Sũ luận*, Paris and Saigon: Lá Bói, 1974; 3rd edition, 3 vols., San Jose, California: Lá Bói, 1993

Nguyễn, Tai Thu, et al., editors, *Lịch sử Phật Gíao Viet Nam*, Hanoi: Khoa hoc xa hoi, 1988; as *History of Buddhism in Vietnam*, Hanoi: Social Sciences Publishing House, 1992

Nyanatiloka, Bhikku, *Buddhist Dictionary: Manual of Buddhist Terms and Doctrines*, Colombo: Frewin, 1950; San Francisco: Chinese Materials Center, 1977; 4th edition, Kandy: Buddhist Publication Society, 1980

Sutra Translation Committee of the United States and Canada, *The Seeker's Glossary of Buddhism*, 2nd edition, New York: Sutra Translation Committee of the United States and Canada, 1998

Tâm-Châu, Thích, *Kinh Thập-Thiện*, Nice: Chùa Tù-Quang, 1981

Trân, Trọng Kim, *Việt-Nam Sử lược*, 2 vols., Saigon: Trung tam hoc li eu, Bo giao duc, 1971; Glendale, California: Dai Nam, 1985

Trân, Van Giap, *Le Bouddhisme en Annam: Des Origines au XIIIe Siècle*, Paris: BEFEO, 1995

Vihāra. *See* Temple, Buddhist

Vinaya. *See* Rules, Buddhist (Vinaya)

Virtues, Buddhist

Discussions on virtues and vices comprise an important theme in practical Theravāda Buddhist ethics. In order to classify virtues, human actions were divided into three groups, depending on whether the actions were performed by body, speech, or mind. Within this threefold division the mind was considered the most important factor and the root of all good and bad actions.

In contrast with the teachings of theistic world religions, a salient feature appears in the Buddhist attitude toward virtues. In Buddhism virtues and morals were presented not as divine commands but as attributes to be either avoided or cultivated for one's own and others' benefit. The fundamental guiding principle was that "one who protects oneself protects others; one who protects others protects oneself." Disciplinary precepts in Buddhist monasticism were designed to mold the character of individuals who led lives in community. The middle path recommended avoidance of the two extremes: self-indulgence and self-mortification. In this training the most important monastic virtue was the cultivation of contentment (*appicchatā*) as a practical guide to liberation.

Virtues continued to be a constant theme in the *baṇapot* (preaching) literature of Sinhala Buddhism. Guruḷugōmi's *Amāvatura*, the first and perhaps the greatest of Sinhala Buddhist classics, begins with a buzzword *noviyat hudījana*, announcing that it was composed "for the benefit of uneducated virtuous people." Emphasis on "virtuous" community is important for understanding a new orientation in Sinhala Buddhist literature within the established tradition.

The Sinhala term *hudī*, which derives from the verbal root *sadh* (good, virtuous), refers to a "virtuous person." When Sinhala compound words are made using *hudī*, they imply "virtuousness," as in the case of *hudīkam* (good work). In Pāli a good act (*sādhu*) is always contrasted with a bad act (*asādhu*). The *Dhammapada* (v. 223) recommends winning over the wicked by goodness and maintains that it is "easy to do things that are bad . . . but exceedingly difficult to do things that are good" (v. 163). The *Butsaraṇa* defines *hudīdaham* (teachings of the virtuous) as abstaining from drinking liquor and killing any living beings. These various references to *hudī* in Sinhala and Pāli literature demonstrate that "virtue" was an important functional religious category.

In the Sri Lankan Theravāda Buddhist tradition, several indigenous terms – *kusala* (skillful), *puñña* (meritorious), *satpuruṣa* (virtuous), *hoňda* (good), and *dakṣa* (clever) – were used to characterize virtuous persons and their moral conduct. By identifying a virtuous person as a *satpuruṣa*, immoral conduct was distinguished from moral excellence. For example, in the Sinhala narrative literature the *Jewels of the Doctrine* demonstrates that the goal of Sinhala *baṇakathā* literature was the inculcation of virtues. This emphasis was due to the Theravāda belief that moral and skillful actions lead ultimately to the realization of the soteriological goal, *nirvāṇa*.

Theravāda Buddhism extols the cultivation of the four *brahmavihāras* (divine states): (1) lovingkindness (*mettā*), (2) compassion (*karuṇā*), (3) sympathetic joy (*muditā*), and (4) equanimity (*upekkhā*). In particular lovingkindness has become a practical and functional virtue within Sinhala Buddhism. The *Karaṇīyametta Sutta* outlines meditation on lovingkindness; it is popular as a religious practice among lay Buddhists, the majority of whom know it by heart:

> May all beings be happy and secure! May their minds be contented! Whatever living beings there may be – feeble or strong, tall, stout, or medium, short, small, or large, seen or unseen, those dwelling far or near, those who are born and those who are yet to be born – may all beings, without exception, be happy minded! Let not one deceive another nor despise any person anywhere. In anger or illwill let not one wish any harm to another. Just as a mother would protect her only child even at the risk of her own life, even so let one cultivate a boundless heart towards all beings. Let one's thoughts of boundless love pervade the whole world – above, below and across – without any obstruction, without any hatred, without any enmity.

As a religious virtue compassion reached its climax within Mahāyāna Buddhist traditions. Idealized in the career of the Bodhisattva Avalokiteśvara, compassion prevailed throughout Asia as a virtue that impels one to help those who are in distress. Defined as "the desire to remove what is detrimental to others' happiness," compassion makes one's heart quiver when one sees the pain of others and motivates one to relieve others of their suffering.

In Theravāda practical ethics, *hiri* (moral shame) and *ottappa* (moral fear) are two virtues considered crucial for cultured life. From the Theravāda perspective, virtues arise in an individual only when *hiri* and *ottappa* are present in that person's life. Whereas Buddhaghosa (fifth century) defined *hiri* as the emotional state of "shrinking" from negative action, *ottappa* is the state of "trembling" when one confronts immoral conduct. The emotional state of "moral shame" arises from reflecting that unethical actions do not suit one's status, whereas the emotional state of "moral fear" arises from concern for public opinion. These two psychological emotional states are the foundation for ethical conduct that benefits both oneself and others.

Both Theravāda and Mahāyāna stipulated the *pāramitā*s (perfections) as virtues that lead one to the perfection. Whereas Mahāyāna traditions recommend only six *pāramitā*s, Theravāda traditions have enumerated ten: (1) generosity, (2) morality, (3) renunciation, (4) wisdom, (5) effort, (6) forbearance, (7) truthfulness, (8) persistency, (9) lovingkindness, and (10) equanimity. The Pāli *Jātaka* literature classifies as *pāramitā* the innumerable moral acts of the Buddha in his previous lives as a bodhisattva preparing himself for Buddhahood.

The essential difference in Theravāda and Mahāyāna in their attitudes toward virtue lies in the fact that Theravāda emphasizes morality as the beginning point of self-development, whereas Mahāyāna emphasizes altruistic thoughts and actions even at the cost of one's own attainment.

Mahinda Deegalle

See also Bodhisattva; Body: Buddhist Perspectives; Buddhism: Overview; Deities, Buddhist; Discourses (Sūtras): Mahāyāna; Economic Justice, Buddhist; Economics: Buddhist; Hermits: Buddhist; Holy Men/Holy Women: Buddhist Perspectives; Liturgy: Buddhist; Mahāyāna; Meditation: Buddhist Perspectives; Mountain Monasteries: Buddhist; Novices, Theravādin Rituals for; Origins: Comparative Perspectives; Patrons, Buddhist: China; Peace Movements, Buddhist; Regulations: Buddhist Perspectives; Repentance Rituals, Buddhist; Self-Immolation, Buddhist; Social Services: Buddhist

Further Reading

Aronson, Harvey B., *Love and Sympathy in Theravāda Buddhism*, Delhi: Motilal Banarsidass, 1980

Deegalle, Mahinda, "The Moral Significance of Buddhist Nirvāṇa: The Early Buddhist Model of Perfection," in *Pāli Buddhism* (Curzon Studies in Asian Philosophy), edited by Deegalle and Frank J. Hoffman, Richmond, Surrey: Curzon Press, 1996

Deegalle, Mahinda, "Noviyat Hudījana: Local Consciousness within Disappearing Cosmopolitan Buddhism," in *The 150th Anniversary of Vidyōdaya Pirivena*, Colombo: Vidyōdaya Pirivena, 1999

Dharmasena Thera, *Jewels of the Doctrine: Stories of the Saddharma Ratnāvaliya* (SUNY Series in Buddhist Studies), translated by Ranjini Obeyesekere, Albany: State University of New York Press, 1991

Fu, Charles Wei-hsun, and Sandra A. Wawrytko, editors, *Buddhist Ethics and Modern Society: An International Symposium* (Contributions to the Study of Religion, number 31), New York: Greenwood Press, 1991

Kalupahana, David J., *Ethics in Early Buddhism*, Honolulu: University of Hawaii Press, 1995

Keown, Damien, *The Nature of Buddhist Ethics*, New York: St. Martin's Press, and Houndmills, Basingstoke, Hampshire: Macmillan, 1992

King, Winston Lee, *In the Hope of Nibbāna: An Essay on Theravāda Buddhist Ethics*, LaSalle, Illinois: Open Court, 1964

Premasiri, P.D., "Moral Evaluation in Early Buddhism," *Sri Lanka Journal of the Humanities* 1:1 (1975)

Premasiri, P.D., "Buddhism: Philosophy as a Way of Life," *Sri Lanka Journal of Buddhist Studies* 5 (1996)

Reynolds, Frank E., "Four Modes of Theravāda Action," *Journal of Religious Ethics* 7:1 (1979)

Saddhatissa, H., *Buddhist Ethics: Essence of Buddhism*, London: Allen and Unwin, and New York: Braziller, 1970

Tachibana, Shundo, *The Ethics of Buddhism*, London: Oxford University Press, 1926; 3rd edition, Colombo: Buddha Sahitya Sabha, 1961; London: Curzon Press, and New York: Barnes and Noble, 1975

Vision, Mystical: Eastern Christian

The teaching of the Eastern Christian monastic tradition on mystical vision distinguishes between the common plague of fantasy (the grip that memory and utopian dreaming have on the person) and authentic vision. The journey to mystical vision is described as a pathway that leads through purification (the art of seeing clearly the phenomenal world of creation) and illumina-

Sucevița Monastery, Romania, 16th century, exterior wall painting of the Heavenly Ladder of St. John Climacus. Photo courtesy of Mary Schaefer

tion (the culmination of the human experience in seeing the Uncreated Light) to glorification (having that light illumine the world through the restoration of one's mind). Throughout the monastic literature there are warnings about taking visions literally. Authentic vision, the vision of a restored person, is the way in which a sanctified person sees God's creation. Such vision sees creation clearly as the presence of the kingdom of God always moving toward the fullness of the kingdom of God. Proper vision, proper seeing, is the fruit of the acquisition of the Holy Spirit and results from the healing of the person.

The purpose of the monastic life is to guide men and women along the pathway leading through purification and illumination to glorification. This journey to the restoration of one's being begins with the arduous process of deconditioning. The golden strand of Orthodox psychotherapy, from the Desert Fathers to contemporary elders, provides counsel on discerning the knots in the mind and heart that skew the way in which one sees and understands experience and the life of the world. Evagrius Ponticus (346–399), monk and ascetic, a friend of Gregory of Nazianzus (329/30–389/90), discussed this struggle in his *Praktikos* and *Chapters on Prayer*. It is one of the first discussions of this struggle. His line of teaching is carried forward and developed in the works of Cyril of Jerusalem (c. 313–c. 386), Nemesius of Emesa (late fourth century), Dorotheos of Gaza (c. 500–c. 560–580), the *Philokalia*, John Climacus (before 579–c. 650), Isaac the Syrian (d. c. 700), Symeon the New Theologian (942–1022), Gregory Palamas (c. 1296–1359), and Nicodemos of the Holy Mountain (c. 1749–1809), among others.

This tradition uses texts drawn from the Scripture to speak about the journey from purification through illumination to glorification. It characterizes that journey as the experience of the Last Judgment with its refiner's fire, an experience in which one's conscience accuses one of missing the mark. This judgment takes place within our conscience, according to St. Cyril of Jerusalem. The spiritual father Dorotheos of Gaza speaks of being "reconciled with your accuser on the way." Being reconciled with your conscience is the existential meaning of the Last Judgment. This process of reconciliation, of experiencing the Last Judgment in this life, is the initial step to becoming a whole person.

Training in the art of prayer is the discipline (*askesis*) leading to illumination. Prayer is a discipline of consciousness, of discerning the remnants in our minds and hearts that prevent us from living a Godly life. The traces of memory and desire that hold us in bondage to nostalgia and utopian dreaming must be discerned and offered to the compassionate Father of all creation for healing. This pathway of discernment restores one to one's rightful human nature. Illumination often comes in fleeting moments but, as the spiritual Fathers assure their children, it will grow as the discipline of prayer deepens. With this freedom from clinging to memory and desire, with restored clarity of mind and heart, the person comes to union with the divine.

Symeon the New Theologian describes this third step along the spiritual pathway as glorification. It is participation in the Uncreated Light. It is an experience of the whole person, soul and body together; it takes place within, in the innermost being. Symeon says of his own experience that at first he did not know where he was during the experience of the Divine Light but that, as he came to himself, he realized that he was "there in my tabernacle [body] all the time."

The mystical vision is not a vision of some thing but rather, in Symeon's *apophatic* theology, an experience of God immanently present in the person. Symeon stood in direct opposition to the Scholastic theology of Archbishop Stephen of Nicomedia, the court theologian of Constantinople in his day. Stephen, following the lead of Roman Catholic thinkers, argued for a philosophical theology that could verify the truth and defend the theology of the church. Symeon called for a restoration of theology to its spiritual purpose. The only theology worthy of the name is a theology that helped the faithful experience the Holy Spirit through a journey of purification and restoration.

Within monastic writings the key biblical text on the experience of glorification is the Transfiguration of Christ (Matt. 17, Mark 9, Luke 9). Whereas in the West this text is understood largely as a disclosure of Jesus as God, in the East the emphasis is on the visible manifestation of the transfigured humanity of Jesus. Because this glory is shared by Moses and Elijah, as we see in the text and as it is depicted in iconography, it is more easily understood as a glory to which all human beings may be restored. The Transfiguration on Mount Tabor is the icon of the monastic vocation. It is the goal of the Christian life in Orthodoxy.

Symeon speaks of mystical vision as the uncreated light of God that "shines on us without evening, without change, without alteration, without form." It speaks, works, lives, gives life, and changes into light those whom it illuminates. The glorified person witnesses that "God is light," and those to whom it has been granted to see the divine have all behold Him as light. Those who have received Him as light do so because the light of His glory goes before Him, and it is impossible for Him to appear without light. Those who have not seen His light have not seen Him, for He is the light, and those who have not received the light have not yet received grace. Those who have received grace have received the light of God and have received God, even as Christ Himself, who is the light and has said, "I will live in them and move among them."

The transfiguration experience of Mount Tabor is the experience of grace to which all human beings are called. The grace is to come into union with the divine. There is a sense in which the goal of the monastic life is to experience the transfiguration on the day of resurrection. Being born again, a type of the resurrection, is, in and through the transfiguration, the experience of the Divine Light. In illumination one experiences the Divine Light, but in glorification the Divine Light dwells in one.

The literature on mystical vision is filled with warnings. This pathway is not to be entered lightly or without a guide. One's spiritual state is not measured by the emotional life or how one feels about oneself, God, or the world. The *therapeutea*, those who counsel monastics on their struggles, constantly warn of the danger of illusions, of visions that split the body and soul. Mystical visions are often seen to hamper the journey to mystical vision. The recovery of sight requires the healing of the mind, freeing it from all forms of fantasy and desire. Instead of striving for mystical visions, the Orthodox tradition seeks to help the monastic struggle for purification. Any intention of experiencing the Divine Light will lead to a false vision and darken the heart and mind. The spiritual elders remind the novice that the pure in heart are blessed and will come to see God. There is no need to seek the Divine Light but only to seek purification. Prayer purifies and leads one to the experience of illumination, a glimpse of the Uncreated Light. This might be a fleeting glimpse, but as our desires fade, the desire for prayer grows. The path to mystical vision, that is, to seeing aright, can be taken only by those who are willing to become conscious of what is in their minds and hearts.

David J. Goa

See also Climacus, John, St.; Evagrius Ponticus; Gregory of Nazianzus, St.; Hesychasm; Images: Christian Perspectives; Isaac the Syrian (Isaac of Nineveh), St.; Mount Athos, Greece; Palamas, Gregory, St.; Prayer: Christian Perspectives; Spirituality: Eastern Christian; Symeon the New Theologian, St.; Visual Arts, Eastern Christian: Painting

Further Reading

Puhalo, Lev, *The Soul, the Body, and Death* (Educational Series, Saints Cyril and Methody Society), Chilliwack, British Columbia: Saints Cyril and Methody Society, 1980; 5th edition, Dewdney, British Columbia: Synaxis Press, 1996

Spidlík, Tomás, *The Spirituality of the Christian East: A Systematic Handbook* (Cistercian Studies Series, number 79), translated by Anthony P. Gythiel, Kalamazoo, Michigan: Cistercian Publications, 1986

Vlachos, Hierotheos, *Orthodox Psychotherapy: The Science of the Fathers*, translated by Esther Williams, Levadeia, Greece: Birth of the Theotokos Monastery, 1994

Vision, Mystical: Western Christian

The tradition that we now know as mysticism, or mystical vision, begins in earnest in the late fifth century A.D. in the work of a writer we have come to know as Dionysius (Dionysius the Pseudo-Areopagite, c. 500). In his important work *Mystical Theology*, Dionysius sets up for the reader the basic tenets of mysticism that would develop and flower in the Christian medieval world. A modern audience cannot readily grasp the impact of mysticism and its prevalence among not only theologians but

Jean de Beaumetz (French, active 1361, died 1396), *The Crucifixion with a Carthusian Monk*, c. 1390–1395, tempera on panel, 56.6 x 45.7 cm. The Cleveland Museum of Art, 1999, Leonard C. Hanna Jr., Fund, 1964.454.
Photo courtesy of The Cleveland Museum of Art

also fairly ordinary medieval Christians throughout the period from roughly A.D. 500 to 1500. Although mysticism has continued beyond the medieval period, its nature had to change, necessarily, because of the Renaissance and the Reformation and the ensuing changes in daily devotion, monastic life, and Christianity at large. Later cultures would identify what medieval audiences understood as mysticism to involve prophecy, witchcraft, spiritualism, and even near-death experience. However it might be characterized, the presence of mysticism has helped shape Western Christian spirituality on a number of levels.

The person of Dionysius the Pseudo-Areopagite is unknown to history, but the influence of his work is immeasurable. Although mystical experience had unfolded in the Western Christian world long before his time, it had not yet acquired a name or a character; his *Mystical Theology* established a language through which we can understand the nature of mystical experience. The first Christian mystics were biblical: figures such as Mary, whose experience of God in the Annunciation can be best described as a mystical, transcendent moment; St. Paul on the road to Damascus envisioning Christ and his Way; and even Christ himself, transfigured on the mountaintop in the desert, being characterized as having experience an immanent, divine exchange that is the basis of all mystical experience.

Although mystics come from a variety of backgrounds and perspectives, the basic elements of their experience remain the same. Everyone who claims to have had a mystical experience reports some kind of moment of transcendence, whether brought on by illness, contemplation, trance, or other forms of concentration and prayer. In that moment the mystic experiences what is most often characterized by either the veiled presence of the Divine or even simply an embodied form of Divine love. The titles of the works of mystical writers bear this out: *The Flowing Light of the Godhead*, *The Cloud of Unknowing*, *The Wooing of Our Lord*, and *Revelations of Divine Love*. Whatever takes place in the mystical experience – and that is a question that remains ultimately unanswered – is characterized by the mystic as an experience of overwhelming love and union with the Divine.

Some mystics experience their vision not as a vision at all but more as a conversation or real-life experience. Christina Markyate, for example, was visited by the Christ Child, who stayed with her and spent the day in her home. Margery Kempe (c. 1373–after 1438), sometimes not strictly included as a mystic because her visions border on psychosis, would see Christ everywhere, in everything, and hear his voice almost constantly. A more traditional mystical experience is described by Julian of Norwich (c. 1342–after 1416), who, sick and almost dying, saw a vision of the Virgin Mary and felt the presence of Christ at her bedside repeating the statement that "all shall be well." When she awoke from her sickness, Julian told her companions what had happened to her, and then, in an act that is as much a part of mysticism as the vision itself, she wrote down her thoughts and experiences, becoming thereby not just a mystic but also an author.

The notion that mystics write is central to an understanding of the genre itself. All mystics do not write about their experiences, but many are called to do so by the voice of the vision itself. Even those whose social position would normally preclude written expression are enabled to write through the liberating experience of mysticism. An excellent example of this is Mechthild of Magdeburg (c. 1207–1282). Mechthild experienced a number of mystical visions throughout her life both as a beguine and as a cloistered nun. However, when she turned to write about her experiences, those around her were not encouraging. She was a woman, after all, illiterate in Latin, and her impressions were not, they assumed, weighty enough to fill a book. Still she wrote them down, sometimes dictating her thoughts. Something in the vision itself impelled her to write, and her book *The Flowing Light of the Godhead* is a testament to the nature of Divine love and the power of the authorial spirit to reach beyond circumstance and the oppression of society to speak and be heard.

Mysticism, then, is characterized by a number of common elements, although not all mystics can be said to have experienced them all. These include sickness or unconsciousness, isolation or solitude, and contemplation of a divine image or thought. Once in the appropriate frame of mind, the mystic becomes aware of a Divine presence – a voice, a figure, or a sensation. In that moment the mystic and the Divine know each other, become united in love and spiritual presence, and share a union often characterized in writing as sensual, physical, and very real. However this moment of transcendence might take place – whether the Divine spirit compels the mystic to act or simply appears as a means of consolation and love – the mystic is forever changed and often exerts a powerful influence on her culture.

Another important aspect of this experience is its provenance. A spiritually inclined person might seek mystical union, but it is not won merely through persistence. In order to become a mystic – that is, to share a transcendent moment with the presence of the Divine – one must be chosen. One cannot choose it oneself. Although frustrating to many religious people throughout history, it is this spontaneous, surprising nature of the experience that makes the mystic unique, often ridiculed. The list of those who experienced a transcendent moment of this nature in the medieval world is long: St. Augustine, St. Bonaventure, Richard Rolle, Walter Hilton, St. Hildegard of Bingen, St. Francis, Mechthild of Magdeburg, Marguerite Porete, Julian of Norwich, St. Catherine of Siena, St. Teresa of Avila, and even St. Joan of Arc. Each of these people, in their desire to know God, came to know the Divine in a unique, transcendent way that most humans can never understand. Two people on the previous list died because of their visions and because the society in which they found themselves was unable to accept people with such a sense of individual empowerment and strength. These people died at the stake, Marguerite Porete in 1310 and Joan of Arc in 1431, still proclaiming the validity of their vision and the presence of the Divine in daily human life.

A great number of other issues are associated with mysticism and mystical vision, many of which have come to be studied only recently. The list is long: the impact of gender on the experience of mysticism; the growth of literacy and the vernacular; the use of erotic, sensual language in the expression of mysticism (what is often termed bridal mysticism, or Brautmystik); the impact of social class and position on the expression of mysticism; the influence of Eastern Christian theology and philosophy on the expression of mysticism in the Christian West; the relationship between written and nonwritten experiences of mysticism; and modern understandings/misunderstandings of mysticism. Mystics have existed within Christianity since its inception, as have those who question the validity of the mystical vision. In a sense the reception of the mystic's story does not concern the mystic herself. It is her ability to speak, to tell us what she has seen, often in a language that falls short and cannot fully describe what she has experienced, that matters. Ultimately this may be the point of mystical vision itself – not that one must be understood fully but simply that one must be given a voice and must, at all costs, use it.

SUSANNAH MARY CHEWNING

See also Bonaventure, St.; Devotions, Western Christian; Dialogue, Intermonastic: Christian Perspectives; Gregory I (the Great), St.; Hildegard of Bingen, St.; Images: Buddhist Perspectives; Mystics, German Monastic; Scholastics, Buddhist; Teresa of Avila, St.

Further Reading

Luibhéid, Colm, translator and editor, *Pseudo-Dionysius: The Complete Works* (Classics of Western Spirituality), New York: Paulist Press, and London: SPCK, 1987

McGinn, Bernard, *The Presence of God: A History of Western Christian Mysticism*, 5 vols., New York: Crossroad, 1991–98; London: SCM Press, 1992–

Petroff, Elizabeth, *Body and Soul: Essays on Medieval Women and Mysticism*, New York: Oxford University Press, 1994

Savage, Anne, and Nicholas Watson, *Anchoritic Spirituality: Ancrene Wisse and Associated Works* (Classics of Western Spirituality), New York: Paulist Press, 1991

Szarmach, Paul, editor, *An Introduction to the Medieval Mystics of Europe: Fourteen Original Essays*, Albany: State University of New York Press, 1984

Underhill, Evelyn, *Mysticism: A Study in the Nature and Development of Man's Spiritual Consciousness*, London: Methuen, and New York: Dutton, 1911

Visitandines

On 6 June 1610, Jane de Chantal (1572–1641) and three companions made their way in procession through the streets of provincial Annecy in Savoy to the *Maison de la Galerie*, a residence donated to the women as the site for their new congregation. The community life that they were in the process of inaugurating in this ritual procession was the product of the spiritual friendship of Madame de Chantal, a youthful widow, with Francis de Sales (1567–1622), bishop of Geneva and a charismatic preacher known for his gifts of spiritual direction and his efforts on behalf of a vigorously reforming Catholic Church. In the course of his pastoral practice, Bishop de Sales had become cognizant of the need for a place in the Church for devout women who had a call to a deep life of prayer but who, for a variety of reasons, including family responsibilities, fragile health, handicaps, and age, would be unsuitable candidates for the rigorous contemplative orders, such as the Discalced Carmelites, that were popular at the time. During his travels in Italy, he had become aware of the existence of loosely structured women's congregations under the sponsorship of local bishops that did not necessitate enclosure or formal vows but that allowed women the opportunity for charitable service and spiritual companionship.

His introduction to the widow de Chantal and their subsequent association as spiritual mentor and pupil brought his concerns into focus. Since her husband's tragic death in a 1601 hunting accident, Jane de Chantal had dreamed of dedicating her life to the love of God despite responsibilities as caretaker of her four young children and of the family properties. The foundation of the "Daughters of the Visitation" (in reference to the biblical story of the Virgin Mary to her cousin Elizabeth), soon popularly known as the "Holy Marys," was a response to their shared desires. The particular end of the community was neither strictly contemplative nor wholly active, thus eluding the distinction commonly made concerning Catholic religious communities. Instead, the bishop wrote,

> this congregation having two principal exercises: one: contemplation and prayer, which is practiced principally in the house; the other service of the poor and sick, principally of the same sex, it has appropriately drawn for its Patron Our Lady of the Visitation, since in this mystery the very glorious Virgin made this solemn act of charity toward her neighbor in going to visit Elizabeth, to help during her pregnancy, and nevertheless composed the Canticle of the *Magnificat*, the sweetest, most uplifting, most spiritual, and most contemplative which was ever written. (*Oeuvres*, XXV, 214)

Community life within the early Visitation was modeled on the classic monastic pattern but adapted to suit the needs of the women involved. They recited the "Little Office of Our Lady," a brief form of the Divine Office, and physical asceticism was discouraged, for food was ample, and the living environment and the habit, modeled on widow's garb of the day, were simple but not austere. The day was ordered to include time for prayer, eating, simple work, assembly, spiritual reading, and recreation. All was to be accomplished in a spirit of silence and reflection. At the heart of the community, and its true charism and inner asceticism, was the spiritual practice captured by the motto "*Vive Jesus!*" (Live Jesus!).

Bishop Francis de Sales was a vocal proponent of the idea that the life of Christian devotion should not be reserved for those in vowed religious or clerical life but that it was the birthright of Christians in all walks of life. Devotion was for him first and foremost an interior practice, a matter of allowing one's life to be transformed by and into love. Thus, one must allow the qualities of the loving divine-human heart of Jesus to infuse one's own heart and then be manifest in the particular circumstances of one's life. The scriptural image that informed this spiritual vision was that of Matthew, chapter 11, in which Jesus is portrayed as inviting all to come and learn, for "I am gentle and humble of heart." Thus, de Sales taught the efficacy of the "little virtues," such as humility, simplicity, gentleness, and patience in the life of Christian love. The Visitation was to be an intentional community for women seeking intimacy with God who would embody this hidden life of the gentle Jesus in their relationships with one another and with those in their immediate surroundings. Entrants would take only temporary vows. Enclosure was partial to provide flexibility for members to respond to the needs of their extended families and to minister to the sick and poor of the immediate vicinity. It would also allow a limited number of married women seeking spiritual refreshment to come inside the community for retreat.

A number of years after the original foundation, Jane de Chantal wrote of the life of "living Jesus" in the Visitation to the Sisters at Annecy. Her letter well describes the purpose of and practice within the early congregation:

> Have in your thoughts only Jesus, in your will only the longing for his love, and in your actions have only obedience, submission to his good pleasure by an exact observance of the rule, not only in externals, but much more, in your interior spirit: a spirit of gentle cordiality toward one another, a spirit of recollection of your whole being before our divine Master, and that true sincere humility that makes us gentle as lambs. Finally, strive for that loving union of hearts which brings about a holy peace and the kind of blessing we should expect in the house of God and His Holy Mother. (*Sa Vie et ses oeuvres*, IV, 290–291)

The little congregation gained attention, and soon requests were made to institute foundations outside Savoy. In fact the foundation in Lyons, France, altered the future course of the Visitation. The same flexible life that Monsignor Francis de Sales envisioned for his Diocese of Annecy, Bishop Denis de Marquement could not imagine in his own of Lyons. The controversy came down to the question: Should the Visitation remain a tiny and unique experiment in one locale, or was it the will of God that it spread, even if some of its original components be lost? The controversy resolved itself in the latter direction, and in 1618 the little congregation was transformed into a formal contemplative religious order that observed strict cloister, thus eliminating outside ministry in the neighborhood and disallowing retreats by married women. Despite the canonical change, the interior Visitandine spirit of living the life of the gentle, humble Jesus was retained.

Visitandine methods of spiritual formation, community interaction, and governance were all informed by the central principal of love of God and neighbor and the practice of the little virtues. Recruitment and novitiate training were to be accomplished by "winning hearts" through kindness and maternal solicitude. Superiors were elected only for short periods of time and were to return regularly to the ranks of the ordinary sisters. The mature Visitation community, once foundations were made beyond the confines of the first house, was to be linked not by juridical ties but only by the bonds of love and the observance of the same rules, constitutions, and customs. Each monastery remained autonomous and under the jurisdiction of the local bishop. Neither a centralized governance, a superior general, an apostolic visitor, nor royal oversight was instituted, but the monastery at Annecy and its superior were to serve informally as the symbolic focal point of the union of hearts between the diverse Visitations. Much of Jane de Chantal's later life was dedicated to the establishment of the customs and spiritual direction of the community spirit by which the union of love might be maintained.

The typical form of prayer that came to be associated with the Order was a hidden prayer of intimate union that Jane de Chantal described as a very simple union and simple apprehension of God's presence effected by an abandonment to God's will and providential care. Although in general extraordinary mystical graces were not fostered by the formation within the communities, the first 100 years of Visitandine life did indeed produce a number of women remarkable for their mystical experiences. Most recognizable among them was Margaret Mary Alacoque (1647–1690), a nun of the monastery of Paray-le-Monial whose visions in 1673 to 1675 of Jesus requesting the institution of a monthly Thursday night vigil followed by a Friday of adoration, as well as a yearly feast in honor of His Sacred Heart, came to form the backbone of the public cult to the Sacred Heart.

The Order proved a popular one, especially among the daughters of the upper classes in French society who were its principal entrants. By the time of Jane de Chantal's death in 1641, 87 houses existed throughout France, Piedmont, Lorraine, Switzerland, and Savoy. The peak of the Order's numbers was reached in France in the 1670s. It spread from there to Italy, Poland, Austria, Spain, and Lebanon in the 17th and 18th centuries and to other areas in Europe, Africa, and North and South America in the 19th and 20th centuries.

A variety of economic, political, and social forces adversely affected the Visitation in the centuries after its first rapid expansion. Material poverty plagued many French monasteries in the 17th and 18th centuries and resulted in the closing of some Visitation houses, as well as in abuses of common property and dowries, and in the taking in of pupil-boarders (a practice discouraged by the founders) in others. The French Revolution virtually eliminated the Visitandine presence in the Order's mother country, and although some communities were reestablished in the next century, often teaching or hospital work became the reason for the refounding. Not until the early 20th century were the French Visitandines able to reclaim their contemplative life. Outside France the suppression of religious houses in Bavaria and persecutions in Spain, Italy, Portugal, Mexico, and Poland disrupted Visitation communities during the 19th and early 20th centuries.

In the United States the Order had a unique history. A group of pious women at Georgetown were sponsored by Bishop Leonard Neale (1746–1817) of Baltimore as educators of young girls. They were soon affiliated with the Visitation Order. From there a network of monasteries spread across the United States, all of them with academies for young women as their apostolate. In the 1950s an attempt was made by the Vatican to form the Order into a confederation. This eventually failed, but a system of federations was its legacy. Communication among monasteries, the sharing of material and spiritual resources, and preparation of superiors and novice mistresses are some of the goals of the federations that are still in place.

Following the Second Vatican Council (1962–1965) and its encouragement to religious orders to retrieve their original charisms, all Visitation communities underwent reform. In the United States some of the monasteries continued their teaching apostolates, whereas others returned to the cloistered contemplative life. Worldwide the Little Office of Our Lady was replaced by the breviary, the three-tiered system of sisters that had grown up was abandoned and replaced by a two-tiered system of intern and extern sisters who receive the same formation. The original practice of admitting laywomen into the cloister for brief periods of retreat was reestablished.

At present the Visitandines are known as the cloistered contemplative monastic community of women that cultivates the life of the gentle, humble Jesus, some of whom, like the American houses, sponsor schools. Thus, it is one of the religious orders of the Church that continues to promote the Salesian spiritual tradition founded by Francis de Sales and Jane de Chantal.

Wendy M. Wright

See also Devotions, Western Christian; France: History; Spirituality: Western Christian; Women's Monasteries: Western Christian

Further Reading

Année sainte des religieuses de la Visitation Sainte Marie, 12 vols., Annecy, 1867–1873

Chantal, Jeanne-Françoise Frémyot de, *Correspondance, Edition critique établie et annotée par Soeur Marie-Patricia Burns*, 5 vols., Paris: Cerf/Centre d'études franco-italien, 1986–1993

Devos, Roger, "Le testement spirituel de Sainte Jeanne-Françoise de Chantal et l'affaire du visiteur apostolique," *Revue d'Histoire de la spiritualité* 48 and 49 (1972–1973)

Devos, Roger, *Vie religieuse féminine et société: Les Visitandines aux XVIIe et XVIIIe siècles*, volume 88, Annecy: Mémoires et documents publiés par l'Académie Salésienne, 1973

Francis de Sales and Jane de Chantal: Letters of Spiritual Direction, selected and introduced by Wendy M. Wright and Joseph L. Power, translated by Péronne Marie Thibert, New York: Paulist Press, 1988

Mission et esprit de l'ordre de la Visitation Sainte Marie selon St. François de Sales et Jeanne de Chantal, Annecy, 1979

Oeuvres de Saint François de Sales, Evêque de Genève et Docteur de l'Eglise, Edition complète, d'après les autographes et les éditions originales . . . publiée . . . par les soins des Religieuses de la Visitation du Premier Monastère d'Annecy, 27 vols., Annecy: Niérat, 1892–1964

Ravier, André, *Francis de Sales: Sage and Saint*, translated by Joseph D. Bowler, San Francisco: Ignatius Press, 1988

Ravier, André, *Saint Jeanne de Chantal*, translated by Mary Emily Hamilton, San Francisco: Ignatius Press, 1989

Sainte Jeanne Françoise Frémyot de Chantal: Sa Vie et ses oeuvres, Edition authentique publiée par les soins des Religieuses du Premier Monastère de la Visitation Sainte-Marie d'Annecy, 8 vols., Paris: Plon, 1874–1879

Stopp, Elisabeth, *Madame de Chantal: Portrait of a Saint*, Westminster, Maryland: Newman Press, 1963

Wright, Wendy M., "Jane de Chantal's Guidance of Women: The Community of the Visitation and Womanly Values," in *Modern Christian Spirituality: Methodological and Historical Essays*, edited by Bradley C. Hanson, Atlanta, Georgia: Scholars Press, 1990

Wright, Wendy M., "The Visitation of Holy Mary: The First Years (1610–1618)," in *Religious Orders of the Catholic Reformation*, edited by Richard L. DeMolen, New York: Fordham University Press, 1994

Related Web Site

http://www4.allencol.edu/~salesian.html (International Commission on Salesian Studies)

Visual Arts, Buddhist: China

Buddhism, founded in India in the sixth century B.C., had reached northern China by the first century A.D. Moving first from northwestern India and into Afghanistan, the religion traveled along the overland trade routes, collectively referred to as the Silk Road, through such trading towns as Bezeklik, Turfan, Kuqa, Qyzil, Miran, and Dandan Uiliq, giving Central Asia a major role in the transmission of Buddhism and Buddhist iconography between India and China. Owing to the activity along the Silk Road, the art of this area contains elements from diverse cultures, including those of India, Sassanian Iran, and China. Influenced by the rock-cut cave-temples of India, similar structures were cut into the cliff faces found throughout the region. The conglomerate sandstone was unsuitable for finely detailed sculpture but allowed the art of wall painting to flourish with stunning achievements at the cave-temple sites of Miran, Kuqa, and Bezeklik. However, it was not until the early 20th century that the full glory of this art was brought to light when the Chinese site of Dunhuang, located at the eastern end of the Silk Road, was rediscovered and brought to public attention.

At the oasis city of Dunhuang, on the eastern edge of the Tarim basin, the Central Asian Buddhist media of stone sculpture and wall paintings met Chinese traditions. Writings of travelers, especially those of Buddhist monk Xuanzang (602–664), who journeyed between China and India in the years 629–645, and Sir Marc Aurel Stein (1862–1942), the great British archaeologist and explorer of the early 20th century, tell of the many

Śākyamuni Buddha, colossal image of Cave 3 (Binyangdong), Longmen stone caves, Luoyang, Henan province, China, early fifth century, Northern Wei dynasty.
Photo courtesy of Marylin M. Rhie

artistic splendors encountered. Here, in the barren desert of northwestern Gansu province, far from the metropolitan and political centers of China, are the Magao caves, also known as the Caves of the Thousand Buddhas. Dunhuang was an important pilgrimage site for both travelers along the Silk Road and worshipers who came to view the religious imagery. There were likely more than 1,000 caves here, but today 492 remain. Eventually Dunhuang's importance as a pilgrimage site waned, but it remained a focus for local devotion. The survival of paintings, sculpture, and texts at Dunhuang is due largely to its remoteness and the dry climate of this semi-desert region. The interiors of the caves are covered with polychrome paintings. However, because the stone consists of a gravel conglomerate, carving was not possible. The artists formed their figures on wooden armatures covered with clay that, once dry, was painted. Work here likely began during the first half of the fifth century, but only one cave, Cave 285, contains an inscription with a date, here corresponding to 538–539. Elaborately decorated, the walls are covered with painted scenes showing heaven, narratives of the Buddha's life, and scenes of the Pure Land of the Western Paradise, where followers hoped to be reborn. This cave, with its niches and chapels, was likely inaccessible to pilgrims but rather was used for private meditation by the monks.

The early artists at Dunhuang belonged to a hereditary lineage by which status was transferred from father to son. Although they worked for the state, these artists did not collect wages: their labor was considered a form of taxation. Later, during the Tang dynasty, artists acted as independent contractors and could be paid in cash or goods, such as flour or oil. A painter could also have assistants, and often the monks of the temple worked as advisers or as painters themselves. Extant documents found at Dunhuang reveal that stencils were used for many of the paintings. Made of thick paper with the figures out-

Octagonal 13-storied pagoda at the Famensi, Fufeng county, west of Xi'an (Changan), Shaanxi province, China. An imperial temple containing a finger bone relic of Śākyamuni Buddha in a crypt beneath the pagoda. The temple was founded in the Eastern Han dynasty. The present pagoda (brick, 47 meters in height) was rebuilt over the Tang dynasty crypt in 1579–1606 of the Ming dynasty.
Photo courtesy of Marylin M. Rhie

lined with pinpricks, these stencils were dusted with chalk, thus transferring the image to the plaster wall. The painter could then use these dotted outlines as a guide. This technique streamlined production of religious paintings by allowing a single image to be used several times. It also ensured consistency and precision. The mineral pigments were imported, a fact that attests to the wealth of the period.

In addition to the spectacular wall paintings, Dunhuang is also known for the Buddhist scroll paintings, embroidered textiles, and documents found there. It appears that sometime in the early 11th century, a chapel within one of the caves was cleared of its statuary and filled with many thousands of manuscripts, paintings, textiles, and other objects. It was then plastered over and the surface painted. In 1900 this sealed room was discovered by the Daoist priest Wang Yuanlu, who had come to Dunhuang with the hope of preserving the site and encouraging worshipers to visit. During the restoration of the caves, a crack was found in the plaster wall, revealing the existence of this inner "library cave." Among the items is the world's earliest surviving printed book, a copy of the *Diamond Sūtra*, a key Buddhist text, printed by woodblock in 868. In addition to the text, the work also contains an illustration of the Buddha in three-quarters view accompanied by *luohan*s, guardian figures, and celestial beings. It is now in the British Library in London.

The tradition of cutting stone cave-temples found at Dunhuang was carried eastward beyond the Silk Road into North China proper, where Buddhist art flourished during the religion's formative years. Unlike Dunhuang, whose stone did not allow detailed carvings, the hard rock at the principal sites of Yungang and Longmen was highly suitable for large-scale and detailed sculpture.

The principal cave-temples at Yungang, located near the modern city of Datong, were produced from around 460 until 494 and were part of a program of Buddhist art sponsored by the Toba conquerors who established their dynasty, the Northern Wei (386–535), in North China. Although these rulers were great supporters of Buddhism, there was a brief but intense persecution of the religion between 444 and 451; anyone serving the "barbarian gods" or creating religious images were threatened with death. When the persecution ended the monk Tanyao suggested that as an act of expiation the ruler create a series of cave-temples designed to outdo those of Central Asia and India. These five caves, known as the Tanyao caves after their initiator, established the Wei rulers as the primary supporters of the

Qianfodong (Caves of the Thousand Buddhas) at Matisi (Horse-Hoof Temple), Zhangye, Gansu province, China. Buddhist caves and niches from the fifth century and later.
Photo courtesy of Marylin M. Rhie

Buddhist way. Under their patronage the religion flourished, with the empire supporting more than 13,000 monasteries and temples. In response to this imperial favor, Buddhist leaders formulated doctrines in which the Buddha was equated with the Wei ruler.

These five caves with their Buddhas have been thought to represent the five Wei emperors up to that time, whereas another theory suggests that these five Buddhas, which included the Buddhas of the past, present, and future, were an iconographic means of protecting the Wei Empire. Cave 20 is especially well known for its colossal Buddha measuring nearly 45 feet in height. It is interesting to note that a wooden facade once covered this cave in a fashion similar to that of the cave-temples at Ajaṇṭā in India, although here it was based on early Chinese architectural forms.

The initial work at Yungang was sponsored by the imperial family, but other caves soon came to be constructed owing to the patronage of donors from all strata of society. Between 483 and 490 work was intense, and 53 caves were constructed along the site. Surviving inscriptions tell of donors consisting of monks and nuns, male and female laypeople, court nobles, and commoners.

The caves were carved from the top down, and walls were filled in with smaller sculptures as patrons sponsored them. Little is known of the craftsmen who made the caves. The stone was soft, and often repairs had to be made. In addition some of the caves were protected by wooden structures in front, attached to the rock by mortises. The caves show a variety in both quality and style. When the Wei rulers moved their capital south to Luoyang in 494, work at Yungang stopped, but a new series of cave-temples began at nearby Longmen.

Set along the banks of the Yi River, the limestone cliffs of Longmen are the site of spectacular large-scale carvings. These images are thoroughly Chinese, with much more rounded forms than those at Yungang. The robes of the figures are loose with rhythmically flowing drapery.

Work continued at Longmen for about 400 years and produced more than 1,300 caves. It was under the patronage of the rulers of the Tang dynasty (618–907) that the site reached its ultimate grandeur. The massive figures of the seventh century found at Yungang are here replaced by a group of five figures: typically the Buddha flanked by bodhisattvas and *luohan*s. The Fengxian temple, a cave-shrine begun in 672 and completed in 675, is one cave that illustrates the group of five figures. At one time roofed, the Fengxian temple was constructed under the imperial patronage of Gaozong (r. 650–683) and his wife, Empress Wu, a devout Buddhist and former nun. It was under the now-lost roof that ceremonies were carried out at Longmen. The group at Longmen consists of a large figure of the cosmic Buddha Vairocana, just over 44 feet in height. Legend states that this figure carries the facial features of Wu herself. Flanking the Vairocana Buddha are heavenly kings and guardian figures in dynamic and realistic poses typical of the period. A substantial amount of Wu's private funds were devoted to this colossal project.

Temple Architecture

With Buddhism's rapid growth in the Six Dynasties period (220–589), there arose a need for a vast number of temples and monasteries; architecture thus received particular emphasis. This affected both the sizes of the religious complexes and the buildings that composed them. In the Sui (581–618) and Tang dynasties, the architectural style was set, forming the foundation for temple buildings for subsequent periods.

In general Chinese temple complexes consist of similarly styled buildings that were based on secular forms and differed very little from each other beyond their size and placement. Although they followed nonreligious architecture in their construction and included among their elements distinctive elaborate bracketing, non-load-bearing walls, multiple doors, and tiled roofs with overhanging eaves, it was their function that distinguished them from nonreligious architecture. Buildings were dedicated to specific deities, to certain concepts (such as heaven or hell), or to specific activities, such as the meditation hall or the sūtra library. For the most part these buildings were arranged around a principal north-south axis and faced the south, a traditional orientation for complexes such as imperial palaces.

According to records, several Buddhist monasteries were founded by the end of the second century. The earliest account, which dates to around 190, tells of a Buddhist shrine containing a two-story pavilion surmounted by a mast of nine bronze disks, the whole surrounded by covered galleries that could hold 3,000 people. Although no artifactual evidence exists to support these texts, they do mention several elements that would become central in Chinese monastery layout. Here is the beginning of the Chinese pagoda, based on the Indian stūpa with its several tiers of umbrellas. The layout, too, suggests a connection to India, where the emphasis is on a single architectural structure. The covered galleries appear to be a Chinese contribution that would continue as a characteristic feature.

Typically the buildings were made of wood. Unfortunately the devastating anti-Buddhist persecution of 842–845 destroyed virtually all of China's early Buddhist architecture when 4,600 temples and 40,000 shrines were razed. The earliest extant building, the Nanchan si, dated to 782, is found at Mount Wutai in Shanxi province. Although few examples remain in China, it is in Japan where one finds evidence of early Chinese monastic architecture and layout. The most notable are those of the Hōryū-ji at Nara, a seventh-century complex that was modeled after the traditional Chinese plan of the Six Dynasties period, and the Tōdai-ji, also at Nara, an eighth-century temple influenced by Tang-dynasty monastic architecture. The main elements of the central courtyard, such as that of the Hōryū-ji, are the middle gate, galleries on three sides, a five-story pagoda, and the Buddha hall, known as the *kondō* (golden hall).

The monastic temple complex consisted of two main types of buildings: the pagoda and the temple hall, both of which were influenced by traditional pre-Buddhist wooden structures. The most distinctive is the multistory pagoda. Although often compared to the Indian stūpa, their only common architectural elements are the central mast and tiers of parasols. Early examples can be found inside the caves at Yungang, where a single squared multistory structure was cut from the same stone as the cave proper. Made of solid rock the pagoda allowed the worshiper to circumambulate it in a similar fashion to that of the stūpa of Indian cave-temples. Decorated with carved images along its sides, the stone pagodas had overhanging eaves and roofs carved to imitate tile.

Pagodas were made of a variety of materials, including wood and stone and brick fashioned to imitate wood. An important early brick pagoda can be found in Xi'an, formerly the Tang capital of Chang'an. The Great Wild Goose Pagoda of the early eighth century is based on the square plan popular at the time. This most famous of all Tang pagodas was built in 652 for the home monastery of the pilgrim-monk Xuanzang. Originally it had five stories and reached a height of about 175 feet; several decades later it required a major renovation, and in the years 701–705 two stories were added, increasing its height to 190 feet. Interior stairs allow access to the levels divided by shallow eaves, accentuating the gradual stepping back of each story. Other extant pagodas further reveal both a continued interest in using stone and brick to imitate wood and a desire to construct pagodas on a polygonal rather than a square plan.

Early monasteries were aligned along a central straight axis with the pagoda placed directly behind the inner gate, followed by an image, or Buddha, hall and an assembly hall. In this arrangement the pagoda's importance is emphasized by its prominent position as the first building encountered on entering the temple complex. However, this plan was altered during the Sui and Tang dynasties. Wealthy temples added a second pagoda and placed the pair outside the central courtyard to either side of the image hall, now the building of primary importance, as found at the Tōdai-ji where two seven-story pagodas are placed to the front and to either side of the Great Buddha Hall. This shift away from the main axis reduced the importance of the pagoda, and the image hall took the dominant position. This building was designed in the style of secular architecture, based on the imperial throne hall. After the Tang period many temples did return to a single-pagoda plan, but the pagoda was placed to one side and never again assumed its former position of importance. With the rise of Chan and Amitābha sects, in which there was less emphasis on the use of relics, the pagoda's role was lessened further.

The reduction of the status of the pagoda coincided with the rise in prominence of the image hall. Set atop a high base of stone or brick, these temples relied on posts and lintels in conjunction with a system of brackets to support the tiled roofs that were extraordinarily heavy. With a post-and-lintel system, the wooden brackets reduced and distributed the weight of the roof and transferred it across a horizontal lintel supported by posts. This system was not only efficient but also attractive, and it created a separate visual element between the pillars and the roof. This is especially true of Tang-dynasty architecture, as the wealth of the period encouraged the construction of exceptionally large and impressive structures that typically made use of the heavy and elaborate hip-and-gable style of roof. The roof, in this case, is comprised of two parts: a lower section in which all four sides slant inward and an upper component of gabled roof where only two sides slant inward. An engraving on a stone lintel at the Great Wild Goose Pagoda provides a clear illustration of Tang Buddhist architecture. Elaborate brackets support the roof. Because the walls were non–load bearing, the front of the building was left open, each bay punctuated by pillars with supporting posts visible inside. The stone supports of the pillars were carved with images of lotus flowers, a symbol of Buddhism. Worshipers approached from the front; all the images, including the central Buddha, faced forward. This was a change from previous arrangements, in which the figures were set facing outward in different directions and were circumambulated by the devout. Behind the figures was an interior wall that separated the public space from the private, a necessity for the secret practices of the esoteric sects. This is seen in the main hall of the Foguang si on Mount Wutai, discovered only in the 1930s. Datable to 857 this hall stands 50 feet high and is 123 feet in length and has nine bays. A second extant example is the Great Buddha Hall of the Tōdai-ji in Japan. Over 150 feet in height, it was designed to house a colossal bronze Buddha.

The great persecution of 845 marked the beginning of the decline of Buddhism in China. Monastic wealth was confiscated, bronze items were melted down, and monks and nuns were returned to the lay life. Buddhism survived, but on a much reduced scale. No more great cave-temples were begun in the north, and with the exception of some glorious temples of the 11th to 13th century, the later periods saw no new developments, only changes in the size and elaborateness of the temple buildings, with the addition of more complex bracketing, the elongation of the eaves, and the addition of glazed roof tiles. The great monastic complexes in stone and wood of the Sui and Tang that had developed during this period of growth would not be seen in China again.

Catherine Pagani

See also Humor: Buddhist; Images: Buddhist Perspectives; Manuscript Production: Buddhist; Patrons, Buddhist: China; Stūpa; Worship Space: Buddhist Perspectives

Further Reading

Caswell, James O., *Written and Unwritten: A New History of the Buddhist Caves at Yungang*, Vancouver: University of British Columbia Press, 1988

Prip-Møller, Johannes, *Chinese Buddhist Monasteries: Their Plan and Function as a Setting for Buddhist Monastic Life*, Copenhagen: GEC Gad, 1937; reprint, Hong Kong: Hong Kong University Press, 1967

Stein, Sir Aurel, *Serindia: Detailed Report of Exploration of Central Asia and Westernmost China, Carried on and Described under the Orders of HM Indian Government*, 5 vols., Oxford: Clarendon Press, 1921

Steinhardt, Nancy Shatzman, *Chinese Traditional Architecture*, New York: China Institute in America, 1984

Weidner, Marsha, editor, *Latter Days of the Law: Images of Chinese Buddhism, 850–1850*, Lawrence: Spencer Museum of Art, University of Kansas in association with University of Hawaii Press, 1994

Whitfield, Roderick, and Anne Farrer, *Caves of the Thousand Buddhas: Chinese Art from the Silk Route*, New York: Brazillier, 1990

Visual Arts, Buddhist: India

The first art associated with Buddhism did not appear until the third century B.C. in India and consisted largely of symbolic images associated with the Buddha rather than explicit images of the Buddha himself. Early Buddhism was a missionary religion, and by the fourth century B.C. the notion of the wandering monk was well established. Monks were allowed to settle in one place only for the three months of the monsoon season. As the number of monks grew, these places, intended originally as shelter from the rain, became permanent monasteries. Among the vast amount of art produced are objects associated with the monastic dimension of the religion.

Early Art

Buddhism had existed in India nearly two centuries by the time that Aśoka (r. 272–231 B.C.), the third ruler of the Maurya empire (322–185 B.C.), became a follower of the Buddha. To commemorate his conversion Aśoka began the first large-scale work in stone, erecting throughout his empire at important sites in the Buddha's life a series of stone pillars carved with edicts. Made of cream-colored chunar sandstone, a local material found near the Mauryan capital of Pāṭaliputra, the columns could reach a height of 30 feet. The capitals of the columns are cut from a single piece of stone and are composed of a large inverted bell of lotus petals and frieze surmounted by animals. The best known and best preserved is the column erected at Deer Park, the site of the Buddha's first sermon, where he "Turned the Wheel of the Law." This column is crowned by four addorsed lions seated on a frieze carved with four animals – a lion, an elephant, a bull, and a horse – between which are four wheels. The Buddha is represented symbolically here through the lions (he has been referred to as the lion of his clan), and the wheels are a reference to his first sermon.

In addition to these columns, Aśoka's patronage also extended to rock-cut structures that represent the earliest extant Buddhist architecture. These caves in Bihar were the first in the development of carving shrines into hillsides that was used by both Hindus and Buddhists in India and eventually found its way to central Asia and China as well.

The Stūpa

Although Aśoka's columns contributed to the dissemination of Buddhism, his decision to open the eight original stūpas containing the Buddha's relics proved the most significant. In a move designed to bring the Buddha to his people, Aśoka had the relics redistributed among 84,000 other stūpas in his empire. The stūpa, one of the three main types of Buddhist architecture (the others being the residence hall, or *vihāra*, and the worship hall, or *caitya*), is the most important of the three types in early India and was modeled after earlier burial mounds. Symbolizing the Buddha's *parinirvāṇa* (achievement of nirvāṇa) and thus the Buddha himself, the stūpa was composed of a simple hemispherical main body made of solid earth surmounted by a single pillar of three umbrellas surrounded by a small gate similar to that encircling the stūpa itself. This number 3 stands for the three aspects of Buddhism: the Buddha, the Buddha's Law (dharma), and the Monastic Order (*saṅgha*). The pillar served as the *axis mundi*, or pivot of the universe, and indicated the placement of the relics within the mound. These relics were not meant to be viewed. Thus, the stūpa represented the Buddha and his teaching, and the worshiper made a ritual clockwise circumambulation (*pradakṣina*) around the monument as a form of meditation.

One of the greatest of the early stūpas is that at the monastery of Sāñcī in Madhya Pradesh in central India. Known as the Great Stūpa, it was one of at least three stūpas at this site and in recent times has been carefully restored. The original was erected by Aśoka in the third century B.C. and included a pillar with a lion capital, similar to that at Sārnāth. Between the first century B.C. and the first century A.D., this stūpa was enlarged to twice its original size and faced with local stone and white stucco. A surrounding railing based on wooden prototypes was added to the stūpa both to signify the monument as a sacred site and to mark a path for ritual circumambulation of the stūpa. A second interior path was also added onto the stūpa itself, placed about 15 feet above the ground with a stairway to the south.

Four gateways (*torana*) in the railing mark the four cardinal directions. Each gateway was made of two heavy squared pillars connected by three gently curving architraves between which stood three smaller vertical posts. They are heavily ornamented with low-relief narratives telling of daily life, stories from the life of the Buddha, and tales of the Buddha's previous lives, called *jātaka*. Depiction of such stories provided visitors and pilgrims with easy access to the religion. These are continuous narratives in which the story is told in one flowing scene. These illustrations do not show the Buddha in human form but instead refer to him through symbols, including footprints, an empty throne, and a wheel. It is not known why the artisans chose to depict the Buddha symbolically. Perhaps it was thought inappropriate to depict a being in human form who had freed himself through enlightenment from the confines of his body.

These early richly decorated Buddhist monasteries flourished because of public funding. Important at this time was the notion of *dāna*, or giving, as a means of achieving spiritual merit and thus a higher rebirth, and this is closely connected to the patronage of Buddhist sites. At Sāñcī records tell of over 600 donations made by a cross section of the population from all walks of life. This was an era of a community involvement in which all contributed to the construction of Buddhist monuments.

Unfortunately, one of the most important of the early stūpas exists only in fragments. The stūpa at Bhārhut, dating to around 100 B.C., was once a huge structure, but today only portions of the railings and one of the four *torana*s remain. It has been partially reconstructed by comparing it to the monument at Sāñcī. The importance of these remains lies in their imagery. The *jātaka*s and other stories have been described as a "visual encyclopedia of early art."

Cave Temples and Monasteries

Instead of using natural recesses, cave temples and monasteries in India were cut into the sides of mountains. Adorned with paintings and sculptures, these were early religious centers. Although the technique of cutting into the living rock dates to the third century B.C., it was not until around 100 B.C. that this was practiced on a large scale, first by Buddhists and then later by Hindus around A.D. 600.

Caves were very popular among early Buddhists for a number of reasons. Cool in the summer and dry during the monsoons, caves were first associated with ascetics who sought shelter from severe weather. The Buddha was also said to have meditated in a cave. Caves also offered stability and longevity because they were believed to last a *kalpa*, or cosmic era. The three basic types of caves were the *vihāra*, or monks' residences, where the individual cells surrounded a main assembly area; the larger *caitya*, or worship halls; and the stūpa, which was now moved inside to the rear of the *caitya*.

The first caves temples in India were located in the granite hills near Pāṭaliputra. The early worship halls had two parts: a rounded area to accommodate the stūpa and an outer assembly hall. Many of the architectural elements imitated wood, including doorjambs that sloped inward (a stabilizing construction in wood but unnecessary in stone), carved arches simulating wood, and "raffia" matting that filled in the arches of the doorways.

Caves temples soon spread to other parts of India, and gradually the walls between the circular chamber for the stūpa and the rectangular assembly hall disappeared, resulting in a single rectangular hall with a rounded end, or apse. Interior columns carved from stone marked the path for the ritual circumambulation around the stūpa. This basic plan was followed for the next 1,000 years.

One example is the cave monastery at Bhājā, dating to around 100 B.C., located about 105 miles south of Bombay. Here the *caitya* extends 60 feet into the mountain, and its barrel-vaulted ceiling with ribs imitating wood reaches a height of 29 feet. Plain octagonal columns line the *caitya*, and above the door is a higher arch that serves as a window; beams are seen along its inner surface, again making reference to wooden architecture. At present, the cave is open, but originally it was covered by a wooden facade as evidenced by a series of regular holes made in front of the window. The stone facade on either side of the *caitya* imitates a multistoried building complete with balconies, windows, and figures of men and women who gaze at the scene below. The residential halls for the monks, or *vihāra*, are on either side of the *caitya*. Each of these single-celled rooms opens onto a communal hall and has a raised bed with a pillow, both carved in stone, and a wall niche that housed an oil lamp. Between 6 and 24 monks lived in these *vihāra*.

Further development of the rock-cut *caitya* can be seen at Karle, dating to around A.D. 50 to 75. About 150 years later than that at Bhājā, the plan here is enlarged, with an elaborately carved veranda opening onto a large courtyard. The multistoried façade includes two life-size elephants on the side walls that support it. Included here are six sets of loving couples, known as *mithuna*, depicted larger than life and in high relief, with two more on the facing wall. These are sensuous beings connected to popular notions of fertility: the men have broad shoulders and narrow hips, whereas the women are voluptuous with full, rounded breasts, narrow waists, and curving hips.

The interior of the *caitya* at Karle cuts deep into the side of the mountain. The row of pillars are capped with couples riding animals atop a bell capital. The bases are a squat "vase," a shape derived from wooden architecture in which wood columns of wood were protected from insects and moisture in ceramic pots. At the end of the apse is a large rock-cut stūpa. Like the hall at Bhājā, Karle has a ribbed barrel-vaulted ceiling with a height of 45 feet. Absent are images of the Buddha, whose presence is suggested aniconically.

Caitya such as this one are commonly referred to as rock-cut architecture, but they are perhaps better described as sculpture on a very large scale. No architectural principles are at work here; the rock cutter did not need to worry about structural concerns but rather focused on the overall aesthetics of the cave. These cutters produced their "buildings" by excavating tons of rock from the mountain. They would start with rough markings for the doors and windows, and detailed plans would show the placement of the columns within. The accuracy with which these columns were aligned suggests that a sophisticated system of measurement was in place. At the far end of the *caitya*, a large boulder was left to be carved into a stūpa.

Unfinished caves reveal the technique used in constructing these monuments. Workers started at the ceiling and worked their way down, making scaffolding unneccessary in the early stages. This involved several types of workers at the site at the same time, including rock cutters who did the initial removal of the stone, masons who added details, and sculptors who were responsible for the fine work.

In western India about 20 major and numerous minor cave monasteries exist. These would have been expensive to produce. The early caves, those dating between around 100 B.C and A.D. 200, were made possible by the many contributions from a broad range of society, including rich merchants, housewives, and fishermen. Donations provided a means of accumulating religious merit and were a powerful motivating force.

This was an era of expanding trade routes and of a rising merchant class. The resulting wealth in India found its way to the construction of new caves and embellishment of existing Buddhist monasteries. Monasteries were conveniently located along trade routes, where easy access existed for merchants and traders, both native and foreign, who would not only visit these monastic establishments but provide donations as well. For example, at Karle records reveal that of some of the pillars were made possible through donations from foreign merchants.

In the mid–fifth century royalty took over from commoners as the main patrons, resulting in an increase and renewal in artistic activity. One of the grandest examples of this patronage can be seen at the cave complex of Ajaṇṭā located in the northwest Deccan, dating to the late Gupta period (320–647). A small monastery already existed at Ajaṇṭā in the first century B.C., but this horseshoe-shaped cliff was reoccupied in the fifth to sixth century. In total 29 caves existed at Ajaṇṭā. Two types of buildings are found at these caves: *vihāra* and *caitya*. The *vihāra*, which previously had been residential, now functioned as areas for daily worship and meditation with the addition of a shrine containing a Buddha carved in stone. Painted tales of the Buddha's previous lives covered the walls, and the ceilings were made to look like the heavens. Now the worshiper was surrounded with images to serve as broad visual reminders of the faith.

However, the *caitya* form the most complex constructions at Ajaṇṭā. The frontage was dominated by large arched doorways and projecting porches, with exterior walls crowded with carvings of Buddhas and bodhisattvas. The irregular placement suggests that these sculptures were added as donations came available. The influence of Mahāyāna Buddhism can be seen at this site. The bodhisattva was a new addition to the Buddhist repertoire of images. Differing in meaning from the term used earlier in India to describe Siddhartha prior to his enlightenment, bodhisattvas were now regarded as compassionate beings on the verge of Buddhahood but who choose to remain on this earth to help others. The complexities of Mahāyāna Buddhism also resulted in changes to the stūpa. Although still the point of focus within the worship hall, the stūpa was heightened with the addition of a thick base, an elongated main section, and elaborate umbrellas at the top. Finally, a large image of the Buddha was set between a pair of elaborately carved columns.

The walls and ceilings of the Ajaṇṭā caves are covered with paintings, likely owing to its wealthy patrons. In preparing the surfaces for painting, the walls were left rough and then covered with two layers of mud and finally a smooth layer of lime wash. The paintings were done on the dry wall, not wet plaster as in fresco painting, and thus were not very durable. Red paint outlined the images. Colors included yellow, red, black, white, and green. Although most pigments came from local minerals, the rich blue was derived from lapis lazuli imported from Afghanistan. Unfortunately, these paintings have suffered damage over the centuries from water (the paints are water soluble) and from insects that sought the rice husks in the wall plaster.

The earliest paintings at the site date to the first century B.C., but most were produced in the late fifth and early sixth centuries. Most paintings depict *jātaka* tales, but large individual bodhisattvas and various decorative designs can be found as well. The paintings flow into one another, creating walls that are alive with color. The paintings make use of multiple perspective, although here the figures in the foreground tend to overlap those in the background. Often the Buddha or bodhisattvas are painted larger than their surrounding figures using a convention by which the relative sizes of the figures indicated their importance. Shading and highlighting suggest three-dimensionality. More than one workshop participated in producing these paintings, and stylistic differences between the various workshops can be discerned even within individual caves.

The audience for these paintings would have included patrons, visitors, and the resident monks. Oil lamps would have illuminated the works a portion at a time, and thus visitors would have needed the assistance of the monks to guide them through the images. The latter might also have aided in focusing attention on one virtue at a time. Certainly, textual evidence tells of the importance of paintings as an aid to meditation.

The work at Ajaṇṭā involved a vast amount of labor to cut, carve, sculpt, plaster, and paint the caves. Most sources agree that work in the second phase began in 462, the year that Harishena (r. c. 462–481) came to the throne. Although a Hindu ruler, he and his court were great sponsors of Buddhist art. It has been held that the work continued for the next 150 years, but research by Walter Spink, the leading scholar on the site of Ajaṇṭā, has suggested that the period of activity was intense and brief. Certainly, it would have been difficult for the artists to maintain such a pace. The position of the caves allowed natural daylight for a few short hours a day; even with oil lamps and white cloth reflectors, the working day would not have increased by much. The three months of monsoon rains would also have impeded activity. Still it has been suggested that work was completed within 40 to 60 years. Work appears to have ended suddenly, soon after A.D. 500. This is likely connected to the loss of patronage on the death of Harishena and the end of his dynasty.

At the end of the Gupta period, Buddhist dominance in India declined; the religion and its artistic traditions expanded to other regions, including Southeast Asia and the Far East, while in India Hinduism became the prevailing religion.

CATHERINE PAGANI

See also Ajaṇṭā, India; Bodhisattva; Buddha (Śākyamuni); Deities, Buddhist; Gestures, Buddhist; Images: Buddhist Perspectives; India: Sites; Manuscript Production: Buddhist; Origins: Comparative Perspectives; Stūpa; Worship Space: Buddhist Perspectives

Further Reading

Behl, Benoy K., *The Ajanta Caves: Ancient Paintings of Buddhist India*, London: Thames and Hudson, 1998

Dahmen-Dallapiccola, Anna Libera, editor, *The Stupa: Its Religious, Historical and Architectural Significance*, Wiesbaden: Steiner, 1979

Dehejia, Vidya, *Early Buddhist Rock Temples: A Chronology*, Ithaca, New York: Cornell University Press, 1972; as *Early*

Buddhist Rock Temples: A Chronological Study, London: Thames and Hudson, 1972
Dehejia, Vidya, *Indian Art*, London: Phaidon Press, 1997
Fisher, Robert E., *Buddhist Art and Architecture*, New York: Thames and Hudson, 1993
Spink, Walter, *Ajanta to Ellora*, Bombay: Marg Publications for the Center for South and Southeast Asian Studies, University of Michigan, 1967
Weiner, Sheila L., *Ajanta: Its Place in Buddhist Art*, Berkeley: University of California Press, 1977

Visual Arts, Buddhist: Japan

The Buddhist visual culture of Japan is perhaps the richest and most complete of any Asian country, comprising a continuous tradition of some 1,400 years, extending to the present day. The absence of any significant persecutions has allowed an exceptionally large proportion of the art and architecture to be preserved, thereby fully documenting all genres, including painting, calligraphy, sculpture, ritual objects, and structures. In contrast to India, China, and Korea, where Buddhism is not currently the dominant tradition, Japan remains an essentially Buddhist country, with the result that most of the art still functions within a religious context. This is not to say that Buddhist objects are not found in museums and private collections, but even there they tend to be seen in both religious and aesthetic terms. As a result of this living tradition and the economic prosperity of Japan, Japanese Buddhist art has been very extensively studied and published, allowing scholars to form a comprehensive image of its entire development.

Buddhism entered the Japanese islands from the Korean peninsula during the sixth century, brought primarily by people moving to the islands. Although an official introduction is associated with the year 538 (or 552), it was not until the end of the sixth century that important production is seen in Japan. This initial phase, designated as the Asuka period (c. 590–c. 650), witnessed the extensive patronage of the Soga clan, the dominant political group of the time. Their clan temple, Asukadera, was built between 590 and around 620 and constitutes the first great monastic complex in Japan. Although it is largely destroyed, archaeological excavations have revealed the original plan; additionally, one of its icons, the Asukadera Great Buddha (605–609), still survives, although in damaged condition. Another temple, associated with the early seventh century, Hōryūji, looms very importantly in standard historiography because its buildings and treasures are very well preserved, although we must remember that during the Asukia period the Soga clan temple was far more important that Hōryūji. Among the key monuments housed at Hōryūji is the Shaka Triad in the Golden Hall; this image, usually dated 623, is believed to have been supervised by a man named Tori-busshi, who was also responsible for the Asukadera Great Buddha. These two icons are of gilt bronze, but other Asuka sculptures, such as the Yumedono Kannon and the Kudara Kannon (both at Hōryūji), were carved from wood. In addition to sculpture there are a few works in other media, including the paintings that decorate the surfaces of the Tamamushi Shrine (Hōryūji) and the textile work of the Tenjukoku Shūchō (Chūgūji).

The Asuka period is followed by the Hakuhō period (c. 650–710). In contrast to the rather archaic nature of Buddhist art during the earlier phase, Hakuhō art appears as more developed and mature. In addition during this period there was extensive building of temples, with grand icons, often under direct imperial patronage. Examples of the latter include Kudara Odera (c. 639), Kawaradera (founded c. 660), and Yakushiji (founded c. 680). Although direct evidence is not available, we know from documentary sources that each of these temples housed important, large-scale sculptural icons. Most of the extant monuments are of smaller scale, including a quite large number of gilt-bronze icons. Especially important examples include the famous Yumechigai Kannon (Hōryūji), dated around 700. In distinction to the archaic style of an image such as the Yumedono Kannon, the Yumechigai Kannon displays much fuller modeling of the body, giving the figure a great sense of realism. Another significant example is the Tachibana Shrine Amida Triad, also at Hōryūji.

The first full-scale, permanent capital, Fujiwarakyō, was built toward the end of the Hakuhō period, but it was occupied only between 694 and 710, when the court moved to an even larger capital, Heijōkyō (present-day Nara). The Nara period (710–794) is often considered the golden age of Japanese art, as its temples and monasteries enshrine many of the greatest treasures of the entire tradition. Several of the great temples mentioned in the preceding paragraphs were transferred to the new capital, whereas others were inaugurated there, including Tōdaiji, Saidaiji, and Tōshōdaiji. By the Nara period the central government had extended its authority over much of the country, and Buddhism had become increasingly mature as a result of greater exposure and study. Sculpture continues to be the dominant category during the Nara period, but in contrast to the Asuka-Hakuhō periods, Nara sculpture is extraordinarily varied in materials and techniques, including, in addition to bronze and wood, other forms, such as clay, dry lacquer, and even gold and silver.

Representative of clay sculpture are the figurines that decorate the four sides of the Hōryūji Pagoda (711); these figurines depict, in remarkably realistic form, various members of the Buddhist pantheon. Although they are now uncolored, originally they would have been brilliantly polychromed. A key example of the dry lacquer mode is the figure of Ashura (c. 730) at Kōfukuji. Here, too, we see an extraordinary sense of realism in the faces, one of the keystones of Nara art. Probably the greatest example of gilt-bronze sculpture in all of Asia is the large Yakushi Triad at the Yakushiji, probably made around 720. Wood is represented at a somewhat later period by a large group of images kept at Tōshōdaiji. This multiplicity of material and techniques, combined with the classic beauty and elegance

Hōōdō (Phoenix Hall), Byōdōin, Uji (near Kyoto), Japan, 11th century.
Photo courtesy of John C. Huntington, the Huntington Archive

of Nara sculpture, has been highly valued by critics, both Japanese and foreign.

The most important single monument of Nara sculpture is the Great Buddha of Tōdaiji; regrettably this enormous gilt-bronze image, dedicated in 752, is only a shadow of its original form because of repeated destruction over the centuries. Nevertheless as the culmination of a concentrated period of imperial patronage of Buddhism, it symbolizes the great heights to which the religion had ascended. In fact there was somewhat of a slackening of production during the second half of the century as a result of the enormous expenditures on Tōdaiji and its icons. Also at Tōdaiji is a great treasure house, called the Shōsōin, which contains all the treasures that belonged to Emperor Shōmu, including the ritual objects that were used in the dedication of the Great Buddha.

Painting continues to be relatively rare during the Nara period, although there are a few significant examples. Perhaps most important are the wall paintings, usually dated early Nara, decorating the interior of the Hōryūji Golden Hall. Also important is a small hemp painting representing the deity Kichijōten, kept at Yakushiji.

The imperial capital was next transferred to Heiankyō (present-day Kyoto) and remained there until 1868. The Heian period (794–1180) is ordinarily divided generally into early Heian (ninth to tenth century) and late Heian (11th to 12th century), the two subdivisions quite different in character. Unlike the situation when the capital was moved from Fujiwarakyō to Heijōkyō in 710 and the great monasteries were also transferred, with the move to Heiankyō the great Nara monasteries were required to remain in the old capital, mainly because they were seen as a threat to the secular government. This is not to say that the court was hostile to Buddhism, however, as two great temples, Tōji and Saiji, were established at the new capital, flanking the great central gate. Also highly significant was the introduction of two new schools of Buddhism – Tendai by Saichō and Shingon by Kūkai – for these schools emphasized a type of esoteric practice and imagery that was fundamental for the early Heian period. An additional important factor was the placement of the headquarters of these schools on mountains rather than in the city: Tendai at Mount Hiei, overlooking Kyoto, and Shingon at more distant Mount Kōya. Typical of the esoteric sculpture of the early Heian period is the extensive group of images in the Lecture Hall of Tōji, a Shingon temple associated with Kūkai. Here we see the deities, often nonanthropomorphic, arranged in a three-dimensional *mandara* format. The *mandara*, of course, is more clearly seen in painted versions, where the very numerous deities of the esoteric pantheon are related to one another in a hierarchical schema. Another important tradition in early Heian sculpture is the "pure wood" style, in which images lack polychromy and gilt and the expression of the wood is primary. The standing image of Yakushi, the Medicine Buddha, at Jingoji, Kyoto, is an outstanding example of this mode.

During the late Heian period, the schools already established continued to be of importance, but more emphasis was placed on the doctrines and practices of the Pure Land (Jōdo) tradition. This tendency is reflected in a series of magnificent temples built in the capital; unfortunately all of these have been lost over the centuries, but a good image of their splendor can be gained from the Phoenix Hall of the Byōdōin, a temple in Uji to the south of Kyoto. The Phoenix Hall, shaped like the bird, appears to hover over the lotus pond in front of it, in this way evoking the wonderful Western Paradise of Amida. Within the Hall is a monumental image of Amida, supervised by the sculptor Jōchō and made in the "joined wood" technique, with a layer of gilt to increase its splendor. A highly important provincial expression of a related visual ideology can be found at the Konjikidō of Chūsonji in Iwate prefecture. Painting also flourished during the late Heian period, and these works project a strong sense of luxury and elegance. One of the most important examples is the "Descent of Amida," a tritypch now kept at Mount Kōya that shows the Buddha Amida welcoming newly saved individuals to the Western Paradise.

In contrast to the aristocratic culture of the late Heian period, the subsequent Kamakura period (1180–1336) was dominated by the warrior class, with the result that the arts are of a somewhat different character. Although the imperial court remained in Kyoto, the center of political authority was in distant Kamakura, the location of the Kamakura military government. During the civil wars that preceded the establishment of this new government, some of the great temples of Nara, including Tōdaiji and Kōfukuji, were destroyed during the chaos, and the Kamakura authorities felt obliged to contribute to their reconstruction. For this reason most of the greatest early Kamakura sculptures are found in the old temples of Nara. Members of the Kei school, especially Unkei and Kaikei, and their studios were responsible for many of the key monuments, including such pieces as the portraits of Muchaku and Seshin at Kōfukuji by Unkei and his disciples. Perhaps the most important characteristic of such works is an intensely probing realism, a trait that combines an earlier Nara-period sensibility with the new spirit of the Kamakura period.

Pure Land belief continues to be important, and the sculptor Kaikei produced many representations of the Buddha Amida. The same tendency can be observed in the many painted representations of Amida. Several important religious thinkers, especially Hōnen, Shinran, and Ippen, contributed to the formulation of Pure Land thought and practice, and each had a highly significant impact on the production of art. Especially interesting are the picture scrolls that provide the biographies of these and other religious leaders. The Zen schools, established by monks such as Eisai and Dōgen, achieved their first flourishing during the Kamakura period, although most of the defining art is associated with the following Muromachi period.

Popular Buddhism became central during the Kamakura period as missionaries spread the religion throughout the country. Important in this context is the production of replicated icons, whereby a specific, highly auspicious image served as the model for numerous copies. One example of this tendency is the tradition of the Shaka of Seiryōji (Kyoto), an image made in China in 985, brought to Japan shortly thereafter and then repeatedly copied from the early Kamakura period on. Replications of the Seiryōji Shaka are found in temples throughout Japan and serve as vehicles for the local cults of this deity. Another important example of a replication cult is that of the Zenkōji Amida Triad, centered on the famous temple, Zenkōji, in Nagano.

With the fall of the Kamakura military government, a new shogunate was established by the Ashikaga family, located in Kyoto, thereby once again uniting the imperial court and the secular government. This phase, referred to as the Muromachi period (1336–1573), combined military and aristocratic tendencies to produce a synthesis that is one of the most characteristic expressions of Japanese visual culture. Although the earlier schools remained in place, the Zen school became dominant, especially in elite circles, thereby leading to the production of a great deal of art. Zen, of course, is the Japanese term for the Chinese school referred to as "Chan," and this Chinese connection is critical for an understanding of the nature of Zen art, for the monks associated with Zen monasteries closely modeled their lives on Chinese prototypes. In fact some of the paintings and calligraphies executed by these monks are essentially based on Chinese secular art and thus, strictly speaking, should not be considered in the context of Buddhist art. Nevertheless there are also numerous works that are specifically Buddhist in content.

Zen art is seen most extensively in a group of monasteries in Kyoto and secondarily in a related group in Kamakura. These monasteries are normally constructed with a series of subtemples, each of which has a sand and rock garden, halls for meditation, and often an icon hall. One of the most important categories of Zen painting is the one where Zen riddles, or kōan, are depicted; a famous example is Josetsu's "Catching a Catfish with a Gourd" at Myōshinji. Various other heroes of early Zen history, such as Kanzan and Jittoku, are frequently represented in ink paintings. A different category of painting depicts important prelates of the Zen schools, such as Minchō's "Portrait of Enni" at Tōfukuji. Such portraits were used in memorial services for the deceased master.

Although conventional art history tends to focus almost exclusively on the Zen arts of the Muromachi period, it is important to recognize that there was an extraordinarily extensive production of orthodox Buddhist sculptures during this period. In fact one can say that there are probably more Muromachi sculptures than from any other period, even though these icons are little studied and not highly valued today. There is also a good deal of religious architecture from the Muromachi period in addition to the more famous Zen establishments, such as the Golden Pavilion and the Silver Pavilion in Kyoto.

The short Momoyama period (1573–1615) is not normally thought of in a Buddhist context, for during these decades there was a tremendous burst of activity in the secular arts. This tendency is related to the civil wars and the subsequent unification of the country by a series of powerful warlords, for the large castles constructed by these lords required extensive decoration, usually in the form of large-scale screens with gold backgrounds and brilliant colors. Perhaps the most interesting of the Buddhist monuments was a great temple in Kyoto, Hōkōji, built by one of the greatest unifiers, Toyotomi Hideyoshi, to rival the Great Buddha Hall at Tōdaiji built in the middle of the eighth century. Ironically, whereas the latter had an icon made of bronze, the best that Hideyoshi could do was commission one made of wood and lacquer.

The period of disunity came to an end with the establishment of the Tokugawa military government by Tokugawa Ieyasu; this period is usually referred to by art historians as the Edo period (1615–1868) based on the location of the military capital in the city of Edo (present-day Tokyo). As was the case with the Momoyama period, Edo is not generally conceptualized in terms of Buddhist art, as this period saw the development of numerous genres that have subsequently been seen as central to Japanese visual culture. For example, in painting we see the Literati, or Nanga, school; the Decorative, or Rimpa, school; and the highly popular Ukiyo-e tradition of woodblock prints depicting the activities of the townspeople. Nevertheless Japan was a Buddhist country during these centuries, and there was very extensive production of Buddhist monuments, including paintings, sculptures, and buildings.

Although a great deal of orthodox art was made, art historians have tended to concentrate on the works of a number of somewhat eccentric artists. For example, in painting there are highly interesting pieces by artists such as Hakuin and Sengai. Similarly in the area of sculpture, men such as Enku and Mokujiki traveled throughout Japan preaching their religious messages and making icons for the local people. Whereas the orthodox production can often seem somewhat lifeless, the innovative works by the monk-artists just mentioned must reflect directly the vitality and energy of life during the Edo period.

As mentioned at the beginning of this article, Japan continues to be an essentially Buddhist country to the present day. Even more so than with the Momoyama and Edo periods, there has been a strong tendency among art historians to ignore Buddhist visual culture in the modern period. The strongly anti-Buddhist policies that were in effect during the first few years of the Meiji period (1868–1912) significantly discredited the Buddhist institutions, and it took several decades for Buddhist leaders to revitalize the tradition. Nevertheless Buddhism gradually regained its position in Japanese society, and at present the majority of the population are at least nominally Buddhist, although usually not exclusively so. Many of the temples that they visit and the icons that they worship are of contemporary production, and in fact many people carve Buddhist icons as a pious hobby. In addition exhibitions of Buddhist "art" are highly popular, although there are difficulties in assessing the degree of motivation that the high attendance figures might show.

DONALD F. MCCALLUM

See also Architecture: Structural Monasteries in East Asia; Dōgen, Eisai (Yosai); Ippen; Japan: History; Kōan; Kūkai; Kyoto, Japan; Mount Hiei, Japan; Mount Kōya, Japan; Nagano, Japan; Nara, Japan; Pure Land Buddhism; Saichō; Zen, Arts of

Further Reading

Kurata, Bunsaku, and Yoshiro Tamura, editors, *Art of the Lotus Sutra: Japanese Masterpieces*, translated by Edna B. Crawford, Tokyo: Kosei, 1987
Nishikawa, Kyotaro, and Emily J. Sano, *The Great Age of Japanese Buddhist Sculpture A.D. 600–1300*, Fort Worth, Texas: Kimbell Art Museum, 1982
Paine, Robert Treat, and Alexander Soper, *The Art and Architecture of Japan*, Harmondsworth: Penguin, 1955; 3rd edition, New Haven, Connecticut: Yale University Press, 1981
Saunders, E. Dale, *Mudra: A Study of Symbolic Gestures in Japanese Buddhist Sculpture*, New York: Pantheon, 1960
Snodgrass, Adrian, *The Matrix and Diamond World Mandalas in Shingon Buddhism*, New Delhi: Aditya Prakashan, 1988
Soper, Alexander, *The Evolution of Buddhist Architecture in Japan*, Princeton, New Jersey: Princeton University Press, 1942

Visual Arts, Buddhist: Korea

Among the arts that relate to Buddhism in Korea, painting is one of the most distinctively Korean. Today very few Buddhist paintings pre-date the Koryŏ dynasty (918–1392), and most paintings in Korean temples date from the second half of the Chosŏn dynasty (1392–1910). Buddhist paintings can be divided into three main groups: (1) those mounted as scrolls or stretched over square, wooden frames (*t'aenghwa*); (2) wall paintings (frescoes); and (3) illustrations and illuminated frontispieces in sūtras. During the Koryŏ but likely right from the beginning of Buddhism in Korea, paper stencils have been used to transmit the standard iconographical forms.

Korean Buddhist painting developed its own stylistic and aesthetic vocabulary in the course of history, and already during the Koryŏ it had attained a pronounced local quality that was admired in both China and Japan. When compared with its Chinese and Japanese counterparts, Korean Buddhist painting tends to be more stylized and more conservative in terms of choice of compositions. The human figures are generally slightly squat, and all without exception have round, flat faces, a feature that distinguishes them from the Buddhist paintings in the rest of eastern Asia. In terms of technique and skill, the Buddhist paintings of Koryŏ are extremely refined and delicate, with attention given to even minute details.

Under the Koryŏ dynasty painters of Buddhist subjects were professional painters who worked from their own workshops and who, as in China and Japan, were commissioned by the clergy and wealthy patrons to make votive paintings to be hung

Three-storied four-lion pagoda, Hwaŏmsa, Mount Jiri, Chŏlla-namdo, ninth century, granite, 5.54 meters in height.
Photo courtesy of Marylin M. Rhie

in temple halls. It appears that painters of Buddhist subjects were laypeople as well as members of the clergy, and the craft was handed down from master to disciple.

Surviving Koryŏ paintings reveal that the Amitābha cult enjoyed great popularity. Among the most common themes is the "Pure Land Triad," in which a central Amitābha is flanked by the bodhisattvas Avalokiteśvara and Mahāsthāmaprāpta. Other Pure Land compositions feature the sitting Amitābha surrounded by the group of eight major bodhisattvas, including Avalokiteśvara, Mahāsthāmaprāpta, Kṣitigarbha, Mañjuśrī, Samantabhadra, Vajrapāni, Maitreya, and Sarvānivaraṇaviṣkambī. In addition to these standard Pure Land Triads are a number of paintings that illustrate the *Guan wuliang shou jing* (*Amitayusdhyāna Sūtra*) as well as paintings depicting certain important scenes taken from the Pure Land Scriptures. Examples of the "Willow Kwanseŭm" (Avalokiteśvara) are rather numerous, some of the finest examples of which are now held in collections in Japan. Among the Buddhist painters from the Koryŏ whose names have come down to us is one No Yŏng (fl. 13th to 14th century). From his hand, two paintings are known. No Yŏng's style was apparently continued in the early Chosŏn dynasty.

When compared with the relatively small number of extant Koryŏ Buddhist paintings, a surprisingly large amount of illuminated manuscripts in concertina format as well as block prints are still extant. Especially noteworthy are illustrations associated with the *Avataṃsaka* and *Saddharmapuṇḍarīka* sūtra.

During the Chosŏn period (1392–1910) the number of iconographical types appears to have increased dramatically, although the paintings are much more formalistic than earlier. From the second half of the Chosŏn, extant Buddhist paintings are rather numerous, and although regional differences can be seen in the way certain details and iconographical concepts were interpreted, a fixed range of compositions and typologies was adhered to within all the painting schools.

During the early Chosŏn, Buddhist paintings retained much of the compositional freedom and elegance that characterized

Buddha (probably Amitābha) triad, granite, K'ae-t'aesa (Temple of the Opening of Peace), Mount Yonsan, Nonsan-gun, Ch'ungch'ong-namdo, c. A.D. 936–940, early Koryŏ dynasty.
Photo courtesy of Marylin M. Rhie

A metal statue of Maitreya from the Unified Silla Period (668–918), now housed in the National Museum, Seoul, South Korea. Photo courtesy of John Powers

the Koryŏ *t'aenghwa*, and despite neo-Confucian dominance of the government they were still being commissioned by the court. However, by the middle of the dynasty they gradually became more stylized. Furthermore, the development of a tradition of images and pantheons on wooden blocks, which arose after A.D. 1600, helped to preserve and "freeze" the compositions. At the close of the Chosŏn period, Buddhist paintings came gradually under the influence of folk-painting (*minhwa*), a shift that heralded a decline of the orthodox painting styles.

The number of extant Chosŏn *t'aenghwa* is comparatively large, and many are still hanging above the altars in the temple halls for which they were originally painted. Because each painting corresponds to a particular type of ritual, their function is well documented. Buddhas such as Śākyamuni, Amitābha, Bhaiṣajyaguru, and Vairocana/Rocana are main icons placed above the central altar in the main hall. Individual bodhisattva paintings are normally placed in special halls, whereas *t'aenghwa* featuring arhats, protectors, and so on are placed in connection with secondary altars. Portraits of historical patriarchs and important masters are commonly found in special memorial halls. These portraits normally depict important historical figures in the history of Korean Buddhism, such as Wŏnhyo (617–686), Chinul (1158–1210), and Hyŭjŏng (1524–1604), but also include Indian and Chinese masters. In some of the large monasteries, whole sets of local patriarch paintings can be found. In the famous Songgwang Temple near Sunch'ŏn in South Chŏlla province is a hall devoted to the Sixteen National Masters, who were connected to the temple's history.

Another type of *t'aenghwa* from the Chosŏn is large, painted banner paintings, normally refered to as *kwaebul* (Hanging Buddhas). Most *kwaebul* measure about 32 to 50 feet in length and between about 16 and 19 feet wide. They are painted like the *t'aenghwa*, usually depicting a Buddha tableau, and are displayed outdoors on the Buddha's birthday or on other festival days.

During the Koryŏ esoteric Buddhism influenced ritual practices, and it is from this period that the tradition of "empowering" the *t'aenghwa* arose. This empowerment was effected through a lengthy ritual in the course of which a special cloth bag (*pokchang*) was hung above the painting. The *pokchang* was made in the shape of a frog, a purse, or a round disk that was filled with power objects, such as the five grains, the precious substances, and *dhāraṇīs*.

Many of the Buddhist paintings from the Chosŏn dynasty are dated and often contain a list of donors as well as provenance. In some cases the name of the painter is also given. Usually such data are contained in an inscription placed within a rectangular red cartouche placed in the center bottom of the painting.

It appears that Sŏn (Chan/Zen) Buddhist painting never developed into a distinct form of art during the dynastic period but formed part of the typological vocabulary of the scholar-painter tradition. Not until the late Chosŏn did Sŏn painting and Sŏn calligraphy come into prominence as a tradition of its own.

Henrik H. Sørensen

See also Chan/Zen: Korea; Chinul; Korea: History; Korea: Sites; Patrons, Buddhist: Korea; Manuscript Production: Buddhist; Pure Land Buddhism; Worship Space: Buddhist Perspectives

Further Reading

Barry, Brian, "A Twentieth Century Gold Fish," *Korea Journal* 33:3 (1993)

Hanguk pulgyo misul saron (Essays on the History of Buddhist Art in Korea), edited by Hwang Suyŏng, Seoul: Minjŏk sa, 1987

Hanguk pulhwa ch'obon (Line-Drawings of Korean Buddhist Paintings), Yangsan: Songbo pomulgwan, 1992

Hanguk pulhwa: Hwagi chip (Korean Buddhist Paintings: Collection of Inscriptions on Paintings), edited by Hong Yunsik, Seoul: Karamsa yŏnguso, 1995

Hwang Pyŏngjin, *Hanguk pulhwa tobon* (Line-Diagrams of Korean Buddhist Painting), Seoul: Taehung Kiwik, 1989

Im Yŏngju, *Tanch'ŏng* (Decorative Patterns), Seoul: Taewŏnsa, 1991

Kim Chŏnghŭi, *Chosŏn sidae Chijang Siwang to yŏngu* (A Study of Paintings of Kṣitigarbha and the Ten Kings during the Chosŏn Period), Hanguk munhwa yesul dae kye 4, Seoul: Ilchisa, 1996
Kim Yŏngju, *Chosŏn sidae pulhwa yŏngu* (A Study of Buddhist Paintings during the Chosŏn Period), Seoul: Chisik sanŏmsa, 1986
Korai butsuga (English title: Korean Buddhist Paintings of the Koryŏ Dynasty [918–1392]), Nara: Yamato Bunkakan, 1978
Mellott, Richard L., "A Korean Painting of Avalokiteśvara in the Asian Art Museum of San Francisco," *Orientation* 1 (1987)
Pak Young-Sook, "Kṣitigarbha as Supreme Lord of the Underworld," *Oriental Arts* 23:1 (1977)
Pak Young-Sook, "Illuminated Manuscript of Amitābha Sūtra," *Orientations* 13:2 (1982)
Pak Young-Sook, "Buddhist Themes in Koguryŏ Murals," *Asiatische Studien/Etudes Asiatiques* 44:2 (1990)
Sørensen, Henrik H., "The *t'aenghwa* Tradition in Korean Buddhism," *Korean Culture* 8:4 (1987)
Sørensen, Henrik H., "The Hwaŏm Kyŏng Pyŏnsang To: An Yi Dynasty Buddhist Painting of the Dharma Realm," *Oriental Arts* 34:2 (1988)
Sørensen, Henrik H., *The Iconography of Korean Buddhist Painting*, volume 12, number 9, *Iconography of Religions*, Leiden: Brill, 1989
The Life of Buddha (Korean title: *Sŏkka palsang to*), edited by Zozayong, Seoul: Emilie Museum, 1975
T'ongdo sa ŭi pulhwa (Buddhist Paintings in T'ongdo Temple), Yangsan: Sŏngbo pomulgwan, 1988
Yun Yŏlsu, *Kwaebul* (Buddhist Banner-Paintings), Seoul: Taewŏnsa, 1990

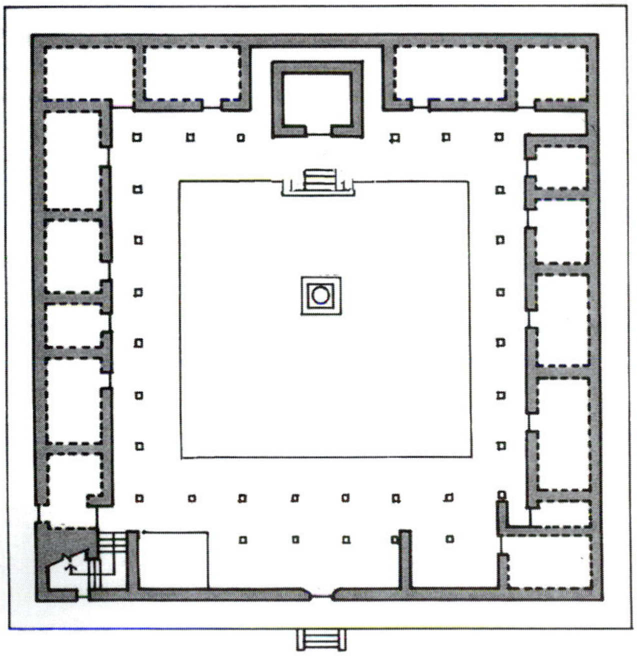

Fig. 1: Idealized ground plan of Bahī in Nepal. Drawing courtesy of Dina Bangdel

Visual Arts, Buddhist: Nepal

Nepal has historically remained a major entrepôt for the transmission of Buddhism and its artistic expression between northeastern India and Tibet. The small fertile Kathmandu Valley, consisting of the three cities of Kathmandu, Patan, and Bhaktapur, is the locus of cultural, artistic, and religious development. Virtually an open-air museum, the valley has more than 500 Buddhist monasteries and numerous temples, giving evidence of the creative genius of the Newars. In fact the term *Nepalese* art in general refers exclusively to the artistic production of the Buddhist Newars of the Kathmandu Valley. Through the centuries these artists have also fulfilled major commissions for the royal Hindu patrons of the valley for centuries.

Buddhism and Hinduism have coexisted in the Kathmandu Valley for more than 2,000 years, and the form of esoteric (Tantric) Buddhism practiced by the Newars has developed some unique features, indicating a blending of the two religions. Newar Buddhism is characterized by a noncelibate monastic tradition, in which the married householders are strictly stratified in a caste-based hierarchy. The monastic community of the Śākyas and Vajrācāryas are the valley's craftsmen, working as carvers of stone, wood, and ivory; as painters; and as highly skilled metal workers. These occupations have led the monastic caste groups to serve as itinerant artists in Tibet and were commissioned to work for Tibetan monasteries in Lhasa, Śākya, and Samye. Historically the Newar artists have been instrumental in the development of Tibetan painting and sculptural style called the *Bal bris* or *Bal mthun* (literally, "Tibetan Nepali" school). The fame of the Buddhist craftsmen even reached the court of imperial China in the 13th century, when Yüan Emperor Genghis Khan invited the Newar artist Aniko (c. 1245–1306) to head the metal casting division at his court.

Although material remains of Nepal's artistic tradition in the valley go back as early as the second century A.D., Buddhist art begins only from the Licchavi period (fourth to ninth century). From this time the Newar Buddhist monasteries served as the focal point for the development of the arts and are still in active use. The basic architectural plan, the pantheon, and iconographic features of the Newar Buddhist monasteries had already been established by the 13th and 14th centuries.

Newar Buddhist Pantheon

The Newar Buddhist pantheon is classed in two broad categories based on its ritual function: exoteric Vajrayāna and esoteric Vajrayāna. Tantric rituals are distinguished through a similar hierarchical classification, and participation is dictated by the practitioner's level of Tantric initiation. Reflective of this ritual hierarchy, Newar Buddhist imagery demonstrates progressively higher and more esoteric levels of Tantric expression. The visual imagery of the Newar Buddhist monasteries articulates this duality.

The exoteric deities constitute the Buddhist deities in their pacific non-Tantric forms, such as the Śākyamuni, the Jina Buddhas (their female counterparts), and numerous bodhisattvas.

Fig. 2: Shrine facade, south wall of the courtyard, Uku bāhā, Patan, Nepal. Photo courtesy of Dina Bangdel

These also include Mahāyāna and Vajrayāna deities, such as Vajrasattva, Dharmadhātu Vāgīśvara Mañjughoṣa, and Caṇḍamahārośana, as well as goddesses Vajrayoginī and Guhyeśvarī. Of these the five Jina Buddhas, represented in their two-armed or multi-armed crowned forms, are the most important in the Newar Buddhist pantheon. This class of exoteric deities can be openly shown in public and propitiated by the entire Buddhist community. Access to worship does not require Tantric initiation.

The second category of deities pertains to the initiated practices of the Newar Buddhist community, in which the esoteric pantheon might not be displayed in public. These constitute the highly esoteric Vajrayāna deities, represented either in fierce multi-armed forms or in sexual union with their female counterparts. The deities, such as Cakrasaṁvara/Vajravārāhī, Yogaṁvara/Jñānaḍākinī, and Hevajra/Nairātmā, relate to the highest class of esoteric Tantric texts (Anuttara Yoga Tantras) and serve as the principal deities of the secret (*āgaṁ*) shrine of the monasteries. Newar Buddhist practitioners are required to receive higher Tantric initiation to participate in the rituals of these esoteric deities, which are invariably performed in secret. This category most often includes female imagery, in which sexual union is used as the metaphor to illustrate the Tantric state of Enlightenment. This class of imagery is a mandatory component of Newar Buddhist architecture.

Monastic Architecture: Bāhā and Bahī

Newar Buddhist architecture is distinguished as *bāhā* and *bahī* institutions based on their socioreligious and structural differences. Etymologically related to the word *vihāra* (way station), they are, by definition, Buddhist monasteries where the monastic community (*saṅgha*) lives. They belong to the Buddhist caste groups of the Vajrācāryas and Śākyas. Newar Buddhist monks are not celibate but have developed a complex socioreligious system of married householders, yet they ideologically retain their ritual status as monks throughout their lives. In the contemporary context the monastic community generally reside outside the monasteries; nonetheless these institutions serve as main ceremonial centers of the community. The rituals performed at the monasteries also provide a means through which Buddhist identity is reaffirmed for the practitioners in a largely Hindu religious environment.

Structurally the *bāhā*s and *bahī*s are required to have three key components: (1) a principal stūpa, along the central axis of the courtyard that is venerated by both the lay community and the members of the monastery; (2) an exoteric shrine to the prin-

Fig. 3: Non-Tantric deity, lower-level shrine, Uku bāhā, Patan, Nepal. Photo courtesy of Dina Bangdel

cipal deity (*kvāḥpāḥ dyaḥ*) of the monastery that is the focus of daily veneration; and (3) an esoteric shrine to a Tantric deity (*āgaṁ dyaḥ*), where entrance is permitted only to initiated members. These architectural elements correlate to the rituals relating to initiation and life-cycle rites of the monastic community. The life-cycle ordination into monkhood is performed in front of the principal stūpa and the exoteric shrine, whereas the esoteric *agam* shrine is used for the higher Tantric initiation rituals.

Bahī Architecture

In terms of its membership patterns and architectural plan, the *bahī* is distinct from the *bāhā*s. Less numerous and located at the periphery of the city boundaries, *bahī* institutions are older and associated with celibate monasticism. A *bahī* is generally a two-story structure built around a quadrangular courtyard, with the main shrine wall opposite the entrance door (Fig. 1). At the center of the courtyard is the principal *caitya*; this serves as the vivifying element of the sacred architecture. The *bahī*'s exoteric shrine is usually located on the first floor, opposite the entrance wall, and houses a non-Tantric deity, such as Śākyamuni, Amitābha, Dipāṅkara, Maitreya, or Avalokiteśvara, whose worship is accessible for all Buddhist practitioners. The third mandatory component is the secret Tantric shrine, situated on the second floor. Entrance into this shrine and the rituals are restricted to the initiated members of the monastic community. The *bahī* structure and shrine facade are relatively simple, without the elaborate visual imagery present in *bāhā* architecture.

Distinctive of *bahī* architecture are the detached exoteric shrine with a circumambulatory passage, the open pillared verandah on side walls, and beyond that a series of small cell-like rooms traditionally used as residences for monks. Prototypes of this ground plan go back to the classic *vihāra* format of caves at Ajaṇṭā and Ellora in western India, indicating a structural continuity that goes back to Indian Buddhism of the fifth century A.D.

Oral tradition confirms the *bahī*s as a separate class of monastery that upholds the Śrāvakayāna path and emphasizes celibate monasticism. As a separate class of monastery, the *bahī*s are not numerous, and their members constitute only 5.4 percent of the Buddhists. *Bahī*s in Patan continue to maintain the memory of a celibate monastic institution, referring to themselves as *brahmācārya bhikṣu* (celibate monks), recalling their former status as celibate monks. Epigraphic evidence as early as the 13th century indicates the development of Newar Buddhist monastic traditions, from celibate monkhood to that of the married householder. The inscriptions referring to the *bahī*s were called "other-worldly forest-dwelling (wandering) monastery" (*nirvāṇika vanaprasta vihāra*), described as being inhabited by celibate monks, whereas *bāhā*s are referred to as "worldly Tantric monastery" (*saṁsārika tāntrika vihāra*) that housed married monks. By the 16th century, inscriptions mention married *brahmācārya bhikṣu*s, indicating that the tradition of celibate monkhood of the *bahī* had already been transformed to that of a householder monk. Dominance of Hinduism in the form of caste hierarchy is generally considered a major factor in the shift from celibate to married monasticism.

Bāhā Architecture

The rich visual imagery and distinctive plan of *bāhā* architecture reflects the ritual needs of the married householder. Whereas *bahī*s have a simple, austere appearance with minimal embellishment, *bāhā*s are elaborate, with a profusion of Mahāyāna and Vajrayāna deities represented on the shrine facade. There are over 500 *bāhā*s, and the major (*mū*) *bāhā*s are built around a quadrangular courtyard, with the entrance door opposite the shrine facade (Fig. 2). The recessed interior courtyard serves as the sacred ritual area, with numerous votive and ritual objects, such as stūpas, maṇḍalas, fire offerings, and *vajra*s, usually placed along an axis to the shrine. As in *bahī*s three components are mandatory in *bāhā* architecture, specifically, the principal *caitya*, the esoteric, and the Tantric *āgaṁ* shrines. Although there might be several votive *caitya*s in the courtyard, the *bāhā* offers special worship to one that is designated as the principal *caitya*, which is consecrated at the time of the *bāhā*'s formal establishment. Both the *bāhā* and the *bahī* structures are designed conceptually around this principal *caitya*, as it generates the

**Fig. 4: Great Stūpa, Svayambhū, Kathmandu Valley, Nepal.
Photo courtesy of Dina Bangdel**

sacred space of the monastery. This *caitya* is morphologically and symbolically identical with the Great Stūpa of Svayambhū, the most important of the Buddhist monuments in the valley. The local cosmogonic myth, the *Svayambhū Purāṇa*, establishes that Svayambhū is also the ontological source of the Newar Buddhist religion.

The main shrine of the monastery is generally a multi-story structure, richly embellished with metal repoussé works and wooden strut figures. The exoteric and esoteric shrines are demarcated in two levels. The lower level houses the non-Tantric exoteric deity, where the shrine and the main image are often lavishly embellished with jewelry, clothing, and other offerings given by the lay community (Fig. 3). The *āgaṁ* shrine most commonly is found above this, marked by the fivefold windows typical of Newar architecture. The upper stories of the shrine facade are supported by decorative struts in which popular iconographic themes include the multi-armed esoteric Buddhas from the Dharmadhātu Maṇḍala and deities associated with auspiciousness or protection, such as the offering goddesses (*Pūjā Devīs*), Pañcarakṣa goddesses, Daśakrodha Bhairava, or the Aṣṭamaṅgala Devīs. The monastery may also have subsidiary shrines to popular Buddhist deities, such as Amoghapāśa Lokeśvara; Nāsādyaḥ, the lord of dance; or Viśvakarma, the patron deity of craftsmen. A shrine to Vajrasattva is mandatory of the monasteries that have Vajrācārya members. The rich imagery of the shrine facade articulates the ideological constructs of Newar Buddhism and signifies the monastic structures as a three-dimensional Buddhist maṇḍala.

Major Iconographic Themes

Certain recurring artistic themes occur in the visual imagery, articulating the complex soteriological methodologies of Newar Buddhism. Three major iconographic themes are consistently present in the visual imagery of Newar Buddhist monasteries and are also significant to the ritual practices. These are the Great Stūpa of Svayambhū (Svayambhū Mahācaitya), the Dharmadhātu Maṇḍala, and Cakrasaṁvara Maṇḍala. These themes reflect their symbolic correlation to the structural components of Newar Buddhist monastic architecture, that is, the principal *caitya*, the exoteric shrine, and the esoteric *āgaṁ* shrine.

The Great Stūpa of Svayambhū (Fig. 4), also known as Svayambhū Dharmadhātu Mahācaitya, is the premier Buddhist monument in the Kathmandu Valley The Great Stūpa defines many features of Newar Buddhist practice as well as religious and ethnic identity. Svayambhū Mahācaitya's significance as the ontological basis of the Newar Buddhism is specifically linked with the local Buddhist cosmogonic legend. Narrated in the sacred history of the site, the *Svayambhū Purāṇa* recounts the emergence of the miraculous Self-Originated Light Form, which was later encased in the stūpa that we know today as the Great Self-Existent Stūpa (Svayambhū Mahācaitya). Svayambhū's preeminence is reiterated in monastic architecture, as the principal *caitya* in the monastery is symbolically identified with Svayambhū, the Ādi, or Primordial, Buddha of Newar Buddhism.

A second iconographic theme that emerges repeatedly in the monasteries is the meditational device of Dharmadhātu Maṇḍala, dedicated to Mañjuśrī. As the root Tantric maṇḍala of Newar Buddhism, the imagery occurs in many permutations: complete freestanding stone or a metal repoussé representation mounted on an octagonal base in strut figures or the tympanum iconography. The central deity is a form of Mañjuśrī, known as Dharmadhātu Vāgīśvara Mañjughoṣa (Speech-Lord of the Dharma-Essence). In Newar Buddhism, Mañjuśrī in this form is identical with the Ādi, or Primordial, Buddha. In this context Mañjuśrī is equated with Svayambhū Mahācaitya.

The third core iconographic component is the Cakrasaṁvara Maṇḍala, whose central figures are Cakrasaṁvara and Vajravārāhī, the archetypal deities of the Tantric *āgaṁ* shrines. Although the imagery related to this esoteric shrine is never displayed in public, the iconography related to the Cakrasaṁvara Maṇḍala is central to the highly technical Tantric meditational practices. The core iconographic themes correlate to the three structural components of Newar Buddhist monastic architecture and articulate a similar hierarchical correlation of the ritual practices.

DINA BANGDEL

See also Cave Temples and Monasteries in India and China; Celibacy: Buddhist; Images: Buddhist Perspectives; Kathmandu Valley, Nepal; Maṇḍala; Mount Meru; Nepal; Stūpa; Topography, Sacred (Buddhist); Vajrayāna Buddhism in Nepal; Visual Arts, Buddhist: Tibet

Further Reading

Bangdel, Dina, "Manifesting the Mandala: A Study of the Core Iconographic Program of Newar Buddhist Monasteries in Nepal," Ph.D. Diss., Ohio State University, 1999

Gail, Adalbert, *Klöster in Nepal: Ikonographie buddhistischer Klöster im Kathmandutal*, Graz: Akademische Druck-u. Verlagsanstalt, 1991

Gellner, David N., *Monk, Householder, and Tantric Priest: Newar Buddhism and Its Hierarchy of Ritual* (Cambridge Studies in Social and Cultural Anthropology, 84), Cambridge and New York: Cambridge University Press, 1992

Gutschow, Niels, *The Nepalese Caitya: 1500 Years of Buddhist Votive Architecture in the Kathmandu Valley* (Monograph Series/Lumbini International Research Institute, 1), Stuttgart: Menges, 1997

Kölver, Bernhard, *Re-Building a Stupa: Architectural Drawings of the Svayambhunath* (Nepalica, 5), Bonn: VGH Wissenschaftsverlag, 1992

Kooij, K.R. Van, "Iconography of the Buddhist Wood-Carvings in a Newar Monastery in Kathmandu (Chusya Baha)," *Journal of the Nepal Research Centre* 1 (1977)

Korn, Wolfgang, *The Traditional Architecture of the Kathmandu Valley* (Bibliotheca Himalayica, series 3, volume 11), Kathmandu: Ratna Pustak Bhandar, 1976

Pal, Pratapaditya, *The Arts of Nepal*, part 1: *Sculpture* (Handbuch der Orientalistik), Leiden: Brill, 1974

Pal, Pratapaditya, *The Arts of Nepal*, part 2: *Painting* (Handbuch der Orientalistik), Leiden: Brill, 1974

Pal, Pratapaditya, *Buddhist Art in Licchavi Nepal*, Bombay: Marg, 1974

Slusser, Mary S., *Nepal Mandala: A Cultural Study of the Kathmandu Valley*, 2 vols., Princeton, New Jersey: Princeton University Press, 1980

Visual Arts, Buddhist: Southeast Asia

1. Thailand and Burma (Myanmar)

A Theravāda Buddhist monastery in Thailand or Burma (Myanmar) commonly consists of a stūpa (Thai, *chedi*; Burmese, *zeidi*) and two great halls: a congregation and ordination hall (Pāli, *uposathaghara*; Thai, *ubosot* or *bot*) and an assembly hall (Pāli, *vihāra*; Thai, *wihan*). The *ubosot*, a large hall with a couple of aisles built on consecrated ground, is considered the most important building of the monastery. It houses Buddha images and accommodates the community when it assembles for religious observances.

The *wihan* is a hall similar in function and plan to the *ubosot*. Here laypeople assemble to listen to sermons and scripture readings. Small monasteries do not have *wihan*, whereas exceptionally large ones have more than one, as, for example, at Wat Chetuphon (also known as Wat Pho) in Bangkok.

The stūpa houses relics of the Buddha, pious monks, or kings. Sometimes a stūpa is filled with Buddha images, gold jewelry, and small votive imagery that monks and laypeople have offered to the temple in hope of accruing merit. The most important examples of visual art in a monastic compound are images of the Buddha. They are considered sacred and are used as objects of devotion and contemplation. Sometimes an image also exemplifies the Theravāda concept of kingship.

The interior walls of the *bot* and *wihan* of Thai and Burmese temples are often illuminated with mural paintings. Typically the murals present scenes from two popular sources: episodes from the life of the Buddha and tales from his previous incarnations (Sanskrit, *Jātakas*). In Burma these two themes are also portrayed on ceramic tiles placed in niches around temples or stūpa bases (e.g., Shwegugyi pagoda). In Thailand another popular theme is the Hindu epic *Rāmāyaṇa* (Thai, *Ramakien*), such as at the Emerald Buddha temple and Wat Pho.

Sculpture

The principal Buddha image in a temple compound in Thailand or Burma is either the one largest in size or, if it is small, the one

Gallery of Buddha images, Phra Boromathat, Chaiya, Thailand, 7th to 13th century. Photo courtesy of John C. Huntington, the Huntington Archive

placed on the highest base in the *ubosot*. It represents Śākyamuni, the historical Buddha. Buddha images are made in several media, the most frequent being wood, metal, stone, and brick covered with several layers of cement, cinnabar, lacquer, and gold. Small images are sometimes made of sandalwood, ivory, or terra cotta (produced by a press-mold technique – commonly used for votive images).

Since the 13th century a Thai Buddha image adopts one of four positions: seated, standing, walking, or reclining. Each position represents an important episode in the life of the Buddha, namely, his enlightenment, the taming of Nalagiri elephant, the descent from the Trāyastriṃśa heaven (where the Buddha went to teach his deceased mother), and his death (*Mahāparinirvāṇa*), respectively. The most common representation of the main Buddha image in extant temples in Thailand and Burma portrays the Buddha seated with his legs crossed in *virāsana* (Thai, *khat smat rap*) and his hands performing the touching-the-earth gesture (*bhūmisparśamudrā*), which represents the moment when Śākyamuni Buddha called the Earth goddess to witness his enlightenment under the Bodhi Tree at Bodh Gayā. The *bhūmisparśamudrā*, with the right hand turned palm downward on the right knee and the left placed palm upward on the lap, has been popularly depicted since the Pala period of India (8th to 12th century). Besides *bhūmisparśamudrā*, another popular hand gesture is *dhyānamudrā*, representing meditation, with both hands placed on the lap with the right hand palm upward on top of the left.

In Thailand the most important Buddha image, for over two centuries, has been Phra Kaeo Morakot (full name Phra Phutthamahāmaṇīratnapaṭimākon, meaning "the great gem statue of the Buddha"), commonly known as the Emerald Buddha. It is situated high up on a gilded altar designed to represent the traditional Hindu aerial chariot (*busabok*) in the *ubosot* of Wat Phra Si Ratana Satsadaram (the Emerald Buddha temple). The Phra Kaeo is rather small and plain. It is seated in *virāsana* with hands in the meditation gesture. As a symbolic enactment of the change of seasons, thrice yearly the king cleans and replaces its heavily adorned costume with an intricate gold robe and colorful jewelry and an elaborate gold hairpiece (for the winter and rainy season) or a crown (for summer). Phra Kaeo Morakot was taken from Vientiane, Laos, in 1778 by General Chakri, who later became King Rama I of the current Thai dynasty.

Generally, in front of the main Buddha image a number of small-size images, in various positions, are placed on lower bases. This is usual in temples in all regions of Thailand and Burma. Note that in Thailand only an odd number of images will be present, as it is believed that Śākyamuni Buddha is always present, making the true number even.

As at Phra Kaeo Morakot in Bangkok, the Mahāmuni (Great Lord) Buddha image is central to contemporary religious life in Mandalay, Burma. The image was created as the palladium of an Arakanese king, Candrasuriya, who is said to have lived at the time of the historical Buddha. The image was originally enshrined in Arakan, a region in lower Burma that is now mainly Muslim. In 1784 Burmese King Bodawpaya conquered Arakan and took the Mahāmuni image to his capital in upper Burma, Amarapura, now known as Mandalay. More than 12 feet tall, the image is made of brass and stands on a block more than six feet high. The Mahāmuni Buddha is seated in *virāsana* with hands in *bhūmisparśamudrā*. It is crowned and clad in royal style with Brahmanic cords and regalia crossing its chest. Every morning at the break of dawn, the face of the Mahāmuni image is washed in an elaborate ritual that attracts large numbers of ethnically diverse local and transregional pilgrims to the temple.

Mural Paintings and Reliefs

Scenes from the life of Śākyamuni Buddha and *Jātaka* themes have been the subject of Buddhist sculpture and painting throughout Asia. Mural paintings are not merely ornamental: their primary function is to teach. Episodes from the Buddha's life are significant because they represent the inspirational story that is the very model for overcoming attachment and ignorance and the attainment of enlightenment. Because of the *ubosot*'s importance, the interior walls are frequently decorated with painting. The murals are arranged along the walls in a virtually unchanging order dictated by the position of the principal image near the far end of the aisle, generally facing to the east (which is the usual orientation of a Thai temple). Typically above the main door(s) of the *ubosot*, opposite the main image, is a painting of the "Victory over Māra and His Army." Here Śākyamuni Buddha is seated under the Bodhi Tree with his hands in the touching-the-earth gesture (*bhūmisparśamudrā*). Bhūmidevī, the Earth Goddess, is shown underneath him holding her hair in the position of flooding the Māra army.

The wall behind the main Buddha image ordinarily depicts the Buddhist cosmology (*triphuṃ*), which lays out the structure of the world, including the heavenly realm and the underworld. The stories depicted on the lateral walls between the windows are adorned with episodes from the life of the Buddha or *Jātaka* themes. As we have seen, the most commonly depicted episodes of the Buddha's life are the four great events: birth, enlightenment, first sermon, and *Mahāparinirvāṇa*. Other popular scenes are the great departure, the miracle of Śrāvasti, the taming of the Nalagiri elephant, and the offering of the monkey.

Depending on the version of the source text, there are between 547 and 550 *Jātaka* stories of previous lives of the Buddha in both animal and human forms. In Thailand the last ten human lives of the Buddha (namely, Temiya, Mahajanaka, Sama, Nimi, Mahosadha, Bhuridatta, Canda-Kumara, Narada, Vidhura-Pandita, and Vessantara) are among the most popular to be portrayed, whether in mural paintings or on smaller objects, such as cloth banners, lacquerware, sūtra cabinets, and illuminated manuscripts. The Vessantara *Jātaka* is considered the most important and is placed most prominently on the wall.

In some temple compounds episodes from the *Rāmāyaṇa* epic are depicted on the gallery walls surrounding the compound (e.g., the Emerald Buddha temple) or on small low-relief panels placed on the walls around the main *wihan* (e.g., Wat Pho). Rāma, the hero of the *Rāmāyaṇa* epic, is a reincarnation of the god Viṣnu, whose duty is to preserve the Universe. Rāma exemplifies the role of the pious king in Southeast Asian countries such as Thailand, Cambodia, and Indonesia.

M.L. Pattaratorn Chirapravati

See also Bangkok, Thailand; Burma (Myanmar); Festivals, Buddhist; Gestures, Buddhist; Novices, Theravādin Rituals for; Stūpa; Thailand

Further Reading

Boisselier, Jean, *Heritage of Thai Sculpture*, New York and Tokyo: Weatherhill, 1975

Boisselier, Jean, *Thai Painting*, translated by Janet Seligman, Tokyo, New York, and San Francisco: Kodansha International, 1976

Schober, Julian, "In the Presence of the Buddha: Ritual Veneration of the Burmese Mahāmuni Image," in *Sacred Biography in the Buddhist Traditions of South and Southeast Asia*, edited by Schober, Honolulu: University of Hawaii Press, 1997

Strachan, Paul, *Pagan: Art and Architecture of Old Burma*, Whiting Bay: Kiscadale, 1989

Woodward, Hiram W., Jr., *The Sacred Sculptures of Thailand: The Alexander B. Griswold Collection, the Walters Art Gallery*, Bangkok: River Books, 1997

Wray, E., C. Rosenfield, D. Bailey, and J. Wray, *Ten Lives of the Buddha: Siamese Temple Paintings and Jataka Tales*, New York and Tokyo: Weatherhill, 1979

2. *Vietnam*

In Vietnam, Buddhist temples are regarded as the hearts of their communities – the cultural centers and the social meeting places. People gather at temples not only for religious practices but also for annual festivals. Geographically the whole country is divided into three parts, each with its own historical and religious backgrounds. Thus, Buddhist temples were also influenced by dynastic periods and specific geographic locations. Temples and monasteries in the three regions – northern, central, and southern – have a distinctive architectural layout, and a number of Buddhist and non-Buddhist deities are honored in the temples. This article discusses the architectural layout, some visual aspects of major deities honored in the temples, and the religious functions.

In the northern region ancient temples are typically oriented toward the south. Main architectural units are laid out symmetrically on a central axis, creating a balanced order. Temples usually consist of an entrance gate, a bell tower, an anterior hall, a central hall, a Buddha hall, a patriarch hall, and a holy mother hall. Two extended corridors enclose the temple's main compound. The abbot's quarters and resident monks' facilities are located in the back, nestled conveniently close to the kitchen, storage, a well, bathrooms, and latrines. There is neither a special hall designated for lectures, meditation, ordination nor a single building dedicated to a particular deity. Overall the divisions of temples are carefully planned to involve the lay community in ritual chanting and devotional practice. All daily services, sacred rituals, ceremonies, and other religious activities take place in three core buildings – the anterior, central, and Buddha halls – which are sometimes referred to as "the Three-Jewel Halls." These three main buildings are considered the religious and architectural "backbone" of the temples.

Furthermore, all major Buddhist deities are enshrined in the core buildings. In the anterior hall are honored sculptures of protecting deities. There are two large Dharma Guardians. One commonly known as a threatening deity has a red face to ward off the evil force, and the other with a benevolent face is believed to protect the good. Ānanda, Buddha's personal attendant, here represented as the Holy Monk, is venerated by the daily ritual of feeding hungry ghosts. Anāthapiṇḍaka, the Buddha's major lay patron, inspires the worshipers about the significance of patronage. Finally the earth deity is worshiped as the protector of land.

The Buddha hall is adorned with statues of major Buddhist deities. They are arranged on the central altar in five tiers. Situated on the uppermost tier are images of the Three-Period Buddhas in gestures of meditation, touching the earth, and teaching. These gestures vary in the sculptures of some temples. The second tier is occupied by images of Buddha Śākyamuni holding a lotus flower in his right hand to indicate that he has transmitted the sacred teaching to Mahākāśyapa. In some temples the statue is flanked by Mahākāśyapa and Ānanda; in other temples the Buddha is attended by Mañjuśrī and Samantabhadra. On the third tier is the Pure Land triad, Amitābha, seated in mediation at the center with Avalokiteśvara and Mahāsthāmaprāpta. The fourth tier singly honors Cundi, a multi-armed form of Avalokiteśvara. The lowermost tier is devoted to the Baby Buddha surrounded by nine dragons and attended by Indian gods, Brahma on the right and Indra on the left. These two deities are depicted in Chinese costumes and often mistaken as the Daoist gods of Northern and Southern Stars. To the right (east) side of the hall is a motherly image of Avalokiteśvara holding a child, popularly known as the Bodhisattva Bestowing a Child. In some ancient temples, such as Tay Phuong and Thay, 16 sculptures of arhats are enshrined in the corridor halls, and stone or wooden images of powerful patrons are honored in the patriarch hall.

Some temples in the northern region have a hall dedicated to the Holy Mother and indigenous deities. Their statues, as images of princesses, are dressed in regal clothes and adorned with artificial jewels. The principal altar in the central hall is adorned with four offerings – candles/light, fresh flowers, fruit, and water. Interestingly, wine and nonvegetarian foods are offered in the holy-mother hall when laypeople gather to perform mediumistic rituals, in which certain spirits borrow a living person's body for teaching.

Temples in the central region, especially in the ancient capital Hue, are known for their beautiful gardens. Well situated in scenic landscapes, temples in Hue usually have a peaceful atmosphere. Only a few bronze sculptures of Buddhas and Bodhisattvas are honored in the main hall. Most numerous are images of the Buddhas of the Three Periods and Śākyamuni Buddha, such as in the Thien Mu and Bao Quoc temples. Other modern temples, such as Tu Dam, have at the main altar only a single image of Śākyamuni, with the right hand in the gesture of fearlessness. Large scenes of the Buddha's five important events – birth, great departure, enlightenment, first sermon, and *parinirvāṇa* – are carved on the upper front walls of the temples. They remind the followers of the Buddha's life. Many ancient temple gardens are dotted with tomb-stūpas of deceased abbots. Compared with the central altars of the temples in the northern region, temples in Hue are less crowded with images.

Buddhist temples in the southern region are more modernized. In the typical temples the nucleus is the main hall, which dominates the entire compound. A large sculpture of Śākyamuni Buddha seated in meditation, underneath a huge painting/tableau of the Bodhi Tree, is the central devotional object. The scene reminds devotees of the Buddha's moment of enlightenment. Followers treat the image respectfully as the living Buddha. In daily practice monks circumambulate the image three times clockwise. The painting wall divides off from the main hall a small part used as the Patriarch altar. Here a painting of Bodhidharma carrying a shoe on a staff is venerated. Pictures of deceased eminent monks and founding abbots are also honored on the altar. Overall the main hall is used for daily chanting, special ceremonies, Dharma lectures, and other religious events. In some well-known temples with two stories, such as Xa Loi and Vinh Nghiem, the ground floor serves as the lecture hall, whereas the upper floor is used for honoring the sculptures of Buddha and Bodhisattvas.

In the southern region the main hall is focused only on the principal image on the central altar. In addition to a large sculpture of Buddha Śākyamuni, a pair of Avalokiteśvara are honored on the right and Kṣitgarbha on the left or of Mahākāśyapa on the right and Ānanda on the left. The images of the two popular Bodhisattvas – Avalokiteśvara, believed to assist the living, and Kṣitigarbha, believed to save the dead from hells – convey the most powerful religious effects.

The most noticeable feature of the southern temples is an outdoor statue of Avalokiteśvara, standing in a lotus or on a dragon's head emerged from a pond or enshrined in a pavilion. The statue is known either as the White Robed or Southern Sea Quan Am.

In general, Vietnamese Buddhist sculptures express a synthetic type of Buddhism, ranging from devotional Pure Land through the meditative dynamics of Chan to esoteric rituals and to indigenous belief. Pure Land imagery is specifically portrayed in sculptures of Amitābha. Chan Buddhist aspects are represented by Śākyamuni Buddha, the 18 arhats, and the portrait sculptures of Bodhidharma and other Chan masters. Tantric practice is seen in the images of the One Thousand-Armed Avalokiteśvara, and Ānanda feeding the hungry ghosts. Indigenous beliefs are presented through images of the holy mothers and local deities.

TRIAN NGUYEN

See also Chan/Zen: Vietnam; Deities, Buddhist; Gardens: Buddhist Perspectives; Gestures, Buddhist; Vietnam; Worship Space: Buddhist Perspectives

Further Reading

Bezacier, Louis, *L'Art Viêtnamien*, Paris: Éditions de l'Union Française, 1955

Ha Van Tan, *Chùa Viêt Nam = Buddhist Temples in Vietnam*, Hanoi: Social Sciences Publishing House, 1993

Trian Nguyen, "Ninh Phuc Temple: A Study of Seventeenth-Century Buddhist Sculpture in Vietnam," Ph.D. Diss., University of California, Berkeley, 1999

Visual Arts, Buddhist: Tibet

Introduction

"Form is emptiness; emptiness also is form. Emptiness is no other than form; form is no other than emptiness."

– *Heart Sūtra of Transcendent Knowledge*

In order to understand the visual arts of Tibetan Buddhism and the way in which those arts relate to the Buddhist monastic community, one must first consider Tibetan Buddhist views of art and its relationship to basic religious presuppositions – in particular to the *trikāya* system. Tibetan Buddhism maintains that there are three (*tri*) bodies (or *kāya*) that comprise the whole of existence. The Dharmakāya, or Dharma body, is considered the adamantine, or unchanging, nature of enlightened mind. It is formless and often referred to as the absolute state of *śūnyatā*, or emptiness. From this emptiness, which is deeply imbued with compassion, emerges the Sambhogakāya, or Bliss body, that radiates the luminous, blissful nature of *śūnyatā*. The third body, the Nirmāṇakāya, is the Form body and traditionally is considered to be the body of the teacher. More generally, however, it is understood as the form manifestation of all things. These three bodies are understood to exist in a fluid, dynamic relationship that is ever changing and never static. In Tibetan paintings, for example of the Kagyü and Sakya lineages, the open, expansive quality of the unknowable Dharmakāya is represented as a Sambhogakāya manifestation of Vajradhara, the Ādi (or Primordial) Buddha. His deep blue color represents the absolute clarity and the skylike expansiveness of the Dharmakāya (Fig. 1). Such standard iconographic forms are presented in the art and are considered to be the form, or *nirmāṇakāya* representation, of absolute emptiness or *śūnyatā*. In the broader sense, then, art, like every manifestation of life, is form that is manifest by enlightened mind and has the vibrant, luminous, and transparent qualities of Sambhogakāya. On this level art is an expression of emptiness as form, and involvement with it helps one to realize the transparent and vibrant nature of existence (for further discussion of Tibetan Buddhist understandings of art, see Rhie and Thurman, 1991).

The relationship between art and the *trikāya* is fundamental to Buddhist practice and informs the lives of monastics, temporary monastics, and the laity, whether they are technical or purely devotional practitioners. However, the depth to which an individual understands this relationship will vary, depending on his or her level of practice.

Historical Role of Monastics in Preserving and Propagating Visual Art

Monastics have played a principal role in the spread of Buddhism throughout the world. The visual arts – an integral component of Buddhism – express the practices and teachings that made their way from northern India and expanded throughout Asia from at least the eighth century. Not surprisingly, then, monastics have played an integral role in the migration, preservation, and development of the practices and teachings that are reflected in the art as well as in the artistic forms and stylistic expressions.

The extant remains corresponding to the First Propagation of Buddhism in Tibet (c. first quarter of the seventh century to the mid–ninth century) are limited in number and relatively uncohesive in style and form. However, works from the Second Propagation (mid– to late tenth century), when studied with extant Tibetan and Indian monastic histories, serve as visual records of monastic migration and the technical practices carried with them. During the Second Propagation, at the behest of would-be students from other lands, great teachers, such as the Indian Paṇḍit Ātīsa, left well-established centers of learning (e.g., Vikramśīla and Nālandā) in what is today eastern India and Bangladesh. Tibetan peoples were no exception, and sought-after teachers from India brought with them the practice traditions as well as the related iconography and aesthetics found in Tibetan art to the present day.

Stylistic categorization of Tibetan art during the early years of the Second Propagation, which corresponds to the development of the gSar ma, or New Schools (three of the four major lineages of Tibetan Buddhism recognized today), is complex. However, despite its complexity, Shar mthun – the style following that of eastern India – influence is evident throughout this period. Fig. 2 shows a detail of Śyāma Tārā from an *Aṣṭasāhasrikā Prajñāpāramitā* palm-leaf manuscript (Sanskrit and Tibetan inscriptions on this manuscript indicate that the book was written by a scribe from Nālandā monastery and traces the manuscript's ownership lineage, indicating that it had been passed from Indian to Tibetan hands; see Huntington, 1990), probably from eastern India or Bangladesh, dating from about the mid–12th century. A Tibetan thangka (Fig. 3), also of Śyāma

Fig. 1: Vajradhara, thangka, cotton support with opaque mineral pigments in water-based (collagen) binder, 23.25 x 32.75 inches, indeterminate region, c. 16th century. The Rezk Collection of Tibetan Art, Southern Alleghenies Museum of Art, #: 94.003.
Photo courtesy of John C. Huntington, the Huntington Archive

Fig. 2: ***Aṣṭasāhasrikā Prajñāpāramitā*** **text, detail of Śyāma Tārā, water-based pigments on talipot palm leaf, approximately 2 3/8 x 22 1/4 inches. The Asia Society, New York, Mr. and Mrs. John D. Rockefeller 3rd Collection (1987.1). Photo courtesy of John C. Huntington, the Huntington Archive**

Tārā and dating from the same period, shows noticeable stylistic similarities. Although the palm-leaf rendering bears nothing of the Tibetan work's detail and elegance, the stylistic relationship between the two is revealed in the rounded treatment of the throne bolster and slightly oval-shaped halo behind the figures' heads. Moreover the lobed rendering of the abdomen and general stylistic treatment is similar in both pieces. Huntington has proposed that certain architectural features, such as the angled roof edges, are Nepali conventions and might indicate that Tibetans commissioned Newari painters to create this piece in an eastern Indian style or that Tibetans were already working in mixed styles by this point (Huntington, 1990). In either case this painting, which shows clear evidence of stylistic propagation, was related to the monastic community. This fact is betrayed by the monk figure located to the proper right of Tārā's outstretched hand, which makes the gesture of *abhayamudra* and grants the absence of fear. Moreover an inscription on the back makes direct reference to one of the five monastic precepts, stating that "[a] monk does no harm to another" (Huntington, 1990). Therefore, from before the 11th to the 12th century, eastern India, with its vibrant monastic centers and fully developed artistic traditions, served as one of three primary artistic sources for Tibetans (Kashmir and China were others), and Tibetan monastics facilitated this relationship by commissioning works intended to be rendered in the eastern Indian or Shar mthun style.

By the late 12th to early 13th century, Muslim conquerors, who displayed little tolerance toward Buddhists, had established control over eastern India. When possible, monastics fleeing India carried with them texts and works of art that served as stylistic and iconographic guides. These works were often paintings that could be rolled up and transported. Metal sculptures, which were more difficult to move, were buried in hordes in an attempt to hide the images and prevent them from being melted down. As bearers of artwork and authorities of codified iconographic traditions, monastics played a significant role in transmitting Buddhist art from eastern India to the Tibetan region.

With the loss of principal Indian centers of learning and artistic schools, Tibetan Buddhists turned to the Newars, the indigenous people of Nepal, with whom they already had a long history of cultural, economic, and social trade, for the production of art. Although Buddhism was known in Nepal long before the 12th century and there is significant evidence that Newar Buddhists had artistic traditions distinguishable from that of eastern India, Tibetan monks (and lay patrons) often requested that the works be created in eastern Indian styles. To fulfill the

Fig. 3: Śyāma Tārā, also known as Aṣṭamahabhaya Tārā and Khadirivani Tārā, Tibet, c. mid–12th to early 13th century, water-based pigments on cotton, height: 20.5 inches, width: 17.25 inches. The Cleveland Museum of Art.
Photo courtesy of John C. Huntington, the Huntington Archive

needs of the Tibetan patrons, many Newari artists, already conversant with Indian art traditions, actively accepted these commissions and traveled with monks to Tibet to create monasteries and train Tibetan artists. An exemplar of these relationships is that of the Newari artist Anige and the Tibetan Sakya monk 'Phags pa. In 1269 Mongol Emperor Kublai Khan ordered 'Phags pa to build a golden stūpa in Tibet. It was the Sakya monk who selected Anige to work on the stūpa, a gesture that helped launch Anige's career, which culminated in his role as the minister of craftsmen in the Mongol courts. To this day Tibetan lamas continue to commission religious paintings and sculptures from Newari artists, a commission that usually includes a specified iconography and artistic style.

Other foreign artistic traditions, prevailing local styles, and indigenous belief systems also influenced the development of Tibetan Buddhist visual arts. Monastics often played key roles in the integration of these traditions, styles, and belief systems into Buddhist methodologies. As Buddhism became established in Tibet, monastics were often asked to deal with meddlesome local deities who caused havoc, and sometimes went so far as to prevent the building of monasteries. Great adepts, many of whom were monastics, subdued these deities and converted them to be protectors of the Dharma. Fig. 4 shows the great Indian teacher Padmasambhava (also known as Guru Rinpoche and Padmakara), who was invited by Tibetan King Trison Detsen to subdue local petulant deities. These deities, once converted, often appear in the art, usually in the bottom registers of paintings. For example, dPal ldan lha mo, a local Tibetan deity converted into a major Buddhist protectress, can be seen to the lower proper right of the refuge tree in Fig. 8.

Tibetan Buddhist monastics contributed to the preservation, propagation, and development of artistic traditions in a variety of ways. As providers of the Buddhist teachings and holders or sustainers of major lineage traditions, monastics acted as liaisons and transmitters of iconographic forms and artistic styles from one region to another. Further, by patronizing artists working in or familiar with eastern Indian stylistic traditions, as well as by commissioning stylistically predetermined artwork and by incorporating both traditional and indigenous elements into the practice and art, monastics played a significant role in dictating the evolution of the visual art traditions.

Today Tibetan Buddhist monks and nuns continue to play an important role in the propagation of artistic styles and, when commissioning a work, will often give the artist pictures or drawing books that guide the creation process. When ordering works, monks are careful to communicate the final destination of a commissioned piece. This is especially important because the quality, iconographic correctness, and overall beauty of an artwork – which is intended to reflect the absolute fluid nature of the *trikāya* – is given greater consideration when it will be used within a practice context or monastic setting.

Monastics as Creators of Art

In Tibetan Buddhism monastics both commission works of art and engage in the creation of the art as part of their practice.

Fig. 4: Padmasambhava, thangka, cotton support with opaque mineral pigments in water-based (collagen) binder exterior, 27.5 x 49.75 inches, interior 23.5 x 34.25 inches, Tibet, indeterminate region, c. 19th century. The Rezk Collection of Tibetan Art, Southern Alleghenies Museum of Art.
Photo courtesy of John C. Huntington, the Huntington Archive

Among the art forms that monastics undertake are sculptures, whether made from mud plaster, wood, concrete, stone, or metal that is largely copper based with additions of tin and zinc; wall paintings; thangkas, i.e. paintings on cloth usually created using mineral or vegetable pigments on a cotton or silk ground; and ephemera, often created for single use such as a festival or ritual.

Generally art created by monastics is not created for "art's sake." More often it is made for ritual and meditational use, and the creation of art is often understood to be part of such practices. For example, the famous Tibetan sand maṇḍalas, a popular and increasingly well known form of art, are practiced by monastic communities (Fig. 5). The Gelukpa sect, headed by the Dalai Lama, is the most well known community to practice this tradition. Sand maṇḍalas are constructed from colored sand that is

Fig. 5: Sand maṇḍala, Spituk Monastery, Ladakh, India.
Photo courtesy of John C. Huntington, the Huntington Archive

placed into hand-size metal funnels, fashioned with ridges on the side. The funnels are rubbed, and the sand is gently poured onto a flat surface that contains an outline of the maṇḍala being created. Sand maṇḍalas, like maṇḍalas painted on Tibetan thangkas, are two-dimensional representations of three-dimensional structures and are understood to be the gem-encrusted palace of Mount Meru, the center of every Buddhist universe.

Monastics create sand maṇḍalas as part of their mindfulness practice and consider their efforts to be compassionate offerings for the well-being of all sentient beings. Once created the maṇḍala becomes the center of ritual practice, and the monastics invoke the "deities" of the maṇḍala, including the five Sambhogakāya Jina Buddhas, their consorts (or *prajnas*), and other protective deities. When the ritual is concluded, the "deities" are asked to leave the maṇḍala, and one of the monks draws several lines through it using his *vajra* (a ritual implement). This practice has proven especially disheartening to many Western museum curators who regularly request to preserve these works of art, although with little success. The creation and subsequent destruction of such artworks is an overt expression of the Buddhist belief in the impermanence of all phenomena, in contrast to the more Western understanding of works of art as hallmarks for posterity. The creation of other art forms that quickly disappear, such as yak butter sculpture (Fig. 6), serve as a further reminder of the impermanent nature of all things. As the butter melts, the notion that all things are transient and ever changing becomes visually apparent.

Monastics in the Art

Great teachers and adepts, many of whom were monastics, constitute one of the most common subject matters in Tibetan art. Appearing in both painting and sculpture, their presence in the art often functions on several different levels. For example, paintings and sculptures of teachers can serve as a reminder to the practitioner of his or her refuge in the three jewels of Buddhism (Buddha, Dharma, and Sangha). Representations of teachers might also function as a visual reference to a particular teaching or important event. Works depicting monastics might also acknowledge a teacher's role as a lineage holder or depict an individual as an exemplar – one who has attained certain perfections, such as an arhat.

Images of Śākyamuni, the historical Buddha, great teacher, and establisher of the monastic community during his lifetime (sixth century B.C.), are among the most frequently seen representations of monastics in art (Fig. 7). In the Tibetan context, where the lineage traditions are well established, root gurus and other teachers also regularly appear. For example, Fig. 8 shows a refuge tree, at the center of which is the great Gelukpa teacher, Tsong Kalpa. The presence of Tsong Kalpa in the center of the refuge tree, with an image of the Buddha at the center of his heart/mind, expresses the unbroken lineage of the teachings. The teacher is respected by the disciple on a level befitting that of the awakened teacher par excellence, Śākyamuni Buddha. Simultaneously this work also refers to the community of practitioners (that create the treelike structure) and the teachings, or Dharma, that were transmitted from this enlightened being.

Fig. 9 shows as the central figure the Indian Paṇḍit Gāyadhāra, an important teacher of the Sakya order, and expresses the teacher's role as part of an unbroken lineage tradition. Gāyadhāra makes the *vitarkamudrā* teaching gesture of discourse with his right hand and holds a text resting in his lap with his left hand. The teaching lineage and the manifestation of the maṇḍala at the time of a specific religious discourse are expressed through the painting's composition. At the top center is Vajradhara, the adamantine, primordial Buddha who is understood to generate the maṇḍala and serves as the source of the teachings. The majority of the figures that surround Gāyadhāra

Fig. 6: Yak butter sculpture, made at Kumbum Monastery, Qinghai, China.
Photo courtesy of John C. Huntington, the Huntington Archive

Fig. 7: Śākyamuni Buddha, Tibet, c. second half of 11th or early 12th century, copper alloy with silver and copper inlays, height: 5 5/8 inches, width: 4 1/4 inches, diameter: 2 1/2 inches. The Asia Society, New York, Mr. and Mrs. John D. Rockefeller 3rd Collection (1979.89). Photo courtesy of John C. Huntington, the Huntington Archive

are clearly labeled and include teachers such as Sarāhā and Āryadeva (located in the upper register directly to the right of Vajradhara). The deities, such as Guhyasamāja Akṣobhya, Amitāyus, and Mañjuśrī, are located within the ring of teachers and refer to initiations or teachings that are part of the lineage tradition (Rhie and Thurman, 1991).

Monasteries also serve as physical expressions of Tibetan Buddhist theory and philosophies. The Potala Palace, former seat of the Dalai Lama and the political and spiritual center of Tibet, is a clear example of the relationship between architecture and Buddhist views of the nature of reality. Potala Palace is formed as a maṇḍalic structure that is simultaneously understood to be Mount Meru, or the center of a Buddhist world (*loka*). Fig. 10 shows the bodhisattva Avalokiteśvara in his Ekadasamukha (11-headed) form as the central figure. Bodhisattvas are compassionate beings who vow to forgo their own *parinirvāṇa* (final cessation) until all sentient beings have attained enlightenment. The Dalai Lama is understood to be an incarnation of Avalokiteśvara – a relationship reiterated visually in this painting that depicts Avalokiteśvara as emanator of Potalaka Paradise. The painting also expresses the *trikāya*, showing

Fig. 8: Tsong Kalpa and the Gelukpa Refuge Tree, Eastern Tibet or Central Regions, late 18th to early 19th century, thangka, water-based pigments on linen, 53 x 37 7/8 inches. Mead Art Museum, Amherst College, Gift of Mrs. George L. Hamilton (1952.25). Photo courtesy of John Bigelow Taylor

Fig. 9: Indian Paṇḍit Gāyadhāra, Guru of Sakya Order, Central Regions, Tibet, probably Tsang, second half of 16th century, thangka, water-based pigments on cotton, 31 x 26 inches. The Zimmerman Family Collection, in Rhie and Thurman, *Wisdom and Compassion* (1991). Photo courtesy of John Bigelow Taylor

Fig. 10: Ekadasamukha ("11-Headed") Avalokiteśvara in Potalaka Paradise thangka, cotton support with opaque mineral pigments in water-based (collagen) binder, 26 x 39.5 inches, painted area only Central Tibet, c. 18th or 19th century, indeterminate style. The Rezk Collection of Tibetan Art, Southern Alleghenies Museum of Art.
Photo courtesy of John C. Huntington, the Huntington Archive

Fig. 11: Cakrasaṁvara and Vajravarahi, 20th century. George Hibbard Collection.
Photo courtesy of John C. Huntington, the Huntington Archive

Sarvāvid Vairocana (Dharmakāya) in the structure's top tier, Amitābha Buddha (Sambhogakāya) directly below him, and Avalokiteśvara (Nirmāṇakāya) as the differentiated form manifestation (see "Ekadashamukha Avalokiteshvara," by Chaya Chandrasekhar, at *http://kaladarshan.arts.ohio-state.edu/exhib/sama/bodh/pgs/T1025.html*). The iteration of paradise realms and other Buddha *loka* in monasteries is also accomplished through the use of elaborate wall paintings that depict key iconographic elements of the realm.

Monastic Initiation and Art

Monastic initiation may involve the linking of the practitioner with a deity, called an *iṣṭadevatā* (chosen deity), through a *samāya* (vow) bond. Some initiations might be part of a lineage tradition's tantric path. One of the most well known Vajrayāna or tantric initiations is that of Cakrasaṁvara, and depictions of this deity are found throughout Tibetan art. Fig. 11 shows the deep blue Cakrasaṁvara in sexual union with his red female consort Vajravarahi, symbolizing the union of *upaya* and *prajna*, or skillful means and transcendent knowledge, into *śūnyatā*, or absolute enlightenment.

Other initiations may be more specifically related to the practitioner's individual path toward enlightenment. In such cases a deity to whom the practitioner is bound might express the practitioner's basic nature or energy. *Iṣṭadevatā*s are generally selected by the teacher (who might or might not be a member of the monastic community) rather than by the practitioner. Following initiation the practitioner might obtain a print, painting, or sculpture of the initiation deity to aid in the visualization process – an activity central to advanced, technical tantric Buddhist practices.

Monasteries as Recipients of Art

Monasteries are often recipients of art. Following an initiation, a practitioner might present an image of the *iṣṭadevatā*, in the form of a painting or sculpture, to a monastery as an offering to the *saṅgha*. Laity and monastics also make offerings of visual art to monasteries to commemorate a special occasion or to accrue merit for a loved one. Tibetan monasteries that have remained undisturbed by violence and theft often contain huge collections of these offerings, and many of the great Tibetan works found in private and public collections today were originally created as offerings to monasteries.

These expressions of generosity are an integral aspect of *dāna* (giving), which is associated with accruing merit (*puṇya*) and central to Buddhism throughout the world. Inscriptions revealing the donor's name and the reason for the donation are often located on the back of a work of art. More prominent identifications often appear in the lower registers of paintings, where donor figures (or the individual who took the initiation) might have themselves included in a painting (Fig. 1).

JANICE M. GLOWSKI

See also Bodhisattva; Deities, Buddhist; Lhasa, Tibet; Liturgy: Buddhist; Maṇḍala; Manuscript Production: Buddhist; Mount Meru; Nālandā, India; Stūpa; Tibetan Lineages; Visual Arts, Buddhist: Nepal; Worship Space: Buddhist Perspectives

Further Reading

Huntington, Susan L., and John C. Huntington, *Leaves from the Bodhi Tree: The Art of Pala India (8th–12th Centuries) and Its International Legacy: The Dayton Art Institute, Dayton, Ohio, 11 November 1989 to 14 January 1990*, Dayton, Ohio: Dayton Art Institute, 1990

Pal, Pratapaditya, *Art of Tibet: A Catalogue of the Los Angeles County Museum of Art Collection*, Los Angeles and Berkeley: Los Angeles County Museum of Art in association with the University of California Press, 1983; expanded edition, 1990

Rhie, Marylin M., and Robert A.F. Thurman, *Wisdom and Compassion: The Sacred Art of Tibet*, London: Thames and Hudson, and New York: Asian Art Museum of San Francisco and Tibet House in association with Abrams, 1991; expanded edition, 1996

Roerich, George N., editor, *The Blue Annals* (Royal Asiatic Society of Bengal, Monograph Series, volume 7), 2 vols., Calcutta: Royal Asiatic Society of Bengal, 1949; 2nd edition, Delhi: Motilal Banarsidass, 1976

Visual Arts, Eastern Christian: Painting

The form of visual art most characteristic of the Christian East is the icon, from the Greek word *eikon*, meaning "image." Usually painted on wooden panels, icons depict Christ, the Virgin Mary, saints, and scenes from biblical narrative. Iconographic representations can also be made from a wide variety of media, such as carved wood or ivory, enamel, or mosaic.

The tradition of icon painting and veneration is identified especially with those Eastern Christian traditions that find their roots in the Byzantine Church (the Balkans, Georgia, and Russia) and is tightly interwoven with the history and spirituality of Eastern Christian monasticism. Monastics were among the staunchest defenders of icons during the iconoclastic controversies in eighth- and ninth-century Byzantium; monastics contributed to the establishment of icon veneration as a central feature of the Eastern Orthodox Church's profession of faith. In addition, in their composition and artistic style, icons reflect a vision of the Christian life that is associated with the efforts of desert ascetics to participate in that life. Accordingly icons are central both to the private contemplative life of individual monastics and, together with frescoes, to the corporate liturgical life of monastic communities.

Art historians have traced some of the stylistic roots of Christian iconography back to late antiquity, to Egyptian funerary art, to the Roman cult of the emperor, as well as to painted panels of gods and goddesses from the Greek mystery religions. In large part because of the widespread destruction of icons during the Byzantine iconoclastic controversies in the eighth and ninth centuries, relatively few icons from before this period have been preserved. Most of the earliest surviving icons are found in the monastery of St. Catherine on Mount Sinai. It is only from the 13th century that considerable numbers of icons are known from various parts of the Orthodox world: the Balkan countries, Russia, and the Near East. However, Orthodox Christians cite the writings of such well-known monastics as Athanasius (c. 296–373), bishop of Alexandria; Basil of Caesarea (c. 330–379); Gregory of Nyssa (c. 330–c. 395); and John Chrysostom (c. 347–407) as testimony to their widespread use in earlier centuries. Despite the growing use of icons following the adoption of Christianity as the religion of the Roman state, icon veneration also had its opponents. Backed in part by the biblical prohibition against the use of "graven images" (Ex. 20:4) and in part by Neoplatonic and Origenist teachings, figures such as Eusebius (c. 260–c. 340), bishop of Caesarea, questioned the possibility of even "delineating" an image of Christ, let alone the propriety of venerating it.

These coexisting pro- and anti-iconic tendencies in Byzantine Christianity flared dramatically during two periods in the eighth (726–787) and ninth century (813–842), forcing iconophiles to articulate a coherent rationale for the use of icons. During these periods of unrest, both of which were instigated mainly by Iconoclastic emperors, conflicts over differing theological visions underlying the religious use of images were complicated by the intricacies of Byzantine imperial and ecclesiastical politics as well as by broader cultural, social, and economic factors, all of which have been addressed extensively by modern scholarship. Despite often diverse interpretations of Iconoclasm, contemporary scholarship appears to agree on two main points: the controversy was a crisis within Byzantine Christianity itself (Brown, 1973), and it was too complex to be explained by such binary oppositions as lay versus hierarchical, monastic versus imperial, or elite versus "popular" (Cormack, 1985; Ringrose, 1979).

Of particular relevance for the history of the icon in its intersection with the history of monasticism is the historian Peter Brown's argument, which sees the Iconoclastic controversy not so much as a debate over art as a debate over the holy in Byzantine society. He turns his attention to the ascetic, the holy man, and studies similarities between his role and that of an icon in believers' lives. The Iconoclasts, in Brown's view, confined the presence of the holy to several symbols – the Eucharist, the church building, and the sign of the Cross – and resisted the centrifugal pull of the holy man and the icon as bearers of the holy outside the hierarchically based sacramental system. Thus, the veneration of icons provided an occasion for ever-present tensions between hierarchical and charismatic authority in the Eastern Orthodox Church to surface.

The result of the Iconoclastic controversies was the formulation of a theology of the icon that has defined the Eastern Orthodox use of images ever since. One of the main spokespersons for the veneration of icons, John of Damascus (c. 655–c. 750), who lived at St. Sabas monastery in Palestine, defended their use on several key points. First, John denied the charge of idolatry. He objected to the Iconoclasts' identification of an image with its human prototype, claiming that in such a case the veneration of icons would indeed be idolatrous. Highlighting instead differences between the two, he cited Basil of Caesarea and maintained that the honor "given to the image is transferred to its prototype." John's distinction between types of worship in the Christian life was also articulated by other iconophiles as well as by the Second Council of Nicaea in 787 in its defense of images: one particular type of worship, adoration, is due to God alone, whereas icons enjoy a relative veneration as remembrances and likenesses.

Second, because the disputes centered in particular on the image of Christ, John grounded the "writing" of icons in the mystery of the Incarnation. Prior to Christ, he maintained, God could not be depicted because he was not seen. But with Jesus, the perfect, living image of the invisible God (Col. 1:15) became visible to the flesh. "I boldly draw an image of the invisible God," John writes, "not as invisible, but as having become visible for our sakes by partaking of flesh and blood" (*On the Divine Images*, 1980). Accordingly in venerating an icon, explained John, one does not worship the matter before one "but the Creator of matter, who became matter for my sake, who willed to take His abode in matter; who worked out my salvation through matter" (*On the Divine Images*). Thus, in his view, to deny the veneration of Christ's image meant to deny the mystery of the Incarnation by means of which God sanctified humanity.

These ideas figured prominently in the Second Council of Nicaea's defense of icon veneration and of the art of iconography, a defense that also focused mainly on the image of Christ. Both Iconophiles and Iconoclasts defended their positions on the basis of Christological beliefs that had been formulated since the fourth century, especially those articulated at the Council of Chalcedon in 451. Eventually recognized as the Seventh Ecumenical Council, the Second Council of Nicaea was summoned by the Iconophile future Empress Irene (797–802) in Nicaea in 787 at the urging of Patriarch Tarasius. According to its *Horos*, icons were of "equal benefit" with the gospel narrative and should be venerated on par with it and with the life-giving Cross. Following another outbreak of Iconoclasm (813–842), the final "triumph" of icons came in 843 (again with the help of an empress, Theodora) with the official reaffirmation of the council of 787. During this period the monastic reformer Theodore of Stoudios (759–826) and Nicephorus (758–828), patriarch of Constantinople, joined John of Damascus as defenders of images and further developed the Christological arguments for the representation of Christ. The final "triumph" of icons is commemorated annually in the Orthodox Church on the first Sunday of Lent.

The Iconoclastic controversies, however, did not produce the final theological word on icons and their veneration. As the Russian Orthodox priest and theologian Sergius Bulgakov (1871–1944) has noted, the dogmatic meaning of the veneration of icons remained (and still remains) open to theological formulation. Another period in the history of Eastern Orthodox theology that greatly influenced Orthodox thinking about and the "writing" of icons, and that situated iconographic art in the broader tradition of Eastern Christian monastic spirituality was the so-called Hesychast controversy during the 14th century. Prompted in part by opposition to a method of unceasing prayer practiced by Byzantine Hesychasts, these debates resulted in the articulation of a theology of divine light and mystical experience.

Through developing a state of unceasing prayer, Hesychasts affirmed, humans could come to experience directly the presence of God in a vision of the divine light. They identified the light they encountered in their contemplative practices with that same light that shone forth from Jesus transfigured on Mount Tabor. As their main spokesperson during the 14th century, Gregory Palamas (c. 1296–1359), noted, divinity manifested itself to the disciples on that mountain as light. This light, he maintained, was "a light without limit, depth, height, or lateral extension" (*The Triads*, 1983). It was eternal and uncreated, a light of revelation that surpasses natural light. Referring to this light as the energies of God, Palamas distinguished them from God's essence that remains inaccessible and unknowable. At the same time God's energies are no less divine than God's essence, as God is "wholly present in each ray of His divinity" (Lossky, 1974). Through his energies God shines forth eternally and penetrates all things in divine self-manifestation, making it possible for humans to know God and to participate in divine life.

According to Palamas, this "knowledge" or "vision" of God by means of divine illumination is neither of the intellect nor of the senses but of the Spirit. Moreover, although experienced through a union of heart and mind, this light or vision of God does not remain confined to the interior realm. Because the human person is a psychosomatic whole, the body too is affected by the internal illumination. Recalling the salvific effect of the Incarnation of the Word of God, Palamas maintained that the light or grace that illumines a person's soul is also transmitted to the body through the soul and enables the body to experience "things divine."

Palamas claimed that God communicates this glory to faithful persons "in proportion to the practice of what is pleasing to God, avoidance of all that is not, assiduity in prayer, and the longing of the entire soul for God" (*The Triads*). Icons, then, testify not only to the divine blessings that make communion with God possible but also to a triumph of the human will and spirit over the numerous obstacles and struggles that plague persons along their path of "ascent." This struggle is expressed in a 12th-century icon depicting the theme of John Climacus' *Divine Ladder*. Icons celebrate those persons who through their life of prayer, charitable acts, and ascetic discipline have been both spiritually and physically transfigured by divine indwelling, who have become likenesses of God and "partakers of the divine nature" (2 Pet. 1:4) as far as is possible. As John of Damascus noted, iconographic depictions of the saints are a hymn of triumph for those who, while humbling the demons, have fought and conquered. Writings that some have attributed to the fourth-century leader of Egyptian monasticism, Macarius of Egypt (c. 300–c. 390), identify the glory that illumines saints in this world with that same glory that later will clothe their bodies after the Resurrection.

Scholars have traced the influence of Hesychasm on art in general in Byzantium during the so-called Palaeologan renaissance and on iconography in particular in Russia, especially on the works of Andrei Rublev and Theophanes the Greek in the 14th and 15th centuries (Alpatov, Goleizovskii). The combined influence of iconophilic thought as it was expressed in the eighth and ninth centuries along with Hesychasm can be seen in the writings of Joseph of Volokolamsk (1439/40–1515), the abbot of Russia's Volokolamsk monastery. Sometimes compared with Byzantium's Theodore of Stoudios, Joseph composed three short treatises in defense of icons in response to a radical religious movement with a prominent iconoclastic bent that arose in northern Russia at the end of the 15th century. Linking the practice of icon veneration with the spiritual rebirth that results from a life of inner prayer, these treatises describe in detail the proper way to adore God both through private prayer and collective worship as well as the role of icons in the adoration of God. In addition to reiterating the traditional defense of icons put forward by the Seventh Ecumenical Council, the treatises also discuss the veneration shown to relics, any church building, the Cross, and the Eucharist.

Icons in the Orthodox tradition not only remind believers about persons and events from sacred history depicted on the image but also facilitate an encounter with the holy for those who pray before them. According to John of Damascus, icons can become a locus of divine presence; they can be filled with grace through prayer addressed to those depicted. Later the Orthodox theologian Sergius Bulgakov would tie such notions of grace and "presence" to an icon's formal liturgical blessing that is performed by ordained clergy. Bulgakov claimed that the blessing of an icon of Christ, Mary, or a particular saint establishes a relationship between the image and its prototype and thereby facilitates a "meeting" between the believer and the person depicted on the image. For Bulgakov a painted image's "iconicity" (*ikonnost'*) is actualized by this blessing.

In the Orthodox tradition icons, along with Holy Scriptures and the Cross, are understood as means of divine revelation and communion with God and thus as having a role in the economy of salvation. The belief in the revelatory nature of icons has a direct bearing on the culture of icons in the Orthodox East. First, it presupposes that art can be revelatory and involve a vision and knowledge of God. Accordingly icon "writing" is understood not so much in terms of individual imagination or talent as in terms of a sacred vocation to which a person is called and in which a person is "trained" through a life of personal prayer, liturgical worship, and fasting in addition to the specifics of iconographic technique. In his treatises in defense of icons, Joseph of Volokolamsk also turned attention to the spiritual education of the iconographer and to the state of his or her heart and mind, emphasizing the organic unity between the spiritual life and its creative expression. Although icon writing is not identified exclusively with the monastic life, given the close association between prayer and the act of icon writing, many icon painters historically have been monastics. In addition iconographers traditionally have realized that their art is not "theirs" – their own private creation – because they convey mainly images of a corporate tradition and are inspired by an ecclesial vision that transcends themselves. Accordingly most iconographers historically have not signed their works.

Second, such a belief means that icons are appreciated not only for what they visually show but also for the effect that they evoke in believers. Powers of healing and spiritual enlightenment have been attributed to many icons, especially to those of the Mother of God. Participants in the Seventh Ecumenical Council went so far as to adduce such experiences associated with icons in order to buttress the legitimacy of the practice of icon veneration in general. For example, they recalled the role played by an icon of the Virgin Mary in the life of the desert ascetic Mary of Egypt. Similarly icons have figured prominently in the lives of many individual monastics as well as of monastic communities. For example, the histories of numerous monasteries in Russia, such as the well-known monastery of the White Lakes in northern Russia in the late 14th century, were associated with particular icons, especially those of Mary. One icon depicts the monastery's founder, monk Cyril, receiving divine inspiration and direction to establish this community during his prolonged prayer before an icon of the Mother of God.

Iconographic representations, especially in the form of frescoes, also play a prominent role in the corporate life of monastic communities through their location in churches and in communal spaces, such as refectories. Here the distinction between icons and monumental fresco decoration becomes evident. Frescoes, although usually sharing the same narrative content as icons, particularly scenes from the lives of Christ and the Virgin, are distinct from painted wooden icons in that they historically have not been objects of direct liturgical veneration or special devotion. Believers, for example, generally neither light candles before them nor kiss them. Aimed mainly at visually depicting sacred history, the arrangement of frescoes in churches usually follows a general theological or narrative schema. At the same time the history of the local monastic or parish community often inspires the choice of images.

VERA SHEVZOV

See also Hesychasm; Holy Men/Holy Women: Christian Perspectives; Hymnographers; Iconoclasm (Controversy); Images: Christian Perspectives; Liturgy: Eastern Christian; Mount Sinai, Egypt; Orthodox Monasticism: Slavic; Palamas, Gregory, St.; Pilgrimages, Christian: Eastern Europe; Spirituality: Eastern Christian; Theology, Eastern Christian; Vision, Mystical: Eastern Christian

Further Reading

Source Texts:

For the acts of the Seventh Ecumenical Council, see Giovan Domenico Mansi, *Sacrorum Conciliorum Nova et Amplissima Collectio*, Paris: Welter, 1900; reprint, Graz: Akademische Druck, 1960. For a translation of the sixth session of this council see Daniel J. Sahas, editor, *Icon and Logos: Sources in Eighth-Century Iconoclasm* (Toronto Medieval Texts and Translations, 4), Buffalo, New York, and London: University of Toronto Press, 1986. For the writings of such well-known iconophiles as John of Damascus, Theodore of Stoudios, and Patriarch Nicephorus relating to icons, see J.-P. Migne, *Patrologiae Cursus Completus, Series Graeca*, Paris, 1860, vols. 94, 99, and 100, respectively. For a collection of texts related to the iconoclastic crisis see Hans-Jürgen Geischer, compiler, *Der byzantinische Bilderstreit* (Texte zur Kirchen- und Theologiegeschichte, 9), Gütersloh: Gütersloher Verlagshaus, 1968. The principal treatises on the use of images can be found in translation: St. John of Damascus, *On the Divine Images: Three Apologies against Those Who Attack the Divine Images*, translated by David Anderson, Crestwood, New York: St. Vladimir's Seminary Press, 1980; 2nd edition, 1994; and St. Theodore the Studite, *On the Holy Icons*, translated by Catharine P. Roth, Crestwood, New York: St. Vladimir's Seminary Press, 1981. For selections from Gregory Palamas' *Triads in Defence of the Holy Hesychasts* see St. Gregory Palamas, *The Triads* (Classics of Western Spirituality), edited by John Meyendorff, translated by Nicholas Gendle, New York: Paulist Press, and London: SPCK, 1983. For a medieval Russian defense of icons see St. Iosif Volotskii, *Poslanie ikonopistsu* (Russkaia mysl' ob ikone), reprint, Moscow: Izobrazitel'noe iskusstvo, 1994.

Studies:

Barasch, Moshe, *Icon: Studies in the History of an Idea*, New York: New York University Press, 1992

Brown, Peter, "A Dark-Age Crisis: Aspects of the Iconoclastic Controversy," *English Historical Review* 346 (January 1973)

Bryer, Anthony, and Judith Herrin, editors, *Iconoclasm: Papers Given at the Ninth Spring Symposium of Byzantine Studies, University of Birmingham, March 1975*, Birmingham, West Midlands: Centre for Byzantine Studies, University of Birmingham, 1977

Bulgakov, Sergei, *Ikona i ikonopochitanie Dogmaticheskii ocherk*, Paris: YMCA Press, 1931

Cormack, Robin, *Writing in Gold: Byzantine Society and Its Icons*, New York: Oxford University Press, and London: Philip, 1985

Kitzinger, E., "The Cult of Images in the Age before Iconoclasm," *Dumbarton Oaks Papers* 8 (1954)

Kostof, Spiro, *Caves of God: The Monastic Environment of Byzantine Cappadocia*, Cambridge, Massachusetts: MIT Press, 1972; as *Caves of God: Cappadocia and Its Churches*, London and New York: Oxford University Press, 1989

Kostsova, A.S., and A.G. Pobedinskaia, editors, *Russkie ikony XVI-nachala XX veka. S izobrazheniem monastyrei i ikh osnovatelei: katalog vystavki*, St. Petersburg: Gos. Ermitazh, 1996

Ladner, G., "The Concept of the Image in the Greek Fathers and the Byzantine Iconoclastic Controversy," *Dumbarton Oaks Papers* 7 (1953)

Lossky, Vladimir, *In the Image and Likeness of God*, Crestwood, New York: St. Vladimir's Seminary Press, 1974; London: Mowbray, 1975

Maguire, Henry, *The Icons of Their Bodies: Saints and Their Images in Byzantium*, Princeton, New Jersey: Princeton University Press, 1996

Meyendorff, J., "Spiritual Trends in Byzantium in the Late Thirteenth and Early Fourteenth Centuries," in *The Kariye Djami* (Bollingen Series, 70), volume 4, edited by P.

Underwood, Princeton, New Jersey: Princeton University Press, 1975
Ouspensky, Léonide, *Theology of the Icon*, translated by Elizabeth Meyendorff, Crestwood, New York: St. Vladimir's Seminary Press, 1978; revised edition, 2 vols., 1992
Parry, Kenneth, *Depicting the Word: Byzantine Iconophile Thought of the Eighth and Ninth Centuries* (The Medieval Mediterranean, volume 12), New York: Brill, 1996
Ringrose, K., "Monks and Society in Iconoclastic Byzantium," *Byzantine Studies/Etudes Byzantines* 6 (1979)
Sherrard, Philip, *The Sacred in Life and Art*, Ipswich, Suffolk: Golgonooza Press, 1990
Weitzmann, Kurt, *The Icon: Holy Images, Sixth to Fourteenth Century*, London: Chatto and Windus, and New York: Braziller, 1978

Visual Arts, Western Christian: Book Arts before the Renaissance

General

For a religion based on Scripture, it was a natural development that Christian production of books in the format of scrolls, codices, or manuscripts would become a major concern for the transmission of the faith. This need for written material encouraged monastic institutions to become involved in its production. The involvement of monastic houses in book production and the book trade also had architectural consequences. Provision had to be made for a place warm enough for the copying of books (scriptorium) and a place to stock the books necessary for studying and praying (*armentarium* and later *bibliotheca*).

The copying of texts was needed for three main purposes: liturgy, study and meditation, and communication. As centuries went by, the variety of liturgical books greatly increased to include evangeliarum, missal, gradual, antiphonary, psalter, benedictional, and sacramental. The importance of *lectio divina*, or meditation on Scripture and Tradition, as described in the Rule of St. Benedict, made the transcription of Bibles, commentaries, and devotional texts a necessity. Contacts cultivated with other monastic or secular institutions necessitated also the presence of a scribe. The production of death rolls that were circulated to other monasteries after the death of an abbot is a case in point.

Monasteries took care of all stages of the production process. Although the production of texts composed by monks of the monastery was part of the work of the scriptorium, this was not its only job. Very often manuscripts were borrowed by one monastery from another to be copied. The parchment needed for the manuscript would be produced in situ. Monks would then copy the volume. For a more attractive presentation of the text, the manuscript could be illuminated with penwork, with foliate or historiated initials, and with marginal decoration using mainly vegetal and mineral pigments that were generally brought in from outside the monastery. Only in very important codices would miniatures be added. In the last stage the book would be bound. It would then enter the library, where manuscripts were at first stored horizontally and sometimes chained to the desks to prevent theft. The various stages in the production process would not necessarily be entrusted to different monks. For example, Hugo, a 13th-century Benedictine monk of the monastery of Oignies on the Sambre River, is known to have copied the text, illustrated the borders, and produced a silver binding for one evangeliarum of his monastery (now at Namur, Sisters of Notre Dame of Namur).

Nearly all monastic orders played a part in the production of manuscripts. Even the Carthusians broke their rule of noncommunication with the outside world by producing books. Cassiodorus (485/90–c. 580) was the first to dwell on the spiritual value of transcribing texts in a scriptorium (*Institutiones Divinarum et Saecularium Litterarum*). Alcuin (c. 740–804) reiterated this idea by saying (*Carmina*) that it is more worthwhile to transcribe books than to work in a vineyard. Until the 13th century monastic scriptoria experienced serious competition only from cathedral chapters, which sometimes ran their own scriptoria. With the rise of the universities, the need for books increased so dramatically that monastic scriptoria were unable to keep up with the demand. Increasingly book production was handed over to professional lay scribes. Toward the end of the Middle Ages, monastic scriptoria had been pushed to the margins of the book trade. However, occasionally the artistic talents of a member of a religious order would play an important role in manuscript production (e.g., Giovanni da Fiesole, O.P., and Cornelia van Wulfschkercke, O.C.). The liturgical complexity and the large size of choral manuscripts used for the Office and for Mass meant that the in-house practice of copying manuscripts often lasted until the 18th century.

The importance of monastic libraries for the transmission of the Christian tradition can hardly be overstated. Until the rise of the universities, most of the intellectual activity in the Western Church was linked with a monastic library. The richess of a library was often the fruit of the private patronage of an abbot. For example, this was the case for Raphael de Mercatellis (d. 1508), abbot of St. Peter's monastery in Ghent, who collected the first humanist library in the Low Countries.

Historical Sketch

The arrival of the first monastic communities in the western Roman Empire went hand in hand with the copying of texts. The first important developments in book production in Western Christianity took place on the outskirts of the western Roman Empire. In the Irish and Northumbrian monasteries, manuscripts were copied from the eighth century on. Around 776 in northern Spain, the monk Beatus of Liébana wrote a commentary on the Apocalypse that would be copied and spectacularly illustrated in all major monastic scriptoria of northern Spain and Aquitaine during the tenth century.

With the spreading of the Benedictine Rule, book production was stepped up. Indeed, of all the monastic orders, it was the Benedictine Order that was to impart the most lasting influence to Western artistic and intellectual culture through its production of manuscripts. The activities of their scriptoria ensured the

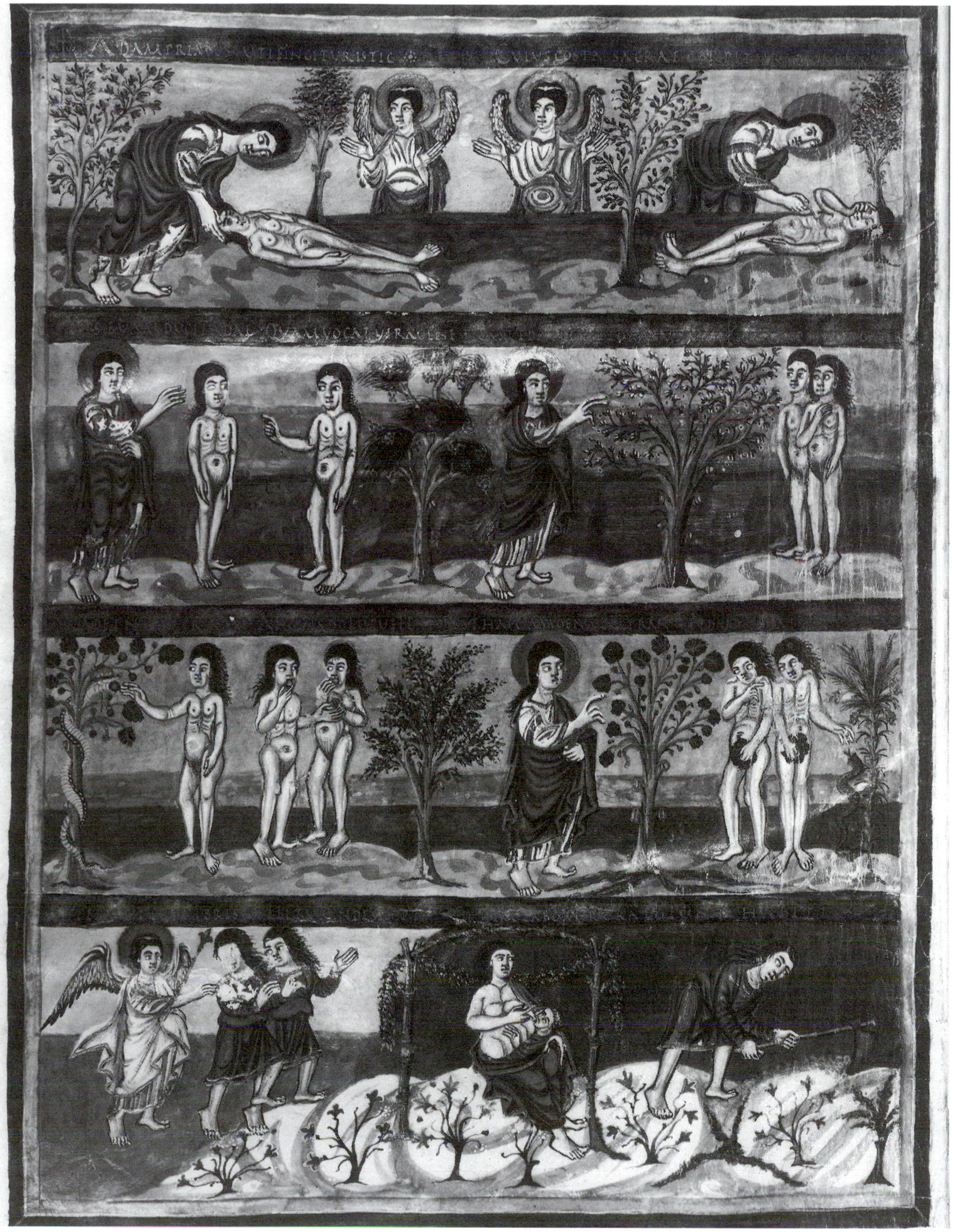

The Story of Adam and Eve, Moutier-Grandval Bible, c. 840. Produced at the Benedictine Abbey of Tours to illustrate the Bible in a text edited by Alcuin.
Photo by permission of the British Library, Additional MS 10546, f.5b.

survival of countless texts and encouraged technical innovations that laid the foundations for later developments in book production. Around 650 the Carolingian minuscle, a script soon adopted throughout Western Europe and imitated at the Renaissance in the *humanistic* script, originated in the monastery of Luxueil (northeastern France). Contacts between monasteries allowed for the circulation of important texts.

The Franciscans played only a minor role in book production because their interpretation of the vow of poverty banned private possession of books. However, this did not prevent the convents from possessing important libraries. By 1230 the Sacro Convento at Assisi had already started to collect books. In places where Franciscans were involved with universities (Paris and Oxford), adequate libraries were organized. Saint James of the March (1393–1476), who belonged to the Observant movement of the Order, relaxed his standards of poverty to allow himself to collect books.

The major orders were not the only ones to produce books. An important example is the Camaldolese monastery of Santa Maria degli Angeli in Florence. During the last quarter of the 14th century, its manuscript production and illumination was seminal for the artistic production of the city. Members of the Order, such as Don Silvestro dei Gherarducci, Don Simone Camaldolese, and Don Lorenzo Monaco, played an important role on the Florentine artistic stage.

ALAIN ARNOULD, O.P.

See also Alcuin; Archives, Western Christian; Assisi, Italy; Camaldolese; Carthusians; Cassiodorus; Celtic Monasticism; Florence, Italy; Images: Christian Perspectives; Ireland; Libraries: Western Christian; St. Gallen, Switzerland

Further Reading

General Works:
de Hamel, C., *A History of Illuminated Manuscripts*, Boston: Godine, and Oxford: Phaidon, 1986
Huyghebaert, Nicolas, *Les documents nécrologiques*, volume 3, Turnhout: Brepols, 1972
McKitterick, R., "The Scriptoria of Merovingian Gaul: A Survey of the Evidence," in *Columbanus and Merovingian Monasticism*, Oxford: BAR, 1981
Williams, John, *The Illustrated Beatus: A Corpus of the Illustrations of the Commentary on the Apocalypse*, 5 vols., London and Langhorne, Pennsylvania: Miller, 1994

Benedictines:
Burke, R.A., "Benedictines as Lovers of Books," *Benedictine Review* 18 (1963)
Lesne, E., "Histoire de la propriété ecclésiastique en France" and "Les livres, 'scriptoria' et les bibliothèques du commencement du VIIIe à la fin du XIe siècle," in *Mémoires et travaux publiés par les professeurs des Facultés catholiques de Lille*, Lille 1938
Newton, Francis, *The Scriptorium and Library at Monte Cassino, 1058–1105*, Cambridge and New York: Cambridge University Press, 1999

Camaldolese:
Bent, George, "The Scriptorium at S. Maria degli Angeli and Fourteenth Century Manuscript Illumination: Don Silvestro dei Gherarducci, Don Lorenzo Monaco and Giovanni del Biondo," *Zeitschrift für Kunstgeschichte* 61 (1992)
Kanter, Laurence, Barbara Boehm, and Carl Strehlke, *Painting and Illumination in Early Renaissance Florence 1300–1450*, New York: Abrams, 1994

Carmelites:
Arnould, Alain, "De la production de miniatures de Cornelia van Wulfschkercke," in *Elementa Historiae Ordinis Praedicatorum*, volume 5, Brussels: Dominicains de Belgique-Sud, 1998

Carthusians:
Gumbert, J.P., *Die Utrechter Kartäuser und ihre Bücher im frühen fünfzehnten Jahrhundert*, Leiden: Brill, 1974
Lehmann, Paul, "Bücherliebe und Bücherpflege bei den Karthäusern," in *Miscellanea Francisco Ehrle*, Rome, 1924

Cistercians:
Zaluska, Yolanda, *L'enluminure et le scriptorium de Cîteaux au XIIe siècle*, Nuits-Saint-Georges: Cîteaux, 1989

Devotio Moderna and Windesheim:
Haverals, M., "De scriptoria en de bibliotheken van de Windesheimers in de Zuidelijke Nederlanden," *Ons Geestelijik Erf* 59:2–3 (1985)
Lourdaux, W., "Het boekenbezit en het boekengebruik bij de Moderne Devoten," *Historia Lovaniensia* 20 (1974)

Dominicans:
Axters, Stephan, "Boekennbezit en boekengebruik in de dertiende eeuw," in *Studia Mediaevalia in honorem admodum Reverendi Patris Raymundi Josephi Matin*, Bruges: Apud Societatem Editricem "De Tempel," 1948
Hamburger, Jeffrey, *The Rothschild Canticles: Art and Mysticism in Flanders and the Rhineland circa 1300*, New Haven, Connecticut: Yale University Press, 1990

Franciscans:
Abate, G., "Manoscritti e bibliothece francescane nel Medio Evo," *Il libro e le bibliotheche* 2 (1950)

Visual Arts, Western Christian: Liturgical Furnishings

The liturgy of the medieval church was spiritually rich and abounded in symbolism. For example, the solemn rite for the High Mass at Cluny in the 11th century was very complicated. Part of the rite included processions before the reading of the gospel and before the offertory. Thus, many acolytes were required at the altar to assist the celebrant, deacon, and subdeacon, and a wide range of liturgical furnishings played a part in fulfilling the ritual.

The liturgy was celebrated in the east end, or presbytery, of the monastic church. The high altar, for the High Mass, stood close to the east wall. The altar, reminiscent of classical tombs, was laid with three linen cloths, symbolizing the shroud of Jesus. A frontal decorated with orphreys (decorated panels) covered the altar front, and even precious metals were used in frontals. A fine example by the ninth-century goldsmith Wolvinus is still in use at the Basilica of St. Ambrogio, Milan.

A tall painted and sculpted reredos, as at Winchester Cathedral and Christchurch Priory (Hants), or a smaller reredos decorated with scenes carved from alabaster, all painted and gilded, stood immediately behind the altar. A common alternative for the reredos was a triptych, such as *Christ on the Cross* by Rogier van der Weyden (c. 1440–1445; in the Kunsthistorisches Museum, Vienna). France excelled in the manufacture of triptychs carved from ivory, such as the 14th-century example in the Musée de Cluny, Paris. In Germany triptychs were often carved from wood, such as *The Altar of the Virgin at Creglingen*, by Tielman Riemenschneider (c. 1500). If a reredos was lacking, the altar would have had curtains to three sides, supported on four riddel posts, often surmounted by winged angels holding candles or else by simple candleholders. The curtains indicated the holiest place in the church.

Behind the altar, aumbries are often found for storing liturgical books and altar furnishings. Either a large cross of precious metals and intricately worked or one carved in ivory, such as *The Bury St. Edmund's Cross* (c. 1150–1190; in the Metropolitan Museum of Art, New York), might have stood on the altar. Before the 13th century any figure on the cross would have symbolized Christ as King, whereas afterward it would have been a crucifix, such as the 12th- to 13th-century French one of Limoges enamel (in the Cleveland Museum of Art, Cleveland). The use of the image of the crucifix was probably due to Franciscan influence. Because the reredos was often decorated with scenes from Christ's Passion and Death, crosses and crucifixes were not always necessary.

Large candlesticks were introduced in the 12th century, often elaborately worked, such as the Gloucester candlestick (in the Victoria and Albert Museum, London). Yet the simplicity of the 13th-century French candlesticks of Limoges enamel work (in the Metropolitan Museum of Art) contrast with the grandeur of that from Gloucester. A cushion or a bookstand of wood or metal would have supported the Missal. The Missal, like all liturgical books, would have been handwritten, often richly decorated and illuminated. It was not unusual for the covers to be silver gilt with precious stones, such as the Lindau Gospels (c. 800; in the Pierpont Morgan Library, New York). A credence table might have stood against the south wall of the presbytery to hold the chalice and paten, the cruets of metal or glass for the water and wine, and other items required for the Mass. Quite often an Easter sepulcher sits to the north of the high altar, either as a simple archway cut into the wall or an ornate piece of liturgical architecture.

At the north end of the altar was a lectern, which in the late Middle Ages would have been in the form of an eagle. There is an excellent rare wooden example at Astbury Church, Cheshire, and at St. Mary, Wiggenhall, Norfolk, is a fine brass lectern of 1518.

During High Mass incense was used to bless the gospel and offering, and thuribles, such as the three 14th-century Italian examples in the National Museum of Scotland, Edinburgh, were used for that purpose. In addition the liturgical setting of the monastic church separated the laity from the presbytery by a pulpitum so that handbells had to be used to signal the different parts of the Mass, such as the consecration and elevation.

Mass was celebrated using a chalice and paten of precious metals, imitating the cup and dish used by Jesus at the Last Supper. A simple chalice by Bertinus (1222; in the Metropolitan Museum of Art) contrasts with an early 15th-century Italian chalice by Piero Martini da Pisa (or Siena; in the Burrel Gallery, Glasgow). When Communion was administered under both kinds, a chalice with two handles was used, such as that of Abbot Suger (in the National Gallery of Art, Washington, D.C.), and golden tubes (like straws) were provided for the laity to drink from the chalice. The miniature of *The Mass of St. Gregory*, Bruges (c. 1520–1530), attributed to Simon Bening (in the J. Paul Getty Museum, Los Angeles), is an excellent depiction of the medieval mass.

From the ninth century on, reservation of the Sacrament became commonplace. The Sacrament was reserved in either a pyx, a ciborium, or a sacrament house. There were different types of pyx, such as the 14th-century Italian silver gilt standing pyx (in the Victoria and Albert Museum), or the 13th-century French hanging pyx in the form of a gilt bronze and enameled eucharistic dove (in the Albright-Knox Museum, Buffalo, New York). Hanging pyxes were common in England and France. The Cluniac abbot Thomas Tervas bought an Italian pyx for his abbey at Paisley.

A ciborium was a small two-story archway on four legs. The lower part held the chalice, the upper part the paten. The sacrament house, which is a special aumbry at or near the altar, was common in Scotland, Portugal, and parts of Italy. One of the finest examples of a sacrament house is that at Auchindoir, Scotland, carved in the form of a monstrance with attendant angels. In Germany and the Low Countries, it became an elaborate piece of liturgical architecture, as at St. Pierre, Louvain.

The sedilia, used by the priest, deacon, and subdeacon during the High Mass, stood close to the high altar on the south side. It was usual for these seats to be ornate liturgical architecture in their own right, as at Furness Abbey, Cumbria. Where there was no sedilia, chairs or stools would have been used.

Vestments worn for Mass in the medieval church carried weighty symbolism and as ceremonial clothing were part of a complex pattern of communication. They emphasized the "special character" of the occasion and indicated the individual roles of the participants. Vestments derived directly from the clothing worn in classical times. Moreover they came to symbolize the Mass itself.

Priests, deacons, and subdeacons wore the amice, a white linen cloth placed around the neck and shoulders, sometimes

Nicholas of Verdun, Verdun Altar, Leopoldskapelle, Klosterneuburg Abbey (Augustinian Canons), Lower Austria, 1181. Photo courtesy of the Austrian National Tourist Office

decorated at one edge. The alb, a full-length white tunic decorated at the neck, cuffs, and hem, was gathered at the waist by a white or colored tasseled cincture. Over that a stole of the same color as the vestments was worn, whereas the deacon wore a stole over his left shoulder and across his chest. The priest, up until the Second Vatican Council (1962–1965), wore a manipule over the left wrist, essentially a smaller version of the stole and of the same color.

The priest then put on the chasuble, a circular outer garment, quite often decorated with orphreys to form a cross. Deacons and subdeacons wore dalmatics and tunicles (knee-length garments with short sleeves) decorated with simple-colored orphreys over the shoulders and across the back and front. At the High Mass the priest or celebrant, deacon, and subdeacons wore matching vestments of the finest materials and richly decorated. The only set of English medieval vestments for the High Mass still extant may have belonged to the Cistercian abbey of Walley in Lancashire (in the Burrel Gallery).

The cope (a large semi-circular vestment) may be worn at Mass by a priest who is not officiating. Its color and rich decoration would be the same as that of the chasuble. The early 14th-century Syon Cope in the Victoria and Albert Museum is a famous example of the *opus anglicanum*. In the time of Pope Innocent III (1198–1216), a set pattern of liturgical colors for the different feasts emerged, although it was not formalized until Pope Pius V (1566–1572) did so in 1570.

The abbot, depending on rank, could wear the miter and ring and carry the crosier, the symbols of the episcopate. The miter, a large, pointed hat with two lappets hanging from the back, could be of three distinct types: jeweled, decorated (but not jeweled), and simple – with the ritual dictating when each would be worn. The crosier could have been of a simple kind carved from wood; one beautifully carved from ivory, such as the 14th-century French example depicting *The Crucifixion* (in the Walters Art Gallery, Baltimore); or one as delicate as the Champlevé enameled example from Limoges, France (c. 1200; in the Metropolitan Museum of Art). A processional cross and candlesticks would also have been used for the entrance and exit, and candles would have been used at the singing of the gospel during the High Mass.

To store the vast array of furnishings required to fulfill the liturgical rituals in a large monastery, various types of cupboards, chests, and cope chests were needed. Cope chests, as their name implies, were used for storing copes and could be a chest of either a half or a quarter circle.

The monks' choir occupied the opposite end of the presbytery from the high altar. Because the west end of the monks' choir stood against the pulpitum, the stalls were in two L-shaped sets. The stalls were usually of two tiers. Early stalls were plain and solid, but by the 13th and 14th centuries the high backs of the upper tiers were occasionally surmounted by canopies of richly carved and delicate tabernacle work, as at Chester Cathedral (c. 1390), whereas the lower stalls had simple bench fronts. The only English monastic choir stalls to survive the Reformation were those of monastic cathedrals, such as Carlisle and Hexham, or those of abbeys, such as Gloucester and Norwich, which became cathedrals.

Beautifully carved choir stalls were standard throughout Europe: the Cathedral of Poitiers still has its 13th-century choir stalls. It was not uncommon for choir stalls to be exported. Dunblane Cathedral, Scotland, has excellent Flemish examples of 1487, and Melrose Abbey also acquired new stalls from Bruges in the 15th century. The fronts of the stalls were often painted, as at Carlisle and Hexham or in the church of the Augustinian Friars of St. Catherine, Krakow, Poland. The misericords underneath the hinged choir seats were often richly carved, as at Ely.

At the east end of the choir stood a large book desk to support the choir books. Handwritten books, perhaps produced in the monastery, were extra large to facilitate easy reading in the poor light and similar to the gradual of St. Alban's Abbey (mid–12th century; in the British Library, London). Beyond this book desk a second eagle lectern was often used.

Although processions played an important role in the eucharistic liturgy of monasteries, they were no less essential in the celebration of the liturgical year – at Easter, Christmas, and other important feasts – when the community would process around the church, go into the cloister by one door, and re-enter the nave by the other. It was not uncommon for the laity to form part of such processions. Copes, dalmatics, and tunicles would have been worn by the officiating clergy, accompanied by acolytes wearing albs and carrying a processional cross, candles, thuribles for incense, decorated banners, and, depending on the feast, perhaps a reliquary. The latter came in all shapes – caskets, miniature churches, and monstrances – usually made from precious metals, decorated and enameled. The shrine of St. Taurinus (mid–13th century), church of St. Taurin, Évreux, is an exceptional example of this art, comprising a miniature cathedral in copper and silver gilt. Reliquaries would often have been central to an altar of pilgrimage, located either in the presbytery or in the nave.

If there was provision in the nave for the laity, the Rood or Jesus altar, as it was known, would have sat before the rood screen. Side chapels and private chapels/chantries, often built with wainscoting, might have had a reredos or painting at the altar provided by a rich benefactor. All these altars would have required the usual altar furnishings. There is also the possibility that a pulpit, richly carved from wood or stone, might have stood in the nave, together with the baptismal font of stone or metal. Dorchester Abbey, Oxfordshire, has a late Norman font of lead, decorated with apostles.

PHILIP E. MCWILLIAMS

See also Abbot: Christian; Clothing: Christian Perspectives; Cluny, France; Liturgy: Western Christian; Manuscript Production: Christian; Office, Daily: Western Christian; Officials: Western Christian; Relics, Christian Monastic; Visual Arts, Western Christian: Sculpture

Further Reading

Calkins, Robert G., *Monuments of Medieval Art*, New York: Dutton, and Oxford: Phaidon Press, 1979

Davies, J.G., editor, *A Dictionary of Liturgy and Worship*, New York: Macmillan, and London: SCM Press, 1972; revised as *The New Westminster Dictionary of Liturgy and Worship*, Philadelphia: Westminster Press, 1986

De Hamel, Christopher, *A History of Illuminated Manuscripts*, Oxford: Phaidon Press, and Boston: Godine, 1986; 2nd edition, London: Phaidon Press, 1994

Dirsztay, Patricia, *Inside Churches: A Guide to Church Furnishings*, London: National Association of Decorative and Fine Arts Societies, 1989; revised edition, 1993

France, James, *The Cistercians in Medieval Art*, Phoenix Mill, Stroud, Gloucestershire: Sutton, 1998

Gibbs, Robert, editor, *Rarer Gifts Than Gold: Fourteenth-Century Art in Scottish Collections: The Burrell Collection, Glasgow Museums and Art Galleries, Pollock Country Park, Glasgow, 28 April–26 June, 1988*, Glasgow: Glasgow University, 1988

Hatje, Ursula, editor, *The Styles of European Art*, London: Thames and Hudson, and New York: Abrams, 1965

Huyghe, René, editor, *Larousse Encyclopaedia of Byzantine and Medieval Art*, London: Hamlyn, 1958; New York: Prometheus Press, 1963; revised edition, New York: Excalibur Books, and London: Hamlyn, 1981

Visual Arts, Western Christian: Painting

Monastic Artists

There has been a long tradition of monastic artists. Most of them remain anonymous, but a few names have survived. The decoration of the monastic buildings, especially in the Benedictine Order, was left mostly to the members of the community, for whom it was considered a spiritual exercise. Among the most famous monastic artists are Fra' Filippo Lippi (1406–1469). He joined the Franciscans in Florence and remained there for 11 years. Because he was totally unsuited for the religious life, he obtained a dispensation and married a nun. The Italian Jesuit Bitti is often considered the best painter of the Americas in the 16th century. He received a mission from his superior to catechize the Indians by his paintings. The artistic tradition was probably most integrated in the Order of Preachers. Famous

Dominican artists can be found equally among the clerical and lay members of the Order. Jacob Griesinger, known as James of Ulm (1407–1491), who was beatified by Leo XII in 1825, made stained-glass windows for the great church of San Petronio in Bologna. Other lay brethren played an important role in the decoration of their own priories. Fra' Damiano Zambelli (1480–1549) produced impressive marquetry for the priory of Bergamo. Other famous Dominican artists include Fra' Bartolomeo Paolo di Jacopo (1472–1517), Fra' Paolino di Antonio del Signoraccio (1488–1547), and Brother Pedron Bedon (1556–1612). Dominican sisters were also involved in the arts. Plautilla Nelli (1523–1588) painted various altarpieces in Florence. This tradition carries on today with brethren such as Kim-En-Joong and Dominicus Carpentier (1938–).

Fra Angelico (Giovanni da Fiesole, c. 1400–1455) is often considered a supreme example of a spiritual artist. He joined the Dominican Observant priory of Fiesole and was later assigned to the San Marco priory in Florence. There he painted frescoes for the cells of each brother as well as for the community rooms. His reputation reached the Vatican, and Pope Eugenius IV (1431–1447) asked him to decorate chapels in the Vatican. Fra Angelico's art is the result of a profound faith and expresses extremely well the ideals set out by the reform movement of his order. He was beatified in 1982 and soon after proclaimed patron of artists by Pope John Paul II.

Monastic Patronage

Abbots and abbesses of important monasteries have long maintained a tradition to have their portrait painted, first mainly on panel and later on canvas. Examples of this custom can be found as early as the 15th century (e.g., Jan Crabbe [d. 1488], O.Cist., abbot of the Benedictine monastery of Ter Doest near Bruges). Later examples can be found for every order or congregation and include portraits by famous artists (e.g., Michael Ophovius, O.P., by P.P. Rubens [1577–1640]). Philippe de Champaigne (1602–1674) maintained regular contact with the Jansenist monastery of Port-Royal near Paris. His paintings of abbess Angélique Arnauld (1591–1661) and other religious of Port-Royal are among the greatest French portraits of the 17th century. Other painters chose to paint monastic figures as a sociological object. Francisco de Zurbarán (1598–1664) painted religious of various orders in Seville.

The decoration of monastic buildings often required commissioning from exterior artists. Many important artists have accepted commissions from monasteries. Rogier van der Weyden (1399–1464) had a son who joined the Carthusians and produced altarpieces for the Carthusian monasteries of Herne and Burgos. Leonardo da Vinci (1452–1519) painted his Last Supper for the Dominican priory of Santa Maria delle Grazie in Milan, and Henri Matisse (1869–1954) decorated the chapel of Dominican Sisters in Vence.

Various periodicals published by religious have dealt with the link between the arts and theology. *L'art sacré* (1935–1969; edited by Alain-Marie Couturier, O.P., and Pie Régamey, O.P.) and *Art d'église* (edited by Frédéric Debuyst, O.S.B.) are examples of attempts to bridge the gap between Christianity and the contemporary arts.

Alain Arnould, O.P.

See also Florence, Italy; Patrons, Christian: Lay

Further Reading

General Works:

Hamburger, Jeffrey, *Nuns as Artists: The Visual Culture of a Medieval Convent*, Berkeley: University of California Press, 1997

Lavergne, Sabine de, *Art sacré et modernité: Les grandes années de la revue "l'Art Sacré,"* Namur: Culture et Verité, 1992

Verdon, Timothy, "Monasticism and Christian Culture," in *Monasticism and the Arts*, edited by Verdon, Syracuse, New York: Syracuse University Press, 1984

Benedictines:

Leclercq, Jean, "Otium Monasticum as a Context for Artistic Creativity," in *Monasticism and the Arts*, edited by Timothy Verdon, Syracuse, New York: Syracuse University Press, 1984

Carthusians:

Girard, Alain, and Daniel Le Blévec, editors, *Les chartreux et l'art: XIVe-XVIIIe siècles: Actes du Xe Colloque international d'histoire et de spiritualité carthusiennes (Villeneuve-lez-Avignon, 15–18 septembre 1988)*, Paris: Cerf, 1989

Cistercians:

Duby, Georges, *Saint Bernard: L'art cistercien*, Paris: Flammarion, 1979

Dominicans:

Alce, Venturino, "Artisti domenicani negli ultimi due secoli," *Arte Cristiana* 82 (1994)

Hood, William, *Fra Angelico at San Marco*, London and New York: BCA, 1993

Marchese, Vincenzo, *Memorie dei più insigni pittori, scultori et architetti domenicani con aggiunta di alcuni scritti intorno le belle arti*, Florence: Presso A. Parenti, 1845

Polli, Vittorio, *Le tarsie di San Bartolomeo in Bergamo del frate Damiano Zambelli, Faber lignarius 1480–1549*, Bergamo: Ferrari, 1995

Norbertines:

De glans van Prémontré: Oude kunst uit Witherenabdijen der Lage Landen, Heverlee: Gemeentebestuur van Heverlee, 1973

Goovaerts, L., *Écrivains, artistes et savants de l'Ordre des Prémontrés*, Brussels: Société belge de librairie, 1899

Visual Arts, Western Christian: Sculpture

In the whole history of Christianity, monastic art never existed as an independent style of its own. Both those monks who created works of art for their monastery and those artists from outside whose work was patronized by a convent followed the same stylistic and iconographic conventions as did contemporary diocesan scriptoria or urban workshops. Nonetheless monastic art set trends for early medieval and Romanesque art, although the products of the courts of the bishops, the kings, and the nobility were of no less importance. At least from the 12th century on, that is, from the emergence of the Gothic style, the mainstream of artistic production was no longer of monastic origin, as urban craftsmen took over the leading position. Because they often created important pieces for monasteries, these objects are taken into account here.

Three categories of sculpture can be established: (1) architectural or monumental sculpture (the chiseled stones form a static part of the building), (2) movable sculpture (statues in stone, wood, metal, and even leather), and (3) applied arts (reliquaries, book covers, liturgical objects, and similar works made of wood, ivory, metal, and so on).

From the early Middle Ages (c. 500–1000), only a few examples of architectural sculpture have been preserved, and these can be illustrated, for example, by the seventh-century capitals of late antique flavor in the crypt of the former abbey of St. Paul in Jouarre. The reading desk of St. Radegunde in the monastery of St. Croix, Poitiers, seems to be the only early medieval wooden piece of applied arts in existence today. Dating from the sixth century, it represents a sort of coarsened Mediterranean style. However, we do not know whether it was made in the monastery or brought from outside, a situation that is typical for nearly all the small objects of religious art found in the treasures of the monasteries. The well-known importance of Hiberno-Saxon style for the early Middle Ages can be demonstrated by the chalice that Duke Tassilo III presented to the monastery of Kremsmünster (Austria) in 777 as well as by some of the contemporary fragments of the marble reliefs preserved in St. John's church in the monastery of Müstair (Switzerland) showing characteristic Irish animal motives. A special case are the many freestanding chiseled crosses that, from the seventh century on, were erected on monastic and ecclesiastical sites in England (Ilkley), Scotland (Ruthwell), and Ireland (Armagh), many of them bearing important bas-reliefs. The Irish high crosses must be understood as products of monastic artists.

Usually we do not have clear information on the social status of the early medieval sculptors, and only a few names are known; the most famous of this epoch certainly is the Benedictine Tuotilo of St. Gall (d. c. 913), who was also a talented musician. We know that he worked both as a goldsmith and as an ivory sculptor; his ivory tablets covering the Evangelium Longum and showing the ascension of the Virgin and the monastery's patron are preserved at St. Gallen, Switzerland. As the celebrated ground plan of this monastery demonstrates, the craftsmen/artists worked within the monastery's walls but without the enclosure. Other convents, such as St. Columban's Bobbio, possessed workshops outside the walls; the artisans must have been slaves or free laymen but not monks. In the early ninth century, Corbie had three foundries of ore and two goldsmiths.

During the central Middle Ages (1000–1200), the situation changed completely. With the construction of many Romanesque monastic stone churches that stand today, many sculptures created for them have been preserved, and many names of sculptors can be found in inscriptions or in historical sources. Although often the epigraphic "XY . . . fecit" does not denote the artist but rather the patron, several Benedictines undoubtedly worked as sculptors. To name some examples from France only, around 1000 a certain fugitive monk from Montier-en-Der (Haute-Marne) called Hugo was renowned as a painter and sculptor. From 1077 to 1081 "Guinamandus monachus" created the tomb of St. Fronto in his monastery Chaise-Dieu. The historian Richer of Senones (Vosges), author of the *Gesta Senonienis ecclesiae*, was a leading sculptor, as he himself designed and chiseled the tombs of a king and of an abbot around 1136. The figures of the mausoleum of St. Lazare (Autun, Musée Rolin) were executed by "Martinus monachus" in the first half of the 12th century. One of the most prominent German artists of the early 12th century was Roger of Helmarshausen, a priest-monk coming from Stablo, who left a book cover and two portable altars. Under the name "Theophilus presbyter," he wrote a famous manual on the technique of applied arts, *Schedula diversarum artium*.

However, during the Gothic period the participation of the religious in art production became insignificant because of the number of lay craftsmen in the towns. Ample documentary evidence shows that now nearly all the major plastic arts of the monasteries were the work of men coming from outside. Of course one or another monk – especially among the *fratres conversi* – might have received training as a sculptor before his conversion or even in the monastery. Thus, one lateral part of the choir stall of the Saxon Premonstratensian church Pöhlde (c. 1285, Hannover, Landesmuseum) shows a tonsured monk in his habit working as lapidary. In the necrology of the abbey of Marbach (Haut-Rhine), a "frater Joannis lapicida" is mentioned in the second half of the 15th century. Bernini's pupil G. Giuliani lived as a *frater conversus* in Heiligenkreuz, O.Cist. (Austria), from 1711 on. However, these were exceptions. Not even most of the great monuments of Romanesque plastic arts made in and for monasteries would have been the work of monks, as we know about lay masters having been invited for that task. In part the collaboration of local monks and lay brothers is probable. However, there seems to be no single monastic sculptor whose fame is comparable to that of the Dominican friar and painter Beato Angelico (1387–1455) or the Carmelite painter Fra Filippo Lippi (c. 1406–1469). Most monastic sculptors, such as Fra Guglielmo da Pisa, O.P. (d. 1313), are known only in local art history.

The most important tasks of high medieval architectural sculpture were the many-figured tympana and historical capitals of the churches and those of the cloisters. In what has been labeled the revival of the monumental plastic arts after the "dark ages," monasteries situated on the frequented pilgrim routes played an important part (although chiseled bas-reliefs belonging to friezes that ornamented church buildings had been known

Romanesque tympanum, south porch, Malmesbury Abbey (Benedictine), 1115–1139. The historian William of Malmesbury (c. 1090–c. 1143) lived here.
Photo courtesy of Chris Schabel

earlier). The art of Cluny III would have been seminal at the end of the 11th century, but only very few of its capitals have survived. An example of a pilgrimage church, belonging to the Cluniac Order, is Vézeley, showing exquisite figural capitals in the nave and the famous tympanum with the Ascension of Christ combined with the Mission of the Apostles (perhaps designed in connection with the preaching of the Second Crusade by St. Bernard of Clairvaux in 1146). The oldest of the historiated cloisters still surviving is that of Moissac (early 12th century). Other than the biblical scenes and saints, a wealth of demonic figures, monsters, and masks are typical of Benedictine architectural sculpture. In England, Italy, Spain, and a bit later in Germany, Benedictine churches showed the same features, even if less frequent and usually of reduced size, for example, Malmesbury Abbey (portal, second half of the 12th century), Monreale (Sicily, historiated cloister, 1175 and more recently), Santo Domingo de Silos (Spain, Christological reliefs, c. late 11th century), and Königslutter in Saxony (cloister, c. 1150).

As regards wooden sculpture, its main tasks were the fashioning of crucifixes, statues of the Virgin ("*sedes sapientiae*") and of the saints, and lecterns. More various were the objects made of metal, for example, chandeliers or antependia (Gross-Comburg, Baden-Württemberg, 1140), portable altars (Fritzlar, Stiftskirche, c. 1160), and reliquaries (shrine of St. Hadelin, Visé, Belgium, 11th to 12th century). All such objects were made for convents of Benedictines or canons; on the contrary the new orders of the monastic reform were not interested in the plastic arts, and St. Bernard's abhorrence of chiseled capitals, as expressed in his "Apologia," will be familiar to all readers. It is only from the 13th century on that sculptures are found in Cistercian monasteries, especially ornamented parts of the architecture and choir stalls (e.g., keystone with dragons in the refectory of Heilsbronn, Baden-Württemberg, c. 1235). At the end of the Middle Ages and in the baroque, stalls like these in Maulbronn (Baden-Württemberg) or Wilhering (Upper Austria), both O.Cist., could have been the pride of any secular church as well.

Although in the earlier development of Gothic art a monastery such as Suger's St. Denis set some of the trends in architecture, the innovative sculpture of this period clearly was developed by the masters of the cathedrals and at the courts of the nobility. From now on until the baroque, the share of monasticism in the plastic arts remains rather insignificant. However, single examples of high quality did exist, such as some of the funeral monuments in the Church of the London Templars (13th century), and works of utmost beauty, such as the prophets made by Claus Sluter around 1400 for the Carthusian monastery of Champmol (Burgundy), but these were enterprises most often initiated not by a convent but by a noble donor who wished to be buried there. This is also true for abbeys with remarkable Renaissance monuments, such as Brou (Ain) (Augustinian Friars), a mausoleum of the Bourbon-Habsburg dynasty. A special invention of the mystical 14th-century Dominican nunneries of southern Germany were the wooden groups of Christ with the sleeping St. John, "Andachtsbilder," intended for meditation (an example is in the Cleveland Museum, c. 1330).

It was the Counter-Reformation that brought a new stream of excellent sculpture into the now often rebuilt monasteries because they had to represent the victorious Roman Church both in architecture and in furnishings. Given the function of many monastic sites as pilgrim centers, impressive altar sculpture was erected above all in southern Germany, the best example of which might be the main altar by Egid Asam (1722/24) in the monastery of Weltenburg, O.S.B. (Bavaria), showing the fight of St. George against the dragon, surrounded by a flood of light falling down from "heaven." It was techniques of the baroque stage that gave life to the ecclesiastical statuary of the time. Other than the churches the libraries of the baroque monasteries, understood as arsenals of spiritual weapons against heresy and disbelief, abounded in splendor; the large allegorical figures by Th. Stammel (c. 1760) in Admont, O.S.B., Styria, illustrate this. Although in the late 17th and 18th centuries the stucco work of Wessobrunn, O.S.B. (Bavaria), gained the widest reputation, only its beginnings stem from the monastery. Notwithstanding a few local exceptions, it is fair to state that in the 19th and 20th centuries the contribution of the monasteries to the sculptural arts has been negligible.

PETER DINZELBACHER

See also Austria; Bobbio, Italy; Cluniacs; Cluny, France; France; Germany; Patrons, Christian: Lay; St. Gallen, Switzerland; Suger

Further Reading

Beaulieu, Michèle, and Victor Beyer, *Dictionnaire des Sculpteurs Français du Moyen Age*, Paris: Picard, 1992

Brinckmann, Albert, *Barockskulptur*, 2 vols., Potsdam: Akademische Verlagsgesellschaft Athenaion MBH, 1917; Berlin-Neubabelsberg: Akademische Verlagsgesellschaft Athenaion MBH, 1919; 2nd edition, 1932

Hearn, Millard F., *Romanesque Sculpture: The Revival of Monumental Stone Sculpture in the Eleventh and Twelfth Centuries*, Ithaca, New York: Cornell University Press, and Oxford: Phaedon, 1981

Legner, Anton, editor, *Ornamenta ecclesiae*, 3 vols., Köln: Stadt Köln, 1900; Köln: Schnütgen-Museum, 1985

Porter, Arthur Kingsley, *Romanesque Sculpture of the Pilgrimage Roads*, 10 vols., Boston: Marshall Jones, 1923

Roth, Helmut, *Kunst und Handwerk im frühen Mittelalter*, Stuttgart: Theiss, 1986

Springer, Anton, "De artificibus laicis et monachis medii aevi," in *Mittheilungen der K.K. Centralkommission zur Erforschung und Erhaltung der Baudenkmale* 7 (1862)

Vocation, Christian

As the Latin root *vocare* ("to call") implies, a vocation is understood in the Christian tradition as the specific calling that each person receives from God. Every human individual is a unique composite of talents, strengths and weaknesses, interests and abilities. Thus, each individual has a unique role to play in the world and can serve and praise God in a unique way. One's vocation is the way of life in which the person can faithfully and authentically express the self as God would will it. It is a response to the creation and gifting that is extended by God. Although as many callings exist as there are persons to follow those, the word *vocation* has often been narrowly associated in English with a vocation to the religious life or has implied that religious service is a "higher" vocation than other callings.

One of the earliest pieces of Christian monastic literature, the *Vita Antonii* (fourth century A.D.), recounts how the young Antony (251?–356) was moved by hearing a reading from Scripture exhorting him to give up all and follow Jesus. The work traces the journey of this man as he gradually comes to realize what that means. His is an actual physical journey from place to deeper place as he deepens his conversation with God. This understanding of the call to deeper relationship is also expressed in the prologue to the Rule of St. Benedict. Benedict (c. 480–c. 550) introduces his teaching by portraying the dialogue whereby God invites a person to spirituality, as stated in Psalm 33:4. "Is there anyone here who yearns for life and desires to see good days?" Benedict has the eager soul answer, "I do," and then God speaks again, inviting the person to walk in God's ways. Benedict says that his own words are addressed to such people, ones who have heard a distinct message for themselves personally and have responded freely to it.

The majority of those who took up Christian monasticism in its early days did so in adulthood and with conscious intent. However, other people took up life in monasteries, especially as this lifestyle became more socially acceptable and even advantageous. Children were often committed to monasteries by their families just as people were committed to arranged marriages or apprenticed to trades at an early age. Others were placed there for care in the absence of family. Although it was generally assumed that they would make a conscious affirmation at a later age, often few suitable alternatives existed were they to decide that they did not feel called to this life. This cultural constraint cannot be dismissed even today, when the rise in vocations in Third World countries and the decline in developed nations at least partially reflects the range of options available to people as regards education and personal development. Yet such a choice involves more than only personal gain and social factors despite what some modern sociologists would contend.

Of course not every religious vocation can be quantified sociologically, and every authentic vocation must contain a strong element of spiritual desire. Especially in cultures in which options for lifestyle are virtually limitless, the fact that some people still choose a monastic vocation affirms their belief that this is a unique and valued choice. Once an adult decision has been made following a lengthy period of discernment and preparation, a monastic vocation is understood to be, like marriage, a commitment made for life unless some extraordinary extenuating circumstances intervene to invalidate the decision.

In modern times as in the beginning, a vocation is considered a conscious, mature response to a perceived calling to a particular way of life that is in keeping with the character and gifts of the individual. When persons feel some attraction to the lifestyle, they generally make contact with a member of the monastic community who serves as a vocation minister, assisting candidates to discern whether this is the lifestyle for them. A period follows in which the candidate and the community becoming acquainted with one another. A majority of communities use some combination of personal visits, recommendations, study, and psychological and physical evaluation in addition to prayer and spiritual guidance in determining whether a person is suited to the way of life.

Each monastic order and each monastery within that order is distinctive because of its history, environment, and the people who inhabit and form it. Some element of vocation draws members to a particular community just as individuals are called not just to the vocation of marriage but to live it out with a particular partner. Like marriage a monastic vocation is more than a career choice. Occupational options within the vocation are many and varied. Some communities live a strictly enclosed life of prayer, contemplation, and manual labor. Others remain in one place but welcome and serve those who come to them by sharing their worship and providing retreats and spiritual direction. Still others engage in a variety of occupations outside the confines of the community although their members live and pray in common.

To take up a vocation is a purposeful and positive action. Contrary to the belief of many, it cannot be a choice made merely out of rejection of other lifestyles or as an escape from the evil world. As Benedict suggests, it is a movement toward something that is seen as good and potentially fulfilling. The monastic vocation involves not only personal prayer, solitude, and contemplation but also the support and challenge of other members of the community. As evidenced in the first stories of Antony and continued as a theme in monastic literature, the community is a model of the peaceable kingdom of the new Eden as well as the continuation of the idealized community of the Acts of the Apostles. Along with the denial of some material and personal goods comes a joy in this life and anticipation of the completion of the coming of the Kingdom. This, then, is a call to be a model of holiness and balance so that individual members might come to peace and fulfillment and others might be led to God through their prayer and example.

JUDITH SUTERA, O.S.B.

See also Antony, St.; Benedict of Nursia, St.; Contemporary Issues: Western Christian; Critiques of Western Christian Monasticism; Initiation: Christian Perspectives; Retreat, Christian; Scholars, Benedictine; Spirituality: Eastern Christian

Further Reading

Athanasius, Saint, *The Life of Antony, and the Letter to Marcellinus*, translated by Robert C. Gregg, New York: Paulist Press, 1980

Boulding, Maria, editor, *A Touch of God: Eight Monastic Journeys*, Still River (now Petersham), Massachusetts: St. Bede's Publications, and London: SPCK, 1982

"A Carthusian," *The Wound of Love: A Carthusian Miscellany*, Kalamazoo, Michigan: Cistercian Publications, and London: Darton, Longman and Todd, 1994

Frank, Karl Suso, *With Greater Liberty: A Short History of Christian Monasticism and Religious Orders*, translated by Joseph Lienhard, Kalamazoo, Michigan: Cistercian Publications, 1993

Fry, Timothy, editor, *RB 80: The Rule of St. Benedict in Latin and English With Notes*, Collegeville, Minnesota: Liturgical Press, 1981

Henry, Patrick, and Donald Swearer, *For the Sake of the World: The Spirit of Buddhist and Christian Monasticism*, Minneapolis, Minnesota: Fortress Press, 1989

Kardong, Terrence, *The Benedictines*, Wilmington, Delaware: Glazier, 1988

Merton, Thomas, *The Monastic Journey*, Mission, Kansas: Sheed, Andrews, and McMeel, and London: Sheldon Press, 1977

Panikkar, Raimundo, *Blessed Simplicity – The Monk as Universal Archetype*, New York: Seabury Press, 1982

Pennington, M. Basil, *The Cistercians*, Collegeville, Minnesota: Liturgical Press, 1992

Rees, Daniel, *Consider Your Call: A Theology of Monastic Life Today*, London: SPCK, 1978; Kalamazoo, Michigan: Cistercian Publications, 1980

Vigilucci, Lino, *Camaldoli: A Journey into Its History and Spirituality*, translated by Peter-Damian Belisle, Trabuco Canyon, California: Source Books, 1995

Vows, Christian. *See* Initiation: Christian Perspectives

W

Walafrid Strabo c. 808–849

German Christian monk, poet, and Abbot of Reichenau

Walafrid (Walahfrid) Strabo, born in the region of Swabia in southwestern Germany, entered the monastery on the island of Reichenau as a young boy and maintained a deep emotional connection to that community throughout his life despite long periods of absence. In 827 he was sent to Fulda to complete his studies under Rabanus Maurus (c. 780–856). Because monks were the principal educators in ninth-century Europe and because Walafrid early on had revealed himself to be an especially talented poet and writer, he was summoned from Fulda to the imperial court to serve as tutor to Louis the Pious' youngest son, Charles the Bald (843–877). Charles later presided over one of the most intense flowerings of the Carolingian renaissance, and the cultured interests of this monarch must owe a great deal to the influence of his teacher.

Louis (814–840) rewarded Walafrid by appointing him abbot of Reichenau in 838. His fellow monks objected to the emperor's act as contrary to their right (previously confirmed by Louis himself) to hold free abbatial elections. When the political chaos of Louis' last years allowed the community at Reichenau to thwart the imperial will, Walafrid was driven into exile and another abbot elected in his place. The monks do not appear to have felt any personal animosity toward Walafrid. Not only did he keep in contact with his monastery but he dedicated to the librarian of Reichenau (one of his former teachers) the major work composed during his exile, the *De exordiis et incrementis quarundam in observationibus ecclesiasticis rerum* ("On the Origin and Development of Some Aspects of the Liturgy"), the earliest known history of the Christian Liturgy. In 842, thanks to the intervention of the abbot of St. Gall, Walafrid was able to return home and resume office. He enjoyed monastic tranquillity for seven years before tragically drowning in the Loire River while traveling on a diplomatic mission for his former royal pupil.

Contemporaries admired Walafrid for both his literary gifts and his theological knowledge. He was often commissioned to edit prestigious texts written by others into a more polished form, as he did for Einhard's biography of Charlemagne. He wrote numerous verse epistles and lyrics, some of which express the qualities of monastic friendship (*amicitia*) with particular beauty and depth. He also served as court poet while tutoring Charles the Bald. The later Middle Ages esteemed him mainly for his saints' lives (especially his *Vita sancti Galli*) and for his works of biblical exegesis, but in and around Lake Constance his poetry was preserved. Two of his best poetic compositions are devoted to describing Reichenau: a shorter piece written at Fulda to convey his longing for the island monastery and a long description of the monastery's garden (*De cultura hortorum*) written while he was abbot. The German humanists rediscovered Walafrid's poetry in the late 15th century, and his verse provides revealing glimpses of the emotional and intellectual outlook of a ninth-century monk. The personal academic notebook (*vademecum*) that he kept throughout his life is also extant, a rare survival identified and described by Bernhard Bischoff.

Scott Wells

See also Alcuin; Botany; Fulda, Germany; Gardens: Christian Perspectives; Germany: History; Hagiography: Western Christian; Hymnographers; Pharmacology; Rabanus Maurus

Biography

Educated at the Abbey of Reichenau, Walafrid "the Squinter" wrote poems there. He studied with Rabanus Maurus at Fulda, and later tutored the future Emperor Charles the Bald. From 839 until his death by drowning in 849 he served as Abbot of Reichenau. He carried on traditions of the Carolingian Renaissance.

Major Works

Visio Wettini
De cultura hortorum
De exordiis et incrementis quarundam in observationibus ecclesiasticis rerum

Further Reading

Bischoff, Bernhard, "Eine Sammelhandschrift Walahfrid Strabos (Cod. Sangall. 878)," in *Mittelalterliche Studien: Ausgewählte Aufsätze zur Schriftkunde und Literaturgeschichte*, volume 2, edited by Bischoff, Stuttgart: Anton Hiersemann, 1966

Borst, Arno, *Mönche am Bodensee: 610–1525*, Sigmaringen: Thorbecke, 1978

Brooke, Martin, "The Prose and Verse Hagiography of Walahfrid Strabo," in *Charlemagne's Heir: New Perspectives on the Reign of Louis the Pious (814–840)*, edited by Peter Godman and Roger Collins, Oxford and New York: Clarendon Press, 1990
Duckett, Eleanor Shipley, *Carolingian Portraits: A Study in the Ninth Century*, Ann Arbor: University of Michigan Press, 1962
Godman, Peter, *Poetry of the Carolingian Renaissance*, London: Duckworth, and Norman: University of Oklahoma Press, 1985
Godman, Peter, *Poets and Emperors: Frankish Politics and Carolingian Poetry*, Oxford and New York: Clarendon Press, 1986
Harting-Correa, Alice L., *Walahfrid Strabo's Libellus de exordiis et incrementis quarundam in observationibus ecclesiasticis rerum: A Translation and Liturgical Commentary*, Leiden and New York: Brill, 1996
Langosch, Karl, and Benedikt Konrad Vollman, "Walahfrid Strabo," in *Verfasserlexikon der deutschen Literatur des Mittelalters* 10:2, Berlin and New York: de Gruyter, 1997
Stoffler, Hans-Dieter, *Der Hortulus des Walahfrid Strabo: Aus dem Kräutergarten des Klosters Reichenau*, Sigmaringen: Thorbecke, 1978; 4th edition, 1996

Waldensian Monasticism. *See* Protestant Monasticism: Waldensian

Wales

Monasticism certainly existed in early Wales, as it is mentioned by Gildas (d. c. 547). Its practices owed much to those of the eastern Mediterranean, the influence of the Desert Fathers apparently reaching Britain via the western sea-routes. Welsh customs thus resembled those of early Irish monasticism but contrasted with those of the disciplined Benedictine congregations of the European Continent. Evidence for early Welsh monasticism occurs in a preface on penance attributed to Gildas and a Latin *Life of St. Samson of Dol* (d. 565). Both texts emphasize manual work, obedience to a rule, and austerity. A tendency toward eremitism is indicated by such isolated monastic sites as Burry Holms in west Glamorgan and Caldy Island off the coast of southwestern Wales.

By the 11th century the most powerful monastic communities in Wales included Llancarfan and Llantwit in Glamorgan, St. Davids in southwestern Wales, Llanbadarn near Aberystwyth, and Tywyn and Clynnog in northwestern Wales. These monasteries, in Welsh called *clas* (plural, *clasau*), attracted criticism from 12th-century reformers. Their monks were allowed to marry, and property rights were transmitted hereditarily. The St. Davids community even included the married bishop Sulien (1011–1091), whose son Rhygyfarch (d. 1099) became a famous scholar and scribe.

East end, Tintern Abbey (Cistercian), Gwent, Wales, late 13th century, suppressed 1536.
Photo courtesy of Chris Schabel

Site of the Cistercian Abbey of Valle Crucis, Llangollen, Clwyd, Wales, 13th–14th century.
Photo courtesy of Chris Schabel

Llanthony Priory (Augustinian Canons), Gwent, Wales, 13th century.
Photo courtesy of Chris Schabel

When the Normans began their gradual conquest of Wales in the late 11th century, they founded monasteries in the regions they controlled (the March). Monasteries were established as well in areas that, until the death of Prince Llywelyn in 1282, remained under native Welsh rule. The surviving *clasau* were also refounded on conventional lines. Thus, in the Norman zone were established Benedictine priories at Brecon (c. 1110) and Ewenni (1141) and Cistercian abbeys at Neath (1130), Tintern (1131), and Margam (1147). All these houses were in southern Wales, they proved consistently hostile to the native Welsh, and their monks were largely or entirely French- or English-speaking. They contrast with such houses in independent Wales as the Cistercian abbey of Strata Florida (founded 1164) near Aberystwyth and the Premonstratensian abbey of Talley (before 1197) in western Wales. Strata Florida remained strongly Welsh in spirit, with a scriptorium active in Latin and Welsh. As for the *clasau*, the last to go was that on the remote, rocky island of Bardsey, off the coast of northwestern Wales. Encountered by Gerald of Wales in 1188 (and described in his *Itinerary of Wales*), it was refounded in the 13th century for the Augustinian Canons.

When the friars reached Wales, they established houses in both the March and independent Wales, as the Cistercians had done before them. The Franciscans of Llanfaes on Anglesey (founded before 1245) were closely associated with the diplomatic and political negotiations of the last native princes. The friars also had literary interests. Brother Madog ap Gwallter composed a Welsh Christmas lyric (often translated) that is worthy of St. Francis (1181/82–1226) himself, whereas a Dominican friar wrote the prose *Ymborth yr Enaid* (Food of the Soul), a mystical treatise resembling the work of Walter Hilton (c. 1343–1396) or Dame Julian of Norwich (c. 1342–after 1416).

The decline of regular life in late medieval Wales is often emphasized. Medieval Wales was not a richly endowed country, and Welsh monasteries, besides the normal economic and spiritual problems of the age, suffered destruction and loss in times of rebellion, especially that of Owen Glendower (d. 1416). Inherent poverty and medieval destruction have been compounded by postdissolution loss. Thus, Daniel Huws comments that although in the early 14th century Margam abbey possessed 242 manuscripts of theology alone, not a single one survives. On the other hand, he notes that the abbey archive is the fullest monastic archive in Britain to have come down to us.

At the dissolution of the monasteries (1536–1539), 47 religious houses existed in Wales. The most numerous were the

Cistercians (13 houses), followed by the Benedictines (eight), Tironians (three), and Cluniacs (one). The Augustinian Canons had six houses, the Premonstratensians two. There were five Dominican friaries, three Franciscan, one Carmelite, and one Austin; one house of the Knights of St. John; one convent of Benedictine nuns, and two of Cistercian nuns.

The regular life in post-Reformation Wales is represented by Augustine Baker (1575–1641), active at Abergavenny in southeastern Wales, and by the Jesuit college at Cwm near Monmouth, founded in 1622 by John Salusbury (1575–1625) but closed down in 1678–1679 by John Croft, Protestant bishop of Hereford. Abergavenny, together with Holywell in northeastern Wales, remained a Recusant stronghold, but Welsh Catholicism was generally at a low ebb until the 19th century.

In 1848 the Jesuits founded the college of St. Beuno near St. Asaph in northeastern Wales (the poet G.M. Hopkins [1844–1889] studied there in 1874–1877). In 1869 Fr. Ignatius (the Rev. Joseph Leycester Lyne, 1837–1908) established an Anglican monastic community at Capel-y-ffin (near the old Augustinian priory of Llanthony in the mountains of southeastern Wales), where his tomb is the center of a cult. Another Anglican Benedictine community, established on Caldy Island in 1906, converted wholesale to Rome in 1913. It left in 1928 for Prinknash, Gloucestershire, and was replaced in 1929 by Cistercian monks from Scourmont, Belgium. Thus, at Caldy the Welsh monastic tradition has come full circle, as inscribed stones there attest to the presence of an early Christian community. Since 1990 Cistercian nuns have resided at Holy Cross abbey, Whitland, in southwestern Wales. The Benedictine abbey at Belmont (founded 1859), near Hereford, is ecclesiastically in Wales but physically in England.

Andrew Breeze

See also Anglican Monasticism; Baker, Augustine; David, St.; Desert Fathers; Dissolution of Monasteries: England, Ireland, and Wales; Ireland: History; Julian of Norwich

Further Reading

Bowen, Emrys George, *Saints, Seaways and Settlements in the Celtic Lands*, Cardiff: University of Wales Press, 1977
Breeze, Andrew C., *Medieval Welsh Literature*, Dublin and Portland, Oregon: Four Courts Press, 1997
Cowley, Frederick G., *The Monastic Order in South Wales 1066–1349*, Cardiff: University of Wales Press, 1977
Davies, R.R., *Conquest, Coexistence, and Change: Wales 1063–1415*, Oxford: Clarendon Press, 1987
Davies, Wendy, *Wales in the Early Middle Ages*, Atlantic Highlands, New Jersey: Humanities Press, and Leicester: Leicester University Press, 1982
Huws, Daniel, "The Medieval Manuscript," in *A Nation and Its Books: A History of the Book in Wales*, edited by Philip Henry Jones and Eiluned Rees, Aberystwyth: National Library of Wales, 1998
Jenkins, Philip, *A History of Modern Wales 1536–1990*, New York and London: Longman, 1992
Lewis, J.M., and David H. Williams, *The White Monks in Wales*, Cardiff: National Museum of Wales, 1976
Lloyd, John Edward, Robert Thomas Jenkins, and William Llewelyn Davies, editors, *The Dictionary of Welsh Biography Down to 1940*, London: Honourable Society of Cymmrodorion, 1959
Rees, William, *An Historical Atlas of Wales from Early to Modern Times*, London: Faber and Faber, 1951
Williams, Glanmor, *The Welsh Church from Conquest to Reformation*, Cardiff: University of Wales Press, 1976; Fayetteville: University of Arkansas Press, 1993
Williams, Glanmor, *Wales and the Reformation*, Cardiff: University of Wales Press, 1997

Warrior Monks: Buddhist

"Monk" armies attached to Buddhist temples and Shintō shrines played a major political role from the middle of the 11th century to the end of the 16th century in Japan. Referred to as *sōhei* or *shūto* in Japanese literature (warrior, soldier, or militant monks), scores of these "armies" operated as a phenomenon of Japanese religious and secular life from the breakdown of central authority after the ninth century to the destruction of the Enryaku-ji north of Kyoto by the warlord Oda Nobunaga in 1571 and the disarming of the populace by the Tokugawa rulers in the early 17th century.

The growth of landholdings into large family estates (*shōen*) resulted from the Nara government's inability to control either its land allotment plan or the geographic expansion of the population. Controls on temples were unenforced, and their land acquisitions went on apace. Decades of fighting the Ezo or Emishi (presumably Ainu) in the north had reached an impasse, but improvements in army recruiting and training by the end of the eighth century and new leadership in the early ninth century brought the war to a conclusion. At one time more than 30,000 troops had been stationed in the northern battle zone, and countless service personnel supported the extended supply lines connecting the frontier posts.

Thousands of young men whose only training and experience had been in warfare were freed from conscript duty. Some attached themselves as security guards to estates and temples, ultimately taking on the character of small armies. With time their function changed from territorial protection to implementing political policy as they undertook alliances with local lords, struggled for favor with or coerced the central government, and attempted to suppress rival sects. Any issue could trigger blows, such as appointments, succession questions, and land claims.

The first record of a temple dispute that saw the deployment of an armed group concerns the Kōfuku-ji in Nara in 968, and around 970 the Gion shrine in Kyoto put its militant monks into action. By the middle of the 11th century, raids on Kyoto from the Enryaku-ji on Mount Hiei were fairly commonplace. Emperor Shirakawa (r. 1073–1086) lamented that the three elements over which he had no control were the Kamo River, gambling, and warrior monks. Tendai temple warrior monks, motivated by their traditional sectarian hostility to the old mainline Nara temples, terrorized Kyoto for centuries, chalking up a history of massive destruction. Nichiren sect temples, because of their priests' antigovernment and belligerent attitude, were a common enemy, and Zen temples were also a major target, notwithstanding their patronage by the samurai and Hōjō and Ashikaga ruling families. The shōgun was frequently forced to compromise with warrior monks' unreasonable demands, caught in the dilemma of often needing their support and intimidated by the fear of antagonizing the deities that the temples honored. Until the entire country was thrown into the chaos of civil war from around 1400, the warrior monks tilted politics in their favor.

The largest armies were apparently kept by the Kōfuku-ji in Nara, the old Fujiwara family temple; the Enryaku-ji on Mount Hiei northeast of Kyoto, the prominent Tendai sect temple built there to protect the city from the evil spirits that always attack from that direction; and Onjō-ji (or Mii-dera) in Otsu, a Tendai branch temple near Lake Biwa that claimed an earlier founding than the Enryaku-ji. Shintō shrines recorded in medieval history as being involved in militant politics were Gion (or Yasaka shrine) on the east side of Kyoto, a shrine with disastrous Mount Hiei connections, its structures all requiring rebuilding around the middle of the 17th century; Kitano shrine in northwest Kyoto, dedicated to Sugawara Michizane, the Fujiwara's rival politician (who died in exile in Kyushu in 903), the buildings fully reconstructed in the early years of the same century; Hiroshi shrine in Otsu city, too closely allied with the Enryaku-ji and burned in 1571, never regaining much prominence; and the Kumano shrine and its famous sacred waterfalls – more properly three shrines – at the southern tip of the Kii peninsula in Wakayama prefecture, the well-known pilgrimage site of medieval times. Its relative physical remoteness from Kyoto and Nara politics stood to its advantage.

In terms of numbers a night raid on Nichiren Lotus sect (Hokke-shū) temples from the Enryaku-ji, for example, might muster about 3,000 warrior monks descending on northern Kyoto, but it is said that at one point some 20,000 monks from the Enryaku-ji and an equal number from the Kōfuku-ji were ready to join battle. Kyoto was to be protected by preventing the Nara monks from crossing the Kizu River. Practiced only in hit-and-run tactics, warrior monks found pitched contests a form of engagement to be avoided.

A thrusting pole arm, known as *naginata*, became the symbol of the warrior monks, borrowed from the standard foot soldier's arsenal used from the 11th to the 15th century. This wooden pole between about four and eight feet in length had a slightly curved iron blade of no more than two and a half inches extending from its end. Eventually women were trained in its use. Most of these "monks" made little pretense of religious involvement other than shaving their heads, and they now appear to have been little more than riffraff living off the spoils of plunder and arson. They were, in fact, notoriously cowardly fighters, quite unable to stand up to the troops of any of the warlords. They sallied out of their sacred precincts, making spectacular use of their religious symbols that, to the ordinary folk, seemed inviolable and untouchable. Portable shrines were carried into Kyoto from the Enryaku-ji – the direction known to the citizenry as the "gate of hell." The local people's fear of even being near the shrines paralyzed whole blocks of the city where the shrines were left.

Relations with Jōdo Shinshū reached irreparable enmity when Mount Hiei monks were able to force the expulsion from Kyoto of Priest Rennyo in 1465, the eighth abbot of the sect's chief temple, Hongan-ji, and burn the buildings. When the headquarters of the sect were moved several times, in each new location the followers successfully converted the local peasantry through their existing agricultural organizations.

These militant peasant uprisings comprised the most persistent opposition to Oda Nobunaga (1534–1582), the virtual unifier of the country. He fought them on several fronts from the 1550s. Known as the *ikkō ikki* revolts, scattered in many provinces (in particular the present-day prefectures of Osaka, Aichi, Mie, and Fukui), they allied themselves with any warlord who opposed the current central leadership. Nobunaga torched the Hongan-ji and slaughtered the major participants in the revolts. The Enryaku-ji monks sheltered Asai and Asakura forces then being pursued by Oda Nobunaga's troops, making the temple on Mount Hiei the target for his revenge. In 1571 he set fire to the 3,000 buildings of the Enryaku-ji and killed the roughly 3,000 defenders, thereby closing the final chapter on the activities of the warrior monks.

J. EDWARD KIDDER, JR.

See also Japan: History; Kyoto, Japan; Mount Hiei, Japan; Nara, Japan; Nation-Building and Japanese Buddhism; Prophethood, Japanese Buddhist; Zen, Arts of

Further Reading

Elison, George, "Enryakuji, Burning of," in *Kōdansha Encyclopedia of Japan*, volume 2, Tokyo and New York: Kōdansha International, 1983

Hurst, Cameron, "Warrior Monks," in *Kōdansha Encyclopedia of Japan*, volume 8, Tokyo and New York: Kōdansha International, 1983

Lamont, H.G., "Temmon Hokke Rebellion," in *Kōdansha Encyclopedia of Japan*, volume 7, Tokyo and New York: Kōdansha International, 1983

"Oda Nobunaga (1534–1582)," in *Kōdansha Encyclopedia of Japan*, volume 6, Tokyo and New York: Kōdansha International, 1983

Sansom, George, *A History of Japan to 1334*, Stanford, California: Stanford University Press, 1958

Saunders, Dale, *Buddhism in Japan*, Philadelphia: University of Pennsylvania Press, 1964

Warrior Monks: Christian

The fall of Jerusalem to a crusading army of European knights in 1099 virtually completed the Christian conquest of the Holy Land. Pilgrims flocked in increasing numbers from Europe to Palestine to see the sacred sites associated with the life and death of Jesus. However, Muslim highwaymen were often waiting on the roads inland from the coast to rob, kidnap, and murder unwary travelers.

When local Christian authorities proved unable to provide the troops needed to patrol the pilgrim routes, a new type of Christian soldier, the military monk, appeared in the early 12th century. Two congregations of soldier-monks, the Templars and the Hospitallers, assumed primary responsibility. They would be joined at the end of the 12th century by the Teutonic Knights.

The curious fusion of monastic piety and discipline with military activity reflected a long-developing Christian idea of Holy War. In the mid-1120s the renowned Cistercian abbot Bernard of Clairvaux (1090–1153) consummated the link of warfare with monastic piety. Inspired by an encounter with Templars in Europe, Bernard became convinced that fighting Christ's enemies in a holy cause was a just and highly commendable way of saving one's soul. Why not combine, then, the religious dedication and discipline of the monk with a military career? Just as labor in the fields and prayer in the cloister comprised basic

East end with Percy Chapel, Tynemouth Abbey (Benedictine), Northumbria, England, 15th century. The fortified abbey stands on a cliff above the North Sea.
Photo courtesy of Chris Schabel

Southwest corner of the inner walls, Crac des Chevaliers (Hospitallers), Syria, with glacis and moat, first half of the 13th century.
Photo courtesy of Chris Schabel

ways of traditional monks to salvation, so wielding the sword against the infidel offered another path to redemption for monks with military skills. Bernard hoped to resuscitate an ideal of Christian knighthood badly tarnished by the sometimes appalling conduct of crusader knights intent mainly on personal gain and self-aggrandizement.

The Templars originated in 1118 in the commitment of a few former French crusaders to serve as escorts for pilgrims to the Christian holy places. Because their first residence stood on the site reputedly that of the ancient Hebrew Temple of Solomon, the new confraternity became the "Poor Knights of Christ and the Temple of Solomon" or simply "Templars." Their responsibility for the defense of pilgrims would soon expand to include defense of the Holy Land in general wherever Christian dominion was threatened. In 1128 the Templars were recognized as a new monastic order based on a rule drafted in part by Bernard of Clairvaux. Shortly thereafter the pope exempted the Templars from any authority but his own.

When not on campaign Templars were to follow a rigorous monastic regimen. Required were permanent monastic vows of

Gallery or cloister viewed from the east, Crac des Chevaliers (Hospitallers), Syria, first half of the 13th century.
Photo courtesy of Chris Schabel

chastity, personal poverty, and absolute obedience to superiors. Also required was recitation of a modified daily office of prayers and chapel attendance. All were to reside in barracks dormitories and observe silence at meals. The rule also specified the conduct of Templars in the field, including care of their horses and weapons. All knights were to wear over their armor a white tunic marked with the distinctive red cross of the order.

As with the other military orders, there were three classes of Templars: the mounted knight-monks who usually were of noble birth, sergeants of bourgeois background who served as infantrymen or as stewards, and noncombatant priest-chaplains who conducted religious services. In short the Templar knight-monks and the sergeants remained laymen despite living under full monastic discipline.

Meanwhile Templar fortunes were greatly enhanced by donations of land and money in the European homeland. By the mid–12th century Templar monastic "commanderies" stretched across Western Christendom and became key foundations for training recruits and collecting money to support the Templar enterprise overseas. In turn this growth required an elaborate hierarchy of Templar officials, headed by an elected master-general and his deputies. Ironically, the very wealth and extent of the Templar establishment would help to cause its eventual downfall.

On the other hand the Order of the Knights of St. John of the Hospital of Jerusalem (Hospitallers) originated, as the name suggests, in the treatment of the sick in the holy city. Only gradually and apparently in imitation of the Templars did the Hospitallers become militarized. By the mid-1130s they had adopted a monastic-military rule and an organization very similar to that of the Templars.

From this point on Templars and Hospitallers formed the core of crusader armies and castle garrisons, a professional elite of disciplined, highly motivated shock troops who fought in the many battles against the Muslim powers in Palestine. The military monks proved far superior to the short-term feudal levies and mercenaries that made up most of the crusader armies of the day. Ultimately, however, the military monks were too few and the power of a resurgent Islam too formidable to prevent the collapse of the crusader empire in the Near East. The fall of the coastal citadel of Acre in 1291 ended the Western Christian hold on Palestine.

With the Holy Land lost, the Templars concentrated their energies on building their base of power and wealth in Europe. They initiated the most important international banking operation of the day, pioneering, for example, the use of "letters of credit," or checks, and making large, high-interest loans to European governments.

Rock-cut moat of Templar Castle (later held by the Hospitallers) at Gastria, north of Famagusta, Cyprus, early 13th century. Photo courtesy of Chris Schabel

Just after 1300 one of these governments, that of the ambitious French King Phillip IV (1285–1314), resolved to break the financial monopoly of the Templar commanderies for the economic benefit of the French crown. A series of trials of leading Templar officials followed in France on the basis of flimsy but highly incendiary morals charges. The grim process culminated in 1312 with the burning at the stake of the defiant last Templar grand master, Jacques de Molay. Two years earlier the Templar Order had been suppressed by Pope Clement V (1305–1314), who had been intimidated by the French king. The papacy was the only superior authority acknowledged by the Templars.

Templar holdings around Europe were seized by local authorities or redistributed to the Hospitallers, who had managed through their continuing charitable activities to avoid much of the animosity leveled against the Templars. By the time of its demise, the Templar Order, whose original motto was "poverty and humility," was widely perceived as embodying nearly the opposite of these virtues.

The Hospitallers met a different fate. Their sustaining purpose after Palestine was the defense of various islands of the eastern Mediterranean against Muslim expansion. Only with Napoleon's capture of Malta in 1806, more than five centuries after the fall of Acre, did the military mission of the Hospitallers end. Their charitable activities continue down to the present under the name "Knights of Malta."

Meanwhile the Teutonic Knights, the third and last of the major military orders founded in the Holy Land, had gone on to a fertile new field of operation in far northeastern Europe. During the 14th and 15th centuries, these Germanic warrior monks conquered and converted to Christianity the native populations of Prussia and Livonia dwelling along the chilly Baltic coastlands (Livonia encompassed what would become the modern lands of Latvia, Lithuania, and Estonia).

Extensive German colonization followed, especially in East Prussia, in a fashion that transformed this remote region into another outpost of the Western Christian world. The Teutonic Knights survived until 1809 when Napoleon dissolved the Order as a military force. It survives as a charitable order centered in Austria.

Finally the medieval tradition of the warrior monk found still another remarkable manifestation in various military orders founded in 12th-century Spain and Portugal. Between 1150 and 1500 the congregations of Calatrava and Santiago would serve as notably effective instruments of Spanish and Portuguese Christian princes in their reconquest of the Iberian Peninsula from the Muslims. Then, having achieved their prime objective, the Iberian orders were demilitarized.

By 1500, if not before, it was obvious that the idea of Christian holy war, like the crusading idea generally, had lost the power to inspire. The stirring ideal of devoting one's military skills to Christ's service in a holy cause sealed through monastic vows was born in a highly charged spiritual environment that no longer existed. Yet despite the obvious failure and disillusionment of the warrior monks in the Holy Land, their brethren

The Twin Churches of the Templars (on the left) and of the Hospitallers (on the right), Famagusta, Cyprus, c. 1300.
Photo courtesy of Chris Schabel

elsewhere, especially in Prussia and Spain, had attained extraordinary successes.

Other societies, such as Japan, had nurtured elite warrior castes, but only the medieval Christian West generated a class of professional soldiers who became monks in order to fight a holy war.

DONALD D. SULLIVAN

See also Antonians; Bernard of Clairvaux, St.; Crusades; Hospitallers (Knights of Malta since 1530); Israel/Palestine; Jerusalem, Israel; Mercedarians; Pilgrimages, Christian: Near East; Spain; Templars; Teutonic Order

Further Reading

Barber, Malcolm, *The Trial of the Templars*, Cambridge and New York: Cambridge University Press, 1978
Barber, Malcolm, *The New Knighthood: A History of the Order of the Temple*, Cambridge and New York: Cambridge University Press, 1994
Benninghoven, Friedrich, *Unter Kreuz und Adler: Der deutschen Orden im Mittelalter*, Mainz: Hase and Koehler, 1990
Christiansen, Eric, *The Northern Crusades: The Baltic and the Catholic Frontier, 1100–1525*, London and New York: Macmillan, 1980
Forley, Alan, *The Military Orders: From the Twelfth to the Early Fourteenth Centuries*, Toronto and Buffalo, New York: University of Toronto Press, 1992
King, Edwin, *The Knights Hospitallers in the Holy Land*, London: Methuen, 1931
Lomax, Derek W., *Los ordenes militares en la Península ibérica durante la Edad Media*, Salamanca: KADMOS, 1976
Nicholson, Helen, *Templars, Hospitallers, and Teutonic Knights: Images of the Military Orders, 1128–1291*, Leicester and New York: Leicester University Press, 1995
Seward, Desmond, *The Monks of War: The Military Religious Orders*, London: Eyre Methuen, and Hamden, Connecticut: Shoestring Press, 1972; 2nd edition, London and New York: Penguin, 1995

Wat. *See* Temple, Buddhist

Welfare. *See* Social Services

Western Buddhism. *See* Buddhism: Western

Whitby, England

Modern pilgrim-tourists who scale the cliffs high above the North Sea at the town of Whitby (Yorkshire) find themselves not only in the impressive 13th-century ruins of the abbey church but on the site of the most famous Anglo-Saxon ecclesiastical council. Here at Streoneshalh (Danish Whitby), King Oswy (642–670) of Northumbria founded a double house for men and women. This was the largest of the 12 monasteries that he vowed in return for victory over King Penda of Mercia. Hilda (614–680), abbess of Hartlepool, came as abbess in 657. In 664 Oswy, apparently encouraged by his son, Alchfrith, called a council to resolve the principal difference – Easter dating – separating his own Celtic Christians of Iona and Ireland from the Roman Christians of his queen, Eanflaed, from Kent. Members of the royal family celebrated Easter on two different days. On behalf of the Celts, Bishop Colman (d. 676) of Lindisfarne cited St. John the Apostle, Bishop Cedd of the East Saxons, and the pre-Nicene Anatolius of Laodicea as his authorities for allowing Easter to coincide occasionally with the Jewish Passover. Because the leading Roman hierarch, the Frankish-born Bishop Agilbert of Wessex, was less acquainted with English, Wilfrid (634–709) of Ripon spoke for Rome, claiming that Anatolius had been misunderstood and that he himself spoke for St. Peter and Rome. At this point Colman admitted St. Peter's precedence, and Oswy, "smiling," decided for St. Peter lest when he die the gatekeeper of Heaven who holds the keys "may turn his back on me." Colman retired to Iona, resigning his bishopric. Although England was now largely united in Easter dating, Celtic practices continued for a time on Iona and in Ireland.

In time the greatest monastery in northeastern England, Whitby also grew as an intellectual and cultural center. It witnessed the birth of English poetry through its cowherd-poet Caedmon (fl. 670). Six bishops were educated there, and the earliest *Life of Pope Gregory the Great* (590–604) was written at Whitby. After Hilda's death in 680, Oswy's wife, Eanflaed, and then his daughter, Ælfflaed, succeeded as abbess.

Destroyed around 867 in the Danish attacks, Whitby was deserted until it was reestablished more than 200 years later. Between 1076 and 1080, Reinfrid, a monk of Evesham but also *miles strenuissimus*, settled with companions on the site on land given by the Norman Lord William Percy. A secession soon formed St. Mary's Abbey, York. Whitby changed from priory to abbey in the early 12th century and became Yorkshire's third-wealthiest Benedictine house, partly because King Henry I (1100–1135) gave it income from the port of Whitby and the wrecks there. Its great church, now in ruins, was built in the early 13th century; the present west end and part of the north nave wall date from a 14th-century addition. Medieval records range from declaring that the rule was kept *salubriter et stricte* to describing a quarreling house (in existence from 1365 to 1366) that required Edward III' (1327–1377) intervention. Whitby was suppressed by Henry VIII (1509–1547) on 14 December 1543, its abbot retiring with pensions of £66.13s. 4d.; there were 22 monks at the suppression.

Three modern excavations (one from 1920 to 1925, one in 1958, and one in 1989) have uncovered much of the abbey and its precincts, with varying interpretations. The abbey is now in the care of the Department of the Environment, and a visitor shop has recently been constructed.

WILLIAM A. CHANEY

See also England; Hilda, St.; Lindisfarne/Holy Isle, England

Further Reading

Butler, Lionel, and Chris Given-Wilson, *Medieval Monasteries of Great Britain*, London: Joseph, 1979
Johnson, Mark, "The Saxon Monastery at Whitby: Past, Present, Future," in *In Search of Cult: Archaeological Investigations in Honour of Philip Rahtz*, edited by Martin Carver, Woodbridge, Suffolk, and Rochester, New York: Boydell Press, 1993
Knowles, David, *The Religious Orders in England*, 3 vols., Cambridge: Cambridge University Press, 1948; New York: Cambridge University Press, 1976
Knowles, David, *The Monastic Order in England*, Cambridge: Cambridge University Press, 1949; New York: Cambridge University Press, 1976
Knowles, David, *Bare Ruined Choirs: The Dissolution of the English Monasteries*, Cambridge: Cambridge University Press, 1976
Lefroy, W. Chambers, *The Ruined Abbeys of Yorkshire*, London: Seeley, Jackson, and Hall, 1883; New York: Seeley, 1891
Peers, Charles, and C.A. Ralegh Radford, "The Saxon Monastery of Whitby," *Archaeologia* 89 (1943)
Woodward, G.W.O., *The Dissolution of the Monasteries*, New York: Walker, and London: Blandford Press, 1966
Young, George, *A History of Whitby and Streoneshalh Abbey*, 2 vols., Whitby: Clark and Medd, 1817

White Canons. *See* Augustinian Canons

Wilfrid, St. 634–709

English Bishop of York and promoter of Roman Christianity in Northern England

Born to a Northumbrian noble family, at age 14 Wilfrid entered the monastery of Lindisfarne during the abbacy of the Irishman Aidan (634–651). In 652 he went to the Kentish royal court and in 653 to Rome. His Roman stay determined his career. He became a supporter of Roman ecclesiastical usage in preference to the Irish. In 654 he moved to Lyons, living with Bishop Annemundus and receiving the monastic tonsure. After the bishop's murder (658), Wilfrid made his way back to England (659).

Alchfrith, son of the Northumbrian King Oswy (642–670), patronized Wilfrid and gave him the newly founded monastery of Ripon (and expelled the Irish monks already there). By 664 Wilfrid had been ordained and became the leading spokesperson for the Romanizing contingent at the Synod of Whitby (664), when Oswy decided to follow Roman rather than Celtic ecclesiastical practices and to patronize Romanized, Benedictine monasticism rather than the Irish type.

Within a year Wilfrid had become bishop of York. The See of Canterbury being vacant, he went to Gaul for consecration, only to have Oswy, then quarreling with Alchfrith, give the See of York to Chad (d. 672) in Wilfrid's absence. He returned to the monastery of Ripon but even while there still tried to carry out episcopal functions.

Archbishop Theodore of Canterbury (668–690) deposed Chad and restored Wilfrid (669), who ruled peacefully but in some splendor. He traveled with an entourage of 120, built churches, and founded monasteries, such as Hexham. In 678 King Ecgfrith (670–685) joined with Theodore to break up the diocese of York and curtail Wilfrid's power. The resourceful Wilfrid left England to evangelize among the pagan Frisians and then went to Rome to appeal his case (679). The following year Pope Agatho (678–681) decided in his favor. The victorious Wilfrid returned home, only to find that Ecgfrith simply ignored the papal decision and even imprisoned Wilfrid, releasing him only when he agreed to exile.

From 681 to 686 Wilfrid evangelized among pagans in southern England and founded the monastery of Selsey, returning to

Northumbria after Ecgfrith's death. He reconciled with Theodore, and in 686 King Aldfrith (685–705) restored him to York, now a much smaller diocese than when he had previously been bishop. Wilfrid ruled quietly until 691, when history repeated itself: he quarreled with the king and went into exile in southern England. However, he did manage to retain authority over the churches and monasteries he had founded. In 703 Aldfrith tried to deny those foundations their endowments. The aged Wilfrid went to Rome to appeal successfully to Pope John VI (701–705). He returned to England shortly before Aldfrith's death; King Osred (705–716) allowed him to settled in Northumbria. He died in 709.

A difficult, imperious man, Wilfrid held few monastic values but founded several monasteries, all of which spread the use of the Benedictine Rule and Roman practices in England as well as enhanced Wilfrid's personal sway. He played a key role in the supplanting of Celtic practices. His disciple, the priest Eddius Stephanus, wrote his *Vita* around 720, and Wilfrid plays a large role in the Venerable Bede's *Ecclesiastical History* (731).

JOSEPH F. KELLY

See also Celtic Monasticism; England: History; Lindisfarne/Holy Isle, England; Netherlands; Whitby, England; Willibrord, St.

Biography

Born into Celtic Christianity in Northumbria, Wilfrid abandoned it for the Roman usage at Canterbury and after 653 visited Rome and Lyons. As Abbot of Ripon, he led the campaign for Roman customs at the Synod of Whitby (664). His tenure as Bishop of York (666–703) was interrupted several times by rival claimants, as well as by his own preference for the abbey of Ripon. He did much to establish Roman practice in the North of England.

Further Reading

Colgrave, Bertram, editor, *Bede's Ecclesiastical History of the English People*, Oxford: Clarendon Press, 1969 (Latin text, with translation and notes)

Farmer, D.H., "Saint Wilfrid," in *Saint Wilfrid at Hexham*, edited by D.P. Kirby, Newcastle upon Tyne: Oriel, 1974

Fletcher, Richard, *Who's Who in Roman Britain and Anglo-Saxon England*, London: Shepheard-Walwyn, 1989; Chicago: St. James Press, 1989 (capsule biographies of major figures of Wilfrid's era)

Foley, William T., *Images of Sanctity in Eddius Stephanus' Life of Bishop Wilfrid, an Early English Saint's Life*, Lewiston, New York: Edwin Mellen Press, 1992

Kirby, D.P., *Saint Wilfrid at Hexham*, Newcastle upon Tyne: Oriel, 1974

Kirby, D.P., "Bede, Eddius Stephanus, and the *Life of Wilfrid*," *English Historical Review* 98 (1983)

Mayr-Harting, Henry, *The Coming of Christianity to Anglo-Saxon England*, London: Batsford, 1972; as *The Coming of Christianity to England*, New York: Schocken Books, 1972

Stephanus, Eddius, *The Life of Bishop Wilfrid*, edited and translated by Bertram Colgrave, Cambridge and New York: Cambridge University Press, 1927 (Latin text, with translation and notes)

Whitelock, Dorothy, editor, *English Historical Documents, I: 597-1042*, London: Eyre, 1979

William of Hirsau c. 1026–1091

German scholar, abbot of Hirsau, and monastic reformer

William of Hirsau was brought up from an early age at St. Emmeram, Regensburg, a Benedictine abbey reformed by Gorze (near Metz) in the tenth century. There William came into contact with Otloh (1010–c. 1070), the erudite author of many treatises about the religious life of an intensely personal character, such as the *Liber visionum* and *Libellus de tentationibus suis*. Like Otloh, William was keenly aware both of the importance of education and of the demands of the religious life. Two treatises of William are known from the early part of his career, both written as literary dialogues between William and Otloh: a *De musica* and an *Astronomica*, of which only the prologue survives. William was not afraid to question the authority of Boethius (c. 480–c. 524), Odo of Cluny (c. 879–942), and even Guido of Arezzo on music. Bernhold of Constance (c. 1050–1100) reports that he devised a natural clock modeled on a celestial hemisphere and demonstrated how to establish the solstice and equinox "by sure experiments" as well as correcting many common errors in chant (*Chronicon*, Monumenta Germaniae Historica V, 451).

William was a charismatic figure who immersed himself in the cause of religious reform. At Regensburg he befriended Ulrich of Zell (d. 1093), who became a monk of Cluny sometime after 1063, when a new bishop came into office for whom Ulrich had little sympathy. William shared with Otloh a strong dislike of the tendency for German ecclesiastics to be politically subservient to secular authority. In 1069 William left St. Emmeram to become abbot of Hirsau in the southwestern part of the empire. A few years later William traveled to Rome to obtain protection for Hirsau from Pope Gregory VII (1073–1085). William played a crucial role in establishing Hirsau as a central focus for the reform movement. Critics of Hirsau complained that its monks were stirring up division through their preaching.

From Hirsau William founded or reformed many monastic houses throughout Germany, including the abbeys of St. George and St. Gregory in the Black Forest, Zwiefalten, Schaffhausen, Peterhausen, and many others. Between 1079 and 1183 William asked Ulrich to send him a record of the customs of Cluny to help him draw up his own monastic constitutions for Hirsau. In his introduction to the customs of Cluny, Ulrich singles out William as having transformed the observance of the monastic life throughout Germany. Where previously so many communities had been weighed down by the presence of crippled and handicapped monks who had been placed there solely by parents eager to avoid taking responsibility for them, monks living in communities reformed by William set new standards of religious zeal (*Patrologia Latina* 149.635–636). William was remembered for his close interest in the poor and for urging both women and men to pursue the religious life and for not presenting himself as a great feudal abbot. The houses that he reformed remained free to develop their own liturgical identity.

CONSTANT J. MEWS

See also Cluny, Abbots of; German Benedictine Reform, Medieval; Germany: History; Gregory VII; Liturgists, German Monastic; Music: Christian Perspectives

Biography

William grew up in the abbey of St. Emmeram in Regensburg, where he wrote on music and astronomy. In 1069 William became abbot of Hirsau (west of Stuttgart), which he elevated into a center of Pope Gregory VII's reform movement. William adapted Cluniac customs for the many monasteries that he founded in Germany.

Major Works

Astronomica (Praefatio), in *Patrologia Latina* 150.1639–1642
Constitutiones Hirsaugienses, in *Patrologia Latina* 150.927–1146
Wilhelmi Hirsaugensis Musica, edited by D. Harbison, 1975

Further Reading

Bernhold of Constance, *Chronicon*, edited by George Pertz, Monumenta Germaniae Historica, Scriptores V, Hannover: Hiersemann, 1844
Bischoff, Bernard, "Wilhelm von Hirsau," in *Die Deutsche Literatur des Mittelalters: Verfasserlexikon*, volume 4, edited by Karl Langosch, Berlin: de Gruyter, 1953
Bultot, Robert, "'Quadrivium,' 'natura' et 'ingenium naturale' chez Guillaume d'Hirsau (d. 1091)," *Rivista di filosofia neoscolastica* 70:1 (1978)
Haimo, *Vita Willihelmi abbatis Hirsaugiensis*, edited by Wilhelm Wattenbach, Monumenta Germaniae Historica, Scriptores XII, Hannover: Hiersemann, 1856
Jakobs, Hermann, *Die Hirsauer, Ihre Ausbreitung und Rechtsstellung im Zeitalter des Investiturstreites*, Cologne: Böhlau, 1961
Schreiner, Klaus, editor, *Hirsau, St. Peter und Paul, 1091–1991*, Stuttgart: Kommissionsverlag, Konrad Theiss, 1991

Willibrord, St. 658–739

English Christian monk, priest, and missionary to Frisia

Willibrord was born of a noble Northumbrian family in 658 during a time of religious and ascetic fervor in Northumbria. Willibrord's father, Wilgils, presented the boy as an oblate to the monastery of Ripon and himself withdrew into solitude, building a cell near the mouth of the Humber River. He was soon joined by a number of disciples, and a small monastery flourished there for several generations. At Ripon Willibrord came under the authority of Wilfrid (634–709), its second abbot. A royal foundation originally staffed by monks from the Irish monastic settlement on Iona, Ripon had been handed over to Wilfrid in 661. He zealously promoted Roman ecclesiastical organization, law, and liturgical observance and in 664 decisively influenced the outcome of the Synod of Whitby, at which the Northumbrians adopted Roman customs in preference to those of the Irish Church. Subsequently Wilfrid was appointed bishop of York but remained abbot of Ripon, ruling through a representative. Under his influence the liturgical celebrations and ceremonial were patterned on Roman observance. Because his cultural investments were architectural rather than academic, Ripon was famous for its buildings but did not rank among the first centers of scholarly learning. No detailed information exists regarding the daily monastic routine at Ripon. Wilfrid later claimed to have been the first to introduce the Rule of St. Benedict to Anglo-Saxon England, but it is impossible to prove its use at this early date.

In his 20th year Willibrord entered on the second stage of his formation; he left Ripon for Ireland, where he spent 12 years and was ordained priest in the monastery at Rath Melgisi under Egbert, another Northumbrian. Willibrord was attracted to Ireland by the fame of its flourishing schools and the saintly lives of its monks. The second half of the seventh century was a time of great Irish influence in both secular and sacred learning, especially in the fields of law, grammar, patristics, and hagiography. Inspired by the Irish ascetic ideal of the *peregrinatio pro Christo*, St. Egbert (d. 729) had made several attempts to cross the English Channel to preach to the heathen Frisians. Being prevented from setting out himself, he proceeded to recruit others for these ventures. In 690 Willibrord crossed to Frisia (modern Low Countries) with 11 companions. They presented themselves at the court of Pepin II (687–714), Frankish mayor of the palace, to obtain support and protection. Pepin assigned Utrecht as their mission base. In 695 he sent Willibrord to Rome to be consecrated archbishop for the Frisians, with Utrecht as his episcopal see. Not only did Willibrord's missionary travels cover the present-day Netherlands from Frisia to Brabant (he is venerated as the "Apostle of the Netherlands") but he and his disciples ventured as far afield as Denmark and Heligoland. In these outposts the mission had no immediate success, but he brought 30 youths back with him, presumably to train them as missionaries for the future.

Throughout his life Willibrord worked closely with Pepin and his successors. In 698 he accepted a church and monastery at Echternach (now in Luxembourg). In 704 he handed this property over to Pepin II and his wife to receive it back from them with additional grants, assurances of protection, and an exhortation to loyalty. During the following decade Willibrord was given other monasteries centered on the Meuse region. A number of these properties lay outside the boundaries of his own diocese and were instead linked through Willibrord's personal relationship with the ruling house. In effect Willibrord accepted Pepin as his liege lord and aided him in creating a "sacred landscape" in middle Austrasia, underpinning secular rule by leadership in the spiritual realm. The strong monastic presence built up by Willibrord strengthened the Church in this locality for many centuries as both a missionary and a cultural force.

Although Willibrord never returned to England, he was never out of touch with his homeland. Northumbrian missionaries joined him in Frisia, among them some members of his own family. The bonds of kinship and Anglo-Saxon inheritance rights helped give stability and continuity to Willibrord's foundations. Beornrad, one of his successors at Echternach who commissioned his biography from Alcuin (c. 740–804), was a relative, as was Alcuin himself, who had inherited the monastery founded by Willibrord's father. In the *Ecclesiastical History* the Venerable Bede (c. 673–735) speaks of Willibrord with great veneration. He had heard of him through his diocesan bishop Acca, a mutual friend, who together with Wilfrid had visited Willibrord on a journey to Rome. Bede highlights Willibrord's Irish training as the background to his missionary enterprises but interestingly makes no reference to his years at Ripon.

Recent scholarship has discussed in detail the "Irish legacy" that Willibrord might have bequeathed to his monasteries. It is likely that Willibrord continued to recruit from among the Irish ascetics. The learning for which the Irish schools were famous was assiduously fostered, especially at Echternach. Its flourishing scriptorium produced Willibrord's Calendar, written between 700 and 720 in Insular script. This commemorates the Irish saints Brigid, Patrick, and Colum Cille as well as the Northumbrians Egfrid, Oswald, and Edwin. Other surviving fragments employ the "Irish hand," and some show Old Irish glosses, even beyond the first generation of scribes. Side by side with evidence of Irish influence is an integration with Frankish and Roman Church customs and structures, as shown in the organization of the Frisian Church and the choice of typically Frankish dedications. Research into the musical tradition at Echternach points to a library rich in liturgical sources and containing most of the important theoretical works known to the Irish and Frankish Churches; its "music school" had a far-reaching influence well into the High Middle Ages. The monastery of Echternach, in whose spiritual and scholarly formation Willibrord's integrating genius is most clearly evident, has proven to be his most lasting monastic legacy. A period of decline in the 14th century was followed by a renewed religious flowering. The monastic community was eventually dispersed in the 19th century, yet the inspiration of its founder continues to make this, his burial place, an important focus for prayer and pilgrimage as well as for academic endeavor.

NIKOLA PROKSCH O.S.B.

See also Bede, St.; Belgium; Boniface, St.; Echternach, Luxembourg; Missionaries: Christian; Netherlands; Whitby, England; Wilfrid, St.

Biography

The "Apostle of Frisia" was born in Northumbria and educated under St. Wilfrid. Between 678 and 690 he lived in a religious community in Ireland, where he was ordained. In 690 he traveled with some companions to West Frisia (now the Netherlands), and three years later received papal support for his mission there. Consecrated Bishop of the Frisians in 695, he established a cathedral near Utrecht and also the monastery of Echternach (Luxembourg) in 698. Willibrord labored for another 40 years, traveling as far as Denmark and receiving assistance from St. Boniface.

Further Reading

Angenendt, Arnold, "Willibrord im Dienste der Karolinger," *Annalen des historischen Vereins für den Niederrhein* 175 (1973)

Goetzinger, N., editor, *Willibrordus: Echternacher Festschrift zur XII. Jahrhundertfeier des Todes des Heiligen, Willibrord*, Luxembourg: Sankt Paulus Druckerei, 1940

Kiesel, Georges, and Jean Schroeder, editors, *Willibrord, Apostel der Niederlande: Gründer der Abtei Echternach: Gedenkgabe zum 1250: Todestag des angelsächsischen Missionars*, Luxembourg: Editions Saint-Paul, 1990

Levison, Wilhelm, "St. Willibrord and His Place in History," *Durham University Journal* 32 (1939–1940)

Ó Cróinín, Dáibhí, "Rath Melgisi, Willibrord, and the Earliest Echternach Manuscripts," *Peritia* 3 (1984)

Richter, Michael, "Der irische Hintergrund der angelsächsischen Mission," in *Die Iren und Europa im frühen Mittelalter*, volume 1, edited by Heinz Löwe, Stuttgart: Veröffentlichungen des Europazentrums Tübingen, 1982

Schroeder, Jean, "Zu den Beziehungen zwischen Echternach und England/Irland im Frühmittelalter," *Hémecht* 31 (1979)

Wagner, Robert, "Zur Frühgeschichte des Willibrordus-Klosters in Echternach," *Hémecht* 37 (1985)

Wampach, Camillus, *Sankt Willibrord, Sein Leben und Lebenswerk*, Luxembourg: Sankt Paulus Druckerei, 1953

Willibrord en het begin van Nederland, Exhibition Catalogue, Utrecht: Museum Catharijneconvent, 1995

Wilson, H.A., *The Calendar of St. Willibrord*, London: Harrison, 1918

Wimmer, Boniface 1809–1887

Bavarian Benedictine missionary to North America

Boniface Wimmer, O.S.B., missionary, archabbot, and founder of St. Vincent Archabbey, the first Benedictine monastery in North America, was born in Thalmassing, Bavaria, on 14 January 1809. The first child of Peter and Elizabeth Lang, his second wife, Wimmer was baptized Sebastian. He displayed a talent for learning and an interest in the priesthood, and his parents sent him to Regensburg to study classics and theology. Wimmer entered the diocesan seminary at Regensburg in 1826 and a year later enrolled at the University of Munich to continue theological studies. For a time Wimmer contemplated the study of law but decided to pursue his priestly vocation. Bishop George Michael Wittmann ordained Wimmer to the priesthood on 1 August 1831, in Regensburg Cathedral.

After serving as a curate at the Marian shrine in Altötting (1831–1832), Wimmer obtained his bishop's permission in December 1832 to enter the novitiate at the restored Benedictine monastery of St. Michael's at Metten. Boniface, as he was known in religion, made solemn vows on 29 December 1833. After several assignments throughout Bavaria, Wimmer was sent to Munich, where he became professor of Latin and Greek at the Ludwigs-Gymnasium and prefect at the boarding school associated with the college. While at Munich, Wimmer, nicknamed *Projektenmacher* (a "plan maker" or "visionary"), became interested in missionary work among German immigrants in the United States. At first, his superior at Metten, Abbot Gregory Scherr, refused Wimmer permission, but he persisted in making plans. He received the abbot's permission in 1846 and began to prepare for his journey. King Ludwig I (1825–1848) of Bavaria and the *Ludwig Missionsverein*, established by royal decree in 1838, offered Wimmer assistance for the new monastery. He had already received support from Father Peter Henry Lemke, a German missionary then working in Carrolltown in western Pennsylvania, and an offer of land that Wimmer could purchase.

Wimmer, four students for the priesthood, and 14 candidates who wanted to become lay brothers departed from Rotterdam on 10 August 1846, and arrived in New York City on 15 September. Wimmer went to Carrolltown but found the land there unsuitable for farming. Michael O'Connor, the bishop of Pittsburgh, after a meeting with Wimmer, offered him property called Sportsman's Hall, approximately 60 miles from Pittsburgh. Because of the fertile soil and the proximity to a proposed railway line, Wimmer accepted Bishop O'Connor's offer. He left Carrolltown and settled at the present site of St. Vincent Archabbey on 18 October 1846. Six days later, he invested candidates for monastic life with the Benedictine habit.

The Right Reverend Boniface Wimmer, O.S.B.
Photo courtesy of the Photograph Collection of Saint Vincent Archabbey

In addition to parochial work in the area and plans to educate both German-speaking students and clergy who would minister to the growing number of immigrants from Germany, Wimmer began to establish a monastic regime in western Pennsylvania. Candidates soon arrived at the young monastery. In 1847 Father Peter Lechner, O.S.B., from Scheyern Abbey in Bavaria, brought 17 candidates for the lay brotherhood to St. Vincent, and in 1852 Wimmer's Benedictine community numbered more than 115 monks. In the same year, Rome raised Wimmer's monastery to the rank of a canonical priory. In 1855, Pope Pius IX (1846–1878) established the American Cassinese Congregation with Boniface Wimmer as its president, made St. Vincent an abbey, and appointed Wimmer abbot for three years. In 1858 Wimmer was canonically elected abbot, and in 1866 Rome designated him abbot and president of the congregation for life.

By 1856, 188 monks were affiliated with St. Vincent. In addition to work near the monastery, monks from St. Vincent established small priories in Pennsylvaina: Carrolltown, Indiana, and St. Mary's (Elk County), where three sisters from St. Walburga in Eichstätt established a community in 1852 with Wimmer's help. Soon, bishops throughout the United States asked Wimmer to establish monastic communities within their dioceses. In 1856, Abbot Boniface sent monks to Minnesota. Communities were later founded in Kansas (1857), New Jersey (1857), and North Carolina (1876). Wimmer also had plans for Benedictine sisters in the United States who would help the monks in missionary work. The abbot wanted to establish independent communities of sisters under the supervision of the president of the American Cassinese Congregation. Wimmer claimed authority over the Benedictine sisters in the United States, but some including Benedicta Riepp (1825–1862) resisted. On 6 December 1859, the Holy See decreed that the local diocesan bishop and not the president of the American Cassinese Congregation had ecclesiastical jurisdiction over the sisterhoods.

Abbot Boniface rapidly became recognized as a leading American churchman. He was present at the Seventh Provincial Council of Baltimore (1849), where he was recognized as "provincial of Benedictines," and at the First and Second Plenary Councils of Baltimore (1852 and 1866, respectively). As president of the American Cassinese Congregation, Wimmer attended the First Vatican Council (1869–1870), where he supported papal infallibility. On 29 December 1883, the 50th anniversary of his profession, Pope Leo XIII (1878–1903) gave Wimmer the Cappa Magna and the title archabbot for life. Wimmer failed in his attempts to open a house of studies for American Benedictines in Rome, but he was influential in the reestablishment in Rome of Sant' Anselmo, which reopened in 1888 as an international house of studies for Benedictines. He also supported Leo XIII's plan to unite all Benedictines in an international confederation.

Wimmer died on 8 December 1887, and was buried in the monastery's cemetery. His first four foundations had become independent abbeys. At St. Vincent the college and seminary were thriving, and a network of parishes staffed by Benedictines was flourishing. Wimmer's work among immigrants – German, Polish, Slovak, and Irish – and former slaves is also praiseworthy. Historian John Tracy Ellis called him the greatest American missionary of the 19th century. Recognizing Wimmer's contributions to American Catholicism and his accomplishments at St. Vincent, the *New York Herald* (9 December 1887) stated, "His acts of kindness and of charity extended to all classes and conditions of society, and there is scarcely a poor family in all the region round about the monastery that, at some time or another, has not been the recipient of his bounty."

RENE KOLLAR

See also Benedictines: General or Male; Christianity: Overview; Libraries: Western Christian; Riepp, Benedicta (Sybilla); Schools and Universities, Benedictine; United States: Western Christian

Biography

Born and educated in Bavaria, Wimmer studied in Regensburg, where he was ordained in 1831. In 1832 he entered the Benedictine monastery at Metten, Bavaria. In 1846 he came with several companions to found a monastery in Carrolltown, Pennsylvania, but moved to Latrobe, where the bishop of Pittsburgh had donated land. Wimmer served as archabbot of St. Vincent Archabbey, founding Benedictine parishes and monasteries throughout the United States, including Saint John's Abbey and University at Collegeville, Minnesota. He received funding from Bavaria, not least from its controversial King Ludwig I (1825–1848).

Further Reading

Barry, Colman J., "Boniface Wimmer, Pioneer of the American Benedictines," *The Catholic Historical Review* 41:3 (1955)

Fellner, Felix, "Archabbot Boniface Wimmer as an Educator," *The National Benedictine Educational Association Bulletin* 25:2 (1942)

Fellner, Felix, *Abbot Boniface and His Monks* (mimeographed copy of typewritten manuscript), 5 vols., Latrobe, Pennsylvania: St. Vincent Archabbey, 1956

Mathäser, Willibald, *Bonifaz Wimmer O.S.B. und König Ludwig I. von Bayern*, Munich: Priester-Missionsbund, 1937

Moosmüller, Oswald, *St. Vincenz in Pennsylvanien*, New York: F. Pustet, 1873

Moosmüller, Oswald, *Bonifaz Wimmer, Erzabt von St. Vincent in Pennsylvanien*, New York: Benziger, 1891

Oetgen, Jerome, *An American Abbot: Boniface Wimmer, O.S.B., 1809–1887*, Latrobe, Pennsylvania: Archabbey Press, 1976; revised edition, Washington, D.C.: Catholic University of America Press, 1997

Rippinger, Joel, *The Benedictine Order in the United States: An Interpretive History*, Collegeville, Minnesota: Liturgical Press, 1990

Wolter, Maurus 1825–1890

German Benedictine theologian and advocate of liturgical revival

Maurus Wolter was born in Bonn on 4 July 1825. One of 14 children, he was given the name Rudolph at baptism. On completion of his *Gymnasium* studies, he entered the University of Bonn, where he was awarded a doctorate in philosophy in 1849. Shortly after this he entered the Cologne diocesan seminary and was ordained a priest for that diocese on 3 September 1850. He spent six years as a diocesan priest, serving as rector of the diocesan schools at Jülich and Aachen. In this period he came under the influence of Austrian theologian Anton Günther (1783–1863), who was a center of opposition to Enlightenment ideas and who expressed hope that the Benedictine Order would take the lead in spearheading a return to a Catholic culture. Emergence of this interest of Wolter coincided with the election of another follower of Günther, Simplicio Pappalettere, as abbot of the monastery of St. Paul-outside-the-Walls in Rome. The abbot promised a welcome to any Germans who would enter his novitiate and help him raise the level of the monastery's monastic observance and scholarly reputation.

Rudolph Wolter accepted the invitation in 1856. He made his novitiate in Perugia and then returned to Rome, where he professed vows for the abbey of St. Paul on 15 November 1857, taking the monastic name Maurus. While in Rome, Maurus Wolter began lecturing in theology. He was also appointed spiritual director of Princess Katherine of Hohenzollern by Pope Pius IX (1846–1878). Princess Katherine, a widow, had expressed an interest in founding a convent in Germany. When Abbot Pappalettere left St. Paul for Monte Cassino, Wolter saw the promise of his monastic vision dim. Thus, when Princess Katherine offered Wolter the old Augustinian Abbey of Beuron in the Danube valley as a site for a new monastery, he promptly accepted the offer, and conventual life began at Beuron in May 1863.

Wolter's monastic model was the Abbey of Solesmes. He had visited Abbot Prosper Guéranger (1805–1875) at Solesmes in 1862 and was convinced that just such a model of monastic liturgical observance and return to the sources would serve Beuron well. Wolter saw his abbey as a counter to Austrian and Swiss monasteries, which at that time were much involved in the work of maintaining schools and parishes.

In 1868 the priory of Beuron was raised to the rank of abbey and Wolter appointed as its first abbot. In that same year Wolter became a leading figure in a meeting of abbots and priors of Benedictine houses of Europe held at Salzburg, Austria. As a result of discussions at this meeting and at a subsequent one between Wolter and Guéranger, fundamental principles took shape for the monastic revival that was under way in Europe. Wolter became a spokesman for this revival in a number of significant works associated with his name. Likely his most influential work was the *Praecipua Ordinis monastici Elementa* (1880; *The Principles of Monasticism*), a one-volume synthesis of monastic and

Church writings. He was also responsible for starting the Beuronese nuns, modeled after the Solesmes-inspired Congregation of St. Cécile in France.

In 1875 Beuron's monastic life was compromised by the Kulturkampf. The monks were forced to leave Germany and remained in exile for 12 years. Partially in reaction to that, Wolter made new monastic foundations in Belgium (Maredsous), England (Erdington), Austria (Seckau), and Prague (Emmaus). A steady number of new recruits entered these foundations, especially lay brothers.

Maurus Wolter died in 1890. His monastic vision of a rich liturgical life based on a return to the sources of monastic tradition was received and expanded by his brother and successor as archabbot at Beuron, Placidus Wolter (1828–1908). Unlike its French counterpart at Solesmes, Beuron was more integrated into the general life of the Church in Germany. The abbeys of Maria Laach and Maredsous and the figures of Raphael Walzer, Idelfons Herwegen (1874–1946), Gérard von Caloen, Hildebrand de Hemptinne, and Columba Marmion (1858–1923), built on Wolter's legacy of scholarship and a return to an authentic monastic observance. In turn they left a lasting imprint on the monastic map of Europe in the 19th and 20th centuries.

Joel A. Rippinger, O.S.B.

See also Abbot Primate, Benedictine; Beuron, Germany; Guéranger, Prosper; Liturgical Movement 1830–1980; Liturgy: Western Christian; Plainchant; Solesmes, France

Biography

Born and educated in Bonn, Germany, Maurus Wolter served a diocesan priest before joining the Benedictine Abbey of St. Paul-outside-the-Walls (Rome) in 1857. From there he moved to found the priory (later abbey) at Beuron, Germany, in 1863. Collaborating with Prosper Guéranger of Solesmes, France, Maurus Wolter, like his brother Placidus, was a leader in the 19th-century liturgical and artistic revival.

Major Work

Praecipua Ordinis monastici Elementa, 1880; as *The Principles of Monasticism*, translated, edited, and annotated by Bernard A. Sause, 1962

Further Reading

Uttenweiler, Justin, *Maurus Wolter: Dem Gründer Beurons, zum 100. Geburtstag, 1825–4. Juni–1925: Erinnerungen und Studien: Mit sieben Vollbildern in Kunstdruck*, Beuron, Hohenzollern: Beuroner Kuntschule, 1925

Wolter, Placidus 1828–1908

German Benedictine promoter of liturgy and the Beuronese school of religious art

Ernst Wolter was born in 1828 in Bonn, Germany, one of 14 children. He was ordained a priest for the archdiocese of Cologne but soon was attracted to European circles promoting the Catholic restoration of religious life. This led him in 1852 to enter the monastery of St. Paul-outside-the-Walls in Rome. He was joined in this enterprise by his brothers Rudolph and Carl. The former was to become, as Maurus Wolter (1825–1890), the first superior of Beuron. The latter was to become professed as Hildebrand, only to die two years after making his profession. Ernst himself took the religious name Placidus. In 1863 he was the companion of his brother Maurus in establishing the foundation of the Benedictine monastery of Beuron in southwestern Germany. In these years Placidus Wolter had much interaction with Abbot Prosper Guéranger (1805–1875) of Solesmes. He spent several years living at Solesmes, finding in it a monastic model that he would strive to emulate for the rest of his life.

As a sign of confidence in his brother's leadership, Maurus appointed Placidus the superior of Beuron's first monastic foundation of Maredsous in Belgium. Benefiting from a gift of prop-

Cloister, St. Paul-outside-the-Walls (Benedictine), Rome, Italy, 13th century. Placidus Wolter lived here 1852–1863 and was joined by his brother Maurus 1857–1863 before both left to establish Beuron. Photo courtesy of Mary Schaefer

erty given by the Desclée family, Maredsous began in 1872 and acquired more importance when Beuron was suppressed in 1875 under the German Kulturkampf. Placidus was named the first abbot of Maredsous in 1878. During his years at Maredsous, he was instrumental in furthering the work of liturgical research that was later carried on by the Beuronese communities of Mont César in Louvain and Maria Laach in Germany. In these years he also engaged in an extensive correspondence with other monastic figures in Europe and North America. He made two trips to Rome (1882–1883) to secure approval of the constitutions of the Beuronese Congregation. On the death of Maurus in 1890, Placidus succeeded him as archabbot of Beuron, remaining in that position until 1908, tirelessly promoting a return to a rigorous monastic observance and a high standard of liturgical life. He was instrumental in giving support to the Beuronese school of religious painting and sculpture under such monastic artists as Desiderius Lenz (1832–1928) and Gabriel Wüger. Moreover, he was responsible for the expansion of the Beuronese Congregation to Brazil and Portugal and its ongoing growth throughout Europe.

At the end of his life, Placidus Wolter stood at the center of those supporting Pope Leo XIII's (1878–1903) plans to centralize the Confederation of Benedictines throughout the world. He was also responsible for promoting Beuronese influence at the Benedictine College of St. Anselmo in Rome, where the first two abbot primates were Beuronese monks. The Beuronese vision of monasticism that had been faithfully transmitted by Wolter for almost half a century did not cease with his death in 1908 but soon pervaded Benedictine houses throughout the world through the channels of its international network.

JOEL A. RIPPINGER, O.S.B.

See also Abbot Primate, Benedictine; Beuron, Germany; Guéranger, Prosper; Liturgical Movement 1830–1980; Liturgy: Western Christian; Plainchant; Solesmes, France

Biography

A younger brother of Maurus Wolter, Placidus followed his brother to Rome and then to Beuron. From there he lived for several years at Solesmes, before becoming in 1872 prior of Beuron's earliest daughter house at Maredsous, Belgium. From 1890 to 1908 Placidus succeeded Maurus as Abbot of Beuron. He promoted liturgical life and the Beuronese school of painting.

Further Reading

Beuron 1863–1963: Festschrift zum hundertjährigen Bestehen der Erzabtei St. Martin, Beuron/Hohenzollern: Beuroner Kunstverlag, 1963
Oer, Sebastian von, *Erzabt Placidus Wolter: Ein Lebensbild*, Freiburg/Breisgau and St. Louis, Missouri: Herder, 1909
Rees, Daniel, "Benedictine Revival in the Nineteenth Century," in *Benedict's Disciples*, edited by David H. Farmer, Leominster: Wright, 1980; Harrisburg, Pennsylvania: Gracewing, 1995

Women's Monasteries: Buddhist

In dealing with Buddhist women's monasteries, we need to distinguish between Buddhist nuns according to Buddhist law and women who live like Buddhist nuns but who are, according to Buddhist law, not nuns. A Buddhist nun (Sanskrit, *bhikṣuṇī*; Pāli, *bhikkhunī*) is a woman who has received both the lower (Sanskrit, *pravrajyā*; Pāli, *pabbajjā*) and higher (Sanskrit, *upasaṃpadā*; Pāli, *upasampadā*) ordination in the Buddhist community (*saṅgha*). She must live according to the rules laid down in the law book for monastics (i.e., the Vinaya). Various Buddhist schools that arose and died out in the course of time developed an ordination tradition for nuns with their own Vinaya. From these schools only the nuns' ordination tradition of the Dharmaguptaka school in China has survived until today, and nuns of this tradition can be found in China, Taiwan, and Korea. All other "nuns" who are not ordained in this ordination line are not nuns, but *anāgārikā*s, that is, women who give up the worldly life and live according to a chosen number of the ten rules valid for novices. The Theravāda countries Sri Lanka, Burma, and Thailand no longer have fully ordained nuns. This has probably been the case since the tenth century. The present-day "nuns" in Sri Lanka call themselves *dasa sil mātāva* or *dasa sil māeniyō* (ten-precept mother), those in Thailand *maeji*, and those in Burma *tilashin* (one who possesses morality). These "nuns" may live as they like because they are not bound by the Vinaya. Nevertheless, many of them live in nunneries and behave like *bhikṣuṇī*s.

In the beginning of Buddhism, nuns were few, and living in nunneries was certainly not obligatory. In contrast to monks nuns were not allowed to live at the foot of a tree, and the five types of additional abodes granted to monks (*vihāra*, *aḍḍhayoga*, *pāsāda*, *hammiya*, and *guhā*) were also not permitted for them. Nuns could live in sheds, in newly built or private houses, and in nunneries with at least one accompanying nun. In the course of time, Buddhists gained more adherents and consequently greater support. Based on the rule that nuns have to live in settlements, nunneries were built only where a settlement already existed (thus, caves, used frequently as abodes by monks, because they were located outside of settlements, were out of the question for nuns). This basic rule was observed by various Buddhist schools in different regions and for a long period of time. This is demonstrated by an inscription from India (Junnar, Maharashtra, c. second century A.D.) in which the erection of a nunnery within the town for the nuns of the school of the Dharmottariya is mentioned and, insofar as Sri Lanka is concerned, in the chronicle Mahāvaṃsa (sixth century A.D.) and in its commentary (c. tenth century A.D.). In the two latter texts, nunneries within townships are under discussion.

The Buddhist canonical texts do not contain descriptions of nunneries but only of monasteries. The Pāli word *upassaya*, used for the nunnery, is defined by the old commentary in the Vinayapiṭaka as "house" (*ghara*) for one or several nuns. As is the case with the monks' monasteries, the nunneries will have

The Hokkeji nunnery, Nara, Japan, founded eighth century A.D., Tempyo (Nara) period. Photo courtesy of Marylin M. Rhie

varied in size and shape. Important nunneries, such as the Upāsikavihāra, the first nunnery erected in Anurādhapura in Sri Lanka, received greater support and thus grew to become larger complexes (12 buildings were added to the original *vihāra*) than nunneries in some distant villages. Because of the rule that nuns must live in a settlement within a monks' residence (*āvāsa*) inhabited by at least one monk, nunneries were always close to monasteries (albeit strictly separated), and if a monastery was abandoned, the depending nunnery could not continue to subsist, mainly because the nuns' community depended on the monk's community for several legal acts as well as for the instruction of the nuns.

Buddhist nunneries consist of two parts: a center for worship represented by the stūpa, or *caitya*, later also a temple with an image of the Buddha (in Sri Lanka additionally the Bodhi Tree), and the abode for nuns (*vihāra*) with all the appertaining buildings (see the following discussion). The stūpa (a mound, or tumulus, originally with a funerary association) developed in Buddhism to become the main object of worship. It was erected over the bodily relics of the Buddha, his main disciples, and of other eminent scholars; over objects believed to have been used by the Buddha; or at places commemorative of certain incidents of the Buddha's life. In nunneries usually a stūpa was erected for Ānanda, the cousin of the Buddha and one of his eminent scholars, because Ānanda had undertaken to convince the Buddha to allow the foundation of the nuns' community. The strict separation of cultic center and abode was given up in the course of time. At least from the fourth century A.D. on, shrine rooms were included in the living quarters, and in the seventh to eighth century A.D. the image house became the center around which the cells for monks or nuns were built.

The residential abodes in great monasteries were comprised of the following: a bathing room (Sanskrit, *jantāgāra*; Pāli, *jantāghara*); a toilet (Sanskrit, *varcaḥkuṭi*; Pāli, *vaccakuṭi*); a kitchen (Sanskrit, *agniśālā*; Pāli, *aggisālā*); a well (Pāli, *udapānasālā*); store houses for food, clothes, juridical papers, and so on (Sanskrit, *koṣṭhika*; Pāli, *koṭṭhaka* or *maṇḍapa*); a store for items that could be accepted by monastics only through the mediation of laypersons (Sanskrit, *kalpiyakuṭi*; Pāli, *kappiyakuṭi*); a cloister (Sanskrit, *caṅkrama*; Pāli, *caṅkama*); an assembly hall (Sanskrit, *upasthānaśālā*; Pāli, *upaṭṭhānasālā*); a dining hall (Sanskrit, *upāhāraśālā*; Pāli, *bhattagga*, *bhattasālā*, or *bhojanasālā*); and a pool (Sanskrit, *puṣkariṇī*; Pāli, *pokkharaṇī*). Places for different legal acts and ceremonies performed by the Buddhist community – that is, a place for ordination (*upasaṃpadamaṇḍala* or *upasampadāmālaka*) or for the observance (Sanskrit, *poṣathapamukha*; Pāli, *uposathagāra*) – were included in the monastic compound. Whereas the earliest monasteries (cave monasteries of the third century B.C.) were of irregular shape, a certain standard type with few variants had developed in the second century B.C. From a mostly square, sometimes apsidial main room three or more cells branched off, each with one

A nun sweeping the veranda of the living quarters at Daewon-sa Monastery, North Chŏlla, South Korea.
Photo courtesy of John Powers

or two beds. Later a veranda, supported by columns, was placed in front of the main room, and the monasteries often had two stories.

Not only do we have no descriptions of nunneries, but no building excavated has been definitely identified as nunnery. Nevertheless, the rules for nuns permit us to draw some conclusions. Because it was forbidden for nuns to use a bathroom (they had to bathe at a public bathing place for women), we can assume that bathrooms were not a part of nunneries, at least as long as this rule was observed. The same holds true for the toilet, which was also forbidden for nuns. They had to relieve themselves in a special construction "open underneath and covered on top" to prevent any privacy.

Because the nuns' community (*bhikṣuṇīsaṅgha*) was an autonomous unit, it had a ceremonial boundary (*sīmā*) of its own that enclosed the nunnery. The nuns performed several legal acts and ceremonies at least partly in their nunnery, including the nuns' ordination and the ceremony of inviting each other (Sanskrit, *pravāraṇā*; Pāli, *pavāraṇā*). Thus, places for the performance of such legal acts or ceremonies must also have been part of a nunnery.

From about the second century B.C. to the fourth century A.D., India must have had centers of nuns in and around Bhārhut and Sāñcī (Madhya Pradesh); in Pauni, Kanherī, Kuḍā, Nāsik, and Karlā (Maharashtra); in Mathurā, Sārnāth, and Sāṃkāśya (Uttar Pradesh); and in Amarāvatī (Andhra Pradesh). A great number of inscriptions show nuns from these areas as donors, making it highly probable that nunneries existed there. In the seventh century A.D., nuns lived in Nālandā (eastern India), the world-famous monastic university. It is not known whether they dwelled in a nunnery or whether they only had separate quarters within the monastery. In the sixth to eighth century A.D., three nunneries existed in Valabhī (Gujarat) that were linked together to an administrative unit (the Yakṣasūravihāramaṇḍala). Thereafter, references to nuns are rare. It is not known when the nuns' ordination tradition died out in India.

The administration of a nunnery was based on the general rules for life in the community. The regular inhabitants were graduated according to their status into nuns (*bhikṣuṇī*), female "probationer" (*śikṣamāṇā*; Pāli, *sikkhamānā*), and novices (*śrāmaṇerikā*; Pāli, *sāmaṇerī*). Only the nuns had full rights. Within the different classes the age of ordination was decisive, as was competence in later centuries, according to the Chinese pilgrims Hsüan-tsang and I-ching (seventh century A.D.). Many of the tasks within the community were conferred on nuns who previously had been appointed to the relevant post. Legal decisions were reached by the entire nuns' community within a nunnery. Each nun had an equal right to vote. Originally, a head of a monastery or nunnery was not provided. Because it has been proven that in the seventh century A.D. monasteries had a head (normally the monk with the highest age of ordination) and sometimes also a very competent monk, it can be assumed that the development in nunneries was similar.

Nuns, like monks, had to live from alms. Thus, their livelihoods depended mainly on the laypeople's generosity. Consequently, the economic welfare of nunneries fluctuated with growth or decline in the respect that resident nuns received from the society. Donations to nunneries included supplies of food, clothes, and other requisites as well as gifts of land and buildings. Whether a nunnery became self-sufficient depended on the type and number of donations. As we can see from inscriptional material, monasteries that attracted patronage of kings and royal households received larger donations of land, villages, and so on and thereby became rich landowners. For nunneries this is documented in Valabhī (Gujarat), where Duḍḍā, the sister of a Maitraka ruler, founded three nunneries that attracted large numbers of donations. If nuns owned private wealth (and some did, as the great number of inscriptions in India naming nuns as donors show), this could also improve the status of the nunnery. However, nunneries were generally not as secure as monasteries, perhaps a result of the inferior role that women played in society. According to the Chinese pilgrim I-ching, who lived in eastern India for several years in the seventh century A.D., supply to the female members of the Order was very small at his time, and many monasteries had no special supply of food for the nuns. Thus, it seems that some nunneries were not able to maintain their nuns.

The present-day nuns in China and Taiwan often live together with monks in one temple, albeit in separate quarters. Both groups have their own building, including a kitchen and a dharma hall. In China nunneries where laywomen and nuns live together exist as well. An abbess heads the nunneries. In Korea monasteries and nunneries are strictly separated. However, nuns have converted many abandoned monasteries into nunneries. Like the monasteries the nunneries are mainly self-sufficient, growing their own vegetables and grain.

PETRA KIEFFER-PÜLZ

See also Anurādhapura, Sri Lanka; Buddhist Schools/Traditions: Japan; Economics: Buddhist; Gender Studies: Buddhist Perspectives; Mahāpajāpatī Gotamī; Monasticism, Definitions of: Buddhist Perspectives; Nālandā, India; Origins: Comparative Perspectives; Repentance Rituals, Buddhist; Rules, Buddhist (Vinaya): Historical; Sexuality: Buddhist Perspectives; Taiwan; Ten-Precept Mothers as Theravādin Nuns

Further Reading

Hüsken, Ute, *Die Vorschriften für die buddhistische Nonnengemeinde im Vinaya-Piṭaka der Theravadin*, Berlin: Reimer, 1997

Karma, Lekshe Tsomo, *Sakyadhītā: Daughters of the Buddha*, Ithaca, New York: Snow Lions, 1988

Kieffer-Pülz, Petra, "Die buddhistische Gemeinde," in *Der indische Buddhismus und seine Verzweigungen*, Stuttgart: Kohlhammer, 1999

Plutat, Birte, "Ordained Women in Buddhism: Survey and Present State of Research," M.A. Thesis, Hamburg, 1993

Tsai, Kathryn, translator, *Lives of the Nuns: Biographies of Chinese Buddhist Nuns from the Fourth to Sixth Centuries*, Honolulu: University of Hawaii Press, 1994

Women's Monasteries: Eastern Christian

Eastern and Western Christian monasteries for women have common ancestors in fourth-century communities in Egypt and Asia Minor and among Syriac-speaking Christians in the Near East. Women's monasteries in these areas and other areas in the Eastern Christian tradition retained many features of the earliest models into the modern period. Although the emergence of monastic orders shaped women's experience in the West, each monastery in the East might have a unique rule written by its founder.

The Eastern Christian tradition includes the ancient Greek and non-Greek family of churches that emerged in the eastern Roman Empire and spread from there. The group includes those who accept or reject the decrees of the Council of Chalcedon of 451 regarding the divine and human natures of Christ. Among the Chalcedonians are the Greek and Russian Orthodox, whose roots are in Constantinople, and the Georgians, Maronites, and Melkites. Among the non-Chalcedonians (also known as Monophysites) are the Coptic Orthodox, Syrian Orthodox, Armenian Apostolic, Ethiopian Orthodox, and Nestorians.

The *Life of Antony* implies that in the third century groups of female virgins were living together in Egyptian villages, dedicated to prayer and asceticism. By the early fourth century, a women's monastery was part of the Pachomian system, which included a formal rule. Shenoute of Atripe (c. 350–465) directed both men's and women's houses in Upper Egypt according to the same rule. The women's house was closer to a village and practiced domestic crafts (e.g., cloth making) rather than agriculture. In Asia Minor, Macrina (c. 327–380), the sister of Basil of Caesarea (329–379), began as a home-based ascetic and later directed a women's monastery guided by Basil's rules. Double monasteries – neighboring men's and women's houses led by one person according to the same rule – developed early in this area and endured into the ninth century. The Syriac sources suggest that vowed ascetics (*benai qeiama*), both men and women, remained in the towns and played a special role in the local church in the third and fourth centuries. Cenobitic monasticism appears in these sources in the fourth century, but evidence for women's monasteries is scarce, for the home-based asceticism seems to have dominated for some time.

As areas on or beyond the borders of the eastern Roman Empire were Christianized in the fourth and fifth centuries, monasteries were founded that followed the patterns established in Egypt and Syria. Thus, Armenia, Georgia, and Persian territory have evidence of women's monasteries along Syrian lines. Ethiopia was Christianized under various influences, but Egyptian models (especially from Pachomian sources) guided the early development of monasticism.

The acceptance or nonacceptance of the decrees of Chalcedon in 451 divided the Church in the East; later the Muslim domination that began in the seventh century created additional fault lines. Women's monasteries in the East developed in ways that reflect their placement in relation to these boundaries.

On the Chalcedonian side, in the Byzantine Empire centered on Constantinople, women's monasteries were about 15 percent of the total. *Typika* (documents setting out the organization, behavior, and liturgical practice in a cenobitic monastery) survive for six convents, each of which housed about 30 nuns, divided between choir and housekeeping sisters. Strict enclosure was prescribed, and necessary contacts with men (e.g., priests) were tightly controlled. Most convents were in cities, as the holy mountains either prohibited (Athos and Meteora) or discouraged women. Little evidence of intellectual activity exists; rather women engaged in crafts, such as cloth making. The life of seclusion and domestic labor in the convent was similar to the life of other Byzantine women, but the convent did provide a refuge for women who were sick or widowed and for those with an ascetic vocation. This pattern endured among the Greek Orthodox after the fall of Constantinople (1453) and was emulated by other Chalcedonian churches before and after the rise of Islam.

Women's monasteries in Russia were especially influenced by the Byzantine model. The first missionaries to Russia were monks, and mass conversion took place in the tenth century; monasteries were in place in the 11th century. Women's monasteries are poorly documented in the early period, but, as in Byzantium, it is known that they were often founded by wealthy patrons and served as a refuge for unmarried women and aristo-

Nuns, Voronet Monastery, Romania, 16th century.
Photo courtesy of Mary Schaefer

cratic widows. When the government confiscated monastic property in 1764, women's houses decreased from 203 (in 1762) to 67 (in 1764). However, a contemplative revival prompted the founding of 283 new women's monasteries between 1764 and 1907. These were self-supporting cenobitic houses, often in rural areas, that seemed to express women's need for autonomy as the modernization of Russia proceeded. Other Orthodox groups under the influence of the Moscow patriarch (e.g., Bulgaria and Serbia) developed similarly. The autocephalous Church of Georgia, although initially very close to Armenia in belief and practice, accepted the definition of Chalcedon in 608 and was then influenced by Byzantine monasticism.

Other Chalcedonian churches in the Near East are the Melkites (from *malko*, Syriac for "king") and the Maronites in Lebanon. The Melkites include Greek Orthodox and Greek Catholics allied to the patriarchates of Antioch, Alexandria, and Jerusalem. Women's monasteries in this community followed Byzantine models until Roman Catholic influence was felt in the 18th century and the Salvatorians founded an order of nuns. Similarly the Maronites moved toward closer union with Rome in the 17th century, and this was followed by the introduction of Latin religious orders for women. An interesting exception is Hindiye Anne Ajeymi (1727–1798), a Maronite woman mystic who founded a new order devoted to the Sacred Heart. She came into conflict with both local and Vatican religious authorities, and the order was disbanded.

The non-Chalcedonian (or Monophysite) churches, already theologically distinct, became still more isolated after the rise of Islam. Among the Syrian Orthodox and Coptic Orthodox, women's monasteries followed the early models but experienced decline as Christians became a small minority in the region. In the Syrian Church female monastic communities disappeared in the 17th century, but a small modern revival is demonstrated (c. 1988) by the presence of a few nuns near men's communities, performing household tasks and teaching catechism to girls. After centuries of persecution and decline, Egypt has seen a stronger revival (c. 1996) and now has both houses of contemplative nuns and the "Daughters of St. Mary," who are active in charitable work.

The Nestorian, or East Syrian, Church began on the frontier between the Roman and Persian Empires but sought refuge in Persian territory when it rejected the decrees of the Councils of

Monastery of the Intercession (Pokrovsky Monastery), Suzdal, Russia, 15th century. The wife of Tsar Basil III (1505–1533) and the wife of Peter the Great (1689–1725) retired as nuns here.
Photo courtesy of Robert E. Jones

Ephesus (431) and Chalcedon (451). Women's monasteries followed the Syrian Orthodox pattern, and Nestorian missionaries spread monastic practice eastward to central Asia, India, and China. However, centuries of religious and political pressure reduced the Nestorian Church (c. 1965) to a small presence in a few villages near Lake Urmia in Iran.

The Armenian Apostolic and Ethiopian Orthodox churches (both non-Chalcedonian) were less affected by the Islamic empires. Monasticism was present in Armenia in the fourth century, perhaps introduced from Syria, and by the ninth to tenth century monasteries were founded by great families, as in Byzantium. Women's monasteries gradually disappeared in Armenia; however, the Armenian Church in Lebanon (c. 1994) included a women's monastery operating an orphanage. Ethiopia received early influence from both the Syrian and the Egyptian monastic traditions and then developed independently. Significant growth in monasticism occurred in the 13th and 14th centuries and remained strong into the modern period. In 1970, 800 men's monasteries, usually paired with a women's house, existed. Each monastery had about 15 monks or nuns, organized along either cenobitic or anchoritic lines. Young, unmarried women (or men) and older widows could enter the monastery. The revolution that ended the Ethiopian monarchy in 1974 altered the religious landscape as well, as most Church property was confiscated in 1975.

Each national, ethnic, or linguistic tradition within Eastern Christianity had women's monasteries at some stage in its history. From common origins each monastic tradition evolved in a different way because of the complicated theological and political history of the region.

JANET TIMBIE

See also Armenia; Desert Mothers; Egypt; Ethiopia; Macrina, St.; Maronites; Mount Athos, Greece; Origins: Eastern Christian; Orthodox Monasticism: Byzantine; Romania; Russia: History; Serbia; Shenoute of Atripe; Syria; Transvestite Saints

Further Reading

Abrahamse, Dorothy, "Women's Monasteries in the Middle Byzantine Period," *Byzantinische Forschungen* 9 (1985)

Atiya, Aziz S., *A History of Eastern Christianity*, Notre Dame, Indiana: University of Notre Dame Press, and London: Methuen, 1968; enlarged and updated edition, Millwood, New York: Kraus Reprint, 1980

Cannuyer, Christian, *Les Coptes* (Fils d'Abraham), Turnhout: Brepols, 1990; enlarged and updated edition, 1996

Dick, Ignace, *Les Melkites: grecs-orthodoxes et grecs catholiques des patriarcats d'Antioche, d'Alexandrie et de Jérusalem* (Fils d'Abraham), Turnhout: Brepols, 1994

Doorn-Harder, Pieternella van, *Contemporary Coptic Nuns* (Studies in Comparative Religion), Columbia: University of South Carolina Press, 1995

Frey, J.M., "Cenobitisme féminin ancien dans les Églises syriennes," *L'Orient Syrien* 10 (1965)

Makhlouf, Avril M., "Hindiya Anne Ajeymi in Her Ecclesiastical and Political Situation," *Parole de l'Orient* 16 (1990–1991)

Meehan, Brenda, "Popular Piety, Local Initiative, and the Founding of Women's Religious Communities in Russia, 1764–1907," in *Seeking God: The Recovery of Religious Identity in Orthodox Russia, Ukraine, and Georgia*, edited by Stephen Batalden, De Kalb: Northern Illinois University Press, 1993
Peltean, Grigor, *Les Arméniens* (Fils d'Abraham), Maredsous: Brepols, 1994
Sélis, Claude, *Les Syriens orthodoxes et catholiques* (Fils d'Abraham), Liège: Brepols, 1988
Stoffregen-Pedersen, Kirsten, *Les Éthiopiens* (Fils d'Abraham), Turnhout: Brepols, 1990
Talbot, Alice-Mary, "A Comparison of the Monastic Experience of Byzantine Men and Women," *Greek Orthodox Theological Review* 30 (1985)
Van Doorn-Harder, Pieternella, *Contemporary Coptic Nuns*, Columbia: University of South Carolina Press, 1995

Women's Monasteries: Western Christian

The first indication we have of the existence of a woman's monastery is when Antony (251?–356) brought his sister to live with nuns before he began his own life as a Desert Father. Palladius (c. 364–420/30) tells us of many Desert Mothers and claims that 20,000 women ascetic lived in Oxyrhynchus. If the term *monastery* is reserved for places where women lived contemplative, cenobitic lives according to a rule, then the first known monastery is that of Tabennesis, where Mary, sister of Pachomius (c. 290–346), presided. The first women's monastery in the West was established in Rome when Marcella (d. c. 410) turned her Aventine Hill palace into a convent around 354. The women associated with this Roman Circle became the founders of numerous other monasteries in Rome and the Holy Land. Association with this group inspired Melanie the Elder (d. c. 410) to establish a male and a female monastery near the Mount of Olives and Paula (347–404) to found the same in Bethlehem. Paula's women's monastery became a beacon throughout the Mediterranean, for the sources tell us of a male emissary from Africa, a married couple from Spain, and a bishop from Eleutheropolis who came to observe it to found monasteries in their own land modeled on Paula's.

Fleeting references are made to women's monasteries existing in Bologna, Verona, Marseilles, and near Lake Geneva during the fourth and fifth centuries, but the first area in the West that supported women's monasteries on a large scale was Ireland. Brigit of Kildare (fourth or fifth century) is believed to be responsible for the spread of women's monasteries there, many of which were double monasteries. From the beginning these monasteries educated their own members, and some established extern schools for boys and girls; Ita's monastery at

Warming room off the cloister, Lacock Abbey (Augustinian Canonesses), Wiltshire, England, c. 1232–1238. Photo courtesy of Chris Schabel

Chapter house, Lacock Abbey (Augustinian Canonesses), Wiltshire, England, c. 1232–1238. Photo courtesy of Chris Schabel

Cluain-Credhuil educated so many future bishops that Ita became known as the foster mother of Irish saints. Double monasteries were also founded in Spain during this period, although here the monasteries were often composed of whole families. In Merovingian Gaul female monasteries enjoyed special prominence. The Monastery of St. John was dedicated in 512 under the leadership of Caesaria of Arles (c. 470–542), and during the next century it was famous as an ecclesiastical center and a repository for the *Rule for Nuns.* The only other monastery known to adopt the *Rule for Nuns* was Radegunde's (c. 518–587) Holy Cross Monastery. A double monastery, Holy Cross was a spiritual, intellectual, and political center during Radegunde's abbacy. After Radegunde's death it fell on hard times and was the site of the most infamous women's monastic rebellion in the early Middle Ages. Other Merovingian double monasteries attained prominence as well, especially through their schools. The Venerable Bede (c. 673–735) mentions the monasteries of Brie, Chelles, and Andalys as places so well known for education that many English parents sent their daughters there.

Although women's monasteries came somewhat later to England, when they did they nurtured many influential abbesses. The most famous was Hilda (614–680), under whose leadership the monastery of Whitby hosted the Synod of 664. The double monasteries of Ely, Folkstone, Sheppy, Barking, Minster-in-Thanet, and Wimbourne thrived until the Viking invasions put an end to this golden age but not before many women left England to establish monasteries in Germany. Lioba (d. c. 782), Boniface's coworker, founded numerous German mission stations that eventually became monasteries, and Walburga (c. 710–779) changed a male monastery at Heidenheim into a double monastery where Latin, Greek, mathematics, and music were taught. During the ninth and tenth centuries, northern Germany witnessed the establishment of four exceptional women's monasteries: Herford, Essem, Quedlinburg, and Gandersheim. Gandersheim, home of Hrosthwitha (c. 932–1000), was the cultural center of ninth-century Saxony.

The male monastic revival that originated with Cluny was not mirrored in female monasticism, but the second phase of the revival gave birth to many great monasteries. Heloise's (c. 1100–1163/64) Paraclete was the mother house of a small order of self-governing monasteries, and Fontevraud was the mother house of the largest federation of women's monasteries. Santa Maria la Real Monastery at Las Huelgas was the mother house for all Spanish Cistercian monasteries; it selected its own chaplains and held court to decide civil and matrimonial cases in its jurisdiction. The period also saw some monasteries attain prominence through saintly and competent abbesses, such as Hildegard of Bingen's (1098–1179) St. Disibod Monastery and Clare of Assisi's (1193/94–1253) St. Damiano Monastery. The great women mystics of Helfta made their monastery a center of spirituality for centuries.

The late Middle Ages witnessed Birgitta of Sweden's (c. 1303–1373) Holy Savior monasteries, and Colette of Corbie's (1381–1447) reform Franciscan monasteries infused enclosed, contemplative life with new energy, but the pre-Reformation and Reformation era really belonged to monasteries that encouraged social services, such as the monasteries of the Oblates of Tor de Specchi and the Ursulines. Nevertheless, the most influential monastery of the 16th century was contemplative: Teresa of Avila's (1515–1582) Monastery of St. Joseph. From this monastery a reform movement spread throughout the West among both male and female houses. Madame Acarie (1566–1618), a powerful founding member of the French school of spirituality, believed herself to be directly inspired by Teresa and established the Parisian Monastery of the Incarnation in full imitation of Teresa's monastery. However, no monastery of the era was of more historical note than the Monastery of Port-Royal-des-Champs. Here the heated controversies of Jansenism festered until during the second half of the 17th century they enveloped the French political and intellectual elite. In the end the monastery was destroyed, and all remaining nuns were dispersed by 1711.

By the 18th century the question of whether new orders of nuns had to reside in enclosed monasteries was resolved in fact if not in theory, and the answer was no. The papacy remained legislatively silent on the issues until 1900, when *Conditiae Christo* acknowledged the validity of active orders whose members lived not in monasteries but in nonenclosed convents. Smaller convents for women engaged in the apostolate became common and gradually replaced monasteries in the laity's mind as the center for women's spiritual leadership. Other political and cultural events also contributed to the passing of the institution of the monastery. The English dissolution of all monasteries during the 16th century was followed by similar legislation from the French National Assembly in 1790. Only after the passing of much time were a few monasteries to reappear in these countries, and never were they to regain their former visibility and prestige. Likewise, when Europe began to Christianize non-Western lands, monasteries were established occasionally but remained less visible and prestigious than convents. Women's monasteries still have the ability to make a statement to society – one need think only of the controversy provoked by the recent foundation of a Carmelite monastery at Auschwitz – but it is a contemplative, silent statement in a world filled with strident voices.

PATRICIA RANFT

See also Benedictines: Female; Brigit, St.; Carmelites: Female; Cistercians: Female; Clare of Assisi, St.; Claustration (Cloister), Rules of; Desert Mothers; Dominicans: Female; Double Houses, Western Christian; Egypt; Fontevraud, France; France: History; Franciscans: Female; Heloise; Hermits: Western Christian; Hilda, St.; Historiography, Recent: Western Christian; Hrosthwitha; Ireland: History; Israel/Palestine; Lay Brothers and Lay Sisters, Christian; Liturgy: Western Christian; Monastery, Christian; Monastics and the World, Medieval; Poland; Recluses, Western Christian; Reformation; Teresa of Avila, St.; Visitandines

Further Reading

Bateson, Mary, "Origin and Early History of Double Monasteries," *Royal Historical Society Transactions* 13 (1890)

Biver, Paul, and Marie-Louise Biver, *Abbayes, monastères, couvents de femmes a Paris: Des origines à la fin du XVIIIe Siècle*, Presses universitaires de France, 1975

Eckenstein, Lina, *Women under Monasticism: Chapters on Saint-Lore and Convent Life Between* A.D. *500 and* A.D. *1500*, Cambridge: University Press, 1896

Escholier, Marc, *Port-Royal: The Drama of the Jansenists*, New York: Hawthorne Books, 1968

Gilchrist, Roberta, *Gender and Material Culture: The Archaeology of Religious Women*, London: Routledge, 1994

Hamburger, Jeffrey F., *Nuns as Artists: The Visual Culture of a Medieval Convent*, Berkeley: University of California Press, 1997

Macleish, Andrew, editor, *The Medieval Monastery*, St. Cloud, Minnesota: North Star Press, 1988

Ranft, Patricia, *Women and the Religious Life in Premodern Europe*, London: Macmillan, 1996; New York: St. Martin's Press, 1997

Rapley, Elizabeth, *The Dévotes: Women and Church in Seventeenth-Century France*, Montreal and Buffalo, New York: McGill-Queens University Press, 1990

Reynes, Geneviève, *Couvents de femmes*, Paris: Fayard, 1987

Thompson, Sally, *Women Religious: The Founding of English Nunneries after the Norman Conquest*, Oxford: Clarendon Press, and New York: Oxford University Press, 1991

Wŏnhyo 617–686

Buddhist scholar-monk and patriarch of Korean Buddhism

Wŏnhyo is undoubtedly the most famous scholar and promulgator of Buddhist faith in the 1,600-year history of Buddhism in Korea. He did not found or directly shape any major monastic order during his lifetime in Silla, yet he has been revered as a patriarch of different sects during the Koryŏ period and afterward. His influence on Korean, Chinese, and Japanese Buddhist philosophical schools persists into the present with renewed interest in the analysis and translation of his works into modern languages.

The details of Wŏnhyo's life as we know it from Chinese hagiographical sources and the *Samguk Yusa* (Legends and Histories of the Three Kingdoms) are sketchy. His career is said to be consistent with his syncretic philosophy of the nondifferentiation of absolute and conventional truth in both theory and practice. His position was enhanced by his legendary personal illumination in an old tomb as well as by his deep study of the entire corpus of Chinese Buddhist scriptures and commentaries available to him in Korea in the seventh century. About 100 works are attributed to him, but only 23 are extant, of which 15 are complete and the rest fragmentary. Among the most influential are his famous thesis on the reconciliation of doctrinal controversies called *Simmun hwajaeng-non* (Treatise on Ten Approaches to the Harmonization of Disputes), which was translated into Sanskrit in India by disciples of the logician Dignāga; his important *Taesŭng kisillon-so* (Commentary on the Treatise of the Awakening of Faith in the Mahāyāna), which bridged Mādhyamika and Yogācāra thought and influenced eastern Asian Mahāyāna thinking profoundly; his incomplete *Hwaŏmgyŏng-so* (Commentary on the Avataṃsaka Sūtra) and *Hwaŏm chongyo* (Thematic Essentials of the Avataṃsaka); and finally, but certainly not least, his *Kŭmgang sammaegyŏng-non* or *Vajrasamādhisūtra-śāstra* (Commentary on the Sūtra of Adamantine Absorption), which lays out systematically the path of all Mahāyāna practice, chapter by chapter, to realize the "fountainhead of the tathāgatagarbha" as nondual reality or "one taste."

Assumed to be ordained a monk in youth within just 100 years of Buddhism's official recognition by the Silla kingdom, Wŏnhyo later became infamous for having contravened the monastic rule of celibacy by fathering a son by a widowed princess. He taught that the Vinaya (monastic precepts) had to be interpreted flexibly and situationally, guided by enlightened discernment that allowed a maximum of "unhindered action" (*mu-ae haeng*) as an expression of the undifferentiated aspects of the One Mind. Unconfined by monastic vows after his liaison, he chose to travel widely about the Korean countryside and spread belief in the Pure Land and devotional practices among common peasant folk while entertaining them with colorful songs and dances. He was also notorious for visiting taverns or brothels without hesitation and for consorting with the most despised of classes yet invariably making appeals to Buddhist faith without discrimination of social rank or the distinction between ordained clergy and lay believers.

Wŏnhyo is distinguished in Korea as a nationalist icon because he never left his home country to study overseas as did other Korean scholar-monks of renown. Wŏnhyo's monastic and philosophical legacy is continued through the efforts of the contemporary Wŏnhyo Order, based in Pusan, which is devoted to the research and publication of Wŏnhyo's writings and practical, religious ideals.

FRANK M. TEDESCO

See also Buddhist Schools/Traditions: Korea; Chinul; Korea: History; Korea: Sites

Biography

An itinerant scholar-monk who broke vows to father a son, Wŏnhyo is revered as the patriarch of many sects of Korean Buddhism. He never studied abroad and spent much time spreading devotional practices among the peasants. Of his more than 100 writings, only 15 survive in their entirety. His emphasis on reconciling doctrinal disputes through syncretism has pervaded Korean Buddhism ever since.

Major Works

Simmun hwajaeng-non (Treatise on Ten Approaches to the Harmonization of Disputes); as *Wŏnhyo ui hwajaeng sasang yŏn'gu = Wŏnhyo's Theory of Harmonization*, translated by Poban O, 1989

Taesŭng kisillon-so (Commentary on the Treatise of the Awakening of Faith in the Mahāyāna); for translation, see Sung-bae Park entry in Further Reading section

Hwaŏmgyŏng-so (Commentary on the Avataṃsaka Sūtra)

Hwaŏm chongyo (Thematic Essentials of the Avataṃsaka)

Kŭmgang sammaegyŏng-non (Commentary on the Sūtra of Adamantine Absorption); portions translated by Robert Buswell appear in *Sourcebook of Korean Civilization*, volume 1, 1993

Further Reading

Buswell, Robert E., *The Formation of Ch'an Ideology in China and Korea: The Vajrasamādhi-Sūtra, a Buddhist Apocryphon* (Princeton Library of Asian Translations), Princeton, New Jersey: Princeton University Press, 1989

Iryon, *Samguk Yusa: Legends and History of the Three Kingdoms of Ancient Korea*, translated by Tae Hung Ha and Grafton K. Mintz, Seoul: Yonsei University Press, 1972

Kim, Sang-hyŏn, *Yŏksa ro ingnun Wŏnhyo*, Seoul: Koryowon, 1994

Ko, Ik-chin, "Wonhyo and the Foundation of Korean Buddhism," *Korea Journal* 21:8 (1981)

Lee, Léo, *Le Maître Wŏn-hyo de Sil-la du VIIe siècle: Sa vie, ses écrits, son apostolat*, Seoul: Librairie Catholique, 1986

Nam, Dong-shin (Nam Tong-sin), *Wŏnhyo*, Seoul: Saenuri, 1999

Pak Chong-hong, "Wonhyo's Philosophical Thought," in *Assimilation of Buddhism in Korea: Religious Maturity and Innovation in the Silla Dynasty* (Studies in Korean Religions and Culture, volume 4), edited by Lewis R. Lancaster and Chai-Shin Yu, Berkeley, California: Asian Humanities Press, 1991

Park, Sung-bae, "Wonhyo's Commentaries on the *Awakening of Faith in Mahayana*," Ph.D. diss., University of California at Berkeley, 1979

Pulgyo Chongi Munhwa Yŏnguso, *Wŏnhyo, ku- i widaehan saeng-ae*, Seoul: Pulgyo Ch'unch'usa, 1999

Rhi, Ki-yong, *Wŏnhyo sasang*, volume 1: *Segyegwan*, Seoul: Hongbobwon, 1967

Rhi, Ki-yong (Yi Ki-yŏng), "Wonhyo and His Thought," in *Main Currents in Korean Thought*, Arch Cape, Oregon: Pace International Research, 1983

Related Web Site

http://www.human.toyogakuen-u.ac.jp/~acmuller/budkor/WonhyoTranslation.htm (Wŏnhyo Translation Project)

Worship Space: Buddhist Perspectives

India

No extant freestanding temples (*vihāras*) remain from the classical period. Thus, most of our knowledge of buildings for ritual purposes is based on conjecture as provided by surviving ground plans as well as by textual sources. However, a number of cave-temples can still be found in the central parts of the subcontinent, including those at Ajaṇṭā, Karle, and Ellora.

Southeast Asia

In the Southeast Asian countries, the large temples feature large, almost palatial halls with a rectangular ground plan for the worship of Buddhas that are placed on low altars. Both the Buddha images in the temple halls and the members of the ordained *saṅgha* are the focus of worship. The monks are normally worshiped by the laypeople in a special hall, where the monks sit on a low platform meant to distinguish them from the laity. The jungle *vihāras* often consist of wall-less buildings. Because of the tropical climate that pervades Sri Lanka, Thailand, Burma, Cambodia, and Vietnam, much religious activity takes place outdoors.

Central Asia

None of the freestanding Buddhist temples and shrines in western or eastern Turkestan (roughly covered by the present-day Xinjiang province) as reported by the Chinese pilgrim-monks of the medieval period has survived. Now only ruins remain. It appears that Gandhāran Buddhist *vihāras* served as models for the early central Asian temples and monasteries. In accordance with this norm, an open temple court was surrounded by monks' cells flanking the inner walls. In the earliest freestanding temples in the Tarim basin, the temples contain several separate courts surrounded by walls and often feature several types of stūpas.

In the later period monasteries were often situated on the edge of ravines and made of freestanding structures built of mud-brick. Narrow, rectangular caves were dug into the sandy cliffs. Most of the caves were meant for worship and contained both central altars and a passage for circumambulation.

In the ruined towns near Turfan, the remains of more than 15 temples have been identified. Most of these have rectangular ground plans divided into an inner main court and a small secondary court. A flight of stairs leads to the entrance at the end of the high, walled enclosure. The main courts may feature a square "tower-stūpa" containing tiered niches that originally held Buddha images.

In addition to temple halls, the Mongolians worship at an outdoor shrine, the *oboo*, which is a primitive type of altar consisting of a large pile of rocks surrounded by several smaller piles placed at the four cardinal points. The central *oboo* is adorned by flags and pieces of cloth in variegated colors, some with printed payers. Originally the *oboo* was the locus for shamanistic rituals but later was incorporated into Lamaism.

Interior, Kannondo, Byōdō-in, Uji (near Kyoto), Japan, 11th century. This Pure Land temple of Kannon (Kwanyin) centers on lay people. Photo courtesy of John C. Huntington, the Huntington Archive

Tibet

Temples are normally constructed on the basis of a strictly symmetrical ground plan. Undoubtedly this characteristic is connected with the fact that temples and sanctuaries are envisaged as three-dimensional maṇḍalas (cosmic diagrams). Large monasteries feature a number of halls dedicated to the worship of a given deity or guru. The Buddhas and other holy images are placed on high altars that often hold a large number of images in bronze and painted clay. Temple courtyards accommodate large communal rituals, such as New Year's celebration and other important events. Cave shrines, usually quite small, are important to the Tibetan tradition and are usually locations at which an important saint, such as Padmasambhava (fl. eighth century) or Milarepa (1040–1123), lived. Stūpas are important points of worship, and the devotees circumambulate them. This ceremony often takes place in conjunction with the turning of multiple prayer wheels set in rows along the base of the stūpa. It is not uncommon for temples to have been built around a central stūpa, as is the case in Gyantse and elsewhere.

China

The temples contains several halls of worship, each designed for the worship of a given Buddha, bodhisattva, or other deity. Altars constitute the focus of worship in these halls and usually consist of a large platform, made of stone or wood, raised three to six feet above the floor. Altars often feature a lower table for offerings and ritual paraphernalia in front. The altars are sometimes tiered to accommodate Buddhas, bodhisattvas, and arhats in accordance with their spiritual rank. Buddhist altars are adorned with streamers and embroidered banners made of silk. The use of wooden superstructures on the altars became popular as early as the Song dynasty (960–1279). During the Yuan (1279–1368) and the Ming dynasties (1368–1644), Buddhist altars attained a certain uniformity with a standardized design and decoration. Lamaist types of altars were introduced during the period of Mongol domination and generally show strong Tibetan features.

Japan

The ground plans of most Japanese temples are strictly symmetrical and contain several halls, each of which is dedicated to a particular ceremonial function. It is common for a temple to contain one or sometimes two pagodas. In addition to the main altar, often built as a large boxlike structure within the hall, many buildings are divided into a holy area and a secular area. Only the Buddhist clergy are allowed into the sanctified area. It is also normal for the main deity on the altar to be screened from the view of the laity and shown publicly only on special occasions. The organization and layout of ritual spaces vary greatly according to each Buddhist school. Shinto shrines and Shintoistic "holy spots," such as waterfalls, rocks, and trees, are often found in association with larger Buddhist temples.

Korea

Close observance to geomancy (*p'ungsu*) is normally practiced in connection with the layout of temples and location of stūpas. Thus, they often display an irregular layout that is meant to harmonize with the surrounding landscape. Here the temple halls bear some resemblance to those found in premodern China. However, the main images on the altars nearly always are supplemented by a large votive painting (*taenghwa*) depicting the same Buddha or deity. In addition the halls are decorated in complex patterns and bright colors, much like those found in Lamaist temples. The courtyards serve as worship space during the celebration of major Buddhist festivals, such as the Buddha's birthday or other important events involving the lay community. All Korean temples feature a hall in which the gods of the Great Bear/Great Dipper are worshiped. A small hall is dedicated to the worship of the Mountain God, a distinct shamanistic element not found in China or Japan.

HENRIK H. SØRENSEN

See also Asia, Central; China; Maṇḍala; Milarepa; Mountain Monasteries, Buddhist; Padmasambhava; Syncretism in Japan, Buddhist; Tibet; Visual Arts, Buddhist: Nepal

Further Reading

Bechert, Heinz, and Richard Gombrich, editor, *The World of Buddhism*, London: Thames and Hudson, and New York: Facts on File, 1984

Chugoku bukkyō no ryo (A Journey of Chinese Buddhism), 5 vols., Kyoto: Meishu shuppan, 1980

Franz, H.G., "Stupa, Tempel und Umgang. Kultbauten des Buddhismus und Hinduismus in Süd- und Zentralasien," *Kunsthistorisches Jahrbuch Graz* 14 (1979)

Hong, Yun-sik, *Yŏngsan chae* (English subtitle: The Yongsanjae Ritual), Seoul: Taewansa, 1989

Ooka, Minoru, *Temples of Nara and Their Art*, New York: Weatherhill, 1973

Prip-Møller, J., *Chinese Buddhist Monasteries*, London: Oxford University Press, 1937; 2nd edition, Hong Kong: Hong Kong University Press, 1968

Sin, Yŏnghŭn, editor, *Sawŏn kŏnch'ŭk*, Seoul: Han'guk burit'aenik'o hoesa, 1989

Sørensen, Henrik H., *The Iconography of Korean Buddhist Painting*, Leiden and New York: E.J. Brill, 1989

Suzuki, Kakichi, *Early Buddhist Architecture in Japan*, Tokyo and New York: Kodansha, 1980

Takeuchi Yoshinori et al., editors, *Buddhist Spirituality: Indian, Southeast Asian, Tibetan, Early Chinese*, New York: Crossroad, 1993; London: SCM Press, 1994

Whitfield, R., and Anne Farrer, *Caves of the Thousand Buddhas: Chinese Art from the Silk Route*, London: British Museum Publications, and New York: George Braziller, 1990

Zhongguo simiao daguan (English subtitle: A Panoramic View of the Temples in China), Beijing: Beijing Yanshan chuban she, 1990

Zwalf, W., editor, *Buddhism: Art and Faith*, London: British Museum Publications, and New York: Macmillan, 1985

Worship Space: Christian Perspectives

By definition a Christian worship service, or liturgy, is an act of prayer engaged in by a community of believers to acknowledge and show honor to the triune God. It is the public ritual prayer in which the Church engages to honor God and to sanctify its members. Worship services include rites of initiating persons into the Church (baptism, chrismation/confirmation); the celebration of the Lord's Supper, or the Eucharist; the daily praise of God through the Liturgy of the Hours (sometimes called the Divine Office); and other, occasional services, such as rites for religious profession, funerals, dedicating a church building, and other sacramental rituals as determined by particular churches. These latter can include rites for penance (or confession), anointing the sick, ordination, and marriage.

In contemporary Roman Catholic Christianity, any act of liturgy requires that the spaces where the liturgy takes place be designed to foster the people's engagement in worship. Thus, to speak of a Christian worship space is to speak mainly of a building where the liturgy is celebrated by a particular congregation. Only in a derivative sense are Christian worship spaces intended to be shrines or places for personal devotions. However, a shrine, understood as a place where a saint is buried (e.g., St. Peter's Basilica in Rome) or a place of pilgrimage, is an obvious location for liturgy to be conducted and worship carried out. Of particular importance here is the distinction made in the patristic era (but based on the New Testament, specifically the Epistles of St. Paul) between "church" as a community of baptized Christians and the building where the gathered church community engages in acts of liturgy and worship.

Almost all contemporary Roman Catholic liturgical books and Church teaching require that the configuration of church buildings support the engagement of the congregation in the act of liturgy. For example, the *Constitution on the Sacred Liturgy* (1963) from the Second Vatican Council (1962–1965) states clearly that when churches are built or renovated, they should be well suited to celebrating the liturgy and thereby to fostering the active participation of the congregation (n. 124). The *Constitution* then goes on to require that the bishops of local territories (and, by extension, the leaders of religious orders and congregations) make appropriate recommendations on how worship spaces should be reconfigured to conform with the demands of the revised liturgy. For example, in the United States the National Conference of Bishops issued a document in 1978 that contained guidelines for implementing this vision of the *Constitution* as expressed in the liturgical rites revised after that coun-

Discalced Carmelite nuns at a prayer service in their chapel in Little Rock, Arkansas. Photo courtesy of Jim Young

cil. Titled *Environment and Art in Catholic Worship* and soon to be republished as *Holy Dwelling*, this document has exerted a great impact on how American Catholic church communities have configured their worship spaces.

Celebration of the recently revised liturgy for the Eucharist requires that the altar be located in a place of prominence where the officiant (priest or bishop) can face the congregation from behind it. The altar table is to be freestanding to allow liturgical ministers to walk around it during the service (e.g., to incense it). Along with their Protestant brethren, Roman Catholics today have come to reemphasize the proclamation of the word at all liturgical services, especially the Eucharist. This requires the location of an *ambo* (to use the more technical term for *lectern* or *pulpit*) in a place that is easily accessible for all readers and from which the Scriptures are proclaimed and the Psalm response to the first reading is sung (as well as the *Exsultet* at the Easter vigil). The chair or bench on which the officiant sits for part of the liturgy (e.g., to listen to the readings) is also emphasized as an important locus within the worship space. When it is a chair used by the bishop in his cathedral, this chair is called a *cathedra*. Thus, the bishop's church is called a *cathedral*.

It is necessary to differentiate among Christian worship spaces so as to denote the variety of communities that worship in them. This is to say that parish communities would legitimately emphasize the baptismal font as the place where new Christians are "made, not born" (to use Tertullian's phrase). Today most fonts are placed at or near the door of the church building to signify entrance into the faith community of the church. More recently designed worship spaces commonly accommodate immersion in water as a more complete sign of baptismal washing than infusion or pouring water only. Such fonts are a permanent feature of parish church buildings and are used especially at the Easter vigil as well as on Sundays for baptismal liturgies on their own or at occasional Eucharists when baptisms take place at Mass. All these practices indicate the prominence that should be given to the place used for Christian initiation in parish churches.

The act of celebrating the Liturgy of the Eucharist and the distribution of Communion to the sick led to the custom in Roman Catholicism of reserving the Eucharist in a tabernacle within the worship space. Devotion to the Eucharist reserved in the tabernacle is not meant to supplant the Eucharistic action, nor is it to replace the act of the Eucharist itself. Although Eucharistic adoration is a legitimate extension of the liturgy, the tabernacle should not compete with the main altar. Thus, it is preferably located in a "chapel of reservation" set apart from the main body of the church. (See the 1967 document *Eucharisticum mysterium*, n. 43.)

When it comes to monastic worship spaces, one of the defining characteristics must be the location and design of the choir. Thus, the monks' commitment to the public celebration of the Liturgy of the Hours (termed the *opus Dei* in the Rule of St. Benedict) is reflected in the types of worship spaces in monasteries. Sometimes such spaces are freestanding abbey churches; at other times they are more modest worship spaces within the larger perimeter of the monastery itself.

The active engagement of monks in the liturgy in general and in the Liturgy of the Hours in particular is to be served by the design of the worship space. No one ideal form of choir exists as long as whatever is used facilitates the celebration of the hours in common. Provision must be made in choir for the various postures that monastics adopt when singing the hours: standing, sitting, kneeling, processing, and so on. Most often this means that each monastic has his or her own choir "stall" placed alongside a number of others in rows. Normally, such a configuration implies that two sets of rows of stalls be on either side of the choir and that each stall contain a movable seat, a shelf for Divine Office (and other) books, a slanted stand on which to place the Office book during the hours, and a movable kneeler. The rationale for a seat that can be placed upright or down is to allow the monastic to stand after each Psalm or part of the hour so that he or she can bow during the singing of the doxology ("Glory be to the Father, and to the Son and to the Holy Spirit . . ."). The rationale for a movable kneeler is for the worshippers to kneel on occasion (depending on local or community custom) for some intercessions during the hours and for an individual monastic's choice to kneel before or after the celebration of an hour of communal prayer.

Normally, such monastic choir stalls situate the monastery's superiors (abbot, prior, and so on) among the members of the choir (albeit in assigned seats normally at the back of the choir). This also allows the function of leading the Office to be shared among all the community, both ordained and nonordained. Most often this leader is designated weekly, and his or her title is *hebdomidarius*. However, on occasion a superior or a member of the community would lead the community by presiding at an hour of the Office from a special chair (normally the one used for the Eucharist), an action that would add particular solemnity to that hour, for example, on Sunday or during a feast day's evening prayer.

Kevin W. Irwin

See also Architecture: Eastern Christian Monasteries; Architecture: Western Christian Monasteries; Beuron, Germany; Church Councils, Recent Catholic; Cluny, France; Collegeville, Minnesota; Liturgy: Western Christian; Office, Daily: Western Christian

Further Reading

Abruzzini, Eugenio, "Architettura," in *Nuovo dizionario di liturgia*, Rome: Edizioni Paoline, 1988

Arte e Liturgia: L'arte sacra a trent'anni dal Concilio, Milan: San Paolo, 1993

Boyer, Mark G., *The Liturgical Environment: What the Documents Say*, Collegeville, Minnesota: Liturgical Press, 1990

Conant, Kenneth, *Carolingian and Romanesque Architecture, 800 to 1200*, Baltimore, Maryland, and Harmondsworth, Middlesex: Penguin, 1959

Environment and Art in Catholic Worship, Washington, D.C.: National Conference of Catholic Bishops, 1978

Huffman, Walker S., and S. Anita Stauffer, *Where We Worship*, Minneapolis, Minnesota: Augsburg, 1987

Krautheimer, R., *Early Christian and Byzantine Architecture*, Harmondsworth, Middlesex: Penguin, 1967; Baltimore, Maryland: Penguin, 1975

Lopez Martin, Julian, "El lugar de la celebración," in *La Liturgia della Iglesia*, Madrid: Biblioteca de Autores Cristianos, 1994

Lukken, Gerard, and Mark Searle, *Semiotics and Church Architecture: Applying the Semiotics of A.J. Greimas and the Paris School to the Analysis of Church Buildings*, Kampen, Netherlands: Kok Pharos, 1993

Settimana regionale di liturgia pastorale, *Gli spazi della celebrazione rituale*, Milan: Edizioni O.P., 1984

White, James F., *Protestant Worship and Church Architecture: Theological and Historical Considerations*, New York: Oxford University Press, 1964

Y

Yeshe Tsogyel eighth century A.D.

Legendary Tibetan Buddhist consort of Padmasambhava, teacher, and composer of *terma*

Western accounts of Tibetan Buddhism rarely mention Yeshe Tsogyel, but in traditional Tibetan sacred histories and hagiography, she is quite important, especially to practitioners, both monastic and lay, in the Nyingma lineage. Along with her consort Padmasambhava, she is one of the more important figures in the story of how Buddhism was established in Tibet in the eighth century, at least according to traditional accounts. Like her consort Padmasambhava she is a miraculous being from her conception to her death, and, like him, her dharmic accomplishments are profound, and she had many students. In addition, like her consort Padmasambhava, she left many *terma* (hidden treasure) texts to be discovered at later times when they would be needed to help revitalize Buddhism. Yet despite these obvious parallels to her male counterpart, Western accounts of Tibetan Buddhism do not even discuss whether a historical woman exists behind this sacred myth model, whereas most Western historians posit some historical reality behind the wondrous tales about Padmasambhava.

Not only does her traditional life story make her an important colleague of Padmasambhava, but her sacred biography also parallels that of the Buddha in many ways. Her biography narrates that when she was conceived both her mother and her father experienced wondrous visions and that when she was born she had unusual abilities. It was predicted immediately that she would become either a great religious teacher or the wife of an emperor. Her parents assumed that she should become the wife of an emperor and were determined to find a suitable marriage for her. She resisted conventional marriage and actually escaped from her first one, but after she was eventually captured, she was indeed married to the emperor against her wishes.

However, at this point her fortunes turned, for Padmasambhava had just been invited to Tibet to tame local deities who were disrupting the building of the first Buddhist monastery in Tibet. The emperor to whom Yeshe Tsogyel was now married wished to learn Vajrayāna teachings from Padmasambhava. Padmasambhava had recognized that Yeshe Tsogyel was an emanation of a Tantric deity in human form and that she needed to be trained in Vajrayāna practices in order for her to realize her true potential and to help others attain enlightenment. Indeed her sacred biography also tells the story of how this supernatural being took human form and was born as the wondrous baby about whom it was predicted that she would become either an important religious teacher or the wife of an emperor. Recognizing Tsogyel's true nature, Padmasambhava told the emperor that part of the price for his own initiation would be to relinquish Tsogyel to Padmasambhava.

Yeshe Tsogyel then undertook the arduous training process that is required of anyone, even an emanation of an supernatural being in human form, who wishes to attain Buddhahood. Indeed even Padmasambhava, renowned in Tibet as a "second Buddha," had undergone this process earlier in India. As she progressed in her journey, she became more a colleague to Padmasambhava than his student. Although she is often said to be his consort, in the context of Vajrayāna Buddhism a consort is more like what westerners think of as a colleague. Eventually she also became a teacher in her own right and attracted many students, both male and female, both monastic and lay. She is especially associated with certain teachings and practices of Vajrakilaya, a *yidam* (meditation deity) whose practice is undertaken to overcome obstacles.

However, in traditional stories Yeshe Tsogyel's most important long-term impact on Tibetan Buddhism lay in her role as someone who composed and hid *terma*, both with Padmasambhava and by herself. These texts, said to be written in a code that could be deciphered only by a special person, known as a *terton* (finder of *terma* texts), are considered by some lineages of Tibetan Buddhism to be as crucial as the initial transmission of Buddhism to Tibet. For those who value *terma* as authentic teachings, they are regarded as extremely reliable because they convey the fresh, untrammeled word of the guru, uncorrupted by misunderstandings or mistakes in transmission. And all traditional accounts of the source of these *terma* credit Yeshe Tsogyel, along with Padmasambhava, for them. In fact because she lived on for many, many years after Padmasambhava had left Tibet and had a prodigious memory for the teachings that she had received, she is credited with recording and hiding many teachings that Padmasambhava had not written down. Thus, in this traditional account many of the teachings of the highly revered Guru Rinpoche (precious master) are available only through Yeshe Tsogyel, his colleague and consort.

The differences between Western and traditional Tibetan accounts are revealing. Regardless of whether a historical woman exists behind the stories of Yeshe Tsogyel, the traditional accounts, with a keen sense of the balance between masculine and feminine, credit Yeshe Tsogyel with a crucial role in establishing Buddhism in Tibet. The prestige ascribed to her in her role as recorder and hider of *terma* texts is even more significant, both to monastic and lay practitioners who recognize the validity of *terma*. In most Western academic histories of Tibetan Buddhism, one searches in vain in the index for an entry "Yeshe Tsogyel."

RITA M. GROSS

See also Tibetan Lineages: Nyingma

Biography

Known entirely through legend or sacred biography, Yeshe Tsogyel functions as the consort of the historical Padmasambhava. Like him she too concealed texts (*terma*) for discovery in future ages.

Further Reading

Bdud-joms, Jigs-bral-ye-ses-rdo-rje, *The Nyingma School of Tibetan Buddhism: Its Fundamentals and History*, 2 vols., Boston: Wisdom, 1991

Dowman, Keith, translator, *Sky Dancer: The Secret Life and Songs of the Lady Yeshe Tsogyel*, London and Boston: Routledge and Kegan Paul, 1984

Gross, Rita M., "Yeshe Tsogyel: Enlightened Consort, Great Teacher, Female Role Model," in *Feminine Ground: Essays on Women and Tibet*, edited by Janis Dean Willis, Ithaca, New York: Snow Lion, 1989

Snying-po, Nam-mkha i, *Mother of Knowledge: The Enlightenment of Ye-shes mTsho-rgyal*, Berkeley, California: Dharma, 1983

Yosai. *See* Eisai (Yosai)

Yugoslavia. *See* Croatia; Serbia

Z

Zen. *See* Chan/Zen; Zen and the West

Zen, Arts of

"Zen art" describes artifact, process, and tradition, challenging monastic/lay boundaries and ultimately the sacred/profane distinction itself. In describing arts of Zen, this article discusses a range of cultural concerns: (1) origins within Chinese religions; (2) rise of indigenous Chinese forms of Buddhism, especially the Chan lineages; (3) Zen monastic use of the arts in Japan after the 11th century; (4) relationship between Zen realization (satori) and creativity; (5) development of Japanese secular lineages of art, craft, and martial arts; and (6) late 19th- and 20th-century nativist interpretation of these arts within the Japanese response to the challenges of colonialism and modernization by the West.

Origins

The Japanese Zen utilization of the arts had its origins: (1) in the early Chinese Daoist emphasis on the spiritual dimensions of craft and art (as epitomized in the episode "Prince Wen-Hui and His Cook" in chapter 3 of *Chuang-tzu*, "The Secret of Caring for Life") – a process of acclimatization, mastering technique, and intuiting and adjusting to the twists and changes of the flow of reality (*dao*) as one works and creates; (2) in the gradual sixth-century Sinicization of Indian and central Asian Buddhism, especially a fusion of this Daoist working of the phenomenal with Indian Mahāyāna ontology (the collapse of dichotomy between suffering/enlightenment [saṃsāra/nirvāṇa]); and (3) in how the Mahāyāna *Wreath of Flowers* sūtra's premise that the "very universe itself *is* the Dharma" (*dharmadhātu*) becomes *the* experience of the Buddha's enlightenment and was interpreted by the Chinese Hua-yen Buddhist school to embrace the interrelationship and interpenetration of all creatures and phenomena in the universe. Simply put, if ignorance and suffering *just as they are* comprise enlightenment, then any action with its products has the potential to be enlightening and to be an expression of the wisdom and compassion of enlightenment.

Chan Lineages

Although the stage was set by the social intercourse and cross-fertilization of early non-Chinese and then native Buddhists with Daoists and Confucian literati during the Eastern Chin (317–420) through the Sui (581–618) dynasties, it would be the budding Chan practice traditions during the Tang dynasty (618–907) that produced a sophisticated relationship between meditative experience and artistic expression. This combined the Daoist dimension in using speech, gesture, body language, and the performance of simple tasks (now for master/disciple interaction) with a Confucian dimension of locating practice as a communal effort in the monastery involved monastic/Buddhist laity and monastic/non-Buddhist literati social intercourse beyond. A range of motives such as propagation, need for patronage, public debates, and exchanges with non-Buddhists, friendship, and so on defined the extramonastic intercourse of Chinese Buddhists, especially such Tang dynasty Chan monks as Shen-hsiu (c. 606–706), P'u-chi (651–739), and Tsung-mi (780–841). Many important Sung and Yüan dynasty Chan monks had extensive ties to political elites and to powerful lay followers and patrons, making constant use of poetry, essay, correspondence, calligraphy, and ink-wash painting (and inscriptions). Major Sung dynasty religious and literary movements and debates beyond Buddhism readily influenced monk/lay intercourse. The Northern Sung Lin-chi Chan monk Chüeh-fan Hui-hung (1071–1128) created a hybrid of Chan practice, Buddhist scriptural study, and secular literature called "literary Zen" (*wen-tzu Ch'an*); yet at almost exactly the same time there emerged the quite famous observation attributed to the Lin-chi school Yün-men lineage Chan master Fa-hsiu (1047–1100) by his disciple Ta-hui Tsung-kao (1089–1163):

> Once, upon the occasion of a snowfall, Ch'an master Yüan-t'ung Hsiu [Fa-hsiu] observed that whenever it snows it becomes quite easy to see that there are three kinds of monks. The best sort remain in the monks' hall in seated meditation. The middling sort grind ink and trim their brushes so they may write snow poems. The worse sort huddle about the brazier talking of warm things to eat.

Chan traditions soon promoted a public image aptly summarized by the epitome "an extraordinary transmission beyond doctrines – no dependence upon or establishing of words or letters": (1) as practice toward abrupt realization (Chinese, *wu*; Japanese, *satori*) unlike other systematic path (*mārga*)-based Indian and Chinese Buddhist schools, (2) as a non-scripture-based direct master/disciple existential encounter, and (3) as an unmediated, nonsymbolic "pure" experience of realization based on an intuitive awareness of reality. However, the essential Chinese culture of Confucian literacy and Daoist creativity proved irresistible, so Sung dynasty Chan readily adopted secular pursuits, such as the use of words and letters in religious practice in two ways: (1) to evaluate progress toward realization and (2) to demonstrate realization and cultural creativity in social contexts beyond the monastery.

Zen Monastic Arts

The scene shifted to Japan in the late 12th century, with the fall of the Sung dynasty to the Mongols and the displacement of the imperial court by a new warrior power throughout Japan. Use of such arts in recently imported Zen practice was initially informal (i.e., not defined within its monastic standards [Chinese, *ching-kuei*; Japanese, *shingi*]), yet such applications quickly escalated during the early Kamakura period as refugee Chinese Sung masters were installed in Zen monasteries built and patronized by a warrior elite in the new northern capital of Kamakura. Of necessity the context of practice emphasized forms of expression other than spoken vernacular Chinese language between Sung Chan master and Japanese lay practitioner. This context included the mainland Chan use of the kōan written case over oral exchanges and the so-called warrior kōans emphasizing existential characteristics of danger, sudden response, strategy common to the warrior lifestyle, gesture and body language, and so on. Especially popular was the Lin-chi school Yün-men lineage founder Yün-men's (864–949) "one word barrier" (Chinese, *i-tzu-kuan*; Japanese, *ichiji-kan*) style of short, sharp ("one-word"), incisive, and highly expressive answers to disciples' questions. In Kamakura Zen this experience stimulated sudden, unpremeditated, energetic responses, often as abrupt as Yün-men's Chan model. In the next generation a quite accomplished native Japanese Rinzai master, Shūhō Myōchō (1282–1337) – one who never went to China or practiced directly under a Sung Chan master – created a new densely compacted style of master/disciple interview response by emphasizing the *hua-t'ou* (Japanese, *watō*) or capping phrase (a pithy concentrated symbolic kōan epitome). (Shūhō would also found the greatest of Zen monasteries for the development of Zen and the arts, Daitokuji, in Kyoto.) Dependence on words and symbols grew.

Intercourse soon developed in early medieval Japan along the lines of the Sung Chinese Chan/literati model, between a highly formalized monastic structure supervised by the warrior government and known as the two Five Mountain systems (Japanese, *gozan*; five major Rinzai Zen monasteries each in Kamakura and in Kyoto) and political, court, religious (other Buddhist schools and non-Buddhist shrines), literary, artistic, and aesthetic realms. Monks from several Kyoto-based Five Mountain monasteries (especially Tenryūji) were engaged by warrior shōgunal governments during the Ashikaga and Muromachi periods to lead diplomatic, commercial, and cultural missions to the Chinese mainland, bringing back new trends in Chinese language, literature, calligraphy, art, official document styles, and so on (which naturally placed these monks in high social demand). At this time the Zen relationship to the arts was highly eclectic, mixing genre and styles in a variety of literati situations – as used by *bunjin-sō*, or "literati-monks." One commonly known social activity involved the use of the landscape arts: the *shigajiku* poem-and-ink-wash painting scrolls in which a painting was created for or during a unique occasion and on which noted individuals calligraphed original verse inscriptions, quotations, and so on. An early Chinese Buddhist form appropriated and popularized by Sung Chan masters that became extremely widespread in Japan was *mo-chi* (Japanese, *bokuseki*), "ink traces," initially a master's authentification certificate (Chinese, *yin-ching*; Japanese, *inka*) to a disciple written in an orthodox style. By the 12th century the Japanese Zen world came to favor much more highly personal, irregular, and eccentric styles of calligraphy written by Chan and Zen masters.

Satori and Creativity

The relationship between Zen practice and the creativity that produces specific artistic results and enables appreciation and understanding is anchored in the Zen process of realization. It is a process that involves a master assigning or locating a specific challenge for a disciple (whether through informal questioning, assignment of a kōan case, request for demonstration, comment on observed daily behavior, and so on). The disciple begins to work with the challenge in daily sitting meditation (*zazen*) as well as carrying it over into all the more complex forms of meditation that comprise the monastic schedule (walking, chanting, eating, working, and begging meditations). Energy accumulates from the use of ordinary self-identity-based intellect- and emotion-driven coping strategies in attempting to meet the challenge. Results of endless frustration with logical contradiction, with the overall worthlessness of intellect, with powerlessness of self, and with psychophysical exhaustion begin to merge to form an introspective focus slowly concentrated into one great existential doubt. Often the challenge is reduced or concentrated into a specific symbol (a word, image, or crucial phrase [*hua-t'ou*]) that develops into tension with the "great doubt" that ultimately should explode into the experience of realization. The tradition also speaks of the possibility of such spiritual phenomena as (1) the master's compassion and transference of merit providing a psychic opportunity for the disciple's existential leap into realization; (2) a disciple's realization as a "plugging in" to a continuous transsymbolic, spiritual experience of enlightenment reaching back through the tradition to the Buddha that enables the disciple to participate in an enlightening process ("tracing back the radiance emanating from the [enlightened] mind," or *hui-kuang fan-chao*) and to understand completely the original intention of an enlightened master (i.e., of a kōan's creator) and thus to see how previously realized masters have created Zen expressions and Zen actions and now to create or use such language or act before one's master; and (3) to thus be able to penetrate any subsequent challenge assigned by a master with the enlightened mind by intuitively and unpremeditatedly creating a new expression from among all equivalent elements of experience interrelated in the "universe-as-the-Dharma" (*dharmadhātu*) or by using some extant symbol, phrase, or image as an existentially new response.

The classic description of how an enlightened mind creates is the explanation of enlightenment in action written by the medieval Rinzai master Takuan Sōhō in his early 17th-century letters to the warrior Yagyū Munenori. This depiction of the Zen No-mind (no "ordinary, deluded, clinging heart/mind") in terms of Japanese swordsmanship has been termed the most understandable explanation of enlightenment in Japanese Zen. Here the life-and-death contest of the sword is an ultimate test of the heightening of the perceptive process and the functioning of the Zen "No-mind" – a physical context of instantaneous tension between the total absorption in concentration necessary for success and the total lack of attachment to concentration necessary for maximum flexibility of response. Takuan's theory of creativity suggests that artistic concentration must be developed as a perfectly "equal" attention to all the factors that comprise a creating (environmental characteristics, tools and materials used, technical and stylistic potential, the doer's own awareness of past efforts, successes, failures, criticisms, motivations, and so on). All relevant factors must be made equally significant by the performer (in other words all must be equally important or equally unimportant). If any single factor becomes an object of concern, Takuan explains that the mind "stops" on that factor, even if only momentarily, and the distracted mind is thus ordinary and functions as a subject aware of an object. The precise source of the freedom to create is the Zen "No-mind" of realization that does not become attached to any element in a situation.

Zen practice provides many degrees of concentric complexity in which to decrease and eliminate distraction and attachment so as to develop instead bare attention as equalizing all dharmas in experiencing the flow of reality. The performer must experience the potential in each element of awareness (perception, symbolization, memory, and so on) that constitutes its uniqueness as a distinct element and must at the same time see the creative potential that each element shares because it is present in this creative action. (The performer's awareness of oneself as doer and action being done must also be reduced to nothing more than simply another two of such elements in the creating.) Such characteristics as lack of premeditation, flexibility of response, flow of awareness, and synthesis via equivalence of elements all provide fluidity of physical motion. Simultaneously there must be the same fluidity within the heart/mind so that creating becomes intuitively selecting elements of structure and form during the moment-to-moment changes as reality flows by, experienced as an unobstructed interrelationship of everything.

The process of how realization informs expression is identical for all of the Zen arts, whether those of performance (Nō drama, tea ceremony, linked verse, and swordsmanship [*kendō*]) or product (poetry, calligraphy, ink-wash painting, Zen gardening, and flower arrangement).

Secular Lineages

However, the lapse of at least a century also encouraged the development of several distinct separately formed art traditions, especially by the time of the Ashikaga shōgun Yoshitmitsu (during the cultural era known as the "Kitayama," or "Northern hills," centering around Yoshimitsu's beautiful but dilettantish Temple of the Golden Pavilion [Kinkakuji] in the hills of northern Kyoto). Evidence for such growing distinctiveness shows how these traditions would to some degree imitate the Zen master/disciple training experience: (1) as an apprenticeship based on the monastic learning process of little explicit instruction, the need for increasingly sophisticated observation, and care in ritual imitation and (2) as a lineage emphasizing intuitive grasp of a nondiscursive self-cultivation by means of oral transmission (*kuden*). Afterward authentification often took the form of a ritual initiation evidenced by a codified but dense esoteric chart, diagram, instructional, or "secret text" (*hidensho*). Such distinct trends in Zen and specific arts included *renga*, or linked verse, by the aristocrat Nijō Yoshimoto (1351–1431) and monk-poet Shōtetsu (1381–1459); the early Nō drama movement by playwrights Kan'ami (1332–1384) and his son Zeami (1363–1443); ink-wash landscape monk-painters Shūbun (active c. 1423–1460) and Minchō (1351–1431); a formal tea ceremony being developed by Nōami (1397–1471); and the Zen garden tradition begun by Muso Soseki (1275–1351) at Saihōji and so on. No less important were the Kinkakuji and Tenryūji Sung rock styles and the new landscape ink-wash-derived gardens of Sesshū Tōyō (1420–1506) and the Shingon school's "Rock-setting monks" (*ishitate-sō*) who compiled the *Illustrations for Designing Mountain, Water, and Hillside Field Landscapes* (*Senzui-narabi-ni yagyō no zu*). Significant writers included broad Five Mountains literary tradition monk-poet Zekkai Chūshin (1336–1405) and monk-prose stylist Gidō Shūshin (1325–1388) and Chinese aesthetics and religion monk-scholars Chūhō En'i (1355–1413) and Taihaku Shingen (1358–1415). Two great Rinzai monasteries existed beyond the Five Mountain system: the imperial Zen monasteries of Daitokuji and Myōshinji. The former produced one of the most radical but highly effective Muromachi Rinzai masters, Ikkyū Sōjun (1394–1481), who either instructed as lay Zen practitioners – the ex-emperor Hanazono – or formed friendships with individuals engaged in many of these arts – such as linked-verse master Iio Sōgi (1421–1502), Nō drama/Zen theorist Komparu Zenchiku (1405–1468 – "the fusion of Zen and the Nō drama" [*zen-nō itchi*]), the great tea ceremony theorist Murata Shukō (1422–1502), and Soga school monk-painters beginning with Soga Jasoku (d. c. 1473) at Daitokuji.

Two distinct monk–ink-wash artist ateliers developed during the 14th century: the Shōkokuji lineage in Kyoto and the Kenchōji lineage in Kamakura. Muromachi monk-painters from both would travel to Ming China to study new trends in ink wash; the most famous was Sesshū Tōyō, who studied at both

Shōkokuji and Kenchōji. Sixteenth- and 17th-century monk-painters trained at Daitokuji, either as monk-painters, as monk-literati (Takuan Sōhō [1573–1645], Kōgetsu Sōgan [1574–1463], [Shingon school monk] Shōkadō Shōjō [c. 1584–1639], Seigan Sōi [1588–1661]), or as lay painters (Konoe Nobutada [1565–1614] and Isshi Bunshu [1608–1646]). Several centuries of Rinzai Zen concern with such arts as poetry and ink-wash painting broadened the practice of these arts by noteworthy monk-painters and lay painters of other Buddhist traditions during the Edo period, such as Sōtō Zen monk-painters Fūgai Ekun (1568–1654) and Gesshū Sōko (1618–1696). Later Rinzai monk-artists included Ungo Kiyō (1582–1659) of Myōshinji, Bankei Yōtaku (1622–1693), and the great Rinzai reformer Hakuin Ekaku (1685–1769). Hakuin produced his own group of monk-painters (who carried on his radical brushwork and calligraphy techniques: Tōrei Enji (1721–1792) Suiō Genro (1717–1789), Reigen Etō (1721–1785), Gako (1737–1805), and indirectly Shunsō Shōjū (1750–1839).

A completely different tradition reached Japan with the monk-painters who introduced the Chinese Ōbaku Chan school to Japan in 1620: Yin-yüan Lung-ch'i (1592–1673), Mu-an Hsing-t'ao (1611–1684), Chi-fei (1616–1671), Tu-chan Hsing-jung (1628–1706), Ta-p'eng (1691–1774), and Ts'ao-tung school monk Hsin-yueh (1639–1696) and Japanese nun Ryōnen Genso (1646–1711). Powerful non-Rinzai monk-calligraphers include Jiun Sonja (1718–1804) of the Shingon school and the Sōtō monk Ryōkan (1758–1831). More recent Zen monk-painter/calligraphers have included Rinzai monks Sengai Gibon (1750–1838) and Nantembō Tōjū (1839–1925), Rinzai lay practitioner Yamaoka Tesshū (1836–1888), and contemporary monk-calligrapher and Zen swordsman Ōmori Sōgen.

Nativist Interpretations

The tremendous amount of change that Japan experienced with the forced 1853 ending of its medieval seclusion, the subsequent downfall of the warrior government and restoration of the emperor in 1868, and the race toward Westernization and modernity that included defeating the Chinese in 1895 and the Russians a decade later, the rise of a modern Japanese colonial empire abroad supported by a fascist government at home, and its defeat and the 1945–1952 Allied occupation all challenged cultural and especially religious elements of Japanese identity as never before. Encounter at home and abroad with the West kindled tremendous interest and ferocious debate about the value of Western technology, ideologies, religions, and so on and questioned what indigenous religions meant in light of them. Foreign and native cultures were evaluated, promoted, and criticized energetically by Japanese scholars, popularizers, revivalists, and nativists. Daisetz Teitaro Suzuki (1870–1966), the singular interpreter of Zen and eastern Asian Buddhism, spent a lifetime of journeying back and forth between Japan and the West, attempting to distill an essence of Buddhism in contrast to the monotheistic traditions of the West and to isolate a unique Japanese cultural component in the Zen tradition. He argued that Zen had contributed the basis to the medieval secular arts of the tea ceremony, calligraphy, waka and haiku poetry, ink-wash painting, Nō drama, puppet theater, flower arrangement, gardens, archery and swordsmanship, and even the fundamental social identity of the Japanese in such cultural forms as language, social structure, courtesy, and crafts. His work stimulated several generations of Japanese and Western philosophers, artists, and writers (including the American beat and hippie movements of 1950s and 1960s) to interpret and apply such theorizations to Western art, literature, music, and so on. In the West genuine religious interest combined with such popular cultural phenomena to generate a half century of interest in the meditative and monastic practices of Zen, largely perpetuating Suzuki's own vision. However, recent Western Buddhist scholarship has begun to question the traditional precedents and actual medieval evidence for much of Suzuki's interpretation of Zen and of Zen and the arts. Critics read his theories as a characteristic but modern Japanese adaptation of contemporary Western philosophical thought and as a nativist response to the challenges to Japanese identity that the West posed during the 20th century. This revisionism sees the relationship between Zen and the arts to have been as much Chinese and Korean as Japanese and to have involved mainly sociopolitical motives of survival, patronage seeking, and institutional power. Scholars no longer see Zen as generating purely spiritual expressions of enlightenment, nor as an intuitive creativity emerging from a pure symbolless experience of reality, nor as an initiative based in a uniquely Japanese cultural experience.

DENNIS LISHKA

See also Buddha (Śākyamuni); Buddhist Schools/Traditions: Japan; Eisai (Yosai); Humor: Buddhist; Images: Buddhist Perspectives; Initiation: Buddhist Perspectives; Japan: History; Kōan; Kyoto, Japan; Visual Arts, Buddhist: Japan

Further Reading

Addiss, Stephen, *The Art of Zen: Paintings and Calligraphy by Japanese Monks, 1600–1925*, New York: Abrams, 1989

Gimello, Robert M., "Mārga and Culture: Learning, Letters, and Liberation in Northern Sung Ch'an," in *Paths to Liberation: The Mārga and Its Transformations in Buddhist Thought* (Studies in East Asian Buddhism, number 7), edited by Gimello and Robert E. Buswell, Honolulu: University of Hawaii Press, 1992

Haga, Kōshirō, *Chūsei Zenrin no gakumon oyobi bungaku ni kansuru kenkyū*, Tokyo: Nihon Gakujutsu Shinkokai, 1956

Kuck, Loraine, *The World of the Japanese Garden: From Chinese Origins to Modern Landscape Art*, New York: Walker/Weatherhill, 1968

Lishka, Dennis, "Zen and the Creative Process: The 'Kendō-Zen' Thought of the Rinzai Master Takuan," *Japanese Journal of Religious Studies* 5:2–3 (June–September 1978)

Nishibe, Bunjō, *Zen to cha* (Zen and Tea), Tokyo: Kōdansha, 1972

Parker, Joseph D., *Zen Buddhist Landscape Arts of Early Muromachi Japan (1336–1573)* (SUNY Series in Buddhist Studies), Albany: State University of New York Press, 1999

Pollack, David, *Zen Poems of the Five Mountains* (American Academy of Religion, Studies in Religion, number 37), New York: Crossroad, 1985

Sakaki Bakuzan, *Zen no sho* (The Zen of Calligraphy), Osaka: Sōgensha, 1969

Sharf, Robert H., "The Zen of Japanese Nationalism," in *Curators of the Buddha: The Study of Buddhism under Colonialism*, edited by Donald S. Lopez, Chicago: University of Chicago Press, 1995

Suzuki, Daisetz T., *Zen Buddhism and Its Influence on Japanese Culture* (Ataka Buddhist Library), Kyoto: Eastern Buddhist Society, 1938; revised as *Zen and Japanese Culture* (Bollingen Series, 64), New York: Pantheon Books, and London: Routledge and Kegan Paul, 1959

Zen and the West

1. The West's Encounter with Zen

Contact can be traced back to 1549–1551, when Spanish Jesuit Francis Xavier (1506–1552) spent 27 months in Japan as the first Christian missionary. After he had explained through an interpreter that he had come from India – Xavier had set sail from Goa – Japanese Buddhist priests at first mistook Xavier's strange teachings for those of a Buddhist sect that had not previously entered Japan.

The first contact with a priest of the Zen sect occurred soon after Xavier arrived at the port of Kagoshima on the island of Kyushu. There he befriended Ninshitsu (Bunshō Hagiwara, d. 1556), 15th abbot of the Fukushōji monastery of the Sōtō Zen sect. Observing Zen monks engaged in *zazen* practice at the monastery, Xavier asked Ninshitsu what they were doing. The Zen abbot's famed reply, as described by Xavier, was that some of the monks were calculating contributions received, others contemplating how to obtain better robes, while others were considering recreations and pastimes; in short, nothing really important was thought about.

This early period of Catholic encounters with Zen Buddhists can be summed up by Father Cosmos Torres, who accompanied Xavier to Japan. He wrote that Zen priests insist there is no soul, so that when we die, everything dies; but they are men of great meditation, so it is very difficult to refute them and to make them understand God's law.

Probably the first westerner to "convert" to the Zen sect was Christovão Ferreira (1580–1650), a Portuguese padre and Jesuit mission superior. Under the horrific pressures of Christian persecution, he was tortured until apostasy and then "converted." In 1636 he wrote *Deceit Disclosed* (*Kengi-roku*), a condemnation of the Christian faith. He signed it with a statement that he had formerly been chief padre of Japan and Macao but was now reformed and an adherent of Zen – a bizarre prelude to recent interest in Zen in the West.

During the subsequent period of national isolation (1639–1854), figures such as Engelbert Kaempfer (1651–1716), a German physician employed by a Dutch trading company on the island of Dejima in Nagasaki Harbor, wrote detailed accounts of Zen practice that were smuggled out and became the basis for *History of Japan*, which appeared in a two-volume English translation in 1727–1728.

Twenty-five years after the Meiji Restoration, in 1893, the World's Parliament of Religions was held for 17 days in Chicago. One of the Japanese participants was Sōen Shaku (1859–1919), then head abbot of the Engakuji branch of Rinzai Zen, centered in Kamakura. His main speech was translated in Japan by his lay disciple Teitaro Suzuki, later known throughout the world as D.T. Suzuki (1870–1966).

Although this event over a century ago marks the beginning of Japanese Zen activity in the West, no mention of "Zen" was made by Sōen Shaku in either of his speeches before the Parliament. In his main address he spoke more broadly about the Buddhist doctrine of cause and effect and contrasted it with the notion of a first cause.

During a second trip to the United States in 1905–1906, Sōen Shaku, assisted this time by his disciple D.T. Suzuki, provided relatively traditional opportunities for Zen practice. However, it was in July 1902 that the first Americans spent some months in a Japanese Zen monastery: Sōen Shaku's Engakuji. This small group included Mrs. Alexander Russell from San Francisco, who was instrumental in bringing Sōen Shaku back to the United States a few years later.

Thomas Kirby appears to have been the first westerner ordained as a Zen monk. He was born in England into a Protestant family, became a Roman Catholic priest in Canada, and then traveled to Japan, where he was ordained by Sōen Shaku at Engakuji on 11 July 1915. He fell ill not long after and had to return west but was active in Mahāyāna missionary work before coming back to Japan in 1927.

A number of Sōen Shaku's disciples traveled to the United States around the turn of the 20th century, including D.T. Suzuki in 1897 and Sōkatsu Shaku (1870–1954; adopted son and dharma heir) and Nyogen Senzaki (1876–1958) in 1906.

Lay disciple D.T. Suzuki was sent to the United States by his teacher to assist the author and publisher Paul Carus and ended up staying 11 years. Besides translating, D.T. Suzuki gradually became proficient at writing about Mahāyāna Buddhism, Zen, and Japanese culture. His writings, translations, and lectures introduced much of the Western world to Zen Buddhism.

Later in his life, D.T. Suzuki arranged to have two outstanding Japanese Zen figures visit the West to continue and deepen what he had begun: Shin'ichi Hisamatsu (1889–1980), a lay Zen man and philosopher who lectured at Harvard Divinity School from 1957 to 1958, then traveled through Europe, where he engaged in dialogues with leading thinkers, including C.G. Jung and Martin Heidegger. The other was Zenkei Shibayama (1904–1974), head abbot of the Nanzenji branch of Rinzai Zen, centered in Kyoto. He visited university campuses around the United States on a number of visits from 1965 to 1970.

Sōtō Zen practice took root in the 1960s through the efforts of Shunryū Suzuki, and a popular form of Zen practice combining Rinzai and Sōtō styles, often with a Christian flavor, has taken root in the West based on the Sambō Kyōdan, an independent lay Zen movement in Kamakura. Although nothing approaching the severity of Japanese Rinzai Zen monastic practice can be found in Western Zen centers, there is at present an unresolved tension between prematurely breaking free from Eastern ways on the one hand and attempting to slavishly imitate them on the other. As Zen practice matures in the West, a form appropriate to the time and place will naturally develop as it did in China and elsewhere.

Jeff Shore

Further Reading

Abe, Masao, editor, *A Zen Life: D.T. Suzuki Remembered*, New York: Weatherhill, 1986
Barrows, John Henry, editor, *The World's Parliament of Religions*, Chicago: The Parliament Publishing Company, 1893
Elison, George, *Deus Destroyed: The Image of Christianity in Early Modern Japan*, Cambridge, Massachusetts: Harvard University Press, 1988
Furuta, Shōkin, "Shaku Sōen: The Footsteps of a Modern Japanese Zen Master," *Philosophical Studies of Japan* 8 (1967)
Kaempfer, Engelbert, *The History of Japan*, translated by J.G. Scheuchzer, New York: AMS Press, 1971
Muramoto, Shoji, translator, "The Jung-Hisamatsu Conversation," *The Couch and the Tree: Dialogues in Psychoanalysis and Buddhism*, New York: North Point Press, 1998
Sasaki, Ruth Fuller, *Zen: A Religion*, New York: First Zen Institute of America, 1958
Schurhammer, Georg, *Francis Xavier: His Life, His Times*, translated by M. Joseph Costelloe, Rome: The Jesuit Historical Institute, 1982
Shaku, Sōen, *Zen for Americans*, LaSalle, Illinois: Open Court, 1974 (previously published as *Sermons of a Buddhist Abbot*)
Shore, Jeff, "Japanese Zen & the West: Beginnings," *FAS Society Journal* (Summer 1992)
Suzuki, Shunryū, *Zen Mind, Beginner's Mind*, New York: Weatherhill, 1970

2. *Zen in the Contemporary United States*

Zen Buddhism in the United States can be classified into what Jan Nattier calls "ethnic" and "import" Buddhism; whereas the former is usually associated with one specific ethnic community, the latter has been separated from its cultural context and has quickly become acculturated and Americanized. Tracing itself to various lineages of Japanese Rinzai, Sōtō, Sambō Kyōdan, Korean Kwan Um, and Vietnamese Lam Te Zen Buddhism, American Zen combines traditional and nontraditional teachings. Faithful to their respective traditions, American Zen Buddhists identify as the core of Zen Buddhism either the breakthrough experience of enlightenment in the sense of D.T. Suzuki's satori and Hakuun Yasutani's *kenshō* or, following Shunryū Suzuki, "practice" in the sense of Dōgen's "oneness of practice and enlightenment" (Japanese, *shushō ichinyo*). By the same token American Zen Buddhists disagree over the importance and effectiveness of kōan study and "seated meditation" (Japanese, *zazen*). However, despite these differences it is possible to identify five common features of American Zen, namely, a rejection of metaphysics and rationalistic speculation, an emphasis on personal experience and self-realization, an authentic and empirically verifiable insight beyond linguistic expression, a down-to-earth naturalness and simplicity of life, and an inherent everydayness. This understanding of Zen has been summarized by D.T. Suzuki's notion of a "higher affirmation" beyond the dualistic thinking characteristic of everyday consciousness; by Shunryū Suzuki's observation that Zen is "nothing special"; by Seung Sahn's repeated exhortation "only don't know"; by Thích Nhát Hanh's engaged Buddhism, which argues that "meditation is to be aware of what is going on in our bodies, in our feeling, in our minds, and in the world" and "to equip oneself with the capacity to reintegrate into society"; and by Philip Kapleau's definition of mindfulness as "not leaving light bulbs burning when they are not needed." At the core of these teachings lies the conviction that Zen eradicates the alienation caused by the ego consciousness and the dualities that it constructs, the egotism inherent in individualism, and a complicated and, ultimately, unnatural way of life by "directly pointing to one's mind." At the same time this teaching of Zen was, as Katja Werthmann observes, "detraditionalized" as its teachers emphasized personal experience over scriptures and defined Zen as a "metareligion," that is, as the ultimate core of human existence that transcends any form of sectarianism or dogmatism.

By the same token American Buddhists de- and recontextualized the organizational structure and practice of Zen Buddhism. Traditionally Zen Buddhism constitutes a monastic tradition with institutionalized lineages, hierarchies, priesthood, ordination, rituals, sūtra chanting, and a strict regulation of the monastic life. In addition as a legacy of the *danka* system, which was operative during the Tokugawa period, Zen temples in Japan provide a religious affiliation, institutionalized rites of bereavement, and memorial services. However, although Zen Buddhism exists as a monastic discipline in the United States, it lacks the institutional context of the *bodaiji*, that is, temples that serve households rather than practitioners. Because American practitioners for the most part are, as Shunryū Suzuki observed, neither monks nor lay people but occupy an intermediate role, American Zen has faced the need to create new organizational structures in order to accommodate practitioners who have family- and work-related responsibilities. In response to this demand, Zen Buddhists have either developed Zen centers that combine lay status and communal living on the one side, such as the San Francisco Zen Center of the 1970s, or have adopted churchlike affiliation on the other. By the same token these Zen centers have had to negotiate their degree of acculturation by deciding which of the traditional rituals to embrace and whether to chant sūtras in the English language. In addition from Robert Aitken's support for conscientious objectors and Thích Nhát Hanh's pleas for peace during the Vietnam War to the outreach programs of the New York Zen Center and the Hartford Street Zen Center in the late 1980s, American Zen has emphasized social engagement as a cultural expression of social and ethical responsibility. Similarly American Zen has confronted the demand for gender equality from its very beginning and, more recently, the call for homosexual rights.

One side effect of this twofold decontextualization has been a secularization of Zen and the emergence of what could be called cultural Zen. Cultural Zen isolates the Zen notion of mindfulness not only from its rich monastic and scriptural tradition and but also from its effort to cut off the roots of suffering and to eradicate the self. It interprets the *dokusan* or *sanzen* between master and disciple as a therapeutic session and utilizes meditation as a method of concentration and spiritual growth. Popularized by heroes of the beatnik and hippie generations, such as Allen Ginsberg, Gary Snyder, Jack Kerouac, and Alan Watts, as well as by contemporary megastars such as basketball coach Phil Jackson, Zen has been transformed into a cultural commodity and an instrument of self-improvement and self-help. Cultural Zen has been practiced by therapists, Catholic monastics, and adherents of the New Age movement.

Finally, over the last 100 years, the United States has seen a significant increase in the academic study of Zen Buddhism. Academic works on Zen Buddhism can be roughly divided into three categories: first, the philological and historical study of Zen in the tradition of the 19th-century Sanskritologists, D.T. Suzuki, and Heinrich Dumoulin and, second, the philosophical study of Zen, which, following the works of Nishida Kitarō and contemporary thinkers such as Abe Masao and Yuasa Yasuo, attempts to explore the implication of Zen conceptions for contemporary philosophy. So far particular emphasis has been given to the mind-body problem, the philosophy of time, and Zen's resemblance with contemporary philosophical deconstruction. Third, following Shin'ichi Hisamatsu's dialogue with C.G. Jung and Erich Fromm's enthusiasm for D.T. Suzuki, there is an increasing number of psychologists and, more recently, cognitive scientists and neuroscientists who explore possible affinities between Zen Buddhism and the contemporary science of consciousness.

GEREON KOPF

See also Chan/Zen: Japan; Critiques of Buddhist Monasticism: Japanese; Initiation: Buddhist Perspectives; Kōan; Suzuki, Daisetz Teitaro; United States: Buddhist

Further Reading

Fields, Rick, *How the Swans Came to the Lake: A Narrative History of Buddhism in America*, Boulder, Colorado: Shambhala, 1981; 3rd edition, Boston: Shambhala, 1992

Nattier, Jan, "Buddhism Comes to Mainstreet," *Wilson Quarterly* 21:1 (Spring 1997)

Prebish, Charles, *American Buddhism*, North Scituate, Massachusetts: Duxbury Press, 1979

Prebish, Charles, and Kenneth K. Tanaka, editors, *The Faces of Buddhism in America*, Berkeley: University of California Press, 1998

Tworkov, Helen, *Zen in America: Five Teachers and the Search for an American Buddhism* (Kodansha Globe), New York: Kodansha America, and London: Kodansha International, 1994

Werthmann, Katja, *Zen und Sinn: Westliche Aneignung, Interpretation und Praxis einer buddhistischen Meditation* (Notizen, 38), Frankfurt: Institut für Kulturanthropologie und Europäische Ethnologie der Universität Frankfurt, 1992

Zhiyi (Chih-i) 538–597

Founder of Tiantai Buddhism in China

Zhiyi, whose family name was Chen and first name was De'an, was born in Huarong, Jingzhou (southwest of present-day Qianjiang in Hubei province). The Chinese tradition regards him as the founder and the first patriarch of Tiantai Buddhism, and he was one of the most important monks of sixth-century China. Zhiyi's biography shows many resemblances to that of the historical Buddha Śākyamuni himself. This is illustrative of the importance in Chinese Buddhism that pious hagiographers have imputed to Zhiyi.

When Zhiyi's father lost his official position because of political turmoil at the end of the Liang dynasty (501–556), his family was left destitute. This factor impelled the devout Buddhist Zhiyi, then 17 years old, to make a vow in front of a Buddha statue in the Changsha Temple in Jingzhou to become a Buddhist mendicant. At age 18 he entered the Guoyuan Monastery in Xiangzhou (Hubei province), where he studied under Vinaya master Huikuang. At the age of 20, he was fully ordained.

On Mount Dasu (present-day Huangchuan in Henan province), Zhiyi studied texts on Buddhist meditation and contemplation under the guidance of Huisi. When political instability in the north made Huisi move farther south, Zhiyi stayed behind in the Wuguan Monastery near present-day Nanjing. For eight years he studied the *Mahāprajñāpāramitā* (Great Perfection of Wisdom) and the *Saddharmapuṇḍarīka* (Lotus of the Good Doctrine), the latter scripture becoming the most important scripture for Tiantai Buddhism. This explains why the Tiantai school is often also called the Lotus school. Because the aim of saving all beings is, according to Zhiyi, to be attained only through the *Lotus Sūtra*, he claimed that preaching this text was the main reason that Buddha had come into the world. This claim exemplifies the trend to classify the large number of Chinese translations of Buddhist texts (*jiaopan*) that had begun even before Zhiyi's time. Zhiyi grouped the Buddhist texts into five chronological periods. The first period corresponds to the first three weeks of the Buddha's preaching activity and consists of preaching the *Avataṃsakasūtra*. This sūtra became the basis of the Chinese Huayan school (Flower Garland). This period of the Buddha's preaching activity is the period of the so-called sudden doctrine, in which enlightenment is achieved instantly. However, as people at that moment did not possess all the capacities needed to understand the doctrine correctly, the Buddha shifted to teaching Hīnayāna Buddhism as it is presented in the *Āgama* sūtras. This period lasted for 12 years and was followed by the teaching of elementary Mahāyāna, a period that lasted for eight years, and then by the teaching of the *Mahāprajñāpāramitā*.

Entrance of the Guoqingsi, Tiantaishan, Zhejiang province, China, founded in the Sui dynasty (A.D. 581–618).
Photo courtesy of Marylin M. Rhie

These three periods represent the era of the gradual doctrine. Having taught the *Mahāprajñāpāramitā* for 22 years, the Buddha finally shifted to the teaching of the *Mahāparinirvāṇa* and the *Lotus Sūtra*. This period, that of the secret and the indeterminate doctrines, lasted for the final eight years of the Buddha's life and corresponds to the Mahāyāna idea that the Buddha simultaneously taught the doctrine in different ways to different people, according to their intellectual capacities, thus making sure that every being reached enlightenment. Not only was this classification by Zhiyi accepted in Tiantai circles but it served also as example for the Chinese Huayan school.

In 575, pushed farther south because of the first major persecution of Buddhists that raged under Emperor Wudi (561–578) of the Northern Zhou, Zhiyi arrived at Tiantai Mountain (in present-day Zhejiang province), which for a long time had been considered by Daoists an excellent place of withdrawal from everyday life. As the mountain became the major center of the religion, it gave its name to Tiantai Buddhism.

Tiantai Buddhism is to be seen as a Chinese attempt to devise an eclectic school that incorporates a variety of Buddhist schools as well as indigenous Chinese philosophies. Whether deliberately or not, this eclectic attitude undoubtedly made Buddhism more acceptable to Chinese intellectuals and enjoyed greater sympathy in government institutions. The text that ultimately united all Buddhist doctrines was the *Lotus Sūtra*. Of the six translations made into Chinese of this text, only three remain.

At first Tiantai did not spread to the lay world. Nonetheless, Zhiyi's fame was so great that, in 577, a decree was issued stipulating that all income of a district in the neighborhood be submitted to the monastery. The emperor and laypeople are reported to have attended a lecture by Zhiyi in the presence of Buddhist clergy. The court even invited Zhiyi to stay in the capital, claiming that the Buddhist doctrine would be better served if he set an example for the laity by means of his good influence. The sympathy that Zhiyi enjoyed in the lay world is further illustrated by the fact that, in 581, he succeeded in forbidding fishing on the shore near Tiantai Mountain, a place that had been a traditional fishing area. The throne also gave another name to the Tiantai Monastery: Xiuchan (Cultivation of Meditation).

When Buddhist institutions languished in the first days of the reunification of the Chinese Empire under the Sui dynasty in 589, Zhiyi went to Lushan (Jiangxi province). However, shortly thereafter the emperor asked for Zhiyi's support in restoring Buddhism. The Buddhist faith came to be used as an element in the legitimization of the newly founded dynasty. Since history had shown that Buddhist monasteries often harbored anti-dynastic feelings, this attempt would also assure the emperor of renewed state control over Buddhism.

From Lushan, Zhiyi moved to Yangzhou (in 591) and to Jingzhou (in 592) and returned in 593 to Tiantai Mountain, where he would spend the rest of his life. His works, mainly on the *Lotus Sūtra*, were partly written by himself and partly recorded by the most important of his 32 renown pupils: Guanding (561–632).

BART DESSEIN

See also Buddhist Schools/Traditions: China; China; Discourses (Sūtras): Mahāyāna; Ennin; Prophethood, Japanese Buddhist; Saicho; Tiantai/Tendai

Biography

Known as the third patriarch but actually the founder of Tiantai Buddhism in China, Zhiyi entered a monastery to study with the second patriarch, Huisu. From 575 to 585 and again from 595 until his death, he retired to Mount Tiantai, where he became known as a "man of wisdom" (*zhizhe*). He endeavored to incorporate the bulk of preceding Buddhism into a synthesis. The notion that Chinese Buddhism divides into "five periods and eight schools" has long been attributed to him, but may have emerged later.

Major Work

Liu miao famen (The Six Marvelous Gates of Dharma)

Further Reading

Armstrong, R.C., "The Doctrine of the Tendai School," *Eastern Buddhist* 3 (1924)
Chen, Kenneth, *Buddhism in China: A Historical Survey*, Princeton, New Jersey: Princeton University Press, 1964
de Bary, William Theodore, editor, *Sources of Chinese Tradition*, 2 vols., New York: Columbia University Press, 1960
Hurvitz, Leon, "Chih-i (538–597)," *Mélanges chinois et bouddhiques* 12 (1960–1961)
Miyuki, Mokusen, "Chiao-p'an: An Essential Feature of Chinese Buddhism," in *Bukkyō Shisōshi Ronshū: Yuki kyoju shoju kinen*, Tokyo: Daizushuppan, 1964
Petzold, "The Chinese Tendai Teachings," *Eastern Buddhist* 4 (1927–1928)
Takakusu, Junjirō, *The Essentials of Buddhist Philosophy*, Honolulu: University of Hawaii Press, 1947
Wu, Ju-chün, *T'ien-t'ai Buddhism and Early Madhyamika*, Honolulu: University of Hawaii Press, 1993

Zhuhong (Chu-hung) 1535–1615

Chinese Buddhist monk and advocate of Pure Land Buddhism

Zhuhong, whose family name was Shen, was born in the Renhe district in Hangzhou, Zhejiang province. Having failed in the official examinations and after many of his closest relatives had passed away, he decided to become a monk. As a monk he first settled in the Zhaoqing Monastery in Hangzhou. In 1571 he moved to Yunqi Mountain, west of Hangzhou, where he stayed until his death in 1615.

Beginning in the Tang Dynasty (618–907), communities of adherents of Pure Land Buddhism had existed within greater monastic complexes. These monks lived according to their own system. Also in Zhuhong's time adherents of Pure Land and Chan lived together on Yunqi Mountain. Despite his training with Chan monks, Zhuhong gradually came to favor Pure Land. He claimed that the true doctrine is Pure Land, the aim of which other schools served only to attain. Accordingly, he was not taken up in the Chan genealogy but was only posthumously called the eighth patriarch of Chan.

When Zhuhong is characterized as a "syncretist," this must be interpreted simply as a logical outcome of the fact that many earnest monks of his time no longer saw themselves as descendants of Chan but rather made a personal response to the difficulties with which the Buddhist community of that time had to cope. One of these difficulties was the tendency to secularize the order, and this had led to the commercialization of rites. Also, monasteries had become gathering places for outlaws who were organized in societies such as the White Lotus. In addition, an increasing number of people tried to escape the political turbulence after the fall of the Yuan dynasty by becoming monks. All this had led to a laxist tendency in discipline. Zhuhong blamed this increasing laxist tendency on the fact that Chan monasteries no longer attracted believers. In reaction he advocated strictness in Buddhist discipline. With this aim he no longer accepted the Yuan dynasty's rules, which are said to be traceable to Huaihai (720–814) and which, according to Zhuhong, were so complex that monks spent more time studying them than they spent submitting themselves to the Buddhist doctrine.

Zhuhong was instrumental in the movement toward a lay religion that began in the second half of the Ming dynasty (1368–1644). A major motivation for Buddhism to make itself known to the lay world was that Ming government examinations had drawn most intellectuals away from Buddhism. So as not to lose these people completely, Buddhism assumed the task of having laypeople practice Buddhism in their private lives. A renewed emphasis on strictness in observing Buddhist rules helped to make the Buddhist faith acceptable to Confucianists. Underlying this policy is Zhuhong's theory that Confucianism and Buddhism are complementary. The concept of complementariness served to protect the Buddhist community from renewed laxism.

Zhuhong also left a great impression on laypeople because of his rule forbidding the eating of meat and the slaughtering of animals for sacrifices. Zhuhong saw this rule as the core of the lay movement.

The late Ming dynasty also is the period during which Catholicism started to penetrate China. Zhuhong wrote various works against the Catholics who saw in Buddhism their greatest rival. Zhuhong's books on the subject are collected under the title *Zhuchuang Sanbi* (Final Jottings under a Bamboo Window).

BART DESSEIN

See also Buddhist Schools/Traditions: China; China

Biography

Zhuhong began under the Chinese Ming dynasty as a monk in strict conformity to the Vinaya. Gradually he came to accept all paths as leading to the same goal. Accordingly, he devised a method that combines Pure Land Buddhism's emphasis on reciting the *nembutsu* with Zen Buddhism's use of koan training. This harmonization served lay Buddhists even more readily than monastics and remains popular.

Major Works

Zhuchuang Sanbi (Final Jottings under a Bamboo Window)
Tianshuo Sibian (Four Chapters on the Teachings of Tien; criticizes Christianity and defends Buddhism)

Further Reading

Demiéville, Paul, *Choix d'études sinologiques (1921–1970)*, Leiden: Brill, 1973
Dumoulin, Heinrich, *The Development of Chinese Zen After the Sixth Patriarch in the Light of Mumonkan*, New York: The First Zen Institute of America, 1953
Fung, Yu-lan, *A History of Chinese Philosophy*, 2 vols., Princeton, New Jersey: Princeton University Press, 1952
Hurvitz, Leon, "Chu-hung's One Mind of Pure Land and Ch'an Buddhism," in *Self and Society in Ming Thought*, edited by William Theodore de Bary, New York: Columbia University Press, 1970

Kern, Iso, *Buddhistische Kritik am Christentum im China des 17. Jahrhunderts: Texte von Yu Shunxi (?–1621), Zhuhong (1535–1615), Yuanwu (1566–1642), Tongrong (1593–1679), Xingyuan (1611–1662), Zhixu (1599–1655)*, Bern: Peter Lang, 1992

Wright, Arthur, *Buddhism in Chinese History*, Stanford, California: Stanford University Press, 1959

Yü, Chün-fang, *The Renewal of Buddhism in China: Chu-hung and the Late Ming Synthesis*, New York: Columbia University Press, 1981

GLOSSARY

Buddhist Terms
(glossary prepared by Mark J. Tatz)

Abhidharma (Pāli, *abhidhamma*). Buddhist philosophy in greater detail than Dharma.

Ācārya (Sanskrit; Pāli, *ācariya*). (1) Precept master (*see* Master, Precept). (2) Spiritual master, especially in Tantric Buddhism (*see* Master, Spiritual).

Anātman. *See* No-Self.

Arahant. *See* Arhat.

Arhat (Sanskrit; Pāli, *arahant*). A title for persons, including the Buddha but generally referenced to his disciples, who have attained nirvāṇa. A pre-Buddhist term of uncertain origin, it is variously etymologized by Buddhists as "worthy of worship" and "slayer of the enemy."

Bhikkhu/Bhikkhunī (Pāli; Sanskrit, *bhikṣu/bhikṣuṇī*). Male or female monastic – specifically, a "monk" or "nun" who has undergone ordination in the full set of rules (i.e., not a novice).

Bodhi (Sanskrit). Buddhist "awakening," also translated as "enlightenment" – coreferents wisdom, buddhahood, and so on – the attainment of which makes one a buddha.

Bodhisattva (Sanskrit). (1) Anyone on the path to buddhahood. (2) Someone at an advanced stage of that path, virtually a buddha, who forgoes entry into nirvāṇa in order to help others.

Bodhisattva (Sanskrit; Pāli, *bodhisatta*). An individual whose spiritual goal is buddhahood. Often referenced to those who have attained a high stage, who are virtually buddhas.

Brahman (Sanskrit). The priestly class (caste) in Indian society.

Buddha. A human being who has attained awakening, or enlightenment (Sanskrit, *bodhi*), a coreferent of nirvāṇa.

Buddha, Historical. The Buddha Śākyamuni, who lived in the sixth to fifth century B.C.

Caitya. *See* Cetiya.

Cakravartin. *See* Wheel-Turning King.

Cetiya (Pāli; Sanskrit, *caitya*, also transliterated as *chaitya*). In early Buddhism, an enclosure for a stūpa; later, any sacred structure.

Chaitya. *See* Cetiya.

Chan (Chinese; Japanese, Zen; Korean, Sŏn). A school (later schools) of Buddhism emphasizing meditation praxis.

Circumambulation (Sanskrit, *pradakṣiṇa*). The ritual of circling a sacred object in a clockwise direction.

Compassion (Sanskrit, *karuṇā*). The desire to help all beings, especially to attain nirvāṇa.

Daoism. The pre-Buddhist nature worship and contemplative philosophy of China.

Dependent Origination (Sanskrit, *pratītya-samutpāda*; Pāli, *paticca-samuppāda*; also "codependent arising, the conditional and causal nature of existence"). (1) A set of 12 causally connected stages explaining the process of life, death, and rebirth. (2) In the Mahāyāna, the general relativity or interconnectedness of all dharmas.

Dhamma. *See* Dharma.

Dhāraṇī (Sanskrit). In Mahāyāna and in Tantric Buddhism, a condensation of sūtra text with magical powers.

Dharma (Sanskrit; Pāli, *dhamma*). (1) The teachings of the Buddha on philosophy and spiritual praxis. (2) The way of things, or law of nature, especially dependent origination or relativity. (3) In the plural, the factors composing physical and mental reality; phenomena.

Diamond Vehicle (Sanskrit, Vajrayāna). *See* Tantric Buddhism.

Discipline, Monastic (Sanskrit, Vinaya). (1) The collected rules for Buddhist monks and nuns. In Mahāyāna Buddhism, also applied to the moral code of bodhisattvas. (2) As a general division of the Buddha's teachings, part of the pair "Dharma and Vinaya." (3) As text, one among the "Three Collections" (Sanskrit, Tripiṭaka).

Egui. *See* Hungry Ghost.

Eight Requisites (Sanskrit, *aṣṭa-pariṣkāra*; also translated as "necessities"). The robes, etc., that a monastic is permitted to own.

Eightfold Path. Eight areas of spiritual practice in early Buddhism.

Emptiness. *See* Śūnyatā.

Enlightenment. *See* Nirvāṇa.

Enlightenment, Sudden. *See* Satori.

Esoteric Buddhism (Chinese, *zhenyan*; Japanese, *mikkyō*). The term for Tantric Buddhism in eastern Asia.

Forest-Dwelling (Pāli, *vanavāsi*) **Monks**. Rural, contemplative monks of Theravāda countries.

Gesture (or "seal"; Sanskrit, *mudra*). Symbols made by hand, as in the Indian traditional theater. In Buddhism, primarily in Tantric ritual meditation, gestures signify the physical forms of celestial (*sambhoga-kāya*) buddhas.

Going Forth (Sanskrit, *pravrajyā*; Pāli, *pabbajjā*; also translated as "leaving home"). Renouncing lay life for monasticism; also, in Vinaya, the ceremony for becoming a novice.

Guru (Sanskrit; Tibetan, *bla-ma*, pronounced "la-ma"). A brahmanic term for "spiritual master" adopted into Tantric Buddhism.

Hīnayāna (Sanskrit; literally, "Lesser Vehicle"). Derogatory term, coined by extrapolation from Mahāyāna, sometimes used in sūtras of the Mahāyāna to refer to the earlier schools of Buddhism, including Theravāda.

Hungry Ghost (Sanskrit, *preta*; Chinese, *egui*). A form of rebirth allotted to individuals whose preponderant karma has been created by greed; although these individuals eat and drink, they can never be nourished or satisfied.

Impermanence (Sanskrit, *anitya*; Pāli, *anicca*). The basic Buddhist doctrine of the transitoriness of all things.

Jainism. An Indian school or path to liberation that arose contemporaneously with Buddhism and with similar doctrines and practices.

Jātaka (Sanskrit, Pāli). A genre of story that recounts the past lives of the historical Buddha.

Kaihōgyō (Japanese). Circumambulation, especially of mountains.

Kami (Japanese). The pre-Buddhist Shintō place deities of Japan.

Karma (Sanskrit; Pāli, *kamma*). "Deed," in the sense of (1) actions that determine the nature of one's future, especially in rebirth, or (2) formal acts of the monastic community.

Karuṇā. *See* Compassion.

Kōan (from Japanese; Chinese, *kung-an*). A riddle, insoluble by reason, used as a meditation exercise in some schools of Chan Buddhism.

Lama. *See* Guru.

Mahāsiddha (Sanskrit). Practitioner of Tantric Buddhism.

Mahāyāna (Sanskrit; literally, "Great Vehicle"). A movement of Indian Buddhism, emerging in the early centuries B.C., emphasizing the doctrine of emptiness and the bodhisattva path.

Maṇḍala (Sanskrit). Mainly in Tantric Buddhism, the space of the deity or deities, generally round; a cosmogram of sacred space.

Mantra. Mainly in Tantric Buddhism, a string of words or syllables, usually in Sanskrit, representing the aural essence of the deity or *yidam*.

Master, Precept (Sanskrit, *ācārya*; Pāli, *ācariya*). The senior monk who guides a novice to mastery of the Vinaya rules of conduct. *See also* Ācārya.

Master, Spiritual (also "patriarch"). Especially in Chan Buddhism, a meditation teacher.

Merit (Sanskrit, *puṇya*; Pāli, *puñña*). The karmic residue of performing good deeds; it can improve one's station in this life or those that follow.

Merit, Field of. Those to whom giving alms earns the greatest merit – buddhas, *bhikkhus*, *bhikkhunīs*, and so on.

Merit, Transference of. Mentally and ritually donating accumulated merit to other living beings, itself a highly meritorious activity.

Middle Way (Sanskrit, *madhyamā-pratipada*). (1) Between asceticism and hedonism in lifestyle (i.e., the Eightfold Path). (2) Between essentialism and nihilism in philosophy (i.e., dependent origination).

Mikkyō. *See* Esoteric Buddhism.

Monastery, Buddhist. *See* Vihāra.

Mudra. *See* Gesture.

Nirvāṇa (Sanskrit; Pāli, *nibbāna*). The goal of Buddhist practice, understood as the removal of all ignorance, limitation, and other negativity; surcease of suffering; synonymous with "awakening" or "enlightenment." *See also* Parinirvāṇa.

No-Self (Sanskrit, *anātman*; also "egolessness"). The basic Buddhist doctrine that living beings are empty of any permanent or essential entity – the "soul," "higher self," or "life force" of various theologies. In Mahāyāna, the extension of this doctrine to the absence of any essential nature in the elements (dharmas) of reality.

Ordination (Sanskrit, *upasampadā*). The ceremony for ordaining monks and nuns with the full set of rules. *See also* Bhikkhu/Bhikkhunī.

Pāli. A Middle Indo-Aryan language of about the fifth century B.C. in which the canon of the Theravāda school has been recorded.

Parinirvāṇa. The historical Buddha's entry into final nirvāṇa, counterpart to the death of mortal persons, whereupon he ceases to function in the world.

Paticca-samuppāda. *See* Dependent Origination.

Pavāraṇā (Pāli). *See* Pravāraṇā.

Posadha (Pāli; Sanskrit, *uposatha*) **Ceremony**. The twice-monthly (new- and full-moon) gathering of monks and nuns to recite the Vinaya rules and confess any violations.

Pradakṣiṇa. *See* Circumambulation.

Prajñāpāramitā (Sanskrit, "perfection of wisdom") **Sūtras**. A genre of Mahāyāna sūtras in which wisdom (*prajña*) is understanding that all phenomena (*dharmas*) are empty of any essential nature. These sūtras also elaborate the bodhisattva's path to buddhahood.

Pratītya-samutpāda. *See* Dependent Origination.

Pratyekabuddha (Sanskrit). Legendary hermits, inhabiting the world before the historical Buddha appeared, who gained enlightenment without the formality of a buddha's teaching.

Pravāraṇā (Sanskrit; Pāli, *pavāraṇā*). The ceremony by which monks and nuns at the end of the yearly three-month retreat evaluate their adherence to the Vinaya rules.

Precept Master. *See* Master, Precept.

Preta. *See* Hungry Ghost.

Pure Land. A supernatural land, created by a celestial (or *sambhoga-kāya*) buddha, free from moral defilement and hindrances to meditative concentration, into which beings can be reborn and easily attain nirvāṇa.

Sambhoga-kāya. *See* Three Bodies.

Saṅgha (Sanskrit, "community"; Pāli, *saṃgha*). Narrowly construed, Buddhist monks and nuns. Broadly construed to include the laity (i.e., all Buddhists).

Saṅgharāja (Sanskrit, "king of the community"). In Theravāda Buddhism, a member of the civil bureaucracy, generally appointed by the king, who functions as head of the monastic community.

Satori (Japanese). The Chan Buddhist term for an enlightenment experience. In some schools, it may arrive suddenly, in response to a psychological shock.

Scripture (Buddhist). *See* Sūtra.

Seal. *See* Gesture.

Sesshin (Japanese). In Chan Buddhism, a meditation session or extended retreat.

Shintō (Japanese). The pre-Buddhist nature worship of Japan.

Siddha. *See* Mahāsiddha.

Sŏn. *See* Chan.

Spiritual Master. *See* Master, Spiritual.

Stūpa (Sanskrit). A shrine constructed to house the relics of the historical Buddha and, later, for other relics and sacred items.

Śūnyatā (Sanskrit, "emptiness"). In the "Perfection of Wisdom" sūtras and the Mādhyamaka school of the Mahāyāna, *śūnyatā* refers to the absence of an essential nature (or "inherent existence") in any and all phenomena (*dharma*s). This is also the understanding in the Yogācāra school, where, however, emphasis is placed on the absence of subject/object duality in the awakened mind.

Sūtra (Sanskrit; Pāli, *sutta*). Texts representing the Buddha's teachings on philosophy and spiritual praxis. One among the "Three Collections" (Sanskrit, Tripiṭaka).

Tantric Buddhism (also Esoteric Buddhism, Vajrayāna, or "Diamond Vehicle"). A late Mahāyāna development in India based on a class of texts called "tantras," sometimes antinomian, utilizing magical homologies to attempt a more rapid transformation of self into buddha and environment into pure land.

Ten-Precept Mother (Sinhalese, *dasa sil mātāva*). In Theravāda countries, a woman who takes the vows of novice nuns in the absence of a living tradition of full ordination. "Mother" is intended as a term of respect.

Theravāda (Sanskrit, Sthavīravāda; literally, "School of the Elders"). The earliest surviving school of Indian Buddhism.

Three Baskets. *See* Three Collections.

Three Bodies (Sanskrit, *tri-kāya*). In Mahāyāna, the three forms of a buddha are: (1) Dharma-kāya, "Dharma" or "law" Body, the corpus of the Buddha's teachings; also the nature of things, that is the fruition of the knowing that constitutes buddhahood. (2) Sambhoga-kāya, the "enjoyment," "bliss," or "recompense" body – the perfect, adorned body visible only to advanced bodhisattvas that is the fruition of the merit that constitutes a buddha. (3) Nirmāṇa-kāya (Tibetan, *sprul-sku*, pronounced "tul-ku"), "emanation" or "transformation" body; the variety of forms that a buddha may take in the realm of *saṃsāra* (e.g., the historical Buddha wearing a monk's robes).

Three Collections (Sanskrit, Tripiṭaka; Pāli, Tipiṭaka). The corpus of early Buddhist genres: Vinaya, Sūtra, and Abhidharma.

Three Jewels. The superlatively revered trinity of Buddhism: Buddha, Dharma, and Saṅgha.

Tipiṭaka. *See* Three Collections.

Tri-kāya. *See* Three Bodies.

Tripiṭaka. *See* Three Collections.

Tulku (Tibetan, *sprul-sku*; Sanskrit, *nirmāṇa-kāya*). (1) The "emanation body" of a buddha (*see* Three Bodies). (2) The Tibetan institution of lineage transmission whereby teachers, usually the abbots of monasteries, are successively identified, usually in childhood. Most are considered the emanation of bodhisattvas at various stages of development. The term *living buddhas* is a designation by Chinese nonbelievers, contrasting these with "dead" statuary.

Upasampadā. *See* Ordination.

Uposatha (Sanskrit) **Ceremony**. *See* Posadha Ceremony.

Vajrayāna. *See* Tantric Buddhism.

Vanavāsi. *See* Forest-Dwelling Monks.

Vihāra (Sanskrit, Pāli). A monastery or residence for monks and/or nuns.

Vinaya. *See* Discipline, Monastic.

Wheel-Turning King (Sanskrit, *cakravartin*). A universal emperor.

Wisdom Sūtra. *See* Prajñāpāramitā Sūtras.

Yidam (Tibetan; Sanskrit, *iṣṭadevatā*, "meditation deity"). In Tantric Buddhism, a deity, typically a buddha or bodhisattva, made the object of meditation.

Yogācāra (Sanskrit). One of the two major doctrinal schools of Mahāyāna Buddhism in India, characterized by the view of reality as "mind only" and by exegesis of bodhisattva praxis.

Zen. *See* Chan.

Zhenyan. *See* Esoteric Buddhism.

Christian Terms

(glossary prepared by Annie Shaver-Crandell)

Abbey. The religious body of monks or nuns governed by an abbot or an abbess; also, the buildings used by such a body.

Acolyte. Altar attendant in public worship.

Advowson. The right of presentation to a benefice or church office.

Aisle. Area flanking nave, choir, or transept of church, often separated from it by an arcade.

Ambulatory. An aisle curving around the apse or hemicycle of a church.
Annates. The first year's revenue of a benefice, payable to the one presenting the benefice.
Apse. Semicircular or polygonal termination of a church or chapel, usually containing an altar.
Archivolt. Molding on the face of an arch, surrounding the arch's contour; may be multiple.
Atrium. An open courtyard; in Christian architecture, the court in front of a church.

Baldachin. A freestanding or suspended canopy over an altar, throne, or tomb.
Baptism. A ceremonial immersion in water or application of water as an initiatory rite or sacrament of the Christian Church.
Baptistery. A building or room set aside for baptismal rites.
Barrel Vault. A continuous semicircular or pointed vault resting on walls; an arch extended sideways.
Basilica (from Greek *basilikos*, "royal"). In Christian architecture, a church of longitudinal plan consisting of a high central nave, often lit by clerestory windows, flanked by lower side aisles and an apse at one end of the nave.
Bay. Internal compartment of a building, defined by vertical projection on the side walls or by transverse divisions of the vault or roof; a "box" of space with its defining supports.
Beatification. In the Roman Catholic Church, the act by which the Pope permits the public veneration after death of some faithful Catholic in a particular church, diocese, country, or religious order.
Benedictine Plan. Church plan with a central apse and choir flanked by side aisles terminating in apses.
Benefice. A position or post granted to an ecclesiastic that guarantees a fixed amount of property or income; the income itself.
Benefit of Clergy. Accorded to clergy, monks, and nuns in the Middle Ages, the exemption, from trial by a secular court on being charged with a felony.
Black Letter Days. The lesser saints' days (as distinct from the major festivals), which normally appeared in black in ecclesiastical calendars.
Book of Hours. An abbreviated version of the Divine Office used primarily by the laity for private prayer; it includes a liturgical calendar, the Little Office of the Blessed Virgin, the litany of saints, Penitential Psalms, Office of the Dead, and additional personal prayers.
Breviary. A liturgical book containing the psalms, hymns, prayers, and readings to be recited during daily devotions.
Bull. A formal papal document having a bulla, or seal, attached.
Buttress. A mass of masonry or brickwork built against a wall to give support to a structure and to counter the thrust of a vault.

Calced. Wearing shoes; applied to members of certain religious orders.
Calefactory. The room in a medieval monastery provided with a fireplace. Where it existed it was commonly near the refectory.
Calends. The first day of the month in the ancient Roman calendar, from which the days of the preceding month were counted backward to the ides.
Canon. A member of a chapter of a cathedral or collegiate church.
Canonization. To place in the canon of Christian saints.
Cantor. An officer whose duty is to lead the singing in a church.
Capital. The crowning member of a column or pier.
Cartulary (also Chartulary). A register of charters, title deeds, and so on.
Catchword. A word written at the end (generally in the lower margin) of a manuscript gathering that repeats the first word on the following page, to facilitate arrangement of the gatherings during binding.
Cathedral (from *cathedra*, a bishop's throne). A bishop's church; the principal church of a diocese.
Censer. An incense burner, usually on chains so that it can be swung; also called a thurible.
Chalice. A cup used in the Mass to contain the Eucharistic wine.
Chapter House. The place for an abbot, a prior, or an abbess and members of a monastery or convent to assemble for discussion of business. It is reached from the cloister, to whose eastern side it usually belongs.
Chartulary. *See* Cartulary.
Chevet. The eastern complex of a church, usually composed of the apse, ambulatory, and radiating chapels.
Choir. The part of a church near the main altar, usually at the east end, where divine service is sung; normally reserved for the clergy. In the Romanesque and Gothic periods, the straight bays preceding the eastern apse or hemicycle comprised the choir.
Ciborium. A freestanding or suspended canopy over an altar, throne, or tomb; a vessel for the consecrated host.
Clerestory. Literally, a "clear story"; the part of the nave wall lit by windows that rises above the level of the aisle roof.
Cloister. In a religious institution, an open courtyard surrounded by covered passageways connecting the church with the other monastic buildings; by extension, the monastery or convent in its entirety.
Codex. A book composed of folded sheets sewn along one edge, as distinct from a roll or tablet.
Collegiate Church. A church that has a chapter or college of canons but is not necessarily a cathedral.
Colophon. Literally, "tail-word"; information about the circumstances of the production of a manuscript or printed book, placed at the end of the work.
Compline. *See* Divine Office.
Consuetudenary. *See* Customary.
Convent. Dwelling place of a community of nuns.
Crossing. The space at the intersection of the nave, transepts, and chevet of a church.
Crypt. The vaulted, semi-subterranean story of a church where relics were generally kept in the Middle Ages, usually beneath the apse and choir.
Customary. A book describing the customs – for example, the rituals accompanying liturgical services or monastic discipline – of an ecclesiastical establishment.

Deacon. In hierarchical churches, a member of a clerical order just below that of a priest.
Discalced. Not wearing shoes; applied to members of certain religious orders.
Divine Office. A cycle of daily devotions performed by members of Roman Catholic religious orders and the clergy. The cycle

of eight canonical hours was fixed as follows: matins (approximately 2:30 a.m.), lauds (approximately 5 a.m.), prime (approximately 6 a.m.), tierce (approximately 9 a.m.), sext (approximately noon), nones (approximately 3 p.m.), vespers (approximately 4:30 p.m.), and compline (approximately 6 p.m.).

Enamel. Powdered colored glass fused to a metal surface at a high temperature and then polished.

Epistle Side. *See* Gospel Side.

Eucharist (Greek, "thanksgiving"). The commemoration of Christ's sacrifice on the cross by the consecration and taking of bread and wine, which signify the body and blood of Christ.

Feast. A periodic religious festival commemorating an event or honoring God or a saint. Feasts include Sundays, the weekly commemoration of the Resurrection; movable feasts, such as Easter; and immovable feasts, such as Christmas or the anniversaries of martyrs.

Folio. A sheet of writing material.

Fresco. Painting on damp plaster; the pigment is mixed with limewater so that it may form a bond with the plaster.

Friar. A member of one of the Mendicant orders founded during the Middle Ages, as distinct from a monk attached to a specific locality.

Garth. An open courtyard enclosed by a cloister.

Gathering. Quires or booklets from which a book is formed.

Gospel Side. Referring to the Christian practice of placing separate pulpits for the reading of the Gospel and the Epistle on either side of a church. In an oriented church, the Gospel side was north, the Epistle side south. "Gospel side" or "Epistle side" can clarify locations in a church that is not laid out on an east-west axis.

Gregorian Chant. The plain song or cantus firmus used in the ritual of the Roman Catholic Church.

Groin Vault. Vault formed by the intersection at right angles of two barrel vaults.

Habit. Monastic dress.

Hebdomadary. A member of a church or monastery appointed for one week to sing the chapter Mass and lead in the recitation of the breviary.

Hemicycle. A semicircular structure, especially the east end of a choir.

Historiated. Decorated with a narrative subject.

Host. The bread or wafer consecrated in the celebration of the Eucharist.

Icon. An image of Christ, the Virgin Mary, or a saint venerated in the Eastern Orthodox Church.

Iconography. The symbolic meaning of objects, persons, or events depicted in works of art.

Ides. In the ancient Roman calendar, the 15th day of the months of March, July, and October; the 13th day of the other months.

Indulgence. In the Roman Catholic Church, a partial remission of the temporal punishment still due for sin after absolution (sometimes a reason for undertaking a pilgrimage).

Latin Cross. A cross with one arm longer than the other three.

Lauds. *See* Divine Office.

Lectionary. A liturgical book containing selections from Scripture to be read during the worship service, organized according to the church calendar.

Liber Vitae (Latin, "Book of Life"). List of benefactors.

Martyrium. A church, usually with a centralized plan, built over a site that bears witness to the Christian faith; for example, a church on top of the grave of a martyr.

Martyrology. The official register of Christian martyrs.

Mass (Latin *missa*, referring to the dismissal of the congregation after the service [*Ite, missa est* = Go, you are dismissed]). The central rite of the Christian Church, attended daily by those in religious orders.

Matins. *See* Divine Office.

Misericord (from Latin *misericordia*, "pity" or "compassion"). A bracket on the underside of the seat of a choir stall that, when the seat is tipped up, provides support for the end of the occupant's spine.

Missal. A service book containing the texts necessary for the performance of the Mass, including chants, prayers, and readings, together with ceremonial directions.

Miter. Cap with two points or horns, worn by bishops and some abbots.

Monastery. Dwelling place of a community of monks.

Mortmain (from Latin, *mortua manus*, "dead hand"). The condition of property held without the right to transfer it; the perpetual holding of land, especially by a corporation or charitable trust.

Mosaic. A surface decoration consisting of small colored pieces of glass, ceramic, or stone set in cement or plaster.

Narthex. Large enclosed porch or vestibule at the main entrance of a church.

Nave. The main body, or middle part, lengthwise, of a church interior, extending from the principal entrance to the choir; frequently flanked by aisles.

Necrology. A list of persons who have died.

Nones. (1) In the ancient Roman calendar, the ninth day before the ides, both days included; the seventh of March, May, July, and October, and the fifth of the other months. (2) *See* Divine Office.

Octave. The eighth day after a feast day, counting the feast day as the first.

Octavo. A volume measuring one-eighth the size of a folio.

Oriented. With reference to a church, having the main altar at the east end of the building and the main entrance at the west.

Paleography. The study of ancient written documents and the handwriting in which such documents are executed.

Parvis. (1) Vacant enclosed area in front of a church. (2) A colonnade or portico in front of a church.

Paten. A platter or dish on which the consecrated bread is placed for the celebration of the Eucharist.

Pier. A freestanding masonry support, more massive than a column and usually with a cross-section that is other than circular.

Pilgrimage. A journey from one's residence to a holy place, and return homeward, often for purposes of penitence or healing.
Precentor. *See* Cantor.
Presbytery. The eastern part of the sanctuary of a church, traditionally reserved for the elders (presbyters).
Prime. *See* Divine Office.
Priory. A religious house presided over by a prior or prioress, which might be dependent on an abbey. In Augustinian establishments, the priory is the normal unit.
Program. In complex works of painting or sculpture, the underlying conceptual scheme determining the choice of subject matter or symbolism.
Psalter. A book containing the Psalms. Benedictine monks recited all the Psalms every week.
Pulpitum. A choir screen.
Pyx. A container for the consecrated Host.

Quarto. A volume measuring one-quarter the size of a folio.

Recto. The front side of a folio or leaf, abbreviated as r.
Red Letter Day. Important feast or saint's day, written or printed in red ink on ecclesiastical calendars.
Refectory. The communal eating room in a monastery or convent.
Reliquary. Small container for a sacred relic; usually of a richly decorated precious material, sometimes in the form of a body part.
Reredos. A sculpted or painted screen behind the altar. Also known as a retable.
Retable. *See* Reredos.
Ribbed Vault. A vault with a framework of arches or ribs connecting the supports.
Rubric (from Latin *rubrica*, "red"). A title, chapter heading, or instruction that is not strictly part of the text but which helps to identify the text's components. Red ink was often used for such elements.
Rubricator. A person responsible for supplying the rubrics within a manuscript.

Sacraments. Rites of the Church: Baptism, Confirmation, the Eucharist, Penance, Matrimony, Holy Orders, Extreme Unction.
Sauveté. A medieval community whose limits were marked off by a series of crosses.
Scribe. A person engaged in the physical act of writing books or documents.
Script. The handwriting used in manuscripts.
Scriptorium. A writing room. The term generally refers to the place in a monastery or church where books are made.
Sedilia. Priests' seats next to the altar.
Sext. *See* Divine Office.

Thurible. *See* Censer.
Tonsure. The shaving of all or part of the head for clerics, often regarded as symbolizing the crown of thorns.
Transept. The transverse element of a basilican church.
Translation. The transference of the relics of a saint either from their original place of burial into an altar tomb or shrine, or from one shrine to another.
Triumphal Arch. In a Christian church, the transverse wall at the end of the nave pierced by an arched opening into the sanctuary.
Tympanum. In Romanesque and Gothic architecture, the nonstructural semicircular or pointed-arched wall above a portal and within its enframing arch, often containing relief sculpture.

Use. Refers to liturgy practiced in a particular geographic region or by a particular group of people; a local modification of the standard (especially the Roman) rite.

Vault. Any curved roof made of masonry, based on the principle of the arch (as distinct from a ceiling, which is flat).
Verso. The back of a folio or leaf, abbreviated as v.
Vespers. *See* Divine Office.
Vestments. The distinctive dress worn by the clergy when performing the services of the church.

INDEX

Page numbers in **boldface** indicate article titles; page numbers in *italics* indicate illustrations.

associated with, 1370; initiation, 646, 647; manual labor, 517; missionary efforts, 863; and monasticism's origins, 969, 970, 1188, 1194; Mount Sinai, Egypt, 371, 372, 484, 902; self-mortification by, 1144; and Shenoute of Atripe, 1161; solitude and, 1174; spiritual direction and, 1180; and Welsh monasticism, 1386; *see also* Antony, St.; Evagrius Ponticus; Pachomius, St.

desert harlots, 374

Desert Mothers, **373–75**, 603, 673, 969, 1194, 1407; icon veneration and, 1373; Jerome and, 695, 696; spiritual direction and, 1180, 1181; transvestite virgin saints, 1298

Desiderius (abbot of Monte Cassino). *See* Victor III (pope)

Desprez, V., 799

Deussen, P., 682

Deuteronomy, Book of, 1144, 1189, 1297

Deutsch, Alcuin, *317*, 319, 773

Devadatta, 5, 90, 997, 1119

Devanampiyatissa (king of Anuradhapura), 42, 997, 1198, 1199, 1201; conversion of, 1301

Devaraja, cult of, 26

Devaraja, Lorna, 519

devas, 901, 959

devotio moderna, 322, 323, 915, 1262

devotions, Western Christian, **375–76**; Daily Office and, 952; *lectio divina*, 13, 288, 652, 750–52, *751*, 848, 849–50; to Mary, 375, 521, 1025; pilgrimages and, 1025, 1026; rosary and, 246, 414, 605, 848; Sacred Heart of Jesus, 913; Salesian view as birthright of all Christians, 1335–36

dGe lugs pa. *See* Tibetan lineages: Gelukpa

Dhamekh Stupa, Sarnath, India, 187, *187*, 642, 1019

dhamma. *See* dharma

Dhammacakkappavattana, 911, 966

dhammacariya, 461, 462

Dhammadinna, 389

Dhammananda Vihara, San Francisco, California, 1267

Dhammapada, 393, 911, 1004, 1009, 1329

Dhammapala, 1198

Dhammayietra (Walks for Peace and Reconciliation), 1005, 1006, 1009

Dhammayut Order, 222, 485

dhammayuttika, 1249, 1250

Dharamsala, India (Tibetan), 355, 377, 651, 805, *816*, 1277–78; re-created Tibetan monastic sites, 1278–79, 1280, 1281, 1311

Dharani Sutra, 818

dharanis, 451, 815, 816, 817, 1039, 1040, 1198

dharma, 97, 99, 160, 169, 190, 194, 195–96, 220, 263, **378–79**, 387–88, 393–94, 485, 1119; abhidharma (commentaries), 635, 1129; Asoka as vehicle for, 1248; of Buddha, 187, 188, 189, 194, 197; Buddhaghosa's guides to, 192, 193, 1201; of early schools, 219–20; governance issues and, 537, 538; hagiography and, 563, 564; hierocrats and, 606; laypeople and, 739, 1232; mandala, 810; monastic regulations and, 1065, 1066; Mount Wutai association, 908; music and, 910; as one of three refuges of Buddhism, 1118; religious imagery and, 634–35; sacred topography and, 1297; systematization of, 1129; temple and, 1239

Dharma body. *See* Dharmakaya (Dharma body)

Dharma centers, 709

Dharma Drum monastery, Ching Shan, Taiwan, 651, 1232

Dharma Guardians, 1358

dharma heirs (Zen representatives), 204

dharma meetings, 1232

Dharma Realm Buddhist Association, 652, 1311

Dharma Vijaya Buddhist Vihara, Los Angeles, California, 1311

dharmacakra, 474, 808

Dharmacakra mudra, 808

Dharmadhatu, 17, 8107

Dharmadhatu Mandala, 1354, 1355

Dharmadhatu Vagisvara Manjughosa, 1352; mandala, 1355; *see also* Manjusri

Dharmadhatujnana, 808

Dharma-Flower temple (Fahua Si), Taiwan, 1229

Dharmagupta school, 269, 270, 283, 360, 1401

Dharmaguptakavinaya, 1095, 1096

Dharmakaya (Dharma body), 31, 89, 226, 280, 563, 636, 637, 727–29, 810, 1359, *1360*, 1370

Dharmakirti, 221, 1116

Dharmakirti dormitory, Nepal, 708

Dharmaksema, 269

DharmaNet (Web site), 653

Dharmankara *vihara*, 88

Dharmapala, Anagarika, 203, **379–80**, 642, 918, 1232

Dharmaraja (righteous king), 1117

Dharmaratna, 861

Dharmaruci, 616

Dharmasena Thera, 1239

dharmashastras, 94, 681

Dharmasvamin, 63, 65, 642, 920

Dharmatrata, 160

Dharmottariya, 1401

dhikr, 848

Dhuoda, 604, 1000

dhutanga, 90, 467, 485, 578, 965

dhyana mudra, 532, 808

Dhyana sect, 1327

Dhyanabhadra, 161

dhyanas (meditations), 845, 896, 899, 1326

Diadokos (Diadochus) of Photiki, 460, 469, 799, 1190

diakonika, 948

Dial (journal), 203

dialectics, 1259

Dialogi (Gregory I), 128–32, 139, 268, 361, 551, 565, 570, 603, 670, 672, 699, 831, 836, 872, 1067, 1086, 1113, 1114

dialogue, intermonastic: Buddhist perspectives, **380–81**, 382; contemporary issues, 328–29, 355–56, 380–81; Internet and, 651–53

dialogue, intermonastic: Christian perspectives, 355–56, 380–81, **382–85**, 555, 640; Internet and, 651–54; Keating, 356, 709; Leclercq, 750; meditative practices, 848; Merton, 856–57; Romania and, 1082

Dialogue Interreligieux Monastique, 750

Dialogues (Gregory I). *See Dialogi* (Gregory I)

Dialogues (Sulpicius Severus), 826, 902

Dialogues (Victor III), 1113

Diamond Hill monastery, Cumberland, Rhode Island, 1310–11

Diamond Realm, 688

Diamond Sutra (*Vajrasekhara Sutra*), 160, 451, 615, 688, 727, 818; Dunhuang site print of, 1339

Dianios (bishop of Caesarea), 116

Diatagai ton Hagion Apostolon, 784

Dicta Pirminii (Pirminius), 1030

Dicuil, 671

Didache (Christian text), 92, 470, 769

Diderot, Denis, 39

Didymos the Great, 666

Diederick VI (count), 935

Diego d'Azevedo (bishop), 408, 412–13

Diekmann, Godfrey, 773, 774, 822

Diem regime (South Vietnam), 1143

Dientzenhofer, Johann, 511

Diest, Belgium, 120, 126

Dietmayr, Berthold, 851

Dietrich of Freiberg, 22, 914

Digambara Jains, 308

Digha Nikaya, 332, 393, 776, 1017

Dignaga, 20, 221, 918, 1116, 1410

Dijon, France, 140

Diksmuide, Belgium, 126

Dimas (martyr), 829

Dimbulagala, Sri Lanka, 90, 1201

Dimitri (czarevitch of Russia), 887

diocese: Caesarius of Arles' view of, 233; Canons Regular and, 237; monk-bishops, 878–79; record keeping, 83; territorial abbeys as, 2–4

Diocletian (emperor of Rome), 342, 1079, 1295

Diodore of Tarsus, 290, 931, 932

Dionysios (archbishop of Larisa), 858

Dionysios (archimandrite), 1256

Dionysiou monastery, Mount Athos, Greece, 889, 891

Dionysius (Bulgarian monk), 762

Dionysius (bishop of Alexandria), 580

Dionysius (bishop of Athens), 11, 12

Dionysius Exiguus, 1295

Dionysius the Pseudo-Areopagite, 22, 246, **385–87**, 460, 586, 705, 769, 785, 799, 914, 1130, 1187, 1189, 1217, 1323; apophatic (negative) theology, 1222; on mysticism, 1332, 1334

Dioscorides, 179, 1014

Dioscorus, 434

Dipamkara Atisa, 224

Dipankara Buddha, 1353

Dipavamsa, 43, 802, 803, 861

diptychs (lists of names of Eastern Christian martyrs), 828

directoria, monastic, 1069

NOTES ON ADVISERS AND CONTRIBUTORS

Alexakis, Alexander. Assistant Professor, Department of Religion, Columbia University, New York City. Author of *Codex Parissnus Graecus 115 and Its Archetype* (1996). Contributor to *Dumbarton Oaks Papers*, *Erytheia*, *Annuarium Historiae Conciliorum* (1995), and *Jahrbuch der Öster. Byzantinistik*. **Essay:** Hagiography: Eastern Christian.

Alfeyev, Hilarion. Moscow Patriachate, Department of External Affairs, Danilov Monastery, Moscow. **Essays:** Isaac the Syrian (Isaac of Nineveh), St.; Russia: Recent Changes.

Alldritt, Leslie D. Associate Professor, Department of Religion and Philosophy, Northland College, Ashland, Wisconsin. Contributor to *Masao Abe: A Zen Life of Dialogue* (1998). **Essay:** Kūkai.

Allison, Robert W. Associate Professor, Department of Philosophy and Religion, Bates College, Lewiston, Maine, and Research Associate, Patriarchal Institute for Patristic Studies, Thessaloniki. Board member, Ancient Biblical Manuscripts Center, Claremont, California, and American Byzantine Studies Conference. North American Secretary, The Friends of Mount Athos. Editor, translator, and author of many publications on early Christian literature and thought, Byzantine monasticism, Greek palaeography and codicology, and "manuscript traditions." **Essays:** Libraries: Eastern Christian; Mount Athos, Greece.

Amstutz, Galen. Reischauer Institute of Japanese Studies, Harvard University, Cambridge, Massachusetts. Author of *Interpreting Amida: Orientalism and History in the Study of Pure Land Buddhism* (1997). Contributor to *Japanese Journal of Religious Studies*, *Journal of Chinese Religions*, *Comparative Studies in Society and History*, *Numen*, and *Eastern Buddhist*. **Essays:** Pure Land Buddhism; Rennyo; Shinran.

Anderson, Wendy Love. Doctoral candidate, Divinity School, University of Chicago. **Essay:** Missionaries: Christian.

Appleby, David. Associate Professor, Department of History, United States Naval Academy. Contributor to *Mediaeval Studies*, *Viator Medieval and Renaissance Studies*, *Catholic Historical Review*, *American Benedictine Review*, and *Word and Image*. **Essays:** Benedict of Aniane, St.; Humanism, Christian.

Arnould, Alain, O.P. Author of *De la production de miniatures de Cornelia van Wulfschkercke au couvent des Carmelites de Sion à Bruges* (1998) and *Splendours of Flanders: Late Medieval Art in Cambridge Collection* (with Jean Michel Massing, 1993). Editor of *Elementa Historiae Ordinis Praedicatorum*. Contributor to *Scriptorium*. **Essays:** Visual Arts, Western Christian: Book Arts before the Renaissance; Visual Arts, Western Christian: Painting.

Ashley, Benedict M., O.P. St. Louis Bertrand Priory, St. Louis, Missouri. Author of *Health Care Ethics: A Theological Analysis* (4th edition, 1997), *Justice in the Church: Gender and Participation* (1996), *Spiritual Direction in the Dominican Tradition* (1995), *The Dominicans* (1990), and *Theologies of the Body: Humanist and Christian* (1985). Editor of *Thomas Aquinas, the Gifts of the Spirit: Selected Spiritual Writings* (1995). **Essays:** Death: Christian Perspectives; Laicization of Spirituality: Christian Perspectives; Life Cycle, Christian; Self-Mutilation, Christian.

Auslander, Diane Peters. Doctoral candidate, Graduate Center, City University of New York. **Essay:** Abbess, Christian.

Bangdel, Dina. Assistant Professor, Western Michigan University, Kalamazoo. Author of *Inventory of Stone Sculptures of the Kathmandu Valley* (with Lain Bangdel, 1995). Contributor to *Orientations*. **Essays:** Vajrayāna Buddhism in Nepal; Visual Arts, Buddhist: Nepal.

Baumstein, Paschal, O.S.B. (Adviser). Monk and priest of Belmont Abbey and College Historian, Belmont Abbey College, North Carolina. Author of *Blessing the Years to Come* (1997), *The Art of Michael McInerney* (1997), *A Carolina Cathedral* (1992), and *My Lord of Belmont: A Biography of Leo Haid* (1985). Book editor of *Cistercian Studies Quarterly* (1997–98) and editor of *Crescat* (1977–78, 1979–87). Contributor to numerous Catholic history journals. **Essays:** Abbeys, Territorial; Anselm, St.; Economics: Christian; Haid, Leo Michael; Knowles, M. David; McInerney, Michael Joseph Vincent.

Beliaev, Leonid. Professor and Head of the Department of Moscow Archaeology, Russian Academy of Sciences, Moscow. Author of several books including *Khristianskie Drevnosti* (1998), *Russkoe Srednevekovoe Nadgrobie s 13 po 17 vv.* (1996), and *Drevnie Monastyri Moskvy* (1994). Second editor-in-chief of *Rossiiskaya Arkheologiia* since 1991. Editor of and contributor to many anthologies and journals in the fields of Russian archaeology, history, and architecture. **Essays:** Archaeology: Near East; Archaeology: Russia.

Bell, David N. Professor, Department of Religious Studies, Memorial University of Newfoundland. Author of *Bartholomaei Exoniensis, Contra Fatalitatis Errorem* (1996), *Many Mansions* (1996), *What Nuns Read: Books and Libraries in Medieval English Nunneries* (1995), and other books. Editor of *Cistercian Studies Quarterly* (1988–98) and *Cîteaux: Commentarii Cistercienses* (1986–98). Contributor to numerous anthologies and journals. **Essays:** Cîteaux, France; La Trappe, France; Rancé, Armand-Jean de; Trappists.

Bellenger, Aidan. Monk of Downside Abbey. Author of *Downside: A Pictorial History* (1998), *The French Exiled Clergy in the British Isles* (1986), and *English and Welsh Priests, 1558–1800* (1984). Editor of *The Great Return* (1994), *Fathers in Faith* (1991), and *Letters of Bede Jarrett* (1989). Contributor to *Downside Review*, *Studies in Church History* and a number of other publications. **Essays:** Butler, Cuthbert; Exile, Western Christian.

Belsole, Kurt, O.S.B. Associate Professor, Saint Vincent Seminary, Latrobe, Pennsylvania, and Pontifical Athenaeum of Saint Anselm, Rome. Associate editor, *American Benedictine Review* (1994–) and board member, *Word and Spirit* (1992–98). Contributor to *Word and Spirit*, *Regulae Benedicti Studia*, and *American Benedictine Review*. **Essays:** Beauduin, Lambert; Beuron, Germany; Guéranger, Prosper; Maria Laach, Germany.

Berman, Constance Hoffman. Professor, Department of History, University of Iowa. Author of *The Cistercian Evolution* (1999) and *Medieval Agriculture* (1986). Co-editor of *Words of Medieval Women* (1985).Contributor to *Studies in Cistercian Art and Architecture* (1998), *Cîteaux, Revue Mabillon*, and many other scholarly publications. **Essays:** Agriculture, Western Christian; Cistercians: Female; Cistercians: General or Male; Orders (Religious), Origin of.

Bisson, Thomas N. Henry Charles Lea Professor of Medieval History, Harvard University, Cambridge, Massachusetts. Author of *Tormented Voices: Power, Crisis, and Humanity in Rural Catalonia (1140–1200)* (1998), *The Medieval Crown of Aragon: A Short History* (1986), *Conservation of Coinage* (1979), and *Assemblies and Representation in Languedoc in the Thirteenth Century* (1964). Editor of several publications including *Parliaments, Estates and Representation* (since 1982). Contributor to *Speculum*, *Past and Present*, and *American Historical Review*. **Essay:** France: History.

Black, Jill. South Australian Coordinator, World Community for Christian Meditation, South Australia. Contributor to *Women Priests in Australia* (1987), *Tablet*, and *Furrow*. **Essay:** Main, John.

Blackstone, Kate. Assistant Professor, Department of Religion, University of Manitoba, Winnipeg. Author of *Women in the Footsteps of the Buddha: Struggle for Liberation in the Therigatha* (1998). Contributor to *Journal of Buddhist Ethics* and *Religious Studies News*. **Essay:** Mahāpajāpatī Gotamī.

Bodhi, Bhikkhu. President and editor, Buddhist Publication Society, Kandy, Sri Lanka. Author of *The Middle Length Discourses of the Buddha* (1995), *A Comprehensive Manual of Abhidhamma* (1993), *The Great Discourse on Causation* (1984), and *The Discourse on the All-Embracing Net of Views* (1978). Editor of *The Wheel* (1984–), *Bodhi Leaves* (1984–), and *Great Disciples of the Buddha* (1997). Contributor to *Buddhist Studies Review*, *The Middle Way*, and other journals. **Essays:** Buddhaghosa; Celibacy: Buddhist; Disciples, Early Buddhist; Discourses (Suttas): Theravāda; Theravādin Monks, Modern Western.

Boisvert, Mathieu. Professor and Director of Graduate Studies, Department of Religion, University of Quebec, Montreal. Author of *The Five Aggregates: Understanding Theravada Psychology and Soteriology* (1996). Editor of *Studies in Religion* (1998–99), *Un Monde de religions: Les traditions de l'Inde* (1997), *Religiologiques: Regards nord-américains sur la religion* (1995), and *Critical Review of Books in Religion* (1995). Contributor to many anthologies and journals. **Essays:** Examinations, Theravādin (with Matthew Kosuta); Novices, Theravādin Rituals for; Origins: Comparative Perspectives.

Boland, Vivian, O.P. St. Dominic's Priory, London. Author of *Ideas in God According to Saint Thomas Aquinas* (1996). Contributor to *Dominican Ashram*, *Milltown Studies*, *Religion, Morality, and Public Policy* (1995), and *Doctrine and Life*. **Essays:** Albertus Magnus, St.; Theology, Western Christian: Dominican.

Bradley, Ritamary, S.F.C.C. Professor Emeritus, Department of English, St. Ambrose University. Author of *Not for the Wise* (1994), *Julian's Way* (1993), *In the Jaws of the Bear: Journeys of Transformation by Women Mystics* (1991), and *The 14th-Century English Mystics: A Comprehensive Annotated Bibliography* (with Valerie Lagorio, 1981). Editor of many publications including *Mystics Quarterly* (1974–91). Advisory board member, *Religion and Literature* since 1962. Contributor to numerous scholarly works including *Mysticism and Spirituality in Medieval England* (1997). **Essay:** Julian of Norwich.

Brassard, Francis. Lecturer, Department of Religious Studies, McGill University, Montreal. Author of *The Concept of Bodhicitta in Śāntideva's Bodhicaryāvatāra* (forthcoming). Contributor to *Religiologiques*. **Essays:** Arhat; Councils, Buddhist; Croatia (Hrvatska); Death: Buddhist Perspectives; Pilgrimages, Buddhist.

Bray, Dorothy Ann (Adviser). Associate Professor, Department of English, McGill University, Montreal. Author of *A List of Motifs in the Lives of the Early Irish Saints* (1992). Contributor to numerous books and journals including *Mittelalter Mythen I: Herrscher, Helden, Heilige* (1996), *Viator*, and *Études Celtiques*. **Essay:** Brigit, St.

Breeze, Andrew. Associate Professor, Department of English, University of Navarre, Pamplona. Author of *Medieval Welsh Literature* (1997). Editor of *Selim* (1992–) and *Grove* (1997–). Contributor to many anthologies and journals including *Alfred the Wise* (1997), *From Baudelaire to Lorca* (1996), and *Studi Medievali*. **Essay:** Wales.

Brodman, James W. Professor of History, Department of History, University of Central Arkansas, Conway. Author of *Charity and Welfare: Hospitals and the Poor in Medieval Catalonia* (1998) and *Ransoming Captives in Crusader Spain: The Order of Merced on the Christian-Islamic Frontier* (1986). Editor of *Perceptions of Reality: A Sourcebook for the Social History of Western Civilization* (1980). Contributor to *Tolerance and Intolerance: Social Conflict in the Age of the Crusades* (1998) and other scholarly publications. **Essay:** Mercedarians.

Callahan, Daniel F. Contributor to numerous anthologies and journals including *Medieval Piety and Purity: Essays on Religious Reform and Clerical Celibacy* (1998), *Portraits of Medieval and Renaissance Living: Essays in Memory of David Herlihy* (1996), *Journal of Ecclesiastical History*, and *Haskins Society Journal*. **Essay:** Jerusalem, Israel.

Carbine, Jason A. Graduate student, History of Religions Program, University of Chicago Divinity School. Co-editor of *The Life of Buddhism* (forthcoming). **Essay:** Saṅgha.

Cardman, Francine. Associate Professor of Historical Theology, Weston Jesuit School of Theology, Cambridge, Massachusetts. Translator of *The Preaching of* Augustine (1973). Contributor to numerous history and theology publications including *Encyclopedia of Women and World Religions* (1999), *Readings in Moral Theology* (1996), and *Dictionary of Feminist Theologies* (1996). **Essays:** Desert Mothers; Spirituality: Western Christian.

Carney, Margaret, O.S.F., S.T.D. Dean, School of Franciscan Studies, St. Bonaventure University, St. Bonaventure, New York. Author of *The First Franciscan Woman: Clare of Assisi and Her Form of Life* (1993) and *Commentary Edition: Rule and Life of the Brothers and Sisters of the Third Order Regular of St. Francis* (1982, 1996). Board member of *Greyfriars Review* and *Propositum of IFC-TOR*. Editor of *Cord* (1988–92). Contributor to *Creating a Home: Benchmarks for Church Leadership Roles for Women* (1997) and other scholarly works. **Essay:** Franciscans: Female.

Casey, Michael, O.C.S.O. Tarrawarra Abbey, Victoria, Australia. Author of *Truthful Living* (1998), *The Art of Sacred Reading* (1995), *Undivided Heart* (1994), *A Thirst for God* (1988), and *Towards God* (1988). Editor of *Tjurunga: An Australasian Benedictine Review*. Advisor, *Cistercian Studies Quarterly* (also associate editor) and *Thomas Merton Annual*. Contributor to numerous anthologies and journals. **Essay:** Bernard of Clairvaux, St.

Caswell, James O. Professor, Department of Fine Arts, University of British Columbia, Vancouver. Author of *Written and Unwritten: A New History of the Buddhist Caves at Yungang* (1988) and *The Single Brushstroke: 600 Years of Painting from the Ching Yuan Cha's Collection* (1985). Contributor to *Archaeology*, *Ars Orientalis*, and *Oriental Art*. **Essays:** Architecture: Structural Monasteries in East Asia; Cave Temples and Monasteries in India and China; Patrons, Buddhist: China.

Chandrasekhar, Chaya. Doctoral candidate, Department of Art History, Ohio State University, Columbus. Contributor to *Ars Orientalis* and *Mirrors of the Heart Mind: The Rezk Collection of Tibetan Art*. **Essay:** Architecture: Buddhist Monasteries in Southern Asia (with John C. Huntington).

Chaney, William A. George McKendree Steele Professor of Western Culture, Department of History, Lawrence University, Appleton, Wisconsin. Author of *The Cult of Kingship in Anglo-Saxon England: The Transition from Paganism to Christianity* (1970). Contributor to *In Iure Veritas: Studies in Canon Law in Memory of Schafer Williams* (1991), *The Other Side of Western Civilization* (1984), and *Harvard Theological Review*, and a number of other scholarly publications. **Essay:** Whitby, England.

Chaoul-Reich, M. Alejandro. Graduate student, Department of Religious Studies, Rice University, Houston, Texas. Editor of *Nyam Gyud Ngondro: The Experimental Transmission Part I* (1999) and *Voice of Clear Light* (1994–96). **Essays:** Bön, Influence of; Bön Monasticism.

Chase, Mary Jane. Associate Professor of History, Westminster College, Salt Lake City, Utah. Contributor to *Encyclopedia of the Reformation* and *Sixteeenth Century Journal*. **Essay:** Reformation.

Chewning, Susannah Mary. Instructor of English, Kean University, Union, New Jersey. Contributor to many anthologies and journals including *Literary Representations of Widowhood and Virginity in the Middle Ages* (1999), *An Age of Crisis and Renewal* (1999), and *Mystics Quarterly*. **Essays:** Gender Studies: Christian Perspectives; Solitude: Christian Perspectives; Vision, Mystical: Western Christian.

Chirapravati, M.L. Pattaratorn. Assistant Curator of Southeast Asian Art, Asian Art Museum of San Francisco. Instructor of Asian Art, Art Department, Sonoma State University. Author of *Buddhist Votive Tablets of Thailand c. Sixth Century to the Thirteenth Century* (forthcoming), *Votive Tablets in Thailand: Origin, Styles, and Uses* (1997), *Hexagon II Exhibition Catalog* (1990), and a number of articles on votive tablets and Thai arts. Editor of *Letters of King Chulalongkorn to His Royal Highness Prince Nakhonchasisuradey* (1998). **Essay:** Visual Arts, Buddhist: Southeast Asia.

Chryssavgis, John. Professor, Holy Cross School of Theology, Boston. Author of *The Way of the Fathers* (1998), *Love, Marriage, and Sexuality* (1996), *Repentance and Confession* (1990), *Ascent to Heaven* (1989), and *Fire and Light* (1987). Editor of *Pacifica* (1995–98), *Greek Orthodox Theological Review* (1995–97), *Phronema* (1986–95), and *The Desert Is Alive* (1990). Contributor to *Sobornost*, *St. Vladimir's Theological Quarterly*, *Cistercian Studies Quarterly*, and other journals. **Essays:** Climacus, John, St.; Hesychasm.

Ciolek, T. Matthew (Adviser). Head, Internet Publications Bureau, Research School of Pacific and Asian Studies, Australian National University, Canberra. Co-author of *Wyrzeczysko: A Study of Public Rituals and Ceremonies in Contemporary Poland* (1976). Editor of numerous internet publications including the *Asian Studies* e-journal and virtual library web site (both since 1994). Contributor to many anthologies and journals including *Colloquium on Academic Library Information Resources for Southeast Asian Scholarship* (1997), *The Internet Compendium: Subject Guides to Humanity Resources* (1995), and *IEEE Computer*. **Essay:** Internet, Buddhist and Christian.

Coff, M. Pascaline, O.S.B. Director, Osage-Monastic Ashram, Sand Springs, Oklahoma. Co-founder, Monastic Interreligious Dialogue (MID) USA. Contributor to *Gethsemani Encounter* (1998), *Dialog Der Religionen* (1996), *Review for Religious*, and other publications. **Essay:** Dialogue, Intermonastic: Christian Perspectives.

Cohen, Richard S. Lecturer, Department of History, University of California, San Diego. Editor of *Critical Review of Books in Religion* (1996–98). Contributor to *History of Religions*, *Indo-Iranian Journal*, *Journal of the American Academy of Religion*, and *Chaos and Society* (1995). **Essays:** Ajaṇṭā, India; India: Sites.

Coleman, Simon. Department of Anthropology, University of Durham. Author of *Pilgrimage Past and Present in the World Religions* (with John Eisner, 1995). Editor of *Discovering Anthropology* (1998), *Journal of the Royal Anthropological Institute* (1999–), and *Journal of Marian Studies* (1998–). Contributor to the journals *Religion*, *Journal of Material Culture*, *World Archaeology*, *Sociology of Religion*, *Ethnos*, and the anthologies *Ritual, Performance, Media* (1998) and *Pilgrimage* *in the Middle Ages and Beyond* (1999). **Essays:** Images: Christian Perspectives; Pilgrimages, Christian: Near East.

Collett, Barry (Adviser). Senior Lecturer, Department of History, University of Melbourne. Author of *Wednesdays Closest to the Full Moon: A History of South Gippsland* (1994) and *Italian Benedictine Scholars and the Reformation: The Congregation of Santa Giustina of Padua* (1986). Editor of *A Long and Troubled Pilgrimage: The Correspondence of Marguerite of Navarre and Vittoria Colonna 1540–1545* (2000), *Here Beygneth the Rule of Seynt Benet: Richard Fox's Translation of the Benedictine Rule for Women (1517)* (2000), and *The "De Republica" of Tito Livio Frulovisi 1434* (2000).

Collins, Roger. Research Fellow, Department of History, University of Edinburgh. Author of *Charlemagne* (1998), *Fredegar* (1996), *Early Medieval Europe, 300–1000* (1991), *The Arab Conquest of Spain, 710–797* (1989), and *Early Medieval Spain* (1983, 1995). Editor of *Bede's Ecclesiastical History of the English People* (1994), *Charlemagne's Heir: New Perspectives on the Reign of Louis the Pious* (1991), and *Ideal and Reality in Frankish and Anglo-Saxon Society* (1983). Contributor to scholarly publications including *Journal of Medieval History* and *Early Medieval Dispute Settlement* (1986). **Essays:** Alcuin; Spain: History; Spain: Sites.

Constantelos, Demetrios J. Charles Cooper Townsend, Sr. Distinguished Professor of History and Religion, Emeritus, Richard Stockton College of New Jersey. Author of *Christian Hellenism* (1999), *Poverty, Society, and Philanthropy in the Late Medieval Greek World* (1992), *Byzantine Kleronomia* (1990), *Understanding the Greek Orthodox Church* (1982, 1998), and *Byzantine Philanthropy and Social Welfare* (1968, 1991). Editor of many publications including *Orthodox Theology and Diakonia* (1981), *Greek Orthodox Theological Review* (1965–71), and *Journal of Ecumenical Studies* (1976–). Contributor to *The Parallel Apocrypha* (1997), *The Oxford Companion to the Bible* (1993), and other scholarly works. **Essays:** Basil the Great, St.; Liturgy: Eastern Christian; Social Services: Eastern Christian.

Constas, Nicholas P. Assistant Professor, Department of Theology, Harvard Divinity School, Cambridge, Massachusetts. Assistant editor of *Greek Orthodox Theological Review* (1996–97). Contributor to *Byzantine Defenders of Images* (1998), *The Contentious Triangle* (1998), *Logos*, and *Journal of Early Christian Studies*. **Essay:** Theology, Eastern Christian.

Copsey, Richard, O.Carm. Catholic Chaplain, Aberdeen University, Scotland. **Essays:** Governance: Christian Perspectives; Initiation: Christian Perspectives.

Cornelius, Michael G. Ph.D. candidate, Department of English, University of Rhode Island. Contributor to *The Whispered Watchword*, *Smoke Signals Quarterly*, and *INANNA: A Journal of Women's Studies*. **Essay:** Capuchins.

Coureas, Nicholas. Researcher, Cyprus Research Centre, Nicosia. Author of *The Cartulary of the Cathedral of Holy Wisdom of Nicosia* (with Chris Schabel, 1997) and *The Latin Church in Cyprus, 1195–1312* (1997). Editor of *Cyprus and the Crusades* (with J. Riley-Smith, 1995). Contributor to a number of scholarly works. **Essay:** Cyprus (with Chris Schabel).

Cowdrey, H.E.J. Emeritus Fellow, St. Edmund Hall, Oxford. Author of *Popes and Church Reform in the 11th Century* (2000), *The Crusades and Latin Monasticism, 11th–12th Centuries* (1999), *Pope Gregory VII, 1073–1085* (1998), *Popes, Monks, and Crusaders* (1984), *The Age of Abbot Desiderius: Montecassino, the Papacy, and the Normans in the Eleventh and Early Twelfth Centuries* (1983), *Two Studies in Cluniac History* (1978), *The Epistolae vagantes of Pope Gregory VII* (1972), and *The Cluniacs and the Gregorian Reform* (1970). Contributor to numerous journals including *Studi Medievali*, *Journal of Ecclesiastical History*, and *Studi Gregoriani*. **Essay:** Celibacy: Christian.

Cunningham, Lawrence S. Professor of Theology, University of Notre Dame, Notre Dame, Indiana. Author of *Christian Spirituality* (1996), *Catholic Prayer* (1989), and *The Catholic Faith: An Introduction* (1987). Editor of *Christian Ecumenism* (1998), *A Search for Solitude: The Journals of Thomas Merton* (1996), and *Thomas Merton: Spiritual* Master (1992). Currently, member of the editorial board, *Cistercian Studies Quarterly*, and associate editor, *Horizons*. Contributor to numerous theological publications. **Essay:** Charism.

Curran, Mary Bernard, O.P. Dominican Sisters, St. Cecilia Congregation, Nashville, Tennessee. Author of *Thinkers through Time* (1993) and *Constitutions, St. Cecelia Congregation, Nashville, Tennessee* (1985). Editor of *The Nashville Dominicans* by Sister Rose Marie Masserano (1985). **Essay:** Prayer: Christian Perspectives.

Dandelet, Thomas. Assistant Professor, Department of History, Princeton University, Princeton, New Jersey. Contributor to *Roma Barocco* (1998) and *Journal of Modern History.* **Essays:** Taizé, France; Teresa of Avila, St.

Davis, Cyprian, O.S.B. St. Meinrad Archabbey, and Professor, Church History, St. Meinrad School of Theology, St. Meinrad, Indiana. Author of *History of Black Catholics in the United States* (1990) and *The Church: A Living Heritage* (1981). Coeditor of *Taking Down Our Harps: Black Catholics in the United States* (1998). Contributor to *The Didactic in Context: Essays on Its Text, History, and Transmission* (1995), *Rozanne Elder: U.S. Catholic Historian* (1986, 1988), and *Benedictus: Studies in Honor of St. Benedict of Nursia* (1981). **Essay:** Einsiedeln, Switzerland.

Deal, William E. Severance Associate Professor of the History of Religion and Director, Department of Religion, Case Western Reserve University, Cleveland, Ohio. Area editor, East Asia, *Religious Studies* Review (1997–2000). Contributor to numerous anthologies and journals including *Caring for the Elderly in Japan and the United States: Practices and Policies* (2000), *Religions of Japan in Practice* (1999), *Japanese Journal of Religious*

Studies, and *Religious Studies Review*. **Essays:** Ennin; Mountain Monasteries, Buddhist; Saichō; Tiantai/Tendai: Japan.

Deeg, Max. Department of Comparative History of Religions, University of Würzburg. Author of *Die altindische Etymologie nach dem Verständnis Yāskas und seiner Vorgänger* (1995). Contributor to *Religion im Wandel der Kosmologien* (1999), *Begegnung von Religionen und Kulturen* (1998), and *Nagoya Studies in Indian Culture and Buddhism*. **Essay:** Missionaries: Buddhist.

Deegalle, Mahinda. Foreign Researcher, Japan Society for the Promotion of Science. Numata Visiting Professor in Buddhist Studies, McGill University, Montreal. Author of *Bana Saha Budusamaya* (1997) and *Nirvānaya Saha Sadācāraya* (1986). Contributing editor of *Pāli Buddhism* (1996). Contributor to numerous anthologies and journals including *Buddhist Theology* (1998), *Recent Research in Buddhist Studies* (1997), and *Asiatische Studien*. **Essays:** Asceticism: Buddhist Perspectives; Death Rituals, Buddhist; Marathon Monks; Monasticism, Definitions of: Buddhist Perspectives; Music: Buddhist Perspectives; Sri Lanka: History; Sri Lanka: Recent Changes; Temple, Buddhist; Virtues, Buddhist.

Derwich, Marek. Professor, Department of History, University of Wrocław. Author of *Monastyczym benedyktyński w średniowiecznej Europie i Polsce* (1998), *Benedyktyński klasztor św. Krzyża na Łysej Górze w średniowieczu* (1992), and *Herby, legendy, dawne mity* (1987, 1989). Editor of many publications including *Quaestiones Medii Aevi Novae* (1996–) and *Opera ad historiem monasticiam spectantia* (1995–). Contributor to *Dictionnaire encyclopédique du Moyen Âge* (1997) and a number of other works of scholarship **Essays:** Abbot: Christian; Benedictines: General or Male; Bishops: Jurisdiction and Role; Bruno, St.; Clothing: Christian Perspectives; Czech Republic; Częstochowa (Jasna Góra), Poland; Gualbert, John, St.; Guigo I; Monk-Bishops; Officials: Western Christian; Origins: Western Christian; Patrons, Christian: Royal; Poland; Radegunde, St.; Regulations: Christian Perspectives.

Dessein, Bart. Assistant Professor, Chinese Language and Culture, Ghent National University. Author of *Heart of Scholasticism with Miscellaneous Additions – Samyuktābhidharmahrdaya* (forthcoming) and *Sarvāstivāda Buddhist Scholasticism* (1998). Contributing editor of *Communication and Cognition: The Notion of "Self" in Buddhism* (forthcoming). Contributor to *Asiatische Studien*, *Indian Journal of Buddhist Studies*, and *Encyclopedia of Indian Philosophies*. **Essays:** Huaihai (Huai-hai); Huiyuan (Hui-yüan); Shenxiu (Shen-hsiu); Taixu (T'ai-hsü); Zhiyi (Chih-i); Zhuhong (Chu-hung).

Dilworth, Mark, O.S.B. Abbot Emeritus, Fort Augustus Abbey, Scotland. Author of *Scottish Monasteries in the Late Middle Ages* (1995) and *The Scots in Franconia* (1974). Editor of *Innes Review* (1979–83; board member, 1964–84; 1997–). Board member, *Records of the Scottish Church History Society* (1974–76, 1982–85, 1986–89) and *Scottish History Society* (1979–83). Contributor to anthologies and journals including *The Renaissance in Scotland* (1994) and *Review of Scottish Culture*. **Essays:** Iona, Scotland; Scotland.

Dinzelbacher, Peter. Honorarprofessor, University of Vienna, and Apl. Professor, University of Stuttgart. Author of several books including *Bernhard von Clairvaux* (1998), *Angst im Mittelalter. Teufels-, Todes- und Gotteserfahrung: Mentalitätsgeschichte und Ikonographie* (1996), and *Heilige oder Hexen? Schicksale auffälliger Frauen in Mittelalter und Frühneuzeit* (1995, 1997). Editor of *Kulturgeschichte der christlichen Orden* (1997), *Europäische Mentalitätgeschichte* (1993), and several other works. Contributor to numerous scholarly publications. **Essays:** Austria; Devotions, Western Christian; Hagiography: Western Christian; Vienna, Austria; Visual Arts, Western Christian: Sculpture.

Eden, Bradford Lee. Order of St. Augustine of Canterbury. Musicologist and independent scholar. Board member *The Heroic Age* (1998–). Contributor of many articles to *Encyclopedia of Medieval Folklore* (1999) and *Encyclopedia of Medieval Italy* (1999). **Essays:** Hymnographers; Relics, Christian Monastic; Rome and the Papacy; Solesmes, France.

Egan, Keith J. Aquinas Chair in Catholic Theology, Saint Mary's College, Notre Dame, Indiana. Author of *Christian Spirituality* (1996). Editor of *Master of the Sacred Page* (1997), *Christian Spirituality Bulletin* (1993–), *Land of Carmel* (1991), and *Studies in Spirituality* (1990–). Contributor to *Carmelite Studies*, *Expanding the Borders* (1998), and other journals and collections. **Essays:** Bonaventure, St.; Carmelites: Male; Thérèse of Lisieux, St.

Elkins, Sharon K. Associate Professor, Department of Religion, Wellesley College, Wellesley, Massachusetts. Author of *Holy Women of Twelfth-Century England* (1988). Contributor to *Women's Studies Encyclopedia* (1991), *Distant Echoes* (1984), *Benedictus: Studies in Honor of St. Benedict of Nursia* (1981), and *Church History*. **Essay:** Gilbertines.

Feiss, Hugh, O.S.B. Ascension Priory, Jerome, Idaho. Author of *Monastic Wisdom* (1999), *Commentary on the Parable of the Prodigal Son by Hugh of Saint-Cher* (1996), *Life of Holy Hildegard* (1996), *Hildegard of Bingen, Explanation of the Rule of Benedict* (1990), and *Peter of Celle: Selected Works* (1987). Editor of *American Benedictine Review* (1986–), *Magistra* (1995–), and *Imagining Heaven in the Middle Ages* (1999). Contributor to many publications. **Essays:** Animals, Attitude toward: Christian Perspectives; Baker, Augustine; Bridgettines; Leclercq, Jean; Monasticism, Definitions of: Christian Perspectives; Victorines.

Flanagan, Sabina. Australian Research Council Fellow, History Department, University of Melbourne. Author of *Hildegard of Bingen: A Visionary Life* (1991, 1998) and *Secrets of God: Writings of Hildegard of Bingen* (1996). Contributor to *Journal of Religious History* and several books. **Essay:** Hildegard of Bingen, St.

Flood, Gavin (Adviser). Senior Lecturer, Religious Studies Department, University of Wales, Lampeter. Author of several books including *Beyond Phenomenology: Rethinking the Study of Religion* (1999) and *An Introduction to Hinduism* (1996).

Foard, James H. Professor, Department of Religious Studies, Arizona State University. Editor of *The Pure Land Tradition: History and Development* (1996). Contributor to *Engaged Pure Land Buddhism* (1998), *Revisioning "Kamakura" Buddhism* (1998), *Journal of the American Academy of Religion*, *Communities in Question* (1994), and *Flowing Traces* (1992). **Essay:** Ippen.

France, John. Department of History, University of Wales, Swansea. Author of *Western Warfare in the Age of the Crusade 1000–1300* (1999) and *Victory in the East: A Military History of the First Crusade* (1994). Editor of *The Crusades and Their Sources: Essays Presented to Bernard Hamilton* (1998) and *Rodulfus Glaber Opera* (1989). Contributor to many scholarly works. **Essays:** Cluny, Abbots of; Crusades.

Frankforter, A. Daniel. Professor of Medieval History, School of Humanities and Social Sciences, Pennsylvania State University, Erie–Behrend College. Author of *The Medieval Millennium: An Introduction* (1999), *The Shakespeare Name Dictionary* (1995), *Civilization and Survival* (1988), and *A History of the Christian Movement* (1978). Translator, *The Equality of the Two Sexes*, by Poullain de la Barre (1989). Contributor to journals including *Journal of Women's History*, *Church History*, and *Manuscripta*. **Essays:** Hrosthwitha; Suger.

Frazee, Charles A. Professor of History, Emeritus, California State University, Fullerton. Author of *World History* (2 volumes, 1997), *Princes of the Greek Islands: The Dukes of the Archipelago* (1988), *Catholics and Sultans: The Church and the Ottoman Empire* (1983), and *The Orthodox Church and Independent Greece* (1969). Editor of *Readings in World History* (2 volumes, 1998). Contributor to *Balkan Currents: Studies in the History, Culture, and Society of a Divided Land* (1998), *Seeking God: The Recovery of Religious Identity in Orthodox Russia, Ukraine, and Georgia* (1993), *Catholic Historical Review*, *Studia Monastica*, and *Church History*. **Essays:** Greece; Istanbul, Turkey; Maronites.

Freedman, Paul H. (Adviser). Professor, Department of History, Yale University, New Haven, Connecticut. Author of *Images of the Medieval Peasant* (1999), *Church, Law, and Society in Catalonia, 900–1500* (1994), *The Origins of Peasant Servitude in Medieval Catalonia* (1991), and other books. Editorial board member, *Journal of Medieval History*, *Mediterranean Studies*, and *Medievalia*. Contributor of numerous articles on medieval history and Catalonia to journals and anthologies.

Friedman, Russell L. Editor, Diplomatarium Danicum, Society for Danish Language and Literature, Copenhagen. Editor of special issue of *Vivarium* (forthcoming) and *Medieval Analyses in Language and Cognition* (1999). Contributor to *Vestigia, Imagines, Verba* (1997) and many other scholarly works. **Essay:** Theology, Western Christian: Franciscan.

Funk, Virgil C. President, National Association of Pastoral Musicians, Washington, D.C. Author of *NPM Workbook: Job Descriptions, Contracts, and Salaries*. Editor of *Pastoral Music Magazine* (1997–), *Catholic Music Educator Magazine* (1992–), and works on music and liturgy. Contributor to *Finding Voice to Give God Praise* (1998), *The Encyclopedia of American Catholic History* (1997), and *The New Dictionary of Sacramental Worship* (1990). **Essay:** Liturgical Movement 1830–1980.

Gilley, Sheridan (Adviser). Department of Theology, University of Durham. Author of *Newman and His Age* (1990). Editor of *A History of Religion in Britain: Practice and Belief from Pre-Roman Times to the Present* (with W.J. Sheils, 1994), *The Irish in Britain, 1815–1939* (with Roger Swift, 1989), and several other anthologies.

Glidden, Aelred, O.S.B. St. Gregory's Abbey, Three Rivers, Michigan. Contributor to *Singing God's Praises* (1998) and *Erudition in God's Service* (1987). **Essay:** Abbot Primate, Benedictine.

Glowski, Janice M. (Adviser). Associate Curator, Huntington Archive of Buddhist and Related Art, Ohio State University. **Essay:** Visual Arts, Buddhist: Tibet.

Goa, David J. Curator of Folklife, Provincial Museum of Alberta. Author of *Eastern Christian Ritual: A Bibliography of English Language Sources* (with Anna E. Altmann, 1988). Editor of *The Ukrainian Religious Experience: Tradition and the Canadian Cultural Context* (1989). Contributor to *Heaven on Earth: Orthodox Treasures of Siberia and North America* (1994). **Essays:** Seasons, Liturgical: Eastern Christian; Vision, Mystical: Eastern Christian.

Golitzin, Hieromonk Alexander. Associate Professor, Department of Theology, Marquette University, Milwaukee, Wisconsin. Author of *On the Mystical Life: St. Symeon New Theologian* (1995–97), *Historical Dictionary of the Orthodox Church* (1996), *The Living Witness of the Holy Mountain* (1996), and *Et Introibo ad Altare Dei: The Mystagog of Dionysius Arcopagita* (1994). Contributor to *St. Vladimir's Theological Quarterly*, *Mystics Quarterly*, and *The South Slav Conflict* (1996). **Essays:** Dionysius the Pseudo-Areopagite; Macarian Homilies; Spirituality: Eastern Christian.

Gómez, Luis O. Professor, Department of Asian Languages and Cultures, and Adjunct Professor, Department of Psychology, University of Michigan. Author, *Traces of Awakening* (1999) and *The Land of Bliss* (1996). Co-editor of *Studies in the Literature of the Great* Vehicle (1989), *Barabudur: History and Significance of a Buddhist Monument* (1992), and *Problemas de filosofía* (1975, 1982).General Editor, Buddhist Studies Series, Collegiate Institute for the Study of Buddhist Literature (1986–). Editorial board member of *Estudios de Asia y África* (1998–) and *Journal of the International Association of Buddhist Studies* (1993–). Contributor to *Aryan and Non-Aryan in South Asia* (1998), *Journal of the International Association of Buddhist Studies*, *Ōtanigakuhō* (1995), and *Curators of the Buddha* (1995). **Essays:** Discourses (Sūtras): Mahāyāna; Latin America; Prayer: Buddhist Perspectives; Spirituality: Buddhist.

Gonneau, Pierre. Maître de Conférences, UFR d'Études Slaves, University of Paris-Sorbonne. Author of *Histoire des Slaves ori-*

entaux des origines á 1689: Bibliographie des sources traduites en langues occidentales (1998) and *La Maison de la Sainte Trinité: Un grand monastère russe du Moyen-àgetardif (1345–1533)* (1993). Editor of *Morines et monastères dans les societés de nilé grec et Patin* (1996). Contributor to *Revue des Études Slaves* and other scholarly publications. **Essays:** Maximus the Greek, St.; Moscow, Russia; Pilgrimages, Christian: Eastern Europe; Russia: Sites.

Goorjian, Taline. Graduate student, Department of Religious Studies, Rice University, Houston, Texas. **Essays:** Critiques of Buddhist Monasticism: Indo-Tibetan; Critiques of Buddhist Monasticism: Japanese; Festivals, Buddhist; Travelers: Buddhist.

Gosling, David L. Cambridge Teape Fellow, Clare Hall, University of Cambridge. Author of *A New Earth* (1992), *Doctor Monk* (1986), *Science and Religion in India* (1976). Editor of *Technology from the Underside* (1986), *Science Education and Ethical Values* (1985), and *Nuclear Crisis* (1977). Contributor to *Anthropology and Medicine* (1998). **Essay:** Thailand.

Gow, Andrew. Associate Professor of History, Department of History and Classics, University of Alberta, Edmonton. Author of *The Red Jews: Antisemitism in an Apocalyptic Age, 1200–1600* (1995). Co-editor of *Continuity and Change: Essays in Honor of Heiko Augustinus Oberman on His 70th Birthday* (2000). Translator of *The Reformation: Roots and Ramifications* by Heiko A. Oberman (1994). Editorial board member, Studies in Medieval and Reformation Thought series, E.J. Brill (1999–). Contributor to *Journal of Early Modern History*, *Medieval Encounters*, *Renaissance Quarterly*, and a number of scholarly collections. **Essay:** Dissolution of Monasteries: Continental Europe.

Green, Bernard, O.S.B. Ampleforth Abbey. Author of *The English Benedictine Congregation* (1980). Editor of *Allanson's History of the English Benedictines* (1978). Contributor to *Benedict's Disciples* (1980), *Ampleforth Journal*, and *Downside Review*. **Essays:** Bede, St.; Benedict of Nursia, St.; Casel, Odo; Gregory I (the Great), St.; Hume, Basil.

Grendler, Paul F. Professor of History, Emeritus, University of Toronto. Author of *Books and Schools in the Italian Renaissance* (1995), *Schooling in Renaissance Italy: Literacy and Learning, 1300–1600* (1989), *Culture and Censorship in Late Renaissance Italy and France* (1981), *The Roman Inquisition and the Venetian Press, 1540–1605* (1977), and *Critics of the Italian World 1530–1560: Anton Francesco Doni, Nicolò Franco, and Ortensio Lando* (1969). Editor of *Roman and German Humanism 1450–1550*, by John D'Amico (1993) and *An Italian Renaissance Reader* (1987, 1992). Editor-in-Chief of *The Encyclopedia of the Renaissance* (1999). Editorial board member, *The Collected Works of Erasmus*, University of Toronto Press (1976–). Contributor to many scholarly publications about the Renaissance. **Essay:** Education of Christian Monastics.

Gross, Rita M. Professor of Comparative Studies in Religion, University of Wisconsin–Eau Claire. Author of *Soaring and Settling: Buddhist Perspectives on Contemporary Social and Religious Issues* (1998). *Feminism and Religion: An Introduction* (1996), and *Buddhism after Patriarchy: A Feminist History, Analysis, and Reconstruction of Buddhism* (1993). Co-editor of *Unspoken Worlds: Women's Religious Lives* (forthcoming). Contributor of articles to many journals and collections. **Essays:** Contemporary Issues: Buddhist; Deities, Buddhist; Dharma; Gampopa; Labdron, Machig; Meditation: Buddhist Perspectives; Milarepa; Padmasambhava; Sexuality: Buddhist Perspectives; Yeshe Tsogyel.

Haile, Getatchew. Cataloguer of Oriental Manuscripts and Regents Professor of Medieval History, Saint John's University, Collegeville, Minnesota. Author of *A Catalogue of Ethiopian Manuscripts* (1979, 1985, 1987, and 1993) and *The Different Collections of Nägs' Hymns* (1983). Editor of several publications including *Beauty of the Creation* (1991), *The Epistle of Humanity* (1990), *The Faith of the Unctionists* (1990). Contributor to *Encyclopedia of Africa South of the Sahara* (1997), *The Coptic Encyclopedia* (1991), and other books. **Essay:** Ethiopia.

Hale, Robert, O.S.B. Cam. Prior, New Camaldoli Hermitage, Big Sur, California. Author of *Canterbury and Rome: Sister Churches* (1982), *Il Cosmo e Cristo: Basi di una teologia ecologica* (1974), and *Christ and the Universe: Teilhard de Chardin and the Cosmos* (1973). Editor of *Vita Monastica* (1978–84), *American Benedictine Review* (1984), *Monaci e ecumenismo* (1978), and *Comunità monastica a profezia* (1975). Contributor to *The New Dictionary of Catholic Spirituality* (1993), *Parola e Spirito*, and several other journals. **Essays:** Camaldolese; Damian, Peter, St.

Harris, Elizabeth J. Executive Secretary for Inter-Faith Relations, Methodist Church, Britain. Author of *What Buddhists Believe* (1998), *Ananda Metteyya: The First British Emissary of Buddhism* (1998), and *The Gaze of the Coloniser* (1994). Editor of *Discernment* (1994–). Contributor to journals, including *Dialogue* (Sri Lanka) and *Scottish Journal of Religious Studies*, and book collections, including *Tissa Balasuriya Omi: Felicitation Volume* (1997) and *Windows on Wesley* (1999). **Essays:** Anurādhapura, Sri Lanka; Dharmapāla, Anagārika; Gender Studies: Buddhist Perspectives.

Harris, Ian. Reader in Religious Studies, University College of St. Martin, Lancaster. Author of *The Continuity of Madhyamaka and Yogacārā in Indian Mahāyāna Buddhism* (1991). Editor of *Buddhism and Politics* (1999), *Journal of Buddhist Ethics* (1995–), *Bulletin of the British Association for the Study of Religions* (1994–97), and *Contemporary Religions: A World Guide* (1992). Contributor to the collections *Buddhism and Ecology* (1997), *Oxford Dictionary of World Religions* (1994), and *Attitudes to Nature* (1994), and the journals, *Religion* and *Journal of Buddhist Ethics*. **Essays:** Libraries: Buddhist; Manuscript Production: Buddhist; Nālandā, India.

Hart, Patrick, O.C.S.O. Abbey of Gethsemani, Trappist, Kentucky. Formerly, Thomas Merton's last secretary. Editor of seven volumes of Merton's journals for Harper San Francisco, as well as *The Intimate Merton: His Life from His Journals* (with Jonathan Montaldo, 1999) and other works by and about Merton. **Essays:** Gethsemani, Kentucky; Merton, Thomas.

Hatlie, Peter. University Lecturer, Department of Modern Greek and Byzantine Studies, University of Groningen. Contributor to *Byzantine and Modern Greek Studies*, *Greek, Roman, and Byzantine Studies*, *Dumbarton Oaks Papers*, and other periodicals. **Essay:** Theodore of Stoudios, St.

Hayes, Dawn Marie. Assistant Professor of European History, Iowa College. **Essay:** Protestant Monasticism: Waldensian.

Heirman, Ann. Research Assistant, Fund for Scientific Research, Department of Chinese Language and Culture, University of Ghent. Contributor to *Buddhist Studies Review*, *Études Asiatiques*, *Journal of the International Association of Buddhist Studies*, and *Indian Journal of Buddhist Studies*. **Essays:** Rules, Buddhist (Vinaya): Monks; Rules, Buddhist (Vinaya): Nuns.

Hen, Yitzhak. University Lecturer, Department of History, University of Haifa. Author of *Culture and Religion in Menouingian Gaul,* A.D. 481–751 (1995). Editor of *The Sacramentary of Echternach* (1997). Contributor to *Revue Belge de Philogie et d'Histoire*, *Revue Bénédictine*, *Anglo-Saxon England*, and *Journal of Theological Studies*. **Essays:** Echternach, Luxembourg; Isidore of Seville, St.; Pirminius, St.

Herbel, Richard G., O.S.B. Contributing editor of *The Bride of Christ* (1996–). **Essay:** Protestant Monasticism: Lutheran.

Hester, David Paul. Priest of the Antiochian Orthodox Church, and Pastor of St. George Orthodox Church, Vicksburg, Mississippi. Author of *The Monasticism and Spirituality of the Italo-Greeks* (1992), *Italo-Greek Monastic Spirituality* (1988), and *The Jesus Prayer: A Gift from the Fathers* (1985). Contributor to *St. Vladimir's Theological Quarterly*, *Studia Patristica*, *Bulletin de Saint Sulpice*, and *Patristic and Byzantine Review*. **Essays:** Italo-Greek Monasticism; Paisy Velichkovsky; Sergius of Radonezh, St.

Hillis, Gregory A. Instructor, Department of Religious Studies, University of Virginia. **Essay:** Tibetan Lineages: Nyingma.

Hirschfeld, Yitzhar. Associate Professor, Institute of Archaeology, Hebrew University, Jerusalem. Author of *Roman Bath of Hammat Gader* (1997), *Palestinian House* (1995), *Judean Desert Monasteries* (1992), and *Map of Herodium* (1985). Editor of *Aqueducts in Ancient Palestine* (1989) and *Tiberius* (1987). **Essay:** Food: Christian Perspectives.

Hoffman, Frank J. Assistant Professor, Department of Philosophy, West Chester University, West Chester, Pennsylvania, and visiting scholar, Department of Asian and Middle Eastern Studies, University of Pennsylvania. Author of *Rationality and Mind in Early Buddhism* (1987, 1992). Editor of *Pali Buddhism* (1996).Series editor, Resources in Asian Philosophy and Religion, Greenwood Press. Editorial board member, *Asian Philosophy*. Contributor to *Cultural Otherness and Beyond* (1998), *Companion Encyclopedia of Asian Philosophy* (1997), *Religious Studies*, and other scholarly publications. **Essays:** Aśoka; Buddha (Śākyamuni); Buddhism: Overview; Buddhism: Western (with Brian Williard, Tarek Tannous, Catherine Oravez, and Adam Morris); Buddhology.

Hoffmann, Richard C. Professor of History, York University, Toronto. Author of *Fishers' Craft and Lettered Art* (1997) and *Land, Liberties, and Lordship in a Late Medieval Countryside* (1989). Contributor to such collections as *Managing Water in Medieval Europe* (1999), *The Salt of Common Life* (1994), and journals including *American Historical Review*. **Essay:** Fishing and Fish Culture, Western Christian.

Hollerman, Ephrem (Rita), O.S.B. Associate Professor of Theology, College of Saint Benedict, St. Joseph, Minnesota. Author of *The Reshaping of a Tradition: American Benedictine Women, 1852–1881*. Editor of *American Benedictine Review* (1994–). Contributor to *The Encyclopedia of American Catholic History* (1997). **Essay:** Riepp, Benedicta (Sybilla).

Holt, John. Professor of Religion, Bowdoin College, Brunswick, Maine. Author of *The Religious World of Kirti Sri: Buddhism, Art, and Politics in Late Medieval Sri Lanka* (1996), *Buddha in the Crown: Avalokitesvara in the Buddhist Traditions of Sri Lanka* (1991, 1994), *Discipline: The Canonical Buddhism of the Vinayapitaka* (1981, 1995, 1999), and *A Guide to the Buddhist Religion* (with Frank Reynolds and John Strong, 1981). Translator, *Anagatavamsa Desana: The Sermon of the Chronicle-to-be* (1993). Contributor to numerous anthologies and journals. **Essays:** Kandy, Sri Lanka; Regulations: Buddhist Perspectives; Sri Lanka: Sites.

Hongladarom, Soraj. Assistant Professor, Department of Philosophy, Faculty of Arts, Chulalongkorn University, Bangkok. Author of *Horizons of Philosophy: Knowledge, Philosophy, and Thai Society* (1998) and *Science Education Crisis in Thailand* (1998). Editor of *Journal of Buddhist Studies* (1994–) and *Journal of the Faculty of Arts* (1993–96). Contributor to *Buddhism and Human Rights* (1998) and *APA Newsletter on Computer and Philosophy*. **Essays:** Laicization of Spirituality: Buddhist Perspectives; Timekeeping: Buddhist Perspectives.

Howe, Elizabeth Teresa. Professor of Spanish, Department of Romance Languages, Tufts University, Boston. Author of *Mystical Imagery: Santa Teresa and San Juan de la Cruz* (1988). General editor of Medieval Mysticism series for Peter Lang (1990–98). Editor of *Instruccion de la Mujer Cristiana* by Juan Luis Vives (1993). Contributor to *Feminist Encyclopedia of Spanish Literature* (1999), *Isabel la Catolica* (1999), and other scholarly publications. **Essay:** John of the Cross, St.

Howe, John. Professor, Department of History, Texas Tech University, Lubbock. Author of *Church Reform and Social Change in Eleventh-Century Italy* (1997). Contributor to anthologies and journals including *Varieties of Religious Conversion in the Middle Ages* (1997), *Revue Bénédictine*, *Catholic Historical Review*, and *Cahiers de civilization médiévale*. **Essays:** Oblates; Saints, Italian Benedictine.

Hughes, Kevin L. Assistant Director, Core Humanities Program, Villanova University, Villanova, Pennsylvania. Editor of *2 Thessalonians: Two Medieval Apocalyptic Commentaries* (1999). Contributor to *The Apocalyptic Year 1000* (1999), *American Benedictine Review*, and *Augustinian Studies*. **Essay:** Augustinian Rule.

Huntington, John C. Author of *The Phur-pa: Tibetan Ritual Daggers* (1975) and *Oceanic Art* (exhibition catalog, 1966). Contributor of articles and photographs to many exhibition catalogs, archival publications, book collections, journals, and web publications. **Essays:** Architecture: Buddhist Monasteries in Southern Asia (with Chaya Chandrasekhar); Maṇḍala; Mount Meru; Stūpa.

Hüsken, Ute. Research Assistant, Institute for Indian and Buddhist Studies, Göttingen University. Author of *Die Vorschriften für die buddhistische Nonnegemeinde im Vinaya-Pitaka der Theravaadin* (1997). Contributor to *Journal of the International Association of Buddhist Studies*, *Buddhist Studies*, and other scholar works. **Essay:** Rules, Buddhist (Vinaya): Historical.

Hutchison, Carole A. Independent archaeologist. Author of *The Hermit Monks of Grandmont* (1989). Contributor to *Current Archaeology* (1991). **Essay:** Grandmontines.

Huxley, Andrew. Senior Lecturer in the Laws of Southeast Asia, Law Department, SOAS, University of London. Contributing editor of *Thai Law/Buddhist Law: Essays on the Legal History of Thailand, Laos, and Burma* (1996). Contributor to such journals as *Buddhist Forum*, *Journal of Indian Philosophy*, and *Law and Critique*, and anthologies including *Islamic Family Law* (1990) and *Essays on the Civil Codes of Québec and St. Lucia* (1984). **Essays:** Burma (Myanmar); Rules, Buddhist (Vinaya): Lineage; Taungpila Sayadaw.

Hyers, Conrad. Retired Professor of Comparative Religion, Gustavus Adolphus College, St. Peter, Minnesota. Author of *The Spirituality of Comedy* (1995), *The Laughing Buddha* (1990), *Once-Born, Twice-Born Zen* (1989), *The Meaning of Creation* (1984), and *The Comic Vision and the Christian Faith* (1981). Editor of *Holy Laughter: Essays on Religion in the Comic Perspective* (1969). Contributor to *Religious Pluralism and Truth* (1995) and other book collections. **Essays:** Hakuin; Humor: Buddhist; Humor: Christian.

Irwin, Kevin W. Ordinary Professor of Liturgy and Sacramental Theology, Department of Theology, Catholic University of America, Washington, D.C. Author of many books including *Context and Text: Method in Liturgical Theology* (1994), *Easter: A Guide to Eucharist and Hours* (1991), and *Liturgical Theology: A Primer* (1990). Contributor to *Preserving the Creation* (1994), *A Promise of Presence: Essays in Honor of David N. Power* (1992), *The Thomist*, and a number of other scholarly publications. **Essays:** Lectio Divina; Seasons, Liturgical: Western Christian; Worship Space: Christian Perspectives.

Izbicki, Thomas M. Collection Development Coordinator, Eisenhower Library, Johns Hopkins University, Baltimore, Maryland. Author of *Friars and Jurists: Selected Studies* (1998), *Juan de Torquemada: A Disputation on the Authority of Pope and Council* (1988), and *Protector of the Faith: Cardinal Johannes de Turrecremata and the Defense of the Institutional Church* (1981). Translator of *Conciliarism and Papalism* (with J.H. Burns, 1997). Co-editor of two volumes on Nicholas of Cusa and *Humanity and Divinity in Renaissance and Reformation* (1993). Contributor to journals and collections including *Christian Unity: The Council of Ferrara-Florence 1438/39–1989* (1991). **Essays:** Dominicans: General or Male; Servites; Subiaco, Italy; Thomas Aquinas, St.

Jaffe, Devra. Doctoral student, Department of Religious Studies, Rice University, Houston, Texas. **Essay:** United States: Buddhist.

Janes, Dominic. Research Fellow, Pembroke College, University of Cambridge. Author of *God and Gold in Late Antiquity* (1998). Contributor to *The Community, the Family, and the Saint* (1998), *Early Medieval Europe*, and *Medieval Life*. **Essay:** Cuthbert, St.

Jestice, Phyllis G. Independent scholar. Author of *Wayward Monks and the Religious Revolution of the Eleventh Century* (1997). Contributor to *Medieval Purity and Piety* (1998), *The Joy of Learning and the Love of God: Studies in Honor of Jean Leclercq* (1995), and *Viator*. **Essays:** German Benedictine Reform, Medieval; Gregory VII; Monastics and the World, Medieval; Recluses, Western Christian.

Johnson, Penelope D. (Adviser). Professor of History, New York University, New York City. Author of *Equal in Monastic Profession: Religious Women in Medieval France* (1991) and *Prayer, Patronage, and Power: The Abbey of la Trinité 1032–1187* (1981). Editor of *Selected Reading Lists and Course Outlines from American Colleges and Universities: Medieval History* (1988). Contributor to many works on medieval history, monasticism, and women's studies. **Essay:** Double Houses, Western Christian.

Johnston, Elva. Christ Church, University of Oxford. Contributor to *Die Religion in Geschichte und Gegenwart, vierte Auflage* (forthcoming), *New Dictionary of National Geography* (forthcoming), *Celts and Christians: The Idea of Celtic Christianity* (forthcoming), and *Peritia*. **Essay:** Transvestite Saints.

Johnston, William M. (Editor). Served as Professor of History at University of Massachusetts, Amherst, 1965–99, where he taught Modern European intellectual history and the history of world religions. He can be reached at 369 Rae Street, North Fitzroy, Victoria 3068, Australia. Author of *The Austrian Mind: An Intellectual and Social History, 1848–1938* (1972), *In Search of Italy: Foreign Writers in Northern Italy since 1800* (1987), *Celebrations: The Cult of Anniversaries in Europe and the United States Today* (1991), and *Recent Reference Books in Religion: A Guide for Students, Scholars, Researchers, Buyers, and Readers* (1996).

Jones, Charles B. Assistant Professor, Department of Religion and Religious Education, Catholic University of America, Washington, D.C. Author of *Buddhism in Taiwan: Religion and the State 1660–1990* (1999). Contributor to *Journal of the International Association for Buddhist Studies*, *Journal of Buddhist Ethics*, and *Journal of Chinese Religions*. **Essays:** Nembutsu; Taiwan.

Jones, E.A. St. Anne's College, Oxford. Author of *Hermits and Anchorites of England* (revised edition, forthcoming). Contributor to *Yearbook of Langland Studies*, *English Manuscript*

Studies 1100–1700 (1997), and *Leeds Studies in English*. **Essay:** Hermits: Western Christian.

Jones, Norman L. Professor and Chair, Department of History, and Associate Director, Liberal Arts and Sciences Program, Utah State University, Logan. Author of *The Birth of the Elizabethan Age: England in the 1560s* (1993), *The Parliaments of Elizabethan England* (1990), *God and the Moneylenders: Usury and Law in Early Modern England* (1989), and *Faith by Statute: Parliament and the Settlement of Religion, 1559* (1982). Co-editor of *Interest Groups and Legislation in Elizabethan Parliaments* (special issue of *Parliamentary History*, 1989). **Essay:** Dissolution of Monasteries: England, Ireland, and Wales.

Jorgensen, John. Senior Lecturer, School of Languages and Linguistics, Griffith University, Queensland. Contributor to *Nog'wŏn Sŭnim kohŭi kinyŏm haksulnonch'ong kanhaeng wiwŏn hoe* (1997), *Bulgyo Yongu*, *Korea Observer*, and *Papers on Far Eastern History* (1987). **Essays:** Bodhidharma; Chan/Zen: China; Chan/Zen: Vietnam; China; Hagiography: Buddhist Perspectives; Huineng; Korea: Recent Changes; Mount Wutai, China; Shaolin, China.

Jorgensen, Wayne James. Associate Professor, Department of Church History, Sacred Heart Seminary, Detroit, Michigan. Contributor to *The Oxford Encyclopedia of Reformation* (1996), *Salvation in Christ: A Lutheran-Orthodox Dialogue* (1992), and *St. Vladimir Theological Quarterly*. **Essay:** Orthodox Monasticism: Byzantine.

Jotischky, Andrew. Lecturer in History, Lancaster University. Author of *The Perfection of Solitude: Hermits and Monks in the Crusader States* (1995). Contributor to *The Sabaite Heritage* (2000), *The Christian Heritage of the Holy Land* (1998), *Studies in Church History*, *Levant*, *Cristianesimo nella Storia*, and *Journal of Ecclesiastical History*. **Essay:** Israel/Palestine.

Joyce, Timothy J., O.S.B. Prior, Glastonbury Abbey, Hingham, Massachusetts. Past President, American Benedictine Academy. Author of *Celtic Christianity: A Sacred Tradition, A Vision of Hope* (1998). Editor of *Glastonbury* (1988–) and *American Monastic Newsletter* (1988–94). **Essays:** Columba, St.; Ireland: Sites.

Kabilsingh, Chatsumarn. Associate Professor, Department of Philosophy, Faculty of Liberal Arts, Thammasat University, Bangkok. Author of *Buddhism and Nature Conservation* (1998), *Women and Buddhism* (1997), *Thai Women and Buddhism* (1991), and other books. Editor of *Journal of India Studies* (1998) and several books on religion written in Thai. Contributor to *Gender, Culture, and Religion* (1995) and *Buddhist Behavioral Codes and the Modern World*. **Essay:** Bangkok, Thailand.

Kalas, Veronica. Doctoral candidate, Institute of Fine Arts, New York University, New York City. Contributor to *The Encyclopedia of Early Christian Art and Archaeology* (forthcoming), *Arashtirma Sonuçlari Toplantisi* (forthcoming), *Bir El Knissia at Carthage*, and *Archaeology Odyssey*. **Essay:** Cappadocia, Turkey.

Kavenagh, Terence. Monk, St. Benedict's Monastery, Arcadia, New South Wales. Contributing editor of *Tjurunga: An Australasian Benedictine Review* (1984–90). Contributor to *Inter Fratres* and *Journal of the Australian Catholic Historical Society*. **Essays:** Australia; Congregations, Benedictine; Melk, Austria; Vallombrosans.

Kawamura, Leslie S. Professor, Department of Religious Studies, University of Calgary, Calgary, Alberta. Editor of many works including *Madhyamika and Yogacara: A Study of Mahayana Philosophies* by Nagao Gadjin (also translator, 1991), *The Bodhisattva Doctrine in Buddhism* (1981), and *Buddhist Thought and Asian Civilization: Essays in Honor of Herbert V. Guenther on His Sixtieth Birthday* (with Keith Scott, 1977). **Essay:** Bodhisattva.

Keefer, Sarah Larratt. Associate Professor, Department of English, Trent University. Author of *Psalm-Poem and Psalter-Gloss* (1990) and *The Old English Metrical Psalter* (1979). Co-editor of *New Approaches to Editing Old English Verse* (1998). Contributor to *The Community, the Family, and the Saint* (1998), and a number of scholarly journals. **Essay:** Reform, Tenth-Century Anglo-Saxon Monastic.

Kelly, Joseph F. Professor of Religious Studies, John Carroll University, Cleveland, Ohio. Author of *The World of the Early Christians* (1997), *The Concise Dictionary of Early Christianity* (1992), *Why Is There a New Testament* (1986), and *Scriptores Hiberniae Minores* (1974). Editor of *Journal of Early Christian Studies* (1996–). Contributor many journals including *Vigiliae Christiane*, *Monastic Studies*, and *Journal of Early Christian Studies*. **Essays:** Heretics, Christian; Lérins, France; Wilfrid, St.

Kidder, J. Edward, Jr. Author of many books on the art and history of Japan including *The Art of Japan* (1985), *Early Buddhist Japan* (1972), *Ancient Japan* (1965, 1977), and *Japan before Buddhism* (1959). **Essays:** Buddhist Schools/Traditions: Japan; Fasting: Buddhist; Kyoto, Japan; Nara, Japan; Patrons, Buddhist: Japan; Warrior Monks: Buddhist.

Kieffer-Pülz, Petra. Author of *Die Sīmā Vorschriften zur Regelung der buddhistischen Gemeinde-grenze in älteren buddhistischen Texten* (1992). Editor of *Untersuchungen zur buddhistischen Literatur* (1997), *Bauddha-vidyāsudhākarah: Studies in Honour of H. Bechert* (1997), and many other collections. Contributor to collections and journals including *Journal of Pali and Buddhist Studies* and *Nepal: Past and Present* (1993). **Essays:** Officials: Buddhist; Women's Monasteries: Buddhist.

Kimura, Takeshi. Associate Professor, Faculty of Humanities, Yamaguchi University. Contributor to *Numen*, *Canadian Journal of Native Studies*, *Yamadai Bungaku Kaishi*, *Yamadi Tetsugaku Kenkyū*, and *Shūkyō Kenkyū*. **Essays:** Chan/Zen: Japan; Fujii, Nichidatsu (Nittatsu); Japan: Sites.

King, Sallie B. Professor, Department of Philosophy and Religion, James Madison University, Harrisonburg, Virginia. Author of *Buddha Nature* (1991) and *Passionate Journey: The Spiritual Autobiography of Satomi Myodo* (1987). Editor of *The Sound* *of Liberating Truth* (with Paul Ingram, 1999) and *Engaged Buddhism: Buddhist Liberation Movements in Asia* (with Christopher S. Queen, 1996). Contributor to *Buddhist-Christian Studies and other* journals. **Essays:** Peace Movements, Buddhist; Self-Immolation, Buddhist.

Kinnard, Jacob N. Visiting Assistant Professor, Department of Religion, Northwestern University, Evanston, Illinois. Author of *Imaging Wisdom: Seeing and Knowing in the Art of Indian Buddhism* (1999). Contributor to *Body Matters* (forthcoming), *Journal of the American Academy of Religion*, *Journal of the International Association of Buddhist Studies*, and *Journal of Religion*. **Essay:** Bodh Gayā, India.

Kirchner, Thomas L. Institute for Zen Studies, Hanazono University. Editor of *Zen Buddhism Today* (1996–99) and *Japanese Journal of Religious Studies* (1992–98). Contributor to *Zen Buddhism Today* and *Eastern Buddhist*. **Essay:** Dialogue, Intermonastic: Buddhist Perspectives.

Kleine, Christoph. Lecturer, Marburg University and Freie University, Berlin. Author of *A Multilingual Dictionary of Chinese Buddhism* (1999) and *Hönens Buddhismus des Reinen Landes: Reform, Reformation oder Häresie* (1996). Contributor to *Religionen im Wandel der Kosmologien* (1999), *Japanese Religions*, *Studies in Central and East Asian Buddhism*, and *Zeitschrift für Religionswissenschaft*. **Essays:** Hermits: Buddhist; Holy Men/Holy Women: Buddhist Perspectives.

Kollar, Rene. Professor/Chairperson, Department of History, St. Vincent College, and monk, St. Vincent Archabbey, Latrobe, Pennsylvania. Author of *A Universal Appeal: Aspects of the Revival of Monasticism in the West in the 19th and Early 20th Centuries* (1996), *Abbot Aelred Carlyle, Caldey Island, and the Anglo-Catholic Revival in England* (1995), *The Return of the Benedictines to London: The History of Ealing Abbey from 1896 to Independence* (1990), and *Westminster Cathedral: From Dream to Reality* (1987). Associate editor of *American Benedictine Review* (1990–94). Contributor to *Journal of Welsh Religious History*, *American Benedictine Review*, and other journals. **Essay:** Wimmer, Boniface.

Kopf, Gereon. Assistant Professor, Department of Religion and Philosophy, Luther College, Decorah, Iowa. Author of *Beyond Personal Identity* (forthcoming). Contributor to *The Couch and the Tree* (1998). **Essays:** Mount Hiei, Japan; Nhát Hanh, Thích; Zen and the West.

Kosuta, Matthew. Doctoral student, University of Quebec, Montreal. Contributor to *Religiologiques*. **Essay:** Examinations, Theravādin (with Mathieu Boisvert).

Krawchuk, Andrii S. Faculty of Theology, St. Paul University, Ottawa, Ontario. **Essays:** Kiev (Kyiv), Ukraine; Russia: History; Ukraine.

LaFleur, William R. The E. Dale Saunders Professor in Japanese Studies, Department of Asian and Middle Eastern Studies, University of Pennsylvania, Philadelphia. Author of *Liquid Life: Abortion and Buddhism in Japan* (1994), *Buddhism: A Cultural Perspective* (1988), *The Karma of Words: Buddhism and the Literary Arts in Medieval Japan* (1983), and *Mirror for the Moon: A Selection of Poems by Saigyō (1118–1190)* (1978). Editor of *The Eastern Buddhist*, *Flowing Traces: Buddhism in the Literary and Visual Arts of Japan* (with James Sanford and Masatoshi Nagatomi, 1992), *Dōgen Studies* (1985), and *Zen and Japanese Thought* by Masao Abe (1985). Contributor to many journals and collections of articles. **Essay:** Dōgen.

Lai, Whalen. Professor, Religious Studies Program and East Asian Languages and Culture, University of California, Davis. Co-author of *Buddhismus und Christentum: Geschichte, Konfrontation, Dialog* (1997). Co-editor of *Early Ch'an in China and Tibet* (1983). Contributor of more than 90 articles and chapters to scholarly publications. **Essays:** Economic Justice, Buddhist; Gnostic Cosmogony in Buddhism; Governance: Buddhist Perspectives; Holy Men in Power (Hierocrats), Buddhist; Images: Buddhist Perspectives; Initiation: Buddhist Perspectives; Intercession for the Dead, Buddhist; Master and Pupil: Buddhist Perspectives; Prophethood, Japanese Buddhist; Scholastics, Buddhist; Social Services: Buddhist; Topography, Sacred (Buddhist).

Law, John Easton. Senior Lecturer, Department of History, University of Wales, Swansea. Author of *Italy in the Age of the Renaissance* (with Dennis Hay, 1989). Editor of *Renaissance Studies* (1997–). Contributor to *Transactions of the Royal Historical Society* and *Renaissance Studies*. **Essay:** Florence, Italy.

Lebecq, Stéphane. Professor of Medieval History, Charles-de-Gaulle de Lille University. Author of *L'économie médiévale* (1993), *Les origins franques* (1990), and *Marchands et navigateurs frisons du haut Moyen Age* (1983). Editor of *Les hommes et la mer dans l'Europe du Nord-Ouest de l'Antiquité à nos jours* (1986). Contributor to *Dictionnaire encyclopédique du Moyen Age chrétien* (1997) and other scholarly works. **Essay:** France: Sites.

Lehmberg, Stanford. Professor of History, Emeritus, University of Minnesota. Author of many books including *Cathedrals under Siege* (1996), *The Peoples of the British Isles* (1992), and *The Reformation of Cathedrals* (1988). Editor of *Sir Thomas Elyot, The Book Named the Governor*. Editorial board member of *Anglican and Episcopal History* (1986–) and *Sixteenth Century Journal* (1983–). Contributor to *Anglican Theological Review*. **Essay:** Cathedral Priories (England).

Lewis, Todd T. Associate Professor of Asian Religions, Holy Cross College, Worcester, Massachusetts. Author of *Mahayana Buddhist Texts from Nepal: Narratives and Rituals of Newar Buddhism* (2000) and *A Syllabus of Himalayan History, Anthropology and Religion* (1995). Associate editor of *Himalayan Research Bulletin* (1991–99). Contributor to journals, such as *Journal of the International Association of Buddhist Studies*, and anthologies, including *Selves in Time and Place: Identities, Experience, and History in Nepal* (1998). **Essays:** Kathmandu Valley, Nepal; Nepal: History; Nepal: Sites.

Lindberg, David C. Hilldale Professor of the History of Science, University of Wisconsin–Madison. Author of many books including *Roger Bacon and the Origins of Perspectiva in the Middle*

Ages (1996) and *The Beginnings of Western Science: The European Scientific Tradition in Philosophical, Religious, and Institutional Context, 600 B.C.–A.D. 1450* (1992). Editor of *The Cambridge History of Science* (forthcoming), *Reappraisals of the Scientific Revolution* (1990), and other books. Editorial board member of several journals including *MEDIAEVALIA* (1996–) and *Early Science and Medicine* (1994). Contributor of more than 50 articles to scholarly publications. **Essay:** Bacon, Roger.

Lipschutz, Julianna. Bibliographic Specialist, East Asian Collection, Van Pelt-Dietrich Library Center, University of Pennsylvania, Philadelphia. **Essay:** Repentance Rituals, Buddhist.

Lishka, Dennis. Assistant Professor, Department of Religious Studies, University of Wisconsin–Oshkosh. **Essays:** Eisai (Yosai); Zen, Arts of.

Logan, F. Donald. Emeritus Professor of History, Emmanuel College, Boston. Author of *Runaway Religious in Medieval England c. 1240–1540* (1996), *The Vikings in History* (1983, 1991), and *Excommunication and the Secular Arm in Medieval England* (1969). Contributor to numerous journals including *English Historical Review.* **Essay:** Fugitive Religious.

Madigan, Kevin. Department of History, Catholic Theological Union, Chicago. Contributor to *Journal of Religion*, *Harvard Theological Review*, and *Traditio.* **Essay:** Joachim of Fiore.

Marra, Claudia. Associate Professor, Department of International Culture, Nagasaki Gaikokugo Tanki Daigakv. Contributor to *Nietzsche Jahrbuch V* (1998) and *Nagasaki Gaigo Journal.* **Essay:** Japan: History.

Mathews, Edward G., Jr. Author of *The Armenian Commentary on the Book of Genesis Attributed to Ephrem the Syrian* (1998). Translator, *St. Ephrem the Syrian: Selected Prose Works* (with Joseph P. Amar, 1994). Contributor to *The Book of Genesis in Jewish and Oriental Christian Interpretation* (1997) and several journals. **Essays:** Armenia; Lavra; Nestorian Monasticism; Syria.

McCallum, Donald F. Professor, Department of Art History, University of California, Los Angeles. Author of *Zenkōji and Its Icon* (1994). Editorial board member of *Artibus Asiae* (1994–) and *Journal of Japanese Studies* (1998–). Contributor to *Archives of Asian Art* (1996). **Essays:** Nagano, Japan; Visual Arts, Buddhist: Japan.

McCarty, Steve. Professor, General Education, Kagawa Junior College, Shikoku Island, Japan. Co-author of *Shikoku Bilingual Guidebook* (1993) and *Kagawa* (1988). Editor of *Kagawa Junior College Journal* (1997–) and *WWW Journal of Online Education* (1998–). Contributor to many education journals and collections including *Bairingaru no Sekai* (1999). **Essays:** Mount Kōya, Japan; Shikoku, the Pilgrimage Island of Japan; Syncretism in Japan, Buddhist.

McGuckin, John. Professor of Early Church History, Union Theological Seminary, New York. Author of several books including *St. Cyril of Alexandria: On the Unity of Christ* (1995), *St. Cyril of Alexandria and the Christological Controversy* (1994), and *Byzantium and Other Poems* (1994). Editor of *Pro Ecclesia* (1991–) and *Scripture Bulletin* (1985–90). Contributor to *Studies in Church History*, *Studia Patristica*, and other journals. **Essays:** Gregory of Nazianzus, St.; John of Damascus, St.; Macrina, St.; Pachomius, St.; Shenoute of Atripe.

McLaughlin, Mary Martin. Independent scholar. Author of *Intellectual Freedom and Its Limitations in the University of Paris, Thirteenth and Fourteenth Centuries* (1977). Contributor of many articles on Abelard and Heloise to journals and collections, including *Pierre Abélard, Pierre le Vénérable: Les courants philosophiques, littéraires et artistiques en Occident* (1953) and *Listening to Heloise* (1999). **Essay:** Catherine of Bologna, St.

McMahan, David L. Visiting Assistant Professor, Department of Religion, University of Vermont. Contributor to *Ethics and World Religion: Cross-cultural Case Studies* (1999) and *History of Religions.* **Essays:** Buddhist Schools/Traditions: South Asia; Dharamsala, India (Tibetan); Mahāyāna.

McMahon, Patrick Thomas, O.Carm. Director of the Carmelitana Collection, Washington, D.C., and Lecturer, Washington Theological Union. **Essays:** Carmelites: Female; Theology, Western Christian: Carmelite.

McWilliams, Philip E. Contributor to *Rarer Gifts than Gold: Fourteenth-Century Art in Scottish Collections* (1988). **Essays:** Archaeology: Western Europe; Architecture: Western Christian Monasteries; Augustinian Friars/Hermits; Canons Regular, Origins of; Claustration (Cloister), Rules of; Cluniacs; Cluny, France; Visual Arts, Western Christian: Liturgical Furnishings.

Merkley, Paul A. Professor, Music Department, University of Ottawa, Ottawa, Ontario. Author of several books including *Music and Patronage in the Sforza Court* (with L. Matthews, 1999), *Modal Assignment in Northern Tonaries* (1992), and *The Melodic Tradition of Ambrosian Office Antiphons.* Editor of *Chant and Its Peripheries* (1998) and *Beyond the Moon: Festschrift Luther Dittmer* (1990). Contributor to many scholarly publications including *Journal of Musicology*, *Musica e Storia,* and *The Divine Office in the Latin Middle Ages: Methodology and Source Studies, Regional Developments, Hagiography* (2000). **Essays:** Antonians; Plainchant.

Mews, Constant J. Senior Lecturer, Department of History, Monash University, Melbourne. Author of *The Lost Love Letters of Heloise and Abelard* (1999) and *Peter Abelard* (1995). Editor of *Hildegard of Bingen and Gendered Theology in Judeo-Christian Traditions* (1995) and *Petri Abelardi Opera Theologica III* (1987). Editorial board member of *Journal of Religious History* (1997–) and *Didascalica* (1997–). Contributor to many journals and anthologies. **Essay:** William of Hirsau.

Mills, Frank A. Professor of Celtic Studies, Department of Humanities, Marylhurst University, Portland, Oregon. Editor of *Brigit's Feast: The Journal of Celtic Wisdom, History, Culture, and Folklore* (1997–) and *The Bear Essential* (1997). Contributor to *Brigit's Feast* and *Celtic Heart* (web journal). **Essays:** Botany; Gardens: Christian Perspectives; Hungary; Netherlands; Pharmacology; Switzerland.

Mills, Martin A. Tutorial Fellow, School of African and Asian Studies, University of Sussex. Contributor to *Scottish Journal of Religious Studies* and *Recent Research in Ladakh* (1997). **Essays:** Ladakh, India; Liturgy: Buddhist; Tibetan Lineages: Gelukpa.

Minnich, Nelson H. Professor and Chair, Department of Church History, and Professor, Department of History, Catholic University of America, Washington, D.C. Author of *The Catholic Reformation: Council, Churchmen, and Controversies* (1993) and *The Fifth Lateran Council (1512–17): Studies in Its Membership, Diplomacy, and Proposals for Reform* (1993). Editor of *The Encyclopedia of the Renaissance* and *Studies in Catholic History in Honor of John Tracy Ellis* (1985). Advisory editor, *Catholic Historical Review* (1990–). Contributor to *Annuarium Historiae Concilliorum* and other scholarly publications. **Essay:** Francis of Paola, St.

Mitchell, Margaret M. Associate Professor of New Testament, Divinity School, University of Chicago. Author of *Paul and the Rhetoric of Reconciliation* (1991). Editor of *Journal of Biblical Literature*. Contributor to many religious studies journals including *Journal of Biblical Literature* and *Journal of Early Christian Studies*. **Essay:** Chrysostom, John, St.

Moorhead, John. Reader, Department of History, University of Queensland. Author of several books including *Ambrose* (1999), *Justinian* (1994), and *Suger's Deeds of Louis the Fat* (1992). Corresponding editor, *Early Medieval Europe* (1992–). Contributor to *Historia*, *Byzantion*, and other journals. **Essay:** Symeon the New Theologian, St.

Morris, Adam. Bachelor of Arts in Philosophy, West Chester University, West Chester, Pennsylvania. **Essay:** Buddhism: Western (with Frank J. Hoffman, Brian Williard, Tarek Tannous, and Catherine Oravez).

Nguyen, Trian. Lecturer, University of California at Santa Cruz. **Essay:** Visual Arts, Buddhist: Southeast Asia.

Nicholson, Helen J. Lecturer in Medieval History, School of History and Archaeology, Cardiff University. Author of *Chronicle of the Third Crusade: A Translation of the Itinerarium Peregrinorum et Gesta Regis Ricardi* (1997) and *Templars, Hospitallers, and Teutonic Knights: Images of the Military Orders, 1128–1291* (1993). Contributor to *From Clermont to Jerusalem: The Crusades and Crusader Societies* (1998), *The Military Orders: Fighting for the Faith and Caring for the Sick* (1997), and several history journals. **Essays:** Hospitallers (Knights of Malta since 1530); Templars.

Nietupski, Paul. Assistant Professor, Department of Religious Studies, John Carroll University, Cleveland, Ohio. Author of *Labrang Monastery: A Tibetan Buddhist Monastery at the Crossroads of Four Civilizations* (1998). Contributor to *Journal of Indian Philosophy*. **Essays:** Clothing: Buddhist Perspectives; Hygiene: Buddhist Perspectives; Medicine, Buddhist.

Nolan, Mary Lee. Professor of Geography, Department of Geosciences, Oregon State University, Corvallis. Author of *Christian Pilgrimage in Modern Western Europe* (with Sidney Nolan, 1989). Contributor of many articles on pilgrimage to journals and collections including *Sacred Places, Sacred Spaces: The Geography of Pilgrimages* (1997), *Geographia Religionum* (1994), and *Pilgrimage in Latin America* (1991). **Essay:** Pilgrimages, Christian: Western Europe.

Nuth, Joan M. Associate Professor, Religious Studies Department, John Carroll University, Cleveland, Ohio. Author of *Wisdom's Daughter: The Theology of Julian of Norwich* (1991). Contributor to *The New Dictionary of Catholic Spirituality* (1993), *The Catholic Theological Society of America Proceedings*, *Theological Studies*, and *Cross Currents*. **Essay:** Elizabeth of Schönau.

Nyberg, Tore. Professor, Institute of History and Western Civilization, University of Southern Denmark, Odense University. Author of numerous books including *Birgittinsk festgåva* (1991), *Die Kirche in Skandinavien* (1986), and *Skt. Peters efterfolgere i brydningstider* (1979). Editor of *Birgittiana* (1996–), *Mediaeval Scandinavia* (1970–99), and other works. Contributor to many history and religion publications. **Essays:** Scandinavia; Vadstena, Sweden.

O'Loughlin, Thomas. Lecturer in Theology, Department of Theology and Religious Studies, University of Wales, Lampeter. Author of *Newman: Seeker after Truth* (1988). Editor of *History Ireland* (1994–), *Milltown Studies* (1990–97), and *Proceedings of the Irish Biblical Association* (1993–), *Intercom* (1989–91), and *The Catholic University* by Cardinal Newman (1990). Contributor to a number of anthologies and journals. **Essays:** Anticlericalism: Christian Perspectives; Celtic Monasticism; David, St.; Fasting: Western Christian; Hagiography: Christian Perspectives; Island Monasteries, Christian; Manuscript Production: Christian; Martyrs: Western Christian; Master and Pupil: Christian Perspectives; Penitential Books; St. Gallen, Switzerland.

Opsahl, Erhard P. Teacher, Luther Preparatory School, Watertown, Wisconsin, and retired Colonel, U.S. Army. Contributing editor of *The Online Reference Book for Medieval Studies*. **Essay:** Teutonic Order.

Oravez, Catherine. Graduate student, Department of Philosophy, West Chester University, West Chester, Pennsylvania. **Essay:** Buddhism: Western (with Frank J. Hoffman, Brian Williard, Tarek Tannous, and Adam Morris).

Pagani, Catherine. Associate Professor, Department of Art and Art History, University of Alabama. Author of *The First Emperor of China* (1989). Contributor to numerous anthologies and journals including *Colonialism and the Object* (1998), *Canadian Art Review*, and *Victorian: Style of Empire* (1996). **Essays:** Visual Arts, Buddhist: China; Visual Arts, Buddhist: India.

Papadakis, Aristeides. Department of History, University of Maryland. Author of *Crisis in Byzantium: The Filioque Controversy in the Patriarchate of Gregory II of Cyprus (1283–1289)* (1983, 1996) and *The Christian East and the Rise of the Papacy: The Church 1071–1453* (1994). Contributor to *Traditio*, *Greek*

Orthodox Theological Review, and other scholarly publications. **Essay:** Palamas, Gregory, St.

Parsons, David. Senior Lecturer in Church Archaeology, University of Leicester. Author of *Churches and Chapels: Investigating Places of Worship* (1998), *Raunds Furnells: The Anglo-Saxon Church and Churchyard* (with A. Boddington, 1996), *Architecture and Liturgy in the Early Middle Ages* (1989), and *Books and Buildings: Architectural Description before and after Bede* (1988). Editor of many publications including *Stone: Quarrying and Building in England, A.D. 43–1525* (1990), *Eleanor of Castile, 1290–1990* (1991), and *Transactions of the Leicestershire Archaeological and Historical Society* (1988–). Contributor of many articles to archaeology journals and anthologies. **Essays:** Fulda, Germany; Germany: Sites; St. Riquier, France.

Payton, James R., Jr. Professor of History, Redeemer College. Editor of *Christian Scholar's Review* (1988–91). Contributor to numerous anthologies and journals including *Calvin Theological Journal, Church History, Articles on Calvin and Calvinism* (1992), and *In Honour of John Calvin, 1509–1564* (1987). **Essays:** Gregory of Nyssa, St.; Iconoclasm (Controversy).

Percival, John. Professor of Ancient History, School of History and Archaeology, Cardiff University. Author of *The Reign of Charlemagne* (with H.R. Loyn, 1975) and *The Roman Villa* (1976, 1988). Contributor to *Latomus, Journal of Ecclesiastical History, Fifth-Century Gaul: A Crisis of Identity?* (1992), and other publications. **Essay:** Martin of Tours, St.

Peterson, Michael D. Branch Librarian, Graduate Theological Union Library, Berkeley, California. Co-author of *Historical Dictionary of the Orthodox Church* (1996). Contributor to *Summary of Proceedings: Annual Conference of the American Theological Library Association* (1993, 1995). **Essays:** Elders, Russian Monastic (Startsi); Fasting: Eastern Christian; Mount Sinai, Egypt; New Skete, New York; Office, Daily: Eastern Christian; Philokalia; Seraphim of Sarov, St.

Pietsch, Sigrid. Lecturer on Indo-Tibetan Buddhism/Classical Tibetan Literature, Department of Religious Studies, Rice University, Houston, Texas. **Essays:** Sakya Pandita (Sapen); Tibetan Lineages: Kagyü; Tibetan Lineages: Sakya.

Podskalsky, Gerhard, S.J. Professor of Ancient Church History, Byzantine and Slavic Theology, Philosophisch-theologische Hochschule, St. Georgen, Frankfurt am Main. Author of numerous books including *Theologische Literatur de Mittelalters in Bulgarien und Serbien (865–1459)* (1999) and *Griechische Theologie in der Zeit der Türkenherrschaft (1453–1821)* (1988). Editor of *Amore del Bello* (1991), *La Russie* (1990), and *Una chiesa nella storia* (1989). Contributor to many scholarly publications. **Essay:** Bulgaria.

Popović, Svetlana. Author of *Mileševa Monastery* (1995), *The Cross in the Circle* (1994), and *Tronoša Monastery* (1987). Editor of *Saopštenja of the Institute for the Protection of Historical Monuments–Belgrade* (1985–92). Contributor to journals, including *Canadian Institute of Balkan Studies*, and anthologies, including *Work and Worship at the Theotokos Evergetis 1050–1200* (1997). **Essay:** Serbia.

Porceddu, Laura. Architect, Helsinki. **Essays:** Angkor Wat, Cambodia; Borobudur, Java, Indonesia; Buddhist Schools/Traditions: Southeast Asia; Gardens: Buddhist Perspectives; Lhasa, Tibet.

Postles, Dave. Marc Fitch Research Fellow, University of Leicester. **Essays:** Augustinian Canons; England: History.

Potts, Cassandra. Associate Professor of History, Middlebury College, Middlebury, Vermont. Author of *Monastic Revival and Regional Identity in Early Normandy* (1997). Contributor to anthologies and journals including *Anglo-Normal Political Culture and the 12th-century Renaissance* (1997), *Anglo-Norman Studies*, and *Haskins Society Journal*. **Essay:** Mont-St.-Michel, France.

Powell, James M. Professor Emeritus, Department of History, Syracuse University, Syracuse, New York. Author of *Albertanus of Brescia: The Pursuit of Happiness in the Thirteenth Century* (1992), *Anatomy of a Crusade* (1986), and *Liber Angustalis* (1972). Editor of *Innocent III: Vicar of Christ or Lord of the World?* (1994) and *Muslims under Latin Rule* (1990). Contributor to *Iberia and the Mediterranean World* (1995) and *Military Orders* (1994). **Essays:** Francis of Assisi, St.; Franciscans: General or Male; Trinitarians.

Powers, C. John. Senior Lecturer, Faculty of Asian Studies, Australian National University, Canberra. Author of *Introduction to Tibetan Buddhism* (1995) and *The Yogacara School of Buddhism: A Bibliography* (1991). Coeditor, with James Fieser, of *Scriptures of the East* and *Scriptures of the West* (both 1998). Translator of *Wisdom of Buddha: The Samdhinirmocana Sutra* (1995) and *Two Commentaries on the Samdhinirmocana-Sutra* (1992). **Essays:** Abbot: Buddhist; Patrons, Buddhist: India; Tibet: History; Tibet: Sites.

Price, Richard M. Dean of Studies and Head of the Department of Church History, Heythrop College, University of London. Author of *Augustine* (1997). Translator of Theodoret of Cyrrhus, *A History of the Monks of Syria* (1985). **Essays:** Body: Christian Perspectives; Sexuality: Christian Perspectives; Stylites.

Proksch, Nikola, O.S.B. Contributor to *Monks of England* (1997) and *Hl. Willibald 787–1987* (1987). **Essays:** Boniface, St.; Willibrord, St.

Prokurat, Michael. Assistant Professor, School of Theology, University of St. Thomas, Houston, Texas. Author of *A Historical Dictionary of the Orthodox Church* (1996), *On the Edge of the World* (1992), and *Haggai and Zechariah 1–8: A Form Critical Analysis* (1989). Editor of *Priest's Guide* (1986) and *Parish Bylaws* (1985). Contributor to *Catholic Bible Quarterly* (1989), *St. Vladimir's Theological Quarterly* (1989), and *The Bible in Churches* (1998). **Essays:** Historiography, Recent: Eastern Christian; Joseph of Volokolamsk, St.; Martyrs: Eastern Christian; Nilus of Sora, St.; Orthodox Monasticism: Slavic; Stephen of Perm, St.; Theodosius of Kiev, St.

Ramsey, Boniface, O.P. St. Vincent Ferrer Priory, New York. Author of *John Cassian: The Conferences* (1997), *Ambrose* (1997), *The Sermons of St. Maximus of Turin* (1989), and *Beginning to Read the Fathers* (1985). Contributor to *Encyclopedia of Early Christianity* (1997), *The New Dictionary of Theology* (1987), and several theology journals. **Essays:** Ambrose, St.; Cassian, John; Persecution: Christian Perspectives.

Ranft, Patricia. Professor, Department of History, Central Michigan University, Mount Pleasant. Author of *A Woman's Way to Perfection* (1999), *Women and Spiritual Equality in Christian Tradition* (1998), and *Women and Religious Life in Premodern Europe* (1996). Contributor to *From Cloister to Classroom* (1986) and a number of scholarly journals. **Essays:** Clare of Assisi, St.; Spiritual Direction, Christian; Women's Monasteries: Western Christian.

Rausch, Thomas P., S.J. Professor and Chair of Theological Studies, Loyola Marymount University, Los Angeles. Author of many books including *Catholicism at the Dawn of the Third Millennium* (1996), *Priesthood Today: An Appraisal* (1992), and *Radical Christian Communities* (1990). Editor of *The College Student's Introduction to Theology* (1993). Contributor to *One in Christ*, *Horizons*, *Mid Stream*, *Chicago Studies*, and several anthologies, including *The Exercise of Primacy* (1998). **Essay:** Hospitality, Christian.

Reader, Ian. Scottish Centre for Japanese Studies, University of Stirling. Author of *Religious Violence in Contemporary Japan: The Case of Aum Shinrikyo* (1999), *Practically Religious: Worldly Benefits and the Common Religion of Japan* (with George J. Tanabe, 1998), *A Poisonous Cocktail? Aum Shinrikyo's Path to Violence* (1996), and *Religion in Contemporary Japan* (1991). Editor of *Pilgrimage in Popular Culture* (with Tony Walter, 1993). Advisory board member of *Japanese Journal of Religious Studies* and *Nova Religio*. Contributor to a number of religious studies publications. **Essay:** Aum Shinrikyō.

Rees, Daniel, O.S.B. Downside Abbey. Editor of *Downside Review* (1966–98), *Monks of England* (1997), and *Consider Your Call* (1980). Contributor to collections including *New Dictionary of National Biography* (2000) and *Lexikon für Theologie und Kirche* (1998). **Essays:** Anglican Monasticism; Chapman, John.

Reinders, Eric. Assistant Professor, Department of Religion, Emory University, Atlanta, Georgia. Contributor to *Historical Encyclopedia of World Slavery* (1997), *History of Religions* (1997), and *Numen* (1997). **Essays:** Animals, Attitude toward: Buddhist Perspectives; Anticlericalism: Buddhist Perspectives; Gestures, Buddhist; Pilgrims to India, Chinese.

Renkin, Claire (Photo Editor). Earned a Ph.D. in Italian Renaissance art history at Rutgers University in 1998 with a dissertation on the religious paintings of Correggio. Has worked as a Visiting Lecturer in art history at the University of Massachusetts, Amherst, and as a Graduate Curatorial Intern at the Smith College Museum of Art.

Renna, Thomas. Professor, Department of History, Saginaw Valley State University, University Center, Michigan. Author of *The West in the Early Middle Ages* (1977) and *Church and State in Medieval Europe 1050–1314* (1974). Contributor to numerous journals including *Cistercian Studies*, *Cîteaux*, and *American Benedictine Review*. **Essays:** Caesarius of Arles, St.; Savonarola, Girolamo.

Repp, Martin (Adviser). Associate Director, NCC Center for the Study of Japanese Religions, Kyoto. Author of *Aum Shinrikyo: Ein Kapitel krimineller Religionsgeschichte* (1997) and *Die Transzendierung des Theismus in der Religionsphilosophie Paul Tillichs* (1986). Contributing editor of *Japanese Religions* (1992–). Contributor to *Japanese Christian Review* and other publications. **Essay:** Hōnen.

Reynolds, Frank. Professor of History of Religions and Buddhist Studies, University of Chicago. Author of *Two Wheels of Dhamma* (with Gananath Obeyesekere and Bardwell Smith, 1973). Editor of many books including *Life of Buddhism* (with Jason Carbine, 2000), *Religion and Practical Reason* (with David Tracy, 1994), and *Discourse and Practice* (with David Tracy, 1992). Translator of *Three Worlds according to King Ruang: A Thai Buddhist Cosmology* (1982). Contributor of more than 60 articles to journals, encyclopedias, and collections. **Essays:** Mongkut; Mun, Ajahn.

Rippinger, Joel A., O.S.B. (Adviser). Marmion Abbey, Aurora, Illinois. Author of *The Benedictine Order in the United States* (1989). Associate editor of *American Benedictine Review* (1979–98). Contributing editor of *The Continuing Quest for God* (1982). Board member of *Review for Religious* (1994–98). **Essays:** Wolter, Maurus; Wolter, Placidus.

Roumbalou, Maria. Doctoral researcher, Department of Politics, University of Reading. Contributor to *Encyclopedia of Greece and the Hellenic Tradition* (1999). **Essays:** Hermits: Eastern Christian; Meteora, Thessaly, Greece.

Rubenson, Samuel. Associate Professor, Department of Theology, Lund University. Author of *The Letters of St. Antony* (1990, 1995). Editor of *The Missionary Factor in Ethiopia* (1998) and *Patristica Nordica* (1995, 1998). Contributor to *Between Desert and City* (1997), *The Christian Heritage in the Holy Land* (1995), *Medieval Encounters*, and a number of other books and journals. **Essays:** Antony, St.; Asceticism: Christian Perspectives; Evagrius Ponticus; Origins: Eastern Christian.

Ruffing, Janet K., R.S.M. Associate Professor of Spirituality and Spiritual Direction, Graduate School of Religion and Religious Education, Fordham University, Bronx, New York. Author of *Uncovering Stories of Faith* (1989). Editor of *Essays in Mysticism and Social Transformation* (forthcoming), *The Way* (1993–), *Christian Spirituality Bulletin* (1993–), and *MAST Journal* (1992–98). Contributor to many publications including *Studies in Spirituality*, *Presence*, and *A Handbook of Spirituality for Ministers* (forthcoming). **Essay:** Meditation: Christian Perspectives.

Sagovsky, Nicholas. William Leech Professorial Research Fellow in Applied Christian Theology, University of Newcastle. Author of *"On God's Side": A Life of George Tyrrell* (1990) and *Between Two Worlds: George Tyrrell's Relationship to the Thought of Matthew Arnold* (1983). Associate editor of *Literature and Theology* (1987–90). **Essays:** Aidan, St.; Lindisfarne/ Holy Island, England.

Salgado, Nirmala S. Assistant Professor, Department of Religion, Augustana College, Rock Island, Illinois. Contributor to numerous anthologies and journals including *Women Changing Contemporary Buddhism* (forthcoming), *Nethra*, and *Ethnology*. **Essay:** Ten-Precept Mothers as Theravādin Nuns.

Samuel, Geoffrey. Professor, Department of Sociology and Anthropology, University of Newcastle, New South Wales. Author of *Civilized Shamans: Religion in Tibetan Societies* (1993) and *Mind, Body, and Culture: Anthropology and the Biological Interface* (1990). Editor of *Nature Religion Today* (1998) and *Tantra and Popular Religion in Tibet* (1994). Translator of *The Religions of Tibet* by Giuseppe Tucci (1980) and *The Religions of Mongolia* by Walther Heissig (1980). **Essay:** Buddhist Schools/Traditions: Tibet.

Schabel, Chris. Lecturer, Department of History and Archaeology, University of Cyprus. Author of *The Cartulary of the Cathedral of Holy Wisdom of Nicosia* (with Nicholas Coureas, 1997). Contributor to *Medieval Philosophy* (1998), *Augustiniana*, and *Cahiers de l'Institut du Moyen-Âge Grec et Latin*, and other publications. **Essays:** Cyprus (with Nicholas Coureas); Theology, Western Christian: Augustinian Friars/ Hermits.

Schaefer, Mary M. Professor of Christian Worship, Atlantic School of Theology, Halifax, Nova Scotia. Author of *The Catholic Priesthood: A Liturgically Based Theology of the Pastoral Office* (with J. Frank Henderson, 1990). Editor of *Culture and the Praying Church* by Edward J. Kilmartin (1990) and *Studies in Religion/Sciences Religieuses*. Contributor to *Liturgy for Liturgical Musicians* (1998), *Studies in Religion*, *Worship*, *Liturgical Ministry*, and *Shaping a Priestly People* (1994). **Essays:** India: Christian; Liturgy: Western Christian; Romania (with Silvia Chitimia and Ronald G. Roberson).

Shaffern, Robert W. Assistant Professor of History, University of Scranton, Scranton, Pennsylvania. Contributor to *Catholic Historical Review*, *Diakonia*, *Journal of Medieval History*, *Church History*, and *Bulletin of Medieval Canon Law*. **Essays:** Germany: History; Jansenist Controversy; Liturgists, German Monastic.

Sharf, Robert H. Associate Professor, Department of Asian Languages and Cultures, University of Michigan. Co-editor of *The Living Image* (with Elizabeth Horton Sharf, forthcoming). Editorial board member of *Journal of the International Association for Buddhist Studies*. Contributor to many publications including *Representations*, *Critical Terms for Studies in Religion* (1998), and *Religions of China in Practice* (1996). **Essay:** Suzuki, Daisetz Teitaro.

Shaver-Crandell, Annie. Professor Emeritus, Department of Art, City College of New York, City University of New York. Coauthor of *The Pilgrim's Guide to Santiago de Compostela: Critical Edition* (1998) and *The Pilgrim's Guide to Santiago de Compostela: A Gazetteer* (1995). Contributor to *Cambridge Introduction to the History of Art* (1982). **Essays:** Santiago de Compostela, Spain; Glossary (Christian Terms).

Shevzov, Vera. Assistant Professor, Department of Religion and Biblical Literature, Smith College, Northampton, Massachusetts. Contributor to *Slavic Review* and *Russian Review*. **Essay:** Visual Arts, Eastern Christian: Painting.

Shinohara, Koichi. Professor, Department of Religious Studies, McMaster University, Hamilton, Ontario. Author of *Speaking of Monks* (1994). Editor of several books including *Monks and Magicians* (1989). Contributor to *Journal of the International Association for Buddhist Studies* and the anthology *Images, Miracles, and Authority in Asian Religious Traditions*. **Essay:** Daoxuan (Tao-hsüan).

Shore, Jeff. Professor of Zen Buddhism, Faculty of Letters, Hanazono University, Kyoto. Editor of *FAS Society Journal* (1984–). Contributor to *Masao Abe: A Zen Life of Dialogue* (1998), *Hisamatsu Shin'ichi Chosakushū-Hisamatsu Shin'ichi no Sekai* (1996), *Bulletin of the Faculty of Letters, Hanzono University*, and *1990 Anthology of Fo Kuang Shan International Buddhist Conference*. **Essays:** Kōan; Zen and the West.

Shuck, Glenn W. Doctoral candidate, Department of Religious Studies, Rice University, Houston, Texas. Contributor to *Journal of Religion and Society*. **Essay:** Brewing, Western Christian.

Silber, Ilana Friedrich (Adviser). Department of Sociology, Hebrew University, Jerusalem. Author of *Virtuosity, Charisma, and Social Order: A Comparative Sociological Study of Monasticism in Theravada Buddhism and Medieval Catholicism* (1995). Editor, with S.N. Eisenstadt, of *Knowledge and Society: Studies in the Sociology of Culture Past and Present* (1988).

Silke, John J. Author of *Two Abbots* (1997), *Relics, Refugees, and Rome* (1975), *Kinsale: The Spanish Intervention in Ireland at the End of the Elizabethan Wars* (1970), and *Ireland and Europe, 1559–1607* (1966). Contributor to *A New History of Ireland* (1976), *Eighteenth-Century Ireland* (1994), *Irish Historical Studies*, *Irish Theological Quarterly*, and *Studies in the Renaissance*. **Essays:** Bobbio, Italy; Liturgy: Celtic.

Simons, Walter. Associate Professor, Department of History, Dartmouth College, Dartmouth, New Hampshire. Author of *Béguines et Béguines à Tournai au Bas Moyen Âge* (1988), *Bedelordekloosters in Het Graafschaf Vlaanderen* (1987), and *Stad en Apostolaat* (1987). Contributor to *The Work of Jacques Le Goff and the Challenges of Medieval History* (1997), *Framing Medieval Bodies* (1994), *The Land of Carmel* (1991), and *Women in the Church* (1990). **Essays:** Beghards; Beguines; Belgium: History; Belgium: Sites.

Sinclair, Tom. Assistant Professor, Department of Turkish Studies, University of Cyprus. Author of *Eastern Turkey: An Archi-*

tectural and Archaeological Survey (four volumes, 1987–90). Contributor to *The Art of Syria and the Jazira 1100–1250* (1982) and *Revue des Études Arméniennes*. **Essay:** Architecture: Armenian Monasteries.

Skinner, Mary S. Lecturer, History and Religion, Empire State College, State University of New York, Corning and Rochester, and Lecturer, Religious Studies, Ithaca College, Ithaca, New York. Contributor to *Lay Sanctity, Medieval and Modern: A Search for Models* (2000), *Distant Echoes: Medieval Religious Women* (1984), and *Benedictus: Studies in Honor of St. Benedict* (1981). **Essays:** Benedictines: Female; Holy Men/Holy Women: Christian Perspectives; Patrons, Christian: Lay.

Smith, Katherine Allen. Graduate student, Department of History, New York University, New York City. **Essay:** Lay Brothers and Lay Sisters, Christian.

Sommerfeldt, John R. Professor of History, University of Dallas, Dallas, Texas. Author of several books on Bernard of Clairvaux, including *The Spiritual Teachings of Bernard of Clairvaux* (1991). Editor of *Studiosorum Speculum* (1993), *Bernardus Magister* (1992), *Erudition at God's Service* (1987), *Cistercian Studies Quarterly* (1991–), and a number of other books, series, and journals. Contributor to many collections and journals on religion. **Essay:** Aelred of Rievaulx, St.

Sørensen, Henrik H. Director of the Seminar for Buddhist Studies, Copenhagen, and Oriental arts consultant. Author of *The Buddhist Sculptures at Yuanjuedon in Anyue* (1999) and *The Iconography of Korean Buddhist Paintings* (1989). Editor-in-chief of *Studies in Central and East Asian Religion, Journal of the Seminar for Buddhist Studies* (1988–present) and *SBS Monandraphs* (1994–present). Editor of *Religions in Traditional Korea* (1995) and *Perspectives on Japan and Korea* (1991). Contributor to anthologies and journals. **Essays:** Buddhism: Inculturation; Buddhist Schools/Traditions: China; Buddhist Schools/Traditions: Korea; Daoism: Influence on Buddhism; Esoteric Buddhism in China and Japan; Korea: History; Mantras; Patrons, Buddhist: Korea; Visual Arts, Buddhist: Korea; Worship Space: Buddhist Perspectives.

Stewart, Columba, O.S.B. Associate Professor of Theology, Curator of Research Collections, Saint John's University, Collegeville, Minnesota. Author of *Prayer and Community: The Benedictine Tradition* (1998), *Cassian the Monk* (1998), *Working the Earth of the Heart* (1989), and *The World of the Desert Fathers* (1986). Editorial advisor for *Vox Benedictina/Magistra* (1989–). Contributor to *American Benedictine Review, Christian Spirituality Bulletin, Studia Patristica*, and several anthologies. **Essay:** Desert Fathers.

Stewart, David. Electronic Services Librarian, Princeton Theological Seminary, Princeton, New Jersey. Contributor to *Alive to the Love of God: Essays Presented to James M. Houston* (1998). **Essays:** Archives, Western Christian; Canada; Libraries: Western Christian.

Stoudt, Debra L. Associate Professor of German, Department of Foreign Languages, University of Toledo, Toledo, Ohio. Contributing editor of *Medieval Sermons and Society: Cloister, City, University* (1998). Contributor to *Women Healers and Physicians: Climbing a Long Hill* (1997), *Manuscript Sources of Medieval Medicine* (1994), *Women as Protagonists and Poets in the German Middle Ages* (19910, and *Medieval Studies*. **Essays:** Dominicans: Female; Mystics, German Monastic: Female; Mystics, German Monastic: Male.

Strong, John S. (Adviser). Professor and Chairman, Department of Philosophy and Religion, Bates College, Lewiston, Maine. Author of *The Experience of Buddhism: Sources and Interpretation* (1994), *The Legend and Cult of Upagupta: Sanskrit Buddhism in North India and Southeast Asia* (1991), and other books. Contributor to many popular and scholarly publications including *Atlantic Monthly, Buddhist Sacred Biography in South and Southeast Asia* (1997), and *The Harper Collins Dictionary of Religion*.

Sullivan, Donald D. Associate Professor, Department of History, University of New Mexico. Contributor to *Nicholas Cusa on Christ and the Church* (1996), *Medieval Scholarship* (1995), *American Cusanus Society Quarterly, History Teacher, Classical Journal, Medieval Studies*, and *Journal of Medieval History*. **Essays:** Cathars; Critiques of Western Christian Monasticism; Maurists; Warrior Monks: Christian.

Sutera, Judith, O.S.B. Monastery of Mount St. Scholastica, Atchison, Kansas. Author of *Work of God* (1997) and *True Daughters* (1987). Editor of *Magistra* (1995–) and *Vox Benedictina* (1990–94). Editorial board member of *American Benedictine Review* (1986–). Contributor to *Word and Spirit, American Benedictine Review, Benedictines*, and other journals. **Essays:** More, Gertrude; United States: Western Christian; Vocation, Christian.

Swearer, Donald K. Charles and Harriet Cox McDowell Professor of Religion, Department of Religion, Swarthmore College, Swarthmore, Pennsylvania. Author of several books including *The Buddhist World of Southeast Asia* (1995) and *For the Sake of the World: The Spirit of Buddhist and Christian Monasticism* (1984). Editor of *Journal of Buddhist-Christian Studies* (1981–), *Journal of Ecumenical Studies* (1983–), *Crossroads* (1988–) and other publications. Contributor to collections and journals including *Journal of Religious Ethics, Wilson Quarterly*, and *Inner Peace, World Peace* (1992). **Essay:** Buddhadāsa.

Talbot, Alice-Mary (Adviser). Director of Byzantine Studies, Dumbarton Oaks, Washington, D.C. General editor, Dumbarton Oaks Byzantine Saints' Lives in Translation series and *Dumbarton Oaks Papers*. Executive editor of the *Oxford Dictionary of Byzantium* (1991). Author of *Faith Healing in Late Byzantium: The Posthumous Miracles of the Patriarch Athanasios I of Constantinople* (1983) and *The Correspondence of Athanasius I Patriarch of Constantinople: Letters to the Emperor Andronicus II, Members of the Imperial Family, and Officials* (1975).

Tannous, Tarek. Graduate student, Department of Philosophy, West Chester University, West Chester, Pennsylvania. **Essay:** Buddhism: Western (with Frank J. Hoffman, Brian Williard, Catherine Oravez, and Adam Morris).

Tatz, Mark J. Instructor of Tibetan Language, University of California, Berkeley. Author of *The Skill in Means (Upayakausalya) Sutra* (1994) and *Buddhism and Healing* (1985). Editor and translator of *Nine Prayers for the Prompt Rebirth of the Gyalwa Karmapa* (1985). Contributor to *Tibetan Review*, *Tibet Journal*, *Journal of Buddhist and Tibetan Studies*, and other journals and anthologies. **Essay:** Glossary (Buddhist Terms).

Teasdale, Wayne. Adjunct Professor, Catholic Theological Union, Columbia College, and DePaul University, Chicago. Advisor to Monastic Interreligious Dialogue and coordinator of the Bede Griffiths International Trust. Author of *The Mystic Heart: Discovering a Universal Spirituality in the World's Religions* (1999), *Toward a Christian Vedanta: The Encounter of Hinduism and Christianity according to Bede Griffiths* (1987), and *Essays in Mysticism Explorations into Contemplative Experience* (1982, 1985). Co-editor of *The Community of Religions: Voices and Images of the Parliament of the World's Religions* (1996). Contributor of more than 200 articles to journals and anthologies. **Essays:** Dalai Lama (Tenzin Gyatso); Griffiths, Bede; Keating, Thomas; Le Saux, Henri.

Tedesco, Frank M. Assistant Professor, College of Humanities, Sejong University, Seoul. Editor of *Buddhist Social Welfare in Asia* (1999). Editorial board member, *Korea Journal* (1989–99). Contributor to numerous anthologies and journals, including *Phra Prayudh Payatto Festschrift* (1999) and *Buddhist-Christian Studies*. **Essays:** Chinul; Korea: Sites; Persecution: Buddhist Perspectives; Wŏnhyo.

Tegeder, Vincent, O.S.B. Professor Emeritus of History and Archivist Emeritus, Saint John's University, Collegeville, Minnesota. Abbey Archivist Emeritus, Saint John's Abbey, Collegeville, Minnesota. Contributor to *Encyclopedia of American Catholic History* (1997), *Mississippi Valley Historical Review*, *Minnesota History*, *American Benedictine Review*, and other publications. **Essay:** Collegeville, Minnesota.

Teteriatnikov, Natalia. Curator of Byzantine Photographs and Fieldwork Archives, Dumbarton Oaks, Washington, D.C. Author of *Mosaics of Hagia Sophia, Istanbul: The Fossati Restoration and the Work of the Byzantine Institute* (1998) and *Liturgical Planning of Byzantine Churches in Cappadocia* (1997). Contributor to a number of journals and collections including *Work and Worship at the Thestokos Evergetis 1050–1200* (1997). **Essay:** Architecture: Eastern Christian Monasteries.

Thurman, Robert A.F. (Adviser). Jey Tsong Khapa Professor of Indo-Tibetan Studies, Department of Religion, Columbia University, New York City. Author of *Circling the Sacred Mountain: A Spiritual Adventure through the Himalayas* (with Tad Wise, 1999), *Inner Revolution: Life, Liberty, and the Pursuit of Real* Happiness (1998), *Essential Tibetan Buddhism* (1995), and many other scholarly and popular works. Editor and translator of numerous publications related to Indo-Tibetan philosophy and Buddhism.

Tierney, Mark, O.S.B. Monk, Glenstal Abbey, County Limerick. Author of *Abbot Columba Marmion* (1994), *Ireland since 1870* (1988), *Croke of Cashel* (1976), *Modern Ireland* (1972), and *The Birth of Modern Ireland* (1969). Contributor to *Collectanea Hibernica*, *Education in Ireland*, and *Irish Ecclesiastical Record*. **Essay:** Marmion, Columba.

Timbie, Janet. Research Fellow, Institute of Christian Oriental Research, Catholic University of America, Washington, D.C. Editor and translator of *Testament of Job* (1975). Contributor to numerous anthologies and journals including *Pilgrimage and Holy Space in Late Antique Egypt* (1998), *Roots of Egyptian Christianity* (1986) and *Coptic Encyclopedia*. **Essays:** Egypt; Jerome, St.; Macarius of Alexandria, St.; Melkite Monasticism; Women's Monasteries: Eastern Christian.

Timko, Philip, O.S.B. St. Procopius Abbey. Professor, Department of Religious Studies, Benedictine University, Lisle, Illinois. Associate editor of *American Benedictine Review* (1985–). Contributor to *Monastic Life in the Christian and Hindu Traditions* (1990). **Essays:** Cassiodorus; Dominic, St.; Monastery, Christian.

Tiyavanich, Kamala. Independent scholar and historian of Southeast Asia. Author of *Forest Recollections: Wandering Monks in Twentieth-Century Thailand* (1997). **Essay:** Forest Masters.

Touwaide, Alain. Senior Fellow, Dumbarton Oaks Center for Byzantine Studies, Harvard University, Cambridge, Massachusetts. Author of *La tossicologia a Bisanzio nel X secolo* (1993) and *Farmacopea Araba Medievale* (1992–93). Editor of *History of Byzantine Medicine* (2000), *History of Arabic Medicine* (1994–95), and other books and journals. Contributor to *Antike Naturwissenschaft: Biologie* (1999), *Western Medical Thought* (1998), and a number of journals. **Essay:** Hygiene: Christian Perspectives.

Tucker, John Allen. Associate Professor, Department of History and Philosophy, University of North Florida. Author of *Itō Jinsai's Gomō jigi and the Philosophical Definition of Early Modern Japan* (1998). Editor of *Japan Studies Review* (1997–98). Contributor to numerous anthologies and journals including *Encyclopedia of the History of Sciences, Technology, and Medicine in Non-western Cultures* (1997), *Journal of Japanese Religions*, and *Philosophy East and West*. **Essays:** Critiques of Buddhist Monasticism: Confucian; Nation-Building and Japanese Buddhism.

Tunstall, Lee. Faculty of General Studies, University of Calgary, Calgary, Alberta. Contributor to *Journal of Graduate Education* and *Archivo Ibero-Americano*. **Essays:** Peter of Alcántara, St.; Portugal.

Turner, David, O.S.B. Monk, St. Procopius Abbey, Lisle, Illinois, and Director of Institutional Mission and University Ministry, Benedictine University, Lisle, Illinois. Editor of *Journal of the Catholic Campus Ministry Associations* (1991–98). Contributor to *Human Development*. **Essays:** Christianity: Overview; Schools and Universities, Benedictine.

Vanden Broucke, Pol. Professor, Department of Japanese Language and Culture, University of Ghent. Author of *Hōkyōshō: The Compendium of the Precious Mirror of the Monk Yūkai* (1992). Contributor to *Romanian Journal of Japanese Studies* and *Bulletin of the Research Institute of Esoteric Buddhist Culture*. **Essay:** Chan/Zen: Korea.

Venarde, Bruce L. (Adviser). Associate Professor of History, University of Pittsburgh, Pittsburgh, Pennsylvania. Author of *Women's Monasticism and Medieval Society: Nunneries in France and England, 890–1215* (1997). Contributor to *Portraits of Medieval and Renaissance Living: Essays in Memory of David Herlihy* (1996) and *Provence historique*. **Essays:** Fontevraud, France; Historiography, Recent: Western Christian; Premonstratensian Canons.

Verbist, Peter. Research assistant, Department of History, University of Leuven. **Essay:** Timekeeping: Christian Perspectives.

Vess, Deborah. Director of Interdisciplinary Studies and Associate Professor of History, Georgia College and State University. Oblate of Mt. St. Scholastica, Atchison, Kansas. Founding coeditor of *Magistra: A Journal of Women's Spirituality in History* (1994–98) and editor of *Vox Benedictina* 1992–94). Net review editor of *History Computer Review* (1997–98). Contributor to *Teaching History*, *Proteus*, *Mystics Quarterly*, and other journals. **Essays:** Abelard, Peter; Assisi, Italy; England: Sites; Heloise; Lanfranc; Monte Cassino, Italy.

Vidmar, John C., O.P. Assistant Professor of Church History, Dominican House of Studies, Washington, D.C. Contributor to *Catholic Historical Review* and *Archivum Historicum Societatis Iesu*. **Essay:** Dissolution of Monasteries: Scotland.

Vorenkamp, Dirck. Assistant Professor, Department of Religious Studies, Lawrence University, Appleton, Wisconsin. Contributor to *Journal of Chinese Philosophy* and *Philosophy East and West*. **Essay:** Tiantai/Tendai: China.

Vũ Văn Thái. Tu-Quang Buddhist Order, Montreal. Author of *Theravada Buddhism* (1999), *Salvation in Some Great Religions* (1998), *The Pure-Land Path* (1997), *Emtyness in Rupa* (1996), and *Survey of Vietnamese Buddhism* (1995). Contributing editor of *The Voice of Dharma* (1990–). Contributor to *Nouveau Dialogue* and *The Quoc-Gia Magazine*. **Essay:** Vietnam.

Walsh, Michael J. Librarian, Heythrop College, University of London. Author of *Pope John Paul II: A Biography* (1994), *A Dictionary of Devotions* (1994), *Opus Dei* (1992), *The Tables* (1990), and *The Triumph of the Meek* (1987). Editor of *Lives of the Popes* (1998), *A Commentary on the Catechism of the Catholic Church* (1994), and other books. Contributor to *An Atlas of World Religions* (1999), *Studies in Printing History* (1992), and *Modern Catholicism* (1991). **Essays:** Papacy: Monastic Popes; Papacy: Papal Pronouncements.

Walsh, Michael J. Doctoral candidate, Department of Religious Studies, University of California, Santa Barbara. Contributor to *The Oxford Companion to Archaeology* (1996). **Essay:** Economics: Buddhist.

Ware, Kalistos T. (Adviser). Fellow, Pembroke College, Oxford University. Author of *The Orthodox Way* (1979), *The Orthodox Church* (1964, 1993), and *Eustratios Argenti: A Study of the Greek Church under Turkish Rule* (1964). Editor and translator of *The Philokalia: The Complete Text* (1979) and many other works related to the Orthodox Church.

Warneke, Sara. Formerly a Senior Lecturer in the Department of History and Medieval Studies at Latrobe University, Bendigo, Australia; currently a full-time fiction writer. Author of *Images of the Educational Traveller in Early Modern England* (1995). **Essays:** Social Services: Western Christian; Travelers: Western Christian.

Wathen, Ambrose G. Monk, St. Joseph Abbey, St. Benedict, Louisiana. Author of *Silence: The Meaning of Silence in the Rule of St. Benedict* (1973). Contributor to *Cistercian Studies*, *American Benedictine Review*, *Monastic Studies*, and *Regulae Benedicti Studia*. **Essay:** Scholars, Benedictine.

Weckman, George (Adviser). Assistant Chairman and Associate Professor, Department of Philosophy, Ohio University, Athens. Author of *My Brothers' Place: An American Lutheran Monastery* (1992). Contributor to numerous anthologies and journals including *The Sacred and Its Scholars* (1996) and *Religion and Reductionism: Essays on Eliade, Segal, and the Challenge of the Social Sciences for the Study of Religion* (1994). **Essays:** Ashram, Influence of; Bible Interpretation; Biblical Figures and Practices; Luther, Martin.

Wells, Scott. Department of History, New York University, New York City. **Essays:** Rabanus Maurus; Reichenau; Walafrid Strabo.

Wickham-Smith, Simon. Independent scholar, Oxford. Author of *Few* (1994), *Three Zero* (1993), and *Small Wheels* (1992). Contributor to *Interchange*. **Essays:** Asia, Central; Solitude: Buddhist Perspectives.

Wickstrom, John B. Professor of History, Kalamazoo College, Kalamazoo, Michigan. Contributor to *Studies in Iconography*, *Manuscripta*, and other publications. **Essays:** Carthusians; Office, Daily: Western Christian.

Wiesner-Hanks, Merry (Adviser). Professor and Chair, Department of History, University of Wisconsin–Milwaukee. Author of *Christianity and Sexuality in the Early Modern World: Regulating Desire, Reforming Practice* (2000), *Gender, Church, and State in Early Modern Germany* (1998), *Discovering the Global Past: A Look at the Evidence* (1997), *Women and Gender in Early Modern Europe* (1993), and other books. Editor of *Sixteenth Century Journal*, *Becoming Visible: Women in European History* (third edition, 1998), *Convents Confront the Reformation: Catholic and Protestant Nuns in Germany* (also co-translator, 1996), and *Oxford Encyclopedia of the Reformation* (1995). Contributor to many scholarly publications including *Church History*, *Journal of Women's History*, and *Journal of Medieval and Renaissance Studies*.

Wiles, Royce. Asian History Centre, Faculty of Asian Studies, Australian National University. Translator of *Nirayāvaliyā-suyakkhandha: Uvavigas 8–12 of the Jain Canon* by Jozef Deleu (with J.W. de Jong, 1996). Editor of *Collected Articles of L.A. Schwarzschild on Indo-Aryan 1953–1979* (1991). **Essay:** Jain Monasticism and Buddhist Monasticism.

Willis, Janice D. Professor, Religion Department, Wesleyan University, Middletown, Connecticut. Author of *Enlightened Beings: Life Stories from the Ganden Oral Tradition* (1995), *On Knowing Reality: The Tattvartha Chapter of Asanga's Bodhisattvabhumi* (1979), and *The Diamond Light of the Eastern Dawn: An Introduction to Tibetan Buddhist Meditation* (1972). Editor of *Feminine Ground: Essays on Women in Tibet* (1989). Contributor to *Tibet Journal* and several anthologies. **Essay:** Asaṅga.

Williard, Brian. Graduate student, Department of Philosophy, West Chester University, West Chester, Pennsylvania. **Essay:** Buddhism: Western (with Frank J. Hoffman, Tarek Tannous, Catherine Oravez, and Adam Morris).

Wilson, Liz. Associate Professor, Department of Religion, Miami University, Oxford, Ohio. Author of *Charming Cadavers: Horrific Figurations of the Feminine in Indian Buddhist Hagiographic Literature* (1996). Contributor to *Journal of Feminist Studies in Religion*, *Journal of Indian Philosophy*, and *Union Seminary Quarterly*. **Essays:** Body: Buddhist Perspectives; Food: Buddhist Perspectives.

Wiseman, James A., O.S.B. Associate Professor, Department of Theology, Catholic University of America, Washington, D.C. Editor of *The Gethsemani Encounter: A Dialogue on the Spiritual Life by Buddhist and Christian Monastics* (1998), *Light from Light: An Anthology of Christian Mysticism* (1988), and *John Ruusbroec: The Spiritual Espousals and Other Works* (1985). Contributor to *Christian Spirituality and the Culture of Modernity* (1998) and a number of journals. **Essays:** Church Councils, Recent Catholic; Theology, Western Christian: Benedictine.

Wittberg, Patricia (Adviser). Associate Professor, Department of Sociology, Indiana University, Indianapolis. Author of *Pathways to Re-creating Religious Communities* (1996), *The Rise and Fall of Catholic Religious Orders: A Social Movement Perspective* (1994), and *Creating a Future for Religious Life* (1991). Contributor to *Handbook of Marriage and the Family* (1998), *Encyclopedia of American Catholic History*, *Sociology of Religion*, and several other publications. **Essay:** Contemporary Issues: Western Christian.

Woods, Richard, O.P. Lecturer, Blackfriars Hall, Oxford University, and Lecturer, Institute of Pastoral Studies, Loyola University, Chicago. Author of *Mysticism and Prophecy* (1998), *Christian Spirituality* (1989, 1996), *Eckhart's Way* (1986), *Symbion: Spirituality for a Possible Future* (1983), and *Mysterion: An Approach to Mystical Spirituality* (1981). Editor of several publications including *Presence* (1993–97) and *Spirituality Today* (1986–90). Contributor to *Crossing Boundaries* (1999) and many journals. **Essays:** Columban, St.; Eckhart, Meister; Ireland: History.

Wortley, John. Professor of Mediaeval History, History Department, University of Manitoba, Winnipeg. Translator of *The Spiritually Beneficial Tales of Paul, Bishop of Monembasia and of Other Authors* (1996), *The Spiritual Meadow* by John Moschos (1992), and other works. Editor of *Mosaic* (1974–79). Contributor to several anthologies, including *Work and Worship at the Theotokos Evergetis 1050–1200* (997), and *Peace and War in Byzantium* (1995), and such journals as *International Journal of Aging and Human Development*, *Greek, Roman, and Byzantine Studies*, and *Byzantion*. **Essay:** Sabas, St.

Wright, Wendy M. Professor, Department of Theology, Creighton University, Omaha, Nebraska. Author of *A Retreat with: Francis de Sales, Jane de Chantal and Aelred of Rievaulx* (1996), *Francis de Sales: Introduction to the Devout Life and Treatise on the Love of God* (1993), and *Bond of Perfection: Jeanne de Chantal and François de Sales* (1985). Editor of *Journal of the Society for the Study of Christian Spirituality* (1995–) and a number of other publications. Contributor to many collections including *The Holy Family in Art and Devotion* (1998). **Essay:** Visitandines.

Yorke, Barbara. Reader, Department of History, King Alfred's College, Winchester. Author of *Wessex in the Early Middle Ages* (1995) and *Kings and Kingdoms of Early Anglo-Saxon England* (1990). Editor of *Bishop Aethelwold: His Career and Influence* (1988). Contributor of numerous articles on Anglo-Saxon history. **Essay:** Hilda, St.

Zagano, Phyllis. Co-chair, Roman Catholic Studies, American Academy of Religion. Author of *Holy Saturday: An Argument for the Restoration of the Female Diaconate in the Catholic Church* (2000), *Ita Ford: Missionary Martyr* (1996), and *On Prayer* (1994). Editor of *Twentieth-Century Apostles: Christian Spirituality in Action* (1999), *Things New and Old: Essays on the Anthology of Elizabeth A. Johnson* (with Terrence W. Tilley, 1999), and other books. Editorial board member, *American Journalism* (1984–90) and *American Catholic Philosophical Quarterly* (1984–89). Contributor to a number of books and journals. **Essay:** Schutz, Roger.

Zaleski, Carol (Adviser). Professor and Chair, Department of Religion and Biblical Literature, Smith College, Northampton, Massachusetts. Author of *The Life of the World To Come: Near-Death Experience and Christian Hope* (1996) and *Otherworld Journeys: Accounts of Near-Death Experience in Medieval and Modern Times* (1987, 1989). Editor of *The Book of Heaven: An Anthology of Writings from Ancient to Modern Times* (with Philip Zaleski, 2000). Contributor to *Death, Ecstasy, and Otherworldly Journals* (1995), *Journal of the Psychology of Religion*, *Buddhist-Christian Studies*, and many other scholarly publications.

Zaleski, Philip. Lecturer, Department of Religion and Biblical Studies, Smith College, Northampton, Massachusetts. Author of *Gifts of the Spirit* (1997), *The Benedictines of Petersham* (1996), and *The Recollected Heart* (1995). Editor of *Parabola* (1980–99) and *The Best Spiritual Writing 1998* (1998). **Essay:** Retreat, Christian.

Zieman, Katherine. Assistant Professor, Department of English, Wesleyan University, Middletown, Connecticut. Contributor to *Representations*. **Essay:** Music: Christian Perspectives.